DIRECTORY OF FAMILY ASSOCIATIONS

DIRECTORY OF FAMILY ASSOCIATIONS

3rd Edition

Elizabeth Petty Bentley

INTRODUCTION

The title, *Directory of Family Associations,* is growing increasingly inappropriate for this collection, which I have deliberately not restricted to formally incorporated organizations. I've tried to include any and all U.S. associations, reunions, surname exchanges, significant databases on single surnames or related groups, independent periodicals, and, new to this edition, publishers of family histories. For the first time in this issue, frequency of publication or reunion, subscription or membership costs, and reunion location are included. All information is subject to change, of course, but particularly prices. Telephone area codes, too, are being continually subdivided in response to an unprecedented demand for additional lines. And the post office is eliminating many rural routes in favor of conventional street addresses required by 911 response teams. The book can only be a snapshot of work which is perpetually "in progress."

Inevitably some associations listed here may not be primarily genealogical in nature, focusing more on gathering information about the current generations and maintaining social ties among living family members. I've also included some questionable listings, having adopted the policy of continuing to list organizations which did not reply to my mail questionnaire, as long as my letter was not returned by the post office as undeliverable, even though some letters may have been simply discarded by the post office, despite my request for address correction. I prefer to err on the side of including too many rather than too few, even if a reference may prove disappointing in the end. I've also doubtless overlooked many organizations which should have been included. I hope that anyone with corrections or additions will contact me at the address below for inclusion in future editions. No particular form is necessary; a simple letter will do.

At present, the computer database (including obsolete and foreign organizations) consists of 21,131 items, an increase of more than 20% since the last edition. Of these, 5,266 organizations and 9,767 cross-references appear in the book. Altogether 2,401, or about 45%, of the organizations responded this time to my questionnaire (although about 68% responded for at least one of the three editions). By their very nature, many of these organizations lack the staff to answer mail queries, so in numerous instances I was obliged to rely upon information gleaned from notices appearing in family history journals and newsletters. An asterisk before the entry indicates that the organization responded for either the second or third edition.

I would like to thank Michael Tepper, Editor-in-Chief of Genealogical Publishing Company, Eileen Perkins, the librarians at the Connecticut Valley History Museum and the LDS Family History Library, and the hundreds of nameless correspondents who took the time to supply data for this book, and whose generous encouragement eased the tedium of my task.

Elizabeth Petty Bentley

The Village Bookstore
45 Southwick Road
Westfield, MA 01085
(413) 562-7332; E-mail: wvbs@vgernet.net

DIRECTORY OF FAMILY ASSOCIATIONS

Multi-family Associations

Blossom Press
Blossom Press
PO Box 831
Burns, LA 70041-0831
Phone (504) 893-8726; (504) 657-9560
William R. Stringfield, Owner
(includes Plaquemines Parish, Louisiana,
    families, mainly those which
    originated in the 1700s: Adolph,
    Alberti, Alesich, Alg(h)ero,
    A(e)ncalade, Ancar, Anderson, Angelo,
    Anglada, Ansardi, Armstrong, Bailey,
    Ballay, Ban, Barberot, Baril, Barrois,
    Barthelemy, Bayhi, Becnel, Biaggini,
    Blazio, Bougon, Bowers, Breny
    (Bruney), Brun, Bubrig, Budenich,
    Buel(le), Bujacic(h), Bulot, Buras/
    Burat, Cadro, Cagnolotti, Cappiello,
    Carel, Carlini, Caro, Casbon,
    Catalanotto, Cauvin, Cavalier, Cazezu,
    Chanove, Chartier, Chauppette,
    Chaussier, Chedville, Cheron,
    Chiappetta, Clark, Close, Cognevich,
    Collette, Collin, Colombel,
    Coludrovich, Conaway, Cook,
    Coppola, Cossé, Cossich, Cure,
    Cvitanovich, Daroca, Daubard/Dobard,
    Dazet, DeArmas, Demandre, Demolle,
    Denes(se)/Dennis, Denet/Dinet,
    Despaux, Dimak, Dobson, Dolese,
    Dragon, Dugas/Dugar, Duplessis,
    Durabbe, Dureau, Edgecombe, Elston,
    Fabiano, Farac, Fontenelle, Fortunia,
    Franatovich, Franicevich, Franovich,
    Frederic(k), Frelich, Galmiche,
    Garc(s)ich, Gartoucies, Gasquet,
    Gauthier, Geoffroy, Ghergich,
    Giordano, Girod, Goodman, Granich,
    Gravolet, Groleau, Hallberg, Harris,
    Hatton, Henritzy, Hihar, Hingle, Holy,
    Hoskin, Howard, Howland,
    I(y)ancovich, Jackson, Jacomine,
    Jeanfreau, Johnson, Juricich, Jurjevich,
    Kelly, Kennair, Kiger, Kinkella,
    LaChute, Laë, Lafrance, Lartigue,
    Lassus, Latapie, Latour, Laussade,
    Lee, Lightell/Lytell, Lingoni, Loar,
    Lobrano, Lyons, Machella, Maliden/
    Meladine, Marinovich, Marrero,
    Marshall, Martin, Matulich, Menge,
    Meyer(s), Mialjevich, Miller, Mistich,
    Moizant, Morel, Morgan, Muhoberac,
    Munsterman, O'Brien, Olivier, Olsen,
    Paolini, Patural, Pelas, Pellegal, Perez,
    Perlander, Piacun, Pigniolo(a),
    Plummer, Popich, Purgley,
    Quatrocchio, Quatroy, Ragas, Repath,
    Richarme, Ricouard, Robinson, Rodi,
    Rojas, Rondey, Ronquillo, Rousse,
    Rousselle, Ruiz, Rusich, Rylander, St.
    Ann, St. Philip, Salinovich, Salvant,
    Savoie, Scarabin, Schayot,
    Schoenberger, Scobel, Sercovich,
    Smith, Solis, Soulant, Sousich,
    Squarsich, Stipelcovich, Stockfleth,
    Sylve, Tabony, Taliancich, Toupard,
    Treadaway, Turlich, Valet(te), Veillon,
    Viard, Vidacovich, Vinet, Vogt,
    Vucinovich, Vuskovich, Waltzer,
    Westerfield, Williams, Yuratich,
    Zibilich, Zuvich; Washington and
    Tangipahoa parishes: Bankston,
    Brumfield, Carson, Magee, Stringfield;
    Livingston Parish: Albritton, Barnett,
    Brannon)

CTC Family Association
*CTC Family Association
PO Box 641
Belle Fourche, SD 57717-0641
Phone (605) 892-2891
Shirley B. O'Leary, Genealogical
    Secretary
Pub. *CTC Courier* (Cousin-to-Cousin,
    Coast-to-Coast), annually, donation for
    subscription; (includes Akers, Barton,
    Barnhart, Baughman, Bodine,
    Coughlin, Creegan, Curtiss, Duvall,
    Eshelman, Felten, Foster, Garlick,
    Hanks, Hantz, Hardy, Heldt, Hixson,
    James, Jackson, King, Leopold,
    McClarrinnon, McFarlane,
    McLaughlin, Odell, O'Leary, Radue,
    Ringle, Thompson and Spaulding)

Ellen Payne Odom Genealogy Library
*Ellen Payne Odom Genealogy Library
Moultrie-Colquitt County Library
204 Fifth Street, S.E.
PO Box 1110
Moultrie, GA 31776-1110
Phone (912) 985-6540; (912) 985-0936
    (FAX)
Ann Glass, Irene Godwin and Catherine
    Bryant, Genealogy Librarians; Beth
    Gay, Clan Donald Archives Committee
    Member
Pub. *The Family Tree*, bimonthly, free;
    (collection includes archival and
    genealogical collections from almost
    40 Scots clans)

Folk Family Surname Exchange
*Folk Family Surname Exchange
PO Box 52048
Knoxville, TN 37950-2048
Hester E. Stockton, Owner
(includes surname exchanges on the
    following: Abbott, Adams, Allen,
    Anderson, Anthony, Archer, Armistead,
    Arnold, Ashby, Aubigne, Ausmus,
    Aylett, Bain, Baldwin, Barksdale,
    Barnard, Barnes, Batte, Baumgardner,
    Beverley, Biggers, Bird, Blair, Blake,
    Bowers, Brock, Brooks, Brown,
    Bryant, Burrows, Byrd, Cabbage,
    Campbell, Capps, Carpenter, Carr,
    Carter, Casey, Chapman, Chesnut,
    Clark, Cockman, Collum, Cook,
    Cooksey, Cooper, Coryea, Coryell,
    Cox, Crowd, Cumbie, Cunningham,
    Curl, Curle, Dabney, Daniel, Daniels,
    Davis, Day, Dean, dePons, Dickson,
    Dixon, Dothit, Duncan, Edwards,
    Estell, Eubanks, Ferguson, Field,
    Fields, Finger, Fleming, Fontaine,
    Forbes, Fowler, Freeman, Gardiner,
    Garland, George, Gifford, Goodman,
    Gordon, Graves, Gray, Griffin,
    Gudylouch, Guffie, Hackney, Hall,
    Hargis, Harris, Harrison, Hart, Harvey,
    Hatley, Haynes, Henderson, Henson,
    Herron, Hersent, Hill, Hodges,
    Hopkins, Horsley, Houston, Hums,
    Hunt, Huskey, Ingle, Isbell, Isham,
    Janaway, Jefferson, Jenkins, Johnson,
    Johnston, Jones, Justice, Keate, Keats,
    Keener, Kerr, Keryea, Kilgore, King,
    Kirby, Lakins, Lattimore, Lea, Leach,
    Lee, Lewis, Likins, Lindsay, Love,
    Lunceford, Lunsford, MacKeon,
    Mallory, Marney, Martin, Mass,
    Massie, Maupin, McCarty,
    McCormick, McCowan, McCown,
    McCulloch, McFatridge, McGowan,
    McGown, McMahan, McNutt,
    Meriwether, Michie, Minor, Moore,
    Moorman, Moss, Myrick, Neblett,
    Newberry, Niblet, Nooner, Nowlin,
    Ogle, Oglesby, Oglethorpe, Overton,
    Owenby, Ownby, Painter, Parker,
    Partain, Patterson, Penn, Pennybaker,
    Perry, Pettijohn, Pettus, Piercy, Pillon,
    Pinegar, Plantagenet, Pomfrett,
    Pomroy, Potts, Priddy, Primrose,
    Quarles, Rae, Ragsdale, Rainwater,
    Randall, Randel, Randolph, Ray, Reed,
    Riley, Risinger, Robertson, Roman,
    Rook, Rooke, Rowlett, Rowzee, Rust,
    Samuels, Sanford, Sconce, Scott,
    Secrest, Shelton, Simms, Sims, Smith,
    Spears, Spencer, Standard, Sterling,
    Stinnett, Stockton, Swaim, Swan,
    Taylor, Terrell, Thompson, Tillery,
    Tiner, Toal, Troutman, Tumblin, Tyler,
    Tyner, Ussery, Valentine, Vance,
    Vaughan, Vaughn, Vaus, Vengular, Via,
    Walker, Waller, Warford, Waters,
    Whaley, Whelchel, Whitesides,
    Whitlock, Williams, Winston, Withers,
    Wood, Woods, Yadon, Yates, Yeats and
    Young)

**Genealogical Reference of Upcoming
    Publications**
*Genealogical Reference of Upcoming
    Publications (G.R.O.U.P.)
South 2827 Ivory
Spokane, WA 99203
Phone (509) 624-0533
Laurine Mae Palmerton Logsdon

The Guild of One Name Studies
The Guild of One Name Studies
2204 West Houston
Spokane, WA 99208-4440
Phone (509) 326-2089
Donna Potter Phillips

Links Genealogy Publications
*Links Genealogy Publications
7677 Abaline Way
Sacramento, CA 95823-4224
Phone (916) 428-2245
Iris Carter Jones, Editor
Pub. *Krefeld Immigrants and Their*

Descendants, semiannually, $14.00 per year subscription, free queries for subscribers; (surname registration, family charts computerized for descendants of the 1683 immigrants who settled Germantown in Philadelphia: Aret/Arent(s), Bebber/van Bebber, Bleikers/Blijkers, van Bom/Bon/Bun(n), Bucholtz, DeHaven/in den Hoffe(e), Dewees(e)/DeWeese, Do(o)rs/Daurss/Dohrs, Frey(s), Hendricks, Keurlis/Kurlis, Klinken, Klosterman, Kuster/Custer/Custard, Kunders/Donard/Cunard/Conrad, Lensen, Linderman, Levering, Lucken/Luken/Luyken(s), Neusz/Nice, op de Trap(p), op den Graeff/up de Graeff/Updegrove, Plejtes/Peters, Pastaorius, Rittenhouse/Rittenhuysen, Scherkes, Schumacher/Shoemaker, Seimen/Siemes, Sellen/Cellen/Zellen, Sellers/Cellers, Sivert, Streepers/Streypers, Telnes, Theison/Teison/Tyson, Tennis/Tunes/Tunis/Tunnis, van Aaken, Wil(l)ems/Williams, and allied names of Beal, Cassell/Kassel(l), Copeland, Delaplaine, Duplovys, Garret/Jarrett, Hirst, Jansen/Johnson/Johnston, Jones/Johns, Kyser/Kiser, Loers, Papen, Penn, Pockhoy, Potts, Rutter, Supplees/Souples, Thatcher, Umstead/Umstat(t)d, Wisee, etc.)

The Memorial Foundation of the Germanna Colonies
*The Memorial Foundation of the Germanna Colonies in Virginia, Inc.
PO Box 693
Culpeper, VA 22701
Phone (703) 825-1919; E-mail: RosieMart@aol.com
Rose Marie Martin, Editor and Executive Secretary; William Herndon Martin, President
Pub. *Germanna*, quarterly; *The Germanna Record*, irregularly; (extensive collection of genealogy, history and biography pertaining to the pioneer settlers composing the Germanna Colonies in Virginia, 1714 and 1717, later arrivals and their descendants, including the following families: Aker, Albright, Amberger, Amburger, Ashby, Aylor, Bach, Back, Baker, Ballenger, Barber, Barler, Barlow, Baumgardner, Beer, Bender, Benneger, Beyerback, Blankenbaker, Boehm, Broyles, Brumbach, Brumback, Bungard, Burdyne, Bush, Button, Camper, Carpenter, Castler, Chelf, Christler, Christopher, Clore, Cobbler, Coller, Cook, Coon, Coons, Corber, Cornwell, Crecelieus, Crees, Crest, Crible, Crigler, Crim, Crumber, Cuntz, Darnall, Deal, Deer, Delf, Delph, Diehl, Duncan, Everhart, Farrow, Fick, Finder, Finks, Fishbach, Fishback, Fisher, Fite, Flender, Fleshman, Folg, Frank, Fray, Friesenhagen, Gansler, Garr, Graham,

Haeger, Hager, Hanback, Harnsberger, Heide, Heite, Herndon, Hirsh, Hitt, Hoffman, Holt, Holtzclaw, Hoop, House, Huettenhen, Huffman, Jacoby, Kabler, Kaifer, Kaiffer, Kaines, Kemper, Kerchler, Kerker, Kines, Klug, Kneisler, Koontz, Kooper, Kriebel, Kuenzle, Kyner, Lang, Langenbuehl, Latham, Leach, Leatherer, Leathers, Lederer, Lehman, Lipp, Long, Lotspeich, Lyons, Manspeil, Martin, Mauck, McClure, Michael, Miller, Motz, Moyer, Nay, Newby, Noeh, Nunnamaker, Oehler, Oehlschutt, Ohlschlagel, Patt, Paulitz, Peck, Prosie, Racer, Railsback, Reading, Rector, Rinehart, Riner, Rodeheaver, Rouse, Russell, Schut, Shafer, Sheible, Sheibley, Sheibly, Sinclair, Slaughter, Slucter, Smith, Snyder, Sohlbach, Souther, Spillman, Spilman, Staehr, Stature, Stigler, Stinesyfer, Stoever, Stoltz, Stonecipher, Stover, Stuell, Swindell, Tanner, Tapp, Teter, Thomas, Troller, Tullser, Urbach, Utterback, Utz, VanMeter, Vaught, Vogt, Walke, Walker, Wayland, Wayman, Weaver, Weingart, Whitescarver, Wieland, Wiley, Wilhoit, Willer, Willheit, Yager, Yeager, Young, Yowell, Ziegler, Zimmerman, Zollicoffer)
$10.00 per year membership for individuals, $15.00 per year membership for families, $150.00 life membership

Southwest Mississippi Family Journal
*Southwest Mississippi Family Journal
7024 Morgan Road
Greenwell Springs, LA 70739
Phone (504) 261-5515
Serena Abbess Haymon; Jean Burns
Pub. *Southwest Journal* (includes southwest Mississippi and Greensburg District, Louisiana, surname exchanges)
$20.00 per year membership

Sullivan Surname Exchange
*Sullivan Surname Exchange
835 2B Prairie View Lane
Woodstock, IL 60098
Phone (815) 338-7045
Gary Sullivan
(includes Arthur in Marion County, Ohio; Autry in Missouri; Bailey in Pemiscot County, Missouri; Crider in Indiana; Crumb in Grundy County, Illinois; Dows in Massachusetts; Fleetwood in Indiana, Kentucky and Virginia; Goode in Grundy County, Illinois; Green in Lawrence County, Illinois; Jackson in Humphreys County, Tennessee; Pemiscot County, Missouri; Kibler in La Salle County, Illinois, and Jasper County, Illinois; Langley in Humphreys County, Tennessee; Lee in Adams County, Pennsylvania; Main in Connecticut, New York, Butler County,

Ohio, and Saint Joseph County, Indiana; Masterman in Weld, Maine, Grundy County, Illinois, and La Salle County, Illinois; Michael in Lawrence County, Illinois; Myler in all states; Nash in Culpepper County, Virginia; Nichols in Deering, New Hampshire; Polly in Wayne County, Kentucky; Porter in Grundy County, Illinois; Rider in Virginia; Scott in Culpepper County, Virginia; Shadduck in Clinton County, Iowa; Shick in Lawrence County, Illinois; Shipley in Brown, Bartholomew, Indiana; Smith in Clinton County, Iowa, and Custer County, South Dakota; Snyder in Marion County, Ohio, and Saint Joseph County, Indiana; Weaver in West Virginia; and Zimmerman in Adams County, Pennsylvania)

Surname Sources
*Surname Sources
3131 18th Avenue, South
Minneapolis, MN 55407-1824
Ruth V. McKee, Publisher
(publishes surname marriage lists: Crane and Tyler in New England and the eastern U.S., Babbitt, Halsey, Kendrick/Dendig, Lansing, Ludlam/Ludlow and Perigo/Perrigo; also "Surnames in America" series: Hoffman (includes Hofmann, Huffman, etc.), Dougherty (includes Daugherty, Doherty, etc.), Ludlow (includes Ludlam, Ludlum, etc), Spangler (includes Spengler); "Charts 'n' Notes" series: William Gresham and Sarah Davis of Kentucky and Harrison County, Indiana, with allied surnames of Brownell, Harbison, Hoffman, McGrain, Olson, Rumbley/Rumley and Smith, Aaron Meigs Bean and Margaret Shields from Tennessee, Harrison County, Indiana, and Minnesota, with allied surnames of Clark, Flora, Haight, Williams and Williamson, Rev. Isaac Babbitt (1757–1833) of New England, including direct lines of Cooper, Crane, Ford, Lovell, Morse, Pierce, Tarne, Tisdale, Walker and Whitman families; Prudence May, daughter of Ezra May and Margaret Lyon, wife of Isaac Babbitt, with direct lines of Atkinson, Badcock, Brewer, Bridge, Brooke, Camp, Carter, Cheney, Clarke, Colburn, Deering, Foote, Hedde, Hemingway, Hewes, Holbrook, Leland, Lyon, Polley, Robinson, Ruggles, Whetman and Wightman familmies of New England, Ezra May Babbitt, son of Isaac Babbitt, and Elisabeth Reynolds Tyler, with allied surnames of Beatty, Fiske, Mockridge and Perrigo, William Lyman Perrigo and Betsy Kittler with allied surnames of Avery, Bingham, Gifford and Mudge, Martin B. Perrigo and Lydia Ouderkirk of Tompkins County, New

York, with allied surnames of Babbitt, Booth, Brown, Cobb, Jessup, Pinckney, Rhodes, Stark(s), Warfield and Williams)

Surname Database
*Surname Database
1301 Bradford Road
Oreland, PA 19075-2414
Phone (215) 836-4727
Dale E. Berger, Publisher
(includes varying amounts of material on the following surnames: Bahl, Bast, Bayer, Berger, Bickert, Boyer, Coder, Diel, Dietz, Dilger, Doll, Dromm, Drum, Finck, Fink, Foltz, Frey, Fromm, Gerlach, Giering, Hagel, Hahn, Hartzel, Heffelfinger, Heller, Hertzel, Herzel, Hohenschild, Holler, Hone, Knauer, Knauss, Kohl, Kostenbader, Kresge, Kromer, Laub, Meixell, Mory, Mueller, Muenster, Mumbauer, Newhart, Petty, Rader, Rapp, Rau, Raub, Reinmüller, Rex, Rinker, Ritter, Rodgers, Roeder, Roemer, Rogers, Römer, Schaubel, Scherer, Seip, Sherer, Shoemaker, Shook, Simons, Steiner, Sterner, Stoltz, Stolz, Storze, Strauss, Stuber, Thonymys, Townsend, Transue, Trexler, Voltz, Wagner, Weber, Wuensch and Yost)

United Family Reunion Association
*United Family Reunion Association
7540 South Seeley
PO Box 208411
Chicago, IL 60620-8411
Phone (312) 488-1473
Curtis G. Brasfield, Director
(offers consultant services to help organize family reunions)

Yates Publishing
*Yates Publishing
PO Box 67
Stevensville, MT 59870
Phone (406) 777-3797; E-mail: wyates@montana.com
William A. Yates
(database includes family group sheets on all U.S. families, 1600–1900)

Family Associations by Surname

Aaldericnk (see Poll)

Abbas (see Abbess)

Abbess
*Abbess, Abbiss, Abbas Surname Organization
7024 Morgan Road
Greenwell Springs, LA 70739
Phone (504) 261-5515

Serena Abbess Haymon, Research Director
Pub. *Abbess Journal*, annually (January); (includes families of the U.S. and England)
Free membership and registration on FGS

Abbiss (see Abbess)

Abbot (see MacDuff)

Abbotson (see Macnab)

Abbott (see Folk Family Surname Exchange, Goodenow, MacDuff, Macnab)

Abbott
*Abbott Family
PO Box 688
Goose Creek, SC 29445
Phone (803) 761-4904
Victor Paul Mertrud, Chief Researcher

Abbott
*William Horace Abbott Proposed Family Organization
3109 Ivanhoe
Abilene, TX 79605
Phone (915) 692-1826
Kerry L. Linley

Abboutoun (see MacDuff)

Abbs
*Abbs Surname Organization
1404 "N" Street
Springfield, OR 97477
Phone (541) 747-9793
Barbara Abbs Stockwell
Pub. *Abbs Family Newsletter*, semiannually, $3.00 per year subscription

Abcher (see Abshire)

Abel (see Abell)

Abel
Abel(l)/Able and Related Lines
1525 Youngs Avenue
Sacramento, CA 95838
Ruby Roles

Abell
Branches and Twigs
5139 Hacienda Drive
San Antonio, TX 78233-5424
Nancy L. King, Editor
Pub. *Branches and Twigs*, quarterly, $7.00 per year subscription; (includes Abell, Abel, Able families in America from 1630)

Abendroth
Franz Abendroth Proposed Family Organization
1538 N.W. 60th
Seattle, WA 98107

Phone (206) 784-3644
Kathi Judkins Abendroth

Aber (see Likes)

Abercrombie (see MacDuff, Sneed)

Abercromby (see MacDuff)

Abernethy (see Fraser, Leslie, MacDuff)

Able (see Abel, Abell)

Ables
*William Ables Family Organization
Rt. 4, Box 365B
Fayetteville, TN 37334
Phone (615) 433-6812
Bobby N. Edwards
Pub. *Newsletter* (includes Ables of Lincoln County, Tennessee)

Abney (see Brooks)

Abott
Myron Abott Family Descendants
Shaw's Florist
5370 Nugget Road
Fair Oaks, CA 95628
Mary Lou Shaw

Abscher (see Abshire)

Abshar (see Abshire)

Abshear (see Abshire)

Absheer (see Abshire)

Absheir (see Abshire)

Absher (see Abshire)

Abshier (see Abshire)

Abshir (see Abshire)

Abshire
*The K.A.R.D. Files
19305 S.E. 243rd Place
Kent, WA 98042-4820
Phone (206) 432-1659
Judy K. Dye, Owner
Pub. *Abshire Abstracts*, irregularly, $6.00–$7.00 per volume (Washington residents add 8.2% sales tax); (includes Abcher, Abscher, Abshar, Abshear, Absheer, Absheir, Absher, Abshier, Abshir, Abshur, Apshire, Ipsher)

Abshur (see Abshire)

Acer
*Acer/Acker Family Reunion
1092 Loncar Drive
Rochester Hills, MI 48307-4689
Phone (810) 651-5153
Virginia Platter
(includes descendants of William Acer

and Dorothy Adams, Pittsford, New
York, 1791 to the present)

Acheson (see Kunkel)

Achmutie (see MacDuff)

Achmuty (see MacDuff)

Acker (see Acer)

Acker
*Acker Family Research
11 Hialeah Circle
Odessa, TX 79761
Phone (915) 366-7816
Peggy Elmore
Pub. *Profiles of the Acker Family*

Ackerman (see Covert)

Ackerman
*David Ackerman Descendants (1662)
   Newsletter*
806 Phelps Road
Franklin Lakes, NJ 07417
Phone (201) 444-7888
Charles E. Post, President
Pub. *David Ackerman Descendants
   (1662) Newsletter*, three times per year
$10.00 per year membership

Ackerson
*Association of Ackerson/Eckerson
   Descendants, Inc.
98 East Avenue
Akron, NY 14001
Phone (716) 542-2418
John I. Eckerson, President
Pub. *The Ackerson/Eckerson Newsletter*,
   two to three times per year (includes
   descendants of Thomas Hugesson and
   Sara Brout, married prior to 1644)
$7.00 per year membership

Ackles
Ackles of Ohio
550 West
Rt. 1, Box 165B
Carthage, IN 46115
R. Willey; D. Willey
Pub. *Ackles of Ohio*, annually, free

Ackroyd (see MacDuff)

Acland (see MacDuff)

Acomb
Acomb Reunion
10498 County Road 46
Dansville, NY 14437
Phone (716) 335-5173
Alice M. Acomb

Acree
Acree Foundation, Inc.
3 East Avenue
Lisbon Falls, ME 04252
Phone (207) 353-4900
John L. Stevens

Acres (see Rathbun)

Acton (see Kunkel, Likes)

Acum (see Exum)

Adair (see Hamblin, Maxwell)

Adair
*Charles Newton Adair Family
   Organization
629 West Sixth Drive
Mesa, AZ 85202
Phone (602) 964-7764
Charles S. Adair, Genealogist

Adairs (see Gunnin)

Adam (see Adams, MacDuff)

Adams (see Folk Family Surname
   Exchange, Acer, Barnes, Bowman,
   Likens, Lush, MacDuff, Reeder, Ross,
   Smith)

Adams
*Adams/Powell Reunion
15445 Cobalt #172
Sylmar, CA 91342
Phone (818) 362-3368
Margaret James
(includes descendants of Alexander and
   Kaziah (Neff) Adams of Mansfield,
   Ohio, Jesse and Annie (Husted)
   Adams, and Alonzo and Charlotte
   (Eldred) Powell of southern Michigan)

Adams
Adams Reunion
939 South Comet Avenue
Panama City, FL 32404
Lowell F. Adams, Editor
Pub. *Adams*, quarterly, donation for
   subscription
Reunion in Eufala, Alabama

Adams
The Adams Family Association, Inc.
1294 West Nancy Creek Drive, N.E.
Atlanta, GA 30319-1690
Phone (404) 457-6564
L. H. Adams, Editor
Pub. *The Adams Family Chronicle*,
   quarterly, donation for subscription

Adams
Now and Then
229 South Ridgeland
Oak Park, IL 60302
Phone (708) 383-5652
Robert Adams Gaebler
Pub. *Now and Then*, three times per year,
   free to family members; (includes
   Adams)

Adams
*Adams' Family Reunion
11720 Morrison Road
New Orleans, LA 70128

Phone (504) 242-0324
Patsy White, Chairperson/Historian
$7.00 per year membership; reunion
   every two to three years

Adams
*Christopher Adams Family
   Organization
6 Laurel Road
Brunswick, ME 04011
Phone (207) 725-7615
Clayton R. Adams

Adams
*Adams Database
409 Birchwood Avenue
White Bear Lake, MN 55110
Elizabeth Adams Ebbott, Publisher
(includes descendants of Col. John
   Emery Adams (1780–1840) of Maine,
   Ohio and Iowa; family descends from
   Robert Adams (1602–1682) of
   Newbury, Massachusetts)

Adams
Adams Addenda
9514 Minerva Avenue
Saint Louis, MO 63114-3912
Dorothy Amburgey Griffith, Editor
Pub. *Adams Addenda*, SASE for content
   list of 25 volumes published 1971–
   1995, back issues available

Adams
Adams/Bannister Descendants of North
   Carolina
16064 Strawn Road
La Pine, OR 97739-9762
Bessie Adams

Adams
*Folk Family
PO Box 52048
Knoxville, TN 37950-2048
Hester E. Stockton, Owner; Sarah Jane
   Adams, Editor
Pub. *Adams Families*, quarterly, $15.00
   per year subscription, $5.00 per issue;
   (includes Adam)

Adams
*Mountain Press
4503 Anderson Pike
PO Box 400
Signal Mountain, TN 37377-0400
Phone (423) 886-6369; (423) 886-5312
   FAX
James L. Douthat, Owner
(Adams family of Tennessee)

Adams
*George Rosil Adams Family
   Organization
1599 Monaco Circle
Salt Lake City, UT 84121
Phone (801) 278-7708
Eldon B. Tucker, Jr., M.D.
(includes family originally from West
   Virginia)

Adamson (see Shaw)

Adamson
*The K.A.R.D. Files
19305 S.E. 243rd Place
Kent, WA 98042-4820
Phone (206) 432-1659
Judy K. Dye, Owner
Pub. *Adamson Ancestry*, irregularly,
$6.00–$7.00 per volume (Washington
residents add 8.2% sales tax)

Adarton (see Additon)

Aday
Aday to Remember
11794 Melody Drive
Northglenn, CO 80234-2918
Mildred Y. Aday
Pub. *Aday to Remember*

Adcock (see Jones)

Addie (see MacDuff)

Addington
*The Addington Association
12407 Millstream Drive
Bowie, MD 20715
Phone (301) 464-0435
Jerry Sue Bowersox, Editor
Pub. *The Addington Newsletter*, three
times per year
$5.00 per year membership (1 August to
31 July)

Addington
*Mountain Press
4503 Anderson Pike
PO Box 400
Signal Mountain, TN 37377-0400
Phone (423) 886-6369; (423) 886-5312
FAX
James L. Douthat, Owner
(Addington family of Addington in U.S.
and England)

Addington
Addington Family
615 Windrift Drive
Earlysville, VA 22936
Norman P. Addington, President
(includes descendants of William
Addington (ca 1750–1805) of Virginia)
Reunion

Additon
*Additon Family Reunion
9 Sutton Place
Lewiston, ME 04240
Phone (207) 786-6133; (207) 782-3072
Douglas I. Hodgkin, Secretary
(includes descendants of Thomas
Additon (1794–1869) and Ann Beals
(1802–1871) of Leeds, Maine, and
descendants of Samuel Adarton and
Mary Teague of Hingham,
Massachusetts, who were married in
1723)

Addiville
Addiville-Chappel-Lyell-Lyle Family
Association
2306 Westgate
Houston, TX 77019
Phone (713) 529-2333
Harold Helm
$25.00 plus pedigree and family group
sheets

Adelmann (see Harting)

Adie (see MacDuff)

Adkins (see Bloss, Frasher, Hatfield,
Hynton, Johnson, Wright)

Adnauchtan (see MacDuff)

Adolph (see Blossom Press)

Aencalade (see Blossom Press)

Aery (see Arey)

Agard (see Storrs)

Ager (see Taylor)

Agner (see Eygner)

Agnew (see Douglas)

Agnew
Agnew Association of America
PO Box 691
Petaluma, CA 94953
Phone (707) 762-7473
A. W. Agnew, Convener
Pub. *Agnewsletter*, quarterly
$15.00 per year membership

Ahwahka (see Elmo)

Aiello (see Gratta)

Aignor (see Eygner)

Aiken (see Davis)

Ainger
Ainger, Anger(s), Angier, Auger, Manter
Information Exchange
PO Box 224
Englewood, FL 34295-0224
Mary Anger

Ainsley (see Ansley)

Ainsworth (see Onsager)

Ainsworth
Ainsworth/Gunter Family Reunion
2101 Mike Street
PO Box 844
Winnsboro, LA 71295
Phone (318) 435-6267
Lucille D. Ainsworth, Editor and
Publisher

Pub. *Ainsworth Trading Post*,
semiannually (April 30 and October
31)
$25.00 per year U.S. membership, $35.00
per year foreign membership

Airth (see Graham)

Airwin (see Irwin)

Aister (see Auster)

Aker (see The Memorial Foundation of
the Germanna Colonies)

Akers (see CTC Family Association,
Frasher, Marty)

Akers
Akers-Helm(s)-Malone-Andrews Family
Association
2306 Westgate
Houston, TX 77019
Phone (713) 529-2333
Harold Helm
$25.00 plus pedigree and family group
sheets

Akert
*Akert Family Genealogy Research
Organization
3784 Grove Avenue
Palo Alto, CA 94303
Phone (415) 494-8868; E-mail:
krallen@townsend.com
Kenneth R. Allen
(PAF™ database includes ancestors and
descendants of John Henry Akert
(1836–1907) of Switzerland and Utah)
Non-tax-deductible donation to defray
costs

Akeson (see Marty)

Albaugh (see Stoner)

Albert
Albert Family Newsletter
Rt. 1, Box 41
Houston, MO 65483-9702
Phone (417) 967-2622
Millie Albert Preissle, Editor/Publisher
Pub. *Albert Family Newsletter*,
bimonthly, $8.00 per year subscription,
unlimited free queries; (includes
Albert, Alberts, Allbert, worldwide)

Alberti (see Blossom Press)

Alberts (see Albert)

Albertson (see Album)

Albertson
*Albertson Family Organization
9443 Springville Road
East Otto, NY 14729
Phone (716) 257-9488
Carrie M. Dudley

Albison
*Albison/Albiston Family History
  Association
4065 Berrywood Drive
Eugene, OR 97404-4061
James R. Brann, Family Representative
(PAF™ data bank on MAC™ computer
  includes England to Canada (Ontario)
  to U. Free information exchange)

Albiston (see Albison)

Alborn (see MacDuff)

Alborne (see MacDuff)

Albourn (see MacDuff)

Albourne (see MacDuff)

Albrecht (see Albright)

Albrechtsen (see McCune)

Albright (see The Memorial Foundation
  of the Germanna Colonies, Likes)

Albright
*The Descendants of Joseph Albright/
  Albrecht
1301 Bradford Road
Oreland, PA 19075-2414
Phone (215) 836-4727
Dale E. Berger, Publisher
(includes descendants of Joseph Albright
  who arrived in Philadelphia in 1727
  and settled in what is now Macungie
  Township, Lehigh County,
  Pennsylvania)

Albritton (see Blossom Press)

Albrook (see Holbrook)

Album
*Coryell County, Texas, Research
1408 Leon
Gatesville, TX 76528
Phone (817) 865-7943
Bobbie Watson Ross, Publisher
(includes research and exchange on
  Album, Albertson, Anderson, Barnes,
  Beavers, Bevers, Burrow, Bynum,
  Clack, Clark, Farrar, Farris, Gilbert,
  Halverson, Higgins, Johnson, Maddox,
  McFarland, Meeks, Miles, Moore,
  Nash, Render, Ross, Russell, Savage,
  Smith, Standifer, Tacker, Taylor,
  Thomas, Thornton and Watson)

Alburn (see MacDuff)

Alden (see Heath, Rutherford)

Alden
*Alden Kindred of America, Inc.
105 Alden Street
PO Box 2754
Duxbury, MA 02331-2754
Phone (617) 934-9092

Ellen Hagney, Director
Pub. *Alden Kindred Newsletter*, annually;
  (includes descendants of John and
  Priscilla Alden)
$10.00 per year membership for
  descendants

Alden
*Alden Kindred of America, Inc.
18 Martin's Cove Road
Hingham, MA 02331-2754
Phone (617) 749-9092
Alicia C. Williams, Genealogist
(includes descendants of Pilgrims John
  and Priscilla (Mullins) Alden)
$15.00 application fee, minimum $10.00
  per year membership

Alderson
*Alderson Cousins
127 Topaz Way
San Francisco, CA 94131-2535
David G. Fridley, Editor
Pub. *Alderson Roots and Branches*,
  quarterly
$7.50 per year U.S. membership, $13.00
  per year foreign membership

Alderston (see Hay)

Aldrich (see Heath, Main, Woodrow)

Aldrich
Aldrich Family Organization
535 North Luce Road
Ithaca, MI 48847
Mary E. Strouse

Aldrich
Aldrich Association
716 Sheldon Road
Shortsville, NY 14548
Edna Aldrich, Secretary
(includes Anderson, Bailey, Bard,
  Criswell, Eichler, Frampton, Genung,
  Kober, McClure, Stilson and Webber)

Aldridge (see Gant, Stewart)

Alesich (see Blossom Press)

Alexander (see Baker, Brawley, Collette,
  Jamison, Lush, Mitchell)

Alexander
*Alexander Surname Organization
7705 Ensley Drive, S.W.
Huntsville, AL 35802-2845
Phone (205) 883-0207
Thomas W. Burns

Alexander
Wade-Smith Genealogy Service
Rt. 7, Box 52
Llano, TX 78643
Evelyn Wade
Pub. *Alexander Kin*, quarterly, $5.00 per
  year subscription

Alexander
Alexander
1221 Candice Court
Mesquite, TX 75149
Mary L. House, Editor
Pub. *Alexander*, quarterly, $15.00 per
  year subscription

Alexander
*Topp of the Line
1304 West Cliffwood Court
Spokane, WA 99218-2917
Phone (509) 467-2299
Bette Butcher Topp, Owner/Operator
Pub. *Alexander Agenda*, irregularly,
  $5.50 per issue plus $2.00 postage and
  handling

Alford
*The Alford American Family
  Association
PO Box 1586
Florissant, MO 63031-1586
Phone (314) 831-8648; E-mail:
  72154.1610@compuserve.com
Gilbert K. Alford, Jr., Executive Director
Pub. *AAFA Action*, quarterly; (includes
  Alfred, Alvord, Halford, Olford and
  100+ variations, all locations and time
  periods)
$5.00 registration fee, $16.00 per year
  membership; weekend-long annual
  reunion on the second weekend of
  October, various locations

Alfred (see Alford, MacDuff)

Alger (see Brown)

Algero (see Blossom Press)

Alghero (see Blossom Press)

Alim (see Elam)

Aliot (see Elliott)

Allan (see Allen)

Allan
Lineages
PO Box 1264
Huntington, WV 25714
Pub. *Allan/Allen Family Workbook*,
  semiannually, queries accepted

Allardyce (see Graham)

Allayne (see Allen)

Albert (see Albert)

Allee
Nicholas Allee Descendants
PO Box 347
Friendswood, TX 77546
Phone (713) 482-2839
Ginger Rae Allee
Pub. *Allees All Around, Includes Alley,
  Ally, Allie, Alyea*, quarterly, $15.00 per
  year subscription

Allen (see Folk Family Surname
Exchange, Allan, Corson, Dockery,
Donald, Emery, Franciscus, Gant,
Goodenow, Heath, Mackay, McCune,
McNees, Miller, Nelson, West, Wright)

Allen
Allen
4604 Virginia Loop Road, Apartment
3156-G
Montgomery, AL 36116-4739
Lisa R. Franklin
Pub. *Allen*, quarterly, $10.00 per year
subscription

Allen
Allen Surname Organization
PO Box 505
Los Angeles, CA 90053
Glenn Lukas

Allen
Oak Leaf Publishing
22 Creek Road, #64
Irvine, CA 91714
Pub. *Allen Family Newsletter*, bimonthly,
$10.00 per year subscription

Allen
*William Berry Allen Family
Organization
Orson William Allen Family
Organization
3784 Grove Avenue
Palo Alto, CA 94303
Phone (415) 494-8868; E-mail:
krallen@townsend.com
Kenneth R. Allen
(PAF™ database includes ancestors and
descendants of William Berry Allen
(1882–1955) and Rebecca May
Roundy (1885–1977) of Utah; also
Orson William Allen (1851–1928) of
Utah)
Non-tax-deductible donation to defray
costs

Allen
*The Allens of Little Egypt
8439 Terradell Street
Pico Rivera, CA 90660
Phone (310) 923-7085
Corben Elko Allen, Editor
(includes Allen, Allan, Allin and Allon
descendants of Robert Allin (1664
Ulster County, Northern Ireland–1770
Virginia), through his sons Rhoda/
Rhody (1742 Charles County,
Maryland–1820 Jefferson County,
Illinois) who married Mary Emile
Ransom and Lucinda Overby, George
(1751–) of Pennsylvania and Sumner
County, Tennessee, and Reuben of
Shenandoah County, Virginia)

Allen
*The Allen Family Circle
4906 Ridgeway
Kansas City, MO 64133-2545
Lois T. Allen, Editor

Pub. *The Allen Family Circle*, annually,
$2.30 per issue postpaid, queries
printed

Allen
Elvius Allen Family Organization
720 Curratuck Drive
Raleigh, NC 27609
William Allen

Allen
*Folk Family
PO Box 52048
Knoxville, TN 37950-2048
Hester E. Stockton, Owner; Rachel Allen,
Editor
Pub. *Allen Families*, quarterly, $15.00 per
year subscription, $5.00 per issue;
(includes Allan, Allayne, Allyn)

Allen
*John Allen Family Organization
PO Box 8072
Longview, TX 75607-8072
Ben R. Reynolds

Allen
*Andrew Bickmore Allen and Susannah
Preece Allen Family Organization
Andrew Lee Allen and Clarinda Knapp
(1794) Family Organization
2015 North 1000 East
North Logan, UT 84321
Phone (801) 753-1458
Kaylene A. Griffin, Genealogist
Donation for membership

Allen
Joseph Stewart Allen Family
Organization
1852 East 3990 South, Apartment B
Salt Lake City, UT 84124
(includes descendants of Joseph Stewart
Allen 1806 and Lucy Diantha Morley
1815)

Allen
*Allens of the Southern States
4865 152nd Place, S.E.
Bellevue, WA 98006-3604
Phone (206) 641-1069
Norma C. Miller
(includes descendants of Robert Allen of
New Kent County, Virginia, in 1698)

Allen
*The Family History of George A. Allen
and Jane Campbell
2216 26th Avenue
Cameron, WI 54822
Phone (715) 234-3392
Richard A. Huehn, Publisher

Allen
*Descendants of George Hunt and Mary
Ogilvie Allen
5886 Scenic Drive
West Bend, WI 53095
William A. Allen
(includes descendants of George H. Allen

(1780 North Carolina–), to Tennessee
1803)
Reunion every 5 years

Alley (see Frasher)

Allin (see Allen)

Allis (see Ellis)

Allison (see Macpherson)

Allison
*Allison Family Reunion
Rt. 1, Box 28
Newbury, IN 47449
Phone (812) 863-7324
Wana Hasler, Family Genealogist
(includes descendants of Joseph Allison
(1792 Pennsylvania–1873 Daviess
County, Indiana) and Mary Ragsdale
(1800 South Carolina–1869 Daviess
County, Indiana))

Allison
*Allison Family Association
10095 County Road 5120
Rolla, MO 65401
Phone (314) 341-3549; (573) 364-5310;
E-mail: sandy@rollanet.org
Sandy Allison, Chairman
Pub. *Allison History*, annually;
Newsletter, quarterly; (includes
descendants of Alfred Allison (1808–)
of Nicholas County, Kentucky; Greene
County, Indiana; Vermilion County,
Illinois; Bourbon County, Kentucky;
and Phelps County, Missouri; also
allied lines of Arthur, Baker, Hendrick,
Leonard and Putnam)
Biennial reunion on the third weekend of
July in odd-numbered years

Allison
*COMGENES
209 North Bayard Street (for UPS only)
PO Box 1581
Silver City, NM 88062
Barbara Holley Rock, Owner
(includes Allison, Blackburn(e), Bryan(t),
Harper, Holley, Officer, Sharp(e),
Tabor, Tubb(s) Clearinghouse)

Allison
*Allison and Allied Families Association
3534 Bear Hollow Road
Whites Creek, TN 37189
Phone (615) 876-0644
Vickey Setters, Family Historian
Pub. *Traces in the Sand*, quarterly
$10.00 per year membership; annual
reunion in July at the Harmony
Primitive Baptist Church, Eva,
Alabama

Allison
*Family Research
11 West 1780 North
Orem, UT 84057
Phone (801) 224-9315

Kelli Clark Sanders
(includes research on Samuel Allison
    (1811 Christian, Kentucky–) and
    Nancy Porterfield (1828 Pennsylvania–),
    James Dexter Clark (1854 Illinois–)
    and Gula Elma Pearce, John
    Porterfield (1795 Pennsylvania–) and
    Elizabeth Thompson (1811–), Starling
    Hill (1803 Kentucky–) and Elizabeth
    Bassett (ca 1803–), Jacob Hadley
    (1800 North Carolina–) and Massie
    Bray (1806 Indiana–))

Allmon (see Chaffin)

Allon (see Allen)

Alloway
Alloway Family Association
855 Greenway Court
Derby, KS 67037
H. Jay Alloway

Allred (see Holden)

Allred
Allred Family Organization, Inc.
6726 South 1405 East
Salt Lake City, UT 84121
Phone (801) 943-5049
Gary D. Allred, President
Reunion

Allred
Ruben Warren Allred Family
    Organization
1852 East 3990 South, Apartment B
Salt Lake City, UT 84124
(includes descendants of Ruben Warren
    Allred 1815 and Lucy Ann Butler
    1814)

Allsop (see Alsop)

Allsop
Allsop Ancestors
2035 Prince Drive
Naples, FL 33942
Phone (813) 566-2246
Elizabeth A. Grissinger, Assistant Editor
Pub. *Allsop Ancestors*, quarterly, $5.25
    per year subscription, published in
    England

Allsopp (see Alsop)

Allstatt (see Allstott)

Allston (see Austin)

Allstott
Allstott/Allstatt/Altstadt/Alstadt
6537 Hummingbird Street
Ventura, CA 93003
Phone (805) 650-3747
Jerry L. Allstott, Publisher

Allsup (see Alsop)

Allton (see Alton)

Allton
Allton-Alton Association
614 North Plum Street
Wellington, KS 67152-3559
Lois Burke Allton
Pub. *Allton-Alton Association Newsletter*,
    semiannually
$2.00 per year membership

Allumbaugh
Allumbaugh-Alumbaugh Newsletter
PO Box 122
Harrington, WA 99134-0122
Donna Alumbaugh
Pub. *Allumbaugh-Alumbaugh Newsletter*,
    annually, $3.00 per year subscription

Ally (see Cian)

Allyn (see Allen)

Almy
*Almy Family
17835 S.W. Shasta Trail
Tualatin, OR 97062
Phone (503) 691-2090
Merwin F. Almy
Pub. *Almy Family Newsletter*, quarterly,
    contribution for subscription; (includes
    descendants of William Almy,
    immigrant of about 1628)

Alpach (see Merier)

Alrich (see Alrichs)

Alrichs
*Peter Alrichs Foundation
Alricks (Alrich) Family Organization
248 Upper Gulph Road
Radnor, PA 19087
Phone (215) 688-7532
William M. Alrich, Executive Secretary
Pub. *Newsletter*, irregularly; (includes
    descendants of Peter Alrichs (–1697
    New Castle, Delaware) and his wife,
    Marie Wessels)
$25.00 per year membership

Alricks (see Alrichs)

Alsbrook (see Holbrook)

Alsebrook (see Holbrook)

Alsep (see Alsop)

Alsept (see Alsop)

Alsip (see Alsop)

Alsobrook (see Holbrook)

Alsop
*Alsop's Tables
Rt. 1, Box 433-B (2515 Cayce Road)
Byhalia, MS 38611
Jerry David Alsup, Publisher
(includes Allsop, Allsopp, Allsup, Alsep,
    Alsept, Alsip, Alsopp, Alsup, with

allied lines: Blackwell, Crooke, Feake,
    Hazard, McIntosh, Rossiter, Sackett,
    Simpkins, Underhill, Wandell, Wardell
    and Wright)

Alsopp (see Alsop)

Alstadt (see Allstott, Dietlein)

Alsup (see Alsop)

Altemose
*Altemose Family Database
1301 Bradford Road
Oreland, PA 19075-2414
Phone (215) 836-4727
Dale E. Berger, Publisher
(includes Altemus, Altemose and Altimus
    settlers of Monroe and Indiana
    counties, Pennsylvania, descendants of
    Hans Peter Altomus who arrived in
    America in 1740)

Altemus (see Altemose)

Alten
*Alten-Von Alten
Box 517
Addison, IL 60101
Phone (630) 543-7899
James Bestman, Publisher
(includes the Hannover, Germany Von
    Alten family and the Lathwehren,
    Germany, Alten family)

Altenbach
*Altenbach/Altenback/Altenbaugh
    Family Clearinghouse
6330 Blackfoot Drive
Helena, MT 59601
Alene Altenbach Stoner
(includes large database of Altenbach,
    with various spellings)

Altenback (see Altenbach)

Altenbaugh (see Altenbach)

Altimus (see Altemose)

Altomus (see Altemose, Serfass)

Alton (see Allton)

Alton
*Alton, Allton, Aulton Family
    Association
15510 Laurel Ridge Road
Dumfries, VA 22026
Phone (703) 670-4842; E-mail:
    ccalton@aol.com; website: http://
    members.aol.com/altonnews/
    aaaafn.htm
Cecil C. Alton, Publisher
Pub. *Newsletter*, quarterly; (database
    includes 12,500 related descendants)
$15.00 per year membership

Altstadt (see Allstott, Dietlein)

Alumbaugh (see Allumbaugh)

Alvis
*Alvis Database
PO Box 425
Hydro, OK 73048
Edward Arthur Alvis and Katherine Alvis
  Patterson, Editors
Pub. *Alvis Exchange*, quarterly, $15.00
  subscription for six issues

Alvord (see Alford)

Alyot (see Elliott)

Amadon
Amadon/Amidon Family Reunion
PO Box 361
Island Pond, VT 05846
Irma Young, Secretary

Amazeen (see Gerade)

Amberger (see The Memorial
  Foundation of the Germanna Colonies,
  see Amburgey)

Ambergey (see Amburgey)

Amburger (see The Memorial
  Foundation of the Germanna Colonies)

Amburgey (see Dean)

Amburgey
*Amburgey Family Association
HC 81, Box 362
Mallie, KY 41836
Phone (606) 642-3842
Lucille Combs
Pub. *Amburgey News*, $3.00 per year
  subscription; (includes Amberger,
  Ambergey, Amburgy, Burgy from
  1650, from Germany to the U.S.)
$4.00 per year membership for families

Amburgy (see Amburgey)

Amdahl
Amdahl Family Records
Fillmore, ND 58333
Sena Amdahl Rendahl
Pub. *Amdahl Family Records*

Amerski (see Hamersky)

Ames (see Eames)

Ames
Ghost of the Past
PO Box 526
Christoval, TX 76935-0526
Jim C. Ames
Pub. *Ghost of the Past, An Ames Family
  Newsletter (Ames, Eames, Amis, Ems)*,
  quarterly, $20.00 per year subscription

Amick (see Emerick)

Amick
*John Amick Family Organization
PO Box 311
Bedford, WY 83112
Phone (307) 883-2730
Jerry Mower

Amidon (see Amadon)

Amis (see Ames)

Ammons
Ammons
3800 South County Road 1185
Midland, TX 79706-6429
Phone (915) 684-6955
Joan Cervenka Cobb, Genealogist and
  Author
(includes research on Ammons,
  Armstrong, Cervenka, Cobb (Kopp),
  Coppedge, Croskery, Crumpton, Isbell,
  Kernodle, Lain, Machu, Ray, Robison,
  Schackelford, Schumacher and
  Wilson)

Amours (see MacDuff)

Amsbaugh
Any Amsbaugh Ancestors?
PO Box 1035
North Highlands, CA 95660-1035
Phone (916) 991-4165
Sally Seaman Williams, Editor
Pub. *Any Amsbaugh Ancestors?*,
  irregularly, $5.00 per issue

Amsbaugh
Amsbaugh Family Association
Rt. 1, Box 23
Menlo, IA 50164
Sherry Foresman
Pub. *Amsbaugh Family Association*

Ancalade (see Blossom Press)

Ancar (see Blossom Press)

Anderpont (see Johnson)

Anders (see Andis)

Andersdatter
*Anne Marie Andersdatter Family
  Organization
1623 North Harrison
Pocatello, ID 83204
Phone (208) 232-3385
Wanda M. Jorgensen

Anderson (see Blossom Press, Folk
  Family Surname Exchange, Album,
  Aldrich, Bosher, Chattan, Corson,
  Davis, Emery, Garner, Goodenow,
  Lush, McCune, Oney, Ross, Scott,
  Williams, Wright)

Anderson
*Grant Larson Anderson Family
  Organization
24182 El Tiradore Circle

Mission Viejo, CA 92691
Phone (714) 837-8916
Robert Dean Bledsoe

Anderson
Clan Anderson Society, Ltd.
1947 Kensington High Street
Lilburn, GA 30247
Phone (404) 972-6804
James N. Anderson, Membership
  Chairman

Anderson
Courier Publications
PO Box 1284
Natchitoches, LA 71458-1284
Annette Carpenter Womack
Pub. *Anderson Family Courier*, quarterly,
  $12.50 per year subscription

Anderson
Anderson's Reunion
223 West Katy
Cushing, OK 74023
William Anderson

Anderson
Anderson Family Newsletter
332 Shady Lane
Azle, TX 76020
Peggy Teague Logan
Pub. *Anderson Family Newsletter*,
  quarterly, $20.00 per year subscription,
  free queries

Andes (see Andis)

Andes
Andes Family Reunion
1240 Mayflower
Ridgecrest, CA 93555
Phone (619) 375-8260
Bonnie Andes

Andess (see Andis)

Andis
Andis Ancestry
13659 East Park Street
Whittier, CA 90601
Cheska Wheatley
Pub. *Andis Ancestry (Andes, Anders,
  Andris, Andess)*, quarterly, free to
  contributors, $15.00 per year
  subscription

Andison (see Ross)

Andlauer
*Andlauer Family Association
3929 Milton Drive
Independence, MO 64055-4043
Phone (816) 373-5309
Robert L. Grover, President
(includes descendants of Anthony
  "Anton" Andlauer (1818 Kappel am
  Rhein, Germany–) and Lenora
  Bauman (1818 Kappel am Rhein,
  Germany–))

Andreani
*Andreani Surname Organization
3 Brazill Lane
Whitehall, MT 59759
Phone (406) 287-3369
Lindia Roggia Lovshin

Andreossi
Andreossi/Giorgi/Gemigani/Ungarretti/
  Prucheti/Pera Italian Collaboration
PO Box 15926
Austin, TX 78761
H. J. Andreozzi

Andrew (see Ross)

Andrews (see Akers, Barnes, Burnham,
  Golding, McConnell, McCune, Ross)

Andrews
*Wirth and Associates
9524 West Pomona Drive
Baton Rouge, LA 70815
Phone (504) 925-8878
Dot Wise Wirth, Editor
Pub. *Frederick Andrews Kith & Kindred*,
  quarterly, $25.00 per year subscription
(database includes all Andrews in
  America prior to 1840 in addition to
  descendants of Frederick Andrews (ca
  1800–1845))
Annual reunion on the Saturday
  following the 4th of July in Cuthbert,
  Randolph County, Georgia

Andrews
*Kinseeker Publications
5697 Old Maple Trail
PO Box 184
Grawn, MI 49637
E-mail: AB064@taverse.lib.mi.us
Victoria Wilson, Editor
Pub. *The Family Series: Andrews*,
  irregularly, $6.50 per issue

Andrews
Andrews-Ragsdale-Malone-Poindexter
  Family Association
2306 Westgate
Houston, TX 77019
Phone (713) 529-2333
Harold Helm
$25.00 plus pedigree and family group
  sheets

Andris (see Andis)

Andrus (see Bouton)

Andson (see MacDuff)

Angelf (see Angeli)

Angeli
Angeli/Angelf Family Organization
Rt. 3, Box 123
Trinity, NC 27370
Cheryl Burrow

Angell
*Thomas Angell Family Association
35 Hodsell Street
Cranston, RI 02910
Phone (401) 467-7594
Mrs. Harold P. Williams, Registrar
$1.00 per year membership, $25.00 life
  membership

Angelo (see Blossom Press)

Anger (see Ainger)

Angier (see Ainger)

Anglada (see Blossom Press)

Angley (see Ansley)

Angus (see MacInnes)

Ankers
*The Ankers of Virginia
5941 Oakdale Road
McLean, VA 22101
Phone (703) 536-5875
Robert E. Ankers, Publisher
(includes descendants of immigrants to
  Maryland in 1630)

Annal (see MacDuff)

Annesley (see Ansley)

Ansardi (see Blossom Press)

Ansel
*Ansel Surname Organization
PO Box 304
Reamstown, PA 17567
Phone (215) 267-2140
Terry Lee Ansel
(includes Ansel from 1752 to the present
  in Lancaster County, Pennsylvania,
  Loudoun County, Virginia, and Ohio;
  also Young from 1790 to the present in
  Lancaster County, Pennsylvania)

Ansley
*Ansley Family Association
1800 Forest Drive
Camden, SC 29020
Phone (803) 432-8075
Bill Ansley, Publications Committee
Pub. *Ansley Reunion Newsletter*,
  semiannually, $5.00 per year
  subscription; (includes Ainsley,
  Angley, Annesley, Ansley, etc.,
  families of North America)

Anson (see MacDuff)

Anstruther (see MacDuff)

Anthes
Lake Creek Pioneer Family Picnic
5500 Lost Creek Road
Eagle Point, OR 97524
Phone (503) 826-7213
Shirley Stone

(includes Anthes, Baldwin, Bradley,
  Charley, Conley, Downing, Elder,
  Farlow, Fox, Gano, Gardner, Grissom,
  Hanley, Heckathorn, Hoefft, Klingle,
  Messal, Meyer, Miller, Moore,
  Nichols, Nickell, Nussbaum, Nygren,
  Pankey, Peck, Plymale, Ragsdale,
  Randles, Ratrie, Short, Sidley,
  Swingle, Tonn, Tyrell, Walch,
  Wilkerson and Wyant families)

Anthony (see Folk Family Surname
  Exchange, MacDuff)

Antley
*Southern Families
12241 Lakeview Drive
Edinboro, PA 16412
Phone (814) 734-7220
Eugene Brevard Antley
(researching Antley, Brevard, Brewton,
  Gambrel and Pevey)

Apáthy
*Apáthy (nagytoti and Voldorf-Dombosi,
  Transylvania/Hungary) Ancestors
  Association (AAA)
191 Selma Avenue
Englewood, FL 34223-3830
Phone (941) 474-4774; E-mail:
  LesApathy@aol.com
László Béla Apáthy, III (USAF Res.)
Pub. *Apáthy Ancestors (Transylvania,
  Hungary & Beyond)* (includes Apáthy
  and Apáti (1270–present), Sebesy and
  Sebesi (1400–present), Ugron (1480–
  present))
Reunion

Apáti (see Apáthy)

Apgar
Apgar Family Reunion
416 Runyon Avenue
Middlesex, NJ 08846
George Apgar, Jr.

Apgar
*Apgar Association
3632 U.S. Highway 22
Somerville, NJ 08876-3455
Wayne Dilts, Editor
Pub. *Apgar Association Family
  Newsletter*, annually

Aplegarth (see Applegate)

Aplegate (see Applegate)

Apperson
Apperson/Epperson Family Organization
Rt. 3, Box 123
Trinity, NC 27370
Cheryl Burrow

Applebe (see Applebee)

Applebee (see Appleby)

Applebee
Applebee Family Data
942 Hatch Street
Cincinnati, OH 45202
Phone (513) 369-0957
W. Thomas Applebee
Pub. *AppleB Family Director*, annually;
(reaching out to other Applebee/bey/by
lines; especially descendants of
Thomas Applebe (1629–1690) of
Gravesend, New Amsterdam, Rye,
Connecticut, Hempstead, Long Island,
and Woodbury, Connecticut, and his
wife Elizabeth Osborne, daughter of
William Osborne of Mad Nan's Neck,
Hempstead, Long Island)

Applebey (see Applebee)

Appleby (see Applebee)

Appleby
*Appleby Heritage Association
PO Box 5069
Elko, NV 89802
Dorothy Appleby Turner
Pub. *Appleby Newsletter* (database
includes over 6,000 names)

Appleby
*Appleby/Applebee Family
PO Box 688
Goose Creek, SC 29445
Phone (803) 761-4904
Victor Paul Mertrud, Chief Researcher

Applegate
Old Time Publications
10828 Oakbrook Drive
Omaha, NE 68154-2437
Peggy Wallingford Butherus
Pub. *Applegate Ancestry (Aplegate,
Aplegarth, Applgate, etc.)*

Appler
Appler Family Newsletter
10417 New Bedford Court, N.E.
Lehigh Acres, FL 33936-7253
Phone (941) 368-6373
Charles Ross Appler, Editor/Publisher
Pub. *Appler Family Newsletter*, quarterly,
$7.00 per year subscription; (includes
Appler, Hyde, Lambert and Winter
from the mid-1700s, Frederick County,
Maryland)

Appleton (see Emery)

Applgate (see Applegate)

Appling (see Scott)

Appling
The Appling Herald
2130 Road 12, N.W.
Quincy, WA 98848
Alcenia Appling, Publisher
Pub. *The Appling Herald*

Apsher (see Abshire)

Apstan (see Edenfield)

Arbogast (see Buzzard, Kahler)

Arbogast
*Arbogast Reunion
1666 Ticonderoga Court
Titusville, FL 32796
Edward D. Arbogast, Sr.
(includes descendants of brothers,
Nichodemus and George Washington
Arbogast, great grandsons of Michael
Arbogast, Sr.)

Arbogast
*Descendants of Henry Harmon
Arbogast
1090 West Ridgeway
Hermiston, OR 97838
Bud Arbogast
Annual reunion on the second Sunday of
August at Umatilla, Oregon

Arbogast
*The Annual Arbogast Reunion
622 East Second Street
Miller, SD 57362
Wilda Arbogast Waring
(includes descendants of David Arbogast)
Annual reunion during the last week of
June at the city park in Miller, South
Dakota

Arbogast
*Arbogast Database
121 Yorktown Road
Franklin, TN 37064-3277
Phone (615) 591-7032
Charles Joseph Eades
(includes over 22,000 descendants of
Michael Arbogast (ca 1734–1812),
Revolutionary War veteran, with a few
lines to the eleventh generation)

Arbogast
*Arbogast Reunion
HCR-03, Box 1A
Millboro, VA 24460
Betty Arbogast Haddis
(includes descendants of Abraham Pryor
Arbogast, the line of the son Henry,
and allied families from the Highland
and Augusta County area of Virginia)
Annual reunion on the second Sunday of
August at Natural Chimneys, Augusta
County, Virginia

Arbogast
*Arbogast Reunion
Rt. 1, Box 73-A
Kerens, WV 26276
Phone (304) 745-4285
Henry Clarence Arbogast
(includes descendants of Samuel Henry
Arbogast, third great-grandson of
Michael Arbogast, Sr., through his son
John)
Annual reunion on the Sunday before
Labor Day at the residence of Clarence
Arbogast on Pleasant Run near Kerens
in Randolph County, West Virginia

Archbald (see Archibald)

Archbold (see Archibald)

Archdeacon (see Cian)

Archer (see Folk Family Surname
Exchange, Corson)

Archer
Archer Family Newsletter
655 Bennett Circle Drive
Cottage Grove, OR 97424
Phone (503) 942-2873
Arlene Arthur Smith
Pub. *Archer Family Newsletter*

Archer
*The Archer Association
PO Box 6233
McLean, VA 22106
Phone (703) 264-1372
George W. Archer, Editor and Publisher

Archibald (see MacPherson)

Archibald
*Clan Archibald Family Association
8 Westwood Lane
Belleair, FL 34616-1619
Elbert L. Archibald, President
Pub. *Archibald Clan Newsletter*,
quarterly; (includes Archbald,
Archbold, etc.)
$10.00 per year membership; annual
reunion on the last Sunday of June in
Morocco, Indiana

Archibald
*William Russell Archibald Family
Organization
68 West 300 North
Malad, ID 83252
Phone (208) 766-4466
Sarah A. Bush

Archibald
Archibald Clan Clearinghouse
302 South Wilson
Hillsboro, KS 67063
Peggy Goertzen
Pub. *Archibald Clan Newsletter*,
quarterly, $10.00 per year subscription

Arderne (see MacDuff)

Ardist (see MacDuff)

Ardnot (see MacDuff)

Ardnott (see MacDuff)

Ardoin (see Johnson)

Ardross (see MacDuff)

Arduthie (see MacDuff)

Arduthy (see MacDuff)

Arends
Arends, Arend Kasper (Honken) Family
   Association
Rt. 1, Box 137
Stanhope, IA 50246
Jane Arends

Arent (see Links Genealogy
   Publications)

Arents (see Links Genealogy
   Publications)

Aret (see Links Genealogy Publications)

Arewine (see Irwin)

Arey
*Peter Arey (Ihrig) Family Organization
450 West Lockwood
Webster Groves, MO 63119
Phone (314) 968-1033
Harriet Arey Davidson
(includes Arey of Rowan and Iredell
   counties, North Carolina, and Ihrig of
   Germany (Baden Mosbach area), also
   Earry, Arry, Aery in America)

Argeropulus (see Garner)

Armand (see Johnson)

Armbruster
*Armbruster-Schapbach Family
21 Wynoka Street
Pittsburgh, PA 15210
Phone (412) 881-3818
Mary Agnes Armbruster, Publisher
(includes Armbrusters from Schapbach
   Roman Catholic Parish, Wuertemberg,
   Germany, especially descendants of
   Ferdinand Armbruster, Sr., (1829 St.
   Bartholomew's, Oberwolfach, Baden,
   Germany–1871 Allegheny County,
   Pennsylvania) and Magdalena Dieterle
   (1833 Baden, Germany–), daughter of
   Ignaz and Magdalena, also related
   surnames of Hilley, Kelleher, Kunkel
   and Normile)

Armistead (see Folk Family Surname
   Exchange)

Arms
Phone (see Gerade)

Armstrong (see Blossom Press,
   Ammons, Gant, McCune, Taylor)

Armstrong
Armstrong Bulletin Board
1516 Avenida Selva
Fullerton, CA 92633-1531
Phone (714) 871-5767
Fred W. Field, Editor
Pub. *Armstrong Bulletin Board*, quarterly,
   $6.00 per year subscription, free
   sample issue, free queries

Armstrong
Armstrong Clan Society, Inc.
RR 2, Box 326
Chaplin, SC 29036
Charles H. Armstrong, Jr., President
Pub. *Armstrong Chronicles*, quarterly
   (spring, summer, fall and winter),
   $18.00 per year subscription
$20.00 per year family membership

Armstrong
*William Armstrong and Jane Penman
   and Emma Staples Organization
2421 North 750 East
Provo, UT 84604-4014
Phone (801) 375-4390
Margaret Talbot, Research Coordinator
(includes descendants of William
   Hutchinson (1826–1871) and his
   wives, Jane Penman (1828–1864) and
   Emma Staples (although not doing
   Staples research); also allied surnames
   of Hamilton, Hepburn, King, Lindsay,
   McFarlane, McVicar, McQueen,
   Stevenson and Stirling of Lanark,
   Scotland, and Glasgow)

Armstrong
*Joseph Andrew Armstrong Family
   Organization
10675 South 1120 East
Sandy, UT 84094
Phone (801) 571-2844
Milton Glynn Armstrong

Armstrong
*Armstrong Clan Association
9811 N.E. 91st Avenue
Vancouver, WA 98662-1935
Phone (206) 256-5299
William S. Armstrong, Clan Archivist
Pub. *The Armstrong News*, at least
   semiannually
$12.50 per year membership, $5.00 per
   year membership for seniors, $10.00
   entrance fee

Arnaud (see Johnson)

Arner (see Orner)

Arnest (see Earnest)

Arnett (see Ribble)

Arnett
*Arnett History
465 Sunset Terrace
Cedar Park, TX 78513
Phone (512) 259-4796
Joseph Carroll, Publisher
(includes descendants of Daniel Arnett
   (ca 1780–))

Arney
Henry Arney of Indiana Organization
1604 Longfellow Street
McLean, VA 22101
Georgia E. Benefiel

Arnold (see Folk Family Surname
   Exchange, Frantz, McConnell, Ross,
   Stoner)

Arnold
Arnold Reunion
5100 Dorset Avenue, #206
Chevy Chase, MD 20815-5461
Ann A. Hennings
(includes descendants of Lt. John
   Arnolds (1782–1863))

Arnold
Arnold Family Association of the South
2481 Eaton Gate Road
Bridgewater, MA 02324
Pub. *Arnold Family Association of the
   South Quarterly*
$11.00 per year membership

Arnold
*Kinseeker Publications
5697 Old Maple Trail
PO Box 184
Grawn, MI 49637
E-mail: AB064@taverse.lib.mi.us
Victoria Wilson, Editor
Pub. *Arnold Ancestry*, quarterly, $7.50
   per year subscription

Arnold
*Arnold Family
501 North Smith
Vinita, OK 74301
Dorothy Nix
No cost, send FGS and SASE

Arnold
Ira Seth Arnold Family Organization
6908 La Manga
Dallas, TX 75248
Phone (214) 387-2623
Dennis T. Griggs

Arnold
Arnold Family Association of the South
1655 Imperial Crown
Houston, TX 77043
Mrs. Marian C. Ledgerwood
Pub. *Arnold Family Association of the
   South Annual News*
$10.00 per year membership

Arnsbarger (see Arnsparger)

Arnsparger
*The Arnsparger Family Association
PO Box 6046
Florence, KY 41022-6046
E-mail: cpjk34a@prodigy.com
Ralph Arnsparger
(includes Arnsbarger, Arnsperger,
   Arnspiger, Ernsberger, Ernsperger,
   etc.)

Arnsperger (see Arnsparger)

Arnspiger (see Arnsparger)

Arrant (see Richerson)

Arrington
Arrington Family Organization
PO Box 249
Lanett, AL 36863
Lynda Eller
Pub. *Arrington Clearing House*

Arroll (see Hay)

Arrowsmith (see Gregor)

Arroyo
*Birchler Arroyo Associates, Inc.
3248 Greenfield Road
Berkley, MI 48072
E-mail: ArroyoR@aol.com
Rodney L. Arroyo, Publisher
(Arroyo and Veloz families from
Venezuela to the United States)
Reunion every three years, usually in
Florida and Georgia

Arry (see Arey)

Arseneau (see Johnson)

Arter (see Farver)

Arterbury (see Atterbury)

Arthur (see Sullivan Surname Exchange,
Allison, MacArthur)

Arthur
*The Arthur Family
4902 Lindsey Lane
Richmond Heights, OH 44143-2930
Phone (216) 381-2459
James A. Bowman, Jr., M.D.,
Corresponding Secretary
(Scotch-Irish descendants from
Drumbane, a sub-denomination of
Balymoghan Beg, County
Londonderry, Ireland, and Belfast from
the late eighteenth century; allied
families: Bartels, Behrens, Betzing,
Black, Booth, Bowman, Brady,
Carlisle, Chase, Doyle, Dunn, Faith,
Gilmore, Hartwig, Herrmann, Hoehn,
Hottenroth, Humes, James, Jessup,
Kelley, Kenning, Lowris, Lyttle, Maag,
McKee, McKeown, Morris, Riess,
Robinson, Rogers, Schade, Simpson,
Spence, Spissman, Starke, Steele,
Taylor, Templeton, Thomson, Tischer,
Walker and Wheway)
Biennial reunion in the Birmingham,
Alabama area

Arthur
Arthur Family Newsletter
655 Bennett Circle Drive
Cottage Grove, OR 97424
Phone (503) 942-2873
Arlene Arthur Smith
Pub. *Arthur Family Newsletter*, quarterly,
$5.00 per year subscription

Arvinge (see Irwin)

Arvon (see Irwin)

Arwine (see Irwin)

Asbell (see Isbell)

Ascher
*Mountain Press
4503 Anderson Pike
PO Box 400
Signal Mountain, TN 37377-0400
Phone (423) 886-6369; (423) 886-5312
FAX
James L. Douthat, Owner
(Ascher family in America to about
1860)

Ash
*Ash Exchange
100 Coalfield Drive
Coal City, IL 60416
Phone (815) 634-8028
Deborah Youskevtch

Ash
Ash/Ashe Exchange
139 Saunders Road
Hampton, VA 23666
Elizabeth Ash Evans

Ashbridge (see Woolley)

Ashby (see Folk Family Surname
Exchange, The Memorial Foundation
of the Germanna Colonies)

Ashby
*William Ashby Family Database
979 East 500 North
Lehi, UT 84043
Phone (801) 768-9666
Dora F. Ashby
(computer database on descendants of
William Ashby 1692 Medbourne,
Leics., England, through William
Ashby 1854 of Leicester, Leics.,
England, and later of Spanish Fork,
Utah, and his wife Sarah E. Markham;
also Samuel Ashby and his wife Emma
Priscilla Clayson)

Ashcomb (see Rutherford)

Ashcroft (see MacDuff)

Ashdown (see McCune)

Ashe (see Ash, Dockery)

Ashenfelter
*Ashenfelter of York Co., PA Association
13200 Doty Avenue, #220
Hawthorne, CA 90250
Elayne Alexander, Head of Research

Ashford (see Underwood)

Ashley (see Gant, Wright)

Ashley
*Ashley/Evans Family Organization
1132 North Tela Drive
Oklahoma City, OK 73127-4308
Phone (405) 789-2842
Pauline Carlton Fletcher, Secretary and
Genealogist
(computer database uses Quinsept™,
PAF™ and Reunion™)
Annual reunion

Ashlock (see Scott)

Ashton (see MacDuff)

Astheimer (see Lambert)

Astin (see Austin)

Atchison (see Etchison)

Atchley
*Atchley/Harden Family Association
914 Hillcrest
Enid, OK 73701
Phone (405) 234-5135
Wayne D. Atchley, D.C., Editor
Pub. *Newsletter*, annually (July);
(includes descendants of John Atchley
(1849 Clermont County, Ohio-Union
County, New Mexico), grandson of
John Atchley and Sarah Shumard of
Middlesex County, New Jersey, and
John's wife Martha "Jane" Harden
(1850 Clermont County–),
granddaughter of Peter Harden of New
Jersey)
Reunion every three years on the last
weekend of July in years evenly
divisible by three in Albuquerque,
New Mexico

Ater (see Ator)

Atha (see Athy)

Atherstone (see MacDuff)

Atherton (see MacDuff)

Atherton
*Atherton Families in Genesee County,
Michigan
5634 Caminito Isla
La Jolla, CA 92037-7224
Phone (619) 454-1769
Anne Hait Christian, Publisher

Athey (see Athy)

Athon (see Athy)

Athon
*Athon Surname Organization
4819 S.W. 18th
Topeka, KS 66604
Phone (913) 273-2569
Ms. Bobbie L. Athon

Athuson
Athuson Family Organization
535 North Luce Road
Ithaca, MI 48847
Mary E. Strouse

Athy
*The Athy Tribe of Galway
3834 Overbrook Lane
Houston, TX 77027
Phone (713) 622-1480
Lawrence F. Athy,Jr
Pub. *Newsletter of the Athy Tribe of Galway*, irregularly, about twice a year; (includes Athy, Athey, Atha, Athon descendants of Captain George Athy (1642 Galway, Ireland–1710 Maryland), and descendant branches: Creel, Dawkins, Leach, Oden, Robey, Staige, Strode and Talbot)

Atkins (see Wright)

Atkinson (see Surname Sources, Gant)

Atkinson
Atkinson Family Organization
535 North Luce Road
Ithaca, MI 48847
Mary E. Strouse

Ator
*Ator Surname Organization
11 West 300 South
Farmington, UT 84025
Phone (801) 451-2904
Bradford N. Ator, Manager
Pub. *Ater/Ator Family Newsletter*, semiannually (March and September)
Donation for membership

Atteberry (see Atterbury)

Attebery (see Atterbury)

Atterberry (see Atterbury, Corson)

Atterbury
Atterbury Family Organization
2112 East Johns Avenue
Decatur, IL 62521
Wanda Wood

Atterbury
*Atterberry Family Association
728 Crescent Circle
Midwest City, OK 73110-1502
Voncille Attebery Winter, Director
Pub. *Atterbury-Arterbury-Atterberry-Atteberry-Attebery*, quarterly
$5.00 per year membership; annual reunion in August

Atwood
Claudette's
3962 Xenwood Avenue, S.
Saint Louis Park, MN 55416-2842
Claudette Atwood Maerz
Pub. *Atwood Ancestors*, semiannually, $8.00 per year subscription

Atwood
*Atwood Descendants
1712 Stonehaven Drive
Las Vegas, NV 89108-2033
Phone (702) 648-8608
Elizabeth A. Logan
(primarily descendants of Stephen of Eastham, Massachusetts, but includes others)
Will check files for SASE

Aubigne (see Folk Family Surname Exchange)

Auchinloick (see Graham)

Auchmutie (see MacDuff)

Auchmuty (see MacDuff)

Aucoin (see Johnson)

Aue (see Hay)

Auger (see Ainger)

Augeron
*Augeron, Sur le Bayou LaFourche
Rt. 1, Box 168
Lockport, LA 70374
Phone (504) 532-5981
The Marquis de Endelegard
Pub. *Les Planteur de la Louisiane*, semiannually; (includes Augernon (Orgeron), Boudreaux, Cevallos, Gautreaux, Gros, LeBlanc, Plaisance and Trosclair)

Auldson (see MacDuff)

Ault (see Buzzard, Preator)

Aulton (see Alton)

Auner (see Orner)

Aurand
*Aurand (Aurant) Family Association
921 Trailwood Drive
Raleigh, NC 27606
Phone (919) 851-6782
Leonard W. Aurand
Pub. *Newsletter*, three or four times per year
$5.00 per year membership

Aurant (see Aurand)

Aurner (see Orner)

Ausmus (see Folk Family Surname Exchange)

Austen (see Austin)

Auster
*Auster Surname Association
8505 Glenview Avenue
Takoma Park, MD 20912
Phone (301) 89-6621; (301) 589-1366 FAX

Barbara Levitz, Family Genealogist
(includes descendants of Auster family from Galicia, Stanslav (Ivano-Frankivsk), Vienna (Wien), Brody, Israel; also Oster, Aister)

Austin (see Goodenow, Keith, Likes)

Austin
*Austin Families Association of America, Inc.
1 Shorter Circle
Rome, GA 30165-4257
Phone (706) 290-0432
Barbara W. Austin, Secretary-Treasurer
Pub. *Austin Association Newsletter*, quarterly; (includes various spellings: Astin, Allston)
$15.00 per year membership

Austin
*Austins of America Genealogical Society
23 Allen Farm Lane
Concord, MA 01742
Phone (508) 369-8591
Dr. Michael E. Austin, Editor
Pub. *Austins of America*, semiannually, queries published free of charge
$6.50 per year membership

Austin
*Austin/Carroll/Carson/Darnell Family Organization
1132 North Tela Drive
Oklahoma City, OK 73127-4308
Phone (405) 789-2842
Pauline Carlton Fletcher, Secretary and Genealogist
(computer database uses Quinsept™, PAF™ and Reunion™)

Austin
*Austin-Larkins Association
2939 Olive
Eugene, OR 97405
Phone (503) 343-7856
Arliene Adams, Historian
(includes descendants of William E. Larkins (1794 Tennessee–1850 Clackamas County, Oregon), son of James, married 1814 in Somerset County, Pennsylvania, to Rachel Reed (1796 Pennsylvania–Molalla, Oregon), daughter of Jeremiah Reed, son of John Reed, and William and Rachel's daughter who married Henry Austin (earlier spelled Austen); also Rachel's maternal line: Strawn)

Austin
Austin-Larkins Family Association
3065 N.E. 124th
Bellevue, WA 98005
Jacqueline Smelser

Auterey (see Autry)

Autery (see Autry)

Auton (see Bagby)

Autrey (see Autry)

Autry (see Sullivan Surname Exchange)

Autry
*Autry Family Association
Rt. 1, Box 106-B
Thomasville, AL 36784
Phone (205) 385-2503
Milton W. Autrey, Treasurer/Coordinator
Pub. *AFA Bulletin*, quarterly; (includes
   Aut(e)r(e)y)
$15.00 per year membership

Auxier
*The Auxier Family
890 Winchester Road
Memphis, TN 38116
Phone (901) 396-4979 (home); (901)
   948-9881 (work); (901) 345-0551
   FAX; E-mail: memdave@netten.net
Dr. Dave Auxier, Author and Editor
Pub. *The Auxier Family Newsletter*
Reunion on the fourth of July weekend
   2000 at Paintsville, Kentucky

Aven (see MacDuff)

Averill
*Averill Family Organization
711 Kensington Avenue
Flint, MI 48503
Phone (313) 234-8574
Phyllis S. Kitson
Pub. *Averill Argos*, quarterly, free

Averill
*Gideon Averill Descendants'
   Organization
10017 11th Avenue, N.W.
Seattle, WA 98177-5201
Phone (206) 782-1139
Mildred Eaton, Genealogy Compiler
(includes Preston, Connecticut, 1792–
   1800; Erie County, Pennsylvania,
   1800–1825; Chautauqua County, New
   York, 1825–1833; Scott County, Iowa,
   1833–1900; Moline, Illinois, 1900–
   1912; and points west)

Avery (see Surname Sources, Barnes,
   Shurtleff)

Avery
*The Dedham Avery Heritage Journal
2402 West 16th Street, Space C-1
Yuma, AZ 85364
Phone (520) 782-0778
Ethel Avery Griffing, Editor
Pub. *The Dedham Avery Heritage
   Journal*, annually, from $6.00 per
   issue; (includes information on the
   descendants of Dr. William Avery who
   arrived in Dedham, Massachusetts, in
   1650, and of Richard Warren,
   Mayflower passenger; also information
   on Rev. John Avery, first pastor (1609)
   at Truro, Massachusetts; George[8]

Avery, Revolutionary veteran and his
descendants)

Avery
*Avery Memorial Association
PO Box 7245
Groton, CT 06340
Phone (203) 536-2698
Catherine Dey Leary, President
Pub. *Avery Newsletter*, semiannually;
   (includes descendants of Christopher
   Avery and his only son, James Avery
   (1650–1700), of England, Gloucester,
   Massachusetts, Pequot (New London,
   Connecticut, and Groton, Connecticut)
$3.00 per year membership, $50.00 life
   membership

Avery
*George Avery Database
712 South Point Drive
Schaumburg, IL 60193
Phone (708) 351-2777
Tom Benson
(includes data on descendants of all
   twelve children of George[8] Avery,
   Revolutionary veteran)

Avery
Avery
2150 Meadowlark Road
Manhattan, KS 66502-4557
Martha Streeter
Pub. *Avery*, annually, $10.00 per year
   subscription

Avery
*Avery Family of Dedham, MA (Kansas
   Branch)
2900 Lakewood Drive
Manhattan, KS 66502
Phone (913) 539-6935
Richard (Dick) Elkins

Avril (see Maier)

Awalt
Awalt Ancestors
PO Box 368
Garden Valley, CA 95633-0368
Suzanne Awalt

Axsom
*Axsom Association of America
1707 Greenridge Circle South
Jacksonville, FL 32259
Phone (904) 287-4629
Larry Earl Axsom
Pub. *Newsletter*, quarterly, $10.00 per
   year subscription; (includes
   descendants of Joseph H. Axsom
   (1778–1833); database contains
   information on over 3,000
   descendants)

Axson (see Exum)

Axtell (see Goodenow)

Axum (see Exum)

Ay (see Hay)

Aye (see Hay)

Ayer (see Corson; Hay)

Ayers (see Louden)

Ayers
*The Ayers Family
327 Duke Road, #3
Lexington, KY 40502
Azuba R. Ward, Publisher
(includes descendants of William Eayers
   of Londonderry, New Hampshire)

Ayers
*Ayers Surname Organization
3 Brazill Lane
Whitehall, MT 59759
Phone (406) 287-3369
Lindia Roggia Lovshin

Aylett (see Folk Family Surname
   Exchange)

Aylor (see The Memorial Foundation of
   the Germanna Colonies)

Aymand (see Johnson)

Aymond (see Johnson)

Ayres
*Ayres and Lockwood Family
   Genealogies
3 Windham Drive
Simsbury, CT 06070
Thomas Ayres

Ayson (see Macnachton, Shaw)

Ayton (see MacDuff)

Babb (see Clark)

Babb
*Babb Family Association News & Notes
12217 Shadetree Lane
Laurel, MD 20708-2814
Phone (301) 776-6138
Jean A. Sargent, Editor
Pub. *Babb Family Association News &
   Notes*, semiannually, $8.00 for three-
   year subscription
Reunion every three years

Babbitt (see Surname Sources)

Babcock
Babcock Family Newsletter
PO Box 13548
Saint Louis, MO 63138
Maryann Schirker
Pub. *Babcock Family Newsletter*

Baber
*Baber(s) Family Association
PO Box 1614
San Marcos, CA 92079
Phone (619) 727-4586
Diane Baber
$3.00 for name search of records, $2.50
for each of five volumes of family
pedigree charts

Babers (see Baber)

Babin (see Johnson)

Babineaux (see Johnson)

Bacastow (see Backenstoss)

Baccach (see Cian)

Bach (see The Memorial Foundation of
the Germanna Colonies)

Bachand (see Bashaw)

Bachman (see McCune)

Bachus (see Baccus)

Back (see The Memorial Foundation of
the Germanna Colonies)

Backensto (see Backenstoss)

Backenstoe (see Backenstoss)

Backenstoes (see Backenstoss)

Backenstos (see Backenstoss)

Backenstose (see Backenstoss)

Backenstoss (see Backenstoss)

Backenstoss
*Backenstoss Family Association of
America
32 Holly Drive
Woodbury, NJ 08096-3316
Phone (609) 845-4058; (609) 368-5578
(summer months)
Elwood B. Backensto, Historian
Pub. *Backenstoss Family Association of
America*, annually; (includes
Bacastow, Backensto, Backenstoe,
Backenstoes, Backenstos, Backenstose,
Backenstoss, Backenstow, Bagenstoes,
Bagenstos, Bagenstose, Bagenstoss,
Baggenstos, Baggenstoss)
$2.00 per year membership; annual
reunion in Pennsylvania

Backenstow (see Backenstoss)

Backus (see Reynolds)

Bacon (see Goodenow, Likes)

Bacon
*Bacon Families Association
200 Wyndemere Circle, Apartment
W-201
Wheaton, IL 60187-2433
John W. Hammersmith, President
Pub. *Quarterly*
$10.00 per year membership (beginning
in October)

Bacon
Bringin' Home the Bacon
9615 England
Overland Park, KS 66212
Jonathan Bacon
Pub., *Bringin' Home the Bacon*

Bacon
*Bacon Family of Delmarva Peninsula
Rt. 2, Box 187
Morgantown, PA 19543
Phone (215) 286-9857
Fred L. Williams, III

Bacus (see Baccus)

Badcock (see Surname Sources)

Badeau (see Johnson)

Badger (see Bower)

Badger
Badger Family Newsletter
215 Joe White Street
Rockwell, TX 75087
Joan McNeil
Pub. *Badger Family Newsletter*

Badgett
*Badgett Family Depository
2103 Harrison Avenue, N.W., #2
Olympia, WA 98502
Phone (206) 439-9934
Audrey Badgett
(includes all Badgett families, any area)

Badgley (see McRae)

Bading (see Schaffer)

Baeill (see Bell)

Baer (see Bear, Rowe)

Baer
The Baer Family Newsletter
3-978 SR 18-R2
Deshler, OH 43516
Phone (419) 278-7386
Connie Petersen, Editor
Pub. *The Baer Family Newsletter*,
bimonthly, $9.00 per year subscription;
(includes Bear, Bar, etc.)

Bagby
Bagby/Auton/Aughton Family in
America
3789 Greene Road
Burlington, KY 41005

Emma C. Auton McPheron
Biennial reunion

Bagenstoes (see Backenstoss)

Bagenstos (see Backenstoss)

Bagenstose (see Backenstoss)

Bagenstoss (see Backenstoss)

Baggenstos (see Backenstoss)

Baggenstoss (see Backenstoss)

Baggett (see Gibson, Scott)

Baggett
*Descendants of Nicholas Baggett
PO Box 178
Washington Grove, MD 20880
Phone (301) 948-0133
Diane Baggett Bender
(includes descendants of Nicholas (1715
Virginia) of Isle of Wight, Virginia,
and North Carolina)

Baggs
*Baggs Database
45865 Michell Lane
Indio, CA 92201-3780
Helen Free VanderBeek
(deals exclusively with families from
Hampshire, England)
$1.00 plus SASE for search

Bagley (see Bickmore, Brinton,
McClure, Merier)

Bagley
*Bagley Clearinghouse
207 Auburn Drive
Dalton, GA 30720
Phone (706) 278-1504
Joseph Wiley Reid
(1400–1890 period; also allied families
of Joyce, Nance, Prichard, Suggs and
White)

Bagwell (see Priddy)

Bagwell
*Bagwell Family Association
1009 Loyola
Perryton, TX 79070
Phone (806) 435-2323
Christine Bagwell Bell

Bahl (see Surname Database)

Bahr
*Albert Andrew Bahr Family
Organization
3305 Cobble Creek Lane
Heber, UT 84032
Phone (801) 654-3623
Ronda Rose, Secretary-Treasurer
Pub. *Bahr Newsletter*, semiannually;
(includes Bahr, Butt, Jackson,
Goodwin)
$5.00 per year membership; biennial
reunion

Bail (see Bell)

Bailes (see Bell)

Bailey (see Blossom Press, Sullivan Surname Exchange, Aldrich, Heath, McCune, Rice, Wigelius)

Bailey
Henry Bailey and Mercy Colvin Descendants
6081 Chad Drive
Newcastle, CA 95658-9543
Jackie Selden Riley

Bailey
*Annual Bailey Reunions
84 Tremont Street
Duxbury, MA 02332-4731
Phone (617) 934-2930
Sandra J. White, O.D., Secretary
Pub. (includes descendants of Thomas Ward Bailey (1809–1868) and Cynthia Chandler (1811–1894) of Kingston, Massachusetts)
Annual reunion on the first Sunday of August at Great Herring Pond, Plymouth, Massachusetts

Bailey
*The Journey Through Life of William & Melvina Bailey and Their Family of Needham, Mass.
1141 Meadow Glen
Lansing, MI 48917
Phone (517) 321-0551
Shirley Bailey, Publisher

Bailey
*Bailey, Bayley, Etc.
453 N.W. 171st Road
Warrensburg, MO 64093-7425
Phone (816) 747-0464
Donna Beers, Editor
Pub. *Bailey Roots in the North*, quarterly, $15.00 per year subscription; *Southern Baileys*, quarterly, $15.00 per year subscription; (database includes over 45,000 names)

Bailey
*Bailey Family Association
2750 South Maryland Parkway
PO Box 15070
Las Vegas, NV 89114
Phone (702) 732-2233 (business);
   (702) 225-5599 (home);
   (702) 731-2813 (FAX)
Patricia A. Saye-Barcus, Family Representative
Pub. *The Bailey Mailer*, quarterly, $5.00 per year subscription; (includes related families of Kerr, Lapsley, McKee and Stone)
$20.00 per year membership

Bailey
Surnames, Limited
RR 3, Box 59
Muleshoe, TX 79347-9208

Pub. *Bailey Lines*, published as material is collected, $8.00 per issue

Bailey
*Jim Mar Publications
1130 Pine Canyon Road
PO Box 430
Midway, UT 84049-0430
Phone (801) 654-4332
Marge Gardner, Publisher
Pub. *Bailey Connections*, semiannually (June and December), $15.00 per year subscription, $25.00 for two years subscription

Baill (see Bell)

Baillie
*House of Baillie U.S.A.
114 Meadow Wood Drive
Lexington, SC 29073
Phone (803) 356-1409; E-mail:
   AA101286@dasher.sc.edu
Art Bailie, Convenor
(includes descendants of the Baillies of Lanarkshire, Scotland, also Bailie of Northern Ireland)

Bailliou (see Bilyeu)

Bailor
*Bailor-Baylor Family Association
6603 Kensington Avenue East
Richmond Heights, CA 94805-2054
Phone (510) 237-7240 (phone and FAX);
   E-mail: tdewitt@creative.net
Dorothy Swinson DeWitt Baldwin, Coordinator
(includes Bealer, Beeler, Behler, Beller and Boehler, early spelling variants)

Bails (see Bell)

Bain (see Folk Family Surname Exchange, MacBean, Mackay, McRae)

Bain
*Bain Surname Organization
3 Brazill Lane
Whitehall, MT 59759
Phone (406) 287-3369
Lindia Roggia Lovshin

Bain
Bain-Baine
1221 Candice Court
Mesquite, TX 75149
Mary L. House, Editor
Pub. *Bain-Baine*, quarterly, $12.00 per year subscription

Bainbridge (see Hall, Reeder)

Baine (see Bain, MacBean)

Baines (see MacBean)

Bair (see Byars)

Bair
*Bair Surname Organization
John Bair Family Organization
PO Box 149
218 South Third West
Bancroft, ID 83217
Phone (208) 648-7809
Janet B. Tolman

Baird (see Louden, NaeSmith)

Baird
*Baird/Beard Surname Organization
John Rice Baird Family Organization
511 Gaylord
Pueblo, CO 81004
Phone (719) 543-0549
Virginia Baird Penaluna Haling

Baird
Baird Family Society Worldwide
2050 Rockledge Drive
Rockledge, FL 32955-5326
Mrs. Byron O. Baird, Convener
Pub. *The Gryphon*, quarterly; (includes Bard)
$15.00 per year membership

Baird
Francis Baird and Esther Eagles Descendants
Rt. 1, Box 472
Pinebush, NY 12566
Phone (914) 361-5577
Jim Baird

Bairfield (see Barfield)

Bairnes (see Barnes)

Bairs (see Byars)

Bait (see MacDuff)

Baits (see MacDuff)

Baker (see The Memorial Foundation of the Germanna Colonies, Allison, Covert, Goodenow, Heath, Lambert, Lund, Nash, Newton, Spradling, Stoner, Wright)

Baker
*Baker
10508 Lincoln Trail
Fairview Heights, IL 62208-1912
Warren Baker

Baker
Baker Family Newsletter International
326 Panhorst
Staunton, IL 62088-1829
Crystal Jensen
Pub. *Baker Family Newsletter International*, annually, $15.00 per year subscription in the U.S., $22.00 per year subscription in Europe

Baker
Baker Family Newsletter
1112 Greentree Court
Lexington, KY 40502
Gwen B. Tippie
Pub. *Baker Family Newsletter*

Baker
Baker/Yaple/Dumond/Coy/Comstock/
 Comfort/Smith/Brown/Davis/Cahill/
 Flavin/Hitchcock/Alexander/Dickensen
 Family Organization
117 North Filmore Avenue
Wagoner, OK 74467-4300
Edward Baker

Baksht (see Israelite)

Bakst (see Israelite)

Balbirnie (see MacDuff)

Balbirny (see MacDuff)

Balcanquall (see MacDuff)

Balcanwell (see MacDuff)

Balcaskie (see MacDuff)

Balcasky (see MacDuff)

Balch (see Carpenter)

Balcomie (see MacDuff)

Balcomy (see MacDuff)

Baldennie (see MacDuff)

Baldenny (see MacDuff)

Balderson
Balderson/Balderston/Balderstone
 International Family Reunion
 Association
600 Francis Drive
Lafayette, CA 94549
Cathy Presta, International Secretary/
 Treasurer
Pub. *Balderdashes*, three times per year
$15.00 per year membership

Baldman
Hungarian Genealogical Newsletter
PO Box 13548
Saint Louis, MO 63138
Maryann Schirker
Pub. *Hungarian Genealogical Newsletter*
 (*Baldman/Friez/Horvath/Siklost/Staub/
 Tinya/Toth/Weisz*)

Baldwin (see Folk Family Surname
 Exchange, Anthes, Williams)

Baldwin
*Topp of the Line
1304 West Cliffwood Court
Spokane, WA 99218-2917
Phone (509) 467-2299

Bette Butcher Topp, Owner/Operator
Pub. *Baldwin By-Lines*, irregularly, $5.50
 per issue plus $2.00 postage and
 handling

Bale (see Beall, Bell)

Bale
Bale Family Organization
1620 Ethridge, N.E.
Olympia, WA 98506
Mary Lee Bale Rose

Bales (see Bell)

Balfour (see MacDuff)

Balgarvie (see MacDuff)

Balgarvy (see MacDuff)

Balich (see Kreger)

Baliew (see Bilyeu)

Balkenwall (see MacDuff)

Ball (see Bell, Hatfield, Kahler,
 Newmyer, Ross, Rothenberger)

Ball
*Ball Database
667 Virginia Avenue
East Lansing, MI 48823
Phone (517) 337-0709
Joseph L. Druse
(includes all Balls of North America)

Ball
Claudette's
3962 Xenwood Avenue, S.
Saint Louis Park, MN 55416-2842
Claudette Atwood Maerz
Pub. *Ball Beginnings*, quarterly, $14.00
 per year subscription

Ballangee (see Bloss)

Ballantyne (see Stewart)

Ballard (see MacDuff)

Ballardie (see MacDuff)

Ballardy (see MacDuff)

Ballay (see Blossom Press)

Ballcanwall (see MacDuff)

Ballengee (see Russell)

Ballenger (see The Memorial
 Foundation of the Germanna Colonies)

Ballenwall (see MacDuff)

Ballew (see Bilyeu)

Ballew
*Ballew Family Association of America,
 Inc.
2711 Leslie Drive, N.E.
Atlanta, GA 30345
Phone (404) 491-0664
Tom Ballew, Executive Advisory
 Committee
Pub. *The Ballew Family Journal*
$10.00 per year membership dues,
 $25.00 membership fee

Ballewen (see Graham)

Ballingall (see MacDuff)

Ballingshall (see MacDuff)

Balloo (see Bilyeu)

Ballou (see Bilyeu)

Ballow (see Bilyeu)

Balmahay (see MacDuff)

Balmakin (see MacDuff)

Balneaves (see Murray)

Balogh
Balogh
557 East 600 South
Provo, UT 84606
Louis Balogh
Pub. *Balogh*, semiannually

Balou (see Bilyeu)

Balram (see MacDuff)

Balthaser
*Balthaser Family
RR 1, Box 218
Bernville, PA 19506
Phone (610) 488-6861
Gloria Balthaser Kramer
(includes descendants of John Jacob
 Balthaser and Mary Magdalena Greth)

Balthazar (see Paxton)

Balvaird (see MacDuff)

Balwearie (see MacDuff)

Balweary (see MacDuff)

Ban (see Blossom Press)

Banbury
*Banbury Family of Pasadena California
 Research Group
5076 Midas Avenue
Rocklin, CA 95677-2277
Ronald L. Bassett, Family Representative

Bancroft
Bancroft Newsletter
6180 Merrywood Drive
Rocklin, CA 95677-3421

Kathleen Stewart
Pub. *Bancroft Newsletter*, quarterly
(February, May, August and
November), $12.00 per year
subscription

Bandy (see Strain)

Bane (see MacBean, Moser)

Bangall (see Bangle)

Bangle
Bangle/Bangall Family Association
3730 Humboldt
Topeka, KS 66609
H. M. Thomas

Banks (see Baughman, Newcomb)

Bankson (see Bankston)

Bankston (see Blossom Press)

Bankston
Blossom Press
PO Box 831
Burns, LA 70041-0831
Phone (504) 893-8726; (504) 657-9560
William R. Stringfield, Owner
(includes Bankston/Bankson surname
and all those who descend from the
family of that origin from the late
1600s in Philadelphia)

Bannatie (see MacDuff)

Bannaty (see MacDuff)

Bannerman (see Forbes)

Bannister (see Adams)

Bannon (see Reynolds)

Banta
Banta Pioneers
Rt. 4, V118
Viroqua, WI 54665
Phone (608) 637-2003
Elsa M. Banta
Pub. *Banta Pioneers*

Banther (see Grice)

Banton (see Rutherford)

Banvard (see Goodenow)

Banz
*The Banz Family Organization
2140 West 300 North
West Point, UT 84015
Phone (801) 773-4388
Fred Banz
(includes research in the U.S. and
Switzerland)

Bar (see Baer, Bear)

Barber (see The Memorial Foundation
of the Germanna Colonies, Behnke,
Dunbar, Newton)

Barber
Barber-Raffe-Johnson-Moses Family
Association
2306 Westgate
Houston, TX 77019
Phone (713) 529-2333
Harold Helm
$25.00 plus pedigree and family group
sheets for membership

Barberot (see Blossom Press)

Barblett (see Clark)

Barbuto (see Gratta)

Barclay (see Lemon, MacDuff)

Barclay
Clan Barclay Society, U.S.A.
2602 Royal Court
Helena, AL 35080
Phone (205) 985-9499
John L. Barclay, President

Barcus
*Barcus Family Association
2750 South Maryland Parkway
PO Box 15070
Las Vegas, NV 89114
Phone (702) 732-2233 (business); (702)
225-5599 (home); (702) 731-2813
(FAX)
Patricia A. Saye-Barcus, Family
Representative
Pub. *The Barcus Barker*, quarterly, $5.00
per year subscription
$20.00 per year membership

Bard (see Aldrich, Baird, Weimar)

Bardfield (see Barfield)

Bardin (see Waltermire)

Barefield (see Barfield)

Barfield (see Moody)

Barfield
*Barfield Family Association
935 Countryside Drive, Apartment #103
Palatine, IL 60067-1927
Phone (847) 776-1848
H. Harvey Barfield, III
Pub. *The Barfield Family Historical
Review*, quarterly, $10.00 per year
subscription; (includes all variations of
Barfield: Bairfield, Bardfield,
Barefield, Bearfield, etc.)

Barger (see Likes)

Barger
John and Catharine Barger Family
Association
1604 Longfellow Street
McLean, VA 22101
Georgia E. Benefiel

Bargman
Bargman-Barrickman-Barkman Family
2905 North Kilbourne
East Chicago, IL 60647
June B. Barekman

Baril (see Blossom Press)

Barker (see Brooks, Corson, Covert,
Pittman, Woodrow)

Barker
*Barkers of VA, NC, SC, GA, AL
2711 Seabreeze Court
Orlando, FL 32805
Phone (407) 425-6942
Col. Clifton O. Duty (USA Ret.) or Jean
Barker Duty
SASE

Barker
Barker-Joslyn Family Tree Climber
9615 England
Overland Park, KS 66212
Jonathan Bacon
Pub. *Barker-Joslyn Family Tree Climber*,
irregularly, free

Barkheimer (see Dooley)

Barkman (see Bargman)

Barksdale (see Folk Family Surname
Exchange, Reid)

Barler (see The Memorial Foundation of
the Germanna Colonies)

Barlette (see Eaves)

Barlow (see The Memorial Foundation
of the Germanna Colonies, Holden)

Barlow
*Barlow of Barlow Family Association
840 East Gunn Road
Rochester, MI 48306
Edson L. Barlow
Pub. *Barlow of Barlow*, quarterly
$10.00 per year membership

Barlow
*Israel Barlow Family Association
PO Box 966
Bountiful, UT 84011-0966
Ronald C. Barlow, Treasurer

Barn (see Barnes)

Barnard (see Folk Family Surname
Exchange)

Barnard
*Barnards' Cousins
1345 Westmoreland Avenue
Syracuse, NY 13210-3436
Phone (315) 472-3539
Ed Barnard, Family Genealogist
(database includes descendants of
    Bartholomew Barnard 1627, Francis
    Barnard 1617, Robert Bartlett 1603,
    Thomas Bingham, I, 1556, Rev.
    Richard Bourne 1610, Andries Bradt
    1585, Jonas "Seignor" Bronck 1610,
    Benjamin Butterfield 1616, Thomas
    Carrier, Sr., 1641, John[1] Church 1335,
    Nicholas Cottrell, Sr., 1590, Elder John
    Crandall 1609, Richard Dana 1617,
    Andries De Vos 1600, Thomas Dewey,
    I, 1616, Jonathan Fairbanks, Jr., 1640,
    Samuel Faulkner, Sr., 1700, Simon
    Fiske, Sr., 1462, Mathew Ford, Sr.,
    1661, Reginald Foster 1595, Robert
    Gage, Sr., 1685, Richard "Goodman"
    Gale 1618, Thomas Gibbs, Sr., 1618,
    John Glazier, Sr., 1637, Robert
    Goodell (Goodale) 1570, John
    Greenman 1603, Casper Jacobse
    Hallenbeck 1625, Andrew Hallett, Sr.,
    1580, Mayor James Hill, Sr., 1550, Lt.
    Edward "Freeman" Howe 1575, Henry
    Howland, Sr., 1568, Henry Ingalls
    1480, Richard Mann, Sr., 1622, John
    Marcy, Sr., 1662, Thomas Merrill
    1450, Roger Morey, Sr., 1600, Robert
    Morse 1486, Deacon Joseph Mygatt
    1596, Isaac/Richard Newton 1575,
    John Nutting, Sr., 1630, John Peirce
    (Pers) 1588, Johannes Petrie 1664,
    Johannes Pruyn 1614, John Roote
    1580, Sylvester Salisbury, Sr., 1629,
    Thomas Sanders 1618, John Shatswell
    1574, John Sherman 1400, Lawrence
    Southwick 1594, Major Abraham
    Staats 1640, William Stilson 1601,
    William Swift, I, 1596, Wessel ten
    Broeck 1612, William/John Towne
    1572, John Treat/Trott 1480, Joseph
    Underwood, Sr., 1614, Martin G. Van
    Bergen 1660, Dirck Van Vechten 1600,
    Bastien Visscher 1595, "Mr" Richard
    Warren 1580, Mathew Webster 1570,
    Major William Whiting 1612, Thomas
    Wickwarre 1500, Thomas Wilbore
    1482, Joshua Winsor 1619, Jan
    Thomas Witbeck 1635, John Young,
    Sr., 1630)
$50.00 deposit for search

Barnard
Barnard Lines
19033 46th Avenue, South
Seattle, WA 98188
Bill Barnard
Pub. *Barnard Lines*

Barne (see Johnson)

Barner
Barner Family
2086 Yorktown
Ann Arbor, MI 48105

Leroy E. Barner, Editor
Pub. *Barner Family Newsletter*, annually

Barner
Barner Family Newsletter
1063 Beech Avenue
Hershey, PA 17033
Elaine Barner
Pub. *Barner Family Newsletter*

Barnes (see Folk Family Surname
    Exchange, Album, Gant, Goodenow,
    Gunnin, Johnson, Rutherford, Saye,
    Wigelius)

Barnes
*Samuel Barnes Family Organization
1822 Granada Drive
Concord, CA 94519
Phone (415) 685-2333
Gary A. Barnes

Barnes
*Thomas Barnes of Hartford,
    Connecticut, from 1615
794 Chestnut Drive
Fairfield, CA 94533-1465
Phone (707) 422-1794
Frederic W. and Edna Barnes, Publisher
(includes descendants and allied
    surnames of Adams, Andrews, Avery,
    Beall, Beavens, Beebe, Bement,
    Bronson, Brown, Clark, Day, Foote,
    Gaylord, Hart, Hayes, Heist, Johnson,
    Jones, Langdon, Lee, Lewis, Miller,
    Moore, Munson, Neal, Painter, Potter,
    Rice, Ripley, Root, Scoville, Smith,
    Tuttle, Warner, Webster, Williams,
    Wing and Woodruff)

Barnes
*Thomas Barnes Family Genealogy
804 60th Street
West Des Moines, IA 50266
Phone (515) 225-1553
Rev. Josephine A. Barnes

Barnes
Family Tree Genealogical Society
450 Potter Street
Wauseon, OH 43567
Phone (419) 335-6485
Howard V. Fausey, Editor
Pub. *Barnes Family Quarterly* (February,
    May, August and November), $12.00
    per year subscription; *Director of
    Barnes Family Researchers*,
    semiannually (June and November),
    $8.00 per issue, postpaid (price varies)

Barnes
Barnes-Barns-Boernes-Bairnes Family
    Association
2306 Westgate
Houston, TX 77019
Phone (713) 529-2333
Harold Helm
$25.00 plus pedigree and family group
    sheets for membership

Barnes
*The K.A.R.D. Files
19305 S.E. 243rd Place
Kent, WA 98042-4820
Phone (206) 432-1659
Judy K. Dye, Owner
Pub. *Barnes Bulletin 2.0*, irregularly,
    $6.00–$7.00 per volume (Washington
    residents add 8.2% sales tax);
    (includes Barn, Barns)

Barnes
Pence Publications
11009 East Third Avenue, #93
Spokane, WA 99206-6501
Maxine E. Pence, Editor
Pub. *Barnes Bulletin*, irregularly, $6.00
    per issue

Barnet
*John Calob Barnet Family Organization
    (proposed)
3894 West Spring Mountain, #8
Las Vegas, NV 89102
Phone (702) 876-1659
Mary Barkan

Barnett (see Blossom Press, Lush,
    Smilie)

Barnett
*Barnett Clearinghouse
6358 South Josephine Way
Littleton, CO 80121
Phone (303) 794-0348
Joanne E. Martin
(families from New York State,
    Pennsylvania, Canada or New England
    and migrations beyond)
$3.00 search fee, plus copy costs and
    postage

Barnett
Craig Junction Publishers
PO Box 242
Craigmont, ID 83523-0242
Marsha Wilson Bovey
Pub. *The Barnett Source*, quarterly,
    $15.00 per year subscription

Barnett
Santa Fe Trail Ranch
Rt. 2
Dodge City, KS 67801
Mrs. Guy D. Josserand
Pub. *Barnett Family Publication*

Barnett
Barnett
3025 Princess Lane
Plano, TX 875074
Dawn Barnett
Pub. *Barnett*, three times per year, $15.00
    per year subscription

Barney (see Conlee, Nelson)

Barney
*The Barney Family Historical
  Association
7361 Silver Pine Drive
Springfield, VA 22153
Phone (703) 451-3916
William Clifford Barney, President,
  Founder and Editor
Pub. *The Barney Family News*, quarterly
  (March, June, September and
  December); (mainly descendants of
  Jacob Barney who came to Salem,
  Massachusetts, in 1634 from England;
  also William Barney who came to
  Baltimore in 1695 from England)
$8.00 per year membership, $12.00 for
  two years membership, $24.00 for five
  years membership; annual reunions in
  Idaho and West Virginia

Barngrover
Barngrover-Berngruber Newsletter
3908 Sparkle Street
Norman, OK 73072
Andree C. Swanson
Pub. *Barngrover-Berngruber Newsletter*,
  quarterly, $5.00 per year subscription

Barnhart (see CTC Family Association,
  Frantz)

Barnheiser (see Hisle)

Barnhill (see Deyarmond)

Barnhill
*Barnhill Family
PO Box 22621
Knoxville, TN 37933
A. Virgil Barnhill, Publisher

Barnhisle (see Hisle)

Barns (see Barnes)

Barnwell
*Barnwell Family 1760–1920
2281 Warren Street
Eugene, OR 97405
Phone (503) 686-8074
Leon R. Barnwell, Director

Baron (see Wright)

Barret (see MacDuff)

Barrett (see Newton)

Barrett
Barrett Family Newsletter
PO Box 13548
Saint Louis, MO 63138
Maryann Schirker
Pub. *Barrett Family Newsletter*,
  quarterly, $25.00 per year subscription

Barrett
Grin and Barrett
472 Hilton Drive
Madison, WI 53711-1149

Kathryn Bush
Pub. *Grin and Barrett*, irregularly, $2.00
  per issue

Barrickman (see Bargman)

Barrie (see Lagesse)

Barrie
*Norbert Barrie Family Organization
PO Box 45
Turton, SD 57477
Phone (605) 897-6528
Richard L. Barrie, Historian
Annual reunion on the last Sunday of
  June at Turton, South Dakota, in odd-
  numbered years and in the Seattle,
  Washington, area on even-numbered
  years

Barringer (see Moser)

Barringer
*Barringer Family Association
15035 29th Avenue, South
Seattle, WA 98188
Phone (206) 243-8057
Donna Burkert Grothaus
Free membership

Barrois (see Blossom Press)

Barron (see MacDuff, McCurdy)

Barron
Family Heritage Publications
1886 Rice Boulevard
Fairborn, OH 45324-3158
Pub. *Barron Family Newsletter*,
  bimonthly

Barrow (see Charlesworth)

Barry
*Mary Julia Barry Family Organization
PO Box 1860
Studio City, CA 91614
Phone (818) 980-1005; E-mail:
  AP471@lafn.org
Karen Mohr

Bartee
Bartee News
2841 Paso Del Robles
San Marcos, TX 78666
Phone (512) 396-6182
Linda Mearse, Editor
Pub. *Bartee News*, three times per year,
  $12.00 per year subscription
Reunion

Bartels (see Arthur)

Barthelemy (see Blossom Press)

Bartholomew (see Leslie)

Bartleson
*Bartlesons of Grand Chain
132 West Inglewood
Broken Arrow, OK 74011-5025
Phone (918) 455-6660
Marvin V. Layman, Editor
Pub. *Newsletter* (includes descendants of
  John Bartleson and Mary Chapman,
  who traveled from Ohio to Grand
  Chain, Illinois, in 1843)

Bartlet (see Lambert)

Bartlett (see Barnard, Davis, Dewitt,
  Stockbridge, Wright)

Bartlett
"Bits A History"
PO Box 516
Mount Hope, KS 67108
Patsy Sutton
Pub. *Bartlett-Hardesty*

Bartlett
Descendants of Robert Bartlett
98 Sumersea Road
Mashpee, MA 02649
Mrs. G. Gordon Bartlett, Jr.
$10.00 per year membership; annual
  reunion on the last Saturday of July in
  Plymouth, Massachusetts area

Bartling (see Mower)

Barton (see CTC Family Association)

Barton
The Barton Banner
12600 Bissonnet A4-407
Houston, TX 77099
Dede D. Mercer, Publisher
Pub. *The Barton Banner*, bimonthly,
  $20.00 per year subscription; (all
  variations of the surname, worldwide)

Barton
Barton
South 2707 Rhyolite Road
Spokane, WA 99203
Phone (509) 747-6969
Jean Jones Holder
Pub. *Barton*

Bartram (see Frasher, Jackson)

Barwick
Barwick Branches
PO Box 69
Grandin, FL 32138
Laura Tully
Pub. *Barwick Branches*, quarterly
  (January, April, July and October),
  $15.00 per year subscription

Basham
Basham Clearinghouse
10352 White Rock Circle
Dallas, TX 75238
Phone (214) 348-1403
L. Malcolm Basham
Pub. *The Basham Family*, free

Bashaw
Bashaw/Bachand Newsletter
6180 Merrywood Drive
Rocklin, CA 95677-3421
Kathleen Stewart
Pub. *Bashaw/Bachand Newsletter*,
    quarterly, $12.00 per year subscription

Bashor (see Frantz)

Basillie (see MacDuff)

Basilly (see MacDuff)

Bass (see Gant, Heath, Rutherford)

Bass
Southern Bass
PO Box 733
Pine Mountain, GA 31822-0733
Lea L. Dowd
Pub. *Southern Bass*

Bassett (see Allison)

Bassett
*Bassett/Walker/Puffer Research Group
5076 Midas Avenue
Rocklin, CA 95677-2277
Ronald L. Bassett, Family Representative
(includes lines from the Davis County,
    Iowa, area)

Bassett
*Lorin Elias Bassett Family Organization
1055 East Hillcrest Drive
Springville, UT 84663
Phone (801) 489-6298
Irvin Gene Bassett, President
Pub. *Research Report*, annually, $12.00
    per issue; (includes descendants of
    Loren Elias Bassett (1809) and his two
    wives, Rachel English (1813) and
    Huldah Dimrus Vaughn (1808))

Bast (see Surname Database)

Batchelder (see Newton)

Batchelder
The Epistle
PO Box 2782
Kennebunkport, ME 04046-2782
Rosemary E. Bachelor
Pub. *The Epistle*, quarterly

Batchelder
*Pioneer Publication
PO Box 1179
Tum Tum, WA 99034-1179
Phone (509) 276-9841
Shirley Penna-Oakes
Pub. *Batchelder Review*, irregularly,
    $6.00 per issue plus $1.75 postage for
    1–3 books, 50¢ for each additional
    book

Batchelor (see Williams)

Bate (see Nell)

Bateman
Bateman Family Association
Lebo Rt., Box 211
West Plains, MO 65775
Erman Bateman
Pub. *Bateman Datum*, annually

Bateman
*Bateman Connection
24 North Manheim Boulevard
New Paltz, NY 12561-1218
Phone (914) 255-8537
Paul F. Bateman
(computer data bank)

Bateman
*Henry and Martha Elizabeth (Brackley)
    Bateman Family Organization
4045 Liberty Avenue
Ogden, UT 84403-2942
Phone (801) 393-7459
C. Diane Baxter, Publisher

Bater
*Bater Surname Organization
1820 West 600 North
Howe, IN 46746
Phone (219) 562-3066
Ann Bowerman Dunkel
Pub. *Newsletter*, annually, free
Annual reunion on the third Sunday of
    August in Michigan

Bates (see Hall, Sinyard, Turner)

Bates
*Caleb Bates Family Organization
    (Kentucky and Indiana)
29 East Portland Avenue
Vincennes, IN 47591
Phone (812) 882-9371
Richard Carl Rodgers, II, Historian/
    Archivist
(archival facility collects information on
    all descendants and ancestors of the
    family in computer database;
    descendants of Caleb Bates (1782
    Virginia–1835 Blue River Township,
    Harrison County, Indiana) and wives
    "Caty" Patterson and Margaret
    "Peggy" Lowden/Louden (1786
    County Antrim, Ireland–1852 Blue
    River Township))

Bates
*William M. Bates (1817–1895) of
    Peasmarsh, East Sussex, England
570 East Main Street
Gaylord, MI 49735
Phone (517) 732-6035
M. J. Luzenski, Publisher

Bates
The Bates Family of Old Virginia
Bates Society of Old Virginia
PO Box 9134, Bellevue Station
Richmond, VA 23227
Wayne Witt Bates
Pub. *Bates Booster*, bimonthly
$10.00 per year membership

Bates
*Thompson G. Bates Family
    Organization
2315 Crescent Avenue
Casper, WY 82604
Phone (307) 237-3966
William Bates
(includes descendants of Thompson G.
    Bates and Jane Whitlock (ca 1807–
    1877))

Batey (see Hutchison)

Batiste (see Hatfield)

Batte (see Folk Family Surname
    Exchange)

Baty (see MacBeth)

Baudet (see Beaudet)

Baudoin (see Baudouin)

Baudouin
*Pierre Baudouin Family Association
903 Chatsworth Circle
Austin, TX 78704-5230
Phone (512) 442-7932
Jack R. Sodke
(includes Baudoin, Baudouin, Bowden,
    Bowdoin, Bowdon, Bowdown, Sodke
    of Virginia, Maryland, Pennsylvania,
    Ohio, Tennessee, and Quaker families
    in North Carolina; over 15,000 on
    computer database)
$5.00 per search, 50¢ per page for copies

Baudreau
*Urbain Baudreau Graveline
    Genealogical Association, Inc.
382 Main Street
PO Box 191
Palmer, MA 01069
Phone (413) 283-8378
Robert Graveline, President
Pub. *The Descendants* (includes
    Baudreau 1653 Montreal, Graveline
    1699 Mobile, Alabama)
$12.00 per year membership

Bauer (see Bower, Hegner)

Bauersachs
Bauersachs/Bowersox Genealogical
    Society
1025 Margaret Street
Des Plaines, IL 60016
Phone (312) 296-3758
Tom and Jan Bowersox
Pub. *Homesteads*, quarterly, cost varies

Baughan (see Pierce)

Baughman (see CTC Family
    Association)

Baughman
Baughman/Banks/Puckett/Talbert/
    Hanvey Link
89 Bucyrus Drive
Buffalo, NY 14228
C. Elaine White Diodate

Bauguess (see Boggess)

Baum (see Leland)

Bauman (see Andlauer, Frantz)

Baumann (see Bowman)

Baumgardner (see Folk Family
    Surname Exchange, The Memorial
    Foundation of the Germanna Colonies,
    Lambert)

Baun (see Vaughn)

Bauscher (see Boucher)

Bausher (see Boucher)

Bautz
*Bautz Descendants
1313 West Paradise Court
Milwaukee, WI 53209
Phone (414) 228-8477
Elynn Lee Bautz, Publisher
Pub. *Bautz Family Newsletter*, annually
    (Christmas); (includes descendants of
    Wendelin (1803–1889) and Magdalena
    (1797–1886) Bautz who came to the
    U.S. from Haigerloch in Hohenzollern
    in 1854, settled in Milwaukee County
    in 1856; especially interested in lost
    lines of Maria Bautz who married
    Thimothy Daly in New York City, had
    at least one son, and died young)
Reunion

Bavaird (see Bovaird)

Baxter (see Hallam, MacMillan,
    McClellan)

Baxter
Baxter
120 West Boardwalk Place
Park Ridge, IL 60068-6202
Hugh W. Baxter, Editor
Pub. *Baxter*, three times per year, $6.00
    per year subscription

Bayard (see Fadner)

Bayer (see Surname Database, Boyer,
    Byars)

Bayers (see Byars)

Bayhi (see Blossom Press)

Bayle (see Bell)

Bayles (see Bell)

Baylor (see Bailor)

Bayn (see MacBean)

Bayne (see Kincannon, MacBean,
    Mackay)

Bayre (see Byars)

Bayres (see Byars)

Bays
Bays Family Association
Rt. 2, #36 Cindy Lane
Stillwater, OK 74074
Evelyn Pepmiller
Pub. *Bays Family Association Newsletter*

Beach (see Oney, Rothenberger)

Beach
Beach-Beech
744 West Livingston
Highland, MI 48357
Eugene H. Beach, Jr.
Pub. *Beach-Beech*, quarterly, $14.00 per
    year subscription

Beachler (see Frantz)

Beagrie (see Hay)

Beal (see Links Genealogy Publications,
    Beall, Bell, Freeman)

Beale (see Beall, Bell)

Beale
*Beale Family History
8529 Spalding Drive
Richmond, VA 23229
Phone (804) 741-1836
B. DeRoy Beale

Bealer (see Bailor)

Beales (see Bell)

Beall (see Barnes, Bell)

Beall
*Beall Family Association
c/o Paperweight Printing
326 S.E. 82nd Avenue
Portland, OR 97216
Phone (503) 235-7569
William R. Beall, III, Editor
Pub. *The Beall News*, quarterly, $10.00
    per year subscription; (includes Beall,
    Beale, Beal, Beals, Bale, Bell, etc., all
    states plus Scotland and England,
    1600s to 1800s+)

Bealles (see Bell)

Bealls (see Bell)

Bealmer (see Likes)

Beals (see Additon, Beall, Bell)

Beals
*The Beals Family Reunion
15341 West Esthner
Goddard, KS 67052-9755
Cliff and Ellen Chambers

Beaman (see Beeman, Moody)

Beaman
*The Beaman Museum
2036 West Side Drive
Rochester, NY 14624
Phone (716) 594-2401
Kenneth P. Beaman, Curator
(includes Beaman, Beamon, Beaumont,
    Beeman, Beman, Bement, Olcott,
    Shepard, Tuttle and Wakely)

Beamon (see Beaman)

Bean (see Surname Sources, Likes,
    MacBean, Reeder)

Bean
*Southern Bean Association
6133 Mary Elizabeth Cove
Memphis, TN 38134
Phone (901) 388-6736
Bettye S. Reed, Past President
Pub. *The Beanstalk*, quarterly, $15.00 per
    year subscription; (includes Bean,
    Beene, Been, Bain, Beane, etc., with
    southern roots or connections)
Annual meeting

Bean
James Bean Family Organization
313 East 2020 North
Provo, UT 84601
Phone (801) 374-5328
Arlene B. Meservy

Bean
*William Bean Family Organization
36 North "B" Street
Saint Albans, WV 25177
Phone (304) 727-6533
Fannie B. Beane
(includes descendants of William Bean of
    Monroe County, West Virginia)

Beane (see Bean, MacBean)

Bear (see Baer)

Bear
Bear Family Newsletter
PO Box 5775
Woodland Park, CO 80866-5775
Phone (719) 687-6167
Beth Horton, Editor
Pub. *Bear Family Newsletter*, bimonthly,
    $10.00 per year subscription; (includes
    all spellings: Baer, Bar, etc.)

Beard (see Clark, Underwood)

Beard
Beard/Wilson/Boutwell Reunion
PO Box 91
Bethany, LA 71007
Phone (318) 938-7755
B. Gibbs; Margie Dawson Gibbs

Beard
The Beard Family of Greene County,
   Mississippi
136 Cedar Oak Drive
Clinton, MS 39206
Douglas A. Copeland, Family
   Representative
Reunion

Beard
Beard Family Association
2810 Thousand Oaks Drive, #163
San Antonio, TX 78232-4108
Mrs. Jackie Morgan

Beardsley (see Brothers)

Bearfield (see Barfield)

Bearsley (see Heath)

Beath (see Gillean, MacBeth)

Beaton (see Gillean, MacBeth, MacDuff)

Beatty (see Surname Sources,
   Cunningham)

Beaty (see Burlingame, MacBeth, Price)

Beauchat (see Likes)

Beaudet
*Beaudet Surname Organization
865 Amwell Road
Flemington, NJ 08822-3902
John E. Boudette
(database includes 4500 Beaudet,
   Beaudette, Bodet, Bodett Boudette
   descendants of Jean Baudet (1648–
   1714) and Marie Grandin of Quebec,
   Canada)
$20.00 for an index of interconnected
   marriages on computer, trees are free if
   located

Beaudette (see Beaudet)

Beaumont (see Beaman, MacDuff)

Beaumont
Old Time Publications
10828 Oakbrook Drive
Omaha, NE 68154-2437
Peggy Wallingford Butherus
Pub. *Beaumont Branches*, $5.50 plus
   $1.25 postage and handling per issue
   (Washington residents add 7.8%
   sales tax)

Beauvais
The Beauvais Family Association
21 Gilman Terrace
Sioux City, IA 51104
Phone (712) 277-0140;
   (800) 831-4815 (days)
Thomas A. Beauvais, Editor
Pub. *The Beauvais Family Newsletter*,
   quarterly (March, June, September and
   December), $15.00 per year
   subscription; (includes descendants of
   Jacques St. Gemme dit Beauvais and
   Jeanne Solde who were married in
   Montreal in 1653)

Beauvois (see Lagesse)

Beaven (see Rutherford)

Beavens (see Barnes)

Beaver (see Dockery)

Beavers (see Album)

Beavers
Beavers/Riddle Family Organization
6529 66th Street
Columbus, NE 68601
Mrs. A. Hoeman

Bebber (see Links Genealogy
   Publications)

Bechtel (see Bechtol, Beghtol, Mininger)

Beck (see Cian)

Beck
Johan Martin Beck Family Society
Rt. 1, Box 458
Clayton, IN 46118
Roger Beck

Becker (see Cole, Koehn, Lambert)

Becker
*Bell Enterprises
PO Box 10328
Spokane, WA 99209
Phone (509) 327-2761
Mary Ann L. Vanzandt Bell, Owner,
   Publisher
Pub. *Becker Banner*, published as time
   and material permits, $6.00 plus $1.25
   postage per issue

Beckham
Beckham-Daniel-Self-DePriest
   Organization
2306 Westgate
Houston, TX 77019
Phone (713) 529-2333
Harold Helm
$25.00 plus pedigree and family group
   sheets for membership

Beckwith
*Beckwith Newsletter
PO Box 1565
Stillwater, OK 74076-1565
Phone (405) 377-9066
Mahlon G. Erickson, Editor
Pub. *Beckwith Newsletter*, quarterly,
   $20.00 per year subscription; (includes
   Beckwith/Beckworth)

Beckworth (see Beckwith)

Becnel (see Blossom Press)

Beddingfield (see Moser)

Beddy (see Cian)

Bedell (see Cummings)

Bedford (see Lush)

Bedford
*Bedford Family Registry
4845 Castle Road
La Canada, CA 91011-1305
Phone (818) 248-6553; E-mail:
   ao@845lafn.org
Luetta Bedford Kirker, Leader
Free exchange of information, donations
   for supplies and searches accepted, can
   do quick search for your connection

Bedingfield (see Hill)

Bedson (see MacDuff)

Bee (see MacBean)

Beean (see MacBean)

Beebe (see Barnes)

Beebe
Beebe Connection
538 CR 801, Rt. 3
Ashland, OH 44805
Mary Beebe, Editor
Pub. *Beebe Connection*, quarterly

Beech (see Beach)

Beecher (see Stowe)

Beedle (see Rutherford)

Beeker (see Cummings)

Beel (see Bell)

Beele (see Bell)

Beeler (see Bailor)

Beeles (see Bell)

Beels (see Bell)

Beeman (see Beaman)

Beeman
*B'Man Family Association
607 East Market
Searcy, AR 72143
Phone (501) 268-3179
Ruth E. Browning, Editor
Pub. *B'man Family Newsletter*, at least
semiannually; (includes Beaman,
Beeman, Beman, Bemen, Bemon, etc.,
all spellings of B'man)
$10.00 per year membership

Been (see Bean, MacBean)

Beene (see Bean, MacBean)

Beer (see The Memorial Foundation of
the Germanna Colonies, Lemon)

Beers
*Regan Genealogical Publishing
Company
PO Box 592
Palatine, IL 60078-0592
Mary Louise Regan, Editor
Pub. *Beers Bulletin (A Newsletter)*,
quarterly, $10.00 per year subscription;
(includes persons of Beers English
ancestry, especially those settling in
New England in the 17th century, but
some later ones also)

Beery (see Stoner)

Beezley
*Beezley Family
PO Box 645
Oxnard, CA 93032-0645
Phone (805) 487-2144; (805) 487-2800
FAX
Gilbert G. Beezley
Pub. *Family News*, annually, voluntary
contribution for subscription; (includes
descendants of John Anderson Beezley
and Lecy Ellen Hays of Rolla,
Missouri, married ca 1856–57,
divorced 1901)

Behel (see Bell)

Behler (see Bailor)

Behnke (see Sager)

Behnke
*Lloyd Publishing
49 Bianca Lane, #54
Watsonville, CA 95076
Lloyd Walter Clark Hoagland, Editor
(includes research on related families:
Behnke, Barber, Brahler, McEntee,
Morosic, Orman, Teare and Walton,
mostly in England, Germany and
Nebraska)

Behr (see Lemon, Rowe)

Behrens (see Arthur)

Behrn (see Rutherford)

Behunin
Isaac Morton Behunin Family
Association
756 East Vine Street
Murray, UT 84107-6502
William Clyde Behunin, President

Behunin
Associated Behunin Family Associations
756 East Vine Street
Murray, UT 84107-6502
William Clyde Behunin, Chairman
Genealogical Research Committees

Beidler (see Lambert)

Beier (see Boyer)

Beil (see Bell)

Beill (see Bell)

Beils (see Bell)

Beiter (see Hegner)

Beitzel
*Beitzel Family of Garrett County,
Maryland
120 Hedgewood Drive
Greenbelt, MD 20770
Phone (301) 441-3718
Florence Harris Abel, Publisher

Bel (see Bell)

Belanger (see Johnson)

Belden (see Dunbar)

Belew (see Bilyeu)

Belfrage (see MacDuff)

Belieu (see Bilyeu)

Beliew (see Bilyeu)

Belk (see Brawley, Davis)

Belknap (see Fowlkes, Wright)

Bell (see Beall, Corson, Dobie, Douglas,
Lynch, MacMillan, Newton, Robinson)

Bell
*Bell Family Association (Tennessee)
100 Andrews Avenue
Springdale, AR 72754-2502
Phone (501) 750-1496 (Secretary)
E. R. Bell, President; Bonnie Bell,
Secretary
Pub. *Bell Tie-ins*, annually; (includes
descendants of the immigrant, William
Bell, Augusta County, Virginia, Knox
County, Tennessee, and Bell County,
Texas)
$5.00 per year membership

Bell
Bell Family Society
11932 Arthur Drive
Anaheim, CA 92804
John Bell

Bell
*Bell Family Association of the United
States
3102 Lakeshore Boulevard
Jacksonville, FL 32210
Phone (904) 387-4669
Grace Bell Rogers, First Vice-President;
Col. William H. Bell, President
Pub. *Bell-a-Peal*, quarterly; (includes
Baeill, Bail, Bailes, Baill, Bails, Bale,
Bales, Ball, Bayle, Bayles, Beal,
Beale, Beales, Beall, Bealles, Bealls,
Beals, Beel, Beele, Beeles, Beels,
Behel, Beil, Beill, Beils, Bel, Biehl,
Biel, Biels, Bihel, Bile, Biles, Bill)
$15.00 per year membership, plus
additional one-time $10.00 computer
entry fee for ancestor charts from new
members

Bell
*Bell Surname Organization
3 Brazill Lane
Whitehall, MT 59759
Phone (406) 287-3369
Lindia Roggia Lovshin

Bell
*Bell Family Reunion of Mifflin County,
Pennsylvania
6835 Gorsten Street
Philadelphia, PA 19119
Mark Frazier Lloyd, Historian

Bell
*The Three Bells
1321 Gum Tree
Huffman, TX 77336
Phone (713) 324-3797
Molly Bateman Reigard, Editor
Pub. *The Three Bells*, quarterly, $15.00
per year subscription; (includes Beall,
Beal(e), etc., anywhere)

Bell
*Clan Bell Descendants, Inc.
PO Box 451
Springfield, VT 05156
Phone (802) 885-3151
Irving Bell, Executive Director Emeritus
and Editor
Pub. *Bell Chimes*, bimonthly; (includes
Bell, Beal, Beale and related families)
$25.00 per year membership (includes
membership in American-Scottish
Alliance)

Bell
*Our Bells of St. André del Misuri
449 Old Dominion Road
Colville, WA 99114
Weir H. and Ethel Bell, Publisher
(includes descendants of William and
Barbara Bell who re-settled by 1798

near St. André, a new town on the
Missouri River)

Beller (see Bailor)

Bellon*
*Bellon Family Organization
3150 South 7700 West
Magna, UT 84044
Phone (801) 250-5603
Jolene Simmons
(includes descendants of Francois
    Augustine Bellon and Mary Ann
    Nickerson)

Bellue (see Bilyeu)

Belmore (see Garstin)

Belongia
*Belongia/Champau Family Reunion
1208 North Tenth Avenue
Wausau, WI 54401
Phone (715) 675-6836
Cynthia Guenther
(includes descendants of John Belongia
    and Christine Champau)

Belote
*Isaac Belote Family Organization
145 Warren Avenue
Rochester, NY 14618
Phone (716) 442-6813
Joan Wilson
Pub. *The Belote Newsletter*, annually,
    free to family members, donation for
    non-family member subscription

Belshe
*Belshe Family Association
Rt. 5, Box 775
Warrensburg, MO 64093
John F. Belshe
(includes descendants of Robert Belshe,
    Esq., and Elizabeth Green, who
    resided in Miller County, Missouri,
    1838)
Annual reunion on Memorial Day
    weekend in Eldon, Missouri

Beltone (see MacBeth)

Belue (see Bilyeu)

Belyew (see Bilyeu)

Belyou (see Bilyeu)

Beman (see Beaman, Beeman)

Bemen (see Beeman)

Bement (see Barnes, Beaman)

Bemon (see Beeman)

Bender (see The Memorial Foundation
    of the Germanna Colonies)

Benedict (see Catlow, Hoyt)

Benedict
Benedict
PO Box 335
Nuevo, CA 92567-0035
Sheila Benedict, C.G.R.S.
Pub. *Benedict*, quarterly, $12.00 per year
    subscription
Annual reunion on the first Sunday of
    August in Earleville, New York

Benedict
*Benedict Family History News
718 South 35th Street
Galesburg, MI 49053
Phone (616) 665-9697
Mary Benedict Grindol, Editor
Pub. *Benedict Family History News*
    (includes descendants of Thomas
    Benedict, who arrived in
    Massachusetts from England about
    1638, later moving to Long Island and
    Connecticut)

Benefiel
*Benefiel Family
Rt. 1, Box 92
Cherokee, OK 73728
Phone (405) 596-2912
James W. Stout

Benefiel
John Wesley Benefiel Family Reunion
1604 Longfellow Street
McLean, VA 22101
Wiley Benefiel

Benge (see Emery)

Benington (see Bennington)

Benison (see MacDuff)

Beniston (see MacDuff)

Benistone (see MacDuff)

Benn (see Ketchum)

Benn
*Benn/Bain Family Reunion
3162 Madeira Avenue
Costa Mesa, CA 92626-2324
Phone (714) 957-0135; (714) 957-6234
    (FAX)
Doris G. Emerson
(includes descendants of Hugh and
    Elizabeth (Scott) Benn, married ca
    1750, of Old Albany County, New
    York)

Benneger (see The Memorial Foundation
    of the Germanna Colonies)

Bennett (see Carpenter, Clark, Corson,
    Goodenow, Heath, Holden, McCune)

Bennett
*Thomas Turner Bennett Organization
16837 Strain Road
Baton Rouge, LA 70726
Phone (504) 275-4281

Jimmy Bennett
(includes registration of descendants of
    Thomas Turner Bennett of Louisiana
    and Mississippi; PAF™ database)

Bennett
*The Bennett Exchange Newsletter
17 Breeman Street
Albany, NY 12205-4928
Phone (518) 869-5260
Beverly Bennett Baumann
Pub. *The Bennett Exchange Newsletter*,
    quarterly; (includes all Bennetts
    everywhere)
$10.50 plus $2.20 postage per year
    membership

Bennett
Wilson Family Record Depository
169 Melody Lane
Tonawanda, NY 14150-9109
Robert J. Wilson
Pub. *Bennett*, quarterly, $25.00 per year
    subscription

Bennett
*Mountain Press
4503 Anderson Pike
PO Box 400
Signal Mountain, TN 37377-0400
Phone (423) 886-6369; (423) 886-5312
    FAX
James L. Douthat, Owner
(Bennett family of Franklin County,
    Tennessee)

Bennett
*Isabella Jane Bennett Family
    Organization
Joshua Bennett Family Organization
2230 North 4000 West
Delta, UT 84624
Phone (801) 864-3674
Nancy B. Fowles

Bennington
*DCF, Inc.
14623 North 49th Place
Scottsdale, AZ 85254-2207
Phone (602) 953-1392
Janna Bennington Larson
Pub. *Bennington Bulletin*, quarterly,
    $10.00 per year subscription; (includes
    comprehensive surname database on
    all U.S. and some foreign Bennington,
    Benington and Binningtons)

Bennison (see MacDuff)

Benoit (see Johnson)

Benson (see Golding)

Benson
Texas Data Books
2410 47th Street
Lubbock, TX 79412
Christine Knox Wood, C.G.
Pub. *Benson Magazine of Research*,
    semiannually, $16.25 per year
    subscription

Benson
*John Jeremiah Benson Family
  Organization
PO Box 9493
Brea, CA 92622
Phone (714) 257-1102
Bryan Nilsen
Pub. *Benson Standard Bearer*, annually

Bent (see Goodenow)

Bentheim
*History of a Family Dispersed
5471 South Hyde Park Boulevard, #8B
Chicago, IL 60615-5830
Phone (312) 667-5471
Mrs. Marion Mayer, Publisher
(includes Jewish-German families,
  Bentheim from Bickenbach, Feitler
  from Seeheim, Frohman from
  Reinheim, Metzger from Mains-
  Weisenau, Steiermann from Biblis, and
  Sussman from Alsbach)

Bentley (see Nettles)

Benton (see Holden)

Bentsen (see Welch)

Berendsen
*Berendsen Database
152 Rockwood Road
Florham Park, NJ 07932
Phone (201) 966-1862
Peter B. Berendsen

Bergen (see Middaugh)

Berger (see Surname Database)

Bergkamp
*Johann Gerhard and Anna Marie
  Bergkamp Genealogy
3709 North State Road 17
Murdock, KS 67111-8911
Phone (316) 297-3978
M. Irene Bergkamp

Berkler
*Berkler Family Association
824 West Fifth Street
Storm Lake, IA 50588-1636
Phone (712) 732-3671
Marjorie M. Berkler Miller, President
(includes descendants of brothers Frank
  and Henry Berkler, who came to the
  U.S. in 1853 to escape military service
  in the Duchy of Hesse-Darmstadt,
  Germany)
Reunion

Bernard (see Berner, Bodine, Cian,
  Johnson, Lambeth)

Berner (see MacDuff)

Berner
*John and Margarette Berner/Burner/
  Bernard Family Association
Rt. 1, Box 123-B
Colfax, WA 99111
Phone (509) 397-3751
Heidi L. Dowling

Berngruber (see Barngrover)

Bernhard
*Bernhard Family Organization
PO Box 2127
Orem, UT 84059-2127
Phone (801) 221-0603
Lynn Jeffrey Bernhard, Family Historian
(includes descendants and ancestors of
  George Peter Bernhard (1804
  Weingarten, Rheinfalz, Germany–1876
  Jonesboro, Illinois) and Susanna
  Messerschmitt (1821 Boebingen,
  Rheinfalz–), and allied families:
  Beisel, Scharf and Zuber; database of
  all Bernhard names in America)

Berrett
*Robert Berrett Family Organization
676 East 2550 North
Ogden, UT 84414
Phone (801) 782-9662
Elwood D. Berrett
(includes descendants of Robert Berrett
  and wife 1604)

Berrie (see Forbes)

Berry (see Forbes)

Berry
Berry
1232 Carlotta Avenue
Berkeley, CA 94707-2707
Dorothy A. Koenig
Pub. *Berry*, quarterly, $10.00 per year
  subscription

Berry
Berry Reunion
53 Lazy River Road
Cloverdale, IN 46120
Francis I. Berry, President
(of German descent)

Berry
*Berry Surname Organization
Highway 87 North
PO Box 340
Burkeville, TX 75932
Phone (409) 565-4751
Helen Rogers Skelton

Berry
*Pioneer Publication
PO Box 1179
Tum Tum, WA 99034-1179
Phone (509) 276-9841
Shirley Penna-Oakes
Pub. *Berry By-Lines*, irregularly, $6.00
  per issue plus $1.75 postage for 1–3
  books, 50¢ for each additional book

Berryman (see Eaves)

Bert
Bert/Burt
6180 Merrywood Drive
Rocklin, CA 95677-3421
Kathleen Stewart
Pub. *Bert/Burt*, quarterly (February, May,
  August and November), $12.00 per
  year subscription

Berthiaume (see Lagesse)

Berton (see Burton)

Bertram (see Buttram, Lambert)

Berwick
*Berwick Branches
7701 Chester Avenue
Northfield, MN 55057
Phone (612) 652-2949
Hazel Berwick Harvey

Bescharde (see Lagesse)

Bessey (see Corson)

Besson (see Rutherford)

Bestman
*The Bestman House on Ballard Road
Box 517
Addison, IL 60101
Phone (630) 543-7899
James Bestman, Publisher
(includes research on descendants of
  Hans Henrich Bestmann (1828–1892
  Germany) and Katharina Dorothea
  Wrage (1832–1888 Germany) from
  Struvenhutten, Germany; Hans Hinrich
  Jaacks (1802–1880 Germany) and
  Catharina Graeve (ca 1807–1882
  Germany) from Wahlstedt, Germany,
  probably Hof No. 5; Johann Greve
  (1823–1900 U.S.) from Wahlstedt,
  Germany, and his wives Sophia
  Christina Luthje (1833–1869) and
  Anna Landahl (–1915 U.S.))

Bestmann (see Bestman)

Betchtel
*Betchtel Family Association
3652 Fernway Drive
Montgomery, AL 36111-3344
Phone (334) 281-1762
Col. Robert W. Betchtel, President
Pub. *Update*, at least biannually, $5.00
  per issue subscription; (includes
  descendants of Samuel W. Betchtel
  (1807 Virginia–1868 Moorefield
  Township, Clark County, Ohio) and
  Christena Sager (1810 Virginia–1844
  Tremont City, Clark County, Ohio))
$15.00 per year membership; reunion
  every six years

Beth (see MacBean)

Bethany (see Cowart)

Bethke (see Evans)

Bethune (see MacBeth, MacDuff)

Betz (see Buechele)

Betzing (see Arthur)

Bevard (see Bovaird)

Bevard
*Bevard Family Organization
7974 Hillsboro Court
Pleasanton, CA 94588-3618
Phone (510) 846-1153
Dorothy Horn Bevard

Beveridge (see MacDuff)

Beverley (see Folk Family Surname
   Exchange, Beverly)

Beverly
*Tejas Publications and Research
2507 Tannehill Drive
Houston, TX 77008-3052
Phone (713) 864-6862; (713) 864-3540
   FAX
Trevia Wooster Beverly, Editor
Pub. *Beverly Family Records*, quarterly,
   $20.00 per year subscription; (includes
   Beverley)

Bevers (see Album)

Beverwych (see Ouderkerk)

Bevier
Bevier-Etling Family Association
717 Maiden Choice Lane, Apartment T07
Baltimore, MD 21228-6113
Phone (410) 732-3444 (work)
Louis Witt, President
$7.00 per year membership

Bevill (see Bosher)

Bevins (see Hatfield)

Bewell (see Lush)

Bewley (see Graves)

Bewley
Bewley Reunion (OK, TX)
32 Oakridge Road
Burleson, TX 76028
Mrs. Milton Watson

Beydler (see Lambert)

Beyer (see Boyer)

Beyerback (see The Memorial
   Foundation of the Germanna Colonies)

Beyerlein
*Beyerlein Family Association
15602 22nd Court, S.E.
Mill Creek, WA 98012
Phone (206) 337-6778
Doug Beyerlein
Pub. *Beyerlein Beginnings*, infrequently,
   $18.00 per issue

Biaggini (see Blossom Press)

Bialac
*Bialac Surname Organization
199 Commodore Drive
Milledgeville, GA 31061
Phone (912) 968-7425
Richard Bialac

Bias (see Byars, Cowart)

Bibee (see Bybee)

Bibee
*William W. Bibee Family Organization
1174 Glorieta Drive
Salt Lake City, UT 84106
Phone (801) 485-0584
Colleen Bibee Hansen
(includes descendants of William W.
   Bibee (1804–1845 Cocke County,
   Tennessee) and Peggy (Mariah) O'Neil
   (1805 Virginia–1844 Cocke County,
   Tennessee))

Bice
Bice Family in America
801 Bangor Drive
Fort Worth, TX 76116
Phone (817) 244-4100
Ernest Gordon Bice
Pub. *Bice Family Bulletin*

Bickers
Uriah Bickers Memorial Association
407 West 200 South
Hyrum, UT 84319
Phone (801) 245-6726
Robert L. Bickers, Vice President
(includes Bickers, all lines, all states;
   association named for Uriah and
   Debby Henry Bickers of Grant County,
   Kentucky)
Free membership; annual reunion on the
   second Sunday of August at White
   Chapel, Holbrook, Grant County,
   Kentucky

Bickert (see Surname Database)

Bickford (see Corson)

Bickford
Bickford Newsletter
230 North Street, B-33
Buffalo, NY 14201
Pub. *Bickford Newsletter*, quarterly,
   queries accepted

Bickmore
Bickmore Family Reunion
PO Box 1147
La Quinta, CA 92253
Virginia Olsen
Pub. *Bickmore Newsletter*

Bickmore
*William Bickmore and Christena
   Bagley (1799) Family Organization
2015 North 1000 East
North Logan, UT 84321
Phone (801) 753-1458
Kaylene A. Griffin, Genealogist

Bicknell (see Williams)

Bicksler
Bicksler-Bixler Newsletter
PO Box 144
Bernville, PA 19506
E. M. Bixler
Pub. *Bicksler-Bixler Newsletter*

Biddle (see Cranston)

Bidlack (see Bidlake)

Bidlake
*Bidlake/Bidlack Family Association
1709 Cherokee Road
Ann Arbor, MI 48104-4448
Phone (313) 662-5080
Dr. Russell E. Bidlack, Editor
Pub. *Bidlake/Bidlack Periodical*,
   annually; (U.S.)
$5.00 per year membership

Bidwell
*Bidwell Family Association, Inc.
6586 Fields Ertel Road
Cincinnati, OH 45241
Faith B. Heath, Secretary
Pub. *Bidwell Family Association
   Newsletter*, quarterly
$15.00 per year membership for families;
   annual reunion

Bieder (see Burnham)

Biederman (see Nettles)

Biedermann (see Nettles)

Biehl (see Bell)

Biel (see Bell)

Biels (see Bell)

Bierce
*Bierce Surname Organization
Augustine Bierce Family Organization
1724 Chestnut Boulevard
Cuyahoga Falls, OH 44223
Phone (216) 920-1222
Fern Clemens Bierce

Bigaouette
*Bigaouette/Thomas Surname
   Organization
13995 220th Street, East
Hastings, MN 55033
Phone (612) 437-8761
Shirley Bigaouette Cuyler
(includes descendants of John-Baptiste
   Thomas dit Bigaouette and wife
   Catherine of Canada and Minnesota
   1860)

Bigbie
Bigbie and Allied Families Quarterly
PO Box 210
Kirtland, NM 87417-0210
Gayle Bigbie Teverbaugh
Pub. *Bigbie and Allied Families
   Quarterly*

Bigelow (see Goodenow)

Bigelow
*The Bigelow Society, Inc.
PO Box 4115
Flint, MI 48504
Pub. *The Forge*, quarterly; (includes
   descendants of John Biglo (Bigelow)
   and Mary (Warren) Big(e)lo(w),
   married 1642; mainly serving the U.S.
   and Canada)
$20.00 suggested donation per year
   membership; annual reunion in July

Biggar
*Clifton James Biggar Family
   Organization
9443 Springville Road
East Otto, NY 14729
Phone (716) 257-9488
Carrie M. Dudley

Biggers (see Folk Family Surname
   Exchange)

Biggs (see Heath, Stoner)

Biggs
*Thomas Biggs Family Organization
1152 North Forest
Mesa, AZ 85203
Phone (602) 969-0112
Judy Nelson

Biggs
*Biggs Research
Rt. 2, Box 166
Frederick, OK 73542-9666
Phone (405) 335-5132 (after 7:00 P.M.)
George M. Biggs
(includes research on George Biggs, who
   came from England in 1881, the son of
   Tabez, and George's wife, Susan)

Bigham
*Bigham/Bingham
1500 Sylvan Drive, #105
Hurst, TX 76053
Phone (817) 282-8749
Sibyl S. Graham, Author

Biglow (see Bigelow)

Bihel (see Bell)

Bile (see Bell)

Biles (see Bell, Reeder)

Biljouw (see Bilyeu)

Bill (see Bell)

Bill
*Bill(s) Family Research
511 South, Park Road, Apartment #133
Spokane, WA 99212-0551
Phone (509) 891-9577
John Lothrop Cobb

Billeadeau (see Johnson)

Billeau (see Bilyeu)

Billiew (see Bilyeu)

Billingsley (see Corder)

Billingsley
*The K.A.R.D. Files
19305 S.E. 243rd Place
Kent, WA 98042-4820
Phone (206) 432-1659
Judy K. Dye, Owner
Pub. *Billingsley Yesterday and Today*,
   irregularly, $6.00–$7.00 per volume
   (Washington residents add 8.2% sales
   tax)

Billington (see Nelson)

Billiou (see Bilyeu)

Billow
*Billow Database
26007 Atherton
Laguna Hills, CA 92653
Phone (714) 643-3492
Carmen Miesen Bussard

Bills (see Bill, Nell)

Billue (see Bilyeu)

Billups
Billups Bulletin
PO Box 151
Hurst, IL 62949
Phone (618) 987-2006
Bill Wyatt, Editor
Pub. *Billups Bulletin*, quarterly, $20.00
   per year subscription

Billyeu (see Bilyeu)

Bilyeu (see Bilyeu)

Bilyeu
*Family Publications
5628 60th Drive, N.E.
Marysville, WA 98270-9509
Phone E-mail: cxwp57a@prodigy.com

Rose Caudle Terry, Publisher
Pub. *Bilyeu By You*, two to four times per
   year, $8.95 per volume subscription,
   plus $1.50 postage per order; (includes
   Bailliou, Baliew, Ballew, Balloo,
   Ballou, Ballow, Balou, Belew, Belieu,
   Beliew, Bellue, Belue, Belyeu, Belyew,
   Belyou, Biljouw, Billeau, Billiew,
   Billiou, Billue, Billyeu, Bilyeu,
   Bilyew, Bilyou, Blu, Boileau, etc., all
   spellings, all nationalities)

Bilyew (see Bilyeu)

Bilyou (see Bilyeu)

Binder
*Charles Henry Binder Family
   Organization
511 Gaylord
Pueblo, CO 81004
Phone (719) 543-0549
Virginia Baird Penaluna Haling

Bingham (see Surname Sources,
   Barnard)

Bingham
Bingham
30 Highfield Drive
Lee, MA 01238
Garth and Karen Story
Pub. *Bingham*

Bingham
Bingham Researchers
2226 Kehrsglen Court
Chesterfield, MO 63005
Phone (314) 532-1578 (home); (314)
   694-3616 (work)
Barry Bingham
Pub. *Bingham Researchers*, biannually,
   $5.00 per issue; (includes all Bingham
   families in the U.S.); *Newsletter for
   the Descendants of James Bingham,
   County Down, Northern Ireland*,
   annually, free

Bingham
Bingham Chronicle
501 West Sharbauer Drive, #30
Midland, TX 79705
Everett F. Bingham
Pub. *Bingham Chronicle*, $5.00 per year
   subscription

Binion (see Dean)

Binkerhoff (see Newcomb)

Binkley (see Moser)

Binkley
Binkley Family Association
437 Martin Avenue
Mount Joy, PA 17552
Vershenda Oberholtzer

Binnie (see MacBean)

Binning (see McCune)

Binnington (see Bennington)

Birch (see Chamberlain)

Birch
Thomas Erskine Birch Family Newsletter
805 West 16th Street
Upland, CA 91786
Isabel Whitney
Pub. *Thomas Erskine Birch Family
   Newsletter*

Birchfield
*Birchfield/Burchfield Clearinghouse
4515 16th Avenue
Rock Island, IL 61204
Phone (309) 786-7888
Mrs. L. Sutton
Free exchange for FGS

Birckhead (see Holden)

Bird (see Folk Family Surname
   Exchange)

Bird
*Bird Family Association
PO Box 308E
Spring Valley, OH 45370-0308
James Bird

Bird
*Folk Family
PO Box 52048
Knoxville, TN 37950-2048
Hester E. Stockton, Owner; Sarah E.
   Bird, Editor
Pub. *Bird Branches*, quarterly, $15.00 per
   year subscription, $5.00 per issue;
   (includes Burd/Byrd)

Birds
Birds Family (KY)
Star Rt., Box 18
Clovis, NM 88101
W. A. Kilmer

Birdsall
Birdsall/Birdsell Family Association
PO Box 11154
Greenwich, CT 06831
Mrs. Clifford A. Birdsell
Pub. *Birdsall Bulletin*, three times per
   year
$12.00 per year membership, $15.00 per
   year overseas membership

Birdsell (see Birdsall)

Birky (see Covert)

Birman
*Birman Surname Organization
199 Commodore Drive
Milledgeville, GA 31061
Phone (912) 968-7425
Richard Bialac

Birrell (see Burrell)

Bisbee
*Bisbee Family Association
65481 C.R. 376 Van Auken Lake
Bangor, MI 49013
Phone (616) 621-4641
Viola Bisbee Drake, Vice President
Pub. *Bisbee Family Connection*, three
   times per year; (includes descendants
   of Elisha Bisbee who ran the ferry in
   1645 on the North River, between
   Marshfield and Norwell,
   Massachusetts, presumed to be the son
   of Thomas Besbeech of Sandwich,
   Kent, England, immigrated 1634/5,
   settled Scituate, Massachusetts)
$15.00 per year membership; biennial
   reunion

Bishop (see Kettenring, McRae, Moser)

Bishop
*Ira D. Bishop Collection on the Bishop
   Families of America
South Suburban Genealogical and
   Historical Society
320 East 161st Place
PO Box 96
South Holland, IL 60473
Phone (708) 333-9474
Alice DeBoer, Librarian
$10.00 search fee by mail

Bishop
Bishop Surname Exchange
22540 Lake Boulevard
Saint Clair Shores, MI 48082
John Bishop

Bishoppe (see McRae)

Bisset (see Fraser)

Bissett (see Macnachton)

Bissie (see MacDuff)

Bissy (see MacDuff)

Bitzer
*Johannes Bitzer/Bizer and Katharine
   Haigis Family Organization
143 Pastors Walk
Monroe, CT 06468-1008
Norma Heyse

Bivins (see Wheeler)

Bixby
*Bixby Family Reunion
1627 Highway 1
Fairfield, IA 52556-8947
Phone (515) 472-2363
Charlotte M. Fleig

Bixler (see Bicksler)

Bizer (see Bitzer)

Bjornhjell (see Thorson)

Blabirn (see MacDuff)

Blaburn (see MacDuff)

Black (see Arthur, Campbell, Gillean,
   Gregor, Lambert, Petersen, Pruitt,
   Watkins)

Black
*Black/Gibson Family Association
8505 Glenview Avenue
Takoma Park, MD 20912
Phone (301) 89-6621; (301) 589-1366
   FAX
M. Sandra Reeves
(restricted to descendants of Samuel
   Black and Polly Gibson (ca 1800–) of
   South Carolina and Alabama; also
   Brasfield, Glover, Peak and Robinson)

Black
*Joseph Smith Black Family
   Organization
Peter Thompson Black Family
   Organization
2230 North 4000 West
Delta, UT 84624
Phone (801) 864-3674
Nancy B. Fowles

Blackbourn (see Blackburn)

Blackbourne
*Blackbourne Family Reunion
1535 Wilshire Road
Fallbrook, CA 92028-9221
Phone (619) 439-5432 (area code 760
   beginning 22 March 1997)
Jennie B. Moyer
(includes descendants of Thomas and
   Sarah Foster Blackbourne, who
   migrated to Mecklenburg County,
   Virginia, in the mid-1700s, with their
   children: Elizabeth, Peter, Mary Anne,
   Charlotte, Mary Asford, Clement)

Blackburn (see Allison, Clark, Hatfield,
   Parker, Underwood)

Blackburn
*Blackburn Family Association
300 East 17th Avenue, Apartment 1219
Denver, CO 80203-1223
Kevin R. Howley, President
Pub. *Blackburn Beginnings*, quarterly
$10.00 per year membership

Blackburn
*Blackburn Family Organization
27894 Gail Drive
Warren, MI 48093-4984
Dorothy Challacombe Rowell

Blackburn
*Blackburn/Blackbourn Reunion
413 North Jackson Street
Cuba City, WI 53807
Phone (608) 744-2724

Roger L. Blackbourn, President
(includes descendants of George and
Martha (Nevitt) Blackbourn and
Richard and Mary Anne (Houghton)
Blackbourn who emigrated from
Lincolnshire, England, to Grant
County, Wisconsin Territory, and
Wayne County, New York, in
1844–45)

Blackburn
*Blackburn/Blackbourn Family Updated
Report
202 South Segoe Road
Madison, WI 53705-4939
Phone (608) 233-1506
Donald E. and Ruth A. Duxbury,
Compilers/Publishers
(includes ancestors and descendants of
George and Martha (Nevitt)
Blackbourn and Richard and Mary
Anne (Houghton) Blackbourn of
Lincolnshire, England, and Wisconsin
Territory from 1759)

Blackburne (see Allison)

Blackham
*John Moroni Blackham Family
Organization
PO Box 383
Lehi, UT 84043
Verona Blackham Balle

Blackhurst
*Blackhurst Burner Reunion
PO Box 184
Greenbank, WV 24944
Phone (304) 456-4815
Robert Sheets
(includes families of Jabez Blackhurst of
Tunstall, England, who emigrated to
America in 1886, and Abraham Burner
who migrated to Pocahontas County,
West Virginia (Virginia) in 1787)
Biennial reunion on the last weekend of
July in odd-numbered years at Cass,
Pocahontas County, West Virginia

Blackistone (see Carley)

Blackketter
Blackketter Family Association
PO Box 229
Blackwell, OK 74631
Phone (405) 363-3535
Jim Menzer, President
Pub. *Blackketter Family Association*,
irregularly
$10.00 per year membership; biennial
reunion

Blacklock (see Douglas)

Blackman
*Ellison Blackman Family Organization
3229 Murphy Mill Road
Dolthan, AL 36303
Phone (205) 792-8483
Willie Floyd Blackman

Blackmore
*Blackmore Clearinghouse
Rt. 1, Box 47
Marble Falls, TX 78654
Phone (512) 693-2532
Peggy Blackmore Tombs, Family
Representative

Blackstock (see Douglas, Maxwell)

Blackwelder (see Brawley)

Blackwell (see Alsop)

Blackwell
Blackwell Researcher
West 2416 Johannsen Road
Spokane, WA 99218
Phone (509) 466-2211
Eugene Blackwell, Editor
Pub. *Blackwell Researcher*, quarterly,
$8.00 per year subscription; (includes
Blackwell families from 1645 to the
present)

Blackwood (see Douglas)

Blackwood
*Blackwood Family Association
3708 Grady Street
Fort Worth, TX 76119
Phone (817) 535-7207
Anne Bucklin Frost

Blair (see Folk Family Surname
Exchange, Cian, Graham)

Blair
*Blair-Moffett Families of California
166 Villa Avenue
Clovis, CA 93612
Bryan Walter, Genealogist and Historian
Pub. *Blair-Moffett Families*, every 10
years, $15.00 per issue; (includes
descendants of James Hamilton
Moffett (1787–1852 southwest
Missouri) and his wives, Nancy Smith
and Charlotte Bunn Mayfield, and of
Rev. Jonathan Blair and his second
wife, Nancy Mayfield Moffett)
Annual reunion on the first Saturday
after Mothers' Day at Mooney Grove,
Visalia, Tulare County, California

Blair
*Thomas Blair Family Organization
747 Lovell Avenue
Roseville, MN 55113
Phone (612) 484-4178
Florence Hart Carr
Pub. *The Blair Family Newsletter*,
annually, contribution for subscription;
(includes descendants of Thomas Blair,
pioneer from Argyllshire (1856) to
Minnesota)

Blair
*Blair Society for Genealogical
Research/Clan Blair Society
5 Nichols Road
Convent Station, NJ 07960-4609
Phone (201) 538-6367
Preston E. Groome, Compiler
Pub. *Blairlin & Blairtrees*, biannually,
usually in odd-numbered years, $25.00
per issue subscription

Blair
*Clan Blair Society
103 Stuart Court
Summerville, SC 29483-1986
Norman D. Blair, President
Pub. *Blair Bruidhinn*, quarterly
$20.00 per year membership

Blair
Blair Reunion
1350 Huntcliff Court
Milford, MI 48380
Nancy Schaffer, Editor

Blair
*Blair Society for Genealogical Research
486 Larkspur Lane
Chambersburg, PA 17201
Phone (717) 264-8927
Mona J. Mattingly, Editor
Pub. *The Blair Family Magazine*,
quarterly
$15.00 per year membership

Blair
Blair Newsletter
PO Box 272341
Houston, TX 77077-2341
Kathleen B. Rheman
Pub. *Blair Newsletter*

Blaisdel (see Corson)

Blaisdell
*Blaisdell Family National Association
PO Box 337
York, ME 03909
Pub. *Blaisdell Papers*, semiannually,
$10.00 per year subscription; (includes
descendants of Ralf Bleasdale who
landed at Pemaquid, Maine, in 1635,
and other Blaisdell families who do
not connect to Ralph (1.1))
Annual reunion

Blake (see Folk Family Surname
Exchange, Corson, Lush)

Blake
*Folk Family
PO Box 52048
Knoxville, TN 37950-2048
Hester E. Stockton, Owner; Sara and
Peter Blake, Editors
Pub. *Blake Banner*, quarterly, $15.00 per
year subscription, $5.00 per issue;
(includes Blakeley, Blakly, Bleak)

Blake
*Blake Surname Organization
Benjamin Frederick Blake Family
    Organization
165 East 200 South
Saint George, UT 84770
Phone (801) 628-6284
Roberta Blake Barnum
(deals exclusively with the Blakes of
    southern England and American
    descendants of Ben F. Blake)

Blakeburn (see Hutchison)

Blakeley (see Blake, Stewart, Warren)

Blakely
*The K.A.R.D. Files
19305 S.E. 243rd Place
Kent, WA 98042-4820
Phone (206) 432-1659
Judy K. Dye, Owner
Pub. *Blakely Bandwagon*, irregularly,
    $6.00–$7.00 per volume (Washington
    residents add 8.2% sales tax)

Blakenbaker (see The Memorial
    Foundation of the Germanna Colonies)

Blakey
Blakey/Blakley/White Family
2702 Locust Street
Saint Joseph, MO 64507
Susan A. Blakley

Blakley (see Blakey)

Blakley
Blakley Family Organization
2612 Geneso Road
Avon, NY 14414
Kenneth E. Blakley

Blakly (see Blake)

Blalock (see Douglas, Foster, Neville)

Blalock
Blalock/Grimmett Family Association
6421 U.S. Highway 31
Hanceville, AL 35077
Delton D. Blalock

Blalock
John Milton Blalock Historical Society
    Family Organization
PO Box 518
Liberty, MS 39645

Blalock
*Blalock, Blaylock Clans
Rt. 1, Box 1280
Ripley, OK 74062
Phone (918) 372-4405
Colleen Blaylock Green

Blanc
Blanc Surname Exchange
174 Hunter Lane
Lake Havasu City, AZ 86403

Phone (520) 680-6078;
    (520) 680-7821 FAX
Donald R. Blanc

Blanchard (see Johnson, Usher)

Blanche (see Likes)

Bland (see Cowart)

Bland
Bland Family Newsletter
250 Roycroft Boulevard
Buffalo, NY 14226-4820
Charles L. Bland
Pub. *Bland Family Newsletter, "Among
    Cousins"*, bimonthly, $18.00 per year
    subscription

Bland
Bland Family Reunion
1118 Sayles Boulevard
Abilene, TX 79605
Marjorie Sayles

Blankenship (see Hatfield)

Blanks
*Blanks Family History
8529 Spalding Drive
Richmond, VA 23229
Phone (804) 741-1836
B. DeRoy Beale

Blanshan (see Crispell)

Blantin (see Blanton)

Blanton (see Huskey)

Blanton
Blanton Quarterly Bulletin
509 Commanche Trail
Frankfort, KY 40601-1751
Joy Van Curon Blanton, Editor and
    Publisher
Pub. *Blanton Quarterly Bulletin*, $10.00
    per year subscription, $3.50 per issue;
    (includes Blantin, Blantoun, etc.)

Blanton
*The Worldwide Blanton Convention
111 Magnolia Street
Upton, KY 42784
Phone (502) 369-7763
Col. Rudolph D. Blanton, CEO and
    Secretary
Annual reunion on the third weekend of
    September

Blanton
Blanton-Scurlock-Wareing-Gray Family
    Association
2306 Westgate
Houston, TX 77019
Phone (713) 529-2333
Harold Helm
$25.00 plus pedigree and family group
    sheets for membership

Blantoun (see Blanton)

Blasingame (see Blassingame)

Blasingim (see Blassingame)

Blassingame
*Blassingame Family Archive
501 West Gandy Street
PO Box 131
Denison, TX 75020-0131
Phone (214) 465-5005; (903) 465-6366
W. Doak Blassingame, M.D., Publisher
(includes Blasingame, Blasingim,
    Blassingame, Blassingham, Blassingim
    and related names)

Blassingham (see Blassingame)

Blassingim (see Blassingame)

Blattenberger
*Blattenberger/Plattenberger Family
1301 Bradford Road
Oreland, PA 19075-2414
Phone (215) 836-4727
Dale E. Berger, Genealogist/Historian
Pub. *Newsletter*, quarterly; (includes
    descendants of Johannes and Barbara
    (Palmer) Blattenberger who arrived in
    Philadelphia in 1743 from the
    Bavarian community of "Hof
    Plattenburg" and settled in Warwick
    Township, Lancaster County,
    Pennsylvania)
Reunion

Blauvelt
Blauvelt News
3040 Kishner Drive, Apartment 315
Las Vegas, NV 89109
Phone (702) 734-8489
Mrs. G. Allen Lovell, Editor and
    Publisher
Pub. *Blauvelt News*, three times per year,
    $2.00 per year subscription

Blauvelt
*Association of Blauvelt Descendants
685 Terrace Heights
Wyckoff, NJ 07481
Phone Susan B. Heilmann, President
    (201) 891-0753

Blauvelt
*Association of Blauvelt Descendants
10462 Cricket Hill Drive
Barboursville, VA 22923
Jean C. Anderson, Secretary-Editor
Pub. *The Blauvelt News*, quarterly, $4.00
    per year subscription
$5.00 per year membership

Blaw (see Blue, MacDuff)

Blawein (see Blue)

Blaylock (see Blalock, Foster)

Blazer
Blazer Picnic
110 Midway Drive
McKees Rocks, PA 15024
Robert Blazier

Blazio (see Blossom Press)

Bleak (see Blake)

Bledsoe
Bledsoe Family Quarterly
5843 Royal Crest Drive
Dallas, TX 75230
Banks McLauren, Jr., Editor and
Publisher
Pub. *Bledsoe Family Quarterly*

Bledsoe
Bledsoe Family Historical Society
1810 Aisquith Road
Richmond, VA 23229
Phone (804) 282-1544
Robert C. "Bob" Siegfried, President

Bleikers (see Links Genealogy
Publications)

Blencowe
*Blencowe Families Association
550 North Darlington Street
South San Gabriel, CA 91770-4312
Phone (818) 280-2506
Helen Blincoe Simpson, Secretary
Pub. *Newsletter*, quarterly; (includes
Blincoe, most common spelling in the
U.S.)
$8.00 per year membership; biennial
reunion

Blessing (see Towne)

Blessington (see Lemon)

Bleuler (see Moales)

Blew (see Blue)

Blewster (see Bluster)

Bleything (see Blythling)

Blickenstaff (see Frantz)

Blijkers (see Links Genealogy
Publications)

Blincoe (see Blencowe)

Bliss (see Wright)

Bliss
Bliss Family of America
2719 S.W. Riven Dell
Lake Oswego, OR 97034
Pub. *Blissful Notes*, irregularly

Blitch (see Dubberly)

Bloberger (see McLouth)

Blocher (see Frantz)

Blockley
*Blockley Surname Organization
William Blockley Family Organization
5546 North Fork Road
Deming, WA 98244
Phone (206) 592-5693
Wilna J. Blockley-Baisden

Blodgett (see Fuller)

Blois
*Blois Family History
729 South Columbia Drive
Woodburn, OR 97071
Phone (503) 982-2110
Ralph S. Blois, Publisher
(any Blois, Bloyce, Bloys, Bloice, or
Deblois, anywhere, any time; database
includes several family lines and
thousands of names)

Blood (see Cian, Ferriss)

Bloss
*Bloss-Pyles-Ross-Sellards Family
History
4031 Grand Avenue
Deland, FL 32720
Phone (904) 985-4046
Harry L. Sellards,Jr., Publisher
(includes related families: Adkins,
Ballangee, Booth, Ferguson, Lewis,
Napier, Queen, Scalf and Smith)

Bloss
Descendants of Valentine Bloss
614 Rothbury Lane
Louisville, KY 40243
Frank Bloss
Pub. *Newsletter* (includes descendants of
Valentine Bloss, Revolutionary soldier,
who died in West Virginia)

Bloss
Descendants of (Georg) Conrad Bloss
9939 Palmerston Road
Richmond, VA 23236
Earl Savage
Pub. computerized newsletter (includes
descendants of (Georg) Conrad Bloss
(1728–1774) from near Elkton,
Virginia)

Blosser (see Stewart)

Blossom Press (see Multi-family
Associations)

Blott (see Clark)

Blow (see MacDuff)

Bloyd (see Newmyer)

Blu (see Bilyeu, Blue)

Blucker (see Kahler)

Blue (see Gregor, MacMillan)

Bluemel (see Stevens)

Blum (see Israelite)

Blund (see MacDuff)

Blunden (see Newcomb)

Blunden
*Blunden Family History Society
7052 Fallbrook Court
New Port Richey, FL 34655-4204
Phone (813) 376-4619
Mrs. America M. Carlson, Historian

Blunt (see MacDuff)

Bluster
Bluster/Blewster Exchange
830 Crestwood, Box 830
El Dorado, AR 71730
Phone (501) 862-2505
W. C. Blewster

Blythling
*Blything Database
3199 West Boulevard
Cleveland, OH 44111-2821
Phone (216) 631-7407
Bob Ghinder
(includes Blything (sometimes spelled
Bleything), located primarily in
Indiana, New Jersey and England)

B'Man (see Beeman)

Boadway
*Boadway/Boardway/Boudway/Budway
Family Clearinghouse
40 Jackson Street
Sanford, ME 04073-3131
Phone (207) 324-4875
Roland Rhoades, Jr., President
Free registration

Boardway (see Boadway)

Boarman (see Rutherford)

Boatman
Boatman Family Association
734 Quapaw
Enid, OK 73701
Phone (405) 234-3496
Opal London Cox
Pub. *Boatman Newsletter*, irregularly

Boatwright (see Gilleland)

Bobley (see Jelly)

Bobo (see Golding, Haynes, Stewart)

Bobo
*Bobo Family Association
358 South Main Street, #18
Orange, CA 92668-3876
Phone (714) 978-2904;
(714) 978-0747 FAX

Charles H. (Chuck) Bobo, Secretary
Pub. *The Bobo Roots-Cellar*, quarterly,
$15.00 per year subscription; (includes
descendants of Israel Bobo (ca 1780
Prince William County, Virginia–)
and Margaret Graham (1780
Pennsylvania–))
$25.00 per year membership

Bobst (see Pabst)

Bockova
*Josefa Bockova Family Organization
3684 Townley Road
Shaker Heights, OH 44122-5120
Phone (216) 751-8601
Donald Allen Zak
(of Bohemia from 1650 to the present)

Boddie
Boddie Family Reunion and Research
7226 Beaufort Way
Shreveport, LA 71129
Bibbit Pierce

Bodeker
*Bodeker Family
609 Spruce Avenue
Tillamook, OR 97141-2859
Phone (503) 842-2497
Willard R. Berry, Editor-Publisher
Pub. *Bodeker Family Newsletter*, once or
twice per year, $2.00 per year
subscription, restricted to family
members; (includes descendants of
William Bodeker (1816 Germany–
1871 Bergholtz, New York), his first
wife, Kristine Schaper, who died in
Germany, and his second wife, Louise
(Schleger) Gombert)
Annual reunion on the third Saturday of
August at Mill City, Oregon

Bodensteiner
*John Carl Bodensteiner Family
Organization
Saint Lucas, IA 52166
Mrs. L. Kuennen

Bodet (see Beaudet)

Bodett (see Beaudet)

Bodewes (see Olthaus)

Bodine (see CTC Family Association,
Graves)

Bodine
*Jean Bodine Family Organization
333 Center Street
Evanston, WY 82930
Phone (307) 789-2893
Harry L. Bodine
(includes related families of Tueller-
Kunz (Switzerland-Utah), Rogers-
Shepherd (England-Utah), Miller-
Stephens (New Jersey), Rouse-Reed-
Bernard)

Boehler (see Bailor)

Boehm (see The Memorial Foundation
of the Germanna Colonies, Böhm)

Boehm
*Boehm Family Reunion
335 West Shackley Street
PO Box 75
Geneva, IN 46740
Phone (219) 368-7352
Ruth Brown

Boehmer (see Miehls)

Boelke (see Klewer)

Boeplen (see Stabler)

Boernes (see Barnes)

Boettcher (see Sager)

Boftz (see Johnson)

Bogan
Bogan Family Association
107 Noweta
Lake Kiowa, TX 76240
Helen Bogan Platt

Bogardus (see Nelson)

Bogardus
Bogardus Cousins
521 West Main Street
Grand Ledge, MI 48837
Warren Coon
Pub. *Bogardus Cousins*

Bogardus
*Anneke Jans and Everardus Bogardus
Descendants Association
1121 Linhof Road
Wilmington, OH 45177-2917
Phone (513) 382-3803
William Brower Bogardus, Family
Representative
Pub. *"Dear Cousin" Letter*, unscheduled
but usually at least twice per year, free;
(extensive library permits research on
virtually all Colonial families of early
New York and New Jersey up to about
1800, especially Bogardus, Brouwer,
Brower, Brewer)

Boges (see Newberry)

Bogges (see Boggess)

Boggess
*Boggess Family Association
1410 Lamar Drive
Richmond, TX 77469
Phone (713) 341-5257
Ronald Lee Boggess; Bitsy Barr, Editor
Pub. *Boggess Family Association
Newsletter*, semiannually; (includes
Boggis, Bogges, Bauguess)
$12.00 per year membership; annual
reunion in various places

Boggis (see Boggess)

Boggs (see Clark, Dean)

Boggs
Boggs Newsletter
396 Taylor Road
Stow, MA 01775
Alice C. Grady
Pub. *Boggs Newsletter*, quarterly, $12.00
per year subscription

Bogle (see MacDuff)

Bogwell (see Newton)

Bohannon (see Kettenring)

Bohanon (see Buchanan)

Bohart
Bohart Family Reunion
12060 Cortona Way
San Diego, CA 92128
Philip Bohart

Böhm
*John Francis Böhm (Boehm) Family
Organization
7680 Lowell Boulevard
Westminster, CO 80030
Phone (303) 429-0158
Wynona Joyce Bohm

Bohm
*William Lizenbery Family Organization
7680 Lowell Boulevard
Westminster, CO 80030
Phone (303) 429-0158
Wynona Joyce Bohm

Bohr (see Lauer)

Bohrer (see Borror)

Boii (see Boyer)

Boileau (see Bilyeu)

Boland (see Cian)

Boles
The Boles-Bole, Boal, Boyle Record
61 Gloucester Street
Clifton Park, NY 12065
David B. Boles
Pub. *The Boles-Bole, Boal, Boyle Record*,
quarterly, $10.00 per year subscription,
queries accepted

Bon (see Links Genealogy Publications)

Bonaker (see Clark)

Bonar (see Brothers, Graham)

Bonass (see Cian)

Bond (see McLouth)

Bond
*Moses Bond Family Organization
29 East Portland Avenue
Vincennes, IN 47591
Phone (812) 882-9371
Richard Carl Rodgers, II, Historian/
Archivist
(archival facility collects information on
all descendants and ancestors of the
family in computer database;
descendants of Moses Bond (1794
Holston River area, Hawkins County,
Tennessee–1880 Hire Township,
McDonough County, Illinois), son of
John Bond and Susannah Wade of
Virginia, and wife Eleanor Ward (1799
Washington County, Kentucky–1876
Hire Township))

Bond
*Bond Reunion
82 Damon Avenue
Melrose, MA 02176
Phone (617) 665-4664
Theodore S. Bond, Editor
Pub. *Bond Family Newsletter* (includes
descendants of William Bond (1754
Plymouth, Devon–) and Hannah
Cranch (1746 Kingsbridge, Devon–))

Bond
Bond Family Reunion
710 Bond Road
Lebanon, TN 37090
(includes anyone with Bond lineage, but
especially descendants of Robert
Henry Bond (1854–))
Reunion at the Cedars of Lebanon State
Park, Lebanon, Tennessee

Bond
The Bond Family Tales and Trails
PO Box 34
Frannie, WY 82423
Clarence Lee Bond, Editor
Pub. *The Bond Family Tales and Trails*,
quarterly (January, April, July and
October), $15.00 per year subscription;
(includes all branches of the Bond
family, with variant spellings: Bonde,
Bondi, Bonds, etc.)

Bonde (see Bond)

Bondi (see Bond)

Bondick (see Johnson)

Bonds (see Bond)

Bondurant
*Bondurant Family Association
170 Windsor Court
Athens, GA 30606
Phone (706) 613-0030
Mary Bondurant Warren, Editor
Pub. *B.F.A. Newsletter*, quarterly, $10.00
per year subscription; (includes
descendants of Jean Pierre (John Peter)
Bondurant (1677 France–1734
Virginia))

Bone (see Cian)

Bone
Fragments: Bone
419 North Larchmont Boulevard, Suite
277
Los Angeles, CA 90004
Pub. *Fragments: Bone*, bimonthly,
$12.00 per year subscription

Bonet (see Bonnete)

Boney
*Boney/Stutts Family Organization
PO Box 702
Cameron, TX 76520
Phone (817) 697-2321
Melba Boney Wells, Secretary
(includes descendants of James Boney
and Penelope Wells and of George
Stutts, who first married Martha and
second married Penelope Jones; also
researching Benjamin Franklin Stewart
(son of Hamilton Stewart and Joanna
Jacoway) and Susan Caroline Jones, of
Neshoba County, Mississippi)

Bonholzer (see Miehls)

Bonk
Geike (Guy) Bonk Family
Rt. 1, Box 137
Stanhope, IA 50246
Jane Arends

Bonnar (see Graham)

Bonnell (see Bunnell)

Bonner (see Graham)

Bonnet (see Bonnete, Bunnett)

Bonnete
*Bonnet(t)e and Kin Family
314 East Glenwood Road
Lake Forest, IL 60045-3020
Phone (847) 234-4804
Dr. Howard T. Bonnett, Editor
Pub. *Bonnet/Bonnettes and Kin*,
irregularly; (includes Bonet, Bonnett)
Donation for membership

Bonnett (see Bonnete)

Bonnett
Bonnett Clearinghouse
Rt. 1, Box 192
Monmouth, IL 61462
James E. and Sharon L. Todd

Bonnette (see Bonnete, Johnson)

Bontein (see Graham)

Bonthron (see MacDuff)

Bonthrone (see MacDuff)

Bontine (see Graham)

Boodry
*Boodry Family Organization
15388 Road 4, N.W.
Quincy, WA 98848
Maxine Read
(includes Boodry-William Peterson and
Maren Hanson)

Book (see Franciscus, MacDuff)

Booker
Booker
PO Box 210
Dover, AR 72837

Boone (see Custer, Gant, Rutherford)

Boone
*The Boone Family Association of the
Southwest
PO Box 2575
Peoria, AZ 85380-2575
Phone (602) 935-1230
Rev. Cynthia Ann Wilson Parks, Editor
and Historian
Pub. *Boone's Desert Sky*, bimonthly
$10.00 per year membership for families

Boone
*Boone Family Association of California
19248 Rockridge Way
Sonora, CA 95370
Phone (209) 532-6266
Mary K. Boone, Editor and Treasurer
Pub. *Boone's Sierra Echoes*, quarterly
$15.00 per year membership for families

Boone
*The Boone Family Association of Cal-
Mont in Missouri
8580 Farley
Overland Park, KS 66212-4626
Phone (913) 383-0221
Dorothy Boone Graham
Pub. *The CAL-MONT News*, quarterly
(July, November, January and April);
(includes a branch of the family of
George[3] Boone who came from
England in 1717 and settled in
Pennsylvania, includes mostly the
descendants of Daniel[5] and his younger
brother George[5] Boone, sons of Squire[4]
Boone and Sarah Morgan, who came
to Missouri Territory 1818–1820, and
settled along the county line between
Callaway and Montgomery counties,
1818–1820; interested in descendants
and history of their part in opening up
the country west of the Mississippi
River from 1820, especially the family
of John Linville[6] Boone, son of
George[5] Boone and Ann Linville)
$5.00 per year membership; annual
reunion on the second Sunday of June
at the Williamsburg Community
Center, Williamsburg, Callaway
County, Missouri (off I-70)

Boone
*The Daniel Boone and Frontier Families
   Research Association
HCR 62, Box 113
Hermann, MO 65041
Ken Kamper, Historian
Pub. *History and Genealogy Research
   Letter*, quarterly; (includes Boone
   family, Byran family, and families
   associated with Boone, 1750–1820)
$5.00 per year membership for
   individuals, $7.50 per year
   membership for families

Boone
Daniel Boone Ancestral Lines
PO Box 13548
Saint Louis, MO 63138
Maryann Schirker
Pub. *Daniel Boone Ancestral Lines*,
   quarterly, $25.00 per year subscription

Boose
*Boose Family
2352 Tyrone Road
Westminster, MD 21158-2636
Phone (410) 857-4964
Evelyne E. Boose
(includes Booze, Buse, Buss and related
   families: Coon, Crouse, Dayhoof,
   Delphey, Eichelberger, Fair, Favorite,
   Frauenfelter, Frownfelder, Groff, Hull
   (German), Wantz, Weant, Wentz and
   Weygandt)

Boosey (see MacDuff)

Boosie (see MacDuff)

Booth (see Surname Sources, Arthur,
   Bloss, Jackson)

Boothe
Association of Boothe Descendants
Boothe Memorial Park Museum
(Main Street and Putney—location)
165 Chapel Street (mailing address)
Stratford, CT 06497
Bessie Burton, Director of Volunteers
Pub. *Newsletter*

Booze (see Boose)

Booze
Booze Family Reunion
PO Box 709
Lahoma, OK 73754
Jack Booze

Boozer (see Garner)

Borchardt
*Borchardt Family History
202 South Segoe Road
Madison, WI 53705-4939
Phone (608) 233-1506
Donald E. and Ruth A. Duxbury,
   Compilers/Publishers
(includes ancestors and descendants of

William and Augusta (Radloff)
   Borchardt of Pommern, Prussia, and
   Wisconsin from 1832)

Borchens (see Kelm)

Borchert (see Rothenberger)

Bordelon (see Johnson)

Borden (see McRae, Wright)

Borden
*Borden Genealogical Society
5968 Nachoochee Trail
Flowery Branch, GA 30542-3133
Donald W. Borden

Borders
*Borders Families
235 Sotir Street
Fort Walton Beach, FL 32548-4263
Phone (904) 862-1500
William Steve Borders
(includes Borders in America)
Free exchange

Borel
The Borel Family Newsletter
429 Page Bacon Road, Suite 140
Mary Esther, FL 32569
Pub. *The Borel Family Newsletter*,
   quarterly, $12.00 per year subscription

Borell (see Burrell)

Borgan (see Cian)

Borgo
*Borgo Press
PO Box 2845
San Bernardino, CA 92406
Phone (909) 884-5813; (909) 888-4942
   FAX
Michael Burgess, Publisher
Pub. *Borgo Family Histories (a
   publishing series, not open to the
   general public for submissions)*,
   irregularly, price varies

Borgstadt (see Borgstedt)

Borgstedt
*Johann Heinrich Borgstedt/Borgstadt
   Family
Rt. 3, Box 190
Concordia, MO 64020-9505
Phone (816) 463-7523
Mrs. Buddy Samuels, Compiler
(includes descendants of Johann Heinrich
   Borgstedt and Catherine Marie
   Borgstedt/Borgstadt, born Westphalia,
   Germany 1820)
Three copies of your line's data and
   share of reunion costs for membership;
   reunion

Borland
*Thomas Borland Family Organization
1 Kingsbridge Place
Pueblo, CO 81001
Phone (719) 542-2779
Mrs. John E. Chenoweth, Jr.

Born (see Kelley)

Borror
Borror's Corners
15525 Menominee Drive
Plymouth, IN 46563-9794
Phone (219) 936-7628
Lillian Borror Kenney, Editor/Secretary
Pub. *Borror's Corners*, three times per
   year, $6.00 per year subscription;
   (includes Bohrer, Boyer)
Reunion

Borthwick
Clan Borthwick Association
25 Lafayette Street
Calais, ME 04619
Phone (207) 454-3886
Joseph T. Borthwick, Secretary for North
   America

Bosher
*John Bosher Family Organization
PO Box 1314
Chester, VA 23831-8314
Phone (804) 748-6456
Carson Gary Bosher
(includes related families: Anderson,
   Bevill, Bowden, Byrd, Chenault,
   Clark, Coleman, Doss, Dowdy,
   Drewry, Drinkwater, Edwards, Eubank,
   Gunn, Henshaw, Holland, Hudgens,
   Lowry, Martin, Meadow, Perkinson,
   Stewart, Wheeler, Whitlock, Williams,
   Wood, dating back to 1612)

Boswell (see MacDuff)

Bosworth (see Bozarth)

Botek (see Israelite)

Botkin (see Clark)

Botsford
*The Botsford Family Historical
   Association
601 Main Street
PO Box 271
Plymouth, CT 06782-0271
Phone (860) 283-9884
Janet Elton, Editor
Pub. *Band of Botsford Bulletin*,
   semiannually; (includes descendants of
   Henry and Elizabeth Botsford)
$10.00 per year membership

Bottoms
*Bottoms Family Organization
Coleman Research Agency
241 North Vine Street, Apartment 1104E
Salt Lake City, UT 84103-1945
Marlene McCormick Coleman
(includes all Bottoms families)

Bouchard
Bouchard Family Newsletter
PO Box 13548
Saint Louis, MO 63138
Maryann Schirker
Pub. *Bouchard Family Newsletter*,
    quarterly, $25.00 per year subscription

Boucher
Boucher Family Newsletter
PO Box 2414
Cridersville, OH 45806
J. Bowsher
Pub. *Boucher Family Newsletter*, three
    times per year, $3.00 per year
    subscription; (Bowsher, Baus(c)her,
    Bousher, etc.)

Boudette (see Beaudet)

Boudreau (see Johnson)

Boudreaux (see Augeron)

Boudway (see Boadway)

Bougon (see Blossom Press)

Boule (see Prohaska)

Bouley (see Prohaska)

Bouligny
*The Bouligny Foundation
331 Doucet Road
Lafayette, LA 70503
Phone (318) 988-0930 (home); (318)
    984-2030 (work); (318) 988-4067 FAX
Dan Bouligny
Pub. *Newsletter*, at least annually
(organized to make and promote
    historical studies of the life, times, and
    family of Don Francisco Bouligny
    (1736–1800))

Bouquet
Bouquet-Buckey
Whispering Oaks
5821 Rowland Hill Road
Cascade, MD 21719-1939
Phone (301) 416-2660
Victor Gebhart, President
Pub. *Bouquet-Buckey*, annually, $2.00 per
    issue

Bourchard (see Bushore)

Bourg (see Johnson)

Bourgeois (see Johnson)

Bourland
Bourland/Loving Reunion
305 Paradise Lane
Granite City, IL 62040
Mrs. R. Huff

Bourland
The Bourland-Loving Bulletin
40269 Highway 373
Hamilton, MS 39746

Helen Crawford, Editor
Pub. *The Bourland-Loving Bulletin*,
    quarterly, $20.00 per year subscription

Bourne (see Barnard, Smith)

Bousher (see Boucher)

Boutcher (see Runyan)

Boutelle (see Main)

Bouton
*Bouton Family Organization
171 Main Street
Newington, CT 06111
Phone (203) 666-9566
John F. Bolles, III
(includes descendants of Capt. Daniel
    Bouton (1743–1820) and Sarah Andrus
    (1745–1828) of South Salem, New
    York)

Bouton
Bouton/Ohlson Family Organization
15 North 700 East
Orem, UT 84057
Mrs. D. Bouton Rock

Boutwell (see Beard)

Bovaird
Bovaird/Bavaird/Bovard/Bevard/Bravard/
    Brevard/Broward Research
    Cooperative
8650 Heather Run Drive, South
Jacksonville, FL 32256-9529
Marianne Herold McNair
Pub. *Bovaird/Bavaird/Bovard/Bevard/
    Bravard/Brevard/Broward Research
    Cooperative*
$25.00 one-time membership fee,
    includes all back issues of newsletters

Bovard (see Bovaird)

Bovee (see Fadner)

Bowater
*Bowater Surname Organization
PO Box 8072
Longview, TX 75607-8072
Ben R. Reynolds

Bowden (see Baudouin, Bosher, Corson)

Bowdoin (see Baudouin)

Bowdon (see Baudouin)

Bowdown (see Bowdouin)

Bowen (see Cian, Rutherford, Scott,
    Smith)

Bowen
Bowen
3894 Williams Street
Clarkston, GA 30021

Debbie Jacobs
Pub. *Bowen*, four or five times per year,
    $4.00 per year subscription

Bowen
Bowen Family Reunion
PO Box 309
Wellington, TX 79095
H. L. Bowen

Bower (see Gregor)

Bower
Bower Family Newsletter
325 West Hickam Drive
Columbia, MO 65203
Phone (314) 442-1498
Janice Tompkins, Editor
Pub. *Bower Family Newsletter*, annually,
    $5.00 per year subscription; (includes
    descendants of David and Susan
    Badger Bower, also Steven Gottlieb
    Bower (Bauer), who came to U.S. in
    1838)
Annual reunion in June

Bowerbank
*John Bowerbank Family Organization
1152 North Forest
Mesa, AZ 85203
Phone (602) 969-0112
Judy Nelson

Bowers (see Blossom Press, Folk Family
    Surname Exchange, Joyner)

Bowers
*Bowers Surname Organization
Evan Bowers Family Organization
4723 West Marconi Avenue
Glendale, AZ 85306
Phone (602) 843-2812
David L. Bowers

Bowers
The Bowers Family Historical Review
935 Countryside Drive, Apartment #103
Palatine, IL 60067-1927
Phone (847) 776-1848
H. Harvey Barfield, III
Pub. *The Bowers Family Historical
    Review*

Bowersox (see Bauersachs, Eisenhauer)

Bowles (see Wiler)

Bowlin (see Louden)

Bowlin
Bowlin Family Organization
Rt. 2
Indianola, IA 50125
Molly Bowlin

Bowmaker (see Gregor)

Bowman (see Arthur, Campbell,
    Johnson, MacDuff, Miehls, Stoner)

Bowman
*Alpheus Bowman Family
PO Box 1312
Muskagon, MI 49443
Claude B. Mitchell, Jr., Family Historian
(includes descendants of Alpheus
Bowman (1817–) and Huldah B.
Adams (1821–1904) and of his uncle
Alpheus Bowman (1795–))

Bowman
Bowman/Baumann Family Association
PO Box 141
Midland, TX 79702-0141
Phone (915) 682-0509
Priscilla A. Milburn, Organizer
Pub. *Bowman/Baumann Family
Newsletter*, quarterly

Bowsher (see Boucher)

Bowsie (see MacDuff)

Bowsy (see MacDuff)

Bowyer (see Boyer)

Boyce (see Forbes)

Boyce
*Boyce Surname Organization
3176 S.E. Villa Carmel Drive
Port Orchard, WA 98366
Phone (206) 876-0833
Linda Marx Terry

Boyd (see Brown, Caskey, Davis, Frantz,
Futral, Stewart)

Boyd
Boyd
61 West Sutter Road
Paradise, CA 95969
Mary Dell Wallace
Pub. *Boyd*, three times per year, no set
fee for subscription

Boyd
Clan Boyd
750 San Fernando Street
San Diego, CA 92106
Mrs. W. R. Goddard

Boyd
*The House of Boyd Society
PO Box 539
Mount Morris, MI 48458
Phone (810) 687-1033
Richard G. Boyd
Pub. *The Dean Road*, quarterly, $10.00
per year membership. Branch: **Pacific
Region**, Phyllis Boyd Laborde,
Chairman, 1182 Camino Vallecito,
Lafayette, CA 94549, *Newsletter*, three
times per year

Boyd
Boyds and Their Branches
PO Box 180193
Richland, MS 39218

Patsy B. Robinson
Pub. *Boyds and Their Branches*

Boyd
The Boyd Family Foundation
PO Box 183
Boydton, VA 23917
Mary Ann Boyd Dettinger, President
Pub. *Newsletter*, as needed, donation for
subscription; (includes descendants of
Alexander and Ann (Swepson) Boyd)

Boydston (see Womack)

Boyer (see Surname Database, Borror,
Goodenow, Welch)

Boyer
Boyer/Murphy Reunion
1405 East Kelly
Peoria Heights, IL 61614
Phone (309) 682-9620
Mrs. Lois B. Lipka, Family Historian

Boyer
*The Association of American Boyers,
Inc.
990 East Philadelphia Street
York, PA 17403
Phone (717) 843-8339
Donald A. Boyer, Historian
Pub. *American Boyers*, biannually,
$45.00 per volume; (includes Bayer,
Beier, Beyer, Bowyer, Boyers, Byer
and Byers); *Boyer Roots: The Annual
Newsletter of the Association of
American Boyers, Inc.*, annually;
(includes Boii as well as other
variations)
$5.00 per year membership, includes
annual newsletter, $50.00 life
membership; annual reunion on the
fourth Saturday of July at Boyertown
Park, Boyertown, Pennsylvania

Boyers (see Boyer)

Boyes (see Forbes)

Boyet (see Boyt)

Boyete (see Boyt)

Boyett (see Boyt)

Boyette (see Boyt)

Boyle
Boyle Family Letter
Rt. 3, Box 136
Stover, MO 65078-9420
Joan Semona Boyle
Pub. *Boyle Family Letter*, quarterly

Boynton (see Burrup)

Boyt
*Boyt/e-Boyet/t/e Association
4808 East Garland Street
Anaheim, CA 92807-1005

Phone (714) 779-8336
Wendy Bebout Elliot, C.G., C.G.L.,
President
Pub. *Boyt/e-Boyet/t/e Newsletter*,
quarterly; (includes families from
Southside Virginia 1690s, North
Carolina and the rest of the southern
states 1750s-1850s)
$12.00 per year membership, unlimited
free queries to members

Boyte (see Boyt)

Boyter (see MacDuff)

Bozard (see Bozarth)

Bozarth
Bozarth Beacon
38518 Kickbush Lane
Springfield, OR 97478-9641
Phone (503) 746-9736
Gayle Rose Mark, Editor/Publisher
Pub. *Bozarth Beacon*, quarterly, $12.00
per year subscription; (includes
Bosworth, Bozard, Bozier and
Bozorth)

Bozier (see Bozarth)

Bozman (see Newton)

Bozorth (see Bozarth)

Brabazon
Brabazon Family Association
118 Cheryl Drive
New Albany, IN 47150

Bracchitta
*Andrea Bracchitta Family Organization
PO Box 2856
Jackson, WY 83001
Phone (307) 733-5647
Margo D. Morey

Bracewell (see Braswell)

Bracken (see Powell)

Brackett
*Brackett Family Reunion
RR 1, Box 49L
Mountain Home, AR 72653-9705
Phone (501) 481-5245
Nola Brackett
(includes descendants of Cyrus Brackett
(1787 Vermont?–1858) and Lucy
Chase (1798 Winchendon,
Massachusetts–1862), daughter of
Charles and Hannah Stuart (Stewart)
Chase)

Brackley (see Bateman)

Brackmann
The Red Barn
1901 West Adams Road
Macomb, IL 61455
Phone (309) 833-5741

Sidney Crowcroft, Editor
Pub. *The Red Barn, A Brackmann
Newsletter*, every three years, $5.00
per issue

Bradburn
Bradburn Family
210 Fourth North Street
PO Box 954
Saint Johns, AZ 85936
Phone (602) 337-2096
Shawn Bradburn Brown

Braddy (see Lynch)

Braden (see Lemon)

Braden
*Braden Bunch
4906 Ridgeway
Kansas City, MO 64133-2545
Lois T. Allen
(clearinghouse for information on the
Braden surname)
SASE for details

Braden
*Love Is Love Forevermore
1743 Blodgett Road
Mount Vernon, WA 98273
Phone (360) 428-0319
Janet K. Armbrust
(includes descendants of William and
Euphemia (Jackson) Braden of Decatur
County, Indiana)

Bradford (see Marshall, Williams)

Bradford
*Society of Descendants of Governor
William Bradford of Plymouth Colony
Governor William Bradford Compact
Society
5204 Kenwood Avenue
Chevy Chase, MD 20815-6604
Phone (301) 654-7233
Mrs. L. W. Pogue, Historian
Pub. *Bradford Compact Newsletter*,
annually (spring)

Bradley (see Anthes, Elford, Heath,
Henrie, Lynch)

Bradley
John Bradley Family Exchange
627 Coolidge Street
Davis, CA 95616
Phone (916) 753-3685
Marilyn Bradley Roberts
(includes database on John and Phebe
(Holloway) Bradley of Cumberland
County, Virginia 1718–1783)

Bradley
*The Bradley Society
7 East 14th Street, Suite 21-G
New York, NY 10003-3115
Phone (212) 989-6881
Frederick W. Bradley, Editor
Pub. *Journal*

Bradley
*Robert Bruce Bradley Family
Organization
PO Box 183
Benton, WI 53803
Phone (608) 759-2755
Lynne Bradley Montgomery, Genealogist

Bradshaw (see McKee)

Bradshaw
Genealogical and Historical News
369 East 900 South, Suite 247
Salt Lake City, UT 84111
R. D. Bradshaw, Editor
Pub. *Bradshaw-Bratcher Letter*,
quarterly, $5.00 per year subscription

Bradshaw
Bradshaw in America
Rt. 1, Box 24
Broadacres
Robstown, TX 78380
Mr. C. M. Bradshaw
Pub. *Bradshaw in America*, quarterly,
$3.00 per year subscription

Bradt (see Barnard)

Bradt
*Bradt Historians
PO Box 186
Mechanicville, NY 12118-0186
Phone (518) 664-6058
Tom Ryan
(includes Bratt, Brott, Vanderzee)
Reunion every five years

Bradt
Bradt Family News
10287 Silverado Circle
Bradenton, FL 34202-4039
E-mail: CompuServe 74651,155
Ken Bradt, Editor
Pub. *Bradt Family News*, three times per
year, $6.00 per year subscription,
queries accepted; (not to be confused
with Brandt)

Bradway
*Bradway/Broadway Family
1119 Hedgewood Lane
Niskayuna, NY 12309-4602
Phone (518) 377-8938
Bette Innes Bradway, C.G.
Exchange of data

Brady (see Arthur)

Braffett
Braffett
138 Depot Road
Hollis, NH 03049-6580
Donald Braffitt
Pub. *Braffett*, irregularly, free

Bragg
*Bragg Family
707 Ringgold Drive
Nashville, TN 37207
Emma W. Bragg, Ph.D.

Brahler (see Behnke)

Brainard
*Brainard-Brainerd-Braynard Family
Association
813 S.W. Alder Street, #700
Portland, OR 97205-3115
Phone (503) 243-2652
Richard D. Brainard, Family Historian,
Publisher and Editor
Pub. *Daniel Brainerd Society Newsletter*,
quarterly
$18.00 per year membership

Brainerd (see Brainard)

Brake
*Brake Association
300 Greenglade Avenue
Worthington, OH 43085-2223
Phone (614) 888-1236
Henrietta Nichols
Pub. *The Brake Bugle*, quarterly
$10.00 per year membership

Brakey (see Breakey)

Bramlett (see Wright)

Brammer (see Foley)

Brammer
Brammer Branches
M.E.U. Box 20
FPO Seattle, WA 98762
Charles D. Brammer
Pub. *Brammer Branches*, quarterly, $8.00
per year subscription

Brammier
*Brammier/Morris Family Reunion
10507 South Corley Drive
Whittier, CA 90604-1114
Phone (310) 693-7611
Bonnie Morris

Branchaud (see Brancheau)

Brancheau
*Brancheau-Branchaud Family
Association
27909 Youngberry Drive
Saugus, CA 91350
Phone (805) 296-8740
Douglas J. Miller

Brand
Pence Publications
11009 East Third Avenue, #67
Spokane, WA 99206-5294
Maxine E. Pence, Editor
Pub. *Brand(t) Names*, irregularly, $6.00
per issue

Brandenburg (see Sager)

Brandin (see MacDuff)

Brandon (see Christopher, MacDuff)

Brandon
Brandon Branches Newsletter
1405 Woodcrest Drive
Knoxville, TN 37918
Phyllis Norman Brandon
Pub. *Brandon Branches Newsletter*,
　quarterly, $8.00 per year subscription

Brandt (see Brand, Harting)

Brangan
*James Warren Brangan Family
　Organization
PO Box 1860
Studio City, CA 91614
Phone (818) 980-1005; E-mail:
　AP471@lafn.org
Karen Mohr

Brann
*Brann/Brawn Family History
　Association
4065 Berrywood Drive
Eugene, OR 97404-4061
James R. Brann, Family Representative
　(PAF™ data bank of 8,000 ancestors with
　2,000 familes on MAC™ computer
　includes all dates and places)
Free information exchange

Brannan (see Emery)

Brannon (see Blossom Press)

Brantley (see Brawley)

Brantley
*Brantley Association of America
5245 Moon Road
Powder Springs, GA 30073
Phone (770) 943-4677
J. Kenneth Brantley, Founder/Editor
Pub. *Brantley Association Semi-Annual
　Report*
$17.50 per year membership; reunion

Brantley
Surnames, Limited
RR 3, Box 59
Muleshoe, TX 79347-9208
Pub. *Brantley Newsletter*, published as
　material is collected, $8.00 per issue

Brasfield (see Black)

Brashear (see Brasher, Kettenring)

Brashears (see Brasher, Kettenring,
　Smith)

Brasher
Br(e)ashe(a)r(s) Family Branches
3110 N.E. 11th Street
Mineral Wells, TX 76067-4128
Arzella Brashear Spear
Pub. *Br(e)ashe(a)r(s) Family Branches*,
　monthly, $20.00 per year subscription

Brashers (see Brasher)

Brasseaux (see Johnson)

Brassieur (see Job)

Braswell (see Lynch)

Braswell
Braswell Branches
PO Box 3793
Santa Cruz, CA 95063
E-mail: NonaW@aol.com
Nona Williams, Editor
Pub. *Braswell Branches*, quarterly,
　$15.00 per year subscription, queries
　accepted (includes Bracewell)

Bratcher (see Bradshaw)

Bratt (see Bradt)

Brattain
Fragments: Brattain/Bratton
419 North Larchmont Boulevard, Suite
　277
Los Angeles, CA 90004
Pub. *Fragments: Brattain/Bratton*,
　bimonthly, $12.00 per year
　subscription

Bratthaver (see Mesenbring)

Bratton (see Brattain)

Braun (see Broun, Horning)

Braune (see Broun)

Bravard (see Bovaird)

Brawley
*Brawley Book
PO Box 340
Fairview, NC 28730
Doris G. Chandler
(includes descendants of Neil Braley/
　Brawley who left Ireland and came to
　Rowan County, North Carolina, and
　was later joined by the William A. I.
　Brawley family which settled nearby;
　allied surnames: Alexander, Belk,
　Blackwelder, Brantley, chandler, Cook,
　Davis, Gabriel, Gibson, Goldsmith,
　Goodman, Greene, Harwell, Holland,
　Hutto, Jackson, Jenkins, Johnson,
　Lipe, McCoy, McKay, McLaughlin,
　McNeely, Miller, Mills, Moore,
　Morrison, Morrow, Oliphant,
　Overcash, Parker, Radford, Robbins,
　Rogers, Rumple, Sherrill, Shoemaker,
　Smith, Thompson, Troutman, White,
　Woods, Young, etc.)

Brawn (see Brann)

Bray (see Allison, Corder, Newton)

Bray
*Bray Nostalgia
PO Box 325
Elwood, NE 68937

Cheryl Clark
Pub. *Bray Nostalgia*, three times per
　year; (includes families of Kansas,
　North Carolina, Iowa, Indiana)
$10.00 per year membership

Braynard (see Brainard)

Brazeale (see Burazeale)

Brazelton
Brazelton Newsletter
974 Eastland Avenue
Akron, OH 44305-1312
Dorothy Dittmer
Pub. *Brazelton Newsletter*, quarterly,
　$10.00 per year subscription

Bread (see MacDuff)

Breakey
*Breakey/Brakey/Breakly/DeBrequet
　Exchange
32 Commane Road
Baldwinsville, NY 13027
Marilyn J. Breakey, Historian

Breakly (see Breakey)

Breashear (see Brasher)

Breashears (see Brasher)

Breasher (see Brasher)

Breashers (see Brasher)

Breathitt (see McNees)

Breaux (see Johnson)

Breckenridge (see Douglas)

Breckler
Christopher Breckler Family Association
120 South Lebanon Street
Bryan, OH 43506
Don Wordkoetter

Breeden (see Breeding)

Breeding
*Breeding/Breeden Genealogical
　Exchange
8311 Braesview Lane
Houston, TX 77071-1231
Phone (713) 777-8920
Bruce A. Breeding, Editor
Pub. *Breeding/Breeden Genealogical
　Exchange*, semiannually, $15.00 per
　year subscription

Brees (see McRae)

Brees
Elias and Deborah Brees Ancestors
31 West Street
Berea, OH 44017
Ira Brees

Breese (see Fadner)

Breeze (see Hays)

Brehm
*Lloyd Publishing
49 Bianca Lane, #54
Watsonville, CA 95076
Lloyd Walter Clark Hoagland, Editor
(includes research on related families:
    Brehm, Butherus, Dietz, Kock/Cook,
    Heirsekorn, Miller and Yost, mostly in
    Germany, Russia and Nebraska)

Brehon (see Cian)

Breidenbach (see Stewart)

Breillatt
Philip Paull Breillatt Family Association
933 Highland Road
Muldelein, IL 60060
Dr. Julian P. Breillatt

Brellsford
Brellsford Newsletter
11044 Berrypick Lane
Columbia, MD 21044
Karen Brellsford
Pub. *Brellsford Newsletter*

Brengel (see Brengle)

Brengle
Brengle Branches
6619 Pheasant Road, Rt. 1, #16
Baltimore, MD 21220
Phone (410) 335-3948
Charles Brengle
Pub. *Brengle Branches*, quarterly, $12.00
    per year subscription; (includes
    Brengel, Bringle, Pringle)

Brennan (see Dwyer)

Brennand
*Brennand Family Association
PO Box 3447
Arlington, WA 98223-3447
Phone (360) 658-1000
Ruth Whetnall, President

Brenon (see Cian)

Brenton
*Brenton Surname Organization
North 4702 Madison
Spokane, WA 99205
Phone (509) 325-2246
Chester F. Brenton

Brentzer (see Brinser)

Breny (see Blossom Press)

Breseman (see Rothenberger)

Bressler (see Presley)

Bretz (see Wert)

Brevard (see Antley, Bovaird)

Brewer (see Surname Sources,
    Bogardus, Gregor)

Brewer
The Paint Rock Valley Brewers (AL and
    TN) Reunion
4315 Hunt Drive, N.W.
Huntsville, AL 35816
Phone (205) 837-6532
Roy Brewer

Brewer
*Brewer Family History
1170 Ripley Court
Muscatine, IA 52761-9579
Phone (319) 263-0879
June Brewer Welsch, Publisher
(includes Lewis and Agatha (Holland)
    Brewer of Grayson County, Virginia)

Brewer
The Wayne and Lawrence County,
    Tennessee, Brewer Reunion
Rt. 1, Box 99
Cypress Inn, TN 38452
Phone (615) 724-9029
Evelyn Brewer

Brewer
Brewer Researcher
600 Eastbrook Road
Estill Springs, TN 37330-3490
Phone (615) 649-2444
James H. Brewer
Pub. *Brewer Researcher*, quarterly, $3.00
    per year subscription

Brewster (see Fraser)

Brewster
*Elder Brewster Society
1119 Hedgewood Lane
Niskayuna, NY 12309-4602
Phone (518) 377-8938
Bette I. Bradway, Historian
Pub. *The Elder Brewster Press*, annually
$12.00 per year application fee in the
    U.S.

Brewster
Great Oak Press of Virginia
Box 6541
Falls Church, VA 22046
Phone (703) 560-6347
Robert B. Sherwood, Publisher
(publisher of book on Pilgrim, William
    Brewster)

Brewton (see Antley)

Breyfoggel
*Julia Ann Breyfoggel Family
    Organization
3176 S.E. Villa Carmel Drive
Port Orchard, WA 98366
Phone (206) 876-0833
Linda Marx Terry

Brian (see Bryan)

Brice (see Bruce)

Bricker
*Pioneer Publication
PO Box 1179
Tum Tum, WA 99034-1179
Phone (509) 276-9841
Shirley Penna-Oakes
Pub. *Bricker Branches*, irregularly, $6.00
    per issue plus $1.75 postage for 1–3
    books, 50¢ for each additional book

Bridge (see Surname Sources)

Bridges (see Towne)

Bridges
The Bridges Between Us
4 Capital Drive
Washingtonville, NY 10992-1342
Pub. *The Bridges Between Us*,
    semiannually

Bridgum (see Catlow)

Brien (see Bryan)

Bright (see Upchurch)

Bright
Bright Family Association
PO Box 184
Oxbow, NY 13671
Edward Bright

Brightbill (see McCanna)

Brightman (see Likes)

Brightwell
Brightwell Family Association
8177 Turn Loop Road
Glen Burnie, MD 21061-1113
Mrs. Avlyn Dodd Conley
Pub. *Brightwell Beings*

Briles (see Broyles)

Brill
*Martin Brill Family Organization
PO Box 311
Bedford, WY 83112
Phone (307) 883-2730
Jerry Mower
(includes descendants of Martin Brill
    (1710 Germany–1791 Lovettsville,
    Virginia))

Brimberry
*Brimberry Family Association
1365 Lesley Court
Santa Maria, CA 93454
Phone (805) 922-4313; (805) 346-1156
    FAX; E-mail: ccsd62B@prodigy.com
    or 72103,2257@compuserve.com
Tina Peddie, President
(includes Brynberg)

Bringle (see Brengle)

Brinker (see Wofford)

Brinkerhoff
Brin(c)kerhoff History
3020 Dellwood Drive
Kokomo, IN 46902
Phone (317) 453-0980
Donald E. Brinkerhoff
Pub. *Supplement to the Brin(c)kerhoffs of
America*, every ten years; (includes
descendants of Joris Dircksen
Brinckerhoff, born in 1604 in Vorden,
Holland, arrived with his family in
New Amsterdam in 1641)
Reunion

Brinkmann
*Herman Heinrich Brinkmann Family
Organization
2506 Mansfield Drive
Des Moines, IA 50317
Phone (515) 262-0707
Thomas C. Boelling

Brinser
Brinser/Brentzer Descendants
419 East King Street, #G-K
Lancaster, PA 17602-3083
Phone (717) 393-0849
Richard V. Brinser

Brinton
*The Brinton Family Association, Inc.
PO Box 283
Rockland, DE 19732
Phone (302) 478-2853
Mel Brinton, Editor
Pub. *Brinton Descendants Newsletter*,
three times per year; (includes
descendants of William and Ann
(Bagley) Brinton who immigrated in
1684)
$10.00 per year membership, $5.00 per
year membership for senior citizens

Brinton
*Brinton Family
647 Summit House
West Chester, PA 19382
Phone (610) 696-8050
L. Brinton
Pub. *Newsletter*, quarterly
$20.00 per year membership

Brion
*Brion Reunion
PO Box 587
O'Neil, NE 68763
Phone (402) 336-2259
Lois Schafer

Brisco (see Grant)

Bristol
*Bristol Family Association, Inc.
420 South Stone Street
West Suffield, CT 06093
Phone (203) 668-5554

Alan Hefflon, Co-genealogist
Pub. *Newsletter*, semiannually; (includes
descendants of Henry Bristol, New
Haven colonist)
$5.00 per year membership

Britt (see Lynch)

Brittain (see Lush)

Brittain
*Brit'n Genealogy Clearing House
2751 East Wilshire Drive
Salt Lake City, UT 84109
Phone (801) 485-4249
Janice Pilling Brittain, Editor
Pub. *Brittain/Britton Newsletter*, $8.00
per year subscription

Brittenburg
*Brittenburg Surname Organization
6750 East Main Street, #106
Mesa, AZ 85205-9049
Warren D. Steffey

Brittingham
Brittingham Post
2143 Harmony Lane
Jamison, PA 18929
Phone (215) 343-6838
Janet R. Brittingham, Publisher
Pub. *Brittingham Post*, quarterly, $15.00
per year subscription

Britton (see Brittain)

Brixey
The Brixey Bulletin
2818 Landershire Lane
Garland, TX 75044-5974
Phone (214) 495-4410; (214) 495-1569
FAX; E-mail: jwylie@metronet.com or
CIS: 72730,1426
Barbara Brixey Wylie, Editor
Pub. *The Brixey Bulletin*, quarterly,
$15.00 per year subscription, queries
accepted; (includes variant spellings)
Several regional reunions

Brizendine
*Mountain Press
4503 Anderson Pike
PO Box 400
Signal Mountain, TN 37377-0400
Phone (423) 886-6369; (423) 886-5312
FAX
James L. Douthat, Owner
(William Brizendine family, primarily in
lower middle Tennessee)

Broad (see Chamberlain)

Broadaway
*John H. Broadaway Family
Organization
1147 West 1500 South
Vernal, UT 84078
Phone (801) 789-5768
Mrs. Jacque B. Johnson

(includes descendants of John H.
Broadaway (1828 Tennessee?–) and
Mariah A. Follis (1830 Tennessee?–),
married 1848 in Lynnville, Giles
County, Tennessee)
Biennial reunion in odd-numbered years
on the first or second weekend of
August

Broadbent
*Broadbent Database
45865 Michell Lane
Indio, CA 92201-3780
Helen Free VanderBeek
(deals exclusively with families from
Yorkshire, England)
$1.00 plus SASE for search

Broadfoot
Broadfoot-Seaton-Seton-Redmond
Family Association
2306 Westgate
Houston, TX 77019
Phone (713) 529-2333
Harold Helm
$25.00 plus pedigree and family group
sheets for membership

Broadhead (see McCune)

Broadwater (see Stanton)

Broadway (see Bradway)

Broady (see Evitt)

Broase (see Bruce)

Brobeck
Brobeck/Brubeck Family of Virginia
320 Seven Oaks Drive
Knoxville, TN 37922
Irma Hansard

Brocher (see Lahey)

Brock (see Folk Family Surname
Exchange)

Brockett (see Newton)

Brockway
*Brockway/Wolston Family Information
Exchange
8750 S.W. 200 Street
Miami, FL 33157
Phone (305) 238-0880
Walter R. Brockway, Acting Coordinator
Pub. *The Wolston Brockway Family
Information Exchange*, quarterly,
$11.00 per year subscription

Broderson (see Elsebuch)

Brodhead
*Brodhead Family Association
PO Box 66
Port Ewen, NY 12466
Phone (914) 331-0615
Jean M. Smith, Corresponding Secretary

Pub. *Capt. Daniel Brodhead, His Wife Ann Tye and Their Descendants*; *Newsletter*, four to six times per year; (includes DePuy and Lapala) $15.00 per year membership

Brodie
Clan Brodie Association
2601 South Braeswood, #701
Houston, TX 77025
Edward F. Brodie, National Convenor and Chieftain

Brodnax
*Brodnax Surname Organization
10462 East Grandeur Avenue
Baton Rouge, LA 70815-4889
Phone (504) 924-3738
Mary Anne Brodnax Massengale
(includes descendants of Edward Brooking Brodnas (1778 Virginia–1861 Newton County, Georgia) and Frances Vivian Brooking; allied family of Revolutionary War veteran, John Dearing (1746–1822) and Anne Jett of Culpeper County, Virginia; Richard Kennon of "Conjurer's Neck," came to Virginia before 1670, settled in Henrico County, Virginia, married Elizabeth Worsham, daughter of William Worsham (–1661 Virginia) and Elizabeth Littlebury; John Stovall, Sr. (ca 1700 Henrico County, Virginia–1781 Granville County, North Carolina) and Dorcas; Dr. William E. Dearing (1820 Georgia–1853 Athens, Georgia) and Carolyn E. Stovall (1821 Georgia–); John Lewis and Elizabeth Warner)

Brog (see MacDuff)

Broida
*Broida Family Association
5 Ladue Court
Saint Louis, MO 63141
Ann Greenstein
Pub. *Broida Family News*, about once every four years; (includes Broida, originally Karklinsky, from Aisheshuk, Lithuania)
$10.00 per year membership

Broiles (see Broyles)

Brokaw (see Covert)

Brokke (see Ostrem)

Broman (see Wigelius)

Bronaugh (see Grant)

Bronck (see Barnard)

Bronson (see Barnes)

Brood (see Lush)

Brook (see Brooks)

Brooke (see Surname Sources, Brooks)

Brooken (see Brooking)

Brookens (see Brooking)

Brookes (see Brooks)

Brookin (see Brooking)

Brooking (see Brodnax)

Brooking
*The Brooking Society, American Chapter
7539 Juler
Cincinnati, OH 45243
Alma Linn
Pub. *The Brooking Line*, three times per year (January, May and September), $10.00 per year subscription to one address in the U.S. or Canada; (includes Brooking, Brooken, Brookin, Brookings, Brookens, Brookins, etc.)

Brooking
Edwin Elliot Brooking Descendants
PO Box 282
White River, SD 57579
Phone (605) 259-3479
Mrs. J. Vos

Brookings (see Brooking)

Brookins (see Brooking)

Brooks (see Folk Family Surname Exchange, Chamberlain, Goodenow, Ross, Steele)

Brooks
*The Brooks of Berrien County
921 South Hill Avenue
DeLand, FL 32724
Phone (904) 734-7455
Lorna Jean Brooks Hagstrom
(includes Brooks-Lewis family and allied families of Abney, Barker, Cook, Ellis, Riley, Stone and Thomason)

Brooks
*The Brooks Historical Library
878 Mitch Drive
Gardnerville, NV 89410-8940
Phone (702) 265-1909; E-mail: DixieLeeNV@aol.com
Dixie L. Judge, Editor
Pub. *The Brooks Historian*, quarterly (January, April, July and October), $14.00 per year subscription; (includes Brook(e)/Brooke(s) anywhere, any time)

Brooks
Brooks Family Reunion
13231 N.W. McNamee Road
Portland, OR 97231
Virginia Luethe
(includes descendants of David Brooks and Jane Morgan, who came to Oregon from Iowa, via San Francisco)

Brooks
*Brooks Family Bulletin
1717 South Angeline Street
Seattle, WA 98108
Phone (206) 762-0957
Mrs. Glen D. Preston
Pub. *Brooks Family Bulletin*

Brookshire (see Williams)

Broon (see Broun)

Broone (see Broun)

Brorn (see Roberts)

Brothers
*Brothers Surname Organization
430 Maple Way
Woodside, CA 94062
Phone (415) 365-4644
William P. Brothers
(includes the families of brothers, Swan, Bonar/Reeves, Beardsley)

Brotherton
*Brotherton-Hunters
2727 East 53rd Avenue, #H-207
Spokane, WA 99223-7999
Robert E. (Bob) Brotherton, Secretary-Treasurer
Pub. *The Brotherton Family Tie*, quarterly (November, February, May and August), $10.00 donation per year subscription; (includes all Brothertons and their spouses)

Brott (see Bradt)

Brough
*Brough/Malkin/Nielsen/Wilson/Willson Family Organization
87 Cedarwood Avenue
Duarte, CA 91010
Phone (818) 359-3575
Faye B. Nielsen

Brouillion (see Merier)

Broun (see MacMillan)

Broun
*Clan Broun Society
101 Oak Island Street
Revere, MA 02151-1542
Phone (617) 923-5558 (weekdays)
Major James L. Brown, President
Pub. *Knop Err*, quarterly; (includes Braun, Braune, Broon, Broone, Broun, Brown, Browne, Brownlee, Brownlow, Brownrigg, Brownson, Brun, Brune, Brunson, Le Brun (1040), etc.)
$10.00 per year membership, $200.00 life membership

Broussard (see Johnson)

Brout (see Hugesson)

Brouwer (see Bogardus)

Brovont (see Frantz)

Broward (see Bovaird)

Brower (see Bogardus, Stoner)

Brown (see Family Publications, Folk
Family Surname Exchange, Surname
Sources, Baker, Barnes, Broun, Clark,
Douglas, Emery, Gerade, Golding,
Goodenow, Heath, Lush, MacDuff,
MacMillan, Marshall, Nienow,
Phillips, Stoner, Wright)

Brown
*Wendel Brown and Descendants
714 South Hillward Avenue
West Covina, CA 91791-2711
Phone (818) 339-3851
Georgia Morgan

Brown
*Brown Association
181 Margarite Road
Middletown, CT 06457
Phone (203) 347-0176
Daisy Zdanowicz Paskiewicz

Brown
*The Descendants of William Henry
Brown*
935 Countryside Drive, Apartment #103
Palatine, IL 60067-1927
Phone (847) 776-1848
H. Harvey Barfield, III
Pub. *The Descendants of William Henry
Brown of Effingham County, Illinois,
Historical Review*

Brown
Brown/Murray Family Organization
Rt. 1
Liscomb, IA 50148
A. Harmon

Brown
*Brown Ancestry
PO Box 32192
Mountain Village, AK 99632
Pat Darling
(includes descendants of George and
Christian (Hibbert) Browne of
Salisbury, England, and sons, Henry,
William and George of Salisbury,
Massachusetts, 1638)

Brown
Claudette's
3962 Xenwood Avenue, S.
Saint Louis Park, MN 55416-2842
Claudette Atwood Maerz
Pub. *Brown Family Helper*, semiannually

Brown
Brown-Warner Descendants Association
801 Fieldcrest Drive
Washington, MO 63090
Dorothy Brown Hill

Brown
*Tactical Edge Emporium
19 Terrace Street
Keene, NH 03431
Phone (603) 352-0194 BBS
Hal Gordon Brown, Editor
Pub. *Brown Family News and
Genealogical Society*, three times per
year; (BBS: 1200, 2400, 4800, 9600,
14.4K, 19.2K Baud; accepts PAF™
records in GEDCOM™ export file on
diskette; free queries (10 lines if typed,
100 lines if submitted on IBM
compatible disk, 200 lines if uploaded
to BBS; computer-scanned photos also
available for download in .tif and .gif
graphics format)
$10.00 per year membership

Brown
*Brown Inlaw Defensive Union (BIDU)
376 Lighthouse Drive
Manahawkin, NJ 08050-2327
Phone (609) 597-8965; E-mail:
BJack8965@aol.com
Barbara Steinersen Jackson
(includes descendants of Henry W.
Brown (1846–1893) who descended
from Rev. Chad Browne of
Providence, Rhode Island; related
surnames: Alger (New York and
Vermont), Chesebrough (Connecticut
and New York), Hiscock (New York
and Vermont), Jackson (Albany and
Rensselaer, New York), Mueller (New
Jersey and Switzerland), Perkins
(Connecticut, Massachusetts and
Vermont), Steinersen (New York and
Norway), and Stiles (Albany and
Rensselaer, New York))

Brown
*Brown Surname Organization
56 Chestnut
Wayne, NJ 07470
Phone (201) 694-8723
Lucille Dillinger Alexander

Brown
*Yankee Brown Family Reunion
306 North Street
Chardon, OH 44024
Phone (216) 286-6649
Annual reunion on the third Saturday of
August at Wilder Field Pavilion, Irvin,
Pennsylvania

Brown
*Dr. Joel Brown Descendants and
Related Families
230 Hamilton Avenue
Olean, NY 14760-1762
Phone (716) 372-2158
Ellsworth L. Brown

Brown
Brown-Probst Reunion
342 James Avenue, Apartment A3
Mansfield, OH 44907-1950
Gene Probst
Annual reunion

Brown
*Futral Genealogy Trails
#6 Wonderland Lane
Carthage, TN 37030
Jenny Futral, Entrepreneur
(publishes Georgia marriage record
booklets on the following surnames:
Brown, Coleman, Cox, Daniel,
Daugherty-Daughtery-Doughtery-
Doughtry, Griffin, Greer, Grier,
Harper, Hendrick-Hendricks-Hendrix,
House, Jackson, Jones, Kea-Key-Keys,
Kendrick-Kendricks-Kendrix, Miller,
Moore, Neal-Neall-Nial-Niel, Rogers
and Smith)

Brown
*Brown Reunion
PO Box 52048
Knoxville, TN 37950-2048
Hester E. Stockton
(includes descendants of Elijah Brown
and Lucinda Tiner)
Annual reunion in June at the Red River
Valley Fairgrounds, Paris, Texas

Brown
*Brown-Stanton-Evans-Sherman
Families
2620 MacArthur
Waco, TX 76708
Phone (817) 776-2632
Shepherd Spencer Neville Brown
(includes collateral lines: Carpenter,
Childow, Coutanche, Darrah, Dossett,
Franklin, Hoxie, Lillington, Miller,
Paterson, Pilkington, Porter, Potts,
Sterne, etc.)

Brown
*David Alma Brown Family
Organization
4275 White Way
Salt Lake City, UT 84124
Phone (801) 277-4783
Calvin Reed Brown

Brown
*Brown Family Reunion
3902 West Galena
Milwaukee, WI 53208
Phone (44) 344-0563
Guy Porth
(includes descendants of Buel and Rhoda
(Edwards) Brown of New York and
Milwaukee, Wisconsin, and related
families of Burbank, Follett, Keene,
Shoff/Schoff, Stevens and White)

Browne (see Broun, Brown, Clark,
Wright)

Brownell (see Surname Sources)

Brownell
Albert Henry Brownell Family
Organization
290 Mountain View
Grand Junction, CO 81503
Wanda Standley

Brownfield
Brownfield Gleanings
16661 Townhouse Drive
Tustin, CA 92680
Phone (714) 543-5882
Florence E. Brownfield, Editor
Pub. *Brownfield Gleanings*, quarterly,
    $9.00 per year subscription

Browning (see Hatfield, McCoy,
    Sawyer)

Browning
Browning Browsing in Kentucky
1516 Elliot Drive
Jeffersonville, IN 47130
Mary Rucker Snyder
Pub. *Browning Browsing in Kentucky*

Brownlee (see Broun, Douglas)

Brownlow (see Broun)

Brownrigg (see Broun)

Brownson (see Broun)

Broyles (see The Memorial Foundation
    of the Germanna Colonies)

Broyles
Broyles Family Newsletter
302 Woodland Hills Road
Clinton, TN 37716-5934
Phone (423) 457-5866
John K. Broyles,Sr.
Pub. *Broyles Family Newsletter (Briles,
    Broiles, Broyles, etc.)*, bimonthly,
    $12.00 per year subscription, $20.00
    for two-year subscription
additional $2.00 for membership

Brubaker (see Frantz)

Brubaker
Brubaker Family Association
245 North Fulton Street
Strassburg, PA 17579
Lois Ann Zook

Brubeck (see Brobeck)

Bruce (see Lemon, Packard)

Bruce
Family of Bruce Society in America
Division of Descendants of Robert the
    Bruce World Wide
"Banner House"
(PO Box 716, Banner Elk, NC 28604—
    address May to November)
320 North Madison Avenue
Clearwater, FL 34615
Phone (704) 898-4385 (North Carolina);
    (813) 446-7404 (Florida)
H. G. C. Hill, Founder and Chairman

Bruce
*The Bruce Family Historical Society
The Royal Bruce Society
PO Box 724511
Atlanta, GA 31139
Michael von Stambach-Bruce, Chairman
Pub. *The Bruce Journal*, quarterly,
    $17.50 per year subscription only;
    (includes Bruce, Brice, Broase,
    de Brus)
$15.00 membership registration, $20.00
    per year membership

Bruce
Bruce International U.S.A. Branch
880 Western Drive
Bloomington, IN 47401
Phone (812) 339-4239
Rex A. Bruce, President

Bruchette (see Joy)

Brucker
*Johann Adam Brucker and His
    American Descendants
5000 Alabama Street, #21
El Paso, TX 79930-2638
Phone (915) 564-4512
Mrs. Wallace H. Brucker, Publisher
(includes descendants of Johann Adam
    Brucker (1787 Hesse-Darmstadt–) and
    his wife, Rosalie Reitzi of Austria, and
    their children: John Francis, Ferdinand
    and his wife Margaretta Zechmeister,
    Anna and her husbands Nicholaus
    Webber and Frederick Neumann, both
    of Detroit, and Charles/Karl and his
    wife Elizabeth Mrkwiczka)

Bruen (see Kelly, Williams)

Brumage
*Brumage—Brummage
3743 Neward Drive
Napa, CA 94558
Virginia Brumage Wakeman, Author

Brumbach (see The Memorial
    Foundation of the Germanna Colonies)

Brumback (see The Memorial
    Foundation of the Germanna Colonies)

Brumfield (see Blossom Press)

Brummage (see Brumage)

Brun (see Blossom Press, Broun)

Brune (see Broun)

Bruney (see Blossom Press)

Brunner
*Frederick Brunner (1835–) and Pauline
    Debrot Family from Switzerland
335 West Shackley Street
PO Box 75
Geneva, IN 46740
Phone (219) 368-7352
Ruth Brown

Brunson (see Broun)

Bruss (see Sager)

Bryan (see Allison, Boone, Cian)

Bryan
Oak Leaf Publishing
22 Creek Road, #64
Irvine, CA 91714
Pub. *Bryan(t) Family Newsletter*,
    bimonthly, $10.00 per year
    subscription

Bryan
*The Sept of the Knight de Bryan
Clans of Ireland, Dublin
Tor Bryan on the Sea
5936 Tulane Street
San Diego, CA 92122
Phone (619) 458-4234
The Hon. Knight de Bryan, Charles
    Bryant-Abraham, Ph.D.
(includes honorary members and
    descendants of the Anglo-Irish Bryans
    of Colonial America, ascendant to
    Lady Alice Needham Bryan and
    Justice William Bryan II, son of
    Colonel William Smith Bryan, 3rd
    Knight Banneret de Bryan (arrived
    Virginia Colony before 1655),
    grandson of Sir Francis Bryan, knight
    banneret, Lord Marshall (–1550) of
    Ireland, and Lady Joan Fitzgerald)

Bryan
*The John Bryan Family-Joseph Clark
    Family
282 Grant Avenue
Hatfield, PA 19446
Steven B. Morris, Sr.
(includes descendants of William
    Jennings Bryan; surnames of Bryan
    and Hawthorne, etc.; descendants of
    Joseph Clark)

Bryan
*Bryan-Bryant-Brien-O'Brien-O'Bryant-
    Brian-Bryen*
10794 Morning Glory
Dallas, TX 75229
Pub. *Bryan-Bryant-Brien-O'Brien-
    O'Bryant-Brian-Bryen*, quarterly,
    $10.00 per year subscription

Bryan
*Williamite Brance, Scotch-Irish Bryans
6003 233rd Place, S.W.
Mountlake Terrace, WA 98043
The Chevalier Lynn G. Bryan,
    Ardseanchai

Bryant (see Folk Family Surname
    Exchange, Allison, Bryan, Cian,
    Farrington)

Bryant
Kenma Publishing Company
1911 Conlin Avenue
Evansville, IN 47714-4248

Kenneth Gene Lindsay
Pub. *Bryant Backtrails*, quarterly, $12.95
    per year subscription

Bryant
Bryant Family Organization
4011 West 95th Street Terrace
Overland Park, KS 66207
Cleo Bryant

Bryen (see Bryan)

Brymer
Brymer Clearinghouse
PO Box 2868
Harbor, OR 97415
Raymond Brymer

Brynberg (see Brimberry)

Bryson (see Archer, Price)

Bryson
*Mount Pulaski Township Historical
    Society
PO Box 12
Mount Pulaski, IL 62548-0012
Phone (217) 792-5565 (President); (217)
    792-3966 (Editor)
Waneta Stephens, President; Dorothy
    Curtis, Editor
Pub. *Mt. Pulaski Township Historical
    Society* (includes research on the
    following families: Archer, Bryson,
    Febus, Keehler, Peddycourt, Sebring,
    Spence and Stephens)
$15.00 per year membership for
    individuals, $25.00 per year
    membership for couples, $150.00 life
    membership, $225.00 life membership
    for couples

Bubolz (see Sager)

Bubrig (see Blossom Press)

Buchan
*Buchan Clan Association
5334 Lakeside Drive
Greendale, WI 53129
Phone (414) 421-3021
Nancy L. Buchan, U.S.A. Representative
Pub. *Newsletter*, three to four times per
    year
$4.00 per year membership

Buchanan (see Thompson)

Buchanan
Buchanan Reunion
62 Elaine Circle
Fort Oglethorpe, GA 30742-3858
Hazel Warren

Buchanan
Clan Buchanan Society in America, Inc.
PO Box 1110
Moultrie, GA 31776-1110
Pub. *The Buchanan Banner*, three to four
    times per year; (includes Bohanon,

Coleman, Cormack, Cousland, Dewar,
Donleavy, Dove, Dow, Gibb, Gibbon,
Gibby, Gibson, Gilbert, Gilbertson,
Harper, Kinkaid, Leavy, Lennie,
Macaldonich, Macalman, Macandeoir,
Macaslan, Macauselan, MacCalman,
MacCalmont, MacCammond,
MacCasland, MacColman,
MacColwan, MacCommon,
MacCormack, MacCoubrey,
MacCruiter, MacCubbie, MacCubbin,
MacDonleavy, MacGeorge,
MacGibbon, MacGilbert,
MacGreusich, MacGubbin, MacInally,
MacIndeor, MacIndoe, MacKibb,
MacKinlay, MacMaster, MacMaurice,
MacMorris, MacMurchie,
MacMurphy, MacNeur, MacQuat,
MacQuattiey, MacQuinten, MacWattie,
MacWhirter, MacWhorter, Masters,
MaWhitty, Morrice, Morris, Morrison,
Murchie, Murchison, Richardson,
Risk, Rusk, Spittal, Walter, Wason,
Waters, Watson, Watt, Watters, Weir,
Yuill, Yule, Zuill, etc.)

Buchanan
*Buchanan Clearinghouse
1056 West Water Street
Berne, IN 46711
Phone (219) 589-3477
Judith Burkhardt
Pub. *Buchanan Clearinghouse*
$5.00 plus FGS submission for life
    membership

Buchanan
*Buchanan Genealogical Group
711 Bellevue
Clinton, MS 39056-3821
Phone (601) 924-7511; E-mail:
    GeBuchanan@aol.com
Gerald Buchanan

Bucher (see Tallent)

Bucher
*Bucher Family Association
210 Cliff Turn
Falling Waters, WV 25419-9530
Phone (304) 274-3104
Larry D. Kump

Buchholz (see Garner)

Buchlyrie (see Graham)

Bucholtz (see Links Genealogy
    Publications)

Buck (see Franciscus, Richardson)

Buck
*Compu-Chart
363 South Park Victoria Drive
Milpitas, CA 95035-5708
Phone (408) 262-1051
Paula Perkins Mortensen
Pub. *Buck Surname Booklets*, irregularly,
    $7.00 per volume

Buck
*George H. Buck Family Organization
William Buck Family Organization
7712 Buck Street
North Richland Hills, TX 76180
Phone (817) 485-3792
Ken Mason

Buckelew
*Buckelew Traces
PO Box 9
Nursery, TX 77976
Phone (512) 575-0860
Gerry Green
Pub. *Buckelew Traces*, irregularly, $5.75
    per issue (except #7 & #8)

Buckeridge (see Buckridge)

Buckland
*Krans-Buckland Family Association
    Library
PO Box 1025
North Highlands, CA 95660-1025
Phone (916) 332-4359
Joyce Buckland, President
(Buckland family worldwide)

Buckland
*Buckland-Bucklin Family Association
3708 Grady Street
Fort Worth, TX 76119
Phone (817) 535-7207
Anne Bucklin Frost
Free membership

Bucklin (see Buckland)

Buckmaster (see Burrow)

Buckner
*The Buckner Newsletter
8857 Revere Run
West Chester, OH 45069-3626
Betty Ann Smiddy-Buckner
Pub. *The Buckner Newsletter*, quarterly,
    $10.00 per year subscription

Buckridge
Buck(e)ridge Database
49 Seaside Avenue
Westbrook, CT 06498
Phone (203) 399-9273
Margaret Buckridge Bock

Budenich (see Blossom Press)

Budway (see Boadway)

Buechele
*The Buechele-Kirchner History
232 Mont Eagle
Milford, MI 48381
Phone (810) 684-0650
Ruth Buechele Doerr, Publisher
(includes descendants of Herman
    Buechele and Mary Rehklau, German
    immigrants, and of Michael Kirchner,
    German immigrant, and Barbara Betz)

Buel (see Blossom Press)

Buel
*Buel Surname Organization
2845 North 72nd Street
Milwaukee, WI 53210
Phone (414) 778-1224; (414) 2109 FAX
Maralyn A. Wellauer
(includes families from Switzerland)

Buell (see Hinshaw)

Buell
Buell-Buhl-Eldridge-Cook Family
  Association
2306 Westgate
Houston, TX 77019
Phone (713) 529-2333
Harold Helm
$25.00 plus pedigree and family group
  sheets for membership

Buell
*Descendants of William Buell Who
  Came to America from England About
  1631
14203 Sixth Avenue, South
Seattle, WA 98168
Phone (206) 243-0609
Estella Wilcox, Publisher

Buelle (see Blossom Press)

Buffham
Buffham Surname Organization
Heman Robert Buffam Family
  Organization
114 Trevethan Avenue
Santa Cruz, CA 95062
Floyd D. P. Oydegaard

Buffington (see Way)

Buffington
*The Buffington Family History
  Foundation, Inc.
1042 Lipscomb Lake Road
Pendergrass, GA 30567
Phone (770) 534-6028
Ralph M. Buffington, C.E.O.

Buffington
*Buffington Family Reunion
4273 North 67th Street
Harrisburg, PA 17111
Verna Balsbaugh, Director

Bufford (see Clark)

Buffum
*Buffum Family Association, Inc.
86 Woodland Terrace
Buffalo, NY 14225-2035
Phone (716) 837-9766
H. Curtiss Buffum, Treasurer
Pub. *Buffum Family Association*, three
  times per year; (includes descendants
  of Robert Buffum (ca 1590 Yorkshire,
  England–) and wife, Thomasine Ward-
  Thompson)
$6.00 per year membership

Buford (see Hallam)

Buford
*Buford Surname Organization
1575 230th Street
Donnellson, IA 52625
Phone (319) 835-5233
Charles W. Buford

Bugbee
*Bugbee Family
11700 Dinwiddie Drive
Rockville, MD 20852
Jane Farrell Burgess, Publisher
(includes books on Bugbee, Estep,
  Gaston, Greeley, Householder and
  Janney surnames, research on
  Maryland, Virginia, District of
  Columbia and Pennsylvania records)

Buhl (see Buell)

Buie
Buie Exchange
3828 Heywood
Fort Worth, TX 76107
S. Buie

Buik (see MacDuff)

Buis (see Byars)

Buist (see MacDuff)

Bujacic (see Blossom Press)

Bujacich (see Blossom Press)

Bulger (see Corson)

Bull (see Clark)

Bullard (see Robinson)

Bullard
*The International Bullard Family
  Newsletter*
2203 Aspen Drive
Alamogordo, NM 88310
Shirley L. Mofield
Pub. *The International Bullard Family
  Newsletter*, quarterly (spring, summer,
  fall and winter), $7.00 per year
  subscription

Buller (see Johnson)

Bullough (see Holden)

Bulot (see Blossom Press)

Bumgardner
Bumgardner Association
8201 Navarre Parkway, #B205
Navarre Beach, FL 32566
Phone (904) 939-1014
Florence Collins Bumgardner, President
Annual reunion

Bumgarner (see Flippin)

Bun (see Links Genealogy Publications)

Bunch (see Newberry)

Buncle (see MacDuff)

Bundy (see Covert)

Bunet (see Bunnett)

Bungard (see The Memorial Foundation
  of the Germanna Colonies)

Bunker (see Mosher)

Bunker
*The Bunker Family Association of
  America
9 Sommerset Road
Turnersville, NJ 08012-2122
Phone (609) 589-6140; E-mail: mary-
  gene.page@omnibbs.com
Gil Bunker, President
Pub. *The Bunker Banner*, quarterly;
  (22,000 Bunker names on computer
  files)
$15.00 per year membership, $17.00 per
  year foreign membership; annual
  reunion in June

Bunkle (see MacDuff)

Bunn (see Links Genealogy
  Publications)

Bunnell
Bunnell Foundation
PO Box 16434
Portland, OR 97216
David A. Bunnell
Pub. *Bunnell Foundation Newsletter*

Bunnell
The Bunnell/Bonnell Newsletter
PO Box 62
Laceyville, PA 18623-0062
Phone (717) 869-2325
William R. Austin, Editor
Pub. *The Bunnell/Bonnell Newsletter*,
  quarterly, $12.00 per year subscription
  (except free to libraries and historical
  societies), queries accepted; (includes
  Bunnell/Bonnell and variations,
  anywhere, but primarily in the U.S.
  and Canada)

Bunnett
*Bunnett Queries
608 Arroyo Seco
Santa Cruz, CA 95060-3148
Phone (408) 423-3852
Sara A. Bunnett
(includes Bunnett, all dates, worldwide,
  often spelled Bonnet or Bunet prior to
  1800; members of the Guild of One-
  Name Studies)

Buntain (see Graham)

Buntin (see Graham)

Bunting (see Graham)

Bunton
William Bunton Descendants
Rt. 1, Box 210
Butler, TN 37640
E. Bunton

Bunyan (see Likes)

Bunyard
*Bunyard Database
70 Ridgecrest Road
Kentfield, CA 94904-2746
Phone (415) 924-4040; E-mail:
    cdgg47a@prodigy.com
Mary Cole
(includes descendants of James Beal
    Bunyard (1744 St. Batolph
    Bishopsgate, London, England–1817
    Ashe County, North Carolina) and
    Hannah)

Buras (see Blossom Press)

Burat (see Blossom Press)

Burbanck (see Burbank)

Burbank (see Brown)

Burbank
*Burbank-Burbanck Family
80 East Street
Bristol, VT 05443
John R. Burbank, Editor and Publisher
Pub. *Burbank Banner*, two to three times
    per year, $1.50 per issue

Burch (see Newmyer)

Burch
*Burch Family Reunion
500 Greenbriar Lane
Bedford, TX 76021
Phone (817) 498-3464
George Armentrout, Publisher
Pub. *Burch Newsletter*, annually (July),
    donation for subscription; (includes
    descendants of Richard Burch and
    Mary Anne Crisp of Persons County,
    North Carolina, 1780)

Burcher (see Kerr)

Burchet (see Hatfield)

Burchfield (see Birchfield)

Burckhardt (see Stabler)

Burd (see Bird)

Burdeau
*Family Research
416 Rockhill Avenue
Dayton, OH 45429-2628
Richard Bordeaux Walker
(includes descendants of Capt. Joseph
    Theodore Burdeau (1817–1881),

steamboat captain of St. Louis,
    Missouri, and New Orleans, Louisiana,
    and his wife Catharine Gwathmey
    (1822–1911))

Burden (see Rice)

Burdett (see Burdick)

Burdett
Burdett/Burdette Family Organization
PO Box 750491
Dayton, OH 45475-0491
Phyllis Brown Miller
Exchange service for SASE

Burdick
*The Burdick International Ancestry
    Library
2317 Riverbluff Parkway, #249
Sarasota, FL 34231-5032
Phone (941) 922-7931
Frank P. Mueller, A.G., Executive
    Director, Vice-President, Treasurer and
    Secretary
(a one-name society for the Burdick
    surname only)

Burdyne (see The Memorial Foundation
    of the Germanna Colonies)

Burge
Burge-Hodges-Lathum-Daunt Family
    Association
2306 Westgate
Houston, TX 77019
Phone (713) 529-2333
Harold Helm
$25.00 plus pedigree and family group
    sheets for membership

Burger (see Stoner)

Burgess (see Cian, Holden, Hyatt,
    MacFaddien, Smith, Warren)

Burgess
*Burgess Family Association and
    Burgess Clearinghouse
PO Box 45184
Boise, ID 83711
Phone (208) 376-7090
Susan Mortensen
Pub. *Burgess Bulletin*, quarterly
$15.00 per year membership

Burgoyne
*Edward Burgoyne Family Organization
694 South 300 East
Cedar City, UT 84720
Phone (801) 586-3036
Dr. Paul Burgoyne

Burgy (see Amburgey)

Burhans
*Burhans Reunion
PO Box 314
Lockport, NY 14095-0314
Phone (716) 433-9300

Bill Burhans, President; Barbara
    Nowack, Historian; Craig Nowack,
    Editor
Pub. *Branch Burhans*, three or four times
    per year; (includes Burhans in America
    since 1660)
$5.00 per year membership

Burhart (see McCanna)

Burington (see Burrington)

Burket
Burket(t)/Burkitt Newsletter
104 Quail Lane
Wake Village, TX 75501-5784
Juanita Russette
Pub. *Burket(t)/Burkitt Newsletter*

Burkett (see Burket)

Burkett
*George Maxwell Burkett Family
    Organization Family Reunion
1204 Linden Street
Dallas Center, IA 50063
Glenn S. Paul, Historian
Reunion in the Methodist Church
    basement, Dallas Center, Iowa

Burkett
Burkett Family Organization
201 Maxwell Lane
Newport News, VA 23606
Mrs. A. Burke Chiesa

Burkhart (see Womack)

Burkhead
*Burkhead Surname Organization
PO Box 157
White Mills, KY 42788
Phone (502) 862-4540
Oren R. White

Burkinsham (see Gooch)

Burkinshaw
*Burkinshaw Surname Organization
67 East Carlson Avenue
Midvale, UT 84047
Phone (801) 255-2494
Burke T. Wells

Burkitt (see Burket)

Burleson
*Burleson Family Association
10555 Le Mans Drive
Dallas, TX 75238
Phone (214) 348-0668
Helen Burleson Kelso, Editor
Pub. *Burleson Family Bulletin*, quarterly
$15.00 per year membership

Burlingame
Burlingame Reunion
16923 Norwood Road
Sandy Springs, MD 20860-1112
Charlene Beaty Bailey

Pub. *Beaty-Burlingame*, three or four
times per year, $15.00 per year
subscription
(includes descendants of Jeremiah
Burlingame (1824, Clinton, New
York–) and Eliza Warner (1830
Livingston County, New York–),
settled in Clinton, Minnesota)

Burlison
Aaron Burlison Descendants
3251 East Fairpoint Street
Pasadena, CA 91107
Dr. O. C. Burlison

Burnam (see Burnham)

Burnam
*Burnam Family of Northwest Missouri
3103 Fishing Hole Road
Flemington, MO 65650
Phone (417) 253-8102; (816) 452-4666
Gloria Fancler Doty
(ancestors and descendants of Joel F. and
Tabitha Harris Burnam)
Annual reunion on the first Saturday of
October

Burner (see Berner, Blackhurst)

Burnett
Burnett Society
1232 North Harrison Avenue
Fresno, CA 93728-1543
Phone (209) 266-2306
Mary B. Dunklee, Secretary-Treasurer
Pub. *The Breagh Burnett Gazette*,
quarterly
$20.00 per year membership

Burnett
*Burnett Family Genealogy Association,
Inc.
3891 Commander Drive
Chamblee, GA 30341-0016
Phone (404) 455-6445
Thomas Robley Burnett, Editor
Pub. *Burnett Family Newsletter*,
quarterly, $15.00 per year U.S.
subscription, $20.00 per year foreign
subscription via surface mail, $25.00
per year foreign subscription via
airmail

Burnett
Clan Burnett, Inc.
13506 Vixen Lane
Oklahoma City, OK 73131
Phone (405) 478-3730
John Burnett, President
Pub. *The Banner*

Burnette (see Holden)

Burnham
*Deacon John Burnham of Ipswich and
Ebenezer Martin of Rehoboth,
Massachusetts
10450 Lottsford Road, Apartment 1117
Mitchellville, MD 20721-2746

Phone (303) 925-7232
Elisabeth P. Martin, Author
(includes descendants of John Burnham,
including Ebenezer who moved to
Connecticut, Joseph who fought in the
Revolution, and Alba who went west
to New York and Ohio; also Martins
from Revolutionary soldier, Ebenezer
to Jarvis who settled in western New
York State, and his son Leonard who
married Louisa Burnham and went to
Ohio; also allied families: Andrews,
Bieder, Colwell, Durkee, Holt,
Loomis, Mason, Montgomery, Scott,
Snow, Varney and Waters)

Burnham
Burnham Family Lineage Charts
315 Castlegate Road
Pittsburgh, PA 15221
Phone (412) 241-3029
Walter J. Burnham
Pub. *Burnham Family Lineage Charts*,
annually, $32.00 per issue; (includes
Burnam)

Burnham
James Burnham Descendants
5141 South 2175 West, #1
Roy, UT 84067-3420
B. Larimore

Burns (see Gregor, Lemon)

Burns
*Burns Surname Organization
7705 Ensley Drive, S.W.
Huntsville, AL 35802-2845
Phone (205) 883-0207
Thomas W. Burns

Burns
Burns Family of Prince Edward Island
and New England
Rt. 5, Box 53
Laconia, NH 03246
S. Theall

Burnside
Burnside Bulletin
201 South Corona Street
Denver, CO 80209
David F. Sorey
Pub. *Burnside Bulletin*

Burr (see Ross)

Burr
*Burr Research
613 Bostwick
Nacogdoches, TX 75961
Phone (409) 564-7478
Berry Fagan Burr, Publisher

Burrell
*Burrell and Allied Families
1335 Monterey Drive
Broomfield, CO 80020
Phone (303) 469-9015
John F. Wecker

(includes surname exchange on Burrell,
Center, Chastain, Denton, Pruitt and
Waters of South Carolina, North
Carolina and Georgia)

Burrell
*Burrell/Burrill Family Association
PO Box 31402
Seattle, WA 98103-1402
Phone (206) 782-9250
Barbara Burrill, Editor
Pub. *Burrill/Burrill News*, quarterly;
(includes Birrell, Borell, Burwell, etc.)
$10.00 per year membership

Burress
Watson Genealogical Services
PO Box 772
Jal, NM 88252
Pub. *Burress/Burrows/Burroughs
Researchers*, quarterly

Burrill (see Burrell)

Burrington
Burrington-Burington
6432 Tanager Lane
Eden Prairie, MN 55346-1806
Zoe Matthews
Pub. *Burrington-Burington*, quarterly,
$10.00 per year subscription

Burris (see Cranston, Lush)

Burroughs (see Burress, Cranston,
Newman, Reeder)

Burrow (see Album)

Burrow
*Burrow/Clark/Buckmaster
Rt. 3, Box 190
Concordia, MO 64020-9505
Phone (816) 463-7523
Mrs. Buddy Samuels
Periodic reunion, Labor Day week in
Concordia, Missouri

Burrow
Burrow Family Organization
Rt. 3, Box 123
Trinity, NC 27370
Cheryl Burrow

Burrows (see Folk Family Surname
Exchange, Burress)

Burrup
*William and Hannah Maria Byington
Burrup Family Organization
6602 West King Valley Road
West Valley City, UT 84120
Phone (801) 250-9017
Jay G. Burrup, Genealogist
Pub. *Newsletter*, irregularly; (includes all
Burrups, worldwide, but especially
from Dymock, Gloucestershire,
England, ca 1560s; also Byingtons and
connections with William and John
Boynton of Rowley, Massachusetts, in
1530s)

Burt (see Bert, MacDuff, Oliver)

Burten (see Burton)

Burtin (see Burton)

Burton (see Jelly, Nelson)

Burton
*Burton Family Organization (Burten/
   Burtin/Berton)
653 Perrshing Drive
Walnut Creek, CA 94596
A. Maxim Coppage, Publisher
Pub. *Burton Families Quarterly*
   $10.00 per year membership

Burton
*Burton Family Reunion Association
   (Descendants of John Pleasant Burton
   and Suzannah Stamper)
7224 Southeast Street
Indianapolis, IN 46227
Phone (317) 881-1352
Emalou Burton Garten, Secretary
Pub. *Burton Bits 'n' Business*, quarterly,
   $5.00 per year subscription

Burton
*Burton Data
3126 Cleveland Avenue
Kansas City, MO 64128
Minnie Burton Bell

Burttram (see Buttram)

Burwell (see Burrell)

Busby (see Nickerson)

Busby
Busby Family Association
2946 Firethorn Drive
Tuscaloosa, AL 35405
Carol Bryan

Busby
Busby Family Association
630-B Colquitt Road
Terrell, TX 75160
Miss Essie N. Busby

Busch (see Mingus)

Buschmeyer (see Likes)

Buse (see Boose)

Bush (see The Memorial Foundation of
   the Germanna Colonies, McCune,
   Neville, Wright)

Bush
Bush/Hall/Meek Families
PO Box 965
Syracuse, KS 67878
Mrs. C. E. Jones

Bush
Bush, The Anglican: A New England
   Species
PO Box 1538
Wichita, KS 67201-1538
Lela Eitel

Bush
*Topp of the Line
1304 West Cliffwood Court
Spokane, WA 99218-2917
Phone (509) 467-2299
Bette Butcher Topp, Owner/Operator
Pub. *Bush Branches*, irregularly, $5.50
   per issue plus $2.00 postage and
   handling

Bushby (see Hutchison)

Bushman (see Rothenberger)

Bushong (see Clark)

Bushong
*Bushong Family Association
4649 Yarmouth Lane
Youngstown, OH 44512-1749
Phone (330) 782-8380
Carol Willsey Bell, C.G., Editor
Pub. *Bushong Bulletin*, quarterly
   $10.00 per year membership

Bushore
Vital Bushore (Bourchard)-Marie Anne
   Trahan of Indiana Family Association
3515 Avenue C
Kearney, NE 68847
Mary Janet Nordhues

Bushyaeger
Bushyaeger Branches Newsletter
602 Forest Lake Drive
Brea, CA 92621
Alfaretta Mastro
Pub. *Bushyaeger Branches Newsletter*,
   three times per year

Bushyeager
Bushyeager Roots and Branches
105 Marble Drive
Bridgeville, PA 15017
Mrs. Donald Bushyager

Buskirk (see Van Buskirk)

Buss (see Boose, Likes)

Bussel (see Rutherford)

Buswell (see Catlow)

Butcher
*Topp of the Line
1304 West Cliffwood Court
Spokane, WA 99218-2917
Phone (509) 467-2299
Bette Butcher Topp, Owner/Operator
Pub. *Butcher Block*, irregularly, $5.50 per
   issue plus $2.00 postage and handling

Butherus (see Brehm)

Butler (see Allred, Cian, Carpenter,
   Cook, Corson, Dawson, Duncan,
   Ingram, Job, Lynch, Priddy, Thayer)

Butler
*Abel Butler Family Organization
571 East Second Street North
Joseph City, AZ 86032
Phone (602) 288-3598
Luella S. Foree

Butler
Butler Society (North American Region)
26 North Street, #119
East Douglas, MA 01516-2002
Carolyn A. Murphy
Pub. *Butler Family Journal*

Butler
*Kinseeker Publications
5697 Old Maple Trail
PO Box 184
Grawn, MI 49637
Phone E-mail: AB064@taverse.lib.mi.us
Victoria Wilson, Editor
Pub. *The Family Series: Butler*,
   irregularly, $6.50 per year subscription

Butrum (see Buttram)

Butson
Butson Family Newsletter
3140 Montevideo Drive
San Ramon, CA 94583
Wesley Johnston
Pub. *Butson Family Newsletter*,
   semiannually, $8.00 per year
   subscription

Butt (see Worch)

Butterbaugh (see Putterbaugh)

Buttercase (see MacDuff)

Butterfield (see Barnard)

Butterfield
*Butterfield Clearinghouse and Exchange
10306 Park Avenue
Santee, CA 92071
Phone (619) 448-9355
Dr. Claude W. Butterfield
Free exchange

Button (see The Memorial Foundation of
   the Germanna Colonies, Fuller)

Buttram
*Buttram Family Association
RR 1, Box 668
Haleyville, AL 35565-9721
Phone (205) 486-3840
Gus M. Buttram, Editor
Pub. *Buttram Kith and Kin*, quarterly
   (winter, spring, summer and fall),
   $10.00 per year subscription; (includes

Buttram, Butrum, Bertram, Burttram
and other spellings)
Reunion

Butts (see Hicks)

Butts
Butts Newsletter
611 Clyde Court
San Marcos, TX 78666-2840
Bill Butts
Pub. *Butts Newsletter* (Butt, Butz),
quarterly, $5.00 per year subscription

Buwalda
*Gerritt Buwalda Family Organization
3560 Wright Avenue
Saint Ann, MO 63074
Phone (314) 429-6646
Bruce F. Buwalda

Buxkemper (see Hoelscher)

Buyer (see Byars)

Buyers (see Byars)

Buyor (see Byars)

Buzan (see LaRue)

Buzzard
*Buzzard and Alt Families
PO Box 353
San Luis Obispo, CA 93406
Monte P. Buzzard, Publisher
(includes descendants of Henry Buzzard
and Elizabeth Alt, married 1760, of
Virginia (now West Virginia), and
other Buzzard and Alt (Ault) families,
with collateral families: Arbogast,
Chestnut, Grimes, Hull, Radabaugh
and Zickafoose)

Buzzell (see Corson)

Byar (see Byars)

Byars (see Byers, Scott)

Byars
Byars, Byers Enquirer
Rt. 1, Box 123A
Buffalo, TX 75831
Phone (214) 322-5462
Clovis Byars Herring
Pub. *Byars, Byers Family Enquirer*,
quarterly, $15.00 per year subscription;
(includes Bair, Bairs, Bayer, Bayers,
Bayre, Bayres, Bias, Buis, Buyer,
Buyers, Buyor, Byar, Byer, Byre,
Byres and all variants)

Bybee
Bybee/Bibee Family Association
1604 Longfellow Street
McLean, VA 22101
Georgia E. Benefiel

Byer (see Boyer, Byars)

Byerly
*The Byerly Family of the Valley of
Virginia
8503 Spring Hollow Drive
Richmond, VA 23227-1227
Phone (804) 262-8855
John Franklin Byerly, Jr., Author
(includes descendants of Joseph Byerly
who arrived in Philadelphia in 1752,
moved to Western Maryland and
finally settled in Rockingham County,
Virginia, about 1783)

Byers (see Boyer, Byars, Lindsay)

Byers
Byers/Byars Family Report
2108 Denfield Lane
Childress, TX 79201
Pub. *Byers/Byars Family Report*

Byington (see Burrup)

Bynum (see Album)

Byran (see Byrom)

Byrd (see Folk Family Surname
Exchange, Bird, Bosher, Lambert,
Smity)

Byre (see Byars)

Byres (see Byars)

Byrom
Byrom-Byrum-Byran-O'Brien Family
Association
2306 Westgate
Houston, TX 77019
Phone (713) 529-2333
Harold Helm
$25.00 plus pedigree and family group
sheets for membership

Byron
*Byron Surname Organization
186 Range Hill Road
Poland Spring, ME 04274
Phone (207) 998-4615
Ronda A. Watson

Byrum (see Byrom)

Cabbage (see Folk Family Surname
Exchange)

Cabbage
*Folk Family
PO Box 52048
Knoxville, TN 37950-2048
Hester E. Stockton, Owner; Wilda
Cabbage, Editor
Pub. *Cabbage Patches*, quarterly, $15.00
per year subscription, $5.00 per issue;
(includes Cubbage)

Cabbage
*Cabbage/Cabage Surname Organization
Rt. 2, Box 97A
Washburn, TN 37888
Phone (423) 497-2287
John Verlin Cabage
Pub. *Annual*
Annual reunion in Tennesse in even-
numbered years and in places
Cabbages have settled in odd-
numbered years

Cable (see Coble, Dawson)

Cade
*Cade Family Reunion
167 San Jose Court
Vacaville, CA 95688
Phone (707) 446-2901
Ann Cade Phelps

Cadro (see Blossom Press)

Cagle
Cagle Journal of Historical Inquiry
PO Box 5342
Little Rock, AR 72215
Phone (501) 224-3819
John G. Cagle, Editor
Pub. *Cagle Journal of Historical Inquiry*,
monthly, $12.00 per year subscription

Cagnolotti (see Blossom Press)

Cahan (see Mosler)

Cahill (see Baker)

Cahill
*Cahill Cooperative
2050 Cedar Johnson Road
West Branch, IA 52358-8630
Phone (319) 643-2829
James Q. Cahill; Rosalie M. Cahill
Pub. *Cahill Cooperative Newsletter*,
quarterly, $6.00 per year subscription,
index 1987–1995 $5.00; (database
includes over 300 Cahill family
backgrounds, and similar spellings)

Cahill
Cahill Family Depository
12711 Westwood Lane
PO Box 37494
Omaha, NE 68137
Phone (402) 334-5550
John M. Cahill
Free database registration and queries
answered

Cahoon (see Colquhoun)

Cail
Cail, Cale, Kahl, Kale, Kehl Family
Association
124 Rudolph
Caldwell, ID 83605
Edwin A. Hemry, Vice President

Cain (see Garren, Hoster)

Cain
Cain
318 Jamaica Drive
San Antonio, TX 78227
Phone (512) 674-2535
Richard Cain Winegar, Editor
Pub. *Cain*, quarterly, $7.00 per year
     subscription

Caird (see Gregor)

Cairer
*Cairer Reunion
Rt. 3, Box 190
Concordia, MO 64020-9505
Phone (816) 463-7523
Mrs. Buddy Samuels
(includes descendants of William Henry
     Carrier (–1893) and Catherine Yankee
     of Shenandoah Valley, Virginia, to
     Missouri and Oklahoma; allied
     families of Jones, Sheets, Thompson,
     Wyatt and Zollicker)
Annual reunion on the Sunday after
     Labor Day at Liberty Park, Sedalia,
     Missouri

Cairns (see Hyatt)

Caison (see Cason)

Calbreath (see Galbraith)

Calcote (see Callicot)

Caldwell (see Looney)

Caldwell
*John Augustus Caldwell Family
     Organization
10042 Lubao Avenue
Chatsworth, CA 91311-3517
Phone (818) 349-3169
Charles A. Cartwright-Frank

Caldwell
Andrew and Martha Caldwell
     Descendants Reunion
101 Evergreen Way
Hartford City, IN 47348
Phone (317) 348-3044
Mrs. R. Lewis Scott
(18th century residents of Drumore
     Township, Lancaster County,
     Pennsylvania)

Cale (see Cail)

Calef
*Family Research
416 Rockhill Avenue
Dayton, OH 45429-2628
Richard Bordeaux Walker
(includes ancestry and descendants of
     Cutting Stevens Calef (1796–1823)
     and Martha Howard Paine of
     Washington, Vermont)

Calhoun (see Colquhoun)

Calhoun
*Calhoun Family Research Society
PO Box 233
Athens, AL 35612

Calico (see Callicot)

Calk
Calk Newsletter
Rt. 1, Box 13
Stoutland, MO 65567
Phone (417) 286-3987
Wayne Calk, Family Representative
Pub. *Calk Newsletter*, quarterly, $10.00
     per year subscription

Calkins (see Heath)

Call (see Koll)

Callahan (see Coffman)

Callaway
*The Callaway Family Association, Inc.
1350 South York Street
Denver, CO 80210
Phone (303) 777-7354
Martha Callaway Winkler, Assistant
     Secretary
Pub. *The Callaway Journal*, annually
     (September)
$20.00 per year membership for
     individuals, $30.00 per year joint
     membership, $40.00 per year
     supporting membership, $350.00 life
     membership; annual reunion in
     October

Callaway
*Callaway Family Association, Inc.
62 Buffalo Ridge Drive
Unicoi, TN 37692
Phone (615) 743-6613
Mrs. Sherman Williams, Genealogist
Pub. *The Callaway Journal*, annually;
     Callaway Communique, three times
     per year; (includes all Callaways (and
     variant spellings), any dates,
     worldwide)
$15.00 per year membership

Callegan (see Wright)

Callen (see Wright)

Callendar (see Gregor, Kylander)

Callette (see Collette)

Calley (see MacDuff)

Callicott
*The Callicott Family in America
PO Box 8387
Saint Petersburg, FL 33738
John T. Callicotte, Editor
Pub. *Newsletter* (includes surname
     variations, Calcote, Calico, Callicotte,
     Callicutt, etc.)

Callicotte (see Callicot)

Callicutt (see Callicot)

Callihan (see Dean)

Callis
Callis Family Newsletter
Rt. 11, Box 166
Jonesborough, TN 37659
Mildred Kozsuch
Pub. *Callis Family Newsletter*, quarterly,
     $4.00 per year subscription

Callison
*Joseph Callison Family Organization
2789 West 12075 South
Riverton, UT 84065-7630
Kairlee D. Graham, President
(includes descendants of Joseph Callison
     (1776 Virginia–1834 Adair County,
     Kentucky) and Susannah Dawson
     (1777 Virginia–1823 Adair County,
     Kentucky), daughter of John Dawson
     and Charity Watkins)

Call
The Call Family Newsletter
Rt. 1, Box 354
Lenoir, NC 28645
William Sherman call
Pub. *The Call Family Newsletter*

Calloway (see Hanes, Holden)

Callum (see Gregor, Kane)

Calmes (see Richardson)

Calmes
*Genealogical Society of Versailles
PO Box 65013
Lubbock, TX 79464-5013
Phone (806) 793-8104
C. James Calmes, Secretary-Treasurer
Pub. *Calmes Notes*, quarterly
$10.00 per year membership; annual
     reunion in June in Lexington, KY

Calvert (see Egerton)

Calvert
Old Time Publications
10828 Oakbrook Drive
Omaha, NE 68154-2437
Peggy Wallingford Butherus
Pub. *Calvert Connections*, $5.50 plus
     $1.25 postage & handling per issue
     (Washington residents add 7.8% sales
     tax)

Calvie (see MacDuff)

Calvin
Calvin/Colvin Family
64 East Elkin Street
Sonora, CA 95370-5628
Marilyn R. Solari

Calvin
*Calvin Family Association
2317 Louisiana Avenue
Deer Park, TX 77536-3811
Phone (713) 476-4715
Donnie Calvin
Pub. *Calvin Connections Past & Present*, semiannually (January and May), free to family members; (includes descendants of William Henry Calvin (1823 Virginia–1885 Burleson County, Texas) and Annie Paula Morgan (1839–1912))
Reunion

Calvy (see MacDuff)

Cambell (see McCune)

Cambo (see MacDuff)

Cambron (see Osborn, White)

Camden (see Montgomery)

Cameron (see MacDuff, Scott, Stewart)

Cameron
Clan Cameron Association of North America
Stone Mountain Branch
946 Hargett Court
Stone Mountain, GA 30083
H. F. Cameron
Pub. *The Charter*, quarterly
$15.00 per year membership

Cameron
*Clan Cameron Association of North America
Grandfather Mountain Branch
PO Drawer 19764
Raleigh, NC 27619-9764
Phone (919) 876-2100
Tom Badger, Treasurer
Pub. *The Cameron Piper*, quarterly; (includes Cameron, Clark, Taylor, Stronach, Clarke, east coast of U.S.)
$15.00 to $20.00 per year membership

Cameron
Cameron Clan of North America
3065 Granville Drive
Raleigh, NC 27609
D. Cameron

Cameron
*Clan Cameron of Ohio
4876 Thomas Boulevard
Geneva, OH 44041
Phone (216) 466-4227
Terry Cameron, President
Pub. *Cameron Drummer*, quarterly; (includes Cameron and all family septs, not primarily genealogical, lists calendar of events in northern Ohio)
$7.00 per year membership

Camfield (see Canfield)

Camp (see Surname Sources, Miller)

Camp
Camp Family Association
4200 Oak Knoll Drive
Carmichael, CA 95608-2634
Barbara Farris, Editor
Pub. *Camp Bulletin*, quarterly
$8.00 per year membership

Campbell (see Folk Family Surname Exchange, Allen, Cranston, Goodenow, Holden, Johnson, Kunkel, McCanna)

Campbell
*James Washington Campbell Family Organization
4840 Wyandot
Denver, CO 80221
Phone (303) 433-2769
Mary E. Tudder, Family Genealogist
(includes Campbell, Logan, Bowman of North Carolina 1700s, Maryland 1765, Tennessee 1773, Missouri 1843, Texas 1870, Colorado 1898)
SASE

Campbell
Campbell
3911 Covert Road
Pontiac, MI 48054
Edmond Campbell
Pub. *Campbell*, quarterly, $14.00 per year subscription

Campbell
*Campbell Reunion Association
26 Colby Street
Keene, NH 03431-4303
Phone (603) 352-2466 (Secretary)
Mrs. Albert G. Clark, Secretary; Richard T. Campbell, President
(includes descendants of Henry Campbell and Martha Black, who arrived in Watertown, Massachusetts, in 1733 and settled in Windham, New Hampshire, particularly descendants of Albert W. Campbell and Josephine Louella (Johnson) Campbell, born in Windham, New Hampshire, settlers of Charlestown, New Hampshire)
$2.00 per year membership; annual reunion on the second Sunday of August in Langdon or Acworth

Campbell
*Folk Family
PO Box 52048
Knoxville, TN 37950-2048
Hester E. Stockton, Owner; Julie and Joe Campbell, Editors
Pub. *Campbell Clans*, quarterly, $15.00 per year subscription, $5.00 per issue

Campbell
Campbell-Gamble-Rose-Gambol Family Association
2306 Westgate
Houston, TX 77019
Phone (713) 529-2333

Harold Helm
$25.00 plus pedigree and family group sheets for membership

Campbell
The Clan Campbell Society, U.S.A.
343 West Patrick Circle
Melbourne, FL 32901
Phone (407) 723-1957
Scott V. Campbell
Pub. *Clan Campbell Society (USA) Journal*, quarterly
$20.00 per year membership

Campbell
*Pioneer Publication
PO Box 1179
Tum Tum, WA 99034-1179
Phone (509) 276-9841
Shirley Penna-Oakes
Pub. *Campbell Connections*, irregularly, $6.00 per issue plus $1.75 postage for 1–3 books, 50¢ for each additional book

Campbell
Campbell Contacts in America
416 JF Townline Road
Janesville, WI 53545
Phone (608) 756-2495
Chris A. Campbell, Editor
Pub. *Campbell Contacts in America*, quarterly (March, June, September and December), $15.00 per year subscription, $18.00 per year includes Regis+Tree service (a database containing the ancestral information of early Campbell families from across America)

Camper (see The Memorial Foundation of the Germanna Colonies, Cowart)

Campfield (see Canfield)

Canaday (see Kennedy)

Canamore
Canamore Family
7161 Kalkaska Drive
Davison, MI 48423
G. Canamore

Canfield (see Kenfield)

Canfield
*Canfield Family Association
1144 North Gordon
Wichita, KS 67203
Phone (316) 942-7120
Genevieve (Canfield) Martinson, Organizing Editor
Pub. *Canfield Family Association Publication*, quarterly, $8.00 per year U.S. subscription, $14.00 (U.S. funds) per year foreign subscription, $4.00 per year subscription for libraries; (includes Camfield, Campfield, anywhere, any time frame)

Canfield
*Canfield Exchange
PO Box 154
Ontario, NY 14519
Jean C. Denison
(includes all Camfield, Campfield, Canfield, especially descendants of Matthew and Sarah (Treat) Camfield/ Canfield (1604–1673) New Haven, Connecticut, Newark, New Jersey)
No charge

Canine (see Cunning, Jones)

Cannadie (see Kennedy)

Cannady (see Cowart)

Cannady
Cannady Family Association
4508 Embleton Drive
Raleigh, NC 27612
E. Tissot

Canney (see Corson)

Cannon
Cannon Surname Organization
James Cannon Family Organization
PO Box 15926
Austin, TX 78761
H. J. Andreozzi

Cannon
*John Wesley Cannon Family
 Organization
Lillie Jane Cannon Family Organization
10042 Lubao Avenue
Chatsworth, CA 91311-3517
Phone (818) 349-3169
Charles A. Cartwright-Frank

Cant (see Douglas, MacDuff)

Canterbury
*Canterbury Database
26007 Atherton
Laguna Hills, CA 92653
Phone (714) 643-3492
Carmen Miesen Bussard

Cantrell (see Jones)

Cantrell
*Cantrell Family Organization
7974 Hillsboro Court
Pleasanton, CA 94588-3618
Phone (510) 846-1153
Dorothy Horn Bevard

Cantrell
Cantrell
1221 Candice Court
Mesquite, TX 75149
Mary L. House, Editor
Pub. *Cantrell*, quarterly, $15.00 per year subscription

Cantrill
Cantrill-Latham-Cayce-Walton Family
 Association
2306 Westgate
Houston, TX 77019
Phone (713) 529-2333
Harold Helm
$25.00 plus pedigree and family group sheets for membership

Cantwell
*Cantwell-Conteville Family Association
3402 Fairlawn Drive
Glenview, IL 60025
Phone (708) 729-0301
Henry V. Cantwell, Editor of *A Cantwell Tapestry*
Pub. *A Cantwell Tapestry*, annually, $15.00; *CCFA Newsletter*, semiannually, $10.00 per year subscription; (includes descendants of Capt. Edmund Cantwell and Mary de Haes of 17th century Delaware, and Herluin and Herleve de Conteville in 11th century Normandy)

Capeheart (see Gebhard)

Capers (see Reynolds)

Caplinger
Caplinger Family Association
3157 Meadow Wood Drive
Springfield, OH 45505
J. L. Caplinger

Capoot
*Capoot Surname Organization
1862 Brooksedge
Germantown, TN 38138
Phone (901) 756-6510
Wayne Capoot

Cappiello (see Blossom Press)

Capps (see Folk Family Surname
 Exchange, Cowart)

Capps
*Capps Family
3617 Link Road
Greensboro, NC 27405
Phone (910) 621-4695
K. Paul Holt, Family History Compiler
(includes descendants of Robert R. Capps (1805–1891) of Orange (now Alamance) County, North Carolina)

Capps
*Folk Family
PO Box 52048
Knoxville, TN 37950-2048
Hester E. Stockton, Owner; Ollie Capps, Editor
Pub. *Capps Families*, quarterly, $15.00 per year subscription, $5.00 per issue

Car
*Car-Kerr Clearing House
Rt. 2, 104 New Bridge Road
Salem, NJ 08079

Phone (609) 935-5015
Beverly Carr Stanley, Editor
Pub. *Carr-Kerr Clearing House Genealogical Periodical*, quarterly, $15.00 per year subscription, free queries; (includes Scot-Irish families in Pennsylvania, North Carolina, Virginia, Kentucky and Tennessee, of interchangeable spellings)

Caracoff (see Kirshop)

Caraher
*Caraher Family History Society
O Carragher Clan Association
142 Rexford Street
Sistersville, WV 26175-1628
Pub. *Caraher Family History Society Journal*, annually
$25.00 per year membership, $15.00 per year associate membership

Cardwell (see McNees, Reynolds)

Carel (see Blossom Press)

Caret
*Caret/Carette Family History
 Association
4065 Berrywood Drive
Eugene, OR 97404-4061
James R. Brann, Family Representative
(PAF™ data bank on MAC™ computer includes Quebec to Maine)
Free information exchange

Carette (see Caret)

Carey (see Kelly, Newton)

Cargo (see Gross)

Caricoff (see Kirshop)

Carley (see Corley)

Carley
Carley Database
7804 Moorland Lane
Bethesda, MD 20814
Phone (301) 652-5836
William S. Carley
(database includes information on Blackistone, Carley, Carson, Mahon, Robinet, Steele, Warden and Wheatley families)

Carlini (see Blossom Press)

Carlisle (see Arthur, Lynch)

Carlson (see Klewer)

Carlton
*Carlton/Reed Family Organization
1132 North Tela Drive
Oklahoma City, OK 73127-4308
Phone (405) 789-2842
Pauline Carlton Fletcher, Secretary and Genealogist

(computer database uses Quinsept™, PAF™ and Reunion™)
Annual reunion

Carmen (see LaRue)

Carment (see MacDuff)

Carmichael (see MacDougall, Pye, Stewart)

Carmichael
*Archibald McDonald Carmichael
  Family Organization
511 Gaylord
Pueblo, CO 81004
Phone (719) 543-0549
Virginia Baird Penaluna Haling

Carmichael
*Clan Carmichael, USA
2591 Rocky Springs Drive
Marietta, GA 30062
Phone (404) 971-0484
Alana Carmichael Nigro, Secretary/
  Treasurer
Pub. *The Eagle Gate* (USA),
  semiannually; *Brokenspear*
  (International)
$15.00 per year membership in Clan
  Carmichael, USA, $35.00 per year full
  membership, including Clan
  Carmichael, International

Carmouche (see Neville)

Carn
*Carn Surname Organization
803 Bel Mar Drive
Ogden, UT 84403
Phone (801) 392-0154
Eunice R. Carn, Family Genealogist
(includes descendants of Reginald Albert
  Carn and Eunice Carn, who were
  married in 1938 in Salt Lake City,
  Utah)
$5.00 per year membership

Carnbee (see MacDuff)

Carnbie (see MacDuff)

Carnegie
Carnegie Clan Society
15113 Rosecroft Road
Rockville, MD 20853
Phone (301) 929-1165
W. Richard Lomax, Secretary U.S.
  Branch

Carneil (see MacDuff)

Carney
*Carney Family Association
7413 South Kingston
Tulsa, OK 74136
Phone (918) 496-9078
Mrs. J. Burdick
(Carney of Ulster County, New York, ca
  1770–1820)

Carney
The Carney Chronicles Newsletter
839 Battery Lane
Nashville, TN 37220
June Carney Pollard, Editor
Pub. *The Carney Chronicles Newsletter*
  (includes Kearney)

Carnie (see Cian, Leslie)

Carnrike
Carnrike Family Association
8156 Sun Vista Way
Orlando, FL 32822
Phone (305) 273-0305
Dr. David M. Carnrike
Pub. *Carnrike Past Times*, irregularly

Caro (see Blossom Press, Karow)

Carpenter (see Folk Family Surname
  Exchange, The Memorial Foundation
  of the Germanna Colonies, Brown,
  Corson, Goodenow, Heath, Johnson,
  Lus, Wright)

Carpenter
Hapsburg Press
PO Box 173
Broomfield, CO 80038-0173
Barbara Inman Beall, Editor
Pub. *Carpenter*, five times per year,
  $10.00 per year subscription

Carpenter
*Carpenter and Related Family
  Association
PO Box 1356
Bowling Green, KY 42102-1356
Phone (502) 842-7803 (between 6:00
  P.M. and 7:30 P.M. only)
James Ausie Carpenter, Author
Pub. *Carpenter and Related Family
  Historical Journal*, quarterly; (includes
  Balch, Bennett, Butler, Carpenter,
  Etheredge, Evans, Ferguson, Kerby,
  Sanders, Yates and others)
$30.00 per year membership

Carpenter
Courier Publications
PO Box 1284
Natchitoches, LA 71458-1284
Annette Carpenter Womack
Pub. *Carpenter Family Courier*,
  quarterly, $12.50 per year subscription

Carpenter
Old Time Publications
10828 Oakbrook Drive
Omaha, NE 68154-2437
Peggy Wallingford Butherus
Pub. *Carpenter Chronicles*, $5.50 plus
  $1.25 postage & handling per issue
  (Washington residents add 7.8% sales
  tax)

Carpenter
*Topp of the Line
1304 West Cliffwood Court
Spokane, WA 99218-2917

Phone (509) 467-2299
Bette Butcher Topp, Owner/Operator
Pub. *Carpenter Chronicles*, irregularly,
  $5.50 per issue plus $2.00 postage and
  handling

Carper
*Carper Family Association
4918 Sudley Road
Catharpin, VA 22018
Phone (703) 754-2665
Janice M. Carper
(includes Carper from 1700 to the
  present)
Queries welcome

Carper
*Carper Family Association
10110 Farmington Drive
Fairfax, VA 22030
Lois Marbert

Carr (see Folk Family Surname
  Exchange, Catlow, Covert, Kerr)

Carr
Carr Surname Newsletter
18002 North 12th Street, #30
Phoenix, AZ 85022
Nani Mercer Neal
Pub. *Carr Surname Newsletter*, quarterly,
  $20.00 per year subscription

Carr
Missing Links
Rt. 4, Box 184
Saint Maries, ID 83861
Pub. *Carr Milestones*, quarterly, $8.50
  per year subscription

Carr
*Carr-Loker Society
309 East Moore Street
Blue Springs, MO 64014
Phone (816) 229-4096
Lawrence L. Loker, President
Pub. *Carr-Loker Chronology*, quarterly,
  $3.00 per issue, $10.00 per year
  subscription

Carr
*Folk Family
PO Box 52048
Knoxville, TN 37950-2048
Hester E. Stockton, Owner; Ann W. Carr,
  Editor
Pub. *Carr/Kerr Chronicle*, quarterly,
  $15.00 per year subscription, $5.00 per
  issue; (includes Kear and Ker
  (Scottish))

Carre (see Kerr)

Carrick (see Karrick, Kennedy)

Carrier (see Barnard, Cairer, Johnson)

Carrier
*Carrier Information Bank
PO Box 2
Frankfort, IL 62896
Phone (618) 937-1912
James T. Carrier

Carriere (see Johnson)

Carrigue (see Carrigues)

Carrigues
*Carrigues (Carrigue, Carrigus) Family/
    Cousins
Route 1, Cragston
Highland Falls, NY 10928-9801
Phone (914) 446-5198
Patricia Wright Strati
Pub. *Branches & Roots*, quarterly, $7.50
    per year subscription from Nancy
    Schaefer, Editor, 49 Showers Drive, A
    142, Mountain View, CA 94040;
    (French Huguenots with connections to
    Charlemagne and European royalty)
Reunion

Carrigus (see Carrigues)

Carro (see Karow)

Carroll (see Austin, Cian, Levi)

Carroll
*Kinseeker Publications
5697 Old Maple Trail
PO Box 184
Grawn, MI 49637
E-mail: AB064@taverse.lib.mi.us
Victoria Wilson, Editor
Pub. *Carroll Cables*, quarterly, $10.00
    per year subscription

Carroll
*Carroll Family Organization
PO Box 660
Beaufort, SC 29901
Phone (803) 524-5860
Lenore B. Stevenson, Secretary
(includes descendants from the family
    which emigrated from County
    Tipperary, Ireland, about 1848 and
    settled in Charleston, South Carolina,
    having one branch which stayed in the
    south and another which migrated to
    the midwest and west)

Carroll
*Carroll History
465 Sunset Terrace
Cedar Park, TX 78513
Phone (512) 259-4796
Joseph Carroll, Publisher
(includes descendants of Timothy Carroll
    (ca 1775 Virginia–))

Carrow (see Karow)

Carrson (see Carson)

Carruthers
*Carruthers Clan Society
227 Old Zion Road
North East, MD 21901
Phone (410) 658-5482
R. Crothers, Historian

Carson (see Blossom Press, Austin,
    Carley, Macpherson, MacPherson,
    McAllister)

Carson
*Our Carson Cousins
1243 Shenandoah Drive
Boise, ID 83712-7454
Phone (208) 344-6136
Ruby L. Ewart, Editor
Pub. *Our Carson Cousins*, quarterly with
    annual consolidated index, $8.00 per
    calendar year subscription

Carson
Carson Family Organization
27894 Gail Drive
Warren, MI 48093-4984
Dorothy Challacombe Rowell

Carson
Carson Clearinghouse
983 S.W. 177th Terrace
Aloha, OR 97006-7524
Paige Lindley
Pub. *Our Carson Cousins*, quarterly,
    $10.00 per year subscription

Carson
Carson-Karson-Carrson-Kerr Family
    Association
2306 Westgate
Houston, TX 77019
Phone (713) 529-2333
Harold Helm
$25.00 plus pedigree and family group
    sheets for membership

Carson
*George Carson Family History
    Association
1480 Edison Street
Salt Lake City, UT 84115
Phone (801) 485-0976; Website:
    HTTP:2//www.utw.com~gnat/
    CARSON/CARSON.HTML
Nat Carson, President
Pub. *Bulletin*, annually; (includes
    descendants of George Carson
    (1792–))
Annual reunion on the Saturday nearest
    the 17th of July at the Stage Coach Inn
    State Park in Fairfield, Utah

Carstairs (see MacDuff)

Carstarphen (see Forrester)

Carte (see Cian)

Carter (see Folk Family Surname
    Exchange, Surname Sources, Cian,
    Frasher, Hatfield, McCune, Wright)

Carter
Data Unlimited
4941 Syracuse Drive
Oxnard, CA 93033
Jeanne Hicks, Researcher

Carter
The Carter Files
155 175th Terrace North, Apartment 3
Redington Shores, FL 33708
Karen Parks DiNardo, Director
(database includes northern and southern
    Carter families)
$1.00 plus SASE for search

Carter
*Carter Clearinghouse
207 Auburn Drive
Dalton, GA 30720
Phone (706) 278-1504
Joseph Wiley Reid
(1400–1890 period)

Carter
*Kinseeker Publications
5697 Old Maple Trail
PO Box 184
Grawn, MI 49637
E-mail: AB064@taverse.lib.mi.us
Victoria Wilson, Editor
Pub. *The Family Series: Carter*,
    irregularly, $6.50 per year subscription

Cartie (see Cian)

Cartmel
*Cartmel-Cartmell-Cartmill Family
    Quarterly and Association
PO Box 463
Auburn, ME 04212-0463
Phone (207) 783-1378
William Patrick Cartmel, Director
Pub. *Cartmel-Cartmell-Cartmill Family
    Quarterly*, $18.95 per year
    subscription; (clearinghouse for these
    surnames around the world)

Cartmell (see Cartmel)

Cartmill (see Cartmel)

Cartwright (see Clark, Henson)

Cartwright
*Charles Reason Cartwright Family
    Organization
10042 Lubao Avenue
Chatsworth, CA 91311-3517
Phone (818) 349-3169
Charles A. Cartwright-Frank

Carty (see Cian)

Carver
*John Carver Family Organization
6602 West King Valley Road
West Valley City, UT 84120
Phone (801) 250-9017
Jay G. Burrup, Genealogist

Pub. *Carver Crier*, irregularly; (includes John Carver (1822 Clifford Parish, Herefordshire, England–1912 Plain City, Utah) immigrated to U.S.A. in 1850)

Caryl (see Newton)

Casbon (see Blossom Press)

Case (see Wright)

Case
Emanuel Case and Eliz. Lee Descendants
324 Roberts Road
Tom's River, NJ 08753
V. Hill

Case
The Brief Case
PO Box 98234
Tacoma, WA 98499
Phone (206) 531-2520
Glenda E. Thayer, Editor
Pub. *The Brief Case*, quarterly

Casebolt
*Casebolt Family Organization
Coleman Research Agency
241 North Vine Street, Apartment 1104E
Salt Lake City, UT 84103-1945
Marlene McCormick Coleman
Pub. *Casebolt Quarterly* (includes all Casebolt families)
$16.00 per year membership

Casedy (see Cassidy)

Casey (see Folk Family Surname Exchange, Helm)

Casey
Casey-Green-Wayne-Clinton Family Association
2306 Westgate
Houston, TX 77019
Phone (713) 529-2333
Harold Helm
$25.00 plus pedigree and family group sheets for membership

Cash (see Cowart)

Cashiday (see Cassidy)

Cashion
Cashion
3417 West LaCrosse
Spokane, WA 99205
Joanne Cashion
$6.00 per year membership

Cashner (see Kershner)

Casiday (see Cassidy)

Caskey
*Caskey Family
101 Mattek Avenue
DeKalb, IL 60115

Phone (815) 756-5107
Kathryn Frey
(includes John Caskey, born ca 1850–1860, also Boyd, Frey, Lauer and Wilson)

Cason
*Cason Family Association
PO Box 88393
Atlanta, GA 30356-8393
Phone (770) 394-2109
William "R" Cason
Pub. *Cason (Caison/Cayson) Association* (do not confuse with Carson family)

Cassell (see Links Genealogy Publications, Cian)

Cassell
*The Cassell Family Organization
1572 South 50 West
Orem, UT 84058
Phone (801) 225-3153
Sandra E. Cassell Erickson, Secretary
Pub. *Cassell Family Newsletter*, semiannually, free; (includes descendants of Harry Elliott Cassell (1873–) of Fredericktown, Ohio, and Hyla Belle Clark (1876–) of Morrow County, Ohio)

Cassels (see Castle, Kennedy)

Cassidy
*Nexus Publications
PO Box 1849
Port Townsend, WA 98368
Lynn Wood, Editor
Pub. *Cassidy Nexus*, quarterly, $20.00 per year subscription; (includes Casiday, Cashiday, Casedy, etc.)

Cassillis (see Kennedy)

Casteel (see Friend)

Caster (see Castor)

Castillo
Oak Leaf Publishing
22 Creek Road, #64
Irvine, CA 91714
Pub. *Castillo Family Newsletter*, bimonthly, $8.00 per year subscription

Castle (see Hynton)

Castleberry
Castleberry Cousins
418 S.E. Lacreole Drive, #1
Dallas, OR 97338-1615
Gwen L. Salsig
Pub. *Castleberry Cousins*, quarterly, $10.00 per year subscription

Castleman (see LaRue)

Castler (see The Memorial Foundation of the Germanna Colonies)

Castleton (see McCune)

Casto (see Parsons)

Casto
*Casto(e) Family Reunion
Rt. 12, Box 66
Bentonville, AR 72712
Phone (501) 273-1281
Winnie Springer-Bell
Pub. *Casto(e) Newsletter*, two or three times per year, donation to cover cost of materials and postage; (includes descendants of Tennessee and Georgia residents, John George Castoe (1816 Virginia–1916 Arkansas) and his wife, Jestern Coots (1816 Tennessee–Arkansas), a Cherokee Indian, whose heritage names were Coots, Goins and Sinnes)
Annual reunion at various locations

Casto
*Casto Surname Organization
53 North First West
PO Box 468
Monroe, UT 84754
Phone (801) 527-4475
Ina Hunt Tuft

Casto
*Casto-Eakle Family Gathering
2000 Williams Avenue
Clarksburg, WV 26301
Phone (304) 623-2674
Nancy Casto Scardina, Family Historian
Pub. *Casto/Eakle Family Newsletter*, annually, donation for subscription; (includes Casto of Upsher County, West Virginia, pre-1809; Eakle of Highland County, Virginia, pre-1809, Suddarth of Albemarle County, Virginia; Cutright of Upsher County, West Virginia, pre-1809)
Reunion

Castor (see Custer)

Castor
*Castor Genealogical Society
John George Castor (Gerster) Descendants Reunion
5681 Middle Road, Rt. 2
Horseheads, NY 14845
Phone (607) 739-1070
Richard J. Castor; Diana W. Castor, Secretary
(includes descendants of Hans George Gerster, who came from Basel, Switzerland, to the Philadelphia area in 1736)

Castor
The Castor Association of America
2103 Plantation Drive
Richmond, TX 77469
Phone (713) 342-5033
Charles E. Scholer, Editor
Pub. *The News-Caster*, quarterly; (Caster, Castor, Custard, Custer, Gerster,

Kaster, Kastor, Keister, Kester, Kiester, Kister, Koester, Koster, Kuester, Kustard, Kuster, Kusterd)
$10.00 initial year membership, $8.00 per year renewal membership; reunion

Caswell
*Caswell Surname Organization
310 Lakeview Drive
Grand Prairie, TX 75051-4916
Phone (214) 262-6074
Noreen E. Haler, Correspondent
(compiling all mentions of Caswell surname)
$10.00 per query, plus LSASE

Catalanotto (see Blossom Press)

Cates (see Cate)

Catesby (see McRae)

Catherman (see Kattermann)

Cathey (see Mcfie)

Cathey
*Cathey Reunion Association
102 Cloverbrook Court
Jamestown, NC 27282
Phone (910) 454-4121
Boyt H. Cathey, Editor
Pub. *Cathey Kith and Kin*, annually, $5.00 per year subscription; (includes a computer database of over 20,000 names: Cathey, Cathie, Cathy, McCathie)
Biennial reunion in odd-numbered years on the first Sunday of August in the Charlotte, North Carolina, area

Cathie (see Cathey, MacDuffee, Macfie)

Cathy (see Cathey)

Catlett (see Marshall)

Catlin
Catlin Reunion
Rt. 2, Box 220A
Saint Elmo, IL 62458
Phone (618) 829-3863
Fleeta Williams Guffey

Catlow
*Catlow/Whitney Family Organization
222 Frances Lane
Barrington, IL 60010-4916
Phone (847) 382-2621
Gloria Bauer Heramb, Family Historian
(includes descendants of Edward Catlow(e) and Anne of England ca 1800, and of their son, John Edward Catlow (1822 Burnley, Lancashire, England–) and Elizabeth Kitson (1823 England–); descendants of Thomas Whitney and Mary Roach of England, 1600s and of their son, Henry Whitney, and Sarah Ketcham of Connecticut; allied names: Thomas

Benedict, Mary Bridgum, Isaac Buswell, George Carr, Philip Challis, Aquila Chase, John Chesley, Robert Clement(s), Magdeline Debont, Lemuel Delano, Reuben Dolittle, Phebe Gill, Elizabeth Greenhalf, John Gregory, John Gretor, Asa Harris, Mary Hilton, Mercy Jelly, Edward Ketchem, Wright Kitson, Joseph Loomis, Abraham Morrill (Morrell), Thomas Oliver, Richard Olmstead, Henry Perkins, Elihu Phillips, Joseph Pike, George Rockenbach, William Sargent, Thomas Seers (Sears), Richard Smith, Elizabeth Spear, William Vandevert, Susan Weed, Dominick Wheeler and George Whitcomb)
Annual reunion on the second Sunday of August in Barrington, Illinois

Catlowe (see Catlow)

Caton
*Caton Family Association
212 Sunset Place
Farmington, NM 87401
Phone (505) 327-9501 (home); (505) 599-0288 (work)
Barbara Caton, Secretary and Treasurer
(includes descendants of Thomas Caton (ca 1810–1863) and Elizabeth Lowrey (1804–1883) of Virginia and Missouri)
$10.00 per year membership for families

Catron (see Gibson, Kettenring)

Cattanach (see Chattan, Macpherson, MacPherson)

Cattermole (see Sherbon)

Cattron (see Gibson)

Cauble
Cauble Reunion
2905 Sentinel Drive
Midland, TX 79701
Julia Cauble Smith, Editor
Pub. *Cauble*, quarterly, $10.00 per year subscription; (includes descendants of Peter and Mary Ann Rotan)

Caudell (see Cordell)

Caudill (see Dean)

Caufield
*Caufield Family Association
PO Box 1860
Studio City, CA 91614
Phone (818) 980-1005; E-mail: AP471@lafn.org
Karen Mohr
(includes research on ancestors and descendants of James Caufield/ Caulfield (1820 parish of Moor, County Roscommon, Ireland–1920 New York) and wife Margaret McKeown)

Cauley (see Corley)

Caulfield (see Caufield)

Caupol (see Coble)

Causey (see Johnson)

Cauvel (see Coble)

Cauvin (see Blossom Press)

Cavalier (see Blossom Press)

Cavan (see Douglas)

Caven (see Cavin)

Cavens (see Cavin)

Cavens
Cavens/Cavins Reunion
Rt. 1, Box 394A
Mount Vernon, IL 62864-9770
Stella Mayes

Cavers (see Douglas)

Cavett
*Cavett/Cavitt Exchange
1416 Gregory Way
Roseville, CA 95661-3505
Billie Cavitt Smith

Cavin
Cavin(s)/Caven(s) Reunion
3331 West 600 South
Jonesboro, IN 46938
Barbara Smith
Pub. *Cavins, Cavens Newsletter*, three times per year, $12.00 per year subscription

Cavins (see Cavens, Cavin)

Cavitt (see Cavett)

Caw (see Stewart)

Cawley (see Corley)

Cayce (see Cantrill)

Cayley (see Cian)

Caylor
*Abraham Caylor Family Organization
26 Kirkwood Lane
Chatham, IL 62629
Phone (217) 483-4377
Mablean Mounkara

Caylor
Caylor Clan
Rt. 1, Box 100
Webb, IA 51366
Valerie Cross

Cays (see Keyes)

Cayson (see Cason)

Cazezu (see Blossom Press)

Cazier (see McCune)

Cell
*Cell(e)/Sell(s) Family Association
2912 12th Street, S.E.
Puyallup, WA 98374-1308
Phone (206) 841-3087
Carolyn Cell Choppin, Editor
Pub. *Celle Newsletter*, quarterly, $2.00
per year subscription, $5.00 for three
years subscription; (includes all Cell,
Gsell, Sell(s), Sill(s), Seal(e), Zell(e),
etc., families of Pennsylvania-German
origin)

Cellar (see Sellers)

Celle (see Cell)

Cellen (see Links Genealogy
Publications)

Cellers (see Links Genealogy
Publications)

Center (see Burrell)

Center
Center/Senter Family Tree
Department of Speech Communications
Ball State University
Muncie, IN 47306
Don B. Center
Pub. *Center/Senter Family Tree*

Centilli
*Ernest Henry Centilli Family
Organization
11206 Ramsdell Drive, N.E.
Rockford, MI 49341
Phone (616) 866-4763
Sandi Centilli Alkire

Ceras (see MacDuff)

Ceres (see MacDuff)

Certain (see Jones)

Cervenka (see Ammons)

Ceubal (see Coble)

Ceubol (see Coble)

Cevallos (see Augeron)

Chadbourne
*The Chadbourne Family Association
HCR 72, Box 8350
Chadbourne's Ridge
North Waterborough, ME 04061-9612
Phone (207) 284-6484
Ted Chadbourne, Genealogical Research;
Kitty Chadbourne, President

Pub. *The Pied Cow*, semiannually;
(primarily, but not exclusively, dealing
with descendants of William
Chadbourne and Elizabeth Sparry, who
landed in Berwick, Maine, in 1634)
$10.00 per year membership for
individuals, $15.00 per year
membership for households, $100.00
life membership; Bibliography says
Pied Cow-Chadbourne Family
Association Newsletter (v.1–, 1983–),
3x.

Chadderdon
Chadderdon/Chatterton Family Reunion
Rt. 1, Box 153 1A
Vernon Center, NY 13477
Helen Chadderdon

Chadwell (see Phillips)

Chaffin (see Dillard)

Chaffin
Chaffin/Allmon Family Organization
4500 Neeley
Midland, TX 79707
Mrs. L. Baker

Chaffin
Chaffin-Chafin-Chalfin-Chalfant-Chapin
1408 North Cheyenne Drive
Richardson, TX 75080
Mary Hall-Marshall
Pub. *Chaffin-Chafin-Chalfin-Chalfant-
Chapin*, quarterly, $15.00 per year
subscription

Chafin (see Chaffin)

Chaillé
*The Chaillés in France and America
1927 Wolf Laurel Drive
Sun City Center, FL 33573-6423
Phone (813) 633-3220
Jack H. Chaille, Author
(includes descendants of Bonaventure
Chaillé born about 1600, whose family
eventually settled on the Eastern Shore
of Maryland)

Chalfant (see Chaffin)

Chalfin (see Chaffin)

Challacombe
Challacombe Family Organization
27894 Gail Drive
Warren, MI 48093-4984
Dorothy Challacombe Rowell

Challenor
*Challenor Family Association
13033 Caminito Dos Amantes
San Diego, CA 92128-1722
Phone (619) 438-8428
Charles Whitlock Rockett

Challis (see Catlow)

Chamberlain (see Davis)

Chamberlain
Chamberlain Index
571 Gablian Street
Los Altos, CA 94022
Mrs. Glenn Chamberlain
Pub. *Chamberlain Index*

Chamberlain
*Chamberlain Association of America
PO Box 151
East Haddam, CT 06423-0151
Alison C. Ainsworth
Pub. *Chamberlain Association News*,
irregularly; (includes 30+ spellings)

Chamberlain
*Thomas Chamberlain Family
Organization, Inc.
147 North 200 East
Orem, UT 84057-5516
Phone (801) 225-2598; E-mail:
JonNBev@aol.com
Jonathan M. Chamberlain, Genealogist
(includes descendants and ancestors of
Thomas Chamberlain and Hannah
Whale (1821 and 1826 Winterbourne,
Berks, England); also allied surnames:
Birch, Broad, Brooks, Cook, Pickett
and Whale, all of Berkshire, England,
before 1821)
$5.00 per year membership

Chamberlain
Chamberlain Chain
West 2206 Borden Road
Spokane, WA 99204-9668
Phone (509) 448-9263
Carolyn Wilson Weidner, Editor/
Compiler
Pub. *Chamberlain Chain*, irregularly,
$5.75 plus $1.75 postage per issue;
(any spelling of Chamberlain)

Chamberlin (see Goodenow)

Chambers (see Dockery, Newberry)

Chambers
Claudette's
3962 Xenwood Avenue, S.
Saint Louis Park, MN 55416-2842
Claudette Atwood Maerz
Pub. *Chambers Helping Chambers*,
quarterly, $14.00 per year subscription

Chambers
*Chambers Surname Organization
3 Brazill Lane
Whitehall, MT 59759
Phone (406) 287-3369
Lindia Roggia Lovshin

Chambers
Chambers Family Reunion
3239 North Main Street
Findlay, OH 45840

Chambless
Herring Enterprises
PO Box 232
Morrow, GA 30260
Pub. *Chambless Quarterly*

Champe
*Champe Surname Organization
333 Center Street
Evanston, WY 82930
Phone (307) 789-2893
Harry L. Bodine

Champion
Champion Family Reunion
325 West Hickam Drive
Columbia, MO 65203-9142
Janice Bower Tompkins

Champlin (see Kettwig)

Chandler (see Bailey, Brawley, Cowart, Johnson)

Chandler
Chandler Collections
Rt. 2, Box 671
Grangeville, ID 83530-9635
Phone (208) 983-0515
Anne Long
Pub. *Chandler Collections*, irregularly, $6.50 per issue (Idaho residents add 5% sales tax)

Chandler
*Chandler Research
2069 East Yale Avenue
Salt Lake City, UT 84108-1905
Phone (801) 582-3668
Preston Woolley Parkinson, Family Historian

Chaney
*Chaney and Allied Families
7550 North 16th Street, Apartment 204-1
Phoenix, AZ 85020-4613
Delma McCourt, Publisher
(database includes Cheyney, Cheyne, etc., of Maryland and Ohio; allied families of Clark, Fivecoat, Lyle, Morgan, Rea and Sparrow)

Chaney
Chaney Family
HC 69, Box 38
Atkinson, NE 68713
Pat Wax

Chaney
*Samuel Chaney Family Organization
PO Box 141
Wessington Springs, SD 57382
Phone (605) 539-9087
D. Cynthia Chaney

Chanove (see Blossom Press)

Chapin (see Chaffin)

Chapman (see Folk Family Surname Exchange, Emery, Hatfield, Waterous)

Chapman
The Chapman Forum
PO Box 154
San Luis Rey, CA 92068-0154
Phone (619) 757-7050
Amelia Chapman Painter, Editor
Pub. *The Chapman Forum: A Newsletter for the descendants of Isaiah Monroe Chapman, Senior and Wife Prudence Ann Slaughter* (anticipates a broadening of research interest)

Chapman
*John Chapman Family Organization
4060 North East Drive
Jackson, MS 39211
Phone (601) 366-2180
Elsie Chapman Edmonds
$20.00 membership

Chapman
Chapman Family Association
770 South Post Oak Lane, Suite 435
Houston, TX 77056-1913

Chapman
Chapman-Hubbard-Griffin-Watkins Family Association
2306 Westgate
Houston, TX 77019
Phone (713) 529-2333
Harold Helm
$25.00 plus pedigree and family group sheets for membership

Chappal
Chappal Family Association
1717 Avenue B
Scottsbluff, NE 69361
Mary E. Anders
Pub. *Chappal Family Association Newsletter*

Chappel (see Addiville)

Chappell (see Fuller)

Charbonneau
Charbonneau Connection
9040 Farley Road
Pinckney, MI 48169
Phone (313) 878-3680
Milton E. Charboneau, Editor and Publisher
Pub. *Charbonneau Connection*, quarterly, $7.00 per year subscription; (includes all spelling variations: Sharbono, etc.)

Charlebois
*The Charlebois/Shalibo Family Association
712 N.W. 95th Terrace
Gainesville, FL 32607
Phone (352) 332-2065; (352) 392-2161 ext. 164
Mitchell E. Sapp

Charles (see Hatfield)

Charlesworth
John Thomas Charlesworth Family Organization
Joseph Charlesworth Family Organization
Thomas Charlesworth Family Organization
1852 East 3990 South, Apartment B
Salt Lake City, UT 84124
Karen Renee Cox
(includes descendants of Thomas Charlesworth 1824 and Alice Barrow 1827)

Charley (see Anthes)

Charter
Charter Connections
1934 Keith Court
Wichita, KS 67212
Diane Charter Baughman
Pub. *Charter Connections*, quarterly, $10.00 per year subscription

Chartier (see Blossom Press)

Chartier
*Chartier Family Association (U.S.A.)
5190 S.W. Dover Lane
Portland, OR 97225
Phone (503) 245-4377
Vernon L. Chartier, Chairman
Pub. *Actualités Historiques Chartier* (in French), semiannually
$15.00 (Canadian funds) per year membership

Chase (see Arthur, Brackett, Catlow, Dunbar, Hyatt, Pierce, Wright)

Chase
*The Reunion of the Descendants of Chase Purinton
RFD 1, Box 4280
Bristol, VT 05443
Phone (802) 453-3254
Harold L. Purinton, President
Pub. *Newsletter*, semiannually
Donation for membership; reunion on the Saturday before the last Saturday of August at Burnham Hall, Lincoln, VT

Chastain (see Burrell)

Chastain
*Pierre Chastain Family Association, Inc.
912 Sprague Road
Indianapolis, IN 46217
Phone (317) 786-1601
Violet Cook, Membership
Pub. *The Chestnut Tree*, quarterly; (includes Chastain, Chasteen, Chastine and other spellings)
$15.00 per year membership, $150.00 life membership; annual reunion on the last weekend of October

Chasteen (see Chastain)

Chastek (see McLouth)

Chastine (see Chastain)

Chatard
*Chatard Family Organization
3040 North 45th East
Idaho Falls, ID 83401-1935
Dixie Walker Young
Pub. *Chatard Family Journal*, irregularly, donation for subscription; (includes descendants of Pierre Francois Chatard and Louise Hélène Joullain-Dupuis (1700s, France, French West Indies and America))

Chatelain (see Johnson)

Chattan
Chattan Clan Association (Overseas)
2001 Park Place, #900
Birmingham, AL 35203-2759
Mrs. J. Sizemore

Chattan
*Clan Chattan
49 Blanca Lane, #626
Watsonville, CA 95076-2158
Ella A. Prince
Pub. *Paw Prints*, quarterly; (includes Anderson, Cattanach, Davidson, Farquharson, MacAndrews, MacBean, MacGillivray, MacIntyres of Badenoch, MacKintosh, MacLeans of Dochgarroch, MacPhail, MacPherson, MacQueen, MacThomas, Shaw, Smith (Gow), Tarril)
$15.00 per year membership for individuals, $20.00 per year membership for families, $25.00 per year for sustaining membership, $325.00 life membership

Chatterton (see Chadderdon)

Chattle (see Parkinson)

Chaudoin
*Chaudoin's of Virginia
331 Mesa Verde Street
Vallejo, CA 94589
Phone (707) 557-4718
Gloria Smith
(includes descendants of Francis Chaudoin (1722–1799) and Sarah Weaver (1730–1785))

Chauppette (see Blossom Press)

Chaussier (see Blossom Press)

Chavous
*Chavous Family Reunion and Research
304 West Ninth Street
Louisville, GA 30434
Phone (912) 625-7673
Leroy Lewis

Cheaney
*Cheaney Surname Organization
15788 Riverside
Livonia, MI 48154
Phone (313) 464-7955
Mary F. Cheaney Mauch, Researcher
(includes descendants of William Cheaney, who married Susannah Crutcher, 1778, Essex County, Virginia)

Cheatham (see Jones)

Chedville (see Blossom Press)

Cheeseman (see Cheesman)

Cheesman
*Cheesman/Cheeseman Family Reunion
1514 South Fernandez Avenue
Arlington Heights, IL 60005-3547
David Cheesman, Historian and Correspondence Chairman
Pub. *Cheesman Family Heritage Newsletter*, annually, free with proof of relationship and LSASE; (includes Cheesman, Cheeseman, Chesman, Chessman, Chisman and variations)
Annual reunion usually on the first Sunday of August in the region of northwestern Indiana (usually Carroll, Fountain, Fulton and Tippecanoe counties, Indiana)

Chelden (see Sheldon)

Cheldon (see Sheldon)

Cheldun (see Sheldon)

Chelf (see The Memorial Foundation of the Germanna Colonies)

Chelm (see Kellum)

Chelton (see Sheldon)

Cheltun (see Sheldon)

Chenault (see Bosher)

Chenault
*Chenault Family National Association
907 Jennifer Lane
Driftwood, TX 78619
D. O. Chenault, Jr., President
Pub. *Newsletter* (includes descendants of Estienne Chenault)
Free membership; annual reunion

Chenault
Chen(n)ault/Shinault/Shinall Reunion Association
1118 Curlew Court
San Antonio, TX 78213-2009
Phone (210) 344-4626
Deurene Oates Morgan
(includes descendants of Claire Lee Chennault, b. 1893 in Commerce, Texas)

Chenevert (see Johnson)

Cheney (see Surname Sources, Fitzwater)

Chennault (see Chenault)

Chenoweth
*The Chenoweth Family in America
701 Hard Scuffle Court
Bowling Green, KY 42103
Phone (502) 843-2118
Richard C. Harris, Publisher

Cherniken (see Jernigan)

Cheron (see Blossom Press)

Cherrington
*Cherrington Family Reunion
638 First Avenue
Gallipolis, OH 45631-1215
Phone (614) 446-1775
Henrietta Cherrington Evans, Historian and Secretary-Treasurer
Annual reunion on the third Sunday of July in Gallia County, Ohio

Cherry (see Stone)

Chesebrough (see Brown)

Chesley (see Catlow)

Chesman (see Cheesman)

Chesnut (see Folk Family Surname Exchange)

Chesnutt
*Chesnutt Family
333 Chadwyck Drive
Danville, VA 24541-3306
Phone (804) 793-1744
A. Ray Griffin,Jr.
(includes Chesnutt of Isle of Wight, Virginia and eastern North Carolina from 1690)

Chessman (see Cheesman)

Chester (see Cole, Frazier)

Chestnut (see Buzzard)

Chew
Chew Family
6619 Pheasant Road, Rt. 1, #16
Baltimore, MD 21220
Phone (410) 335-3948
Frances Brengle, Editor
Pub. *Chew Family*, quarterly, $15.00 per year subscription

Cheyne (see Chaney, Sutherland)

Cheyney (see Chaney)

Chiappetta (see Blossom Press)

Chidester (see Holden)

Chilcoat (see Turner)

Child
*Child(e) Family History Organization
3787 Jackson Avenue
Ogden, UT 84403
Phone (801) 392-5384
Paul L. Child, D.D.S., Kt. Arminger,
    President
(interested in ancestors and descendants
    of Child(e) immigrants from England
    to New England prior to 1680,
    including Benjamin, Richard, John,
    Joseph, Richard and Joyhn Childe of
    Roxbury, Watertown, Barnstable, and
    Boston, Massachusetts)

Childears (see Childress)

Childen (see Sheldon)

Childers (see Childress)

Childers
Childers/Childress Family Association
1428 South Roanoke
Springfield, MO 65807-1822
Frances Curry, Treasurer

Childin (see Sheldon)

Childon (see Sheldon)

Childow (see Brown)

Childres (see Childress)

Childress (see Childers, Lush, Main)

Childress
*Childress/Childers Family Organization
1321 Gum Tree
Huffman, TX 77336
Phone (713) 324-3797
Molly Bateman Reigard, Editor
Pub. *Childress Chatter*, quarterly;
    (Childers, Childears, Childres, etc.,
    anywhere)
$15.00 per year membership

Childs (see Likes)

Childun (see Sheldon)

Chiles (see Golding)

Chilson
Chilson
117 Harvard Lane
Seal Beach, CA 90740
Susan M. Roe
Pub. *Chilson*, quarterly, $10.00 per year
    subscription

Chilten (see Sheldon)

Chilton (see Covert, Sheldon)

Chiltun (see Sheldon)

Chipman
Chipman Quarterly
2868 Harrison Street
San Francisco, CA 94110
Larry Burnett
Pub. *Chipman Quarterly* (includes
    descendants of Perez Chipman of
    Delaware)

Chippendale
*Chippendale Surname Organization
2701 Milo Way
Salt Lake City, UT 84117
Phone (801) 277-1453
LaVerne A. Diehl
(includes descendants of Peter
    Chippendale and Ann Helme
    Chippendale (1814 Lancashire,
    England–) of Preston, Lancashire,
    England; Alice Chippendale, 1843;
    Richard Chippendale and Nancy
    Sharples Chippendale, married 1798 in
    Rishton, Blackburn, Lancashire,
    England)

Chisholm (see Chism)

Chisholm
*Clan Chisholm Society in America
PO Box 1091
Keene, NH 03431
Phone (603) 357-5003
Mrs. Val Chisholm Perry, Chairman
Pub. *Clan Chisholm Newsletter
    (American Branch)*, semiannually;
    (includes Chisham, Chisum, Chism,
    etc.); *Clan Chisholm Journal*, annually
    by parent society in Scotland
$10.00 per year membership, $3.50 per
    year membership under 18

Chism (see Chisholm)

Chism
Chism Family Association
3705 S. 48th
PO Box 6323
Lincoln, NE 68506-0323
James Chism
Pub. *James Chism of Virginia
    Association Newsletter*

Chisman (see Cheesman)

Chisum (see Chisholm)

Chittenden
*Chittenden Family
2 Buxton Avenue
Middletown Springs, VT 05757
Phone (802) 235-2302
Frances B. Krouse
Pub. *Informal Newsletter*, annually
    (January); *Reunion Reminder*, annually
    (July)
Annual reunion on the first Sunday of
    August

Chlerich (see Macpherson)

Choate (see Priddy)

Choate
*The Choates in America, Inc.
21 Vine Street
Melrose, MA 02176-3119
Phone (617) 662-6127
David P. Choate, President
Pub. *Newsletter* (includes descendants of
    John Choate of Ipswich,
    Massachusetts, 1643)
$15.00 per year membership (beginning
    1 August), plus $10.00 new-member
    fee; annual reunion in July or August

Cholden (see Sheldon)

Choldin (see Sheldon)

Choldun (see Sheldon)

Cholochwost
Cholochwost/Holochwost Family
    Association
2804 Florida Avenue
Baltimore, MD 21227
Phone (410) 789-1719
Thomas L. Hollowak
Pub. *Cholochwost/Holochwost Family
    Association Newsletter*, semiannually
$5.00 per year membership

Choplin
Choplin Family Organization
Rt. 3, Box 123
Trinity, NC 27370
Cheryl Burrow

Chopp
In Search of the Chopp-Guibord Family
9615 England
Overland Park, KS 66212
Jonathan Bacon
Pub. *In Search of the Chopp-Guibord
    Family*, irregularly, free

Chorum (see Corum)

Choules (see Mower)

Choyce
*Choyce Family Reunion
837 Laurel Street
Delanco, NJ 08075-4625
Phone (609) 461-4034
Richard E. Choyce, Historian
Pub. *Newsletter*, annually, no charge to
    Choyces or descendants

Chrisley (see Christley)

Chrislip (see Christlieb)

Chrisman (see Guthrie, Richardson)

Chrismon
*Chrismon Family Director
4138 Sudbury Road
Charlotte, NC 28205
Phone (704) 568-1477
Roger Lee Chrismon

Christ (see Crist)

Christal (see Crystal)

Christensen (see Lush, McCune, Sorensen)

Christensen
*The Henry Bockholdt Christensen
Family Organization
936 West Pages Lane
West Bountiful, UT 84087-1803
Phone (801) 292-5830
Halvor Miller Olsen, Representative-
Administrator
(includes descendants of Henry
Bockholdt Christensen (1835 Nodoger,
Randers, Denmark–), came to Utah in
1862)

Christenson (see Kunkel)

Christian
Christian Bulletin
PO Box 206
Chillicothe, MO 64601
Elizabeth Prather Ellsberry
Pub. *Christian Bulletin*, irregularly

Christie (see MacDuff)

Christler (see The Memorial Foundation
of the Germanna Colonies)

Christley
*Christley/Chrisley Family Association
922 South Coleman
Tooele, UT 84074
Phone (801) 882-2323
Nancy F. Byrd
Pub. *Christley Family Newsletter*,
semiannually; (includes descendants of
Henry Crisley and Mary Jones of
Wythe County, Virginia, pre-1815)
$20.00 per year membership

Christlieb
Christlieb/Crislip/Chrislip Family
Association
12016 Midlake Drive
Dallas, TX 75318
Phone (214) 341-0598
Marjorie Heater Herring, Association
Representative
Pub. *Jacob's Ladder (includes Christlieb,
Chrislip, Crislip)*, quarterly
$10.00 per year membership

Christmas
*Christmas Tree Surname Organization
7024 Morgan Road
Greenwell Springs, LA 70739
Phone (504) 261-5515
Serena Abbess Haymon, Editor/Founder
Pub. *Christmas Tree* (includes all
spellings of the South)
Free membership and registration on
FGS

Christmas
Christmas Family Workbook
1160 N.E. Grant Street
Hillsboro, OR 97124-3433
Ginger Christmas
Pub. *Christmas Family Workbook*,
annually

Christopher (see The Memorial
Foundation of the Germanna Colonies)

Christopher
*Christopher Family Association
3779 Northview Lane
Dallas, TX 75229-2737
Phone (214) 358-2729
Shirley Christopher Romine, Historian/
Editor
Pub. *Christopher Newsletter and Journal*
(includes descendants of John
Christopher (1814 or 1815–) and his
wives, Mary Lawson and Delila Walls;
related families of Brandon, King and
Ryan; database on Roots III™)
Annual reunion on the Saturday after
Labor Day weekend

Christy (see MacDuff)

Chronster (see Garner)

Chrystal (see Crystal)

Chubb (see Griffin)

Chumley (see Cowart)

Chun
Chun
6619 Pheasant Road, Rt. 1, #16
Baltimore, MD 21220
Phone (410) 335-3948
Frances Brengle, Editor
Pub. *Chun*, quarterly, $15.00 per year
subscription

Chunn
Chunn Surname Organization
1785 North 1500 East
Provo, UT 84604
Phone (801) 374-1777
Helen Clegg, Genealogist

Church (see Barnard)

Church
*Kinseeker Publications
5697 Old Maple Trail
PO Box 184
Grawn, MI 49637
E-mail: AB064@taverse.lib.mi.us
Victoria Wilson, Editor
Pub. *Church Family Chronicles*,
quarterly, $10.00 per year subscription

Churchill (see Goodenow, Powell)

Churchwell (see Corson)

Churchyard
*The Churchyard Family
1783 Hawaii Circle
Costa Mesa, CA 92626-2015
Phone (714) 540-5022
Jim Churchyard
(informal information exchange includes
Churchyard family from Suffolk
County, England)

Chute
Chute Family Newsletter
42 East Logan Avenue
Westerville, OH 43081
Edith Heise
Pub. *Chute Family Newsletter*, $15.00
per year subscription

Cian
*Clan Cian Services
PO Box 30823
Stockton, CA 95213-0823
Phone (209) 464-4655 (phone and FAX)
Eli F. J. O'Carroll, Chief Clan Cian
(Carroll)
Pub. *Seabhach Abu'*, irregularly, $20.00
per year subscription; (includes septs
or branches that trace to O'Carroll of
Eile' (Ely): MacAlary, Ally,
Archdeacon, MacArthur, MacAuliffe,
MacAwliff, Baccach, O'Bannan, Beck,
Beddy, O'Behan, O'Beice, Bernard,
Blair, Blood, Boland, Bonass, Bone,
Borgan, Bowen, MacBrady, O'Brady,
Brehon, O'Brenan, O'Brennan,
Brenon, O'Breslin, O'Briain, O'Brien,
O'Brocain, MacBroodin, Bryan,
Bryant, Burgess, Butler, O'Cahalan,
O'Cahill, O'Callaghan, O'Carney,
Carnie, O'Carol, Carroll, MacCarroll,
O'Carroll, O'Carry, Carte, Carter,
MacCarthy, MacCarthy-Welply,
O'Carthy, Cartie, MacCartney, Carty,
MacCarvill, O'Casey, Cassell,
O'Castles, MacCaura, Cayley,
MacClanaghan, MacClanchy, Clancie,
Clancy, MacCleary, MacClenaghan,
Clinch, Cochran, Cochrane,
MacCoghlan, O'Coghlen, Coghrane,
Colin, O'Collin, O'Collins,
Colquhoun, Conealy, Coneely,
O'Connell, O'Connelly, O'Connor,
Conroy, MacConry, MacConsidine,
Conway, Coomb, Coombs, Cooney,
MacCorcoran, O'Corcoran, Corey,
Cormac, MacCormac, O'Cormacan,
MacCormack, Cormick, MacCormick,
O'Corra, Correl, Correll, Corril,
Corrill, O'Corry, MacCosgrave,
O'Cosgrave, Costigan, MacCoughlan,
MacCrae, Creagh, Creeth, O'Cronan,
O'Cuill, Culhane, Cullen, O'Cullen,
O'Cullenan, Currie, McCurry,
O'Curry, Dale, O'Dallon, O'Dally,
Danes, Davoren, O'Day, O'Dea,
Deady, Dee, Deering, Delahunt,
Delahunty, O'Dell, O'Dermod,
O'Derry, Devan, O'Dinan, O'Dinerty,
Doan, Donaghy, O'Donnegan,
MacDonnell, O'Donnelly, O'Donocho,

Donogh, O'Donoghy, O'Donohoe, MacDonough, MacDonoughe, O'Donoughe, MacDonovan, O'Dooley, O'Doran, Downey, Downs, O'Druin, Drum, Drumin, Drummond, Duaine, O'Duana, Duane, O'Dullahanty, MacDurkan, Durkin, Dwaine, O'Eark, MacEgan, MacEligod, MacEligodd, McEllcole, MacElligott, Elliott, McEllycuddy, MacEnery, MacEniry, Ercke, Eustace, MacFadden, O'Felan, O'Fercinn, O'Finnegan, Fitch, Fitzpatrick, O'Flanagan, Flattery, Flood, O'Flynn, O'Fogarty, Fullmer, O'Furey, O'Gara, Garville, Geary, Gerry, MacGilfoyle, MacGillicuddy, MacGilpatic, MacGilpatick, MacGilpatrick, Glancy, O'Gleason, Gleeson, Glinn, Glynn, Good, Grace, MacGrade, MacGrady, O'Grady, MacGrath, McGrath, O'Guda, O'Gunning, Haggerty, O'Haithchir, Hall, O'Halley, Hally, O'Hally, Hamilton, Hanagan, O'Hanrahan, O'Hara, O'Hare, Harley, O'Hay, Hayes, Healy, Hearne, Hefferan, O'Heffernan, O'Hegarty, O'Hehir, Hely, Hely-Hutchinson, Henaghan, Henehan, O'Henery, MacHenry, O'Heron, Heyfron, O'Hickey, Hinnegan, Hog, O'Hogan, Hogg, Hogge, O'Hora, Hughes, Hunt, O'Hurley, MacInnery, Kaneely, O'Karrell, Karwell, O'Kearney, O'Keeffe, MacKeely, O'Keely, Keily, McKelgol, O'Kelleher, Keller, Kellie, Kellies, Kelliey, Kellys, Kenealy, O'Kennedy, MacKeogh, Keohe, Kerny, Kielty, Kiely, Killeen, Kinneally, Knight, McKynery, MacLanaghan, Lane, Laney, O'Lanigan, MacLawson, O'Leary, Leddy, Lehan, Lehane, Le Poer, O'Liddy, Loftus, O'Lonergan, O'Loughnan, Lunergan, O'Lynch, MacLysaght, Magan, Maglin, Maguire, Maher, MacMahon, O'Mahoney, O'Mahony, Mannery, O'Maolin, O'Mara, O'Meagher, O'Meara, O'Meehan, O'Moloney, O'Moore, Moriarty, Morris, Muldowney, Muriarty, Murtagh, MacNamara, Neeney, O'Neil, O'Neill, MacNevin, MacNevins, O'Noonan, Odel, Ogan, Ostagain, Ougan, Owens, MacPadden, MacPadine, Parogan, Parrican, Patchy, Mulpatrick, O'Patten, Pennfeather, Perkin, Perkins, Plunket, Plunkett, Powell, Power, Purcell, Quaile, Quain, O'Quill, Quilty, O'Quin, O'Quinlevan, O'Quirk, O'Quirke, MacRaghnall, O'Regan, Reynolds, Ring, Roan, Roughan, O'Ryan, MacScanlan, O'Scanlan, O'Scully, MacSeartha, O'Seasnain, O'Sexton, O'Shanahan, O'Shannon, MacSheedy, O'Sheedy, Sheera, MacShera, Silk, Silke, O'Slattery, O'Spealain, O'Spellan, O'Spellman, O'Spillan, O'Spillane, Spilman, Spollen, Stack, Stapleton,

Stewart, Stone, Storey, Stuart, O'Sullivan, Sutton, Tamany, Tavney, O'Tirney, Torrens, O'Tracey, Trasey and Wolf)
$40.00 life membership

Cigarroa
Cigarroa-Yanez Family Organization
4249 South 3290 West
West Valley City, UT 84119
Phone (801) 964-9374
Isabel Cigarroa Glade

Cilurzo (see Gratta)

Circle (see Zirkle)

Cisco (see Francisco)

Clack (see Album)

Claflin (see MacLachlan, Newton)

Clamage
*Family Ties
19355 Sherman Way, Unit 1
Reseda, CA 91335-3560
Phone (818) 772-1941; (800) 772-1942;
   (818) 772-8816 FAX
Richard H. Hoffman
Pub. *Clamage, Clemage, Clenowich, Klemitz & Klimist Family Ties Newsletter*, three times per year, SASE for sample issue; (Jewish specialty)

Clancie (see Cian)

Clancy (see Cian, Thompson)

Clapp (see Klapp)

Claridge (see McCune)

Clark (see Blossom Press, Folk Family Surname Exchange, Surname Sources, Album, Allison, Barnes, Burrow, Bosher, Bryan, Cameron, Cassell, Chaney, Clarke, Corson, Fuller, Goodenow, Gregor, Heath, Johnson, Lush, MacDuff, Macpherson, MacPherson, Mitchell, Nelson, Newton, Ross, Smith, Wright)

Clark
*Clark Surname Organization
7348 Aldea Avenue
Van Nuys, CA 91406
Phone (818) 344-1378
Louis M. Clark

Clark
*Lloyd Publishing
49 Bianca Lane, #54
Watsonville, CA 95076
Lloyd Walter Clark Hoagland, Editor
(includes descendants of John Clark (1612–1648 New Haven) from Ipswich, County Suffolk, England, of New Haven, Connecticut, and related families: Babb, Barblett, Beard,

Bennett, Blackburn, Blott, Boggs, Bonaker, Botkin, Brown, Browne, Bufford, Bull, Bushong, Cartwright, Cornwall, Crown, Deane, Devine, Dolbere, Dougherty, Dwight, Farrell, Flint, Francis, Fuller, Gillett, Goodwin, Hale, Hall, Harris, Hawke, Hesser, Hinsdale, Hoar, Hough, Howse, Koch, Lambert, Lamberton, Lane, Lemaster, Lichtenstein, Lothrop, Love, Lyman, McHenry, Michell, Morgenson, Newton, Partridge, Peck, Pinson, Plumb, Pomeroy, Poppy, Randolph, Rankin, Rich, Richardson, Roehr, Rose, Sampson, Seals, Sheldon, Sherman, Smith, Spence, Stokes, Strong, Taintor, Teas, Tappin, Tong, Umfraville, Ward, Warriner, Watts, Welch, White, Woodford and Young)

Clark
The Clark Clarion
633 East 13th Street
Bowling Green, KY 42101-2531
Editor
Pub. *The Clark Clarion*, quarterly, $8.00 per calendar year subscription; (includes Clarke, Clerke)

Clark
Kentucky Clark Quarterly
633 East 13th Street
Bowling Green, KY 42101-2351
Ruth C. Lanphear
Pub. *Kentucky Clark Quarterly*, $8.50 per year subscription, free queries

Clark
*Society of Scottish Clarks
1946 A Wickland Drive
Lexington, KY 40505
Phone (606) 293-0823
Elissa H. Perry, President
Pub. *An Clerich*, three times per year
$10.00 per year membership for individuals, $15.00 per year membership for families

Clark
Clark-Williams Reunion
27 Gates Road
Princeton, MA 01541-1601
Mr. and Mrs. David Bisbee

Clark
Clark Reunion
421 Tenth Street
Woodward, OK 73801
Bill Clark, President
(primarily descendants of Ira Clark (son of Thomas and Rhoda) and Elizabeth Cullison, but includes some others, where known)

Clark
*Rowland? Clark/Clarke Family Organization
1107 Shady Lane
Manchester, TN 37355
Phone (615) 728-9784
Gene S. Clark

Clark
Clark-Clarke-Clerk-Hollaway Family
    Association
2306 Westgate
Houston, TX 77019
Phone (713) 529-2333
Harold Helm
$25.00 plus pedigree and family group
    sheets for membership

Clark
Clark Family Organization
Rt. 3, Box 86
Jayton, TX 79528
Mrs. J. A. Kidd

Clark
Surnames, Limited
RR 3, Box 59
Muleshoe, TX 79347-9208
Pub. *Clark Connection*, published as
    material is collected, $8.00 per issue

Clark
Clark/Jones Family Reunion
509 Hyde Park
Tyler, TX 75701
Phone (214) 595-0671 (after 6:00 P.M.)
M. D. Dippel

Clark
Clark Lincs Family Association
906 Oakley Street
Kohler, WI 53044-1417
Nancy B. Clark
(includes Clarks from Lincolnshire,
    England)

Clarke (see Surname Sources, Cameron,
    Clark, Macpherson, McRae)

Clarke
*Charles Augustus Clarke Family
    Organization
5144 Mount Jura Court
Marrero, LA 70072
Phone (504) 347-0231
Patricia Clarke Roser

Clarkson (see MacPherson)

Classen
*Classen Family Organization (George
    Classen Family)
PO Box 131
Blue Hill, NE 68930
Phone (402) 756-2771
William (Bill) Classen, President

Classon
Classon Surname Organization
1936 East Fifth Street
Ontario, CA 91764
Greg Legutki

Clausings
Clausings Reunion
855 Appletree Lane
Brookfield, WI 53005
Delores Rauschenberger

Clawson
Clawson Family
140 North Tenth Street
Indiana, PA 15701
Sara Clawson
Pub. *Clawson Family*

Clay (see Lambeth, Stewart)

Clay
Clay Family Association
PO Box 35254
Houston, TX 77035

Claybaugh (see Fisher)

Clayson (see Ashby)

Clayton (see McCune, Reynolds, Smith)

Cleary
*Generations
2983 Bayside Court
Wantagh, NY 11793
Stephen A. Lamb, Editor/Publisher
Pub. *The Cleary News*, sometimes
    quarterly, $15.00 for four issues

Cleaveland (see Cleveland)

Cleaver (see Newmyer)

Cleef (see Van Cleave)

Cleland (see MacLennan)

Clelland (see MacLellan, MacLennan)

Clemage (see Clamage)

Clemant (see Clement)

Clemens (see Clement)

Clement (see Catlow, Corson,
    Newcomb)

Clement
*Clement-Clemant-Clements-Clemmons-
    Clemens*
PO Box 2244
Saratoga, CA 95070-0244
E-mail: suefitz@aol.com
Sue Fitzpatrick
Pub. *Clement-Clemant-Clements-
    Clemmons-Clemens*, quarterly, $10.00
    per year subscription

Clements (see Catlow, Clement,
    McCune, Paulk)

Clements
*Clements Family History
8529 Spalding Drive
Richmond, VA 23229
Phone (804) 741-1836
B. DeRoy Beale

Clemmens (see Horlacher)

Clemmons (see Clement)

Clemson
*Clemson History Associates
554 State Street
Lancaster, PA 17603
Phone (717) 394-8490
Charles R. Clemson, Family Genealogist
(maintains database of all American
    Clemsons with connection to the main
    1699 family or eleven others known)

Clenowich (see Clamage)

Clephane (see MacDuff)

Clerk (see Clark, MacDuff, Macpherson,
    MacPherson, McRae)

Clerke (see Clark, Newton)

Clerks (see Gregor)

Clermund (see Cole)

Cletherow (see Rutherford)

Cleve (see Van Cleave)

Cleveland (see Usher)

Cleveland
Cleveland Family Chronicles
328 Vincent
Salem, IL 62881-1831
Vikki Lyn Cleveland
Pub. *Cleveland Family Chronicles*,
    quarterly, $15.00 per year U.S.
    subscription, $20.00 per year foreign
    subscription

Cleveland
*Family Research
416 Rockhill Avenue
Dayton, OH 45429-2628
Richard Bordeaux Walker
(includes ancestry and descendants of
    Richard Cleveland/Cleaveland (1797–
    1874) and Elizabeth Mead of
    Connecticut, New York State and
    Lemont Township, Cook County,
    Illinois)

Clevenger (see Garner)

Clevenger
Clevenger
717 South Henderson Street
Bloomington, IN 47401-4838
Sarah Clevenger
Pub. *Clevenger*, bimonthly, donation for
    subscription

Clever
Clever
10540 S.E. 28th Street
Bellevue, WA 98004-7459
Melissa and Bob Clausen
Pub. *Clever*, semiannually, $6.00 per
    issue in the U.S., $7.00 per issue in
    Canada

Cleverly (see Hotchkiss)

Clezie
Clezie Clearinghouse
236 Villa Road
Twin Falls, ID 83301-8030
Juvanne Clezie

Cliff (see Hopkin)

Clifford (see Futral, Gerade)

Clift
*Richard Clift Family Organization
8477 Seeno Avenue
Roseville, CA 95678
Phone (916) 791-7354
Maurine Clift Nuttal
(includes descendants of Richard Clift
    (1806 Falmouth, Cornwall, England–)
    and Christian Bottrall Holocombe
    (1816 Mawgan, Cornwall, England–))

Clifton (see Banks)

Clifton
*Clifton Clan
901 Jewell Avenue
Portsmouth, VA 23701-1911
Phone (804) 488-1573
L. Neale Clifton, Family Representative
    and Editor
Pub. *Clifton Clan Chronicle*, quarterly
    (November, February, May and
    August), $12.00 per year subscription,
    no charge for queries; (includes Clifton
    surname, all spellings, in North
    America and Europe)
Reunion

Clinch (see Cian)

Cline (see Hatfield, Moser)

Clinger (see McCune)

Clint (see Dean)

Clinton (see Casey, Night)

Clinton
Clinton-Travis-Robbins-Jenkins Family
    Association
2306 Westgate
Houston, TX 77019
Phone (713) 529-2333
Harold Helm
$25.00 plus pedigree and family group
    sheets for membership

Clodfelter (see Glattfelder)

Cloniger
Cloniger/Kloniger/Gloniger Newsletter
1311 LaClede
Sheridan, WY 82801
Kathryn Popovich
Pub. *Cloniger/Kloniger/Gloniger
    Newsletter*, quarterly

Clooney (see Macpherson)

Clopton
Clopton Family Association
PO Box 322
Pine Plains, NY 12567
Dean H. Clopton, President

Clopton
*Clopton Family Association
PO Box 451224
Houston, TX 77047
Pat Clopton-Wheeler, Publisher
Pub. *Clopton Family Newsletter*, three
    times per year; (includes descendants
    of William and Ann Clopton of New
    Kent County, Virginia, 1673/74)
$10.00 per year membership

Clore (see The Memorial Foundation of
    the Germanna Colonies)

Close (see Blossom Press)

Clotfelter (see Glattfelder)

Clothier (see Heath)

Cloud (see Johnson)

Cloud
Cloud Family Newsletter
1800 Kendra Cove
Austin, TX 78758
Pat Cloud
Pub. *Cloud Family Newsletter*, quarterly,
    $15.00 per year subscription

Cloud
*Cloud Family Association
508 Crestwood Drive
Eastland, TX 76448
Linda Boose, Secretary
Pub. *Cloud Family Journal*, quarterly;
    (includes the Cloud surname,
    regardless of line of descent)
$25.00 per year membership; annual
    reunion in July

Cloud
*Cloud Reunion
PO Box 181
Pharr, TX 78577-0181
Phone (210) 787-2308
David Cloud

Clough (see Gerade)

Clough
*Clough/Clow Family
PO Box 736
Gambrills, MD 21054-9998
Phone (410) 987-1890
Trish Surles, Publisher
(includes family from Queen Anne
    County, Maryland)

Clough
*The John Clough Genealogical Society
75 River Road
Hudson, NH 03051
Phone (603) 883-1368
Bev Cluff Landry, Genealogist
Pub. *Bulletin of the John Clough
    Genealogical Society*, semiannually
    (fall and spring); (includes Cluff and
    Clow)
$10.00 per year membership

Clover (see Harmon)

Clover
The Clover Family Exchange
1861 Cameo Court
Redding, CA 96002
Robert and Marguerite Clover
Pub. *The Clover Family Exchange*, three
    times per year, $10.00 per year
    subscription

Clow (see Clough)

Clowes
*Clowes-Swanson Genealogy
2751 Regency Oaks Boulevard, R302
Clearwater, FL 34619
Lois C. Witherspoon, Author
(includes allied families of Korn, Uhl and
    Thompson)

Cloyes (see Towne)

Cloyse (see Towne)

Cluff (see Clough)

Clugston (see Dunbar)

Clunie (see MacPherson)

Clunn
Clunn Cousins
316 Cokes Drive
Tom's River, NJ 08753
Robert R. Cordell

Cluny (see Macpherson)

Coal (see Cole)

Coale (see Cole)

Coates (see Farnworth)

Coates
Coates Cousins Newsletter
820 Sapphire Drive
Layton, UT 84041
Patricia Irons
Pub. *Coates Cousins Newsletter*, $15.00
    per year subscription

Coatney (see Nettles)

Coatney
*Coatney/Courtney Family Association
809 South Walnut
PO Box 536
Freeman, SD 57029
Phone (605) 925-7186
Carol Peterson
(includes Coatney, Courtney, Cotney, etc.)

Cobaugh (see Coble)

Cobb (see Surname Sources, Ammons, Gwynne, Lindsay)

Cobb
Cobb Publications
1208 Tatum Drive
Alexandria, VA 22307-2007
John E. Cobb, Publisher

Cobb
*Cobb and Hobby Family Research
   (from Banbarg, England)
511 South, Park Road, Apartment #133
Spokane, WA 99212-0551
Phone (509) 891-9577
John Lothrop Cobb

Cobbald (see Coble)

Cobble (see Coble)

Cobbler (see The Memorial Foundation of the Germanna Colonies)

Cobbold (see Coble)

Cobel (see Coble)

Cobel
*John Cobel Family Organization
6922 Montgomery Church Road
Mercersburg, PA 17236
Phone (717) 328-2557
Sybil Coble
(includes Coble, Kobel, Gobel of
   Franklin County, Pennsylvania,
   descendants of Jacob Kobel (1682–
   1731) of Germany)
Annual reunion in August

Coberly
Coberly Tradition
1128 South Delaware Place
Tulsa, OK 74104
Lois Ferguson
Pub. *Coberly Tradition*, semiannually

Cobill (see Coble)

Cobl (see Coble)

Coble
Coble Family Group
Alamance County Historical Association
PO Box 411
Burlington, NC 27215
(includes descendants of Jacob Kobel
   (1682–1731) and his brothers, George

and Nicholas Coble, who went to
North Carolina)

Coble
*Coble Database
3 Spruce Road
Marysville, PA 17053
Phone (717) 975-4656
Ralph M. Coble
(collection of 1000 miscellaneous Coble
   groups, not tied together, primarily in
   Pennsylvania, New York and North
   Carolina, but including all U.S.,
   Germany, France, Switzerland,
   England, Scotland, etc.: Cable, Caupol,
   Cauvel, Ceubal, Ceubol, Cobaugh,
   Cobbald, Cobble, Cobbold, Cobel,
   Cobill, Cobl, Cobleigh, Cobler, Cobyll,
   Colebaugh, Coolbaugh, Covel, Covile,
   Coville, Cyble, Gabel, Gobbel,
   Gobble, Gobel, Göbel, Goble,
   Goebbel, Kable, Kauble, Kobel,
   Köbel, Kobell, Kobelt, Koble, Koebel,
   Kofel, Kolbach, Koolbaugh, Kopal,
   Kopple, Korbel, Koval)

Coble
*Coble Reunion
3 Spruce Road
Marysville, PA 17053
Ralph M. Coble, Historian
(includes Kobel, Cobel)

Cobleigh (see Coble)

Cobler (see Coble)

Cobyll (see Coble)

Cocheran (see Cochran)

Cocheron (see Cochran)

Cochran (see Cian, Cothren, Johnson, Kilgore, Kunkel, Pettigrew, Wood)

Cochran
Cochran/Lewis Descendants (East
   Tennessee)
739 33rd Street
Manhattan Beach, CA 90266
Don Cochran

Cochran
House of Cochran
414 East Seventh
Wellington, KS 67152
Harriet Gooch

Cochran
*Ensign James Cochran Family
   Organization
Rt. 1, Box 195
PO Box 442
Deer River, MN 56636
Phone (218) 246-8863
Teri Ann Cochran Allred, President
Pub. *Cochran Family Newsletter*,
   semiannually; (includes descendants of
   James Cochran (1749–1830) and

Temperance Morgan (1760–1849),
   married 1777)
$5.00 per year membership; reunion

Cochran
Cochran-Cocheron-Cochrane-Kasey
   Family Association
2306 Westgate
Houston, TX 77019
Phone (713) 529-2333
Harold Helm
$25.00 plus pedigree and family group
   sheets for membership

Cochrane (see Cian, Cochran, Cothren, Garner, Pettigrew)

Cock (see MacDuff)

Cocke (see McRae, Neville)

Cockman (see Folk Family Surname Exchange)

Cockram (see Cochran)

Cockran (see Cochran)

Cockrell (see Pettigrew)

Cockrell
The Cockrell Connection
5757 Guhn, #155
Houston, TX 77040
Kay Cockrell Kazmir, Editor
Pub. *The Cockrell Connection*, quarterly,
   $8.00 per year subscription

Cockrum (see Cochran)

Coco (see Johnson)

Coddington
The Coddington Family Registry
231 North 19th Street
Louisville, KY 40203
Phone (502) 896-2738; (502) 584-7423
Charles William Coddington, Editor
Pub. *The Coddington Family Registry*,
   one or two times per year, no
   subscriptions or funds are solicited, but
   requests are honored and all
   correspondence is welcomed,
   additional copies $2.00 each

Coder (see Surname Database)

Coder
*Coder Koder Family from 1550
PO Box 10
Whitney, PA 15693-0010
Richard Glenn Huffman, Publisher

Coe
Coe-Cole-Coen-Coos Family Association
2306 Westgate
Houston, TX 77019
Phone (713) 529-2333
Harold Helm
$25.00 plus pedigree and family group
   sheets for membership

Coe
Coe Chronicles
West 2225 Gardner
Spokane, WA 99201
Jeanne Coe
Pub. *Coe Chronicles*

Coele (see Cooley)

Coen (see Coe)

Coen
*Samuel R. Coen Family Organization
1013 Rudy Avenue
Mattoon, IL 61938
Phone (217) 234-7753
Ruby Overmyer Heldman

Coenen (see Sager)

Coenen
*To Those of the Surname Coenen
506 Fifth Street
Rayville, LA 71269
Phone (318) 728-2305
Henry Alphones Coenen; Jan D. Coenen,
    Editor
(includes descendants of Jules Theophile
    Coenen (J.Q.), b. 1845 in Liau
    (Zuotleeuw), of Brabant Province,
    Belgium, married in 1845 to Anne M.
    Wood in 1866 in Louisville, Kentucky)

Coffeen (see Coffin)

Coffey
*James Coffey Family Database
1411 West 995 North
Lake Village, IN 46349
Phone (219) 992-3579
Ruth Studer

Coffey
Coffey Cousins' Clearinghouse
1416 Green Berry Road
Jefferson City, MO 65101
Phone (314) 635-9057
Bonnie R. Culley, Editor
Pub. *Coffey Cousins Clearinghouse*,
    quarterly (March, June, September and
    December), $8.00 per year U.S.
    subscription, $10.00 per year foreign
    subscription
Annual convention in May

Coffey
*James Bluford Coffey Family
    Organization
1018 Clay Street
Ashland, OR 97520
Phone (503) 488-1087
Marvin D. Coffey
(includes descendants of Edward Coffey
    and Ann Powell, 16?? to 1716)

Coffin
*Barnabas Coffin Family Organization
PO Box 171
Douglas City, CA 96024
Phone (916) 778-3136
Paul Jones

Coffin
Coffin Family Newsletter
8907 Mohawk Lane
Bethesda, MD 20817-3519
Phone (301) 530-2885
David P. Coffin, Editor and Publisher
Pub. *Coffin Family Newsletter*, quarterly,
    $20.00 per year subscription; (includes
    Coffing, Coffeen; database of 20,000
    names, searches made on request)

Coffing (see Coffin)

Coffman (see Cowart)

Coffman
*The Coffman-Callahan Clan of
    Washington County, Ohio
RR 2, Box 177
Marietta, OH 45750
Phone (614) 374-6718
Hugh Coffman
(includes descendants of Jacob Coffman
    and John Callahan, Delaware)

Cogan (see Endicott)

Coghran (see Cothren)

Coghrane (see Cian)

Cognevich (see Blossom Press)

Cogswell
*The Cogswell Family Association, Inc.
1479 Great Plain Avenue
Needham, MA 02192
Phone (617) 444-0852
John H. Cogswell, Treasurer and
    Secretary
Pub. *Cogswell Family Association
    Newsletter*, about quarterly; (includes
    descendants of John and Elizabeth
    Cogswell, arrived in America in 1635
    and settled Ipswich, Massachusetts)
$20.00 per year membership for
    individuals, $30.00 per year
    membership for families

Cohen (see Mosler)

Cohen
Cohen/Gidal Clans
PO Box 157
Knightsen, CA 94548
Carolyn Sherfy

Cohen
*Family Ties
19355 Sherman Way, Unit 1
Reseda, CA 91335-3560
Phone (818) 772-1941; (800) 772-1942;
    (818) 772-8816 FAX
Richard H. Hoffman
Pub. *Cohen, Ostroff, Ostrov & Ostrow
    Family Ties Newsletter*, three times per
    year, SASE for sample issue; (Jewish
    specialty)

Cohoon (see Colquhoun)

Cohran (see Cochran)

Colborn (see Cummings)

Colburn (see Surname Sources)

Colby (see Cummings, Heath)

Cole (see Coe, Golding, Hall, Kunkel,
    Likes, Ross, Willcox)

Cole
*Cole Database
3050 Quail Street
Lakewood, CO 80215-7142
Phone (303) 237-1760
David R. Cole
(includes allied families of Becker,
    Clermund, Cole, Fischer, Fordred,
    Morgan, Müller, Noll, Rademacher,
    Scholl, Schrader and Wagner)

Cole
*Descendants of Daniel Cole Society
PO Box 367
Mahopac Falls, NY 10542
Phone (914) 628-0912
Marilyn Cole Greene, Secretary
Pub. *Descendants of Daniel Cole Society
    Newsletter*, quarterly, $5.00 per year
    subscription; (includes descendants of
    Daniel Cole and wife Ruth Chester)
$10.00 per year membership

Cole
Cole Chronicle
Rt. 1, Box 123A
Buffalo, TX 75831
Phone (214) 322-5462
Clovis Byars Herring
Pub. *Cole Chronicle*, quarterly, $15.00
    per year subscription; (includes Coal,
    Coale, Cool, Cowle, Kole, Khol,
    Khole and all variant spellings)

Colebaugh (see Coble)

Colehour
*Colehour Family (Colhouer/Colehower/
    Colhour)
14120 S.W. 72nd Avenue
Miami, FL 33158
Phone (305) 253-2759
William W. Colehour
Pub. *Newsletter*, quarterly; (includes
    descendants of John and Henry
    Kohlhauer, immigrants to
    Philadelphia)
$8.00 per year membership

Colehower (see Colehour)

Coleman (see Bosher, Brown, Buchanan,
    Cook, Hatfield, Masterson)

Coleman
*Coleman World
1516 Avenida Selva
Fullerton, CA 92633-1531
Phone (714) 871-5767

Fred W. Field, Editor
Pub. *Coleman World*, quarterly, $6.00 per
 year subscription, free sample issue,
 free queries

Coleman
*Nall News Publishing Company
PO Box 2186
Willingboro, NJ 08046-2186
Josephine Crittenberger-Nall, Editor-
 Publisher
Pub. *Irish Coleman Connections*,
 quarterly, $16.00 per year subscription

Coles (see Marshall)

Colewell (see Burnham)

Coley (see Cooley)

Coley
*Coley Family Association
384 Valley Brook Road
Orange, CT 06477-3019
Phone (203) 795-4112; E-mail:
 WCUC79A@prodigy.com
William Booth Coley

Colgate (see Fadner)

Colhouer (see Colehour)

Colhour (see Colehour)

Colin (see Cian)

Collar (see Kahler)

Coller (see The Memorial Foundation of
 the Germanna Colonies)

Collette (see Blossom Press, Lagesse)

Collette
*Collette Family Association
2750 South Maryland Parkway
PO Box 15070
Las Vegas, NV 89114
Phone (702) 732-2233 (business); (702)
 225-5599 (home); (702) 731-2813
 (FAX)
Patricia A. Saye-Barcus, Family
 Representative
Pub. *Call-ette Quarterly*, $5.00 per year
 subscription; (includes related families
 of Alexander, Franklin, Lovell and
 Reed)
$20.00 per year membership

Colley (see Cooley, Corley, Johnston)

Collier (see Donnachaidh, MacDuff)

Collin (see Blossom Press)

Collings (see Collins, Garner)

Collingwood (see Rutherford)

Collingwood
*Collingwood Surname Organization
768 Tamarack Drive
San Rafael, CA 94903-3722
Phone (415) 479-2472
Jack R. Collingwood
(includes Collingwood families in
 England from 1279 to the present and
 in America from ca 1621 to the
 present)

Collins (see Dunbar, Goodenow, Joy,
 Lush, McCune, Rogers, Rutland)

Collins
Collins Chronicles
2190 Camino Largo Drive
Chino Hills, CA 91709
Trish Elliott Collins
Pub. *Collins Chronicles*

Collins
*Descendants of Perry Lee Collins
2424 Nebraska Court
Kansas City, KS 66102
Phone (913) 371-2648
Rick Yarnell, Editor; Helen Collins
 Bailey, Chairwoman
Pub. *The Collins Caller*, two or three
 times per year, free; (includes
 descendants of Perry Lee and Sarah
 Jane (Lankford) Collins, married 1860
 in Sevier County, Tennessee)
Biennial reunion on odd-numbered years
 in Houston, Missouri, or Madisonville,
 Tennessee

Collins
*John Collins 1784 of Varky
1248 Clintonville Road
Paris, KY 40361-9117
Phone (606) 987-4587
Helen Collins Hadden, Publisher

Collins
*Collins/Collings Surname Organization
 and Newsletter
1671 Monitor Avenue
Baton Rouge, LA 70817
Phone (504) 756-2322
Shirley Craig, Publisher/Researcher
Pub. *Calling Collins·Collings*, quarterly;
 (includes descendants of William
 Elston Collins/Collings (1758
 Pennsylvania–))
$15.50 per year membership

Collins
*Moses Collins Family Organization
7902 Edgemoor
Houston, TX 77036
Phone (713) 774-7881
Dr. A. O. Collins
(includes descendants of Moses Collins,
 founder of New Albany, Mississippi, in
 1840)

Collis (see Lush)

Collum (see Folk Family Surname
 Exchange)

Collum
*Collum-Cumbie-Emery McCormick
 Families Reunion
PO Box 52048
Knoxville, TN 37950-2048
Hester E. Stockton
(includes descendants of John Williams
 Cumbie and Talitha Jane Harry)
Annual reunion in June at the Red River
 Valley Fairgrounds, Paris, Texas

Collums (see Lemon)

Colmery
Colmery Cousins Reunion
1002 Hemlock Cove
Brandon, MS 39042-7614
Bess Colmery Varnado

Colombel (see Blossom Press)

Colpitts (see Weatherbee)

Colquhoun (see Cian, McCown)

Colquhoun
Clan Colquhoun Society of North
 America
245 Lincoln Street
Savannah, GA 31401
L. A. Roberts, Treasurer
Pub. *Clan Colquhoun Newsletter*,
 quarterly, $10.00 per year membership;
 (includes Calhoun, Cahoon, Cohoon,
 Cowan, Cowen, McCowan,
 McClintock, Kilpatrick, Kirkpatrick,
 Ingram, Laing)

Colson (see Corson)

Colson
*Corson/Colson Family History
 Association
PO Box 1837
Leesburg, VA 22075
Stanton Darnbrook Colson, Publisher
Pub. *Colson's Corner*, quarterly;
 (supplement to *Corson Cousins*)
$10.00 per year membership

Colt (see Hitchcock)

Colton
*Surname Publications
900 Todhunter Street, #4
Broderick, CA 95605
Phone (916) 373-1262
Verna Ellis, Editor
Pub. *Colton Clarion*, semiannually,
 $10.00 per year subscription

Coludrovich (see Blossom Press)

Colver (see Culver)

Colver
*Colver/Culver Reunion and Depository
4168 Woodland Street
Santa Maria, CA 93455-3356
Phone (805) 937-3518
Valerie Dyer Giorgi

Colvin (see Calvin, Bailey, Lush)

Colyear (see Donnachaidh, MacDuff)

Combich (see Stewart)

Combie (see MacThomas, Stewart)

Combs (see Hyatt)

Combs
Alfred T. Combs Memorial Association
PO Box 4
Clayhole, KY 41317
Delton Blalock
Pub. *Alfred T. Combs Memorial Association Newsletter*

Combs
Hardin Combs Family Association (Kentucky)
1604 Longfellow Street
McLean, VA 22101
Georgia E. Benefiel

Comer (see Kunkel)

Comer
*Comer Family Organization
PO Box 8072
Longview, TX 75607-8072
Ben R. Reynolds

Comerford (see Drury)

Comfort (see Baker, McKune)

Comines
*Comines Reunion
PO Box 4
Vienna, NJ 07880
Phone (908) 637-4565
George W. Cummins
(information on about 1700+ persons, descendants of Christeen and Jacob Comines (Cummins), who arrived in Philadelphia aboard *The Good Ship Molly* from Rotterdam in 1741)

Commeaux (see Johnson)

Compton (see Rowe)

Compton
*Compton Surname Organization
William Compton Family Organization
17051 N.W. 29th Avenue
Miami, FL 33056
Phone (305) 621-8207
Beulah Compton Jackson
(includes descendants of William Compton (1622–1679))

Compton
*Family Reunion
545 East Mount Vernon Boulevard
Mount Vernon, MO 65712
Phone (417) 466-2422; (417) 466-2512
Lem Compton
Biennial reunion in odd-numbered years

Comrie (see Gregor)

Comstock (see Baker)

Con (see Hay)

Conacher (see MacDougall, Stewart)

Conan (see Cunning)

Conand (see Cunning)

Conant (see Cunning)

Conaway (see Blossom Press)

Condit (see Goodenow)

Condon
*Generations
2983 Bayside Court
Wantagh, NY 11793
Stephen A. Lamb, Editor/Publisher
Pub. *Condon House Newsletter*, sometimes quarterly, $15.00 for four issues

Conealy (see Cian)

Coneely (see Cian)

Conerty (see Smith)

Conger (see Powell)

Conger
*Conger Confab
PO Box 447
Janesville, IA 50647
Phone (319) 397-2206
Maxine Leonard
Pub. *Conger Confab*, quarterly, $6.00 per year subscription

Conghlan (see Lahey)

Conine (see Jones)

Coninges (see Cunning)

Conings (see Cunning)

Coningus (see Cunning)

Conkle (see Kunkel)

Conklin
*Conklin Family Organization
9443 Springville Road
East Otto, NY 14729
Phone (716) 257-9488
Carrie M. Dudley

Conlay (see Stewart)

Conlee
Conlee Family Reunion
1019 S.E. 37th
Portland, OR 97214
Phone (503) 235-2968

Joan Loop
(includes descendants of James Reuben Conlee and Susan Ann Barney, who arrived in Yamhill County, Oregon, in 1853)

Conley (see Anthes, Hickman)

Conn (see Hay)

Connan (see Cunning)

Connely
*Thomas Connely Family Organization
5967 Rosinante Run
Columbia, MD 21045
Phone (410) 730-8566
Roger R. Connelly
(includes descendants of Thomas Connely and Margaret Walker, raised a large family in Augusta County, Virginia, both died there in 1794)

Conner (see Franklin)

Conning (see Cunning)

Connochie (see Donnachaidh)

Connors (see Corson)

Conochie (see Donnachaidh)

Conover (see Van Kouwenhoven)

Conrad (see Links Genealogy Publications, Emery, Rutherford)

Conroy (see Cian)

Conroy
Conroy Surname Organization
6180 Merrywood Drive
Rocklin, CA 95677-3421
Kathleen Stewart

Constable (see Hay)

Conteville (see Cantwell)

Conway (see Cian)

Conyers (see Graham)

Conynges (see Cunning)

Cook (see Blossom Press, Folk Family Surname Exchange, The Memorial Foundation of the Germanna Colonies, Brawley, Brehm, Brooks, Buell, Chamberlain, Corson, Davis, Holden, Likes, McCune, Ross, Wright)

Cook
*Cook-Reid-Stalling Family Association
3146 Marola Court
Lafayette, CA 94549-4115
Phone (510) 935-5731; (510) 947-1632 FAX
Mrs. Chris Adams, President

Pub. *Cook-Reid-Stalling Family Association*, three times per year, free queries; (includes families from southern Alabama, ancestors from Virginia, South Carolina, North Carolina and Georgia, allied surnames of Butler, Coleman, Hampton, Knight, Lee and Moseley)
$10.00 per year membership; annual meeting in September or October in the South

Cook
*Leonard E. W. Cook Organization
10780 South Union Road
Manteca, CA 95336
Phone (209) 983-0222
Rosalee Thomsen, Genealogist
(includes descendants of Leonard E. W. Cook (ca 1816 New York–) and his wife, Hester A. Hewett (ca 1819 Ohio–))

Cook
Quantic, Inc.
542 Cascade Circle, #104
PO Box 180993
Casselberry, FL 32718-0993
Phone (407) 339-3557
Carl A. Patin, Editor
Pub. *Cook's Crier*, quarterly, $20.00 per year subscription

Cook
Phineas Wolcott Cook Family Organization
1334 Maple Lane
Provo, UT 84604
Pub. *Phineas Wolcott Cook Family Organization Newsletter*, irregularly

Cook
*Cook-McConnell Family Organization
Coleman Research Agency
241 North Vine Street, Apartment 1104E
Salt Lake City, UT 84103-1945
Marlene McCormick Coleman
(includes families from Oregon, Tennessee, North Carolina, Pennsylvania and Ireland)

Cooke (see Corson)

Cooksey (see Folk Family Surname Exchange, Kunkel)

Cool (see Cole)

Coolbath (see Corson)

Coolbaugh (see Coble)

Cooley
*Cooley Family Association of America
1106 North Eagle Lake Drive
Kalamazoo, MI 49009-8428
Edna L. Smith Farthing, President
Pub. *Cooley Communique*, five times per year; (includes descendants of Benjamin Cooley who settled in

Longmeadow, Massachusetts, about 1640; Cornelius Coele of Holland, settled in New York State, descendants named Cooley and Coolley; Samuel Coley, one of the first settlers of Milford, Connecticut; Peter Cooley who sailed from London and settled in Virginia just prior to the Revolution; Abraham Cooley who came to New York State about 1780 and moved to North Carolina and later Virginia; also variant spellings Cowley, Colley, Cully and Culy, etc.)
$5.00 per year membership, $5.00 initiation fee; biennial reunion

Cooley
*Cooley Cousins: Descendants of Timothy Goode Cooley
4256 Botanical Avenue, Apartment 6
Saint Louis, MO 63110
Phone (314) 771-3592
Dale L. Walker, Editor
Pub. *Cooley Cousins*, irregularly, free; (includes descendants of Timothy G. Cooley (1810–1893) and Lucinda Mullinix (1816–1899))

Coolidge (see Newton)

Coolley (see Cooley, Pannill)

Coomb (see Cian)

Coombs (see Cian, McCune)

Coombs
Family Matters
3903 Capital Boulevard, Suite 119
Raleigh, NC 27604
Christine Werenko
Coombs, quarterly, $16.00 per year subscription

Coombs
*Mark Anthony Coombs Family Organization
3396 Lorraine Circle
Salt Lake City, UT 84106
Phone (801) 467-1113
Sandra Dawn Brimhall, Vice President and Assistant Genealogist
Pub. *Counterpoint*, annually; (includes descendants of Antoine Coombs, who came from France in the mid 1500s and settled in Maine)
$15.00 per year membership per wage earner

Coon (see The Memorial Foundation of the Germanna Colonies, Boose, Garner)

Cooney (see Cian)

Coonfield
*The Coonfield Connection
1217 Grandview Road
Bartlesville, OK 74006-5006
Phone (918) 333-0028
Jeanette Dittmeyer Yokley

Coons (see The Memorial Foundation of the Germanna Colonies)

Coons
*Coons Reunion
129 Tremont
Baltimore, OH 43105
George Stilwell
(restricted to descendants of John Coons-Kuntz, son of George W. Coons of Union County, Ohio, whose two sons probably decided on the spelling Koontz in opposition to the Civil War)
Annual reunion during the last week of June at the Johnson Park in Baltimore, Ohio

Cooper (see Folk Family Surname Exchange, Surname Sources, Goodenow, Hewitt, MacDuff, Powell, Scott, Shurtleff, Speakman)

Cooper
*Coopers of Izard County, Arkansas
350 East Charles Street
Batesville, AR 72501
Phone (501) 793-7725
Mary Cooper Miller, Historian
(includes descendants of Coopers who arrived in Izard County, Arkansas, in 1848 from Bedford County, Tennessee)
Reunion at the Izard County Senior Citizens Center

Cooper
*Kinseeker Publications
5697 Old Maple Trail
PO Box 184
Grawn, MI 49637
E-mail: AB064@taverse.lib.mi.us
Victoria Wilson, Editor
Pub. *Cooper Collection*, quarterly, $10.00 per year subscription

Cooper
*History and Genealogy of the Cooper Family
1301 Bradford Road
Oreland, PA 19075-2414
Phone (215) 836-4727
Dale E. Berger, Publisher
(includes descendants of the immigrants Wilhelm and Gertrude Kupper who settled in Upper Saucon Township, Lehigh County, Pennsylvania)

Cooper
Cooper-Nantooth-Hughes-Montgomery Family Association
2306 Westgate
Houston, TX 77019
Phone (713) 529-2333
Harold Helm
$25.00 plus pedigree and family group sheets for membership

Coos (see Coe)

Coots (see Casto)

Cope (see Nettles)

Copeland (see Links Genealogy Publications)

Copeland
*Copeland/Sewell/Morgan Family Organization
1132 North Tela Drive
Oklahoma City, OK 73127-4308
Phone (405) 789-2842
Pauline Carlton Fletcher, Secretary and Genealogist
(computer database uses Quinsept™, PAF™ and Reunion™)
Annual reunion

Copeland
Olsen Enterprises
3931 South 238th
Kent, WA 98032
Pub. *Copeland*, quarterly, $14.00 per year subscription; (England and New England)

Copley (see Jackson)

Coppage (see Coppock)

Coppage
*Coppage, Coppedge Family Newsletter
653 Perrshing Drive
Walnut Creek, CA 94596
A. Maxim Coppage, Publisher
Pub. *Coppage, Coppedge Family Newsletter*, semiannually

Coppedge (see Ammons, Coppage)

Coppick (see Coppock)

Coppock (see Woolley)

Coppock
Coppock Family Organization
2162 Montgomery Road
Thousand Oaks, CA 91360
Joyce Haskell

Coppock
Coppock-Coppick, Koheck-Coppage Family Association
2306 Westgate
Houston, TX 77019
Phone (713) 529-2333
Harold Helm
$25.00 plus pedigree and family group sheets for membership

Coppola (see Blossom Press)

Corbally (see Corbly)

Corber (see The Memorial Foundation of the Germanna Colonies)

Corbet (see Ross)

Corbett (see Dunbar, Ross)

Corbie (see MacDuff)

Corbin (see Main)

Corbin
*Corbin Family Research
10315 Lagrange Road
Louisville, KY 40223-1226
Phone (502) 245-7317
Kenneth C. Corbin

Corbley (see Corbly)

Corbly
*John Corbly Descendants Association, Greene Co., Pa.
415 West State
Pendleton, IN 46064
Leola Wright Murphy, Recording Secretary
Pub. *Corbly Descendants News Letter*, annually (December), no charge; (includes Corbally, Corbley, Corbly)
Annual reunion on the fourth Sunday of June at John Corbly Memorial Baptist Church, Garards Fort, Pennsylvania

Corby (see MacDuff)

Corcoran (see Cochran, Cothren)

Cord (see McCord)

Cordell
Cordell Family Association
Wooten Road, Rt. 4, Box 155
Ringgold, GA 30736
Elizabeth Beeler
Pub. *Newsletter*

Cordell
Cordell-Caudell
6109 Pythian Road
Harrison, TN 37341
Vicki Griffey
Pub. *Cordell-Caudell*, three times per year, $10.00 per year subscription

Corder (see Cornelius)

Corder
Corder-Bray-Taylor-Billingsley Family Association
2306 Westgate
Houston, TX 77019
Phone (713) 529-2333
Harold Helm
$25.00 plus pedigree and family group sheets for membership

Corderman (see Kattermann)

Cordes
*Cordes and Sandau Families
503 Fairview Avenue
Saint Louis, MO 63119-1850
Marie Strippgen Holtz, Publisher
(includes descendants of Heinrich Cordes and Marie Sophie Höft, married 1890, Gifhorn, Germany; Christian Sandau and Dorothea Geffers, married 1881, Neudorf-Platendorf, Germany)

Corell (see Coryell)

Corey (see Cian, Currie, Cory)

Coriell (see Coryell)

Corle (see Corley)

Corlew
Corlew Clearinghouse
16938 Westside Highway, S.W.
Vashon, WA 98070
Jan Irish Nelson
Pub. *Corlew Clues*

Corley
*Corley Quarterly
6415 Enfield Avenue
Reseda, CA 91335
Phone (818) 708-0384
Troy Kathleen Corley, Publisher and Editor
Pub. *Corley Quarterly*, $10.00 per year subscription, free queries; (includes Corley and its variations, such as Carley, Cauley, Cawley, Colley, Corle and Curley)

Corley
Corley Family Organization
1101 North Taylor
Decatur, IL 62522
Mrs. K. Corley

Corley
*Valentine Corley Family Organization
608 Hunter
Kilgore, TX 75662
Phone (214) 984-7564
Ila Gatons Eckstadt

Corliss (see Witham)

Cormac (see Cian)

Cormack (see Buchanan)

Cormick (see Cian)

Corn
The Exchange
1068 Pinewood Drive
Sparks, NV 89434
Phone (702) 331-3520
Charles W. Barnum

Cornelison (see Cornelius)

Cornelius
Cornelius-Corder-Cornelison-Franklin Family Association
2306 Westgate
Houston, TX 77019
Phone (713) 529-2333
Harold Helm
$25.00 plus pedigree and family group sheets for membership

Cornell
The Cornell Crier
12600 Bissonnet A4-407
Houston, TX 77099
Dede D. Mercer, Publisher
Pub. *The Cornell Crier*, semiannually,
$20.00 per year subscription; (all
variations of the surname, worldwide)

Cornett
Cornett Family Reunion
Stover, MO 65078
Claude Cornett

Corning
*Corning Family History Association
1525 Cambridge Drive
Longmont, CO 80501-2330
Phone (303) 776-3662; (303) 776-5264
FAX
Robert Nathan Corning, Correspondent
Pub. *The Corning Connection*,
bimonthly; $12.00 per year
subscription; (includes descendants of
Samuel Corning I (1616 England–
1694), immigrated to Massachusetts)

Cornum
*Jens Christensen Cornum Family
Organization
311 Main Street, North
Sanford, CO 81151
Phone (303) 274-5261
Marilee Cornum Vannoy

Cornwall (see Clark, Helmer, Wright)

Cornwell (see The Memorial Foundation
of the Germanna Colonies, Dockery)

Corporon (see Johnson)

Correl (see Cian, Coryell)

Correll (see Cian, Coryell)

Corrie (see Cory)

Corriell (see Coryell)

Corril (see Cian)

Corrill (see Cian)

Corry
*The Corry Family Genealogical Society,
Inc.
4416 Briers Place
Stone Mountain, GA 30083
Phone (404) 292-5699
Mildred S. Ezell
Pub. *The Corry Family Genealogical
Society, Inc. Newsletter*
$5.00 per year membership for
individuals

Corson
*TAL Publications
PO Box 1837
Leesburg, VA 22075

(includes descendants of Cornelius
Cursonwhit/Corson of Dover, New
Hampshire, Corson and Colson
families of Maine and New
Hampshire, and allied families: Allen,
Anderson, Archer, Atterberry, Ayer,
Barker, Bell, Bennett, Bessey,
Bickford, Blaisdel, Blake, Bowden,
Bulger, Butler, Buzzell, Canney,
Carpenter, Churchwell, Clark,
Clement, Connors, Cook(e), Coolbath,
Cowell, Cunningham, Davis, Demeritt,
Dore/Dorr, Downing, Downs,
Dumphe, Dutton, Ellis, Emerson,
Favour, Feavaugh, Flint, Forest,
Freeman, Garland, George, Gerrish,
Goodwin, Gowen, Grant, Green,
Guptill, Hall, Hanford, Harlow, Hatch,
Hayes, Heath, Hobbs, Hodgdon/
Hodson, Hoitt, Horn(e), Howard,
Hussey, Johnson, Jones, Kelton,
Kingsley, Langton, Leighton, Lewis,
Libby, Locke, Look, Lord, Lowell,
Lyons, McCall, McDuffee, McIntire,
Means, Miles, Miller, Mitchell, Moore,
Morang, Morris, Morse, Nash, Nason,
Nichols, Nute, Odlin, Overstreet, Page,
Penny, Perkins, Phillips, Pitts, Potter,
Quimby, Ransom, Redman, Remick,
Richards, Ricker, Roberts, Ross,
Russell, Sabin(e), Sampson, Sanborn,
Shell, Skaggs, Small, Smith, Staples,
Stim(p)son, Stith, Swain, Tibbet(t)s,
Tilton, Treat, Trippe, Turner, Tuttle,
Varguson, Wallingford, Walton,
Wasson, Watkins, Webber, Webster,
Weld, Wentworth, Wil(l)ey, Wingate,
Witt and Young)

Corson
*Corson/Colson Family History
Association
9311-P Golden Way Court
Richmond, VA 23294
Phone (804) 747-8180
Iverne Corson Rinehart, Secretary-
Treasurer
Pub. *Corson Cousins*, quarterly, $5.00
per year subscription; (includes
alternate spellings)
$5.00 per year membership (does not
include periodical)

Cortnor (see Wheeler)

Corum (see Simpson)

Corum
William and Richard Corum/Chorum
Family Association
1604 Longfellow Street
McLean, VA 22101
Georgia E. Benefiel

Cory
*Cory Family Society
1123 North Cambrian
Bremerton, WA 98312
Phone (206) 377-1512
Maxine Hester, Membership

Pub. *Cory Family Newsletter*, quarterly;
(includes Cory, Corey, Corrie, etc.)
$10.00 per year per membership for
families; annual reunion in various
locations

Coryea (see Folk Family Surname
Exchange)

Coryel (see Coryell)

Coryell (see Folk Family Surname
Exchange)

Coryell
Coryell Newsletter
PO Box 662
Santa Barbara, CA 93102-0662
Phone (805) 965-3749
N. Burr Coryell, Editor
Pub. *Coryell Newsletter*, occassionally
(about twice per year), $1.00 donation
per issue; (includes Corell, Coriell,
Correl, Correll, Corriell, Coryel,
Coryell, Currell, Koriel, Querelle)

Coshun (see Covert)

Coskrey (see Kinsey)

Cossé (see Blossom Press)

Cossich (see Blossom Press)

Costáles
Costáles Spanish Family Association
1516 Mesa Avenue
Colorado Springs, CO 80906
Phone (719) 473-0122
Colonel Dennis F. Keegan
Pub. *Branches off the Laurel*
(descendants of Bernardo Costales, born
in the mid-1700s in the Asturias
Region of Spain)

Costello
*Nall News Publishing Company
PO Box 2186
Willingboro, NJ 08046-2186
Josephine Crittenberger-Nall, Editor-
Publisher
Pub. *Costello Cousins*, quarterly, $16.00
per year subscription

Costigan (see Cian)

Costley
James Daniel Costley Family
Organization
1729 Grant Avenue
Ogden, UT 84404
Phone (801) 394-6864
Roberta Costley Palmer
Pub. *Costley Family News Bulletin*,
semiannually

Cotherman (see Kattermann)

Cothran (see Cothren)

Cothran
Sam Cothran Family Organization
65 Phillips Drive
Decatur, IL 62521
Phone (217) 428-0613
Paul D. Cothern

Cothren
The Family Connection
730 East Grand Avenue
Pomona, CA 91766-3643
Jim and Beverly Cothren
Pub. *The Family Connection of the
   Cothren-Cochran(e) Surname*, three
   times per year, $15.00 per year
   subscription; (includes Cothran,
   Coghran, Corcoran, etc.)

Cotney (see Coatney)

Cottam
*Cottam Family Organization
5370 Nugget Road
Fair Oaks, CA 95628
Phone (916) 961-5271
Robert K. Shaw; William and Ellen
   Gallagher

Cotterman (see Kattermann)

Cotton (see MacDuff)

Cottrell (see Barnard, Tanner)

Cottrell
*Cottrell Exchange
17580 Redbud
Hesperia, CA 92345
Phone (619) 244-2483
Lorraine Cottrell Moffat

Couch
The Couch Genealogist
12600 Bissonnet A4-407
Houston, TX 77099
Dede D. Mercer, Publisher
Pub. *The Couch Genealogist*,
   semiannually, $20.00 per year
   subscription; (all variations of the
   surname, all over the world)

Couey
Couey Family Association of Alabama
5664 Crooked Finger Road
Scott's Mill, OR 97375
Phone (503) 873-4274
Edward H. Couey, Historian
Unpublished Couey Family Manuscript
   available for copying cost

Coughlin (see CTC Family Association)

Coughran (see Cochran)

Coulthard (see Dobie)

Council (see Lynch)

Countryman
*Countryman-Wood Family History
35 Robinwood Road
Trumbull, CT 06611
Phone (203) 375-1796
Robert Wood

Coupar (see MacDuff)

Couparer (see MacDuff)

Coupe (see Robinson)

Court (see Likes)

Courtenay (see Lynch)

Courtney (see Coatney, Nettles,
   Pennington)

Courtney
Courtney Chronicles
1217 Fifth Street
Pawnee, IL 62558
Stanley G. Courtney
Pub. *Courtney Chronicles*, quarterly,
   $10.00 per year subscription

Courtney
*Thomas Courtney Family Organization
1599 Monaco Circle
Salt Lake City, UT 84121
Phone (801) 278-7708
Eldon B. Tucker, Jr., M.D.
(includes family originally from West
   Virginia)

Cousar (see MacFaddien)

Cousland (see Buchanan)

Coutanche (see Brown)

Couvillion (see Johnson)

Covel (see Coble)

Coventry
Coventry Family Organization
8865 East Baseline, #421
Mesa, AZ 85208
Joan Coventry Mueller
Reunion

Cover (see Stoner)

Coverstone
Coverstone/Vencell Clearinghouse
1833 South 246th Place
Des Moines, WA 98198
Peggy Coverstone Vencill

Covert (see Joy)

Covert
*Covert Surname Organization
Morris Covert Family Organization
4723 West Marconi Avenue
Glendale, AZ 85306
Phone (602) 843-2812
David L. Bowers

Covert
*Covert Family Association
303 West Violet Street
Tampa, FL 33603
Phone (813) 238-3816
Diane Covert Broderick, Editor
Pub. *Covert Activities Newsletter*,
   quarterly; (surname research and
   exchange service)
$5.00 per year membership

Covert
*Covert Books
627 Grant Place
Frederick, MD 21702
Phone (301) 694-9554; (301) 619-2018;
   (301) 619-3320 FAX
Norman M. Covert, President; Rev.
   Harry M. Covert, Jr., Vice President
(includes genealogy of Covert, Goodson,
   Dey, Barker, Triplett and allied
   families from 1607: Ackerman, Birky,
   Brokaw, Coshun, Cushing, DeRapaljie,
   Dillman, Duckworth, Dye, Fairfax,
   Gilbert, Hegeman, Housel, Houshill,
   Mason, Massey, Nash, Neill, Tebbs,
   Tillery, Trousdell, Washington, Wev,
   Whiteman, etc.)

Covert
*Octopus Ancestries Collection
535 N.E. Birchwood Terrace
Hillsboro, OR 97124
Phone (503) 640-2975
Itlana Hewitt
(includes descendants of Sylvanus Covert
   from 1750, Turston (The Fleming) De
   Whitney from 1170, Henry S. Distin
   from 1827, James Chilton from 1563,
   John Bundy from 1617, John Odell
   from 1771, Joannes (Duehr) Dehr from
   1750, Edmond Baker from 1653, John
   Crane from 1731, Margre from Sant,
   Richard Carr from 1666, Thomas Sant
   from 1540)

Covey
Covey Cousins
PO Box 54127
Phoenix, AZ 85078-4127
Phone (602) 971-2068
Rita Wilburn Ackerman, B.A.
Pub. *Covey Cousins*, quarterly, $10.00
   per year subscription

Covile (see Coble)

Coville (see Coble)

Cowan (see Colquhoun, MacDougall)

Coward (see Cowart)

Coward
Coward Family Newsletter
2140 Marion Street
Birmingham, AL 35226-3012
Trudy Adams, Editor
Pub. *Coward Family Newsletter*,
   semiannually; (started by descendants

of Nathan Coward (1818–1909) and
his wives, Jane Rogers (1820–1885)
and Sophia Hedden (1869–1922);
expanded to include descendants of
brothers and uncles of Nathan;
includes Cowherd)

Cowart
*Cowart Family Clearinghouse
10601 S.W. 83rd Avenue
Miami, FL 33156
Phone (305) 274-0231
Willard Splan "Bill" Kemper
(includes Bethany, Bias, Bland, Camper,
Cannady, Capps, Cash, Chandler,
Chumley, Coffman, Coward, Dilbeck,
Dunagan, Dunnigan, Foster, Fowler,
Guire, Hill, Hunter, Kauffman,
Keen(e)y, Kemper, Ken(n)edy,
Laughenor(e), Lothenor(e),
Loughenor(e), Lovell, Markham,
Marshall, Martin, McGee, Morgan,
Neel(e)y, Nelson, Palmer, Penion,
Pennington, Petty, Pinion, Ramsey,
Shelton, Smith, Vines, Walden,
Weaver, Whittenburg, Williams,
Wittenburg, Worley)

Cowdery (see Reeder)

Cowdery
*The Cowdery Family Association: A
Surname Association
(836 East 5300 South, Suite D—location)
4851 South 600 West (mailing address)
Ogden, UT 84405-6008
Phone (801) 476-0723
John A. Reeder, C.I.
(includes descendants of William
Cowdry (1602 Weymouth, England–))

Cowell (see Corson)

Cowen (see Colquhoun)

Cowgill (see Cranston)

Cowgill
*Cowgill Cousins Club
1300 Seminole Street, A #10
West Plains, MO 65775-3800
Beatrice E. Cowgill
Pub. *Cowgill Cousins Newsletter*, three
or four times per year
$5.00 per year membership; biennial
reunion usually in June of odd-
numbered years

Cowgill
Cowgill Cousins
109 Linden
Cambridge, OH 43725
Wilbert Cowgill

Cowherd (see Coward)

Cowie (see Fraser)

Cowing (see Cummings)

Cowle (see Cole)

Cowles
*Cowles Family Association
1717 South Angeline Street
Seattle, WA 98108
Phone (206) 762-0957
Mrs. Glen D. Preston
Pub. *Brooks Family Bulletin*

Cowley (see Cooley)

Cowley
*Charles Cowley Family Organization
155 East 100 South
Venice, UT 84701
Enid Jamison, Record Keeper
(includes descendants of Charles Cowley
(1800 Isle of Man, England–) and Ann
Killip (1815 Isle of Man, England–))
$10.00 per year membership for families

Cowper (see MacDuff)

Cowran (see Cochran)

Cox (see Folk Family Surname
Exchange, Brown, Dean, Elder, Friend,
Goodenow, Guthrie, Mowreader,
Nelson)

Cox
James Cox and Anna Downer
Descendants
302 Burkesville Street
Columbia, KY 42728
Bonnie Trubbe

Cox
Joseph and Mary (Rue) Cox Family
Association
6703 Holdrege Street
Lincoln, NE 68505
Phone (402) 466-1818
Ruth Anna Hicks

Cox
*Ambrose and Sarah (Sally) Reed Cox
Reunion
PO Box 186
Southmont, NC 27351-0186
Phone (704) 798-2401
Mr. Elza B. Cox, Editor
Pub. *Cox-Phillips Family Newsletter*,
quarterly, $12.00 per year subscription;
Cox-Phillips Bulletin, irregularly;
(includes Quesenberry)
Annual reunion at the Ambrose Cox
Memorial Park, Indian Valley, Virginia

Cox
Cox Surname Organization
Arthur Cox Family Organization
Franklin Cox Family Organization
1852 East 3990 South, Apartment B
Salt Lake City, UT 84124
Karen Renee Cox
(includes descendants of Arthur Cox
1866 and Amanda Funk 1869, and
Frederick Walter Cox 1812 and Sally
Emeline Whiting 1817)

Cox
*Voice Cox Reunion
PO Box 236
Dublin, VA 24084
Phone (703) 674-6915
Col. and Mrs. Dallas L. Cox
(includes descendants of Voice P. Cox
and Narcissis Duncan-Cox)
Annual reunion at the Appalachian
Power picnic area in Dublin, Virginia

Cox
Cox Reunion
Rt. 2, Box 83
Pulaski, VA 24301
Phone (703) 980-1208
Hazel Cox
(includes descendants of Voice P. and
Narcissis Duncan Cox)

Cox
*Palouse Publications
S.E. 310 Camino
Pullman, WA 99163-2206
Phone (509) 334-1732
Janet Margolis Damm
Pub. *Cox Heritage*, irregularly, as enough
material is collected, $5.00 plus $1.50
postage (Washington residents add 47¢
tax)

Coy (see Baker)

Cozier
Cozier Clearinghouse
58 Stony Ridge
Asheville, NC 28804-1854

Crabb
Crabb Newsletter
14104 Piedras Road, N.E.
Albuquerque, NM 87123-2323
Phone (505) 299-8386
Richard D. Prall, Editor
Pub. *Crabb Newsletter*, quarterly, $12.00
per year subscription; (Crabb and
allied families, including a number of
immigrants to the thirteen colonies,
with the Prince George's County,
Maryland, and the Westmoreland
County, Virginia immigrants founding
the largest branches of the Crabbs
living today)

Crabtree (see Jackson)

Crabtree
Crabtree Family Association
PO Box 556
Ahwahnee, CA 93601
Belinda Crabtree Brown

Crabtree
*Crabtree Family
34755 Highway 190
Springville, CA 93265
Phone (209) 539-3792
Marilyn Meredith, Author

Crae (see MacRae)

Craford (see Crawford)

Craft
Craft/Hill/Haynes/Harris Family
  Organization
2015 Orchard Avenue
McMinnville, OR 97218
Phone (503) 472-2038
Darlene Robins

Craig
*Craig Clan of America
43779 Valley Road
Decatur, MI 49045-8905
Phone (616) 423-8639
Ann Burton, Editor-Publisher
Pub. *Craig Links, Dedicated to the
  Uniting of the Craigs of America*,
  quarterly, $15.50 per year subscription;
  (includes any spelling)

Craig
*Craig Creatures
PO Box 1872
Dodge City, KS 67801-1872
Laura Tasset Koehn, President
(includes research on Robert Henry Craig
  and Nettie W. Mosley family)

Craigo
*Craigo Surname Organization
56 Chestnut
Wayne, NJ 07470
Phone (201) 694-8723
Lucille Dillinger Alexander

Crail (see MacDuff, Wright)

Crain (see Crane)

Craine (see Crane)

Crale (see MacDuff)

Cram (see MacDuff)

Cramb (see MacDuff)

Crambie (see MacDuff)

Cramby (see MacDuff)

Cramond (see Gregor)

Cranch (see Bond)

Crandall (see Barnard)

Crandall
*Crandall Family Association
PO Box 1234
Hudson, NY 12534-0308
Phone (518) 943-2981
Earl P. Crandall, Editor
Pub. *Crandall Corner*, quarterly, $10.00
  per year subscription for members only
  from PO Box 1472, Westerly, Rhode
  Island 02891; (includes descendants of
  Elder John Crandall (ca 1609–1676) of
  Westerly, Rhode Island)

Crane (see Surname Sources, Covert,
  Ross, Willcocks)

Crane
Crane Flock
21 Poinsettia Drive
Fort Myers, FL 33905
Phone (941) 693-2343
Edith C. Breker, Publisher
Pub. *Crane Flock, The Crane Family
  Newletter*, quarterly, $8.00 per year
  subscription; (includes Crain, Craine,
  Crayne, Krane, etc.)

Crane
Crane Surname Organization
PO Box 995
Alexandria, MN 56308
Phone (612) 763-5666
Charles N. Crane
Pub. *Crane Family Bulletin*

Crane
Crane-Craine Bulletin
PO Box 206
Chillicothe, MO 64601
Elizabeth Prather Ellsberry
Pub. *Crane-Craine Bulletin*, irregularly

Crane
*Crane Surname Organization
56 Chestnut
Wayne, NJ 07470
Phone (201) 694-8723
Lucille Dillinger Alexander

Crankshaw
*Crankshaw Family Organization
33 N.E. 25th Street, Apartment 1
Wilton Manors, FL 33305
David C. Crankshaw
Pub. *Crankshaw Newsletter*, quarterly;
  (includes all Crankshaws, worldwide,
  especially U.S., U.K., South Africa,
  New Zealand, Australia and France,
  including Samuel William Crankshaw
  (1797–1864) and Hazael Crankshaw
  (1846–1927); database on PAF™)
$2.00 per year membership

Cranston
*Cranston Exchange
4251 Niblick
Fair Oaks, CA 95628
Phone (916) 961-0879
Mary Anne Scarlett McDaniel
(also researches Biddle, Burris,
  Burroughs, Campbell, Cowgill,
  Hamilton, Lippincott, Scarlett)

Cranston
*The Cranston Society
2633 Hopi Drive
Melbourne, FL 32935
Phone (407) 254-8509
Col. E. J. Cranston, Convener
Pub. *The Vigilant Crane*, quarterly
$10.00 per year membership for
  individuals, $15.00 per year
  membership for families

Cranston
Cranston Family Newsletter
PO Box 729
Elkader, IA 52043
David Cranston
Pub. *Cranston Family Newsletter*

Crary (see MacQuarrie, McCrary)

Crary
The Crary Family Society
94 Birch Road
Westfield, MA 01085
Phone (413) 533-8257; (413) 535-0350
  FAX; E-mail: jnesbitt@crocker.com
James Fash Nesbitt

Cratser (see Lair)

Crauswell (see Banks)

Craven
*Thomas Craven Family Organization
PO Box 26183
Salt Lake City, UT 84126
Phone (801) 272-3928
Willis S. Whittlesey, III

Cravens (see Thompson)

Craver
*Craver-Harrington
164 Carriage Park
West Seneca, NY 14224
Phone (716) 674-0695
Patricia A. Haug
(database includes descendants of Anna
  M. Craver and Luke James
  Harrington)

Crawford (see Daley, Decker, Lindsay)

Crawford
Crawford Surname Organization
18 Chapel Hill Drive
Napa, CA 94559-2148
Nancy Miller

Crawford
*Crawford Family Reunion
2496 Highway 215
Buffalo, MO 65622-9016
Phone (417) 267-2433
Jack Crawford, President
(includes descendants of Benjamin
  Crawford (1823 Kentucky–1895
  Missouri) and Rebecca Williams (1820
  Kentucky–1895 Missouri))

Crawford
*Whisler Creations, Publisher
121 South 168
Seattle, WA 98148-1611
Phone (206) 244-9277
Wilton M. Whisler, Editor
Pub. *The Crawford Exchange*, quarterly,
  $15.00 per year U.S. subscription,
  $19.00 (U.S. funds) foreign
  subscription; (includes Crawford and
  all variants, e.g. Craford, Croford,

Crufurd in North America and the British Isles)

Craycroft (see Rutherford)

Crayne (see Crane)

Crays (see Lair)

Crayse (see Lair)

Creabill (see Lambert)

Creagh (see Cian)

Crecelieus (see The Memorial Foundation of the Germanna Colonies)

Cree (see MacRae, Worch)

Cree
Cree Family History Society
603 East Cranbrook Road
Cockeysville, MD 21030
R. H. Cree
Pub. *Cree Family History*

Creech (see Dean, MacDuff)

Creech
Creech Country
1243 Shenandoah Drive
Boise, ID 83712-7454
Phone (208) 344-6136
Ruby L. Ewart, Editor
Pub. *Creech Country*, quarterly with annual consolidated index, $8.00 per calendar year subscription

Creed
*Creed Surname Organization
Rt. 2, Box 175
Floydada, TX 79235
Phone (806) 983-2633
Sue Lovell

Creed
*Creed Family Association
2832 Andiron Lane
Vienna, VA 22180
Phone (703) 560-8006
Nyla Creed DePauk
Pub. *Creed Genealogy Newsletter*, quarterly
$10.00 per year membership

Creegan (see CTC Family Association)

Creekmore
*Creekmore Family Association
15502 MacArthur
Redford, MI 48239
Phone (606) 354-2811 Treasurer
Jan Belew Howell, President; Helen S. Smith, Editor; Anna Mary Creekmore, Treasurer
Pub. *Creekmore Cousins*, semiannually (April and October), $10.00 per year subscription to Anna Mary Creekmore,

Treasurer, General Delivery, Strunk, KY 42649; annual reunion at Cumberland Falls, State Resort, Kentucky; primarily on Robert and Ballentine Creekmore, born in Norfolk County, Virginia, died in Whitley County, Kentucky)

Creel (see Athy, MacDuff)

Crees (see The Memorial Foundation of the Germanna Colonies)

Creeth (see Cian)

Crego
*Crego Family
12 Mount Airy Road
Basking Ridge, NJ 07920-2017
Phone (908) 766-2653
Roy Crego
Pub. *Update to a Selective History of the Crego Family*, annually, free to purchasers of *A Selective History of the Crego Family*

Creighton (see Rennison)

Crepeau
*Crepeau Surname Database
13442 93rd Avenue, North
Maple Grove, MN 55369-9740
Phone (612) 494-6694
Sherry Constans-Kaiserlik

Cresap
Cresap Society
3905 North Chadam Lane, #1A
Muncie, IN 47304-5256
Jeff Harris, Secretary/Treasurer
Pub. *Cresap Society "Bulletin"*, quarterly
$6.00 per year membership for individuals, $10.00 per year membership for families

Crespel (see Crispell)

Cress (see Crist)

Crest (see The Memorial Foundation of the Germanna Colonies)

Cretho (see Mattern)

Crews
From Generation to Generation
Rt. 1, Box 147
Buncombe, IL 62912
Melody Tellor, Editor
Pub. *Crews News*, quarterly, $15.00 per year subscription

Crews
Crews Cousins
9141 Covey Hollow Court
Charlotte, NC 28210-7997
Mrs. Ann W. Crews

Creyts
Creyts-Wait Family Association
9968 Wilson Road
Eaton Rapids, MI 48827
Mrs. Henry Creyts

Crible (see The Memorial Foundation of the Germanna Colonies)

Crickbaum (see Kriegbaum)

Crider (see Arthur)

Crigler (see The Memorial Foundation of the Germanna Colonies)

Crile (see Crowl)

Crill (see Frantz)

Crim (see The Memorial Foundation of the Germanna Colonies)

Crimmond (see Gregor)

Cripe (see Frantz)

Cripe
Cripe Family Association
7542 Stewart Avenue
Los Angeles, CA 90045-1050
Jann Cripe, Genealogist
Pub. *Cripe Family Newsletter*, quarterly

Crippen
*Crippen Family Newsletter
PO Box 340
Hancock, MD 21750-0340
Phone (301) 678-6999; E-mail: fanfare@intrepid.net
Donna Younkin Logan, Publisher
Pub. *Crippen-Crippen Family Journal*, quarterly, $15.00 per year subscription; (all Crippen, Crippin, Grippen and Grippin family lines)

Crippen
Crippen Family Newsletter
8210 North Seven Mile
Mesick, MI 49668
Jolene Kelly Pillars
Pub. *Crippen Family Newsletter*, quarterly, $18.00 per year subscription, $3.50 for a sample issue

Crippin (see Crippen)

Crisley (see Christley)

Crislip (see Christlieb)

Crisp (see Burch)

Crisp
*Phillip Heritage House
605 Benton
Missoula, MT 59801
Phone (406) 543-3495
Ruth Phillip, MAS R.G.
Pub. *Crisp Newsletter*, annually, $5.00 per year subscription

Crisp
Crisp Family Reunion
PO Box 246
Port Royal, VA 22535-0246
David R. Crisp
(all Crisps, nationwide)

Crispell (see Oney)

Crispell
*The Crispell Family Association
(Huguenot Historical Society, New Paltz, New York)
PO Box 1194
Kingston, NY 12402
Phone (914) 339-5279
Lewis J. Crispell, President
(includes descendants of Anthony[1] Crispell (Crespel) (1635 Artois, France–1707 Ulster County, New York) and his two wives, Marie Blanshan (1640 Armentiers, France-) and Petronella Lamann (DuMond))
$10.00 per year membership; annual reunion on the third Saturday of August, 10:00 A.M. at the Huguenot Historical Society

Crispell
*The Crispell Family Reunion (PA Branch)
42 Hedge Road
Levittown, PA 19056
Phone (215) 949-3312
Dr. Albert J. Crispell
(includes descendants of Thomas[5] Crispell (Salomon[4], Jan[3], John[2], Anthony[1]) (1795 Ulster County, New York–1861 Wyoming County, Pennsylvania) and his two wives, Sarah Weckes (1795–1823) and Emilie Devoe (1806–))
Donation for membership; reunion on the second Saturday of August, at Dymond Grove (Behing Methodist Church), Route 29, Noxen, Pennsylvania

Crispell
Crispell Database
PO Box 35
Tafton, PA 18464-0035
Phone (717) 226-4721; E-mail: Compuserve 73130,30
Sharon S. Robinson

Criss (see Crist)

Crist (see Frantz, MacLachlan)

Crist
*Rolandus Crist Family Organization
26 Kirkwood Lane
Chatham, IL 62629
Phone (217) 483-4377
Mablean Mounkara

Crist
*Crist Update
26220 Price Strongs Road
Vinton, OH 45686-8905

Phone (614) 669-4005
Marguerite Crist Calvin
Pub. *Crist Update*, quarterly, $10.00 per year subscription; (includes all spellings: Cress, Criss, Christ, Gress, Kreis, Kress, etc.)

Cristofaro (see Gratta)

Criswell (see Aldrich)

Critchlow (see Williams)

Crite (see Likes)

Crittenden
Crittenden Family Association
114 Longmeadow
Lindenhurst, IL 60046
Betty Keough Burns
Reunion in Losantville, Indiana

Crocheron
Crocheron Family Organization
4114 Woodhaven
Houston, TX 77025-5719
Lucia C. Greer
Pub. *Crocheron Family Newsletter*, three times per year, free

Croesen (see Crusan)

Croford (see Crawford)

Croft
*John and Amelia Mitchell Croft Family Organization
3385 South Bluff Road
Syracuse, UT 84075
Phone (801) 773-0531
Allen S. Willie, Assistant
(includes descendants of early 1860 pioneers from England, settled in Morgan, Morgan County, Utah)

Crole (see Crowl)

Croley (see Louden)

Crolius
*Crolius Exchange
88 Hickory Street, #2
Norwich, CT 06360
Phone (860) 886-1345; (860) 886-2953 FAX; E-mail: KFitzpa661@aol.com or 104150,2635 (CompuServe)
Katherine Fitzpatrick

Croll (see Crowl)

Crolley
*Duncan C. Crolley Family Organization
941 Hilltop Drive
Clearfield, UT 84015
Phone (801) 773-5667
John (Jerry) Boseman, Genealogist

Crombie (see Goodenow)

Cromer (see Rolston)

Cron (see Cronn)

Cronics (see Gunnin)

Cronin (see Lemon)

Cronn
*Cronn-Sears Reunion
PO Box E
Cedar, KS 67628-0178
Phone (913) 697-2643
Doris M. Sears Swank, Family Historian
(includes descendants of Jesse (possibly the son of John Sears and Anna Wheeler/Whistler) and his wife, Margaret Ellen Cox, of Pulaski and Whitley counties, Kentucky, about 1800–1860, and their two sons, Alva and Otto, who married Cronn sisters, variant spellings: Cron and Kron)
Donation for membership; annual meeting on the Sunday of Memorial Day weekend

Crook (see Reynolds)

Crook
*The Crook Clan
2 Laura Lane
Conway, AR 72032-2414
Phone (501) 513-4310; E-mail: Loucrook@aol.com
LTC Louis (Lou) M. Crook, Jr., USA, Ret.
Pub. *The Crook Clan*, semiannually, $25.00 per year subscription and database access; (includes research on the Crook, Crooke and Crooks families)

Crook
Crook(e)/Crooks Quarterly
252 Meadowbrook
DeRidder, LA 70634
Pub. *Crook(e)/Crooks Quarterly*

Crooke (see Alsop, Crook)

Crooks (see Crook)

Cropp
*Cropp Family Organization
757 Gypsy Lane
Pittsburgh, PA 15228-2448
Phone (412) 531-4121
Ruth Cropp King
Pub. *The Cropp Family in America*, annually; (newsletter update of book published in 1987)

Crosby (see Walker)

Crose
Christian Crose Family Newsletter
5907 Walton Avenue
Camp Springs, MD 20023
Henry A. Hamann
Pub. *Christian Crose Family Newsletter*, irregularly

Croskery (see Ammons)

Cross (see Neville)

Cross
Cross Connections
1630 Victor Way
Modesto, CA 95351
Phone (209) 523-7683
Nadien Cross Marlett
Pub. *Cross Connections*, irregularly,
$6.50 per year (Idaho residents add
5% sales tax)

Cross
Cross Collections
Rt. 2, Box 671
Grangeville, ID 83530-9635
Phone (208) 983-0515
Anne Long
Pub. *Cross Collections*, irregularly, $6.50
per year (Idaho residents add 5% sales
tax)

Cross
Cross Connections
Rt. 1, Box 100
Webb, IA 51366
Valerie Cross

Cross
Cross Family Association
62 Peony Street, S.W.
Grand Rapids, MI 49508
Sandra J. Elliott
Pub. *Cross Notebook*

Crossman
*The Crossman Society
2984 S.E. Aspen Street
Port Orchard, WA 98366
Phone (360) 871-5694
Andrea D. MacDonald

Crosswaite (see Golding)

Crosthwait (see Golding)

Crotty
*Crotty Family Organization
2342 Coventry Lane
Daleville, VA 24083
Phone (703) 992-1292
Gene Crotty, Family Historian
$10.00 per year membership

Crotzer (see Lair)

Crouch
*Jonathan G. Crouch Family
Organization
531 East 1050 North
Bountiful, UT 84010
Phone (801) 292-8774
Colleen C. Uhl

Crouse (see Boose)

Crouse
The Crouse/Krause Connection
536 N.E. 908th Place
Kansas City, MO 64155
Norma Sollman, Editor
Pub. *The Crouse/Krause Connection*,
quarterly, $15.00 per year subscription,
free queries; (all spellings)

Crover
*Crover Family Reunion
17161 South Potter Road
Oregon City, OR 97045-8836
Barbara Crover Reed
(includes descendants of George W.
Crover/Grover (1753 Burlington, New
Jersey–1814 Stoughton,
Massachusetts) and his wife, Sarah
(Smith) Stone (1757–))
Annual reunion in July

Crow (see Crowl, Ross, Wright)

Crow
*Our James Crow
9640 Walmer
Overland Park, KS 66212-1554
Phone (913) 648-8725; E-mail:
JoanCGRS@aol.com
Joan Kusek, C.G.R.S., Publisher
(includes descendants of James Crow,
Revolutionary War veteran from
Virginia)

Crow
Crow-Crowe
6584 Red Fox Road
Reynoldsburg, OH 43068-1631
Amy Crow
Pub. *Crow-Crowe*, quarterly, $10.00 per
year subscription

Crowd (see Folk Family Surname
Exchange)

Crowe (see Crow, Crowl, Ross)

Crowel (see Crowl)

Crowell (see Crowl)

Crowl (see Mueller)

Crowl
*Crowl Name Association
9603 Bel Glade Street
Fairfax, VA 22031-1105
Phone (703) 281-9562
Linda Gail Komar, Editor/Membership
Pub. *Crowl Connections*, quarterly,
$12.00 per year subscription, $4.00
each for back issues; (includes Crile,
Crole, Croll, Crow(e), Crowel,
Crowell, Croyle, Crull, Cryle, Kroh,
Kroll, etc., all like-sounding spellings;
includes two lines back to Germany)

Crowley (see Louden)

Crown (see Clark)

Crowner (see Likes)

Crowther (see Gregor)

Crowton
*Thomas Crowton Family Organization
45 East 500 North
Salt Lake City, UT 84103
Phone (801) 363-3272
Paul A. Hanks
(database includes Crowton from 1600 to
the present in England and the U.S.)

Croy (see Ross)

Croyle (see Crowl)

Crufurd (see Crawford)

Cruickshank (see Stewart)

Cruickshanks (see Stewart)

Crull (see Crowl)

Crumb (see Sullivan Surname
Exchange)

Crumber (see The Memorial Foundation
of the Germanna Colonies)

Crump (see Mower)

Crump
Crump Family Newsletter
1347 Woodland
Wichita, KS 67203
Beth Shearer Johnson
Pub. *Crump Family Newsletter*, quarterly,
$4.00 per year subscription

Crumpacker (see Stoner)

Crumpton (see Ammons)

Crumrine
*Crumrine Family Reunion
15440 S.E. Rhone Court
Portland, OR 97236
Phone (503) 761-7337
Kathryn V. Morehead
Pub. *Crumrine Family History*, $5.00 per
year subscription; (includes
descendants of John Crumrine and
Mary Ullery, who came to Oregon
from Abilene, Kansas)

Crusan
*Garret Crusan Descendants Database
Rt. 3, Box 125
Saegertown, PA 16433
M. Marie Metzgar
(includes descendants of Garret Crusan
and Rebecca Mitchell 1790–1840,
Pennsylvania; descendants of Garret
Dircksen Croesen and Nelltje Jans
Staats 1650 to date, New York City to
wherever; spelling variations: Cruson,
Croesen, Cruser, Kivasen)

Cruser (see Crusan)

Cruson (see Crusan)

Crutcher (see Cheaney)

Cryle (see Crowl)

Crystal
Crystal (Chrystal-Christal) Family
    Association
Rt. 1, Box 229K
Sedalia, MO 65301
Mrs. James Crystal

CTC Family Association (see Multi-
family Associations)

Cubbage (see Cabbage)

Cubbin (see McCubbin)

Cudworth
*Cudworth Surname Organization
PO Box 937
Holbrook, AZ 86025
Phone (602) 524-6037
Dorothy Williams
(includes descendants of Gen. James
    Cudworth (1610–1682) and Mary
    Masham (1606–1674))

Cuffe (see MacDuff)

Cuillard
*Russel and Mary Cuillard Family
    Organization
6273 Anastasia Avenue
Simi Valley, CA 93063
Phone (805) 522-3828
Thomas Cuillard

Culberson
Culberson/Culbertson Family Association
6428 Arthur Drive
Fort Worth, TX 76134
R. Culbertson

Culbertson (see Culberson, Lemon)

Culbreath (see Galbraith)

Culhane (see Cian)

Cullan (see Dwyer)

Cullen (see Cian)

Cullins
*The Cullins Family Historical Review
935 Countryside Drive, Apartment #103
Palatine, IL 60067-1927
Phone (847) 776-1848
H. Harvey Barfield, III
Pub. *The Cullins Family Historical
    Review*

Cullom (see Cullum)

Cullum
Cullums Synonymous
PO Box 861905
Plano, TX 75086-1905
David Cullum
Pub. *Cullums Synonymous*, quarterly,
    free; (includes Cullum and Cullom)

Cully (see Cooley)

Culpepper
*Culpepper Surname Organization
Francis Gillespie Culpepper Family
    Organization
620 Carlton Road
Pensacola, FL 32534-1108
Phone (904) 474-4780
Walter C. Otto, Jr.

Culross (see MacDuff)

Culver (see Colver)

Culver
*Culver/Colver Family Association
4168 Woodland Street
Santa Maria, CA 93455-3356
Phone (805) 937-3518
Valerie Dyer Giorgi, Author/Publisher
(includes descendants of Edward Colver
    (Culver), who emigrated from England
    to Massachusetts in 1635, buried in
    Groton, Connecticut)

Culver
*Culver Database
152 Rockwood Road
Florham Park, NJ 07932
Phone (201) 966-1862
Peter B. Berendsen

Culver
Culver/Colver Crossings
1675 East Sunset Road
Cedar City, UT 84720
Phone (801) 586-4507
Ann Wilcken
Pub. *Culver/Colver Crossings*,
    irregularly, donation for subscription

Culy (see Cooley)

Cumbie (see Folk Family Surname
    Exchange, Collum)

Cummings (see Sawyer)

Cummings
*Seth and Della Cummings Family
    Association
928 North Humboldt Avenue
Ontario, CA 91764-3024
Phone (909) 395-0661
Helen A. Cummings Lynch
(includes all ancestral lines: Bedell,
    Beecker, Colborn, Colby, Cowing,
    Dunker, Gould, Homeston, Kirby,
    Mayerhoffer, Muzzy, Space/Spies,
    Stahl, Stetson, Tressler and Vaughan)

Annual reunion on the third Sunday of
    July in Owosso, Michigan

Cummings
*Seagull Productions
West 1818 Nora
Spokane, WA 99205
Phone (509) 326-6066
Nancy Cummings Smith
Pub. *Cummings and Goings*, irregularly,
    $5.00 per issue plus $1.00 postage

Cummins (see Comines)

Cunard (see Links Genealogy
    Publications)

Cundiff
*Cundiff Surname Organization
5892 West 10620 North
Highland
American Fork, UT 84003-9591
Phone (801) 756-0155
Grant H. Iverson

Cunlen (see Cunning)

Cunnane (see Cunning)

Cunneln (see Cunning)

Cunnieson (see Cunning)

Cunnin (see Cunning)

Cunning
*Cunning Clan Association
3824 Lanewood Drive
Des Moines, IA 50311
Phone (515) 255-4594
Willis L. Cunning, President
(includes Canine, Conan, Conand,
    Conant, Coninges, Conings, Coningus,
    Connan, Conning, Conynges, Cunlen,
    Cunnane, Cunneln, Cunnieson,
    Cunnin, Cunningson, Gunning,
    Gunnison, Kenning, Kennison,
    Kenyon (Anglicized version in
    Ireland), Kinning, Kinnison,
    MacCanich, MacChoning, MacConich,
    MacConing, MacConochar,
    MacConochie, MacConquchar,
    MacCuning, MacCunneain,
    MacGunyon, Mahoning, McCanish,
    McConkie)

Cunningham (see Folk Family Surname
    Exchange, Corson, Elder, Gant,
    Lemon, Porterfield)

Cunningham
The Cunningham Lair
PO Box 3793
Santa Cruz, CA 95063
E-mail: NonaW@aol.com
Nona Williams, Editor
Pub. *The Cunningham Lair*, quarterly,
    $15.00 per year subscription, queries
    accepted

Cunningham
The Lair
8980 North Skyline Drive
Floyds Knobs, IN 47119
Phone (812) 949-7903
Bonny E. Wise, Editor
Pub. *The Lair*, three times per year,
$10.00 per year subscription

Cunningham
Clan Cunningham Society of America
5441 Mockingbird Drive
Knoxville, TN 37919
Phone (615) 584-2903
David M. Pickens, Membership
Secretary

Cunningham
*Cunningham, Gatlin, Beatty, Stiger,
Murray Surname Organization
5341 Whitney Lane
Amarillo, TX 79110
Phone (806) 359-1012
Clyde A. Murray, Coordinator
(clearinghouse includes Cunningham of
Virginia and Kentucky; Gatlin of
Georgia; Beatty of Pennsylvania;
Stiger of Pennsylvania; Murray of
Vermont, New York and Michigan)

Cunningham
Mathes Cunningham Family
Organization
3925 Thistle Lane
Fort Worth, TX 76109
S. C. Arrant

Cunningson (see Cunning)

Cunnison (see Donnachaidh)

Cuntz (see The Memorial Foundation of
the Germanna Colonies)

Cure (see Blossom Press)

Curl (see Folk Family Surname
Exchange)

Curle (see Folk Family Surname
Exchange)

Curley (see Corley)

Curnalia
*Curnalia Family of New York State
PO Box 67
Columbia, CT 06237-0067
Phone (203) 228-0080
Mrs. Marion Rosebrooks Emmons,
Family Researcher

Curnock (see Woolley)

Curnutte
*Curnutte and Phillips Reunion
8587 Ridge Road
Dittmer, MO 63023
Phone (314) 285-2359
Lucille Curnutte, Genealogist

(includes descendants of Caleb Harlan
Phillips and Mary; James Henderson
Curnutte and Mary E. (Gentry)
Curnutte)
Annual reunion on the first Sunday of
June in Oswego, Labette County,
Kansas

Currell (see Coryell)

Currey (see Currie, Gaskill)

Currie (see Cian, Gregor, MacPherson)

Currie
*The Clan Currie Society
PO Box 541
Summit, NJ 07902-0541
Phone (908) 273-3509; Website: http://
www.discribe.ca/world/scotland/clans/
html
Robert Currie, Clan Commander
Pub. *Inspire to Victory: The Journal of
the Clan Currie Society* (includes
Corey, Currey, Curry, MacCorey,
MacCurrie, MacCurry, MacMhuirrich,
MacVarich, McCurrey, McCurrie and
McCurry)
$20.00 per year membership, $200.00
life membership

Currier (see Gerade, Macpherson)

Currin
*The Currins of Granville County, North
Carolina
9920 N.E. 120th Street
Okeechobee, FL 34972-7453
Frances Scroggins Wheeler, Publisher
(includes descendants of Thomas Cirrin
who was born in Ireland, died in 1730
and was buried in Old Trinity
Churchyard, New York City, and some
of whose descendants ended up in
Granville County, North Carolina (via
Louisa County, Virginia) about 1765)

Curry (see Currie, Macpherson)

Curry
Curry Clearinghouse
Rt. 1, Box 192
Monmouth, IL 61462
James E. and Sharon L. Todd
Pub. *Curry Critters*, quarterly, $10.00 per
year subscription

Curry
*Curry Surname Organization
Highway 87 North
PO Box 340
Burkeville, TX 75932
Phone (409) 565-4751
Helen Rogers Skelton

Cursonwhit (see Corson)

Curtice (see Curtis)

Curtis (see Goodenow, Ross, Rowe)

Curtis
Moses (1840) and Emily Curtis Family
Organization
5505 Towers Street
Torrance, CA 90503
V. Vaughn

Curtis
*The John and Elizabeth Curtis/Curtiss
Society
131 Lake Road
Ontario, NY 14519-9311
Phone (716) 265-0621
Barbara C. Weaver, President
Pub. *Curtis/s Chronicle*, quarterly; (an
extensive archives related to the
surname and a computerized database
approaching 100,000 entries; all
variants: especially Curtiss and
Curtice)
$10.00 per year membership for
individuals (calendar year), $15.00 per
year membership for couples, $150.00
life membership; annual meeting; free
research, no charge for queries in the
quarterly

Curtis
Wilson Family Record Depository
169 Melody Lane
Tonawanda, NY 14150-9109
Robert J. Wilson
Pub. *Curtis*, quarterly, $25.00 per year
subscription

Curtiss (see CTC Family Association,
Curtis)

Curwen (see Irwin)

Curwing (see Irwin)

Curwings (see Irwin)

Cushing (see Covert)

Cusick
*John Cusick Family Association
9603 Bel Glade Street
Fairfax, VA 22031-1105
Phone (703) 281-9562
Linda Gail Komar, Historian
(includes descendants of John Cusick (ca
1790 Saint Mary's County, Maryland–)
and Sarah Tippett, to Ohio by 1815)
Reunion every three years (in years
evenly divisible by three) in
Steubenville, Ohio

Custard (see Links Genealogy
Publications, Castor, Custer)

Custard
*Custard Family Database
1301 Bradford Road
Oreland, PA 19075-2414
Phone (215) 836-4727
Dale E. Berger, Publisher

Custer (see Links Genealogy
Publications, Castor)

Custer
Shields Publishing Company
PO Box 43
Palos Verdes Estates, CA 90274
Mary Ann Shields
Pub. *Custer Chronicles (Custard/Koster/
Castor, Etc.)*, three times per year,
$10.00 per year subscription

Custer
*Arnold Custer Family
5892 West 10620 North
Highland
American Fork, UT 84003-9591
Phone (801) 756-0155
Ina M. Custer Iverson
(includes descendants of Arnold Custer
(1755 Shenandoah Valley, Virginia–),
son of William Custer, and Arnold's
wife, Elizabeth Shoell/Scholl, daughter
of William Scholl and Leah Morgan,
possibly relatives of Daniel Boone's
mother)

Cutchin (see Lynch)

Cutler (see Goodenow)

Cutright (see Casto)

Cvitanovich (see Blossom Press)

Cyble (see Coble)

Cypherts (see Fenstermaker)

Dabinot (see Newberry)

Dabney (see Folk Family Surname
Exchange, Louden)

Dabney
*Folk Family
PO Box 52048
Knoxville, TN 37950-2048
Hester E. Stockton, Owner; Suzanne
Dabney, Editor
Pub. *Dabney Families*, quarterly, $15.00
per year subscription, $5.00 per issue;
(includes d'Aubigne)

D'Abonneville (see De Bonville)

Daehler (see Dahler)

Dafft
Dafft/Daft Family Newsletter
1605 Cottonwood Road
Carrollton, TX 75006-3856
Phone (214) 466-0336
Mr. Dafft
Pub. *Dafft/Daft Family Newsletter*,
annually, $5.00 per year subscription

Daft (see Dafft)

Dagenhart
Dagenhart Family Association
1323 Alabama Street
Vallejo, CA 94590

Phone (707) 643-7443
Betty Dagenhart Heryford
(includes Dagerhardt, Daggerhart,
Degenhard(t) and related lines)

Dagerhardt (see Dagenhart)

Dagert (see Lagesse)

Dages (see Lagesse)

Dagesse (see Lagesse)

Dagest (see Lagesse)

Daggerhart (see Dagenhart)

Dagner (see Kelm)

da Hay (see Hay)

da Haya (see Hay)

Dahler
*Dahler/Daehler Reunion
Rt. 1, Box 139
Mason, WI 54856
Phone (715) 765-4597; E-mail:
cjwilson@win.bright.net
Carol Jones Wilson
Pub. *Newsletter*, published during
reunion years
Reunion

Dahrs (see Tyson)

Dail (see Dale)

Dailey (see Da Lee)

Daines
*Elias Royal Daines Family Picnic
Reunion
100 Center Drive
Silver Lake, KS 66539
Virginia Dain Jackson
Annual reunion at Gage Park Zoo
Shelterhouse

Dajes (see Lagesse)

Dajesse (see Lagesse)

Dalbec
*Dalbec/Dolbec Surname Database
13442 93rd Avenue, North
Maple Grove, MN 55369-9740
Phone (612) 494-6694
Sherry Constans-Kaiserlik

Dalbey (see Dalby)

Dalchau (see Farrington)

Dale (see Cian, Richardson)

Dale
*The Dale Library
The Noble Order of Dale
101 North Seventh Street, Suite 120
Phoenix, AZ 85034-1054

Phone (602) 253-7446
Dr. Donald Karl Smith Dale
Pub. *Searching for the Hidden Dale*,
$5.00 per volume, $15.00 for four
consecutive volumes; (includes Dail,
Daley, Deal, Deale, Diehle, Dial,
Dyall, etc.)
two first class stamps required, plus FGS
and pedigree with inquiries

Dale
*Dale Surname Organization
56 Chestnut
Wayne, NJ 07470
Phone (201) 694-8723
Lucille Dillinger Alexander

Da Lee
*DaLee Family Organization
1810 Linwood Boulevard
Oklahoma City, OK 73106-2626
Phone (405) 232-8843; (405) 232-8844
FAX
Martha Da Lee Haidek, Editor
Pub. *The Da Lee Newsletter*, quarterly
(February, May, August and
November); (includes Daly, Daley,
Dailey)
$10.00 per year membership

Daley (see Dale, Da Lee)

Daley
*Daley-Crawford Surname Exchange
605 Fir Street
Coulee Dam, WA 99116
Phone (509) 633-2208
Jean Daley Gwynn, Compiler
(includes surnames Daley, Crawford,
Dean, Hart, Hulin, O'Toole-
Richardson, Purdy and Wildey, all of
New York State)

Dalgetty (see MacDuff)

Dalhousie (see Ramsay)

Dallin (see McCune)

Dalton (see Pigg, Ryther)

Dalton
*Bell Enterprises
PO Box 10328
Spokane, WA 99209
Phone (509) 327-2761
Mary Ann L. Vanzandt Bell, Owner,
Publisher
Pub. *Dalton Data*, irregularly, $6.00 plus
$1.25 postage per issue

Daly (see Bautz, Da Lee)

Dalziel
*Clan Dalziel
1208 Fairview Drive
Columbia, SC 29205
Phone (803) 254-3334
Jack MacLean Dalziel, Petitioner for the
titles Earl of Carnwath, Baron Dalziel,
Dalziel of that Ilk

Dament (see Dement)

Dameron
*Dameron-Damron Family Association
203 East Portland
Springfield, MO 65807
Phone (417) 862-7121
Mary Dameron Shearholdt, Secretary-
Treasurer
Pub. *The Dameron-Damron Family
Newsletter*, semiannually (mid-March
and mid-September); (computer
database includes Dameron and
Damron, any time, any place)
$7.50 per year membership; annual
reunion

Damkroger (see Siems)

Damon
Oak Leaf Publishing
22 Creek Road, #64
Irvine, CA 91714
Pub. *Damon Family Newsletter*,
bimonthly, $10.00 per year
subscription

Damon
Damon/Demming Database
120 Van Meter Drive
Amherst, MA 01002
Richard A. Damon

Damron (see Dameron)

Dana (see Barnard)

Dance
*Leroy Dance Family Organization
123 East Loma Vista Drive
Tempe, AZ 85282
Phone (602) 967-6230
Norene Dance Thomas

Danes (see Cian)

Daniel (see Folk Family Surname
Exchange, Beckham, Brown, McCune,
Scott)

Daniel
Daniel Discoverer and Documenter
5580 La Jolla Boulevard, #343
La Jolla, CA 92037
Connie Daniels Graves
Pub. *Daniel Discoverer and Documenter*,
quarterly, $7.00 per year subscription

Daniel
*Daniel Family Reunion
2943 Appling Drive
Chamblee, GA 30341-5113
Phone (404) 455-9348
Wayne W. Daniel
Pub. *Daniel Family Newsletter*, annually,
$1.00 per issue; (includes descendants
of Isaac B. Daniel and Elizabeth
Lovvorn)
Annual reunion on the first Sunday of
August in Tallapoosa, Georgia

Daniel
*Daniel Clearinghouse
207 Auburn Drive
Dalton, GA 30720
Phone (706) 278-1504
Joseph Wiley Reid
(1400–1890 period)

Daniel
*Angele Fernande Daniel Family
Organization
24 Reynolds Drive
Eatontown, NJ 07724-2324
Phone (908) 542-0770
Jacqueline F. Fernandez, President
Pub. *Newsletter* (includes husband, Emile
Gantois (1896–), father, Pierre Marie
Daniel, and mother, Berthe Sonzay
(1877–), daughter of Emile Adolph
Sonzay and Therese Antoinette Gruot
(1861–), all of Paris, France)

Daniel
*Folk Family
PO Box 52048
Knoxville, TN 37950-2048
Hester E. Stockton, Owner; MaryAnna
Daniel, Editor
Pub. *Daniel/Daniels Families*, quarterly,
$15.00 per year subscription, $5.00 per
issue; (includes Dannile)

Daniels (see Folk Family Surname
Exchange, Daniel)

Dannenberg
Dannenberg
9452 East Conquistadores Drive
Scottsdale, AZ 85255
Arnold M. Gavin
Pub. *Dannenberg*, monthly, free with
submission of family information

Dannenmueller
*Dannenmueller Family Association
1039 Highway "W"
Warrenton, MO 63383
Phone (314) 456-4610
Dorey Schrick
Pub. *Annual Newsletter*
$2.00 per year membership

Danner (see Dohner, Stoner)

Dannewitz
*Dannewitz Family Organization
84 Granada Drive
Los Alamos, NM 87544
Phone (505) 672-3226
Margie Dannewitz

Dannile (see Daniel)

Darbonne
*Darbonne Surname Organization
1156 Murphy Lane
Moab, UT 84532
Phone (801) 259-5001
Dina L. Darbonne

Darling
*Darling Data Bank
PO Box 71
Akutan, AK 99553
Phone (907) 698-2350
Virginia Darling

Darlington (see Ribble)

Darnall (see The Memorial Foundation
of the Germanna Colonies, McRae)

Darnall
Darnall/Darnell Family Association
8177 Turn Loop Road
Glen Burnie, MD 20161-1113
Mrs. Avlyn Dodd Conley
Pub. *Darnall-Darnell-Dawn to Dusk*,
quarterly
$10.00 per year membership

Darnell (see Austin, Darnall, Lemon,
McRae)

Daroca (see Blossom Press)

Darrah (see Brown)

Darrell (see Dorrill)

Darris
Darris Family Association
14696 Hidden Cove Lane
Florissant, MO 63034
W. Darris

Darrow
Darrow Family Association
603 North Green Street
Anna, IL 62906
Bill Huelson

Darsie (see MacDuff)

Darsy (see MacDuff)

Dart (see McCurdy)

Daub
*Daub Family Reunion
230 Swatara Circle
Jonestown, PA 17038-9729
Phone (717) 865-0520; (717) 865-0520
FAX; E-mail: jbeidler@nbn.net
Jim M. Beidler, Historian
Pub. *Daub Digest: News and notes about
the Lebanon County family Daub*,
three times per year, $5.00 per year
subscription; (targeted for but not
exclusive to descendants of Johann
Daub and Anna Catharina Mermilo)
Annual reunion on the third Sunday of
August in Lebanon County,
Pennsylvania

Daubard (see Blossom Press)

Daubenspeck
*Daubenspeck-Doverspike Families
 Exchange
51 Forbus Street
Poughkeepsie, NY 12603
Phone (914) 473-3757; E-mail:
 cco@sebridge.org
Christine Crawford-Oppenheimer
(extensive database on this surname)
No charge for sharing information

d'Aubigne (see Dabney)

Daugherty (see Surname Sources,
 Brown, Dougherty)

Daughtery (see Brown)

Daunt (see Burge)

Daurss (see Links Genealogy
 Publications)

Daut (see Doutt)

Dautt (see Doutt)

Davald (see Duvall)

Davenport (see Hatfield)

Davenport
Old Time Publications
10828 Oakbrook Drive
Omaha, NE 68154-2437
Peggy Wallingford Butherus
Pub. *Davenport Times*, $5.50 plus $1.25
 postage & handling per issue
 (Washington residents add 7.8% sales
 tax); (includes Devenport, Deavenport,
 Dovenport, etc.)

Davenport
The Davenport Newsletter
3510 McMillan
Tyler, TX 75701
Phone (214) 597-6412
Gene Davenport, Editor
Pub. *The Davenport Newsletter*,
 quarterly, $9.00 per year subscription

David
*David Family Organization
8810 Lagrima de Oro Road, N.E.
Albuquerque, NM 87111
Phone (505) 298-5050
Frederick Wilhelm Haury, Jr.
(includes related families of McKennon
 and Morgan)

Davids (see Gonsalus-Duk)

Davids
*James Henry Davids Family
 Organization
1990 Bittern Drive
Idaho Falls, ID 83406
Phone (208) 523-4744
Phoebe Davids Gilchrist

Davidson (see Family Publications,
 Chattan, Dockery)

Davidson
*Clan Davidson Society
4523 Holliston Road
Atlanta, GA 30360
Phone (404) 457-1692
Andrew S. Davis, President
Pub. *The Sporran*, three times per year
$15.00 per year membership

Davies (see Davis, Neville)

Davis (see Family Publications, Folk
 Family Surname Exchange, Surname
 Sources, Baker, Brawley, Corson,
 Dawson, Dockery, Eaves, Ellett, Fuller,
 Gant, Goodenow, Hatfield, Heath,
 Johnson, Kelty, Lemon, Lush,
 McCune, McGee, Newton, Pack,
 Rutherford, Tingler, Willard, Wright)

Davis
Davis Surname Newsletter
18002 North 12th Street, #30
Phoenix, AZ 85022
Nani Mercer Neal
Pub. *Davis Surname Newsletter*,
 quarterly, $20.00 per year subscription

Davis
Digging for Davis
4041 Pedley Road, #18
Riverside, CA 92509
Phone (714) 685-8936
Frances R. Nelson
Pub. *Digging for Davis*

Davis
*Descendants of Samuel Davis
10528 Lower Azusa Road, #162
El Monte, CA 91731-1296
Phone (818) 309-0764
Richard R. Dietz
Pub. *Diggin' for Davises*, quarterly,
 $10.00 per year subscription, queries
 free to subscribers; (includes
 descendants of Samuel Davis, I, of Isle
 of Wight County, Virginia)

Davis
John Davis of Derby, Connecticut,
 Association
c/o Masonic Home
PO Box 70
Wallingford, CT 06492-7001
R. G. Davis

Davis
*James Hyrum Davis Family
 Organization
2047 Inkom Road
Inkom, ID 83245
Phone (208) 775-3609
Arnold L. Davis
No charge

Davis
*Robert Davis and Joseph Bartlett
 Research
375 Harrison
Twin Falls, ID 83301
Phone (208) 733-9015
Vera Bartlett Metz, Researcher
(includes research on Robert Davis,
 father of Henry Jackson Davis (ca
 1760 North Carolina or Virginia–), and
 Joseph Bartlett and Millicent Rice ca
 1760 Virginia; and other progenitors:
 John Belk and Susannah Chamberlain
 ca 1740 Virginia and North Carolina;
 Isaac West and Susannah Anderson ca
 1704 North Carolina; Lawrence
 Anderson and Mae Kirkpatrick ca
 1705 Scotland; Thomas Tittsworth and
 Martha Morgan ca 1820 Tennessee;
 William McNabb and Betty Aiken ca
 1730 Scotland; Anthony and Elizabeth
 Hughes ca 1700 Virginia; William
 Chamberlain and Mary Hughes ca
 1710 North Carolina, Ephriam Leath
 and Barbara Job ca 1732 Virginia;
 Richard Johnson, father of John
 Johnson ca 1750 Tennessee; George
 and Isabella Boyd ca 1690 Ireland;
 William Boyd and Mary Wasson ca
 1761 North Carolina)

Davis
Samuel H. Davis Family Organization
115 Carriage Hill
Macomb, IL 61455
S. M. Meyer

Davis
*The Descendants of Samuel and Jane
 Cook Davis, Inc.
Rosemont Plantation
PO Box 814
Woodville, MS 39669
Phone (601) 888-6809
Ernesto Caldeira, Executive Director
Pub. *The Davis Family Newsletter*,
 quarterly, $10.00 per year subscription

Davis
Davis Clearing House, Inc.
1916 North Signal Hills Drive
Kirkwood, MO 63122
Phone (314) 965-6245
Dorothy Davis Smith

Davis
*Henry William Davis Family
 Organization
7472 Silver Circle
West Jordan, UT 84084
Phone (801) 566-1083
Joseph F. Buchanan, President
(the family name Davis was used only
 since the late 1800s, prior to that it was
 Davies, of Welsh origin)

Davis
*Days of Our Davis
9935 Kingston Farm Road
Kingston, WA 98346

Louise Burt, Publisher
(includes descendants of James Davis
and Nancy Norton, daughter of John
and Mary Ann; especially James' son,
John, and his descendants from Hardy
County, West Virginia and Knox and
Allen counties, Ohio)

Davison (see Family Publications)

Davoren (see Cian)

Dawes (see Newton)

Dawes
*John W. Dawes Family Association
1535 Macken Avenue
Crescent City, CA 95531
Phone (707) 464-3026
Ken B. Knudsen, Editor and Treasurer
Pub. *Dawes Family Newsletter*, quarterly
$8.00 per year membership; reunion

Dawes
Dawes
259 East Avenue
Greenville, PA 16125
Ardath Dawes, Editor
Pub. *Dawes*, quarterly, $8.00 per year
subscription; (includes descendants of
John W. Dawes)

Dawkins (see Athy)

Dawley
*Dawley Family Association
2834 "L" Avenue
National City, CA 91950-7539
Phone (619) 474-4065
Raymond A. Dawley
(includes Dawley family of early
Connecticut, Massachusetts, New
York, Rhode Island, Iowa and Ohio)

Dawson (see Callison, Lush, McCune)

Dawson
*Descendants of Edward Pratt and Mary
Elizabeth Butler Dawson
8220 Toloso Road
Atascadero, CA 93422-4852
Phone (805) 466-4075
Shirley D. Smith
(includes descendants of Edward Pratt
Dawson and Mary Elizabeth Butler
who were married in 1849 in
Southampton, England; Levis and
Mary Dean Pyle, Alexander John
Robert Archibald and Frances Maria
Stubbs Stewart)
Reunion when the fourth of July falls on
a weekend

Dawson
Dawson-Mercer/Cable-Davis Family of
Illinois
624 North Harrison
Fresno, CA 93728
F. Dawson

Dawson
*Dawson Family Organization
11845 Newsom Drive
Baton Rouge, LA 70811-1160
Phone (504) 775-5383 (no collect calls)
Sallie M. Pattin, Family Genealogist
(includes descendants of William
Dawson and Dinah McCormick)

Dawson
Dawson/Richardson Family Reunion
PO Box 91
Bethany, LA 71007
Phone (318) 938-7755
B. Gibbs; Margie Dawson Gibbs

Dawty (see Doughty)

Day (see Folk Family Surname
Exchange, Barnes, Goodenow,
McCune, Newton, Stowe)

D'Ay (see Hay)

Day
Day Family Society of America
3000 13th Avenue, South, #1
Birmingham, AL 35025
Miss V. W. Day

Day
Day Family Association
1448 State Street
Veazie, ME 04401-7003
Freeland Jones, President
Pub. *Day Family News*, quarterly
(March, June, September and
December); (includes descendants of
Anthony Day and Susanna Machett)
$3.00 per year membership for
individuals, $2.00 per year
membership for senior citizens; annual
reunion on the third Sunday of July

D'Aye (see Hay)

Dayhoof (see Boose)

Dayton (see Rothenberger)

Dazet (see Blossom Press)

Deady (see Cian)

Deal (see The Memorial Foundation of
the Germanna Colonies, Dale)

Deale (see Dale)

de Aliot (see Elliott)

Deam (see Diehm)

Dean (see Folk Family Surname
Exchange, Daley, Dawson, Ross)

Dean
*Dean and Creech Reunion
6770 U.S. 60E
Morehead, KY 40351
Phone (606) 784-9145

Lloyd Dean, Co-chairman
Pub. *Dean & Creech Newsletter*,
annually (includes descendants of
James H. Dean and Nancy Fields
Dean, who came to Carter County,
Kentucky, from Scott County, Virginia,
in 1862; allied families: Amburgey,
Binion, Boggs, Callihan, Caudill,
Clint, Cox, Fultz, Hall, Kegley, Kelley,
Lewis, Lyons, Mabry, Mocabees,
Perry, Plank, Smith, Sparks, Tabor,
Tackett, Thomas, Wells, Williams,
Wynn)
Annual reunion

Dean
*Dean/Deane: The Washington Forbears
10 West 74th Street, Apartment #1-A
New York, NY 10023
Phone (212) 877-1291
Hugh Deane

Dean
*William Dean of Dedham,
Massachusetts, Family
PO Box 115
Westerville, NY 13486
Phone (315) 827-4606
Howard J. Dean

Deane (see Clark, Dean)

Deans (see Moody)

Dearborn (see Jelly)

Dearing (see Brodnax)

Dearing
*Dearing Reunion
3444 North Wolters
Fresno, CA 93726-5922
Phone (209) 224-9503
Betty V. Dearing, Family Historian
Biennial reunion

De Arman (see DeArman)

DeArman
*DeArman, De Arman Database
2525 Nantucket, #4
Houston, TX 77057
Phone (713) 782-1557; (713) 782-0231
FAX; E-mail: cfbn41a@prodigy.com
or PFite16816@aol.com
Pat Fite

DeArmas (see Blossom Press)

Deas (see Ross)

Deatherage (see Richardson)

Deaton
*Deaton Surname Organization
5251 Old Canton Road
Jackson, MS 39211
Phone (601) 956-5405
Dolores Deaton Nader
(includes all U.S. Deaton families)

Deavenport (see Davenport)

Deboi (see Olthaus)

Debolt
Debolt Family Association
2011 Tam Court
Simi Valley, CA 93063
Phone (805) 584-0860
Amelya Sandt

Debont (see Catlow)

De Bonville
*DeBonville/Labonville/D'Abonneville/
PalinBonville Association
68 Kings Highway, Unit #23
Hampton, NH 03842
Richard DeBonville, Publisher
Pub. *From Good City*, biannually (spring)

DeBrequet (see Breakey)

Debrot (see Brunner)

de Brus (see Bruce)

de Bryan (see Bryan)

DeBülow (see vonBülow)

De Catesby (see McRae)

DeCew (see DeCou)

Deck
*Deck Family Organization
1132 North Tela Drive
Oklahoma City, OK 73127-4308
Phone (405) 789-2842
Pauline Carlton Fletcher, Secretary and
Genealogist
(computer database uses Quinsept™,
PAF™ and Reunion™)

Decker
*Z. B. Decker, Jr., Family Organization
PO Box 46
Thatcher, AZ 85552
Phone (602) 428-3278
Rey M. Decker

Decker
Decker-Crawford and Allied Families
11280 West 20th Avenue, #24
Lakewood, CO 80215
Marilynn Munn Strand
Pub. *Decker-Crawford Newsletter*,
quarterly
Reunion on Labor Day weekend in
Macomb, Ilinois

DeCoe (see DeCou)

de Conteville (see Cantwell)

DeCou
*DeCou/DeCow/DeCoux/DeCew
Families
314 East Glenwood Road
Lake Forest, IL 60045-3020

Phone (847) 234-4804
Mrs. Howard T. Bonnett, Secretary-
Treasurer
(includes DeCoe and DeCow)
Donation for membership; annual
reunion in June or July in
Independence, Kansas

DeCoursey
*Robert L. DeCoursey Family
Organization
1819 South Polouse Street
Kennewick, WA 99337-3547
Phone (509) 586-0219
Dale L. DeCoursey, President
(includes descendants of William
DeCoursey (1756) and Elizabeth Irvin
(1759))

DeCoux (see DeCou)

DeCow (see DeCou)

Dee (see Cian, Dye)

Deem (see Lemon, McCanna)

Deer (see The Memorial Foundation of
the Germanna Colonies)

Deering (see Surname Sources, Cian)

Dees
*Dees Family Association
PO Box 453
Elenora Street
Hillsboro, NM 88042
Delores Springer

Deeter
Pro Temp, Inc.
PO Box 154
Nooksack, WA 98276
Marilyn A. and Ron Deeter, Editors
Pub. *Deeter Connection*, semiannually,
$17.00 per year subscription

DeFrance (see Ribble)

DeGarma
DeGarma Clearinghouse
25 Glyndon Drive, #A3
Reisterstown, MD 21136-2025
Dolly Huff

Degenhard (see Dagenhart)

Degenhardt (see Dagenhart)

de Haes (see Cantwell)

Dehart (see MacDuff)

de Haven (see Havens)

De Haven (see Links Genealogy
Publications, Havens)

DeHaven
*DeHaven Club
913 Chasewood
Denton, TX 76205-8203
Phone (817) 387-9993
Dorothy W. Bertine, President and CEO
Pub. *DeHaven Club Newsletter*, three
times per year; *Directory*, annually;
(includes descendants of Evert and
Elizabeth Schibbauerr DeHaven (In
den Hoffe), 1698 to Germantown,
Pennsylvania, 1702 to Whitpaine and
Perkiomen/Skippack townships,
Pennsylvania; more than 650 families
listed in a National DeHaven Family
Registry begun in 1894; related
families of Levering, Op den Graeff,
Pawling and Supplee)
$10.00 per year membership, free
exchange of information; biennial
reunion plus Area Chapter reunions
and meetings

De Hay (see Hay)

De Haya (see Hay)

deHerwyne (see Irwin)

Dehr (see Covert)

Dei (see Dye, McCleave)

Deibler (see Wert)

deIrevigne (see Irwin)

deIruwyn (see Irwin)

deIrwin (see Irwin)

deIrwyn (see Irwin)

De Jong
Berend De Jong Family
PO Box 1
Wheaton, IL 60189
Phone (708) 668-0705
Kenneth B. De Jong

Dekko (see Johnson)

de La Beche (see Rothenberger)

De La Chaumette
*De La Chaumette Random Notes
39 North Williams Street
Newark, OH 43055-4141
Phone (614) 344-9643
Virgil D. Close
Pub. *De La Chaumette Random Notes
(Delashmutt/Delashmet/Delashmitt/
Lashmet and other related families)*,
irregularly, $4.00 for three issues;
(especially Elias Delashmutt (–1778)
and his wife, Elizabeth Nelson (–1785/
6) of Frederick County, Maryland)

DeLacy
*The DeLacy, Lacey, Lacy Family from
1066
2011 Ashman
Midland, MI 48640
Phone (517) 835-4259
Gerard C. Lacey

delaGarde (see Gard)

Delahaney (see Leland)

de la Hay (see Hay)

de la Haye (see Hay)

Delahunt (see Cian)

Delahunty (see Cian)

De la Montagne
*Society of Descendants of De la
Montagne (La Montagne)
3657 West Nichols
Springfield, MO 65803
Phone (417) 831-6140
Lois Stewart, Editor
Pub. *Descendants of Johannes De la
Montagne Newsletter*, quarterly,
$10.00 per year subscription; (includes
Mantanya, Mintonye, Montaney,
Montanye variations)
$15.00 per year membership

Delaney (see Moody)

DeLaney (see Perkins)

Delano (see Catlow)

Delaplaine (see Links Genealogy
Publications)

Delashaw
Delashaw/Dilleshaw Family Reunion
6234 South Fulton Avenue
Tulsa, OK 74136
Phone (918) 493-2670
Sandra Delashaw Warden
Annual reunion

Delashmet (see De La Chaumette)

Delashmitt (see De La Chaumette)

Delashmutt (see De La Chaumette)

Delashmutt
Elias Delashmutt and Margaret Taliferro
Descendants
PO Box 122
Whiting, IA 51063
L. S. Walker

DeLaughter
*DeLaughter Family Association
12002 Pleasant Forest Drive
Little Rock, AR 72212
Phone (501) 227-9480
Nolan DeLaughter, Chairman

(includes DeLaughter, Gaston, Pace,
Traylor and Wardlaw families of South
Carolina, Alabama, and Georgia, prior
to 1850)

De Lay
De Lay International Genealogical
Foundation
4723 Deeboyar Avenue
Lakewood, CA 90712
Phone (213) 423-8953
Leonard A. DeLay

DeLee (see Neville)

Delf (see The Memorial Foundation of
the Germanna Colonies)

Delgatie (see Hay)

Dellahay (see Hay)

Dellinger (see Moser)

Deloach (see Lynch)

DeLong
DeLong Family Organization
22916 Carlow Road
Torrance, CA 90505
Phone (310) 378-3574
Charlene DeLong

Delph (see The Memorial Foundation of
the Germanna Colonies)

Delphey (see Boose)

De Mache (see Dimoush)

Demandre (see Blossom Press)

De Ment (see Dement)

Dement
*Dement Family Association
1400 Bluefield Drive
Florissant, MO 63033-2104
Marilyn Holmes, Newsletter Editor
Pub. *Bits of Dements*, quarterly; (includes
Dament, Dement, De Ment, Deming,
Demint, Demond, Demont, Diamen,
Diamon, Diamond, Dimand, Diment,
Dimint, Dimmon, Dimon, Dimond, Du
Mont, Dyment, Dymond)
$15.00 per year membership; national
reunion in July in Bossier City,
Louisiana

Demeritt (see Corson)

de Mévius (see Movius)

de Mill (see Funk)

Deming (see Dement)

Demint (see Dement)

Demming (see Damon)

Demolle (see Blossom Press)

Demond (see Dement)

Demont (see Dement, Smith)

Demott
Demott
401 Tuxedo Drive
Thomasville, GA 31792
Annette Stewart
Pub. *Demott*, quarterly, $10.00 per year
subscription

De Mouch (see Dimoush)

Dempsterton (see MacDuff)

Demsher (see McCune)

Demuth (see Lemon)

DeMuth (see Demuth)

Demuth
Demuth-DeMuth
1115 Fifth Avenue
Worthington, MN 56187-2403
Patrick Demuth
Pub. *Demuth-DeMuth*, quarterly, $1.25
per issue

Denbow
Denbow
63 Morris Avenue
Athens, OH 45701-1939
Carl Denbow
Pub. *Denbow*, quarterly, $9.00 per year
subscription
Reunion

Dendig (see Surname Sources)

Deneen (see Dineen)

Denes (see Blossom Press)

Denesse (see Blossom Press)

Denet (see Blossom Press)

Denger (see Dinger)

Dengert (see Dinger)

Denig
Denig Information Center
RR 1, Box 101-B
Fruitvale, TX 75127
Beverly Bates

Denison (see Kahler)

Denison
*The Denison Society, Inc.
Denison Homestead, Pequot-Sepos Road
PO Box 42
Mystic, CT 06355
Phone (203) 536-9248
Anne Collier, Membership Chairman

Pub. *Denison Newsletter*, semiannually; (includes descendants of Captain George Denison, an early settler of New London County, Connecticut, and Lady Ann Borodell Denison)
$10.00 per year membership for individuals, $5.00 per year membership for individuals under age 18, $20.00 per year membership for families, $200.00 life membership

Denkins (see Dinkins)

Denlinger (see Frantz)

Dennard
*Dennard Heritage II
5422 Fairdale Lane
Houston, TX 77056-6607
Norris Dennard, Editor
SASE

Denney (see Nettles)

Denney
*Descendants of Allison and Emma Denney
10020 Artesia Drive
Shreveport, LA 71115
Phone (318) 797-0442
Robert E. Pitts

Dennis (see Blossom Press)

Dennison (see Gregor)

Denniston (see Stewart)

Dennler (see Schwend)

Denoon (see Ross)

Denson (see Gregor)

Denton (see Burrell)

deOrvin (see Irwin)

DePartee (see Holden)

de Plessis (see Hay)

de Pollock (see Pollock)

dePons (see Folk Family Surname Exchange)

De Prael (see Prall)

DePraelles (see Prall)

de Praulle (see Prall)

DePriest (see Beckham)

DePuy (see Brodhead)

DeRapaljie (see Covert)

DeRaulin (see Raulin)

Derham (see Lush)

Derk (see Wert)

Deroun
*The Deroun Diplomat
12600 Bissonnet A4-407
Houston, TX 77099
Dede D. Mercer, Publisher
Pub. *The Deroun Diplomat*, annually, $20.00 per year subscription; (all variations of the surname, all over the world)

Derrick (see Wert)

Derry
Derry Family Organization
535 North Luce Road
Ithaca, MI 48847
Mary E. Strouse

Descant (see Johnson)

Des Hay (see Hay)

Deshays (see Hay)

DeShazo
DeShazo Newsletter
212 Kings Forest Drive
Leeds, AL 35094
Bob and Patsy DeShazo
Pub. *DeShazo Newsletter*

DeShazo
DeShazo Newsletter
520 Forrest Avenue
Lodi, CA 95240
Shirley E. Buirch
Pub. *DeShazo Newsletter*, quarterly

Deshotels (see Johnson)

Deskins (see Hatfield)

Desmerits (see Johnson)

de Somerville (see Somerville)

Despain (see Reynolds)

Despaux (see Blossom Press)

DeSpiegelaere (see Heath)

Dessaint
*International Dessaint Family Association
94 Birch Road
Westfield, MA 01085
Phone (413) 533-8257; (413) 535-0350 FAX; E-mail: jnesbitt@crocker.com
James Fash Nesbitt, U.S. Representative

deStockton (see Stockton)

Detamore
*Detamore Family Genealogy Group
411 South Richland
Olney, IL 62450
Phone (618) 392-2437
Karl Mehnert, Genealogy Coordinator
Pub. *More and More Detamores*, irregularly, contribution for subscription; (includes descendants of Christian Detamore, 1790 Rockingham County, Virginia)

Detelante (see Detillion)

Detering
Detering-Williams-Laney-Fagen Family Association
2306 Westgate
Houston, TX 77019
Phone (713) 529-2333
Harold Helm
$25.00 plus pedigree and family group sheets for membership

Detillion
*La Famille Detillion
2136 Appaloosa Lane
Arcata, CA 95521
Phone (707) 822-4085
Olive E. Kuchel Vieira
(includes descendants of Louis Detelante and Maria Louisa, researching Detelante/Detillion family of Ohio and Washington)

Deuchars (see Lindsay)

Deul (see Duvall)

deValer (see Waller)

Devall (see Duvall)

Devalut (see Duvall)

Devan (see Cian)

Devault (see Dewald, Duvall)

Devenport (see Davenport)

Deville (see Johnson)

Devine (see Clark)

Devine
*Devine/Falvey/Sheehy/Stack Clan
6394 South 6000 West Road
Chebanse, IL 60922-9712
Doris Devine, Publisher
Pub. *Devine/Falvey/Sheehy/Stack Clan*, annually; (includes Devine of New London, Connecticut, 1846–47, and Falvey of Richmond, Virginia, 1855)
Periodical meeting

Devoe (see Crispell)

Devol (see Duvall)

DeVolland (see Volland)

De Vos (see Barnard)

Devoto (see Marre)

Dewald
*Dewald Clearinghouse
9190 Oak Leaf Way
Granite Bay, CA 95746
Phone (916) 791-0405
Linus Joseph Dewald
Pub. *Dewald Newsletter*, semiannually,
$25.00 per year subscription; (includes
all phonetic variations: Dewald,
DeWalt, Devault, Dawalt, etc.)

Dewall (see Duvall)

Dewalt (see Dewald)

DeWalt (see Dewald)

Dewalt
*Dewalt Family Database
1301 Bradford Road
Oreland, PA 19075-2414
Phone (215) 836-4727
Dale E. Berger, Publisher

Dewar (see Buchanan, Macnab,
Menzies)

Dewees (see Links Genealogy
Publications)

Dewees
Dewees-Deweese
PO Box 4304
Salem, OR 97302
Ted D. Deweese
Pub. *Dewees-Deweese*, bimonthly,
$30.00 per year subscription
Reunion

Deweese (see Links Genealogy
Publications, Dewees)

DeWeese (see Links Genealogy
Publications)

Dewell (see Duvall)

Dewey (see Barnard)

De Whitney (see Covert)

Dewhurst
Dewhurst Family Association
PO Box 520
Ramona, CA 92065-0520
Roger Dewhurst

De Witt (see Friend)

De Witt
*De Witt, Monmouth and Middlesex
Counties, New Jersey
6603 Kensington Avenue East
Richmond Heights, CA 94805-2054

Phone (510) 237-7240 (phone and FAX);
E-mail: tdewitt@creative.net
Dorothy Swinson DeWitt Baldwin,
Coordinator

De Witt
De Witt Family Organization
535 North Luce Road
Ithaca, MI 48847
Mary E. Strouse

Dewitt
*Dewitt and Bartlett Reunion
146 North Lennox
Casper, WY 82601
Stella Lofink

Dey (see Covert, Dye)

Deyarmond
*Deyarmond Surname Organization
48 Clark Road
Chester, NH 03036
Phone (603) 887-3820
Michelle E. Scott, Chairperson
(includes descendants of Alexander
Deyarmond (1735 Donegal County,
Ireland–) and Mary Barnhill, parents
of Robert, who settled in Upper
Stewiacke, Nova Scotia, Canada)

Deye (see Dye)

Deyo
Deyo Family Association
(Huguenot Historical Society)
8 Town Road
PO Box 141
Mount Marion, NY 12456
Esther Deyo Aldridge

deYrewyne (see Irwin)

Dhigh (see Dye)

Dhye (see Dye)

Di (see Dye)

Dial (see Dale, Rowe)

Diamen (see Dement)

Diamon (see Dement)

Diamond (see Dement)

Dibbs (see MacDuff)

Dichtel (see Dichtl)

Dichtl
*Dichtl Surname Organization
41 Pineview Lane
Boulder, CO 80302-9414
Phone (303) 705-0702
Rudolph J. Dichtl
(includes Dichtl and Dichtel from 1840
to the present in the U.S. and from
before 1840 to the present in
Germany)

Dick
Dick Surname Newsletter
18002 North 12th Street, #30
Phoenix, AZ 85022
Nani Mercer Neal
Pub. *Dick Surname Newsletter*, three
times per year, $20.00 per year
subscription; (includes Dickerson,
Dickinson, Dickson, Dixon, Dixson,
etc.)

Dickensen (see Baker)

Dickenson (see Newton)

Dickerson (see Dick)

Dickey (see Douglas, Ross, Stewart)

Dickinson (see Dick)

Dickinson
*Nathaniel Dickinson Family Association
1124 Longmeadow Street
Longmeadow, MA 01106
Phone (413) 567-6079
Robert Magovern
Pub. *Newsletter*, semiannually, donation
for subscription; (includes descendants
of Nathaniel Dickinson (1600 Ely,
England–1676 Hadley,
Massachusetts))

Dickinson
*Dickinson Family Database
PO Box 2127
Orem, UT 84059-2127
Phone (801) 221-0603
Lynn Jeffrey Bernhard
(includes descendants of Nathaniel
Dickinson plus English relatives)

Dickson (see Folk Family Surname
Exchange, Dick, Dixon, Heath, Keith)

Die (see Dye)

Dieball
Descendants of Fred and Jane Dieball of
Germany, Missouri and Oklahoma
4286 Deborah Street
Simi Valley, CA 93063
Martha Wright

Dieboldt (see Mueller)

Diebolt (see Mueller)

Diedrich (see O'Brien)

Dieffenbach
Dieffenbach Family
218 North Maple Street
Elizabethtown, PA 17022
Ray J. Dieffenbach
Pub. *Dieffenbach Family*

Diehl (see The Memorial Foundation of
the Germanna Colonies, Lambert,
Stoner)

Diehle (see Dale)

Diehm
Diehm/Deam Family Organization
4116 Meadowcroft Road
Kettering, OH 45429
Pat Frappier

Diel (see Surname Database, Lambert)

Dienemann (see Thienemann)

Dierhing (see Herd)

Dieterle (see Armbruster)

Dietlein
Assumption Abbey
PO Box A
Richardton, ND 58652
Phone (701) 974-3315
Damian Dietlein
(includes ancestors of Philipp Dietlein
    and Christina Eckstein, of John
    Heembrock (Hembrock) and Maria
    Altstadt (Altstadt), and descendants of
    their siblings as well as two other
    Dietlein families of unconfirmed
    relationship)

Dietwiler
German-Swiss Newsletter
PO Box 13548
Saint Louis, MO 63138
Maryann Schirker
Pub. *German-Swiss Newsletter*
    (*Dietwiler/Fechter/Schicker/Hahn/Eck/*
    Schmitz/Kuhlman/Rower/Redre)

Dietz (see Surname Database, Brehm)

Dietz
*The Dietz Database
10528 Lower Azusa Road, #162
El Monte, CA 91731-1296
Phone (818) 309-0764
Richard R. Dietz
(includes Dietze and Diez)

Dietze (see Dietz)

Diez (see Dietz)

Diff
*Diff Clan
3168 Dolly Ridge Drive
Birmingham, AL 35243
Phone (205) 967-1506
T. Earl Diffee, President
Pub. *Family Newsletter*, two to three
    times per year; (includes Diffee, Diffie,
    Diffey, Diffy)
$10.00 per year membership

Diffee (see Diff)

Diffey (see Diff)

Diffie (see Diff)

Diffy (see Diff)

Digh (see Dye)

Dikeman (see Dyckman)

Dilbeck (see Cowart)

Dilday
*Charles Dilday Family Organization
PO Box 2856
Jackson, WY 83001
Phone (307) 733-5647
Margo D. Morey

Dilger (see Surname Database)

Dillard (see Rutherford, Tate)

Dillard
*Dillard Family
PO Box 1923
Athens, GA 30603
Phone (706) 353-1283
Jim Hawkins
(includes descendants of Fielding Dillard
    II (1815–1896) and America Frances
    Chaffin (1826–1909) of Cherokee
    Corner, Oglethorpe County, Georgia)

Dillard
*Dillard Doorways
12600 Bissonnet A4-407
Houston, TX 77099
Dede D. Mercer, Publisher
Pub. *Dillard Doorways*, bimonthly,
    $20.00 per year subscription; (all
    variations of the surname, all over the
    world)

Dillard
*The Dillard Family Association
218 Indian Trail
Anderson, SC 29625
Rachel Dillard Scott, Secretary
Pub. *The Dillard Annual*, annually;
    (includes descendants of John Dillard
    (1755–1842) of Culpeper and
    Pittsylvania counties, Virginia,
    Washington County, Tennessee,
    Buncombe County, North Carolina,
    and Rabun County, Georgia; interested
    in all Dillards and maintains a
    repository in the Rabun County
    Library in Clayton, Georgia)
$8.00 per year membership; annual
    reunion on the second weekend of
    June at Dillard, Georgia

Dilleshaw (see Delashaw)

Dilley (see Wright)

Dillinger
*Dillinger Surname Organization
56 Chestnut
Wayne, NJ 07470
Phone (201) 694-8723
Lucille Dillinger Alexander

Dillman (see Covert)

Dillon (see Johnson)

Dillon
*John Dillon Family Organization
William John Dillon Family Organization
15600 Cannon Drive
Los Gatos, CA 95030
Phone (408) 354-3064
Carole J. Freitas

Dilworth (see Woolley)

Dilworth
Dilworth Southern Association
5411 West El Camino del Cerro
Tucson, AZ 85745
Phone (602) 745-7223
Mary Jane S. Marsh, Chairman
Pub. *Family Letter*, donation for copying
    and postage

Dimak (see Blossom Press)

Dimand (see Dement)

Dimbter (see Kahler)

Diment (see Dement)

Dimint (see Dement)

Dimmit
Dimmit Family Association
420 South Madison Avenue, #315
Pasadena, CA 91101
Phone (818) 792-1466
Dr. Richard B. Miller

Dimmon (see Dement)

Dimon (see Dement)

Dimond (see Dement)

Dineer
*The Dineen/Dinneen Information
    Exchange
914 East Lemon Street, #214
Tempe, AZ 85281
Phone (602) 517-5071
Tom Baker
Pub. *The Dineen/Dinneen Information
    Exchange* (includes variant spellings:
    Deneen, O'Deneen, O'Dineen,
    O'Dinneen)

Dinet (see Blossom Press)

Dinger
Dinger Family Newsletter
PO Box 124
Fredericksburg, PA 17026
Peter Dinger
Pub. *Dinger Family Newsletter*
    (Denger(t))

Dingwall (see Ross)

Dinkins
Dinkins-Dockins-Denkins-Dunkin
Family Association
2306 Westgate
Houston, TX 77019
Phone (713) 529-2333
Harold Helm
$25.00 plus pedigree and family group
sheets for membership

Dinneen (see Dineen)

Dinnes (see Innes)

Dinsmore (see Murray)

Dinwiddie (see Maxwell)

Dinwoodie (see Maxwell)

Disbrow
Disbrow Family Descendants
48 Sweetbay Lane
Orlando, FL 32811-1028
A. Gantz

Disbrow
Disbrow Family Newsletter
435 North Franklin
Sioux Falls, SD 57103
Cash Disbrow, Editor
Pub. *Disbrow Family Newsletter*,
quarterly, $8.00 per year subscription

Dishart (see MacDuff)

Disney
*Normandy Heritage Publishing
Company
1618 Inglis Lane
San Jose, CA 95118
Phone (408) 266-4807
Patricia Disney McKenzie, Publisher and
Editor
Pub. *The Disney Chronicles From
Colonial Time To Present*, quarterly
(February, May, August and
November), $16.00 per year
subscription

Disney
Disney Family Bulletin
Rt. 1, Box 23
Menlo, IA 50164
Sherry Foresman
Pub. *Disney Family Bulletin*, quarterly,
$10.00 per year subscription

Distin (see Covert)

Dittman
*Dittman Surname Organization
199 Commodore Drive
Milledgeville, GA 31061
Phone (912) 968-7425
Richard Bialac

Dittmann
*Carl G. Dittmann Family Organization
620 North Edmunds
Mitchell, SD 57301

Phone (605) 996-5448
Mrs. E. T. Goldammer, Family Historian
(includes descendants of Carl G. (1858–)
and Minnie Roemer (1864–) Dittmann,
who were married in 1884 in Stassfurt,
Germany, and came to the U.S. in
1893)
Annual reunion at Hitchcock Park,
Mitchell, South Dakota

Dittmer (see Wiese)

Dix (see Rothenberger)

Dixon (see Folk Family Surname
Exchange, Dick, Keith, Lush)

Dixon
*Dixon/Dixson/Dickson Family
Newsletter*
1708 Keysville Road South
Keymar, MD 21757
Phone (301) 775-2256; E-mail:
TCouzins@aol.com
Richard Dixon Couzins
Pub. *Dixon/Dixson/Dickson Family
Newsletter*, quarterly, $5.00 per year
subscription; (over 18,000 Dixons
prior to 1900)

Dixon
Dixon Family Organization
120 Prince Lane
Las Vegas, NV 89110
Zylphia Shaw

Dixon
Dixon Family Association
PO Box 966
Liberty, NC 27298-0966
Warren Dixon, Jr.

Dixson (see Dick, Dixon)

D'Marney (see Marney)

D'Maupin (see Maupin)

Doan (see Cian)

Doan
*Doan/Doane Family Reunion
2709 S.E. Taylor, #6
Portland, OR 97214
Elaine Smith
(includes descendants of Joseph Branson
Doan (of Pennsylvania, to Illinois in
1866) and his wife Hannah Jane
Carpenter, who came to Rainier,
Oregon, in 1884, or of Rev. Nehemiah
Doane, who came to Oregon from
Massachusetts in 1849; also Donne)

Doane (see Doan, Wright)

Doane
Doane Family Association
PO Box 392
Essex, CT 06426

Doane
The Doane Family Association
PO Box 43
Alcoa, TN 37701-0043
Thomas Kirchoff
Pub. *Doane Doin's and Diggin's*

Doane
*The Doane Family Association of
America, Inc.
1044 South Ironwood Road
Sterling, VA 20164-5111
Katherine Blair Hartman, National
Historian
Pub. *Doane, A Publication of the Doane
Family Association of America, Inc.*
(for descendants of John Doane, who
came to Plymouth in 1629 and settled
in Eastham, Massachusetts)
$10.00 per year membership for
individuals, $25.00 per year
membership for families, $50.00 life
membership; biennial reunion

Dobard (see Blossom Press)

Dobbie (see Donnachaidh)

Dobbin (see Donnachaidh)

Dobbins
Dobbins Family Organization
Rt. 3, Box 123
Trinity, NC 27370
Cheryl Burrow

Dobbins
Dobbins Files
PO Box 114
Cartwright, OK 74731
Clara Nash
Pub. *Dobbins Files*, quarterly, $8.00 per
year subscription

Dobie (see Donnachaidh)

Dobie
*The Dobie Clan of North America
20001 Ridge Road
North Royalton, OH 44133
Phone (216) 237-6657
George N. Dobie, II, Editor
Pub. *The Dobie Connection*,
semiannually; (includes Dobie family
heritage and Scottish origins and
contemporary North American history;
Robert (1716–1760) of Scotland to
William (1777-1835) of Virginia and
Texas, William (1724–1772) and Jean
Bell of Dumfries, Scotland; John
(1718–1807) and Mary Glover of
Hardbush, Scotland; William (about
1750) and Mary Murdoch of Dumfries;
Alexander (1762–1826) and Ann Swan
of Woodside, Scotland; William
(1789–1850) and Mary Coulthard of
Dumfries and Ontario; Alexander
(1817–1904) and Maria Willey of
Aleidon County, Michigan; David
(1819–1914) and Flora McRae of
Annan, Scotland, and Ontario)

$10.00 per year membership; annual reunion

Dobieson (see Donnachaidh)

Dobinson (see Donnachaidh)

Dobson (see Blossom Press, Donald, Donnachaidh)

Dochart (see Gregor)

Docherty (see Gregor)

Dochnahl
Dochnahl
827 Chervil Court
Chula Vista, CA 91910-6611
Janice B. Heller
Pub. *Dochnahl*, three times per year, $10.00 per year subscription

Dockery
*Dockery Family Association, Inc.
Rt. 3, Box 94
Murphy, NC 28906-9313
Phone (704) 837-7617 phone and FAX; E-mail: dfassoc@grove.net; Website: http://www.tib.com/dfai
William G. "Bill" Allen, President
Pub. *Hanging Dog Echoes*, annually (June); (includes surnames: Allen, Ashe, Beaver, Chambers, Cornwell, Davidson, Davis, Dockery, Farmer, Fricks, Garrett, Gentry, Graves, Hampton, Hembree, Johnson, Kephart, Killian, Lonsford, Lovingood, Lunsford, McDonald, Miller, Mills, Palmer, Panther, Peebles, Postell, Radford, Roberts, Rose, Sneed, Weeks, Whitener and Woody)
$7.00 per year membership; annual reunion on the second weekend of September at the Historic J. C. Cambell Folk School, Brasstown, Cherokee County, North Carolina

Dockins (see Dinkins)

Dodd (see MacDuff)

Dodd
Dodd Diggins
8177 Turn Loop Road
Glen Burnie, MD 21061-1113
Mrs. Avlyn Dodd Conley
Pub. *Dodd Diggins*, quarterly, $7.00 per year subscription

Dodds (see MacDuff)

Dodenhoff
*Dodenhoff Database
20310 Delight Street
Canyon Country, CA 91351
Phone (805) 252-7795
Charlene Dodenhoff Patterson
(includes all Dodenhoffs who came to America, including Peter Dodenhoff (1572–1623) and his wife, Susanna

Wessel (1590–1627), of Danzig, West Prussia (Germany))

Dodge (see Goodenow)

Dodge
*The Dodge Family Association
5960 Caminito Yucatan
San Diego, CA 92108-2434
Phone (619) 282-4246
Col. Robert L. Dodge, USAF Ret., President
(includes database for all Dodge family histories)
$10.00 per year membership; annual reunion on the last Saturday of January in southern California, on a Saturday in June or July in the Seattle, Washington, area, on the last Saturday of September in Ipswich, Massachusetts, and on the last day of October in northern California

Dodge
Dodge & Allied Families Surname Organization
PO Box 1452
Las Vegas, NV 89125
George S. Dodge, II
Pub. *Dodge & Allied Families Surname Organization Quarterly Newsletter*
$11.00 per year membership

Dodge
Dodge Memorial Society
301 Roselawn Boulevard
Green Bay, WI 54301

Dodson (see Wolverton)

Doeckel
*Doeckel-Schnigter Descendants
2028 45th Street
Rock Island, IL 61201
Phone (309) 788-6217 (Lehan); (309) 762-0332 (May)
Joan E. Doeckel-Lehan; Mary E. Doeckel-May
Pub. *Family/Reunion Newsletter*, annually; (includes descendants of Frederich Ernst Doeckel and Mathilda H. Schnigter)
Annual reunion

Doering (see McKenzie)

Doherty (see Surname Sources)

Dohner
*Dohner Family Surname Exchange
40701 Rancho de la Vista Rd., #68
Palmdale, CA 93550
Phone (805) 943-3416
Dudley H. Dohner
(includes Danner, Doner, Donner variations)

Dohrs (see Links Genealogy Publications)

Doiron (see Johnson)

Dolan
*Dolan Family
1009 Burlington Beach Road
Valparaiso, IN 46383
Phone (219) 462-6661
Armida Sharpin

Dolbere (see Clark)

Dolby (see Dalby)

Dolese (see Blossom Press)

Dolittle (see Catlow)

Doll (see Surname Database)

Dolph
*Dolph Association
351 Farnum Road
Medina, PA 19063
Phone (215) 566-0964
Carol Maginnis, President
(published book that includes Dolph 1729–1995, U.S.)

Domgaard (see Holden)

Domsieffer (see Lemon)

Donachie (see Donnachaidh)

Donaghy (see Cian, Donnachaidh)

Donahoe
Nexus Publications
2207 N.E. 12th Street
Renton, WA 98056
Lynn Wood, Editor
Pub. *Donahoe Nexus*, quarterly, $20.00 per year subscription; (includes Donoho, Donahue, Donoghue, etc.)

Donahue (see Donahoe)

Donald
Donald/Dobson/Allen/Flower Family Organization
750 Terraine Avenue
Long Beach, CA 90804
E. Donald

Donald
*The Clan Donald Archives
Ellen Payne Odom Genealogy Library
Moultrie-Colquitt County Library
204 Fifth Street, S.E.
PO Box 1110
Moultrie, GA 31776
Phone (912) 985-6540; (912) 985-0936 (FAX)
Ann Glass, Irene Godwin and Catherine Bryant, Genealogy Librarians; Beth Gay, Clan Donald Archives Committee Member and Editor of *The Family Tree*
Pub. *The Family Tree*, bimonthly, no subscription charge, contributions appreciated; *By Sea By Land*,

semiannually (spring/summer and fall/winter); (includes MacDonald or recognized sept name) $20.00 per year membership, $250.00 life membership

Donald
*Clan Donald, U.S.A., Inc.
220 Lincoln Street
Downers Grove, IL 60515
Phone (708) 969-1151
Marvin G. Ronaldson, F.S.A. Scot, National Secretary
Pub. *By Sea By Land*, semiannually (spring/summer and fall/winter)
Branches: **California**, Ms. Nancy Bauer, Commissioner, PO Box 1077, Glen Ellen, CA 95442-1077, (707) 996-5003; **Central Pacific**, Donald S. Spence, Commissioner, 25 Circle Drive, Apartment A, Tilburon, CA 94920, (415) 381-2576; **Central South**, Maj. Wayne H. Thompson, USAF Ret., Commissioner, 311 North Sixth Street, Weatherford, OK 73096, (405) 772-6169; **Great Lakes**, Charles R. LaSalle, Commissioner, 3241 Luce Road, Flushing, MI 48433, (810) 732-7002; **Mid-East**, S. Edward Weary, Commissioner, 9921 Marquand Drive, Burke, VA 22015, (703) 978-7155; **Mid-South**, James McBride, Mid-South Commissioner, 5003 Sunset Bluff, Huntsville, AL 35803, (205) 881-5237; **Midwest/Great Plains**, Bruce A. MacDonald, Commissioner, 12959 Homestead Drive, White Bear Lake, MN 55110, (612) 426-4532; **New England**, Kenneth D. MacDonald, Commissioner, 873 Chestnut Street, Waban, MA 02168, (617) 969-6423; **Northeast Atlantic**, James Gammon, Commissioner, PO Box 347, Newfoundland, NJ 07435, (201) 697-3763; **North Pacific**, Mrs. Gloria McQuesten Walker, Commissioner, 33513 18th Avenue South, Federal Way, WA 80127, (206) 838-2925; **Northwest**, Francis R. McDonald, F.S.A. Scot, Commissioner, 4511 Bluebird Lane, Laramie, WY 82070, (307) 745-8645; **Southeast**, Mrs. Mary Jane Gibbons, Southeast Commissioner, 17 Glenview Dr., N.E., Rome, GA 30160, (706) 235-7229; **South Pacific**, Alan MacDonald, South Pacific Commissioner, 15572 View Ridge Lane, Granada Hills, CA 91344, (818) 684-2476; **Southwest**, James M. Johnston, Commissioner, 7076 Miller Ct., Littleton, CO 80127, (303) 972-8646
$20.00 per year membership, $250.00 life membership

Donally (see Donley)

Donard (see Links Genealogy Publications)

Donavant (see Dunnavant)

Donelly (see Donley)

Doner (see Dohner)

Donleavy (see Buchanan)

Donlevy (see Stewart)

Donley
The Donley Directory
12600 Bissonnet A4-407
Houston, TX 77099
Dede D. Mercer, Publisher
Pub. *The Donley Directory*, semiannually, $20.00 per year subscription; (includes all variations of the surname: Donally, Donelly, etc., worldwide)

Donnachaidh
Clan Donnachaidh Society
PO Box 493
Brisbane, CA 94005-0493
Phone (510) 782-8818 after 6:30 P.M. or on weekends
Marjorie Robertson Hale, International Vice Chairman
Pub. *Clan Annual* (includes Collier, Colyear, Connochie, Conochie, Cunnison, Dobbie, Dobbin, Dobie, Dobieson, Dobinson, Dobson, Donachie, Donaghy, Duncan, Duncanson, Dunnachie, Hobson, Inches, Kynoch, MacConachie, MacConchie, MacConechy, MacConnochie, MacCullich, MacDonachie, MacGlashan, MacIver, MacIvor, MacJames, MacLagan, MacOnachie, MacOnich, MacRobbie, MacRobert, MacRoberts, MacRobie, MacWilliam, McInroy, Reed, Reid, Robbie, Roberts, Robertson, Robison, Robson, Roy, Stark, Tonnochy).
Branches: **Arizona**, Philip Donnachie, President, 4342 West Bunkhouse Road, Bridlewood Ranch, AZ 85741, (602) 744-2635; **California (Northern)**, James M. Robertson, 1203 Cameron Lane, Daly City, CA 94014, (415) 586-6357; **California (Southern)**, Mrs. J. Selmer Robertson, President, 10615 Atlanta Avenue, Northridge, CA 91326, (818) 360-4349 (*Faigh Corrie*); **Florida**, David L. Reid, 1143 Crown Drive, Jacksonville, FL 32221, (904) 781-0628; **Illinois**, Joanne R. Reid, 2201 South Highland, Apartment 6L, Lombard, IL 60148, (708) 495-8234; **Michigan**, Edward W. Robinson, 8188 Potter Road, Davidson, MI 48423, (313) 653-4275; **Mid-Atlantic States**, James E. Fargo, 7506 Willowbrook, Fairfax Station, VA 22039, (703) 978-7268, *Robertson's Rant*; **Mid-South States**, David M. Moore, 1507 Miller Farms Road, Germantown, TN 38138, (901) 754-8468; **New England States**, Alistair Duncan, 17 Mallard Road, Acton, MA 01720, (508) 263-0916,

Donnachaidh Doings; **Ohio**, Gretchen Koons, 1212 Central Avenue, Sandusky, OH 44870; **Oklahoma**, Dean Robertson, 340 S.W. 14th Street, Prior, OK 74361; **Pacific Northwest States**, June Wilber, 262 East 68th Street, Tacoma, WA 98404, (206) 472-2044; **Rocky Mountain States**, Curtis W. Roberts, 1037 Hazel Court, Denver, CO 80204, (303) 825-5734; **South**, C. J. Mashburn, 165 Bay Colt Road, Alpharetta, GA 30201, *Donnaichaidh Dispatch: The Newsletter of the Clan Donnachaidh Society of the South*; **Texas**, Nancy C. R. T. Bishop, President, 2700 Kessler Avenue, Midland, TX 79701, (915) 697-2476.
$16.00 per year membership, plus branch dues

Donne (see Doan)

Donner (see Dohner)

Donner
*To America
2650 North Lakeview, #1010
Chicago, IL 60614
Raymond K. Donner, Editor/Author
(includes the Albert Donner and Henrietta Oehler family which originated in the area near Zeitz, Germany and was part of the Saxon migration to Missouri in 1858, and later moved to Chicago)

Donogh (see Cian)

Donoghue (see Donahoe)

Donoho (see Donahoe)

Donshea
*Donshea Family Association
PO Box 1860
Studio City, CA 91614
Phone (818) 980-1005; E-mail: AP471@lafn.org
Karen Mohr
(includes the Donshea family of Scotland, Ireland and England, with possible variants: Donshee, Dunshea, Dunsheath, Dunshee; descendants of James Harvey Donshea (1823 Ireland-1876 New York) and wives Mary (–New York) and Rosetta Willis of Westchester, New York)

Donshee (see Donshea)

Dooley
Family Limbs
6423 S.E. 97th Avenue
Portland, OR 97266-4529
Shirley L. Bodak
Pub. *Dooley/Duley Family Newsletter*

Dooley
*Alfred Brady Dooley Family Organization

105 South 350 East
North Salt Lake, UT 84054
Phone (801) 292-6161
Carol Lucile Forsey
(includes Dooley, Harvey, Eddy,
   Barkheimer families of Ohio and
   Indiana, 1850)

Doolittle
Doolittles of America
23204 Falena Avenue
Torrance, CA 90501
Mrs. Jackie Shelhart

Doolittle
*Doolittles of America, Inc.
46537 Hollymead Place
Sterling, VA 22075
Linda Huxta, Treasurer
Biennial reunion

Doom
*Doom Research Network
2108 Grace Street
Fort Worth, TX 76111-2816
Merle Ganier

Door
*Door-Dorr Surname Organization
5721 Antietam Drive
Sarasota, FL 34231-4903
Phone (813) 924-9170
Charles Delmar Townsend

Doors (see Links Genealogy
   Publications, Tyson)

Dooty
*Dooty/Duty Family Reunion
PO Box 116
Moberly, MO 65270-0116
Phone (816) 263-7576; E-mail:
   kcecyr@mcmsys.com
Karl Rice, Genealogist
(includes descendants of William Duty,
   born 1788 Chatham County, North
   Carolina)

Dopp
Dopp Family Newsletter
301 Windcrest Drive
San Antonio, TX 78239
David C. Dopp, Editor-in-chief
Pub. *Dopp Family Newsletter*, quarterly,
   $10.00 per year subscription; (includes
   descendants of New York immigrant
   1710, and Pennsylvania, Canada and
   Louisiana immigrant families)

Dopp
*Those Utah Dopps
4045 Liberty Avenue
Ogden, UT 84403-2942
Phone (801) 393-7459
C. Diane Baxter, Publisher
(includes descendants of Peter Dopp
   (1808 Charleston, New York–) and his
   four wives; also allied families of
   Henry Marston (1841 Norton,
   Gloucester, England–), settled in

Kaysville, Utah; John Martin Johnson
(1853 Wilkesboro, North Carolina–)
and Ellen Penelope Inscore; Jacob
Flickinger (1836–1891 Meadville,
Crawford County, Pennsylvania), son
of Jacob Flickinger, and the younger
Jacob's wife, Elizabeth)

Dore (see Corson)

Dorland
*Dorland Family Research Group
1254 University
San Jose, CA 95126
Phone (408) 298-2494
Jerry T. Estruth, Secretary
Pub. *The Dorland Newsletter*, irregularly,
   free

Dorman
Dorman/McDorman Family Association
14 West Mountain Lane
Grand Prairie, TX 75051
Beth Dorman

Dorney
Dorney (Turni)
Whispering Oaks
5821 Rowland Hill Road
Cascade, MD 21719-1939
Phone (301) 416-2660
Victor Gebhart, President
Pub. *Dorney (Turni)*, annually, $2.00 per
   issue

Dorr (see Door, Corson)

Dorrell (see Dorrill)

Dorrill
*The Dorrill-Dorrell-Darrell Society
"An International Surname Forum"
156 Lewiston Road
Grovetown, GA 30813
Phone (404) 863-2863
James Stewart Dorrill, Director and
   Editor
Pub. *The Dorrill-Dorrell-Darrell File*,
   three times per year (January, May and
   September), $5.00 per issue
$13.00 per year membership

Dors (see Links Genealogy Publications)

Dorsey (see LaRue)

Dorsey*California
Dorsey Dreams
20245 Serrano Road "A"
Apple Valley, CA 92307
Lois Colette Dorsey Bennington
Pub. *Dorsey Dreams, Our Dorsey Family
   Newsletter*, quarterly, $12.00 per
   volume subscription

Dorsey
Dorsey
RR 3, Box 2103B
Benton City, WA 99320-9772
E-mail: KTWS63A@prodigy.com

Donavon D. Dorsey
Pub. *Dorsey*, quarterly, $20.00 per year
   subscription
Reunion

D'Orvin (see Irwin)

Dorwart (see Sabin)

Dorwin (see Kunkel)

Doshier (see Scott)

Doss (see Bosher)

Doss
*Doss Surname Organization
718 North 900 West, #206
Salt Lake City, UT 84116
Phone (801) 531-2529
Frank D. Elkins
(clearinghouse for Doss information,
   1600–1850, Virginia, Tennessee and
   Texas)

Dossett (see Brown)

Dostal
Dostal Family Organization
2926 Perla
Newport Beach, CA 92660-3529
M. Dostal

Doster (see Hoster)

Dothage
Dothage Family Association
2850 Oledel Road
Saint Louis, MO 63125
C. Ramsey

Dothit (see Folk Family Surname
   Exchange)

Dotson (see Hatfield)

Dott (see MacDuff)

Dotterman
Dotterman Family Newsletter
77 Hollow Road
Quarryville, PA 17566-9491
Harry Hoffman
Pub. *Dotterman Family Newsletter*

Doty (see Doughty, Parker)

Doty
*The Pilgrim Edward Doty Society
155 Argyle Road
Brooklyn, NY 11218
Phone (718) 282-7707
Edward G. Doty, Governor
Pub. *The Pilgrim Edward Doty Society
   Newsletter*, three times per year
   (March, July and November), $1.00
   per issue; (includes descendants of
   Edward Doty, who arrived on the
   Mayflower in 1620)
$10.00 per year membership

Douberley
*William and Zachariah B. Douberley
Descendants
3606 Starwood Trail, S.W.
Lilburn, GA 30247-2448
Frank L. Perry, Jr., EdD.
Annual reunion on the second Sunday of
June at Ebenezer Cemetery, Lake City,
Florida

Doud
*Doud Reunion
10531 Cemetery Road
Canaseraga, NY 14822
Mrs. Harold Carney

Dougall (see MacDougall)

Dougan
*Neal Dougan-Theodorus Scowden
Family Organization
PO Box 6
Aultman, PA 15713
Phone (412) 726-5653
Richard F. Dougan
(includes descendants of Neal Dougan
(1800–1847) of Butler, Pennsylvania,
or Theodorus Scowden (1754–1832) of
Meadville, Pennsylvania)

Dougherty (see Surname Sources, Clark)

Dougherty
Dougherty Reunion (Descendants of Dan
and Pat Dougherty (OH))
PO Box 16
Woodsfield, OH 43793
Georgia Brown
Pub. *Dougherty-Daugherty Roots &
News*, semiannually (June and
December), $3.00 per year
subscription

Doughtery (see Brown)

Doughtry (see Brown)

Doughty (see Hopfensperger, Taylor)

Doughty
*The Doughty Family Association
PO Box 203
Mays Landing, NJ 08330
Phone (609) 625-7561
Clarence E. Doughty, Editor
Pub. *The Doughty Tree*, quarterly, free
fifty-word query for cooperative or
sustaining members, 6¢ per word for
active members and non-members;
(includes Dowty, Dowdy, Dawty, Doty,
etc.)
$12.00 per year membership

Douglas (see Douglass, Ogan)

Douglas
*Clan Douglas Society of North
America, Ltd.
National Office, Archivist, Treasurer
701 Montgomery Highway #209
Birmingham, AL 35216-1833

Phone (205) 822-9670
Gilbert F. Douglas, Jr., M.D., FSA (Scot),
Archivist
Pub. *Newsletter (Dubh Ghlase)*,
bimonthly; (includes Agnew, Bell,
Blacklock, Blackstock, Blackwood,
Blalock, Breckenridge, Brown,
Brownlee, Cant, Cavan, Cavers,
Dickey, Drysdale, Forest, Forrester,
Foster, Gilpatric, Glendinning, Glenn,
Inglis, Kent, Kilgore, Kilpatrick,
Kirkland, Kirkpatrick, Lockerby,
Lockery, MacGuffey, MacGuffock,
McKittrick, Morton, Sandilands,
Sandlin, Soule, Sterett, Symington,
Troup, Young, etc.)
$15.00 per year membership in the U.S.,
$20.00 per year membership in
Canada, $21.00 per year membership
in Australia; annual meeting on the
second full weekend of July in
Linville, North Carolina, during the
Grandfather Mountain Highland
Games and Gathering of Scottish
Clans

Douglass (see Nelson)

Douglass
*Douglass-Woofter Union
2101 Atoka Drive
Orlando, FL 32839
W. Wilson White, Author
(includes descendants of Alvin and Dora
(Woofter) Douglass from 1813)

Douglass
Douglass Family Organization
Coleman Research Agency
241 North Vine Street, Apartment 1104E
Salt Lake City, UT 84103-1945
Ronald Douglass Coleman
(includes Douglas/Douglass families
from Ireland)

Dousman
*Dousman History
1608 West Parkside Drive
Peoria, IL 61606
Linda Gates Sahn

Douthard (see Douthit)

Douthert (see Douthit)

Douthett (see Douthit)

Douthird (see Douthit)

Douthit
*Douthit Ancestry
1530 Harrison Avenue
Boulder, CO 80303-1121
Jan Douthit Weir, Editor
Pub. *Douthit Ancestry*, semiannually;
(includes Douthard, Douthert,
Douthett, Douthird, Douthitt,
Douthwaite, etc.)

Douthitt (see Douthit)

Douthwaite (see Douthit)

Doutt
*Doutt Dialogues
340 Hazel Avenue
Saint Louis, MO 63119-4267
Phone (314) 962-0025
Frances Doutt Smith
Pub. *Doutt Dialogues, A Newsletter for
The Family Doutt*, quarterly, free;
(includes descendants of John Doutt
(1788–Butler County, Pennsylvania);
Daut, Dautt, Doutt, Doutts, etc.)

Doutts (see Doutt)

Dove (see Buchanan)

Dovenport (see Davenport)

Doverspike (see Daubenspeck)

Dow (see Buchanan)

Dowd (see Doud)

Dowden (see Underwood)

Dowden
Dowden
Whispering Oaks
5821 Rowland Hill Road
Cascade, MD 21719-1939
Phone (301) 416-2660
Victor Gebhart, President
Pub. *Dowden*, annually, $2.00 per issue

Dowdy (see Bosher, Doughty)

Dowie (see Gregor)

Dowis (see Rowe, Usher)

Downen
*Downen Family Exchange
4009 Terrace Drive
Annandale, VA 22003
Robert Downen
Pub. *Newsletter*, semiannually, no charge;
(surname exchange, any location)

Downer (see Cox)

Downey (see Cian, Richardson)

Downey
*Urial Downey Family Organization
36 S.W. Crescent Drive
Mount Vernon, IL 62864
Phone (618) 244-3795
Herbert Griswold Downey

Downie (see Lindsay)

Downing (see Anthes, Corson, Dunbar)

Downing
*The Downing Family Historical Society
   of America (DFHSA)
2400 Pleasant Grove Road
Lansing, MI 48910
Phone (517) 484-1290
Ross W. Downing, Membership
   Chairman
Pub. *The Downing Family Historical
   Society of America Newsletter*,
   quarterly
$10.00 per year membership

Downlap (see Dunlop)

Downman (see Thorn)

Downs (see Cian, Corson)

Dows (see Sullivan Surname Exchange)

Dowty (see Doughty)

Doyle (see Arthur, Wright)

Doyle
Doyle Descendants
199 Diamond Spring Road
Denville, NJ 07834-2911
Clark Neal

Doyle
Doyle Diary
PO Box 4477
Casper, WY 82604
Michael Doyle
Pub. *Doyle Diary*, quarterly, $12.00 per
   year subscription

Dozier
Dozier Family Association
2011 Tam Court
Simi Valley, CA 93063
Phone (805) 584-0860
Amelya Sandt

Drach (see Orebaugh)

Drader (see Heath)

Dragaud (see Dragoo)

Dragon (see Blossom Press)

Dragoo
*The Dragoo Family Association
   (HC 74, Box 61, Alma, WV 26320—
   May to December address)
Rt. 4, Box 376 (January to April address)
Hawthorne, FL 32640
Phone (313) 781-9013 Assistant Editor
Louise Dragoo Sinclair, Editor; Carol
   Van Sickle, Assistant Editor
Pub. *Dragoo Family News*, quarterly;
   (includes Dragaud, which became
   Dragoo in America: Pierre Dragaud
   (1669–1712) and Elizabeth Tavaude
   (1669–?), Huguenots from Saintonge,
   France, married in Bristol, England, in
   1699, said to have come to Staten
   Island in 1700)

$8.00 per year membership; biennial
   reunion in even-numbered years

Drake (see Emery, Lynch, Newton,
   Wright)

Drake
Samuel Drake and Derick VanVliet
   Family Reunion
PO Box 857
Mundelein, IL 60060
Mrs. Henry Moulton

Drake
*Sarah Abbe Drake Family Organization
10143 Farrington
Saint Louis, MO 63137-2008
Phone (314) 867-3876
Evelyn J. Brakensiek

Draper
Draper Family Organization
528 East Forest
Brigham City, UT 84302
Phone (801) 723-2535
Jeanne B. Wilson, President
Pub. *Down Draper Lane*, semiannually
$20.00 per year membership

Drawdy (see Drody)

Dray (see Garner)

Dremon (see Drummon)

Drennan
Drennan Exchange (Drinnan/Drennen/
   Drinan)
2502 Lakewood Drive
Valdosta, GA 31602-2107
L. G. English

Drennen (see Drennan)

Drewry (see Bosher)

Drewry
*George and Elizabeth (Pepper) Drewry
   Descendants
4 Pinewood Gardens SMW
Homosassa, FL 34446
Phone (352) 382-1298
Mrs. R. W. Rogers,Jr.
(includes about 600 descendants of
   George Drewry (1769–1840) and
   Elizabeth Pepper (1776–1863) from
   Lincolnshire, England, 1817 to Prince
   Edward County, Ontario, with
   descendants to the U.S.)

Drictoni (see McCune)

Driggs
Driggs Family of America
115 South Lafayette Boulevard,
   Suite 512
South Bend, IN 46601-1542
Harry S. Driggs
Free membership

Drinan (see Drennan)

Drinkwater (see Bosher)

Drinnan (see Drennan)

Dripps (see Drips)

Drips
*Drips/Dripps Family Association
7000 "Y" Street
Lincoln, NE 68505-2101
Phone (402) 464-1436; E-mail:
   adrips@unlinfo.unl.edu
Allen Dripps

Driscal (see O'Driscoll)

Driscoll (see O'Driscoll)

Driskell (see O'Driscoll)

Driskill (see O'Driscoll)

Dritt (see Tritt)

Droddy (see Drody)

Drody
Trendy Publications, Inc.
4528 Wyndale Avenue, S.W.
Roanoke, VA 24018
Phone (703) 989-9402
Margaret Drody Thompson, President-
   Editor-Publisher
Pub. *Drody Family Newsletter (Droddy/
   Drawdy, etc.)*, annually, $10.00 per
   year subscription

Droke
*Droke Family Association
2143 Camden Avenue
Los Angeles, CA 90025
Phone (310) 478-5476
Alfred B. Droke
Pub. *Yearly Report*, free

Dromm (see Surname Database)

Drouillard (see Lagesse)

Drugge
*The Drugge Family Organization
2555 West 15000 South
Bluffdale, UT 84065
Phone (801) 254-1095
Margareta Soderquist, A.G.

Drum (see Surname Database, Cian)

Drumaguhassle (see Graham)

Drumelizior (see Hay)

Drumin (see Cian)

Drummon
*Drummons of PA Association
13200 Doty Avenue, #220
Hawthorne, CA 90250

Elayne Alexander, Head of Research
(includes Dremon, Drummons)

Drummond (see Banks, Cian)

Drummons (see Drummon)

Drury
*Drury Database
431 South Center Street
Bensenville, IL 60106
Phone (630) 595-3573
Linda Lightholder Kmiecik
(includes descendants of Samuel (ca
1770–1824), son of Nicholas and
Catharina (Schmidt) Drury of Albany,
New York, and Samuel's wife, Hannah
Drury, of Vermont, New York and
Kentucky; also descendants of Hugh[1]
Drury of New England to about 1850)

Drury
*Drury National Reunion
5 Woodland Drive
Boonton, NJ 07005-9741
Phone (201) 334-4622
Jeanne Drury Otto, Executive Vice
President
(includes descendants of Roger (Rodger)
Drury (1819–1885) and Ann
Comerford (1830–1871) of Roxbury,
Massachusetts)

Dryden
Thomas Dryden Family Organization
7109 East 53rd Place
Tulsa, OK 74145-7749
Phone (918) 622-2018
Jane Dryden Weinert

Drysdale (see Douglas)

Duaine (see Cian)

Duane (see Cian)

Duarte
Duarte Family Association
27 Lucile
Arcadia, CA 91006
Phone (213) 447-8035
Vickie Duarte Cordova

Dubberly
*Manning Jasper Dubberly, Robert T.
Wolfe & Emma Blitch Descendants
3606 Starwood Trail, S.W.
Lilburn, GA 30247-2448
Frank L. Perry, Jr., EdD.
Annual reunion on the second Saturday
of October at Laura Walker Park,
Waycross, Georgia

Dubberly
*Joseph Allen Dubberly Descendants
3606 Starwood Trail, S.W.
Lilburn, GA 30247-2448
Frank L. Perry, Jr., EdD.
Annual reunion on the second Saturday
of October at Laura Walker Park,
Waycross, Georgia

Dubhghlase (see Douglas)

Dublin (see Hardwick)

Dubois
*Dubois Family Association
242–22 54th Avenue
Douglaston, NY 11362
Phone (914) 255-9050
William M. Haines

DuBois
DuBois Family Association
The Huguenot Historical Society
PO Box 339
New Paltz, NY 12561-0339

Duchray (see Graham)

Duck (see Jay)

Duckworth (see Covert)

Ducote (see Johnson)

Dudek
Dudek Family Association
22520 Lincoln
Saint Clair Shores, MI 48082
Richard J. Jacob

Duehr (see Covert)

Duel (see Duvall)

Duelge
*Karl August Wilhelm Duelge/Diilge
Family Organization
311 Copa De Oro Drive
Brea, CA 92621
Phone (714) 491-3364
Barbara Renick
(includes descendants of Karl August
Wilhelm Duelge (1830 Muenchendorf,
Pommern, Germany–1903 Prussia))

Duell (see Duvall)

Duesing
*Duesing Daze
PO Box 1872
Dodge City, KS 67801-1872
Laura Tasset Koehn, President
(includes research on Gerhard Joseph
Duesing and Anna Christine Wolbers)

Dufacius (see Macfie)

Duff (see MacDuff)

Duffee (see MacDuffee)

Duffus (see Sutherland)

Duffy (see Macfie)

Dugalston (see Graham)

Dugan
Oak Leaf Publishing
22 Creek Road, #64
Irvine, CA 91714
Pub. *Dugan Family Newsletter*,
bimonthly, $10.00 per year
subscription

Dugar (see Blossom Press)

duGard (see Gard)

Dugas (see Blossom Press)

Duggan (see Frazier)

Duhan
Duhan Reunion
25 North Spruce Street
Batavia, NY 14020
Mr. and Mrs. Joseph Welch

Duhlap (see Dunlop)

Duhnemann (see Thienemann)

Duilach (see Stewart)

Duk (see Gonsalus)

Dulany
*Dulany Database
PO Box 95
Eastville, IL 60518
Phone (815) 246-9626
Ann A. Hecathorn
(includes descendants of Preston and
Susan Hutson Dulany from 1800
especially in White and Van Buren
counties, Tennessee, Jefferson County,
Illinois and northeastern Oklahoma)

Dulap (see Dunlop)

Dulape (see Dunlop)

Duley (see Dooley)

Dulon (see Dulong)

DuLong (see Dulong)

Dulong
*Dulong Family Registry
959 Oxford Street
Berkley, MI 48072-2011
Phone (810) 541-2894; E-mail:
dulongj@oeonline.com; Website: http:/
/oeonline.com/~dulongj/dulong.html
John P. Dulong, Ph.D., Coordinator
(includes all Dulong, DuLong or Dulon
families, especially the descendants of
Richard Dulong, a Montréal innkeeper,
1718–1787, the ancestor of the
majority of DuLong descendants in
North America; PAF™ database
includes about 133 Dulong
descendants)

Duman
*Duman Clearinghouse
1605 Holly
Gering, NE 69341
Phone (308) 436-5617
Shirley Weihing

Dumas (see Lagesse)

Dumford
*Dumford Surname Organization
11 West 300 South
Farmington, UT 84025
Phone (801) 451-2904
Bradford N. Ator

Dummer
*The Dummer Family in America
PO Box 44102
Washington, DC 20026-4102
David A. Dummer
Pub. *The Dummer Family in America*
    (includes the Dummers and related
    families in the U.S. and Canada; also a
    central repository for all known
    genealogical and historical information
    about these families)

Dumond (see Baker)

DuMond (see Crispell)

Du Mont (see Dement)

Dumphe (see Corson)

Dunagan (see Cowart)

Dunahay
Dunahay "Kith-Kin" Newsletter
4513 Lake Haven Boulevard
Sebring, FL 33872
Phone (813) 382-2522
Lowell V. Dunahay, Editor
Pub. *Dunahay "Kith-Kin" Newsletter*,
    semiannually (May and November),
    $5.00 per year subscription

Dunbar (see MacDuff)

Dunbar
*Descendants of Thomas Dunbar
801 Sequoia Avenue
Millbrae, CA 94030
Phone (415) 697-9410
Thomas M. Brocher, Publisher
(includes descendants of Thomas Dunbar
    (1764 Westerly, Rhode Island–1839
    Blandford, Massachusetts) and Eunice
    Barber (1767–1857) of Westerly,
    Rhode Island, Hartland, Connecticut,
    and Blandford, Massachusetts, and
    collateral Belden and Downing
    families, especially Elisha Belden
    (1796–after 1870) and Martha Collins
    (1803–1828) of Wethersfield,
    Connecticut, and Joshua Downing (ca
    1769 New Hampshire–1858 Deering,
    New Hampshire) and Patience Chase
    (1768 Kensington, New Hampshire–
    1844 Deering, New Hampshire))

Dunbar
Dunbar
6180 Merrywood Drive
Rocklin, CA 95677-3421
Kathleen Stewart
Pub. *Dunbar*, quarterly, $12.00 per year
    subscription

Dunbar
Clan Dunbar
5205 South Highway 77
Cameron, TX 76520-9516
Tom Lawhon, Editor
Pub. *Lion & Thistle*, quarterly; (includes
    descendants of Gospatric, Earl of
    Dunbar and March, including
    Clugston, Corbett, Dundas, Gray,
    Herying, Home, Nesbit, Nevill,
    Strickland, Washington, etc.)

Dunbar
*Dunbar Research
PO Box 743
Fall City, WA 98024
Phone (206) 222-6940
Audrey Allan Schroeder, Researcher-
    Publisher

Duncan (see Folk Family Surname
    Exchange, The Memorial Foundation
    of the Germanna Colonies, Cox,
    Donnachaidh, Layman, Massey,
    McRae)

Duncan
*Duncan Surname Association
5938 S.E. 45th Street
Tecumseh, KS 66542-9743
Phone (913) 379-5585; E-mail:
    wad@tyrell.net; Homepage: http://
    www.tyrell.net/~wad/dsa/dsa.htm
Wes A. Duncan
Pub. *Duncan Association Newsletter*,
    quarterly (March, June, September and
    December), $10.00 per year
    subscription; (largest database of
    Duncan research material in the U.S.
    includes Duncan, Dunkin, etc., all
    spelling variations in the U.S. prior to
    1850)
$25.00 life membership includes a one-
    year subscription

Duncan
*Kinseeker Publications
5697 Old Maple Trail
PO Box 184
Grawn, MI 49637
E-mail: AB064@taverse.lib.mi.us
Victoria Wilson, Editor
Pub. *The Family Series: Duncan*,
    irregularly, $6.50 per year subscription

Duncan
Duncan/Butler Family Association
1410 Chester Drive
Grand Prairie, TX 75050
Phone (214) 262-4425
Marcie Bridges

Duncanson (see Donnachaidh)

Dundas (see Dunbar)

Dunham (see Potts)

Dunham
*Dunham Family Organization
(address withheld upon request)
Pub. *Dunham Dispatch*, bimonthly, free;
    (includes descendants of Deacon John
    Dunham (1589–1669))

Dunham
Steven Dunham and Mary Jane Fostert of
    Wisconsin Family Association
31108 Third Avenue, Trailer 301
Black Diamond, WA 98010-9708
Arthur Brown

Dunkelberger
Dunkelbergers in America
4701 Saint George Street
Reading, PA 19606
Phone (215) 779-3464
Jackie Nein Flamm, Historian
Pub. *Dunkelbergers in America*, annually
    (April), $10.00 per year subscription

Dunker (see Cummings)

Dunkin (see Dinkins)

Dunlap (see Dunlop)

Dunlape (see Dunlop)

Dunlop
*Dunlop-Dunlap Family Society
104 Lewis
Billings, MT 59101
Phone (406) 256-0031
Ella Dunlap Patte, Director-Genealogist
Pub. *Merito*, quarterly; (includes all
    Dunlop-Dunlap, worldwide)
$25.00 per year membership

Dunlop
Dunlop/Duhlap Family Society
6519 Burlwood Road
Charlotte, NC 28211-5605
Phone (704) 366-5938
Elizabeth W. Girard, President
Pub. *Merito*, quarterly; (includes Delap,
    Downlap, Dulap, Dulape, Dunlap,
    Dunlape, Dunlope, Dunloup)
$15.00 per year membership

Dunlope (see Dunlop)

Dunloup (see Dunlop)

Dunn (see Arthur, Goodenow, Leland,
    Newcomb)

Dunn
From Generation to Generation
Rt. 1, Box 147
Buncombe, IL 62912
Melody Tellor, Editor

Pub. *Dunn Descendants*, quarterly,
$15.00 per year subscription

Dunn
*Dunn Database
368 Terebet Court
Edgewood, KY 41017
Phone (606) 331-4525
Gerald C. Dunn
(master index with 160,000 names,
including Dunns in the 1850 and 1860
census)
Free searches for FGS and LSASE

Dunn
*William Gallimore Dunn Family
Organization
712 East 675 North
American Fork, UT 84003
Phone (801) 756-7584
Val Dunn
(includes descendants of William
Gallimore Dunn and Jane Milner of
Staffordshire, England, about 1800)

Dunnachie (see Donnachaidh)

Dunnavant
*Dunnavant/Donavant Family
Association
3929 Milton Drive
Independence, MO 64055-4043
Phone (816) 373-5309
Robert L. Grover, President
(includes descendants of W.C. Dunnavant
(1803 Virginia–) and Mary Waddle
(1806 Grainer County, Tennessee–))

Dunnigan (see Cowart)

Dunning
James P. Dunning Descendants Reunion
1420 Greenwich Lane
Janesville, WI 53545
D. Davis

Dunseith (see Newmyer)

Dunseth (see Newmyer)

Dunshea (see Donshea)

Dunsheath (see Donshea)

Dunshee (see Donshea)

Dunsieth (see Newmyer)

Dunsmore (see Murray)

Dunstan (see MacDuff)

Dunwell (see Witter)

Duplessis (see Blossom Press)

Duplissey (see Johnson)

Duplovys (see Links Genealogy
Publications)

Dupplin (see Hay)

Du Prael (see Prall)

Dupre (see Johnson)

Dupree (see Harvey)

Dupy
Dupy Family Newsletter
2102 Racine Avenue
Burlington, IA 52601-2249
Timothy S. Dupy
Pub. *Dupy Family Newsletter*

Durabbe (see Blossom Press)

Durant (see Smith)

DuRant (see MacFaddien)

Dureau (see Blossom Press)

Durfee (see Stevens)

Durgy (see Durkee)

Durham
Durham Descendants
5389 Evanston
Indianapolis, IN 46220-3444
Phone (317) 253-5831
H. Suzanne O'Brien

Durham
John and Martha Durham Descendants
6301 Mackey
Merriam, KS 66202
Dorothy Early

Durham
Durham-Phillips Newsletter
17720 New Market Road
Dearborn, MO 64439-9720
Lois J. Phillips Foster
Pub. *Durham-Phillips Newsletter*,
annually (January)

Durie (see MacDuff)

Durkee (see Burnham)

Durkee
*Society of Genealogy of Durkee
3753 East 15th Street
Long Beach, CA 90804-2943
Phone (310) 494-2836
Bernice B. Gunderson, Editor
Pub. *The Durkee Family Newsletter*,
quarterly, $7.50 per year subscription,
$10.00 per year first class subscription,
$9.00 per year subscription in Canada,
$12.00 per year subscription
elsewhere; (any Durkee family,
including families of Durkee daughters
and descendants of immigrant William
Durgy, who arrived at Ipswich,
Massachusetts, in 1663)

Durkin (see Cian)

Durst (see Stanton)

Durtschi
*Edward Durtschi Family Organization
383 East 1800 South
Orem, UT 84058
Phone (801) 224-1609
Mrs. Phillip D. Harris, Durtschi Family
Genealogist
Annual reunion

Dussler (see Johnson)

Dutcher
Dutcher and Perry Clan
Rt. 1, Box 94B
Osawatomie, KS 66064
Linda Troutman

Duthie (see Ross)

Du Trieux
*Phillipe Du Trieux Descendants
Association
5602 Kingsway West
Cincinnati, OH 45215
Mrs. Maurice Butterfield
Pub. *Philippe Du Trieux Descendants
Newsletter*, quarterly, $10.00 per year
subscription in the U.S., $10.00 per
year subscription in Canada; (includes
Truax, Truex)

Dutson (see Jenkins)

Dutson
*John William Dutson Family
Organization
1055 East Hillcrest Drive
Springville, UT 84663
Phone (801) 489-6298
Nel Lo H. Bassett, A.G., Researcher
Pub. *Research Report*, biannually, $10.00
per year membership; (ancestry of
John William Dutson (1828) of
Herefordshire, England)

Dutton (see Corson)

Dutton
*Dutton-Davis, Jackson-Doane
Educational, Historical and Memorial
Foundation, Inc.
521 Caroline Street
Janesville, WI 53545
Phone (608) 754-8067
Deborah A. Dutton, Editor
Pub. *Newsletter of the Davis Family: For
the Descendants of Daniel Davis*,
quarterly; *Jackson Family*, quarterly

Duty
*Duty in America Family Organization
2711 Seabreeze Court
Orlando, FL 32805
Phone (407) 425-6942
Col. Clifton O. Duty (USA Ret.) or Jean
Barker Duty
(of Arkansas, Illinois, Indiana,
Massachusetts, Missouri, North

Carolina, Tennessee, Texas, Virginia
and West Virginia)
SASE

Duval (see Scadlock)

DuVal (see Duvall)

Duvall (see CTC Family Association)

Duvall
*Mareen Duvall Descendants Society
3580 South River Terrace
Edgewater, MD 21037-3245
Phone (410) 798-4531
Barrett L. McKown, Registrar
Pub. *Duvall Newsletter*, semiannually;
(Duvall of Maryland)
$6.00 per year membership, $2.00
application fee

Duvall
Duvall Data
587 Johnson Road
Chillicothe, OH 45601
Phone (614) 775-2344
Lillian Duvall Kepp
Pub. *Duvall Data*, quarterly (June,
September, December and March),
$20.00 per year membership; (includes
Davald, Deul, Devall, Devalut,
Devault, Devol, Dewall, Dewell, Duel,
Duell, DuVal, etc.)

Du Vernet
*Henri Jacques DuVernet Family
Organization
6025 Riverwood Drive
Atlanta, GA 30328-3732
Phone (404) 256-1925; E-mail:
74761.2054@compuserve.com
Roger M. Scovil
(includes descendants of Henry Jacques
Du Vernet de la Vallee, born 1676)

Duxbury
*Duxbury Family History
202 South Segoe Road
Madison, WI 53705-4939
Phone (608) 233-1506
Donald E. and Ruth A. Duxbury,
Compilers/Publishers
(includes ancestors and descendants of
Luke and Jane (Pickles) Duxbury of
Lancashire, England, Rhode Island and
Wisconsin from 1696)

Duyts (see Rutherford)

Dwaine (see Cian)

Dwight (see Clark)

Dwyer
Dwyer/Rooney/Cullan/Brennan Lineage
Collaboration
PO Box 15926
Austin, TX 78761
H. J. Andreozzi

Dy (see Dye)

Dyall (see Dale)

Dyar
Dyar/Dyer Reunion
6227 Prairie Road
Springfield, OH 45502
Bernard Dyar

Dyckman
*Dyckman/Dikeman/Dykeman Family
Association
13650 North Frontage Road, #334
Yuma, AZ 85367
Marjorie Dikeman Chamberlain
Pub. *Dyckman, Dikeman, Dykeman (3-D
Data) Newsletter*, quarterly; (includes
descendants of Johannes and Maria
(Bosyns) Dyckman, immigrants to
New Amsterdam in 1651)
$12.00 per year membership

Dye (see Covert, Lagesse)

Dye
*The K.A.R.D. Files
19305 S.E. 243rd Place
Kent, WA 98042-4820
Phone (206) 432-1659
Judy K. Dye, Owner
Pub. *Dye Data*, irregularly, $6.00–$7.00
per volume (Washington residents add
8.2% sales tax); (includes D'Yee, Dee,
Dei, Dey, Deye, Dhigh, Dhye, Di, Die,
Digh, Dy, etc.)

D'Yee (see Dye)

Dyer (see Dyar, Eaves, Phillips,
Rutherford)

Dyer
*Hebron Dyer Descendants: Pioneer of
Ohio
822 Camino De Los Padres
Tucson, AZ 85718
Phone (520) 297-6585
Leallah Franklin, Publisher

Dyer
Dyer Exchange
2705 Newton
Silver Spring, MD 20902
Mrs. G. Dyer Melander

Dyer
Dyer Search
1629 18th Avenue, N.W.
New Brighton, MN 55112
Alice Dyer Finley, Editor
Pub. *Dyer Search, For Promoting and
Reporting Research on the Surname
Dyer and Its Variant Spellings*,
quarterly, $12.00 per year subscription

Dykeman (see Dyckman)

Dyment (see Dement)

Dymond (see Dement)

Dysart (see MacDuff)

Dyshart (see MacDuff)

Eachus (see Way)

Ead (see Eads)

Eadds (see Eads)

Eade (see Eads)

Eades (see Eads)

Eads
*Eads Ancestry Researchers (EAR)
2691 Montague Drive
Galesburg, IL 61401-1253
Phone (309) 344-5116
Mary Lou Delahunt
(open to all researching Eads, Edds lines)
No membership fee but SASE
appreciated for exchange; annual
meeting

Eads
*Eads Family in America
2209 East Carriage Lane, #39
Salt Lake City, UT 84117-4419
Phone (801) 272-6514
William A. Eads, Sr., President/Editor
Pub. *Eads Family in America*,
semiannually, $10.00 per year
subscription; (includes Ead, Eadds,
Eade, Eades, Edds, Edes, Eeds, etc.)
Periodic reunions and annual conference
of Eads Family Researchers on the last
Friday and Saturday of April

Eager (see Newton)

Eagle (see Ekell)

Eagle
Eagle Newsletter
1724 Greer Drive, West
Newark, OH 43055-1457
Ronna Eyman Eagle
Pub. *Eagle Newsletter*, quarterly;
(includes Egle and Egli)

Eagles (see Baird)

Eakin
Eakin Family Association
61331 Todd-Smith Road
Grass Valley, OR 97029-3068
Emma Smith

Eakle (see Casto, Ekell)

Eames (see Ames)

Eames
*Eames/Ames Family
4524 K Avenue
Meriden, IA 51037
Phone (712) 443-8274
June J. Ames, Genealogist and Historian

Earewin (see Irwin)

Earhart
*Earhart Genealogy
315 Castlegate Road
Pittsburgh, PA 15221
Phone (412) 241-3029
Walter J. Burnham

Early
Early Family Association
525 Ivy Way
Garland, TX 75043
Henry Early

Earnest
Earnest's Family Association
Rt. 1, Box 14
Lilly, PA 15938
James E. Earnest

Earnest
*Earnest Surname Organization
5341 Whitney Lane
Amarillo, TX 79110
Phone (806) 359-1012
Sylvia D. Murray, A.G., Coordinator
(includes Earnest in Germany and
    Pennsylvania)

Earnest
*Earnest/Ernest/Earnist/Arnest Family
    Exchange
4407 51st Avenue, N.E.
Seattle, WA 98105-4932
Phone (206) 522-9269
John E. Ernest, Family Genealogist
(a single surname study, including
    exhaustive list of the descendants of
    William Earnest who came to Isle of
    Wight County, Virginia, in the early
    1600s)

Earnist (see Earnest)

Earnst
Free Exchange—All Ernsts
209 Cresthaven Drive
Vincennes, IN 47591-3854
Terry L. Earnst, Family Historian

Earry (see Arey)

Earven (see Irwin)

Earwen (see Irwin)

Earwin (see Irwin)

Earwing (see Irwin)

Easey
*Easey Newsletter
2626 Forest Lane
Sarasota, FL 34231
Phone (813) 922-1222
Hazelle Easey
Pub. *Easey Newsletter*, bimonthly, $13.00
    per year subscription

Easlick
Easlick/Eastlick/Eslick Newsletter
1372 Bobwhite Avenue
Sunnyvale, CA 94087
Jessie Easlick Alexander
Pub. *Easlick/Eastlick/Eslick Newsletter*,
    quarterly, $12.00 per year subscription

Easson (see Macnachton)

East (see McNeil)

East
East Wind
902 Pintail Lane
Wausau, WI 54401-7141
Joanne A. Baker, Editor
Pub. *East Wind*, semiannually (May and
    November), $5.00 per year
    subscription

Eastep (see Estep)

Easter
Easter Family Organization (IA and OH)
7413 Chestnut Court
Woodridge, IL 60515
Ellen Collins

Easterday (see Ostertag)

Easterling
Easterling Reunion
PO Box 129
Brinkley, AR 72021
L. Mitchell

Easterling
*Easterling Family Genealogical Society,
    Inc.
1126 Pearl Valley Road
Wesson, MS 39191-9361
Phone (601) 894-2642; (601) 894-2642
    FAX
Letson E. Easterling, Sr., President
Pub. *Easterling Family Newsletter*,
    quarterly
$15.00 per year membership, $150.00
    life membership; reunion and annual
    membership meeting in August or
    September

Eastham (see Richardson)

Eastlick (see Easlick)

Eastman
*Eastman Family Reunion
PO Box 147
Nashotah, WI 53058-0147
Phone (414) 646-8183
Susan M. Hopfensperger

Eastwood
Judson Eastwood Family Database
1411 West 995 North
Lake Village, IN 46349
Phone (219) 992-3579
Ruth Studer

Easty (see Towne)

Eaton (see Goodenow, MacDuff,
    Nelson)

Eaton
Eaton Embers
1500 N.W. 18th
Oklahoma City, OK 73106
Gerald Hoover
Pub. *Eaton Embers*, quarterly, $5.50 per
    year subscription

Eaves
Eaves/Eves Family Organization
112 East Hanna Street
Tampa, FL 33604
Doris Barnes
(includes descendants of Jon Eaves, from
    England to Virginia 1636, and related
    families: Barlette, Berryman, Justice,
    Davis, Dyer, Lee, Lewis, Graves,
    Hampton, Pruit, Yancey, etc.)
$7.00 per year membership; reunion
    during the first week of August

Eaves
*The National Eaves Family Association
902 Antlers Drive
Sumter, SC 29150
Phone (803) 469-8383
James M. Eaves, Eaves Family
    Genealogist
Pub. *Newsletter*, three times per year;
    (includes descendants of Jon Eaves
    who immigrated to Virginia in 1636,
    especially through his son William)
$7.00 per year membership; annual
    reunion

Eayers (see Ayers)

Ebbott
*Ebbott Database
409 Birchwood Avenue
White Bear Lake, MN 55110
Elizabeth Adams Ebbott, Publisher
(includes Ebbott family worldwide,
    especially the family known to have
    originated in Cornwall with
    descendants in the U.S., Canada,
    Australia, New Zealand and South
    Africa)

Echols (see Futral)

Eck (see Dietwiler)

Eck
Eck Family Newsletter
520 Forrest Avenue
Lodi, CA 95240
Shirley E. Buirch
Pub. *Eck Family Newsletter (der
    Familien-name Eck)*, quarterly, $7.00
    per year subscription

Eck
Eck Family Newsletter
PO Box 13548
Saint Louis, MO 63138

Maryann Schirker
Pub. *Eck Family Newsletter*, quarterly,
    $25.00 per year subscription

Eckerson (see Ackerson)

Eckhart (see Kunkel)

Eckstein (see Dietlein)

Eddens
The Eddens Family Association
Rt. 8, Box 99
Florence, AL 35630
Phone (205) 766-9652
Frank Lee Eddens,Jr.

Edds (see Eads)

Edds (see Eads)

Eddy (see Dooley)

Eddy
*Eddy Family Association
PO Box 354
Duxbury, MA 02331
Phone (617) 934-6058 (Executive
    Secretary and Editor); (203) 666-9833
    (Genealogist)
Sylvia Breck, Executive Secretary and
    Editor; Mac Desmond, Genealogist
Pub. *The Eddy Family Association
    Bulletin*, annually
$2.00 per year associate membership,
    $5.00 per year supporting membership,
    $25.00 per year sustaining
    membership, $100.00 life membership

Eddy
*Eddy Homestead
Middleborough, MA 02346
Thomas A. C. Eddy
Pub. *Eddy Homestead*, semiannually

Edelen (see Rutherford)

Edelen
Edelen Family Association
PO Box 3304
Shreveport, LA 71103
Mildred L. Watkins, Editor
Pub. *Edelen Family Newsletter*,
    bimonthly

Edenfield
Edenfield Genealogical Society
PO Box 6996
Warner Robins, GA 31095
Paul A. Edenfield, Editor
Pub. *Edenfield Genealogical Society
    Newsletter* (includes descendants of
    David Edenfield (1761–1856),
    Revolutionary soldier from South
    Carolina, and Elizabeth Apstan (1769–
    1859), settled in Emanuel County,
    Georgia, after the Revolution)

Ederington (see Ethington)

Edes (see Eads)

Edgar (see Maxwell)

Edgar
*Edgar Clearing House
HC 3, Box 3400
Boss, MO 65440
Loeta Crews
(includes Edgar and Edger, all times, all
    places)

Edge (see Hall)

Edgecombe (see Blossom Press)

Edgerton (see Hammond)

Edick (see Meigs)

Edison (see Eidson)

Edler
Edler-Morosini Newsletter
12402 Woodthorpe Lane
Houston, TX 77024-4109
Phone (713) 461-7437
Avis Moore Rupert, Editor
Pub. *Edler-Morosini Newsletter*,
    semiannually, $3.00 per year
    subscription; (includes descendants of
    Hermann Joseph Edler (1821–1892)
    from Hesse-Kassel in 1846, and his
    wife Christina Jahraus (1827–1896)
    from Baden; also Napoleon Victor
    Morosini (1808–1849) from Italy, and
    his wife Marie Madeleine Kobloth
    (1808–1905) of Obernai, France)

Edmiston (see Edmondson)

Edmonds (see Hyatt)

Edmonson
*The Edmondson Family Association
4747 Westminster Circle
Eagan, MN 55122-2756
Oran David Edmonson
Pub. *Edmondson Family Association
    Bulletin*, quarterly (January, April, July
    and October); (includes any of 13
    spellings: Edmundson, Edmiston,
    Edmonston, etc.)
$6.00 per year membership

Edmonston (see Edmondson)

Edmunds
Edmunds' Newsletter
4246 32nd Avenue, South
Minneapolis, MN 55406
Jann Marie Foster
Pub. *Edmunds' Newsletter*, three times
    per year (March, July and November),
    $10.00 per year subscription

Edmundson (see Edmondson, Lynch)

Ednie (see MacDuff)

Edny (see MacDuff)

Edrington (see Ethington)

Edson (see Eidson, Packard)

Edson
*Edson Genealogical Association
1309 Lulu Street
Trenton, MO 64683-1816
E-mail: EGA9@aol.com
Gene Edson
Pub. *Edsonian: Journal of the Edson
    Genealogical Association*, quarterly,
    with annual index
$12.00 per year regular membership,
    $5.00 per year library membership,
    $6.00 per year junior membership,
    $25.00 per year promotional
    membership, $50.00 per year donor
    membership, $100.00 per year patron
    membership

Edward (see Goodenow)

Edwards (see Folk Family Surname
    Exchange, Bosher, Kunkel, Newton,
    Riggle)

Edwards
*Edwards Family Association
935 Countryside Drive, Apartment #103
Palatine, IL 60067-1927
Phone (847) 776-1848
H. Harvey Barfield, III
Pub. *The Edwards Family Historical
    Review*, quarterly, $10.00 per year
    subscription; (specifically those
    Edwardses and their descendants who
    either resided in Ashe County, North
    Carolina, and Grayson County,
    Virginia, in the late 1700s or who
    migrated to Clay County, Illinois, by
    way of Lawrence County and Owen
    County, Indiana, during the early
    1800s)

Edwards
Conley Publications
PO Box 2617
Laurel, MD 20708
Elaine Nelson, Editor
Pub. *The Edwards Journal*, quarterly,
    $12.00 per year subscription

Edwards
*John Edwards (Canadian) Family
    Organization
412 Main Street
Acton, MA 01720
Phone (617) 263-8259
Judith Wetherbee Peterson

Edwards
*Kinseeker Publications
5697 Old Maple Trail
PO Box 184
Grawn, MI 49637
E-mail: AB064@taverse.lib.mi.us
Victoria Wilson, Editor

Pub. *The Family Series: Edwards*, irregularly, $6.50 per year subscription

Edwards
*Edwards Family History
202 South Segoe Road
Madison, WI 53705-4939
Phone (608) 233-1506
Donald E. and Ruth A. Duxbury, Compilers/Publishers
(includes ancestors and descendants of John and Anne (Tabb) Edwards of Cornwall, England, and Wisconsin Territory from 1679)

Eeds (see Eads)

Eells
*The Eells Family Association
35 Townsend Street
Walton, NY 13856
Phone (607) 865-5686
Dr. Walter E. Eells, Editor
Pub. *The Eells Family Association Bulletin*, quarterly; (includes Ells)
$15.00 per year membership, $150.00 life membership

Egard (see Storrs)

Egelston
Egelston/Eggleston Families
Rt. 1, Box 127A
Hazelhurst, MS 39083
Jim Eggleston Haddock

Egerton
*Egerton/Calvert Family Database
10743 Harding Road
Laurel, MD 20723-1288
Phone (301) 725-1624
Lawrence T. Fadner
(includes descendants of Maryland Lords Baltimore only)

Eggert
*Eggert Surname Organization
2413-B Burleson Court
Austin, TX 78741-5603
Phone (512) 462-3951
Gerald O. Eggert

Eggleston (see Egelston)

Eggleston
*Eggleston Surname File
1454 Goldrush Avenue
Melbourne, FL 32940
Phone (407) 242-9318
Elsie Ernst Treadwell

Egle (see Eagle)

Egli (see Eagle)

Egnor (see Eygner)

Eibl
*Eibl Surname Organization
41 Pineview Lane
Boulder, CO 80302-9414

Phone (303) 705-0702
Rudolph J. Dichtl

Eichelberger (see Boose)

Eichelman
Eichelman Clan Diggers Association
1212 North Taylor
Little Rock, AR 72205
Phone (501) 663-0886
Carol Ann Eichelman, Head Clan Digger
(includes Eickelman, Eickelmann, Ikelman and Ikelmann)

Eichen (see Lemon)

Eichler (see Aldrich)

Eichton (see Heath)

Eickelman (see Eichelman)

Eickelmann (see Eichelman)

Eidson
*The Eidson Newsletter
607 West Columbia
Weatherford, TX 76086
Phone (817) 594-4740
Mrs. Jack L. Eidson, Editor
Pub. *The Eidson Newsletter*, semiannually, $5.00 per year subscription; (includes Itson, Hitson, Hittson, Edson, Edison)

Eikenberry (see Frantz)

Eiman (see Einman)

Einman
Einman, Eiman, Eyman, Iman, One Man's Family
1724 Greer Drive, West
Newark, OH 43055-1457
Ronna Eyman Eagle
Pub. *Einman, Eiman, Eyman, Iman, One Man's Family*, quarterly, $12.00 per year subscription

Eipper
*Eipper Family Reunion
150 North Main
Lombard, IL 60148
Phone (708) 627-1421
Florence Eipper Stout, Editor
Pub. *The Eipper Kin-ship*, free
Donation for membership

Eirich (see Irick)

Eirich
Eirich (Eyerich/Irick) Family Association
1024 Apollo Way
Sacramento, CA 95822-1709
Phone (916) 448-1030
Donnadeane D. Depew

Eirryn (see Irwin)

Eirven (see Irwin)

Eirvin (see Irwin)

Eirving (see Irwin)

Eirvyn (see Irwin)

Eirwin (see Irwin)

Eisenhauer
*Eisenhauer-Bowersox-Kline Family Reunion Association
195 Eloise Drive
Benton Harbor, MI 49022
Phone (616) 926-8156
Donald J. Stuck, Secretary-Historian
Pub. *Annual Newsletter and Reunion Announcement*, annually (June or July), free; (includes families from Snyder County, Pennsylvania and Michigan, etc.)
Donation for membership

Eisenstadt (see Israelite)

Eisloeffel
*Eisloeffel Family Reunion
5108 Concordia Road
Belleville, IL 62223
Phone (618) 277-7005
Marsden Eisloeffel
Pub. *Eisloeffel Family Newsletter*, once or twice per year, probably $5.00 per year subscription; (includes descendants of Johann Karl Eisenlöffel, who married Marie Margaretha Lutzky in Mandel, Southwest Germany, on 16 November 1811, and came to the U.S. with five children in 1843)
Reunion about every three years at various locations throughout the south and midwest

Ekes
Henry Ekes Family Reunion
212 North Cumberland Street
Metairie, LA 70003
Bobby Henriques

Elam (see Nickels)

Elam
Elam-Ellams, Helem, Alim Family Association
2306 Westgate
Houston, TX 77019
Phone (713) 529-2333
Harold Helm
$25.00 plus pedigree and family group sheets

Elbert (see Montague)

Elder (see Anthes)

Elder
Elder Family Newsletter
4320 Alden Drive
Indianapolis, IN 46241
Christine Elder

Pub. *Elder Family Newsletter*, quarterly, $6.00 per year subscription

Elder
*Elder Family Newsletter
PO Box 340
Hancock, MD 21750-0340
Phone (301) 678-6999; E-mail: fanfare@intrepid.net
Donna Younkin Logan, Publisher
Pub. *Elder Family Newsletter*, quarterly, $15.00 per year subscription; (includes all Elder families prior to the 1900s, in the U.S. and abroad)

Elder
Elder Family Homecoming
4603 Oakcliffe Road
Greensboro, NC 27406
James W. Elder

Elder
*Genealogy of the Elder Clan
1636 Utah Avenue
San Angelo, TX 76904
Phone (915) 942-9499
Lee M. Elder
(includes over 45,000 names in database: Elder, Cox, Cunningham, Hundley, Sockwell and Weatherford)

Eldred (see Adams)

Eldredge (see McCune)

Eldridge (see Buell)

Eldridge
Eldridge Family Organization
4521 Saviers Road
Oxnard, CA 93033
Phone (805) 483-1227
Florence Eldridge
Annual reunion at Lake Lopez, CA

Eldridge
*Descendants of Levi Eldridge (1806–1877) and Allied Families
PO Box 54736
Cincinnati, OH 45254-0736
Vicki M. Watkins, Publisher
(includes descendants of Levi Eldridge (Virginia–) of southeastern Kentucky)

Eler (see Eller)

Elett (see Elliott)

Elford (see Bradley)

Eliot (see Elliott)

Eliott (see Elliott)

Elkins
The Elkins Eagle
Rt. 1, Box 123A
Buffalo, TX 75831
Phone (214) 322-5462
Clovis Byars Herring

Pub. *The Elkins Eagle*, quarterly, $15.00 per year subscription

Ellams (see Elam)

Ellar (see Eller)

Elledge (see Rutherford)

Ellen Payne Odom Genealogy Library (see Multi-family Associations)

Eller
William Alexander Eller Family Association
PO Box 36
Rockwell, NC 28138
Mrs. Jordan

Eller
*The Eller Family Association
Rt. 2, Box 145-D
Whittier, NC 28789
Phone (704) 586-8844
Dr. J. Gerald Eller, Editor
Pub. *The Eller Chronicles*, quarterly (February, May, August and November); (includes Eler, Ellar, Ellor, Ohler)
$15.00 per year membership; biennial conference the third week of July in odd-numbered years

Elles (see Ellis)

Ellet (see Elliott)

Ellett
*Ellett Family
(Rt. 2, Bertram, TX—location)
PO Box 45 (mailing address)
Burnet, TX 78611
Phone (512) 756-4452
Jessie Ellett
(includes descendants of John Vinson Ellett and Elizabeth Warden Ellett, 1873 Burnet County, 1870 Sherman, Texas, earlier Pennsylvania; John and Jane Elliott (Ellett) of Collin County, Texas, 1843 (Peter's Colony); also Davis, Elliott, Estepp, Gibbs, Ousley, Ray, Warden and others)

Ellice (see Ellis)

Elliet (see Elliott)

Elliff (see Ellis)

Elliff
*The Elliff Families Centennial Reunion
RR 1, Box 460-A
Dewey, OK 74029-9770
Phone (918) 534-1672
Kenneth Mickelson, Publisher
(includes descendants of John Elliff (1735–1800) and Charity Garrett who were married circa 1770 in Chowan County, North Carolina)

Elliot (see Elliott)

Elliot
Elliot Clan Society, U.S.A.
3200 Habersham Road, N.W.
Atlanta, GA 30305
Phone (404) 233-1883
James Elliott, Jr., President

Elliott (see Cian, Ellett, Lambert, Saye, Warren)

Elliott
Elliott Reunion (Descendants of Comfort and Martha)
991 Leisure World
Mesa, AZ 85206-2444
Loren S. Elliott

Elliott
Elliott Family Quarterly
2190 Camino Largo Drive
Chino Hills, CA 91709
Trish Elliott Collins
Pub. *Elliott Family Quarterly*, $14.00 per year subscription

Elliott
Elliott Clearinghouse
62 Peony Street, S.W.
Grand Rapids, MI 49508
Sandra J. Elliott
Pub. *Elliott Empire*, quarterly, $10.00 per year subscription; (includes Aliot, Alyot, de Aliot, Elett, Eliot, Eliott, Ellet, Elliet, Elliot, Ellot, Elott, Elyot, Elyotte, Eyllyott and Lelliott)

Elliott
Elliott Clan Association
7100 Friendly Road
Guilford College, NC 27410
A. Elliott

Elliott
*Elliott 'n' Kin
815 Hartsook Boulevard
Roanoke, VA 24014-4321
Phone (540) 427-1535
John Burrows, Editor
Pub. *Elliott 'n' Kin*, quarterly (February, May, August and November), $11.00 per year subscription (calendar year), $16.00 per year foreign subscription; (for all Elliotts, all spellings, everywhere)

Ellis (see Brooks, Corson, Graves, Holden, Likes, Macpherson, MacPherson, Millet)

Ellis
Ellis Family Researcher
8941 Balboa Road
Northridge, CA 91325
Gretchen Martin
Pub. *Ellis Inquiries*, quarterly, $10.00 per year subscription

Ellis
Ellis
6626 South 76 E Avenue
Tulsa, OK 74133
Jack E. Westbrook
Pub. *Ellis*, irregularly, no charge

Ellis
*Ellis Cousins Nationwide
1201 Maple Street
Friona, TX 79035
Phone (806) 247-3053
Bill and Carol Ellis, Co-editors
Pub. *The Ellis Cousins Newsletter*,
quarterly (January, April, July and
October), $16.00 per year subscription
in the U.S., $19.00 per year
subscription outside the U.S., annual
index $4.00; (includes all Elles, Allis,
Ellice, Elliff families in the U.S. and
Canada)

Ellison (see Macpherson, MacPherson)

Ellor (see Eller)

Ellot (see Elliott)

Ells (see Eells)

Ellzey (see Elsey)

Elmer (see McCune)

Elmo
Elmo-Elmore-Ahwahka-Helmo Family
Association
2306 Westgate
Houston, TX 77019
Phone (713) 529-2333
Harold Helm
$25.00 plus pedigree and family group
sheets

Elmore (see Elmo, Emery)

Elmwood (see Pricer)

Elott (see Elliott)

Elrod (see Scott)

Elsbree
*Ephraim Elsbree Family Association
2330 259th Avenue, N.E.
Redmond, WA 98053-9009
Phone (206) 836-8110; E-mail:
elsbree@msn.com
John E. Elsbree

Elsea (see Elsey)

Elsebuch
Elsebuch/Broderson Association and
Affiliated Family
5356 Hillmont Avenue
Los Angeles, CA 90041
Phone (213) 257-1014
Marie E. Northrup

Elsey
*Elsey Family Association
1566 Lejeune Avenue
Lincoln Park, MI 48146-2141
Carol Elsey, Vice President and
Librarian; Stella Mercer, Director and
Acting Editor
Pub. *Elsey Echoes*, quarterly, $10.00 per
year subscription, free queries;
(includes various spellings: Elzey,
Elsea, Ellzey, Elza, Elzea, etc.)

Elston (see Blossom Press)

Elswick
Elswick Family Association
Rt. 2, Box 302 A
Staunton, VA 24401
Rev. A. Elswick

Elvain (see MacBean)

Elvaine (see MacBean)

Elvane (see MacBean)

Elvayne (see MacBean)

Elveen (see MacBean)

Elverson (see Welch)

Elwain (see MacBean)

Elwane (see MacBean)

Elwayne (see MacBean)

Elwee (see MacBean)

Elwell (see Lush)

Elwood
Elwood Echoes
West 5917 Crosscut Road
Deer Park, WA 99006
Phone (509) 276-2550
Margaret Burdega
Pub. *Elwood Echoes*, irregularly, $6.00
plus $1.25 postage and handling per
volume

Ely (see MacDuff)

Ely
*Lorania Ely Family Organization
PO Box 171
Douglas City, CA 96024
Phone (916) 778-3136
Paul Jones

Elyot (see Elliott)

Elyotte (see Elliott)

Elza (see Elsey)

Elzea (see Elsey)

Elzey (see Elsey)

Emanuel
*Emanuel Family Genealogy
213 Mill Stream Drive
Huntsville, AL 35806
Phone (205) 837-7487
Garvin Emanuel, Family Genealogist
(includes Emmanuel, Manuel)

Emde
Emde Family Organization
5600 Dorrell Lane
Las Vegas, NV 89106
Phone (702) 645-9024
Patricia Hall Emde

Emerer (see Emery)

Emerich (see Emerick)

Emerich
By the Name of Emerich
6870 Mad River Road
Dayton, OH 45459
Kenneth D. Hains
Pub. *By the Name of Emerich*

Emerick
The Ohio Connection
PO Box 14296
Dayton, OH 45413-0296
Phone (513) 436-2990
Ann Fenley
Pub. *Emerick Family Newsletter*,
quarterly, $16.00 per year subscription,
back issues $17.00 per year, $6.00 per
issue; (Amick, Emerich, Emick, Emig,
Emmerich, Emmerick, Emrich and
Emrick)

Emerson (see Corson, Heath)

Emerson
*English Roots of the Haverhill and
Ipswich Emersons
115 Warner Avenue
Roslyn Heights, NY 11577
Phone (516) 671-5454
Ralph S. Emerson, M.D., Editor

Emery (see Collum, Goodenow, Heath)

Emery
Eugene Emery Senior Organization
Star Route Box 19
Albion, ID 83311
Phone (208) 673-5356
Dorothy Clark
(includes family of Eugene and Ida Gray
Emery, also Hunter and Kniskern
surnames)
Biennial reunion in odd-numbered years

Emery
*Futral Genealogy Trails
#6 Wonderland Lane
Carthage, TN 37030
Jenny Futral, Entrepreneur
(includes research on Emery-Brown-
Hollon (not Holland)-Drake, with
allied lines: Allen, Anderson,

Appleton, Brannan, Chapman, Elmore, Langford, McCullough, Millwayne, Morgan, Mosely, Pope, Rambo, Rawls, Sturdivant, Summers, Turner and Wilson; also John Benge, third husband of Quatie (nee Nancy) Conrad, who previously married Alexander Brown and Archibald Fields)

Emfield
*Emfield Historical Society
4628 Sawtooth Lane
Chubbuck, ID 83202-2637
Phone (208) 238-0135
Eric Karl Emfield, Editor
Pub. *Emfield Historical Society Newsletter*, semiannually, free; (includes Empfield, Endfield, Infield and phonetic variations)

Emick (see Emerick)

Emig (see Emerick)

Emmanuel (see Emanuel)

Emmanuel
Emmanuel Bulletin
3605 Lakewood Road, N.W.
Huntsville, AL 35801
Mr. Emmanuel
Pub. *Emmanuel Bulletin*

Emmerich (see Emerick)

Emmerick (see Emerick)

Emmert
Emmert Family Association
1613 Rutledge Street
Madison, WI 53704
Nancy Emmert

Emory (see Emery)

Empfield (see Emfield)

Emrich (see Emerick)

Emrick (see Emerick)

Ems (see Ames)

Endfield (see Emfield)

Endries
Endries Family Reunion
11 West Barbie Rand Boulevard
Hilbert, WI 54129
Mary Liebzeit
(includes descendants of Joseph and Anna Endries)

Engel (see Stoner)

Engelbrecht (see Sager)

Engelmann
*Engelmann-Hilgard Family Association
"Sandcastle"
1 Sac Street
PO Box C
Frankfort, MI 49635-1119
Phone (616) 352-5097
Mary E. Armstrong, Family Historian
(includes descendants of Friedrich Theodor Engelmann (1779–1854) and Elizabeth Kipp (Illinois), and Erasmus Theodor Engelmann (1730–1802) and Anna Margaretha Hartmann (1742–1825) (Bacharach, Germany))
Annual meeting and picnic on the second Saturday of June at the family cemetery in Shiloh Valley, Illinois

Engie (see Smith)

Englar (see Stoner)

Engle (see Stanton)

English (see Bassett, Garner, Newmyer)

English
*English Family Association
731 Firing Center Road
Yakima, WA 98901
Phone (509) 248-3672
Bette Schlagel Rogers, Family Historian/ Reunion Organizer
(includes descendants of William English from Ireland to Ontario, Canada, before 1822; family to Wisconsin and Washington State)
Reunion

Engren (see Nelson)

Engstrom (see McCune)

Ennis (see Innes)

Enoch (see Friend)

Enrick (see Gunn)

Enslee (see Inslee)

Ensley (see Inslee)

Ensminger
*Ensminger Families of Alsace and America
702 Irving Avenue
Royal Oak, MI 48067-2879
Phone (810) 543-3065; E-mail: an563Wdetroit.freenet.org; Website: http://www.geocities.com/Paris/1947/ and http://www.grfn.org/
Brendan Wehrung, Secretary
(includes Ensminger of Waldnambach and Diemeringen)

Enterline (see Wert)

Entriken (see Way)

Eorvin (see Irwin)

Eorwine (see Irwin)

Epperson (see Apperson)

Epps (see MacFaddien)

Erbine (see Irwin)

Ercke (see Cian)

Erdweins (see Erdwins)

Erdwins
*Erdwins Reunited
Rt. 3, Box 190
Concordia, MO 64020-9505
Phone (816) 463-7523
Mrs. Buddy Samuels, Compiler
(includes descendants of Henry William Erwins (Erdweins) and Anna Meyer (1820–1900) of Breman, Germany, and Royal, Illinois; also Minnesota, Iowa, Missouri, Kansas, Nebraska, California, Oklahoma and Florida; related families of Fruehling, Hess, Hutton and others)
Share of reunion expenses, submission of photos and family history; reunion on the first Sunday of June at Sedalia Steakhouse

Erenvine (see Irwin)

Erenwine (see Irwin)

Erevein (see Irwin)

Erevin (see Irwin)

Erevine (see Irwin)

Erewynis (see Irwin)

Erickson (see Lush)

Erin (see Irwin)

Erin-Feine (see Irwin)

Erinfeiner (see Irwin)

Erin-Veine (see Irwin)

Erinvine (see Irwin)

Erisman (see Hawbaker)

Eriveen (see Irwin)

Eriven (see Irwin)

Erivin (see Irwin)

Ernest (see Earnest)

Ernsberger (see Arnsparger)

Ernsperger (see Arnsparger)

Ernwine (see Irwin)

Erouard (see Heroy)

Erroll (see Hay)

Errvin (see Irwin)

Errving (see Irwin)

Erskine (see Gregor, MacDuff)

Eruing (see Irwin)

Eruini (see Irwin)

Ervan (see Irwin)

Erven (see Irwin)

Ervening (see Irwin)

Ervens (see Irwin)

Ervewin (see Irwin)

Ervien (see Irwin)

Ervin (see Irwin)

Ervine (see Irwin)

Erving (see Irwin)

Ervinge (see Irwin)

Ervington (see Irwin)

Ervinlet (see Irwin)

Ervinlott (see Irwin)

Ervinne (see Irwin)

Ervinton (see Irwin)

Ervion (see Irwin)

Ervwin (see Irwin)

Ervwyn (see Irwin)

Erwane (see Irwin)

Erwein (see Irwin)

Erweng (see Irwin)

Erwin (see Irwin, Wigelius)

Erwin
*Issac Erwin Family Organization
James and Agnes Erwin Family
 Organization
c/o Guardian Angels
391 Trolley Square
Salt Lake City, UT 84102
Phone (801) 521-6248
Nita Kemsley

Erwine (see Irwin)

Erwing (see Irwin)

Erwinn (see Irwin)

Erwinne (see Irwin)

Erwins (see Erdwins, Irwin)

Erwinski (see Irwin)

Erwinss (see Irwin)

Erwvin (see Irwin)

Erwyn (see Irwin)

Erwyne (see Irwin)

Eryvine (see Irwin)

Eryvino (see Irwin)

Eryvinus (see Irwin)

Eryvyne (see Irwin)

Erywen (see Irwin)

Esbank (see Graham)

Esch
Esch Estates
4140 South Fitzner Road
Greenville, MI 48838
Phone (616) 754-7404
Elda Esch Dickinson

Eshbach (see Likes)

Eshelman (see CTC Family Association)

Eskridge (see Stevens)

Eslick (see Easlick)

Essary (see Jay)

Esson (see Shaw)

Estell (see Folk Family Surname
 Exchange)

Estep (see Bugbee)

Estep
*Estep Family Association
12206 Brisbane Avenue
Dallas, TX 75234-6528
Phone (214) 241-2739;
 (214) 620-1416 FAX
Nova A. Lemons, Historian and Editor
Pub. *Estep Family Journal*, quarterly;
 (includes Eastep)
$10.00 per calendar year membership

Estepp (see Ellett)

Esterholdt (see McCune)

Estes
*Estes Surname Organization
56 Chestnut
Wayne, NJ 07470
Phone (201) 694-8723
Lucille Dillinger Alexander

Estey (see Towne)

Estey
*Estey Family Reunion Association
6835 Fisher Road
Ontario, NY 14519-9709
Phone (315) 524-8394
James F. Roome, Historian and
 Genealogist
Annual meeting since 1909

Esty (see Towne)

Etchingham (see Van Trump)

Etchison
Etchison/Eytcheson/Atchison Family
 Organization
2905 North Kilbourne
East Chicago, IL 60647
June B. Barekman
Pub. *Etchison Family Newsletter*

Etheredge (see Carpenter)

Etherington (see Ethington)

Etling (see Bevier)

Etling
*Etling Clearinghouse
1605 Holly
Gering, NE 69341
Phone (308) 436-5617
Shirley Weihing

Eton
The Francis Eton Society
60 Sheridan Street
Brockton, MA 02402-2852
James Hoban, Genealogist

Etter (see Newton)

Eubank (see Bosher)

Eubanks (see Folk Family Surname
 Exchange)

Euervinus (see Irwin)

Eurich (see Irick)

Eurini (see Irwin)

Eurwings (see Irwin)

Eustace (see Cian)

Evans (see Ashley, Brown, Carpenter,
 Heath, Layman, McCune, Newton,
 Pessner)

Evans
Evans-Erwin Family Reunion
1315 S.E. 18th Terrace
Cape Coral, FL 33904
Lillian Stewart

Evans
*Evans Surname Organization
Daniel Evans Family Organization
1013 Rudy Avenue
Mattoon, IL 61938
Phone (217) 234-7753
Ruby Overmyer Heldman

Evans
Evans Ancestors
1112 Greentree Court
Lexington, KY 40502
Gwen B. Tippie and Gwendolyn Garrison
Pub. *Evans Ancestors*

Evans
Evans Ancestory
Rt. 2, Box 280
Sheldon, MO 64784
Wilma Lathrop
Pub. *Evans Ancestory*, three times per
    year, $13.50 per year subscription

Evans
*John Morgan Evans of Merthyr Tydfil
Rt. 1, 260 Meadow View Drive
Butte, MT 59701
Phone (406) 494-3066
Robert Evans

Evans
*Henry George Evans 1831–1906
PO Box 105
Joplin, MT 59531
Barbara Cady
(includes wives Anna Ramsey, Missouri
    Pool, Amelia Bethke, Henrietta Bethke
    and their families)
Reunion

Evans
*International Genealogical Exchange
    Service
Surname Linking
67 Emerald Street, #403
Keene, NH 03431-3626
Richard C. Evans, Sr., Researcher
(emphasis on John and Robert Evans, ca
    1630, Dover, New Hampshire)

Evans
*Seagull Productions
West 1818 Nora
Spokane, WA 99205
Phone (509) 326-6066
Nancy Cummings Smith
Pub. *Everything Evans*, irregularly, $5.00
    per issue plus $1.00 postage

Evanson
*Evanson/Knudsen Family Organization
John Henry Evenson Family
    Organization
2941 South Palmetto Circle
Saint George, UT 84770

Phone (801) 628-0215
Nephi N. Evenson

Everett
Claude Everett and Lillie Sellers Family
    Organization
3419 West 80th Avenue
Anchorage, AK 99502
Phone (907) 243-4502
Mrs. D. L. Sherwood, Genealogist
Pub. *Everett Journal*, annually; (includes
    Sellers and Witham)
$15.00 per year membership

Everhart (see The Memorial Foundation
    of the Germanna Colonies)

Eves (see Eaves)

Evitt
Family Histories
270 Iven Avenue, 2-C
Saint David's, PA 19087
Phone (610) 293-0365
Thomas Jack Hockett
(Virginia and other locations: Evitt,
    Helton, McNew (also Maryland);
    White/Wight (Maryland/Virginia);
    Broady (Virginia); Snead (Virginia);
    Jackson (Virginia/Tennessee/Kentucky/
    North Carolina); Hunt)

Ewell
*The Ewell Family National Historical
    and Genealogical Society
3654 West 3965 South
West Valley City, UT 84120
Phone (801) 968-9976
VaLene Ewell Collings, President

Ewen (see Holden, Rutherford)

Ewen
Ewen Clan Society
413 N.W. 48th Street
Oklahoma City, OK 73118
Michael Ewen

Ewing (see Underwood)

Ewing
*Kinseeker Publications
5697 Old Maple Trail
PO Box 184
Grawn, MI 49637
E-mail: AB064@taverse.lib.mi.us
Victoria Wilson, Editor
Pub. *Ewing Exchange*, quarterly, $10.00
    per year subscription

Exum
*Exum Family Exchange
40607 Highway 50 East
Pueblo, CO 81006-9322
Phone (719) 948-4481
June M. Hatton, Founder
Pub. *Exum Exchange (includes Acum,
    Axson, Axum, Exunn, etc.)*, quarterly

Exunn (see Exum)

Eyanson (see Premm)

Eyerich (see Eirich)

Eyerin (see Fleck)

Eygner
Eygner Family Association (Agner/
    Aignor/Egner/Egnor)
21 Locust Drive
Rt. 1, Box 212X
Lake Valhalla
Cold Spring, NY 10516
Phone (914) 265-2373
Ms. Roberta Stanulewich Schwartz,
    Family Representative
Pub. *The Eygner Eagle*, semiannually,
    $2.50 per issue
$10.00 per year membership

Eyllyott (see Elliott)

Eyman (see Einman)

Eytcheson (see Etchison)

Ezell
Ezell Family Organization
Rt. 6, Box 233
McAlester, OK 74501
Nancy Culhane Ezell

Faatz
Faatz Family Association
2143 Blair Street
Salt Lake City, UT 84115
Joye Cummings, Family Representative

Fabiano (see Blossom Press)

Fabul'a (see Fabula)

Fabula
Fabula Family Newsletter
5497 Coral Reef Avenue
La Jolla, CA 92037
Phone (619) 270-1333
Andrew G. Fabula
Pub. *Fabula Family Newsletter*,
    semiannually, free to contributors;
    (includes Fabulya and Fabul'a)

Fabulya (see Fabula)

Face
*Face Family of America
12517 Petersburg Street
Chester, VA 23831
Phone (804) 748-2414
Edward J. Face

Fadner
*Fadner/Bovee/Trever Family Database
10743 Harding Road
Laurel, MD 20723-1288
Phone (301) 725-1624
Lawrence T. Fadner

(database of more than 16,000 names, including ancestors and descendants Samuel Finley Breese Morse, the inventor of the telegraph, and associated family names of Breese, Colgate and Griswold; separate database for John Moss (later changed to Morse), including family name, Bayard)

Fagan
Fagan Clan Flyer
PO Box 26095
San Diego, CA 92196
Phone (619) 566-0148
Michael R. Fagan
Pub. *Fagan Clan Flyer*, irregularly; (includes descendants of Michael Fagan, immigrant)

Fagan
*Fagan/Feagin/Fagon Family Association
7 Pleasant Court
Kirkwood, MO 63122-3936
Nancy H. Ragsdale, Vice President and Genealogist
(includes descendants of Patrick Fagan/ Feagin and families of Ohio-Missouri, Indiana, etc. 1700s, New Jersey-South Carolina-Alabama to the present, also Fagin)

Fagan
Fagan Reunion
17205 S.W. Johnson
Beaverton, OR 97006
Nancy Havill
(includes descendants of John Fagan and Mary Ann Morgan, of Tangent, Linn County, Oregon)

Fagen (see Detering)

Fagin (see Fagan)

Fagon (see Fagan)

Faherty (see Harting)

Fahler (see Fehler)

Fahrney
*The Fahrney Re-Union Association
8507 Mapleville Road
Boonsboro, MD 21713-1844
Phone (301) 663-3516
Omer M. Long, Historian
(includes descendants of Dr. Peter Fahrney (1767–1837) of San Mar, Maryland)
Annual reunion on the second Saturday of August at Fahrney Keedy Memorial Home for the Aged, San Mar, Maryland

Failor (see Fehler)

Fair (see Boose, Pharr, Ross)

Fairbanks (see Barnard)

Fairbanks
*Fairbanks Family in America
511 East Street
Dedham, MA 01026-3060
Phone (617) 326-1170
Clarence or Betty Buckley, Curators
Pub. *The Homestead Courier*, quarterly; (includes descendants of Jonathan and Grace Fairbanks of Dedham, Massachusetts)
$20.00 per year membership, $500.00 life membership; annual reunion on the third Saturday of August in odd-numbered years, and on the third Saturday of July in even-numbered years

Fairbanks
Fairbanks
2209 Second Street
White Bear Lake, MN 55110
Jo Emerson
Pub. *Fairbanks*, quarterly, $12.00 per year subscription

Fairfax (see Covert)

Fairfield (see MacDuff)

Fairfoul (see MacDuff)

Fairfull (see MacDuff)

Fairrington (see Farrington)

Faith (see Arthur)

Fajfer
*Fajfer Surname Organization
199 Commodore Drive
Milledgeville, GA 31061
Phone (912) 968-7425
Richard Bialac

Falconburg
Falconburg Family Association
518 South Albany
Yuma, CO 80759
Mrs. H. J. Falconburg, Family Representative

Falconer (see Keith)

Faler (see Fehler)

Falk (see Drone)

Falkenburg (see Van Valkenburg)

Falkenburgh (see Van Valkenburg)

Falkner (see Friend)

Falor (see Fehler)

Falvey (see Devine)

Fambrough
Fambrough Family Society
133 S.E. Graham Street
Port Charlotte, FL 33952
Mary Fambrough

Fambrough
Fambrough Family Society of America
4411 Ram Court
Houston, TX 77072
Jean Moritz, Publicity
Pub. *Newsletter*
$5.00 per year membership plus $3.00 for the first year

Family Publications
*Family Publications
PO Box 463
Auburn, ME 04212-0463
Phone (207) 783-1378
William Patrick Cartmel, Director
Pub. *Family Pictorial and Biographical* (a series featuring a different surname each issue: Brown, Davis/Davison/ Davidson, Johnson, Jones, Martin, Miller, Smith, Williams/Williamson)

Fancher
Fancher Exchange
Rt. 2
Taluga, OK 73167
Mary Briggs

Fanckboner (see Fangboner)

Fangboner
*Fangboner/Fanckboner/Fankboner Family Association
121 North Howard
Croswell, MI 48422
Phone (810) 679-3176
Michael Jackson, President/Archivist

Fankboner (see Fangboner)

Fankhauser
*Fankhauser-Funkhouser Family Association of America
PO Box 284
Haviland, KS 67059
Phone (316) 862-5310
Lloyd L. Fankhouser
Pub. *Newsletter of the Fankhauser-Funkhouser Family Association of America*, three times per year (January, May and September); (includes descendants of Hans zum Fanghus (ca 1375) of Trub-Fankhaus, Canton of Bern, Switzerland, also Frankhouser variant spelling)
$3.00 per year membership

Farac (see Blossom Press)

Farefull (see MacDuff)

Farlow (see Anthes)

Farmer (see Dockery, Loop, MacDuff)

Farnes
*Farnes Isacke Shackleton Association
1451 South Main Street
Bountiful, UT 84010-5135
Barbara F. Nebeker
(includes descendants of John Burnside
    Fanres and Ann Isacke, John
    Shackleton and Susanah Isace)

Farnworth
*George Farnworth Family Organization
136 South 3000 West
West Point, UT 84015
Phone (801) 773-5891
Joy Timbrel, Family Researcher
(includes descendants of George
    Farnworth (1818 Landrethum le Nord,
    Pas-de-Calais, France–) and his wife,
    Susanna Coates (1836 Chesterfield,
    Derby, England–))
Annual reunion in July

Farquarson
*The Clan Farquarson Society
Rt. 1, Box 59
Cape Girardeau, MO 63701
Rev. Fred H. Faughn, Newsletter Editor
Pub. *The Cairn*, bimonthly
$12.00 per year membership for
    individuals, $15.00 per year
    membership for families, $10.00 per
    year honorary membership

Farquharson (see Chattan, MacDuff)

Farr (see Pharr)

Farr
*Winslow Farr Sr., Family Organization,
    Inc.
26561 Campesino
Mission Viejo, CA 92691
Phone (714) 582-1852; (714) 348-9586
    FAX
David J. Farr, President
Pub. *Newsletter*, semiannually (June and
    January); (includes descendants of
    Winslow Farr (1794 New Hampshire–
    1865 Utah) and Olive Hovey Freeman)
$15.00 per year membership; reunion in
    Utah

Farr
*Julius E. Farr Family Organization
301 Las Flores Avenue
Modesto, CA 95354
Phone (209) 523-3634
Mileta Farr Kilroy, Family Historian and
    Secretary
Pub. *Newsletter*, annually
Occasional reunions

Farr
*Pioneer Publication
PO Box 1179
Tum Tum, WA 99034-1179
Phone (509) 276-9841
Shirley Penna-Oakes
Pub. *Farr Footnotes*, irregularly, $6.00
    per issue plus $1.75 postage for 1–3
    books, 50¢ for each additional book

Farrar (see Album)

Farrell (see Clark)

Farrelly
Farrelly Family Association
808 Jaydee Avenue
Baltimore, MD 21222
Richard J. Farrelly

Farren (see Ferrin)

Farrington
*Farrington Families of the South
13822 Methuen Green
Dallas, TX 75240-5829
Phone (214) 690-1312
Margaret F. Jagmin, Publisher
(includes Farrington, Fearington,
    Fairrington families in North Carolina,
    South Carolina, Tennessee,
    Mississippi, Texas, Indiana, Oklahoma,
    Illinois, Arkansas, Virginia and
    Missouri, and allied lines of Bryant
    (Illinois, Missouri, Texas), Dalchau-
    Lehmberg-Trott (Alabama, Texas),
    Gross, Le Gros and Groce
    (Pennsylvania, North Carolina,
    Kentucky, others), Graham (North
    Carolina, Missouri), Lord (Illinois,
    Nebraska, Texas), Jagmin (Poland,
    Lithuania, Wisconsin, Texas), Morgan
    (Torquay, England, Texas, Missouri),
    Smith and Telford-Lott (North
    Carolina, South Carolina, Mississippi,
    Texas), Swaim (Pennsylvania, North
    Carolina, others), Taylor (New York,
    Pennsylvania, North Carolina) and
    Whittemore (New York, Mississippi,
    Wisconsin, Texas) families)

Farris (see Album, Lemon)

Farrow (see The Memorial Foundation
    of the Germanna Colonies, Gotham)

Farver
Farver/Arter Family Organization
171 North Risket Road
Bayport, MI 48720
Helen Wichert

Fast
Fast Family Reunion (Descendants of
    Nicklaus Fast)
831 County Road 40
Nova, OH 44859
Richard Fox

Faught
Faught Findings
950 Maison Drive, Apartment 122
Athens, GA 30605-3150
Don Fortner
Pub. *Faught Findings*, quarterly, $3.00
    per year subscription

Faulconer
*Faulconer Family History
5200 Oakborne Drive
Kettering, OH 45440

Phone (513) 439-2029
James G. Faulconer

Fauler (see Fowler)

Faulkner (see Barnard, Forkner)

Faupel
*Faupel Family
1009 Burlington Beach Road
Valparaiso, IN 46383
Phone (219) 462-6661
Armida Sharpin

Faure (see Fore)

Faust (see Foust, McCune)

Faust
*FAust/FOust Family and Allied
    Families
3982 Trotwood Drive
Lake Havasu City, AZ 86406
Phone (520) 680-6257
Donald Judson Foust, President
Pub. *FAust/FOust Family Forum:
    Preserving and Printing Genealogy
    and History For Future Generations*,
    quarterly, $20.00 per year membership

Fautz (see Foust)

Favorite (see Boose)

Favour (see Corson)

Fawsler
Fawsler Family Organization
6475 Warner Street
Allendale, MI 49401
Robert Fawsler

Fay (see Wright)

Fay
Oak Leaf Publishing
22 Creek Road, #64
Irvine, CA 91714
Pub. *Fay Family Newsletter*, bimonthly,
    $10.00 per year subscription

Fazio (see Toronto)

Feagin (see Fagan)

Feake (see Alsop)

Fear (see Ross)

Fearing
*Fearing Surname Organization
John Fearing Family Organization
558 Little Piney Island Drive
Fernandina Beach, FL 32034
Phone (904) 277-3536
Jeri James
Donation for membership

Fearington (see Farrington)

Fearn (see Ross)

Feathers (see MacDuff)

Featherston (see MacDuff)

Featherston
Featherston Findings
227 Maryhill Road, Lot 10
Pineville, LA 71360-4168
Joyce Featherston Hawkins
Pub. *Featherston Findings*, irregularly,
  $7.50 per issue

Featherstone (see Hutchison, MacDuff)

Featherstone
The Featherstone Families
7911 Yancey Drive
Falls Church, VA 22042
Phone (202) 736-1726
Gene Hyden, Editor
Pub. *The Featherstone Families*,
  quarterly, $12.00 per year subscription

Feavaugh (see Corson)

Febus (see Archer)

Fechter (see Dietwiler)

Federith (see Sutherland)

Fee (see MacDuffee, Macfie)

Feeback
Feeback Folks
20015 Mullen Road
Belton, MO 64012
Suzanne Grimes
Pub. *Feeback Folks*

Feeney (see McCanna)

Fehler
Fehler/Failor/Falor/Fahler Clearinghouse
8118 Whitsett Avenue
North Hollywood, CA 91605
H. M. Ball
Pub. *Fehler Newsletter* (Falor, Faler,
  Failor, Fetler, etc.)

Feitler (see Bentheim)

Felbrigg (see Philbrick)

Feldie (see MacDuff)

Feldy (see MacDuff)

Felps (see Phelps)

Felten (see CTC Family Association)

Feltl (see McLouth)

Felton
*Felton Family Association, Est. 1988
7791 Macleay Road, S.E.
Salem, OR 97301

Phone (503) 370-9028
Cora Felton Anderson, Family Historian
Pub. *Felton Family Association
  Newsletter*, bimonthly; (includes
  descendants of Nathaniel Felton who
  came to Salem, Massachusetts, in
  1633, and of Richard Felton who came
  to the Virginia/Georgia area in 1670)
$10.00 per year membership for
  individuals, $15.00 per year
  membership for families, $250.00 life
  membership

Felts (see Phelps)

Felty
*Felty (Feltz, Veltz, Velty, Valentine)
  Family
335 West Shackley Street
PO Box 75
Geneva, IN 46740
Phone (219) 368-7352
Ruth Brown
(includes descendants of William
  Christian Felty (1848 Fairfield County,
  Ohio–1906 Adams County, Indiana)
  and Sarah Walker; and Charles Felty)

Feltz (see Felty)

Fendley (see Scott)

Fenex (see Fenix)

Fenix (see Helm)

Fenix
Fenix-Fenex-Phoenix-Fenwick Family
  Association
2306 Westgate
Houston, TX 77019
Phone (713) 529-2333
Harold Helm
$25.00 plus pedigree and family group
  sheets membership

Fenniger (see Place)

Fenstermaker
Fenstermaker/Cypherts Family
  Association
4223 Hackett Avenue
Lakewood, CA 90713
Roy Fenstermaker
Pub. *Fenstermaker News Notes*, quarterly
$3.00 per year membership

Fenton
The F.I.G. Tree News
718 Kensington Lane
Mansfield, TX 76063-2819
Leslie E. Fenton, Editor
Pub. *The F.I.G. (Fenton International
  Genealogy) Tree News*, quarterly,
  donation for subscription

Fenwick (see Fenix)

Feree (see Free)

Fergie (see Fergusson)

Fergus (see Fergusson)

Fergushill (see Fergusson)

Ferguson (see Folk Family Surname
  Exchange, Bloss, Carpenter, Frasher,
  Jackson, Rodgers)

Ferguson
*George Cochran Ferguson Family
  Organization
2620 Forrest Court
Fremont, CA 94536-5233
Phone (510) 796-5978
Wayne S. Ferguson, President
(includes descendants of George Cochran
  Ferguson (1824 Airdrie, Lanark,
  Scotland–), who was married in 1850
  in London, Middlesex, England, to
  Elizabeth Batten (1830 Plymouth,
  Devon, England–))
Costs vary with type of membership

Ferguson
Fragments: Ferguson
419 North Larchmont Boulevard, Suite
  277
Los Angeles, CA 90004
Pub. *Fragments: Ferguson*, bimonthly,
  $12.00 per year subscription

Ferguson
*Kinseeker Publications
5697 Old Maple Trail
PO Box 184
Grawn, MI 49637
E-mail: AB064@taverse.lib.mi.us
Victoria Wilson, Editor
Pub. *Ferguson Files*, quarterly, $10.00
  per year subscription

Ferguson
*Ferguson Family History
8529 Spalding Drive
Richmond, VA 23229
Phone (804) 741-1836
B. DeRoy Beale

Fergussill (see Fergusson)

Fergusson
*Clan Fergusson Society of North
  America
151 Pine Forest Drive
Lawrenceville, GA 30245-6029
Phone (770) 963-5432
Kathryn F. Henneberg
Pub. *The Bee Line*, semiannually;
  (includes Fergie, Fergus, Fergushill,
  Fergussill, Ferrie, Ferries, Ferris,
  Forgan, Forgie, Grevsack, Hardie,
  Hardy, Keddie, Keddle, Ketchen, Kidd,
  Kiddie, Kydd, MacAdie, MacCade,
  MacErries, MacFergus,
  MacFhearghuis, MacFirries,
  MacHerries, MacInlay, MacIrish,
  MacKeddie, MacKerras, MacKersey,
  MacKestan, MacMagnus, MacTavert)

$20.00 per year membership, $10.00
initiation fee

Ferner (see Verner)

Fernie (see MacDuff)

Ferny (see MacDuff)

Fero (see Fiero)

Ferrell
*Ferrell Surname Organization
7818 North Matanzas Street
Tampa, FL 33614
Phone (813) 935-4338
Rosalie Ferrell Jaszczak

Ferren (see Ferrin)

Ferrie (see Fergusson)

Ferries (see Fergusson)

Ferrin
Ferrin-Farren-Ferren
PO Box 40002
Tucson, AZ 85717
Pub. *Ferrin-Farren-Ferren* (includes
   descendants of Capt. Jonathan Farren),
   three times per year, $15.00 per year
   subscription

Ferrin
The Ferrin Family Newsletter
3857 South 3660 West
West Valley City, UT 84120
Phone (801) 967-0392
Michael J. Ferrin, Secretary/Treasurer
Pub. *The Ferrin Family Newsletter*, once
   or twice per year, $10.00 per year
   subscription; (includes Farren, Ferren)

Ferris (see Fergusson, Hatfield,
   McCune)

Ferriss
*Zachariah Ferriss Family Organization
711 Kensington Avenue
Flint, MI 48503
Phone (313) 234-8574
Phyllis S. Kitson
Pub. *Zachariah Ferriss Chronicles*,
   monthly, free; (includes descendants of
   Zachariah Ferriss (–1710) and Sarah
   Blood Ferriss)

Ferry
*Ferry Family History Association
4065 Berrywood Drive
Eugene, OR 97404-4061
James R. Brann, Family Representative
(PAF™ data bank on MAC™ computer
   includes County Donegal, Ireland, to
   U.S.)
Free information exchange

Ferson (see MacPherson)

Fesmire
Fesmire Family Association
PO Box 212
McComb, MS 39648
Alice Khalid

Fessler (see Gross)

Fetler (see Fehler)

Fetro (see Hoster)

Fetterhoff (see Wert)

Fetters (see MacDuff)

Fick (see The Memorial Foundation of
   the Germanna Colonies)

Fickling (see Hughes)

Fidkin
*John Fidkin Family Organization
45 East 500 North
Salt Lake City, UT 84103
Phone (801) 363-3272
Paul A. Hanks
(database includes Fidkin from 1600 to
   the present in England and the U.S.)

Field (see Folk Family Surname
   Exchange, Fields, Rutherford)

Fields (see Folk Family Surname
   Exchange, Emery)

Fields
Fields Family Findings
4740 Roosevelt Avenue
Sacramento, CA 95820-4522
Mary A. Thomas, Editor
Pub. *Fields Family Findings*, quarterly,
   $20.00 per year subscription; (includes
   Field and Fields)

Fiero
Fiero/Fero Family Association
2534 Rambling Court
Vienna, VA 22180
Phone (703) 938-3158
Patricia Shank, Genealogist

Fife (see Heath, MacDuff)

Fife
*Randolph Wilson Fife Family
   Organization
819 College Avenue
Norman, OK 73069
Phone (405) 321-4361
James D Fife, President
Pub. *The R. W. Fife Family Letter*,
   bimonthly

Fike (see Hopkin)

Filbee (see Filby)

Filbey (see Filby)

Filbrick (see Philbrick)

Filbrun (see Frantz)

Filby
Filby Newsletter
PO Box 413
Savage, MD 20763-0413
Phone (301) 792-7051
P. William Filby, Editor
Pub. *Filby Newsletter*, irregularly,
   donation for subscription; (includes
   Filbee, Filbey and Philby)

Filby
Filby-Filbey-Filbee Philby Family
301 East Meyer Boulevard
Kansas City, MO 64113

Fillingame (see Fillingim)

Fillingham (see Fillingim)

Fillingim
Fillingim-Fullingim-Fillingame-
   Fillingham Exchange
PO Box 636
Janesville, CA 96114-0636
Wendy Dolphay

Fillmore (see Newton)

Fimpel
Fimpel/Fimple Family Factor
6503 Darby Way Road
Spring, TX 77389
Mrs. Joyce Bagley

Fimple (see Fimpel, Rowe)

Fimreite (see Velline)

Fincham (see Finchum)

Finchum
*Finchum/Fincham/Flinchum Families
278 West 870 North
Logan, UT 84321
Phone (801) 753-8233
Willis Arnold Finchum
Pub. *Fincham/Flinchum/Finchum
   Newsletter*, annually, donation for
   subscription

Finck (see Surname Database, Kinney)

Finder (see The Memorial Foundation of
   the Germanna Colonies)

Findley (see Putman)

Fine (see Phillips)

Fine
Fine Lines
1836 North Kibby Road
Merced, CA 95340-9335
Phone (209) 722-4717
Betty McCollum Padilla, Editor

Pub. *Fine Lines*, quarterly, $5.00 per year subscription; (includes Fine, Fines families and descendants)

Finefrock
Finefrock Clearinghouse
28411 59th Avenue, South
Kent, WA 98032
Phone (206) 852-4557
Carolle Berry

Fines (see Fine)

Finger (see Folk Family Surname Exchange)

Fingry (see Graham)

Finical (see Kunkel)

Fink (see Surname Database, Hoster, McKee)

Finks (see The Memorial Foundation of the Germanna Colonies)

Finley
Finley Findings International
PO Box 314
Wynne, AR 72396-0314
Timothy John Kessler
Pub. *Finley Findings International*, bimonthly, $20.00 per year subscription; (includes Finlay, Findlay)

Finnell
*Finnell Database
3917 Heritage Hills Drive, #104
Bloomington, MN 55437-2626
Arthur Louis Finnell

Finnerty
*Finnerty Family
1600 Century Avenue
Odessa, TX 79762
Phone (915) 362-6290
Ruthelle Harrison Finnerty

Finney
*John Finney Family Organization
1819 Severn Hill Lane
Severn, MD 21144
Bruce and Diane Phinney

Finnick (see MacDuff)

Finnock (see MacDuff)

Firman (see Reeder)

Firmin (see Johnson, Nelson)

Fischbach (see Lemon)

Fischer (see Cole, Fisher)

Fischer
Fischers of Los Angeles County Family Association
PO Box 460
Livermore, CA 94550
T. Reitter

Fish (see Hicks, Possien)

Fish
*Lauri-Lines
South 2827 Ivory
Spokane, WA 99203
Phone (509) 624-0533
Laurine Mae Palmerton Logsdon
Pub. *Fish Families—Records and Lines*, irregularly, $6.00 plus $1.75 postage and handling ($2.75 foreign postage and handling), (Washington state residents add 63¢ tax)

Fishbach (see The Memorial Foundation of the Germanna Colonies)

Fishback (see The Memorial Foundation of the Germanna Colonies)

Fishel (see Hoster)

Fisher (see The Memorial Foundation of the Germanna Colonies, McCune, Nell, Nettles, Stoner)

Fisher
Fisher Facts
6059 Emery Street
Riverside, CA 92509
Betty L. Pennington
Pub. *Fisher Facts*, quarterly, $6.00 per year subscription

Fisher
Charles Fisher and Mary Harris and Eliz. Claybaugh Fisher Family Organization
Benjamin Fisher and Fodena Royce Family Organization
PO Box 954
Ketchum, ID 83340
B. Higbee

Fisher
*Frederick Joseph and Mary Ann (Triplett) Fisher Family Reunion
Rt. 1, Box 64
Worden, MT 59088
Phone (406) 967-4723
Shirley Fisher, Family Historian

Fisher
Fisher Family Reunion
PO Box 236
Underwood, ND 58576
M. Brown

Fisher
Fisher Families
3960-E German Road
Kettle Falls, WA 99141-9402
Phone (509) 738-6731
Susan Gallyon Dechant

Pub. *Fisher Families*, irregularly; $7.00 postpaid per issue; (includes Fischer and Visser)

Fisk
*Ancestors and Progeny of Hiram Fisk(e) and Diantha Russell
1123 North Myers Street
Burbank, CA 91506-1214
Phone (818) 848-2855
Martha S. Hutchins, Publisher

Fisk
*Fisk(e) Family Association
2215 Anderson
Manhattan, KS 66502
Elaine Fisk Baxter, Secretary
Pub. *Fisk(e) Family Association*, usually once or twice per year
$9.00 per year membership (includes two issues)

Fisk
*Fisk Family Organization
33 N.E. 25th Street, Apartment 1
Wilton Manors, FL 33305
David C. Crankshaw
Pub. *Fisk Family Flyer*, annually; (includes descendants of Solomon Fisk (1773–1857); database on PAF™)

Fiske (see Surname Sources, Barnard, Fisk, Woodrow)

Fitch (see Cian)

Fitch
*Descendants of Rev. James Fitch, 1622–1702
4 Canal Park, #712
Cambridge, MA 02141
Phone (617) 494-4882
John T. Fitch

Fitch
*Fitch Family Collection
1387 Emery Street
Salt Lake City, UT 84104
Phone (801) 972-2341
Patricia M. Geisler
(includes much information from colonial period to mid-1800s)

Fite (see The Memorial Foundation of the Germanna Colonies)

Fite
*Fite Database
2525 Nantucket, #4
Houston, TX 77057
Phone (713) 782-1557; (713) 782-0231 FAX; E-mail: cfbn41a@prodigy.com or PFite16816@aol.com
Pat Fite

Fitts
Fitts/Fitz/Fittz Project
51 North Main Street
Newmarket, NH 03857
Phone (603) 659-3652
Sylvia Fitts Getchell

Fittz (see Fitts)

Fitz (see Fitts)

Fitzgerald (see Bryan)

Fitzgerald
*John Morgan Fitzgerald Family
    Organization
2586 Dillard Road
Bowling Green, KY 42104
Phone (502) 781-6427
Judith Anne Gover Waddell

Fitzhugh
*Fitzhugh Surname Organization
1616 Sheridan Road #2E
Wilmette, IL 60091
Phone (847) 853-0133
Robert Fitzhugh Steinhoff
(includes family of Colonel William
    Fitzhugh)

Fitzpatrick (see Cian)

Fitzwater
*Fitzwater Database
70 Ridgecrest Road
Kentfield, CA 94904-2746
Phone (415) 924-4040; E-mail:
    cdgg47a@prodigy.com
Mary Cole
(includes descendants of Thomas
    Fitzwater (–1699 Philadelphia,
    Pennsylvania) and Mary Cheney (–on
    the *Welcome*))

Fitzwater
Fitzwater Family Organization
Rt. 9, Box 1320
Bucyrus, MO 65444
George Fitzwater

Fivecoat (see Chaney)

Flack (see Rutherford)

Flagg
*Flagg Genealogical Collection
357 Red Fox Trail
Rock Hill, SC 29730
Phone (803) 324-8606
Sharon Nowery
Pub. *Flagg Family Newsletter*, quarterly,
    free

Flake
*Descendants of Adam Flake Reunion
Rt. 3, Box 106
Franklin, IN 46131
Phone (317) 878-4793
Jeanne Short

Flanary (see Stone)

Flanders (see Heath)

Flanigan
*Thomas Flanigan Family Organization
13174 South 5700 West
Herriman, UT 84065
Phone (801) 254-6140
Mrs. Jackie F. Robinson
(includes Emanuel Flanigan, ca 1785,
    Ireland)

Flaningam (see Flanningham)

Flannery (see Waterous)

Flanningham
*George Flanningham Family
    Organization
3227 East Stewart Road, Rt. 10
Midland, MI 48640
Phone (517) 835-3227
Mr. Ora Ley Flaningam
Pub. *Flaningam Descendants Newsletter*,
    annually, free; (includes descendants of
    Patrick (1680–1713) and Elizabeth
    (1680–1765) Flanningham, and George
    (1711–1770) and Sarah Jennings
    (1720–1767) Flaningam)

Flatt
Flatt Family Organization
Rural Delivery, Rt. 550
PO Box 143
Warriors Mark, PA 16877
Phone (814) 632-3680; (814) 684-2884
Beverly Flatt Getz

Flatt
*Flatt Surname Organization
1015 East 2050 North
North Logan, UT 84341
Phone (801) 752-8439
Legrand E. Reeder

Flattery (see Cian)

Flavin (see Baker)

Fleck
*Fleck Family Descendants
9746-61 Avenue, South
Seattle, WA 98118
Phone (206) 722-8771
Lorraine J. Fleck McQuade
(includes descendants of Josephus Fleck
    (ca 1731–1779 Wingen, Alsace,
    France) and first wife, Catherine
    Barbara Eyerin (–1757))

Fleetwood (see Sullivan Surname
    Exchange)

Fleig
*Fleig Family Reunion
1627 Highway 1
Fairfield, IA 52556-8947
Phone (515) 472-2363
Charlotte M. Fleig
Pub. *Fleig Newsletter*, annually, free to
    members
Donation for membership; annual
    reunion on the third Saturday of July
    in Rubio, Washington County, Iowa

Fleischer (see Flesher)

Fleisher (see Flesher)

Fleming (see Folk Family Surname
    Exchange, McCune, Murray)

Flemming (see Wiese)

Flender (see The Memorial Foundation
    of the Germanna Colonies)

Flerey (see Flora)

Flescher (see Flesher)

Fleshman (see The Memorial
    Foundation of the Germanna Colonies)

Fletcher (see Goodenow, Gregor,
    Williams)

Fletcher
Fletcher Family Research Bulletin
627 Polk 412
Mena, AR 71953
Marilyn Bridge Brown, Editor
Pub. *Fletcher Family Research Bulletin*,
    quarterly, $15.00 per year subscription

Fletcher
Fletcher Family Association
5151 Burning Tree Circle
Stuart, FL 34997
Ewin Fletcher

Fletcher
*Fletcher/Wilson/Hindman Family
    Organization
1132 North Tela Drive
Oklahoma City, OK 73127-4308
Phone (405) 789-2842
Pauline Carlton Fletcher, Secretary and
    Genealogist
(computer database uses Quinsept™,
    PAF™ and Reunion™)
Annual reunion

Fleure (see Flora)

Fleuree (see Flora)

Fleurey (see Flora)

Fleurie (see Flora)

Fleury (see Flora)

Flewellen (see Llewellyn)

Flickinger (see Dopp)

Fligg (see Joy)

Flinchum (see Finchum)

Flint (see Clark, Corson, Flynt)

Flippen (see Flippin)

Flippin
Flippin-Bumgarner Family Organization
112 North Harrill
Wagoner, OK 74467
Mable Flippin

Flippin
*Flippin Family Association
12206 Brisbane Avenue
Dallas, TX 75234-6528
Phone (214) 241-2739; (214) 620-1416
  FAX
Nova A. Lemons, Historian and Editor
Pub. *Flipping Flippins*, quarterly
  (February, May, August and
  November); (includes Flippen and
  Flipping)
$15.00 per calendar year membership

Flipping (see Flippin)

Flisk (see MacDuff)

Fliske (see MacDuff)

Flockhart (see MacDuff)

Flockhert (see MacDuff)

Flohri (see Flora)

Flood (see Cian)

Flood
*Nall News Publishing Company
PO Box 2186
Willingboro, NJ 08046-2186
Josephine Crittenberger-Nall, Editor-
  Publisher
Pub. *Flood Families*, quarterly, $16.00
  per year subscription

Floore (see Flora)

Flooree (see Flora)

Floorey (see Flora)

Flora (see Surname Sources, Frantz,
  Stoner)

Flora
Flora-Flory-Fleury Family Newsletter
300 Birch Street
Grandview, WA 98930-1328
Phone (509) 882-3973
Bill Flory, Editor
Pub. *Flora-Flory-Fleury Family
  Newsletter*, quarterly, $5.00 per year
  subscription; (includes descendants of
  Joseph Fleury (1682 Palatinate,
  Germany–1741 Lancaster,
  Pennsylvania) and wife, Mary;
  additional alternate spellings: Flerey,
  Fleure, Fleuree, Fleurey, Fleurie,
  Flohri, Floore, Flooree, Floorey,
  Florah, Floray, Florea, Florey, Flori,
  Floriey, Florin, Florry, Flouri, Flowrah,
  Flowry, Flurie and Flury)

Florah (see Flora)

Floray (see Flora)

Florea (see Flora)

Florey (see Flora)

Flori (see Flora)

Floriey (see Flora)

Florin (see Flora)

Florry (see Flora)

Flory (see Flora, Frantz, Stoner)

Flouri (see Flora)

Flower (see Donald)

Flowers
Flowers-Pieper-Jenett-Gilbert Family
  Association
2306 Westgate
Houston, TX 77019
Phone (713) 529-2333
Harold Helm
$25.00 plus pedigree and family group
  sheets membership

Flowrah (see Flora)

Flowry (see Flora)

Floyd
*Milton John Floyd Family Organization
8255 South Krameria Way
Englewood, CO 80112
Phone (303) 290-0998
Mr. Dana M. Floyd
Free membership

Flucker (see MacDuff)

Flurie (see Flora)

Flury (see Flora)

Flynn (see Griffin)

Flynn
*Nall News Publishing Company
PO Box 2186
Willingboro, NJ 08046-2186
Josephine Crittenberger-Nall, Editor-
  Publisher
Pub. *Flynn Flyer*, quarterly, $16.00 per
  year subscription

Flynt
Flynt-Flint
7 Northlake Road
Columbia, SC 29223-5909
Dorothy C. Flynt
Pub. *Flynt-Flint*, quarterly, $6.00 per
  year subscription

Foard (see Fore)

Fogel
Fogel/Fogle Clearinghouse
Rt. 1, Box 192
Monmouth, IL 61462
James E. and Sharon L. Todd

Fogle (see Fogel)

Fogleman
*Fogleman Surname Organization
3 Brazill Lane
Whitehall, MT 59759
Phone (406) 287-3369
Lindia Roggia Lovshin

Fogler (see Payson)

Folcord (see Heath)

Folds
Folds Family Association
109 Oak Way Street
Eatonton, GA 31024
Phone (706) 485-6810
E. V. Knight, Jr.

Foley
Foley Findings
1720 Santa Maria Place
Orlando, FL 32806
Phone (407) 894-6895
Loretta Fiebrandt
Pub. *Foley Findings*, quarterly (June,
  August, November and March), $20.00
  per year subscription; (includes entire
  U.S. to the present)

Foley
*Foley Family Researchers
210 East 21st Street
Oak Grove, MO 64075
Phone (816) 690-3490
Everett W. Johnson
Pub. *Yearly Reunion Newsletter*
  (restricted to descendants of Capt.
  Richard B. Foley (1819–1881), son of
  James (1796–1859 Mercer County,
  West Virginia) and Judith (Thomas)
  Foley of Patrick County, Virginia, and
  Capt. Richard's wife, Parshandatha
  McAlexander, of Patrick County,
  Virginia, to Mercer County, West
  Virginia, about 1853; also descendants
  of Rosa Bell Foley Brammer, daughter
  of Richard Foley; also Johnsons from
  the same area)
Reunion

Folg (see The Memorial Foundation of
  the Germanna Colonies)

Follett (see Brown)

Folsom
Folsom Family Association
4000 Larkston Drive
Charlotte, NC 28226
Pub. *Folsom Family Association Annual
  Report*

Foltz (see Surname Database)

Fontain (see Fontaine)

Fontaine (see Folk Family Surname Exchange, Johnson)

Fontaine
*Folk Family
PO Box 52048
Knoxville, TN 37950-2048
Hester E. Stockton, Owner; Mary Anne Fontaine, Editor
Pub. *Fontaine Families*, quarterly, $15.00 per year subscription, $5.00 per issue; (includes Fontain, Fountain)

Fontenelle (see Blossom Press)

Fontenot (see Johnson)

Fonvielle (see Fonville)

Fonville
Fonville Family Findings
1937 South Main Street
Orem, UT 84058-7409
Phone (801) 225-7218
Judith W. Hansen, Editor
Pub. *Fonville Family Findings*, quarterly, $8.00 per year subscription; (includes all descendants of John Fonvielle (1672–1741), French Hugenot of Craven County, North Carolina)

Foos
Foos Family Association
PO Box 363
La Rue, OH 43332
Lea Foos Jenkins

Foote (see Surname Sources, Barnes, Foot, Wright)

Foote
*The Foote Family Association of America
12 Dutton Avenue
Fair Haven, VT 05743
Phone (802) 265-2021
Dorothy B. Offensend, Editor and Genealogist
Pub. *Footeprints*, quarterly; (includes descendants of any Foote)
$15.00 membership for two years

Foote
*The Foote Family Association of North America
22622 S.E. 47th Court
Issaquah, WA 98027
Phone (206) 392-7494
Helen Raid, President
Pub. *Footnotes*, three times per year
$10.00 per year membership

Forbes (see Folk Family Surname Exchange, Heath)

Forbes
*Clan Forbes Society
PO Box 1118
Alexandria, VA 22313
Murray Forbes, President; Ronald W. Pearson, Secretary/Treasurer
Pub. *Clan Forbes Newsletter*, quarterly; (includes septs: Bannerman, Berrie, Berry, Boyce, Boyes, Fordyce, Lumsden, Macouat, Macowat, MacQuattie, MacWatt, Mechie, Mekie, Meldrum, Michie, Middleton, Walter, Walters, Waters, Watson, Watt, Watters, Wattie, Watts)
$15.00 per year membership, $200.00 life membership

Forbey (see Forby)

Forby
*Forby Family History Society
12550 West Idaho Drive
Lakewood, CO 80228-3826
Phone (303) 988-3787
George Forby
(includes Forbey)
Triannual reunion

Ford (see Surname Sources, Barnard, Fore, Newton)

Fordney (see Fortney)

Fordred (see Cole)

Fordyce (see Forbes)

Fore
*Fore Reunion
PO Box 401
Midland, NC 28107
Bertie Fore Smith, President

Fore
*Fore Reunion
Rt. 1, Box 417
Charlotte Court House, VA 23923-9891
Phone (804) 248-5754
Rev. Cecil Robert Taylor, Founder, Publisher, Editor and Head of Reunion Committee
Pub. *Fore Front* (covers all Fores with roots in Virginia, also Foard, Ford, Foree, Forey, descendants of French Huguenots named Faure)
$12.95 per year subscription; annual reunion at the Beale Memorial Presbyterian Church Social Hall in Pamplin, Virginia

Foree (see Fore)

Foreman (see Johnson, Zebert)

Forest (see Corson, Douglas, Forrester, Johnson)

Forester (see Forrester)

Forester
Forester (Richardson, Roberts) Family Reunion
1008 Winged Foot Drive
Mitchellville, MD 20716
Kathy Mull, Secretary

Forey (see Fore)

Forgan (see Fergusson, MacDuff)

Forgey (see Reynolds)

Forgie (see Fergusson)

Forister (see Forrester)

Forkner
*Forkner Clan
2610 Yadon Road
Manhattan, MT 59741-8020
Phone (406) 284-3396
Mona Forkner Paulas
Pub. *Forkner Newsletter*, quarterly, $12.00 per year subscription; (includes Fortner and Faulkner)

Forman (see Johnson)

Forrest (see Forrester)

Forrest
Forrest Family Reunion
Rt. 2, Box 60
Poplar Bluff, MO 63901
Mrs. F. Baker

Forrester (see Douglas, MacBeth)

Forrester
Clan Forrester Society, Inc.
3070 Georgia Highway 81, S.W.
Loganville, GA 30249
Phone (404) 466-8134
E. Jerald Forrester, President
Pub. *Corstorphine Journal*, quarterly, $10.00 per year membership for individuals, $15.00 per year membership for families; (includes Forrister, Forester, Forister, Forster, Foster, Forrest, Forest, Carstarphen, etc.)

Forrester
Forrester Family Reunion
59 Roberts Street
Portland, ME 04102
Una Bentley

Forret (see MacDuff)

Forrister (see Forrester)

Forster (see Forrester)

Forster
*Forster Foster and their Royal Descendants
2625 North Sixth Street
Abilene, TX 79603-7259

Phone (915) 673-3918
Gerneva Foster Dennis, Publisher

Forsyth
Clan Forsyth of America, Inc.
4667 Dolphin Drive
Lake Worth, FL 33463
Phone (407) 439-5693
Percy G. Forsyth, President

Forsythe (see Newton)

Fortenberry (see Haynes)

Fortin (see Lagesse)

Fortinet (see Fortney)

Fortineux (see Fortney)

Fortna (see Fortney)

Fortner (see Forkner)

Fortney
*Fortney-Fortna Genealogy Family, Inc.
323 State Route 7
Coolville, OH 45723
E-mail: DeanM10529@aol.com
Dean L. McKnight, Editor
Pub. *The Fortineux Family News*
   (includes Fordney, Fortinet, Fortineux,
   Fortna, Fortney (which is most popular
   and numerous), Furtney, plus 32 other
   variant spellings)
$10.00 per year membership for
   individuals, $20.00 per year
   contributing membership, $25.00 per
   year sustaining membership; reunion

Fortunia (see Blossom Press)

Foshee
Foshee Families of America
PO Box 704
Platteville, CO 80651
Velma Lowman Foshee
Pub. *Foshee Families of America
   Newsletter*, quarterly
$10.00 per year membership

Foskett (see Goodenow)

Foss
*Foss Family Reunion
PO Box 664
Hanover, NH 03755
Phone (603) 643-5447
Connie Stiles, Genealogy Compiler
(includes descendants of John Foss
   (ca 1634–ca 1710) and Mary Berry
   (ca 1636–after 1710) of Rye, New
   Hampshire)
$5.00 per year membership for families
   living under one roof; annual reunion
   on the first Sunday after Labor Day at
   Camp Foss, Rt. 126, Strafford, New
   Hampshire

Foster (see CTC Family Association,
   Barnard, Cowart, Douglas, Forrester,
   Forster, Golding, Goodenow, Heath)

Foster
Foster
4604 Virginia Loop Road, Apartment
   3156-G
Montgomery, AL 36116-4739
Lisa R. Franklin
Pub. *Foster*, quarterly, $10.00 per year
   subscription

Foster
*Foster Family of Virginia
10012 Penfold Court
Potomac, MD 20854-2157
Patricia F. Elton, Author and Publisher
(includes John Yancey Foster of Hat
   Creek, Campbell County, Virginia)

Foster
*Foster/Bla(y)lock Family Organization
1132 North Tela Drive
Oklahoma City, OK 73127-4308
Phone (405) 789-2842
Pauline Carlton Fletcher, Secretary and
   Genealogist
(computer database uses Quinsept™,
   PAF™ and Reunion™)
Annual reunion

Fostert (see Dunham)

Fotheringham (see Lindsay)

Fountain (see Fontaine)

Fournier
*Fournier Family
PO Box 688
Goose Creek, SC 29445
Phone (803) 761-4904
Victor Paul Mertrud, Chief Researcher

Foust (see Faust)

Foust
*Foust/Faust/Fouts/Fautz Family
   Exchange
Rt. 1, Box 195
Williamsville, MO 63967
Phone (314) 998-2327
Gretta White, Researcher
$10.00 per year membership

Fouts (see Foust, Ray)

Fowler (see Folk Family Surname
   Exchange, Cowart, Phillips)

Fowler
*Kinseeker Publications
5697 Old Maple Trail
PO Box 184
Grawn, MI 49637
E-mail: AB064@taverse.lib.mi.us
Victoria Wilson, Editor
Pub. *The Family Series: Fowler*,
   irregularly, $6.50 per year subscription

Fowler
*Folk Family
PO Box 52048
Knoxville, TN 37950-2048
Hester E. Stockton, Owner; Martha E.
   Fowler, Editor
Pub. *Fowler Families*, quarterly, $15.00
   per year subscription, $5.00 per issue;
   (includes Fauler)

Fowlkes
*Bee Hive Press
1916 Maryland Parkway
Las Vegas, NV 89104-3106
Phone (702) 878-1742
Richard B. Taylor
(includes microfiche of records of
   Fowlkes, Belknap and the Taylor
   family of Lincolnshire, England)

Fox (see Anthes)

Fox
Fox Family Facts
PO Box 1035
North Highlands, CA 95660-1035
Phone (916) 991-4165
Sally Seaman Williams, Editor
Pub. *Fox Family Facts*, irregularly, $6.00
   per issue

Fox
*Fox Surname Organization
199 Commodore Drive
Milledgeville, GA 31061
Phone (912) 968-7425
Richard Bialac

Fox
*The Annual Fox/Smith Reunion
245 Inca Road
Industry, IL 61440
Phone (309) 254-3230
Barbara Black Lawyer
Annual reunion in June at the fire hall in
   Good Hope, McDonough County,
   Illinois

Frable
*Frable/Fravel Family Reunion
376 Valley Park South
Bethlehem, PA 18018
Phone (610) 867-0100
Ann C. Frabel, Genealogist
Annual reunion on the third Sunday of
   August at the West End Fairgrounds,
   off Route 209, Gilbert, Pennsylvania

Frady
Frady
4895 Cool Springs Drive
Reno, NV 89509
Steve Frady
Pub. *Frady*, three times per year,
   donation for subscription

Frakes (see Garner)

Frame
*Frame Database
Box 1299
Ellensburg, WA 98926-1299
Warren Louis "Tuck" Forsythe
(includes 500 to 1,000 pre-1830 Scribner
    descendants of Ohio and Pennsylvania)

Frampton (see Aldrich)

Franatovich (see Blossom Press)

France (see Stewart)

France
*Michael France Family Organization
56 Chestnut
Wayne, NJ 07470
Phone (201) 694-8723
Lucille Dillinger Alexander

Francis (see Clark, France, MacDuff,
    Stewart)

Francis
Francis Exchange
503 Morehead Street
Chadron, NE 69337-2540
Mary Osborn Hemmingsen
Pub. *Francis Exchange*, quarterly, $7.00
    per year subscription

Francisco (see Franciscus)

Francisco
Francisco Researcher
1454 Springleaf Circle, S.E.
Smyrna, GA 30080
Rick Dodds
Pub. *Francisco Researcher*, five times
    per year, $15.00 per year subscription;
    (includes Cisco, Sisko, Fransoy,
    Franciscuss, Franser, etc.)

Franciscus
*Franciscus Family Foundation
68 Ojeda Street
Condado, PR 00907
Phone (809) 728-7777;
    (809) 728-0715 FAX
John Allen Franciscus, President and
    Editor; Jan Johnson, Secretary
Pub. *O-US* (an update to the book *The
    House of Franciscus* and *A History of
    the United States According to
    Franciscus and Related Families*;
    includes descendants of Christophel
    Franciscus (1680 Germany–), arrived
    in Pennsylvania in 1710, Francisco and
    related families: Allen, Book/Buck,
    Grover, Jung/Young, La Farge,
    Lightner, Lindsay, Mullunphy,
    Ostertag, Simmons, Stoutzenberger,
    Taylor, Thompson, Wellman and
    Whitney found predominantly in
    Pennsylvania, Virginia, West Virginia,
    Kentucky, Tennessee, Missouri and
    Montana through the early to mid
    1800s)

Franicevich (see Blossom Press)

Frank (see The Memorial Foundation of
    the Germanna Colonies)

Frankhauser (see Movius)

Frankhouse (see Movius)

Frankhouser (see Fankhauser)

Franklin (see Brown, Collette,
    Cornelius, Miller, Mower)

Franklin
Franklin Fireplace
118 Fairview Avenue
Warrensburg, MO 64093
Betty Williams
Pub. *Franklin Fireplace*, quarterly, $7.00
    per year subscription

Franklin
Franklin Family Reunion
7755 S.W. 84th Avenue
Portland, OR 97223
Phone (503) 246-1617
Verlie L. Johnston
(includes descendants of Josiah Franklin
    (New Jersey or Delaware–) and Sarah
    Conner (West Virginia–), who arrived
    in Oregon in 1847)
Reunion

Franklin
*Franklin Family Researchers United
736 Dogwood Street
Jasper, TX 75951-5826
Elaine Franklin Giddens, Co-founder
Pub. *Franklin Family Researchers
    United*, quarterly (January, April, July
    and October), $6.00 per issue, free
    queries with Franklin connection
$20.00 per year membership

Franks (see Likes)

Franks
*Franks Clan Association
685 Morgantown Street
Uniontown, PA 15401
Phone (412) 438-2926
Ruth Franks, President

Franovich (see Blossom Press)

Franser (see Francisco)

Fransoy (see Francisco)

Frantz
*Frantz Database
PO Box 2076
Lancaster, CA 93539-2076
Phone (805) 949-6236
Lorraine Frantz Edwards
(includes over 32,000 Frantz and
    collateral lines, including descendants
    of immigrant Michael Fantz (1687–
    1748) and related surnames: Arnold,

Barnhart, Bashor, Bauman, Beachler,
Blickenstaff, Blocher, Boyd, Brovont,
Brubaker, Crill, Cripe, Crist,
Denlinger, Eikenberry, Filbrun, Flora,
Flory, Funderberg, Garber, Garst,
Grisso, Hamm, Heaston, Heck, Hirt,
Houtz, Hufford, Karns, King, Kinzie,
Landes, Lavy, Metzger, Miller, Montel,
Neff, Neher, Ohmart, Peters, Royer,
Shoup, Shull, Skiles, Snell,
Studebaker, Tridle, Ulery, Vaniman,
Wagoner, Wenger, Yoder and Zug)

Frantz
*(Matthias) Frantz Clan
40 Klahr Road
Bethel, PA 19507
Phone (717) 933-8238
Caleb Frantz, Liaison
(includes descendants of Christian
    Frantz, who emigrated from St. Jacobs
    Parish, Basel, Switzerland, 1732)
No membership fee

Frarey (see Frary)

Frary
*Frary Family Association
10615 Mosquero Drive
Port Richey, FL 34668-3034
Phone (813) 863-7815
Anne Frary Lepak, Historian/Genealogist
    and Compiler of *Frary Family
    Journal*; Grace L. Frary, Editor of
    Frary Family Newsletter
Pub. *Frary Family Newsletter*,
    semiannually; *Frary Family Journal*,
    biannually in odd-numbered years,
    (supplements of *Frary Family in
    America*); (includes Frary and Frarey
    descendants of John Frary (–1675) and
    wife Prudence Townsend (1601–1690/
    1), who came from Norwich, England,
    in 1637 and settled in Dedham and
    Medfield, Massachusetts)
$6.00 per year membership; biennial
    reunion in even-numbered years in
    Deerfield, Massachusetts

Fraser (see MacFaddien)

Fraser
*The Clan Fraser Society of North
    America
4268 Green Meadow Lane
Chico, CA 95973
Phone (916) 894-1111 (8:00-5:00 PST)
Gordon Fraser, Secretary
Pub. *Nessy*, semiannually; (includes
    Abernethy, Bisset, Brewster, Cowie,
    Frisell, Gilruth, Grewar, MacIlriach,
    MacTavish, Oliver, Simpson, Tweedie)
$20.00 per year membership

Frasher
*Frasher/Frazier Family History
4031 Grand Avenue
DeLand, FL 32720
Phone (904) 985-4046
Harry L. Sellards, Jr., Publisher

(includes descendants of Micajah Frasher and his wife Susan Hamilton; Joshua Davidson Frazier family from South Carolina and Tennessee; related families: Adkins, Akers, Alley, Bartram, Carter, Ferguson, Frasure, Lowe, Maynard, Napier, Perry, Smith, Thompson, Webb, Wellman and Wilson)

Frasure (see Frasher)

Frauenfelter (see Boose)

Fravel (see Frable)

Frawley
*Frawley Family History Association
4065 Berrywood Drive
Eugene, OR 97404-4061
James R. Brann, Family Representative
(PAF™ data bank on MAC™ computer includes County Clare, Ireland, to U.S.)
Free information exchange

Fray (see The Memorial Foundation of the Germanna Colonies)

Frazee (see Sidwell)

Frazee
John Frazee Family Organization
Rt. 3, Box 134
6644 Baker Road #47
Shelby, OH 44875
Phylis Hughes Frazee

Frazee
Frazee-Frazier Families/Queries
565 S.E. South Street
Pullman, WA 99163-2333
Marilu VonBargen
Pub. *Frazee-Frazier Families/Queries*

Frazer (see Frazier)

Frazier (see Frasher, Frazee)

Frazier
*Frazier Database
2802 North 32nd Place
Phoenix, AZ 85008-1237
Phone (602) 955-8345
Kent Davis Myrick
(database includes about 40,000 people, any spelling, time or place)

Frazier
*Frazier/Shockney/Zondervan/Swank Reunion
5007 West 14th Street
Speedway, IN 46224-6503
Phone (317) 243-0107
Elizabeth Swank Frazier

Frazier
*Frazier Research
PO Box 360
Anton, TX 79313
Phone (806) 997-2951

Wanda Frazier Harrell, Genealogist
(includes descendants of Richard Frazier and Wesley Chester)

Frazier
*The Harry Hugh Frazier Family Association
PO Box 1306
Seguin, TX 78156-1306
Theresa Frazier Crump
Pub. *Frazier Footnotes*, quarterly, queries accepted; (includes Frazier and related families of Duggan, Holmes, Simpson and Smith

Frazier
*Frazier Surname Organization
3037 Navajo Lane
Provo, UT 84604
Phone (801) 375-1516
Garth F. Frazier, Family Historian
(includes descendants of George Thomas Frazer (ca 1736 Scotland/North Carolina) or any Thomas Frazier who came to the southern states during the colonial period)

Frederic (see Blossom Press)

Frederick (see Blossom Press)

Frederick
*Frederick Surname Organization
Sebastian Frederick, Sr., Family Organization
17051 N.W. 29th Avenue
Miami, FL 33056
Phone (305) 621-8207
Beulah Compton Jackson
(includes descendants of Sebastian Frederick, Sr. (–1787), and wife Mary)

Frederick
Frederick Forerunners
3803 MacNicholas Avenue
Cincinnati, OH 45236
Phone (513) 791-2240; (513) 395-3509 Voice mail
Jean Nathan, Editor
Pub. *Frederick Forerunners*, quarterly (June, September, December and March), $10.00 per year subscription; (includes Frederick, Frederickson and various spellings)

Frederick
*David Frederick Family Organization
PO Box 425
Duchesne, UT 84021
Phone (801) 738-5340
Nellie P. Lang
(includes descendants of David Ira Frederick and Mary Ann Winner, married 1828)

Frederick
*Lineage Search Associates
7315 Colts Neck Road
Mechanicsville, VA 23111-4233

Phone (804) 730-7414 (8:00 A.M.–10:00 P.M.); (800) 728-1935;
E-mail: pollockme@aol.com
Michael E. Pollock, Editor
Pub. *Frederick Findings*, quarterly, $21.00 per year subscription

Frederickson (see Frederick)

Fredrickson (see Goodenow)

Free
*Free Database
45865 Michell Lane
Indio, CA 92201-3780
Helen Free VanderBeek
(deals exclusively with families from the South, Illinois, Idaho, California, or Utah)
$1.00 plus SASE for search

Free
Born Free
1247 Live Oak Boulevard
Yuba City, CA 95991
Patricia E. Gaither
Pub. *Born Free*, at least semiannually, $8.00 per year subscription; (Frei and Feree)

Free
Absalom Pennington Free Family Organization
152 North 130 East
Orem, UT 84057-5506
Eugene and Evelyn Gibbons
Pub. *Free Family News*

Freeborn
The Freeborn Family Organization
518 Alahmar Street
Alhambra, CA 91801

Freeland
Freeland and Allied Families
220 Fourth Street
Del Mar, CA 92014
Barney French Freeland
Pub. *The Freeland and Allied Families*, irregularly, $3.50 per issue

Freeland
*Freeland and Allied Families
5112 Huisache
Bellaire, TX 77401
Phone (713) 667-4190
Bernard R. Freeland, Publisher
(includes descendants of Jesse Engles Freeland (Greene County, Pennsylvania–), migrated to Marion County, West Virginia, during the Civil War, married Elmina Matilda Straight; also associated families, including foreign countries)

Freelove
*Freelove Surname Organization
Morris Freelove Family Organization
28253 Stillwater Drive
Menifee, CA 92584

Phone (909) 672-9488
Linda R. Freelove Arnold
(includes Freelove surname and
    descendants of Morris Freelove and
    Elizabeth Wilbore, who married 1680/
    81 Portsmouth, Rhode Island)

Freeman (see Folk Family Surname
    Exchange, Corson, Farr, Garner, Heath,
    Moser, Rutherford)

Freeman
John Freeman Family Organization
1852 East 3990 South, Apartment B
Salt Lake City, UT 84124
Karen Renee Cox
(includes descendants of John Freeman
    1804 and Nancy Beal Smoot 1807)

Freer
*Freer-Low Family Association
(Huguenot Historical Society)
22 North Oakwood Terrace
New Paltz, NY 12561
Phone (914) 255-1612
Richard A. Percy
Pub. *News and Reviews*

Freer
*Freer Family Reunion
1311 East 41st Street
Erie, PA 16504-2509
Phone (814) 825-3248 (unlisted)
Alice M. Freer Henneberry

Frei (see Free, Frey)

Freiling
Freiling-Sliger-Matlock-Owens Family
    Association
2306 Westgate
Houston, TX 77019
Phone (713) 529-2333
Harold Helm
$25.00 plus pedigree and family group
    sheets membership

Frelich (see Blossom Press)

French (see Nelson, Newton)

French
*French Family Association
521 River View Drive
San Jose, CA 95111-2661
Mara French
Pub. *The Frenchline*, quarterly
$15.00 per year membership for
    individuals in the U.S.

French
French Family Newsletter
PO Box 13548
Saint Louis, MO 63138
Maryann Schirker
Pub. *French Family Newsletter*

Frensley
*Frensley Family Trust
10714 Charlene Drive
Fairdale, KY 40118

Phone (502) 368-1056
Dolores Stone Hall, Historian
Pub. *Frensley Family Newsletter*

Freshwater
*Freshwater Family Association
74 Jose Gaspar Drive
North Fort Myers, FL 33917-2932
Phone (813) 995-6476
Jim Freshwater, President
(includes Freshwater back to early
    England)
Annual reunion in Delaware, Ohio

Fressley (see MacDuff)

Fresslie (see MacDuff)

Frest
Fretz Reunion
PO Box 42
Milford Square, PA 18935
Loretta A. Rosenberger
Reunion at the Deep Run Mennonite
    West Church in Perkasie, Pennsylvania

Fretz
Fretz Family Association
RMC 21, Route 152, #654
Sellersville, PA 18960
Mrs. Stanley Fretz, Secretary
Pub. *FRETZLETTER*, quarterly
$4.00 donation per year for membership
    (August)

Freund
Freund Family Fest
1605 North Park
McHenry, IL 60050
B. Guasch

Frey (see Links Genealogy Publications,
    Surname Database, Caskey)

Frey
Frey Surname Organization
12171 Country Lane
Santa Ana, CA 92705
Phone (714) 544-0680
Mr. Larue Frey
(includes Frei)

Frey
*Frey-Frye-Fry Family Association
White School Road
Rt. 1, Box 710
Honey Brook, PA 19344-9753
Phone (215) 273-3241
James E. Frey, President
Pub. *Journal* (includes descendants of
    Heinrich Frey of 1684)
$10.00 per year membership

Frey
*Pennsylvania-German Frey/Fry Family
107 West Sunhill Road
Manheim, PA 17545
Phone (717) 665-5869
D. Ernest Weinhold

(especially descendants of the very early
    immigrants who settled in Lancaster
    County, Pennsylvania and nearby
    areas)
Annual reunion on the fourth Sunday of
    July, Lititz Springs Park, along Rt.
    501, Lititz, PA

Freyberkova
*Marie Freyberkova Family Organization
3684 Townley Road
Shaker Heights, OH 44122-5120
Phone (216) 751-8601
Donald Allen Zak
(of Bohemia from 1650 to the present)

Freys (see Links Genealogy
    Publications)

Fricks (see Dockery)

Friederich
*The Friederich Family in America
PO Box 09787
Columbus, OH 43209
Jay Randall Worch, D.D.S., Publisher

Friedman
*Friedman Surname Organization
199 Commodore Drive
Milledgeville, GA 31061
Phone (912) 968-7425
Richard Bialac

Friend
*Friend Family Association of America
First and Maple Streets
PO Box 96
Friendsville, MD 21531
Phone (301) 746-5615 (Librarian)
Ina C. Hicks, Librarian
Pub. *Friendship News*, three times per
    year (January, May and September);
    (includes southwest Pennsylvania,
    northwest West Virginia, western
    Maryland; related lines: Casteel, Cox,
    DeWitt, Enoch, Falkner, Savage, Sines
    and Skidmore)
$15.00 per year membership; biennial
    reunion

Frierson (see Gipson, MacFaddien)

Frierson
*America's Friersons Ancestry Bureau
    (AFAB)
PO Box 130969
Birmingham, AL 35213-0969
Phone (205) 967-3437;
    (205) 967-7525 FAX
Meade Frierson, III
Pub. *America's Friersons Ancestry Book
    Supplements*, free; (includes
    descendants of Scotch-Irish
    immigrants)

Friesenhagen (see The Memorial
    Foundation of the Germanna Colonies)

Friez (see Baldman)

Frisbie
*Frisbie-Frisbee Family Association of
    America, Inc.
770 Rosslare Place
Crown Point, IN 46307-2981
Phone (219) 663-4045
Elizabeth Frisbie Goodlad, Secretary
Pub. *Bulletin of Frisbie-Frisbee Family
    Association of America*, quarterly;
    (includes descendants of Edward
    Frisbie of Branford (ca 1621–1690),
    settled Branford, Connecticut about
    1644)
$20.00 per year membership for
    individuals (from July 1)

Frisbie
*Levi Collins Frisbie Family
    Organization
PO Box 26183
Salt Lake City, UT 84126
Phone (801) 272-3928
Willis S. Whittlesey, III

Frisell (see Fraser)

Fritts
Fritts/Fritz Family Newsletter
2801 Park Center Drive, A-1109
Alexandria, VA 22302-1431
Phone (703) 931-5834
Greg and Patti Fritts
Pub. *Fritts/Fritz Family Newsletter*,
    annually, donation for subscription

Fritz (see Fritts)

Frodsham (see MacDuff)

Froeschle
*Froeschle-Uptegrove Family
    Association
3100 Turner Road, S.E., #180
Salem, OR 97302
Phone (503) 399-8966
Ed Froeschle, Family Historian
Free membership

Fromm (see Surname Database)

Frost (see Goodenow, Sheldon)

Frost
Frost Family Association
2665 Orchard Street
Soquel, CA 95073
Debbie Fulmer, Editor
Pub. *Frost on the Vine*, two to three times
    per year
$10.00 per year membership

Frost
*The Frost Reunion
730 Cherokee Boulevard
Knoxville, TN 37919
Phone (615) 524-7887
Marihall Frost

(includes families from California,
    Georgia, Ohio and Tennessee,
    descendants of the Frosts of Bedford
    County, Tennessee)

Frost
*Frost Family Association
3708 Grady Street
Fort Worth, TX 76119
Phone (817) 535-7207
Anne Bucklin Frost

Frownfelder (see Boose)

Fruehling (see Erdwins)

Fry (see Frey)

Fryar
Fryar Family Reunion
3325 Fryar Road
Gibsonville, NC 27249-9737
Phone (919) 697-9088
Janice Fryar Buckner
Pub. *Fryar Family History*

Frye (see Frey)

Fryer (see Ross)

Fuerst
Fuerst Family Association
PO Box 1113
Point Roberts, WA 98281
Janet M. Schreiber

Fugate
*Fugate Clearinghouse
(PO Box 517, Wright City, MO 63390—
    May to October address)
1081 West Wild Dune Lane (October to
    May address)
Tucson, AZ 85737-6912
Phone (520) 797-0643 (October to May);
    (314) 745-2867 (May to October)
Mary D. Fugate, C.G.R.S., Editor
Pub. *Fugate Family Newsletter*,
    quarterly, $12.50 per year subscription;
    (includes Fugit, Fugett, etc.)

Fugate
Fugate-Fugit-Fugett-Frigate Newsletter
Rt. 1, Box 318A
Mission, TX 78572
Mrs. Denis Gaines
Pub. *Fugate-Fugit-Fugett-Frigate
    Newsletter*, quarterly, $5.00 per year
    subscription

Fugett (see Fugate)

Fugit (see Fugate)

Fulciniti (see Gratta)

Fulghum (see Fulgham)

Fulgham
*Fulgham-Fulghum Family Association
4831 Avon Lane
Jacksonville, FL 32210-7505

Dr. James E. Fulghum, Historian
Pub. *Fulgham-Fulghum Family Facts*
$10.00 per year membership; annual
    reunion

Fulk (see Likes)

Fullbright (see Miller)

Fuller (see Clark, Stewart, Wright)

Fuller
Elijah Knapp Fuller Family Organization,
    Inc.
349 East Park
Gilbert, AZ 85234
Velma A. Fuller, Secretary

Fuller
*Descendants of Thomas Fuller
9190 Oak Leaf Way
Granite Bay, CA 95746
Phone (916) 791-0405
Linus Joseph Dewald
(includes descendants of Thomas Fuller,
    who immigrated ca 1635 at Dedham,
    Massachusetts)

Fuller
*Fuller Data Bank
Morganton, GA 30560-0419
John Beattie Fuller, Jr.
(includes all Fuller ancestors, except
    New England, free computer searches,
    exchanges, printouts)

Fuller
Missing Links
Rt. 4, Box 184
Saint Maries, ID 83861
Pub. *Fuller Findings—Allied Clark/
    Davis/Blodgett Family News*, quarterly,
    $8.50 per year subscription

Fuller
Fuller
HCR 69, Box 675
Friendship, ME 04547
Mary Lee Merrill, Governor
Pub. *Fuller*, three times per year, $2.00
    per issue to non-members
$10.00 per year membership; reunion

Fuller
Fuller-Button Family News
718 South 35th Street
Galesburg, MI 49053
Phone (616) 665-9697
Mary Benedict Grindol, Editor
Pub. *Fuller-Button Family News*,
    quarterly; (includes descendants of
    George William Fuller of New York
    and Michigan, and James Ambrose
    Button of New York, Michigan and
    Nebraska)

Fuller
*Elijah K. Fuller Family Record
6612 North Grove Avenue
Oklahoma City, OK 73132
Phone (405) 721-5687

Gerald R. Fuller, D.V.M.
(includes descendants of Elijah K. Fuller,
    son of Cornelius who married Zilpha
    Knapp, grandson of John (son of
    Cornelius and Patience Chappel Fuller)
    and John's wife Dorcas (daughter of
    Amos and Margaret Phelps Fuller),
    third-great-grandson of Edward Fuller
    of *Mayflower*)

Fullerton (see Stewart)

Fullick
*Fullick Reunion
1203 Hooker Road
Sequim, WA 98382
Phone (206) 683-2521
Virginia Edwards
(includes descendants of Charles Albert
    Fullick and Margaret Alice Simpson
    Fullick, who left Yorkshire, England,
    in 1881; also Albert F. Fullick, Bertha
    (Fullick) Henry, Thomas George
    Fullick, Ernest C. Fullick, or Simpson
    Leland Fullick)

Fullingim (see Fillingim)

Fullmer (see Cian)

Fulton (see Loop)

Fulton
The Fulton Family Letter
505 Nottingham Drive
Chambersburg, PA 17201-8750
Robert Fulton
Pub. *The Fulton Family Letter*, quarterly,
    $10.00 per year subscription

Fultz (see Dean)

Funderberg (see Frantz)

Funderburk (see Vail)

Funderhide (see McCanna)

Funk (see Cox, Stoner)

Funk
Daniel Buckley Funk Family
    Organization
1852 East 3990 South, Apartment B
Salt Lake City, UT 84124
Karen Renee Cox
(includes descendants of Daniel Buckley
    Funk 1820 and Mariah DeMill 1820)

Funkhouser (see Fankhauser)

Fuqua
*The Fuqua Family Foundation
PO Box 260068
Littleton, CO 80163-0068
Phone (303) 470-0882
Frank Fuqua, President
Pub. *Fuqua Foundation News*, quarterly;
    (database includes over 27,000
    connected family members, plus

information regarding thousands of
individuals who have not yet been
connected, most descended from
Guillaume Fouquet who lived in
colonial Virginia in the 1600s, many
spelling variations)
$15.00 per year membership

Fuqua
*Fuqua(y) Family Association (FFA)
343 Chamberlain Drive
Lexington, KY 40517-1601
Phone (606) 273-7814 (P.M.)
Mary Louise Fuqua McAskill, Family
    Representative and President
Pub. *Fuqua(y) Family Association
    Newsletter*, quarterly, $10.00 per year
    membership
Annual reunion on the Saturday of Labor
    Day weekend in Lafayette, Tennessee

Fuquay (see Fuqua)

Furman (see Hyatt)

Furnell
*Benjamin Furnell Family Organization
3813C Del Ray
Jefferson City, MO 65109
Phone (573) 893-8397
Deborah Furnell

Furse
*Albert Arthur Furse Family
    Organization
3125 North 575 East
North Ogden, UT 84414
Phone (801) 782-5302
Alberta J. Roberts, Genealogy Chairman
(includes descendants of Albert Arthur
    Furse and Pleasance Taylor of Norfolk,
    England, prior to 1865)
Optional membership dues

Furtney (see Fortney)

Fury (see Nienow)

Fuselier (see Johnson)

Futcher
*Futcher Surname Organization
9493 83rd Street, South
Cottage Grove, MN 55016-3494
Mr. and Mrs. J. S. Futcher
(includes any and all Futcher families,
    everywhere)

Futral
*Futral Genealogy Trails
#6 Wonderland Lane
Carthage, TN 37030-9546
Jenny Futral, Entrepreneur
Pub. *Ancestors-Descendants of Futral,
    Clifford, Watkins, Wood—with Allied
    Lines: Boyd, Echols, Gay, Glass,
    Henry, McClanahan, McClurkin,
    McDaniel, O'Menhundro, Pinson,
    Reynolds, Smith . . .*, semiannually

(April and October), $15.00 per year
    subscription; (includes Futrelle and
    Futrel)

Futrel (see Futral)

Futrelle (see Futral)

Fyall (see MacDuff)

Fyfe (see MacDuff)

Fyffe (see MacDuff)

Fyler
Fyler Family Reunion
47 Woodchuck Hill Road
West Simsbury, CT 06092
Phone (203) 658-4211
Wadsworth T. Fyler

Gaar (see Crisler)

Gabbard
Gabbard/Gabbert Family Newsletter
Rt. 1, Box 1122
Bois D'Arc, MO 65612
Phone (417) 672-2631
Marjorie A. Greer
Pub. *Gabbard/Gabbert Family
    Newsletter*, quarterly (March, June,
    September and December), $12.00 per
    year subscription

Gabbert (see Gabbard)

Gabel (see Coble)

Gabler
*Gabler Family Association
470 Acoma Boulevard, South, #114
Lake Havasu City, AZ 86406-7786
David H. Gabler, Editor
Pub. *Gabler Family Newsletter*, annually,
    $5.00 plus 90¢ postage per issue

Gabriel (see Brawley)

Gadberry (see Mayberry)

Gadsden (see Thorn)

Gadtka (see Gatkie)

Gaede (see Pessner)

Gaedtke (see Gatkie)

Gaertner (see Sahnow)

Gaffney
*McLaughlin Publications
PO Box 1342
Jackson, CA 95642
Leslie McLaughlin, Editor
Pub. *The Gaffney Seanache*, annually,
    $25.00 per issue postpaid

Gafford
*Gafford Family Association
29801 Highview Circle
San Juan Capistrano, CA 92675
Phone (714) 661-4808; (714) 661-8408;
    (714) 499-5575 (FAX)
Rachel Hayward, Editor and Publisher
Pub. *Gafford*, quarterly, $10.00 per year
    subscription; (for all Gafford families,
    everywhere, including Giffard,
    Gifford, etc., and related families)
$25.00 per year membership

Gafford
Gafford Reunion
101 Maplewood Drive
Rome, GA 30161
Dr. A. V. Gafford
(includes descendants of Stephen
    Gafford)
Annual reunion

Gage (see Barnard, Smith)

Gage
*Gage Exchange
29 Seminole Court
Winter Haven, FL 33881
Phone (813) 294-2496
John A. Gage
Pub. *Gage Family Newsletter*, quarterly,
    $8.00 per year subscription

Gaggioni (see Giorgi)

Gagnier
Gagnier/Gunter Newsletter
236 Villa Road
Twin Falls, ID 83301-8030
Juvanne Clezie

Gailey
*Marlin Gailey Family Organization
3333 South 1000 West
Syracuse, UT 84075
Phone (801) 776-2461
Michael L. Gailey, Secretary/Treasurer

Gair (see Gregor)

Galbraith
*Clan Galbraith Association of North
    America
PO Box 1332
Muskogee, OK 74402
Phone (918) 682-3494 (work); (918)
    682-9889 (home)
Glenn E. Smith, President
Pub. *The Red Tower*, quarterly; (includes
    Gilbreath, Gilreath, Calbreath,
    Culbreath, Kilbreath, etc.)
$15.00 per year membership

Galbraith
Redtower
12004 Fingerboard Road
Monrovia, MD 21770
Scott Galbraith
Pub. *Redtower*, quarterly

Galbreath
Galbreath Genealogy
14 Bonanza
Centralia, IL 62801
Phone (618) 532-0704
Joseph W. Galbreath
Pub. *Galbreath Genealogy*

Galche (see Gunn)

Gale (see Barnard)

Gallagher
*Thomas Clifford Gallagher Family
    Organization
869 E, 750 Road
Lawrence, KS 66047
Phone (913) 748-0904
Joanne Ridgway Powell

Gallard (see MacDuff)

Gallie (see Gunn)

Galloway (see Rothenberger)

Gallup (see Joy, MacQuarrie)

Galmiche (see Blossom Press)

Galrig (see MacDuff)

Galt (see Gault)

Galvin (see McRae)

Gamberlen (see Kimberlin)

Gamble (see Campbell)

Gambler (see Powers)

Gambol (see Campbell)

Gambrel (see Antley)

Gange
*Gange Surname Organization
1257 North Main Street
Centerville, UT 84014-1107
Phone (801) 298-1029
David Bruce Gange

Gann (see Hardwick)

Gann
*Gann Historical Society and Library,
    Inc.
104 Saddle Run Court
Macon, GA 31210
Gayle A. Gann, Membership Chairman
Pub. *Gann Gazette*, quarterly; (includes
    Gan, Ganne, Ghan, Ghann, etc.)
$15.00 per year membership for
    individuals (beginning July 1), $25.00
    per year membership for households;
    annual reunion on the third weekend of
    June

Gano (see Anthes)

Gansler (see The Memorial Foundation
    of the Germanna Colonies)

Gant (see Moser, Sager)

Gant
Ganttrees
55441 Firestone
La Quinta, CA 92253
Clifford Gant, Co-editor
Pub. *Ganttrees*, quarterly, $10.00 per
    year subscription to Ben Gantt, Co-
    editor, 12319 Perthshire, Houston, TX
    77024; (includes ancestry and
    descendants of the Gant, Gantt, Gaunt,
    Gent, Ghent and Jent families of early
    America with emphasis on John[1] Gant
    (ca 1713–1783) of Virginia and North
    Carolina; major allied families in
    North and South Carolina: Aldridge,
    Armstrong, Ashley, Atkinson, Bass,
    Boone, Cunningham, Davis, Garrison,
    Harbour, Harper, Hill, Jordan, Judge,
    Lollar, Martin, Norwood, Perkins,
    Phillips, Pratt, Ray, Rippy, Shearin,
    Shirley, Simmons, Thomas, Thornton,
    Townley, Wakefield, Wilhoit and
    Wood; in Isle of Wight County,
    Virginia: Thomas Allen, John B.
    Barnes, John Gurndy, Ambrose
    Hadley, Thomas and John Howell,
    Edward, Mathew, Francis and
    Albrighton Jones, Sampson Lanier,
    William Newton, Christopher
    Reynolds, John Turner, Henry Vaughn,
    Richard Vick, Richard, George and
    Arthur Washington, Nicholas Williams
    and Oliver Woodward)

Gant
Gant/Gaunt Clearinghouse
444 Cold Springs Road
Virginia Beach, VA 23454

Gantois (see Daniel)

Gantz
Gantz Family Clearinghouse
77 Hollow Road
Quarryville, PA 17566-9491
Harry Hoffman

Ganz
*Josef Ganz Family Organization
29490 Robert Drive
Livonia, MI 48150
Barbara Komar

Garard
Fragments: Garard/Gerrard
419 North Larchmont Boulevard,
    Suite 277
Los Angeles, CA 90004
Pub. *Fragments: Garard/Gerrard*,
    bimonthly, $12.00 per year
    subscription

Garber (see Frantz, Gerber, Stoner,
    Wampler)

Garcich (see Blossom Press)

Garcsich (see Blossom Press)

Gard
*Gard, Guard, delaGarde, duGard, Garde
   Research
2072 Aeneas Cr. Road
PO Box 82
Malo, WA 99150-0082
Margie Gard Gray, Editor

Garde (see Gard)

Gardener (see Gardner)

Gardens (see Garner)

Gardiner (see Folk Family Surname
   Exchange, Gardner, Rutherford)

Gardner (see Anthes, Rogers, Saye)

Gardner
*Gardner Clearinghouse
207 Auburn Drive
Dalton, GA 30720
Phone (706) 278-1504
Joseph Wiley Reid
(1400–1890 period)

Gardner
*Gardner Gardiner Gardener Garner
   Newsletter*
5 Anderson Court
West Bay Shore, Long Island, NY 11706-
   7701
Phone (516) 665-7693; E-mail:
   SUE12632@aol.com
Sue Gardner Shreve, Publisher and
   Compiler
Pub. *Gardner Gardiner Gardener Garner
   Newsletter*, semiannually (June and
   December), $16.00 per year
   subscription, free queries to
   subscribers

Gardner
*Jim Mar Publications
1130 Pine Canyon Road
PO Box 430
Midway, UT 84049-0430
Phone (801) 654-4332
Marge Gardner, Publisher
Pub. *Gardner Family News*,
   semiannually (June and December),
   $15.00 per year subscription, $25.00
   for two years subscription; (includes
   Gardener, Gardiner and Garner)

Garinger (see Garringer)

Garland (see Folk Family Surname
   Exchange, Corson)

Garland
Garland Family Research Association
80 Danton Street
San Francisco, CA 94112
D. Kindred

Garland
*Garland Family Research Association
12522 Georgia Road
Otto, NC 28763
Phone (704) 369-9546
George and Julia Garland
Pub. *Newsletter*
Annual meeting on the first or second
   weekend of May in various locations

Garland
*Folk Family
PO Box 52048
Knoxville, TN 37950-2048
Hester E. Stockton, Owner; Thomas C.
   Garland, Editor
Pub. *Garland Gazette*, quarterly, $15.00
   per year subscription, $5.00 per issue

Garlick (see CTC Family Association)

Garmon
Garmon Newsletter
28111 Mountain Meadow Road
Escondido, CA 92026
Patricia Scott Garmon
Pub. *Garmon Newsletter*, bimonthly,
   $5.00 per year subscription

Garner (see Gardner)

Garner
*Our Legacy
Rt. 1, Box 132
Lepwai, ID 83540
Phone (208) 843-2152
Barbara Benscoter
(includes the Garner-Thain Family of
   Idaho from 1895, with allied families
   of Anderson, Argeropulus, Boozer,
   Buchholz, Chronster, Clevenger,
   Cochrane, Collings, Coon, Dray,
   English, Frakes, Freeman, Gardens,
   Geddes, Genscoter, Gentry, Goodlow,
   Grindstaff, Hall, Harness, Hathaway,
   Herinanus, Humphrey, Ironside,
   Jackson, Keene, Larsen, Leeper,
   Lorimer, Mater, Matticks, Maxwell,
   McCall, McClain, McCoy, McCurrack,
   McFadden, McGilvery, Melvear,
   Newby, Newton, Noel, Norris, Pell,
   Ramey, Richey, Rush, Still, Stout,
   Tayler, Turner, Watson and Wells)

Garner
*Garner Family History Association
4065 Berrywood Drive
Eugene, OR 97404-4061
James R. Brann, Family Representative
(PAF™ data bank on MAC™ computer
   includes England to U.S.)
Free information exchange

Garner
Raking for Garner Newsletter
701 Lobo Street
Cedar Park, TX 78613
Helen Smothers Swenson
Pub. *Raking for Garner Newsletter*, three
   times per year, $14.00 per year
   subscription

Garnet (see Golding)

Garr (see The Memorial Foundation of
   the Germanna Colonies, Crisler)

Garr
Garr Reunion (John and Nancy Young
   Descendants)
1801 Fair Street
Chillicothe, MO 64601-1226
Richard Garr

Garra (see Hay)

Garrad (see Hay)

Garren
*Garren Family Reunion Organization
433 Summit Chase Drive
Valrico, FL 33594
Phone (813) 685-2544
Scott L. Peeler, Jr., Original Organizer/
   Director
(includes descendants of John Wesley
   Garren (1841–1927) and his first wife,
   Elizabeth J. Cain (1842–1928), mixed-
   blood Cherokee Indian family from
   East Tennessee and northeastern
   Oklahoma, and his second wife, Lydia
   Splitlog, of the Seneca Nation)
Reunion every five years at Corntassel
   Cumberland Presbyterian Church and
   Cemetery in Monroe County, near
   Madisonville, Tennessee (late June
   1997)

Garren
*Garren Heritage Association
380 Corbly Drive, #11
Henderson, NC 28739
Elaine M. Gilbert
Pub. *Garren*, quarterly, $20.00 per year
   subscription; (includes all Garrens)
Annual reunion on the fourth Saturday of
   August in Hoopers Creek Township,
   Fletcher, North Carolina

Garret (see Links Genealogy
   Publications)

Garretson (see Lambert)

Garrett (see Dockery, Elliff, Rickett)

Garrett
Garrett
803 South Buckeye Avenue
Abilene, KS 67410-3211
Cathy Wood
Pub. *Garrett*, quarterly, $20.00 per year
   subscription

Garringer
*Garringer Family Reunion
4 Willis Court
Washington Court House, OH 43160
Phone (614) 335-0229
M. Caroline Shaper, Historian-
   Genealogist

(includes Garinger, Geringer, Gerringer, descendants of David and Barbara Geringer/Garinger 1769 Maryland, Virginia and West Virginia)

Garrison (see Gant)

Garrison
Andrew Jackson Garrison Broken Branches
PO Box 389
612 Amanda Street
Arbuckle, CA 95912
Phone (916) 476-2769
Peter and Janice Spyres
Pub. *Andrew Jackson Garrison Broken Branches*

Garrison
*Isaac Garrison Family Association, Inc.
5567 Ecton Road
Winchester, KY 40391
Phone (606) 842-3028
Edwanna Garrison Chenault, Executive Secretary
Pub. *The Garrison Gazette*, semiannually, contribution of $5.00 per year minimum; (includes descendants of Isaac Garrison 1732–1836)
Biennial reunion in even-numbered years

Garrow (see Hay, Stewart)

Garson
*Garson Families Association
13033 Caminito Dos Amantes
San Diego, CA 92128-1722
Phone (619) 438-8428
Charles Whitlock Rockett

Garst (see Frantz)

Garstin
*The Garstin Family Organization
2945 S.E. Brian Street
Hillsboro, OR 97123
Phone (503) 648-2945;
   (503) 640-0810 (work)
David J. Garstin
(includes White and Belmore families)

Gartoucies (see Blossom Press)

Garvey
*Search and Strategy
PO Box 4153
Mountain View, CA 94040
Phone (415) 967-2017
Sandra Ryder Shafer, Publisher
(includes Garvey family history)

Garvey
*The Garvey Family Association
PO Box 6046
Florence, KY 41022-6046
E-mail: cpjk34a@prodigy.com
Ralph Arnsparger

Garville (see Cian)

Garvin
*Samuel Garvin Family Organization
319 B Avenue South
Mount Vernon, IA 52314
Phone (319) 895-8301
Paul L. Garvin
(includes descendants of Samuel Garvin (1799–1849) and Nancy Hanen (1805–1849))

Gasaway (see Gassaway)

Gaskill
*Gaskill Ghosts
PO Box 1872
Dodge City, KS 67801-1872
Laura Tasset Koehn, President
(includes research on Claude E. Gaskill and Myrtle Irene Currey)

Gaspard (see Johnson)

Gasquet (see Blossom Press)

Gass (see Womack)

Gassaway (see Rutherford)

Gassaway
*Genealogical History of the Gassaway Family
PO Box 85
Lexington, MO 64067-0085
Phone (816) 259-2641
Mrs. Kenneth Rutherford, Publisher
(includes descendants of Col. Nicholas Gassaway and other lines not yet proven as his descendants: Berry Gazzaway of Georgia, John Gordon Gazaway of Georgia, Nicholas Gassaway of Indiana, John W. Gazaway, John T. Gazaway, Philip N. Gazaway, John Gassaway, Samuel Gassaway, William Gazaway, Thomas Gazaway and Samuel Gasaway, and the female lines of Sophia (Gassaway) Springs, Frances (Gassaway) Taylor and Nancy (Gassaway) Shipman)

Gastineau
Gastineau Newsletter
435 Hargis Lane
Eubank, KY 42567
Mrs. Harold Gastineau
Pub. *Gastineau Newsletter*

Gaston (see Bugbee, DeLaughter)

Gates
*Gates Surname Organization
7705 Ensley Drive, S.W.
Huntsville, AL 35802-2845
Phone (205) 883-0207
Thomas W. Burns

Gates
*Gates Family Research Center
2716 Melbourne Road
Springfield, MO 65804-5212
Phone (417) 887-6912

Robert C. Gates, President and Corresponding Secretary
(Gates surname database with free query service)

Gates
*Pioneer Publication
PO Box 1179
Tum Tum, WA 99034-1179
Phone (509) 276-9841
Shirley Penna-Oakes
Pub. *Gates Gazette*, irregularly, $6.00 per issue plus $1.75 postage for 1–3 books, 50¢ for each additional book

Gatkie
*Gatkie Surname Organization
150 Brown Street
Saint Clair, MI 48079-4882
Phone (810) 329-9359
George M. Roberts
(includes Gatkie, Gaedtke, Gadtka families of U.S.A., Ontario, and Germany)

Gatlin (see Cunningham)

Gatten (see Likes)

Gatton
Gatton Newsletter
PO Box 365
Beech Bottom, WV 26030
James McKittrick
Pub. *Gatton Newsletter*

Gaudet (see Johnson)

Gauger (see Sager)

Gaulche (see Gunn)

Gault
Gault/Galt Exchange
175 West Bidwell
Battle Creek, MI 49015
Phone (616) 973-7540
Robert E. Gault

Gault
*Gault Family Association
4614 Manchester Road
Akron, OH 44319
Marilyn Gault Brasaemle

Gaunson (see Gunn)

Gaunt (see Gant)

Gaus (see Horkheimer)

Gause (see Goodenow)

Gauss (see Horkheimer)

Gauthier (see Blossom Press)

Gautreaux (see Augeron)

Gautrot (see Johnson)

Gavin
Gavin
9452 East Conquistadores Drive
Scottsdale, AZ 85255
Arnold M. Gavin
Pub. *Gavin*, monthly, free with
submission of family information

Gawan (see Gowen)

Gawans (see Gowen)

Gay (see Futral)

Gaylord (see Barnes)

Gaylord
*Gaylord Family Organization
3275 Blue Ridge Circle
Stockton, CA 95219-3502
Phone (209) 477-7216
Barry C. Wood
(includes exchange of information,
descendants of William Gaylord
(1589–1673))

Gazaway (see Gassaway)

Gazzaway (see Gassaway)

Gear (see Geer)

Gearing
*Frederick August Gearing Family
Organization
511 Gaylord
Pueblo, CO 81004
Phone (719) 543-0549
Virginia Baird Penaluna Haling

Geary (see Cian)

Gebeheart (see Gebhard)

Gebert (see Gebhard)

Gebhard (see Pessner)

Gebhard
*Gebhard Family Society International
Whispering Oaks
5821 Rowland Hill Road
Cascade, MD 21719-1939
Phone (301) 416-2660
Victor Gebhart, President
Pub. *Newsletter—Gebhard Family
Society International*, quarterly, $6.00
per year U.S. subscription, $8.00 per
year foreign subscription; (includes
variations Capeheart, Gebeheart (the
medieval given name), the
Pennsylvania-Dutch Gebert, Gebhardt,
Gebhart, Gephart, Keephart, Kephart
and allied families of von Dollonstein
and von Lichtenstein)

Gebhard
*Gebhard Family Society of America
Whispering Oaks
5821 Rowland Hill Road
Cascade, MD 21719-1939

Phone (301) 416-2660
Victor Gebhart, President
Pub. *Newsletter—Gebhard Family
Society of America*, quarterly, $6.00
per year U.S. subscription, $8.00 per
year foreign subscription

Gebhardt (see Gebhard)

Gebhart (see Gebhard)

Gebhtol
*Beghtol-Bechtel Family
804 60th Street
West Des Moines, IA 50266
Phone (515) 225-1553
Rev. Josephine A. Barnes

Gedd (see MacDuff)

Geddes (see Garner)

Geddes
*William Geddes Family Organization
6602 West King Valley Road
West Valley City, UT 84120
Phone (801) 250-9017
Jay G. Burrup, President and Co-
Genealogist
Pub. *Geddes Gazette*, annually; (includes
descendants of William Geddes (1832
Newtown-Hamilton, Armagh, Ireland–
1899 Plain City, Utah) immigrated to
the U.S. from Glasgow, Scotland, in
1854)

Geer
*The Geer Family Association
PO Box 88
Lebanon, CT 06249
Phone (407) 668-8580
Harold N. Geer, President
Pub. *The Geer Family Association
Newsletter*, three times per year;
(includes persons who can trace their
ancestry or relationship to George or
Thomas Geer of Ledyard, Connecticut,
in the 1600s, as shown in the
Publication, *The Geer Genealogy* by
Walter Geer (1923), or to other Geer;
spelling variations: Geer, Gear, Gere
and Geere)
$15.00 per year membership; national
reunion every three years

Geer
Geer (Gere/Gear) Family Association
PO Box 343
Georgetown, ME 04548
Judy A. Ewing, Newsletter Editor
Pub. *Geer (Gere/Gear) Family
Association Newsletter*, three times per
year
$15.00 per year membership

Geere (see Geer)

Geeseman (see Skinner)

Geffers (see Cordes

Gehret (see Miehls)

Geisberger (see Hall)

Geissinger
*Charles Geissinger Family Organization
PO Box 311
Bedford, WY 83112
Phone (307) 883-2730
Jerry Mower

Gelding (see Lemon)

Gellie (see MacDuff)

Gelly (see MacDuff)

Gelm (see Kellum)

Gemigani (see Andreossi)

**Genealogical Reference of Upcoming
Publications (G.R.O.U.P.)** (see Multi-
family Associations)

Genning (see Jennings)

Genning (see Jennings)

Gennings (see Jennings)

Gennins (see Jennings)

Genscoter (see Garner)

Gentry (see Curnutte, Dockery, Garner,
Wright)

Gentry
Gentry Family Organization
Rt. 3, Box 123
Trinity, NC 27370
Cheryl Burrow

Gentry
*Gentry Family Gazette and Genealogy
Exchange*
6151 Tompkins Drive
McLean, VA 22101
Phone (703) 356-9370
Dick Gentry, Editor
Pub. *Gentry Family Gazette and
Genealogy Exchange*, bimonthly
$25.00 first-year membership, $20.00 per
year renewal membership

Genung (see Aldrich)

Genz
Genz
Whispering Oaks
5821 Rowland Hill Road
Cascade, MD 21719-1939
Phone (301) 416-2660
Victor Gebhart, President
Pub. *Genz*, annually, $2.00 per issue

Geoffroy (see Blossom Press)

George (see Folk Family Surname
Exchange, Corson, Ross)

George
*George Family Database
1301 Bradford Road
Oreland, PA 19075-2414
Phone (215) 836-4727
Dale E. Berger, Publisher

Georgeson (see Gunn)

Gephart (see Gebhard)

Gerade
*Ancestors and Descendants of Warren
  Capers Gerade and Pearl Eva Gibson
5222 Mitchell Street
Alexandria, VA 22312
Phone (703) 354-3830
William A. Gerade
(includes allied families: Amazeen,
  Arms, Brown, Clifford, Clough,
  Currier, Hawks, Trefethen and
  Woodworth, early families in New
  England)

Gerber (see Repass)

Gerber
Gerber/Garber Family Reunion
2288 Locust Drive
Lansdale, PA 19446

Gerberich
Gerberich Family Association
Rt. 2
Jonestown, PA 17038
Mrs. William Ludwig

Gerdine (see Golding)

Gere (see Geer)

Geren (see Geurin)

Geringer (see Garringer)

Gerlach (see Surname Database)

Gerlitz (see Leinweber)

Gerow
*Gerow Family Association
Huguenot Historical Society
18 Brodhead Avenue
PO Box 339
New Paltz, NY 12561-0339
Phone (914) 255-1660
Kenneth E. Hasbrouck, Sr., President
Pub. *Giraud-Gerow Family in America*
$10.00 per year membership

Gerrard (see Garard)

Gerringer (see Garringer)

Gerrish (see Corson)

Gerrish
*Gerrish Exchange
PO Box 896
Ukiah, CA 95482-0896

Phone (707) 462-0454;
  (707) 462-0454 FAX
Douglass Graem Adams
(includes descendants of William Gerrish
  (1617–1687), founder of Newbury,
  Massachusetts)

Gerron (see Geurin)

Gerry (see Cian)

Gerry
*The Elbridge Gerry Family
282 Grant Avenue
Hatfield, PA 19446
Steven B. Morris, Sr.
(Signer of the Declaration of
  Independence)

Gerster (see Castor)

Gerth
Gerth Family Organization
4075 East 28th Street
Highland, CA 92376
Elna Gerth

Gest
Gest-Guest Quarterly
2101 Hayes Road, #1409
Houston, TX 77077
Henry G. Guest, Jr., Coordinating Editor
Pub. *Gest-Guest Quarterly*, three times
  per year; $10.00 for two years
  subscription (six issues or 48 pages),
  $14.00 for two years subscription
  outside the U.S. and Canada (includes
  Gist, Guess, etc.)

Getchell
Getchell Project
51 North Main Street
Newmarket, NH 03857
Phone (603) 659-3652
Sylvia Fitts Getchell

Gette (see Jett)

Gettings
*Gettings-Gowins Family Association
4201 Wildflower Circle
Wichita, KS 67210
Phone (316) 529-0438
J. Robert Thurman, Historian
Pub. *Newsletter*, annually
Annual reunion on the third Saturday of
  August in Canton, Oklahoma

Gettys
Gettys Clan
7850 Beardsley Road
Galion, OH 44833
Doris Bibler

Getz
*Getz Family Reunion
PO Box 143
Brodheadsville, PA 18322
Phone (717) 992-7406
Patricia Ann Frable, President

Annual reunion on the second Saturday
  of August at the West End Fairgrounds,
  off Route 209, Gilbert, Pennsylvania

Geurin
Geurin Gazette
457A Manzanita Avenue
Santa Cruz, CA 95062
Mr. Geurin
Pub. *Geurin Gazette*, monthly; (includes
  Geren, Gerron, Gourant, Guerrant,
  etc.)

Geyer
*Geyer Family Association
PO Box 1860
Studio City, CA 91614
Phone (818) 980-1005; E-mail:
  AP471@lafn.org
Karen Mohr
(includes descendants of Frederick W.
  Geyer (1808–1880 New York) and
  Margaret (1813–1889 New York), both
  Germans from Russia)

Geyer
*The Geyer Society of America, Inc.
PO Box 270396
Corpus Christi, TX 78427-0396
Phone (512) 850-9268
Carl P. Geyer, President
Pub. *The Geyer Newsletter*, annually, free
  subscription; (includes descendants of
  Johann Joseph Geyer (1744–before
  1816) of Garnsdorf, Germany in the
  old Kingdom of Saxony, former East
  Germany; one database lists 3,029
  related families from the U.S. and/or
  Germany, mostly not named Geyer;
  second database lists about 3,000
  Geyers (18 spellings), whose
  relationship is undetermined)
$25.00 per year membership; annual
  reunion on 8 October in Waco, Texas,
  limited to members

G'Feller (see Meyer)

Ghergich (see Blossom Press)

Gheri
*Gheri Surname Organization
3 Brazill Lane
Whitehall, MT 59759
Phone (406) 287-3369
Lindia Roggia Lovshin

Gibb (see Buchanan)

Gibbes (see Rutherford)

Gibbon (see Buchanan)

Gibbons (see McRae)

Gibbons
*Joshua Gibbons Family Association
Calgon Corporation, Box 1346
Pittsburgh, PA 15230
Phone (412) 494-8585

Donald L. Gibbon
Pub. *Newsletter*, occasionally; (includes descendants of Joshua Gibbons, of Currituck County, North Carolina, 1790–1800, also Gibbon)

Gibbs (see Barnard, Ellett, Likes)

Gibbs
Gibbs-Johnson
PO Box 706
Boulder, CO 80306-0706
Betty L. Gibbs
Pub. *Gibbs-Johnson*, quarterly, $10.00 per year subscription
Reunion

Gibbs
From Generation to Generation
Rt. 1, Box 147
Buncombe, IL 62912
Melody Tellor, Editor
Pub. *Gibbs Gathering*, quarterly, $15.00 per year subscription

Gibbs
Gibbs Family Newsletter
1131 Clinton
Des Moines, IA 50313
Lenore Gibbs Freeman
Pub. *Gibbs Family Newsletter*, quarterly, $20.00 per year subscription; (includes descendants of Solomon Gibbs and Rebecca Gibson)

Gibbs
Gibbs Family Organization
Rt. 2, Box 50
State Center, IA 50247
Juanita Gibbs, Historian
Pub. *Gibbs Newsletter*
Reunion

Gibbs
*The Gibbs Family
116 Crescent Drive
Mount Sterling, KY 40353
Phone (606) 498-1076
Vernon L. Gibbs

Gibbs
Gibbs and Shadowens Reunion
PO Box 91
Bethany, LA 71007
Phone (318) 938-7755
B. Gibbs; Margie Dawson Gibbs

Gibby (see Buchanan)

Giberson (see Newcomb)

Gibson (see Black, Brawley, Buchanan, Endicott, Gibbs, Gipson, Jacoby, Lambert, MacDuff)

Gibson
*Gibson Descendants Reunion
6923 Cypress Road, 13-A
Plantation, FL 33317-0307
Phone (305) 472-6806

Marguerite R. VanEtten, R.D.
(includes allied lines of Baggett, Kettering (Cattron, Catron, Kotron, etc.), Kilgore, Lurkey, Marquart, Nickols, Reece and Van Hooser)

Gibson
*Kinseeker Publications
5697 Old Maple Trail
PO Box 184
Grawn, MI 49637
E-mail: AB064@taverse.lib.mi.us
Victoria Wilson, Editor
Pub. *Gathering Gibsons*, quarterly, $10.00 per year subscription; (includes Gipson)

Gidal (see Cohen)

Giddens
Giddens Family Associations
PO Box 4153
Chapel Hill, NC 27515
Phone (919) 968-3963
Lynn Giddens
Pub. *Giddens Newsletter*, about quarterly
Donation for membership

Giddings
*Giddings Surname Organization
George Giddings Family Organization
1820 East Jensen Street
Mesa, AZ 85203-2843
Phone (602) 969-2707
Dr. C. Bland Giddings

Gideon
*Gideon Family Association
160 West Dunedin Road
Columbus, OH 43214-4006
Phone (614) 263-4232
Mark R. Gideon, Corresponding Secretary
$5.00 per year membership

Gidney
*George Gidney Family Organization
4214 South Morris Street
Taylorsville, UT 84119
Phone (801) 967-8957
John E. Gidney
(includes descendants of George Gidney, b. 1837, Sharrington, Norfolk, England)
Donation for membership

Giering (see Surname Database)

Giffels
Giffels Gleanings
1887 Yallup Road, Rt. 4
Saint Johns, MI 48879
Phone (517) 224-7807
Arlene Lowe Lounds
Pub. *Giffels Gleanings*, semiannually, $2.00 per issue

Gifford (see Folk Family Surname Exchange, Surname Sources, Hay)

Gifford
Gifford Family
532 South 670 East
Orem, UT 84058
Phone (801) 224-4241
Sylvia M. Gifford

Gikchrist (see MacLachlan)

Gilbert (see Album, Buchanan, Covert, Flowers, Moser, Nasby)

Gilbert
Gilbert Genealogy
3923 Harrison Street
Kansas City, MO 64110
Phone (816) 753-3789
Larry D. Gilbert
Pub. *Gilbert Genealogy*, quarterly, $8.00 per year subscription

Gilbert
*Gilbert Surname Organization
2204 West Houston
Spokane, WA 99208-4440
Phone (509) 326-2089
Donna Potter Phillips
Pub. *Gilbert Gallery*, irregularly, $7.00 per issue, free queries; (includes anyone of the surname, any place, any time)

Gilbertson (see Buchanan)

Gilbreath (see Galbraith)

Gilchrest (see MacLachlan)

Gilchris (see MacLachlan)

Gilchrist (see MacLachlan)

Gilchrist
*Neil Gilchrist Family Organization
1990 Bittern Drive
Idaho Falls, ID 83406
Phone (208) 523-4744
Phoebe Davids Gilchrist

Gilday (see Gildea)

Gildea
*Gildea/Gilday Family History Association
4065 Berrywood Drive
Eugene, OR 97404-4061
James R. Brann, Family Representative
(PAF™ data bank on MAC™ computer includes County Clare, Ireland, to U.S.)
Free information exchange

Gildersleeve (see McKune)

Gile
*Gile/Guile/Guiles/Guyle Surname Association
138 Hillandale Farm Road
(Off Southard Road)
Saratoga Springs, NY 12866

Phone (604) 477-8006
John Gile, c/o Alice Zetterstrom

Giles (see Neville)

Gilfallan (see Macnab)

Gilfillan (see MacLellan)

Gilkchrist (see MacLachlan)

Gilkerson (see Rutherford)

Gill (see Catlow)

Gill
*Isaac Gill Family Organization
35 Cavalcade Circle
Sacramento, CA 95831
Phone (916) 424-2583
Gordon H. Gill
(includes descendants of Isaac Gill, 1820,
   Wooster, Wayne County, Ohio)

Gill
*The Wyatt and Maude Gill Family
3230 South Concourse Drive
Mount Pleasant, MI 48858-9131
Rev. David H. Gill, Publisher

Gillanders (see Ross)

Gillaspie
Elijah and Mary Rabun Gillaspie Family
2534 East A Street
Torrington, WY 82240-2022
Marilyn Gillaspie Glandt

Gillean
*Clan Gillean Association, USA (The
   MacLeans)
804 Pecan, Suite #8
McAllen, TX 79501
Phone (512) 631-1905
Robert C. Rankin, President
Pub. *The Pipings of MacLean*, quarterly;
   (affiliated with the Clan MacLean
   Association in Scotland; includes
   MacLean, MacLain(e), MacLane, etc.,
   or any septs: Beath, Beaton, Black,
   Huei, Lain, Lean, MacBeath, MacBee,
   MacBeth, MacCormick, MacCraken,
   MacFayden, MacGillivray, MacVey,
   Padon, Patton, Peden, Rankan, etc.)
$25.00 initial-year membership, $15.00
   per year membership thereafter

Gillechreiste (see MacLachlan)

Gilleland (see MacLellan)

Gilleland
*Gill(e)(i)land Researchers
11863 207th Street
Lakewood, CA 90715
Phone (310) 402-6062
Rebecca Howser

Gilleland
*Gilleland Endowment, Inc.
940 Bacacita Farms Road
Abilene, TX 79602
Phone (915) 698-0824
Patricia Gilleland Young,
   Correspondence Secretary
Pub. *The Gilleland Endowment, Inc.,
   Newsletter*, about twice per year, free;
   (primarily descendants of Daniel
   Gilleland (1795–1873) and Precilla
   (Boatwright) to Texas 1821)

Gillenchreist (see MacLachlan)

Gillespie (see MacDuff, Macpherson,
MacPherson)

Gillespie
*John Gillespie Family Organization,
   1770–1812 of Chester County, South
   Carolina
HCR 62, Box 113A
Flippin, AR 72634-9710
Phone (501) 453-5286
Charlene Gillespie Deutsch, Compiler

Gillespie
*Gillespie Clan Society
1300 East 109th Street
Kansas City, MO 64131-3585
Phone (816) 942-5497
La Roux K. Gillespie, Editor
Pub. *Gillespie Clan Newsletter*, quarterly,
   $10.00 per year subscription, $12.00
   with index

Gillespie
*Elijah Gillespie Family Organization
7650 Fairview Road
Tillamook, OR 97141
Phone (503) 842-6036
Orella Chadwick

Gillet
Gillet, Gillette, Gillett Pride 'n' Joy
1103 West First
McCook, NE 69001
Phone (308) 345-5358
B. E. Gillett, Editor
Pub. *Gillet, Gillette, Gillett Pride 'n' Joy*,
   quarterly, $10.00 per year subscription,
   $12.00 per year foreign subscription

Gillett (see Clark, Gillet)

Gillette (see Gillet, Johnson)

Gillette
*Gillette Historical Society
PO Box 3028
Sonora, CA 95370
Robert Charles Gillette, President
Pub. *Gillette Gazette*, irregularly;
   (includes any information related to
   the surname Gillette, of all dates and
   places)

Gilley
*Gillie/Gilley Family Organization
1480 Edison Street
Salt Lake City, UT 84115
Phone (801) 485-0976
Pamela Gillie Carson, President
(includes research in Henry County,
   Virginia, and Rockingham County,
   North Carolina)

Gilliam
Cockerill Publishing Company
PO Box 196612
Anchorage, AK 99519-6612
Pub. *Gilliam Communique*, quarterly

Gilliam
Gilliam Clan
2330 Greenglade Road, N.E.
Atlanta, GA 30455
David L. Smith
Pub. *Gilliam Clan*, quarterly, $5.00 per
   year subscription; (includes
   descendants of Epaphroditus Gilliam)

Gillian (see MacLennan)

Gillie (see Macpherson, MacPherson)

Gillies (see Macpherson, MacPherson)

Gillilman (see MacLennan)

Gilliman (see MacLennan)

Gilling (see Jennings)

Gillis (see MacPherson)

Gills (see MacGill)

Gilman (see Wright)

Gilmer (see Gilmore)

Gilmore (see Arthur)

Gilmore
*Master Copy
3522 Twin City Highway
Groves, TX 77619
Phone (409) 963-2679
William R. Gilmore
Pub. *Gilmore, Gilmer, Gilmour
   Genealogical News Letter*, annually,
   free to owners of *Collection of
   Newsletters* ($34.95) and to 100 top
   genealogical libraries

Gilmour (see Gilmore)

Gilpatric (see Douglas)

Gilpatrick (see Kirkpatrick)

Gilray (see MacGillivray)

Gilreath (see Galbraith)

Gilroy (see MacGillivray)

Gilruth (see Fraser)

Gilson
*John William Gilson Family
   Organization
895 North 200 West
Pleasant Grove, UT 84062
Phone (801) 785-1002
James N. Gilson, Family Representative
(includes descendants of John William
   Gilson and Anna Lovisca Hepworth,
   who were married in 1899 in Utah)
No cost

Gilstrap
*Gilstrap Family Association
1921 North Harrison
San Angelo, TX 76901
Phone (915) 949-0792
Marcus Gilstrap
(includes descendants of Thomas
   (ca 1710) and Hanna Gilstrap, Peter
   Gilstrap (ca 1735), Benjamin Gilstrap
   (ca 1766), Jesse Momfort Gilstrap
   (1791), Guilford Gilstrap (1822),
   William Isaac Gilstrap (1864))

Gilvray (see MacGillivray)

Gingrich (see Heath)

Ginning (see Jennings)

Ginnings (see Jennings)

Ginnins (see Jennings)

Giordano (see Blossom Press)

Giorgi (see Andreossi)

Giorgi
*Giorgi Family of Gordevio, Ticino,
   Switzerland
4168 Woodland Street
Santa Maria, CA 93455-3356
Phone (805) 937-3518
Valerie Dyer Giorgi, Author/Publisher
(includes descendants of Carlo Giorgi,
   the father of Giuseppe Giorgi who
   married Guiseppina Gaggioni in 1856
   and had ten children, four of whom
   came to America)

Gipson (see Gibson)

Gipson
*The Sidney Levi Gipson Family
   Association
PO Box 1306
Seguin, TX 78156-1306
Theresa Frazier Crump, President
Pub. *Gipson Gazette*, quarterly, queries
   accepted; (includes Gibson/Gipson and
   related families of Frierson, Jones and
   Smith)

Girardot (see Kellett)

Girdner
Girdner Family Association
1311 North Parkland Avenue
Claremore, OK 74017
Pub. *Girdner Gatherings*

Girod (see Blossom Press)

Gish (see Stoner)

Gish
Gish Families of America
2398 Spruce Street
Carlsbad, CA 92008

Gist (see Gest)

Gitelson
Gitelson-Kamaiko Foundation
845 West End Avenue
New York, NY 10025
Pub. *Magnet*, irregularly

Gladden (see Miller)

Gladfelter (see Glattfelder)

Glancy (see Cian)

Glas (see MacDuff)

Glasco
*La Colline
Rt. 4, Box 4819
Quitman, TX 75783
Faye G. Boucher
(includes descendants of Jesse Martin
   Glasco (1818 Tennessee–1886 Upshur
   County, Texas) and Louisa Mitchell
   Earp (1823 Alabama–1907 Upsher
   County, Texas))

Glascock (see Lush)

Glasgow (see Gregor)

Glasgow
*The Glasgow Family Association
117 Sunnyside Drive
Greenwood, SC 29646
Phone (864) 223-3047
Spencer L. Glasgow
(principally descendants of Robert
   Glasgow and Rachel Wilson or
   Willson Glasgow of Ballykeel, County
   Antrim, Northern Ireland, from 1727,
   originally from Scotland)
Free membership; annual reunion on the
   second Sunday of June in Newberry,
   South Carolina

Glass (see Futral, Stewart)

Glass
Glass Family Association
Rt. 2, Box 206
Golconda, IL 62938
Marie Bannon

Glass
Glass
1221 Candice Court
Mesquite, TX 75149
Mary L. House, Editor
Pub. *Glass*, quarterly, $10.00 per year
   subscription

Glatfelter (see Glattfelder)

Glattfelder
*The Casper Glattfelder Association of
   America, Inc.
3376 Appleford Way
York, PA 17402
Jack O. Gladfelter, Secretary
Pub. *Newsletter*, two or three times per
   year; (includes descendants of Capser
   Glattfelder (1709 Glattfelden,
   Switzerland–1775 York County, PA),
   immigrated to Pennsylvania 1743;
   variant spelling: Clodfelter, Clotfelter,
   Gladfelter, Glatfelter, Glotfelty)
Free membership; annual reunion on the
   last Sunday of July at Heimwald Park
   in rural York County, Pennsylvania

Glawson
*Glawson Clearinghouse
207 Auburn Drive
Dalton, GA 30720
Phone (706) 278-1504
Joseph Wiley Reid
(1400–1890 period)

Glazier (see Barnard)

Gleason
*Gleason Reunions and Research
5721 West Washington Boulevard
Milwaukee, WI 53208
Phone (414) 258-9349
John Gleeson (Ceannaire)
Pub. *The Gleesheet*, biannually
   (December of odd-numbered years),
   $5.00 per issue; (includes Gleeson)

Gledhill (see Lush)

Gleeson (see Cian, Gleason)

Gleeson
Michael Gleeson and Anora Hogan
   (Ontario) Family Organization
PO Box 157
Knightsen, CA 94548
Carolyn Sherfy

Glendenning (see Hoggatt)

Glendinning (see Douglas)

Glenn (see Douglas, Rutherford)

Glenn
Glenn Gleanings
2203 Aquila's Delight
Fallston, MD 21047
Bette Brengle-Poole
Pub. *Glenn Gleanings*, quarterly, $15.00
   per year subscription

Glenn
*Nall News Publishing Company
PO Box 2186
Willingboro, NJ 08046-2186
Josephine Crittenberger-Nall, Editor-
Publisher
Pub. *Southern Glenn Gleanings*,
quarterly, $16.00 per year subscription

Glenny (see Graham)

Glerum
*Dutch Ancestors: The Glerums
5318 Chelsea Street
LaJolla, CA 92037
Phone (619) 488-2123
Meg Thompson, Genealogist, Author and
Publisher

Glinn (see Cian)

Glisson
*Thomas Glisson Family Organization
1599 Monaco Circle
Salt Lake City, UT 84121
Phone (801) 278-7708
Eldon B. Tucker, Jr., M.D.
(includes family originally from West
Virginia)

Gloniger (see Cloniger)

Glotfelty (see Glattfelder)

Glover (see Black, Dobie)

Glover
*Glover Family Association
2070 Burnt Hickory Road
Marietta, GA 30064
Phone (770) 428-2525
Jim Glover, Editor
Pub. *Glover Family Association
Newsletter*, quarterly
$12.50 per year membership

Glynn (see Cian)

Goad
*The Goads—A Frontier Family
1730 Fairmeadows Drive
Bettendorf, IA 52722
Phone (319) 355-7942
Kenneth F. Haas, Publisher
(includes Goad, Goard, Gourd
descendants of Abraham and Katherine
(Williams) Goad, ca 1675–1735,
Richmond County, Virginia)

Goan (see Gowen)

Goans (see Gowen)

Goard (see Goad)

Goates
*William Goates Family Organization
3051 West 3800 South
West Valley City, UT 84119
Phone (801) 968-3442

Kenneth Joseph Goates, Publisher
(includes descendants of William Goates,
Sr. (1817–1895), Cambridgeshire,
England, to Utah, and wife, Susan
Larkin)

Gobbel (see Coble)

Gobble (see Coble)

Gobble
*Gobble Family Organization
7818 East Almond Street
Tucson, AZ 85730
Phone (520) 790-3463
Victor C. Parsons, Historian
Pub. *Turkey Talk*, semiannually (fall and
spring); (includes descendants of
James B. Gobble (1836 Virginia–1900
Val Verde County, Texas) and Phoebe
A. McKay (1840 Newton County,
Missouri–1910 Val Verde County,
Texas)
Annual reunion on a weekend of June

Gobel (see Coble)

Göbel (see Coble)

Goble (see Jacoby, McIlraith, Powell)

Goble
*Goble Surname Organization
2310 Juniper Court
Golden, CO 80401-8087
Phone (303) 526-1319
Terence T. Quirke, Jr., Ph.D., C.G.,
Proprietor

Gochenour
Gochenour
4901 Arborgate Drive
Arlington, TX 76017-1049
William A. Gochenour, Jr.
Pub. *Gochenour*, three times per year,
$5.00 per year subscription
Reunion

Godard (see Goddard)

Godbee
Godbee Family Association
1330 Ellison Bridge Road
Sardis, GA 30456
Phone (912) 569-4192
Willard Godbee,Sr.
Pub. *The Brier Creek Banner*,
semimonthly
$14.00 per year membership

Goddard
*The Goddard Association of America
118 South Volutsia
Wichita, KS 67211-2038
Phone (316) 682-4942
Kathryn Goddard Myer, Editor/Executive
Secretary
Pub. *The Goddard Newsletter*, quarterly
(February, May, August and
November), $7.50 per year

subscription; (includes all spellings of
Goddard/Godard)
$10.00 per year membership for
individuals, $15.00 per year
membership for husband/wife, $20.00
per year membership for families

Godeau (see Johnson)

Godfrey (see Rothenberger)

Godfrey
*The James Godfrey and Fannie Alice
Jones Family Organization
1064 West 13th South
Salt Lake City, UT 84104
Margery Austin Gold
Reunion

Godfrey
*Godfrey Cousins Family Reunion
124 North Franklin
Whitewater, WI 53190
Judith Triebold
(includes descendants of Thomas
Godfrey and John Godfrey)
Annual reunion in August or September
at Johnstown, Rock County, Wisconsin

Godman (see Goodman)

Goebbel (see Coble)

Goede (see Pessner)

Goen (see Gowen)

Goens (see Gowen)

Goetz (see Honaker)

Goff
*Goff/Gough Family Association
8624 Wimbledon Drive
Knoxville, TN 37923
Phone (423) 690-2432
Bob B. Goff, Editor
Pub. *Goffs/Goughs, Their Ancestors and
Descendants*, quarterly
$10.00 per calendar year membership

Goin (see Gowen)

Goine (see Gowen)

Goines (see Gowen)

Going (see Gowen)

Goings (see Gowen, Gowings)

Goins (see Casto)

Goins (see Gowen)

Goins
*Goins Family
PO Box 3336
McAllen, TX 78502
Phone (210) 687-2609
Patricia J. Sharkey

Golden (see Golding, Hull, MacDuff)

Golden
*Golden Surname Organization
53 North First West
PO Box 468
Monroe, UT 84754
Phone (801) 527-4475
Ina Hunt Tuft

Golden
Golden Family Association
PO Box 742
Falls Church, VA 22046
Thomas Golden

Goldenstein
*Goldenstein Family Organization
RR 2, Box 256
Red Cloud, NE 68970
Phone (402) 746-2279
Mrs. Betty Krueger, Secretary

Goldhahn
Goldhahn Family Newsletter
4823 Jerome Avenue
Skokie, IL 60077
Phone (847) 675-5550
Charlotte Wiedman, Editor
Pub. *Goldhahn Family Newsletter*,
    semiannually (March and September),
    donation for subscription

Golding
*The Golding Family Foundation
1131 C Golfview Drive
Carmel, IL 46032
Dwight R. Owens, Editor
Pub. *Golding Nuggets*, quarterly;
    (includes descendants of William
    Golding (ca 1704–ca 1782) and
    Elizabeth Foster; also allied families:
    Andrews, Bobo, Brown, Chiles, Cole,
    Crosswaite, Crosthwait, Foster, Garnet,
    Gerdine, Golden, Golding, Goulding,
    Griffin, Haney, Hunter, Leonard,
    Ligon, Long, McGowen, Motes,
    Nichols, Nickles, Overby, Owen(s),
    Pearson, Phillips, Pinson, Putman,
    Reid, Snow, Tinsley, Tolleson,
    Waldrip, Waldrop, Williams, Wilmoth,
    Wood(s), Woodson, Workman, Young)
$10.00 per year membership (beginning
    in January); biennial reunion

Golding
*William Golding (1805) Family
    Organization
1895 North 285 East
Orem, UT 84057
Phone (801) 225-7375
Carma M. Golding
(includes descendants of William
    Golding (1805 South Carolina–) and
    Elizabeth Lawrence)
Cost for materials only

Goldmänn (see Hoster)

Goldsberry
*The Goldsberry Family Research Group
8775 Mockingbird Lane
Cincinnati, OH 45231-4758
Phone (513) 931-7269 (P.M.); E-mail:
    ausberry@tso.cin.ix.net
Eric E. Hovemeyer, Archivist/Compiler
Pub. *GFRG Newsletter*, published on
    demand and as needed for research;
    (includes Goldsberry family, any time
    and any place, primarily sent via E-
    mail, but available in hard copy for the
    cost of reproduction and mailing)

Goldsmith (see Brawley)

Gollan (see MacDuff)

Golliher
*Golliher/Trent Reunion
111 North Lincoln Street
Kahoka, MO 63445
Phone (816) 727-2472
Lila Ferguson
(includes descendants of James Golliher
    (1808 Kentucky–1884 Burden,
    Kansas) and his wife, Catherine Jewett
    (1814 Illinois–1899 Burden, Kansas);
    Pleasant Trent (1810 Kentucky–), son
    of Benjamin and Mary, and Pleasant's
    wife, Mary J. Pearman (1812 Hardin
    County, Kentucky–), daughter of
    Samuel Pearman and Nancy Shelton)

Golz
*Golz Family Reunion
PO Box 147
Nashotah, WI 53058-0147
Phone (414) 646-8183
Susan M. Hopfensperger

Gombert (see Bodeker)

Gomminger (see Mouser)

Gonsalus-Duk
*Emanuel Gonsalus-Duk and His
    Descendants: Working Papers*
611 East 980 Road
Baldwin, KS 66006
Phone (913) 842-4437
Ann S. Johnson
Pub. *Emanuel Gonsalus-Duk and His
    Descendants: Working Papers*,
    irregularly; (includes descendants of
    Emanuel Gonsalus-Duk (ca 1660–ca
    1752) and his wives, Marritje Davids
    and Rebecca Westfall)

Gooch
*The Gooch Family Library
222 Alexandria Drive
Macon, GA 31210
Phone (912) 477-6790
Cecil Daniels, Editor
Pub. *The Gooch Family*, quarterly,
    $10.00 per year subscription
    (beginning in July); (any spelling)
Annual reunion on the fourth Sunday of
    July at Mount Airy Church, Mount
    Airy Church Road, Suches, Georgia

Gooch
*William Edmund Gooch and Anne
    Burkinsham (1816) Family
    Organization
2015 North 1000 East
North Logan, UT 84321
Phone (801) 753-1458
Kaylene A. Griffin, Genealogist

Good (see Cian, Stoner)

Good
*Good Surname Organization
150 Brown Street
Saint Clair, MI 48079-4882
Phone (810) 329-9359
George M. Roberts
(includes Good and Goode families of
    Ontario and U.S.A.)

Good
The Good(e) Family Association
935 S. Court Street, Apartment 48
Circleville, OH 43113
Phillip Good, Family Historian
Pub. *Good News*, quarterly
$10.00 per year membership; reunion

Goodale (see Barnard)

Goode (see Sullivan Surname Exchange,
    Good, Stewart)

Goode
W. S. Dawson Company
PO Box 62823
Virginia Beach, VA 23466
C. W. Tazewell
Pub. *Goode*, quarterly, $2.00 per issue

Goodell (see Barnard, Pasko)

Goodenough (see Goodenow)

Goodenow
*Goodenow-Goodenough-Doodnowe-
    Doogno-Goodinow*
101 Fourth Street, N.E.
Union, IA 52175
Miriam Colvin West, Editor
Pub. *Goodenow-Goodenough-
    Doodnowe-Doogno-Goodinow*
$20.00 per year membership

Goodenow
*Goodenow Family Association
Rt. 2, Box 718
Sheperdstown, WV 25443-9403
Phone (304) 876-2008
Theodore J. F. Banvard, Corresponding
    Secretary
Pub. *Goodenows' Ghosts*, quarterly;
    (includes Goodenough, Goodno,
    Goodnough, Goodnow, especially
    Sudbury, Massachusetts, family;
    30,000-name database; allied families:
    Abbott, Allen, Anderson, Austin,
    Axtell, Bacon, Baker, Banvard,
    Barnes, Bennett, Bent, Bigelow, Boyer,
    Brooks, Brown, Campbell, Carpenter,

Chamberlin, Churchill, Clark, Collins, Condit, Cooper, Cox, Crombie, Curtis, Cutler, Davis, Day, Dodge, Dunn, Eaton, Edward, Emery, Fletcher, Foskett, Foster, Fredrickson, Frost, Gause, Green, Griffin, Hall, Hamilton, Hanson, Hatstat, Hayden, Hern, Hess, Hunt, Jackson, Jenkins, Johnson, Jones, Koch, Lane, Lawton, LeBarron, Martin, Maynard, McEdward, Miles, Miller, Moore, Morse, Nelson, Newton, Nims, Ostrin, Palmer, Parmenter, Pendleton, Peterson, Phillips, Potter, Powers, Pratt, Read, Rice, Rich, Robinson, Rowley, Slider, Smith, Starkey, Stoddard, Stone, Taylor, Thompson, VanEpps, Walker, Warner, Wells, White, Wilcox, Williams, Winslow and Young)
$20.00 per year membership for families, $50.00 supporting membership, $75.00 sustaining membership, $200.00 life membership, optional $25.00 initiation fee encouraged; reunion in even-numbered years

Goodin
Goodin News
411 Avondale Road
Huntington, WV 25705-1524
Melinda Vance, Family Representative
Pub. *Goodin News*

Goodinow (see Goodenow)

Goodknight (see Goodnight)

Goodlap (see MacDuff)

Goodlet (see MacDuff)

Goodlow (see Garner)

Goodman (see Blossom Press, Folk Family Surname Exchange, Brawley)

Goodman
*Folk Family
PO Box 52048
Knoxville, TN 37950-2048
Hester E. Stockton, Owner; Ellen Elizabeth Goodman, Editor
Pub. *Goodman Families*, quarterly, $15.00 per year subscription, $5.00 per issue; (includes Godman, Guttmann)

Goodman
*Goodman Gathering
PO Box 52048
Knoxville, TN 37950-2048
Hester E. Stockton
(includes descendants of Charles Goodman and Eliz. Horsley of Albemarle County, Virginia)
Annual reunion in June at the Red River Valley Fairgrounds, Paris, Texas

Goodman
*Isaiah Goodman Family Organization
2353 West Bueno Vista
West Jordan, UT 84084

Phone (801) 561-3724; E-mail: michael.goodman@m.k12.ut.us
Michael L. Goodman
Pub. *Goodman "Treesearch" Notes*, irregularly (quarterly/semiannually); (includes descendants of Isaiah H. Goodman (1826–1906) of Kentucky and Callaway County, Missouri, and descendants of Mariah Snell (1826–1876) of Callaway County, Missouri)
$5.00 per year membership

Goodman
Goodman Family Association
14333 Aldengate Road
Midlothian, VA 23113
Anne Hale Kellam
Pub. *Goodman Family Gazette*, quarterly

Goodnight
Good(k)night/Gut(d)knecht Family Organization
1007 Baffin Lane
Houston, TX 77090-1214
Veda G. Jones

Goodno (see Goodenow)

Goodnough (see Goodenow)

Goodnow (see Goodenow)

Goodnowe (see Goodenow)

Goodrich
Goodrich Family Association
7 Lake Shore Drive
Cary, IL 60013
Ginny Farrell
Pub. *Goodrich Gospel*, quarterly

Goodrich
*The Goodrich Family in America
315 East 68th Street
New York, NY 10021
Dr. Joyce Goodrich

Goodrum (see Tidwell)

Goodsir (see MacDuff)

Goodson (see Covert)

Goodwiley (see MacDuff)

Goodwilie (see MacDuff)

Goodwin (see Clark, Corson, Heath, Warren)

Goodwin
*The Goodwin Family Organization
39 Lost Trail
Roswell, NM 88201-9509
Phone (505) 625-0961
Alice B. Goodwin Sharp, President and Corresponding Secretary
Pub. *The Goodwin News*, semiannually (April and October), $15.00 per year subscription; (includes all Goodwin families, worldwide)

$3.00 per year membership (publication not included); annual reunion at the First Federated Church, South Berwick, Maine

Goodyear (see MacDuff)

Gookin
*Gookin Surname Research
2838 Evergreen Avenue, N.E.
Salem, OR 97303
Phone (503) 585-2985
Richard N. Gookins
(Gookin and Gookins)

Gookins (see Gookin)

Goolar (see Westerfield)

Gold
*Goold Surname Organization
7 Sweden Hill Road
Brockport, NY 14420-2517
Roy Goold
(includes descendants of Thomas Goold (1630–1690) of Salem, Massachusetts)

Goolsby
Goolsby Family Association
6004 S.W. Second Street
Des Moines, IA 50315
Robert La Freddo

Goon (see Gowen)

Goons (see Gowen)

Gorball
Gorball, Gorble, Gorbel Family Newsletter
PO Box 48
Lander, WY 82520-0048
Coleen Coleman
Pub. *Gorball, Gorble, Gorbel Family Newsletter*

Gorbel (see Gorball)

Gorbet (see Gorbett)

Gorbett
Gorbett/Gorbet Family Association
1516 North Carlton
Farmington, NM 87401

Gorble (see Gorball)

Gorby
*National Gorby Association (N.G.A.)
8165 South Mill Road
Spanish Fork, UT 84660
Phone (801) 798-2651
Jennings C. Fish, President
Pub. *Gorby Roots*, quarterly
$4.00 per year membership

Gordon (see Folk Family Surname Exchange, McRae)

Gordon
*House of Gordon (United States
   Branch)
PO Box 3827 CRS
Johnson City, TN 37601
Phone (615) 283-4505
Charles O. Gordon, President
Pub. *House of Gordon Newsletter*
$10.00 per year U.S. Branch membership

Gordy (see Sidwell)

Gore (see Underwood, Wiler)

Gore
Gore Gazette
411 Avondale Road
Huntington, WV 25705-1524
Melinda Vance, Family Representative
Pub. *Gore Gazette*

Gorham
Gorham Grandparents
920 Lexington Street
Hemet, CA 92545-5330
Carole J. Reddoch
Pub. *Gorham Grandparents*, quarterly,
   $15.00 per year subscription

Gorley (see MacDuff)

Gorley
*Gorley/Gourlay Family Association
109 Oak Way Street
Eatonton, GA 31024
Phone (706) 485-6810
E. V. Knight, Jr.

Gorlie (see MacDuff)

Gorman (see Kelly)

Gorouard (see Johnson)

Gorrell (see Lambert)

Gorton (see Lush)

Goslin (see Gosnell)

Gosman (see MacDuff)

Gosnell
Gosnell Feathers
1776 Forest Park Drive
Anchorage, AK 99517
Phone (907) 278-9147
Gloria Banks Rankin, Compiler
Pub. *Gosnell Feathers*, three times per
   year (September, January and May/
   June), $13.50 per year subscription;
   (includes Goslin, Gossnold, Gossnald
   and related families)

Gosnell
*Gosnell Family Ancestors
59 Marseille Place
Sicklerville, NJ 08081
Phone (609) 629-6910
June A. Gosnell Freed

Pub. *Our Folks*, quarterly, $20.00 per
   year subscription

Goss (see Scadlock)

Gosselin
*Association des Familles Gosselin, Inc.
600 West 22nd Street
Odessa, TX 79761
Lorraine Gosselin Harrison, United
   States Representative
(includes descendants of Gabriel
   Gosselin, who arrived in New France
   (now Quebec) from Comberay,
   Normandy, France, settled on Ile
   d'Orleans about 1650, married 1653
   near Silley, Quebec, to Françoise
   Lelievre from Nancy, Lorraine,
   France)

Gossler
Gossler Family Association
414 S.E. 45th
Portland, OR 97215
Phone (503) 639-1981
Walter N. Gossler,Jr.

Gossman (see MacDuff)

Gossnald (see Gosnell)

Gossnold (see Gosnell)

Gotham
*Gotham Ties Family Association
12 Estacada Road
Santa Fe, NM 87505
Phone (505) 983-6496
Ken Rhines, Editor
Pub. *Gotham Ties*, bimonthly; (Gotham
   surname in general and related
   families: Farrow, Guthrie, Howe,
   Kendall, Keyes, Latimer and Rhines)
$8.00 per year membership

Gotto (see Pannill)

Goudey (see Macpherson)

Goudie (see Macpherson)

Gough (see Goff, Kane)

Gould (see Cummings)

Gould
*Samuel Gould Family Organization
340 East Balboa Drive
Tempe, AZ 85282
Phone (602) 966-0961
Barbara B. and Bryce W. Obray

Goulding (see Golding)

Gourant (see Geurin)

Gourd (see Goad)

Gourdin
*The Gourdin Books
6323 Early Red Court
Columbia, MD 21045-4499
J. Raymond Gourdin, Publisher and
   Author
Pub. *The Gourdin(e) Family Newsletter*,
   quarterly; (a French-African-American
   Family from South Carolina
Reunion

Gourdine (see Gourdin)

Gourlay (see Gorley, MacDuff)

Gourley (see MacDuff, Merier)

Gow (see Chattan, Gregor, MacDuff,
   Macpherson, MacPherson)

Gowan (see Macpherson, MacPherson)

Gowans (see Gowen)

Gowdie (see MacPherson)

Gowen (see Corson)

Gowen
*Gowen Research Foundation
5708 Gary Avenue
Lubbuck, TX 79413
Phone (806) 795-8758; (806) 795-9694;
   (806) 795-2005 (electronic library)
Arlee Gowen, President and Editor
Pub. *Gowen Research Foundation
   Newsletter*, monthly, $12.50 per year
   subscription; (includes Gawan, Goan,
   Goen, Goin, Goine, Going, Goon,
   Gowan, Gowin, Goyen, Goyne, plus
   plurals)

Gower
*The Gower History
2076 Valley View Road
Joelton, TN 37080
Phone (615) 876-7797
Mary Solomon, Publisher
(also researching Humphrey, McPherson,
   Norman, Solomon lines)

Gowin (see Gowen)

Gowings
Martin and Terry Gowings/Goings
   Family Organization
1604 Longfellow Street
McLean, VA 22101
Georgia E. Benefiel

Gowins (see Gettings, Gowen)

Goyen (see Gowen)

Goyens (see Gowen)

Goyne (see Gowen)

Goynes (see Gowen)

Grabeal
Grabeal Surname Organization
John Peter Graybeal, Sr., Family
    Organization
HC 71, Box 372
Jeremiah, KY 41826
Phone (606) 633-2166
Joy S. Adams

Grabill (see Lambert)

Grace (see Cian, McIlraith)

Grace
*Grace Surname Organization
2310 Juniper Court
Golden, CO 80401-8087
Phone (303) 526-1319
Terence T. Quirke, Jr., Ph.D., C.G.,
    Proprietor

Grad
*Grad Family Reunion
22 Haven Road
Wellesley Hills, MA 02181-2405
Phone (617) 237-1800
Dr. Eli Grad
Pub. *Grad Family Newsletter*, quarterly,
    donation for subscription

Gradeless
*Gradeless/Grayless Computerized Data
    Exchange
1721 Edgewood Avenue
Racine, WI 53404-2306
Phone (414) 634-2824; E-mail:
    DrG@execpc.com; Website: http://
    www.execpc.com/~drg
Dr. Donald E. Gradeless
(includes 5,000+ names on descendants
    of Timothy Grayless (–1743
    Maryland))

Grady
*Grady Surname Organization
3 Brazill Lane
Whitehall, MT 59759
Phone (406) 287-3369
Lindia Roggia Lovshin

Graef (see Schaffer)

Graetz
*Graetz Surname Organization
199 Commodore Drive
Milledgeville, GA 31061
Phone (912) 968-7425
Richard Bialac

Graeve (see Bestman)

Graf (see Groff)

Graf
*The Graf(f) Gazette
12600 Bissonnet A4-407
Houston, TX 77099
Dede D. Mercer, Publisher

Pub. *The Graf(f) Gazette*, semiannually,
    $20.00 per year subscription; (includes
    all variations of the surname,
    worldwide)

Graff (see Graf)

Graff
Graff Newsletter
927 East Seventh Street
Salt Lake City, UT 84102
E. G. Luken
Pub. *Graff Newsletter*

Graffunder (see Grawunder)

Gragg (see Gregg)

Graham (see The Memorial Foundation
    of the Germanna Colonies, Farrington,
    McCullah, Thompson)

Graham
Graham Clan Society
6708 Hillcroft Place
Oxon Hill, MD 20022
H. Graham

Graham
*Kinseeker Publications
5697 Old Maple Trail
PO Box 184
Grawn, MI 49637
Phone E-mail: AB064@taverse.lib.mi.us
Victoria Wilson, Editor
Pub. *Graham Group*, quarterly, $10.00
    per year subscription

Graham
*The Elliot Harold Graham Family
3230 South Concourse Drive
Mount Pleasant, MI 48858-9131
Rev. David H. Gill, Publisher

Graham
*Clan Graham Society, Inc.
1228 Kensington Drive
High Point, NC 27262
Phone (910) 885-5789; E-mail:
    71116.702@compuserve.com
Robert H. Howard, Membership Vice
    President
Pub. *Clan Graham News*, quarterly;
    (includes septs: Airth, Allardyce,
    Auchinloick (Kilpatrich), Ballewen,
    Blair, Bonar, Bonnar, Bonner, Bontein,
    Bontine, Buchlyrie, Buntain, Buntin,
    Bunting, Conyers, Drumaguhassle,
    Duchray, Dugalston, Esbank, Fingry,
    Glenny, Hadden, Haldane, Lingo,
    MacGibbon, MacGilvernock,
    MacIlvern, MacShille, Menteith,
    Montrose, Monzie, Orchille, Pitcairn,
    Pyatt, Pye, Pyott, Rednock, and
    Sirowan)
$15.00 per year membership for
    individuals, $20.00 per year
    membership for families

Graham
*Graham Family Association
118 Yosemite Drive
San Antonio, TX 78232-1323
Phone (210) 494-2772
Edw. A. Graham
No cost

Graham
William Graham and Mary Puckett
    Association
Rt. 3, Box 14
Pomeroy, WA 99347
K. Fitzsimmons

Gralla
*Gralla Surname Organization
5663 West 11200 North
Highland, UT 84003
Phone (801) 756-2713
Sonja Nishimoto, A.G., Family
    Genealogist and Historian
Pub. *Gralla Family Newsletter*,
    semiannually, free; (of Poland)

Gramse
*Gramse/Gramsey Reunion
10422 South 47th Street
Phoenix, AZ 85044
Phone (602) 893-3690
Evelyn Gramse White

Grandin (see Beaudet)

Grandstaff (see Grindstaff)

Grange
*Grange Surname Organization
435 Grandview Avenue
Novato, CA 94947
Phone (415) 892-9025
Sonja Jensen
(includes descendants of William and
    Elizabeth Newell Grange)

Granger (see Johnson)

Granich (see Blossom Press)

Grann (see Harmon)

Granson (see Gunn)

Grant (see Corson)

Grant
Grant Gleanings
Rt. 2, Box 671
Grangeville, ID 83530-9635
Phone (208) 983-0515
Anne Long
Pub. *Grant Gleanings*, irregularly, $6.50
    per year (Idaho residents add 5% sales
    tax)

Grant
Grant/Lee Association (IL, KY, IN)
607 North Logan Street
Marion, IL 62959
A. Grant

Grant
Clan Grant Society
4177 Circle Court
Williamsville, NY 14221
Anne Grant-Knapp
Pub. *Clan Grant Society*

Grant
*Amzi Neely Grant and Descendants
1225 Peden Bridge Road
Chester, SC 29706-8596
Mrs. Wm. F. White
(includes descendants of Amzi Neely
    Grant and his wives, Elizabeth Geneva
    Grant Grant and Marie Louise Olds
    Grant, of Chester, Chester County,
    South Carolina)

Grant
*Edith Roxy Grant Family Organization
4302 Hollow Hill
San Antonio, TX 78217
Phone (210) 653-2542
Col. Francis W. Boldway

Grant
*The Descendants of William and
    Elizabeth Grant
771 North 500 East
Logan, UT 84321
Phone (801) 753-8668
Dianne Clem Hirschi, Publisher
(includes descendants of William Grant
    who immigrated to Virginia about
    1690 from Scotland, and his three sons
    and two daughters, especially John
    Grant who married Margaret
    Bronaugh; also interested in Matthew
    Leeper and Amyteer, who left Virginia
    and settled in Barren County,
    Kentucky, in 1800; Jacob Roller and
    Patsy Brisco, who left Virginia and
    settled in Benton County, Arkansas, in
    1824; Johann Conrad Klemm and
    Maria Catherina, who left Ittlingen,
    Germany, and settled in Montgomery
    County, Pennsylvania, in the 1750s;
    James Heard, who settled in Union
    County, Ohio, from Berkeley County,
    Virginia, about 1800; Hugh Smith and
    Rachel Stockton, who left Virginia and
    settled in Barren County, Kentucky, in
    1800)

Grasser
*Grasser Surname Exchange
3385 South Bluff Road
Syracuse, UT 84075
Phone (801) 773-0531
Helga Reber Willie, Researcher

Grasty
*Grasty Surname Organization
1686 East Ardenwood Court
Concord, CA 94521
Phone (510) 685-3414
Dee Merritt
(includes Grasty, McCaslin and Wilsey)
Free

Gratta
The International Society of Gratta
    Families Worldwide
PO Box 15334
Hattiesburg, MS 39404-5334
Phone (601) 288-3191; (601) 288-3191
    FAX
David M. Gratta, Director
Pub. *Newsletter*, semiannually to
    quarterly (includes allied surnames of
    Aiello, Barbuto, Cilurzo, Cristofaro,
    Fulciniti, Iannino, Notaro, Politano,
    Rosano and Truglia)

Grave (see Graves)

Graveline (see Baudreau)

Graves (see Folk Family Surname
    Exchange, Dockery, Eaves, Job)

Graves
*Wells Genealogical Research
4504 Fox Creek Drive
Crystal Lake, IL 60012-1870
Phone (815) 455-9055
Ann L. Wells, Publisher
Pub. *Graves Researcher*, quarterly,
    $12.00 per year subscription in the
    U.S., $16.00 per year subscription in
    Canada, $18.00 or £20 per year
    subscription elsewhere, queries $5.00
    from non-subscribers; (includes all
    Graves, no restrictions)

Graves
*The Graves Family Association
261 South Street
Wrentham, MA 02093-1504
Phone (508) 384-8084; E-mail:
    kgraves239@aol.com; Website: http://
    www.andrews.edu/~calkins/
    gravesfa.html
Kenneth Vance Graves
Pub. *The Graves Family Newsletter*,
    bimonthly; (includes Greaves, Grave)
$20.00 per year membership in the U.S.
    and Canada, $30.00 per year foreign
    membership, $40.00 per year
    sustaining membership, $600.00 life
    membership; biennial national reunion
    in even-numbered years, usually in
    September; annual New England
    reunion, usually in June; annual
    Virginia reunion

Graves
Graves-Bewley Reunion
1515 S.W. Hume Court
Portland, OR 97219
Phone (503) 244-2545
Edna King
(includes descendants of Col. James B.
    Graves and Diana Newton, who came
    to Oregon in 1847 from Virginia,
    Kentucky and Missouri; or of John W.
    Bewley and Catherine Ellis, who came
    to Oregon in 1847 from Tennessee,
    Indiana and Missouri)

Gravius (see Simmon)

Gravolet (see Blossom Press)

Grawunder
*The Grawunder & Graffunder
    Connection
13108 Penn Avenue
Burnsville, MN 55337
Phone (612) 890-3240
Gladys Grovender and Linnea
    Grovender, Co-Editors
Pub. *The Grawunder & Graffunder
    Connection*, semiannually, $5.00 per
    volume subscription; (includes variant
    spellings)

Gray (see Folk Family Surname
    Exchange, Blanton, Dunbar, Emery,
    Gregor, Heath, Job, MacDuff, Stewart,
    Sutherland)

Gray
Gray Family Newsletter
520 East Griffiths Road
Santa Ana, CA 92707
Linda Lee Ferguson
Pub. *Gray Family Newsletter*

Gray
*Charles Monroe Gray Family
    Organization
Almo, ID 83312
Phone (208) 824-5536
Janis C. Durfee
(includes descendants of C. M. and Sarah
    Stephenson Gray, 1830–1898 Daviess
    County, Missouri, to Albion, Idaho;
    also John-James Stephenson, 1744–
    1821, Simpson County, Kentucky, to
    Clay County, Missouri)
Meeting every third year in Albion, Idaho

Gray
*Kinseeker Publications
5697 Old Maple Trail
PO Box 184
Grawn, MI 49637
E-mail: AB064@taverse.lib.mi.us
Victoria Wilson, Editor
Pub. *Getting Gray*, quarterly, $10.00 per
    year subscription, $2.50 for sample
    issue

Gray
Gray-Grey
1221 Candice Court
Mesquite, TX 75149
Mary L. House, Editor
Pub. *Gray-Grey*, quarterly, $20.00 per
    year subscription

Gray
*Gray/Posey Family Organization
1107 West Thomas
Pasadina, TX 77506
Phone (713) 472-3582
Fred E. Gray, Historian
No fixed annual membership fee, average
    $25.00

Graybill (see Stoner)

Grayless (see Gradeless)

Grayson (see Gregor)

Grayson
*Grayson Family Association
302 Randall Road, #208
Geneva, IL 60134-4204
Dr. Richard R. Grayson

Greagory (see MacDuff)

Grear
*Grear Ghosts
PO Box 1872
Dodge City, KS 67801-1872
Laura Tasset Koehn, President
(includes research on Ely Samuel Grear
and Amanda Francis Jackson)

Greathouse (see Sawyer)

Greathouse
*John Greathouse Family Organization
PO Box 205
Lynndyl, UT 84640
Mary Greathouse

Greaves (see Graves)

Gree (see Rutherford)

Greeg (see McRae)

Greeley (see Bugbee)

Green (see Sullivan Surname Exchange,
Belshe, Casey, Corson, Goodenow,
Gregor, Johnson, Nelson, Paxton,
Pryor, Reeder)

Green
The Gregath Publishing Company
PO Box 505
Wyandotte, OK 74370
Phone (800) 955-5232
Fredrea Gregath Cook
Pub. *The Green Family Quarterly*,
$15.00 per year subscription

Green
Green/Greene Genealogy
Rt. 2, Box 671
Grangeville, ID 83530-9635
Phone (208) 983-0515
Anne Long
Pub. *Green/Greene Genealogy*,
irregularly, $6.50 per year subscription
(Idaho residents add 5% sales tax)

Green
From Generation to Generation
Rt. 1, Box 147
Buncombe, IL 62912
Melody Tellor, Editor
Pub. *Green Group*, quarterly, $15.00 per
year subscription

Green
Kenma Publishing Company
1911 Conlin Avenue
Evansville, IN 47714-4248
Kenneth Gene Lindsay
Pub. *Green Gravevine*, quarterly, $12.95
per year subscription

Green
Green Surname Organization
John C. Green Family Organization
William Harvey Green Family
Organization
5389 Evanston
Indianapolis, IN 46220-3444
Phone (317) 253-5831
H. Suzanne O'Brien

Green
Green(e)
PO Box 1461
Ashland, KY 41105-1461
Charles A. Barker
Pub. *Greene(e)*, quarterly, $15.00 per
year subscription

Green
The Green Family Quarterly
18435 South Mission Hills
Baton Rouge, LA 70810
Phone (504) 756-2303
Alton T. Moran, Editor-Publisher
Pub. *The Green Family Quarterly*,
$15.00 per year subscription

Green
Courier Publications
PO Box 1284
Natchitoches, LA 71458-1284
Annette Carpenter Womack
Pub. *Green Family Courier*, quarterly,
$12.50 per year subscription

Green
Green Register
5 Rand Road
North Barnstead, NH 03225
Phone (603) 776-6996
Richard Herbert Tivey
Pub. *Green Register*, quarterly, $35.00
per year subscription
$50.00 per year active membership

Green
Jeduthan Green(e) Descendants
160 Northern Pines Road
Gansevoort, NY 12831
Phone (518) 587-0321
Karen Ufford Campola, Historian
Annual reunion in July

Green
Green(e) Family Association
2118 Goliad Road, #109-A
San Antonio, TX 78223-3220
Charlene Ives Nelson
Pub. *Greenleaves*, quarterly; (includes
Greene)
$10.00 per year membership

Green
*Jared Green-Deloretta Harris Family
947 McClelland
Salt Lake City, UT 84105
Phone (801) 359-5762
Judith G. Ison, Accredited Genealogist
(includes descendants of Jared Green
(1856 Cedar City, Utah–) and
Deloretta Harris (1856 Kaysville,
Utah–))
$25.00 per year membership

Green
*Philip Schuyler Green Family
1102 S.W. Trenton
Seattle, WA 98106-2423
Phone (206) 767-3413
Myrtle Prohaska
(includes Greene)

Greenaway (see Greenway)

Greene (see Brawley, Green, Greenway,
McCanna, McCune, Rutherford)

Greene
*Jeremiah Greene Family Organization
6002 Tolmie Drive, N.E.
Olympia, WA 98516
Phone (206) 456-0271
Linnea R. Brewer

Greenhalf (see Catlow)

Greenlaw
*Greenlaw/Pineo Family Organization
2230 North 4000 West
Delta, UT 84624
Phone (801) 864-3674
Nancy B. Fowles
(includes descendants of John Alfred
Greenlaw and Deborah Pineo of
Princeton, Maine)

Greenleaf (see Heath)

Greenlee (see Montgomery)

Greenlee
Greenlee Gazette
2130 Road 12, N.W.
Quincy, WA 98848
Alcenia Appling, Publisher
Pub. *Greenlee Gazette*, quarterly, $10.00
per year subscription

Greenman (see Barnard)

Greenslit (see Wright)

Greenway
*Greenway/Greenaway Family
Association
10 Munroe Road
Lexington, MA 02173
Phone (617) 862-6528
Robert C. Stuart Greenway, M.A.
$10.00 per year membership

Greenway
Greenway-Greenaway-Greene-Harrison
  Family Association
2306 Westgate
Houston, TX 77019
Phone (713) 529-2333
Harold Helm
$25.00 plus pedigree and family group
  sheets membership

Greenwell
*House of Greenwell (Worldwide)
3422 Rogers Drive
Fayetteville, NC 28303-3959
Phone (910) 867-2607
Dr. Charles W. A. Greenwell, Patriarch
Pub. *Greenwell News Letter*,
  semiannually, $2.00 per year
  subscription

Greenwood (see Lagesse)

Greer (see Brown, Gregor)

Greer
The Greer Family Genealogical Society
  of the Southern States
1068 Pinewood Drive
Sparks, NV 89434
Phone (702) 331-3520
Charles W. Barnum, President

Greer
Greer Family Reunion
Phone (615) 626-3695; (606) 678-5641;
  (313) 241-3757
(includes descendants of William W.
  Greer of Claiborne County, Tennessee,
  and of Isaac Greer who migrated to
  Kentucky)
Reunion at Springdale Elementary
  School, Tazewell, Tennessee

Greer
*Greer Surname Organization
11 West 300 South
Farmington, UT 84025
Phone (801) 451-2904
Bradford N. Ator

Gregg (see Gregor, MacDuff, McRae)

Gregg
William Gregg/Gragg and Nancy Holder
  (1829) Association
5505 Towers Street
Torrance, CA 90503
V. Vaughn

Gregg
*Gregg Family Society
PO Box 4585
Topeka, KS 66604-0585
Phone (913) 266-9058
Ms. Lee Nichols, Genealogist
(includes affiliated names: Hadley and
  McCay)

Gregor (see MacDuff)

Gregor
*The Clan Gregor Society of Scotland,
  Western USA Chapter
PO Box 1423
Stockton, CA 95201
Phone (408) 633-2112
Richard Magruder, Treasurer
Pub. *Griogarach*, quarterly; (includes
  MacGregor, McGregor and septs)
$29.00 per year membership

Gregor
*The Clan Gregor Society, Southeast
  U.S. Chapter
PO Box 393
Stone Mountain, GA 30083
Phone (404) 292-5588
Inez Gregory Boothe, C.G.S., Secretary
Pub. *Newsletters from Scotland and the
  U.S. Chapter* (includes Greer, Gregor,
  Gregory, MacGregor and septs)

Gregor
Gregor Clan Society of America
1109 Crowfoot Lane
Silver Spring, MD 20904

Gregor
*The Clan Gregor Society, New England
  Chapter, Inc.
PO Box 190
Boylston, MA 01505
Phone (617) 322-6271
George W. MacGregor, Chairman of
  Council
Pub. *The Sheep Stealer's Gazette*,
  bimonthly, $10.00 per year
  subscription; (includes MacGregor and
  over 100 related surnames and septs,
  Rob Roy MacGregor connections;
  serves New England, New York,
  Pennsylvania, New Jersey, Delaware
  and Maryland)
$25.00 per year membership for
  individuals, $40.00 per year
  membership for families

Gregor
*American Clan Gregor Society
249A South Lake Shore Drive
Whispering Pines, NC 28327
Phone (919) 949-3119
Joseph C. Tichy, Assistant Chieftain
Pub. *Yearbook of ACGS*, annually

Gregor
*Clan Gregor Center and Foundation
20770 Lake Road
Rocky River, OH 44116
Phone (216) 333-1008
Margaret M. Frost, Vice President
Pub. *The Quaich*, about three times per
  year; (includes Arrowsmith, Black,
  Blue, Bower, Bowmaker, Brewer,
  Burns, Caird, Callendar, Callum,
  Clark, Clerks, Comrie, Cramond,
  Crimmond, Crowther, Currie,
  Dennison, Denson, Dochart, Docherty,
  Dowie, Erskine, Fletcher, Gair,
  Glasgow, Gow, Gray, Grayson, Green,
  Greer, Gregg, Gregor, Gregorson,
  Gregory, Gregson, Greig, Grewar,
  Grey, Greyson, Grier, Grierson,
  Grieve, Grigg, Grigor, Grimmond,
  Gruer, Johnstone, King, Kirkpatrick,
  Kirkwood, Laikie, Leckie, Lecky,
  Leith, Livingston, Lockie, MacAdam,
  MacAinsh, MacAldowie, MacAlester,
  MacAlister, MacAlpine, MacAngus,
  MacAnish, MacAnsh, MacAra,
  MacAree, MacCainsh, MacCance,
  MacChoiter, MacClerich,
  MacConachie, MacCondach,
  MacCondochie, MacCrimmon,
  MacCrouther, MacDiarmid, MacEwan,
  MacGeach, MacGeorge, MacGregor,
  MacGrewar, MacGrigor, MacGrouther,
  MacGruder, MacGruer, MacGruther,
  MacIldowie, MacIlduff, MacIlduy,
  MacIlroy, MacInnes, MacInstalker,
  MacIntyre, MacLeister, MacLiver,
  MacNay, MacNea, MacNee,
  MacNeice, MacNeish, MacNess,
  MacNey, MacNie, MacNiesh,
  MacNocaird, MacNucator, MacPeter,
  MacPetrie, MacPhatridge, MacQueen,
  MacQwan, MacWilliam, Magrew,
  Malloch, Millar, Neilson, Neish,
  Nelson, Nice, Nish, Nucator, Orr,
  Paisley, Paterson, Pattullo, Pearson,
  Peat, Peter, Peterkin, Peters, Peterson,
  Petrie, Renfrew, Riddoch, Roy,
  Skinner, Slessor, Stalker, Sterling,
  Stringer, Taylor, Turner, Walker,
  Weliver, White, Whyte, Wilson)
$30.00 per year membership

Gregor
*Clan Gregor Society, Great Lakes
  Chapter
Clan Gregor Center and Foundation
22677 Peachtree Lane
Rocky River, OH 44116
Phone (216) 333-4098
Jean Skinner Anderson, Chairman
(includes Gregor, MacGregor, Greer,
  Greig, etc.)
$20.00 per year membership for
  individuals, $35.00 per year
  membership for families

Gregor
*The American Southwest Chapter, Clan
  Gregor Society
10550 Valley Forge, #225
Houston, TX 77042
Phone (713) 952-7142
Barbara Zoe Alexander, Secretary
(includes members of Clan Gregor,
  Scotland, and associated septs, in
  Louisiana, Texas, Oklahoma, Arkansas
  and New Mexico)
$25.00 per year membership for
  individuals, $40.00 per year
  membership for families

Gregorcik (see Hribar)

Gregorson (see Gregor)

Gregory (see Catlow, Gregor, Joy, Stone, Wright)

Gregory
*Family Research
416 Rockhill Avenue
Dayton, OH 45429-2628
Richard Bordeaux Walker
(includes ancestry and descendants of Daniel Gregory (–1847) and Sarah Lamont of Ashtabula, Allen and Auglaize counties, Ohio, and Marshall and Peoria counties, Illinois)

Gregson (see Gregor)

Greig (see Gregor, MacDuff)

Gremillion (see Johnson)

Grems
Grems Family Association
612
Schenectady, NY 12305-1518
Mandalay D. Grems

Grenelle
*Grenelle Family Association
Cayuga Lake MHP Box D6
Moravia, NY 13118
Richard C. Grinnell, President
Pub. *GFA Official Newsletter*, three times per year

Gresham (see Surname Sources)

Greshewick
Greshewick Surname Organization
1936 East Fifth Street
Ontario, CA 91764
Greg Legutki

Gress (see Crist, Kress)

Greth (see Balthaser)

Gretory (see Catlow)

Greve (see Bestman)

Grevsack (see Fergusson)

Grewar (see Fraser, Gregor)

Grey (see Gray, Gregor)

Greyson (see Gregor)

Grice
Grice Family Reunion
404 South East Street
Guymon, OK 73942
Nancy Grice Stewart
(includes descendants of Jane Banther and Lawson MacKell Grice of North Carolina, Georgia and Oklahoma)

Griepp (see Sager)

Griepp
*Descendants of Gottfried and Wilhelmina Griepp and their Hintz and Rathke Kinships
3505 Coolheights Drive
Rancho Palos Verdes, CA 90275
Frank and Muriel Griepp, Publisher

Griepp
Griepp Reunion
207 North Main Street
Clintonville, WI 54929
Phone (715) 828-3471
Fern Habeck Bernhardt, Secretary
Annual reunion in Shawano, Wisconsin

Grier (see Brown, Gregor)

Grier
*Grier and Company
144 Downing Street
Denver, CO 80218-3917
Phone (303) 744-8416
William M. Grier, Jr., Publisher

Grierson (see Gregor)

Griesemer (see Griesmer)

Griesemer
*Griesemer Family Association
PO Box 814
Lompoc, CA 93438-0814
Phone (805) 736-9637
Albert C. Hardy, Jr., Vice-President/ Editor
Pub. *The Thistle*, semiannually, $3.00 per year subscription; (includes Griesemer, Grismore, Grisamore and 23 other spellings)
Annual reunion on the last Sunday of August in Mohnton, PA

Griesmer
Griesmer-Griesemer Family Organization
10813 Dale Avenue
Cleveland, OH 44111
Howard Griesmer

Grieve (see Gregor)

Griffee
Griffee Family Association
Rt. 1, Box 197
Engadine, MI 49827
Ann Griffee

Griffen
*Griffen Family
158 Ashdown Road
Ballston Lake, NY 12019
Phone (518) 399-5013
Jane Meader Nye, Secretary
Pub. *Newsletter*, annually
$10.00 per year membership

Griffin (see Folk Family Surname Exchange, Brown, Chapman, Golding, Goodenow, Miller)

Griffin
*Kinseeker Publications
5697 Old Maple Trail
PO Box 184
Grawn, MI 49637
E-mail: AB064@taverse.lib.mi.us
Victoria Wilson, Editor
Pub. *The Family Series: Griffin*, irregularly, $6.50 per year subscription

Griffin
*The Irish Griffins
2776 County Road 27
Bellevue, OH 44811
Phone (419) 483-2363
Kate L. Jett
(includes associated names of Sheehan, Flynn and Chubb, 1849 immigrants to America from Ireland)

Griffin
*Griffin Family
333 Chadwyck Drive
Danville, VA 24541-3306
Phone (804) 793-1744
A. Ray Griffin, Jr.
(includes Griffin of eastern North Carolina from 1728)

Griffith
*Griffith Clearinghouse
40 Hillsdale Drive
Council Bluffs, IA 51503-0552
Phone (712) 323-4303
Howard G. Griffith

Griffith
*Griffith Family
333 Chadwyck Drive
Danville, VA 24541-3306
Phone (804) 793-1744
A. Ray Griffin, Jr.
(includes Griffith of the Eastern Shore of Virginia, 1644–1727)

Grigg (see Gregor)

Griggs
Griggs Pioneers
6908 La Manga
Dallas, TX 75248
Phone (214) 387-2623
Dennis T. Griggs
Pub. *Griggs Pioneers*, monthly, $12.00 per year subscription

Grigor (see Gregor)

Grigsby (see Worch)

Grigsby
*National Grigsby Family Society, Southwest Chapter
906 Pecan Street
Crossett, AR 71635
Phone (501) 364-3776
Hoy C. Grigsby, Editor
Pub. *Southwest Chapter Newsletterr, The National Grigsby Family Society*, quarterly (March, June, September and

December), free to public libraries, otherwise restricted to members

Grigsby
*National Grigsby Family Society
10138 Valley Forge
Houston, TX 77042
Phone (713) 789-5766
Margaret Grigsby Mottley, Administrator
Pub. *National Grigsby Family Society Newsletter*, quarterly
$15.00 per year for membership

Grill
*Pennsylvania-German Grill/Krill Family
107 West Sunhill Road
Mannheim, PA 17545
Phone (717) 665-5869
D. Ernest Weinhold
(especially descendants of the very early immigrants who settled in northeast Lancaster County, Pennsylvania, and nearby areas)

Grimes (see Buzzard)

Grimes
Family Limbs
6423 S.E. 97th Avenue
Portland, OR 97266-4529
Shirley L. Bodak
Pub. *Grimes Family Newsletter*, ten times per year, $6.00 per year subscription

Grimmett (see Blalock)

Grimmond (see Gregor)

Grindle (see Maize)

Grindstaff (see Garner)

Grindstaff
Grindstaff/Grandstaff Family
PO Box 692
Sierra Vista, AZ 85635
Catherine J. Siegle

Grinnell
Grinnell Family Association of America
2122 North 63rd Street
Seattle, WA 98103
Betty Grinnell, Reunion Information

Grippen (see Crippen)

Grippin (see Crippen)

Grisso (see Frantz)

Grissom (see Anthes)

Griswold (see Fadner, Wright)

Griswold
Griswold Family Association of America
Rural Delivery, Box 139
Chatham, NY 12037
Esther French, Genealogist

Pub. *Griswold Family of England & America*, irregularly
$10.00 per year membership; annual reunion on the first weekend of October in New England

Grizzle
Grizzle Family Organization
1229 Tanager
Garland, TX 75042
Linda Barnes

Groberg
*Groberg Surname Organization
390 Lincoln Drive
Idaho Falls, ID 83401-4161
Phone (208) 522-3185
Mary Jane Groberg Fritzen

Groce (see Farrington)

Groendyke
Groendyke-Shields Kuzzin's
4930 Del Mar #205
San Diego, CA 92107
Pub. *Groendyke-Shields Kuzzin's*, semiannually

Groesbeck (see McCune)

Groeschel (see Schulze)

Groff (see Boose, Hoster, Welch)

Groff
*The Groff History Associates
(151 Cherry Hill Road, Ronks, PA 17572—location)
713 Columbia Avenue (mailing address)
Lancaster, PA 17603
Phone (717) 392-8252
Clyde L. Groff, A.G., Vice President
(includes some 55 spellings of the name: Graf, Groff, Grove, etc., especially lines of Groffs who came to Pennsylvania from 1710 on)
No membership fee; reunion every three years

Grogan (see Lemon)

Groleau (see Blossom Press)

Gros (see Augeron)

Grosnick
*The Grosnick Family History
1370 County T
Amherst Junction, WI 55407
Edward R. Seefelt, Author and Publisher

Grospitch
Grospitch Family Reunion
3188 West 138th Street
Cleveland, OH 44111
R. Grospitch

Gross (see Farrington, Richardson, Zebert)

Gross
Frank Gross and Catharine Cargo Reunion
1440 Hemingway Road
Lake Orion, MI 48035
Mrs. Schultz

Gross
Gross and Fessler
9719 Mary Avenue, N.W.
Seattle, WA 98117-2334
Phone (206) 784-8403
Mary E. Peters

Grothaus
Grothaus Family Organization
PO Box 93
Dickinson, TX 77539
C. Riley

Ground
Ground/Grounds Family History Association
3612 Marin Drive
Irvine, CA 92714
James H. Ground, President

Grounds (see Ground)

Grove (see Groff)

Grover (see Crover, Franciscus, Kettwig)

Grover
*Grover Family Organization
3929 Milton Drive
Independence, MO 64055-4043
Phone (816) 373-5309
Robert L. Grover, President
(includes descendants of Thomas Grover (1514 Chesham, Buckinghamshire, England–) and Elizabeth Wilks (1516 Hughley, Shropshire, England–))

Groves (see McConnell)

Grueb (see Sager)

Gruer (see Gregor)

Grumann (see Lahey)

Grunewald (see Nelson)

Gruot (see Daniel)

Gsell (see Cell)

Gualmay (see Gwaltney)

Gualtney (see Gwaltney)

Guard (see Gard)

Guckian (see Hackett)

Gudylouch (see Folk Family Surname Exchange)

Guello (see Guillot)

Guellow (see Guillot)

Guerrant (see Geurin)

Guess (see Gest)

Guess
Guess-Guest
401 Tuxedo Drive
Thomasville, GA 31792
Annette Stewart
Pub. *Guess-Guest*, quarterly, $10.00 per
year subscription

Guest (see Gest, Guess, Stone)

Guffie (see Folk Family Surname
Exchange)

Guffins (see Gunnin)

Guibord (see Chopp)

Guidry (see Johnson)

Guild
*Guild Reunion
1620 Guild Road
Woodland, WA 98674
Phone (360) 225-8752
Grace Davis
(includes descendants of Peter Guild and
Elizabeth Richardson, who came to
Oregon in 1847 from Erie Township,
Whiteside County, Illinois)

The Guild of One Name Studies (see
Multi-family Associations)

Guile (see Gile)

Guiles (see Gile)

Guilford
*Guilford Resource
2710 East Adams Avenue
Orange, CA 92667-6240
Joan S. Guilford, Publisher

Guillet (see Johnson)

Guillo (see Guillot)

Guillot (see Johnson)

Guillot
*Guillot/Guillo(w) Surname
Organization
Francois Guillot/Guello(w) Family
Organization
412 Main Street
Acton, MA 01720
Phone (617) 263-8259
Judith Wetherbee Peterson

Guillow (see Guillot)

Guire (see Cowart)

Guise (see Keyes)

Guittard (see McCune)

Gulick
*Gulick Family Association
295 Mohawk Road
Owens Cross Roads, AL 35763
Phone (205) 518-9964
Paul I. Gulick, Editor
Pub. *Gulick/Hulick Family Newsletter*,
quarterly (January, April, July and
November), $7.50 per year
subscription, $1.70 per issue, queries
answered free with SASE; (includes
Gulick and Hulick lines back to the
1600s and some allied lines to 1000)

Gull (see Dickinson)

Gulledge
Gulledge Family Association
209 South Cheery Street, Apartment 8
Kernersville, NC 27284

Gulley
*Gulley Family of America, Inc.
297 Constance Place
Harrison, OH 45030
Phone (513) 367-9868
Frank J. Gulley, President
Pub. *Gulley Newsletter*, three times per
year; (includes all Gully or Gulley
families and descendants in the
colonies and from Europe)
$25.00 per year membership; biennial
reunion in October of odd-numbered
years in Saint Louis, Missouri

Gullick
*Gullick Family Association
PO Box 33
Ferris, TX 75125
Phone (214) 544-3988
Dennis Turner
(includes Gullick in all of the U.S.)
$25.00 per year plus FGS/ancestor chart
membership

Gully (see Gulley)

Gumbertin (see Guthrie)

Gunckel (see Kunkel)

Gunion (see Gunnin)

Gunkel (see Kunkel)

Gunn (see Bosher, James, Sheldon)

Gunn
*Clan Gunn Society of North America
210 D Street
Fremont, CA 94536-2808
Phone (510) 793-7756
H. Al Gunn, Secretary for Membership
Pub. *Gunn Salute*, quarterly; (includes
Enrick, Galche, Gallie, Gaulche,
Gaunson, Georgeson, Granson,
Henderson, Inrig, Jameson, Jamieson,
Johnson, Kean, Keene, MacComas,
MacCorkill, MacCorkle, Maccullie,
MacIan, MacKames, MacKeamish,
MacKean, MacMains, MacManus,
Macomish, MacRob, MacWilliam,
Magnus, Main, Mann, Manson,
Manus, Neilson, Nelson, Robinson,
Robison, Robson, Sandison, Swan,
Swann, Swanney, Swanson, Will,
Williamson, Wills, Wilson, Wylie,
Wyllie)
$10.00 per year membership for
individuals, $15.00 per year
membership for families

Gunn
*Gunn Family Association
1365 Lesley Court
Santa Maria, CA 93454
Phone (805) 922-4313; (805) 346-1156
FAX; E-mail: ccsd62B@prodigy.com
or 72103,2257@compuserve.com
Tina Peddie, President
(includes Gunn in the southern states
from the 1600s to the present)

Gunn
Pan Gunn Society of North America
4286 Cedar Ridge Trail
Stone Mountain, GA 30083
Pub. *Gunn Salute*, quarterly

Gunnin
*Gunnin Family Association
3131 Old Jonesboro Road
PO Box 82371
Hapeville, GA 30354
Phone (404) 767-8449
Helen Gunnin Mishasek, Author
(includes O'Gunning to Gunning to
Gunnin to Gunion and related families:
Adairs, Barnes, Cronics, Guffins,
Hardy, Huff, McPherson, Lords,
Richey/Ritches, etc.)
Annual reunion on the last Sunday of
July at the home of Ray Gunnin,
Treasurer, 8715 Skitts Mountain Road,
Lula, Georgia 30554, (770) 983-9893

Gunning (see Cunning, Gunnin)

Gunnison (see Cunning)

Gunter (see Ainsworth, Gagnier)

Guptill (see Corson)

Gurndy (see Gant)

Gurney
*Gurney Family Clearinghouse
2117 Puualii Place
Honolulu, HI 96822
Jean Gurney Rigler
Free exchange for SASE

Guse (see Sager)

Guss
*Guss Lines
315 Ronnie Road
Golden, CO 80403-9757
Phone (303) 642-3261
Willa I. Guss
(includes descendants of Charles Guss
    (1732–1794) and Mary Shunk (1741–
    1821) of Chester County,
    Pennsylvania)
Biennial reunion in Harlan, Shelby
    County, Iowa

Gustafson (see Heath)

Gustin (see Holden)

Gutdknecht (see Goodnight)

Guthery
*Guthery Family of Alabama
370 East Archwood Avenue
Akron, OH 44301
Phone (216) 773-1757
Ima Gene Boyd

Guthrey (see Guthrie)

Guthrie (see Gotham)

Guthrie
*Clan Guthrie-USA, Inc.
PO Box 2981
Pittsfield, MA 01202
Phone (413) 442-9815
Harry L. Guthrie, President
Pub. *Clan Guthrie Newsletter*, quarterly;
    (also Guthrie, Guthrey, Guthry, Gutry,
    etc., of that Ilk genealogy database)
$20.00 per year membership

Guthrie
*Thomas Guthrie Family Organization
39 South 300 East
Orem, UT 84058-5536
Phone (801) 225-4161
R. E. Evans
(includes descendants of Thomas
    Guthrey, 1796 Virginia, and Catherine
    Cox, 1804 Virginia; also Chrisman,
    Thomas and Spradling families in
    Tennessee; also Jacob Jenni, 1683,
    Catharine Gumbertin, married in 1708
    in Bötzingen, Freiburg, Baden,
    Germany, but came from Switzerland;
    also Johann George Jenne/Yaney and
    Yaney respository)

Guthry (see Guthrie)

Gutknecht (see Goodnight)

Gutry (see Guthrie)

Guttmann (see Goodman)

Guy (see Harris)

Guy
Ben Guy Family Database
1411 West 995 North
Lake Village, IN 46349
Phone (219) 992-3579
Ruth Studer

Guyle (see Gile)

Guyman
Isaiah Guyman Family Association
1785 North 1500 East
Provo, UT 84604
Phone (801) 374-1777
Helen Clegg, Genealogist
$2.00 per year membership, plus
    expected donation for research

Guymon
*Guymon Family Organization of
    Southern Illinois
327 Frances Avenue
Peoria, IL 61614
Phone (309) 693-0005
Mrs. Harry E. Bauder, Family Historian
Pub. *The Guymon Gazette*, annually
    (March); (includes descendants of
    Isaiah Guymon (first listed with Martin
    Armstrong in a 1774 tax list in Surry
    County, North Carolina) and his wife,
    Elizabeth Flinn (Flynn, etc.), the
    granddaughter of Laughlin Flinn,
    immigrant from Ireland to Lunenburg
    County, Virginia)

Guyon (see Paradis)

Gwaltney
*Gwaltney Clearinghouse
1810 Linwood Boulevard
Oklahoma City, OK 73106-2626
Phone (405) 232-8843; (405) 232-8844
    FAX
Martha Da Lee Haidek
(includes descendants of Thomas
    Gualmay of Surry and Isle of Wight
    counties, Virginia, includes Gualtney,
    Gwartney, etc.)

Gwartney (see Gwaltney)

Gwathmey (see Burdeau)

Gwynn (see Gwynne)

Gwynne
*Benjamin Gwynne and Maria Cobb
    Descendants Reunion
605 Fir Street
Coulee Dam, WA 99116
Phone (509) 633-2208
Carl E. Gwynn
(includes surnames Gwynn, Gwynne,
    Cobb, Harvey and Latta)
Biennial reunion on the third weekend of
    July in Thermolpolis, Wyoming

Gye (see Newton)

Haas (see House)

Haasen (see Thorson)

Habeck (see Sager)

Hack
*Hack Family Association
2523 Paxton Street
Woodbridge, VA 22192-3414
Phone (703) 497-4888
Randy L. Hack
(includes Hilton, Roberts, Smith, Stone
    and Tower families)

Hackett (see MacDuff)

Hackett
Hackett Heirlooms
2523 Fair Oaks Road
Decatur, GA 30033-1418
Patricia Hackett Nicola
Pub. *Hackett Heirlooms*, quarterly,
    $10.00 per year subscription;
    (Guckian)

Hackleman
Hackleman
729 Grapevine Highway, Suite 204
Hurst, TX 76054-2805
Pat Clark
Pub. *Hackleman*, three times per year,
    $10.00 per year subscription
Reunion

Hackler
*Hackler Reunion
Rt. 1, Box 622
Galax, VA 24333
Phone (540) 236-2012
Katherine Hackler, Historian

Hackney (see Folk Family Surname
    Exchange)

Haddad (see Heath)

Hadden (see Graham)

Hadden
*Samuel Hadden 1744 and His
    Descendants in Utah and Kentucky
1248 Clintonville Road
Paris, KY 40361-9117
Phone (606) 987-4587
Helen Collins Hadden, Publisher

Haden (see Heydon)

Hadley (see Allison, Gant, Gregg)

Haefene (see Havens)

Haefner
*Generations
2983 Bayside Court
Wantagh, NY 11793
Stephen A. Lamb, Editor/Publisher
Pub. *Haefner Journal*, sometimes
    quarterly, $15.00 for four issues;
    (includes Marschhauser)

Haeger (see The Memorial Foundation of the Germanna Colonies)

Haeger (see The Memorial Foundation of the Germanna Colonies)

Haessig
Jacob Haessig Family Association
29825 Cuthbert Road
Malibu, CA 90265
Phone (213) 457-7829
C. Haessig

Hafen (see Havens)

Haff
*Haff Family in America
402 Lee Avenue
Endwell, NY 13760-3344
Phone (607) 754-0156
Robert M. Haff

Haffey (see Macfie)

Haga
*The Haga-Helgøy Families
983 Venus Way
Livermore, CA 94550-6345
Phone (510) 455-5059; E-mail:
    enokh@aol.com
Enoch Haga, Publisher
(includes some families originating in the
    Stavanger area of Norway, with
    descendants in Norway, Australia,
    Canada and the U.S.)

Hagan (see Rutherford)

Hagart (see Ross)

Hagel (see Surname Database)

Hagen
*The Hagen Family Reunion
834 North Third Street
Stayton, OR 97383
Olga Hagen Stuart
Annual reunion on the first weekend of
    September in Salem

Hagenbuch
Hagenbuch Family Newsletter
821 West Siddonsburg Road
Dillsburg, PA 17019
Phone (717) 432-8911
Mark O. Hagenbuch, Editor
Pub. *Hagenbuch Family Newsletter (The
    Beech Grove)*, semiannually, $4.00 per
    year subscription

Hagenbush
Hagenbush Family Organization
Rt. 1, Box 401
Milton, PA 17847
Mark O. Hagenbush, Editor

Hager (see The Memorial Foundation of
    the Germanna Colonies, Taylor)

Hagerman
Joseph Hagerman Family Reunion
221 Church Street
Le Suer, MN 56058
M. Nyblom

Hagert (see Heath)

Hagerty (see Lemon, Weaver)

Haggard
*Haggard Family Database
205 Oakdale Avenue
Pawtucket, RI 02860
Phone (401) 725-9850
Clinton R. Haggard

Haggart (see Ross)

Haggerty (see Cian)

Hague (see Lush)

Hagy (see Wilfong)

Hahn (see Surname Database, Dietwiler,
    Lush)

Hahn
Hahn Reunion
4185 Greenwood Drive
Bethlehem, PA 18017-9689
Lucy Hahn Stackhouse
(includes descendants of Peter Philip
    Hahn and Angel Haufman)
Annual reunion in Pen Argyl,
    Pennsylvania

Haible (see Hively)

Haier (see Hire)

Haight (see Surname Sources, Hoyt)

Haight
*Horton David Haight and Louisa
    Leavitt Haight Family Organization
1550 East 1220 North
Logan, UT 84341
Phone (801) 752-4035
Gary Haight Richardson, President

Haigis (see Bitzer)

Hail (see Jones)

Hainer (see Hayner)

Haines (see Haynes, Henn)

Hair
*Arthur Hair Family Organization, 1850
    of Illinois
HCR 62, Box 113A
Flippin, AR 72634-9710
Phone (501) 453-5286
Charlene Gillespie Deutsch, Compiler

Haire (see Hire)

Hal (see Howell)

Halbert (see Holbert)

Halbert
Halbert History Association
7 Summit Lane
Gray Summit, MO 63039-1109
K. Moore

Halbrook (see Holbrook)

Halbrooks (see Holbrook)

Haldane (see Graham)

Haldeman
Haldeman Reunion
6770 U.S. 60E
Morehead, KY 40351
Phone (606) 784-9145
Lloyd Dean, Co-chairman

Hale (see Clark, Howell, Jones, Newton)

Hale
Hale Family Association
14333 Aldengate Road
Midlothian, VA 23113
Anne Hale Kellam
Pub. *Hale Family Newsletter*, quarterly

Hale
Hale Heritage Newsletter
PO Box 6282
Norfolk, VA 23508
Mark Hale
Pub. *Hale Heritage Newsletter*, $10.00
    per year subscription

Hales
*The Hales Family History Society
5990 North Calle Kino
Tucson, AZ 85704-1704
Phone (602) 888-9199
Kenneth Glyn Hales, Founder
Pub. *The Hales Newsletter—New Series*,
    quarterly (spring, summer, fall and
    winter); (includes all Hales (not Hale)
    surnames, U.S., Canada, U.K.)
$6.00 per year active membership,
    $12.00 per year contributing
    membership, $25.00 per year
    sustaining membership

Halfhill
Peter Halfhill Association
215 East North Street
Corydon, IA 50060
V. Cobb

Halford (see Alford)

Haliburton (see MacDuff)

Haling
*Elmer Haling Family Organization
511 Gaylord
Pueblo, CO 81004
Phone (719) 543-0549

Virginia Baird Penaluna Haling
(includes descendants of Edwin Nelson
   Haling and Emma Sauve, Afrain Sauve
   Haling and Wyenie Montpetit, Charles
   Nelson Haling and Cordelia Truax)

Halkett (see MacDuff)

Hall (see Folk Family Surname
   Exchange, Bush, Cian, Clark, Corson,
   Dean, Garner, Goodenow, Heath,
   Holmes, Hutchison, Lambert, Lush,
   Nienow, Rutherford)

Hall
*Hall Family Reunion
4785 Topaz Drive
Colorado Springs, CO 80918
Andy Bistline of LaTunita
Annual reunion

Hall
Hall Family Clearinghouse
1015 West Bearss Avenue, Lot 82
Tampa, FL 33613-1135
Ethel M. Patrick

Hall
*Hall-Wiedeman Family and Reunion
356 Meadowrue Lane
Batavia, IL 60510
Phone (630) 879-5909
Ralph N. Hall
(includes descendants of Francis and
   Sarah (Bainbridge) Hall of
   Pennsylvania and New Jersey, and
   descendants of Xavier and Kreszenz
   (Geisberger) Wiedemann of Bavaria,
   Germany, and Kansas)

Hall
The Back Log
108 Balmoral Drive, East
Oxon Hill, MD 20745
Phone (301) 839-3694
Alton P. Hall, Editor and Publisher
Pub. *The Back Log*, three times per year
   (November/December, March/April
   and July/August), $3.00 per year
   subscription; (includes Cole, Hall,
   Henderson, Herron, Rayburn, Thrash
   and Wright)

Hall
*Kinseeker Publications
5697 Old Maple Trail
PO Box 184
Grawn, MI 49637
E-mail: AB064@taverse.lib.mi.us
Victoria Wilson, Editor
Pub. *Hunting Hall*, quarterly, $10.00 per
   year subscription, $2.50 for sample
   issue

Hall
Hall-Lewis-Lancaster-Modesett Family
   Association
2306 Westgate
Houston, TX 77019
Phone (713) 529-2333

Harold Helm
$25.00 plus pedigree and family group
   sheets

Hall
*John Hall and Sarah Edge and Mary
   Bates Organization
2421 North 750 East
Provo, UT 84604-4014
Phone (801) 375-4390
Margaret Fawson Talbot, Committee
   Member
(includes descendants of John Hall
   (1786–1852) and his wives, Sarah
   Edge (1790–before 1825) and Mary
   Bates (1802–1885); also allied
   surnames of Jackson, Harrison,
   Lancaster, Montford, Oxley, Sanders,
   Sheldon and Slane of Derbyshire,
   Staffordshire, Birmingham and
   Warwickshire, England)
$30.00 per year membership

Hall
*Thomas Hall Family Organization
1599 Monaco Circle
Salt Lake City, UT 84121
Phone (801) 278-7708
Eldon B. Tucker, Jr., M.D.
(includes family originally from West
   Virginia)

Hallam
*Hallam/Hallum Family Association
300 Greenglade Avenue
Worthington, OH 43085-2223
Phone (614) 888-1236
Henrietta Nichols

Hallam
Hallam-Baxter-Buford-Helmoldus
   Family Association
2306 Westgate
Houston, TX 77019
Phone (713) 529-2333
Harold Helm
$25.00 plus pedigree and family group
   sheets

Hallberg (see Blossom Press)

Hallenbeck (see Barnard)

Hallett (see Barnard)

Halliburton (see Rutherford)

Halliburton
*Genealogical History of the Halliburton
   Family
PO Box 85
Lexington, MO 64067-0085
Phone (816) 259-2641
Mrs. Kenneth Rutherford, Publisher
(includes the ancient family of
   Halliburton in Scotland, tracing some
   descendants to the Province of Canada
   and Colonial America, especially
   David Halliburton (–1767 Orange
   County, North Carolina))

Hallmark
Hallmark
526 Caravaca Drive
Garland, TX 75043
William O. Hallmark
Pub. *Hallmark*, quarterly, $5.00 per year
   subscription
Annual reunion, usually in October, in
   Gonzales, Texas

Hallock
*Hallock Family Association
4 Woodland Drive
Severna Park, MD 21146
Marion Adams

Hallock
*Hallock Family Network
23 Briar Hill Lane
Waltham, MA 02154-8107
Phone (617) 899-7712; (603) 432-0777
   FAX; (516) 298-5292 (Hallockville
   Farm Museum and Folk Life Center)
Georgie Ann Hallock, Editor
Pub. *Hallock Family Connections*,
   quarterly; (includes descendants of
   William Hallock of Southhold,
   Riverhead, Long Island, said to be the
   son of most elusive Peter)
$7.00 per year membership; annual
   reunion at Hallockville Farm Museum
   and Folk Life Center, 6038 Sound
   Avenue, Riverhead, NY 11901

Hallum (see Hallam)

Hally (see Cian)

Halsell
Halsell Family Research
846 Garfield Avenue
Salt Lake City, UT 84105
Phone (801) 485-4782
Roger K. Halsell
Pub. *Halsells and Their Families*,
   semiannually, $5.00 per year
   subscription

Halsey (see Surname Sources)

Halstead (see Bradley)

Halton (see Paxton)

Halverson (see Album, McCune)

Hamblen
The Hamblen Connector
4432 Carya Square
Columbus, IN 47201
Phone (812) 342-0017
John W. Hamblen, Editor and Publisher
Pub. *The Hamblen Connector*, quarterly,
   $10.00 per year subscription; (includes
   Hamblin, Hamlen, Hamlin, etc.)

Hambleton (see Hamilton)

Hamblin (see Hamblen)

Hamblin
*William Clyde and Reva Fern Mangum
   Hamblin Family Organization
2532 Smith Road
American Falls, ID 83211
Phone (208) 226-7854
Linda H. Wiese, Secretary
(includes allied surnames of Adair,
   Johnson and Mangum)

Hambright (see Schindel)

Hamby (see Louden)

Hamelin (see Johnson)

Hamelton (see Hamilton)

Hamerske (see Hamersky)

Hamerski (see Hamersky)

Hamersky
*Hamersky and Allied Families
   Newsletter*
PO Box 1334
San Diego, CA 92112-1334
Michael D. Hamersky
Pub. *Hamersky and Allied Families
   Newsletter (Hammersky, Hamersky,
   Hamerski)*, bimonthly, $7.50 per year
   subscription, $12.00 per year foreign
   subscription; (includes Hamerski of
   West Prussia/Poland, Hamersky of
   Moravia, Hammersky of Kansas,
   Hamerske, Amerski and Hamorski,
   plus Germanic lines of Dold,
   Rennenger, Schurmann, Walk and
   affiliated families of Connecticut,
   Illinois, Indiana, Iowa, Kansas,
   Massachusetts, Michigan, Minnesota,
   Missouri, Nebraska, New Jersey, New
   York, Ohio, Pennsylvania and
   Wisconsin)

Hames
*Hames Heritage
14515 Wunderlich Drive, #211
Houston, TX 77069
Phone (713) 583-8878
Loubeth R. Hames, Publisher

Hamilton (see Armstrong, Cian,
   Cranston, Frasher, Goodenow,
   McClure, Poe, Stoner, Woodrow)

Hamilton
*Hamilton National Genealogical
   Society, Inc. (HNGS)
215 S.W. 20th Terrace
Oak Grove, MO 64075-9248
Phone (816) 690-7768; E-mail:
   larry.hamilton@passport.com
Lawrence M. Hamilton, Editor; Ann B.
   Hamilton, Director of Operations
Pub. *The Connector of the Hamilton
   National Genealogical Society, Inc.*,
   monthly; (includes Hambleton,
   Hamelton worldwide)
$20.00 per year membership

Hamilton
*Clan Hamilton Society
PO Box 71881
Charleston, SC 29415-1881
Phone (803) 873-2430
Philip G. Dixon, Secretary
Pub. *The Review*, quarterly
$15.00 per year membership

Hamilton
*The Fifer's Clan
5219 Eighth Avenue, N.E.
Aberdeen, SD 57401-8181
Phone (605) 226-2358
Dr. James Edward Hamilton
(includes descendants of William
   Anderson Hamilton (1829–1905),
   Civil War veteran and musician from
   Wake County, North Carolina)

Hamlen (see Hamblen)

Hamlin (see Hamblen, Woodrow)

Hamm (see Frantz, Ross, Schindel)

Hamman
The Phillip Hamman Echo
PO Box 486
Arab, AL 35016
Phone (205) 586-4151
Ralph Hammond, Founder
Pub. *The Phillip Hamman Echo*, two or
   three times per year, donation for
   subscription

Hammer
*Hammer-Mink (Alwois)
840 Fourth Street
Moline, IL 61265
Rock Island, IL 61201
Phone (309) 762-0332
Mary E. Doeckel-May, Secretary/
   President
(includes descendants of Andreas
   Hamme and Johann David Mink)
Annual reunion on the third Sunday of
   August in Rock Island, Illinois

Hammer
Hammer Family Reunion
2817 77th Street
Urbandale, IA 50322
Nicoe Hart
(includes descendants of Adam Hammer
   of Newton, Iowa)
Annual reunion on the fourth Sunday of
   June at the Country Club in Union,
   Iowa

Hammer
Hammer Family Reunion
PO Box 387
Pilot Rock, OR 97868
Mozelle Ryan
Annual reunion each July in Eugene,
   Oregon

Hammerling (see Kettwig)

Hammersky (see Hamersky)

Hammond (see Hinshaw)

Hammond
Hammond Herald
11626 South Goldendale Drive
La Merada, CA 90638
Ina Ruth Hammond King
Pub. *Hammond Herald*, quarterly, $12.00
   per year subscription

Hammond
*Stephen Hammond Family Organization
211 South Rhode Island Avenue
Mason City, IA 50401-4234
Phone (515) 424-1317
Ruth M. Umbarger, President
Pub. *Hammond Heritage*, irregularly;
   (includes descendants of Stephen
   Hammond (1764–1847) and Lorancy
   E. Edgerton (1788–1850) of Rhode
   Island, Connecticut and New York)

Hammond
*Hammond Family Association
PO Box 6545
North Augusta, SC 29841
Phone (803) 279-7632
Pub. *Newsletter*, irregularly; (includes
   descendants of Martin Hammond,
   immigrant from London to Virginia)

Hammontree
Michigan Hammontree Quaestors
1237 Lakeshore Drive
Boyne City, MI 49712
Nancy Hammontree
No membership fee, donation taken at
   reunions

Hamner
Hamner Reunion
6232 Derwent Road
Richmond, VA 23225
Mrs. N. Langford

Hamor (see Haymore)

Hamore (see Haymore)

Hamorski (see Hamersky)

Hampt
Hampt Hunters
935 North Warren
Oklahoma City, OK 73107
R. Hamp

Hampton (see Cook, Dockery, Eaves)

Hanagan (see Cian)

Hanback (see The Memorial Foundation
   of the Germanna Colonies)

Hanby (see Job)

Hancock (see Heath)

Hancock
*The Hancock Family of England and
   America
726 Jura Way
Sunnyvale, CA 94087
Arvil Dale Hancock
(includes descendants of William
   Hancock (1580–1622))

Hancock
Hancock
3394 Areca Palm Avenue
Melbourne, FL 32901
Wilam Ingersoll, Editor
Pub. *Hancock*, quarterly, $16.00 per year
Reunion on the last Saturday of
   September

Hand
*Hand Clearinghouse
207 Auburn Drive
Dalton, GA 30720
Phone (706) 278-1504
Joseph Wiley Reid
(1400–1890 period)

Hand
*Hand Family Reunion
206 North Sixth Street
Petersburg, IN 47567
Kevin Myers, Secretary
(ancestors and descendants of Aaron
   Hand (1770–1839) of North Carolina
   and Jackson County, Indiana)

Hand
Courier Publications
PO Box 1284
Natchitoches, LA 71458-1284
Annette Carpenter Womack
Pub. *Hand Family Courier*, quarterly,
   $12.50 per year subscription

Hanen (see Garvin)

Haner (see Hayner)

Hanes (see Haynes, Moore)

Hanes
James Hanes and Jemina Calloway
   Family
921 Thunderbird Drive
El Paso, TX 79912
Mrs. J. Wilbanks

Haney (see Golding)

Haney
*Haney Family Association
717 Pahaquarry Street
Belvidere, NJ 07823
Phone (908) 475-2942
Grace Sassaman, Historian
(includes descendants of Jacob Heaney
   (1713 Tinicum Township, Bucks
   County–1801) and Catherine
   Weisbecker (1722–1803); also Michael
   Heaney/Haney and Simon Heaney/
   Haney, Revolutionary War veterans)

Annual reunion on the third Saturday of
   July at Kellers Church (Lutheran)

Hanford (see Corson)

Hanks (see CTC Family Association,
   Wolverton)

Hanks
Hanks Historical Review
PO Box 191
Monroe, OH 45050
Barbara Baber, Editor/Publisher
Pub. *Hanks Historical Review*, three
   times per year, $10.00 per year
   subscription, free queries for
   subscribers; (ancestors and
   descendants of Thomas and John
   Hanks of England, settled on the
   James River in Virginia by 1618, and
   allied families of Harper, Lincoln and
   Shipley)

Hanks
Hanks Historical Review
PO Box 191
Monroe, OH 45050
E-mail: baber2@aol.com
Pub. *Hanks Historical Review*, three
   times per year (January, May and
   September), $10.00 per year
   subscription, free queries for
   subscribers; (all Hanks families from
   England to America and westward)

Hanley (see Anthes)

Hanline (see Henlein)

Hanna (see Leland)

Hanna
*Hanna, Hannay, Hannah Clan Society
   (U.S.A.)
The Manse
Oak Hill, OH 45656
Phone (614) 682-7507
Rev. James A. M. Hanna, National
   Convener
Pub. *Clan Hanna/Hannay/Hannah
   Newsletter*, semiannually (spring and
   autumn)

Hanna
Hanna Herald
West 5917 Crosscut Road
Deer Park, WA 99006
Phone (509) 276-2550
Margaret Burdega
Pub. *Hanna Herald*, irregularly, $6.00
   plus $1.25 postage and handling per
   volume

Hannah (see Hanna, Kunkel)

Hannan (see Wagner)

Hannay (see Hanna, MacDuff)

Hannon (see Waterous)

Hannum
Hannum Reunion
9725 27 Hwy. No. Lot 53-N
Davenport, FL 33837
Irma D. Thompson, Historian

Hanor (see Hayner)

Hansard
Hansard Family Register
320 Seven Oaks Drive
Knoxville, TN 37922
Irma Hansard

Hansen (see Larsen, McCune, Peterson,
   Sorenson)

Hansen
*Sophus Frederick Hansen Family
   Organization
8686 Beauxart Circle
Sacramento, CA 95828
Phone (916) 689-4644
Donna Glasser, President
(includes descendants of Sophus
   Frederick Hansen and wife, Hannah
   Salina Wadsworth)

Hanson (see Goodenow, Heath, Hopkin,
   Nell)

Hanson
Hanson, Henson, Hinson, Hynson
   Research Associates
2300 Oxford
Bryan, TX 77802
Maxine Miller, Treasurer

Hanson
Hanson/Henson/Hinson/Hynson Family
   Research Association
2722 Hazel
Texarkana, TX 75503
J. J. Schefflin, Editor
Pub. *Hanson, Henson, Hinson, Hynson
   Research Associates Newsletter*

Hantz (see CTC Family Association)

Hanvey (see Baughman)

Happy
*James Happy Family Organization
11617 Gravelly Lake Drive
Tacoma, WA 98499
Phone (206) 588-2585
Cyrus Happy, III
(includes descendants of James Happy
   and Mary Burgin (of Appoquinimink
   Hundred, Delaware), married about
   1770)
No membership cost

Harber (see Harbour)

Harbin
*Harbin Clearinghouse
1290 23rd N.E.
Salem, OR 97301
Phone (503) 585-9129

Joan Marie Salzmann
Pub. *Harbin Newsletter*, quarterly, $15.00
  per year subscription

Harbison (see Surname Sources, Wright)

Harbor (see Harbour)

Harbour (see Gant)

Harbour
*Jeremiah Dale Harbour Family
  Organization
56 Chestnut
Wayne, NJ 07470
Phone (201) 694-8723
Lucille Dillinger Alexander

Harbour
*The Harbour-Witt Family Association,
  Inc.
7904 Joliet Avenue
Lubbock, TX 79423-1720
Phone (806) 795-5136
Bettye Atkins Cartwright, Editor
Pub. *The Harbour-Witt Family
  Association Bulletin*, quarterly, $12.00
  per year membership; (includes
  descendants of Thomas Harbour and
  Sarah Witt of Virginia, all spellings:
  Harber, Harbor, Whit, Whitt, etc.)

Hardcastle (see Jackson)

Hardee (see Hardwick)

Hardeman (see Stone)

Hardeman
Hardeman-McClure
7513 Collingwood Street
Sacramento, CA 95822
Ellener Hardeman Howell
Pub. *Hardeman-McClure*, three times per
  year, $10.00 per year subscription

Harden
Harden/Hardin/Harding Family
  Association
350 Broadway
Enon, OH 45323
N. Hardin

Harden
*Harden, Hardin, Harding Family
  Association
Rt. 1, Box 2290
Crewe, VA 23930
Mr. J. Oran Hardin, Editor
Pub. *Harden, Hardin, Harrding
  Newsletter*, quarterly; (also
  computerized repository)
$15.00 per year membership

Harden
Harden/Hardin Family Quarterly
7600 129th Avenue, S.E., #40
Renton, WA 98055
Delgar Clyde Harden
Pub. *Harden/Hardin Family Quarterly*

Hardesty (see Bartlett)

Hardesty
*Charles Hardesty Family Organization
2789 West 12075 South
Riverton, UT 84065-7630
Kairlee D. Graham
(includes descendants of Charles
  Hardesty (1768 Talbot County,
  Maryland–after 1843 Washington
  County, Kentucky), son of John
  Hardisty, and Charles' wife, Ann
  "Nancy" Fowler (ca 1770 Virginia–ca
  1850 Washington County, Kentucky))

Hardgrave (see Hargrave)

Hardgrove (see Hargrove)

Hardie (see Fergusson, MacDuff)

Hardie
*The Thornhill Foundation
PO Box 1988
Mobile, AL 36633-1988
Phone (205) 432-7682
William H. Hardie, President
Pub. *Thornhill Newsletter*, biannually;
  (Hardie family)
$25.00 per year membership

Hardin (see Harden, LaRue)

Hardin
Courier Publications
PO Box 1284
Natchitoches, LA 71458-1284
Annette Carpenter Womack
Pub. *Hardin Family Courier*, quarterly,
  $12.50 per year subscription

Harding (see Harden, Heckmann,
  Rutherford)

Harding
*William Harding Family Organization
200 Los Robles Way
Woodland, CA 95695
Phone (916) 666-5493
William L. Marble

Harding
*Pennsylvania-German Harding/Harting/
  Hartung Family
107 West Sunhill Road
Manheim, PA 17545
Phone (717) 665-5869
D. Ernest Weinhold
(especially descendants of the very early
  immigrants who settled in northeast
  Lancaster County, Pennsylvania, and
  nearby areas)

Hardisty (see Hardesty)

Hardman (see Kunkel)

Hardwick
*Liberty P. Hardwick Family
  Organization
1126 East Cedar Street
Angleton, TX 77515-5802
Phone (409) 849-6227
M. Warren Hardwick, M.D.
Pub. *Roots, Branches, Leaves, Hardwick
  Edition* (includes Hardwick, Stepp,
  Gann, Vincent, Warren, Sewell,
  Hardee, Walker, Dublin, Strickland)

Hardwick
*Hardwick Hunting
101 Rainbow Drive, #643
Rt. 5, Box 310-0677-643
Livingston, TX 77351
Shirley Hornbeck, Editor
Pub. *Hardwick Hunting*, annually, $20.00
  per year subscription; (database
  includes all Hardwick families)
Search costs vary with problem and
  requirements

Hardy (see CTC Family Association,
  Fergusson, Gunnin, MacDuff)

Hardy
*Hardy Family Association of America
70 Fairfield Drive
Concord, NH 03301-5279
Cora H. Morse, Secretary/Treasurer

Hare (see Kunkel)

Harford
*Adeline Harford Family Organization
PO Box 171
Douglas City, CA 96024
Phone (916) 778-3136
Paul Jones

Harger
*George Washington Harger Family
  Organization
2131 First Avenue, S.W.
Cedar Rapids, IA 52404
Phone (319) 365-8237
Jon R. Kime
Pub. *Harger Heritage*, quarterly;
  (includes descendants of Julia Ann
  Harger Williams (1851–1918))

Hargis (see Folk Family Surname
  Exchange)

Hargrave (see Hargrove)

Hargrave
Hargrave Family Association
  (Hardgrave/Hargreave/Hartgrave)
10603 Parkfield
Austin, TX 78758
S. Hargrave
Pub. *Hargrave Family Newsletter*

Hargreave (see Hargrave)

Hargrove
Hargrove/Hargrave Clan
7600 129th Avenue, S.E., #40
Renton, WA 98055
Lois Harden
Pub. *Hargrove Newsletter (Hartgrove/ Hardgrove)*

Harkness
Harkness Family Society
218 Butts Hollow Road
Dover Plains, NY 12522
S. K. Harkness

Harlan (see Underwood)

Harler
Harler's Heirline
47 Hardy Road
Levittown, PA 19056
E-mail: Ed.Harler@blackboard.com
Edwin C. Harler, Jr.
Pub. *Harler's Heirline*, irregularly, participation in research required for receipt of magazine; (for Harler surname and related lines)

Harless
*Harless Family Association
595 Camellia Way
Los Altos, CA 94024
Phone (415) 948-0477
William Harless, Publisher; Carol Harless, Editor
Pub. *Harless Family Association Bulletin*, semiannually (June and December); (includes descendants of Johan Philip Harless and Margaretha Price)
$5.00 per year membership, $10.00 research contribution

Harley (see Cian)

Harlocher (see Herlacker)

Harlow (see Corson)

Harlow
*Harlow Family Association, Inc. (Harlow Old Fort House, Plymouth, MA—location)
26 Deerpath Lane (mailing address)
Westfield, MA 01085
Phone Ann Harlow, Secretary
(413) 568-6995
Pub. *Harlow Happenings*, semiannually (June and December); (includes descendants of Sgt. William (ca 1624 England–1691) of Plymouth, Massachusetts, from ca 1646)
$5.00 initial membership fee, $10.00 per year membership dues, $75.00 life membership

Harmason (see Harmison)

Harmer
Harmer Family Newsletter
18115 S.E. 416th Street
Enumclaw, WA 98022
Dale Harmer
Pub. *Harmer Family Newsletter*, quarterly

Harmison
Harmison/Harmason Search Committee
940 Stanford Avenue, #203
Baton Rouge, LA 70808
Mrs. S. P. Singhal

Harmon (see Vaughn)

Harmon
*The Harmon-Rudland-Hellstrom-Grann Lines
3588 Walter Drive
Slidell, LA 70458
Phone (504) 649-3119
Marshall Larry Johnson, Sr., Chief Genealogist
(includes descendants of Francis Harmon (1590s England–) and William David Rudland (ca 1840s England–), also Clover, Grann and Hellstrom surnames)

Harness (see Garner)

Harney
Harney Family Association
6696 Hollow Dale Drive, Suite B
Salt Lake City, UT 84121-2709
Linda Harney MacDonald
Pub. *Harney Update*, quarterly, free; (all Harney families, worldwide)

Harnish
Harnish Family Newsletter
77 Hollow Road
Quarryville, PA 17566-9491
Harry Hoffman
Pub. *Harnish Family Newsletter*

Harnsberger (see The Memorial Foundation of the Germanna Colonies)

Harp
Harp Notes
4349 Eaglewood
Shreveport, LA 71119
Fran Nash
Pub. *Harp Notes*, quarterly

Harper (see Allison, Brown, Buchanan, Gant, Hanks, Rutherford)

Harper
*Harper Reunion
36800 Highway 41
Pearl River, LA 70452
Lottie Harper
(restricted to descendants of John Harper and his wife, Mary Frances (Fanney) of Washington Parish, Louisiana)
Annual reunion near Pearl River, Louisiana

Harper
*Kinseeker Publications
5697 Old Maple Trail
PO Box 184
Grawn, MI 49637
E-mail: AB064@taverse.lib.mi.us
Victoria Wilson, Editor
Pub. *The Family Series: Harper*, irregularly, $6.50 per year subscription

Harper
Harper Family Association
Rt. 3
Princeton, MO 64673
Carol Branam

Harpole
*Harpole Cousins
720 Cromwell Street
West Point, MS 39773
Phone (601) 494-3320
B. C. or Agnes Harpole
(includes Harpole (1738), Sargent and Middleton families)

Harr
*Harr Family Organization
141 Oak Street
Blountville, TN 37617-9254
Phone (615) 323-5590
Joe C. Harr, Sr.

Harrel (see Herrell)

Harrell (see Herrell)

Harrell
Harrell
2937 Coral Strip Parkway
Gulf Breeze, FL 32561-2633
Florence Moore
Pub. *Harrell*, quarterly, $10.00 per year subscription

Harrell
*Harrell Family Association
PO Box 360
Anton, TX 79313
Phone (806) 997-2951
Wanda Frazier Harrell, Secretary
Pub. *Harrell Family News—Family of James Harrell from 1826 and Sarah Ann Elizabeth Wallingsford b. 1837*, annually, $1.00 per year subscription; (includes Harrel, Harrell and Harrold)
Annual reunion at the home of W. R. and Wanda Harrell in Anton, Texas

Harriman
*Harriman Family Association
(70 Circle Drive, Port Orange, FL 32127- address Nov 1 to May 1)
PO Box 1478
Bucksport, ME 04416
Phone (207) 469-2174 (Maine); (904) 788-3303 (Florida)
Leland W. Lowell, Treasurer
Pub. *Harriman Family Association Newsletter*, semiannually (usually January and May); (includes

descendants of Leonard and Margaret Harriman, early settlers of Rowley, Massachusetts)
$10.00 per year membership for individuals, $15.00 per year membership for families

Harrington (see Craver, Packard)

Harrington
Harrington Family Society
2317 Casey Avenue
Las Vegas, NV 89119
Richard A. Walkow, Editor
Pub. *Harrington News*, semiannually; (includes descendants of Jeremiah Harrington of Dunmanway, County Cork, Ireland)

Harris (see Blossom Press, Folk Family Surname Exchange, Burnam, Catlow, Clark, Craft, Fisher, Green, Lush, McCune, Newton, Rowe, Rutherford, Strain, Wolverton, Wright)

Harris
Harris Hunters
PO Box 539
Mount Morris, MI 48458-0539
Phone (810) 687-1033
Richard G. Boyd
Pub. *Harris Hunters*, quarterly, $12.50 per year subscription

Harris
*Gideon Harris Family Reunion
PO Box 1912
Nettleton, MS 38858
Phone (601) 963-1181
Lewis D. Harris, President
(includes descendants of Gideon Harris (1772 Prince Edward County, Virginia–1860 Marshall County, Tennessee), a descendant of Capt. Thomas Harris (1586–1658) of Jamestown Colony)
Annual reunion on the second weekend of August at Columbia, Tennessee in even-numbered years and at Adamsville, Tennessee in odd-numbered years

Harris
*James David Harris Reunion
1040 East McCanse
Springfield, MO 65803-3613
Phone (417) 833-2814
Glen Gohr, Editor
(includes descendants of James David Harris (1871 Harris County, Tennessee–1938), a descendant of Capt. Thomas Harris (1586–1658) of Jamestown Colony, and James' wife Docia Bell Pyron (1872–1944))
Annual reunion in June or July in various locations in Texas, Oklahoma, Louisiana and Colorado

Harris
Annual Reunion of the Descendants of Evans and Henrietta Guy Harris
PO Box 381
Smithfield, OH 43948
Phone (614) 733-7960
Frances Michele Freeman, Historian
Pub. *Harris Family Newsletter*, annually, free
Annual reunion on Labor Day in Smithfield, Ohio

Harrison (see Folk Family Surname Exchange, Greenway, Hall, Hylton, Joyner, Moody, Neville, Reynolds)

Harrison
Harrison Heritage
2816 Sloat Road
Pebble Beach, CA 93953
Ruth Harrison Jones
Pub. *Harrison Heritage*, quarterly, $10.00 per year subscription

Harrison
John Harrison Family Newsletter
805 West 16th Street
Upland, CA 91786
Isabel Whitney
Pub. *John Harrison Family Newsletter*

Harrison
*Kinseeker Publications
5697 Old Maple Trail
PO Box 184
Grawn, MI 49637
E-mail: AB064@taverse.lib.mi.us
Victoria Wilson, Editor
Pub. *The Family Series: Harrison*, irregularly, $6.50 per year subscription

Harrison
The Harrison Herald
12600 Bissonnet A4-407
Houston, TX 77099
Dede D. Mercer, Publisher
Pub. *The Harrison Herald*, semiannually; $20.00 per year subscription; (all variations of the surname, worldwide)

Harrison
Harrison/Pounds Reunion
Rt. 3, Box 67
Jayton, TX 79528
Mrs. Harrison

Harrison
*Edward and John Harrison Family
1400 Linlier Drive
Virginia Beach, VA 23451
Phone (804) 425-1852
William A. Stokes

Harrod (see McCune)

Harrold (see Harrell, Howell)

Harrow (see Lambert)

Harrower (see MacDuff)

Harry (see Collum, Richards)

Harshbarger
*Harshbarger Association
975 East 6600 South, #64
Ogden, UT 84405-9702
Donald L. Harshbarger
Free membership

Hart (see Folk Family Surname Exchange, Barnes, Daley, Hatfield, Hines, Moser)

Hart
Hart
PO Box 453
Lincoln, MA 01773
Phone (617) 259-9908 FAX
Dan and Linda Hart
Pub. *Hart*, bimonthly, $15.00 per year subscription, $3.00 per issue

Hart
*Hart Family Research Association
15875 Interurban Road
Platte City, MO 64079-9185
Phone (816) 858-3599
Betty N. Soper, Editor
Pub. *Hart Lines Newsletter*, three times per year, $10.00 per year subscription; (especially descendants of John Hart of Bucks County, Pennsylvania, through his son, Thomas Hart, The Elder, of Pennsylvania, Virginia, North Carolina and South Carolina)

Harter (see Newton)

Hartgrave (see Hargrave)

Hartgrove (see Hargrove)

Harting (see Harding)

Harting
*The Harting Family Association
1135 Washington Avenue
Albany, CA 94706-1625
Phone (510) 524-1410; (510) 524-1140; E-mail: hartingp@aol.com or pharting,103726.1333@compuserve.com
Paul Harting
Pub. *Harting Across the USA*, annually; (includes ancestors back to 1683, and descendants of Harting immigrants from Kleinenbremen (Porta Westfalica/ Weserbergland near Minden/ Buckeburg), Germany to New Minden, Illinois in 1854; allied surnames of Adelmann, Brandt, Faherty and Hoeinghaus)
$10.00 per year membership

Hartle (see Underwood)

Hartley
Thomas Hartley Family Reunion
41 Beaver Street
High Bridge, NJ 08829
Mrs. Repka

Hartman (see Engelmann, Johnson)

Hartpence
*Hartpence Family
4174 Fairfax Drive
Columbus, OH 43220-4525
Phone (614) 451-0803
Esther Leonard Heer, Editor
(includes descendants of Johannes
    Eberhart Pence and Hannah Kitchen of
    New Jersey in the mid 1700s; surname
    became Hartpence after the
    Revolutionary time period; some of the
    family went to Ohio, Indiana and
    Missouri in the early to mid 1800s and
    further west)
Annual reunion on the second Sunday of
    September at the Boundary Methodist
    Church, near Edison, Morrow County,
    Ohio

Hartshorn
Hartshorn Reunion
5319 North Jackson
Kansas City, MO 64119

Hartshorn
*Hartshorn Family Association
1204 Fourth Street Drive, S.E.
Conover, NC 28613-1827
Phone (704) 464-4981
Derick S. Hartshorn,III, President
Pub. *Hartshorn Hotline*, quarterly;
    (includes Hartshorn/e-Hartson U.S./
    England to the present)
$10.00 per year membership; annual
    reunion

Hartshorne (see Hartshorn)

Hartson (see Hartshorn)

Hartt (see Newcomb)

Hartung (see Harding)

Hartwell (see Mueller)

Hartwig (see Arthur)

Hartzel (see Surname Database)

Harvey (see Folk Family Surname
    Exchange, Dooley, Gwynne, Keith,
    McAllister, Reid, Usher, Wright)

Harvey
*Franklin Brister Harvey Family
    Organization
3541 Tracy Drive
Santa Clara, CA 95051
Phone (408) 248-1612
Susan McGhie, Family Genealogist
(includes descendants of Peter Ivey
    Harvey (ca 1778 England–ca 1871
    Pearl River, Mississippi) and Mary
    Ann Dupree (1795 Alabama–1850
    Mississippi)
$15.00 per year membership

Harwell (see Brawley)

Harwell
*Harwell Descendants Reunion
5048 North Bernard Street
Chicago, IL 60625-4916
Phone (312) 463-7693
Albert L. Harwell, Editor
Pub. *The Harwell Researcher*, quarterly,
    $15.00 per year subscription

Hasbrouck
Hasbrouck Family Association
(Huguenot Historical Society)
16 Shelley Court
Plainview, NY 11803
Phone (516) 931-5112
Robert C. Hasbrouck, President
$10.00 per year membership

Haseltine
*Haseltine Database
70 Ridgecrest Road
Kentfield, CA 94904-2746
Phone (415) 924-4040; E-mail:
    cdgg47a@prodigy.com
Mary Cole
(includes descendants of Robert
    Haseltine/Hazeltine/Hazelton/
    Hesseltine (ca 1609/10 Knedlington,
    Howden, East York, England–1674
    Bradford, Massachusetts) and his wife
    Ann)

Hash
Hash Family Historian
PO Box 235
Grass Valley, CA 95945
Phone (916) 273-9600
Richard O. Johnson, Editor
Pub. *Hash Family Historian*, quarterly,
    $8.00 per year subscription

Haskell
International Haskell Family Association
3005 Lee Lane
Covington, KY 41017-2619
Allan Haskell
Pub. *Haskell Journal*, quarterly
$7.00 per year membership

Haskell
*Haskell Family Association
200 Brightdale Road
Timonium, MD 21093-3001
Phone (410) 252-1576
Mrs. Marion S. Anderson, Secretary/
    Historian
Pub. *Haskell Journal*, three times per
    year
$15.00 per year membership; reunion

Hasness (see Kunkel)

Hassebrock
Hassebrock Library
Rt. 1, Box 49
Kenney, IL 61749
Alfred and Doretta Hassebrock
(includes descendants of the Hassebrocks
    from Westrup, Germany)

Hassebrock
Hassebrocks of Tichelwarf
Rt. 1, Box 137
Stanhope, IA 50246
Jane Arends

Hassinger (see Unger)

Hastings
Hastings Family Organization
PO Box 30
Elnora, IN 47529
S. E. Hastings

Hastings
Hastings Family Organization
PO Box 585
Clarksville, TN 37040
Jill Hastings Johnson

Hastings
*Name Game Enterprises
4204 South Conklin Street
Spokane, WA 99203-6235
Phone (509) 747-4903
Mrs. E. Dale Hastin Smith
Pub. *Hastings Herald*, irregularly, $5.75
    plus $2.00 postage and handling per
    issue

Hatch (see Corson)

Hatch
*The Hatch Family
327 Duke Road, #3
Lexington, KY 40502
Azuba R. Ward, Publisher
(includes descendants of Thoms Hatch of
    Barnstable, Massachusetts)

Hatch
*Orin Hatch and Maria Thompson
    (1830) Family Organization
2015 North 1000 East
North Logan, UT 84321
Phone (801) 753-1458
Kaylene A. Griffin, Genealogist

Hatch
*Hatch Surname Organization
795 Bel Mar Drive
Ogden, UT 84403
Phone (800) 393-0278
Dale Hatch

Hatcher (see Wright)

Hatchet (see Wright)

Hatchett (see MacDuff)

Hatfield (see Lambert, Likes)

Hatfield
*Hatfield Family History
4031 Grand Avenue
DeLand, FL 32720
Phone (904) 985-4046
Harry L. Sellards, Jr., Publisher

(includes Hatfield-Phillips Families of
Eastern Kentucky and Southwestern
West Virginia, especially descendants
of George and Nancy Jane Whitt
Hatfield and related families: Ball,
Bevins, Blackburn, Blankenship,
Chapman, Charles, Deskins, Dotson,
Coleman, Justice, Lowe, McCoy,
Musick, Ratliff, Reynolds, Runyon,
Scott, Smith, Varney and Williamson;
also descendants of George Goff
Hatfield (1715–) and John Hatfield
(1717–) and Hatfield families of
Virginia, West Virginia, Kentucky,
Tennessee and many other states,
mainly descendants of Joseph Hatfield
(1739–1832) and Captain Andrew
Hatfield (1737–1813), John Hatfield
(1773–1838) and Edward Hatfield
(1770–) and related families: Adkins,
Blackburn, Blankenship, Browning,
Carter, Cline, Coleman, Davis, Dotson,
Hart, Johnson, Justice, Kennedy,
Maynard, McCoy, Miller, Morgan,
Mounts, Runyon, Scott, Thompson,
Toler and Varney)

Hatfield
*Hatfield Cousins—Oregon Branch
4055 N.W. Carlton Court
Portland, OR 97229
Evelyn Hatfield Hunt
(includes descendants of John C. and
Beatrice Johnson Hatfield, descendants
of Tilman and Mathilda Burchet
Johnson)
Biennial reunion in even-numbered years
in Hillsboro, Oregon

Hatfield
Wade-Smith Genealogy Service
Rt. 7, Box 52
Llano, TX 78643
Evelyn Wade
Pub. *Hatfield Clan Newsletter*, quarterly,
$10.00 per year subscription

Hatfield
Hatfield and Lichfield
PO Box 925
La Verkin, UT 84775
Phone (801) 635-4675
Robert B. Lichfield
(includes descendants of John Hatfield
and Dorthy Sarah Jennison-Lichfield-
Batiste-Ferris-Hatfield of Belper,
Derbyshire, England; John Hatfield
and Elizabeth Street; Thomas Hatfield
and either Martha Davenport or
Martha Hunt)

Hathaway (see Garner, Masterson)

Hathaway
*Hathaway Family Association
3102 Royal Troon
Woodstock, GA 30189-6894
Phone (770) 516-1590
Ruth Hathaway Keightley, Genealogist

Pub. *Hathaway Family Association*,
quarterly
$10.00 per year membership

Hatleli (see Ostrem)

Hatley (see Folk Family Surname
Exchange)

Hatstat (see Goodenow)

Hatt
Hatt Family Organization
4552 Trails Drive
Sarasota, FL 34232-3749
William S. Hatt

Hatten (see Hatton)

Hatten
Hatten Reunion (Descendants of
Absolum Hatten of North Carolina)
Wiggins, MS 39577
Ona Mae Willingham, Secretary

Hatton (see Blossom Press, Rutherford)

Hatton
Hatton Heritage Association
1451 Sandy Lane
Clearwater, FL 34615-2044
Phone (813) 442-2683
Walter E. Hatton, Ph.D., Director
Pub. *Hatton Family Newsletter*, quarterly,
$7.00 per year subscription; (includes
Hatten)
Donation for membership

Hauer (see Hire)

Hauer
Hauer
Whispering Oaks
5821 Rowland Hill Road
Cascade, MD 21719-1939
Phone (301) 416-2660
Victor Gebhart, President
Pub. *Hauer*, annually, $2.00 per issue

Haufman (see Hahn)

Hauger
Hauger Family Reunion
119 North Alleghany Street
Cumberland, MD 21502
Stephan Lawson

Haugh (see MacDuff)

Haulbrook (see Holbrook)

Haulbrooks (see Holbrook)

Haun
*Haun Surname Organization
16117 West Lake Burrell Drive
Lutz, FL 33549
Phone (813) 972-2725

John W. Palm
Pub. *Haun Herald*, semiannually, free;
(includes descendants of Frank Henry
Haun, Cincinnati, Ohio)
Annual reunion on Peaks of Otter,
Virginia

Haupt (see Houp)

Haury
*Frederick Wilhelm Haury Family
Organization
8810 Lagrima de Oro Road, N.E.
Albuquerque, NM 87111
Phone (505) 298-5050
Frederick Wilhelm Haury, Jr.
(includes related families of Smith and
McKenzie)

Haus
*Palatine Descendants of 1709
44 Sunbeam Way
Rancho Cordove, CA 95670
Phone (916) 635-2841
Richard James House

Haushower (see Hoschar)

Havan (see Havens)

Havans (see Havens)

Havekost (see McLouth)

Havekost
*Havekost Reunion
5950 North Stony Creek Road
Monroe, MI 48161
Phone (313) 289-1236
Brent Havekost, Historian
(includes descendants of Johann
Havekost (1615–))
Annual reunion in Monroe, Michigan

Haven (see Havens)

Havens
Havens Harbor
PO Box 246
Snohomish, WA 98290
Phone (206) 338-2165
JoAnn Havens Wright, Editor/Owner
Pub. *Havens Harbor*, quarterly (January,
April, July and October), $28.00 per
year subscription, $6.25 per issue;
(includes De Haven, de Haven,
Haefene, Hafen, Havan, Havans,
Haven, Havince, Havings, Havins,
Havn, Havre, Heaven and Heavens
from the 1600s to the present)

Haviland
*Haviland Family Organization
19662 Westover Avenue
Rocky River, OH 44116
Phone (216) 331-6444
Richard J. Haviland, President
(research on Haviland family names)
Free research

Havince (see Havens)

Havings (see Havens)

Havins (see Havens)

Havlik
*Havlik/Zeleny Clearinghouse
1177 Deerfield Place
Highland Park, IL 60035
Phone (708) 433-0351
Nancy Jo Stein, Coordinator

Havn (see Havens)

Havre (see Havens)

Hawbaker
*John Hawbaker/Elizabeth Erisman
   Family
PO Box 207
Hershey, PA 17033-0207
Phone (717) 533-5662
Gary T. Hawbaker
Pub. *Newsletter*

Hawes
*Clair L. Hawes Family Organization
3019 South Birch Circle
Saint George, UT 84770
Phone (801) 673-8366
Gary T. Hawes
No charge

Hawk (see MacDuff)

Hawk
*History and Record of the Hawk Family
Box 123
Ellsworth, KS 67439
Phone (913) 472-3751
Louise Fulton, Publisher

Hawk
*Hawk Family Reunion
444 Roosevelt Avenue
Glendora, NJ 08029
Phone (609) 939-1890
Atwood James Shupp, Historian
Annual reunion on the fourth Sunday of
   July at Macungie Memorial Park,
   Macungie, Pennsylvania

Hawke (see Clark, MacDuff)

Hawkes (see MacDuff)

Hawkes
*Adam Hawkes Family Association, Inc.
3600 Lester Court
Lilburn, GA 30247
Phone (404) 985-9285
Susan Hawkes Cook, Historian/Registrar
Pub. *Hawkes Happenings: Newsletter of
   the Adam Hawkes Family Association,
   Inc.*, semiannually, $4.00 per year
   subscription; (includes Hawkes and
   Hawks families in the U.S., 1630 to
   the present)
$6.00 per year membership, $2.00
   application fee

Hawkes
*Adam Hawkes Family Association
65 Centre Street
Danvers, MA 01923
Phone (508) 774-7342
Cynthia Hawkes Meehan, President
Pub. *Hawkes Happenings*, semiannually;
   (includes descendants Adam Hawkes
   of Saugus, Massachusetts)
Annual meeting on the last Saturday of
   July

Hawkins
Hawkins Heritage
15051 Humphrey Circle
Irvine, CA 92714
Phone (714) 551-5099
Joan George, Membership Chairman
Pub. *Hawkins Heritage*, three times per
   year (April, August and November);
   (mostly, but not limited to, southern/
   western Hawkins, especially James
   and Margaret Hawkins (1769 Virginia)
   and John R. Hawkins (1791 Virginia))
$12.00 per year membership for
   individuals, $20.00 per year
   contributing membership

Hawkins
Hawkins
Whispering Oaks
5821 Rowland Hill Road
Cascade, MD 21719-1939
Phone (301) 416-2660
Victor Gebhart, President
Pub. *Hawkins*, annually, $2.00 per issue

Hawkins
*The Hawkins Association
PO Box 2392
Setauket, NY 11733
Phone (516) 567-4979
Sue Carmiencke, Genealogist
Pub. *The Hawkins Newsletter*,
   semiannually; (includes descendants of
   Robert and Mary Hawkins of
   Charlestown, Massachusetts (1635),
   and their sons Zackariah Hawkins of
   Setauket, New York, and Joseph of
   Derby, Connecticut)
$10.00 per year membership for
   individuals or families

Hawks (see Gerade, Hawkes, MacDuff,
   Reeves)

Hawley
*Society of the Hawley Family
12 Colony Road
Westport, CT 06880
Phone (203) 226-8836
Joseph S. Hawley, President
Pub. *Hawley Bulletin*, irregularly (one or
   more per year)
$5.00 per year membership for
   individuals, $10.00 for three years for
   individuals, $7.50 per year
   membership for families, $15.00 for
   three years membership for families

Haworth
Haworth Family Newsletter
921 North Center Street
Terre Haute, IN 47807
LaVerne A. Hughes
Pub. *Haworth Family Newsletter*,
   monthly

Haworth
Old Time Publications
10828 Oakbrook Drive
Omaha, NE 68154-2437
Peggy Wallingford Butherus
Pub. *Haworth Association (Hayworth)*

Haws
Haws/Luttrell/Templeton/Mayberry
   Family Organization
PO Box 928
Wrangell, AK 99929
Phone (907) 874-3640; (907) 874-2102
Barbara Angerman

Haws
*John Franklin Haws Family Ancestral
   Organization
165 North Ninth East
Brigham City, UT 84302
Phone (801) 723-8069
Dr. John Claud Haws, Genealogical
   Chairman
(includes descendants of Minnie and
   Frank Haws of Escalante, Utah, early
   1900s)
Annual reunion on the first Saturday of
   August

Haws
*Gilberth Haws and Hannah Whitcomb
   Family Organization
448 Barlow
Clearfield, UT 84015
Phone (801) 776-2551
Richard L. Scott
$15.00 per year membership

Hawsey
Hawsey-Higdon-Mixson Reunion
206 Vicki Leigh Avenue
Fort Walton Beach, FL 32548
Cecelia Lindegreen, Treasurer

Hawson (see Hay)

Hawthorne (see Bryan, Simkins)

Haxton (see Keith)

Hay (see Hayes, MacDuff, Shurtleff)

Hay
*Clan Hay Society, American Branch
521 Shenango Road
Beaver Falls, PA 15010
Phone (412) 846-6883
David E. Hays, Genealogy Coordinator
Pub. *Hay Happenings* (not primarily
   genealogical, includes Alderston,
   Arroll, Aue, Ay, Aye, Ayer, Beagrie,
   Con, Conn, Constable, da Hay, da

Haya, D'Ay, D'Aye, De Hay, De Haya, de la Hay, de la Haye, Delgatie, Dellahay, de Plessis, Des Hay, Deshays, Drumelizior, Dupplin, Erroll, Garra, Garrad, Garrow, Gifford, Hawson, Hay, Hayburn, Hayden, Haydock, Haye, Hayens, Hayes, Hayfield, Hayhoe, Hayhow, Haylees, Haylor, Hayne, Haynes, Haynie, Hays, Hayson, Hayston, Haystoun, Hayter, Hayton, Haytor, Hayward, Haywood, Hea, Hey, Heyes, Kellour, Kinnoull, Kinsman, Laxfirth, Leith, Lockerwort, MacGaradh, MacGarra, MacGarrow, MacHay, McArra, O'Garra, O'Garrow, O'Hay, O'Hea, Peebles, Peeples, Peoples, Slains, Turriff, Tweeddale, Yester and certain families of King, Ley, Ritchie and Watson)

Hayburn (see Hay)

Haycraft
Haycraft Family Association
PO Box 193
Lewisville, MN 56060
Dean and Bernice Haycraft, Publishers
Pub. *Haycraft Heritage News*, quarterly (March, June, September and December)
$10.00 per year membership

Hayden (see Goodenow, Hay, Heydon, Rutherford)

Haydock (see Hay)

Haydon (see Ames, Heydon)

Haye (see Hay)

Hayens (see Hay)

Hayes (see Barnes, Cian, Corson, Johnson, McRae, Rand, Williams)

Hayes
*Hayes of America Herald
22 Water Edge Road
Keeseville, NY 12944
James T. Hays, Editor
Pub. *Hayes of America Herald*, quarterly, $12.00 per year subscription; (includes Hays, Hay, etc.)

Hayfield (see Hay)

Hayhoe (see Hay)

Hayhow (see Hay)

Haylees (see Hay)

Haylor (see Hay)

Hayman
*Haymans of the Eastern Shore of Maryland 1666–1800
1387 Stonecreek Road
Annapolis, MD 21403

Douglass F. Hayman, Jr., Author and Publisher
(includes all descendants from Henry Hayman (–1685 Somerset County) and his wife Elinor)

Haymon
*Haymon Surname Organization
7024 Morgan Road
Greenwell Springs, LA 70739
Phone (504) 261-5515
Serena Abbess Haymon, Research Editor
Pub. *Haymon Grapevine*, annually (September); (includes descendants of Henry and Rebecca Haymon of Louisiana, Georgia and Virginia)
FGS registration

Haymore
Haymore Family of North America
4518 Clearwater Drive
Corpus Christi, TX 78413
C. Lemond
Pub. *Haymore Family of North America*

Haymore
Haymore Family Organization
Coleman Research Agency
241 North Vine Street, Apartment 1104E
Salt Lake City, UT 84103-1945
Ronald Douglass Coleman
(includes Haymore, Hamor, Hamore families)

Hayne (see Hay)

Hayner
Hayner Family News
2361 S.E. 10th Street
Pompano Beach, FL 33062
Mrs. Clifford N. Hayner
Pub. *Hayner Family News*, fifteen times per year

Hayner
*The Hayner Family Association
PO Box 3523
Reston, VA 22090
Diane Haner Anderson, Secretary
Pub. *The Hayner Family News*, quarterly; (includes Hainer, Haner, Hanor, Heiner, Hener, Hohner, descendants of Johannes Haner and Catharina Monsieur (or Mussier) of the Palatine area of Germany and East Camp (now Germantown), New York, 1710)
$5.00 per year membership

Haynes (see Folk Family Surname Exchange, Craft, Hay, Lawrence, Newton)

Haynes
*Haynes-McDonald Heritage Quest
3026 Brittany Place
Anchorage, AK 99504
John L. Haynes
Pub. *Haynes-McDonald Heritage Quest* (includes Haynes and related surnames: Bobo, Fortenberry,

Kimberline, McDonald, McMullan, Moore, Neese, Perkins, Rainwater, Skelton, Stowers, White and Woolley)

Haynes
*Haynes Family Association
330 Gralake
Ann Arbor, MI 48103-2025
Phone (313) 769-4437
Paul D. Haynes
Pub. *Chronicle of the Haynes Family Association* (includes Haines and Hanes)
$10.00 per volume of four issues

Haynie (see Hay)

Hays (see Hay, Rand)

Hays
*Hays and Breeze Ancestors
7613 Buffalo Grove Road
Loves Park, IL 61111
Phone (815) 633-0711
Eugene T. Hays

Hayson (see Hay)

Hayston (see Hay)

Haystoun (see Hay)

Hayter (see Hay)

Hayton (see Hay)

Haytor (see Hay)

Hayward (see Hay, Heath)

Hayward
*Hayward Surname Organization
Rt. 1, Box 350
Poland Spring, ME 04274
Phone (207) 998-4615
Ronda A. Watson

Haywood (see Hay)

Hayworth (see Haworth)

Hazard (see Alsop)

Hazelbaker
The Hazelbaker News
61 Waterman Avenue
Coldwater, MI 49036
Phone (517) 279-7875
Randall S. Hazelbaker, Editor
Pub. *The Hazelbaker News*, annually, 50¢ per issue to cover postage

Hazelbaker
*Hazelbaker Families
1 Davis Street
PO Box 154
Grove, OK 74344
Phone (918) 786-2360
Imogene Sawvell Davis

Hazelrigg
The Richard K. Hazelrigg Family
  Association
1525 South Home Avenue
Independence, MO 64052
Phone (816) 461-5725
Alan B. Hazelrigg
Pub. *Hazelrigg Family Newsletter*

Hazelrigg
Hazelrigg Family Newsletter
5024 Norfleet Avenue
Independence, MO 64055-5669
Teresa J. Miller
Pub. *Hazelrigg Family Newsletter*, one or
  two times per year, $5.00 per year
  subscription

Hazeltine (see Haseltine)

Hazelton (see Haseltine, Johnson)

Hazelton
Hazelton
41136 Highway 228
Sweet Home, OR 97386
Phone (503) 367-4406
Ralph W. Hazelton
Pub. *Hazelton* (includes descendants of
  Charles Hazelton (1866 Ossian, Iowa–
  1947 Newport Oregon) and Frank R.
  Hazelton (1832 Vermont–1900
  Remmington, Wisconsin))

Hazelwood (see Lush)

Hazen
*Daniel Hazen, U.E.L. Family
  Association
1 Forest View Drive
Cumberland, RI 02864
Phone (401) 333-3128
Ross W. McCurdy, President
Pub. *Hazen Family Association
  Newsletter*, semiannually; (includes
  descendants of United Empire Loyalist
  Daniel Hazen, of Walsingham,
  Ontario, 1755–1845)
$7.00 per year U.S. membership, $8.00
  per year Canadian membership

Hea (see Hay)

Heacock
*Heacock Surname Organization
150 Brown Street
Saint Clair, MI 48079-4882
Phone (810) 329-9359
George M. Roberts
(includes families of Ontario and U.S.A.)

Head (see Stone)

Head
Head
6162 South Poplar
Englewood, CO 80111
Phone (303) 740-9051
Betty Lue Jones
Pub. *Head*, semiannually, free

Heald
*Heald Family Association
250 Robinson Road
Cave Junction, OR 97523-9719
Phone (503) 592-3203
Jack W. Heald, President
(largest collection in the U.S. of Heald
  genealogical materials, including
  descendants of John Heald (1615–),
  immigrated 1635, and Samuel Heald
  (1668–), a Quaker, immigrated 1703)

Healy (see Cian)

Heaney (see Haney)

Heap (see Mouser)

Heard (see Grant)

Hearne (see Cian)

Heasley
*Heasley Family Association
423 11th Street
PO Box 297
Franklin, PA 16323
Phone (814) 437-5263
Ruth R. Heasley, Editor and Genealogist
Pub. *The Little House of Heasley*,
  annually
$5.00 per year membership

Heaston (see Frantz)

Heath (see Corson, Holden, Job)

Heath
*Bartholomew Heath of Haverhill,
  Massachusetts, and William Heath of
  Roxbury, Massachusetts
4168 Woodland Street
Santa Maria, CA 93455-3356
Phone (805) 937-3518
Valerie Dyer Giorgi, Author/Publisher
(includes descendants of Bartholomew
  Heath (ca 1615, England-) and Hannah
  Moyce, daughter of Joseph and
  Hannah Folcord, with allied lines of
  Allen, Bailey, Baker, Bradley, Brown,
  Calkins, Colby, Davis, Drader,
  Emerson, Emery, Fife, Flanders,
  Forbes, Freeman, Goodwin, Gray,
  Haddad, Hancock, Howard, Hughes,
  Huntington, Johnson, Keniston,
  Lobdell, Lyons, Magoon, Mann,
  Mason, Merrill, Miller, Moore, Morse,
  Nichols, North, Page, Paige, Paris,
  Parker, Phegley, Phillips, Ramsey,
  Randall, Reed, Roach, Roberts, Ross,
  Sargent, Schad, Shaver, Smith,
  Stevens, Stiles, Stratton, Taisey,
  Thompson, Watts, Welch, White,
  Williams and Wolf; William Heath and
  additional allied lines of Alden,
  Aldrich, Bass, Bearsley, Bennett,
  Biggs, Carpenter, Clark, Clothier,
  DeSpiegelaere, Dickson, Eichton,
  Evans, Foster, Gingrich, Gustafson,
  Hagert, Hall, Hanson, Hayward,

Hengel, Hinman, Hofmann, Hosteland,
  Howse, Jeffers, Jenniges, Lewis,
  Lipetzky, May, McGill, Mussack,
  Olson, Palmer, Parmely, Pattison, Port,
  Riley, Sackett, Saxby, Sherwin, Soule,
  Stilwell, Vogt, Ward, Welder, Whitford,
  Wicks, Wille, Woodson and Zulauf)

Heath
Heath Reunion
643 Sixth Avenue, N.E.
Dawson, GA 31742
Derrell Heath
Annual reunion at the Heath Family
  Cemetery off Georgia Highway 90,
  between Talbotton and Junction City,
  Georgia

Heath
Heath Family Association
9401 Belfort Road
Richmond, VA 23229
Phone (804) 741-0362
B. R. Heath

Heatherwick (see MacDuff)

Heatherwyck (see MacDuff)

Heaven (see Havens)

Heavens (see Havens)

Hebard (see Hubbard)

Hebner
David William Hebner and Martha
  Martin Descendants
2843 Electric Avenue
Port Huron, MI 48060
William Ford Hebner,III

Hebson
*William Hebson Family Organization
1152 North Forest
Mesa, AZ 85203
Phone (602) 969-0112
Judy Nelson

Heck (see Frantz)

Heckathorn (see Anthes)

Heckel (see Lahey)

Heckmann
*William Jacob Heckmann Family
  Organization
200 Los Robles Way
Woodland, CA 95695
Phone (916) 666-5493
William L. Marble
(includes descendants of William J.
  Heckmann (1861 New York City-) and
  Mary Jane Harding (1856
  Wandsworth, Surrey, England-))

Hedde (see Surname Sources)

Hedden (see Coward)

Hedlund
*Jenny Fredrika Hedlund Family
   Organization
2555 West 15000 South
Bluffdale, UT 84065
Phone (801) 254-1095
Margareta Soderquist, A.G.

Hedrick (see Hetrick, Smith)

Heeke
*The Heeke Family in Indiana
367 Nottinghill Court
Indianapolis, IN 46234-2667
Sharon H. Kennedy, Publisher
(includes Heekes (pronounced *he-key*)
   from Westalen, Germany, and later
   Jasper, Dubois County, Indiana)

Heembrock (see Dietlein)

Heeter
Sebastian Heeter Family Organization
7519 15th Avenue
Kenosha, WI 53140
Terry Heeter
Pub. *Heeter Connections*

Heffelfinger (see Surname Database)

Hefferan (see Cian)

Hefferon (see Wright)

Heflin
Heflin Hemlock
107 Madison Hills Boulevard
Richmond, KY 40475-8728
Donald Lee Heflin
Pub. *Heflin Hemlock*, monthly, $1.00 per
   year subscription

Hefner
The Hefner Handbook
12600 Bissonnet A4-407
Houston, TX 77099
Dede D. Mercer, Publisher
Pub. *The Hefner Handbook*,
   semiannually, $20.00 per year
   subscription; (includes all variations of
   the surname, all over the world)

Hegeman (see Covert)

Hegner (see Miehls)

Hegner
*The Ancestors and Descendants of
   George Hegner and Regina Herrmann
232 Mont Eagle
Milford, MI 48381
Phone (810) 684-0650
Ruth Buchele Doerr, Publisher
(includes descendants of George Hegner
   and Regina Herrmann through Wen
   Leopold Hegner and Elizabeth
   VonGaelhausen, Catherine Hegner and
   Ignatius Beiter, Mary Ann Hegner and
   George Miehls, Cecelia Hegner and
   Martin Wingerter, and allied family of
   Bauer)

Heiby
*John Philip Heiby Family Organization
5649 Campanile Court
Toledo, OH 43615
Phone (419) 531-6158
Warren R. Monday, President
Annual reunion on the third Sunday of
   August in Aumiller Park, Bucyrus,
   Ohio

Heide (see The Memorial Foundation of
   the Germanna Colonies)

Heier (see Hire)

Heimann (see Heymann)

Heimbach (see Lemon)

Heimbach
*Heimbach Reunion
9501 Fourth Place
Lorton, VA 22079
Phone (703) 883-8231 (daytime); (703)
   690-7488 (home)
Paul J. Heimbach, President and Editor
Pub. *Heimbach Herald*, semiannually
   (spring and fall), $6.00 per year
   subscription, queries free to
   subscribers; (newsletter of the
   Heimbach Reunion, Snyder County,
   Pennsylvania)

Heiner (see Hayner, Whitfield)

Heiney (see Van Trump)

Heinlein (see Henline)

Heiny (see Van Trump)

Heir (see Hire)

Heirsekorn (see Brehm)

Heist (see Barnes)

Heite (see The Memorial Foundation of
   the Germanna Colonies, Lemon)

Heldt (see CTC Family Association)

Helem (see Elam)

Helgeson
Helgeson Family Organization
22916 Carlow Road
Torrance, CA 90505
Phone (310) 378-3574
Charlene DeLong

Helgøy (see Haga)

Heller
*BGM Publications
28635 Old Hideaway Road
Cary, IL 60013-9726
Phone (847) 639-2400
Betty G. Massman, Editor and Publisher

Pub. *The Heller Helper*, quarterly, $18.00
   per year subscription; (over 350
   separate and distinct Heller families
   identified, including 18th-century
   immigrants, John Christoph Heller and
   Berndt Heller)

Hellstrom (see Harmon)

Hellums (see Helm)

Helm (see Akers, LaRue, Turner)

Helm
Helm(s)/Casey/Porterfield/Fenix/Phoenix
   Family Organization
c/o Princeton Club
15 West 43rd Street
New York, NY 10036
Hal Helm

Helm
Helm-Helms-Hellums-Nelms Family
   Association
2306 Westgate
Houston, TX 77019
Phone (713) 529-2333
Harold Helm
$25.00 plus pedigree and family group
   sheets

Helmer
*Helmer Research Group
RR 1, Box 134A
Allenwood, PA 17810-9605
Barbara Stabley, Family Historian
(source for the German surname Helmer
   and for the families of Frederick
   Helmer (1816 Wurtemberg,
   Germany–) and daughter Lydia Helmer
   (1847 Philadelphia–1915 Williamsport,
   Pennsylvania) married Joseph Kurtz
   (1845 Wurtemberg–1905 Lycoming
   County, Pennsylvania), and son
   George Helmer (1858 Philadelphia–
   after 1915 Philadelphia) married Kate
   Cornwall)

Helmo (see Elmo)

Helmoldus (see Hallam)

Helms (see Akers, Helm)

Helmsley (see Roades)

Helsey
Helsey Family Reunion
803 McKinley Avenue
Kellogg, ID 83837
D. Helsey

Helton (see Evitt)

Hely (see Cian)

Hely-Hutchinson (see Cian)

Hembree (see Dockery, Louden)

Hemingway (see Surname Sources)

Hemingway
*Hemingway Book Committee
708 Oxford Road
Ypsilanti, MI 48197
Phone (313) 483-1395
Mary L. Liskow
(interested in descendants of Ralph
   Hemingway (–1684) and Elizabeth
   Hewes (1604–1684) of Roxbury,
   Massachusetts, 1634, published book
   on sixth generation descendant Isaac
   (1762–), and wife Elizabeth Hewes)
Annual reunion

Hemmick
Hemmick Exchange
2111 Lawndale Drive
San Antonio, TX 78205
Clarence Hemmick

Hemphill
*Hemphill Historical Society
1403 Torbert Drive
West Point, MS 39773
Phone (770) 924-7342;
   (770) 591-7052 FAX
Sue Hemphill Melcher, Secretary
(includes descendants of John Hemphill
   (1715–1792) and Margaret Ramsey
   (1730–1802))
$15.00 per year membership; annual
   reunion in June

Hempson (see Thorn)

Henaghan (see Cian)

Hencely
Hencely Family Association
Rt. 1, Box 185
Marianna, FL 32445
Charles Hencely

Henchman (see Hinchman)

Hendershot
Hendershot Family Association
101 Jo Ann Drive
Archbald, PA 18403
Phone (717) 383-1402
Karen Gaughan

Henderson (see Folk Family Surname
   Exchange, Gunn, Hall, Lush,
   MacDuff)

Henderson
Clan Henderson Society of the United
   States and Canada
57 South Hedley Street
Buffalo, NY 14206
Phone (716) 892-1627
Harold M. Henderson, Secretary-
   Treasurer
Pub. *An Canach* (The Cottongrass)

Henderson
*Henderson Peek Family Reunion
119 Pinewood Drive
Greer, SC 29651
Phone (864) 877-2424
Robert H. Henderson, Family Historian
(includes descendants of Thomas
   Henderson (–1806 South Carolina) and
   his wife Frances (–1811 South
   Carolina), and John Peek (ca 1700–)
   and his wife Ann)
Donation for membership; annual
   reunion on the third Sunday of July in
   Franklin, North Carolina

Henderson
Henderson Heritage
PO Box 2272
Leesburg, VA 22075
Pub. *Henderson Heritage*

Henderson
*Bell Enterprises
PO Box 10328
Spokane, WA 99209
Phone (509) 327-2761
Mary Ann L. Vanzandt Bell, Owner,
   Publisher
Pub. *Henderson Highlights*, irregularly,
   $6.00 plus $1.25 postage per issue

Hendren
*Hendren Surname Organization
626 McConwell
Memphis, TN 38112-1822
Phone (901) 458-3554
Lucile Hendren Cox
(includes Hendren of Ireland, Virginia,
   North Carolina and Tennessee

Hendrick (see Allison, Brown, Reinbold,
   Wright)

Hendrick
Hunting Hendrick, Hendricks, Hendrix
901 Old Galveston Road
Alvin, TX 77511
Grace Hendricks Atwood
Pub. *Hunting Hendrick, Hendricks,
   Hendrix*, quarterly, $8.00 per year
   subscription

Hendricks (see Links Genealogy
   Publications, Brown, Hendrick,
   Reinbold)

Hendrickson (see Reeder)

Hendrickson
Nexus Publications
2207 N.E. 12th Street
Renton, WA 98056
Lynn Wood, Editor
Pub. *Hendrickson Nexus*, quarterly,
   $20.00 per year subscription

Hendrie (see Macnachton)

Hendrix (see Brown, Hendrick)

Hendry (see Macnachton)

Henehan (see Cian)

Hener (see Hayner)

Henery
Henery Family Reunion
PO Box 803
Marietta, OH 45750
Sharon Gardner, Vice President

Hengel (see Heath)

Henke (see Van Buren)

Henkel
Henkel-Hinkle
Whispering Oaks
5821 Rowland Hill Road
Cascade, MD 21719-1939
Phone (301) 416-2660
Victor Gebhart, President
Pub. *Henkel-Hinkle*, annually, $2.00 per
   issue

Henlein
*The Henlein-Heinlein Family
   Association
11502 Grace Terrace
Indianapolis, IN 46236-8834
Phone (317) 823-2376
Enid I. Beihold
Pub. *Henlein-Heinlein Chanticleer*
   (includes Henline, Hanline, Heinlein,
   all spellings)

Henline (see Henlein)

Henn
Henn/Haines Family Organization
1000 South 1000 East
Mapleton, UT 84663

Henneman
Henneman Family Reunion
260 Sagerman Avenue
Vandergriff, PA 15690
William Henneman

Hennen (see Lambert)

Henrie
Daniel Henrie Family Organization
1852 East 3990 South, Apartment B
Salt Lake City, UT 84124
Karen Renee Cox
(includes descendants of Daniel Henrie
   (1825) and Amanda Bradley (1829))

Henritzy (see Blossom Press)

Henry (see Bickers, Fullick, Futral,
   Locke)

Henry
Patrick Henry Allied Families of Virginia
Rt. 2, Box 1300
Stuart, VA 24171
Phone (703) 930-2978
Joan F. Forbes, Executive Secretary

Henshaw (see Bosher)

Hensley
Hunting Hensleys
6875 East Middletown Road
Waldron, IN 46182-9739
Phone (317) 525-9532
Judy Borton, Editor
Pub. *Hunting Hensleys*, quarterly, $10.00
per calender year subscription

Henson (see Folk Family Surname
Exchange, Hanson)

Henson
Henson/Cartwright Cousins
801 Camp Street
Kilgore, TX 75662
Faye Pool

Henton
George Henton of Berks County,
Pennsylvania
1024 Apollo Way
Sacramento, CA 95822-1709
Phone (916) 448-1030
Donnadeane D. Depew, Secretary
Pub. *Newsletter*, irregularly, $5.00 per
issue

Hepburn (see Armstrong)

Hepburn
Hepburn Family Society
10 Towne Lane
Centerreach, NY 11720
Phone (516) 732-2572
Patrick J. Hepburn

Hepworth (see Gilson)

Hepworth
*Joseph Hepworth and Mary Hirst
Family Organization
1055 East Hillcrest Drive
Springville, UT 84663
Phone (801) 489-6298
Nel Lo H. Bassett, A.G., Researcher
Pub. *Hepworth-Hirst Family Newsletter*,
biannually; *Research Report*, annually;
(includes ancestry of Joseph Hepworth
(1816) and his wife, Mary Hirst (1820)
of West Yorkshire, England)
$12.00 per year membership

Herbert (see Hubbard)

Herbnain (see Irwin)

Herd
Andrew Jackson Herd and Mary
Dierhing Family Association
Daniel B. Herd and Mary Ann
Kretzmeier Association
8626 Splitlog
Kansas City, KS 66112
Phone (913) 299-9522
Helen L. Looper

Herinanus (see Garner)

Herl
*Herl Surname Organization
6750 East Main Street, #106
Mesa, AZ 85205-9049
Warren D. Steffey

Herlacher
Herlacher Herald
19341 Knotty Pine Way
Monument, CO 80132
Phone (719) 481-2875
Ruth H. Christian
Pub. *Herlacher Herald*, quarterly, $10.00
per year subscription; (Harlocher,
Herlocher and Horlacher)

Herlocher (see Herlacher)

Hermanski
Hermanski Exchange
Rt. 2
Taluga, OK 73167
Mary Briggs

Hern (see Goodenow)

Herndon (see The Memorial Foundation
of the Germanna Colonies, Banks)

Herndon
*Herndon Family of Virginia
613 Bostwick
Nacogdoches, TX 75961
Phone (409) 564-7478
Berry Fagan Burr, Publisher

Herold (see Rentsch)

Heron (see McCune, McKitrick)

Heroy
*Heroy Family Clearinghouse
Rt. 2, Box 33, Lyon Road
Bainbridge, NY 13733
Phone (607) 967-8015
Eleanor Munk
(extensive card file includes Erouard,
which was Anglicized to Heroy about
1765)

Herran (see McCune)

Herrell
Herrell/Herrill/Harrell Messenger
13101 La Paloma Road
Los Altos Hills, CA 94022-3334
Phone (415) 941-3434; E-mail:
CHMarch@aol.com
Carol Hodge March, Editor/Publisher
Pub. *Herrell/Herrill/Harrell Messenger*,
quarterly, $7.50 per year subscription,
$2.00 per issue; (includes descendants
of John Herrell and Martha Roberts of
Virginia, North Carolina, Tennessee,
1780–1830)

Herries (see Maxwell)

Herrill (see Herrell)

Herring (see Parish)

Herring
Herring Family Archives
850 Doty
Centralia, MO 65240
Dr. J. P. Herring

Herrington
*Herrington Family Association
PO Box 361
Mount Olive, MS 39119
Phone (601) 797-3334
Sandra E. Boyd
(includes descendants of Enoch
Herrington (ca 1800–1850, possibly
the son of William Herrington, who
was in Mississippi by 1812) and
Harriet Stuckey Herrington (ca 1804–
1880 Mississippi); and especially all
Herringtons in Mississippi prior to
1840)

Herriott
Herriott Heritage Association
1709 Gentry Square Lane, #105
Champaign, IL 61821-5964
Dean Herriott

Herrmann (see Arthur, Hegner)

Herrold (see Maier)

Herrold
*Charles E. Herrold Family Organization
313 West Hill Street
Wabash, IN 46992
Phone (219) 563-6901
Thomas L. Herrold, Sr.

Herron (see Folk Family Surname
Exchange, Hall)

Hersent (see Folk Family Surname
Exchange)

Hersey
Hersey Family Association
2 Drawbridge Road
Westford, MA 01886
Stephen E. Hersey

Hershour (see Hoschar)

Hertzel (see Surname Database)

Hervey (see Keith, Newton)

Hervey
Hervey Families of America Bulletin
8910 Brae Acres Road
Houston, TX 77074
Joyce P. Hervey
Pub. *Hervey Families of America
Bulletin*, quarterly, $10.00 per year
subscription

Herwynd (see Irwin)

Herying (see Dunbar)

Herzel (see Surname Database)

Heskett (see McCune)

Hess (see Erdwins, Goodenow, Lush, Millet, Stoner)

Hess
Hess/Kirk of Virginia to Indiana
2905 North Kilbourne
East Chicago, IL 60647
June B. Barekman

Hess
*Hess Family Association
PO Box 335
Owenton, KY 40359-0335
Doris Shell Gill, Editor
Pub. *Hess Family Newsletter*, biannually;
(includes descendants of Martin Hess
and Mary Ann Wood)
Annual reunion in August

Hesse (see McCune)

Hesseltine (see Haseltine)

Hesser (see Clark)

Hesslar (see Lemon)

Hester (see Banks)

Hester
Hester Newsletter
16 Smith Garrison Road
Newmarket, NH 03857
Lucile V. Novak, Editor
Pub. *Hester Newsletter*, quarterly, $6.00
per year subscription

Heston
Heston Historian
9377 Chatham Street
Allen Park, MI 48101
John P. Heston
Pub. *Heston Historian*, quarterly

Hetrick
*Descendants of Christopher Hetrick
2610 Lark Avenue
Altoona, PA 16602
Phone (814) 944-0194
Betty Hetrick Boslet, Historian-
Genealogist
(includes descendants of Christopher
Hetrick, who immigrated to America
in 1738 on the ship *Robert and Alice*,
Philadelphia, with brothers George and
Peter, the latter of whom was in the
Revolutionary War and whose
descendants spell their name Hedrick)

Hettrick (see Pittenger)

Heuer (see Hire)

Hewes (see Surname Sources,
Hemingway)

Hewett (see Rutherford)

Hewitt (see Main)

Hewitt
Hewitt-Matheny Family
221 S.E. 12th Avenue, Apartment 8
Hillsboro, OR 97123-4392
Julie Jones
(includes descendants of the Hewitt,
Matheny, Cooper and Kirkwood
families, early Oregon pioneers of
Yamhill County)
Annual reunion

Hey (see Hay)

Heydon
*Heydon/Hayden/Hyden Family
Association
7911 Yancey Drive
Falls Church, VA 22042
Phone (202) 736-1726
Gene Hyden, Editor
Pub. *The Heydon-Hayden-Hyden
Families*, quarterly; (includes Haydon,
Haden, Hiden, Hiten, Hyten)
$15.00 per year regular membership,
$25.00 and up, contributing
membership

Heyer (see Hire)

Heyes (see Hay)

Heyfron (see Cian)

Heyle
*Heÿle/Hiley of Germany and South
Carolina Family Association
109 Oak Way Street
Eatonton, GA 31024
Phone (706) 485-6810
E. V. Knight, Jr.

Heymann
*Heymann Historical Society
PO Box 241
Monroeville, OH 44847
Phone (419) 465-2633
John P. Seaman, Sr., President
Pub. *November Newsletter*, annually,
free; (includes Heimann)

Heyseau (see Hisaw)

Heywood
*John Heywood and Families
203 Las Marias Drive, S.E.
Rio Rancho, NM 87124-1317
Frieda Heywood Massara
(includes descendants of John Heywood
(ca 1634–1700/01) of Concord,
Massachusetts)

Hiatt
Hiatt/Hyatt Family Newsletter
2801 Gardenia Way
Columbus, GA 31906
Florence Hiatt
Pub. *Hiatt/Hyatt Family Newsletter*

Hibbard (see Hubbard)

Hibbard
*The Hibbard Family Association
801 Pinebrook Court
Alpharetta, GA 30201-1335
Phone (404) 475-2099
ElizaBeth Queen-McKee
Pub. *The Hibbard Family Gazette*
(includes Hebbard, Hubbard)

Hibberd (see Pessner)

Hibbert (see Brown)

Hice (see Hise)

Hickenbottom (see Higginbotham)

Hickman
Hickman/Speed/Werli/Conley Family
Organization
22916 Carlow Road
Torrance, CA 90505
Phone (310) 378-3574
Charlene DeLong

Hicks (see Hyatt, Kettenring, Lush)

Hicks
Hicks Newsletter II
8900 Leatham Avenue
Fair Oaks, CA 95628
Phone (916) 965-4773
Virginia Hicks, Editor
Pub. *Hicks Newsletter II*, quarterly,
$15.00 per year subscription; (includes
Hix)

Hicks
*Hicks/Wenlock Database
45865 Michell Lane
Indio, CA 92201-3780
Helen Free VanderBeek
(deals exclusively with families from
Essex, England)
$1.00 plus SASE for search

Hicks
Hicks Happenings
850 New Middletown Road, N.E.
Corydon, IN 47112
Phone (812) 738-3470
Shirley M. McKim, Editor
Pub. *Hicks Happenings*, quarterly, $5.00
per year subscription; (includes
descendants of Elva Bayard Hicks
(1892–) and wife Eva Gertrude Catt
(1892–), all of Pike County, Indiana)

Hicks
*Hicks Ancestry
1115 N.E. Orchard Drive
Pullman, WA 99163
Phone (509) 332-5612
Mildred B. Stout, Publisher
(includes descendants of John Hicks, Sr.
(1768?–), probably from the family in

Guilford, Vermont, who came from Rehoboth, Massachusetts, married Elizabeth Butts of Canterbury, Connecticut, allied with the family of Joshua Hicks of Sutton, Massachusetts, who served in the Revolutionary War, and with Caroline Fish)

Hicks
Hicks
Rt. 2, Box 195A
Branchland, WV 25506
N. L. Sanders
Pub. *Hicks*, quarterly, $21.20 per year subscription

Hiden (see Heydon)

Hier (see Hire)

Hierewine (see Irwin)

Hieronymus
Hieronymus Family of America (Romeus/Rhonemus)
1106 Jefferson Street
Greenwood, SC 29646
Al Heironemus

Higdon (see Hawsey)

Higdon
*The Higdon Family Association, Inc.
PO Box 26008
Alexandria, VA 22314
Phone (703) 548-7200
Frank B. Higdon, Treasurer
Pub. *Higdon Family Newsletter*, monthly $15.00 per year membership

Higganbottom
Higganbottom Organization
833 East Rosebriar
Springfield, MO 65807
R. L. Higgenbottom

Higginbotham (see Von Bargen)

Higginbotham
*Higginbotham Descendants
PO Box 1153
Bruceville, TX 76630-1153
Phone (817) 859-5337
Earl Higginbotham, Publisher
(includes descendants of Moses Higginbotham and Frances Kyle of Amherst County, Virginia, also Hickenbottom and Higinbotham variations, mainly of the south, plus Texas and Missouri)

Higginson
*The Higginsons of Shropshire
983 Venus Way
Livermore, CA 94550-6345
Phone (510) 455-5059; E-mail: enokh@aol.com
Enoch Haga, Publisher
(includes descendants in America, especially Idaho)

Higgs
Higgs Heritage
South 2707 Rhyolite Road
Spokane, WA 99203
Phone (509) 747-6969
Jean Jones Holder
Pub. *Higgs Heritage*, $5.00 per year subscription

High
*The High Family Association
PO Box 5841
Columbia, SC 29250
Phone (803) 782-9595
Lake E. High, Jr., Editor
Pub. *Newsletter*, semiannually, free to family members; (includes descendants of the English High family which settled in Surry County, Virginia, in the 1660s; Thomas High (1647–1688) and Hannah Clements (ca 1654–ca 1693), immigrant ancestors)

Higher (see Hire)

Highmiller
Highmiller Family Association
1332 Ronald Road
Springfield, OH 45503
P. David Highmiller

Highsaw (see Hisaw)

Hight (see Hoyt)

Hightower
The Hightower News
Communications Department, Indiana State University
Terre Haute, IN 47809
Phone (812) 234-0754; E-mail: cmhigh@ruby.indstate.edu or NikonPaul.aol.com; Webiste: www=http://hightower.indstate.edu
Paul Hightower
Pub. *The Hightower News*, annually (summer), $5.00 for two-year subscription

Higinbotham (see Higginbotham)

Higley (see Lush)

Hihar (see Blossom Press)

Hil (see Hill)

Hilborn
*Hilborn Surname Organization
7705 Ensley Drive, S.W.
Huntsville, AL 35802-2845
Phone (205) 883-0207
Thomas W. Burns

Hildebrand (see Looney)

Hildreth
*Hildreth Family Association
30 Rockefeller Plaza, 44th Floor
New York, NY 10112

Ronald B. Hildreth, President
Pub. *Hildreth Highlights*

Hiley (see Heÿle)

Hill (see Folk Family Surname Exchange, Allison, Barnard, Cowart, Craft, Gant, Jelly, McCune, Scott, Wright)

Hill
Zion Hill and Solomon Bedingfield Descendants
Rt. 6, Box 740
Guthrie, OK 73044
J. D. Hill

Hill
Hill Trails-Branches-Trees
Box 2455 C.S.
Pullman, WA 99165
Marilu VonBargen
Pub. *Hill Trails-Branches-Trees*

Hillery (see Armbruster)

Hillman
*Charles Lewis Hillman Family Organization
Rt. 4, Box 118
Floresville, TX 78114
Phone (512) 393-2417
Irma M. Meyr
(includes any Hillman family, especially in southern states)
Free exchange

Hills (see Jelly, Millet)

Hillsdon (see Thorn)

Hils (see Hill)

Hilton (see Catlow, Hack)

Himmelberger (see Nelson)

Hinchman
Hinchman/Henchman
Boxton Road
Groton, MA 01450
Pub. *Hinchman/Henchman*

Hinckley
The Tower
539 Kapahula Avenue
Honolulu, HI 96815
Rev. Robert J. Goode, Jr.
Pub. *The Tower*, quarterly, $10.00 per year subscription; (for descendants of Elder Samuel Hinckley of Barnstable, Massachusetts, 1639)

Hinckley
*Hinckley—Heritage and History
6049 Wrigley Way
Fort Worth, TX 76133-3533
Phone (817) 292-3942
E. Charles Hinckley, Author and Compiler

(includes descendants of Samuel[1] (1587–1662) and Mary Hinckley of Barnstable, Massachusetts, also Hinkley and Hingley spellings in the U.S. and U.K.)

Hindman (see Fletcher)

Hinds (see Likes)

Hiner (see Whitfield)

Hiner
Hiner Reunion Association of Texas
5543 Meadow Creek Lane
Houston, TX 77017-6707
John Hensel
Pub. *Hiner News Bulletin*, three times per year, $5.00 per year subscription

Hines (see Scott)

Hines
*Hines Haze
PO Box 1872
Dodge City, KS 67801-1872
Laura Tasset Koehn, President
(includes research on James D. Hines and Margaret Belle Mason family)

Hines
Hines-Trammel-Hart-McPherson Family Association
2306 Westgate
Houston, TX 77019
Phone (713) 529-2333
Harold Helm
$25.00 plus pedigree and family group sheets membership

Hingle (see Blossom Press)

Hingley (see Hinckley)

Hinkley (see Hinckley)

Hinman (see Heath)

Hinman
*Hinman Family Association
2263 East Leonora Street
Mesa, AZ 85213-2260
Phone (602) 890-2827
Milton E. Hinman
Pub. *Hinman Heritage*, quarterly; (includes descendants of Sgt. Edward Hinman of Stratford, Connecticut, and John Hinman of Virginia)
$10.00 per year regular membership, $15.00 or more sustaining membership

Hinman
Hinman Family Association
337 North 725 East
North Salt Lake, UT 84054-3130
Arlene Hinman
Pub. *Hinman Newsletter*, quarterly, $10.00 per year subscription

Hinnegan (see Cian)

Hinsdale (see Clark)

Hinshaw
Hinshaw/Inkshaw Family Organization
Rt. 3, Box 123
Trinity, NC 27370
Cheryl Burrow

Hinshaw
Hinshaw-Buell Reunion
1019 S.E. 37th
Portland, OR 97214
Phone (503) 235-2968
Joan Loop
(includes descendants of Isaac Hinshaw and Mellissa Buell, or Elias Buell and Sarah Hammond, all of whom settled in Polk County, Oregon before 1850)
Reunion

Hinson (see Hanson)

Hinton (see Hynton)

Hinton
Surnames, Limited
RR 3, Box 59
Muleshoe, TX 79347-9208
Pub. *Hints on Hintons*, irregularly, $8.00 per issue

Hintz (see Gottfried)

Hipp (see Hipps)

Hipps
Hipps/Hipp Clearinghouse
1601 Rim Road
El Paso, TX 79902

Hire
*Hire Family Organization (Heier/Haier/Hier/Heyer/Hyer)
2434 Banyon Drive
Beavercreek, OH 45431
Sasha Hire Stanley, Editor/Family Representative
Pub. *Hire-O-Glyphics*, quarterly, $5.00 per year subscription, free queries; (includes Haier, Haire, Hauer, Heier, Heir, Heuer, Heyer, Higher, Hyer and other variant spellings in the U.S. and Canada, especially descendants of John William Hier/Hire and Elizabeth Ott)
Free membership; annual Hier-Ott reunion in July

Hirevigne (see Irwin)

Hirewine (see Irwin)

Hirschel (see Kutsch)

Hirsh (see The Memorial Foundation of the Germanna Colonies)

Hirst (see Links Genealogy Publications, Hepworth)

Hirt (see Frantz)

Hisaw
*Hisaw Family Association
6411 South Quay Court
Littleton, CO 80123
Phone (303) 972-9073
Susan Hollis
Pub. *Hisaw Family Newsletter (Including Also Heyseau, Highsaw, Hysaw and Hyso)*, semiannually
$5.00 per year membership

Hiscock (see Brown)

Hise (see Kunkel)

Hise
*Hise/Hice Family Association
6413 Windsor Lane
San Jose, CA 95129
Phone (408) 253-6579
Millie Hise Biren
Pub. *Hise Newsletter*, quarterly
$5.00 per year membership

Hisle
*Hisle/Hysell (Barnhisle/Barnheiser)
2649 Briarwood Drive
San Jose, CA 95125
Corinne Hisle
Pub. *Hisle/Hysell (Barnhisle/Barnheiser)*

Hissem (see Lambert)

Hitchcock (see Baker)

Hitchcock
*Julius William Hitchcock Family Organization
PO Box 24
Buhl, ID 83316
Phone (208) 543-4138
Ricardo G. Hitchcock
(includes descendants of Julius William Hitchcock (1819 Waterford, Erie County, Pennsylvania–) and Heneretta Gilbert Colt (1818 Waterford–), plus 5000-name index to collection of 600 pedigree charts and family group sheets on the Hitchcock surname)

Hite (see Richardson, Sawyer)

Hite
Hite
6801 West 100 South
Andrews, IN 46702
Kenneth D. Baker
Pub. *Hite*, quarterly, $7.00 per year subscription

Hite
Hite Family Association
102 Shady Meadow Circle
Cary, NC 27513
Phone (919) 467-2950
John L. Hite, President
Pub. *Hite Family Association Newsletter*, semiannually, $10.00 per year subscription

Hiten (see Heydon)

Hiter (see Rutherford)

Hitson (see Eidson)

Hitt (see The Memorial Foundation of the Germanna Colonies)

Hitt
*Hitt and All Allied Families
1400 S.W. Shorewood Drive
Dunnellon, FL 34431-3882
Phone (352) 489-7190
Maurice Hitt, Jr.

Hittson (see Eidson)

Hiveley (see Hively)

Hively
Hively Family Newsletter
375 Manor Road
Red Lion, PA 17356-9245
Phone (717) 244-7358
David P. Hively
Pub. *Hively Family Newsletter*, three times per year, $12.00 per year subscription; (includes Haible and Hiveley)

Hix (see Hicks)

Hixson (see CTC Family Association)

Hoag (see Miles)

Hoag
Hoag Family
PO Box 6163
Los Osos, CA 93412
Phone (805) 528-8013
Rosemary Sylvester Flamion

Hoar (see Clark)

Hoard
Hoard Family Organization
535 North Luce Road
Ithaca, MI 48847
Mary E. Strouse

Hobart (see Hubbard)

Hobbs (see Corson)

Hobby (see Cobb)

Hobert (see Hubbard)

Hobson (see Donnachaidh)

Hobson
*Hobson Family Data Exchange
5805 Warwick Place
Columbus, GA 31904
Phone (706) 323-6273 (home);
(706) 596-3643 (work)
Jay W. Hobson

(computer data base of over 25,000 people)
No charge

Hochstedler (see Hochstetler)

Hochstetler
*Jacob Hochstetler Family Association, Inc.
1008 College Avenue
Goshen, IN 46526
Phone (219) 533-7819
Daniel E. Hochstetler
Pub. *H/H/H Family Newsletter*, quarterly; (includes descendants of Jacob Hochstetler (1712–1776), Swiss/German immigrant of 1738 to Berks County, Pennsylvania; main spellings: Hochstetler, Hostetler, Hochstedler)
$7.00 per year membership; reunion every five years

Hockett (see Hoggatt)

Hockett
*Hockett History
465 Sunset Terrace
Cedar Park, TX 78513
Phone (512) 259-4796
Joseph Carroll, Publisher
(includes descendants of John V. Hockett (ca 1782 Virginia–))

Hodapp
*Hodapp Surname Organization
5341 Whitney Lane
Amarillo, TX 79110
Phone (806) 359-1012
Sylvia D. Murray, A.G., Coordinator
(includes Hodapp of Minnesota and Germany)

Hodgdon (see Corson)

Hodge (see Lessey, Saye, Stewart)

Hodgen (see LaRue)

Hodges (see Folk Family Surname Exchange, Burge, Hodgin)

Hodges
*Hodges Family Association
14850 23 Mile Road
Albion, MI 49224
Phone (517) 629-2345
Shirley J. Hodges, Secretary
Pub. *The Hodges Family Newsletter*, quarterly
$15.00 per year membership

Hodges
Lineages
PO Box 1264
Huntington, WV 25714
Pub. *Hodges Family Newsletter*, semiannually, queries accepted

Hodgin
Hodgin-Hodges
1221 Candice Court
Mesquite, TX 75149
Mary L. House, Editor
Pub. *Hodgin-Hodges*, quarterly, $12.00 per year subscription

Hodgson
Jonathon Hodgson Descendants
480 West 13
Eureka, KS 67045
C. Hodgson

Hodson (see Corson)

Hoefft (see Anthes)

Hoefler
*Hoefler Family Association
1039 Highway "W"
Warrenton, MO 63383
Phone (314) 456-4610
Dorey Hoefler Schrick
Pub. *Ho(e)fler Herald - USA: Hoefler Family Association Newsletter Dedicated to researching and preserving Hoefler Family History*, $1.00 per issue
$2.00 per year membership

Hoehn (see Arthur)

Hoehn
*The Hoehn Family
4902 Lindsey Lane
Richmond Heights, OH 44143-2930
Phone (216) 381-2459
James A. Bowman, Jr., M.D., Corresponding Secretary
(includes antecedents to early 18th century in Wuerttemberg, Germany)

Hoeinghaus (see Harting)

Hoekstras
*Hoekstras of Jelsum Foundation
358 South Naranja Avenue
Port Saint Lucie, FL 34983
Phone (407) 871-0410
Mrs. Jitske Bergman-Smith
Pub. *News of the Family Circle*, semiannually; (published in Dutch but mailed to U.S. and Canada about a month after original publication with an English translation, includes the Hoekstra descendants from Jelsum (Friesland), Netherlands, in both male and female lines of 17th-century ancestor)
$5.00 per year membership

Hoelscher
*Hoelscher-Buxkemper Family
106 Ranchland
San Antonio, TX 78213-2305
Phone (210) 344-7229
Theresa G. Gold, Family Historian
Pub. *Newsletter*, biannually, free to family members; (includes descendants

of Anton and Mary Katherine
Hoelscher, 1846 immigrants to Texas
from Germany)
Biennial reunion in even-numbered years

Hoffer
Mathias Hoffer Descendants
PO Box 392
Elizabethtown, PA 17022-0392
Audrey Gates Risser
Pub. *Hoffer Happenings*, quarterly, $4.00
per year subscription

Hoffert (see Nelson)

Hoffman (see The Memorial Foundation
of the Germanna Colonies, Surname
Sources, Wert)

Hoffman
Hoffman Happenings
7443 East Crescent
Mesa, AZ 85208
Phone (602) 981-1933
Naomi Martineau, Publisher
Pub. *Hoffman Happenings*, quarterly,
$15.00 per year subscription; (includes
Huffman)

Hoffman
*Family Ties
19355 Sherman Way, Unit 1
Reseda, CA 91335-3560
Phone (818) 772-1941; (800) 772-1942;
(818) 772-8816 FAX
Richard H. Hoffman
Pub. *Hoffman & Volvoski Family Ties
Newsletter*, three times per year, SASE
for sample issue; (Jewish specialty)

Hoffman
Hoffman
Whispering Oaks
5821 Rowland Hill Road
Cascade, MD 21719-1939
Phone (301) 416-2660
Victor Gebhart, President
Pub. *Hoffman*, annually, $2.00 per issue

Hoffman
*Surname Sources
Hoffman/Huffman Database
3131 18th Avenue, South
Minneapolis, MN 55407-1824
Ruth V. McKee, Publisher
Pub. *Hoffman Newsletter*, quarterly,
$20.00 per year subscription

Hoffman
Hoffman Family Clearinghouse
77 Hollow Road
Quarryville, PA 17566-9491
Harry Hoffman
Pub. *Hoffman Family Newsletter*

Hoffses
Hoffses Family Newsletter
480 East Haines Boulevard
Lake Alfred, FL 33850
Phone (941) 956-2289

William J. Hoffses, Publisher
Pub. *Hoffses Family Newsletter*,
quarterly, $5.00 per year subscription

Hoffses
*Hoffses Family History
467 Friendship Road
Waldoboro, ME 04572
Phone (207) 832-7942; (617) 661-5866
Keith E. Hoffses

Hofler (see Hoefler)

Hofman (see Silverstein)

Hofmann (see Surname Sources, Heath)

Höft (see Cordes)

Hog (see Cian)

Hogan (see Gleeson, McCanna, Paulk)

Hogan
Hogan Family Searchers
206 North Thayer Street
Ann Arbor, MI 48104
Joseph Hogan

Hogan
*Hogan Family Association
6212 Vista Verde
Las Vegas, NV 89102
Phone (702) 871-7241
Carol A. Hogan, President
Pub. *Hogan Family Association Research
Quarterly*
$5.00 per year membership

Hogard
*Hogard Search Group
3927 Fernwood
Davenport, IA 52807-2339
Phone (319) 359-8676
R. W. Hogard, Sr., President
(includes descendants of John Hogard
and his wife Elizabeth, who were from
Virginia and moved to Livingston
County, Kentucky, about 1811;
includes Hogard ancestors from
northeast Holland and/or Germay
about 1740–1790 and descendants in
Kansas, Oklahoma, Oregon,
Tennessee, Missouri and New Jersey)

Hogarth (see MacDuff)

Hogg (see Cian)

Hogg
Hogg Reunion
1020 west Oak Drive
Yukon, OK 73099
Carol Knuppel
$15.00 per year membership

Hoggard (see MacDuff)

Hoggart (see MacDuff)

Hoggatt
William T. Hoggatt Family Association
411 West South Street
Yates Center, KS 66783-1671
John Hoggatt

Hoggatt
*Hoggatt/Hockett Family Assocation
13890 S.W. 114th Avenue
Tigard, OR 97223-3772
Phone (503) 639-5505; (503) 684-0849;
E-mail: kenhoggatt@aol.com
Ken and Phyllis Ferrara Hogatt
Pub. *Quarterly*, $13.50 per year
subscription; (includes Quakers Philip
Hoggatt (1687 England–1783 North
Carolina) and Mary Glendenning
(1698 Scotland–1780 North Carolina))

Hogge (see Cian)

Hoggs
Wilson Family Record Depository
169 Melody Lane
Tonawanda, NY 14150-9109
Robert J. Wilson
Pub. *Hoggs*, quarterly, $25.00 per year
subscription

Hohenschild (see Surname Database)

Hohner (see Hayner)

Hoit (see Hoyt)

Hoitt (see Corson, Hoyt)

Hoke (see Moser, Reid)

Holben
Holben Family Gleanings
PO Box 171
Cedar Crest, NM 87008
Richard Holbein
Pub. *Holben Family Gleanings*

Holbert
Holbert/Halbert Family Association
PO Box 78
Rineyville, KY 40162
Phone (502) 877-2475
Shelby Jackson Bewley
Pub. *Holbert Herald*

Holbrook (see Surname Sources,
McCune, Reynolds, Wright)

Holbrook
*The Holbrook Report
357 Snake Meadow Hill Road
Sterling, CT 06377
Phone (860) 564-7660
J. C. Halbrooks
Pub. *The Holbrook Report*, irregularly,
free upon receipt of family line
information of inquirer; (includes
Halbrook, Halbrooks, Haulbrook,
Haulbrooks, Holbrooks, Holdbrook,
Albrook, Alsbrook, Alsebrook,
Alsobrook, etc., any time, worldwide)

Holbrooks (see Holbrook)

Holcomb
*Lucy E. Holcomb Family Organization
7712 Buck Street
North Richland Hills, TX 76180
Phone (817) 485-3792
Ken Mason

Holdbrook (see Holbrook)

Holden (see Paxton)

Holden
*Anna Jane Holden—Her Ancestors and
   Descendants
PO Box 1411
Ukiah, CA 95482
Viettia Newcomb, Publisher
(twenty-two generations of Anna Jane's
   direct line, including allied lines of
   Allred, Barlow, Bennett, Benton,
   Birckhead, Bullough, Burgess,
   Burnette, Calloway, Campbell,
   Chidester, Cook, DePartee, Domgaard,
   Ellis, Ewen, Gustin, Heath, Knight,
   Mangum, Mears, Mortimore, Mott,
   Nickerson, Ostberg, Osterberg, Owen,
   Parrish, Parry, Raine, Rowland,
   Russell, Sampson, Smithson, Spalding,
   Sproul, Stevens, Talbott, Taylor,
   Wallace, etc.; also researching Joshua
   Holden (1800 North Carolina–1862
   Nephi City, Utah) and Mary Talley
   (1802–1851 Bluffbranch,
   Pottawatomie County, Iowa))

Holder (see Gregg)

Holebrook (see Wright)

Holeman
*Holeman/Holman Newsletter
10785 Illinois Highway 78
Kewanee, IL 61443
Phone (309) 853-8095
Roger and Merry Ann Malcolm, Editors
Pub. *Holeman/Holman Newsletter*,
   quarterly, $4.00 per year subscription

Holland (see Bosher, Brawley, Brewer,
   LaRue)

Holland
*Holland Surname Organization
Gabriel Holland Family Organization
175 Thornton Drive
Fayetteville, GA 30214-3824
Phone (770) 719-1754
Jeanette H. Austin

Hollaway (see Clark)

Holleman (see Holliman)

Hollen
*Hollen Family Association
3018 Leado Avenue
Des Moines, IA 50310-5211
Phone (515) 255-8798

Raymond E. Bond, Treasurer
Pub. *Hollen Family Newsletter*, quarterly
   (March, June, September and
   December); (includes descendants of
   Joseph and Margaret Hollen (ca 1777
   Pannsylvania–))
$10.00 per year membership for
   individuals, $15.00 per year
   membership for families; biennial
   reunion in odd-numbered years

Holler (see Surname Database)

Holley (see Allison)

Holley
*James Hyrum Holley Family
   Organization
1623 North Harrison
Pocatello, ID 83204
Phone (208) 232-3385
Wanda M. Jorgensen

Holliman
*Holliman (Holliman/Holleman/
   Hollomon/Hollyman) Family
   Association
1365 Lesley Court
Santa Maria, CA 93454
Phone (805) 922-4313; (805) 346-1156
   FAX; E-mail: ccsd62B@prodigy.com
   or 72103,2257@compuserve.com
Tina Peddie, President
(includes descendants of Christopher
   Hollyman and wife Mary (Gray?), who
   probably came from England and
   resided in Isle of Wight County,
   Virginia, in the early to mid-1700s)

Hollinger (see Hullinger)

Hollingshead (see Smith)

Hollingshead
*Hollingshead Database
45865 Michell Lane
Indio, CA 92201-3780
Helen Free VanderBeek
(deals exclusively with families from
   Canada)
$1.00 plus SASE for search

Hollingsworth
Hollingsworth Register
21532 Appaloosa Court
Canyon Lake, CA 92587-7628
Harry Hollingsworth, C.G., R.G.
Pub. *Hollingsworth Register*, quarterly
   (March, June, September and
   December), $10.00 per year
   subscription

Hollinshead
*Hollinshead Family Association
109 Oak Way Street
Eatonton, GA 31024
Phone (706) 485-6810
E. V. Knight, Jr.

Hollis (see Tidwell)

Hollis
*Hollis (SC, AL, LA, VA) Family
   Organization
2711 Seabreeze Court
Orlando, FL 32805
Phone (407) 425-6942
Col. Clifton O. Duty (USA Ret.) or Jean
   Barker Duty

Hollomon (see Holliman)

Hollon (see Emery)

Holloway
*Holloway/Ralston Family Association
7650 Fairview Road
Tillamook, OR 97141
Phone (503) 842-6036
Orella Chadwick

Hollowell
*Palouse Publications
S.E. 310 Camino
Pullman, WA 99163-2206
Phone (509) 334-1732
Janet Margolis Damm
Pub. *Hollowell Heritage*
irregularly, $5.00 plus $1.50 postage
   (Washington residents add 47¢ tax)

Hollyman (see Holliman)

Holman (see Holeman, Millet)

Holmes (see Frazier, Hughes, Lemon,
   Rutherford)

Holmes
S. Adelbert Holmes and Emma Witter
   Descendants
PO Box 157
Knightsen, CA 94548
Carolyn Sherfy

Holmes
*The Holmes Family Reunion
5634 Caminito Isla
La Jolla, CA 92037-7224
Phone (619) 454-1769
Anne Hait Christian
Pub. *The Search*, bimonthly, $7.00 per
   year subscription; (includes
   descendants of William Holmes and
   Alice Setchfield, who emigrated from
   Whittlesey, Cambridgeshire, England,
   in 1849, and of William Setchfield and
   Eliza S. Hall; and allied families in
   Livingston County, Michigan)

Holmes
Holmes Family Newsletter
801 Gillaspie Drive, #130
Boulder, CO 80303
Fern Maynard
Pub. *Holmes Family Newsletter, For and
   About the Descendants of William M.
   Holmes (1715–1758) and Honor Wells
   (1724–1816) Married Baltimore 1740*,
   donation for subscription

Holmes
*Greatorex Surname Organization
1869 South Fairway Drive
Pocatello, ID 83201
Phone (208) 232-5777
Brent Michael Holmes

Holmes
*Robert Holmes Family Organization
1869 South Fairway Drive
Pocatello, ID 83201
Phone (208) 232-5777
Brent Michael Holmes

Holmqvist
*Carl Richard Holmqvist Family
    Organization
2555 West 15000 South
Bluffdale, UT 84065
Phone (801) 254-1095
Margareta Soderquist, A.G.

Holochvort
Holochvort Family Association
2804 Florida Avenue
Baltimore, MD 21227
Phone (410) 789-1719
Thomas L. Hollowak

Holochwost (see Cholochwost)

Holocombe (see Clift)

Holsaert (see Hulse)

Holt (see The Memorial Foundation of
    the Germanna Colonies, Burnham)

Holt
*Matthew Eugene Holt Family
    Organization
1503 Seventh Street, North
Nampa, ID 83687
Phone (208) 466-5348
Madge Holt Koudelka, Genealogist
(includes the family of Matthew Eugene
    Holt (1879 Utah–1964 Utah), a
    descendant of Robert Holt (1697
    Askerwell, Dorset, England–1765
    Broadwindsor, Dorset, England))
25¢ per sheet for large FGS or pedigree
    chart

Holt
*Holt Association of America
79 Diamond Hill Road
Candia, NH 03034
Phone (603) 483-8293
Russell E. Holt, President
Pub. *Holt Happenings*, annually;
    (includes descendants of Nicholas and
    William Holt)
$5.00 per year membership, $50.00 life
    membership

Holt
*Isabella Jane Holt Family Organization
2230 North 4000 West
Delta, UT 84624

Phone (801) 864-3674
Nancy B. Fowles

Holte
*Holte Surname Organization
5341 Whitney Lane
Amarillo, TX 79110
Phone (806) 359-1012
Sylvia D. Murray, A.G., Coordinator
(includes Holte of North Dakota, Canada
    and Norway)

Holter
George Holter, Jr., Family Reunion
31988 Court Street Road
Racine, OH 45771
K. Werry

Holtfort (see Strippgen)

Holton
*Holton Family Association
1069 Piper Sonoma Street
Eugene, OR 97404
Phone (541) 461-7328
Joan Hunter, Historian/Genealogist
(includes descendants of William Holton
    (1610 England–1691 Northampton,
    Massachusetts) and wife Mary,
    emigrated to Boston in 1634, lived
    possibly in Cambridge, definitely in
    Hartford, Connecticut, and
    Northampton, Massachusetts)

Holtz
*Holtz Surname Organization
199 Commodore Drive
Milledgeville, GA 31061
Phone (912) 968-7425
Richard Bialac

Holtz
*Our Holtz Family Then and Now
503 Fairview Avenue
Saint Louis, MO 63119-1850
Marie Strippgen Holtz, Publisher
(includes descendants of Paul Holtz and
    Wilhelmina Schultz, married 1914,
    Ankalam, Germany)

Holtzclaw (see The Memorial
    Foundation of the Germanna Colonies)

Holtzer (see Likes)

Holtzhauer
Holtzhauer/Holzover Family Association
18748 Collins Street
Tarzana, CA 91356
L. Jones

Holway
*Joseph Holway of Sandwich, Mass
2936 Knoll Circle
Ellicott City, MD 21043
Phone (410) 461-0592
James Malcolm Holway, Publisher

Holy (see Blossom Press)

Holzover (see Holtzhauer)

Home (see Dunbar, MacDuff)

Home
Clan Home/Hume Society
2721 Mae Loma Court
Orlando, FL 32806
Phone (407) 898-6047
Albert C. Eaton, President

Homeston (see Cummings)

Honaker
*The National Association of Hans Jacob
    "Honegger" Honaker Families
PO Box 3636
Alexandria, VA 22302-9998
Phone (703) 751-7321
Thomas G. Hanlin, Vice President
Pub. *Honaker Family Newsletter*
    (includes descendants of the 1749
    Swiss immigrant who married Maria
    Goetz and lived in Pennsylvania,
    Maryland and finally Virginia)
$10.00 per year membership for
    individuals, $15.00 per year
    membership for families at one
    address; annual reunion on the second
    Saturday of August

Hone (see Surname Database)

Honeyman (see MacDuff)

Honeywell
*Honeywell (Hunnewell) Family
    Association
785 Island Way
Clearwater, FL 34630-1816
Phone (813) 461-4244
A. Parks Honeywell, Editor
Pub. *Honeywell Heritage*, quarterly
$20.00 per year membership; annual
    reunion at Theresa, Jefferson County,
    New York

Honken (see Arends)

Honnold
*Honnold Organization
Rt. 1, Box 91
Kansas, IL 61933
Phone (217) 948-5229
Chester W. Fell, Family Representative
Annual reunion on the third Monday of
    July in Kansas, Illinois

Hood (see Scott)

Hood
Hapsburg Press
PO Box 173
Broomfield, CO 80038-0173
Barbara Inman Beall, Editor
Pub. *Hood*, five times per year, $10.00
    per year subscription

Hook (see Hooks)

Hooke (see Hook, Hooks)

Hooker (see Stowe)

Hooker
*Hooker Family Reunion
175 East Delaware Place, #5618
Chicago, IL 60611-1726
Phone (312) 751-0250
David L. Hooker
(includes descendants of John Orton
    Hooker (1840–1916))
Annual reunion

Hooks (see Hook)

Hooks
*Hooks Family Association
5800 Swarthmore Drive
College Park, MD 20740-2633
Phone (301) 345-8066; (703) 256-2336
    Helen Smith
Mary Ruth Stultz, Editor/Publisher
Pub. *Hook-Hooke-Hooks-Houck-Hux
    Family Chronicles*, semiannually
    (spring and fall), $10.00 per year
    subscription; (includes Hooks in
    Virginia 1600s, North Carolina 1700s,
    and from there south and west;
    Hook(e) primarily New England, north
    and west; all spelling variations)
Annual reunion

Hoop (see The Memorial Foundation of
the Germanna Colonies)

Hoopengardner (see Hoopingarner)

Hoopengarner (see Hoopingarner)

Hoopes
*The Hoopes Family Organization, Inc.
910 Delaware Street
Berkeley, CA 94710
Phone (510) 841-7713
Zan H. Turner, Secretary
Pub. *Hoopes Family Newsletter*,
    semiannually (March and October)
$12.00 per year sustaining membership

Hoopes
*Hoopes-Hoops Surname Organization
6612 North Grove Avenue
Oklahoma City, OK 73132
Phone (405) 721-5687
Gerald R. Fuller, D.V.M.

Hoopingarner
Hoopingarner Family Newsletter
39 North 300 East
Monroe, UT 84754
Lovena M. Hamblen
Pub. *Hoopingarner, Hoopengarner,
    Hopingardner, Hoopengardner Family
    Newsletter*, quarterly

Hoops (see Hoopes)

Hoover (see Stoner)

Hoover
Hoover/Huber Family Genealogical
    Association
PO Box 12
Elk Grove, CA 95759-0012
Phone (916) 686-6946
Henry Hoover, Publisher/Editor
Pub. *Hoover Histories*, quarterly
$15.00 per year membership

Hoover
Non-profit FGS Exchange: Hoover
    Surname
Hoover Exchange
2305 East Indian Trail
Chandler, OK 74834
Gerald Hoover

Hoover
Happenings
PO Box 471291
Tulsa, OK 74147
Linnie Hoover Howell
Pub. *Happenings*, irregularly, $16.00 per
    volume subscription; (includes Hoover,
    Huber, Hover surname)

Hope (see MacDuff)

Hopfensperger
*Hopfensperger-Doughty Family
    Reunion
PO Box 147
Nashotah, WI 53058-0147
Phone (414) 646-8183
Susan M. Hopfensperger

Hopingardner (see Hoopingarner)

Hopka (see Likes)

Hopkin
*Hopkin, Jubb, Cliff, Johnson, Lane,
    Fike, Richardson Database
998 Bloomington Drive South
Saint George, UT 84790-7585
Phone (801) 673-6314
Carolyn Reinbold
(includes descendants of Robert Hopkin
    and Sarah Palmer, ca 1755 in Bole,
    Nottinghamshire, England; William
    and Mary Jubb (1767–) of
    Beckingham, Nottinghamshire,
    England; Joseph Cliff and wife Sarah
    (ca 1710–) of Beckingham,
    Nottinghamshire, England; John
    Johnson and Mary Hanson (1754–) of
    Gringley-on-the-Hill, Nottinghamshire,
    England; John and Elizabeth Lane (ca
    1700–) of Wheatley, Nottinghamshire,
    England; John and Elizabeth Fike of
    Granville County, North Carolina;
    John and Nancy Richardson of
    Maryland, North Carolina, Tennessee
    and Illinois)

Hopkins (see Folk Family Surname
    Exchange, Hoshaw, Lynch)

Hopkins
Dennis Hopkins (1760 NC) Family
    Organization
1422 Alpowa
Moscow, ID 83843
B. Jackson

Hopper
Hapsburg Press
PO Box 173
Broomfield, CO 80038-0173
Barbara Inman Beall, Editor
Pub. *Hopper*, five times per year, $10.00
    per year subscription

Hopper
Hopper Family Reunion
Rt. 1, Box 17
Ranger, GA 30734
J. W. Hopper

Hopper
Hopper Researchers Clearinghouse
PO Box 7324, University Station
Provo, UT 84602
Irene E. Johnson
Pub. *Hopper Journal*, $10.00 per year
    subscription

Hopperstad (see Ostrem)

Hopson (see Nelson)

Horan
Horan Family Association
2700 Chariot Lane
Olympia Fields, IL 60461
J. Cunningham

Horkheimer
*Johann Horkheimer and Mary Gaus(s)
    Family Organization
18980 Glen Kerry Drive
Brookfield, WI 53045
Phone (414) 782-1329
Maureen O'Hara Horkheimer
(includes descendants of Horkheimer and
    Gaus/Gauss 1856 to the present in
    Prairie du Chien, Wisconsin, especially
    of Johann Horkheimer (Wildbad,
    Wüerttemberg, Germany–), married
    Mary Gaus 1819)

Horlacher (see Herlacher)

Horlacher
*Dr. Jacob Horlacher and Susannah
    Clemmens Descendants
19341 Knotty Pine Way
Monument, CO 80132
Phone (719) 481-2875
Ruth H. Christian

Horn (see Corson, Thorn, Wright)

Horn
*Bythel Horn Family Organization
7974 Hillsboro Court
Pleasanton, CA 94588-3618
Phone (510) 846-1153
Dorothy Horn Bevard

Horn
Horn History
14352 Anola Street
Whittier, CA 90604
Charles Horn

Horn
*Horn(e) Database
11 Wilcher Drive
Laurel, MS 39440
Phone (601) 428-4777
Rachel Baughman Horne
(includes more than 20,000 names and
fifty years of research on Horn(e)s in
southern states)

Hornbeck
*Hornbeck Hunting
101 Rainbow Drive, #643
Rt. 5, Box 310-0677-643
Livingston, TX 77351
Shirley Hornbeck, Editor
Pub. *Hornbeck Hunting*, annually, $20.00
per year subscription; (database
includes all Hornbeck families)
Search costs vary with problem and
requirements

Hornby (see Lush)

Horne (see Corson, Horn)

Horner
*Horner Surname Organization
1671 Monitor Avenue
Baton Rouge, LA 70817
Phone (504) 756-2322
Shirley Craig

Horning
*Jacob Horning Family Organization
1665 Hartland Woods Drive
Howell, MI 48843-9044
Phone (313) 632-5763
Kathleen Horning
(includes Hornung, Horning, Wacker,
Walker, Braun, Marquardt surnames,
Wurtemburg, Germany, to the U.S.)

Hornung (see Horning)

Horowitz (see Israelite)

Horsburgh (see MacDuff)

Horsley (see Folk Family Surname
Exchange, Goodman)

Horst (see Hursh)

Horton (see Ross)

Horton
*Horton Family Association
173 Gallia Sardis Road
Oak Hill, OH 45656-9678
Phone (614) 682-6745
Perry Horton, Corresponding Secretary

Horton
*Seagull Productions
West 1818 Nora
Spokane, WA 99205
Phone (509) 326-6066
Nancy Cummings Smith
Pub. *Horton Happenings*, irregularly,
$5.00 per issue plus $1.00 postage

Horvath (see Baldman)

Hoschaar (see Hoschar)

Hoschar
Hoschar Family Letter
PO Box 266
Savannah, MO 64485
John Hoshor
Pub. *Hoschar-Hoshour-Hoschaar-
Hoschauer-Hoshauer-Hushaw-Hoshor-
Hoshaw Family Letter*

Hoschar
*Hoschar/Hoschaar/Hoshour/Hoschauer/
Hershour/Haushower/Hushower/
Hoshor/Hoshaw/Hosier, etc., Family
Reunion
PO Box 155
Adamstown, PA 19501
Phone (215) 484-4732
Florence M. Palsgrove, Historian
Pub. *Hoschaar Family Association*,
quarterly, $5.00 per year subscription

Hoschauer (see Hoschar)

Hosfeld
Hosfeld Heritage
7010 Foster Street
Morton Grove, IL 60053-1212
Corinne Hosfeld Smith, Editor
Pub. *Hosfeld Heritage*, bimonthly, free;
(includes Hosfelt and Hosfield)
Annual reunion on the second Sunday of
June in Newburg, PA

Hosfelt (see Hosfeld)

Hosfield (see Hosfield)

Hoshauer (see Hoschar)

Hoshaw (see Hoschar)

Hoshaw
*Manerva Clementine Hoshaw Family
Organization
2702 Hamilton Lane
Grants Pass, OR 97527
Phone (503) 474-7872
Faith Holden
(includes descendants of Manerva
Clementine Hoshaw; also Mayfield
Hushaw, who was married in 1841 in
Barry County, Missouri, to Frances
Hopkins)

Hoshor (see Hoschar)

Hoshour (see Hoschar)

Hosier (see Hoschar)

Hoskin (see Blossom Press)

Hosmer (see Newton)

Hosteland (see Heath)

Hoster
*Pennsylvania-German Hoster Family
107 West Sunhill Road
Manheim, PA 17545
Phone (717) 665-5869
D. Ernest Weinhold
(especially descendants of the very early
immigrants who settled in northeast
Lancaster County, Pennsylvania, and
nearby areas)

Hoster
*Hoster Family Club
1600 South Eads Street, #134 South
Arlington, VA 22202
Phone (703) 521-9156
Col. Charles Stewart Hoster, USAF
(Ret.), Archivist/President
Pub. *Acorns to Oak Leaves: Hoster
Family Newsletter* (includes Hosters of
West Germany, also Cain, Doster,
Fetro, Fink, Fishel, Goldmänn, Groff,
Keiser, Livengood, Nelson, Ort/Orth,
Reigart, Remick, Schwartz, Stewart,
Strohm, Youse)
No cost

Hostetler (see Hochstetler)

Hostetter
Hostetter Family Association
108 Village Road
Orwingsburg, PA 17961
Richard L. Hostetter, President
Reunion in Lancaster County, PA

Hotchkiss
*Hotchkiss Family Association, Inc.
36 Beach Drive
Prospect, CT 06712-1603
Phone (203) 758-5423
Joan A. Johnson, Corresponding
Secretary and Editor
Pub. *Hotchkiss Family Association
Newsletter*, annually; (includes
descendants of Samuel Hotchkiss
(ca 1622 Doddington, England–1663
New Haven, Connecticut), probably
the son of John and Margaret (Nevett)
Hotchkiss, and husband of Elizabeth
Cleverly (–1681 New Haven))
$10.00 per year membership; annual
reunion, usually on the first Saturday
of August

Hottel
*Hottel-Keller Memorial, Inc.
PO Box 33
Toms Brook, VA 22660-0033
Phone (540) 984-8881
Jane Markley Madigan, Membership
Secretary

Pub. *The Hottel-Keller Voice*, quarterly
$10.00 per year membership for
individuals, $15.00 per year
membership for households, $200.00
life membership

Hottenroth (see Arthur)

Houck (see Hauck, Hook, Huyck)

Houck
*David Houck Family Organization
3176 S.E. Villa Carmel Drive
Port Orchard, WA 98366
Phone (206) 876-0833
Linda Marx Terry

Hough (see Clark)

Houghmann
Houghmann
Whispering Oaks
5821 Rowland Hill Road
Cascade, MD 21719-1939
Phone (301) 416-2660
Victor Gebhart, President
Pub. *Houghmann*, annually, $2.00 per
issue

Houghton (see Blackburn, Wright)

Houle (see Lagesse, Therrien)

Houp
Houp/Houpe/Houpt/Haupt Reunion
PO Box 232
Alma, AR 72921
J. Randall Houp
Pub. *Houp, Houpe, Houpt Family
Historian Quarterly*, $5.00 per year
subscription

Houpe (see Houp)

Houpt (see Houp)

House (see The Memorial Foundation of
the Germanna Colonies, Brown)

House
House Surname Organization
5245 Moon Road
Powder Springs, GA 30073
Phone (770) 943-4677
Linda Hendrick Brantley

House
House Family Newsletter
1221 Candice Court
Mesquite, TX 75149
Mary L. House, Editor
Pub. *House Family Newsletter (includes
Haas, Howse, Howze, etc.)*, monthly,
$20.00 per year subscription, queries
free to members, $1.00 to non-
members

Householder (see Bugbee)

Housel (see Covert)

Houshill (see Covert)

Housley (see Owsley)

Houston (see Folk Family Surname
Exchange, Huston)

Houtz (see Frantz)

Hovdesven (see Nygaard)

Hover (see Hoover)

Hovey (see Farr)

Howard (see Blossom Press, Corson,
Heath, Lynch, Rosenberger)

Howard
The Howard Historian
4441 Ormond Trace
Marietta, GA 30066-1611
Phone (404) 926-4010
Curt Howard, Editor
Pub. *The Howard Historian*, three times
per year, $12.00 per year subscription;
(on the Howard surname)

Howard
James Benjamin Howard Family
Organization
Rt. 4
Hickman, KY 42050
M. Howard Adams

Howard
Howard/Ruby Roots Foundation
8430 Old Forge
Southaven, MS 38671
W. Ruby

Howard
Howard
2904 S.E. 35th Avenue
Portland, OR 97202-1802
Barbara Howard
Pub. *Howard*, three times per year, $6.00
per issue

Howe (see Barnard, Gotham, Newton)

Howe
*Howe Genealogies Update
6143 Peachtree Street
Kalamazoo, MI 49002-2741
Rev. H. Walter Yoder, Editor
Pub. *Update of the Howe Genealogies*,
available on computer disk
Queries answered if accompanied by
pedigree chart, SASE and $1.00

Howel
Family Limbs
6423 S.E. 97th Avenue
Portland, OR 97266-4529
Shirley L. Bodak
Pub. *Howel/Howell Family Newsletter*,
ten times per year

Howell (see Gant, Howel, Job, Lynch,
Reeder, Wright)

Howell
Howell
PO Box 5351
Walnut Creek, CA 94596-1351
Ruth Howell Thomson
Pub. *Howell*, three times per year, $5.00
per year subscription

Howell
Howell-Hal-Hale-Harrold Family
Association
2306 Westgate
Houston, TX 77019
Phone (713) 529-2333
Harold Helm
$25.00 plus pedigree and family group
sheets membership

Howell
*Bell Enterprises
PO Box 10328
Spokane, WA 99209
Phone (509) 327-2761
Mary Ann L. Vanzandt Bell, Owner,
Publisher
Pub. *Howell Lines*, irregularly, $6.00 plus
$1.25 postage per issue

Howenstine
*Howenstine Family Reunion
9764 North 300 West
Huntington, IN 46750-9726
Glen E. Howenstine, Publisher and
Reunion Treasurer
Pub. *Howenstine Reunion*, annually, free;
(includes Hauenstein and Howenstein)
Annual reunion

Howes (see Linnell)

Howes
*Howes Family Association
504 White Hall Circle
Hampton, VA 23669
Phone (804) 851-2963
Lewis L. Howes, President
Pub. *Howes Family Association
Newsletter*, quarterly
$12.00 per year membership

Howk (see Huyck)

Howkins
*The Howkins Book
2466 Frankson Avenue
Rochester Hills, MI 48307-4632
Phone (810) 852-8575; E-
mail:fhowkins@tln.lib.mi.us
Frederick R. Howkins, Publisher

Howland (see Blossom Press, Barnard,
McLouth)

Howland
The Pilgrim John Howland Society
65 North Street
Yarmouth, ME 04096
Mrs. Bernard J. Elfring, Registrar
Pub. *Howland Quarterly*
$2.00 per year membership

Hows (see Rogers)

Howse (see Clark, Heath, House)

Howze (see House)

Hoxie (see Brown)

Hoxsey
Our Hoxsey Family Connections
6206 North Hamilton Road
Peoria, IL 61614
Phone (309) 691-3680
Gerald R. Steffy
Pub. *Our Hoxsey Family Connections*
    (includes Lodowick Hoxsey)

Hoy
The Hoy Family Newsletter
718 Gouldman Lane
Great Falls, VA 22066
Phone (703) 759-4073
James Hoy, Editor
Pub. *The Hoy Family Newsletter*,
    semiannually, $10.00 per year

Hoyt
*Hoyt Family Organization
171 Main Street
Newington, CT 06111
Phone (203) 666-9566
John F. Bolles, III
(includes descendants of Dr. Abner Hoyt
    (–1797) and Phebe Benedict of South
    Salem, New York)

Hoyt
*Hoyt Family Association
360 Watson Road
Paducah, KY 42003-8978
Phone (502) 898-8168; (408) 624-7765
    FAX (research editor)
Roy F. Olson, Jr., President, Editor and
    Publisher
Pub. *Hoyt's Issue*, semiannually (April
    and October); (includes Hoit, Hoitt,
    Haight, Hight, etc., descendants of
    John[1] Hoyt of Amesbury/Salisbury,
    Massachusetts, and Simon[1] Hoyt of
    Massachusetts and Connecticut
    lineage)
$15.00 per year membership, $18.00 per
    year Canadian membership; $3.00
    search fee plus two third-class postage
    stamps and envelopes to research
    editor, Anne Hoyt Sanford, 25225
    Stewart Place, Carmel, CA 93923

Hrenchir
*Hrenchir Family Association
3441 S.E. 77th Street
Berryton, KS 66409
Phone (913) 862-0225
Joan M. Hrenchir, Secretary
Pub. *The Hrenchir News*, one or two
    times per year
Annual reunion on the first Sunday of
    May in Magetta, Kansas

Hribar
*Hribor/Gregorcik Surname Organization
Anton Hribar Family Organization
33516 170 Avenue, S.E.
Auburn, WA 98092
Phone (206) 833-7229
Mary H. Smith

Hribor (see Hribar)

Hubbard (see Chapman)

Hubbard
Hubbard Family Reunion
PO Box 374
Bonanza, OR 97623-0374
Mrs. L. Hubbard

Hubbard
Hubbard Surname Organization
Charles Wesley Hubbard Family
    Organization
1729 Grant Avenue
Ogden, UT 84404
Phone (801) 394-6864
Roberta Costley Palmer

Hubbard
*The Hubbard Families Association
Upper Valley Road
PO Box 34
Jeffersonville, VT 05464
Phone (802) 644-2995
Jane R. Hubbard
Pub. *Hubbard Families Association
    Newsletter*, monthly; (includes data
    base of over 350,000 names, with
    substantial information on George
    Hubbard (Guilford, Connecticut),
    George Hubbard (Middletown,
    Connecticut), Edmund Hobart
    (Hingham, Massachusetts), Philip
    Hubbard (Maine), Robert Hibbard
    (Salisbury, England), Hebard, Herbert,
    Hobert, Hubbart, etc.)
$15.00 per year U.S. membership, $20.00
    per year Canadian membership,
    includes free search of data base

Hubbart (see Hubbard)

Hubbel (see Hubbell)

Hubbell
*The Hubbell Family Historical Society
2051 East McDaniel Street
PO Box 3813 GS
Springfield, MO 65808-3813
Clifton H. Hubbell, President
Pub. *Annually*, annually (fall); *Family
    Notes*, semiannually (spring and fall);
    (includes Hubbel, Hubble, Hubel,
    Huble)
$15.00 per year membership for couples,
    $50.00 per year contributing
    membership, $100.00 per year
    participating membership, $10.00 per
    year membership for societies and
    libraries

Hubble (see Hubbell)

Hubel (see Hubbell)

Huber (see Hoover)

Huber
*John Francis Huber Family
    Organization
3553 Berne Road
Hamburg, PA 19526-8987
Gloria C. Hartzell
(includes descendants of John Francis
    Huber (ca 1718–after 1787) and Maria
    Elizabeth (ca 1720–probably after
    1790), of Pennsylvania)

Huble (see Hubbell)

Huckstep
*Huckstep Surname Organization
11 West 300 South
Farmington, UT 84025
Phone (801) 451-2904
Bradford N. Ator

Huddleston
Huddleston Family Clearinghouse
1221 Herzel Avenue
Lancaster, CA 93535-4378
Donald L. Cordell

Huddleston
Huddleston Heritage Queries
Box 2455 C.S.
Pullman, WA 99165
Marily VonBargen
Pub. *Huddleston Heritage Queries*

Hudgens (see Bosher)

Hudgins (see Wheeler)

Hudlow
*Hudlow-Marchell-Ronk-Showalter
    Families*
4301 Deer Lakes
Wichita, KS 67210-1650
Brenda Robertson
Pub. *Hudlow-Marchell-Ronk-Showalter
    Families*, semiannually

Hudnal (see Lynch)

Hudson
*Hudson Family Association
232 Loop Drive
Slidell, LA 70458-1320
Phone (504) 643-0633
Lucile Backes Hudson, Treasurer and
    Membership Secretary
Pub. *Bulletin Hudsoniana*, quarterly;
    (includes all Hudson, Hutson,
    Heudson, Hodson and other variant
    spellings on a computer database of
    more than 70,000 pages of data)
$20.00 per year membership for
    individuals, $25.00 per year
    membership for households; annual
    reunion

Huebotter
*Huebotter Family Organization
2634 Associated Road, Apartment #A110
Fullerton, CA 92635
Phone (714) 990-5946
Nancy M. Huebotter, President
Pub. *Huebotter Family Newsletter*

Huefner (see McCune)

Huei (see Gillean)

Huettenhen (see The Memorial
Foundation of the Germanna Colonies)

Huey (see Way)

Huey
*Huey Surname Organization
PO Box 553
Valley Forge, PA 19481-0553
Phone (610) 933-1308;
(610) 889-9753 FAX
Richard M. Huey, Secretary
(includes Pennsylvania families, from
1730 to the present)

Huff (see Gunnin)

Huffer
*Huffer Family
27 Autumn Leaf Drive
Thousand Oaks, CA 91360
Phone (805) 495-6209
Charles B. Huffer
(includes Huffers of Pennsylvania,
Virginia, Ohio, Indiana, Illinois)

Huffman (see The Memorial Foundation
of the Germanna Colonies, Surname
Sources, Hoffman, Nelson)

Hufford (see Frantz)

Huffschmidt
*Huffschmidt/Huffsmith Surname
Specialty
1301 Bradford Road
Oreland, PA 19075-2414
Phone (215) 836-4727
Dale E. Berger, Publisher
(includes descendants of Peter and Anna
Maria Huffschmidt who arrived in
Philadelphia in 1750 and settled in
Monroe County, Pennsylvania)

Hufstetler (see Sidwell)

Hufstutler (see Sidwell)

Hug (see MacDuff)

Hugesson (see Ackerson)

Huggan (see MacDuff)

Hughes (see Cian, Cooper, Davis, Heath,
Lambert, Newton)

Hughes
*George Hughes Family Organization
14168 Ceazar Road
PO Box 837
Gonzales, LA 70737
Phone (504) 644-1899
Ronnie Hughes
(includes Fickling, Holmes and Kirchen
families)

Hughes
Hughes, A First Family of West Virginia
119 South Toussaint-Portage Road
Oak Harbor, OH 43449
Twila Smith
Pub. *Hughes Heritage*, quarterly, $12.00
per year subscription

Hughes
William Richard Hughes Reunion
Rt. 3, Box 134
6644 Baker Road #47
Shelby, OH 44875
Phylis Hughes Frazee

Huit (see Moser)

Hulce (see Hulse)

Hulet
*Francis Edgar Hulet Family
Organization
1106 East 1400 North
Terreton, ID 83450
Phone (208) 663-4460
Dorothy H. Pincock, Family Genealogist

Hulick (see Gulick)

Hulin (see Daley)

Hull (see Boose, Buzzard, Lush, McRae)

Hull
*Hull Database
19259 Harleigh Drive
Saratoga, CA 95070-5145
Phone (408) 867-2677
Robert E. Hull
(extended Hull family computer database
includes ancestors and descendants of
George Hull of Crewkerne, Somerset,
England, Dorchester, Massachusetts,
and Windsor and Fairfield,
Connecticut, and his wife Thamzen
Michell, and of George's brother, the
Rev. Joseph Hull; descendants of Ezra
Hull of Athens County, Ohio;
descendants of Fred H. Hull and his
wife Margaret Lush of Gainesville,
Florida; descendants of Richard Hull
of New Haven, Connecticut; etc.)

Hull
Hull/Golden Reunion
221 South 13th
Independence, KS 67301
L. Hull

Hull
*Hull Surname Organization
150 Brown Street
Saint Clair, MI 48079-4882
Phone (810) 329-9359
George M. Roberts
(includes families of U.S.A. and Canada)

Hull
Hull Family Register
4411 Ram Court
Houston, TX 77072
Jean Moritz, Publicity
Pub. *Hull Family Register*

Hull
*Hull Family Association
PO Box 2066
Merrifield, VA 22116-2066
Phone (703) 280-5627
Col. Robert L. Hull, Secretary
Pub. *Hull Family Newsletter*, three times
per year; *Hull Family Association
Journal*, three times per year; *Hull
Family Association Book of Member
Lineages*, irregularly
$15.00 for first-year membership
includes all three publications, $10.00
per year renewal membership; annual
meeting and family reunion

Hullah (see Jackson)

Hullett
Hullett Herald
2787 Brisa Bland
Arroyo Grande, CA 93420
Pub. *Hullett Herald*, quarterly, $5.00 per
year subscription

Hullinger
Hullinger/Hollinger Family Association
1739 Bella Vista
Cincinnati, OH 45237
Bob Hullinger

Huls (see Hulse)

Hulse
*Hulse Surname Organization
30 Pleasant Street
Colebrook, NH 03576
Phone (603) 237-4039
Granvyl Hulse
(includes Hulse, Hulce, Huls, Hulseheart
and Holsaert, also pre-1850 Hults and
Hultz)

Hulseheart (see Hulse)

Hulsey
*Hulsey Family Organization
7974 Hillsboro Court
Pleasanton, CA 94588-3618
Phone (510) 846-1153
Dorothy Horn Bevard

Hults (see Hulse)

Hultz (see Hulse)

Hume (see Home, MacDuff)

Humes (see Arthur)

Humphrey (see Garner, Gower, Pessner, Sawyer)

Humphrey
*Humphrey Family Association
701 Mountain Trail
Warrior, AL 35180
Phone (205) 647-3485
Robert L. Humphrey, Editor
Pub. *Humphrey Family Quarterly*,
(January, April, July and October)
$12.00 per year U.S. membership, $15.00
per year foreign membership

Humphrey
*Frederick Griswold Humphrey Family
Association
225 Cherry Brook Road
Canton Center, CT 06020
Riuth L. Humphrey, Historian
(includes descendants of Frederick
Griswold Humphrey, 1856–1934)
Annual reunion on the third Sunday of
August

Humphrey
Humphrey Family Quarterly
337 North 725 East
North Salt Lake, UT 84054-3130
Arlene Hinman
Pub. *Humphrey Family Quarterly*

Humphreys (see Rutherford)

Humphreys
Humphreys Family Reunion
14765 Waldo Hills Drive, S.E.
Sublimity, OR 97385
Robert Humphreys
(includes descendants of Thomas Melvin
Humphreys, who came to Oregon in
1853)

Humphries
Pelham Humphries Heirs Association
PO Box 1023
Johnson City, TN 37605
Roy Feathers, President
(includes descendants of Pelham
Humphries, William and Leasy
Hudson Humphries)
$50.00 per year membership

Hums (see Folk Family Surname
Exchange)

Hundley (see Elder)

Hungate
Hungate Family Historical Society, Inc.
PO Box 127
Bowersville, GA 30516
Lloyd A. Hungate, Executive Vice
President
Pub. *Hungate Family Historical Society
Journal*, quarterly

Hunnewell (see Honeywell)

Hunsberger
*The Hunsberger-Huntsberger Family
Association
211 Cedar Avenue
Holmes, PA 19043
Phone (610) 532-9240
Sylvia L. Hunsberger, President
Pub. *The Hunsberger Family Newsletter*,
three or four times per year; (all
Hunsberger-Huntsberger variations,
especially descendants, of brothers
Hans, Jacob and Ulrich of Franconia,
Pennsylvania, 1720, or to Peter H. of
Lancaster County, Pennsylvania, 1727)
$5.00 per year membership for adults,
$35.00 life membership

Hunsucker (see Moser)

Hunt (see Folk Family Surname
Exchange, Cian, Evitt, Goodenow,
Hatfield, Reeder, Rosenberger, Wright)

Hunt
Hunt Family Association
PO Box 2480
Hot Springs, AR 71914
J. O. Dunn

Hunt
Hunt Family Reunion (Descendants of
John and Eliz. Hunt)
24 Sycamore Lane
Palmyra, PA 17078
Phone (717) 838-1935
Edward M. Hunt

Hunt
*Family Research Associates
502 Church Street
Willow Grove, PA 19090-2701
Phone (215) 659-8048
Mitchell J. Hunt
Pub. untitled publications come out
irregularly, costs for duplication of
material provided; (includes research
on Hunt families of America)

Hunt
Hunt Family Foundation International
150 West 1950 South
Bountiful, UT 84010
Mrs. B. A. Page

Hunt
Roots Dugout
3328 SR 530 N.E.
Arlington, WA 98223
Pub. *Hunt Heritage*, irregularly, $6.00
per year subscription

Hunter (see Cowart, Emery, Golding,
Lush, Massey, Stewart)

Hunter
*The Hunter Clan Association, USA
3645 Kingshill Road
Birmingham, AL 35223-1423

Charles M. Hunter, Clan Officer, U.S.A.
Pub. *Clan Hunter News*, semiannually
$20.00–$30.00 per year membership

Hunter
Hunter
6180 Merrywood Drive
Rocklin, CA 95677-3421
Kathleen Stewart
Pub. *Hunter*, quarterly (February, May,
August and November), $12.00 per
year subscription

Hunters (see Brotherton)

Huntington (see Heath)

Huntington
*Henry Huntington Family Organization
1774 Country Club Drive
Logan, UT 84321
Phone (801) 753-6924
Joyce Elfrena Kalanquin

Huntley (see Smith)

Huntley
*Huntley National Association
154 West Belle Avenue
Saint Charles, MI 48655
Phone (517) 865-9025
Evelyn R. Simon, Corresponding
Secretary
Pub. *Spring Bulletin*, annually; (includes
descendants of immigrant John
Huntley of Lyme, Connecticut, and
Rev. Thomas Huntley, patriot of Anson
County, North Carolina)
$5.00 per year membership, $10.00
sustaining membership; reunion in Old
Saybrook, Connecticut

Huntress
*Sons and Daughters of George Huntress
PO Box 597
Federal Road
Kegar Falls, ME 04047
Mrs. Clifford Wallace, President
(includes descendants of George
Huntress, who came to Portsmouth,
New Hampshire, about 1650)
$1.00 per year membership

Huntsberger (see Hunsberger)

Huntsman (see Leavitt, Rutherford)

Huntsman
*Huntsman Surname Organization
10315 South 1540 West
South Jordan, UT 84095
Phone (801) 254-3532
Betty Barney Farnsworth

Hurd (see McCune)

Hurley (see Newberry)

Hursh
Hursh/Hurst Quarterly
2040 East 200 North
Rexburg, ID 83440
Phone (208) 356-3528
Sally Hursh Nef
Pub. *Hursh/Hurst Quarterly*

Hursh
Hursh-Horst Family Organization
526 North Edgewood Avenue
La Grange, IL 60525-5510
Ruth Peterson Hursh
Pub. *Hursh, Horst Family Organization Quarterly*
$10.00 per year membership

Hurst (see Hursh)

Hurven (see Irwin)

Hushaw (see Hoschar, Hoshaw)

Hushower (see Hoschar)

Huskey (see Folk Family Surname Exchange)

Huskey
*The Huskey Surname Organization and History Society
67 Craggy Avenue, West
PO Box 1712
Asheville, NC 28802
Phone (704) 252-8910
Naaman O. Huskey, President
(includes descendants of Dave (David) Huskey (ca 1854 or 1859 North Carolina or Tennessee) and Jane Blanton (1854 Rutherford County, North Carolina))
Free

Hussey (see Brown, Corson)

Husted (see Adams)

Huston
Huston Family of Southwest Ohio
5463 Schiering Drive
Fairfield, OH 45014
Frank Steig, Jr.

Huston
Huston Family Reunion Picnic
2229 East Burnside, #133
Portland, OR 97030
Mae Vasey Huston
(includes descendants of Joel Bradshaw and Catherine "Kitty" (Houston) Huston, who came to Oregon from Tennessee, via Latlarge, Henderson County, Illinois, in 1853)
Reunion

Huston
Surnames Limited
RR 3, Box 59
Muleshoe, TX 79347-9208
Pub. *Huston Newsletter*, irregularly, $8.00 per issue

Hutchens
Hutchens/Hutchins Family
1606 Third Street
Garden City, KS 67846-4506
Phone (316) 276-6713
Rita Hineman Townsend

Hutchenson (see Wright)

Hutcheson
*The Hutcheson Chronicles
Seminary Plaza #408
Red Wing, MN 55066
Phone (612) 388-1435; E-mail: mhutch@win.bright.net
Margaret Hutcheson, Publisher
(includes descendants of William and Margaret (Weir) Hutcheson, came from Northern Ireland in the early 1790s, settled in Parker Township, Butler County, Pennsylvania, with descendants in Pennsylvania, Florida, Minnesota, the Dakotas, California, etc.)

Hutchins (see Hutchens)

Hutchinson (see Rutherford)

Hutchison
William Hutchison and Jane Penman Organization
2421 North 750 East
Provo, UT 84604-4014
Phone (801) 375-4390
Margaret Fawson Talbot, Research Coordinator
Pub. *Newsletter*, annually (December); (includes allied surnames of Batey, Blakeburn, Bushby, Featherstone, Hall, Leighton, Short, Teasdale and Whitfield of Northumberland, England)
$30.00 donation per year membership

Hutto (see Brawley)

Hutton (see Erdwins, McCanna)

Hutton
*Alexander Hamilton Hutton, Sr., Family Organization
6945 South 3420 West
West Jordan, UT 84084-1713
Phone (801) 966-6585
Gerald Hutton
(includes descendants of Alexander Hamilton Hutton, Sr. (1810 Newery, County Down, Ireland–) and his wife, Hanna Jane (Ireland–))

Hutzler (see Johnson)

Hux (see Hook)

Huyck
*Huyck/Howk/Houck Family
PO Box 11
Medina, WA 98039
Phone (206) 454-3714
Sylvia E. Wilson, Publisher

Hyatt (see Hiatt, Lynch)

Hyatt
*Hyatt Family Organization
5892 West 10620 North
Highland
American Fork, UT 84003-9591
Phone (801) 756-0155
Ina M. Custer Iverson
(includes Hyatt and Pierce families of New York)

Hyatt
*Clarence Edmund Hyatt Family Organization
261 West 1200 North
Bountiful, UT 84010
Phone (801) 295-2670
Anita Hyatt Davis, Genealogist
(also researching Phillips, Cairns, Furman, Lanfear, Burgess, Savage, Streator, Edmonds, Chase, Hicks, Stone, Sperry, Combs and Woodhouse of New England, New York, Pennsylvania and Ohio)

Hyde (see Appler, Lynch, Rutherford, Sawyer)

Hyde
Hyde Family Association
PO Box 992
Guthrie, OK 73044
Esther Waner
Pub. *Hyde Family Swap*

Hyden (see Heydon)

Hyer (see Hire)

Hylton
*Riley Harrison Hylton Descendants
3264 Eastpointe Drive
Franklin, IN 46131
Phone (317) 736-8525
Karen Sue Hylton Hargis
Reunion at Franklin, Indiana

Hylton
*The Ira Slusher Hylton Descendants
Rt. 2, Box 506
Floyd, VA 24091
Phone (540) 745-2314
Maynard G. Hylton

Hynson (see Hanson)

Hynton
*Hynton-Hinton-Stone-Reeder-Stevens-Castle-Adkins Family Genealogy
PO Box 566
Morehead, KY 40351
Phone (606) 784-7012
Leroy C. Hinton, Author

Hyre (see Stoner)

Hysaw (see Hisaw)

Hysell (see Hisle)

Hyso (see Hisaw)

Hyten (see Heydon)

Iancovich (see Blossom Press)

Iannino (see Gratta)

I'anson (see Premm)

Iarwin (see Irwin)

Ickus (see Kunkel)

Ieriven (see Irwin)

Iervine (see Irwin)

Ihrig (see Arey)

Ikelman (see Eichelman)

Ikelmann (see Eichelman)

Iliff (see MacDuff)

Iliff
Iliff Genealogist
2906 Stoneybrook Drive
Bowie, MD 20715
George E. Russell
Pub. *Iliff Genealogist*

Illiffe (see MacDuff)

Ilsley (see Inslee)

Iman (see Einman)

Imfeld (see Kunkel)

Immichenhain (see Ortstadt)

Inch (see Innes, MacInnes)

Inches (see Donnachaidh)

in den Hoffe (see Links Genealogy
Publications)

in den Hoffee (see Links Genealogy
Publications)

Infield (see Emfield)

Ingalls (see Barnard)

Ingalls
Ingalls Inquirer
5640 West Chadwick Road
DeWitt, MI 48820
Phone (517) 669-3219
Arlene Ingalls Schrader
Pub. *Ingalls Inquirer*, three times per
year, $6.00 per year subscription;
(includes Ingell, Ingles, Inglis, Ingle,
Engel)

Ingle (see Folk Family Surname
Exchange)

Ingledew
*Ingledew Surname Organization
3594 South 700 East
Salt Lake City, UT 84106
Phone (801) 466-5958
Carolyn Ingledew Royce

Ingli (see Rothenberger)

Inglis (see Douglas)

Inglis
*William Henry Inglis Family
Organization
818 S.W. 120th
Seattle, WA 98146
Phone (206) 244-1331
William V. Ingalls

Ingraham (see Hiscock)

Ingram (see Colquhoun, Hiscock,
Rutherford)

Ingram
Ingram Inklings
7049 North Fox Point Drive
Peoria, IL 61614-2231
Phone (309) 692-7898; E-mail:
adlof@ix.netcom.com
Deborah Ingram Adlof, Editor and
Compiler
Pub. *Ingram Inklings*, semiannually,
15.00 per year subscription, $8.50 per
issue

Ingram
*Ingram-Ingrum Connection Reunion
2226 Kehrsglen Court
Chesterfield, MO 63005
Phone (314) 532-1578 (home); (314)
694-3616 (work)
Barry Bingham
Pub. *Newsletter for the Descendants of
Jonas Ingram and Melinda Butler*,
annually, free; (includes descendants of
Jonas Ingram, who lived in Kentucky
in the early 1800s, and Melinda Butler,
who moved to middle Tennessee in the
early 1800s)

Ingrum (see Ingram)

Ingwerson
Frederick Ingwerson and Marian
VonBellor Association
1608 McGraw Drive
Ponca City, OK 74601-2951
Mrs. C. Mitchell

Inie (see Innes)

Inks (see Newcomb)

Inkshaw (see Hinshaw)

Inman
*Inman Newsletter
18002 North 12th Street, #30
Phoenix, AZ 85022

Nani Mercer Neal
Pub. *Inman Newsletter*, every three to
four months, $20.00 per year
subscription

Inman
*Inman Clearinghouse
1328 East Hermosa Drive
Tempe, AZ 85282-5719
Phone (602) 491-2877
Gloria Kay Vandiver Inman
(includes spelling variations such as
Innman, Inmann, etc.)

Inman
*John Peter Inman Family Organization
PO Box 171
Douglas City, CA 96024
Phone (916) 778-3136
Paul Jones

Inman
Hapsburg Press
PO Box 173
Broomfield, CO 80038-0173
Barbara Inman Beall, Editor
Pub. *Inman*, five times per year, $10.00
per year subscription

Inman
Inman Family Association
129 Garden Drive
Montgomery, IL 60538
Phone (312) 897-0934
Ruth L. May
Pub. *Inman Family Association
Newsletter*

Inmann (see Inman)

Innes
*Innes Clan Society
1280 Mariposa Drive
Brea, CA 92621
Phone (714) 671-5982
Frances Ferrier Hanks, Genealogist
Pub. *The Bullrush*, quarterly; (includes
septs: Dinnes, Ennis, Inch, Inie, Innis,
Macrob, Mactary, Marnoch, Maver,
Mavor, Middleton, Mill, Milnes,
Mitchell, Mitchelson, Oynie, Redford,
Reidford, Wilson and Yunie)
$15.00 per year membership, $25.00 per
year sustaining membership

Innis (see Innes)

Innman (see Inman)

Inrig (see Gunn)

Inscoe (see Insco)

Inscore (see Dopp)

Inslee
Inslee Family Organization
Inslee Association
601 West 17th Street
Ada, OK 74820

Phyllis Mullikin Inslee, Historian
Pub. *Inslee Index*, semiannually, $5.00
    per year subscription; (includes Ilsley,
    Insley, Enslee, Ensley)

Insley (see Inslee)

Ipsher (see Abshire)

Ireton
*Family History and Genealogy Center
1300 East 109th Street
Kansas City, MO 64131-3585
Phone (816) 942-5497
La Roux K. Gillespie, Editor
Pub. *Ireton News*, quarterly, $10.00 per
    year subscription, $12.00 per year
    subscription with index

Irevigne (see Irwin)

Irevin (see Irwin)

Irewin (see Irwin)

Irewing (see Irwin)

Irewyne (see Irwin)

Irick (see Eirich)

Irick
Irick (Eirich, Eurich) Family Association
1024 Apollo Way
Sacramento, CA 95822-1709
Phone (916) 448-1030
Donnadeane D. Depew
Pub. *Newsletter*, irregularly

Irin (see Irwin)

Irish
Irish/Irishe/Iryshe Surname Association
4375 Weber River Drive, Lot 35
Ogden, UT 84405
Phone (801) 392-8726
Mrs. John H. Payne
Pub. *Irish Inquirer, A Surname
    Genealogical Periodical*, semiannually
$6.00 per year membership

Iriving (see Irwin)

Irn (see Irwin)

Ironside (see Garner)

Ironson (see Premm)

Irrein (see Irwin)

Irrewin (see Irwin)

Irrewine (see Irwin)

Irrewing (see Irwin)

Irrewings (see Irwin)

Irrin (see Irwin)

Irruein (see Irwin)

Irruen (see Irwin)

Irruin (see Irwin)

Irruings (see Irwin)

Irruwin (see Irwin)

Irruwing (see Irwin)

Irruwingus (see Irwin)

Irruwyng (see Irwin)

Irrwin (see Irwin)

Irrwing (see Irwin)

Irrwynnis (see Irwin)

Irueyn (see Irwin)

Iruiin (see Irwin)

Iruin (see Irwin)

Iruine (see Irwin)

Iruing (see Irwin)

Iruvine (see Irwin)

Iruwyn (see Irwin)

Iruwyne (see Irwin)

Iruyn (see Irwin)

Iruyne (see Irwin)

Irvaine (see Irwin)

Irvainston (see Irwin)

Irvane (see Irwin)

Irvein (see Irwin)

Irveing (see Irwin)

Irven (see Irwin)

Irvene (see Irwin)

Irveyn (see Irwin)

Irvin (see DeCoursey, Irwin)

Irvine (see Irwin)

Irvinee (see Irwin)

Irviner (see Irwin)

Irvines (see Irwin)

Irviney (see Irwin)

Irving (see Irwin)

Irvinge (see Irwin)

Irvings (see Irwin)

Irvington (see Irwin)

Irvinn (see Irwin)

Irvins (see Irwin)

Irvinscow (see Irwin)

Irvinson (see Irwin)

Irvinus (see Irwin)

Irvon (see Irwin)

Irvun (see Irwin)

Irvyerins (see Irwin)

Irvying (see Irwin)

Irvyn (see Irwin)

Irwain (see Irwin)

Irwan (see Irwin)

Irwayne (see Irwin)

Irwaynes (see Irwin)

Irwein (see Irwin)

Irweing (see Irwin)

Irwen (see Irwin)

Irwenis (see Irwin)

Irwien (see Irwin)

Irwin (see Lush)

Irwin
*Irwin Family Reunion Association
    (Descendants of William Jared Irwin)
100 Willow Spring Road
Wilmington, DE 19807
Patricia Lesky

Irwin
*Clan Irwin Association
226 1750th Avenue
Mount Pulaski, IL 62548-6635
Phone (217) 792-5226
Guy Irvin, Chairman
Pub. *Holly Leaf Chronicle*, quarterly;
    (includes Airwin, Arewine, Arvinge,
    Arvon, Arwine, Curwen, Curwing,
    Curwings, deHerwyne, deIrevigne,
    deIruwyn, deIrwin, deIrwyn, deOrvin,
    deYrewyne, D'Orvin, Earewin,
    Earven, Earwen, Earwin, Earwing,
    Eirryn, Eirven, Eirvin, Eirving, Eirvyn,

Eirwin, Eorvin, Eorwine, Erbine,
Erenvine, Erenwine, Erevein, Erevin,
Erevine, Erewynis, Erin, Erin-Feine,
Erinfeiner, Erin-Veine, Erinvine,
Eriveen, Eriven, Erivin, Ernwine,
Errvin, Errving, Eruing, Eruini, Ervan,
Erven, Ervening, Ervens, Ervewin,
Ervien, Ervin, Ervine, Erving, Ervinge,
Ervington, Ervinlet, Ervinlott, Ervinne,
Ervinton, Ervion, Ervwin, Ervwyn,
Erwane, Erwein, Erweng, Erwin,
Erwine, Erwing, Erwinn, Erwinne,
Erwins, Erwinski, Erwinss, Erwvin,
Erwyn, Erwyne, Eryvine, Eryvino,
Eryvinus, Eryvyne, Erywen,
Euervinus, Eurini, Eurwings,
Herbnain, Herwynd, Hierewine,
Hirevigne, Hirewine, Hurven, Iarwin,
Ieriven, Iervine, Irevigne, Irevin,
Irewin, Irewing, Irewyn, Irewyne, Irin,
Iriving, Irn, Irrein, Irrewin, Irrewine,
Irrewing, Irrewings, Irrin, Irruein,
Irruen, Irruin, Irruings, Irruwin,
Irruwing, Irruwingus, Irruwyng,
Irrwin, Irrwing, Irrwynnis, Irueyn,
Iruiin, Iruin, Iruine, Iruing, Iruvine,
Iruwyn, Iruwyne, Iruyn, Iruyne,
Irvaine, Irvainston, Irvane, Irvein,
Irveing, Irven, Irvene, Irveyn, Irvin,
Irvine, Irvinee, Irviner, Irvines, Irviney,
Irving, Irvinge, Irvings, Irvington,
Irvinn, Irvins, Irvinscow, Irvinson,
Irvinus, Irvon, Irvun, Irvyerins,
Irvying, Irvyn, Irwain, Irwan, Irwayne,
Irwaynes, Irwein, Irweing, Irwen,
Irwenis, Irwien, Irwine, Irwing,
Irwinge, Irwinger, Irwingh, Irwington,
Irwingus, Irwinn, Irwins, Irwintin,
Irwintire, Irwinturner, Irwirn, Irwon,
Irwoney, Irwony, Irwyn, Irwyne,
Irwyng, Irwynn, Irwynnis, Irynagio,
MacIrwin, McIrwin, Oerin, Oeryn,
Orruein, Orvine, Orvington, Orwin,
Ourine, Ouron, Ourren, Owyrn,
Uirvine, Uirwin, Urewens, Urewing,
Urowrin, Urrwine, Uruin, Urven,
Urvens, Urvin, Urvine, Urwain,
Urwaine, Urwan, Urwayne, Urwen,
Urwenn, Urwens, Urwin, Urwine,
Urwing, Urwins, Urwung, Urwyng,
Varven, Varvin, Varvine, Vervine,
Verwayn, Vrowing, Vruing, Vruving,
Vruvinn, Vrvin, Vrvynn, Vrwayn,
Vrwayne, Vrwen, Vrwin, Vrwine,
Vrwing, Vryne, Yearven, Yirwing,
Yivewing, Yrein, Yrewing, Yrvin,
Yrwen, Yrwens, Yrwin, Yrwing,
Yrwyne, etc.)
$15.00 per year membership

Irwine (see Irwin)

Irwing (see Irwin)

Irwinge (see Irwin)

Irwinger (see Irwin)

Irwingh (see Irwin)

Irwington (see Irwin)

Irwingus (see Irwin)

Irwinn (see Irwin)

Irwins (see Irwin)

Irwintin (see Irwin)

Irwintire (see Irwin)

Irwinturner (see Irwin)

Irwirn (see Irwin)

Irwon (see Irwin)

Irwoney (see Irwin)

Irwony (see Irwin)

Irwyn (see Irwin)

Irwyne (see Irwin)

Irwyng (see Irwin)

Irwynn (see Irwin)

Irwynnis (see Irwin)

Irynagio (see Irwin)

Isaacks (see Reeder)

Isaacson (see Tillman)

Isace (see Farnes)

Isacke (see Farnes)

Isbel (see Harvey)

Isbell (see Folk Family Surname
Exchange, Ammons, Lambert)

Isbell
*Folk Family
PO Box 52048
Knoxville, TN 37950-2048
Hester E. Stockton, Owner; Mary Agnes
Isbell, Editor
Pub. *Isbell Inquires*, quarterly, $15.00 per
year subscription, $5.00 per issue;
(includes Asbell and Isbill)

Isbill (see Isbell)

Isch (see Ish)

Ish
Ish/Isch Exchange
9855 Cape Arago Highway
Coos Bay, OR 97420
Phone (503) 888-9444
Ms. M. H. Mosher

Isham (see Folk Family Surname
Exchange, Isom)

Isles (see Wooten)

Isom
Isom-Isham
401 Tuxedo Drive
Thomasville, GA 31792
Annette Stewart
Pub. *Isom-Isham*, quarterly, $10.00 per
year subscription

Israel
*Israel Family Reunion
17890 Highway 68 West
Crossville, AL 35962
Phone (205) 528-7216
Willard A. Israel, Historian
(includes descendants of Soloman Israel
and Mary Johnston)

Israel
*Israel Association
HC 65, Box 113
Wauneta, NE 69045
Phone (308) 394-5511
Pat Kitt
Annual reunion on the first Sunday of
August

Israeli (see Israelite)

Israelit (see Israelite)

Israelite
*Israelite-Eisenstadt Family Database
9341 Chelsea Drive South
Fort Lauderdale, FL 33324-6282
Phone (954) 472-5455 (phone and FAX);
E-mail:
koosh@bcfreenet.seflin.lib.fl.us
Bernard I. Kouchel
(includes Israeli, Israelit, Lurie, Baksht,
Bakst, Blum, Botek, Horowitz,
Klotzkin, Kouchel, Litt, Marcus,
Nelson, Rosenblum, Schaiman,
Shimenson, Simenson, Singer,
Volinsky and variant spellings)

Israelovitch
*Israelovitch Family Association
8505 Glenview Avenue
Takoma Park, MD 20912
Phone (301) 89-6621; (301) 589-1366
FAX
Barbara Levitz
(includes descendants of Israelovitch
family from Novogrudok
(Navahrudak), now Belarus; also
Israelowitcz, Isralowitcz, Levitch,
Levitt, Levitts and Levitz,)

Israelowitcz (see Israelovitch)

Isralowitcz (see Israelovitch)

Itson (see Eidson)

Iverson
*Victor Moses Iverson Family
  Organization
5892 West 10620 North
Highland
American Fork, UT 84003-9591
Phone (801) 756-0155
Grant H. Iverson

Ives
Ives Index
2118 Goliad Road, #109-A
San Antonio, TX 78223-3220
Charlene Ives Nelson
Pub. *Ives Index*, quarterly, $10.00 per
  year subscription

Ivory
Ivory Family Association
5313 Penguin Circle
Salt Lake City, UT 84117-7356
George Ivory

Iyancovich (see Blossom Press)

Izatt (see MacDuff)

Izzett (see MacDuff)

Jaacks (see Bestman)

Jack
Jack Newsletter
12825 Lillian Place, N.E.
Albuquerque, NM 87112
Phone (505) 293-3258; E-mail:
  charwil@nmia.com
Charlee Wilson
Pub. *Jack Newsletter*, semiannually,
  $5.00 per year suscription,
  complimentary issue for two stamps,
  free queries; (includes Jack, Jacks,
  Jacques and Jaques, all locations)

Jacks (see Jack)

Jackson (see Blossom Press, CTC
  Family Association, Sullivan Surname
  Exchange, Braden, Brawley, Brown,
  Evitt, Garner, Goodenow, Hall,
  Johnson, Lambert, Stewart)

Jackson
*Jackson-Thompson-Lett-Copley-
  Wilson-Williamson Family History
4031 Grand Avenue
DeLand, FL 32720
Phone (904) 985-4046
Harry L. Sellards, Jr., Publisher
(includes related families: Adkins,
  Bartram, Booth, Crabtree, Ferguson,
  Osborn, Smith, Webb and Wellman)

Jackson
*Jackson-Cowley Family Tree
376 Lighthouse Drive
Manahawkin, NJ 08050-2327
Phone (609) 547-8965
Tom Jackson, Founder

(sharing information on Jackson, Cowley,
  Hardcastle, Sharphouse, Hullah)
SASE

Jaco (see Wright)

Jacob (see McCune)

Jacob
Jacob Family Association
22520 Lincoln
Saint Clair Shores, MI 48082
Richard J. Jacob

Jacobson (see Lush)

Jacoby (see The Memorial Foundation
  of the Germanna Colonies)

Jacoby
*Jacoby/Goble/Gibson/Tiller Family
  Association
114 Mariae Lane
O'Fallon, MO 63366
Phone (314) 240-3335
Betty Maude Gibson

Jacomine (see Blossom Press)

Jacoway (see Boney)

Jacques (see Jack)

Jaeger (see Pellien)

Jagger (see Usher)

Jagmin (see Farrington)

Jahnke
Jahnke
Whispering Oaks
5821 Rowland Hill Road
Cascade, MD 21719-1939
Phone (301) 416-2660
Victor Gebhart, President
Pub. *Jahnke*, annually, $2.00 per issue

Jahraus (see Edler)

Jahrhau (see Pessner)

Jameison (see James)

James (see CTC Family Association,
  Arthur, LaRue, Miller, Wright)

James
*James Family Association
18002 North 12th Street, #30
Phoenix, AZ 85022
Nani Mercer Neal
Pub. *James Surname Newsletter*,
  quarterly, $20.00 per year subscription

James
*Hollis James Descendants: Pioneer of
  Ohio
822 Camino De Los Padres
Tucson, AZ 85718

Phone (520) 297-6585
Leallah Franklin, Publisher

James
James/Sills/Pierce Family Reunion
1204 Clay Street
Winnfield, LA 71483-2956
W. L. Sowers

James
*James History
643 Highland Drive
Eden, NC 27288
Phone (910) 623-3655
Dee James, Publisher
(includes Reuben James family from
  1755)

James
James Family Reunion
1729 East Frontier Terrace
Mustang, OK 73064
Loreta West

James
James Family Reunion
2029 Harris Road
Knoxville, TN 37924
Polly Arnett

James
James-Jameson-Jameison-Gunn Family
  Association
2306 Westgate
Houston, TX 77019
Phone (713) 529-2333
Harold Helm
$25.00 plus pedigree and family group
  sheets for membership

James
*Victor Hough James Family
  Organization
2767 Brinton Way
Layton, UT 84040
Phone (801) 546-3828
Franklin H. Ayrton

Jameson (see Gunn, James, Scott)

Jamieson (see Gunn, Stewart)

Jamison (see Kunkel, Walker)

Jamison
Jamison-Alexander-Steele-White Family
  Association
2306 Westgate
Houston, TX 77019
Phone (713) 529-2333
Harold Helm
$25.00 plus pedigree and family group
  sheets for membership

Jamnik (see Kadunc)

Janaway (see Folk Family Surname
  Exchange)

Janczewski
Janczewski Database
PO Box 35
Tafton, PA 18464-0035
Phone (717) 226-4721; E-mail:
    Compuserve 73130,30
Sharon S. Robinson

Janney (see Bugbee)

Janney
*Janney Journal
PO Box 413
Duchesne, UT 84021
Susan Janney Wight
Pub. Janney Journal, quarterly, $6.00 per
    year subscription

Janosik (see Wright)

Janota
*John Janota Family Organization
3684 Townley Road
Shaker Heights, OH 44122-5120
Phone (216) 751-8601
Donald Allen Zak
(includes descendants of John Janota of
    Bohemia from 1650 to the present)

Jans (see Bogardus, Rutherford)

Jansen (see Links Genealogy
    Publications, Rutherford)

Janson (see Johnson)

Jaques (see Jack, Ross)

Jaques
*JFA
967 Spindle Hill Road
Wolcott, CT 06716
Pat Jacques
(genealogy of the Jaques family)

Jaquith
*Jaquith Family Association
PO Box 511
Brawley, CA 92227
Phone (619) 344-3520
George Jaquith, President Emeritus
(includes descendants of Abraham
    Jaquith, 1643, Charlestown,
    Massachusetts)

Jardine
Clan Jardine
21951 Cosalo Street
Mission Viejo, CA 92691
Bill J. Cook, Commissioner for U.S.A.
Pub. Clanline, annually; (Jardine of
    Applegirth)
Branches: **Arizona**, Ralph R. Jardine,
    Convener, 10226 Highwood Lane, Sun
    City, AZ 85373; **Central States**, Sue
    Jardine-Orr, Convener, 9130
    Forestview Drive, Temperance, MI
    48182; **Florida**, Tom P. Jardine,
    Convener, 2476 Pacer Lane, South,

Cocoa, FL 32926; **Mountain States**,
Donald M. Jardine, Convener, PO Box
105, Markleeville, CA 96120, (916)
694-2209; **Northeastern States**,
George J. Jardine, Convener, 431
Greenview Road, Turnersville, NJ
08012; **Northern California**, Jerry
Jardine, Convener, 900 Broderick
Street, #11, San Francisco, CA 94115,
(415) 567-5853; **Northern States**,
Marion Hayward, Convener, 57
Riverdale Road, Concord, MA 01742;
Southern States, R. Andrew Jardine,
Convener, PO Box 61540, New
Orleans, LA 70161, (504) 586-5495
£5 per year membership, £60 life
membership to Sir Alec Jardine, Ash
House, Thwaites, Millom, Cumbria
LA18 5HY, England

Jardine
*Jardine Clan Society, Northeastern
    States Branch
24 Lyndon Lane
Ashland, MA 01721
Shirley Jardine, Genealogist/Historian
Pub. The Jardine Clan Society of the
    Northeastern States Clanline, from
    Scotland Newsletter, annually
$15.00 per year membership (includes
    dues to Scotland)

Jardine
*Frank and Ada Jardine Family
    Organization
1020 South Davis Boulevard
Bountiful, UT 84010
Phone (801) 295-8115
Betty Jardine Tingey
(restricted to descendants of Walter
    Jardine and Fanny Isabella Stubbings
    of Northampton, England; also Jardine,
    Percival and Stubbings families of
    Northampton, England, Jardine family
    of Scotland, Scott family of Scotland,
    1700s and 1800s)

Jarnigen (see Jernigan)

Jarrell
Jarrell Newsletter
2810 Thousand Oaks Drive, #163
San Antonio, TX 78232-4108
Mrs. Jackie Morgan
Pub. Jarrell Newsletter, three times per
    year, $10.00 per year subscription

Jarrett (see Links Genealogy
    Publications, Scadlock)

Jarvis (see Newmyer)

Jarvis
Fields Jarvis Family (born
    Westmoreland, VA)
25 North Center
Trenton, UT 84338
Gerri L. Ball

Jay
*Jay Family Association—West
4406 Moffett Road
Ceres, CA 95307-9427
Phone (209) 538-3613
Loretta Jay Davis, Editor
Pub. Jay News, annually; (includes
    collection of material for surnames of
    Duck, Essary, Taber and Wareham)
$7.00 life membership

Jeancomme (see Johnson)

Jeanconne (see Johnson)

Jeanfreau (see Blossom Press)

Jeanson (see Johnson)

Jeansonne (see Johnson)

Jeardoe
*The Jeardoe Journal
PO Box 85
Glenwood, IA 51534-0085
C. J. Mohney White
Pub. The Jeardoe Journal, quarterly,
    $6.00 per year subscription (beginning
    January)

Jeffcoat (see King)

Jeffers (see Heath)

Jefferson (see Folk Family Surname
    Exchange, Nelson)

Jefferson
*The Monticello Association
3701 Old Gun Road, East
Midlothian, VA 23113
Phone (804) 272-2046
Gerald Morgan, Jr., Secretary
Pub. Annual Report (includes lineal
    descendants of Thomas Jefferson,
    primarily interested in preserving the
    graveyard at Monticello)

Jeffery (see MacDuff)

Jefford
*Thomas Harvey Jefford Family
708 South East Drive
Greenfield, IN 46140
Phone (317) 462-9651
Richard Deane Jefford, II
(includes Jefford and Burgener surnames,
    data on IBM™ PAF™)

Jeffries
*Jeffries Reunion
Country Court Trailer Park
1101 Pocahontas, Trailer #18
Palmyra, MO 63461
Marjorie J. Westmoreland

Jelks (see McRae)

Jelley (see Jelly)

Jellings (see Jennings)

Jelly (see Catlow)

Jelly
*Jelly's Works of Memories
322 West Columbia Street
Weatherford, TX 76086-4052
Phone (817) 599-0874
Arthur Hill Jelly
(includes Bobley, Burton, Dearborn, Hill,
   Hills, Jelley, Loflin, Mathew, Mathieu,
   Stokes, Tigner and Yeaple surnames)

Jen (see Jensen)

Jenett (see Flowers)

Jenings (see Jennings)

Jenkins (see Folk Family Surname
   Exchange, Brawley, Clinton,
   Goodenow, Jennings, McCune, Nettles,
   Rutherford)

Jenkins
*Joseph Sanford Jenkins Descendants
   Association
19341 Knotty Pine Way
Monument, CO 80132
Phone (719) 481-2875
Ruth H. Christian

Jenkins
*Caroline Geneva Jenkins Family
   Organization
1055 East Hillcrest Drive
Springville, UT 84663
Phone (801) 489-6298
Nel Lo H. Bassett, A.G., Researcher
Pub. *Research Report*, biannually;
   (includes ancestry of Caroline Geneva
   Jenkins (1802) of London, England,
   wife of John William Dutson (1828))
$12.00 per year membership

Jenne (see Guthrie)

Jenner
*Jenner Surname Organization
1780 Panay Circle
Costa Mesa, CA 92626
Phone (714) 979-8672
David Lane Walden

Jenni (see Guthrie)

Jenniges (see Heath)

Jenning (see Jennings)

Jennings (see Flanningham, Leavitt,
   Moody)

Jennings
*Jennings Branch
2920 Highcrest Road
Rockford, IL 61107
Eileen Kimber, Author

Jennings
*Jennings Newsletter
PO Box 245
Novinger, MO 63559
Phone (816) 488-6616; (816) 488-6885
   FAX; E-mail:
   Jethomas@Vax2.Rain.Gen.MO.Us
Janet E. Thomas, Publisher/Owner
Pub. *Jennings Newsletter*, three times per
   year (February, June and October),
   $15.00 per year subscription in the
   U.S., $18.00 per year subscription
   outside the U.S.; (for the Jennings
   lineage, with all variations of spelling:
   Genning, Gennings, Gennins, Gilling,
   Ginning, Ginnings, Ginnins, Jellings,
   Jenings, Jenkins, Jenning, Jennins,
   Jilling, Jining, Jinnings and Jinnins)

Jennings
*Jennings Surname Organization
200 Walnut Hill Avenue, #4
Hillsboro, TX 76645-9521
Phone (817) 582-8988
Thomas E. Jennings

Jennins (see Jennings)

Jennison (see Hatfield)

Jensen (see Lush)

Jensen
*Jens Christian Jensen Family
   Organization
944 Hillview Road
Brigham City, UT 84302
Phone (801) 723-7405
Daniel Myron Wheatley

Jernigan
*Nall News Publishing Company
PO Box 2186
Willingboro, NJ 08046-2186
Josephine Crittenberger-Nall, Editor-
   Publisher
Pub. *Jernigan Journal*, quarterly, $16.00
   per year subscription

Jernigan
Jernigan-Journagan-Cherniken-Jarnigen
   Family Association
2306 Westgate
Houston, TX 77019
Phone (713) 529-2333
Harold Helm
$25.00 plus pedigree and family group
   sheets for membership

Jespersen (see Sorenson)

Jesse
August Jesse Family Association
9750 Parktree Way
Elk Grove, CA 95624
Brooklea Lutton

Jesse
*Jesse Family Database
4851 Royce Road
Irvine, CA 92715-2233
Phone (714) 786-7293
Harry and Bev Jesse Shuptrine
(includes more than U.S. 5,500
   descendants of William Morgan Jesse
   and Mary Ann Parker, both born in
   Cumberland County, Virginia, 1798
   and 1802, a founding family of the city
   of Mexico, Missouri)

Jessup (see Surname Sources, Arthur)

Jester
*Jester Family Reunion
6029 Route 88
Finleyville, PA 15332
Phone (412) 348-6544
Jean Jester Livingston
No fee except SASE for search of large
   files, biennial reunion in even-
   numbered years

Jestrab (see McCanna)

Jett (see Brodnax, Rutherford)

Jett
*Jett Set Family Association
2776 County Road 27
Bellevue, OH 44811
Phone (419) 483-2363
Kate L. Jett
Pub. *"Jett Set" Family Newsletter*,
   quarterly; (includes all Gette, Jett and
   Jette families, everywhere, and related
   families: McCarty, Stowe, Phyllips,
   Lentz and Thompkins)
$7.00 per year membership

Jette (see Jett)

Jewett (see Golliher)

Jewett
*Jewett/Pearl Family Reunion Group of
   Connecticut
PO Box 67
Columbia, CT 06237-0067
Phone (203) 228-0080
Mrs. Marion Rosebrooks Emmons,
   Family Researcher

Jewett
*The Jewett Family of America, Inc.
PO Box 254
Rowley, MA 01969
Phone (423) 539-6685
Ms. Lee Jewett Petry, Historian
Pub. *Year Book*, annually (December);
   Newsletter, three times per year
   (March, June and September);
   (includes Jewitt, Jouett, Juett, etc.)

Jewitt (see Jewett)

Jewitt
Jewitt Family Reunion
15769 Meyers
Detroit, MI 48227
M. Lindsay

Jilling (see Jennings)

Jimison (see Kunkel)

Jining (see Jennings)

Jinnin (see Jennings)

Jinnings (see Jennings)

Jnlin (see Rothenberger)

Job (see Davis)

Job
Job(e) Journal
3804 Carpenter Avenue
Studio City, CA 91604
Phone (818) 766-9092 FAX
Bill Jobe
Pub. *Job(e) Journal*, quarterly, $15.00
    per year subscription; (includes Jobe
    (1620 Wales), Pearson (1790 South
    Carolina), Thomas (1606 Virginia),
    Howell, Satterfield, Wilson, Butler,
    Graves, and family heads born before
    1600 and lived in Virginia: Brassieur,
    Gray, Hanby, Heath, Marshall, Sanders
    and Tatum)

Jobe (see Job)

Joffrion (see Johnson)

Johansen (see Johnson, Peterson)

Johns (see Links Genealogy
    Publications)

Johnson (see Blossom Press, Family
    Publications, Folk Family Surname
    Exchange, Links Genealogy
    Publications, Album, Barber, Barnes,
    Brawley, Campbell, Corson, Davis,
    Dockery, Dopp, Foley, Gibbs,
    Goodenow, Gunn, Hamblin, Hatfield,
    Heath, Hopkin, Johnston, Lush, Millet,
    Moody, Rothenberger, Rutherford,
    Stoner, Wright)

Johnson
*Johnson Association
181 Margarite Road
Middletown, CT 06457
Phone (203) 347-0176
Daisy Zdanowicz Paskiewicz

Johnson
Descendants of Peter Johnson
2251 Sagamore Hills Drive
Decatur, GA 30033
Albert Sydney Johnson
Pub. *Descendants of Peter Johnson*

Johnson
*Johnson-Sinsabaugh Family Association
4201 Wildflower Circle
Wichita, KS 67210
Phone (316) 529-0438
Dianne Stark Thurman, Historian
Pub. *Newsletter*, annually; (includes
    Hiram and Nancy, from Orange
    County, New York, to Kansas)
Annual reunion on the first Sunday of
    August in Eureka, Kansas

Johnson
*Genealogy of the Johnsons and Related
    Families
1302 Estelle Street
Hattiesburg, MS 39402-2719
Phone (601) 268-3300
Floyd E. Johnson, Publisher
(includes the Johnson, Janson,
    Jeancomme, Jeanconne, Jeanson and
    Jeansonne, family with roots from
    Norway to Scotland, to Acadia
    (Canada), to the New England states,
    to Louisiana, and related families:
    Anderpont, Ardoin, Armand, Arnaud,
    Arseneau, Aucoin, Aymand, Aymond,
    Babin, Babineaux, Badeau, Belanger,
    Benoit, Bernard, Billeadeau,
    Blanchard, Boftz, Bondick, Bonnette,
    Bordelon, Boudreau, Bourg,
    Bourgeois, Bowman, Brasseaux,
    Breaux, Broussard, Buller, Campbell,
    Carpenter, Carrier, Carriere, Causey,
    Chandler, Chatelain, Chenevert, Clark,
    Cloud, Cochran, Coco, Commeaux,
    Corporon, Couvillion, Davis, Dekko,
    Descant, Deshotels, Desmerits,
    Deville, Doiron, Ducote, Duplissey,
    Dupre, Dussler, Firmin, Fontaine,
    Fontenot, Foreman, Forest, Forman,
    Fuselier, Gaspard, Gaudet, Gautrot,
    Gillette, Godeau, Gorouard, Granger,
    Green, Gremillion, Guidry, Guillet,
    Guillot, Hamelin, Hartman, Hayes,
    Hazelton, Hutzler, Jackson, Joffrion,
    Jones, Juneau, Kelley, Laborde,
    Labourg, LaCombe, Lacour, Lafleur,
    LaHaye, Landerneau, Landry,
    Langlois, LeBlanc, LeClair, Ledoux,
    Leger, Lejeune, Lemoine, Long, Lord,
    Manuel, Marcotte, Martin, Mathews,
    Mayes, McCarter, Mellason, Miller,
    Moreau, Mouton, Nezat, Norman,
    Nugent, Olivo, Ortego, Patin, Perron,
    Pitre, Plauche, Ponthieu, Porche, Poret,
    Powers, Prejean, Prudhomme,
    Quinteros, Rabalais, Ragsdale,
    Ragsdille, Randel, Randolph, Reed,
    Remel, Riche, Rider, Ritter, Roberson,
    Robichaud, Robicheaux, Robinson,
    Rousseau, Roy, St. Romain, Saucier,
    Savoye, Scallon, Schexnayder,
    Simouneau, Smith, Soileau, Stone,
    Sylvester, Tassin, Tate, Therriot,
    Thibodeaux, Trahan, Vidrine, White,
    Whittington, Wilkerson, Woodruff,
    Young, Zimmer and many more)

Johnson
*Johnson Clan of Missouri
Genealogical Recorder
PO Box 252
Booneville, MO 65233-0252
Phone (816) 882-2478
Clyde G. Johnson, Chieftain

Johnson
*Peter Wilhelm Johnson Family
    Organization
34701 Knox Butte Road, East
Albany, OR 97321
Phone (541) 926-5964
Kristine Hansen, President; LeRoy
    Hansen
(includes descendants of Peter Wilhelm
    Johnson/Wilhelm Peter Johansen
    (1888–) and his wife, Alta Rasmussen,
    of Denmark, Brown County,
    Wisconsin, in 1908)

Johnson
Johnson Herald
648 Salem Heights Avenue, South
Salem, OR 97302-5613
Gerald Johnson
Pub. *Johnson Herald*, monthly

Johnson
*The A. D. Johnson Family Association
930 West Long Avenue
DuBois, PA 15801-1737
Phone (814) 371-2532 (phone and FAX,
    no collect calls accepted, no calls after
    9:00 P.M. Eastern time); E-mail:
    RBT@Penn.com
John S. Walker, President and Family
    Historian
Pub. *Roots, Branches, and Twigs*,
    semiannually, $10.00 per year
    subscription, send SASE with queries;
    (includes descendants, ancestors and
    lateral lines of Capt. Edward Johnson,
    founder of Woburn, Massachusetts, of
    Canterbury, Kent, England, married
    Esther Wheadon of Branford,
    Connecticut; follows to Artemas
    Johnson and Mary Barne(es) of
    Branford, Connecticut (Revolutionary
    War), to Bradford County,
    Pennsylvania, ca 1795–96, forward to
    Clearfield and Huntingdon Counties,
    Pennsylvania; and related Johnson and
    Dillon families of England/Ireland)
Annual reunion on the third Saturday of
    July as close as possible to the home
    of A.D. and Sarah Dillon Johnson

Johnson
Johnson Quarterly
1321 Gum Tree
Huffman, TX 77336
Phone (713) 324-3797
Molly Bateman Reigard, Editor
Pub. *Johnson Quarterly*, $15.00 per year
    subscription; (includes Johns(t)on(e),
    mostly southern lines)

Johnson
Surnames, Limited
RR 3, Box 59
Muleshoe, TX 79347-9208
Pub. *Johnson Newsletter (Southern)*,
    irregularly, $8.00 per issue

Johnson
*Johnson Family Organization
600 Palomino Drive
Evanston, WY 82930
Phone (307) 789-9436
Carl Martin Johnson
(Icelandic family)

Johnston (see Folk Family Surname
    Exchange, Links Genealogy
    Publications, Israel, Johnson, Kahler)

Johnston
*Johnston Family Research
340 Alta Vista, #3
Oakland, CA 94610
Phone (510) 465-5868
Janet Prince

Johnston
Johnstons of Alabama
5038 Lakeshore Drive
Columbia, SC 29206-4403
Anita McCray
Pub. *Johnstons of Alabama*, quarterly,
    $12.00 per year subscription

Johnston
*James Johnston/Ellen E. Pinney Family
    Organization
5246 South 2150 West
Roy, UT 84067
Phone (801) 773-4568
Beverly Sessions, Family Representative
(includes descendants of John Johnston/
    Johnson (1798 London, England) and
    Mary Stuart (1808 Fifeshire,
    Scotland); also John Seager and Sarah
    Colley of Somersetshire, England; also
    John Seger of London, England and
    Switzerland)

Johnston
*Clan Johnston/e in America
11712 Rockaway Lane
Fairfax, VA 22030-7940
Phone (703) 273-2450
William Page Johnston, President
Pub. *Spur and Phoenix*, quarterly
$15.00 per year membership

Johnstone (see Gregor, Johnson,
    Johnston)

Joley (see Joly)

Joly
Jol(e)y Researcher
PO Box 10121
Eugene, OR 97401
Mary L. Henke
Pub. *Jol(e)y Researcher*, quarterly,
    $12.00 per year subscription

Jones (see Family Publications, Folk
    Family Surname Exchange, Links
    Genealogy Publications, Barnes,
    Boney, Brown, Cairer, Camden,
    Christley, Clark, Corson, DuBois,
    Gant, Gipson, Godfrey, Goodenow,
    Johnson, LaRue, Lush, McCune,
    Nelson, Neville, Newmyer, Ogan,
    Reynolds, Rutherford, Stewart)

Jones
Jones
4604 Virginia Loop Road, Apartment
    3156-G
Montgomery, AL 36116-4739
Lisa R. Franklin
Pub. *Jones*, quarterly, $10.00 per year
    subscription

Jones
The Jones Genealogist
2001 First Avenue
Tuscaloosa, AL 35401
Phone (205) 752-7893
Jerry E. Jones, M.D., M.S.
Pub. *The Jones Genealogist*, bimonthly,
    $12.00 per year subscription, $3.00 per
    issue; (focus on Jones in Wales,
    England, Colonial America, Virginia
    and Kentucky, beginning with the
    Jamestown settlements)

Jones
Jones Family Descendants
8626 North Fowler
Clovis, CA 93612
Peggy Glahn

Jones
*Hannibal Jones Family Organization
PO Box 171
Douglas City, CA 96024
Phone (916) 778-3136
Paul Jones

Jones
Oak Leaf Publishing
22 Creek Road, #64
Irvine, CA 91714
Pub. *Jones Family Newsletter*, bimonthly,
    $10.00 per year subscription

Jones
Jones Journeys
4041 Pedley Road, #18
Riverside, CA 92509
Phone (714) 685-8936
Frances R. Nelson, Editor
Pub. *Jones Journeys*, quarterly, $17.00
    per year subscription

Jones
*Genealogy of William Jones, Sr., of
    Granville County, North Carolina (ca
    1735?-1799)
9920 N.E. 120th Street
Okeechobee, FL 34972-7453
Frances Scroggins Wheeler, Publisher

Jones
Jones Junctions
11821 Shirley Street
Omaha, NE 68144-2956
Diane Korten
Pub. *Jones Junctions*, quarterly;
    (a Jones Roots Cellar Plus, and
    database index)
$6.50 per year membership

Jones
*Jacob Jones Family Organization
26 Edgewater Drive
Matawan, NJ 07747
Walter H. Jones
(from 1750 to the present)
Annual reunion on the first Saturday of
    October at Lowes Crossroads United
    Methodist Church, Lowes Crossroads,
    Delaware

Jones
*Jones Surname Organization
56 Chestnut
Wayne, NJ 07470
Phone (201) 694-8723
Lucille Dillinger Alexander

Jones
Jones Family Reunion Association
1016 Washington Street
Roanoke Rapids, NC 27870
Phone (919) 537-3812
Edith J. Brown, Secretary-Treasurer
Pub. *Jones Family Connections*,
    quarterly; (includes the family of
    William Jones (1737–))
$10.00 per year membership

Jones
*Jones Family Association
6132 Silver Fox Trail
Morristown, TN 37814
Phone (423) 581-7066
Sarah Jones Risdahl
(includes descendants of Amasa and Jane
    Canine Jones of Delaware County,
    Ohio, born about 1790; allied names:
    Adcock, Canine/Conine, Cantrell,
    Certain, Cheatham, Hail/Hale, League
    and Stoner)
Annual reunion on the first Sunday of
    May at Jefferson meeting house,
    Smithville, DeKalb County, Tennessee

Jones
*Mountain Press
4503 Anderson Pike
PO Box 400
Signal Mountain, TN 37377-0400
Phone (423) 886-6369; (423) 886-5312
    FAX
James L. Douthat, Owner
(John Jones (1755–1838) of Culpeper
    County, Virginia, and Kanawha
    County, West Virginia)

Jones
*John R. Jones Family Organization
Highway 87 North
PO Box 340
Burkeville, TX 75932
Phone (409) 565-4751
Helen Rogers Skelton

Jones
Genealogical and Historical News
369 East 900 South, Suite 247
Salt Lake City, UT 84111
R. D. Bradshaw, Editor
Pub. *Jones of Virginia Family News-Letter*, quarterly, $10.00 per year subscription

Jones
*Thomas Jones and Letitia Thomas
  Family Organization
781 Seventh Avenue
Salt Lake City, UT 84103
Phone (801) 359-5300
Nellie Jones Brossard, Research
  Specialist
(includes descendants of Thomas Jones
  (1810 Beaumaris, Anglesey, Wales–)
  and Letitia Thomas (1809 Llysfaen,
  Caernarvonshire, North Wales–))
Donation for membership, reunion

Jordan (see Gant, Mitchell, Moore, Wright)

Jordan
*Kinseeker Publications
5697 Old Maple Trail
PO Box 184
Grawn, MI 49637
E-mail: AB064@taverse.lib.mi.us
Victoria Wilson, Editor
Pub. *The Family Series: Jordan*,
  irregularly, $6.50 per year subscription

Jordan
*The Family Jordan—Descendants of
  The Rev. Robert & Sarah Winter
  Jordan
39 Jared Sparks Road
West Willington, CT 06279
David S. Jordan, Editor and President
Pub. *The Jordan*, semiannually; (includes
  descendants of the Rev. Robert and
  Sarah (Winter) Jordan, who arrived in
  Maine in 1640 and settled on
  Richmonds Island, Maine, now Cape
  Elizabeth)
$20.00 per year membership; reunion
  every three years (last one was in
  1995)

Jorger (see Jurger)

Jose (see MacDuff)

Joseph
Joseph Lines
Rt. 2, Box 97
Sullivan, IN 47882
Orland Stanley
Pub. *Joseph Lines*

Josleyn (see Main)

Joslyn (see Barker)

Joss (see MacDuff)

Jouett (see Jewett)

Journagan (see Jernigan)

Joy
*Elias Joy Family Organization
30 North Third East
Soda Springs, ID 83276
Phone (208) 547-3683
Roberta Gaye Gunnell
(includes descendants of Thomas Joy
  (1611) and Joan Gallup (1618), John
  Gallup and Christobell Bruchette
  (1590), and related families of Covert,
  Fligg, Collins and Gregory)

Joyce (see Bagley)

Joyner
*Joyner Family Association
5243 Carpell Avenue
PO Box 18044
Salt Lake City, UT 84118-8044
Phone (801) 964-2825; (801) 964-0551
  (FAX)
George M. McCune, Historian
(for descendants of John William Ashley
  Joyner (1851–1924); and associated
  families: Bowers, Harrison, Mosley,
  Parish, Reed and Walker from North
  Carolina, Virginia and Pennsylvania)

Jubb (see Hopkin)

Judd
Judd Surname Organization
6180 Merrywood Drive
Rocklin, CA 95677-3421
Kathleen Stewart

Judge (see Gant)

Judkins
*Judkins Family Association
1538 N.W. 60th Street
Seattle, WA 98107-2328
Phone (206) 784-3644
Kathi Judkins Abendroth, President
Pub. *Judkins Journal*, quarterly, $4.00
  per back issue
$14.00 per year membership, $200.00
  life membership

Juedes (see Sager)

Juett (see Jewett)

Julian
Julian Jamboree
10552 Parfet Court
Westminster, CO 80021-3521
Pamela S. Forristall
Pub. *Julian Jamboree*

Julien
*Julien Clearinghouse
6603 Kensington Avenue East
Richmond Heights, CA 94805-2054
Phone (510) 237-7240 (phone and FAX);
  E-mail: tdewitt@creative.net
Dorothy Swinson DeWitt Baldwin,
  Coordinator
(includes descendants of Stephen Julien
  (1700 South Carolina–) of South
  Carolina, Maryland and Virginia)

Juneau (see Johnson, Kalanquin)

Jung (see Franciscus, Young)

Jungblut (see Youngblood)

Junghen (see Younkin)

Junk
Junk Breeze
8307 Manor Drive
Fort Wayne, IN 46808
Cletus Junk
Pub. *Junk Breeze*, semiannually

Junkin (see McJunkin)

Junkins
*Junkins Family Association
259 Cider Hill Road
York, ME 03909-5303
Alan D. Junkins, President and Founder
Pub. *Junkins Family Association
  Newsletter*, semiannually, $10.00 per
  year subscription; (includes
  descendants of Robert Junkins (1621–
  1699) of York, Maine)

Jurger
*Jurger/Jorger/Yerger/Yarger
  Clearinghouse
11502 Grace Terrace
Indianapolis, IN 46236-8834
Phone (317) 823-2376
Enid I. Beihold
(includes all spellings)

Juricich (see Blossom Press)

Jurjevich (see Blossom Press)

Justice (see Folk Family Surname
  Exchange, Eaves, Hatfield, Justis,
  Moser)

Justis
*Justis, Justus, Justice for All
220 Northwest Avenue
Swannanoa, NC 28778
Joyce Justus Parris

Justus (see Justis, Moser)

Kabbel (see Kebel)

Kabble (see Kebel)

Kabel (see Kebel)

Kabell (see Kebel)

Kable (see Coble)

Kabler (see The Memorial Foundation of the Germanna Colonies)

Kadunc
*Kadunc/Krompel/Stibernik/Jamnik Surname Organization
33516 170 Avenue, S.E.
Auburn, WA 98092
Phone (206) 833-7229
Mary H. Smith

Kahl (see Cail)

Kahle (see Miehls)

Kahler
*Kahler/Collar Family and In-Laws
6600C River Valley Marina
Little Rock, AR 72212-9711
Phone (501) 868-1775
Grant H. Collar, Jr.
(includes Kahler line beginning 1760 with the marriage of Michael Kahler to Ursula Dimbter at Barzdorf, Bohemia, Austria-Hungary (now the Czech Republic); associated families: Arbogast from 1734 in Germany, Ball/Talbert from 1720 in Virginia, Blucker, Lejon and Thurasson or Turasson from 1743 in Kristianstad and Malmohus, Sweden, Denison from 1554 in England, Johnston from 1788 in Tennessee, Kilian/Killion from 1500 in Germany, McHenry from 1715 in County Antrim, Ireland, Osborn/Osborne from 1780 in Ohio, Piersol from 1748 in Pennsylvania, Sallee from 1718 at Versailles, France, Webb from 1873 in Arkansas)

Kahler
Kahler Clearinghouse
Rt. 1, Box 192
Monmouth, IL 61462
James E. and Sharon L. Todd
Pub. *Newsletter*, quarterly, $10.00 per year subscription

Kaifer (see The Memorial Foundation of the Germanna Colonies)

Kaiffer (see The Memorial Foundation of the Germanna Colonies)

Kaines (see The Memorial Foundation of the Germanna Colonies)

Kalanquin
*François Kalanquin Family Organization
1774 Country Club Drive
Logan, UT 84321
Phone (801) 753-6924
Joyce Elfrena Kalanquin
(includes descendants of François Kalanquin (1821 Frahier, France–) and Kate Juneau)

Kale (see Cail)

Kalloch
*Kalloch Family Society
Fish Point Road
PO Box 75
Orland, ME 04472
Phone (207) 469-7010
Dean R. Mayhew
Pub. *Newsletter*, quarterly; (includes Kalloch, Kallock, Keller, Kelloch, Kellock, Kellough and Killough)
Donation for membership; annual reunion in August

Kalloch
*Kalloch Family Reunion Association
199 Chestnut Street
Andover, MA 01810-1820
Phone (508) 470-1006 (Historian); E-mail: ptemr@aol.com (Historian); (207) 354-2468 (Editor)
Rev. Peter T. Richardson, Historian; Evelyn Kalloch, Editor
Pub. *Newsletter*, annually; (includes Kalloch family of Warren and Knox County, Maine, including variant spellings of Kallock, Kellar, Keller, Kelloch, Kellogh, Kellough or Killough; also descendants of Finley Kelloch (1711–) and Mary Young (1700–1795) of Warren, Maine)

Kallock (see Kalloch)

Kamenah
*Christine Elisabeth Kamenah Family Organization
2506 Mansfield Drive
Des Moines, IA 50317
Phone (515) 262-0707
Thomas C. Boelling

Kammerlich (see Kimberlin)

Kammerling (see Kettwig)

Kanaday (see Kennedy)

Kanady (see Kennedy)

Kane
Kane Family News Notes
1364 Walker Avenue
Baltimore, MD 21239
Phone (410) 323-3883
Agnes K. Callum, Editor
Pub. *Kane Family News Notes*, quarterly, $5.00 per year subscription; (includes Callum and Gough)

Kaneely (see Cian)

Kanne
Kanne/Marzahn/Minske Family Organization
13403 Maywood
Minnetonka, MN 55343
Mrs. L. Benson

Karacoff (see Kirshop)

Karklinsky (see Broida)

Karlentowsky
*Karlentowsky Surname Organization
199 Commodore Drive
Milledgeville, GA 31061
Phone (912) 968-7425
Richard Bialac

Karnaghan (see Carnahan)

Karns (see Frantz)

Karou (see Karow)

Karow
*The K.A.R.D. Files
19305 S.E. 243rd Place
Kent, WA 98042-4820
Phone (206) 432-1659
Judy K. Dye, Owner
Pub. *Karow Knowledge*, irregularly, $6.00–$7.00 per volume (Washington residents add 8.2% sales tax); (includes Caro, Carro, Carrow, Karou, Karrel, Karro and Karow)

Karr (see Kerr)

Karrel (see Karow)

Karrick
*Karrick/Kerrick Family Research
4844 Fairlawn Road
Lyndhurst, OH 44124-1121
Phone (216) 381-4474
Robert Joseph Karrick, F.A.C.G.
(includes all spellings: Carrick, Karrick, Kerrick, from 1001 to the present, from Scotland, England, Ireland and the U.S.; collecting information for a book on the descendants of Hugh Kerrick (–1755 Maryland))

Karro (see Karow)

Karrow (see Karow)

Karschner (see Kershner)

Karshner (see Kershner)

Karson (see Carson)

Karwell (see Cian)

Kasdorf
Kasdorf Kin
RR 1, Box 19A
Parkers Prairie, MN 56361-9702
Douglas M. Holt
Pub. *Kasdorf Kin*, bimonthly (January, March, May, July, September and November), $10.00 per year subscription; (more than 2100 entries in data base)

Kasey (see Cochran)

Kassel (see Links Genealogy
Publications)

Kaster (see Castor)

Kastor (see Castor)

Kate (see Koeth)

Katering (see Kettenring)

Katerman (see Kattermann)

Kates
Kates Kin
29 West Main
PO Box 8
Rarden, OH 45671
Phone (614) 372-6705
Anna Kates Gardner, Editor
Pub. *Kates Kin*, quarterly, no charge to
libraries, societies, families involved in
research, donation for subscription
from others; (includes Cates)

Kates
*Kates Family
RD 3, Box 603 J
Milford, DE 19963
Ruth Kates Peterman
(Delaware family)

Katherman (see Kattermann)

Katron (see Kettenring)

Katterman (see Kattermann)

Kattermann
*K/Catherman Reunion Association of
Mifflinburg, Union County,
Pennsylvania
10910 Larch Avenue
Hagerstown, MD 21740-7809
Paul M. Catherman
Pub. *David Kattermann Family*
(K/Catherman, K/Cotherman,
K/Cotterman, Corderman, Katerman
and Katterman)
Annual reunion on the second Saturday
of July at Mifflinburg

Kauble (see Coble)

Kauffman (see Cowart)

Kaufman (see McKee)

Kaufmann
*Kaufmann Surname Organization
150 Brown Street
Saint Clair, MI 48079-4882
Phone (810) 329-9359
George M. Roberts
(includes families of Germany and
Ontario)

Kautz
Kautz Family Newsletter
6165 Lamda Drive
San Diego, CA 92120-4615
Ollen Kay, Publisher
Pub. *Kautz Family Newsletter*, quarterly,
$3.00 per year subscription for Kautz,
$6.00 per year subscription for others

Kay (see Mackay)

Kay
Kay Family Newsletter
6165 Lamda Drive
San Diego, CA 92120-4615
Ollen Kay, Publisher
Pub. *Kay Family Newsletter*, quarterly,
$3.00 per year subscription for family
members, $6.00 per year subscription
for others

Kay
Kay
26 Paisley Park
Sumter, SC 29150
Dr. James E. Kay
Pub. *Kay*, quarterly, $5.00 per year
subscription
Reunion

Kea (see Brown)

Keach
Keach Newsletter
9001 Highway 1078 South
Henderson, KY 42420
Phone (502) 826-1811
Brenda Keach Hester
Pub. *Keach Newsletter*, quarterly, $5.00
per year subscription

Kean (see Gunn)

Keane
Keane Cousins Family Association
75 Pollard Road
Mountain Lakes, NJ 07046
Clark Neal

Keaner (see Keener)

Kear (see Carr)

Kearl (see McCune)

Kearnes (see Kernes, Kerns)

Kearney (see Carney)

Kearns (see Kerns)

Keate (see Folk Family Surname
Exchange)

Keats (see Folk Family Surname
Exchange)

Keay (see Mackay)

Kebble (see Kebel)

Kebel
Kebel Kinfolk
PO Box 2010
Sparks, NV 89432
Larry Kebel
Pub. *Kebel Kinfolk*, quarterly, $10.00 per
year subscription; (includes Kabbel,
Kabble, Kabel, Kabell, Kebel, Kebble,
Keibel, Kibble, Kobel, Kubel, plus all
surnames that satisfy Soundex K-140)

Keck (see Lush)

Keddie (see Fergusson, MacDuff)

Keddle (see Fergusson)

Kee (see Mackay)

Keefer
Keefer Family Newsletter
42 Circle Creek Court
Lafayette, CA 94549-3214
Phone (415) 944-9967
Eldon G. Keefer, Editor
Pub. *Keefer Family Newsletter*, quarterly,
$8.00 per year subscription; (includes
Keever, Keffer, Keifer, Kiefer, Kieffer,
etc., from Pfalz or Palatinate; most
descended from Huguenot, Thibaud
LeTonnelier, who fled France in 1563
and settled at Kettenheim, near Alzey))

Keefer
*Frederick Keefer Family Organization
315 South Park Avenue
Mercersburg, PA 17236
Phone (717) 328-2938
Jere S. Keefer, Researcher
(maintains database of over 11,000
Keefer/Kiefer/Keffer and related
names, with emphasis on the Frederick
Keefer line)

Keehler (see Archer)

Keen
Highland Rim Keen(e) & Kin
105 East Newcomb Road
Oak Ridge, TN 37830-5358
Phone (423) 483-7549
Edward James Keen, Editor
Pub. *Highland Rim Keen(e) & Kin*,
semiannually (June and December),
$10.00 per year subscription; (includes
descendants of Elisha Keen, born in
Virginia, moved to Tennessee,
Kentucky, North Carolina, Illinois,
Indiana and Missouri; over 50,000
entries on database)
Annual reunion in Indianapolis, Indiana

Keenan (see Kellett)

Keene (see Brown, Garner, Gunn)

Keene
Keene Family Association
PO Box 123
Danville, ME 04223
E. Keene Young

Keener (see Folk Family Surname
   Exchange)

Keener
Keener Family Organization
720 Franklin Street
Burlington, IA 52601-4859
Evelyn Keener Benz
Pub. *Keener Family Newsletter*

Keener
*Folk Family
PO Box 52048
Knoxville, TN 37950-2048
Hester E. Stockton, Owner; Clem
   Keener, Editor
Pub. *Keener Kinfolk*, quarterly, $15.00
   per year subscription, $5.00 per issue;
   (includes Keaner, Keiner and Kuhner)
Annual reunion in June at the Red River
   Valley Fairgrounds, Paris, Texas

Keeney (see Cowart, Kunkel)

Keeney
Keeney Update
PO Box 5519
Charleston, WV 25361
Phone (304) 346-2036
Roscoe C. Keeney, Jr.
Pub. *Keeney Update*, quarterly, donation
   for subscription

Keeny (see Cowart)

Keep
*The Keep Family Society
62 Weston Road
Weston, CT 06883
Phone (203) 227-8103
Donald Bergquist, Vice President
Pub. *Keepsake*, two to three times per
   year; (includes descendants of John
   Keep of Longmeadow)
$10.00 per year membership; annual
   reunion

Keephart (see Gebhard)

Keeran
Keeran Family Association
5301 North Walker
Oklahoma City, OK 73118
Rosa Mary Keeran
Pub. *Keeran Family Association
   Newsletter*

Kees (see Keyes)

Keese (see Keyes)

Keeton
*Keeton Database
152 Rockwood Road
Florham Park, NJ 07932
Phone (201) 966-1862
Peter B. Berendsen

Keever (see Keefer)

Keffer (see Keefer)

Kegley (see Dean)

Kehl (see Cail)

Keibel (see Kebel)

Keifer (see Keefer)

Keily (see Cian)

Keiner (see Keener)

Keise (see Keyes)

Keiser (see Hoster)

Keister (see Castor)

Keister
*Keister Surname Organization
7705 Ensley Drive, S.W.
Huntsville, AL 35802-2845
Phone (205) 883-0207
Thomas W. Burns

Keith (see LaRue, Macpherson, Wright)

Keith
The Keith Clan Society
7530 Goodson Road
Dawsonville, GA 30534-4244
Pub. *Keith & Kin*

Keith
Keith Clan Society
517 Wagstaff Road
Fuquay Varina, NC 27526-9797
Marie S. Keith
(includes septs: Austin, Dickson, Dixon,
   Dickson, Falconer, Harvey, Hervey,
   Haxton, Lumbair, MacKeith, Marshall,
   Urie)

Keith
Clan Keith Society, U.S.A.
1132 Parkinsmill Road
Greenville, SC 29607
Thomas M. Keith, Lt. to Chief-Emeritus

Kelchner (see Keltner, Slagle)

Kelgore (see Kilgore)

Kellam (see Kellum)

Kellar (see Kalloch)

Kelleher (see Armbruster)

Kelleher
*Nall News Publishing Company
PO Box 2186
Willingboro, NJ 08046-2186
Josephine Crittenberger-Nall, Editor-
   Publisher
Pub. *Kelleher Kin*, quarterly, $16.00 per
   year subscription

Keller (see Cian, Hottel, Kalloch, Krick,
   Nienow)

Keller
John P. H. Keller II Family Association
3080 Georgetown Drive
Prescott, AZ 86301
Richard Pearce

Keller
Keller Cousins
1381 City View Drive
Denver, CO 80229
J. A. Keller
Pub. *Keller Cousins*

Keller
*Vitus Keller Family of Talheim, Baden,
   and Descendants Worldwide
183 Springdale Avenue
Wheeling, WV 26003-5515
Phone (304) 242-5176
Thomas G. Wack, Scribe

Kellett
*Boyhood Memories and Family Ties
5 Terrace Drive
Pueblo, CO 81101-1135
Phone (719) 584-2807
James G. Kellett, Publisher
(includes Kellett, Keenan, Girardot and
   Visger families)

Kelley (see Arthur, Dean, Johnson,
   Kelly)

Kelley
*George Washington Kelley Family
   Organization
100 Dundee Drive
Fern Park, FL 32730
Phone (407) 331-0568
Bonnie Lee Ward, Historian
(includes descendants of George
   Washington and Mary Ellen Born
   Kelley)
Reunion in Fayette or Greene County,
   Pennsylvania

Kelley
Kelley Klan
581 North 450 West
Shoshone, ID 83352
Jean Kelley Smith, Secretary

Kelley
Kelley Clan (Descendants of John
   Kelley)
811 South Harrison
McGregor, TX 76657
M. Stearns

Kellie (see Cian)

Kellies (see Cian)

Kelliey (see Cian)

Kelloch (see Kalloch)

Kellock (see Kalloch)

Kellogh (see Kalloch)

Kellough (see Kalloch)

Kellour (see Hay)

Kellum
Kellum-Chelm-Gelm-Kelms Family
Association
2306 Westgate
Houston, TX 77019
Phone (713) 529-2333
Harold Helm
$25.00 plus pedigree and family group
sheets for membership

Kellum
Kellum/Kellam Family Association
14333 Aldengate Road
Midlothian, VA 23113
Anne Hale Kellam

Kelly (see Blossom Press, Reardon)

Kelly
Kelly/Kelley Clearinghouse
Rt. 1, Box 192
Monmouth, IL 61462
James E. and Sharon L. Todd
Pub. *Kelly/Kelley Newsletter*

Kelly
Kelly-Kelley
8210 North Seven Mile
Mesick, MI 49668
Jolene Kelly Pillars
Pub. *Kelly-Kelley*, quarterly, $18.00 per
year subscription

Kelly
Claudette's
3962 Xenwood Avenue, S.
Saint Louis Park, MN 55416-2842
Claudette Atwood Maerz
Pub. *Kell(e)y Kinsfolk*, semiannually
(March and September), $8.00 per year
subscription

Kelly
*Kelly/Bruen/Carey/Gorman Clan
PO Box 343
Pine Beach, NJ 08741-0343
M. Kelly
(pre-1900 Essex County, New Jersey)

Kellys (see Cian)

Kelm
*Kelm-Majesky-Wilts Reunion
PO Box 476
Pohnpee, FM 96941
Phone 011 (691) 320-2319; 011 (691)
320-2345 (FAX); E-mail:
70610,3126@compuserve.com
George Kelm, Secretary
(includes Kelm, Majesky, Wilts, Schmidt,
Borchens and Dagner families,
Germany 1800s)

Kelms (see Kellum)

Kelsey
Kelsey Newsletter
2055 Sierra Road, Apartment 93
Concord, CA 94518-4101
Mason Dutton Kelsey
Pub. *Kelsey (Kelso) Family Bulletin*
(includes descendants of Samuel
Kelso/Kelsey 1720/1796 of Chester
County, South Carolina)

Kelsey
The Kelsey Kindred of America
113 Montoya Drive
Branford, CT 06405-2501
Phone (203) 481-9804
Grace Kelsey Benoit, Secretary
Pub. *The Kelsey Family News Bulletin*,
semiannually; (includes descendants of
William Kelsey (1600), Puritan
immigrant, 1632 from England, one of
the settlers of Cambridge,
Massachusetts, Hartford, Connecticut,
and Clinton, Connecticut)
$5.00 per year membership, $1.00
application fee; annual reunion

Kelso (see Stewart)

Kelso
Kelso Family Association
287 Clark Drive
Cedar Falls, IA 50613
Phone (319) 266-1420
Dorothy S. Kelso, Associate Editor
Pub. *Kelso Correspondence*, quarterly
$8.00 per year membership

Keltner (see Slagle)

Keltner
*The Keltner Family Association
(15026 Fernview, Whittier, CA—
location)
14550 East Broadway (mailing address)
Whittier, CA 90604
Brian Lee Keltner, President
(computerized records of all Keltners
living and deceased, from four origins,
65% being from Michael Kelchner
(Keltner) to America 1733)
$5.00 per year membership for
individuals or family units, $100.00
life membership

Kelton (see Corson)

Kelty
Timothy Joseph Kelty and Idona Irene
Davis Descendants
2212 Tallow Court
Austin, TX 78744
Pat Culpepper

Kelvedon (see Wright)

Kelverstone (see Wright)

Kemble
*Genealogy of the Kemble (Kimble)
Family
1115 N.E. Orchard Drive
Pullman, WA 99163
Phone (509) 332-5612
Kemble Stout, Publisher

Kemmerlein (see Kimberlin)

Kemp (see Page)

Kemp
*Kemps with Roots in the South
210 Avenue M
Abernathy, TX 79311
Phone (806) 298-4048
Jamie Kay Kemp Taylor
Pub. *Kemps with Roots in the South*,
annually, $7.00 per volume

Kemp
*Kemp Family Association
18 Golden Hill Road
Danbury, CT 06811-4633
Robert Young, Secretary and Editor
Pub. *Kemp Files*, quarterly
$8.00 per year membership

Kemper (see The Memorial Foundation
of the Germanna Colonies, Cowart)

Kemperling (see Kimberlin)

Kempsell (see Lush)

Kendall (see Gotham, Kindel, Likes,
Rowe)

Kendall
Oak Leaf Publishing
22 Creek Road, #64
Irvine, CA 91714
Pub. *Kendall Family Newsletter*,
bimonthly, $10.00 per year
subscription

Kendall
Kendall
PO Box 9265
Spokane, WA 99209
Pam Payne
Pub. *Kendall*, quarterly, $6.00 per year
subscription

Kendrick (see Surname Sources, Brown,
Macnachton)

Kendrick
*Kendrick/Morphis Family Organization
1132 North Tela Drive
Oklahoma City, OK 73127-4308
Phone (405) 789-2842
Pauline Carlton Fletcher, Secretary and
Genealogist
(computer database uses Quinsept™,
PAF™ and Reunion™)
Annual reunion

Kendricks (see Brown)

Kendrix (see Brown)

Kenealy (see Cian)

Kenedy (see Cowart, Kennedy)

Kenfield
*Kenfield Family Association
PO Box 1234
Hudson, NY 12534-0308
Phone (518) 943-2981
Earl P. Crandell, Editor
Pub. *Kenfield Kernels*, semiannually,
$8.00 for two-year subscription in the
U.S., $10.00 for two-year subscription
in Canada; (includes Kenfield,
Kentfield and Canfield of central
Massachusetts)

Keniston (see Heath)

Kenluck (see MacDuff)

Kennady (see Weimar)

Kennair (see Blossom Press)

Kennaway (see MacDuff)

Kennedy (see Cowart, Hatfield, Weimar)

Kennedy
*John Kennedy Family Organization
5510 West Pershing Avenue
Glendale, AZ 85304
Phone (602) 978-9309
Elaine Koll Andersen
(includes descendants of John Kennedy
and Margaret Tadlock, married ca
1817 Greene County, Tennessee, ca
1783 of Greene County, Tennessee,
and 1830 of Rush County, Indiana, and
Shelby County, Illinois)
No membership cost

Kennedy
Kennedy Klues
6059 Emery Street
Riverside, CA 92509
Betty L. Pennington
Pub. *Kennedy Klues*, quarterly, $5.00 per
year subscription

Kennedy
*Kennedy Society of America
17271 Via Carmen
San Lorenzo, CA 94580
Phone (510) 278-1264
John Sidney Kennedy, Chieftain
Pub. *The Kennedy Gazette*, quarterly;
(includes Canaday, Cannadie, Carrick,
Cassels, Cassillis, Kanaday, Kanady,
Kenedy, MacUlric and MacWalrich)
$15.00 per year membership

Kennett (see Saye)

Kenney
*John Kenney Family Organization
7455 Donna Avenue
Reseda, CA 91335
Phone (818) 342-4302
Lorene E. Lawrence
(of New York 1850, Kentucky and
Tennessee 1850 or before, Canada
1850, Ireland 1849)

Kenning (see Arthur, Cunning)

Kenning
*David Gerald Kenning Family
Organization
8255 South Krameria Way
Englewood, CO 80112
Phone (303) 290-0998
Mr. Dana M. Floyd
Free membership

Kennison (see Cunning)

Kennon (see Brodnax)

Kennoway (see MacDuff)

Kenrick (see Macnachton)

Kenser (see Wampler)

Kent (see Douglas, Lush)

Kentfield (see Kenfield)

Kenyon (see Cunning)

Keohane
Keohane Sept
455 115th Avenue
Treasure Island, FL 33706
Phone (813) 360-1978
James Keohane

Keohe (see Cian)

Keperling (see Kimberlin)

Kephart (see Dockery, Gebhard)

Keppel (see Rhines)

Keppie (see MacDuff)

Kepple (see Rhines)

Kepple
*Kepple, Klingensmith, Staymates
Association
Jacob Nickolas and Andrew Kepple,
Peter and Philip Klingensmith, Philip
Steinmetz/Statmates Family
Association
921 Elmwood Avenue
McKeesport, PA 15133
Isabel Podolak
Pub. *Announcement*, annually, free;
(includes descendants of Nicholas
Kepple (1724–1804) and Anna Marie
Molly Williams (1736–1821) of
Herletzeheim-Bas-Rin, Germany)

Keppler
*Keppler Surname Organization
1438 Shaner Drive
Pottstown, PA 19464
Phone (215) 326-5301
C. Stanley Stubbe

Ker (see Carr, Kerr)

Kerby (see Carpenter)

Kerby
*Kerby Family Association
1640 South Chicago Avenue
Freeport, IL 61032
Phone (815) 232-8402
Janette Kerby Ayer
Annual reunion on Father's Day at Town
Hall, Glenwood, Missouri

Kerchler (see The Memorial Foundation
of the Germanna Colonies)

Kerchner
*Kerchner Surname Database
East Allen Township
5507 Louise Lane
Northampton, PA 18067-9076
Phone (610) 262-1276;
(610) 837-0700 (business)
Charles F. Kerchner, Jr.
(5,300 names in computer database, will
exchange for SASE, research reports
published on CompuServe's genealogy
forum)

Kerker (see The Memorial Foundation
of the Germanna Colonies)

Kernodle (see Ammons)

Kerns
*Kerns/Kearns/Kearnes Family
Organization
Rt. 1, Box 13
Spalding, NE 68655
Phone (308) 497-2628
C. Esch

Kerny (see Cian)

Kerr (see Folk Family Surname
Exchange, Bailey, Car, Carr, Carson)

Kerr
*Kerr Kinseeker
PO Box 1872
Dodge City, KS 67801-1872
Laura Tasset Koehn, President
(includes research on Jesse Fell Kerr and
Winifred Florence Burcher)

Kerr
Kerr Family Association
1755 Black Oaks Lane
Plymouth, MN 55447
Sally Kerr Edstrom, Secretary
(includes Carr, Carre, Karr and Ker)

Kerr
*Kerr Family Association of North
    America
1004 Lakewood Drive
PO Box 811
Monroe, NC 28110
Phone (704) 283-2985
A. H. Kerr, Jr., Genealogy Director
Pub. *The Border Line*, quarterly;
    (includes Carr, Carre, Karr and Ker,
    over 900 lines in database)
$14.00 per year associate membership

Kerr
*Descendants of Alexander Kerr
1201 Wellington Hills Circle
Salisbury, NC 28147
Phone (704) 636-7817
Hope W. Davis, Publisher
(includes family from Tyrone County,
    Northern Ireland, from the mid-1700s)

Kerr
Kerr/Carr Family Organization
Rt. 3, Box 123
Trinity, NC 27370
Cheryl Burrow

Kerrick (see Karrick)

Kerschner (see Kershner)

Kersey (see Lush)

Kershner
*Kershner Family Association
1449 Fox Run Drive
Charlotte, NC 28212
Phone (704) 535-6025
William E. Kershner, Jr., Editor
Pub. *Kershner Kinfolk*, quarterly;
    (includes Cashner, Karschner,
    Karshner, Kerschner and Kirschner)
$14.00 per year membership

Kershner
*Kershner Family Association
210 Cliff Turn
Falling Waters, WV 25419-9530
Phone (304) 274-3104
Larry D. Kump

Keryea (see Folk Family Surname
    Exchange)

Kesler (see Kessler)

Kesler
*Kesler Surname Organization
Fredrick Kesler Family Organization
4349 Falcon Street
West Valley City, UT 84120-5353
Phone (801) 969-6551
Pricilla K. Roper, Historian
(includes descendants of Frederick
    Kesler and Mary Lindsay of
    Pennsylvania)

Kesslar (see Lemon)

Kessler
Hapsburg Press
PO Box 173
Broomfield, CO 80038-0173
Barbara Inman Beall, Editor
Pub. *Kessler-Wing*, five times per year,
    $10.00 per year subscription

Kessler
*West Virginia Kessler/Kesler Family
    History Center
458 Delaware Avenue
Egg Harbor Township, NJ 08234-5906
Phone (609) 927-6014; (609) 927-5108
    FAX; E-mail: aruba@aol.com
Karen Kessler Cottrill, Historian
Pub. *Kessler Family History Quarterly
    Newsletter*, $10.00 per year
    subscription, free queries

Kessler
Kessler Reunion
5355 Donner Drive
Clinton, OH 44216
Conrad Riffle
Pub. *Kessler*, quarterly, $6.00 per year
    subscription

Kester (see Castor)

Kesterson (see Tidwell)

Ketcham (see Ketchum)

Ketcham
Ketcham(um) Kables
2133 Hermitage Drive
Davison, MI 48423
Ginger Ketchum Stork
Pub. *Ketcham(um) Kables*, quarterly,
    $6.00 per year subscription

Ketchem (see Catlow)

Ketchen (see Fergusson)

Ketchum (see Ketcham, Lunday, Reeder,
    Roades)

Ketchum
*A Gathering of Ketchum Kindred
1743 Blodgett Road
Mount Vernon, WA 98273
Phone (360) 428-0319
Janet K. Armbrust, Publisher
(includes descendants of Benjamin and
    Rhoda (Benn) Ketuchum of Decatur
    County, Indiana; also Ketcham
    spelling)

Ketering (see Kettenring)

Kettenring
Kettenring and Allied Families Reunion
6923 Cypress Road, 13-A
Plantation, FL 33317-2307
Phone (305) 587-7373
Marguerite Van Etten
(includes variant spellings: Ketering,
    Katering, Catron, Katron, etc.; allied

families: Bishop, Bohannon,
    Brashear(s), Hicks, Larkey, Marquart,
    Quillen, Rhea, Schneider, Sluss,
    Vinnirick, Wennrick, Yates, etc.)
Annual reunion

Ketter
*Ketter Family Association
1311 Candlelight Avenue
Duncanville, TX 75137-3318
Phone (214) 298-9576
Paul S. Ketter
Pub. *The Ketter Letter*, irregularly, free
    on receipt of family data; (includes
    950 Ketter, Koetter, Ketterer families,
    dating from 1550)
Reunion every five years in Pittsburgh,
    Pennsylvania

Ketterer (see Ketter)

Kettering (see Gibson)

Kettwig
*Kettwig and Grover Families
PO Box 1411
Ukiah, CA 95482
Viettia Newcomb, Publisher
(includes many descendants of Johann
    Kettwig and Eva Hammerling
    (Kammerling?), Isaac Grover and
    Delight Champlin, and Adam Scharf,
    from Germany, New York to LaSalle
    County, Illinois, Devils Lake, North
    Dakota, and California)

Keurlis (see Links Genealogy
    Publications)

Key (see Brown, Mackay)

Keyes (see Gotham)

Keyes
K(e)y(e)s Newsletter
PO Box 372205
Satellite Beach, FL 32937-0205
Maurice K. Kurtz, Jr.
Pub. *K(e)y(e)s Newsletter*, quarterly,
    $8.00 per year subscription; (includes
    Cays, Guise, Kees, Keese, Keise,
    Keyes, Keys, Kies and Kyes)

Keyes
*Seagull Productions
West 1818 Nora
Spokane, WA 99205
Phone (509) 326-6066
Nancy Cummings Smith
Pub. *Keyes to Your Past*, irregularly,
    $5.00 per issue plus $1.00 postage

Keys (see Brown, Keyes)

Keyt (see Ross)

Khol (see Cole)

Khole (see Cole)

Kib
JERLS Incorporated
PO Box 3551
Richmond, VA 23235
Pub. *Kib's Kousins Newsletter*, quarterly

Kibble (see Kebel)

Kibler (see Sullivan Surname Exchange)

Kichline
*Kichline Family Database
1301 Bradford Road
Oreland, PA 19075-2414
Phone (215) 836-4727
Dale E. Berger, Publisher

Kidd (see Fergusson)

Kidd
*Kidd Family Heritage Publication
14130 S.E. 17th, Suite C-1
Bellevue, WA 98007
Hazel Kidd Lawson, Editor
Pub. *Kidd Family Heritage*, bimonthly,
$22.00 per year subscription

Kiddie (see Fergusson)

Kidwell (see Lemon)

Kidwell
*Kidwell Family Association
2616 Janice Lane
Fort Worth, TX 76112
Phone (817) 451-2386
Billy Dan Kidwell, President
Pub. *Kidwell Family Newsletter*,
quarterly
$7.00 per year membership, annual
reunion in the summer in Ohio/
Kentucky

Kidwiler (see Lemon)

Kie (see Mackay)

Kiefer (see Keefer)

Kieffer (see Keefer, Miehls)

Kielty (see Cian)

Kiely (see Cian)

Kierstede (see Rutherford)

Kies (see Keyes)

Kiester (see Castor)

Kieth
Kieth Clan Society
464 Pinetree Drive, N.E.
Atlanta, GA 30305

Kiger (see Blossom Press)

Kiggins
*Kiggins Exchange
6437 West Arbor Drive
Littleton, CO 80123-3827
Phone (303) 795-1150
Mary Lou King

Kight
Kight Kids of NC, IN, KY
5842 Paddon Circle
San Jose, CA 95123
J. Kight Bliven

Kight
Kight
PO Box 790274
San Antonio, TX 76279-0274
Malcolm L. Kight
Pub. *Kight*, annually, free

Kilander (see Kylander)

Kilbourne (see McKee)

Kilbreath (see Galbraith)

Kilburn (see McGee)

Kilby
Kilby Family Association
Rt. 1, Box G-19
Townsend, DE 19734
D. Kilby

Kilchrist (see MacLachlan)

Kilduff
Kilduff One-name Study
3470 Vista Oaks Drive, Apartment 205
Martinez, CA 94553
Phone (510) 370-6265 FAX
Christi Carter Kilduff, President
(includes Kilduff, worldwide)

Kilgoar (see Kilgore)

Kilgore (see Folk Family Surname
Exchange, Douglas, Gibson, MacDuff)

Kilgore
*Kilgore Family Reunion
13492 Auroa Court
Magalia, CA 95954-9541
Phone (916) 873-6511
Carllene Marek
(includes descendants of George Kilgore
and Elizabeth R. Cochran)
Annual reunion on the third Sunday of
May in Sacramento, California

Kilgore
The Kilgore Clan
106 Mikel Court
Summerville, SC 29485
Doris J. O'Brien
Pub. *The Kilgore Clan*, bimonthly, $7.50
per year subscription

Kilgore
*Folk Family
PO Box 52048
Knoxville, TN 37950-2048
Hester E. Stockton, Owner; Lydia Ann
Kilgore, Editor
Pub. *Kilgore Kith 'n' Kin Newsletter*,
quarterly, $15.00 per year subscription,
$5.00 per issue; (includes Kelgore and
Kilgoar)

Kilgour (see MacDuff)

Kilian (see Kahler)

Killeen (see Cian)

Killgore
*Killgore Surname Organization
Highway 87 North
PO Box 340
Burkeville, TX 75932
Phone (409) 565-4751
Helen Rogers Skelton

Killian (see Dockery, Moser)

Killian
Andreas Killian Family Reunion
1995 Haywood Road
Hendersonville, NC 28739
Dr. W. D. Killian

Killion (see Kahler)

Killip (see Cowley)

Killough (see Kalloch)

Killough
*Killough Family Reunion Association
1335 Brighton Drive
Brighton, CO 80601
Phone (303) 659-3593
Zora Cunninghom , President
Pub. *The Killough Family in Ireland,
Canada and the United States*
$10.00 per year membership for families

Kilmaron (see MacDuff)

Kilmartin (see MacDuff)

Kilner
*Kilner Family Organization
173 Ridgeberry Drive
PO Box 601
Xenia, OH 45385
Phone (513) 372-0783; (513) 372-1698
Arthur R. Kilner, President; (513) 372-
1698 FAX

Kilpatrich (see Graham)

Kilpatrick (see Colquhoun, Douglas,
Kirkpatrick)

Kilts
*The Kilts Family Association
141 Hudson Avenue
Chatham, NY 12037
Phone (518) 392-4544
Herman W. Witthoft, Sr., Publisher
Pub. *Kilts Family Association*, annually
Donation for membership

Kilty (see Reardon)

Kimball (see Powers)

Kimball
Kimball Family Association of Northern
  California
1535 El Cerito Drive
Red Bluff, CA 96080
Elsie Faiman

Kimball
*Kimball Family Association
14 Manson Road
Kittery, ME 03904-5534
Phone (207) 439-2747
Judith A. Kimball, Newsletter Editor;
  George H. Kimball, Jr., Researcher
Pub. *Connections: Kimball Family
  Association Newsletter*, quarterly
  (February, May, August and
  November)
$7.50 per year membership for
  individuals, $10.00 per year
  membership for families

Kimball
*Heber Chase Kimball Family
  Organization
1387 Emery Street
Salt Lake City, UT 84104
Phone (801) 972-2341
Patricia M. Geisler, Chairman
  Genealogical and Historical
  Committee
Pub. *Heber C. Kimball Family News*,
  semiannually, no charge; (includes
  much ancestry of Heber's wife, Vilate
  Murray)

Kimberlein (see Kimberlin)

Kimberlin
The Kimberlin Kobold
7854 Goll Avenue
North Hollywood, CA 91605
Lillian Kimberlin
Pub. *The Kimberlin Kobold*, annually
  (November), $3.00 per year
  subscription; (includes Gamberlen,
  Kammerlich, Kemmerlein,
  Kemperling, Keperling, Kimberlein,
  Kimberlin, Kimerling, Kimmerlin,
  etc.)

Kimberline (see Haynes)

Kimble (see Kemble)

Kimble
*Kimble Family Association
7149 Sutton Drive
Everson, WA 98247
Neil Bancroft
Pub. *Kimble Pursuit*

Kimbro
*Kimbro/Kimbrough Genealogical
  Quarterly*
449 Brockwood Drive
Auburn, AL 36830
Mr. Kimbro
Pub. *Kimbro/Kimbrough Genealogical
  Quarterly*, $6.00 per year subscription

Kimbrough (see Kimbro)

Kimerling (see Kimberlin)

Kimes
Kimes Family Association
12 East 79th Terrace
Kansas City, MO 64114
C. Felten

Kimmel
Kimmel Family Newsletter
325 West Hickam Drive
Columbia, MO 65203
Phone (314) 442-1498
Janice Tompkins, Editor
Pub. *Kimmel Family Newsletter*, two or
  three times per year, $5.00 per year
  subscription; (includes descendants of
  David and Leah Reigel Kimmel and
  related families)
Annual reunion in June

Kimmel
Kimmel/Reeder Family Association
7020 Norma Street
Fort Worth, TX 76112
G. Boney

Kimmerlin (see Kimberlin)

Kincaid
Data Unlimited
4941 Syracuse Drive
Oxnard, CA 93033
Jeanne Hicks, Researcher

Kincaid
Kincaid Clan U.S.A.
3302 Jewell Street
San Diego, CA 92109
Phone (619) 273-7245
Steve Kincaid, President
Pub. *Kincaid Letter, International*,
  quarterly
$10.00 per year membership

Kincaid
*Clan Kincaid
2864 Baylis Court
Ann Arbor, MI 48108-1706
Phone (313) 973-1828 (home)
William H. Kincaid, Clan Secretary
Pub. *The Defender*, quarterly

$10.00 per year membership, $110.00
  life membership

Kindel
*William Kindel Family Organization
111 Shelley Court
Folsom, CA 95630
Phone (916) 985-3179; (916) 985-7972
Fred Kindel
(computer database includes 12,000
  Kindel, Kendall, etc., connections,
  including William Kindel (1783–
  1865), who was married in 1800 in
  Tennessee to Elizabeth Webb (1783
  Tennessee–) of Virginia, Kentucky,
  Tennessee, Mississippi and Arkansas)

Kineardune (see MacDuff)

Kines (see The Memorial Foundation of
  the Germanna Colonies)

King (see CTC Family Association, Folk
  Family Surname Exchange, Armstrong,
  Christopher, DuBois, Frantz, Gregor,
  Hay, Wise)

King
King
6180 Merrywood Drive
Rocklin, CA 95677-3421
Kathleen Stewart
Pub. *King*, quarterly (February, May,
  August and November), $12.00 per
  year subscription

King
*Wallace A. King Family Organization
PO Box 41101
Sacramento, CA 95841
Phone (916) 722-9085
Joan Wadsworth

King
King Family Association
2011 Tam Court
Simi Valley, CA 93063
Phone (805) 584-0860
Amelya Sandt

King
King Family Reunion
Rt. 1, Box 83 B-1
Gaston, SC 29053
Eula Mae Ellis
(includes descendants of Joshua King
  and Barbara Jeffcoat)

King
Partin Publications
230 Wedgewood
Nacogdoches, TX 75961-5326
Pub. *King*, quarterly, $15.00 per year
  subscription

King
*Thomas Jefferson King Family
  Organization
1774 Country Club Drive
Logan, UT 84321

Phone (801) 753-6924
Joyce Elfrena Kalanquin

King
King Kin
323 Cedarcrest Court East
PO Box 779
Napavine, WA 98565-0779
Phone (360) 262-3300
Ruby Simonson McNeill
Pub. *King Kin*, irregularly, $5.75 plus
    $2.00 postage per issue

King
The King Quarterly
1602 East Beech
Yakima, WA 98907
Lou Pero
Pub. *The King Quarterly*, $20.00 per year
    subscription

Kinghorn (see MacDuff)

Kingsbury (see Wigelius)

Kingsley (see Corson, Nelson)

Kinkaid (see Buchanan)

Kinkella (see Blossom Press)

Kinloch (see MacDuff)

Kinlough (see MacDuff)

Kinnaman (see MacDuff)

Kinneally (see Cian)

Kinnear (see MacDuff)

Kinney
*Kinney-Furrow Reunion
PO Box 472
Potomac, IL 61865
Phone (217) 987-6555
Betty J. Kinney, Secretary-Treasurer
(includes descendants of Harvy Kinney
    (1821–1900) and Eliza Jane Furrow
    (1826–1901), who were married in
    1843 in Madison County, Ohio, and
    came to Pilot Township, Vermilion
    County, Illinois, in 1844)
Reunion

Kinney
*Mary Ellen Kinney Family
    Organization
8810 Lagrima de Oro Road, N.E.
Albuquerque, NM 87111
Phone (505) 298-5050
Frederick Wilhelm Haury, Jr.
(includes allied families of Schaff, Finck,
    Wohlgemuth and Schmidt)

Kinney
Kinney Family
PO Box 137
Wasco, OR 97065
Nancy Lanni

Kinning (see Cunning)

Kinninmonth (see MacDuff)

Kinnison (see Cunning)

Kinnoull (see Hay)

Kinross (see MacDuff)

Kinsey
*Kinsey Clearinghouse
775 South 13 Avenue
Brighton, CO 80601
Phone (303) 659-6308
Judy Kinsey Brooks
Pub. *Kinsey's On the Move* (K.O.T.M.),
    quarterly (April, July, October and
    January)
$8.50 per year membership

Kinsey
Kinsey-Coskrey
803 South Buckeye Avenue
Abilene, KS 67410-3211
Cathy Wood
Pub. *Kinsey-Coskrey*, quarterly, $8.00 per
    year subscription
Annual reunion on the first Sunday of
    August

Kinsland
Kinsland Family Newsletter
PO Box 533
Candler, NC 28715
Phone (704) 667-2704
Jean Pressley Warren
Pub. *Kinsland Family Newsletter*,
    bimonthly, $10.00 per year
    subscription; (includes descendants of
    John and Rebecca Simmons Kinsland
    of Haywood County, North Carolina)
Reunion

Kinsman (see Hay)

Kintigh
*Kintigh Family
1011 East Chestnut Avenue
Orange, CA 92667-3830
Phone (714) 637-4250
Dorothy Kintigh Sidfrid
(includes descendants of Alexander and
    Agnes (Moreland) Stewart)

Kinzie (see Frantz)

Kipp (see Engelmann)

Kipp
Kipp Family Organization
Rt. 1, Box 230
Calmar, IA 52132
G. Holthaus

Kiracoff (see Kirshop)

Kirby (see Folk Family Surname
    Exchange, Cummings)

Kirchen (see Hughes)

Kircher
Stammbaum der Familie Kircher
(4817 Hollyview Drive, Vermilion, OH
    44089—location after 1998)
Pfingstweid Strasse 8-B (mailing
    address)
D-6382 Friedrichsdorf 1
Germany
Robert H. Kircher, P.E.
(databank of more than 10,000 Kircher
    families, worldwide from 1306, very
    few born in the U.S. after 1910, no
    spelling variations)

Kirchner (see Buechele)

Kirk (see Hess, Kirkpatrick, Maxwell,
    Nettles)

Kirk
Sampson Kirk and Sarah Sims Family
    Organization
2905 North Kilbourne
East Chicago, IL 60647
June B. Barekman

Kirkaldie (see MacDuff)

Kirkaldy (see MacDuff)

Kirkendale (see Kuykendall)

Kirkham
Kirkham Family Newsletter
405 Cockletown Road
Grafton, VA 23692
Phone (804) 898-5692
Steve Kirkham
Pub. *Kirkham Family Newsletter*, eight
    times a year, $6.00 per year
    subscription

Kirkkaldie (see MacDuff)

Kirkkaldy (see MacDuff)

Kirkland (see Douglas, Maxwell)

Kirkpatrick (see Banks, Colquhoun,
    Davis, Douglas, Gregor)

Kirkpatrick
Kirkpatrick Family Association
492 Glen Street
Glens Falls, NY 12801
Phone (518) 793-2900
Harold Kirkpatrick, M.D., Secretary

Kirkpatrick
*Kirkpatrick Association
PO Box 322
North Syracuse, NY 13212-0322
Phone (315) 458-2263
George M. Kirkpatrick
Pub. *Kirkpatrick Newsletter*, quarterly;
    (includes Gilpatrick, Kilpatrick and
    Kirk)

$8.00 per year sustaining membership, $12.00 per year contributing membership

Kirkwood (see Gregor, Hewitt)

Kirkwood
Kirkwood Newsletter
6180 Merrywood Drive
Rocklin, CA 95677-3421
Kathleen Stewart
Pub. *Kirkwood Newsletter*, quarterly (February, May, August and November), $12.00 per year subscription

Kiron (see Waterous)

Kirschner (see Kershner)

Kirshop
Kirshop/Caracoff/Caricoff/Karacoff/ Kiracoff Family Reunion
Bridgewater Home
Bridgewater, VA 22812
L. Miller

Kiser (see Links Genealogy Publications)

Kiser
Kiser Family Clearinghouse
77 Hollow Road
Quarryville, PA 17566-9491
Harry Hoffman

Kissinger
Kissinger Konnection
North 629 Hilly Road
Merrill, WI 54452
Patti Laessig Zimmerman
Pub. *Kissinger Konnection*

Kistard (see Castor)

Kister (see Castor)

Kistler
*Kistler Family Association (PA)
9437 North 37th Avenue
Phoenix, AZ 85051
Phone (602) 973-5622
Melvin Persons

Kistner
*The Kistner Family
2709 S.E. Taylor, #6
Portland, OR 97214-2971
Elaine Smith
(from the 1700s–present)
LSASE

Kitch (see Wert)

Kitch
Kitch Travelling Notebook
26723 Fairfax Lane
North Olmstead, OH 44070
J. Workman

Kitchel (see Pierson)

Kitchen (see Lynch)

Kitson (see Catlow, Reynolds)

Kittle
Kittle Family Association
PO Box 221
Jefferson, OH 44047-0221
Geraldine Kittle

Kittler (see Surname Sources)

Kivasen (see Crusan)

Kives
*Alexander Kives Family Organization
658 Colonial Club Drive
Harahan, LA 70123
Phone (504) 737-5480
Julius J. Kives

Kizer (see Pack)

Kjærulf
*Anders Kjærulf Family Assocation
358 South Bentley Avenue
Los Angeles, CA 90049
Phone (310) 472-9206
Cap T. Kierulff
Pub. *Kjierulf Family Assocation* (includes database containing 10,000 Kjærulfs from 1450, Denmark)
Reunion every four years in various locations

Klapp
*Pennsylvania-German Klapp/Clapp Family
107 West Sunhill Road
Manheim, PA 17545
Phone (717) 665-5869
D. Ernest Weinhold
(especially descendants of the very early immigrants who settled in northeast Lancaster County, Pennsylvania, and nearby areas)

Klee
Hapsburg Press
PO Box 173
Broomfield, CO 80038-0173
Barbara Inman Beall, Editor
Pub. *Klee*, five times per year, $10.00 per year subscription

Klein (see Moser, Stoner, Wiese)

Kleinfelter (see Kunkel)

Klemitz (see Clamage)

Klemm (see Grant)

Klewer
Missing Links
Rt. 4, Box 184
Saint Maries, ID 83861
Pub. *Klewer News (Allied Schilling/ Boelke/Carlson)*

Klimist (see Clamage)

Kline (see Eisenhauer)

Klinefelter
*Klinefelter Family
PO Box 333
Colona, IL 61241-0333
Phone (309) 792-4579
Norma J. Ogburn

Klingensmith (see Kepple)

Klinger
The Klingers, From the Odenwald, Hesse, Germany, ca 1610–1989
RD 3, Box 307
Stewartstown, PA 17363
Phone (717) 993-6094
Mary Ann Tschopp

Klingle (see Anthes)

Klingman (see Nichols)

Klinken (see Links Genealogy Publications)

Klock (see Smith)

Kloepfer
*George Kloepfer Family Organization
1152 North Forest
Mesa, AZ 85203
Phone (602) 969-0112
R. Duane Nelson

Kloniger (see Cloniger)

Klos (see Mohr)

Klosterman (see Links Genealogy Publications)

Klotzkin (see Israelite)

Klug (see The Memorial Foundation of the Germanna Colonies)

Knapp (see Allen)

Knarr
*Knarr-Knerr-Knorr Family Association
7657 Squirrel Creek Drive
Cincinnati, OH 45247
Larry Knarr, Editor
Pub. *Knarr, Knerr, Knorr Family Newsletter*, bimonthly
$7.50 per year membership

Knauer (see Surname Database)

Knauss (see Surname Database)

Knebel
Knebel Family Reunion
184 Crescent Drive
Granbury, TX 76048
Robert M. Knebel

Knecht (see Knight)

Knechtel
*Knechtel Family
1009 Burlington Beach Road
Valparaiso, IN 46383
Phone (219) 462-6661
Armida Sharpin

Kneisler (see The Memorial Foundation of the Germanna Colonies)

Kneland (see MacLennan)

Knell (see McCune)

Kniffen
*The Grapevine
PO Box 124
Red Bank, NJ 07701-0124
Phone (908) 741-9460;
  (908) 530-2065 FAX
Paul and Joanne Sniffen
Pub. *The Grapevine*, semiannually (spring and fall), postage only for subscription; (includes Kniffen, Sniffen)
Reunion being planned

Knight (see Cian, Cook, Holden, Newton, Night)

Knight
*Knight Match-Up
415 Caicos Drive
Punta Gorda, FL 33950
Betsey Lambert

Knight
Knight Family Association
Jacob Knight Family Reunion
701 Parkview
New Iberia, LA 70560
Terrence Knight Benoit

Knight
*Knight Line
4425 Tustin Court
Bridgeton, MO 63044-1752
Phone (314) 291-7233
Gene D. Knight, Family Historian
Pub. *Knight Line*, quarterly; donation for subscription; (includes descendants of Nathan Kinsman Knight)
Annual reunion

Kniskern (see Emery)

Knoles (see Knowles)

Knott
Knott Ancestors
3490 Brentwood
Beaumont, TX 77706
L. Sanders

Knowles
Knowles-Knoles Family Association
227 Redbud #8
New Braunfels, TX 78130
Joan G. Knowles

Knowles
Knowles
11818 Rockaway Lane
Fairfax, VA 22030
Bob Knowles
Pub. *Knowles*, quarterly, $12.50 per year subscription

Knox
*Just Knox
36 Mustang Road
PO Box 2007
Edgewood, NM 87015
Phone (505) 281-0094 (phone or FAX)
Mary Knox Boles, Researcher
(includes database on descendants of David Knox (1700 County Antrim, Ireland–), Andrew Knox (1728 County Antrim, Ireland–1807) and Isabella White (1731 Philadelphia, Pennsylvania–))

Knuth (see Sager)

Kobascza (see McCallus)

Kobel (see Coble, Kebel)

Köbel (see Coble)

Kobell (see Coble)

Kobelt (see Coble)

Kober (see Aldrich)

Koble (see Coble)

Kobloth (see Edler)

Kobs (see Seefeld)

Koch (see Clark, Goodenow, Reedy)

Koch
Koch Reunion (Wilhelm Koch Descendants)
2613 South Newton Street
Sioux City, IA 51106-3412
J. Winn

Kocher (see Oney)

Kochy
Kochy
Whispering Oaks
5821 Rowland Hill Road
Cascade, MD 21719-1939
Phone (301) 416-2660
Victor Gebhart, President
Pub. *Kochy*, annually, $2.00 per issue

Kock (see Brehm)

Koder (see Coder)

Koebel (see Coble)

Koehn
*Koehn Kindred
PO Box 1872
Dodge City, KS 67801-1872
Laura Tasset Koehn, President
(includes research on Henry B. Koehn and Elizabeth Becker family; Cornelius T. Koehn and Mary Schmidt family)

Koelsch
*Ludwig Koelsch Family Organization
6775 West Rose Canyon Road
Herriman, UT 84065
Phone (801) 254-4629
Sallee Jessop, President

Köenig (see Rebele)

Koester (see Castor)

Koeth
*Koeth-Kate Family
804 60th Street
West Des Moines, IA 50266
Phone (515) 225-1553
Rev. Josephine A. Barnes

Koetter (see Ketter)

Kofel (see Coble)

Koheck (see Coppock)

Koheim (see Kohlheim)

Kohl (see Surname Database)

Kohleim (see Kohlheim)

Kohlenberger
Kohlenberger Family Reunion
210 West White Street
Millstadt, IL 62260
H. Kohlenberger

Kohlhagen
*Kohlhagen Family Genealogy
5 Anderson Court
West Bay Shore, Long Island, NY 11706-7701
Phone (516) 665-7693; E-mail: SUE12632@aol.com
Sue Gardner Shreve, Publisher and Compiler

Kohlmeier
*Kohlmeier Surname Organization
Caroline Dorothea Kohlmeier Family Organization
12 Bonnievale Drive
Bedford, MA 01730
Jim Eggert

Kokkonen
*Kokkonen Family Association
14677 80th Avenue
Evart, MI 49631
John Kokkonen

Pub. *Midsummer Fire*, annually
(December), SASE for sample issue,
no charge for anyone named
Kokkonen

Kolbach (see Coble)

Kole (see Cole)

Kolhoff (see Miehls)

Koll
*Koll/Call Research
5510 West Pershing Avenue
Glendale, AZ 85304
Phone (602) 978-9309
Lee T. Andersen
(includes descendants of Louis Koll and
Isabella Call who were married ca
1867 in Urbana, Champaign County,
Illinois)
No cost

Kollock (see Wiltbank)

Konkel (see Kunkel)

Koolbaugh (see Coble)

Koontz (see The Memorial Foundation
of the Germanna Colonies, Coons)

Kooper (see The Memorial Foundation
of the Germanna Colonies)

Kopal (see Coble)

Kopp (see Ammons)

Kopple (see Coble)

Korbel (see Coble)

Koriel (see Coryell)

Korn (see Clowes)

Kostenbader (see Surname Database)

Koster (see Castor, Custer)

Kothe
Kothe Foundation
12534 S.E. 134
Oklahoma City, OK 73165
Teresa M. Reif, Editor
Pub. *Kothe Foundation Newsletter*,
biannually

Kotherman (see Kattermann)

Kotron (see Gibson)

Kotterman (see Kattermann)

Kouchel (see Israelite)

Koval (see Coble)

Kraemer (see Rothenberger)

Krail (see MacDuff)

Krane (see Crane)

Krause (see Crouse)

Kreachbaum (see Kriegbaum)

Kregal
Kregal/Willenbrock/Willenbrook Family
of Hanover, Germany
Garnaville, IA 52049
Ken Johnson

Kreis (see Crist)

Krenelka
*Ernst Krenelka Family Organization
2011 18th Street, South
Moorhead, MN 56560
Phone (218) 233-1606
Dale D. White

Kresge (see Surname Database)

Kresge
*Kresge Family Reunion
444 Roosevelt Avenue
Glendora, NJ 08029
Phone (609) 939-1890
Atwood James Shupp, Historian
Annual reunion on the third Saturday of
August at West End Fairgrounds, off
Route 209, Gilbert, Pennsylvania

Kress (see Crist)

Kress
*Pennsylvania-German Kress/Gress
Family
107 West Sunhill Road
Manheim, PA 17545
Phone (717) 665-5869
D. Ernest Weinhold
(especially descendants of the very early
immigrants who settled in northeast
Lancaster County, Pennsylvania, and
nearby areas)

Kretzmeier (see Herd)

Krick
*The Krick-Keller Families
983 Venus Way
Livermore, CA 94550-6345
Phone (510) 455-5059; E-mail:
enokh@aol.com
Enoch Haga, Publisher
(includes families originating in
Rheinland-Pfalz (Kaiserslautern) areas
of Germany and in the Alsace
(Mulhouse) area of France, with
descendants in Germany, France and
the U.S.)

Kriebel (see The Memorial Foundation
of the Germanna Colonies)

Kriegbaum
Kriegbaum Heritage
1112 Monroe
Quincy, IL 62301
Carol Krigbaum
Pub. *Kriegbaum Heritage*, quarterly,
$8.00 per year subscription; (includes
Crickbaum, Kreachbaum and
Krigbaum)

Krigbaum (see Kriegbaum)

Krill (see Grill)

Krille (see Pessner)

Kroetch
Kroet(s)ch Family Association
143 Crest Drive
Ephrata, WA 98823
J. Klassen

Kroetsch (see Kroetch)

Kroh (see Crowl)

Kroll (see Crowl)

Krom
*Krom/Wood Family History
35 Robinwood Road
Trumball, CT 06611
Phone (203) 375-1796
Robert Wood

Kromer (see Surname Database)

Krompel
*Krompel-Krampel-Krimpel Surname
Organization
Ludvik Krompel Family Organization
33516 170 Avenue, S.E.
Auburn, WA 98092
Phone (206) 833-7229
Mary H. Smith

Kron (see Cronn)

Krueger (see Sager)

Kruger (see Wright)

Kubel (see Kebel)

Kuenzle (see The Memorial Foundation
of the Germanna Colonies)

Kuester (see Castor)

Kuhlman (see Dietwiler)

Kuhlman
Kuhlman Family Organization
43 S.E. Elliott
Gresham, OR 97030
R. Shupp

Kuhner (see Keener)

Kump
*Kump Klan
210 Cliff Turn
Falling Waters, WV 25419-9530
Phone (304) 274-3104
Larry D. Kump

Kunchel (see Kunkel)

Kunders (see Links Genealogy
Publications)

Kundrat (see Waterous)

Kunkel (see Armbruster)

Kunkel
*Kunkel Database
19834 Squire Drive
Covina, CA 91724-3457
Phone (818) 915-1378
Janet H. Reinhold, Editor
Pub. *The Kunkel-Kunkle-Conkle-Gunkel
Spindle Family Newsletter*, quarterly,
$12.00 per year subscription; (includes
Conkle, Gunckel, Gunkel, Konkel,
Kunkel, Kunkelmann, Kunkle and
Kunkler)

Kunkel
*Our Kunkel Family in America
Genealogical Headquarters
16 Brookside Avenue
Hackettstown, NJ 07840
Phone (201) 852-9199; E-mail:
wescorp@eclipse.net; Website: http://
www.maracorp.com/sawdust
Wallace M. Kunkel, Coordinator
(includes descendants of Huynerich
Kunchel I of Shrewsbury Township,
York County, Pennsylvania, a Hessian
soldier from Flörsbach, Prussia (now
Germany), captured by George
Washington at Trenton, and related
families (1650–1800): Hise, Ickus,
Imfeld, Kleinfelter, Schuster,
Steigerwald, Sunday, Sutten, (1750–
1800): Acton, Campbell, Davis,
Dorwin, Finical, Keeney, Meyers,
Myer, Norman, Peterson, Pierce,
Robinson, Rostock, Way, Whipple,
(1850–1900): Acheson, Christenson,
Cochran, Cole, Comer, Cooksey,
Eckhart, Edwards, Hannah, Hardman,
Hare, Hasness, Heller, Hood, Jamison,
Jimison, Johnson, Loucks, Market,
Martin, McCann, Plamann, Prather,
Proud, Reedy, Rush, Schlotzhauer,
Stephenson, Vogan, Watson; also forty
early Kunkel (Kunkle/Gunkel/Conkle)
families from 1620 (Germany) to Civil
War period only)
$10.00 minimum charge for search and
printout, no queries considered without
SASE

Kunkelmann (see Kunkel)

Kunkle (see Kunkel)

Kunkler (see Kunkel)

Kuntz (see Coons)

Kuntzmann (see Drone)

Kunz (see Bodine)

Kupper (see Cooper)

Kurlis (see Links Genealogy
Publications)

Kurtz (see Helmer)

Kustard (see Castor)

Kuster (see Links Genealogy
Publications, Castor)

Kusterd (see Castor)

Kuykendall
Kuykendall Newsletter
PO Box 1871
Lake Placid, FL 33852
S. Kirkendale
Pub. *Kuykendall Newsletter (Kirkendale,
etc.)*

Kwapis
*Kwapis(z) Surname Exchange
570 East Main Street
Gaylord, MI 49735
Phone (517) 732-6035
M. J. Luzenski, Publisher

Kwapisz (see Kwapis)

Kwiram (see Quiram)

Kwirant (see Quiram)

Kyburz
Kyburz Newsletter
132 Edmund Street
Royal Oak, MI 48073
Carl E. Kyburz
Pub. *Kyburz Newsletter*, semiannually,
$2.00 per year subscription

Kydd (see Fergusson)

Kyes (see Keyes)

Kylander
*Kylander/Kilander Gatherings
838 West Outer Drive
Oak Ridge, TN 37830
Phone (423) 483-3805
Joyce K. Maienschein, Records Secretary
Pub. *Kylander, Kilander/Callendar
Families of America Newsletter*,
biannually; (includes descendants of
Philip Ki/Kylander, Revolutionary War
Soldier)
$5.00 per year membership

Kyle
*Kyle/Lawrence Family Organization
1132 North Tela Drive
Oklahoma City, OK 73127-4308
Phone (405) 789-2842
Pauline Carlton Fletcher, Secretary and
Genealogist
(computer database uses Quinsept™,
PAF™ and Reunion™)
Annual reunion

Kyner (see The Memorial Foundation of
the Germanna Colonies)

Kynnimond (see MacDuff)

Kynoch (see Donnachaidh)

Kyser (see Links Genealogy
Publications)

Laar (see Lair)

Labelle
*Labelle Surname Database
13442 93rd Avenue, North
Maple Grove, MN 55369-9740
Phone (612) 494-6694
Sherry Constans-Kaiserlik

Labonville (see De Bonville)

Laborde (see Johnson)

Labourg (see Johnson)

Labouteaux (see Wimmer)

La Breit (see Widrick)

Lacey (see DeLacy)

Lachie (see MacLachlan)

Lachlainn (see MacLachlan)

Lachlan (see MacLachlan)

Lachlann (see MacLachlan)

Lachlanson (see MacLachlan)

Lachley (see Lashlee)

Lachlieson (see MacLachlan)

LaChute (see Blossom Press)

Lachy (see MacLachlan)

Lackey (see Parker)

Lackey
*Lackey Family Association
1316 Mosslake Drive
Desoto, TX 75115
Phone (214) 383-8824
Sue or Lynn Lackey, Secretary-Treasurer
Pub. *Newsletter*, irregularly; (includes
Lackey, any spelling)
$10.00 per year membership

LaCombe (see Johnson)

Lacour (see Johnson)

Lacy (see DeLacyPye)

Lacy
*Lacy Family Organization
171 Main Street
Newington, CT 06111
Phone (203) 666-9566
John F. Bolles, III
(includes descendants of Joseph Jerome
    Lacy (–1842) and Anna Osborn of
    Trumbull, Connecticut)

Lacy
Lacy Genealogist Newsletter
1040 Druid Drive
Maitland, FL 32751
Lee Lacy
Pub. *Lacy Genealogist Newsletter*

Ladd (see Warren)

Ladd
Ladd Leads
12600 Bissonnet A4-407
Houston, TX 77099
Dede D. Mercer, Publisher
Pub. *Ladd Leads*, semiannually, $20.00
    per year subscription; (all variations of
    the surname, worldwide)

Laë (see Blossom Press)

Laessig
Laessig Letter
North 629 Hilly Road
Merrill, WI 54452
Patti Laessig Zimmerman
Pub. *Laessig Letter*

La Farge (see Franciscus)

LaFlamme
*LaFlamme Family History Association
4065 Berrywood Drive
Eugene, OR 97404-4061
James R. Brann, Family Representative
(PAF™ data bank on MAC™ computer
    includes Quebec to Maine)
Free information exchange

Laflan (see MacLachlan)

Laflen (see MacLachlan)

Lafleur (see Johnson)

Laflin (see MacLachlan)

Lafond (see Lagesse)

Lafrance (see Blossom Press)

La Freddo
La Freddo Genealogical Exchange
6004 S.W. Second Street
Des Moines, IA 50315
Robert LaFreddo

Lagan (see MacLennan)

Lagerstedt
*Lagerstedt Surname Collection
34151 N.E. Electric Road
Corvallis, OR 97333
Phone E-mail: lagersth@ucs.orst.edu
Bert Harry Lagerstedt
(includes large collection of information
    on Lagerstedt descendants from
    Sweden and the U.S.)

Lagess (see Lagesse)

La Gess (see Lagesse)

Lagesse
*Lagesse Family Association
PO Box 45
Turton, SD 57477
Phone (605) 897-6528
Richard L. Barrie, Historian
(includes Dagert, Dages, Dagesse,
    Dagest, Dajes, Dajesse, La Gess,
    Lagesse, La Jess, Lajesse, Larges,
    Largess, descendants of Jean Dagert-
    Dagesse-Lagesse, 1640s)

Lagesse
Lagesse-Dagesse Family Association
104 Begonia
Lake Jackson, TX 77566
Phone (409) 297-7367
Laura LaGess
Pub. *Lagesse/Lagess/Lajess/Larges
    Newsletter*, occasionally, donation for
    subscription; (includes descendants of
    Jean Dagesse and Marie Anne
    Drouillard; associated names: Barrie,
    Beauvois, Berthiaume, Bescharde,
    Collette, Dumas, Dye, Fortin,
    Greenwood, Houle, Lafond, Mannie,
    Nolin, Paradis, Robidoux, Regnier,
    Roy, Simoneau and Viau)

Laggan (see MacLennan)

LaHaye (see Johnson)

Lahaye
*Lahaye/Lepele Family History
    Association
4065 Berrywood Drive
Eugene, OR 97404-4061
James R. Brann, Family Representative
(PAF™ data bank on MAC™ computer
    includes Quebec to Maine)
Free information exchange

Lahey
*Lahey-Grumman-Williamson-Brocher-
    Weber Families of Chippewa,
    Manitowoc, and Sheboygan Counties,
    Wisconsin
801 Sequoia Avenue
Millbrae, CA 94030
Phone (415) 697-9410
Thomas M. Brocher, Historian
(includes descendants of John Lahey
    (ca 1808–after 1880) and Ellen

Conghlan (ca 1813–after 1880) of
    Ireland, Stow, Massachusetts, and Two
    Creeks, Manitowoc County,
    Wisconsin; Johann Grumann (1803–
    1847) and Elizabeth Heckel (ca 1807–
    1855) of Polnisch Wette and
    Markesdorf, Schlesien, Prussia;
    William Williamson (1782–1872) and
    Catherine Morrison (ca 1784–1876) of
    Delting and Gardie, Weisdale,
    Shetland, Scotland; Hans Henrich
    Brocher (1829–1870) of Rethwischer
    Dorf, Holstein, Germany, and Viborg,
    Denmark; Johann Weber (ca 1792–
    1855) and Anna Maria Zehren (ca
    1792–1867) of Butzdorf/Tettingen,
    Krs. Saarburg, Rhineland-Palatinate)

Laikie (see Gregor)

Lain (see Ammons, Gillean, Lane)

Laing (see Colquhoun, MacDuff)

Laing
*The Laing Family
327 Duke Road, #3
Lexington, KY 40502
Azuba R. Ward, Publisher
(includes descendants of John Laing of
    Saratoga County, New York; Thomas
    Laing of Cambridge, Washington
    County, New York; and their nephew,
    James Runciman, all emigrants from
    Langholm, Dumfriesshire, Scotland)

Lair
*Lair, Crays(e), Tosh Families of
    Macoupin Co., IL Family Association
28253 Stillwater Drive
Menifee, CA 92584
Phone (909) 672-9488
Linda R. Freelove Arnold
(includes descendants of Charles Lair
    and Nancy, who came to Macoupin
    County, Illinois, ca 1818–1823;
    William Herrin Crayse and Elizabeth
    Jane Lawson, who came to Macoupin
    County ca 1830; William Tosh and
    Sarah, who came to Macoupin County
    ca 1830)

Lair
Lair Linkage
19400 Glencannon Way
Monument, CO 80132
Phone (719) 481-4635
Valerie L. Lair, Editor-Publisher
Pub. *Lair Linkage (Lair Family
    Newsletter)*, quarterly (March, June,
    September and December), $5.00 per
    year subscription, no queries accepted;
    (includes descendants of Jacob Leher/
    Laar/Lair and Catherine Cratser/
    Crotzer)

Laix (see Likes)

Lajess (see Lagesse)

La Jess (see Lagesse)

Lajesse (see Lagesse)

Lake
*DCF, Inc.
14623 North 49th Place
Scottsdale, AZ 85254-2207
Phone (602) 953-1392
Janna Bennington Larson
Pub. *Lake/Leake Newsletter*, quarterly,
$10.00 per year subscription

Lake
Lake Reunion
103 Balsam Street
Fort Morgan, CO 80701
Herman Keller

Lakins (see Folk Family Surname
Exchange)

Lam
Lam Family Association
1548 Luzerne Street
Reading, PA 19601
Sterling Lamm

Lamann (see Crispell)

Lamb (see Rothenberger)

Lamb
*Generations
2983 Bayside Court
Wantagh, NY 11793
Stephen A. Lamb, Editor/Publisher
Pub. *Lamb's Pastures*, biannually, $20.00
for four issues

Lamb
*Moses Lamb (b. 1793) Family
16934 N.E. 131st Place
Redmond, WA 98052
Phone (206) 881-1785
Mrs. S. Lamb Davis
No cost

Lambert (see Appler, Clark, Likes,
MacDuff, Osborn, Ross, White,
Wright)

Lambert
*Lambert Surname Organization
Philip Lambert Family Organization
6005 West Indianola Avenue
Phoenix, AZ 85033
Phone (602) 846-1544
Watha Lambert

Lambert
*Lambert Family Association
PO Box 64007
Sunnyvale, CA 94088-4007
Randy D. Lambert, Editor and Compiler
Pub. *Lambert/Lamberth Family
Association Newsletter*, semiannually
(January and June)
$10.00 one-time membership fee, $6.00
per year membership renewal

Lambert
*History of the Lambert Family from
Jugenheim in Rheinhessen
5200 Brittany Drive, South, #208
Saint Petersburg, FL 33715-1513
Phone (813) 867-4959
Christene L. Bertram, Author
(includes descendants of Christopher
Lambert (1725 Jugenheim–), son of
Philipp Lampert and Anna Martha
Koenigsmann, arrived in Philadelphia
1749, settled in Winchester, Virginia,
about 1753; related families:
Astheimer, Baker/Becker, Bartlet,
Bertram, Baumgardner, Beydler/
Beidler, Black, Byrd, Diel/Diehl,
Elliott, Garretson, Gibson, Gorrell,
Grabill/Creabill, Hall, Harrow,
Hatfield, Hennen, Hissem, Hughes,
Isbell, Jackson, Larrick, Lowther, Lyle,
Lynch, Mahaney, Maul, Maurer,
Maxwell, Moore, Morris, Morrow,
Mumford, Myers, Noel/Nohl,
Northcraft, Rehlich, Sivey, Smith,
Sonner, Sutphin, Troisi, Trout/Traut,
Walden, Watts, Wendel/Windle, Wenz,
Whitmore, Woofter and Yager/Yeager)

Lamberth (see Lambert)

Lamberton (see Clark)

Lambeth
*Lambeth Family
13319 Belfield Drive
Farmers Branch, TX 75234
Phone (214) 243-5444
Lee D. Lambeth, Executive Director;
A. Jo Lambeth
(includes Lambeth from ca 1690 to the
present, Meredith same dates, of
Virginia, Texas and the South, also
Bernard and Clay)

Lamer (see Lehmer)

Lamkin (see Lampkin)

Lamont (see Gregory)

Lamont
Clan Lamont Society of North America
4121 Bannister Road
Fair Oaks, CA 95628-6914
Daryl J. Turner, Secretary
Pub. *The Lamont Harp*

Lamont
Lamont Clan Society
PO Box 116
Southern Pines, NC 28387
Phone (919) 692-4900; (919) 692-8722
Lamont Brown, Past President
(includes McLauchlin)

La Montagne (see De la Montagne)

Lamoreaux
*D. Tenney Lamoreux Genealogical
Organization
PO Box 301
Gilbert, AZ 85234
Phone (602) 963-9329
Isabelle Lamoreaux H. Cluff
(Lamoreaux/Lamoureux family,
descendants of Joshua Lamoureux
(1739–1830) and Elizabeth Ogden
(1738–?) of New York, New
Brunswick and Toronto, Ontario)
Donation for membership

Lamoureaux (see Lamoreaux)

Lampkin
*The Thomas and Deborah Newcomb
Lampkin Family
427 Washington Street
Dundee, MI 48131
Phone (313) 529-5729
Ella Lamkin Henning
(includes descendants of Thomas
Lampkin (1719/20 Willington,
Connecticut–), possibly a descendant
of David Lampkin, 1654 of
Westmoreland County, Virginia, and
Thomas's wife Deborah Newcomb
Lamkin (1702 Eastham or Truro,
Massachusetts–))

Lampman (see Wright)

Lamson (see Robison)

Lancaster (see Hall, Wheeler)

Lancaster
*Lancasters of Tennessee
2711 Seabreeze Court
Orlando, FL 32805
Phone (407) 425-6942
Col. Clifton O. Duty (USA Ret.) or Jean
Barker Duty

Lance (see Lentz)

Lance
*The Lance-Lantz-Lentz-Lence People,
Inc.
PO Box 39
Nelson, GA 30151
Phone (770) 735-2272;
(770) 479-3069 FAX
Dennis Lance
(includes descendants of four brothers:
Bastian or Sebastian, Dewalt or
Diebolt, Peter and John)
Annual reunion on the second Sunday of
June and the preceding Friday and
Saturday

Lance
Charger
419 West Main
McMinnville, TN 37110
Carolyn Lance
Pub. *Charger*, quarterly; (includes
descendants of John Lentz from

Germany, through James Jasper Lance of Buncombe County, North Carolina, and Warren County, Tennessee)

Lancelot (see Lundsford)

Lancton (see Newton)

Landahl (see Bestman)

Landale (see MacDuff)

Landels (see MacDuff)

Landerneau (see Johnson)

Landers
Landers Family Organization
3110 "Z" Street
Vancouver, WA 98661
Phone (206) 695-7910
Jo Landers
Pub. *Landers' Landings*, bimonthly
$6.00 per year membership

Landes (see Frantz)

Landingham (see Putman)

Landis (see Stoner)

Landreth
Landreths of Nebraska
419 State Street
Sterling, CO 80751
Phone (303) 522-5633
Gladys Landreth Stewart

Landreth
*Landreth Family Association
935 Countryside Drive, Apartment #103
Palatine, IL 60067-1927
Phone (847) 776-1848
H. Harvey Barfield, III
Pub. *The Landreth Family Historical Review*, quarterly, $10.00 per year subscription; (specifically those members of the Landreth family and their descendants who migrated to Clay County, Illinois, from Ashe County, North Carolina, and Grayson County, Virginia, by way of Lawrence County and Owen County, Indiana)

Landrum (see Melton)

Landry (see Johnson)

Landry
Landry Letters
12600 Bissonnet A4-407
Houston, TX 77099
Dede D. Mercer, Publisher
Pub. *Landry Letters*, semiannually, $20.00 per year subscription; (all variations of the surname, worldwide)

Landsman (see MacDuff)

Lane (see Cian, Clark, Goodenow, Hopkin, Montague, Powell, Root, Rowe)

Lane
Lane Family Bulletin
5946 Weimar Avenue
San Jose, CA 95120
Pub. *Lane Family Bulletin*, quarterly

Lane
*Lane Ancestors
10452 S.W. Forest Ridge Place
Beaverton, OR 97007
Phone (503) 644-1120
Sherry Lane Bader, Publisher
Pub. *Lane Ancestors*, quarterly (February, May, August and November), $12.00 per year subscription; (includes Lain and Layne)

Laney (see Cian, Detering)

Laney
*Laney Clan, U.S.A.
3049 Thrush Drive (or 2420 Leewood Boulevard)
Melbourne, FL 32935
Phone (407) 259-9663
Lawrence Laney, Genealogy Research Director
Pub. *Notes 'n Quotes of The Laney Clan, U.S.A.*, two to three times per year
$10.00 per year membership

Lanfear (see Hyatt)

Lang (see The Memorial Foundation of the Germanna Colonies, Leslie, MacDuff)

Langdon (see Barnes)

Langenbuehl (see The Memorial Foundation of the Germanna Colonies)

Langford (see Emery, Lankford)

Langley (see Sullivan Surname Exchange)

Langlois (see Johnson)

Langston
*Samuel Bennett Langston Family Organization
888 East Main
Batesville, AR 72501-3438
Brian R. Langston
Reunion

Langton (see Corson)

Lanier (see Gant)

Lankford (see Parker)

Lankford
Lankford/Langford
6180 Merrywood Drive
Rocklin, CA 95677-3421

Kathleen Stewart
Pub. *Lankford/Langford*, quarterly (February, May, August and November), $12.00 per year subscription

Lansing (see Surname Sources)

Lantz (see Lance, Lentz, Underwood)

Lap
Maise Lap Family Organization
The Galena Territory
6 Horizon Lane
Galena, IL 61036-9258
Barbara Shapiro Alexander

Lapala (see Brodhead)

Lapham
*Lapham Family Organization
711 Kensington Avenue
Flint, MI 48503
Phone (313) 234-8574
Phyllis S. Kitson
Pub. *Lapham Leader*, monthly, free; (includes descendants of John Lapham)

La Pone (see Richie)

Lapsley (see Bailey)

Large
Large Family Letters, Queries
Box 2455 C.S.
Pullman, WA 99165
Marilu VonBargen
Pub. *Large Family Letters, Queries*

Largent
Largent Family Bulletin
955 North Palm
Rialto, CA 92376
Robert Eustice
Pub. *Largent Family Bulletin*, annually

Larges (see Lagesse)

Largess (see Lagesse)

Larkey (see Kettenring)

Larkin (see Newton)

Larkins (see Austin)

Larnach (see Stewart)

Larrick (see Lambert)

Larsen (see Garner, Peterson)

Larsen
Peder Larsen Family Organization
1852 East 3990 South, Apartment B
Salt Lake City, UT 84124
Karen Renee Cox
(includes descendants of Peder Larsen 1817 and Karen Hansen 1815)

Lartigue (see Blossom Press)

LaRue
*LaRue Insights
6805 N.W. 20th Street
Bethany, OK 73008-5803
Don H. Watson, Ph.D.
(includes all LaRue and allied families,
particularly LaRue-Holland and
Watson-James)

LaRue
*Linking LaRues Newsletter
424 Leonard Avenue
Washington, PA 15301
Phone (412) 225-8895
Sandra Thompson Schrader, Editor and
Reunion Coordinator
Pub. *Linking LaRues Newsletter*,
quarterly, $16.00 per year subscription,
free queries to subscribers, $4.00 to
non-subscribers; (includes LaRue,
Buzan, Carmen, Castleman, Helm,
Hodgen, Keith and Rust; book, *LaRue/
Hodgen Directory*, includes LaRue,
Castleman, Dorsey, Hardin, Hodgen,
Jones, Mather and Owings)
Reunion in Elizabethtown, Kentucky

Larussa
*Joseph Larussa Family Organization
124 Walnut Street
Batavia, NY 14020
Phone (716) 343-2648
Lawrence LaRussa, Researcher
(includes family which migrated from
Vallalunga, Sicily, 1904)

Lasater
Olsen Enterprises
3931 South 238th
Kent, WA 98032
Pub. *Lasater*, quarterly, $14.00 per year
subscription; (England and New
England)

Lasher
Lasher Family Association
9132 Country Club Drive
Sun Lakes, AZ 85224
Eileen Lasher Powers
Pub. *Lasher Letter*, quarterly
$6.00 per year membership

Lashlee
*Lashlee Locator
1029 Crestview Drive, East
Atlanta, TX 75551-1833
Phone (903) 796-6750
Jean Gilley, Researcher
Pub. *Lashlee Locator*, quarterly, $8.00
per year subscription; (includes all
Lachley, Lashlee, Lashleigh, Lashley,
Lashly and other spellings)

Lashleigh (see Lashlee)

Lashley (see Lashlee)

Lashly (see Lashlee)

Lashmet (see De La Chaumette)

Lasley
*Morgan Eli Asbury Lasley Family
Organization
2904 Sunset Drive, West
Tacoma, WA 98466
Phone (206) 564-2755
Richard H. Martin

Lassus (see Blossom Press)

Latapie (see Blossom Press)

Latham (see The Memorial Foundation
of the Germanna Colonies, Cantrill,
McRae)

Latham
*Latham Surname Organization
7705 Ensley Drive, S.W.
Huntsville, AL 35802-2845
Phone (205) 883-0207
Thomas W. Burns

Lathrisk (see MacDuff)

Lathrop (see Packard)

Lathum (see Burge)

Latimer (see Gotham, Reynolds)

Latour (see Blossom Press)

Latta (see Gwynne)

Lattimer (see Maxwell)

Lattimore (see Folk Family Surname
Exchange, Maxwell)

Lattimore
Lattimore Family Association
Sitkum Rt., Box 157
Myrtle Point, OR 97458
Phone (503) 572-2621
Esther Lattimore Jenkins

Latty
Latty Family Reunion
Rt. 3, Box 57A
Anderson, MO 64831
Phone (417) 845-6740
Gene Latty

Lau (see Lowe)

Laub (see Surname Database)

Laubach
*Laubach Family Association
2204 Jennings Street
Bethlehem, PA 18017
Phone (610) 866-0823
Katharine C. Laubach
(includes all Laubach descendants, most
of whom are descended from Johann
Christian and Susanna Catharina
(Zimler) Laubach who arrived in

Philadelphia in 1738 from Büdingen,
Hessen, Germany and settled in what
is now Lower Saucon Township,
Northampton County, Pennsylvania)

Laubach
*Laubach Family Database
1301 Bradford Road
Oreland, PA 19075-2414
Phone (215) 836-4727
Dale E. Berger, Publisher

Lauchlan (see MacLachlan)

Laudenslager
Laudenslager Surname Database
East Allen Township
5507 Louise Lane
Northampton, PA 18067-9076
Phone (610) 262-1276;
(610) 837-0700 (business)
Charles F. Kerchner, Jr.

Lauderdale (see Maitland)

Laudon
*Laudon Database
924 18th Avenue, S.E.
Minneapolis, MN 55414
Phone (612) 331-2710; E-mail:
laudo011@maroon.tc.umn.edu
Robert Tallant Laudon, Researcher
(includes Laudons of Minnesota,
especially Carl August Hermann
Laudon (1843 Perleburg,
Brandenburg–1914 Lewiston, Idaho)
and his wife, Friedericke Caroline
Wilhelmine Turban (1848 Putlitz,
Brandenburg–1897 Dover, Minnesota))

Laudon
*Laudon Reunion
420 Worth Street, N.E.
Stewartville, MN 55976
Marguerite Lawrence

Lauer (see Caskey)

Lauer
*Lauer and Bohr Family Association
2450 Clara Bea Lane
Fairfield, OH 45014-3975
Phone (513) 858-1848
David Jeffrey Endres
Pub. *Lauer Lines*, biannually; (includes
descendants and relatives of Nikolas
Lauer (1879 Kaiserslautern, Germany–
1951 Hamilton, Ohio) and Magdalena
Bohr (1882 Saarbrücken, Germany–
1949 Hamilton, Ohio))
Biennial reunion in even-numbered years

Laugenour
*Philip Laugenour Family Organization
548 Second Street
Woodland, CA 95695
Phone (916) 668-1433
Stephen Thomas and Theresa Ann
Laugenour

(includes descendants of Philip
  Laugenour and Philippina Davis,
  married 1823 in Stokes County
  (present-day Forsyth County), North
  Carolina)

Laughenor (see Cowart)

Laughenore (see Cowart)

Laughlan (see MacLachlan)

Laughland (see MacLachlan)

Laughlen (see MacLachlan)

Laughlin (see MacLachlan)

Laughlon (see MacLachlan)

Laughridge (see Lokrig)

Laughton (see Lawton, MacLachlan)

Lauhghlan (see MacLachlan)

Laurenson (see MacDuff)

Laussade (see Blossom Press)

Lauterbach
*Lauterbach Association
4111 South Gate
Lincoln, NE 68506
Phone (402) 489-2916
Wes Lauterbach

Lavender
Lavender Agency
PO Box 884
Bay Minette, AL 36507
Pub. *Lavender Lines*, quarterly, $20.00
  per year subscription

Lavender
Lavender Line
1913 N.E. 17th Way
Fort Lauderdale, FL 33305
Doris Lavender Vilda
Pub. *Lavender Line*, quarterly, $15.00 per
  year subscription

Lavy (see Frantz)

Law (see MacLaren)

Lawerance (see MacLaren)

Lawler (see MacDuff)

Lawrence (see Golding, Kyle, Nettles,
  Rutherford)

Lawrence
*Lawrence Family Reunion
Lawrence-Morris & Allied Family
  Research, Inc.
10507 South Corley Drive
Whittier, CA 90604-1114
Phone (310) 693-7611

Bonnie Morris, Editor
(includes descendants of John and
  Rachael (Payne/Haynes) Lawrence of
  Coshocton, Ohio)
Reunion

Lawrence
*Lawrence Surname Organization
Highway 87 North
PO Box 340
Burkeville, TX 75932
Phone (409) 565-4751
Helen Rogers Skelton

Lawson (see Christopher, Lair, Likes,
  Louden)

Lawson
The League of Lawsons International
468 Alamine Drive
Redding, CA 96003-3766
Mary Alice Lawson
Pub. *The Lawson Letters*, quarterly
$10.00 per year membership

Lawton (see Goodenow, Shurtleff)

Lawton
*Lawton Surname Organization
George William Lawton Family
  Organization
1816 West Pine
Warren, AR 71671
Phone (501) 226-3771
Myrtie Lawton Sedberry

Lawton
Lawton Issue
159 Linwood Avenue
Buffalo, NY 14209-2003
Tony Fusco
Pub. *Lawton Issue*, quarterly, $16.00 per
  year subscription; (includes Laughton
  and Leighton)

Laxfirth (see Hay)

Layman
*Layman Surname Organization
16117 West Lake Burrell Drive
Lutz, FL 33549
Phone (813) 972-2725
John W. Palm
(includes descendants of John Walker
  Layman, Cincinnati, Ohio)

Layman
Layman/Duncan/Evans Family Reunion
6555 Manson Drive
Waterford, MI 48095
Phone (313) 623-6062
Emma L. Smith

Layman
*Lauri-Lines
South 2827 Ivory
Spokane, WA 99203
Phone (509) 624-0533
Laurine Mae Palmerton Logsdon

Pub. *Layman-Lehman Records and Lines*,
  irregularly, $6.00 plus $1.75 postage
  and handling or $2.75 foreign postage
  and handling (Washington State
  residents add 63¢ tax)

Layne (see Lane)

Layton
*Layton Surname Organization
James Layton Family Organization
4723 West Marconi Avenue
Glendale, AZ 85306
Phone (602) 843-2812
David L. Bowers

Layton
Layton Family Reunion
10700 Brunswick Avenue
Kensington, MD 20895
Benjamin Layton
Pub. *Layton Family Reunion*, annually

Lazenby (see Usher)

Lea (see Folk Family Surname
  Exchange)

Lea
Lea-Leahy-O'Leahy-Ley Family
  Association
2306 Westgate
Houston, TX 77019
Phone (713) 529-2333
Harold Helm
$25.00 plus pedigree and family group
  sheets for membership

Leach (see Folk Family Surname
  Exchange, The Memorial Foundation
  of the Germanna Colonies, Athy)

League (see Jones)

Leahy (see Lea)

Leake (see Lake)

Leamer (see Lehmer)

Lean (see Gillean)

Learmonth (see MacDuff)

Leary (see Macpherson, MacPherson)

Lease
Lease Family Exchange
Rt. 2, Box 671
Grangeville, ID 83530-9635
Phone (208) 983-0515
Anne Long

Leask
*Clan Leask Society
303 West Casa Linda
Woodland, CA 95695
Mary Leask Holmes

Leasure
At Leisure with the Leasure-Leisures
2510 Tulane Avenue
Alamogordo, NM 88310-4531
Alta Leasure Carmichael
Pub. *At Leisure with the Leasure-Leisures*, quarterly, $6.00 per year subscription

Leath (see Davis)

Leatherer (see The Memorial Foundation of the Germanna Colonies)

Leathers (see The Memorial Foundation of the Germanna Colonies)

Leaton (see Leeton)

Leavascy (see Livesay)

Leavasey (see Livesay)

Leavitt (see Haight)

Leavitt
*Leavitt-Jennings-Roots & Branches
7901 East Mabel Drive
Tucson, AZ 85715-5107
Phone (520) 298-1368
Edna Jennings Zeavin, Publisher
(includes descendants of Dudley Leavitt and Mary Huntsman, married 1853, and Sherburn Jennings and Sabrina Smith, married 1824)

Leavy (see Buchanan)

Leay (see Stewart)

Le Baron (see Millet)

LeBarron (see Goodenow)

LeBeau (see Levi)

LeBlanc (see Augeron, Johnson)

Lebo (see Levi)

Le Brun (see Broun)

Lechleiter (see Leichleiter)

Lechliter (see Leichleiter)

Leckie (see Gregor)

Lecklider (see Leichleiter)

Leckliter (see Leichleiter)

Lecky (see Gregor)

LeClair (see Johnson)

Ledbetter
*Ledbetter Family Association
16200 Kennedy Road
Los Gatos, CA 95032-6478
Kenneth Haughton

Ledbetter
Ledbetter Cousins Queries
Box 2455 C.S.
Pullman, WA 99165
Marilu VonBargen
Pub. *Ledbetter Cousins Queries*

Leddy (see Cian)

Lederer (see The Memorial Foundation of the Germanna Colonies)

Ledford (see Tidwell)

Ledford
*Ledford Clearinghouse
702 Fouts Avenue
Irving, TX 75061
Phone (214) 790-9030
Mary Ellen Ledford

Ledom
Ledom Clearinghouse
Rt. 1, Box 192
Monmouth, IL 61462
James E. and Sharon L. Todd

Ledoux (see Johnson)

Ledsinger
Ledsinger-Letsinger-Letzinger Family Association
2306 Westgate
Houston, TX 77019
Phone (713) 529-2333
Harold Helm
$25.00 plus pedigree and family group sheets for membership

Lee (see Blossom Press, Folk Family Surname Exchange, Sullivan Surname Exchange, Barnes, Case, Cook, Eaves, Grant, Lemon, Lush, Rand, Wright)

Lee
Lee
6180 Merrywood Drive
Rocklin, CA 95677-3421
Kathleen Stewart
Pub. *Lee*, quarterly, $12.00 per year subscription

Lee
*Lee Cemetery Association
Rt. 3, Box 190
Concordia, MO 64020-9505
Phone (816) 463-7523
Mrs. Buddy Samuels, President
Pub. *Lee Family Researchers Newsletter*, irregularly, $10.00 per year subscription with submission of group sheets or family data, $15.00 per year subscription otherwise; (includes descendants of Richard Lee (175(?)–1819) and Elizabeth Scott(?) (176(?)–1838 Missouri) of Madison County, Kentucky; Lee of Virginia, Kentucky, Missouri, Texas and the west)
Annual meeting on the third Saturday of May

Lee
*Lee Family
108 Worley Drive
Madison Heights, VA 24572
Richard E. Lee

Lee
William and Ephraim Lee Family Association
1604 Longfellow Street
McLean, VA 22101
Georgia E. Benefiel

Lee
*Bell Enterprises
PO Box 10328
Spokane, WA 99209
Phone (509) 327-2761
Mary Ann L. Vanzandt Bell, Owner, Publisher
Pub. *Lee Lines*, irregularly $6.00 plus $1.25 postage per issue

Leebo (see Levi)

Leech (see MacBeth)

Leeper (see Garner, Grant)

Lees (see Macpherson, MacPherson)

Leet (see Leete)

Leet
*The Leet Family Group
5 Pinewood Road
Wilmington, MA 01887-1908
Steven Wayne Leet
(Leete family data base only)

Leete
*Leete Family Association
607 AW Jefferson Street
LaGrange, KY 40031
Marjorie Morgan, President
Pub. *The Leete Legacy*, semiannually (May and November); (includes descendants of Gov. William C. Leete, founder of Guilford Colony and Governor of Connecticut; open to all with surname Leete or Leet)
$8.00 per year membership; reunion

Leethian (see MacDuff)

Leeton
*Leeton, Leaton Surname Organization
7024 Morgan Road
Greenwell Springs, LA 70739
Phone (504) 261-5515
Serena Abbess Haymon, Data Entry
(includes Mississippi, Texas, Tennessee and South Carolina)
Free membership and registration on FGS

Le Fevre
Le Fevre Family Association
(Huguenot Historical Society)
45 North Oakwood Terrace
New Paltz, NY 12561

Phone (914) 255-1538
Mrs. Donald Martin

Leffingwell
*The Leffingwell Record and On
3283 Millerfield Road
Macon, GA 31211
Phone (912) 745-0921
James E. Silz
Free (except costs of copies and postage)

Leftwich
*The Leftwich Family History
 Association
PO Box 40
Hillsborough, NC 27278
Shirley L. Greer, Editor
Pub. *The Leftwich Heritage Newsletter*

Leger (see Johnson)

Le Gros (see Farrington)

Lehan (see Cian)

Lehane (see Cian)

Leher (see Lair)

Lehman (see The Memorial Foundation
 of the Germanna Colonies, Layman)

Lehmberg (see Farrington)

Lehmer
The Lehmer-Leamer-Lamer Newsletter
221 Torrance Avenue
Vestal, NY 13850
Phone (607) 748-6021
Laurence E. Leamer
Pub. *The Lehmer-Leamer-Lamer
 Newsletter*, semiannually (May and
 December), $3.00 per year
 subscription

Lehnherr
*Lehnherrs of Swiss Origins & Their
 Collateral Ties*
3631 South 257th Street
Kent, WA 98032-5669
Robert E. Lehnherr, Editor
Pub. *Lehnherrs of Swiss Origins & Their
 Collateral Ties*

Leiby
Leiby Exchange
1943 Vermont Road
Escondido, CA 92025
Carl Bennett

Leichleiter
*Leichleiter and Variants Family
 Association
4201 Wildflower Circle
Wichita, KS 67210
Phone (316) 529-0438
Dianne Stark Thurman, Historian
Pub. *Leichleiter and Variants (Leckliter,
 Lichlyter, Lechliter, Licklider,
 Lecklider, Lickliter & Lechleiter)
 Newsletter*, semiannually

Membership fee; annual reunion on the
 last full weekend of June in Sullivan,
 Missouri

Leightner (see Lightner)

Leighton (see Corson, Hutchison,
 Lawton, MacDuff)

Leimback (see Lineback)

Leinback (see Lineback)

Leinweber
*Leinweber Family Association
Rt. 1, Box 123-B
Colfax, WA 99111
Phone (509) 397-3751
Heidi L. Dowling, Historian and Reunion
 Chairman
(includes descendants of Joseph
 Leinweber and Elizabeth Gerlitz and
 allied families)
Reunion

Leisure (see Leasure)

Leith (see Gregor, Hay)

Leix (see Likes)

Lejeune (see Johnson)

Lejon (see Kahler)

Leland (see Surname Sources)

Leland
Leland/Roark Clearinghouse (Hanna/
 Dunn/Delahaney/Baum)
623 North View Street
Aurora, IL 60506
S. D. Leland

Lelliott (see Elliott)

Lemaster (see Clark, Patterson)

Lemaster
*Lemaster Family Association
1365 Lesley Court
Santa Maria, CA 93454
Phone (805) 922-4313; (805) 346-1156
 FAX; E-mail: ccsd62B@prodigy.com
Tina Peddie, President
(includes descendants of Abraham and
 Elizabeth Lemaster)

Lembeck (see Mueller)

Lemmon (see Lemon)

Lemmond (see Lemon)

Lemmonds (see Lemon)

Lemmons (see Lemon)

Lemoine (see Johnson)

Lemon
Lem[m]on[d][s] Genealogical Society
43728 27th Street West
Lancaster, CA 93536-5848
Phone (805) 942-5553
Gene C. Lemmon
Pub. *Lem[m]on[d][s] Genealogical
 Society Descendants' Directory*,
 biannually (odd-numbered years)
$20.00 per year active membership

Lemon
The Lemon Tree Press
PO Box 522
Marietta, OH 45750-0522
Phone (614) 373-5697
Marilyn Sims Vadakin and Julia Vadakin
 Lambert, Editors
Pub. *The Lemon Family Tree*, quarterly,
 $14.00 per year subscription; (includes
 Barclay, Behr (Beer), Blessington,
 Braden, Bruce, Burns, Collums,
 Cronin, Culbertson, Cunningham,
 Darnell, Davis, Deem, Demuth,
 Domsieffer, Eichen, Fischbach,
 Gelding, Gilliland, Hagerty, Heimbach,
 Heite, Holmes, Kesslar (Hesslar),
 Kidwell (Kidwiler), Lee, Lemon,
 Martin, Nay, O'Neil, Otterbach, Pulley,
 Robinson, Rod, Schweissfurth, Sims,
 Stribling, Stuell, Thrasher, Tyler
 (Taylor), Wallace, Webb, Wildman,
 Wurmbach and Young)

Lemon
*William Lemon Family Organization
3429 North 950 East
Ogden, UT 84414-1727
Laura L. Spendlove
(includes descendants of William Lemon
 (1849 Acworth, Georgia–) and three
 wives, Louisa Jane Grogan, Martha
 Ella Farris and Alice Shugart, also
 James LeMont (1740 Dumfane,
 Antrim, Ireland–), came to South
 Carolina)
Annual reunion in June in Sulpher
 Springs, Texas

Lemond (see Lemon)

Lemonds (see Newton)

Lemons (see Lemon)

LeMont (see Lemon)

Lenan (see MacLennan)

Lence (see Lance, Lentz)

Lenderman
Gregath Publishing Company
PO Box 1045
Cullman, AL 35056-1045
Pub. *Lenderman Links Newsletter*

Lenington (see Linington)

Lenker (see Wert)

Lennan (see MacLennan)

Lennie (see Buchanan)

Lennon (see MacLennan)

Lennox (see Stewart)

Lensen (see Links Genealogy Publications)

Lent
Lent Van Lent Newsletter
PO Box 2183
Clifton Park, NY 12065
Phone (518) 383-3617
Ruth E. Lent Hand
Pub. *Lent Van Lent Newsletter*, semiannually (June and December), $18.00 per year subscription; (includes descendants of the family that left Holland in 1640 for what is now known as Peekskill, New York, in Halfmoon, Schenectady County, New York, in 1791, and other localities)

Lentron (see MacDuff)

Lentz (see Jett, Lance)

Lentz
Association of Lentz Descendants
807 17th Street, North
Moorhead, MN 56560
Carl William Roder, Secretary

Lentz
Lentz Heritage
5579 Woodduck Circle
Wilmington, NC 28409-3941
John Paul Lentz
Pub. *Lentz Heritage* (includes Lance, Lantz, Lence, Lintz, etc.; descendants of four Lentz brothers from Germany in 1753, settled in Illinois, Georgia, Tennessee and western North Carolina)

Leonard (see Allison, Golding, MacLennan, Tillman)

Leonard
Leonard Lines
318 East Seventh
PO Box 212
Staunton, IL 62088
Phone (618) 635-8506
Cindy Leonard
Pub. *Leonard Lines*, three times per year (August, December and April), $15.00 per year subscription; (includes Leonard and variant spellings)

Leonard
Leonard Family Tree Newsletter
2801 Park Center Drive, A-1109
Alexandria, VA 22302-1431
Phone (703) 931-5834
Greg and Patti Fritts
Pub. *Leonard Family Tree Newsletter*, annually, donation for subscription

Leonerd (see MacLennan)

Leopold (see CTC Family Association)

Leopold
Leopold/Zurier/Shapiro Family Association
The Galena Territory
6 Horizon Lane
Galena, IL 61036-9258
Barbara Shapiro Alexander

Lepele (see Lahaye)

Le Poer (see Cian)

Le Porche
Jacques Le Porche Descendants
1203 Wendell Street
Lake Charles, LA 70601-2068
L. P. Wyatt, Genealogical Researcher
Reunion

Lesh (see Stoner)

Lesher
Lesher Families in America
18310 Florwood Avenue
Torrance, CA 90504
Don Lesher
Pub. *Lesher Families in America*, quarterly

Leslie (see MacDuff)

Leslie
*Clan Leslie Society
612 North Maple Avenue
Ridgway, PA 15853
Bob Leslie, Secretary/Registrar
Pub. *The Griffin*, annually; *The Journal*, annually; *Grip Fast*, bimonthly; (includes septs: Abernethy, Bartholomew, Carnie, Lang, Moore and More)
$15.00 per year membership

Lessels (see MacDuff)

Lessey
*Alanson Lessey and Abigail Hodge Family Organization
171 Main Street
Newington, CT 06111
Phone (203) 666-9566
John F. Bolles, III
(includes descendants of Alanson Lessey (1792–1874 New Fairfield, Connecticut) and Abigail Hodge (1795–1852))

Lessig
*Lessig Family Database
1301 Bradford Road
Oreland, PA 19075-2414
Phone (215) 836-4727
Dale E. Berger, Publisher

Lester (see Millet)

Lester
*Richard Alexander Lester and Mable Marie Young Lester Family Organization
PO Box 1084
Welch, WV 24801
Phone (304) 436-6677
Carrie Marie Lester Smith, President and Secretary
(includes descendants of Richard Alexander Lester (1908 Davy, West Virginia–1974 Beckley, West Virginia) and wife Mable Young (1916 Cabin Creek, West Virginia–1980 Virginia))

Lethan (see MacDuff)

Letourneau (see Parrott)

Letsinger (see Ledsinger)

Lett (see Jackson)

Letzinger (see Ledsinger)

Leu (see Falk)

Leuchars (see MacDuff)

Leuenberger (see Lionberger)

Leupp (see Loop)

Leurs (see MacDuff)

Le Vache (see Veitch)

Levack (see Stewart)

Levasey (see Livesay)

Leven (see MacDuff)

Levering (see Links Genealogy Publications, DeHaven)

Levering
Levering Reunion
7750 County Road 97
Belleville, OH 44813
D. Rhodebach

Levescy (see Livesay)

Levi
*Frederick John Levi Family Organization Trust
501 North Highway 89
PO Box 450
Chino Valley, AZ 86323-0450
Phone (520) 636-0420; (520) 636-0684 FAX; E-mail: Levied@primenet.com
Dewey J. Levie
Pub. *Frederick John Levi Family Newsletter*, two to four times per year, $5.00 contribution per year subscription; (includes LeBeau, Lebo, Leebo, Levie, Levy, Liebau and allied families of Carroll and Whittle of Missouri, Illinois, Iowa, Utah and Essex, Ontario, Canada, from 1800)

Levie (see Levi)

Levin (see Lewin)

Levingston (see Leviston)

Levingstone (see Leviston)

Leviston
Leviston Exchange
1724 Greer Drive, West
Newark, OH 43055-1457
Ronna Eyman Eagle
Pub. *Leviston, Levingston, Levingstone, Livingston, Livingstone Family Exchange*, quarterly

Levitch (see Israelovitch)

Levitt (see Israelovitch)

Levitts (see Israelovitch)

Levitz (see Israelovitch)

Levy (see Levi)

Lewellen (see Llewellyn)

Lewin
*Lewin/Paltiel Family Organization
14547 Titus Street, Suite 207
Panorama City, CA 91402
Phone (818) 785-4282; (818) 762-3652
Hillel Don Lazarus, D.D.S.
(includes Paltiel from Iwie, Byelorussia and Lewin (Levin), Devenishici or Devenishok, Russia (Lithuania))

Lewis (see Folk Family Surname Exchange, Barnes, Bloss, Brodnax, Cochran, Corson, Dean, Eaves, Hall, Heath, Moore, Newcomb, Stewart, Wright)

Lewis
*Henry Lewis Family Association
R.D. 4, Box 404A
Dover, DE 19901
Phone (302) 736-6621
John C. Lewis, Family Historian
Pub. *The Lewis Line*, semiannually, free to immediate family; (includes Lewises from Kent County, Delaware)

Lewis
*Lewis and Clark Publishers
6729 Taylorsville Road
Dayton, OH 45424
Phone (513) 236-5697
Jim Lewis, Publisher
Pub. *Lewis Newsletter*, quarterly (January, April, July and October), $25.00 per year subscription

Lewis
*Lewis/Martin/Palmer/Turner Family Organization
1132 North Tela Drive
Oklahoma City, OK 73127-4308

Phone (405) 789-2842
Pauline Carlton Fletcher, Secretary and Genealogist
(computer database uses Quinsept™, PAF™ and Reunion™)

Lewis
*Ira Dabney Lewis Family Organization
Rt. 1, Box 1570
Athens, TX 75751
Phone (903) 675-2448
Jana Shumate
(includes descendants of Ira Dabney Lewis (1847 Mississippi–1915 Texas) and Mary Elizabeth Perry Lewis (1856 Tennessee–1939 Texas))
Annual reunion in June

Lewis
Lewis Listings
12600 Bissonnet A4-407
Houston, TX 77099
Dede D. Mercer, Publisher
Pub. *Lewis Listings*, semiannually; $20.00 per year subscription; (includes all variations of the surname, worldwide)

Lewis
*Sophia Lewis Family Organization
7712 Buck Street
North Richland Hills, TX 76180
Phone (817) 485-3792
Ken Mason

Lewis
Lewis Lineages
East 13124 Nixon
Spokane, WA 99216
Joanne M. Elliott
Pub. *Lewis Lineages*, irregularly, $8.50 plus $1.00 postage per volume

Lewis
*Pioneer Publication
PO Box 1179
Tum Tum, WA 99034-1179
Phone (509) 276-9841
Shirley Penna-Oakes
Pub. *Lewis Unlimited*, irregularly, $6.00 per issue plus $1.75 postage for 1–3 books, 50¢ for each additional book

Ley (see Hay, Lea)

Ley
*Ley Family of New Jersey
PO Box 460
Livermore, CA 94551
Phone (501) 443-3326
T. Reitter

Leyenberger (see Lionberger)

Libbee (see Libby)

Libby (see Corson, Libbey)

Libby
*The John Libby Family Association
Libby Homestead Corporation
PO Box 11365
Portland, ME 04104
Phone (207) 839-8069 (Secretary)
James F. Libby, President; Robert A. Lindquist, Secretary
Pub. *Litty Newsletter*
$5.00 per year membership, $50.00 life membership; annual reunion on the fourth Saturday of September in Scarborough, Maine

Libby
John Libby Family Association
Libby Homestead Corporation
119 Winn Street
Sumter, SC 29150
Phone (803) 773-7257
Ernest S. "Steve" Libby, Editor
Pub. *John Libby Family Association Newsletter*, semiannually; (includes Libbee, Libbey and other spellings)
$5.00 per year membership, $150.00 life membership; annual reunion on the fourth weekend of September

Lichfield (see Hatfield)

Lichlyter (see Leichleiter)

Lichtenberger (see Schindel)

Lichtenstein (see Clark)

Licklider (see Leichleiter)

Lickliter (see Leichleiter)

Liebau (see Levi)

Liebeskind
*The Liebeskind Family Association
233 Saddle Hill Road
Stamford, CT 06903
Phone (203) 329-9876
Dr. David Liebeskind

Lifsey (see Livesay)

Ligda
*Victor Ligda Family Organization
1129 Valle Vista
Vallejo, CA 94589
Phone (707) 552-4910
Paul Ligda
(includes descendants of Victor Ligda (1832 Moscow, Russia–1902 Oakland, California))

Light
Search Light
Rt. 8
Carmel, NY 10512-9808
Betty M. Light Behr
Pub. *Search Light—The Light (and Variant) Family Newsletter*, quarterly, $7.50 per year subscription in the U.S., $8.50 per year subscription outside the U.S.

Lightell (see Blossom Press)

Lightfoot
Lightfoot Family Association
1330 Kings Highway
Dallas, TX 75208
Phone (214) 946-7985
Mrs. Stanley A. Williams
Pub. *Lightfoot Family Newsletter*,
    quarterly
$10.00 per year membership

Lightholder
*Lightholder Family Association
431 South Center Street
Bensenville, IL 60106
Phone (630) 595-3573
Linda Lightholder Kmiecik
(includes descendants of William and
    Margaret (McGuire) Lightholder, Irish
    famine immigrants from counties
    Dublin, Meath and Westmeath, resided
    in Saratoga County, New York, ca
    1848–1857, in Peoria County, Illinois,
    1860–186?, in McLean County, Illinois
    1870–?, in Livingston County, Illinois,
    1880 to the present)

Lightner (see Franciscus, Stoner)

Lightner
Lightner/Leightner Clearinghouse
2391 Mayfield Street
York, PA 17402

Ligon (see Golding)

Likens
Likens-Adams Family Newsletter
PO Box 133
Cortland, NE 68331
Donna Adams Likens
Pub. *Likens-Adams Family Newsletter*

Likes
*The "Likes" Family Genealogy
1755 West Florida Avenue
Denver, CO 80223
Phone (303) 935-0953
Wm. C. "Chet" Likes, Publisher
(includes descendants of Georga and
    John Laix (Likes), brothers who came
    from Pennsylvania and homesteaded
    Ashland, Ohio, with allied families:
    Aber, Acton, Albright, Austin, Bacon,
    Barger, Bealmer, Bean, Beauchat,
    Blanche, Brightman, Bunyan,
    Buschmeyer, Buss, Childs, Cole,
    Cook, Court, Crite, Crowner, Ellis,
    Eshbach, Franks, Fulk, Gatten, Gibbs,
    Hatfield, Hinds, Holtzer, Hopka,
    Kendall, Lambert, Lawson, Leix,
    Martin, McCorkle, McCurdy,
    McGinte, Miller, Miracle, Montana,
    Newcomer, Newman, Norberg,
    Pollard, Poppy, Raubenolt, Read,
    Richards, Riddle, Rinesmith, Roberts,
    Robey, Roecklein, Roland, Ruffcorn,
    Scheibler, Shaffers, Shick, Shire,

Showalter, Shriver, Smick, Sprinkle,
    Spurgeon, Stagner, Stiffler, Strawn,
    Strouse, Struckers, Swartz, Thomas,
    Trease, Uhl, Van Horn, Waite, Walker,
    Wicoff, Wicuff, Williams, Wolfe,
    Wonse, Young and Zook)

Likins (see Folk Family Surname
    Exchange)

Lile (see Lyle)

Lillard
William (1817) and Lucretia Lillard
    Family Association
5505 Towers Street
Torrance, CA 90503
V. Vaughn

Lillard
*The Lillard Family Association
Rt. 2, Box 147
Benton, TN 37307
Phone (615) 338-5777
Ralph Emerson Lillard, Secretary and
    Treasurer
Pub. *Lillard Lines*, two to three times per
    year
Donation for membership

Lillibridge
*Lillibridge Family Reunion
9610 S.W. 72nd Court
Ocala, FL 34476-7094
Phone (352) 854-7077
John L. Lillibridge
Reunion every three years

Lillington (see Brown)

Lilly
The Lilly Historical and Genealogical
    Society
5267 Big Tyler Road
Charleston, WV 25313
James Richardson
Pub. *The Lilly Letter*

Limbach
Limbach Family Association
6548 Old Vincennes Road
Floyds Knobs, IN 47119
Phone (812) 923-8660
Barbara Limbach Bulleit

Linck
*Linck and Ragatz
121 Northwood Drive
Dayton, TX 77535
Murl M. Linck, Editor

Lincoln (see Hanks, Rowe)

Lincoln
Lincolnlogger News
PO Box 238
Leland, NC 28451
Carol Moore
Pub. *Lincolnlogger News*

Lindbert
*Petter Abrahamson Lindberg Family
    Organization
PO Box 63263
Pipe Creek, TX 78063-3263
Phone (210) 510-4355
Sandra Umina

Linden (see MacLennan)

Linder
*The Linder Quarterly
HC 73, Box 989
Walker, MN 56484
Phone (218) 547-3217
J. Ken Linder, Editor
Pub. *The Linder Quarterly* (includes all
    Linder families, so far 16 separate and
    distinct Linder progenitors from 1565
    to present on computer database)
$5.00 per year membership

Linderman (see Links Genealogy
    Publications)

Linderman
Gregath Publishing Company
PO Box 1045
Cullman, AL 35056-1045
Pub. *Linderman Links*

Linderman
*Linderman Family
25 Kings Boulevard
Shillington, PA 19607
Phone (610) 777-7495
Myrtle L. Council

Lindmeyer
Lindmeyer Searching
1101 South Valley
New Ulm, MN 56073
L. Lindmeyer

Lindon (see MacLennan)

Lindores (see MacDuff)

Lindors (see MacDuff)

Lindsay (see Folk Family Surname
    Exchange, Armstrong, Franciscus,
    Kesler, MacDuff, McAllister)

Lindsay
Clan Lindsay Association of U.S.A., Inc.
4621 Saybrook Drive
Norcross, GA 30093
Ronald Tingle
Pub. *Lindsay Recorder* (includes septs:
    Byers, Cobb, Crawford, Deuchars,
    Downie, Fotheringham, Rhind,
    Summers and Sumner)

Lindsay
Kenma Publishing Company
1911 Conlin Avenue
Evansville, IN 47714-4248
Kenneth Gene Lindsay
Pub. *Lindsay Links & Legacy*, quarterly,
    $12.95 per year subscription

Lindsay
Lindsay Letter
124 East 71st Street
New York, NY 10021
Elliott Stringham
Pub. *Lindsay Letter*

Lindsay
*Folk Family
PO Box 52048
Knoxville, TN 37950-2048
Hester E. Stockton, Owner; William
    Lindsey, Editor
Pub. *Lindsay Letters*, quarterly, $15.00
    per year subscription, $5.00 per issue;
    (includes Lindsey)

Lindsey (see Lindsay, Rigney)

Lineback
Lineback News
5120 Jameson Drive
Columbus, OH 43232
Walt Lineback
Pub. *Lineback (Leinback/Leimback, Etc.)
    News*

Lingo (see Graham)

Lingoni (see Blossom Press)

Linington
Linington-Lenington Lineage
1912 Norwood Lane
Arlington, TX 76013
Phone (817) 275-3660
Lee Roy Lennington, Jr., Family
    Representative

Linn (see Lynn, Rutherford)

Linnell
*Linnell Family Association
PO Box 95
Orangeville, IL 61060
Phone (815) 789-4668
Dick Linnell, Chairman
Pub. *Linnell Family Newsletter*,
    semiannually (October and April);
    (includes descendants of Robert
    Linnell (1584–1662), who took oath of
    fidelity in 1638 in Scituate,
    Massachusetts, and married Penninah
    Howes, daughter of John Howes,
    Eastwell, Kent, England)
$15.00 per year membership for
    individuals, $25.00 per year
    membership for families, $125.00 life
    membership; reunion

Linschoten
*Linschoten Family Organization
177 West 650 North
Vernal, UT 84078
Phone (801) 781-1179
E. James Linschoten
(includes Van Linschoten, Utrecht,
    Netherlands, from ca 1700 to the
    present)

Linse
*Linse Family Association
731 Firing Center Road
Yakima, WA 98901
Phone (509) 248-3672
Bette Schlagel Rogers, Family Historian/
    Reunion Organizer
(includes Linses from Walschleben,
    Prussia, Germany, 1848 to Ontario,
    Wisconsin, South Dakota and
    Washington State)
Reunion

Linton
Linton Research Fund, Inc.
PO Box 792
Fredericksburg, VA 22404-0792
Terry Linton

Lintz (see Lentz)

Linville (see Boone)

Linville
*New Trails!
Box 766
Montpelier, VT 05602
Phone (802) 229-0648
Alice Eichholz, Ph.D., C.G.
Pub. *Linville Roots* (back issues only,
    1984–1992)

Lionberger
Lionberger Reunion (Leyenberger/
    Leuenberger)
PO Box 64
Colusa, IL 62329
Bill Lionberger

Lipe (see Brawley)

Lipetzky (see Heath)

Lipp (see The Memorial Foundation of
    the Germanna Colonies)

Lippard
Lippard Family Association
4744 Princess Lane
Del City, OK 73115
Mark Lippard, President
Annual reunion on the second weekend
    of July

Lippincott (see Cranston, Newmyer)

Lipscomb
*Phillip Heritage House
605 Benton
Missoula, MT 59801
Phone (406) 543-3495
Ruth Phillip, MAS R.G.
Pub. *Lipscomb Newsletter*, annually,
    $5.00 per issue

Lisle (see Stewart)

Lister (see Millet)

Litrel (see Luttrell)

Litrell (see Luttrell)

Litt (see Israelite)

Littell
*Littell Families of America, Inc.
(1219 Kat-Ca-Lani Avenue, Sebring, FL
    33870—location)
PO Box 1019 (mailing address)
Sebring, FL 33871-1019
Phone (941) 471-9387; (941) 471-3839
Judge Noble Keith Littell, President and
    Historian
Pub. *Littell's Living Age*, annually
$7.50 per year membership; annual
    reunion on the weekend nearest July 4,
    usually in Beaver County,
    Pennsylvania

Little (see Moser, Ross, Wright)

Little
The George Little Family Association
20214 Stone Road
Hebron, IN 46341
(Newbury, Massachusetts, 1640)

Little
*The Family of Captain Daniel Little,
    Esq., Inc.
165 Tower Circle Drive
Winston-Salem, NC 27107
Phone (910) 764-1227
Kathleen K. Little, Secretary
Pub. *The Little Bit*, semiannually (spring
    and fall); (includes descendants of
    Capt. Daniel Little (–1775 Rowan
    County, North Carolina) and wife
    Mary, ancestors in Catawba County,
    North Carolina)
$10.00 per year membership, $75.00 life
    membership; national reunion every
    other year (odd-numbered years)

Littlebury (see Brodnax)

Littlefield (see Wolverton)

Littlefield
*Littlefield Clearinghouse and
    Newsletter
PO Box 817
Ogunquit, ME 03907-0817
Phone (207) 646-3753; (207) 646-3753
    (FAX)
Charles Littlefield Seaman, Owner
Pub. *Littlefield Family Newsletter*,
    quarterly (January, April, July and
    October), $12.50 per year subscription
    via First Class mail; (includes
    Littlefield from the 1500s, nationwide)

Littlefield
*Littlefield Family Reunion
HC 30, Box 2380
Lawton, OK 73501
Phone (405) 492-4543
Helen Wolf
(includes descendants of John Monroe
    Littlefield (1859–1959))

Annual reunion on the Sunday before Memorial Day at Fletcher New School Building on the east side, Fletcher, Oklahoma

Littlehale (see Newton)

Littleton
Littleton Clearinghouse
8430 Highway 2 West
Havre, MT 59501
Phone (406) 265-2465
Barbara VanDePete
SASE required, evidence of Littleton connection appreciated

Littreal (see Luttrell)

Littrel (see Luttrell)

Littrell (see Luttrell)

Livascy (see Livesay)

Lively (see Ross)

Lively
*National Association of Lively Families
220 Vinita Circle
Richmond, VA 23233
Phone (804) 784-5500
Mrs. Bobbie Unger, Secretary/Treasurer
Pub. *National Association of Lively Families Quarterly Newsletter*
$15.00 per year membership

Livengood (see Hoster)

Livesay
*Livesay Historical Society
1290 Breckenridge Drive
Jackson, MS 39204
Phone (601) 372-2199
James J. Livesay, Historian
Pub. *Livesay Bulletin*, quarterly, no charge for either subscription or membership; (includes Livesay/Livesey and variant spellings in England, the U.S. and other countries, from 1200 to the present)
Annual reunion for three days in July in different locations

Livesay
*Livesay Historical Society
104 Linden Avenue
Mercersburg, PA 17236
Virginia Smith, Bulletin Editor
Pub. *The Livesay Bulletin*, quarterly; (includes Leavascy, Leavasey, Levasey, Lifsey, Livascy, Livesay, Livesey, Livezey immigrants to the colonies and the U.S. from England)
$10.00 per year membership

Livesey (see Livesay)

Livezey (see Livesay)

Livezey
Livezey Family Association
1871 Hemlock Circle
Abington, PA 19001
Phone (215) 884-8796
Jane Livezey Worley

Livingston (see Gregor, Leviston, MacDougall, Stewart)

Livingston
Livingston
720 Giles Drive, N.E.
Huntsville, AL 35801
Elizabth Whitten
Pub. *Livingston*, quarterly, $8.00 per year subscription

Livingstone (see Leviston, MacDougall, Stewart)

Ljungqvist (see Segerstrom)

Llewellyn
*Llewellyn National Reunion
781 McCarthy Boulevard
Pueblo, CO 81005-9704
Phone (719) 564-2210
Martha Jewett Abbey, Editor and Reunion Coordinator
Pub. *Llewellyn Traces*, quarterly (March, June, September and December) and annual every-name index; (includes Lewellen, Luellen, Flewellen, etc.—more than 150 spellings—immigrants who came to America as early as the first decade of the 17th century, with the earliest Llewellyn recorded at Jamestown)
$25.00 per year membership; biennial reunion in October of odd-numbered years

Llewellyn
Llewellyn Family Association
5118 California Street
Omaha, NE 68132
Don Wilson

Lloyd
Lloyd Exchange
4826 Twin Valley Drive
Austin, TX 78731
James L. Lloyd

Loachridge (see Lokrig)

Loar (see Blossom Press)

Lobban (see MacLennan)

Lobdell (see Heath)

Lobdell
Lobdell
RR 2, Box 194
Patterson, NY 12563
Reginald A. White, Jr.
Pub. *Lobdell*, quarterly, $6.00 per year subscription
Reunion

Lobdell
Lobdell Family Reunion
Rt. 1, Box 153 1A
Vernon Center, NY 13477
Helen Chadderdon

Lobrano (see Blossom Press)

Locard (see Lockhart)

Lochart (see Lockhart)

Lochridge (see Lokrig)

Lockard (see Lockhart)

Locke (see Corson, Reeder)

Locke
*Locke Family Association of Rye, New Hampshire
102 Crooked Spring Road
Chelmsford, MA 01863
Phone (508) 251-4804
Donald P. Hayes, Secretary
Pub. *Locke Sickle & Sword*, quarterly; (specializes in descendants of John Locke of Hampton, New Hampshire, of William Locke of Woburn, Massachusetts, and of Nathaniel Locke of Portsmouth, New Hampshire)
$7.00 per year membership; reunion

Locke
*Locke Surname Organization
7650 Fairview Road
Tillamook, OR 97141-9714
Phone (503) 842-6036
Orella Chadwick, Editor
Pub. *Lookin' for Lockes*, quarterly (February, May, August and November); (includes all except New England Lockes)
$15.00 per year membership; annual reunion in June in Florence, Kentucky

Locke
Locke Family Association
325 Park Avenue
Florence, SC 29501-4738
E. George Wenhold
Pub. *Locke Family Association Newsletter*

Locke
*Mountain Press
4503 Anderson Pike
PO Box 400
Signal Mountain, TN 37377-0400
Phone (423) 886-6369;
(423) 886-5312 FAX
James L. Douthat, Owner
(includes descendants of Thomas and Susanna (Henry) Locke)

Locker
Locker Cousins
550 West
Rt. 1, Box 165B
Carthage, IN 46115

D. Willey
Pub. *Locker Cousins*, annually, free

Lockerby (see Douglas)

Lockert (see Lockhart)

Lockerwort (see Hay)

Lockery (see Douglas)

Lockett (see Lockhart)

Lockhart (see Porterfield, Ross)

Lockhart
The Lockhart Family Association
2476 Bolsover Street, #295
Houston, TX 77005-2518
Roy and Betty Lockhart
Pub. *Lockhart Letters*, quarterly, $5.00
    per issue; (includes Lockert, Lochart,
    Loc(k)ard, Lockett, Lockheart,
    descendants of Walter and Jane Otty
    Lockhart)
Reunion

Lockheart (see Lockhart)

Lockie (see Gregor, Jackman)

Locklan (see MacLachlan)

Lockland (see MacLachlan)

Lockridge (see Lokrig)

Lockwood (see Ayres)

Loers (see Links Genealogy
    Publications)

Loertscher
Loertscher Families International—North
    Central
10571 North County Road 50 East
Lizton, IN 46149
David H. Loertscher

Loertscher
Loertscher Families International—
    Central U.S.
PO Box 0115
Bern, KS 66408-0115
R. Gary Lortscher

Loertscher
Loertscher Families International—
    Eastern
79 Handy Street
Rochester, NY 14611
John J. Lortscher

Loflin (see Jelly)

Loftus (see Cian)

Logan (see Campbell, MacLennan,
    McCune, McRae)

Logan
Logan Surname Organization
6180 Merrywood Drive
Rocklin, CA 95677-3421
Kathleen Stewart

Loggie (see MacDuff)

Logie (see MacDuff)

Lohmeier (see Voss)

Loker (see Carr, Newton)

Lokrig
*Lokrig Family History Association
4913 Reynolds Road
Fort Worth, TX 76180
Phone (817) 498-2423
H. Oscar Lochridge, Co-editor and
    Co-historian
Pub. *The Lock-On*, semiannually
    (January and July); (includes
    Laughridge, Loachridge, Lochridge,
    Lockridge, Lorthridge, Lothridge,
    Lotridge, Lottridge, Loughridge,
    Loughrige and other derivatives of the
    name, of Northern Ireland, Scotland
    and Virginia, 1730 to date, and the
    Carolinas 1750 to date)
$20.00 for two years membership (from
    October 1 of odd-numbered years);
    biennial convention in September of
    odd-numbered years

Lollar (see Gant, Lawler)

Lomas (see Loomis)

Lomax (see Loomis)

Lombard (see Stewart)

Long (see The Memorial Foundation of
    the Germanna Colonies, Golding,
    Johnson, Lush, MacDuff, Perry,
    Stoner, Wright)

Long
*The Long's Root Cellar
6153 S.W. Fifth Street
Margate, FL 33068
Phone (305) 975-7062
Seymour E. Long, Executive Director
(includes database for all Long families)
SASE

Long
*Jonathon Milton Long Family
514 Fall Creek
Huffman, TX 77336
Phone (713) 324-5179 FAX
Susan Long Cowles

Long
Wade-Smith Genealogy Service
Rt. 7, Box 52
Llano, TX 78643
Evelyn Wade
Pub. *Our Long Line*, three times per year,
    $10.00 per year subscription

Longbottom
*Longbottom Family Reunion
1164 Catherine Street
Suffield, OH 44260
Phone (330) 628-4435
Robert A. Longbottom, Family
    Genealogist and Historian
(includes descendants of John
    Longbottom and Mary Ann Hopton
    who immigrated to the U.S. in 1854)
Annual reunion on the weekend before
    the Labor Day weekend in the
    Canfield, Ohio area

Longest (see Lumpkin)

Longley
Longley Family in America
2236 South 77th Street
West Allis, WI 53219
Janneyne L. Gnacinski
Pub. *Longley Family in America
    Newsletter*, quarterly, $3.00 per year
    subscription

Longmire
*Charles Longmire Family Organization
George Longmire Family Organization
William Longmire Family Organization
1718 North Mildred Street
Tacoma, WA 98406
Phone (206) 752-1496
Marie B. Rice, Researcher
(includes descendants of William
    Longmire (–1748/9 King George
    County, Virginia), immigrant from
    England, through his sons Charles
    (–1799) of Washington County,
    Tennessee, George (–1785) of
    Abbeville County, South Carolina, and
    William (–1816) of Granville County,
    North Carolina)

Lonsford (see Dockery)

Look (see Corson)

Look
Look Newsletter
2816 Sloat Road
Pebble Beach, CA 93953
Ruth Harrison Jones
Pub. *Look Newsletter*

Loomis (see Burnham, Catlow)

Loomis
*Loomis Families of America (Lummis/
    Lomas/Lomax/Etc.)
PO Box 17
Denair, CA 95316
Phone (209) 634-3706
Clyde E. Loomis, Families
    Representative
$18.00 per year membership

Looney
*Roots Researchers
East Smith
Springfield, MO 65802

Phone (417) 833-4282
Judith A. McClung, Editor
Pub. *Roots Researchers*, three times per
   year, $6.00 per year subscription;
   (includes Looney, Caldwell,
   Hildebrand and Sweaney)

Loop
*Loop/Lupp/Leupp Family
2 Georgetown Drive
Amherst, NH 03031
Phone (603) 673-9073
Victor L. Bennison

Loop
Loop Family Reunion
1019 S.E. 37th
Portland, OR 97214
Phone (503) 235-2968
Joan Loop
(includes descendants of three brothers,
   John Loop and wife Mary Jane Fulton,
   Adam Loop and wife Amanda
   Norman, and Joseph Loop and wife
   Sarah Farmer, who came to Oregon
   from Tennessee between 1900 and
   1910)
Reunion

Loos (see Wert)

Loppnow (see Sager)

Lorah
*Pennsylvania-German Lorah Family
107 West Sunhill Road
Manheim, PA 17545
Phone (717) 665-5869
D. Ernest Weinhold
(especially descendants of the very early
   immigrants who settled in northeast
   Lancaster County, Pennsylvania, and
   nearby areas)

Lord (see Corson, Farrington, Johnson)

Lord
*Lord Reunion
3131 Old Jonesboro Road
PO Box 82371
Hapeville, GA 30354
Phone (404) 767-8449
Helen Gunnin Mishasek, Author
Annual reunion on the last Saturday of
   September at Black's Creek Baptist
   Church outside of Commerce, Georgia

Lord
*The Sons and Daughters of Nathan
   Lord
55 Lafayette Street
PO Box 954
Yarmouth, ME 04096-0954
Phone (207) 846-4092
Matson M. Lord

Lords (see Gunnin)

Loretan (see Pellien)

Lorimer (see Garner)

Lorne (see Stewart)

Lorthridge (see Lokrig)

Loterell (see Luttrell)

Lothenor (see Cowart)

Lothenore (see Cowart)

Lothridge (see Lokrig)

Lothrop (see Clark)

Lotridge (see Lokrig)

Lotspeich (see The Memorial
   Foundation of the Germanna Colonies)

Lott (see Farrington, Paulk)

Lott
Lott Lineages
PO Box 1035
North Highlands, CA 95660-1035
Phone (916) 991-4165
Sally Seaman Williams, Editor
Pub. *Lott Lineages*, irregularly, $5.50 per
   issue

Lott
Lott Family Newsletter
956 West Pajard Road
Las Cruces, NM 88005-3532
Carol Ainsworth McElligott
Pub. *Lott Family Newsletter*, quarterly,
   $12.00 per year subscription

Lottie (see Wofford)

Lottridge (see Lokrig)

Loucks (see Kunkel, Louks)

Louden (see Bates, MacDuff)

Louden
*The Louden-Thomas-Hamby Reunion
7673 Shields Road
Lewisburg, OH 45338
Phone (513) 962-4909
Shelby Jean Lawson Alexander, Co-
   ordinator
(includes descendants of William Henry
   Louden and allied families of Ayers,
   Baird, Bowlin, Croley, Crowley,
   Dabney, Hembree, Lawson, Loudin,
   Lowden, Muse, Owens, Rains, Siler
   and Walden)
Annual reunion on the last Sunday of
   July at Shelter #2, Indian Mountain
   State Park, Jellico, Tennessee

Loudin (see Louden)

Loudon (see MacDuff)

Louew (see Lowe)

Lough (see Lowe)

Loughenor (see Cowart)

Loughenore (see Cowart)

Loughlan (see MacLachlan)

Loughlin (see MacLachlan)

Loughmiller
*Loughmiller Family Genealogy
   Organization
13715 CR 2216
Tyler, TX 75707-9619
Phone (903) 566-1842
Grover C. Loughmiller, President
(includes descendants and progenitors of
   George Washington Loughmiller of
   McMinn County, Tennessee, ca 1840–
   50s)

Loughrey
Loughrey Families of America
   Association
3830 Sixth Avenue, Apartment 7B
Des Moines, IA 50313-3462
Delores B. Loughrey-Larson, Historian

Loughridge (see Lokrig)

Loughrige (see Lokrig)

Louks
*Louks/Loucks Reunion
1 Forest View Drive
Cumberland, RI 02864
Phone (401) 333-3128
Ross W. McCurdy

Lourwood (see Stone)

Loury (see Lowrey)

Louthan
*Louthan/Louthen Families
1571 Green Valley, N.W.
Orangeburg, SC 29115
Phone (803) 534-4589
Dolores R. Ham
(includes descendants of James
   (–ca 1820 Wythe County, Virginia) and
   Frances Louthan)
Biennial reunion in even-numbered years
   on the first Saturday of July

Louthen (see Louthan)

Love (see Folk Family Surname
   Exchange, Clark, MacKinnon,
   McMillan)

Love
Roots 'n Things
11910 Windmill Road
Colorado Springs, CO 80908-4169
Pat Stubblefield Warner
Pub. *Love Letters*, quarterly, $10.00 per
   year subscription

Loveall (see Lovell)

Lovel (see Lovell)

Lovelace (see Wright)

Lovell (see Surname Sources, Collette, Cowart, McGrath, Richardson)

Lovell
Lovell Lineage (Oxfordshire Lovells)
2301 North Lafayette
Grand Island, NE 68801
Phone (308) 384-0124
Sharon Lovell Gergen
Pub. *Lovell Lineage*, quarterly, $5.00 per year subscription; (includes Loveall, Lovel and Lovil)

Lovell
*Lovell Family Association
12 Leone Road
Tom's River, NJ 08755-6321
Phone (908) 349-8157
Elisabeth Lovell Bowman, C.G.
Pub. *Lovell Family Association Newsletter*, biannually; (includes descendants of Alexander Lovell of Medfield, Massachusetts, 1640)
$3.00 per year membership for individuals, $5.00 per year membership for families; biennial reunion in even-numbered years on the second Sunday of August

Lovil (see Lovell)

Loving (see Bourland)

Loving
Loving Family Association
14333 Aldengate Road
Midlothian, VA 23113
Anne Hale Kellam

Lovingood (see Dockery)

Low (see Freer, Lowe)

Lowden (see Bates, Louden)

Lowe (see Frasher, Hatfield)

Lowe
Lowe-Low-Lau-Louew-Lough
4801 Woodhall
Detroit, MI 48224-2226
Brenda Lowe-Acquaviva
Pub. *Lowe-Low-Lau-Louew-Lough*, quarterly, $16.00 per year subscription

Lowe
*Lowe Database
1887 Yallup Road, Rt. 4
Saint Johns, MI 48879
Phone (517) 224-7807
Arlene Lowe Lounds
(includes descendants of Robert Anthony Lowe (son of Mary McCracken and Thomas Lowe) and Sarah McFarland, Ireland 1800s, Canada after 1840)

Lowell (see Corson)

Lowell
*John Lowell Family Organization
1136 West Lincoln Drive
Pasco, WA 99301-3551
Phone (509) 545-6596
Durward Malcolm Lowell, II

Lowery
Lowery
Whispering Oaks
5821 Rowland Hill Road
Cascade, MD 21719-1939
Phone (301) 416-2660
Victor Gebhart, President
Pub. *Lowery*, annually, $2.00 per issue

Lowrance
Lowrance Family Organization
2305 North Roosevelt Avenue
Springfield, MO 65803-2154
Gayford R. Lowrance, Editor
Pub. *Lowrance Letters*

Lowrance
*Lowrance Database
152 Rockwood Road
Florham Park, NJ 07932
Phone (201) 966-1862
Peter B. Berendsen

Lowrey (see Caton)

Lowrey
*The Thomas and Mary Lowrey Family Association
36 Scotland Avenue
Madison, CT 06443
Phone (203) 245-4769
Marjorie M. Lowrey, Historian
Pub. *Newsletter*, semiannually; (includes descendants of Thomas Lowrey of Northern Ireland and Mary Loury of Scotland, who arrived in Boston ca 1727 on the same ship and were married in 1732 and had six sons: Thomas, John, Nathaniel, David, Samuel and Daniel)
$10.00 per year membership

Lowrey
Lowrey Family Organization
Pattonsburg, MO 64670
Mrs. D. Lowrey

Lowris (see Arthur)

Lowry (see Bosher, MacLaren)

Lowry
Sharon Loury and Associates
128 Royal Drive
Winterville, NC 28590-9103
Sharon Loury
Pub. *The Lowry Quarterly*
$12.00 per year membership

Lowther (see Lambert)

Loy (see Stewart)

Loyall (see Wiese)

Lubcke (see Lubcker)

Lubcker
*Frederick Lubcker Family
3025 Napoleon Avenue
Tampa, FL 33611-5323
Phone (813) 831-0414
Edna Lubcker Gramlich
(database includes Lubcker/Lubcke/Luebecke, Germany to 1870, New York City from 1870 to the present)

Lucas
Lucas Quarterly
2868 Harrison Street
San Francisco, CA 94110
Larry Burnett
Pub. *Lucas Quarterly* (includes descendants of Dennis Lucas of Ontario, Canada)

Lucas
Lucas Ledger
Rt. 2, Box 76
3650 LaPlata Highway
Farmington, NM 87401
Mr. Lucas
Pub. *Lucas Ledger*, quarterly, $10.00 per year subscription

Luce
Luce Lines
166 Sand Pointe Lane
Bay Pointe, CA 94565
Phone (510) 458-4479
Louisa Luce-Horton
Pub. *Luce Lines—Our Family Newsletter*, semiannually, free

Lucken (see Links Genealogy Publications)

Luckens
Links Genealogy Publications
7677 Abaline Way
Sacramento, CA 95823-4224
Phone (916) 428-2245
Iris Carter Jones, Editor
Pub. *Luckens-Luken(s)-Lukin(s)*, quarterly, $7.00 per year subscription

Lucklaw (see MacDuff)

Ludlam (see Surname Sources)

Ludlow (see Surname Sources)

Ludlow
Ludlow Lines
1940 Galveston Street
San Diego, CA 92110
Evelyn R. Noderer, Editor
Pub. *Ludlow Lines*, three times per year

Ludlum (see Surname Sources)

Luebecke (see Lubcker)

Luellen (see Llewellyn)

Lugton (see MacDuff)

Luken (see Links Genealogy
    Publications, Luckens)

Luken
Luken Family History
927 East Seventh Street
Salt Lake City, UT 84102
E. G. Luken
Pub. *Luken Family History*

Lukens (see Luckens)

Lukin (see Luckens)

Lukins (see Luckens)

Lumbair (see Keith)

Lumbert (see Lush)

Lummis (see Loomis)

Lumpkin
*Lumpkin Family Reunion
531 Lockshire Road
Columbia, SC 29210
Phone (803) 772-4788
Dalton A. Parker, Historian (*ex officio*)
(includes descendants of Spencer and
    Dorothy Lumpkin through their two
    sons, Robert Lumpkin (1791–) and
    William Lumpkin (1801–) and his
    second wife Susan Longest (1815–))
Reunion

Lumpkin
*Lumpkin Exchange
16315 Jim Creek Road
Arlington, WA 98223
Michele Heiderer

Lumsden (see Forbes)

Lunceford (see Folk Family Surname
    Exchange, Lundsford)

Lund
*Charley Edwin Lund Family
    Organization
161 West 1500 North
Rexburg, ID 83440
Phone (208) 356-8340
Kay Clark
(includes descendants of Charley Edwin
    Lund (1876 Richmond, Cache County,
    Utah–) and Margaret Lucy Baker
    (1885 Franklin, Oneida County,
    Idaho–))

Lunday (see Lundy)

Lunday
*Lunday/Ketchum History
3628 West Earll Drive

Phoenix, AZ 85019-4243
Phone (602) 278-5225
Fay L. S. Arellano, Publisher
(includes Lunday in Georgia before
    1700, also Ketchum (Delaware Indian)
    in Kansas before 1868)

Lundeen (see Wigelius)

Lundie (see Lundy, MacDuff)

Lundin (see MacDuff, Wigelius)

Lundine (see MacDuff)

Lundsford
Lundsford-Lunceford-Lancelot-Lunsford
    Family Association
2306 Westgate
Houston, TX 77019
Phone (713) 529-2333
Harold Helm
$25.00 plus pedigree and family group
    sheets for membership

Lundy (see MacDuff)

Lundy
Lundy Newsletter
(308 Linderman Avenue—location)
PO Box 2327 (mailing address)
West Monroe, LA 71294
Phone (318) 322-1345
Toni Blain Rodgers, Editor
Pub. *Lundy Newsletter*, quarterly, $12.00
    per year subscription, free queries;
    (includes Lunday and Lundie)

Lunergan (see Cian)

Lunnen
*Thomas Lunnen Family Organization
1780 Siesta Drive
Sandy, UT 84093-6247
Phone (801) 942-6414
Dona Miller West

Lunsford (see Folk Family Surname
    Exchange, Dockery, Lundsford)

Lunt (see McCune)

Lupp (see Loop)

Lupton
The Luptonian
413 Main Street
PO Box 443
Bayboro, NC 28515
Phone (919) 745-7037; (919) 745-3569
David W. Lupton, Editor
Pub. *The Luptonian*, irregularly, free
Reunion

Lurie (see Israelite)

Lurkey (see Gibson)

Lurvey (see Newton)

Lush (see Hull)

Lush
*Lush Database
19259 Harleigh Drive
Saratoga, CA 95070
Phone (408) 867-2677
Robert E. Hull
(includes descendants of Edmund Lush
    of East Knoyle, Wiltshire, England and
    related families of Adams, Alexander,
    Anderson, Barnett, Bedford, Bewell,
    Blake, Brittain, Brood, Brown, Burris,
    Carpenter, Childress, Christensen,
    Clark, Collins, Collis, Colvin, Davis,
    Dawson, Derham, Dixon, Elwell,
    Erickson, Glascock, Gledhill, Gorton,
    Hague, Hahn, Hall, Harris,
    Hazelwood, Henderson, Hess, Hicks,
    Higley, Hornby, Hull, Hunter, Irwin,
    Jacobson, Jensen, Johnson, Jones,
    Keck, Kempsell, Kent, Kersey, Lee,
    Long, Lumbert, Mairs, Mashek,
    Meighbors, Moon, Moore, Morgan,
    Morrill, Munson, Myers, Naugle,
    Nelson, Niece, Olson, Painter, Peers,
    Prior, Prussia, Rankin, Reller, Rice,
    Roberts, Rohde, Rudd, Russell,
    Schmalz, Slininger, Smith, Stearns,
    Stewart, Taylor, Thompson, Uhlendorf,
    Wagner, Walters, Waugh, Welch,
    Wheeler, Wichern, Wilson, Wooldridge
    and Wrigglesworth)

Lute (see Newmyer)

Luteral (see Luttrell)

Luther
*Luther Family Association
2531 Lakeview Street
Lakeland, FL 33801
Phone (813) 665-5788
George A. Luther, Secretary
Pub. *The Luther Family Newsletter*,
    quarterly (February, May, August and
    November); (includes descendants of
    Captain John Luther of the
    Massachusetts Bay Colony, 1630–
    1635, whose sons Samuel and
    Hezekiah were original settlers of
    Swansea)
$10.00 donation per year membership;
    reunion every five years

Luthje (see Beestman)

Luthreal (see Luttrell)

Luthrel (see Luttrell)

Luthrell (see Luttrell)

Lutreal (see Luttrell)

Lutrel (see Luttrell)

Lutrell (see Luttrell)

Luts (see Lutt)

Lutt
Lutt/Lutts/Luts Seekers
RR 1, Box 141
Cedar Point, KS 66843-9733
Phone (316) 273-6411 (A.M.)
Judy Lutt, Historian

Lutteral (see Luttrell)

Lutterel (see Luttrell)

Luttreal (see Luttrell)

Luttreall (see Luttrell)

Luttrel (see Luttrell)

Luttrell (see Haws)

Luttrell
*The K.A.R.D. Files
19305 S.E. 243rd Place
Kent, WA 98042-4820
Phone (206) 432-1659
Judy K. Dye, Owner
Pub. *Luttrell Lineages and Data*,
    irregularly, $6.00–$7.00 per volume
    (Washington State residents add 8.2%
    sales tax); (includes Litrel, Litrell,
    Littreal, Littrel, Littrell, Loterell,
    Luteral, Luthreal, Luthrel, Luthrell,
    Lutreal, Lutrel, Lutrell, Lutteral,
    Lutterel, Luttreal, Luttreall and Luttrel)

Lutts (see Lutt)

Lutz
Lutz Family Organization
22916 Carlow Road
Torrance, CA 90505
Phone (310) 378-3574
Charlene DeLong

Lutz
Lutz Reunion
Rural Delivery
Kempton, PA 19529
Mrs. George Henry

Lutzky (see Eisloeffel)

Luyken (see Links Genealogy
    Publications)

Luykens (see Links Genealogy
    Publications)

Luzynski
*Luzynski Surname Exchange
570 East Main Street
Gaylord, MI 49735
Phone (517) 732-6035
M. J. Luzenski, Publisher

Lybarger
*Lybarger Memorial Association
PO Box 611
Delaware, OH 43015-0611
Lee H. Lybarger, Secretary

Pub. *Lybarger Linkages*, semiannually;
    (includes Lebarger, Leinbarger,
    Leyberger and Lyberger)
$10.00 per year membership

Lyell (see Addiville)

Lyfield (see Newton)

Lyle (see Addiville, Chaney, Lambert,
    Stewart, Wright)

Lyle
Lyle/Lile Family Organization
352 South Belaire
Monett, MO 65708
R. Barekman

Lyman (see Clark)

Lyman
Lyman Reunion
190 Powder Hill Road
Middlefield, CT 06455
Margaret Lyman
(includes descendants of Richard Lyman
    of High Ongar, England, came to
    America in 1631)

Lyman
Lyman
PO Box 9700
Dixon, MO 65459
Ms. Jorn Jamieson
Pub. *Lyman*, quarterly, $9.00 per year
    subscription
Reunion

Lynch (see Lambert)

Lynch
*Lynch Family Association
1712 Clay Street
Fairfield, CA 94533
Phone (707) 422-9297
Del Lynch, Editor
Pub. *Lynch Family Association*,
    quarterly; (includes descendants of
    John Lynch and Mary Moore, 1600s)
$12.00 per year membership for
    individuals, $15.00 per year
    membership for families

Lynch
*Lynch, Parker, Edmundson,
    Satterthwaite, Bradley, Hopkins,
    Cutchin and Taylor Families of
    Edgecombe County, NC
Rt. 3, Box 139
Greenville, NC 27858
Phone (919) 752-8168
W. John Lynch
(includes related families in Edgecombe
    Halifax, Northampton, Bertie, Pitt,
    Martin, Hyde, Beaufort and Hertford
    counties, North Carolina, and in
    Nansemond County, Virginia,
    exclusively: Bell, Boykin, Braddy,
    Braswell, Britt, Butler, Carlisle,
    Council, Courtenay, Deloach, Drake,

Howard, Howell, Hudnal, Hyatt, Hyde,
    Kitchen, Pender, Pittman, Weeks and
    Wells)

Lyndon (see MacLennan)

Lynn
Lynn/Linn Lineage
3510 Turnberry Drive
McHenry, IL 60050-7557
Phone (815) 385-9626
Phyllis J. Bauer, Editor
Pub. *Lynn/Linn Lineage Quarterly*,
    (spring, summer, fall and winter),
    $18.00 per year subscription, $20.00
    (U.S. funds) per year foreign
    subscription, queries free to
    subscribers, queries $3.00 to non-
    subscribers, back issues available

Lyon (see Surname Sources)

Lyon
*Lyon/Lyons Families Association of
    America
524 Mark Lane
Belton, MO 64012-1829
Phone (816) 331-4193
S/T Ted Thomas Lyons
Pub. *The Lyon's Tale*, three times per
    year (January–April, May–August and
    September–December); (includes all
    spellings)
$5.00 per year membership; reunion
    every third year in various locations

Lyons (see Blossom Press, The
    Memorial Foundation of the Germanna
    Colonies, Corson, Dean, Heath, Lyon)

Lytell (see Blossom Press)

Lyttle (see Arthur)

Maag (see Arthur)

MaBaxter (see MacMillan)

Mabee (see Maybee)

Maberry (see Mayberry)

Mabey (see Maybee)

Mabie (see Maybee)

Mabry (see Dean, Mayberry)

Maby (see Maybee)

MacAdam (see Gregor, McAdams)

MacAdams (see McAdams)

MacAdie (see Fergusson)

MacAfee (see Macfie)

MacAfie (see Macfie)

MacAinsh (see Gregor, MacInnes)

MacAlary (see Cian)

Macaldonich (see Buchanan)

MacAldowie (see Gregor)

MacAlenon (see MacLennan)

MacAlester (see Gregor)

MacAlinden (see MacLennan)

MacAlionion (see MacLennan)

MacAlister (see Gregor)

MacAlister
Clan MacAlister Society International
PO Box 4311
Clearlake, CA 95422-4311
Michael Fletcher McAllister, Chairman
Pub. *Fortiter*, bimonthly
$15.00 per year membership

Macalman (see Buchanan)

MacAlonan (see MacLennan)

MacAlpine (see Gregor, McAlpin)

Macandeoir (see Buchanan, Macnab)

MacAndrew (see Ross)

MacAndrews (see Chattan)

MacAngus (see Gregor, MacInnes)

MacAnich (see MacInnes)

MacAninch (see MacInnes)

MacAnish (see Gregor, MacInnes)

MacAnsh (see Gregor)

Macara (see MacRae)

MacAra (see Gregor)

MacAree (see Gregor)

Macarra (see MacRae)

MacArthur (see Cian)

MacArthur
*Clan MacArthur Society of Clan Arthur
24479 Audubon Drive
Brooksville, FL 34601
Phone (904) 796-0170
Christine McA. Ruckdeschel, Secretary
Pub. *The Roundtable*, quarterly; (includes
  Arthur and other spellings)
$15.00 per year membership

Macartney (see MacCartney)

Macaslan (see Buchanan)

Macaulay
Clan Macaulay
PO Box 343
West Union, SC 29696
Phone (803) 638-6945
Alexander S. Macaulay, Representative

MacAuliffe (see Cian)

Macauselan (see Buchanan)

MacAwliff (see Cian)

MacAy (see Shaw)

MacAys (see Macnachton)

MacBain (see MacBean, Mackay)

MacBaine (see MacBean)

MacBaines (see MacBean)

MacBane (see MacBean)

MacBayn (see MacBean)

MacBayne (see MacBean)

MacBean (see Chattan)

MacBean
*The MacBean Clan in North America
The Clan MacBean Foundation
441 Wadsworth Boulevard, Suite 213
Denver, CO 80226
Phone (303) 233-6002 FAX
Raymond L. Heckethorn, Treasurer
Pub. *The Clan Register*, quarterly;
  (includes Bain, Baine, Baines, Bane,
  Bayn, Bayne, Bean, Beane, Bee,
  Beean, Been, Beene, Beth, Binnie,
  Elvain, Elvaine, Elvane, Elvayne,
  Elveen, Elwain, Elwane, Elwayne,
  Elwee, MacBain, MacBaine,
  MacBaines, MacBane, MacBayn,
  MacBayne, MacBeane, MacBee,
  MacBeean, MacBeen, MacBeene,
  MacBinnie, MacElvain, MacElvaine,
  MacElvane, MacElvayne, MacElveen,
  MacElwain, MacElwane,
  MacElwayne, MacElwee, MacIlvain,
  MacIlvaine, MacVain, MacVaine,
  MacVane, MacVayn, MacVayne,
  MacVaynes, MacVean, MacVeane,
  MacVee, MacVeen, MacVeene,
  MacVian, MacWain, MacWaine,
  MacWane, M'Bean, McAlvin,
  McBain, McBaine, McBaines,
  McBane, McBayn, McBayne,
  McBeain, McBean, McBeane,
  McBeath, McBee, McBeean, McBeen,
  McBeene, McBheath, McBinnie,
  McElvain, McElvaine, McElvane,
  McElvayne, McElveen, McElwain,
  McElwane, McElwayne, McElwee,
  McIlvain, McIlvaine, McIlvayne,
  McIlvean, McIlveen, McIlveene,

McIlwain, McIlwane, McIlwee,
  McVain, McVaine, McVane, McVayn,
  McVayne, McVaynes, McVean,
  McVeane, McVee, McVeen, McVeene,
  McVian, McWain, McWaine,
  McWane, Vain, Vaine, Vane, Vayn,
  Vayne, Vaynes, Vean, Veane, Vee,
  Veen, Veene, Vian, Wain, Waine, Wane
  and certain of the MacBeth Clan)
$18.00 per year membership

MacBeane (see MacBean)

MacBeath (see Gillean)

MacBee (see Gillean, MacBean)

MacBeean (see MacBean)

MacBeen (see MacBean)

MacBeene (see MacBean)

MacBeth (see Gillean, MacBean)

MacBeth
*Clan MacBeth Society of North
  America
Indiana Point
Hebron, NH 03241
Phone (603) 744-5559
Fred Firth, President
Pub. *MacBeth Newsletter*, bimonthly;
  (includes Baty, Beath, Beaton, Beaty,
  Beltone, Bethune, Forrester, Leech,
  MacBeth, MacFinlay and McFinlay)
$15.00 per year membership for families

MacBinnie (see MacBean)

MacBrady (see Cian)

MacBrayne (see Macnachton)

MacBroodin (see Cian)

MacCade (see Fergusson)

MacCainsh (see Gregor, MacInnes)

MacCaiodh (see Mackay)

MacCallum
MacCallum/Malcolm Clan Society
1830 Fawsett Road
Winter Park, FL 32789
A. MacCallum

MacCallum
Clan MacCallum/Malcolm Society
403 Kemp Avenue
Roanoke Rapids, NC 27870
Phone (919) 537-0712
Donald A. Malcolm, Treasurer

MacCalman (see Buchanan)

MacCalmont (see Buchanan)

MacCamie (see Stewart)

MacCammond (see Buchanan)

MacCance (see Gregor, MacInnes)

MacCanich (see Cunning)

MacCanish (see MacInnes)

MacCansh (see MacInnes)

MacCants (see MacInnes)

MacCarroll (see Cian)

MacCarson (see Macpherson)

MacCarthy (see Cian)

MacCarthy-Welply (see Cian)

MacCartney (see Cian)

MacCartney
*MacCartney Clan Society
827 Continental Boulevard
Toledo, OH 43607
Phone (419) 536-5690
Kenneth E. MacCartney, Convenor-
    Editor
Pub. *The McCartney Newsletter*,
    quarterly (second series); (includes
    Macartney, MacCartney and
    McCartney families in Scotland,
    Ireland and throughout the world)
$6.00 per year membership

MacCarvill (see Cian)

MacCasland (see Buchanan)

MacCaura (see Cian)

MacCaw (see Mackay, Stewart)

MacCeol (see Macnachton)

MacChlerich (see Macpherson)

MacChlery (see Macpherson)

MacChoiter (see Gregor)

MacChoning (see Cunning)

MacClachlan (see MacLachlan)

MacClachlane (see MacLachlan)

MacClachlen (see MacLachlan)

MacClair (see Macpherson)

MacClanachan (see MacLennan)

MacClanaghan (see Cian)

MacClanchan (see MacLennan)

MacClanchy (see Cian)

MacClaron (see MacLennan)

MacClauchlane (see MacLachlan)

MacClaughlin (see MacLachlan)

MacCleary (see Cian, Macpherson,
    MacPherson)

MacCleish (see Macpherson,
    MacPherson)

MacClelland (see MacLennan)

MacClenaghan (see Cian)

MacClendon (see MacLennan)

MacClennen (see MacLennan)

MacClerich (see Gregor, Macpherson)

MacClooney (see Macpherson)

MacCloonie (see Macpherson)

MacClouchlin (see MacLachlan)

MacCloy (see Stewart)

MacCluney (see Macpherson)

MacClunie (see Macpherson)

MacCluny (see Macpherson)

MacCoghlan (see Cian)

MacColl (see Macnachton, Stewart)

MacColman (see Buchanan)

MacColwan (see Buchanan)

MacComas (see Gunn)

MacCombe (see Stewart)

MacCommon (see Buchanan)

MacConacher (see MacDougall)

MacConachie (see Gregor,
    Donnachaidh)

MacConchie (see Donnachaidh)

MacCondach (see Gregor)

MacCondochie (see Gregor)

MacConechy (see Donnachaidh)

MacConich (see Cunning)

MacConing (see Cunning)

MacConnochie (see Donnachaidh)

MacConochar (see Cunning)

MacConochie (see Cunning)

MacConquchar (see Cunning)

MacConry (see Cian)

MacConsidine (see Cian)

MacCorcoran (see Cian)

MacCorey (see Currie)

MacCorkill (see Gunn)

MacCorkle (see Gunn)

MacCormac (see Cian)

MacCormack (see Buchanan, Cian)

MacCormick (see Cian, Gillean,
    MacLaine)

MacCosgrave (see Cian)

MacCoubrey (see Buchanan)

MacCoughlan (see Cian)

MacCoul (see MacDougall)

MacCowan (see MacDougall)

MacCowis (see Macfie)

MacCoy (see Mackay)

MacCra (see MacRae)

MacCrach (see MacRae)

MacCracken (see Macnachton)

MacCrae (see Cian, MacRae)

MacCraith (see MacRae)

MacCraken (see Gillean)

MacCrary (see McCrary)

MacCraw (see MacRae)

MacCray (see MacRae)

MacCrea (see MacRae)

MacCreath (see MacRae)

MacCree (see MacRae)

MacCrie (see MacRae)

MacCrimmon (see Gregor)

MacCrouther (see Gregor)

MacCrow (see MacRae)

MacCroy (see MacRae)

MacCruiter (see Buchanan)

MacCubbie (see Buchanan)

MacCubbin (see Buchanan)

MacCubbin
MacCubbin Clan Lineage
1305 Poppy Avenue
Pensacola, FL 32507-2238
Sheila L. Martin
Pub. *MacCubbin Clan Lines*, at least
   three times per year
$12.00 per year membership

MacCuish (see Macfie)

MacCullich (see Donnachaidh)

Maccullie (see Gunn)

MacCulloch (see MacDougall)

MacCuning (see Cunning)

MacCunneain (see Cunning)

MacCurrach (see Macpherson,
   MacPherson)

MacCurrie (see Currie, Macpherson)

MacCurry (see Currie, Macpherson,
   MacPherson)

MacDhubsite (see Macfie)

MacDiarmid (see Gregor)

Macdoffy (see Macfie)

MacDolothe (see MacDougall)

MacDonachie (see Donnachaidh)

MacDonald (see Shurtleff)

MacDonleavy (see Buchanan, Stewart)

MacDonnell (see Cian)

MacDonough (see Cian)

MacDonoughe (see Cian)

MacDonovan (see Cian)

MacDougall
Clan MacDougall Society of the United
   States and Canada
15 Partridge Lane
Greenville, SC 29601
Phone (803) 235-2747
George E. McDougall, President
(includes septs: Carmichael, Conacher,
   Cowan, Dougall, Livingston(e),
   MacConacher, MacCoul, MacCowan,
   MacCulloch, MacDolothe,
   MacDougall, MacDowell, MacHowall,
   MacKirchen, MacLucas, MacLucash)

MacDowell (see MacDougall)

Macduff (see MacDuff)

MacDuff
*Clan MacDuff Society of America, Inc.
4528 Greenhill Way
Anderson, IN 46012
Phone (317) 643-2929
Ted McDuffee, Convener
Pub. *Clan MacDuff Newsletter*, quarterly;
   (includes associated surnames:
   Abbot(t), Abboutoun, Abercrombie,
   Abercromby, Abernethy, Achmutie,
   Achmuty, Ackroyd, Acland, Adam(s),
   Ad(d)ie, Adnauchtan, Albo(u)rn(e),
   Alburn, Alfred, Amours, Andson,
   Annal, Anson, Anstruther, Anthony,
   Arderne, Ardist, Ardnot(t), Ardross,
   Arduthie, Arduthy, Ashcroft, Ashton,
   Atherstone, Atherton, Auchmutie,
   Auchmuty, Aughmutie, Aughmuty,
   Auldson, Aven, Ayton, Bait(s),
   Balbirnie, Balbirny, Balcanquall,
   Balcanwell, Balcaskie, Balcasky,
   Balcomie, Balcomy, Baldennie,
   Baldenny, Balfour, Balgarvie,
   Balgarvy, Balkenwall, Ballard,
   Ballardie, Ballardy, Ballcanwall,
   Ballenwall, Ballingall, Ballingshall,
   Balmahay, Balmakin, Balram,
   Balvaird, Balwearie, Balweary,
   Bannatie, Bannaty, Barclay, Barret,
   Barron, Basillie, Basilly, Beaton,
   Beaumont, Bedson, Belfrage,
   Ben(n)ison, Beniston(e), Berner,
   Bethune, Beveridge, Bissie, Bissy,
   Blabirn, Blaburn, Blaw, Blow, Blund,
   Blunt, Bogle, Bonthron(e), Book,
   Boosey, Boosie, Boswell, Bowman,
   Bowsie, Bowsy, Boyter, Brandin,
   Brandon, Bread, Brog, Buik, Buist,
   Buncle, Bunkle, Burt, Buttercase,
   Calley, Calvie, Calvy, Cambo,
   Cameron, Cant, Carment, Carnbee,
   Carnbie, Carneil, Carstairs, Ceras,
   Ceres, Christie, Christy, Clark,
   Clephane, Clerk, Cock, Collier,
   Colyear, Cooper, Corbie, Corby,
   Cotton, Coupar(er), Cowper, Crail,
   Crale, Cram(b), Crambie, Cramby,
   Creech, Creel, Cuffe, Culross,
   Dalgetty, Darsie, Darsy, Dehart,
   Dempsterton, Dibbs, Dishart, Dodd(s),
   Dott, Duff, Dunbar, Dunstan, Durie,
   Dys(h)art, Eaton, Ednie, Edny, Ely,
   Erskine, Fairfield, Fairfoul, Fairfull,
   Farefull, Farmer, Farquharson of
   Invercauld, Feathers, Featherston(e),
   Feldie, Feldy, Fernie, Ferny, Fetters,
   Fife, Finnick, Finnock, Flisk(e),
   Flockhart, Flockhert, Flucker, Forgan,
   Forret, Francis, Fressley, Fresslie,
   Frodsham, Fyall, Fyf(f)e, Gallard,
   Galrig, Gedd, Gellie, Gelly, Gibson,
   Gillespie, Glas, Golden, Gollan,
   Goodlap, Goodlet, Goodsir,
   Goodwiley, Goodwilie, Goodyear,
   Gorley, Gorlie, Gos(s)man, Gourlay,
   Gourley, Gow, Gray, Greagory, Gregg,
   Gregor, Greig, Hackett, Haliburton,
   Halkett, Hannay, Hardie, Hardy,
   Harrower, Hatchett, Haugh,
   Hawk(e)(s), Hay, Heatherwick,
   Heatherwyck, Henderson, Hogarth,
   Hoggard, Hoggart, Home, Honeyman,
   Hope, Horsburgh, Hug, Huggan,
   Hume, Iliff, Illiffe, Izatt, Izzett, Jeffery,
   Jose, Joss, Keddie, Kenluck,
   Kennaway, Kennoway, Keppie,
   Kilgore, Kilgour, Kilmaron, Kilmartin,
   Kineardune, Kinghorn, Kinloch,
   Kinlough, Kinnaman, Kinnear,
   Kinninmonth, Kinross, Kirk(k)aldie,
   Kirk(k)aldy, Krail, Kynnimond, Laing,
   Lambert, Landale, Landels, Landsman,
   Lang, Lathrisk, Laurenson, Lawler,
   Learmonth, Leethian, Leighton,
   Lentron, Leslie, Lessels, Lethan,
   Leuchars, Leurs, Leven, Lindores,
   Lindors, Lindsay, Loggie, Logie,
   Long, Louden, Loudon, Lucklaw,
   Lugton, Lundie, Lundin(e), Lundy,
   Macduff, Macdufson, Macgill,
   Macgough, Machardie, Machardy,
   Machay, Macinross, Mack,
   Mackintosh, Maclundie, Maclundy,
   Macouff, Mactrustie, Mactrusty,
   Maine(s), Malcolm, Mar, Markinch,
   Marr, Masterton, Mather(s), Maynard,
   Mayne(s), Mcduff, Meek(s), Meik,
   Meiklejohn, Meiks, Melburn(e),
   Mentiplay, Merchant, Mergie, Mergy,
   Mires, Mithceison, Moncur,
   Moneypenny, Monypenny, Mortimer,
   Mount(s), Mowbray, Mowbrey,
   Munnoch, Munnock, Murison, Myres,
   Nesbet, Nesbitt, Ness, Nid(d)ie,
   Nid(d)y, Nudie, Nydie, Nydy, Orrick,
   Orrock, Oswald, Pate, Pattie, Pattison,
   Pattullo, Peattie, Peddie, Phin(n),
   Pinkerton, Pitcairn, Pittenweem,
   Playfair, Preston, Primrose, Quarral(s),
   Quarrel(s), Raith, Ramsay, Randall,
   Randell, Randle(s), Randolph,
   Ranle(i)llor, Readie, Ready, Reiach,
   Reith, Rendall, Rendell, Rendle,
   Reuel, Robertson, Royds, Rule,
   Saltoun, Sandford, Sandilands, Sands,
   Scott, Scott of Balweary, Scrimgeour,
   Scrymgeour, Seath, Seggie, Seggy,
   Seybold, Shaw, Shaw of Torclarroch,
   Shearer, Sheerer, Sherar, Shoolbread,
   Sibbald, Sibball, Sibbuld, Sidey, Sidie,
   Silverton, Silvester, Smairt, Smart,
   Speedie, Speedy, Spence, Spens,
   Spess, Spink(s), Spowatt, Squair,
   Squire, Stark, Steuart, Stewart,
   Stirk(s), Stormont, Strang, Strong,
   Stuart, Sylvester, Syras, Tennant,
   Thall(i)on, Theobald, Torbain, Torn,
   Torr, Toshack, Trail(l), Trainer,
   Trainor, Trent, Tullar, Tuller, Tullis,
   Turcan, Tynemouth, Venters, Wakelin,
   Wallach, Walloch, Wardlaw, Wardrop,
   Warren(der), Watchman, Watson,
   Wedderburn, Weems, Weepers, Wells,
   Wellwood, Wemyss, Westburn,
   Westwater, Westwood, Weymes,
   Whitelaw, Whyte-Melville, Wilkie,

Willard, Williamson, Wimbs,
Wim(m)s, Winram, Workman,
Wormet, Wymbs, Wymes, Wyms,
Yellowlees, Yellowley, Yellowlie,
Younger)
$15.00 per year membership for
individuals, $20.00 per year
membership for families (member and
spouse and any children under
eighteen), $5.00 per year for non-
voting membership for individuals
under eighteen

MacDuff
*MacDuff or McDuff Surname
   Organization
John Robertson MacDuff Family
   Organization
639 East 3100 North
North Ogden, UT 84414
Phone (801) 782-4432
Laraye Sheridan

MacDuffee
MacDuffee Clan of America
159 Hester Road
Guyton, GA 31312
Pub. *MacDuffee Clan of America Journal*

MacDuffee
*MacDuffee/Macfie Clan Society of
   America, Inc.
Member Society of the International Clan
   Macfie
239 Kobert Avenue
Lebanon, KY 40033
Phone (502) 692-4255
W. Coleman McDuffee, President
Pub. *Clan Chatter*, quarterly (spring,
   summer, fall and winter); (includes
   Cathie, Duffee, Fee, MacDuffee,
   Macfie, MacFie, MacGuffey,
   MacPhee, Mahaffey, McAfee, etc.)
$20.00 per year membership for
   individuals over 30, $10.00 per year
   membership for individuals 30 and
   under, $150.00 life membership

MacDuffie (see Macfie)

Macdufson (see MacDuff)

MacDurkan (see Cian)

Mace (see Mays)

MacEgan (see Cian)

MacElheran (see Stewart)

MacEligod (see Cian)

MacEligodd (see Cian)

MacElligott (see Cian)

MacElmeel (see MacMillan)

MacElvain (see MacBean)

MacElvaine (see MacBean)

MacElvane (see MacBean)

MacElvayne (see MacBean)

MacElveen (see MacBean)

MacElwain (see MacBean)

MacElwane (see MacBean)

MacElwayne (see MacBean)

MacElwee (see MacBean)

MacEnery (see Cian)

MacEniry (see Cian)

MacErries (see Fergusson)

MacEwan (see Gregor)

MacEwan
Clan MacEwan Association of North
   America
4087 Sunset Lane
Pebble Beach, CA 93953-3049
Robert L. McEwing, High Commissioner
Pub. *MacEwan*

MacEwens (see MacLachlan)

MacEye (see Mackay)

MacFadden (see Cian, MacLaine)

MacFaddien
*MacFaddien Family Society
Rt. 1, Box 28
Sardinia, SC 29143
Phone (803) 473-2643
Norman McFaddin, Sr., President and
   Treasurer
Pub. *The MacFaddien News*, quarterly;
   (family in America since 1730,
   includes Burgess, Cousar, DuRant,
   Epps, Fraser, Frierson, MacFayden,
   McCutchen, McFadden, McFaddin,
   McFadin, McKnight, Montgomery,
   Muldrow, Nelson, Rose, Scarborough,
   Wilson, Witherspoon and Woods)
$10.00 per year membership

MacFarlane
Clan MacFarlane Association of Arrochar
6509 Old Railroad Bed Road
Toney, AL 35773
Chris Scantland, Minister of Publications
Pub. *The Defender*, quarterly
$8.00 per year membership for
   individuals, $12.00 per year
   membership for families

MacFarlane
MacFarlane Clan in the U.S.A. and
   Canada
1 Park Place, #450
Atlanta, GA 30318
I. MacFarlane

MacFarlane
*Clan MacFarlane Society
27-A Maple Street
Essex Junction, VT 05452
Phone (802) 878-8575
Alan Powell, Vice President Membership
Pub. *MacFarlane's Lantern*, quarterly
$12.00 per year membership for
   individuals, $18.00 per year
   membership for families

MacFayden (see Gillean, MacFaddien)

MacFergus (see Fergusson)

MacFhearghuis (see Fergusson)

MacFie (see MacDuffee, Macfie)

Macfie
*International Clan Macfie
102 Cloverbrook Court
Jamestown, NC 27282
Phone (910) 454-4121
Boyt H. Cathey, Chairman of the
   Genealogy Committee
(includes Cathey, Cathie, Dufacius,
   Duffy, Fee, Haffey, MacAfee,
   MacAfie, MacCowis, MacCuish,
   MacDhubsite, Macdoffy, MacDuffie,
   MacFie, MacGuffie, MacHaffie,
   MacPhee, Macphied, Mahaffy,
   Makduffie, Makfeithe, McAfee,
   McAfie, McAphie, McCafferty,
   McCaffrey, McDiffie, McDuffie,
   McDuffy, McFee, McFeithe, McFeye,
   McFie, McGuffie, McIphie, McPhee,
   McPheir, McPhie, M'Duffe, etc.)

Macfie
*Macfie Clan Society of North America
7501 Hickory Ridge Road
Mount Juliet, TN 37122

MacFinlay (see MacBeth)

MacFirries (see Fergusson)

MacGaradh (see Hay)

MacGarra (see Hay)

MacGarrow (see Hay, Stewart)

MacGaw (see Mackay)

MacGeach (see Gregor)

MacGee (see Mackay)

MacGeehee (see Mackay)

MacGeorge (see Buchanan, Gregor)

MacGhee (see Mackay)

MacGhie (see Mackay)

MacGhilc (see MacLachlan)

MacGibbon (see Buchanan, Graham)

MacGilbert (see Buchanan)

MacGilchrist (see MacLachlan)

MacGilfoyle (see Cian)

Macgill (see MacDuff)

MacGill
MacGill Society U.S.A.
35 Treasure Drive
Riverdale, GA 30296
Fred Houston, President
(includes MaGill, McGill, Gills, etc.)

MacGill
MacGill Society
282 Christmas Ridge
Berea, KY 40403
J. Carroll McGill, President

MacGillecrist (see MacLachlan)

MacGillicuddy (see Cian)

MacGillies (see Macpherson)

MacGillilian (see MacLennan)

MacGillis (see MacPherson)

MacGillivoor (see MacGillivray)

MacGillivray (see Chattan, Gillean, MacLaine)

MacGillivray
The Clan MacGillivray
7233 North Denver Avenue
Portland, OR 97217
Phone (503) 286-8740
Bruce P. McGillivray, United States Commissioner
(includes Gilray, Gilroy, Gilvray, MacGillivoor, MacGilroy, MacGilvra, Macgilvray, Macilroy, Macilvrae, Milroy, Roy, etc.)

MacGilpatic (see Cian)

MacGilpatick (see Cian)

MacGilpatrick (see Cian)

MacGilroy (see MacGillivray)

MacGilvernock (see Graham)

MacGilvra (see MacGillivray)

Macgilvray (see MacGillivray)

MacGinnes (see MacInnes)

MacGinnis (see MacInnes)

MacGlachan (see MacLachlan)

MacGlachen (see MacLachlan)

MacGlachland (see MacLachlan)

MacGlachlin (see MacLachlan)

MacGlashan (see Donnachaidh, Stewart)

MacGlauchin (see MacLachlan)

MacGlauchlan (see MacLachlan)

MacGlauchlin (see MacLachlan)

MacGlauchlon (see MacLachlan)

MacGlaughlin (see MacLachlan)

MacGlothin (see MacLachlan)

MacGlothlon (see MacLachlan)

MacGlotten (see MacLachlan)

MacGlottin (see MacLachlan)

MacGloughlan (see MacLachlan)

MacGloughlin (see MacLachlan)

MacGlouthlin (see MacLachlan)

MacGnish (see MacInnes)

MacGouen (see Macpherson)

Macgough (see MacDuff)

MacGoun (see Macpherson)

MacGow (see Macpherson)

MacGowan (see Macpherson, MacPherson)

MacGrade (see Cian)

MacGrady (see Cian)

MacGrath (see Cian, MacRae)

MacGratten (see Macnachton)

MacGraw (see MacRae)

MacGray (see McGray)

MacGregor (see Gregor)

Macgregor
*Grier and Company
144 Downing Street
Denver, CO 80218-3917
Phone (303) 744-8416
William M. Grier, Jr., Publisher

MacGreusich (see Buchanan)

MacGrewar (see Gregor)

MacGrigor (see Gregor)

MacGrouther (see Gregor)

MacGruder (see Gregor)

MacGruer (see Gregor)

MacGruther (see Gregor)

MacGubbin (see Buchanan)

MacGuffey (see Douglas, MacDuffee)

MacGuffie (see Macfie)

MacGuffock (see Douglas)

MacGunyon (see Cunning)

Mach (see Mock)

MacHaffie (see Macfie)

Machardie (see MacDuff)

Machardy (see MacDuff)

Machay (see MacDuff)

MacHay (see Hay, Shaw)

Machella (see Blossom Press)

Machen
Courier Publications
PO Box 1284
Natchitoches, LA 71458-1284
Annette Carpenter Womack
Pub. *Machen Family Courier*, at least three times per year, $12.50 per year subscription

MacHendrie (see Macnachton)

MacHendry (see Macnachton)

MacHenry (see Cian)

MacHerries (see Fergusson)

Machett (see Day)

Machlachlin (see MacLachlan)

MacHlachlin (see MacLachlan)

MacHowall (see MacDougall)

Machray (see MacRae)

Machu (see Ammons)

MacIan (see Gunn)

MacIlchreist (see MacLachlan)

MacIlcrist (see MacLachlan)

MacIldowie (see Gregor)

MacIlduff (see Gregor)

MacIlduy (see Gregor)

MacIll-Christ (see MacLachlan)

MacIllichrist (see MacLachlan)

MacIlriach (see Fraser)

Macilroy (see MacGillivray)

MacIlroy (see Gregor)

MacIlvain (see MacBean)

MacIlvaine (see MacBean)

MacIlvern (see Graham)

Macilvrae (see MacGillivray)

MacInally (see Buchanan)

MacInch (see MacInnes)

MacIndeor (see Buchanan)

MacIndoe (see Buchanan)

MacInlay (see Fergusson)

MacInnery (see Cian)

MacInnes (see Gregor)

MacInnes
*Clan MacInnes Society
8232 Kay Court
Annandale, VA 22003
Phone (703) 560-4371;
    (703) 560-2080 FAX
Mary A. Faulk, Executive Secretary/
    Treasurer/Editor
Pub. *The Thistle and the Bee*, quarterly;
    (includes Angus, Inch, MacAinsh,
    MacAngus, MacAnich, MacAninch,
    MacAnish, MacCainsh, MacCance,
    MacCanish, MacCansh, MacCants,
    MacGinnes, MacGinnis, MacGnish,
    MacInch, MacInnis, MacInnish,
    MacKinnes, MacKinnis, MacKinnish,
    MacMaster, MacMasters, MacNeice,
    MacNeish, MacNesh, MacNess,
    MacNiece, MacNinch, MacNish,
    Magennis, Maginnis, Masters,
    Masterson and all corresponding
    Mc- variations)
$15.00 per year membership for
    individuals, $20.00 per year
    membership for families, $17.50 and
    $22.50 per year membership outside
    the U.S.

MacInnis (see MacInnes)

MacInnish (see MacInnes)

Macinross (see MacDuff)

MacInstalker (see Gregor)

MacIntaylor (see Macnachton)

MacIntire (see MacIntyre)

MacIntosh (see Mackintosh)

MacIntosh
MacIntosh Clan Society
567 Olmstead
Evansville, IN 47711
William Ritchie

Macintosh
Clan Macintosh Washington DC area
2604 Bayview Lane
Silver Spring, MD 20906
Phone (301) 460-4550
Nicholas McIntosh, Convener of North
    America

MacIntyre (see Chattan, Gregor)

MacIntyre
MacIntyre Clan Association
10703 Tenbrook Drive
Silver Spring, MD 20906
Phone (301) 593-7989
Dorothy McIntire, Secretary

MacIntyre
Clan MacIntyre Association
Rt. 1, Box 193-C
Kingsland, TX 78639
Phone (915) 388-3608
Jerry L. McIntyre, Secretary
(includes MacIntire, McEntyre,
    Wright, etc.)

MacIrish (see Fergusson)

MacIrwin (see Irwin)

MacIver (see Donnachaidh)

MacIvor (see Donnachaidh)

MacJames (see Donnachaidh)

Mack (see MacDuff)

MacKai (see Mackay)

MacKames (see Gunn)

MacKay (see Mackay, McKay)

Mackay
Clan Mackay Society of North America
Eastern and Western Regions, USA
23890 Summit Road
Los Gatos, CA 95030
Phone (408) 353-4369
Barbara Paul Fanshier, Convener
(includes Allen, Bain, Bayne, Kay, Keay,
    Kee, Key, Kie, MacBain, MacCaiodh,
    MacCaw, MacCoy, MacEye, MacGaw,
    MacGee, MacGeehee, MacGhee,
    MacGhie, MacKai, Mackay, MacKay,

MacKee, MacKey, MacKie, MacKoy,
    MacPhail, MacQuade, MacQue,
    MacQuey, MacQuoid, MacVail,
    Magee, McCay, McCoy, McFall,
    McGee, McKay, McKee, McKey,
    McKie, McPhail, McQuade, McQuaid,
    Morgan, Neilson, Nelson, Paul,
    Paulson, Pole, Poleson, Pollard, Quay,
    Quey, Reay, Scobie, Williamson)

MacKay
*Clan MacKay Society of USA
52490 Auonelle Street
Granger, IN 46530
Phone (219) 272-4222
Andrew MacKay Betts, President

MacKay
Clan MacKay Society
93 Killam Hill Road
Boxford, MA 01921
Branson A. McKay

MacKclauchlane (see MacLachlan)

MackClenden (see MacLennan)

MacKeamish (see Gunn)

MacKean (see Gunn)

MacKeddie (see Fergusson)

MacKee (see Mackay)

MacKeely (see Cian)

MacKeith (see Keith, Macpherson,
    MacPherson)

Macken (see McCanna)

MacKendrick (see Macnachton)

MacKenrick (see Macnachton)

MacKeogh (see Cian)

MacKeon (see Folk Family Surname
    Exchange, MacLachlan)

MacKeowan (see MacLachlan)

MacKeowen (see MacLachlan)

MacKeowin (see MacLachlan)

MacKeown (see MacLachlan)

MacKerras (see Fergusson)

MacKerron (see Stewart)

MacKersey (see Fergusson)

Mackerwithey (see Withy)

Mackerwithy (see McWethy)

Mackes (see Meckes)

MacKestan (see Fergusson)

MacKewan (see MacLachlan)

MacKewen (see MacLachlan)

MacKewn (see MacLachlan)

MacKey (see Mackay)

Mackey
The James and Mary Mackey Family
PO Box 459
Paris, TX 75460
D. Mackey

Mackey
*Samuel and Phebe Wilkinson Mackey
  Family Organization
295 West Union
Manti, UT 84642
Phone (801) 835-9872; (602) 461-9836
David G. Mackey, Vice President
Pub. *Mackey Family Newsletter*, two to
  three times per year; (includes
  descendants of Samuel Mackey (1800–
  1890) and Phebe Wilkinson (1804–
  1886) Conestoga, Lancaster County,
  Pennsylvania, and Manti, Sanpete
  County, Utah)
Donation for membership

MacKhone (see MacLachlan)

MacKibb (see Buchanan)

MacKie (see Mackay)

Mackie
Mackie Family Association
Rt. 1, Box 193
Nora Springs, IA 50458
Leona Mackie Montag
Pub. *Mackie Family Association
  Newsletter*, quarterly
$5.00 per year membership

Mackie
Mackie Family Association
PO Box 891
Yadkinville, NC 27055
Andrew L. Mackie
Pub. *Mackie Family Association
  Newsletter*, quarterly

MacKilchrist (see MacLachlan)

MacKilligan (see MacLennan)

MacKin (see McCanna)

MacKinlay (see Buchanan)

MacKinnes (see MacInnes)

MacKinney (see MacKinnon)

MacKinning (see MacKinnon)

MacKinnis (see MacInnes)

MacKinnish (see MacInnes)

MacKinnon (see McKinnon)

MacKinnon
*The Clan MacKinnon Society of North
  America, Inc.
4012 Tyndale Drive
Jacksonville, FL 32210
Phone (904) 771-2864
N. Joann MacKinnon Osborne, High
  Commissioner
Pub. *The Shank Bone* (includes septs:
  MacKinney, MacKinning, MacKinven,
  Love, MacMorran)
$15.00 per year membership for
  individuals, $25.00 per year
  membership for families

Mackintosh (see MacDuff)

MacKintosh (see Chattan)

Mackintosh
*Clan Mackintosh of North America
729 Freeport Road
Creighton, PA 15030
Ronand D. Wassel, Secretary
Pub. *Mists of Moigh*, quarterly; (includes
  McIntosh, MacIntosh, Mackintosh and
  Tosh)
$10.00 per year membership for
  individuals, $15.00 per year
  membership for families

MacKinven (see MacKinnon)

MacKirchen (see MacDougall)

Mackittrick (see Maxwell)

MackLandon (see MacLennan)

MacKlawachlane (see MacLachlan)

Macklechreist (see MacLachlan)

MackLenddon (see MacLennan)

MacKlendin (see MacLennan)

MackLendon (see MacLennan)

Macklin (see Mechling)

Macknew (see McNew)

MacKnight (see Macnachton)

MacKown (see MacLachlan)

MacKoy (see Mackay)

MacKuen (see MacLachlan)

MacKuin (see MacLachlan)

MacKune (see MacLachlan)

MacLachan (see MacLachlan)

MacLachen (see MacLachlan)

MacLachian (see MacLachlan)

MacLachin (see MacLachlan)

MacLachine (see MacLachlan)

MacLachlain (see MacLachlan)

MacLachlainn (see MacLachlan)

MacLachlan
*Clan MacLachlan Association of North
  America
PO Drawer 14102
Durham, NC 27709
James A. Finegan, Secretary
Pub. *The Roebuck*, quarterly; (includes
  Claflin, Lachie, Lachlainn, Lachlan,
  Lachlann, Lachlanson, Lachlieson,
  Lachy, Laflan, Laflen, Laflin,
  Lauchlan, Laughlan, Laughland,
  Laughlen, Laughlin, Laughlon,
  Laughton, Lauhghlan, Locklan,
  Lockland, Loughlan, Loughlin,
  M'Clachlane, M'Clachlene,
  M'Claichlan, M'Clauchlan,
  M'Kclachlane, M'Klachlane,
  M'Lauchan, M'Lauchland,
  M'Laughland, M'Lawchtlane,
  MacClachlan, MacClachlane,
  MacClachlen, MacClauchlane,
  MacClaughlin, MacClouchlin,
  MacGlachan, MacGlachen,
  MacGlachland, MacGlachlin,
  MacGlauchin, MacGlauchlan,
  MacGlauchlin, MacGlauchlon,
  MacGlaughlin, MacGlothin,
  MacGlothlon, MacGlotten,
  MacGlottin, MacGloughlan,
  MacGloughlin, MacGlouthlin,
  Machlachlin, MacHlachlin,
  MacKclauchlane, MacKlawachlane,
  MacLachan, MacLachen, MacLachian,
  MacLachin, MacLachine,
  MacLachlain, MacLachlainn,
  MacLachlan, MacLachland,
  MacLachlane, MacLachlann,
  MacLachlen, MacLachlin,
  MacLachline, MacLachlon,
  MacLachlun, MacLackken,
  MacLacklan, MacLacklane,
  MacLacklen, MacLacklin,
  MacLackline, MacLacklon,
  MacLaclan, MacLaflen, MacLaflin,
  MacLaghlan, MacLaghlane,
  MacLaouhlan, MacLauchlain,
  MacLauchlan, MacLauchland,
  MacLauchlane, MacLauchleam,
  MacLauchleine, MacLauchlen,
  MacLauchlin, MacLauchline,
  MacLauchlon, MacLaucklan,
  MacLaughlan, MacLaughland,
  MacLaughlane, MacLaughlen,
  MacLaughlin, MacLaughlon,
  MacLaughlun, MacLaughton,
  MacLauthlan, MacLauthlin,
  MacLawhlan, MacLawlan,
  MacLlauchland, MacLochan,

MacLochlainn, MacLochlan, MacLochlin, MacLochlon, MacLocklan, MacLouchlan, MacLoughlan, MacLoughlin, MacLouthan, MacLuchlayne, Makclachlane, Makclauchlane, Makclotan, Makclowden, Maklawchlan, McClachlan, McClachlane, McClachlen, McClauchlane, McClaughlin, McClouchlin, McGlachan, McGlachen, McGlachland, McGlachlin, McGlauchin, McGlauchlan, McGlauchlin, McGlauchlon, McGlaughlin, McGlothin, McGlothlon, McGlotten, McGlottin, McGloughlan, McGloughlin, McGlouthlin, Mchlachlin, McHlachlin, McKclauchlane, McKlawachlane, McLachan, McLachen, McLachian, McLachin, McLachine, McLachlain, McLachlainn, McLachlan, McLachland, McLachlane, McLachlen, McLachlen, McLachlin, McLachline, McLachlon, McLachlun, McLackken, McLacklan, McLacklane, McLacklen, McLacklin, McLackline, McLacklon, McLaclan, McLaflen, McLaflin, McLaghlan, McLaghlane, McLaouhlan, McLauchlain, McLauchlan, McLauchland, McLauchlane, McLauchleam, McLauchleine, McLauchlen, McLauchlin, McLauchline, McLauchlon, McLaucklan, McLaughlan, McLaughland, McLaughlane, McLaughlen, McLaughlin, McLaughlon, McLaughlun, McLaughton, McLauthin, McLauthlan, McLawhlan, McLawlan, McLlauchland, McLochan, McLochlainn, McLochlan, McLochlin, McLochlon, McLocklan, McLouchlan, McLoughlan, McLoughlin, McLouthan, McLuchlayne, O'Laughlen, O'Laughlin, O'Loughlin, Vclauchlayne; sept Gilchrist: Crist, Gikchrist, Gilchrest, Gilchris, Gilkchrist, Gillenchreist, Gillechreiste, Kilchrist, M'Gilchrist, M'Gilcreist, M'Lecgreist, M'Lechreist, M'Yllecrist, MacGhilc, MacGilchrist, MacGillecrist, MacIlchreist, MacIlcrist, MacIll-Christ, MacIllichrist, MacKilchrist, Macklechreist, Makgilkriste, McGhilc, McGilchrist, McGilleycrist, McIlchreist, McIlcrist, McIll-Christ, McIllichrist, McKilchrist and V'Lechreist; sept MacEwens: MacKeon, MacKeowan, MacKeowen, MacKeowin, MacKeown, MacKewan, MacKewen, MacKewn, MacKhone, MacKown, MacKuen, MacKuin, MacKune, MacOunn, MacOwan, MacOwans, MacOwen, MacOwens, MacOwin, MacOwins, MacQuone, MacQuowen, MacQuowens, Makevin, Makewin, Makewn, McCeun,

McCoan, McCoin, McCoon, McCoun, McCuan, McCuen, McCuidhean, McCuithan, McCuithein, McCune, McCunn, McEoghan, McEroune, McEwan, McEwen, McEwin, McEwing, McGoon, McGruen, McKeon, McKeowan, McKeowen, McKeowin, McKeown, McKewan, McKewen, McKewn, McKhone, McKown, McKuen, McKuin, McKune, McOunn, McOwan, McOwans, McOwen, McOwens, McOwin, McOwins, McQuone, McQuowen, McQuowens, Owen, Owens and VcQuhewin
$20.00 per year membership for families (individuals at same house)

MacLachland (see MacLachlan)

MacLachlane (see MacLachlan)

MacLachlann (see MacLachlan)

MacLachlen (see MacLachlan)

MacLachlin (see MacLachlan)

MacLachline (see MacLachlan)

MacLachlon (see MacLachlan)

MacLachlun (see MacLachlan)

MacLackken (see MacLachlan)

MacLacklan (see MacLachlan)

MacLacklane (see MacLachlan)

MacLacklen (see MacLachlan)

MacLacklin (see MacLachlan)

MacLackline (see MacLachlan)

MacLacklon (see MacLachlan)

MacLaclan (see MacLachlan)

MacLaflen (see MacLachlan)

MacLaflin (see MacLachlan)

MacLagan (see Donnachaidh)

MacLaghlan (see MacLachlan)

MacLaghlane (see MacLachlan)

MacLain (see Gillean)

MacLaine (see Gillean)

MacLaine
*Clan MacLaine of Lochbuie
4744 Casper Drive
Roanoke, VA 24019
Phone (703) 362-4706
Barry W. Hartman, Lieutenant to the Chief

Pub. *The Battleaxe*, quarterly; (includes MacLaine, MacLean, MacCormick, MacFadden, Patton, Huie and MacGillivray)
$15.00 per year membership

MacLamon (see MacLennan)

MacLanaghan (see Cian)

MacLandon (see MacLennan)

MacLane (see Gillean)

MacLaouhlan (see MacLachlan)

Maclaren (see MacLaren)

MacLaren
*Clan MacLaren Society of North America
3632 Lakeside Drive
Louisville, TN 37777
Phone (423) 970-2926
Dr. James B. McLaren, Sr., President and Genealogist
Pub. *MacLaren Standard*, quarterly, (includes Law, Lawerance, Lowry, Maclaren and Patterson)
$25.00 per year membership

MacLauchlain (see MacLachlan)

MacLauchlan (see MacLachlan)

MacLauchland (see MacLachlan)

MacLauchlane (see MacLachlan)

MacLauchleam (see MacLachlan)

MacLauchleine (see MacLachlan)

MacLauchlen (see MacLachlan)

MacLauchlin (see MacLachlan)

MacLauchline (see MacLachlan)

MacLauchlon (see MacLachlan)

MacLaucklan (see MacLachlan)

MacLaughlan (see MacLachlan)

MacLaughland (see MacLachlan)

MacLaughlane (see MacLachlan)

MacLaughlen (see MacLachlan)

MacLaughlin (see MacLachlan)

MacLaughlon (see MacLachlan)

MacLaughlun (see MacLachlan)

MacLaughton (see MacLachlan)

MacLauthlan (see MacLachlan)

MacLauthlin (see MacLachlan)

MacLawhlan (see MacLachlan)

MacLawlan (see MacLachlan)

MacLawson (see Cian)

MacLean (see Chattan, Gillean, MacLaine)

MacLean
MacLean Clan Society of the Carolinas
PO Box 1489
Lumberton, NC 28358
H. MacLean

MacLean
Clan MacLean Association
4536 20th, N.E.
Seattle, WA 98105
Phone (206) 522-4557
Marjorie T. Lev

MacLear (see Macpherson, MacPherson)

MacLeary (see Macpherson, MacPherson)

MacLeay (see Stewart)

MacLees (see Macpherson)

MacLeish (see Macpherson, MacPherson)

MacLeister (see Gregor)

MacLellan (see MacLennan)

MacLellan
*MacLellan Clan in America, Inc.
5230 Angelita Avenue
Dayton, OH 45424-2709
Phone (513) 233-1543
John W. McClellan, Membership Secretary
Pub. *Think On*, quarterly; (includes MacLellan, all spellings, and related surnames such as Clelland, Gilfillan, Gilleland, Gilliland)
$15.00 per year membership

MacLellen (see MacLennan)

MacLenadhan (see MacLennan)

MacLenagan (see MacLennan)

MacLenahan (see MacLennan)

MacLendall (see MacLennan)

MacLenden (see MacLennan)

MacLendon (see MacLennan)

MacLennan
*Clan MacLennan Association of America
765 West Holcomb Lane
Reno, NV 89511
Phone (702) 358-2200
John E. McLennan, M.D., Eoin Mhor of Kintail
Pub. *Furze*, quarterly; (includes Logan, MacLellan, MacLendon and MacLennan)
$35.00 per year membership

MacLennan
*Clan MacLennan Association, USA Branch
(Highland Heritage House, Inc., The Parsonage, Saint George Square—location)
Willtown Bluff (mailing address)
Adams Run, SC 29426
Phone (803) 889-2979
Marilyn Wallace MacLennan Baumeister, National Secretary and Museum Trustee
Pub. *Clan MacLennan Newsletter*, quarterly; (includes MacLennan, its septs and variations: Cleland, Clelland, Gillian, Gilliland, Gillilman, Gilliman, Kneland, Lagan, Laggan, Lenan, Lennan, Lennon, Leonard, Leonerd, Linden, Lindon, Lobban, Logan, Lyndon, MacAlenon, MacAlinden, MacAlionion, MacAlonan, MacClanachan, MacClanchan, MacClaron, MacClelland, MacClendon, MacClennen, MacGillilian, MackClenden, MacKilligan, MackLandon, MackLenddon, MacKlendin, MackLendon, MacLamon, MacLandon, MacLellan, MacLellen, MacLenadhan, MacLenagan, MacLenahan, MacLendall, MacLenden, MacLendon, MacLennan, MacLennon, MacLernon, MacLoran, MacLorinan, MacLyndon, MacWilname, McClenda, McClendal, McClendon, McLendon, McLennon, Meclendon, Winan and Winning)
$20.00 for first year membership, $15.00 per year membership renewal

MacLennon (see MacLennan)

MacLeod
*Clan MacLeod Society, U.S.A., Inc.
7909 Loch Lane
Columbia, SC 29223
Phone (616) 527-2715 (Editor in Ionia, Michigan)
Jack McLeod Stephens, Secretary; Harry E. Boyes, Editor
Pub. *The Clan MacLeod Newsletter*, semiannually
$20.00 per year membership

MacLerie (see Macpherson, MacPherson)

MacLernon (see MacLennan)

MacLew (see Stewart)

MacLewis (see Stewart)

MacLise (see Macpherson, MacPherson)

MacLish (see Macpherson)

MacLiver (see Gregor)

MacLlauchland (see MacLachlan)

MacLochan (see MacLachlan)

MacLochlainn (see MacLachlan)

MacLochlan (see MacLachlan)

MacLochlin (see MacLachlan)

MacLochlon (see MacLachlan)

MacLocklan (see MacLachlan)

MacLoran (see MacLennan)

MacLorinan (see MacLennan)

Maclory (see Macpherson)

MacLouchlan (see MacLachlan)

MacLoughlan (see MacLachlan)

MacLoughlin (see MacLachlan)

MacLouthan (see MacLachlan)

MacLoy (see Stewart)

MacLucas (see MacDougall)

MacLucash (see MacDougall)

MacLuchlayne (see MacLachlan)

Maclundie (see MacDuff)

Maclundy (see MacDuff)

MacLunie (see MacPherson)

MacLyndon (see MacLennan)

MacLysaght (see Cian)

MacMagnus (see Fergusson)

MacMahon (see Cian)

MacMains (see Gunn)

MacManus (see Gunn)

MacMaster (see Buchanan, MacInnes)

MacMasters (see MacInnes)

MacMath (see Macnachton)

MacMaurice (see Buchanan)

MacMeil (see MacMillan)

MacMenzies (see Menzies)

MacMhuirrich (see Currie)

MacMichael (see Stewart)

MacMillan (see Blue)

MacMillan
*Clan MacMillan Society of North
    America
600 Fort Hill Drive
Vicksburg, MS 39180-2134
C. MacMillan
Pub. *Newsletter of Clan MacMillan
    Society of North America*, three times
    per year, free with membership

MacMillan
*Clan MacMillan, Appalachian Branch
1314 40th Avenue
Kenosha, WI 53144
Phone (414) 552-7075
Dottie McMillan, Secretary/Treasurer
Pub. *MacMillan Newsletter*, quarterly;
    (includes Baxter, Bell, Blue, Brown,
    Broun, MaBaxter, MacElmeel,
    MacMeil, MacNamiel, Walker and
    Waulker)
$15.00 per year membership renewal,
    $20.00 for new members; annual
    meeting on the second weekend of
    July at Grandfather Mountain, North
    Carolina

MacMinn (see Menzies)

MacMonies (see Menzies)

MacMorran (see MacKinnon)

MacMorris (see Buchanan)

MacMunn (see Stewart)

MacMurchie (see Buchanan)

MacMurdo (see Macpherson,
    MacPherson)

MacMurdoch (see Macpherson,
    MacPherson)

MacMurdock (see Macpherson)

MacMurich (see MacPherson)

MacMurphy (see Buchanan)

MacMurrich (see Macpherson)

MacMurtrie (see Stewart)

MacNab
Clan MacNab Society of North America
2141 Camino Rey
Fullerton, CA 92633
Phone (714) 525-6544
Joan McNabb, Treasurer

Macnab
Clan Macnab Society
9760 Taft Road
Nunika, MI 49448
C. McNab Fortenbacher, President
(includes septs: Abbotson, Abbott,
    Dewar, Gilfallan and Macandeoir)

MacNachtan (see Macnachton)

Macnachton
*Clan Macnachton Association of North
    America
13028 Avenue La Valencia
Poway, CA 92064
Bonnie McNutt Bradt, Secretary
Pub. *The Red Banner*, quarterly (January,
    April, July and October); (includes
    Ayson, Bissett, Easson, Hendrie,
    Hendry, Kendrick, Kenrick, MacAys,
    MacBrayne, MacCeol, MacColl,
    MacCracken, MacGratten,
    MacHendrie, MacHendry,
    MacIntaylor, MacKendrick,
    MacKenrick, MacKnight, MacMath,
    MacNachtan, MacNaghten,
    MacNaight, MacNair, MacNamell,
    MacNaught, MacNaughtan,
    MacNaughton, MacNayre, MacNeid,
    MacNett, MacNeur, MacNevin,
    MacNicol, MacNight, MacNitt,
    MacNiven, MacNuir, MacNutt,
    MacNuyer, MacQuaker, MacVicker,
    Naughton, Nevin, Nivenson, Nutt,
    Porter, Weir)
$20.00 per year membership, $300.00
    life membership

MacNaghten (see Macnachton)

MacNaight (see Macnachton)

MacNair (see Macnachton)

MacNairn (see Stewart)

MacNamara (see Cian)

MacNamell (see Macnachton)

MacNamiel (see MacMillan)

MacNaught (see Macnachton)

MacNaughtan (see Macnachton)

MacNaughton (see Macnachton)

MacNay (see Gregor)

MacNayre (see Macnachton)

MacNea (see Gregor)

MacNeal (see Macneil)

MacNee (see Gregor)

MacNeice (see Gregor, MacInnes)

MacNeid (see Macnachton)

MacNeil (see Macneil)

MacNeil
*The Clan MacNeil Association of
    America
9420 Trillium Drive
Saint Louis, MO 63126-2840
Cora McNeil Beggs, Genealogist
Pub. *The Galley*, semiannually (spring
    and winter); (includes MacNeal,
    MacNeil, MacNiel, McNeely, McNeil,
    McNeill, Neal, Neilson, etc., all
    spellings, places)
Branches: **Alaska**, Mrs. Larry R.
    Peterson, PO Box 9546, Ketchikan,
    AK 99901; **Carolinas**, John A.
    McNeill, Sr., Commissioner, PO Box
    339, Whitesville, NC 28427; **Florida**,
    Robert A. MacNeille, Commissioner,
    12296 137th Street, North, Largo, FL
    34644; **Great Lakes/Canada**, Carolyn
    R. Neal, Commissioner, 2042 State
    Route 579, Curtice, OH 43412;
    Hawaii, Don W. McNeil,
    Commissioner, 5632 Kamaikui Street,
    Honolulu, HI 96821; **Kentucky/
    Tennessee**, Bruce M. McNeill,
    Commissioner, 3534 Kahlert Avenue,
    Louisville, KY 40215; **Mid-Atlantic**,
    Charles E. MacNeill, Commissioner,
    19105 Canadian Court, Montgomery
    Village, MD 20879; **Mid-West**,
    Donald P. Welling, Rt. 3, Box 298-A,
    Baldwin City, KS 66006; **Mississippi/
    Louisiana**, David L. McNeill, M.D.,
    Commissioner, 4400 General Meyer
    Avenue, #309, New Orleans, LA
    70114; **New England**, Warren E.
    Blake, Commissioner, PO Box 989,
    Jefferson, ME 04348; **Northern
    California**, Edgar E. MacNeill,
    Commissioner, 125 North Walnut, #6,
    Manteca, CA 95336; **Pacific
    Northwest**, Col. John H. Neilson,
    Commissioner, 17830 N.E. Everett
    Court, Portland, OR 97230; **South
    Atlantic**, Louis McNeill Quigley,
    Commissioner, 3008 Forest Lane,
    Oxford, AL 36203; **Southern
    California**, James McNeill Stancil,
    Commissioner, 3642 Mountainview,
    Pasadena, CA 91107; **Tennessee
    Valley**, J. Ralph Payne, F.S.A. Scot,
    113 Moss Street, Glasgow, KY 42141;
    Texas, Howard G. McNeil,
    Commissioner, 4012 Harlanwood, Fort
    Worth, TX 76109; **Wyoming/
    Nebraska**, John V. Hedrick,
    Commissioner, 5304 Eastview Street,
    Cheyenne, WY 82001
$15.00 per year membership

MacNeish (see Gregor, MacInnes)

MacNesh (see MacInnes)

MacNess (see Gregor, MacInnes)

MacNett (see Macnachton)

MacNeur (see Buchanan, Macnachton)

MacNevin (see Cian, Macnachton)

MacNevins (see Cian)

MacNey (see Gregor)

MacNicol (see Macnachton)

MacNicol
*Clan MacNicol The Americas
RR 2 Kerovach Road
Wellfleet, MA 02667
Phone (508) 349-1965
Chenoweth Watson, Membership
   Secretary
Pub. *Sgorr A Bhreac*, quarterly; (includes
   MacNicol, Nicol, Nicolson, etc.).
   Branches: **Australia**, Peter Nicol,
   Counsellor, PO Box 284, Chermside,
   Queensland 4032, Australia, (61)
   07-3502297; **New South Wales**, John
   Nicoll, Counselor, 2 Cameron Avenue,
   Basshill, New South Wales 2197,
   Australia, (61) 2-701682; **Scotland**,
   John A. Nicolson, Commissioner,
   Almond Bank, Viewfield Road,
   Portree, Isle of Skye, Scotland, (44)
   478-2696.
$15.00 per year membership

MacNie (see Gregor)

MacNiece (see MacInnes)

MacNiel (see Macneil)

MacNiesh (see Gregor)

MacNight (see Macnachton)

MacNinch (see MacInnes)

MacNish (see MacInnes)

MacNitt (see Macnachton)

MacNiven (see Macnachton)

MacNocaird (see Gregor)

MacNucator (see Gregor, Stewart)

MacNuir (see Macnachton)

MacNutt (see Macnachton)

MacNuyer (see Macnachton)

MacOmie (see MacThomas)

Macomish (see Gunn)

MacOmish (see MacThomas)

MacOnachie (see Donnachaidh)

MacOnich (see Donnachaidh)

Macouat (see Forbes)

Macouff (see MacDuff)

MacOunn (see MacLachlan)

MacOwan (see MacLachlan)

MacOwans (see MacLachlan)

Macowat (see Forbes)

MacOwen (see MacLachlan)

MacOwens (see MacLachlan)

MacOwin (see MacLachlan)

MacOwins (see MacLachlan)

MacPadden (see Cian)

MacPadine (see Cian)

MacPeter (see Gregor)

MacPetrie (see Gregor)

MacPhail (see Chattan, Mackay)

MacPhatridge (see Gregor)

MacPhee (see MacDuffee, Macfie)

Macpherson (see MacPherson)

MacPherson
MacPherson Clan Association (United
   States Branch)
142 Riverside Drive
The Spruces
Williamstown, MA 01267
H. Armitt
Pub. *The Urlar*, quarterly; (not primarily
   genealogical; includes Macpherson,
   McPherson and septs: Archibald,
   Carson, Cattanach, Clark, Clarkson,
   Clerk, Clunie, Currie, Ellis, Ellison,
   Ferson, Gillespie, Gillie, Gillies, Gillis,
   Gow, Gowan, Gowdie, Leary, Lees,
   MacCleary, MacCleish, MacCurrach,
   MacCurry, MacGillis, MacGowan,
   MacKeith, MacLear, MacLeary,
   MacLeish, MacLerie, MacLise,
   MacLunie, MacMurdo, MacMurdoch,
   MacMurich, MacVail, MacVurich,
   Murdo, Murdock, Murdoson, Parsons,
   Pearson, Pherson and Smith)
$15.00 per year membership

Macpherson
*Clan Macpherson Association, United
   States Branch
227 Amelia
Royal Oak, MI 48073-2659
Phone (313) 588-1623; Website: http://
   www.getnet.com~mhuirich/header.html
James W. McPherson, Membership
   Secretary
Pub. *Creag Dhubh* (international
   publication), annually; *The Urlar* (U.S.
   publication), quarterly; (includes
   Macpherson, MacPherson, McPherson
   (or other spellings) and septs: Allison,
   Archibald, Carson, Cattanach,
   Chlerich, Clark, Clarke, Clarkson,
   Clerk, Clooney, Clunie, Cluny, Currie,
   Currier, Curry, Ellis, Ellison, Ferson,
   Gillespie, Gillie, Gillies, Goudey,
   Goudie, Gow, Gowan, Keith, Leary,
   Lees, MacCarson, MacChlerich,
   MacChlery, MacClair, MacCleary,
   MacCleish, MacClerich, MacClooney,
   MacCloonie, MacCluney, MacClunie,
   MacCluny, MacCurrach, MacCurrie,
   MacCurry, MacGillies, MacGouen,
   MacGoun, MacGow, MacGowan,
   MacKeith, MacLear, MacLeary,
   MacLees, MacLeish, MacLerie,
   MacLise, MacLish, Maclory,
   MacMurdo, MacMurdoch,
   MacMurdock, MacMurrich, MacVail,
   MacVurich, MacVurrich, McCarson,
   McClooney, McCloonie, McCluney,
   McClunie, McCluny, Murdo,
   Murdoch, Murdock, Murdoson,
   Parson, Pearson, Person, Smith)
$20.00 per year membership for
   individuals, $225.00 life membership

MacPherson (see Chattan, Macpherson)

MacPhetridge (see McFatridte)

Macphied (see Macfie)

MacQuade (see Mackay)

MacQuaker (see Macnachton)

MacQuarie
*Clan MacQuarrie—Minnesota
3000 West River Parkway, #207
Minneapolis, MN 55406
Phone (612) 721-1886
Janel K. Harris
(includes descendants of Peter Crary
   (1645–1708) who married Christobel
   Gallup in 1677 in Stonington,
   Connecticut)

MacQuat (see Buchanan)

MacQuattie (see Forbes)

MacQuattiey (see Buchanan)

MacQue (see Mackay)

MacQueen (see Chattan, Gregor)

MacQuey (see Mackay)

MacQuinten (see Buchanan)

MacQuoid (see Mackay)

MacQuone (see MacLachlan)

MacQuowen (see MacLachlan)

MacQuowens (see MacLachlan)

MacQwan (see Gregor)

MacRa (see MacRae)

MacRach (see MacRae)

MacRae
*Clan MacRae Society of North America
3501 Oleander Drive
PO Box 3145
Wilmington, NC 28406
Phone (919) 392-3300; (910) 392-5123
  FAX
Hugh MacRae, II, President Emeritus
Pub. *Sgurr Uaran Newsletter*, four to six
  times per year; (includes Crae, Cree,
  Macara, Macarra, MacCra, MacCrach,
  MacCrae, MacCraith, MacCraw,
  MacCray, MacCrea, MacCreath,
  MacCree, MacCrie, MacCrow,
  MacCroy, MacGrath, MacGraw,
  Machray, MacRa, MacRach,
  MacRaith, MacRath, MacRaw,
  MacRay, MacRie, Rae, Raith, Ray,
  Rea, Reath). Chapters: **Southern
  Highlands** (Maryland, Virginia, West
  Virginia, North Carolina, South
  Carolina, Georgia, Tennessee and
  Kentucky); **New England** (Maine,
  New Hampshire, Vermont,
  Massachusetts, Connecticut and New
  York); **Northern Lights** (Minnesota,
  Wisconsin, Illinois, Missouri, Kansas,
  Nebraska, South Dakota, North Dakota
  and Iowa), c/o Roderick MacRae,
  Chairman, **Clan MacRae Northern
  Lights Chapter**, 1210 West 22nd
  Street, Minneapolis, MN 55405, (612)
  377-0130; **California** (California,
  Nevada, Oregon and Washington).
$30.00 per year membership for
  individuals or families

MacRaghnall (see Cian)

MacRaith (see MacRae)

MacRath (see MacRae)

MacRaw (see MacRae)

MacRay (see MacRae)

MacRie (see MacRae)

Macrob (see Innes)

MacRob (see Gunn, Stewart)

MacRobbie (see Donnachaidh)

MacRobert (see Donnachaidh)

MacRoberts (see Donnachaidh)

MacRobie (see Donnachaidh)

MacScanlan (see Cian)

MacSeartha (see Cian)

MacSheedy (see Cian)

MacShera (see Cian)

MacShille (see Graham)

MacSwene (see McSween)

MacTaggert (see Ross)

Mactary (see Innes)

MacTavert (see Fergusson)

MacTavish (see Fraser)

MacTavish
*Clan MacTavish Association
222 Katherine Avenue
Salinas, CA 93901-3136
Phone (408) 422-4212
Myron McTavish, Secretary
Pub. *Occasionally Published Association
  Newsletter*, irregularly
$5.00 per year membership

MacTear (see Ross)

MacThomas (see Chattan)

MacThomas
MacThomas Family Association
101 Countryside Drive
Hutchison, KS 67501
J. McComb

MacThomas
The Clan MacThomas Society
106 Eighth Street
Milford, PA 18337
John G. McComb, Commissioner, North
  America
(includes Combie, McColm, McComas,
  McComb(e), McCombie, McComie,
  McComish, MacOmie, MacOmish,
  Tam, Thom, Thomas, Thoms,
  Thomson)

MacTier (see Ross)

Mactire
*Clan Mactire (Wolf) Society, Inc.
3987 Indian Lakes Circle
Stone Mountain, GA 30083
Phone (404) 292-6003
Raymond M. McTyre, President
Pub. *Clan Mactire (Wolf) Society*

Newsletter, quarterly (January, April,
  July and October); (includes Mactear,
  Mactier, MacTier, MacTire, Mactyre,
  MacTyre, Mateaar, Matear, McTear,
  McTier, McTire, McTyeir, McTyeire,
  McTyer, McTyier, McTyiere, McTyre,
  McTyree, McTyrie, Tyree, Tyrie, etc.;
  clan dates from legendary chieftain
  Paul Mac/McTyre (1310–1386), "Son
  of Tyre", known as Paul MacTire
  ("Wolf of Ross"))
$10.00 per year membership

Mactrustie (see MacDuff)

Mactrusty (see MacDuff)

MacTyre (see Ross)

MacUlric (see Kennedy)

MacVail (see Mackay, Macpherson,
  MacPherson)

MacVain (see MacBean)

MacVaine (see MacBean)

MacVane (see MacBean)

MacVarich (see Currie)

MacVayn (see MacBean)

MacVayne (see MacBean)

MacVaynes (see MacBean)

MacVean (see MacBean)

MacVeane (see MacBean)

MacVee (see MacBean)

MacVeen (see MacBean)

MacVeene (see MacBean)

MacVey (see Gillean)

MacVian (see MacBean)

MacVicker (see Macnachton)

MacVurich (see Macpherson,
  MacPherson)

MacVurrich (see Macpherson)

MacWain (see MacBean)

MacWaine (see MacBean)

MacWalrich (see Kennedy)

MacWane (see MacBean)

MacWatt (see Forbes)

MacWattie (see Buchanan)

MacWhirter (see Buchanan)

MacWhorter (see Buchanan)

MacWilliam (see Donnachaidh, Gregor, Gunn)

MacWilname (see MacLennan)

Madama
Madama Family Newsletter
104 South Main Street
South Tom's River, NJ 08757
Phone (908) 341-1657
Khadi Antonia Madama
Pub. *Madama Family Newsletter*, $2.00 per year subscription

Madden
Madden Family Newsletter
1101 Wilmington Avenue, Apartment A
Dayton, OH 45420
Phone (513) 293-0779
Mariam W. Schaefer, Editor
Pub. *Madden Family Newsletter*, quarterly (February, May, August and November), $15.00 (U.S. funds) per year for subscription; (includes Madden by any spelling, worldwide)

Maddix (see Ross)

Maddock (see McRae)

Maddox (see Album)

Mader (see Meador)

Mader
*Mader Surname Organization
1257 North Main Street
Centerville, UT 84014-1107
Phone (801) 298-1029
David Bruce Gange

Maennlein (see Shuptrine)

Maes
*Santa Fe to Maes Creek
4801 Hackamore Drive, North
Colorado Springs, CO 80918
Phone (719) 598-7806
Arthur F. Maes, Publisher
(includes Maes(e) family)

Maese (see Maes)

Maevius (see Movius)

Maffatt (see Moffatt)

Maffett (see Moffatt)

Maffitt (see Moffatt)

Magan (see Cian)

Magee (see Blossom Press, Mackay)

Magennis (see MacInnes)

MaGill (see MacGill)

Maginnis (see MacInnes)

Maglin (see Cian)

Magnan
*Magnan Family Association
170 DeSota Place
Macon, GA 31204
Phone (912) 743-9902
Joe Magnan, President
(includes descendants of Jean Baptist Magnan and Susanne Victoire Magnan)

Magnus (see Gunn)

Magny
*Magny Families Association
5 Fieldstone Court
Newburgh, NY 12550
Phone (914) 565-3638 (Historian); (203) 683-8943 (Editor in Windsor, Connecticut)
Kenneth B. Schoomaker, Historian; Dorothy Many, Editor
Pub. *Magny Families Association Newsletter*, semiannually (April and October); (includes Magny, Manee, Maney, Manney, Manny and Many)
$10.00 per year membership

Magoon (see Heath)

Magray (see McGray)

Magrew (see Gregor)

Magruder (see Newmyer)

Maguire (see Cian)

Maguire
*James Francis Maguire (McGuire) Family
2454 West Walnut
Wheatland, WY 82201
Phone (307) 322-2764
Francis McGuire
(includes descendants of James Francis Maguire (McGuire), Sr., of Ireland 1832, and James Francis McGuire, Jr., 1884)

Mahaffey (see MacDuffee)

Mahaffy (see Macfie)

Mahan
Mahan Surname Booklet
East 5509 Ohio Match Road
PO Box 969
Hayden, ID 83835-0969
Phone (208) 772-2068
Linda Pollick Shorb
Pub. *Mahan Surname Booklet*, annually, $6.00 per issue

Mahaney (see Lambert)

Mahaney
*Mahaney-Newlin Reunion
PO Box 267
Mansfield, IL 61854
Phone (217) 489-5221
Nora L. Rogers, Hostess
(includes descendants of Ezra A. Mahaney, I (1816–), who married Ann Eliza Dovel, 1841, Page County, Virginia, primarily through their grandson, Ezra A. Mahaney, II)
Mahaney Homecoming on the weekend nearest October 15 at the old homeplace near Winterrowd, R #1, Dieterich, Illinois

Maher (see Cian)

Mahlander (see Melander)

Mahllander (see Melander)

Mahon (see Carley)

Mahoning (see Cunning)

Maier
*Maier/Avril/Herrold/Zeltner/Vogel/Schwoder Exchange
2609 Hillcrest Avenue, N.W.
Roanoke, VA 24012
Phone (703) 362-2245
M. C. Maier, Researcher

Mailander (see Melander)

Maillander (see Melander)

Main (see Sullivan Surname Exchange, Gunn)

Main
*Nancy L. Childress Services
3709 West Gardenia
Phoenix, AZ 85051-8266
Phone (602) 841-7478
Nancy L. Porter Childress, Owner and Editor
Pub. *Main Gazette*, quarterly, $11.00 per year subscription; (includes Main, Maine, Mayne and allied families of Aldrich, Boutelle, Childress, Corbin, Hewitt, Josleyn, Ostrander and Stukey)

Maine (see MacDuff, Main)

Maines (see MacDuff)

Mains (see Nimmo)

Maintzer (see Mansker)

Mairs (see Lush)

Maitland
*Clan Maitland Society of North America
108 Lawson Road
Scituate, MA 02066-2546
Phone (617) 545-2637

Mary Maitland Kelly, Secretary
Pub. *Newsletter*, six to eight times per
    year plus annually from Chief, $25.00
    U.S. funds per year subscription only;
    (includes Maitland and Lauderdale
    descendants)
$25.00 per year membership for
    individuals, $30.00 per year
    membership for families

Maize
*Maize Maze
PO Box 1872
Dodge City, KS 67801-1872
Laura Tasset Koehn, President
(includes research on Pinkney Maize and
    Susannah Grindle family)

Majesky (see Kelm)

Major
Major Productions (Majors)
PO Box 7357
Tacoma, WA 98407

Majors (see Major, Warren)

Makclachlane (see MacLachlan)

Makclauchlane (see MacLachlan)

Makclotan (see MacLachlan)

Makclowden (see MacLachlan)

Makduffie (see MacFie)

Makevin (see MacLachlan)

Makewin (see MacLachlan)

Makewn (see MacLachlan)

Makfeithe (see Macfie)

Makgilkriste (see MacLachlan)

Maklawchlan (see MacLachlan)

Malby
Malby Family Association
PO Box 922
Three Forks, MT 59752
Phone (406) 285-3467
Bud Malby, Editor
Pub. *The Clan Clamor*, five times per
    year, with an historical supplement
    each April
$11.50 per year membership

Malcolm (see MacCallum, MacDuff)

Maleander (see Melander)

Malender (see Melander)

Maliden (see Blossom Press)

Malinder (see Melander)

Maljander (see Melander)

Malkin (see Brough)

Malleander (see Melander)

Mallender (see Melander)

Mallinder (see Melander)

Malljander (see Melander)

Malloch (see Gregor)

Mallory (see Folk Family Surname
    Exchange)

Mallory
Mallory Memorabilia
12600 Bissonnet A4-407
Houston, TX 77099
Dede D. Mercer, Publisher
Pub. *Mallory Memorabilia*, semiannually,
    $20.00 per year subscription; (all
    variations of the surname, worldwide)

Malloy (see Stewart)

Malluege
Carl and Augusta Malluege Organization
400 North Church Street
Winnsboro, TX 75494
Phone (903) 342-5598
Phyllis Emory Lemon
(includes descendants of Carl and
    Augusta Malluege, who came from
    Prussia about 1869/1870 and settled in
    Merrill, Lincoln County, Wisconsin)

Malone (see Akers, Andrews)

Malory
Malory Multitude
306 Jefferson
Madison, MO 65263
C. Mallory

Malott (see Merlet)

Mancil
Mancil/Taft Family Association
Rt. 1
Pearson, GA 31642
I. Mancell Burkett

Mandel
*Mandel Family Association
PO Box 1860
Studio City, CA 91614
Phone (818) 980-1005; E-mail:
    AP471@lafn.org
Karen Mohr
(includes research on ancestors and
    descendants of Carl Friedrike Johann
    Mandel (1837 Schwerin, Mecklenburg,
    Germany–1880 New York) and Sophie
    Caroline Friedrike Rosenow (1842
    Germany–1904 New York))

Manee (see Magny)

Manes
Manes/Manis Family History
PO Box 33937
San Antonio, TX 78265
Phone (210) 654-9912
Clifford Manis
Pub. *Manes/Manis Family History*

Maney (see Magny)

Mangum (see Hamblin, Holden)

Maniak
Maniak Surname Organization
1936 East Fifth Street
Ontario, CA 91764
Greg Legutki

Manis (see Manes)

Manley
Manley Family Newsletter
171 Nathan Drive
Bohemia, NY 11716
Phone (516) 567-0386
Trudi Manley, Editor
Pub. *Manley Family Newsletter*,
    semiannually (spring/summer and fall/
    winter), $15.00 per year subscription;
    (includes Manly)
Reunion

Manly (see Manley)

Mann (see Barnard, Gunn, Heath,
    Taylor)

Manner
*Manners Across the Years and Lands
2117 San Antonio Avenue
Alameda, CA 94501
Esther Tremain Manners, Publisher
(includes descendants of Alexander
    (O., Theo., Thos.) Manner of
    Kentucky, 1787)

Mannery (see Cian)

Manney (see Magny)

Mannie (see Lagesse)

Manning (see Martin)

Manning
Manning Family Reunion
380 Kick Hill Road
Lebanon, CT 06249
Phone (203) 642-7367
Mr. O. J. Manning
Robinson-Manning annual reunion on the
    third Sunday of August

Mannix
Mannix Family Association
1281 Branchwater Lane
Birmingham, AL 35216
P. McGrath

Manny (see Magny)

Mansberger
Mansberger Family of America
831 Brae Court, N.E.
Palm Bay, FL 32905-4531
P. Mansberger

Mansker
*BGM Publications
28635 Old Hideaway Road
Cary, IL 60013-9726
Phone (847) 639-2400
Betty G. Massman, Editor and Publisher
(research includes Mansker, Minsker,
Maintzer, Meinser)

Manson (see Gunn)

Manspeil (see The Memorial Foundation
of the Germanna Colonies)

Mantanye (see De la Montagne)

Manter (see Ainger)

Mantooth
Mantooth/Mantieth Family Organization
5600 Dorrell Lane
Las Vegas, NV 89106
Phone (702) 645-9024
Patricia Hall Emde

Manuel (see Emanuel, Johnson)

Manus (see Gunn)

Manwaring
*Herbert Manwaring Family
Organization
1623 North Harrison
Pocatello, ID 83204
Phone (208) 232-3385
Wanda M. Jorgensen

Manwell
Manwell Family Organization
PO Box 157
Knightsen, CA 94548
Carolyn Sherfy

Many (see Magny)

Mapes
Mapes Family Association
127 Willys Street
Elmira, NY 14904
Carolyn Mapes

Mar (see MacDuff)

Marble (see DuBois)

Marble
*DuBois/Marble Research
1549 Wilder Street
Thousand Oaks, CA 91362
Phone (805) 496-7184
Jackie DuBois Bergstrom
(includes descendants of Jeremiah
DuBois (1831 Lowville, Lewis
County, New York–1913 Bryan,

Williams County, Ohio) and Mary
Catherine Jones (1833 Hunters Mill,
Fairfax, Virginia–1926 Bryan,
Williams County, Ohio); and Nathaniel
Marble III (1800 Conway, Franklin
County, Massachusetts–1845 Nauvoo,
Hancock County, Illinois) and Mary
Polly King (1802 Shrewsbury,
Monmouth County, New Jersey–1881
Richfield, Sevier County, Utah))

Marchand (see Smith)

Marchand
*Marchand Clearinghouse
Nall News Publishing Company
PO Box 2186
Willingboro, NJ 08046-2186
Josephine Crittenberger-Nall, Editor-
Publisher
Free

Marchant (see Westcott)

Marchell (see Hudlow)

Marcotte (see Johnson)

Marcus (see Israelite)

Marcy (see Barnard)

Marden
Marden Project
51 North Main Street
Newmarket, NH 03857
Phone (603) 659-3652
Sylvia Fitts Getchell

Maring
*Maring/Moehring Surname
Organization
8106 S.E. Carlton Street
Portland, OR 97206
Phone (503) 774-1233
Ellen Maring Benedict
(includes descendants of Nicholas
Mearing and George Mearing of
Morris and Sussex counties, New
Jersey, from 1767, whose descendants
went to Belmont County, Ohio, by
1810)

Marinovich (see Blossom Press)

Mark (see McCurdy)

Market (see Kunkel)

Markham (see Cowart, Ashby)

Markham
Markham Family Organization
490 East 600 South Street
Orem, UT 84058
Phone (801) 224-1167
Jerold E. "Jerry" Molloy
(includes descendants of Stephen
Markham)

Markinch (see MacDuff)

Markley
Markley Reunion
410 Bonshire Road
Akron, OH 44319
D. Markley

Marks (see Schulz)

Marks
*Christian Marks Society
North Road, RR 1 Box 51A
South Ryegate, VT 05069
Phone (802) 429-2346
Vivian G. Nemhauser
Pub. *Christian Marks Society Newsletter*,
annually (if possible), no cost;
(includes descendants of Christian
Marks (1801 or 1798 Lebanon County,
Pennsylvania–))

Markwell
Markwell Family Association
1921 East 208th Street, #60
Spanaway, WA 98387
Mrs. Leonard Kessels
Pub. *Markwell Newsletter*

Marlatt (see Merlet)

Marley
*Marley Family Association
8910 West 62nd Terrace
PO Box 29160
Shawnee Mission, KS 66201
Phone (800) 292-2273;
(913) 362-4627 FAX
Michael D. Frost, Ph.D., Marley Family
Archivist
Pub. *Marley Family Newsletter*,
quarterly; (includes members living
throughout the U.S., mostly
descendants of the Marleys who came
from Europe through Pennsylvania,
reaching Virginia and North Carolina
before the Revolutionary War)
$20.00 per year membership; annual
meeting on the first weekend of
August

Marney (see Folk Family Surname
Exchange)

Marney
*Folk Family
PO Box 52048
Knoxville, TN 37950-2048
Hester E. Stockton, Owner; Polly
Marney Stockton, Editor
Pub. *Marney Monitor*, quarterly, $15.00
per year subscription, $5.00 per issue
(includes D'Marney)

Marnoch (see Innes)

Marois
*The Marois Genealogy
3425 Daisy Crescent
Virginia Beach, VA 23456

Phone (804) 468-5416
Bernice Savigny Foster, Publisher

Marostica
*Marostica Surname Organization
PO Box 442
Rye, CO 81069
Phone (719) 676-4054
Tony Marostica, Coordinator

Marquardt (see Horning)

Marquardt
Marquardt Reunion
Rt. 1, 9501 Snyder Road
Fort Wayne, IN 46773
Constance Marquardt

Marquart (see Gibson, Kettenring)

Marr (see MacDuff)

Marrero (see Blossom Press)

Marrs
*Marrs Family
2405 Marlandwood Road
Temple, TX 76502-2556
Phone (817) 773-3493
William M. Marrs, Family Historian

Marschhauser (see Haefner)

Marshall (see Blossom Press, Cowart, Job, Keith, Nimmo, Way, Zilliox)

Marshall
*Descendants of Albert Stanton Marshall and Almeda Maude McLain of Forbes, North Dakota
1141 Meadow Glen
Lansing, MI 48917
Phone (517) 321-0551
Shirley Bailey, Publisher

Marshall
Marshall Exchange
6419 Bradley Brownlee Road
Burghill, OH 44404
Mary Marshall Brewer, Editor
Pub. *Marshall Exchange*, quarterly, $10.00 per year subscription

Marshall
*Simon Granser Marshall, Sr., Association
1514 Ardmore Place
Kingsport, TN 37664
Phone (615) 378-4172
G. Payne Marshall, Chairman
Pub. *Marshall Newsletter*, annually; (includes descendants of Simon Granger Marshall, Sr. (1791 Surry County, North Carolina–1877))
Donation for membership; annual reunion on the Sunday before Labor Day

Marshall
*George C. Marshall Research Library
VMI Parade
PO Box 1600
Lexington, VA 24450
Phone (703) 463-7103
Archivist-Librarian
(includes Bradford, Brown, Catlett, Coles, Pender, Taliaferro and Tupper families)

Marston (see Dopp, Rogers)

Marston
Marston Family Reunion
2916 West 220th Street
Jordan, MN 55352
Phone (612) 492-6148
Charles R. Marston, Family Representative
$3.00 per year membership

Marte (see Marty)

Marter (see Motter)

Martin (see Blossom Press, Family Publications, Folk Family Surname Exchange, The Memorial Foundation of the Germanna Colonies, Bosher, Burnham, Cowart, Gant, Goodenow, Hebner, Johnson, Kunkel, Lemon, Lewis, Likes, Ross, Wright)

Martin
*Peter and Sarah "Redding" Martin Reunion
7940 South Martinsburg Road
Pekin, IN 47165
Phone (812) 976-3287
Walter K. Martin, President
(includes descendants of Peter Martin (1741 Germantown, Orange County, Virginia–1807 Shelby County, Kentucky) and Sarah "Redding" Martin (ca 1743 Germantown–ca 1830–40 Henry County, Kentucky))
Donation for membership; annual reunion on the Sunday before Labor Day at the Firehouse in Martinsburg, Indiana

Martin
Martin Family News
607 Jerome Street
Marshalltown, IA 50158
Michael E. Martin
Pub. *Martin Family News*, quarterly, $7.00 per year subscription; (includes descendants of Quaker Martins of Chester County, Pennsylvania)

Martin
*Martin Family Registry of Fayette County, Pennsylvania
PO Box 19
Hanover, MD 21076
Phone (410) 796-7265
Marilyn Martin Tolentino, Historian

(includes Martins from 1769 to the present for Fayette County)
Copy costs plus postage

Martin
*Kinseeker Publications
5697 Old Maple Trail
PO Box 184
Grawn, MI 49637
E-mail: AB064@taverse.lib.mi.us
Victoria Wilson, Editor
Pub. *Martin Mysteries*, quarterly, $10.00 per year subscription, $2.50 for sample issue

Martin
Martin
1225 North Chestnut Street
Lansing, MI 48906
Yvonne E. Martin
Pub. *Martin*, quarterly; (includes descendants of Robert and Abigail Parker)
$12.00 per year membership; reunion

Martin
*Phillip Heritage House
605 Benton
Missoula, MT 59801
Phone (406) 543-3495
Ruth Phillip, MAS R.G.
Pub. *Martin Newsletter*, annually, $5.00 per issue

Martin
Moses Martin of Burke/Caldwell County, North Carolina Newsletter
2724 Blowing Rock Boulevard
PO Box 7
Patterson, NC 28661-0007
Phone (704) 758-8373
Linda McGalliard Staley
Pub. *Moses Martin of Burke/Caldwell County, North Carolina Newsletter*, quarterly, $12.00 per year subscription; (includes descendants of Moses Martin (1870, aged 84–) and his wife Jinsey (Virginia–between 1850 and 1860))

Martin
*Micah Martin Family Organization
Rt. 1, Box 803 A
952 Swofford Drive
Cowpens, SC 29330
Phone (803) 463-4576
Dawn M. Cerny, Genealogist
(includes Micah Martin, Mourning, Manning)
$24.00 per year membership

Martin
Martin Family Research
8755 Rexford Dr.
Dallas, TX 75214
Mrs. Michal Martin Farmer

Martin
Partin Publications
230 Wedgewood
Nacogdoches, TX 75961-5326

Pub. *Martin*, quarterly, $18.00 per year subscription

Martin
*John Thomas Martin Family
  Organization
327 Thalia Drive
Newport News, VA 23608-2718
Phone (804) 877-1190; E-mail:
  KEN8893@aol.com
Vernon Kenneth Martin, Historian
(includes descendants of John Thomas
  Martin (ca 1795–ca 1870) and Allie
  Williams (ca 1805–1873) of
  Rutherford County, North Carolina)
Annual reunion on the third Saturday of
  August in Lincolnton, North Carolina

Marty
Marty-Akers-Akeson-Marte Family
  Association
2306 Westgate
Houston, TX 77019
Phone (713) 529-2333
Harold Helm
$25.00 plus pedigree and family group
  sheets for membership

Marum
Multiple Marums
PO Box 42413
Phoenix, AZ 85080-2413
Mrs. Bob DeBreau

Marx
*Marx Surname Organization
3176 S.E. Villa Carmel Drive
Port Orchard, WA 98366
Phone (206) 876-0833
Linda Marx Terry

Marzahn (see Kanne)

Mascraft (see Mascroft)

Mascroft
Mascroft/Mascraft Family Organization
145 Edson Road
Oakham, MA 01068
A. Mascroft, Jr.

Mase (see Mays)

Mashek (see Lush)

Maslen (see Rice)

Masler (see Mosler)

Masner (see Masoner)

Masnor (see Masoner)

Mason (see Burnham, Covert, Heath,
  Otto, Stewart)

Mason
*Compu-Chart
363 South Park Victoria Drive
Milpitas, CA 95035-5708

Phone (408) 262-1051
Paula Perkins Mortensen
Pub. *Mason Family Newsletter*, quarterly,
  $10.00 per year subscription

Mason
*Mason Reunion
Ebenezer Prouty Mason Family
  Organization
8375 Wattsburg Road
Erie, PA 16509
Phone (814) 825-4975
Agnes Lee Mitchell, Historian
Pub. *Newsletter*, annually
Annual reunion at Mad Park, Corry, Erie
  County, Pennsylvania

Mason
*Percy Harvey Mason Family
  Organization
William Henry Mason Family
  Organization
7712 Buck Street
North Richland Hills, TX 76180
Phone (817) 485-3792
Ken Mason

Mason
*George Sterling Mason Family
  Organization
PO Box 352
Tremonton, UT 84337
Phone (801) 257-6197
Dr. Reese B. Mason

Mason
Our Family Books
115 East Rainbow Drive
Bridgewater, VA 22812-1733
Phone (540) 828-4617
Floyd R. Mason, Publisher
(John Mason and Mary Ann Miller of
  Virginia; Matthias Miller and his
  seventeen children; Michael Miller)

Masoner
Masoner Monitor
1122 West Bus. 60/63
Willow Spring, MO 65793-9802
Phone (417) 469-3089
Pub. *Masoner Monitor*, quarterly, $10.00
  per year subscription; (includes
  Masoner, Masner, Masnor and related
  lines)

Mass (see Folk Family Surname
  Exchange)

Massengill (see Stone)

Massey (see Covert)

Massey
*Upcountry Reflections
3736 Chiara Drive
Titusville, FL 32796
Phone (407) 268-2924
Sara Hunter Kellar
(includes Jane Duncan Todd Massey and
  Massey, Duncan and Hunter surnames)

Massey
Massey Family Reunion (James Massey
  Descendants)
16200 East 35th Street
Independence, MO 64055
T. Massey

Massie (see Folk Family Surname
  Exchange)

Masterman (see Sullivan Surname
  Exchange)

Masters (see Buchanan, MacInnes)

Masterson (see MacInnes)

Masterson
*Masterson Family Association
1820 N.E. Jensen Beach Boulevard, #545
Jensen Beach, FL 33457-7234
Phone (407) 288-4606
Larry and Reba Shepard, Co-editors
Pub. *Masterson Family Newsletter and
  Historical Journal*, quarterly, $16.00
  per year subscription; (includes
  Masterson wives: Hathaway, Coleman
  and Tucker)

Masterton (see MacDuff)

Matchett (see Newton)

Mater (see Garner)

Matheny (see Hewitt)

Mather (see LaRue, MacDuff)

Mathers (see MacDuff)

Matheson
Matheson Clan Society
11 West Geyer Lane
Saint Louis, MO 63131

Matheson
*Clan Matheson Society
12126 Rhett Drive
Houston, TX 77024
Phone (713) 465-8519
Lyman W. Matheson, Honorary
  Secretary, U.S.A.
Pub. *Clan Matheson Society Newsletter*,
  annually; (includes Matheson,
  Mathieson, Matheison, Mathison and
  Matthewson descendants of Highland
  Scottish origin)
$7.50 per year membership, $75.00 life
  membership

Mathew (see Jelly)

Mathews (see Johnson, McCune)

Mathews (see McGee)

Mathews
*The Book of Mathews
13615 Debby Street
Van Nuys, CA 91401
Phone (818) 785-0498
John Krizek, Publisher
Pub. *Newsletter* (includes Mathews
family from Welsh settlements in
Pennsylvania to California in the
1850s to distribution throughout the
U.S.)

Mathews
*Mathews Database
152 Rockwood Road
Florham Park, NJ 07932
Phone (201) 966-1862
Peter B. Berendsen

Mathewson (see Matteson)

Mathieu (see Jelly)

Mathorn (see Mattern)

Mathysee
*Mathysee Surname Organization
199 Commodore Drive
Milledgeville, GA 31061
Phone (912) 968-7425
Richard Bialac

Matkin (see Matkins)

Matkins
*Matkins Information Center
3120 Quincy Street
Butte, MT 59701
Phone (406) 494-4126
Robert E. Matkins, Sr., Editor
Pub. *Matkins Journal*, quarterly (January,
April, July and October); (includes all
Matkin(s) family lines in the U.S. and
Canada, and some in England)
$10.00 per year membership

Matlock (see Freiling)

Matney
Matney Family Organization
1307 Maxine
Fort Worth, TX 76117
Opal Bouett

Matson
*Matson Surname Information
8001 Adams
Lincoln, NE 68507
Phone (402) 466-2239
Guy M. Matson, M.D.

Matsov
*Matsov Surname Database
13442 93rd Avenue, North
Maple Grove, MN 55369-9740
Phone (612) 494-6694
Sherry Constans-Kaiserlik

Mattaliano
*Mattaliano Exchange
16315 Jim Creek Road
Arlington, WA 98223
Michele Heiderer

Matter (see Mattern, Motter)

Mattern (see Motter)

Mattern
*Mattern Family Association
2241 Nayland Road
Columbus, OH 43220
Phone (614) 457-9337
Betsy Martin, Historian
(includes Mattern, Matter, Motter and
Mathorn descendants of Johann Adam
Mattern, who came to the U.S. in 1751
on the ship *Edinburg*, and whose son,
George (a.k.a. George Cretho), served
in the Revolutionary War)
Annual meeting at the home of John
Mattern in Harrison County, Ohio

Matteson
*The Matteson Historical Congress of
America, Inc.
61 Cedar Street
Newington, CT 06111
Phone (203) 667-4545
Robert T. Williams, Editor
Pub. *The Mattesonian*, semiannually
(November and May); (includes
descendants of Henry Matteson (1646
England–), immigrated 1666, and
Hannah Parsons, who were married in
1670 in Portsmouth, Rhode Island)
$5.00 per year membership

Matteson
Matteson/Mattison/Mathewson Review
Rt. 2, Box 136, Meads Creek Road
Painted Post, NY 14870
Agnes Brown
Pub. *Matteson/Mattison/Mathewson
Review*

Matthews (see Stowe)

Matticks (see Garner)

Mattison (see Matteson)

Mattocks
Mattocks Relatives, Researchers and
Friends
9345 South Citrus Lane
Sun Lakes, AZ 85248
Don M. Mattocks, Editor-Publisher
Pub. *Mattocks Newsletter*, five times per
year (March, May, July, September and
November), $10.00 per year
subscription

Matulich (see Blossom Press)

Mauck (see The Memorial Foundation
of the Germanna Colonies)

Mauger
*Mauger Surname Organization
Peter Yocum Mauger Family
Organization
PO Box 284
Belgrade, MT 59714-0284
Phone (406) 656-0979
Wallace Cyril Mauger

Mauk (see Mock)

Maul (see Lambert)

Mauldin
Mauldin Family News
8745 East Ninth Street
Tulsa, OK 74112
Phone (918) 835-4118
Dorothy J. Tincup Mauldin
Pub. *Mauldin Family News*, quarterly,
$7.00 per year subscription

Maupin (see Folk Family Surname
Exchange)

Maupin
Maupin Family Organization
1819 North 82nd Street
Kansas City, KS 66112
Phone (913) 299-8850
Dorothy Maupin Shaffett, Secretary

Maupin
*Folk Family
PO Box 52048
Knoxville, TN 37950-2048
Hester E. Stockton, Owner; Gabrielle
Maupin, Editor
Pub. *Maupin Families*, quarterly, $15.00
per year subscription, $5.00 per issue;
(includes D'Maupin)

Maurath
*Maurath Surname Organization
Felix Maurath Family Organization
12 Crestview Terrace
Buffalo Grove, IL 60089
Phone (708) 520-4065
John Louis Maurath

Maurer (see Lambert, Mohr)

Maurer
*John Michael Maurer Family
Organization
PO Box 311
Bedford, WY 83112
Phone (307) 883-2730
Jerry Mower

Maury (see Fontaine)

Mauser (see Mouser)

Mausolf
*Mausolf Family Tree
3284 Piper Road
Alpena, MI 49707
Phone (517) 354-2304
Diane Mausolf Lasek Laseck
(families from Prussia and Poland)

Mauzey
Mauzey/Mauzy/Mozee Family History
  Society
21 Spinning Wheel Road
Hinsdale, IL 60521
A. J. Mauzey

Mauzy (see Mauzey)

Maver (see Innes)

Maverick (see Newton)

Maveus (see Movius)

Mavor (see Innes)

Maw (see Seaton)

MaWhitty (see Buchanan)

Maxam
Maxam Family Association
22529 Lincoln
Saint Clair Shores, MI 48082
Richard J. Jacob

Maxfield
*Maxfield Surname Organization
John Maxfield Family Organization
250 South First East
Hyrum, UT 84319
Phone (801) 245-6984
Dianne Pierson
Charges only for copies

Maxton (see Maxwell)

Maxwell (see Garner, Lambert)

Maxwell
Missing Links
Rt. 4, Box 184
Saint Maries, ID 83861
Pub. *Maxwell News*, quarterly, $7.50 per
  year subscription

Maxwell
*Clan Maxwell Society of the United
  States of America
303 Audubon Boulevard
New Orleans, LA 70125-4124
Phone (504) 866-9753
Murvan M. Maxwell, Chieftain
  (Convener); Edith B. Maxwell,
  Secretary
Pub. *The House of Maxwell*, quarterly;
  (includes Adair, Blackstock,
  Dinwiddie, Dinwoodie, Edgar, Herries,
  Kirk, Kirkland, Lattimer, Lattimore,
  Mackittrick, Maxton, Mescall,
  Monreith, Moss, Nithsdale, Paulk,
  Peacock, Polk, Pollock, Pollok,
  Sturgeon, Wardlaw)
$10.00 per year membership

Maxwell
Clan Maxwell Society of USA
246 DeLee Drive
Kingsport, TN 37663

Phone (615) 239-8426
Laurence Maxwell Long, President

May (see Surname Sources, Heath)

May
Zachariah May and Adelina Moser
  Descendants
840 S.E. Tecumseh Road
Topeka, KS 66605
R. May

Maybee
*Maybee Society
10020 23rd Drive, S.E.
Everett, WA 98208
Phone (206) 337-1369
Belva Perry, Executive Secretary; George
  Martin, President
Pub. *Communicator*, quarterly; (includes
  Maybee, regardless of spelling: Mabee,
  Mabey, Mabie, Maby, Maybee, Van
  Orden, etc.)
$20.00 membership, $10.00 per year
  dues

Mayberry (see Haws, Newcomb)

Mayberry
*Mayberry-Gadberry Reunion/Durant,
  OK
1111 Simpkins Road
Napa, CA 94558
Phone (707) 255-9508
Mrs. Billie Borders, Editor
Pub. *The Berry Pickers*, three to four
  times per year, $4.00 per year
  subscription; (includes Gadberry)

Mayberry
Mayberry/Maberry/Mabry Reunion
2123 Tenth Street, N.W.
Roanoke, VA 24012
Phone (703) 366-9142
Ora Belle McColman
(includes descendants of settler Captain
  Charles Mayberry (Mabry) of Grayson
  (now Carroll) County, Virginia)
Annual reunion at the Dugspur Rescue
  Squad Building, Dugspur, Virginia

Mayer
Mayer Notebook
62 Peony Street, S.W.
Grand Rapids, MI 49508
Sandra J. Elliott
Pub. *Mayer Notebook*

Mayerhoffer (see Cummings)

Mayes (see Johnson)

Mayfield (see Blair)

Mayhugh (see Sams)

Maynard (see Frasher, Goodenow,
  Hatfield, MacDuff, McCune, Nell)

Mayne (see MacDuff, Main)

Maynes (see MacDuff)

Mays
Mays/Mace/Mase Family
1675 Colbrook Road
Lebanon, PA 17042
Pub. *Mays/Mace/Mase*

Mazler (see Mosler, Osborn, White)

Mazur
Mazur Surname Organization
1936 East Fifth Street
Ontario, CA 91764
Greg Legutki

Mazuran
*Mazuran Surname Organization
67 East Carlson Avenue
Midvale, UT 84047
Phone (801) 255-2494
Burke T. Wells

M'Bean (see MacBean)

McAdam (see McAdams)

McAdams
*McAdams Historical Society
14018 Davana Terrace
Sherman Oaks, CA 91423
Phone (818) 789-1086
Joe F. McAdams, Director
Pub. *McAdams Historical Society
  Newsletter*, quarterly; (includes
  MacAdam, MacAdams, McAdam,
  McAdams and McCadam of Ayr,
  Scotland, Northern Ireland (1569 to
  the present) and America (1685 to the
  present))
$10.00 per year membership

McAfee (see MacDuffee, Macfie)

McAfie (see Macfie)

McAinsh (see MacInnes)

McAlexander (see Foley)

McAlister
Clan McAlister/McAllister of America
7654 Rico Road
Palmetto, GA 30268
Barbara W. McAlister
Pub. *Journal*, quarterly
$12.00 per year membership

McAlister
McAlister
Whispering Oaks
5821 Rowland Hill Road
Cascade, MD 21719-1939
Phone (301) 416-2660
Victor Gebhart, President
Pub. *McAlister*, annually, $2.00 per issue

McAllister (see Lane)

McAllister
McAllister Clearinghouse
Rt. 2, Box 235
Pikeville, NC 27863
C. Peele

McAllister
McAllister-Carson-Harvey-Lindsay
    Family Association
2306 Westgate
Houston, TX 77019
Phone (713) 529-2333
Harold Helm
$25.00 plus pedigree and family group
    sheets for membership

McAlpin (see McMillan)

McAlpin
*McAlpin(e) Family Association
8600 Hickory Hill Lane, S.E.
Huntsville, AL 35802
Phone (205) 881-4697
Doris McAlpin Russell, President
(includes McAlpin, McAlpine,
    MacAlpine, McCalpin, etc., throughout
    the U.S., Canada, Australia, New
    Zealand, Scotland, England and other
    countries)
No charge for membership

McAlpin
McAlpin Clan Newsletter
643 Mahaly Avenue
Salisbury, NC 28144
Hal Ervin
Pub. *McAlpin Clan Newsletter* (not
    primarily genealogical)

McAlpine (see McAlpin)

McAlvin (see MacBean)

McAngus (see MacInnes)

McAnich (see MacInnes)

McAninch (see MacInnes)

McAnish (see MacInnes)

McAphie (see Macfie)

McArdle
*McArdle Family Association
PO Box 38
Cassel, CA 96016
Phone (916) 335-4344
Alice J. McArdle
(includes McArdle ancestors of Armagh,
    Northern Ireland; Stewart of Osprey
    Township, Greef County, Ontario,
    Canada)

McArra (see Hay)

McArtor
*McArtor Family Association
935 Countryside Drive, Apartment #103
Palatine, IL 60067-1927

Phone (847) 776-1848
H. Harvey Barfield, III
Pub. *The McArtor Family Historical
    Review*, quarterly, $10.00 per year
    subscription; (specifically includes the
    relatives and descendants of Jonathan
    McArtor (ca 1760–1835 Loudoun
    County, Virginia–))

McBain (see MacBean)

McBaine (see MacBean)

McBaines (see MacBean)

McBane (see MacBean)

McBayn (see MacBean)

McBayne (see MacBean)

McBeain (see MacBean)

McBean (see MacBean)

McBeane (see MacBean)

McBeath (see MacBean)

McBee (see MacBean)

McBeean (see MacBean)

McBeen (see MacBean)

McBeene (see MacBean)

McBheath (see MacBean)

McBinnie (see MacBean)

McBride (see McCune, Underwood,
    Wright)

McBurney (see Simmons)

McBurney
Samuel Fergus McBurney and Ella
    Ramsey Family Organization
4406 Arabella Street
Lakewood, CA 90712
Arthur Barrett
Pub. *McBurney Newsletter*

McBurney
*George Morgan McBurney and Mary
    Patterson Descendants Organization
969 Shamrock Drive
Barnesville, OH 43713
Mrs. M. Hunkler

McBurney
McBurney Family News
PO Box 6577
Corpus Christi, TX 78411
Mr. McBurney
Pub. *McBurney Family News*

McCadam (see McAdams)

McCafferty (see Macfie)

McCaffrey (see Macfie)

McCain
*McCain-Whitehead Family Association
814 West Fifth Street South
Newton, IA 50208
Phone (515) 792-1605
Elaine Richardson, Family Historian
(includes descendants of Lorenzo Dow
    McCain (1817–1864) and Esther
    Whitehead (1818–1895))

McCain
*Albert Alexander McCain Family
    Organization
5892 West 10620 North
Highland
American Fork, UT 84003-9591
Phone (801) 756-0155
Grant H. Iverson

McCainsh (see MacInnes)

McCaleb (see Oliver)

McCall (see Corson, Garner, Paulk)

McCall
*Samuel McCall Family Research
134 West Liberty Road
Slippery Rock, PA 16057
Phone (412) 794-4791
Edith McCall Young
(includes descendants of Samuel McCall
    (1770–1843) and Else McCall)

McCallus
*McCallus Family Council
114 Clinton Street
PO Box 490
Avis, PA 17721-0490
Phone (717) 753-5138
Carl C. McCallus, Chairman
Pub. *Informer*, semiannually, free, but
    available only to lineal descendants;
    (heritage and reunions exclusively for
    lineal descendants of Michael and
    Catherine (Kobascza) McCallus)

McCalpin (see McAlpin)

McCammon (see Sneed)

McCance (see MacInnes)

McCandless
*McCandless Researchers
240 Duffy Road
Slippery Rock, PA 16057
Phone (412) 794-4627
Helen McCandless Staiger
$1.00 plus SASE

McCanish (see Cunning, MacInnes)

McCann (see Kunkel, McCune)

McCann
James McCann Family Association
120 South Lebanon Street
Bryan, OH 43506
Don Wordkoetter

McCanna
*McCanna Family History
2115 Payne Street
Evanston, IL 60201-2561
Blanche R. Childs, Publisher
(includes descendants of Michael
   McCanna and Maria Burhart, whose
   family migrated to Iowa in 1852 and
   subsequently to Minnesota and Dakota
   Territory, with allied families of
   Brightbill, Campbell, Deem, Feeney,
   Funderhide, Greene, Hogan, Hutton,
   Jestrab, Macken, Mackin, McCarthy,
   Neth, Rieder, St. George, Sexton,
   Thomas and Varty)

McCansh (see MacInnes)

McCants (see MacInnes)

McCarson (see Macpherson)

McCarter (see Johnson)

McCarthy (see McCanna)

McCartney (see MacCartney)

McCartney
*The McCartney Newsletter
1228 West Saginaw Street
East Lansing, MI 48823-2432
Clyde A. Chamberlin, Publisher
Pub. *McCartney Newsletter*, quarterly,
   $6.00 per year subscription

McCarty (see Folk Family Surname
   Exchange, Jett, Newberry, Richardson)

McCaslin (see Grasty)

McCathie (see Cathey)

McCauley
*PO Box 5054
Silver City, NM 88062
Phone (505) 538-9001
La Verne H. McCauley

McCay (see Gregg, Mackay)

McCeun (see MacLachlan)

McChord (see McCord)

McClachlan (see MacLachlan)

McClachlane (see MacLachlan)

McClachlen (see MacLachlan)

McClain (see Garner, Wright)

McClanahan (see Futral)

McClanahan
McClanahan Family Reunion
938 Highway 25-32
White Pine, TN 37890
Annie Riner
Annual reunion on the second Sunday of
   August

McClarrinnon (see CTC Family
   Association)

McClauchlane (see MacLachlan)

McClaughlin (see MacLachlan)

McCleary (see McClure)

McCleave
*George McCleave Family Organization
29 East Portland Avenue
Vincennes, IN 47591
Phone (812) 882-9371
Richard Carl Rodgers, II, Historian/
   Archivist
(archival facility collects information on
   all descendants and ancestors of the
   family in computer database;
   descendants of George McCleave
   (ca 1751 Maryland, Delaware or
   Pennsylvania–1824 near Harmony,
   Clark County, Ohio), possibly son of
   George McCleave and Elizabeth
   Portman, and wives Gloria Dei,
   Johannah Notter and Elizabeth
   Straughton)

McClelen (see McClellan)

McClellan
*James McClellan Family Record
6612 North Grove Avenue
Oklahoma City, OK 73132
Phone (405) 721-5687
Gerald R. Fuller, D.V.M.
(includes descendants of James, son of
   Hugh McClellan, Jr. and great-
   grandson of Robert McClelen, who
   was married in 1725 in Lancaster
   County, Pennsylvania, to Margaret
   Baxter)

McClenda (see MacLennan)

McClendal (see MacLennan)

McClendon (see MacLennan)

McClendon
McClendon/McLendon Association
PO Box 6
Ridgecrest, CA 93555
Bennie Edwards

McClenthen (see McClanathan)

McClintock (see Colquhoun)

McClintock
*McClintock Clearinghouse
18901 East Dodge Avenue
Santa Ana, CA 92705

Phone (714) 544-3755
Maureen (McClintock) Rischard
(includes McClintock worldwide, all
   spellings)

McClooney (see Macpherson)

McCloonie (see Macpherson)

McClouchlin (see MacLachlan)

McClug (see Smith)

McCluney (see Macpherson)

McClung
*The McClung Family Association
1431 Parkside Drive
Columbus, IN 47203
Phone (812) 376-3707
H. Randy McClung, Secretary
Pub. *The McClung Family Association
   Journal*, annually (or more often)
$5.00 per year membership

McClung
McClung Surname Organization
East Smith
Springfield, MO 65802
Phone (417) 833-4282
Judith A. McClung

McClunie (see Macpherson)

McCluny (see Macpherson)

McClure (see The Memorial Foundation
   of the Germanna Colonies, Aldrich,
   Hardeman)

McClure
McClure-McCleary-Hamilton-Bagley
   Family Association
2306 Westgate
Houston, TX 77019
Phone (713) 529-2333
Harold Helm
$25.00 plus pedigree and family group
   sheets for membership

McClure
McClure Memento
East 13124 Nixon
Spokane, WA 99216
Joanne M. Elliott
Pub. *McClure Memento*, $8.50 plus $1.00
   postage per issue

McClurg
*McClurg Surname Organization
3 Brazill Lane
Whitehall, MT 59759
Phone (406) 287-3369
Lindia Roggia Lovshin

McClurkin (see Futral)

McCoan (see MacLachlan)

McCoin (see MacLachlan)

McCoin
McCoin-McKaughan Reunion
703 Tanglewood Lane
Kerrville, TX 78028
Minniebell McKaughan Perkins,
  Secretary-Treasurer

McCollor
McCollor/McCollough/McCullough
  Family Association
2404 South 18th Street
Moorhead, MN 56560
K. Stigman

McCollough (see McCollor)

McColm (see MacThomas)

McComas (see MacThomas)

McComb (see MacThomas)

McComb
McComb Family Association
6500 West Charleston Boulevard, #132
Las Vegas, NV 89102-9071
Steve Kushner
Pub. *McCombs Matters*, quarterly
$7.50 per year membership

McCombe (see MacThomas)

McCombich (see Stewart)

McCombie (see MacThomas)

McComie (see MacThomas)

McComish (see MacThomas)

McConkie (see Cunning)

McConnaughey
*McConnaughey Society of America,
  Inc.
5410 South Meridian Street
PO Box 47051
Indianapolis, IN 46227-0051
Phone (317) 786-4363;
  (317) 783-540 (weekdays)
Patricia M. Gregory, Editor and
  Secretary-Treasurer
Pub. *McConnaughey Bulletin*, quarterly;
  (includes McConnaughey and variant
  spellings)
$27.00 per year membership for
  individuals, $22.00 per year
  membership for retired people,
  $150.00 life membership

McConnell (see Cook)

McConnell
McConnell Family Reunion
2105 North Squire Avenue
Tempe, AZ 85281
Marcia B. Croye
(includes related families: Andrews,
  Arnold, Groves, Miller, Swickard and
  Wilson)

McCoon (see MacLachlan)

McCord
*Clan McCord Society
16035 Placer Hill Road
Meadow Vista, CA 95722
Phone (916) 878-8392
Howard McCord, Secretary/Convenor
Pub. *Clan Newsletter*, quarterly;
  (includes McCord, McChord,
  McCourt, Cord and other various
  spellings and their relatives)
$15.00 per year membership, $10.00 one-
  time application fee

McCorkle (see Likes)

McCorkle
The McCorkle and Woolard Clans
PO Box 847
Pahrump, NV 89041
Wayne L. Woolard

McCormick (see Folk Family Surname
  Exchange, Collum, Dawson)

McCormick
McCormick Clan Society
Hasty Road
Laurinsburg, NC 28352
N. McCormick

McCormick
*McCormick-Reid Family Organization
Coleman Research Agency
241 North Vine Street, Apartment 1104E
Salt Lake City, UT 84103-1945
Marlene McCormick Coleman
(includes families from Texas, Alabama,
  South Carolina and County Antrim,
  Ireland)
Free

McCornack
*McCornack Family Organization
5302 North Arrow Drive
Peoria, IL 61614
Phone (309) 691-2847
John McCornack
(includes McNatt)

McCosh
The McCosh Clan
900 N.W. Second
Abilene, KS 67410
Phone (913) 263-1855
Jean McCosh Abeldl

McCoughey (see Mowreader)

McCoun (see MacLachlan)

McCourt (see McCord)

McCowan (see Folk Family Surname
  Exchange, Colquhoun)

McCown (see Folk Family Surname
  Exchange)

McCown
Collier Research
PO Box 371883
El Paso, TX 79937
Phone (915) 595-2725
Timothy P. Biarnesen, Editor
Pub. *McCown Quarterly*, $20.00 per year
  subscription; (includes Colquhoun)

McCoy (see Brawley, Garner, Hatfield,
  Mackay, Sterling)

McCoy
*The William McCoy Family
  Organization
6740 West Paradise Lane
Peoria, AZ 85382
Phone (602) 979-6109
Leslie E. McCoy
(includes descendants of William McCoy
  (1752–1823 Ross County, Ohio) and
  Drusilla Browning (1773–1805 Ross
  County, Ohio))
$10.00 per year membership

McCoy
*Bell Enterprises
PO Box 10328
Spokane, WA 99209
Phone (509) 327-2761
Mary Ann L. Vanzandt Bell, Owner,
  Publisher
Pub. *McCoy Material, Etc.*, irregularly,
  $6.00 plus $1.25 postage per issue

McCracken (see Webster)

McCrary
*McCrary (McCreary) Clan
2216 Parkside Court
Virginia Beach, VA 23454
Ann McCrary, Co-Chair-Reunion
  Committee
Pub. *McCrary (McCreary) "Clan"
  Newsletter*, quarterly, $14.95
  subscription for ten issues, $7.95
  subscription for five issues; (includes
  Crary, MacCrary, McCready,
  McCreery, McCrory and McRay)

McCraw
*U.S. McCraw Family Association
4075 Moffat Road
Mobile, AL 36618
Phone (205) 344-2959
Clinton P. King, Chairman
Pub. *Newsletter*, three to four times per
  year; (includes all U.S. McCraws)
$10.00 per year membership; reunion

McCraw
McCraw Family Reunion
PO Box 255
Warsaw, MO 65355
Elizabeth McCraw Drake

McCraw
McCraw Family Reunion
7400 Crestway, #917
San Antonio, TX 78239
Doris Cobb

McCray (see Smith)

McCrea
*McCrea Network
PO Box 55-8136
Miami, FL 33255
Phone (305) 661-3833
John T. McCrea
Pub. *Newsletter*, irregularly, no cost;
(includes "first in America" McCrea
and McCray families in America up to
about 1850, one of which is the family
of Thomas and Jean (Thomson)
McCrea of Ayrshire, Scotland, who
came to America about 1860, settling
in Illinois and Indiana; the Network is
a small group of family historians
brought together for purposes of
cooperation in research; database
includes about 1800 persons in the
early American group, plus about 1500
from Ayrshire, Scotland)

McCready (see McCrary, Williams)

McCreary (see McCrary)

McCreery (see McCrary)

McCrory (see McCrary)

McCuan (see MacLachlan)

McCubbin
*Clan McCubbin Society
653 Perrshing Drive
Walnut Creek, CA 94596
A. Maxim Coppage, Publisher

McCubbin
*McCubbin, Cubbin-McKibbon Clan
News*
653 Perrshing Drive
Walnut Creek, CA 94596
A. Maxim Coppage, Publisher
Pub. *McCubbin, Cubbin-McKibbon Clan
News*, three times per year (April,
August and December)
$20.00 per year membership

McCue
*James McCue and Esther Swartz
Family Reunion
9603 Bel Glade Street
Fairfax, VA 22031-1105
Phone (703) 281-9562
Linda Gail Komar, Secretary/Treasurer
(includes descendants of James McCue
(1789 Northern Ireland–1846
Tuscarawas County, Ohio), possibly
the son of John McCue, and husband
of Esther Swartz (1791 Lancaster
County, Pennsylvania–1865
Tuscarawas County, Ohio), daughter of
Christian Swartz)
Annual reunion in New Philadelphia,
Tuscarawas County, Ohio

McCuen (see MacLachlan)

McCuidhean (see MacLachlan)

McCuistion
McCuistion-Turk Reunion
433 West Rockwood Street
Rockwood, TN 37854

McCuithan (see MacLachlan)

McCuithein (see MacLachlan)

McCullen
Patrick McCullen Descendants
1755 Smith Crossing
Midland, MI 48640
M. McCullen

McCulley
McCulley Depository
205 Hensel Drive
Bryan, TX 77801
Phone (409) 846-6311
William S. McCulley

McCullie (see Ross)

McCulloch (see Folk Family Surname
Exchange, Reynolds, Ross)

McCullough (see Emery, McCollor)

McCune (see MacLachlan)

McCune
McCune and Allied Families
RR 4, Box 331
Franklin, PA 16323-9721
Phone (814) 432-3720
Marjorie McCune Rodgers

McCune
*McCune Family Association
5243 Carpell Avenue
PO Box 18044
Salt Lake City, UT 84118-8044
Phone (801) 964-2825;
(801) 964-0551 (FAX)
George M. McCune, Historian
Pub. *McCune Family Association
Newsletter*, annually (summer); (for
descendants of Matthew McCune
(1811–1889); and associated families:
Albrechtsen, Allen, Anderson,
Andrews, Armstrong, Ashdown,
Bachman, Bailey, Bennett, Binning,
Broadhead, Bush, Cambell, Carter,
Castleton, Cazier, Christensen,
Claridge, Clayton, Clements, Clinger,
Collins, Cook, Coombs, Dallin,
Daniel, Davis, Dawson, Day, Demsher,
Drictoni, Eldredge, Elmer, Engstrom,
Esterholdt, Evans, Faust, Ferris, Fisher,
Fleming, Greene, Groesbeck, Guittard,
Halverson, Hansen, Harris, Harrod,
Heron, Herran, Heskett, Hesse, Hill,
Holbrook, Huefner, Hurd, Jacob,
Jenkins, Jones, Kearl, Knell, Logan,
Lunt, Mathews, McBride, McCann,
McDonald, McDonnel, McGeehee,
McNamara, Mee, Merrill, Maynard,

Midgley, Miller, Montgomery, Musser,
Nakama, Naylor, Neil, Nelson,
Nielson, Noble, Norman, Osborne,
Osguthorpe, Palmer, Paxman, Pay,
Petersen, Phillips, Price, Porter,
Quealy, Quinn, Rall, Rangila, Rice,
Riddle, Russon, Rymal, Schmidt,
Scott, Scowcroft, Sherman, Sisson,
Smith, Squire, Steed, Tams, Taylor,
Tekulvie, Thompson, Trower, Ure,
Usher, Wait, Weeks, Westmoreland,
Whitaker, Widdison, Wilcox,
Wilkinson, Wolsey, Wood, Woolf and
Young)
$15.00 suggested donation per year
membership

McCunn (see MacLachlan)

McCurdie (see Stewart)

McCurdy (see Likes)

McCurdy
*McCurdy Family of America
Association
2860 South Hudson Street
Denver, CO 80222-6922
David W. MacCurdy, Executive Director
$25.00 per year membership

McCurdy
*Samuel McCurdy Family Association
498 Main Street
West Yarmouth, MA 02673-4841
Ross W. McCurdy, President
Pub. *McCurdy Family Association
Newsletter*, semiannually; (includes
descendants of Samuel McCurdy
(1723–1808) of Surry, New
Hampshire, and allied families:
Barron, Dart and Mark)
$7.00 per year U.S. membership, $8.00
per year Canadian membership

McCurrack (see Garner)

McCurrey (see Currie)

McCurrie (see Currie)

McCurry (see Cian, Currie, Tidwell)

McCutchen (see MacFaddien)

McCutchen
The McCutchen
20 West Jennings Street, #14C
Newburgh, IN 47630-1212
Harry and Mildred McCutchen
Thompson, Editors
Pub. *The McCutchen*, semiannually

McCutchen
McCutchen Family Newsletter
716 C Avenue
Lawton, OK 73501
Jeanne McCutcheon
Pub. *McCutchen Family Newsletter*,
semiannually

McCutchen
*McCutchen Trace Association
25 Troxell Lane
Staunton, VA 24401
Phone (540) 886-5032
Sarah S. Splaun, Secretary-Treasurer
Pub. *McCutchen*, semiannually (spring
  and fall), $7.50 per year subscription;
  (includes McCutcheon, any spelling)
Biennial reunion in odd-numbered years

McCutcheon (see McCutchen)

McDaniel (see Futral, Reynolds)

McDavitt
*George Madison McDavitt Family
  Organization
8524 Ash
Raytown, MO 64138
Phone (816) 358-2670
Dean F. McDavitt
(McDavitt family of Shelby County,
  Kentucky, 1796, of Woodford County,
  Kentucky, 1820, and of Macon County,
  Missouri, 1850)

McDiffie (see Macfie)

McDonald (see Dockery, Donald,
  Haynes, McCune)

McDonald
*McDonald Family Organization
4309 West Second Street
Plainview, TX 79072
Phone (806) 293-1987
Shari Measles
(includes descendants of Harrison
  McDonald (1828 South Carolina–1865
  Wayne County, Missouri), brother of
  Mose, and Harrison's wife Cornelia
  Angeline McGhee (ca 1830
  Tennessee–), and their children
  Florada, Mary Nancy, William Marion,
  James Buck, Alice J. and George T.)

McDonnel (see McCune)

McDonough
*Thomas McDonough Family
  Organization
1599 Monaco Circle
Salt Lake City, UT 84121
Phone (801) 278-7708
Eldon B. Tucker, Jr., M.D.
(includes family originally from West
  Virginia)

McDorman (see Dorman)

McDougal
*William McDougal Family
  Organization
116 West 12th Street
Wayne, NE 68787
Phone (402) 375-1620
Berniece M. Fulton

Mcduff (see MacDuff)

McDuffee (see Corson)

McDuffie (see Macfie)

McDuffy (see Macfie)

McEachern (see Scott)

McEdward (see Goodenow)

McEllcole (see Cian)

McEllycuddy (see Cian)

McElroy
*Robert McElroy Descendants
  Organization
17825 Continental Drive
Brookfield, WI 53045
Phone (414) 781-8215
Jeane Yigit, Family Archivist
(includes family which came to Quebec
  in 1847 from Ireland)

McElvain (see MacBean)

McElvaine (see MacBean)

McElvane (see MacBean)

McElvayne (see MacBean)

McElveen (see MacBean)

McElwain (see MacBean)

McElwane (see MacBean)

McElwayne (see MacBean)

McElwee (see MacBean)

McEntee (see Behnke)

McEntyre (see MacIntyre)

McEoghan (see MacLachlan)

McEroune (see MacLachlan)

McEuen
*McEuen Family Association
4325 Kay Lane
Saint Louis, MO 63123
Phone (314) 631-5831
Ruth Richtermeyer, Editor
Pub. *McEuen Family Association*,
  quarterly (June, September, December
  and March)
$12.00 per year membership

McEver
*McEver Memorial Association
Rt. 3, Box 71
Sallisaw, OK 74955
Phone (918) 775-6816
Byrdia Miller, Corresponding Secretary
Annual reunion at Sallisaw, Oklahoma

McEwan (see MacLachlan)

McEwen (see MacLachlan)

McEwen
Descendants of Robert McEwen and
  Sarah Wilcoxson, Stratford,
  Connecticut
119 Essex Meadows
Essex, CT 06426-1522
Ruth McEwen Coleam

McEwin (see MacLachlan)

McEwing (see MacLachlan)

McFadden (see Garner, MacFaddien)

McFaddin (see MacFaddien)

McFadeyan (see McGee)

McFadin (see MacFaddien)

McFall (see Mackay)

McFarland (see Album)

McFarland
McFarland Family Association
PO Box 37
Albany, TX 76430
Elsa McFarland Turner, Historian

McFarland
Wade-Smith Genealogy Service
Rt. 7, Box 52
Llano, TX 77643
Evelyn Wade
Pub. *McFarland Clan Newsletter*, three
  times per year, queries accepted

McFarland
*William McFarland Family
  Organization
1757 North 1770 East
Mapleton, UT 84664
Phone (801) 489-7858
Dr. Kenneth E. Ainge, President
Pub. *Annual*

McFarlane (see CTC Family
  Association, Armstrong)

McFatridge (see Folk Family Surname
  Exchange)

McFatridge
*McFatridge Family Association
PO Box 52048
Knoxville, TN 37950-2048
J. A. and D. P. McFatridge, Co-Chairs

McFatridge
*Folk Family
PO Box 52048
Knoxville, TN 37950-2048
Hester E. Stockton, Owner and Editor;
  Ell McFatridge, Editor
Pub. *McFatridge Families*, quarterly,
  $15.00 per year subscription, $5.00 per
  issue; (includes MacPhetridge,

McFatridge, McFetridge, McPhedris, McPhetridge clans in America, Ireland and Scotland)
Annual reunion in June at the Red River Valley Fairgrounds, Paris, Texas

McFee (see Macfie)

McFeithe (see Macfie)

McFetridge (see McFatridge)

McFeye (see Macfie)

McFie (see Macfie)

McFinlay (see MacBeth)

McGahan (see McGahen)

McGahen
*McGahen/McGhan/McGhen/McGahn/
McGahan Family Association
575 Stone Jug Road
Lewisberry, PA 17339-9178
Phone (717) 432-2611
Neil V. McGahen
(all branches with optional spelling of the name within family over the years)
Annual reunion in July in Erie County, Pennsylvania, and periodic reunions in Michigan and Alaska

McGahn (see McGahen)

McGalliard
McGalliard Family Newsletter
2724 Blowing Rock Boulevard
PO Box 7
Patterson, NC 28661-0007
Phone (704) 758-8373
Linda McGalliard Staley
Pub. *McGalliard Family Newsletter*, quarterly, $12.00 per year subscription

McGarry
McGarry Newsletter
4099 Pafford Road
Dayton, OH 45405
J. L. McGarry, Sr.
Pub. *McGarry Newsletter*

McGaughey
*McGaughey Surname Organization
137 Lorenzi, South
Las Vegas, NV 89107
Phone (702) 877-2438
Juanita Mae McGaughey Clark

McGee (see Cowart, Mackay, Scott)

McGee
*McGee/Kilburn/Davis/Wakefield/
Stuckey/Mathews/Murchison/
McFadeyan Family Organization
3188 Clark Court
PO Box 266
Placerville, CA 95667
Phone (916) 622-0575

Elinor and Omer McGee, Coordinators
Pub. *Newsletter*, irregularly, free

McGeehee (see McCune)

McGhan (see McGahen)

McGhen (see McGahen)

McGhilc (see MacLachlan)

McGibboney
*McGibboney Family Association
124 Clinto Street
Frankford, KY 40601-1949
Martha A. Hubbard

McGilchrist (see MacLachlan)

McGill (see Heath, MacGill)

McGill
*Mountain Press
4503 Anderson Pike
PO Box 400
Signal Mountain, TN 37377-0400
Phone (423) 886-6369;
(423) 886-5312 FAX
James L. Douthat, Owner
(William McGill of Ireland and North Carolina)

McGilleycrist (see MacLachlan)

McGillivary (see Smith)

McGilvery (see Garner)

McGinnes (see MacInnes)

McGinnis (see MacInnes, McRae)

McGinte (see Likes)

McGirr (see McRae)

McGlachan (see MacLachlan)

McGlachen (see MacLachlan)

McGlachland (see MacLachlan)

McGlachlin (see MacLachlan)

McGlauchin (see MacLachlan)

McGlauchlan (see MacLachlan)

McGlauchlin (see MacLachlan)

McGlauchlon (see MacLachlan)

McGlaughlin (see MacLachlan)

McGlothin (see MacLachlan, Tidwell)

McGlothlon (see MacLachlan)

McGlotten (see MacLachlan)

McGlottin (see MacLachlan)

McGloughlan (see MacLachlan)

McGloughlin (see MacLachlan)

McGlouthlin (see MacLachlan)

McGnish (see MacInnes)

McGoon (see MacLachlan)

McGowan (see Folk Family Surname Exchange)

McGowen (see Golding)

McGown (see Folk Family Surname Exchange)

McGrady
McGrady News
930 South Monaco
PO Box 11337
Denver, CO 80224
Pub. *McGrady News*

McGrady
*McGrady Family Association
5760 Saint Clement Court
Toledo, OH 43613
Phone (419) 472-9538
L. J. McGrady

McGrain (see Surname Sources)

McGrath (see Cian)

McGrath
*McGrath Family Association
Rt. 1, Box 37
Concord, NE 68728
Phone (402) 584-2407
Marlys McGrath Rhodes Rice, Historian
(database includes Lovell, McGrath, Miner, Rhodes, Rice and Toomey of Ireland, Michigan, Iowa, Illinois and New York)
$5.00 per year membership for families, includes reunion dinner; annual reunion on the last Sunday of July in Independence, Iowa, area

McGrath
*McGrath Family Organization
449 Race Track Road
Ho Ho Kus, NJ 07423
Phone (201) 444-0783
Harold D. McGrath

McGraw
McGraw Family Reunion (Francis McGraw Descendants)
RR 1
Richmond, VA 23231-9801
Mrs. C. P. Harland

McGray
McGray Clearinghouse
17 Harrison Street
Roslindale, MA 02131-2101
Phone (617) 323-7751
Claude R. MacGray
Pub. *McGray Family Newsletter*,
    semiannually (April and October);
    (includes MacGray and Magray of
    Maine and Nova Scotia)
$5.00 per year membership

McGregor (see Gregor)

McGregor
McGregor Family Association
2325 Ridge Drive
Northbrook, IL 60062
Larry McGregor

McGruen (see MacLachlan)

McGuffie (see Macfie)

McGuire (see Lightholder, Maguire)

McHenry (see Clark, Kahler)

Mchlachlin (see MacLachlan)

McHlachlin (see MacLachlan)

McIlchreist (see MacLachlan)

McIlcrist (see MacLachlan)

McIlhaney
*James William McIlhaney Family
    Association
4308 South Peoria, #1776
Tulsa, OK 74105
Phone (918) 749-4319
Carol Corbett Ellis

McIll-Christ (see MacLachlan)

McIllichrist (see MacLachlan)

McIlraith
*McIlraith Surname Organization
2310 Juniper Court
Golden, CO 80401-8087
Phone (303) 526-1319
Terence T. Quirke, Jr., Ph.D., C.G.,
    Proprietor
(includes Grace, pre-1900, Sussex,
    England, and Goble pre-1900, Kent
    and Sussex, England)

McIlvain (see MacBean)

McIlvaine (see MacBean)

McIlvayne (see MacBean)

McIlvean (see MacBean)

McIlveen (see MacBean)

McIlveene (see MacBean)

McIlwain (see MacBean)

McIlwane (see MacBean)

McIlwee (see MacBean)

McInch (see MacInnes)

McInnis (see MacInnes)

McInnish (see MacInnes)

McInroy (see Donnachaidh)

McIntire (see Corson)

McIntire
McIntire-Mendenhall Reunion
10808 Santa Anita Terrace
Damascus, MD 20872
Patricia Troth, Secretary
Pub. *Newsletter*, annually; (includes
    descendants of Fidelis McIntire and
    Isabell Mendenhall of Washington
    County, Ohio)

McIntosh (see Alsop, Mackintosh)

McIntosh
*McIntosh Surname Organization
George McIntosh Family Organization
PO Box 284
Belgrade, MT 59714-0284
Phone (406) 656-0979
Irma Jane Mauger

McInvale
*McInvale Surname Organization
Highway 87 North
PO Box 340
Burkeville, TX 75932
Phone (409) 565-4751
Helen Rogers Skelton

McIphie (see Macfie)

McIrwin (see Irwin)

McIver
Trendy Publications, Inc.
4528 Wyndale Avenue, S.W.
Roanoke, VA 24018
Phone (703) 989-9402
Margaret Drody Thompson, President-
    Editor-Publisher
Pub. *The Pipers*, annually, $10.00 per
    issue; (for Scottish-American Clan
    McIver)

McJenkin (see McJunkin)

McJunkin
McJunkin Quarterly
7736 Idlewood Lane
Dallas, TX 75230-3202
Katherine L. McJunkin
Pub. *McJunkin Quarterly, Including
    Junkin, McJunkin, McJenkin*, $11.00
    per year subscription

McKay (see Brawley, Mackay, Mueller)

McKay
Robert McKay Clan Newsletter
5319 Manning Place, N.W.
Washington, DC 20016-5311
Phone (202) 363-3663
Wallace E. and Dorothy Shipp, Editors
Pub. *Robert McKay Clan Newsletter*,
    annually (April), $10.00 average
    donation per year subscription
Annual reunion in June in Virginia

McKay
McKay/MacKay Family Association
11 John Swift Road
Acton, MA 01720
Marian Hogan Oliveros

McKclauchlane (see MacLachlan)

McKee (see Arthur, Bailey, Mackay)

McKee
Mark T. McKee Family Journal
Broken Rocks
Port Austin, MI 48467
Pub. *Mark T. McKee Family Journal*
    (includes Bradshaw, Fink, Kaufman,
    Kilbourne, Thompson, White and
    Witheril)

McKeever
McKeever Cousins Reunion
Rt. 1, Box 8
Macy, IN 46951
Phone (219) 382-3301
Jack W. McKeever

McKelgol (see Cian)

McKenney (see McKinney)

McKennon (see David)

McKenzie (see Haury)

McKenzie
*William McKenzie and Katharine
    Doering Descendants
PO Box 69
Hamilton, KS 66853
Phone (316) 678-3372
P. Reed
Annual reunion in May

McKeon (see MacLachlan)

McKeowan (see MacLachlan)

McKeowen (see MacLachlan)

McKeowin (see MacLachlan)

McKeown (see Arthur, Caufield,
    MacLachlan)

McKerron
*McKerron Surname Organization
Rt. 1, Box 350
Poland Spring, ME 04274

Phone (207) 998-4615
Ronda A. Watson

McKewan (see MacLachlan)

McKewen (see MacLachlan)

McKewn (see MacLachlan)

McKey (see Mackay)

McKhone (see MacLachlan)

McKibbon (see McCubbin)

McKie (see Mackay)

McKilchrist (see MacLachlan)

McKinnes (see MacInnes)

McKinney
*Bridget McKinney Family Organization
PO Box 1860
Studio City, CA 91614
Phone (818) 980-1005; E-mail:
    AP471@lafn.org
Karen Mohr

McKinney
*McKinney Family Association
6201 Lansbrook Lane
Oklahoma City, OK 73132
Phone (405) 722-3077 (phone and FAX)
Barbara Pannage Stanfield, Coordinator
Pub. *McKinney Maze*, semiannually
    (March and September); (includes
    McKenney)
$10.00 per year membership

McKinney
*Daniel McKinney Family Organization
608 Hunter
Kilgore, TX 75662
Phone (214) 984-7564
Ila Gatons Eckstadt

McKinnis (see MacInnes)

McKinnish (see MacInnes)

McKinnon
McKinnon (MacKinnon) Family
    Organization
5394 Hencely Road
Marianna, FL 32445
Charles Hencely

McKitrick
*McKitrick Family Database
998 Bloomington Drive South
Saint George, UT 84790-7585
Phone (801) 673-6314
Carolyn Reinbold
(includes descendants of William
    McKitrick (1724 Ulster, Northern
    Ireland–) and Agnes Heron)

McKittrick (see Douglas)

McKlawachlane (see MacLachlan)

McKnight (see MacFaddien, Weaver)

McKnight
*Licht Publications
490 M Street, S.W., Apartment W604
Washington, DC 20024-2612
Phone (202) 554-2429
Lilla McKnight Licht, Editor and
    Publisher
Pub. *McKnight Newsletter*, quarterly,
    $12.00 per year subscriptions;
    (includes McKnutt, McNaught,
    McNight, McNutt, etc.)

McKnutt (see McKnight)

McKown (see MacLachlan)

McKuen (see MacLachlan)

McKuin (see MacLachlan)

McKune (see MacLachlan)

McKune
*McKune and Comfort Family Reunion
    Organization
1215 Glen Ridge Drive
Glassboro, NJ 08028
Phone (609) 589-7042
Robert B. Taylor, Historian
(includes descendants of Robert McKune
    from Glasgow, Scotland in 1754, John
    and Phoebe Gildersleeve Comfort
    1776)
Donation for membership; annual
    reunion on the second Saturday of
    August in the Binghamton, New York,
    area

McKusick
*McQ6 Family Association, Inc.
PO Box 548
South Orleans, MA 02662
Phone Website: http://www.metrolink.net/
    ~mckusick
Kenneth A. McKusick, M.D., Secretary
    Treasurer
Pub. *Clan Connections*, quarterly, $10.00
    per year membership

McKynery (see Cian)

McLachan (see MacLachlan)

McLachen (see MacLachlan)

McLachian (see MacLachlan)

McLachin (see MacLachlan)

McLachine (see MacLachlan)

McLachlain (see MacLachlan)

McLachlainn (see MacLachlan)

McLachlan (see MacLachlan)

McLachland (see MacLachlan)

McLachlane (see MacLachlan)

M'Clachlane (see MacLachlan)

McLachlann (see MacLachlan)

McLachlen (see MacLachlan)

M'Clachlene (see MacLachlan)

McLachlin (see MacLachlan)

McLachline (see MacLachlan)

McLachlon (see MacLachlan)

McLachlun (see MacLachlan)

McLackken (see MacLachlan)

McLacklan (see MacLachlan)

McLacklane (see MacLachlan)

McLacklen (see MacLachlan)

McLacklin (see MacLachlan)

McLackline (see MacLachlan)

McLacklon (see MacLachlan)

McLaclan (see MacLachlan)

McLaflen (see MacLachlan)

McLaflin (see MacLachlan)

McLaghlan (see MacLachlan)

McLaghlane (see MacLachlan)

M'Claichlan (see MacLachlan)

McLain (see Marshall)

McLain
*Biennial McLain Reunions
4343 Woods Trail, S.W.
Wyoming, MI 49509-6400
Phone (616) 534-0294
Barbara Benson, Historian, Editor and
    Publisher
Pub. *The McLain News*, semiannually
    (May and November); (includes
    descendants of Alexander McLain
    (1839–1921) and Eliza Ann Stover
    (1845–1925) from Forreston, Illinois,
    to Laurens, Iowa)

McLaouhlan (see MacLachlan)

McLaren
Clan McLaren Society of North America,
    Ltd.
5843 Royal Crest Drive
Dallas, TX 75230

Banks McLaurin, Jr., Editor and
  Publisher
Pub. *Clan McLaren Society, USA*,
  quarterly

McLauchlain (see MacLachlan)

McLauchlan (see MacLachlan)

M'Clauchlan (see MacLachlan)

McLauchland (see MacLachlan)

McLauchlane (see MacLachlan)

McLauchleam (see MacLachlan)

McLauchleine (see MacLachlan)

McLauchlen (see MacLachlan)

McLauchlin (see MacLachlan)

McLauchline (see MacLachlan)

McLauchlon (see MacLachlan)

McLaucklan (see MacLachlan)

McLaughlan (see MacLachlan)

McLaughland (see MacLachlan)

McLaughlane (see MacLachlan)

McLaughlen (see MacLachlan)

McLaughlin (see CTC Family
  Association, Brawley, MacLachlan)

McLaughlon (see MacLachlan)

McLaughlun (see MacLachlan)

McLaughton (see MacLachlan)

McLauthin (see MacLachlan)

McLauthlan (see MacLachlan)

McLawhlan (see MacLachlan)

McLawlan (see MacLachlan)

McLellan
McLellan Clan in America
355 Newton Drive
Southern Pines, NC 28387
Hugh McLellan, Convener

McLendon (see McClendon,
  MacLennan)

McLennon (see MacLennan)

McLlauchland (see MacLachlan)

McLochan (see MacLachlan)

McLochlainn (see MacLachlan)

McLochlan (see MacLachlan)

McLochlin (see MacLachlan)

McLochlon (see MacLachlan)

McLocklan (see MacLachlan)

McLouchlan (see MacLachlan)

McLoughlan (see MacLachlan)

McLoughlin (see MacLachlan)

McLouth
*McLouth Database
11397 County Road 219
Tyler, TX 75707-9609
Phone (903) 566-1822
Marilyn Feltl McLouth, Historian
  (includes over 2,600 descendants of
  Lawrence[1] McLouth (1724–) and
  Molly Pratt, also allied families of
  Bloberger, Bond, Chastek, Feltl,
  Havekost, Howland (John of
  Mayflower), Pratt, Roden and
  Schumacher)

McLouth
*McLouth-Pratt Family of America
  Association
11397 County Road 219
Tyler, TX 75707-9609
Phone (903) 566-1822
Marilyn Feltl McLouth, Historian
  (includes descendants of Lawrence[1]
  McLouth (1724–) and Molly Pratt)
Annual reunion in June in Michigan and
  in July in Minnesota

McLouthan (see MacLachlan)

McLuchlayne (see MacLachlan)

McLullich (see Ross)

McMahan (see Folk Family Surname
  Exchange)

McMahan
*Folk Family
PO Box 52048
Knoxville, TN 37950-2048
Hester E. Stockton, Owner; Deborah
  McMahan, Editor
Pub. *McMahan Families*, quarterly,
  $15.00 per year subscription, $5.00 per
  issue; (includes McMahon)

McMahon (see McMahan, Reardon)

McMakin
McMakin Family Organization
902 S.W. Fourth
Marietta, OK 73448
Mary Zachary

McMaster (see MacInnes)

McMasters (see MacInnes)

McMillan
*McMillan-Love-McAlpin Family
  Research (Argyleshire and Paisley,
  Scotland)
511 South, Park Road, Apartment #133
Spokane, WA 99212-0551
Phone (509) 891-9577
John Lothrop Cobb

McMinn
*Joseph McMinn Family Organization
10042 Lubao Avenue
Chatsworth, CA 91311-3517
Phone (818) 349-3169
Charles A. Cartwright-Frank

McMorris
*McMorris of PA Association
13200 Doty Avenue, #220
Hawthorne, CA 90250
Elayne Alexander, Head of Research

McMullan (see Haynes)

McMurry (see Rutherford)

McNabb (see Davis)

McNair
*McNair Memoirs
12600 Bissonnet A4-407
Houston, TX 77099
Dede D. Mercer, Publisher
Pub. *McNair Memoirs*, bimonthly,
  $20.00 per year subscription; (all
  variations of the surname, worldwide)

McNamara (see McCune)

McNatt (see McCornack)

McNatt
Surnames, Limited
RR 3, Box 59
Muleshoe, TX 79347-9208
Pub. *McNatt Ancestry*, irregularly, $8.00
  per issue

McNaught (see McKnight)

McNeely (see Brawley, Macneil)

McNeely
McNeely Mas and Pas
411 Avondale Road
Huntington, WV 25705-1524
Melinda Vance, Family Representative
Pub. *McNeely Mas and Pas*

McNees
*Family Ties from McNees to
  Menees Et Al*
3262 Beach Drive, East
Port Orchard, WA 98366-8116
Marjorie Menees, Secretary/Treasurer
Pub. *Family Ties from McNees to Menees
  Et Al*, three times per year (February,
  June and October), $15.00 per year
  subscription, $6.00 each for back
  issues; (includes descendants of James

McNees (1710 County Antrim, Ireland–) and his wives, Ellen Cardwell Williams Breathitt(?) and Margaret Allen, of Bethel, Pennsylvania)
Reunion

McNeice (see MacInnes)

McNeil (see MacNeil)

McNeil
McNeil Family Association
100 Ferriday Drive
Ferriday, LA 71334-3612
Carolyn Perrault

McNeill (see Macneil)

McNeish (see MacInnes)

McNesh (see MacInnes)

McNess (see MacInnes)

McNew (see Evitt)

McNew
*McNew History
465 Sunset Terrace
Cedar Park, TX 78513
Phone (512) 259-4796
Joseph Carroll, Publisher
(includes descendants of Jeremiah McNew (then Macknew) in Maryland 1668)

McNiece (see MacInnes)

McNight (see McKnight)

McNinch (see MacInnes)

McNish (see MacInnes)

McNutt (see Folk Family Surname Exchange, McKnight)

McOunn (see MacLachlan)

McOwan (see MacLachlan)

McOwans (see MacLachlan)

McOwen (see MacLachlan)

McOwens (see MacLachlan)

McOwin (see MacLachlan)

McOwins (see MacLachlan)

McPhail (see Mackay)

McPhedris (see McFatridge)

McPhee (see Macfie)

McPheir (see Macfie)

McPherson (see Gower, Gunnin, Hines, MacPherson)

McPherson
*McPherson Family
3617 Link Road
Greensboro, NC 27405
Phone (910) 621-4695
K. Paul Holt, Family History Compiler
(includes McPhersons of Old Orange County, North Carolina, especially descendants of Daniel McPherson and Ruth Shires of Chester County, Pennsylvania, who settled in the Orange County area of North Carolina, also William McPherson (1726–1817), of Orange County, North Carolina)

McPhetridge (see McFatridge)

McPhie (see Macfie)

McQuade (see Mackay)

McQuaid (see Mackay)

McQueen (see Armstrong)

McQuivey (see Withy)

McQuone (see MacLachlan)

McQuowen (see MacLachlan)

McQuowens (see MacLachlan)

McRae (see Dobie)

McRae
*McRae Database
Rt. 5, Box 178
Cochran, GA 31014
Phone (912) 934-4343
Robert A. McRae
(includes research on Anthony Badgley (1660 New York), Clark Badgley (1816 Indiana), Catherine Bain (1805 Scotland), Lydia Bishop (1758 North Carolina), Walter Bishoppe (1592 Kent County, England), Henry Borden (1370 England), Benjamin Borden (ca 1730 New England), Timothy Brees (1758 Maryland), Wilburga Catesby (1528 England), Jeremiah Clarke (1605 Kent County, England), John Clerk (1398 Kent County, England), Thomas Cocke (1638 England), Pleasant Cocke (1775 Virginia), Edward Darnall (1671 Maryland), Elizabeth Darnell (1800 Maryland), Phillipp De Catesby (1085 England), David Duncan (1775 Scotland), Jane S. Duncan (1821 Kentucky), James Galvin (1798 Kentucky), Robert Gibbons (1811 Ohio), William Gordon (1770 Virginia), Thomas Gregg/Greeg (1800 Ireland), Zelpha Hayes (1762 North Carolina and Georgia), Richard Hull (1521 Somerset, England), Richard Jelks (1720 Ohio and Northwest Territory), Henry Latham (1100 England), John Latham (1522 Northhamptonshire, England), John

Logan (1790 Kentucky and Virginia), Thomas Maddock (1615 Cheshire, England), Deborah Maddock (1740 New England), Levi McGinnis (1814 New England), Arthur McGirr (1750 Maryland and Scotland), Alexander McRae (1845 Scotland), David Nicholson/Nicolson (1779 Caithness, Scotland), John Park (1834 Ireland), Charlotte Pate (1785 Pennsylvania), William Patten (1754 Virginia and England), William Pleasants (1530 Norfolk County, England), George Pyle (1766 Virginia), Jane Richey (1812 Ireland), Janet Smith (1780 Caithness County, Scotland), Robert Stanton (1599 England), Daniel Stubbs (1685 England), Joseph Stubbs (1762 North Carolina), George W. Trew (1820 Suffolk County, England) and Jerome Weston (1553 England))

McRay (see McCrary)

McSween
*McSween/MacSwene/McSwein Family Organization
412 Main Street
Acton, MA 01720
Phone (617) 263-8259
Judith Wetherbee Peterson

McSwein (see McSween)

McVain (see MacBean)

McVaine (see MacBean)

McVane (see MacBean)

McVay
McVay, McVeigh, McVey Archives Quarterly
12500 John Williams Road
Pascagoula, MS 39581-9042
Mrs. Mickey McVey Paulk
Pub. *McVay, McVeigh, McVey Archives Quarterly*, (April, July, October and January); (includes all spellings)
$20.00 per year membership

McVayn (see MacBean)

McVayne (see MacBean)

McVaynes (see MacBean)

McVean (see MacBean)

McVeane (see MacBean)

McVee (see MacBean)

McVeen (see MacBean)

McVeene (see MacBean)

McVeigh (see McVay)

McVey (see McVay)

McVian (see MacBean)

McVicar (see Armstrong)

McWain (see MacBean)

McWaine (see MacBean)

McWane (see MacBean)

McWethey (see Withy)

McWethy (see Withy)

McWethy
*McWethy Family Genealogy Group
411 South Richland
Olney, IL 62450
Phone (618) 392-2437
Karl Mehnert, Genealogy Coordinator
(includes descendants of James
    Mackerwithy, who was in Dedham in
    1651 and may have been a Scottish
    prisoner-of-war)

McWilliams
*McWilliams Historical Project
PO Box 92
Hillsdale, WY 82060
Phone (307) 547-3424
Jerry McWilliams, Director-Editor
Pub. *Now & Then*, quarterly, $12.00 per
    year subscription

McWithey (see Withy)

McWithy (see Withy)

M'Duffe (see Macfie)

Meacham (see Rand)

Mead (see Cleveland)

Mead
Mead/e Surname Repository
PO Box 18258
Reno, NV 89511
Gisela Stuehrk Mead
$1.00 plus SASE and FGS

Meade (see Mead)

Meader (see Meador, Meadows)

Meader
*The Meader Family Association, Inc.
158 Ashdown Road
Ballston Lake, NY 12019
Phone (518) 399-5013
Jane Meader Nye, Secretary
Pub. *Newsletter*, annually
$10.00 per year membership

Meador (see Meadows)

Meador
Reason Mobley and Sarah Meador
    Family Organization
5505 Towers Street
Torrance, CA 90503
V. Vaughn

Meador
Meador-Meadows-Meader-Mader Family
    Association
2306 Westgate
Houston, TX 77019
Phone (713) 529-2333
Harold Helm
$25.00 plus pedigree and family group
    sheets for membership

Meadow (see Bosher)

Meadows (see Meador)

Meadows
Meadows Heritage National Reunion
1113 West University Avenue
Muncie, IN 47303
Juanita M. Wise, Historian
Pub. *Meadows Heritage Newsletter*,
    quarterly, $5.00 per year subscription;
    (includes Meader, Meador)

Meadows
*Footrints on the James
Box 504
Van Vleck, TX 77482
Phone (409) 245-4885
James W. Richardson
(includes history and genealogy of the
    Meadows and Pemberton family from
    1607)

Means (see Corson, Menzies)

Mears (see Holden)

Measures
*Measures Family Association
PO Box 90054
Nashville, TN 37209
Phone (615) 356-7192
W. Lenard Measures, President
Pub. *Measure's Advisor*, irregularly;
    (includes descendants of Thomas and
    Mary Measures, 1798–1875, Deeping
    Saint James, England)

Mechie (see Forbes)

Mechlin (see Mechling)

Mechling
*The Mechling Historical Association
820 Hunter Lake Drive
Reno, NV 89509-2402
Phone (702) 329-2078
Mary Frances Porter
Pub. *Newsletter*, quarterly; (includes
    Mechlin and Macklin)
$5.00 per year membership; biennial
    reunion in even-numbered years

Mechling
Mechling-Mechlin-Macklin
3456 North 13th Street
Arlington, VA 23103
Carol Mechling Bennett
Pub. *Mechling-Mechlin-Macklin*,
    quarterly, $5.00 per year subscription
Reunion

Meckes
*Meckes Family Database
1301 Bradford Road
Oreland, PA 19075-2414
Phone (215) 836-4727
Dale E. Berger, Genealogist/Historian
(includes descendants of Conrad Meckes/
    Mackes who arrived in Philadelphia in
    1744 from the Pfaltz region of
    Germany, and whose only son,
    Valentine, settled in what is now Ross
    Township, Monroe County,
    Pennsylvania)
Annual reunion

Meclendon (see MacLennan)

Mee (see McCune)

Mee
Lucky Mee Family Organization
PO Drawer 4487
El Paso, TX 79914
Phone (915) 751-7233
Joseph W. Mee, Historian
Pub. *News and Notes (From Mee to
    Mee)*, three times per year (April, July
    and October); *Yearbook*, annually
    (December), $3.00 per issue
$12.00 per year membership includes
    both periodicals

Meece (see Meese)

Meek (see Bush, MacDuff)

Meeker
*Vira Eleanor Meeker Family
    Organization
1223 North Michigan
Caldwell, ID 83605
Phone (208) 459-2400
Marvel L. Loosli

Meeker
Meeker Family Newsletter
1313 Lee Road
Troy, OH 45373-1608
George Meeker

Meeker
*Ezra Meeker Historical Society
(312 Spring Street, Puyallup, WA
    98372—location)
PO Box 103 (mailing address)
Puyallup, WA 98371
Phone (206) 848-1770
J. M. (Andy) Anderson, Administrator
Pub. *Puyallup Valley Heritage*, quarterly
$10.00 per year membership for
    individuals, $20.00 per year

membership for families, $35.00 per year donor membership, $100.00 per year supporting membership; $250.00 per year membership for businesses, $1,000.00 life membership

Meeks (see Album, MacDuff, Ross, Wright)

Meese
*Meese/Meece Family Network
37 Radcliffe Avenue
West Paterson, NJ 07424-2524
Phone (201) 256-5524
Jim Meece
Pub. *Meese/Meece Family Journal*, quarterly, $20.00 plus $1.48 postage per year subscription; (includes Miess and Meiss)

Meiers (see Myers)

Meighbors (see Lush)

Meigs
William Meigs and Catherine Edick Association
11273 Quartz Drive, #30
Auburn, CA 95602-2122
Jackie Selden Riley

Meik (see MacDuff)

Meiklejohn (see MacDuff)

Meiks (see MacDuff)

Mein (see Menzies)

Meine (see Menzies)

Meinser (see Mansker)

Meints
Meints Family
11221 East 75th Street
Raytown, MO 64138
Robert J. Meints

Meiss (see Meese)

Meixell (see Surname Database)

Mekie (see Forbes)

Meladine (see Blossom Press)

Melander
Melander Members
256 Ibis Street
Fort Myers Beach, FL 33931-4518
Tove Melander Stellas
Pub. *Melander Members*, quarterly, $10.00 per year subscription; (includes Mahlander, Mailander, Maleander, Malender, Malinder, Maljander, Melander, Melender, Melinder, Mialander, Milander, Milender, Milinder, Molander, Molender, Molinder, Mulander, Mulandoor,

Mulender, Mulendore, Mulinder, Mulindore plus double *l*'s)

Melanson
Melanson Registry
19460 Placer Hills Road
Colfax, CA 95713-9625
Alfred E. Melanson

Melburn (see MacDuff)

Melburne (see MacDuff)

Meldrum (see Forbes)

Melender (see Melander)

Melinder (see Melander)

Mellander (see Melander)

Mellason (see Johnson)

Mellender (see Melander)

Mellinder (see Melander)

Mellott (see Merlet)

Melrose
*Melrose Surname Organization
860 West Rosewood Court
Ontario, CA 91762
Phone (714) 986-6883
Opal Melrose Callaway, President (includes any Melrose in America and Scotland)

Melrose
*Melrose Family Association
3520 27th Place, West, #423
Seattle, WA 98199
Phone (206) 284-9304
Marcia Melrose, Secretary
Pub. *Who's Who in American Melroses*, quarterly
$5.00 per year membership

Melton (see Milton)

Melvear (see Garner)

The Memorial Foundation of the Germanna Colonies (see Multi-family Associations)

Menden
John Bertram Menden Family Organization
1042 West Mountain View
Mexa, AZ 85201
Phone (602) 834-0186
Fay Menden

Mendenhall (see McIntire)

Mendenhall
*Mendenhall Family Association
400 20th Avenue South
Great Falls, MT 59405

Phone (406) 727-7119; E-mail: 71220.1106@compuserve.com
Jim Mendenhall, Secretary
Pub. *Mendenhall Matters*, quarterly
$10.00 per year membership

Mendenhall
Mendenhall
26 East 83rd Street
Sea Isle City, NJ 08243-1114
Ralph I. Mendenhall
Pub. *Mendenhall*, quarterly, $10.00 per year subscription

Menees (see McNees)

Menge (see Blossom Press)

Menges (see Mingus)

Menges
*Menges Family Association in America
3757 Redthorne Drive
Amelia, OH 45102
Helen Menges Mains

Mennie (see Menzies)

Menning
Menning Family Association
Rt. 2, Box 49
Hampton, IA 50441
Wanda Spainhower

Menteith (see Graham)

Mentieth (see Stewart)

Mentiplay (see MacDuff)

Menzies
Clan Menzies Society, North America
Rt. 1, Box 530
Canton, NC 28716
Phone (704) 648-4255
David A. Mathewes, Convener (U.S.)
Pub. *The Red and White*, irregularly; (includes septs: Dewar, MacMenzies, MacMinn, MacMonies, Means, Mein, Meine, Mennie, Meyners, Minn, Minnus, Monzie)
$24.00 per year membership for individuals, $5.00 per year for junior membership (under 18 years of age)

Mercer (see Dawson)

Mercer
*Mercer and Related Families Database
765 East Wood Duck Circle
Fresno, CA 93720
Phone (209) 434-5212
Dolores Graham Doyle, Publisher

Mercer
*Joseph Frank Mercer Family Organization
9005 Fairglade Drive
Jacksonville, FL 32221
Phone (904) 786-2076

Paul L. Mercer
(includes descendants of Joseph Frank
   Mercer, who married Rosa Adeline
   Lowery, 1885 in Quaker City, Ohio)
$5.00 for reply to inquiries

Mercer
*Mountain Press
4503 Anderson Pike
PO Box 400
Signal Mountain, TN 37377-0400
Phone (423) 886-6369;
   (423) 886-5312 FAX
James L. Douthat, Owner
(Charles Fenton Mercer and his
   empresairo grant in east Texas)

Mercer
The Mercer Family Historian
12600 Bissonnet A4-407
Houston, TX 77099
Dede D. Mercer, Publisher
Pub. *The Mercer Family Historian*,
   semiannually; $20.00 per year
   subscription; (includes all variations of
   the surname, all over the world)

Merchant (see MacDuff)

Meredith (see Lambeth)

Merget
*Suzanne Merget Family Organization
PO Box 1860
Studio City, CA 91614
Phone (818) 980-1005; E-mail:
   AP471@lafn.org
Karen Mohr

Mergie (see MacDuff)

Mergy (see MacDuff)

Mergy
*Mergy Ancestors
223 West First Street
Van Wert, OH 45891-1113
Phone (419) 238-4174
James H. Mergy, Sr.

Merier
*Merier-Gourley-Roark Family
   Organization
"Gourley Hill"
Box 80 Ivy Road
Broxton, GA 31519
Phone (912) 384-1033
Winifred Merier Gourley
(includes Merier, Gourley, Roark, Shell,
   Bagley, Alpach, Pechelux, Brouillion
   families)

Meriwether (see Folk Family Surname
   Exchange)

Meriwether
*The Meriwether Society, Inc.
2075A Lakewood Club Drive, South
Saint Petersburg, FL 33712-4939

Phone (813) 866-9281; E-
   mail:JOglesby@aol.com or
   GenKen@aol.com
Joe M. Oglesby, Editor
Pub. *Meriwether Connections*, quarterly;
   (database contains over 25,000 names,
   including descendants of Nicholas
   Meriwether I (1631–1678) and many
   prominent related families of early
   Virginia, including Anderson, Barker,
   Bathurst, Browne, Burnley, Clemens/
   Clements, Crawford, Holmes, Howard,
   Jefferson, Lewis, Mathews, Minor,
   Oglesby, Overton, Pollard, Taliaferro,
   Terrell, Thornton, Washington,
   Wingfield, etc.)
$15.00 per year membership

Merklin (see Nelson)

Merlet
Descendants of Gedeon Merlet
2924 Kilkenny Court
Davidsonville, MD 21035
Phone (410) 956-4295
Frank Ruff, Newsletter Editor
Pub. *Descendants of Gedeon Merlet*,
   $8.00 per year subscription; (includes
   Malott, Marlatt and Mellott, past and
   present)

Mermilo (see Daub)

Merrick
*Merrick Family of Maryland
1623 12th Avenue
San Francisco, CA 94122
Phone (415) 564-2875
Rev. Fred H. Merrick
(seeking all descendants of Julian
   Merrick, who came with his two sons
   from Southampton, England, to
   Virginia in 1649, especially through
   his descendant, Israel Merrick (1764
   Maryland–1844 Wellsboro,
   Pennsylvania))

Merrill (see Barnard, Heath, McCune,
   Wright)

Merrill
Merrill Roots and Branches
5045 Sequoia Drive
Baton Rouge, LA 70814
Phone (504) 275-2917
Howard and Jean Merrill
Pub. *Merrill Roots and Branches*
$10.00 for search of 40,000+ database

Merrill
The Merrill Newsletter
922 South Westfield Street
Feeding Hills, MA 01030-0274
Phone (413) 789-2363
Dick Listro, Editor
Pub. *The Merrill Newsletter*, quarterly,
   $5.00 per year subscription, $8.00 per
   year subscription with Ancestral

Directory; (includes Merrills, 1600s to
   1900, both Nathaniel of Massachusetts
   and Richard of New York)

Merrill
*Florence Percy Merrill Family
   Organization
7712 Buck Street
North Richland Hills, TX 76180
Phone (817) 485-3792
Ken Mason

Merritt
Merritt
9560 Sunnehanna C101
Pensacola, FL 32514
Robert Merritt Shores
Pub. *Merritt*, three times per year, $20.00
   per year subscription

Merritt
George Merritt (CT) Descendants
   Association
8552 19th Avenue, N.W.
Seattle, WA 98117-3518
G. Merritt

Merryman (see Rutherford)

Mershon (see Reeder)

Mershon
*Association of Descendants of Henri
   Mershon, Inc.
3635 Rosehaven Place
Titusville, FL 32796-2966
Phone (407) 269-5469
William H. Trott
Pub. *Mershon Newsletter*, semiannually
No membership fee

Mertrud
*Mertrud Clan
PO Box 688
Goose Creek, SC 29445
Phone (803) 761-4904
Victor Paul Mertrud, Chief Researcher
(includes Mertrud/Mertrude from 1650 to
   the present)

Mertrude (see Mertrud)

Merwin
*Miles Merwin (1623–97) Association,
   Inc.
1733 Blue Bell Road
Blue Bell, PA 19422-2117
Phone (215) 646-0231
Merwyn R. Buchanan, Genealogist
Pub. *Milestones*, three to four times per
   year; (covers activities of the
   association of the descendants of
   Miles[1] Merwin)
$12.50 per year membership, free to
   libraries; reunion

Mescall (see Maxwell)

Mesenbring
Mesenbring/Bratthaver Reunion
112 South Stark
Bennington, NE 68007
Phone (402) 238-2491 (after 6:00 A.M.)
Dorothy E. Champ
Pub. *Mesenbrink(g) Bulletin*, quarterly
(March, July, September and
December), $10.00 per year
subscription

Mesenbrink (see Mesenbring)

Mesenbrink
*Mesenbrink Genealogical Society
PO Box 299
Dike, IA 50624
Twyla Mesenbrink

Messal (see Anthes)

Messecar
*Messecar Surname Organization
59 Shady Lane
Coventry, CT 06238
Ann L. Messecar
(includes Michiel Mesecar, who arrived
in Dutch New York in 1647, and his
son Johannes (1648–), of New York,
New Jersey and Ontario, Canada)
Costs of photocopies

Messner
*Messner Database
11469 Western Sunset Drive
Dewey, AZ 86327-5731
Phone (520) 772-8616
Col. (Ret) Joseph P. ("Phil") Barnes,
FACG, Family Genealogist
(includes 3,000 names of descendants of
the immigrant, Michael Messner, who
arrived at Philadelphia in 1738, and
Salome Reister)

Metcalf
*Michael Metcalf Family Database
27 Bell Drive
Salem, NH 03079-1304
Phone (603) 893-6487
Paul T. Metcalf
(especially descendants of Michael
Metcalf (1527 Tatterford, Norfolk,
England–1664 Dedham,
Massachusetts) and his wife Sarah
Ellwyn (1593 Heigham, Norfolk,
England–1644 Dedham), immigrated
1637)
Biennial reunion

Metherell
*Metherell Surname Organization
2808 Grants Lake Boulevard, #703
Sugarland, TX 77479
Phone (713) 980-4513
Mrs. B. D. Metherell
(worldwide)
Postage costs

Mettlin (see Robeson)

Metz (see Wert)

Metzgar
Jacob Metzgar and Eliz. Putterbaugh
Family Reunion
2159 State Route 121 North
New Madison, OH 45346
William Metzgar

Metzger (see Bentheim, Frantz, Stabler)

Mevius (see Movius)

Meyer (see Blossom Press, Anthes,
Erdwins, Myers)

Meyer
*Karl Johannes Meyer (1842–1915) and
Anna G'Feller Family from
Switzerland
335 West Shackley Street
PO Box 75
Geneva, IN 46740
Phone (219) 368-7352
Ruth Brown

Meyers (see Blossom Press, Kunkel,
Myers)

Meyers
*Martin L. Meyers Family Reunion
1114 Harvey
Topeka, KS 66604
Phone (913) 272-0649
Eadie Flickinger, President
(includes descendants of Martin L.
Meyers (1815 Somerset County,
Pennsylvania–1895 Brown County,
Kansas) and Sally Witt (1820–1898)
Annual reunion on the first Sunday of
August in Hiawatha, Kansas

Meyners (see Menzies)

M'Gilchrist (see MacLachlan)

M'Gilcreist (see MacLachlan)

Mialander (see Melander)

Mialjevich (see Blossom Press)

Miallander (see Melander)

Michael (see The Memorial Foundation
of the Germanna Colonies, Sullivan
Surname Exchange)

Michael
*Michael Family Reunion
4769 Arcadia Boulevard
Dayton, OH 45432
Phone (513) 254-1686
Mrs. Kenneth Striker, Secretary

Michell (see Clark, Hull)

Michener
*Michener-Worthington Family
Association
40 Fleetwood Avenue, Apartment 4B
Mount Vernon, NY 10552
Phone (914) 428-2360
Anna E. Shaddinger
Pub. *Newsletter*, annually; (includes
descendants of John Michener, who
married Sarah Moore in 1686)
Annual reunion on the fourth Saturday of
June

Michie (see Folk Family Surname
Exchange, Forbes)

Michie
*Folk Family
PO Box 52048
Knoxville, TN 37950-2048
Hester E. Stockton, Owner; Patrick
Michie, Editor
Pub. *Michie Families*, quarterly, $15.00
per year subscription, $5.00 per issue;
(includes Mickey)

Mick
Mick Family Newsletter
6555 Manson Drive
Waterford, MI 48095
Phone (313) 623-6062
Emma L. Smith, Editor
Pub. *Mick Family Newsletter*, quarterly,
$5.00 per year subscription

Mickey (see Michie)

Middag (see Middaugh)

Middagh (see Middaugh)

Middaugh
*Middaugh/Meddaugh/Maddaugh
Surname Organization
150 Brown Street
Saint Clair, MI 48079-4882
Phone (810) 329-9359
George M. Roberts
(includes Middag, Middaugh, Meddaugh
and Maddaugh families of the U.S.,
Ontario and Holland)

Middaugh
*Middaugh Surname Organization
7026 Valley Brook Drive
Charleston, WV 25312
Phone (304) 984-0768
Cherie Middaugh Pauley
(includes all Middaugh, especially
descendants of Aert Anthonisze
(Theunissen) Middagh (ca 1640
Keckop, Utrect, Netherlands–) and his
wife, Breckje Hansen Bergen (chr.
1642 New York))

Middleton (see Forbes, Harpole, Innes)

Midgley (see McCune)

Midkiff (see Rowe)

Miehls (see Hegner)

Miehls
*The Ancestors and Descendants of
  George Miehls and Mary Ann Hegner
232 Mont Eagle
Milford, MI 48381
Phone (810) 684-0650
Ruth Buchele Doerr, Publisher
(includes descendants of George Miehls
  (1818–) and Mary Ann Hegner
  (1826–) through George Miehls, Jr.,
  and Margaret Kieffer, Joseph Miehls
  and Augusta Bowman, Catherine
  Miehls and Clements Pund, Mary
  Anna Miehls and Ignatius Kahle,
  Barbara Miehls and William Kolhoff,
  Clara Miehls and William Henry
  Rowe, Benedict Miehls and Mary
  Boehmer, Frank Miehls and Theresia
  Bonholzer, Theresa Miehls and Elvin
  Rower, and Albert Miehls and Pearl
  Gehret)

Mier (see Myers)

Miess (see Meese)

Mikels (see Endicott)

Miklaszewsky
*Miklaszewsky Surname Organization
3084 Lakeshore Road
Manistee, MI 49660
Donald Harter, Jr.

Milam
*Milam Family Association
1208 North 85th Place
Scottsdale, AZ 85257-4114
Phone (602) 990-7914; E-mail:
  rmwiv@getnet.com; Website: http://
  www.getnet.com/~rmwiv
Robert M. Wilbanks, IV
Pub. *Milam Roots*, bimonthly (January,
  March, May, July, September and
  November), $5.00 per issue, queries
  accepted; *Milam News & Events
  Quarterly*
$8.00 per year membership, includes
  Milam News & Events Quarterly only

Milander (see Melander)

Milburn
*Milburn Family Association
1557 East Garnet
Mesa, AZ 85204
Phone (602) 892-0403
Beverly Murphy
$10.00 per year membership

Milburn
*Milburn Family Association
7357 Admiralty Drive
Canton, MI 48187-1501
Phone (313) 416-9883

Patrick K. Persons
Pub. *Newsletter*, biannually; (includes
  descendants of early Milbourns of
  New Jersey and Virginia)

Milender (see Melander)

Miles (see Album, Corson, Goodenow,
  Rutherford)

Miles
Looking for Miles
72 Dogleg Drive
Meriden, CT 06450
Phone (203) 238-3097
Sylvia Miles Guerin
(includes Hoag)

Miles
Miles/Raley Family Association
3730 Humboldt
Topeka, KS 66609
H. M. Thomas

Milford (see Campbell)

Milican (see Milligan)

Miligan (see Milligan)

Milikan (see Milligan)

Milinder (see Melander)

Mill (see Innes)

Millander (see Melander)

Millar (see Gregor)

Millard
Millard Family Ancestral Lines
PO Box 13548
Saint Louis, MO 63138
Maryann Schirker
Pub. *Millard Family Ancestral Lines*,
  quarterly, $25.00 per year subscription

Milleman (see Milleman)

Milleman
*Milleman Family Organization
9726 Mirage Circle
Garden Grove, CA 92644
Carol R. Austin
(database includes Millemon, Millerman,
  Millermon and Milliman)
Biennial reunion in even-numbered years
  on the fourth of July

Millemon (see Milleman)

Millender (see Melander)

Miller (see Blossom Press, Family
  Publications, The Memorial
  Foundation of the Germanna Colonies,
  Anthes, Barnes, Bodine, Brawley,
  Brehm, Brown, Corson, Dockery,

Frantz, Goodenow, Hatfield, Heath,
  Johnson, Likes, Mason, McConnell,
  McCune, Moser, Olsen, Ross,
  Schindel, Stoner, Taylor, Wert,
  Williams, Woodrow, Wright)

Miller
The Miller Family
204 Crabapple Drive
Sitka, AK 99835
Timothy E. Miller
Pub. *The Miller Family*, bimonthly, $5.00
  per year subscription; (includes Allen,
  Camp, Fullbright, Gladden, Griffin and
  Newman)

Miller
*Henry Miller Family Organization
PO Box 171
Douglas City, CA 96024
Phone (916) 778-3136
Paul Jones

Miller
Miller Monitor
4041 Pedley Road, #18
Riverside, CA 92509
Phone (714) 685-8936
Frances R. Nelson, Editor
Pub. *Miller Monitor*, quarterly, $17.00
  per year subscription

Miller
*James Redman Miller Family
  Organization
29 East Portland Avenue
Vincennes, IN 47591
Phone (812) 882-9371
Richard Carl Rodgers, II, Historian/
  Archivist
(archival facility collects information on
  all descendants and ancestors of the
  family in computer database;
  descendants of James Redman Miller
  (ca 1798 Lincoln County, Kentucky–),
  son of George Miller and Sarah Rice,
  and James' first wife Priscilla Franklin
  (ca 1806 Kentucky–before 1841
  Anderson or Washington County,
  Kentucky), daughter of James Franklin
  and Rhoda Walker, and James' second
  wife Jemima)

Miller
*William R. Miller Family Organization
PO Box 5103 E.K.S.
Johnson City, TN 37603
Phone (615) 929-2847
Mildred A. Holly

Miller
Miller
126 Perkins Extended
Memphis, TN 38117-3125
J. Gerald Miller
Pub. *Miller*, quarterly, $10.00 per year
  subscription

Miller
Genealogical and Historical News
369 East 900 South, Suite 247
Salt Lake City, UT 84111
R. D. Bradshaw, Editor
Pub. *Miller of Virginia Family Newsletter*

Miller
*The Hans Peter Hansen Miller Family
   Organization
936 West Pages Lane
West Bountiful, UT 84087-1803
Phone (801) 292-5830
Halvor Miller Olsen, President and
   Editor
Pub. *Miller Monitor*, annually; (includes
   descendants of Hans Peter Hansen
   Miller (1833 Nekso, Bornhold,
   Denmark–), came to Utah in 1862)
$10.00 per year membership

Miller
*Clell's Cousins
808 Charlotte Street
Fredericksburg, VA 22401
Phone (540) 371-3253
Ruth Fitzgerald
(includes relatives of Clell Miller, who
   was a member of Jesse James' gang)

Miller
Stephan Miller Family Association
   (Tennessee and Missouri)
1604 Longfellow Street
McLean, VA 22101
Georgia E. Benefiel

Miller
Miller Pursuit
7149 Sutton Drive
Everson, WA 98247
Neil Bancroft
Pub. *Miller Pursuit*

Miller
*Miller Family Reunion
PO Box 9223
Casper, WY 82609
Barbara Helwick

Millerman (see Milleman)

Millermon (see Milleman)

Millet
*Alma Wesley Millet (Sr.) Family
   Organization
Millet Heritage Enterprises
M.H.E. Heritage Library
433 South Hobson Street
Mesa, AZ 85204
Phone (602) 964-1613
Mr. Alma W. Millet, Jr., Founder-
   Chairman; A. Wesley Millet, III,
   Family Historian-Researcher; Paul A.
   Millet, Vice Chairman; Paul R. Millet,
   Computer Specialist
(includes related families of Batchelder,
   Beal, Brundage, Chapman, Ellis,
   Green(a)way, Grene(a)way, Hess,

Hills, Holman, Johnson, Lane, Lang,
   Le Baron, Lester, Lister, Martin,
   Peters, Stauffer, etc.)

Millican (see Milligan)

Milligan
Old Time Publications
10828 Oakbrook Drive
Omaha, NE 68154-2437
Peggy Wallingford Butherus
Pub. *Milligan Memories (Miligan,
   Milican, Milikan, Millikan, Millican,
   Mullican, Mullikan, Mulligan, etc.)*

Millikan (see Milligan)

Milliken (see Ross)

Milliman (see Milleman)

Millinder (see Melander)

Million
*Million Families Association
1311 Candlelight Avenue
Duncanville, TX 75137
Phone (214) 298-9576
Dorothy Ketter
Reunion in Lexington, Kentucky, or Glen
   Rose, Texas

Milliron (see Muhleisen)

Millison (see Muhleisen)

Milloy (see Stewart)

Mills (see Brawley, Dockery, Nelson,
   Tanner)

Mills
*Peter Mills Family Organization
713 Main Street
Acton, MA 01720
Phone (508) 263-2037
Helen Schatvet Ullmann

Mills
*George Henry Mills Family
   Organization
9443 Springville Road
East Otto, NY 14729
Phone (716) 257-9488
Carrie M. Dudley

Mills
*Mills Surname Organization
5341 Whitney Lane
Amarillo, TX 79110
Phone (806) 359-1012
Sylvia D. Murray, A.G., Coordinator
(includes Mills of Pennsylvania, West
   Virginia, Ohio and Indiana)

Mills
Collier Research
PO Box 371883
El Paso, TX 79937
Phone (915) 595-2725

Timothy P. Biarnesen, Editor
Pub. *Mills Quarterly*, $20.00 per year
   subscription

Mills
*Milton Crockett Mills Family
   Organization
7712 Buck Street
North Richland Hills, TX 76180
Phone (817) 485-3792
Ken Mason

Mills
*George Mills Family Association
905 West 7110 South
Richfield, UT 84701
Phone (801) 896-8600
LaMar M. Mills
Pub. *George Mills Family Newsletter*,
   bimonthly; (includes descendants of
   George Mills and Caroline Boxall)
$16.95 per year membership

Mills
*George Mills Family Organization
Rt. 1, Box 2168
Hinesburg, VT 05461
Phone (802) 482-3797
Michael Mills
Pub. *Mills Ancestry*, every six weeks,
   $10.00 for 8 issues, $5.00 for 4 issues;
   (includes Mills of Colonial New York,
   New Jersey and Connecticut, and
   various lines descendant, such as Nova
   Scotia)

Millwayne (see Emery)

Milne
*David Milne Family Organization
211 South 100 East
Saint George, UT 84770
Phone (801) 673-2283
Daniel Clark Watson, Jr.

Milner (see Dunn, Potts)

Milnes (see Innes)

Milroy (see MacGillivray)

Miltenberger
*Miltenberger Family Association
10820 Colbert Way
Dallas, TX 75218
Phone (214) 349-5318
The Rev. Gordon Miltenberger
Queries welcome

Minck (see Mink)

Miner (see McGrath, Minor, Oney)

Miner
*Mormon Miner Family Organization
529 West 1600 South
Orem, UT 84058-7319
Phone (801) 224-2297
Louie Jean M. Bahr, Secretary
$10.00 per year membership

Miner
*Albert Miner Family Organization
565 South 200 East
Springville, UT 84663
Phone (801) 489-4126
Richard K. Miner
(includes descendants of Albert Miner
    (1809–1948), New York and Ohio)
$10.00 per year membership

Mingus
*Mingus Family Association
18603 Fourth Avenue, S.W.
Seattle, WA 98166
James L. Powell
Pub. *Mingus Newsletter*, quarterly, free;
    (includes descendants of Johannis
    Menges (Mingus) and Anna Eva
    Busch, 1709 immigrants to New York
    from Germany)

Mininger
*Mininger Mysteries
PO Box 1872
Dodge City, KS 67801-1872
Laura Tasset Koehn, President
(includes research on Hiram Johnson
    Mininger and Catherine Bechtel
    family)

Mink (see Hamme)

Mink
*Mink Family Depository
12N002 Almora Terrace
Elgin, IL 60123
Phone (708) 741-7176
Allan R. Mink
(includes any and all Minck, Mink and
    Minks)

Minkel (see Nienow)

Minks (see Mink)

Minn (see Menzies)

Minnis
Minnis
2125 Tymber Hammock Drive
Jacksonville, FL 32223-1867
Phone (904) 262-9329;
    (904) 268-3912 FAX
M. Lee Minnis, Editor
Pub. *Minnis: Newsletter of the Minnis
    Families of America*

Minnus (see Menzies)

Minor (see Folk Family Surname
    Exchange)

Minor
*Thomas Minor Family Society
815 North 300 West
Provo, UT 84604
Phone (801) 377-8294
O. Geral Wilde, Genealogist

Pub. *The Minor Mirror*, semiannually;
    (includes descendants of Thomas
    Minor (1608–1690) and Grace Palmer
    of Chew Magna, England, and
    Stonington, Connecticut, includes
    Miner)
$10.00 per year membership; biennial
    reunion in odd-numbered years in
    various parts of the U.S., England and
    Canada

Minske (see Kanne)

Minsker (see Mansker)

Mintonye (see De la Montagne)

Miracle (see Likes)

Mires (see MacDuff)

Mischler
Mischler Newsletter
3199 West Boulevard
Cleveland, OH 44111-2821
Phone (216) 631-7407
Bob Ghinder, Editor
Pub. *Mischler Newsletter*, irregularly,
    $20.00 for six issues; (includes
    extensive database of Mischler/Mishler
    families, primarily from the mid-1700s
    to the present, mostly from
    Pennsylvania, Ohio, Indiana, Illinois,
    Oregon, Kansas, Switzerland and
    Canada, and all other related families)

Mistich (see Blossom Press)

Mitchell (see Corson, Croft, Crusan,
    Innes, Ross, Stewart)

Mitchell
*The John Mitchell Family Association
Rt. 1, Box 1250
Stewartstown, PA 17363-8718
Phone (717) 993-2104
Kathryn B. Jordan, Secretary/Treasurer
Pub. *Mitchell Letter*, quarterly; (includes
    descendants of John Mitchell (–1767
    Drumore Township, Lancaster County,
    Pennsylvania) and wife Mary; also
    allied families of Alexander, Clark and
    Jordan)
$10.00 per year membership; biennial
    reunion on the second weekend of
    October in even-numbered years in
    Pennsylvania or Ohio

Mitchell
Mitchell
2619 Cypress Street
Harlingen, TX 78550-8525
Lil Follett-Hall
Pub. *Mitchell*, quarterly, $15.00 per year
    subscription
Reunion

Mitchelson (see Innes, Stewart)

Mithceison (see MacDuff)

Mittelstedt (see Mower)

Mix
*Mix Database
362 Appleblossom Lane
Bay Village, OH 44140
Phone (216) 871-7039
Edwin Chesney
(database includes 13,200 Mix or Mix
    related names, mostly descendants of
    Thomas and Rebecca (Turner) Mix of
    New Haven, Connecticut, in the early
    1640s)

Mixson (see Hawsey)

Mize
Mize Reunion
4172 Hanes Drive
Decatur, GA 30035
Mrs. H. Nix

M'Kclachlane (see MacLachlan)

M'Klachlane (see MacLachlan)

M'Lauchan (see MacLachlan)

M'Lauchland (see MacLachlan)

M'Laughland (see MacLachlan)

M'Lawchtlane (see MacLachlan)

M'Lecgreist (see MacLachlan)

M'Lechreist (see MacLachlan)

Moales
*Family Research
416 Rockhill Avenue
Dayton, OH 45429-2628
Richard Bordeaux Walker
(includes descendants of William Henry
    Moales (–about 1878) and Anna Celina
    Bleuler of Switzerland and New
    Orleans, Louisiana)

Mobius (see Movius)

Möbius (see Movius)

Mocabees (see Dean)

Mochelbost
*Mochelbost Surname Organization
155 South 300 East
Logan, UT 84321
Phone (801) 753-0078
Roger A. Johnson

Mock
Mock Family Reunion
823 Munro Avenue
Rifle, CO 81650
Phone (303) 625-1659
Eldon White, Chairman

Mock
*Mock Family Historian
366 Jacaranda Drive
Danville, CA 94506-2125
Barbara Eichel Dittig, Family
　Representative
Pub. *Newsletter*, quarterly, $10.00 per
　year subscription; (a clearinghouse for
　research on Mock, Mauk, Mach of
　German and Swiss descent)
Reunion

Mockbee
Mockbee Family Organization
6107 N.W. 51st Terrace
Parkville, MO 64151
S. Ames

Mockridge (see Surname Sources)

Modesett (see Hall)

Moeller
Moeller Family Association
4212 N.W. 43rd Place
Oklahoma City, OK 73112
Phone (405) 947-8460
Glona Moeller Bozarth

Moffat
Moffat Clan Society of North America
95 Gallo Road, N.W.
Carrollton, OH 44615
Phone (216) 627-2027
Jack L. Maffett, M.D.

Moffatt
Moffatt Clan Society of North America
PO Box 18
Rosemark, TN 38053
Ralph Moffatt
(includes Maffatt, Maffett, Maffitt,
　Moffatt, Moffett, Moffitt)

Moffett (see Blair, Moffatt)

Moffitt (see Moffatt)

Mogingo
Mogingo, Monzingo, Montzingo
　Depository
205 Hensel Drive
Bryan, TX 77801
Phone (409) 846-6311
William S. McCulley

Mohler
*Mohler Family Reunion
269 Heatherwood Drive
Ephrata, PA 17522
Phone (717) 733-3141
Sarah Mohler, Secretary
(includes descendants of Ludwig Mohler,
　1730, Ephrata, Pennsylvania)
Reunion at Mohler Church of Brethren,
　Eprhata, Pennsylvania

Mohme (see Van Buren)

Mohn
*The Mohn Family History Society of
　Eastern Pennsylvania
Box 47, Shartlesville Road, RD 3
Bernville, PA 19506
Dorothy Mohn
(includes Mohns from Berks County
　towns of Mohnton, Bernville, Mohn's
　Hill, Blattadahl, Reading, etc., and
　Iowa)
Free

Mohney
*The Mohney Line
PO Box 85
Glenwood, IA 51534-0085
C. J. Mohney White
Pub. *The Mohney Line*, quarterly, $3.00
　per year subscription (beginning in
　July)

Mohr
*Johann Martin Mohr Family
　Association
PO Box 1860
Studio City, CA 91614
Phone (818) 980-1005; E-mail:
　AP471@lafn.org
Karen Mohr
Pub. *The Melting Pot: A Genealogy
　Newsletter for Mohr, Moore & Maurer
　Names*, quarterly, $15.00 per year
　subscription; (includes descendants of
　Johann Martin Mohr (1785 Germany–
　1840 Germany) and Juliana Augusta
　Kloss (1795 Germany–1861 New
　York))

Moizant (see Blossom Press)

Mojler (see Mosler)

Mokotoff
*Mokotoff/Mokotow Exchange
507 Crest Drive
Northvale, NJ 07646
Phone (201) 767-1299
Gary Mokotoff
(includes Mokotowski)

Mokotow (see Mokotoff)

Mokotowski (see Mokotoff)

Molander (see Melander)

Molden (see Molen)

Molen
*Molen Family Organization
Molen Surname Organization
9436 Natick Avenue
North Hills, CA 91343
Phone (818) 894-2085
Carol Molen
(includes Molden, Molin, Moreland and
　Moulden variations)

Molenaar (see Rutherford)

Molender (see Melander)

Molin (see Molen)

Molinder (see Melander)

Molines (see Molyneux)

Mollander (see Melander)

Mollender (see Melander)

Mollinder (see Melander)

Molyneux
*International Molyneux Family
　Association
PO Box 10306
Bainbridge Island, WA 98110
Phone (206) 842-6636; E-mail:
　mxworld_us@halcyon.com
Marie Mullenneix Spearman
Pub. *MX World: Newsletter of the
　International Molyneux Family
　Association*, quarterly, $11.00 per year
　membership; (includes Molines,
　Molyns, Moulin, Mulleneaux,
　Mullennix, Mulliner, Mullinix,
　Mullinax, Mulnix, etc., descendants of
　Earls of Sefton)

Molyns (see Molyneux)

Mombauer (see Mumpower)

Monaghan (see Mongan)

Moncrief
Moncrief Family Association
1367 Law Street
San Diego, CA 92109
B. Moncrief

Moncur (see MacDuff)

Monday (see Munday)

Mondy (see Munday)

Monegan (see Mongan)

Money (see Mooney)

Moneyham (see Moody)

Moneypenny (see MacDuff)

Mongan
Mongan Family Association (Monegan/
　Monigan/Monaghan)
10960 North 67th Avenue
Glendale, AZ 85304-3641
R. T. Gill

Monigan (see Mongan)

Monreith (see Maxwell)

Monro (see Munro)

Monroe (see Munro)

Monsieur (see Hayner)

Montag (see Montague)

Montague
Montague Family Organization
Rt. 3, Box 113
Arab, AL 35016
Jerry N. Peddycoart
Pub. *Montague Family News*, quarterly
$10.00 per year membership

Montague
*Montague Surname Organization
69 North Liberty Street
Delaware, OH 43015
Phone (614) 362-1372
Owen F. Tagg
(includes Montague, Tagg and Tague,
   especially William Tagg and Pearl
   Elbert, also Thomas Tague of
   Maryland to Huntingdon County,
   Pennsylvania, prior to 1790; also
   Patrick Tagge, Revolutionary War,
   Philadelphia County, Pennsylvania,
   also William (Tague) Tagg
   (Montague), born in Pennsylvania,
   married 1834 in Jackson County, Ohio,
   to Mary Lane; also John Teague who
   didn't take a warrant for land in
   Northumberland County, Pennsylvania,
   1794 but went to Cincinnatti, Ohio
   1796 under the name of Montag and
   settled in Kentucky)

Montague
Montague/Purcell/Warren Family of
   Pennsylvania and Ireland
PO Box 15926
Austin, TX 78761
H. J. Andreozzi

Montana (see Likes)

Montaney (see De la Montagne)

Montanye (see De la Montagne)

Montel (see Frantz)

Montford (see Hall)

Montgomery (see Burnham, Cooper,
   MacFaddien, McCune)

Montgomery
*Clan Montgomery Society of North
   America, Inc.
Rt. 2, Box 59
Paxton, IL 60957
Phone (217) 379-2479
Betty S. Carlson, Secretary
Pub. *Clan Montgomery Society
   Newsletter*, quarterly
$15.00 per year membership for
   individuals

Montgomery
Montgomery Clan Society
PO Box 354
Kearny, NJ 07032
Phone (201) 997-3403
Joan M. Dunphy

Montgomery
*Joseph Goodbrake Montgomery Family
   Organization
PO Box 183
Benton, WI 53803
Phone (608) 759-2755
Lynne Bradley Montgomery, Genealogist

Montjoy (see Mountjoy)

Montpetit (see Haling)

Montrose (see Graham)

Montzingo (see Mogingo)

Mony (see Mooney)

Monypenny (see MacDuff)

Monzie (see Graham, Menzies)

Monzingo (see Mogingo)

Moodie (see Stewart)

Moody
Moody Newsletter
6180 Merrywood Drive
Rocklin, CA 95677-3421
Kathleen Stewart
Pub. *Moody Newsletter*, quarterly
   (February, May, August and
   November), $12.00 per year
   subscription

Moody
*Moody Family Association
5243 Carpell Avenue
PO Box 18044
Salt Lake City, UT 84118-8044
Phone (801) 964-2825;
   (801) 964-0551 (FAX)
George M. McCune, Historian
(for descendants of John W. Moody
   (1840–1906); and associated families:
   Barfield, Beaman, Deans, Delaney,
   Harrison, Jennings, Johnson,
   Moneyham, Phillips, Pritchard,
   Sadeen, Teacher and Whitley from
   North Carolina, Virginia and
   Pennsylvania)

Moomaw (see Probst)

Moomaw
Moomaw Newsletter
138 South Fifth Street
Greenfield, OH 45123
Pub. *Moomaw Newsletter*, quarterly

Moon (see Lush)

Moon
The Moon Tribune
12600 Bissonnet A4–407
Houston, TX 77099
Dede D. Mercer, Publisher
Pub. *The Moon Tribune*, semiannually;
   $20.00 per year subscription; (includes
   all variations of the surname,
   worldwide)

Moon
*Henry Moon Family Organization
1774 Country Club Drive
Logan, UT 84321
Phone (801) 753-6924
Joyce Elfrena Kalanquin

Mooney
Nexus Publications
2207 N.E. 12th Street
Renton, WA 98056
Lynn Wood, Editor
Pub. *Mooney Nexus*, quarterly, $20.00
   per year subscription; (includes Mony,
   Moony, Money, Muny, etc.)

Moony (see Mooney)

Moor (see Moore, Nicklin)

Moor
Moor Clearinghouse
Rt. 1, Box 192
Monmouth, IL 61462
James E. and Sharon L. Todd

Moore (see Folk Family Surname
   Exchange, Album, Anthes, Barnes,
   Brawley, Brown, Corson, Goodenow,
   Haynes, Heath, Lambert, Leslie, Lush,
   Lynch, Mohr, Richardson, Rutherford,
   Way)

Moore
Moore (Moor) Family of Washington
   County, New York
127 West Glaucus Street, #D
Leucadia, CA 92024
R. Stevenson

Moore
*Wythul Wood Moore Family
1303 North 39th Street
Nampa, ID 83687
Phone (208) 466-5821
Ann Tomlinson

Moore
Joseph Moore and Samuel Veach Hanes
   Family Historian
PO Box 153
West Chicago, IL 60186
Phone (708) 293-3147
Holly S. Sorensen, Family Genealogist
(includes descendants of John Skillman
   Moore, who settled near Watseka,
   Iroquois County, Illinois, in 1831)

Moore
Idens and Frances Reeves Moore Family
Association
PO Box 14566
Baton Rouge, LA 70808
V. Moore
Pub. *Shamrocks and Grits*

Moore
*Kith and Kin Gatherings
430 South Airport Road, East
Traverse City, MI 49686-4832
Phone (616) 946-3507
Brenda K. Wolfgram Moore
Pub. *Moore Mysteries Journal*,
semiannually

Moore
Moore Family Newsletter
PO Box 13548
Saint Louis, MO 63138
Maryann Schirker
Pub. *Moore Family Newsletter*, quarterly,
$25.00 per year subscription

Moore
*Clinton H. Moore Family Reunion
433 Hillcrest Circle
Hendersonville, NC 28792
Phone (704) 692-8685
Frances Myers Reese, Family Historian
(includes descendants of Clinton Houston
Moore (1810 North Carolina–1905
North Carolina) and Sally Shipman
(1813–1897 North Carolina))
Reunion

Moore
Moore/Lewis Family Reunion
1208 Harris
Ardmore, OK 73401
Jean Moore Murphy

Moore
*Mountain Press
4503 Anderson Pike
PO Box 400
Signal Mountain, TN 37377-0400
Phone (423) 886-6369; (423) 886-5312
FAX
James L. Douthat, Owner
(includes the captives of Abb's Valley;
Captain James Moore of Tazewell and
Rockbridge counties, Virginia)

Moore
*Hugh Jordan Moore Family Association
3374 West Bigarade Lane
Taylorsville, UT 84118
Phone (801) 968-4326
Lee Henry Moore
(includes descendants of Henry Moore
(1806 Staffordshire, England–), last
known to be residing in London in
1878, and Frances Elizabeth Jordan
(1809 Wolverhampton, Staffordshire,
England–), daughter of John Jordan
and Susannah Richards)

Moore
Moore Research for Us
323 Cedarcrest Court East
PO Box 779
Napavine, WA 98565-0779
Phone (360) 262-3300
Ruby Simonson McNeill
Pub. *Moore Research for Us*, irregularly,
$5.75 plus $2.00 postage per issue

Moorer
Moorer (Murer) of Lowndes County
Family Association
5504 Overlook Road
Mobile, AL 36618
Mickey Hendricks

Moorman (see Folk Family Surname
Exchange)

Morang (see Corson)

Moray (see Murray)

Morden
Morden
8210 North Seven Mile
Mesick, MI 49668
Jolene Kelly Pillars
Pub. *Morden*, quarterly, $18.00 per year
subscription

More (see Leslie)

More
*John More Association, Inc.
9831 Sidehill Road
North East, PA 16428
Phone (814) 725-4915
Eric More Marshall, President
Pub. *The Historical Journal of the More
Family*, semiannually
$10.00 per year membership per
household

Moreau (see Johnson)

Morehouse
*Clayton Morehouse Family
Organization
2790C Pineridge Drive, N.W.
Walker, MI 49544
Phone (616) 735-9846
Dana D. Lord-Swayze

Morel (see Blossom Press)

Moreland (see Kintigh, Molen)

Moreland
Moreland Muster
PO Box 3793
Santa Cruz, CA 95063
E-mail: NonaW@aol.com
Nona Williams, Editor
Pub. *Moreland Muster*, quarterly, $15.00
per year subscription, queries accepted

Morey (see Barnard)

Morey
*Morey/Mowry Association
Rt. 5, Box 200
Brookville, PA 15825
Phone (814) 328-5205
Helen McKinney
No cost

Morey
The Morey Maximum Reader
12600 Bissonnet A4-407
Houston, TX 77099
Dede D. Mercer, Publisher
Pub. *The Morey Maximum Reader*,
semiannually, $20.00 per year
subscription; (all variations of the
surname, worldwide)

Morgan (see Blossom Press, Boone,
Brooks, Chaney, Cochran, Cole,
Copeland, Cowart, Custer, David,
Davis, Emery, Fagan, Farrington,
Hatfield, Lush, Mackay, Rutherford,
Vaughn, Weimar)

Morgan
Morgan Family Newsletter
PO Box 13548
Saint Louis, MO 63138
Maryann Schirker
Pub. *Morgan Family Newsletter*,
quarterly, $25.00 per year subscription

Morgan
*Mountain Press
4503 Anderson Pike
PO Box 400
Signal Mountain, TN 37377-0400
Phone (423) 886-6369; (423) 886-5312
FAX
James L. Douthat, Owner
(Daniel Morgan)

Morgan
*Lineage Search Associates
7315 Colts Neck Road
Mechanicsville, VA 23111-4233
Phone (804) 730-7414 (8:00 A.M.–
10:00 P.M.); (800) 728-1935; E-mail:
pollockme@aol.com
Michael E. Pollock, President
Pub. *Morgan Migrations*, three times per
year, $18.00 per year subscription,
unlimited free queries for members,
$8.00 each for non-members (includes
a copy of the issue in which the query
appears); (includes Morgen, Morgin)

Morgen (see Morgan)

Morgenson (see Clark)

Morgin (see Morgan)

Morgrage
*Morgrage-Morgridge Clearinghouse
40 Jackson Street
Sanford, ME 04073-3131
Phone (207) 324-4875

Roland Rhoades, Jr., President
(includes descendants of John Morgrage
    of Kittery, Maine)
Registration free

Morgridge (see Morgrage)

Moriarty (see Cian)

Moriarty
*Thomas Moriarty and Associates, Inc.
9836 South Turner Avenue
Evergreen Park, IL 60805-3053
Phone (708) 425-1468;
    (708) 423-6991 FAX
Thomas J. Moriarty
Pub. *The Moriarty Clan Newsletter*,
    semiannually, $6.00 per year
    subscription

Morland (see Richie)

Morley (see Allen)

Morosic (see Behnke)

Morosini (see Edler)

Morphis (see Kendrick)

Morrell (see Catlow)

Morrice (see Buchanan)

Morrill (see Catlow, Lush)

Morris (see Arthur, Brammier,
    Buchanan, Cian, Corson, Lambert,
    Lawrence)

Morris
The Morris Journal
PO Box 535
Farmington, MI 48332
Andrew J. Morris
Pub. *The Morris Journal*, quarterly,
    $20.00 per year subscription

Morris
*Kinseeker Publications
5697 Old Maple Trail
PO Box 184
Grawn, MI 49637
E-mail: AB064@taverse.lib.mi.us
Victoria Wilson, Editor
Pub. *Morris Members*, quarterly, $10.00
    per year subscription

Morris
*Morris Surname Organization
5341 Whitney Lane
Amarillo, TX 79110
Phone (806) 359-1012
Sylvia D. Murray, A.G., Coordinator
(includes Morris of Pennsylvania, West
    Virginia, Ohio and Indiana)

Morris
*William Clayton Morris Family
    Organization
Rt. 6, Box 716
Cleburne, Johnson, TX 76031
Phone (817) 645-0617
Travis Dee Morris
Pub. *Morris' Tree*, biannually; (includes
    Morris family of Tennessee and
    Georgia, from 1814)

Morris
Morris Family Organization (Virginia
    and Missouri)
PO Box 93
Dickenson, TX 77539
C. Riley

Morris
*Eli Morris Family Organization
4956 South 4300 West
Kearns, UT 84118
Phone (801) 968-0440
John Morris Hancock
(includes descendants of Eli Morris (ca
    1790 to 1800 North Carolina–) of
    Pasquotank, Guilford, Rowan and
    Randolph counties)

Morrison (see Brawley, Buchanan,
    Lahey, Witham)

Morrison
Missing Links
Rt. 4, Box 184
Saint Maries, ID 83861
Pub. *Morrison Memories*, quarterly,
    $8.50 per year subscription

Morrison
*Morrison Family
627 S.E. 53rd Avenue
Portland, OR 97215
Phone (503) 236-0742
John Morrison, Researcher
(includes all immigrant lines of
    Morrisons in America)

Morrison
Clan Morrison Society, U.S. and Canada
20111 Sunny Shores Drive
Atascocita, TX 77346
Phone (713) 852-1381

Morrison
The Morrisons
3319 Bedford Forrest Drive
Missouri City, TX 77459
Phone (713) 438-4808
Glenn Morrison, Secretary and Editor
Pub. *The Morrisons* (includes
    descendants of Alexander C. Morrison
    who came to Arkansas from
    Columbus, Georgia, in 1875)
Annual reunion in May in Cleveland
    County, Arkansas

Morrow (see Brawley, Lambert)

Morrow
*Morrow Surname
5 Troy Lane
Bedford, NY 10506
Phone (914) 273-6605
Sharon Tomback

Morse (see Surname Sources, Barnard,
    Corson, Fadner, Goodenow, Heath,
    Wright)

Morse
*The Morse Society
Rt. 2, Box 379
Tilton, NH 03276
Phone (603) 286-4690
Lola L. Morse, President
Pub. *The Morse Family Newsletter*,
    quarterly
$7.50 per year membership for U.S.
    citizens

Morse
*Morse Society
5208 Mallory Drive
Fort Worth, TX 76117
Phone (817) 834-0074
Colleen Morse Elliott, Secretary
Pub. *The Morse Society Newsletter*,
    quarterly; (includes Morse and related
    families, 1636 to the present)
$7.50 per year U.S. membership; $9.00
    per year Canadian membership, annual
    reunion in Massachusetts

Morsman (see Mosman)

Mort
*The Mort Family of America
1721 Edgewood Avenue
Racine, WI 53404-2306
Phone (414) 634-2824; E-mail:
    DrG@execpc.com; Website (coming
    soon: http://www.execpc.com/~drg/
    mort.html)
Dr. Donald E. Gradeless
Pub. *Mort Newsletter* (includes Morts,
    Mortz, computerized data exchange,
    6,000+ names, especially descendants
    of Thomas William Mort)
Annual reunion in Pierceton, Indiana,
    since 1951

Mortensen
*Anders Mortensen Family Organization
4218 Ben View Drive
West Valley City, UT 84120
Phone (801) 969-3670
Eldon H. Walker, President
(includes descendants of Anders
    Mortensen (1834 Dyngby, Odder,
    Aarhus, Denmark–))

Mortimer (see MacDuff)

Mortimore (see Holden)

Morton (see Douglas, Sawyer)

Morton
*Thomas Morton Family Organization, 1770–1804 of Chester County, South Carolina
HCR 62, Box 113A
Flippin, AR 72634-9710
Phone (501) 453-5286
Charlene Gillespie Deutsch, Compiler

Morton
*Palouse Publications
S.E. 310 Camino
Pullman, WA 99163-2206
Phone (509) 334-1732
Janet Margolis Damm
Pub. *Morton Heritage*, irregularly, $5.00 plus $1.50 postage (Washington State residents add 47¢ tax)

Morts (see Mort)

Mortz (see Mort)

Mory (see Surname Database)

Moseley (see Cook)

Moseley
Moseley Database
Rt. 2, Box 47A
Clifton, TX 76634-9608
Thomas Moseley, Jr.

Mosely (see Craig, Emery)

Moser (see May)

Moser
*North Carolina Pioneers
4714 Shady Waters Lane
Birmingham, AL 35243-2634
Phone (205) 969-0437
James Beddingfield
(includes ancestors and descendants of Catawba County pioneer, Leonard Moser (1718 Germany–1782) of Frederick County, Maryland, and Surry County, North Carolina, and Maria Sarah Binkley (1733 Alsace–1820 Surry County, North Carolina), with allied surnames of Barringer, Dellinger, Gilbert, Huit, Mull, Poovey, Setzer, Sigman and Weidner; other Catawba County pioneers, including descendants of Johann Sebastion Klein (1716 Postroff, the Saarwerden–), Cline, Gant, Hoke, Killian, Hunsucker, Little, Miller, Roseman, Pope, Wike and Wilfong; Henderson County pioneers, including Bane, Beddingfield, Bishop, Freeman, Hart, Justice, Justus, Moss and Stepp)

Moser
Moser Family Organization
Rt. 3, Box 123
Trinity, NC 27370
Cheryl Burrow

Moser
*Lydia Moser Family Organization
5241 South 5200 West
Kearns, UT 84118-7024
Phone (801) 968-5916
Lloyd Van Neste Viall

Moses (see Barber, Tillman)

Mosher
*Mosher Family Reunion
5227 Blue Ridge Boulevard
Raytown, MO 64133
Phone (816) 524-4598 (home);
(816) 737-2771 (work)
Bill Stilley
(includes descendants of Asa Mosher, Jr., and Sarah P. Bunker)
Annual reunion

Mosler
*Mosler
8505 Glenview Avenue
Takoma Park, MD 20912
Phone (301) 89-6621; (301) 589-1366 FAX
Barbara Levitz, Family Genealogist
(includes descendants of Mosler family from Vilna (Vilnius) Dolhinov, Dolginova, Lithuania; also Cahan, Cohen, Masler, Mazler and Mojler)

Mosley (see Joyner)

Mosman
Mosman/Mossman/Morsman Reunion
10349 Quail Crown Drive
Naples, FL 33942
Phone (941) 592-0147
Kenneth F. Mosman
Pub. *Newsletter*, irregularly, no charge

Moss (see Folk Family Surname Exchange, Fadner, Maxwell, Moser, Peters)

Moss
*Moss Surname Organization
1671 Monitor Avenue
Baton Rouge, LA 70817
Phone (504) 756-2322
Shirley Craig
(includes descendants of James Moss, b. 1790 Rowan County, North Carolina)

Mossman (see Mosman)

Motes (see Golding)

Motley
American Motley Association
PO Box 708
Valley Forge Office Colony
Valley Forge, PA 19481
Phone (215) 933-1775
Thomas Motley-Freeman, Editor
Pub. *Motley Ancestral Gleanings*, quarterly; *Kinsfolk*
$8.00 per year membership

Motree
Motree Family Association
Rt. 5, Box 53
Laconia, NH 03246
S. Theall

Mott (see Holden)

Motter (see Mattern)

Motter
*Motter/Marter/Matter/Mattern Database
5272 South Skare Court
Rochelle, IL 61068
Phone (815) 562-3745
Ray D. Schwartz
(includes George and Sussanah Motter family from 1778)

Mottron (see Newmyer)

Motz (see The Memorial Foundation of the Germanna Colonies)

Mouat (see Mowat)

Moulden (see Molen)

Moulin (see Molyneux)

Moungey (see Randall)

Mount (see MacDuff)

Mountain
Mountain Family Association
3752 Paraiso Way
La Crescenta, CA 91214
Lee Battaglia

Mountford (see Mower)

Mountjoy
*Mountjoy Data Base
Box 459
Lamesa, TX 79331
Phone (806) 872-3603
Margaret B. Kinsey, C.G.
(includes all Mountjoy, Montjoy, Munjoy in the U.S.)

Mounts (see Hatfield, MacDuff)

Mourning (see Martin)

Mouser (see Nelso)

Mouser
*Johann Frederick Mouser Family Organization
29 East Portland Avenue
Vincennes, IN 47591
Phone (812) 882-9371
Richard Carl Rodgers, II, Historian/Archivist
(archival facility collects information on all descendants and ancestors of the family in computer database; descendants of Johann Frederick Mouser (1740 Charlottenof,

Wuertemberg, German–1799
Lincolnton, Lincoln County, North
Carolina), son of Hans Mouser/Mauser
and Agathia Gomminger, and wife
Frances Heap)

Mout (see Mowat)

Mouton (see Johnson)

Movius
*Movius and Mevius Family Association
PO Box 13774
Sacramento, CA 95853
Phone (916) 753-3206
John Dryden Movius
Pub. *The Movius and Mevius Family
Surname—Recent Discoveries and
Events*, annually; (includes Movius,
Mevius, Maevius, Baron von der
Moevius, Baron de Mévius, von
Mövius, Möbius, Mobius, Maveus and
other transliterations worldwide, also
Frankhouse/Frankhauser, Tuch/Rue
and Sellin (U.S.); especially
descendants of Herr und Ritter
Rambau von der Moevius and wife,
Hedrina von Merkle, ca 1463 from
Duchy of Pomerania; database lists all
Movius and Mevius descendants
worldwide)
$10.00 per year membership

Mowait (see Mowat)

Mowaite (see Mowat)

Mowat (see Sutherland)

Mowat
Mowat Family International
PO Box 9538
Jackson, MS 39206
James Mowat, Secretary-Treasurer
(includes Mowatt, Mout, Mouat, Mowait,
Mowaite, Mwat, etc., derived from the
ancient Monte Alto)

Mowatt (see Mowat)

Mowbray (see MacDuff)

Mowbrey (see MacDuff)

Mower
*Isaac Henry Mower Family
Organization
4868 Navajo Street
Pocatello, ID 83204-3720
Phone (208) 233-2456
Mark L. and Rhoda Hopkins
(includes allied families of Bartling,
Choules, Crump, Franklin, Mittelstedt
and Mountford, from Idaho, Utah,
Pennsylvania, England and Germany)

Mower
*Henry Mower Family Organization
PO Box 311
Bedford, WY 83112

Phone (307) 883-2730
Jerry Mower

Mowreader
Mowreader-Robinson-Cox-McCoughey
Family Organization
15248 S.E. 49th Street
Bellevue, WA 98006
Jack Marcus Mowreader, Family
Representative
Reunion

Mowry (see Morey)

Mowry
*Mowry Family Association
13033 Caminito Dos Amantes
San Diego, CA 92128-1722
Phone (619) 438-8428
Charles Whitlock Rockett

Moyce (see Heath)

Moyer (see The Memorial Foundation of
the Germanna Colonies)

Mozee (see Mauzey)

Mrkwiczka (see Brucker)

Muckler (see Newcomb)

Mudge (see Surname Sources)

Mueller (see Surname Database, Brown,
Stabler)

Mueller
*H. L. Mueller Family
306 North Court Street, #R3
Waukon, IA 52172-1174
Phone (319) 568-2987
Eloise Meyer, Writer
Pub. *H. L. Mueller Family Newsletter*
semiannually; (includes descendants of
H. Ludwig Mueller (1822
Mecklenburg Schwerin, District
Crabow, Village Canow near
Doemitz–) and Dorothea Palas)
Donation for membership

Mueller
*To Cleveland and Away
8848 Music Street
Russell Township
Novelty, OH 44072
Phone (216) 338-3857; (216) 338-5040
FAX
Werner D. Mueller, C.G., Publisher
(includes Mueller, especially ancestors
and descendants of Peter Mueller
(1819–1886), Jacob Mueller/Müller
(1822–1905), Louis Mueller (1823–
1906), all born in Alsenz, Rhineland-
Palatinate, then resided in Cleveland,
Cuyahoga County, Ohio; Reid,
especially Dr. James Sims Reid (1894
Mississippi–1981), resident of the
greater Cleveland, Ohio, area;
Cleveland branches of families named

Crowl, Diebolt (Dieboldt), Hartwell,
Lembeck, McKay, Prindle, Taft and
Weideman)

Muenster (see Surname Database)

Muhleisen
*Muhleisen-Milliron-Millison Families
Exchange
51 Forbus Street
Poughkeepsie, NY 12603
Phone (914) 473-3757; E-mail:
cco@sebridge.org
Christine Crawford-Oppenheimer

Muhoberac (see Blossom Press)

Muir
*Walter Muir (1809) Family
Organization
1895 North 285 East
Orem, UT 84057
Phone (801) 225-7375
Carma M. Golding
(includes descendants of Walter Muir
(1809 Scotland–) and Mary Bell Ross)
Cost for materials only

Mulander (see Melander)

Mulandoor (see Melander)

Muldowney (see Cian)

Muldrow (see MacFaddien)

Mulender (see Melander)

Mulendore (see Melander)

Mulford (see Shaver, Willcocks)

Mulford
Mulfords in America
515 Bonnymeade Drive
Champaign, IL 61821
Phone (217) 359-3457
Joan Black Lund
Pub. *Mulfords in America and Their Kin*,
quarterly

Mulinax (see Reeves)

Mulinder (see Melander)

Mulindore (see Melander)

Mulkey
Mulkey Journal
RR 2, Box 7
Moran, KS 66755-9502
Phone (316) 237-8800
Sandra Everson, Editor
Pub. *Mulkey Journal*, three times per
year, $12.00 per year subscription

Mull (see Moser)

Mullander (see Melander)

Mullandoor (see Melander)

Mullenax (see Pillow)

Mullender (see Melander)

Mullendore (see Melander)

Mulleneaux (see Molyneux)

Mullennix (see Molyneux)

Müller (see Cole, Mueller)

Mullican (see Milligan)

Mullicken
*Robert Mullicken Family Organization
3424 Beth Drive
Mesquite, TX 75150-2141
Phone (214) 270-5465
Terri Mulliken Allen
(includes descendants of Robert
    Mullicken (Mulliken) and Rebekah
    Savory of Bradford, Massachusetts
    from 1680 to the present)

Mulligan (see Milligan)

Mullikan (see Milligan)

Mulliken (see Mullicken)

Mullinax (see Molyneux, Taylor)

Mullinder (see Melander)

Mullindore (see Melander)

Mulliner (see Molyneux)

Mullinix (see Cooley, Molyneux)

Mullins (see Alden, Rutherford)

Mullunphy (see Franciscus)

Mulnix (see Molyneux)

Mulpatrick (see Cian)

Mumaw
*George Mumma Mumaw Family of
    Lancaster and Westmoreland Counties,
    Pennsylvania, from 1732
PO Box 10
Whitney, PA 15693-0010
Richard Glenn Huffman, Publisher

Mumbauer (see Surname Database,
    Mumpower)

Mumbower (see Mumpower)

Mumford (see Lambert)

Mumford
*McCanse Family Association
PO Box 2587
Eugene, OR 97402

Phone (503) 321-5001
Sherrie Styx
Reunion every three years on the west
    coast, Oregon area

Mumford
*Mumford Family Association
PO Box 2587
Eugene, OR 97402
Phone (503) 321-5001
Sherrie Styx
Annual reunion in the midwest

Mumma (see Mumaw)

Mumpower
*Mumpower Family Association
614 North Calvert
Muncie, IN 47303
Phone (317) 288-1888
Joe Mumpower
Pub. *Mumpower Family*, irregularly,
    costs vary; (includes Mombauer,
    Mumbauer and Mumbower)

Munday
*Munday-Mundy-Monday-Mondy
    Family Association
3880 Highway 93, West
Whitefish, MT 59937
Phone (406) 862-2641
Anna Joy Munday Hubble
(database includes thousands of
    Mundays, all spellings, in the U.S.)
Queries answered for copy costs plus
    postage

Mundy (see Munday)

Munjoy (see Mountjoy)

Munn (see Stewart)

Munnoch (see MacDuff)

Munnock (see MacDuff)

Munro
*Clan Munro Association USA, Inc.
11 La Huertas Ridge Road
Placitas, NM 87043
Frances E. Stephens, Editor
Pub. *Munro Eagle*, annually (August),
    $2.50 per issue; *Eagle Flyer*, annually
    (January), $2.00 per issue; (includes
    Munroe, Monro and Monroe)

Munroe (see Munro)

Munson (see Barnes, Lush)

Munson
*Thomas Munson Foundation, Inc.
140 State Line Road
Vestal, NY 13850
Phone (607) 754-4912 (New York);
    (813) 424-2151 (Florida)
Robert E. Munson

Pub. *Thomas Munson Foundation
    Newsletter*, quarterly, $10.00 per year
    subscription; (includes thirteen family
    groups)
$25.00 per year membership

Munsterman (see Blossom Press)

Muntzell
Muntzell Ancestors
4250 Cedarbush
Dallas, TX 75229
Phone (214) 352-7093
Marvelle Awalt Muntzel

Muny (see Mooney)

Murbach
*The Swiss Origin and Genealogy of the
    American Murbachs
18 Alfred Road, West
Merrick, NY 11566-3056
Phone (516) 379-2776
J. Frederick Murbach

Murchie (see Buchanan)

Murchison (see Buchanan, McGee)

Murdo (see Macpherson, MacPherson)

Murdoch (see Macpherson, Dobie)

Murdock (see Macpherson,
    MacPherson)

Murdoson (see Macpherson,
    MacPherson)

Murer (see Moorer)

Murer
Murer Reunion
547 Cedar Street
Chadron, NE 69337
Phone (308) 432-2681
Joe Murer, Family Representative
Reunion

Muriarty (see Cian)

Murison (see MacDuff)

Murphy (see Boyer, Richardson)

Murphy
Murphy Family Organization
22916 Carlow Road
Torrance, CA 90505
Phone (310) 378-3574
Charlene DeLong

Murphy
*Kinseeker Publications
5697 Old Maple Trail
PO Box 184
Grawn, MI 49637
E-mail: AB064@taverse.lib.mi.us
Victoria Wilson, Editor
Pub. *Murphy Mates*, quarterly, $10.00
    per year subscription

Murphy
Pro-Temp, Inc.
PO Box 154
Nooksack, WA 98276
Marilyn A. and Ron Deeter, Editors
Pub. *Murphy Connection*, semiannually,
$17.00 per year subscription

Murray (see Brown, Cunningham,
Kimball, Reardon)

Murray
*Clan Murray Society of North America
803 Evergreen Drive
Wyomissing, PA 19610
Phone (610) 670-1433
Robert W. Murray, President
Pub. *AITIONN*, quarterly; (includes
septs: Balneaves, Dinsmore,
Dunsmore, Fleming, Moray, Murrie,
Neaves, Piper, Pyper, Smail, Smale,
Small, Smeal and Spalding)
$20.00 for first year membership, $15.00
per year membership thereafter

Murrie (see Murray)

Murtagh (see Cian)

Muse (see Louden)

Muse
*Muse Reunion Association, Inc.
3954 West Chapel Road
Aberdeen, MD 21001
Phone (410) 272-3681
Robert T. Muse, Historian
Pub. *Triannual Musings*, three times per
year (December, April and August);
(preparing volume on descendants of
John Muse of Virginia)
$15.00 per year membership for families
(beginning in October); reunion

Musgrave (see Powell)

Musick (see Hatfield)

Mussack (see Heath)

Musselman
Musselman Family Clearinghouse
77 Hollow Road
Quarryville, PA 17566-9491
Harry Hoffman

Mussen (see Musson)

Musser (see McCune)

Mussier (see Hayner)

Musson
*Frederick Musson and Charlotte Tarry
Descendants
1440 Timbergrove Road
Knoxville, TN 37919-8448
Phone (423) 693-7704
Esther Musson Johnson, Ph.D.

Musson
*Musson Surname
PO Box 3035
Edinburg, TX 78540
Phone (210) 381-0132
Robert F. Cell
(includes Musson, Mussen, etc.)

Mustain
Mustain/Mustian/Mustion/Musteen
Family Association
Rt. 2, Box 345
West Plains, MO 65775
O. Harris

Musteen (see Mustain)

Mustian (see Mustain)

Mustion (see Mustain)

Muth (see Nienow)

Muzzy (see Cummings)

Mwat (see Mowat)

Myer (see Kunkel)

Myers (see Lambert, Lush, Stoner)

Myers
*Myers Mine
PO Box 1872
Dodge City, KS 67801-1872
Laura Tasset Koehn, President
(includes research on Irvin Ellsworth
Myers and Elizabeth L. Wagner)

Myers
*Myers/Meiers Clearinghouse
Rt. 4, Box 176
Moravia, NY 13118
Phone (315) 364-8957
Mildred D. Myers
(includes Myers, Mier, Meiers, Meyer
born 1850 or before; will respond to
queries, but only as time allows)
Free

Myers
*Henry Myers and Pheba Parkhurst
Family Association
PO Box 306
Stillwater, OK 74076
J. Myers Kelly

Mygatt (see Barnard)

Mylar (see Miler)

Myler (see Sullivan Surname Exchange)

M'Yllecrist (see MacLachlan)

Mylorie
Mylorie Family Organization
812 Lithuanica Lane
Webster, NY 14580
V. Mylorie

Myres (see MacDuff, Myers)

Myrick (see Folk Family Surname
Exchange)

Naef (see Neff)

NaeSmith
*NaeSmith Genealogical Society of the
United States, Inc.
404 Demper Drive
Jacksonville, FL 32208-4504
Phone (904) 764-0550
John W. NesSmith, Society Compiler
Pub. *Annual Update on New Family
Records* (includes NeeSmith, Nesmith,
NeSmith, Nessmith, NesSmith, also
Scots NaeSmyth and Naismyth,
especially descendants of Michael
NaeSmyth and Elizabeth Baird who
were married in Edinburgh, Scotland,
1544)
Annual meeting on the third weekend of
May at the Regional Library,
Statesboro, Georgia

NaeSmyth (see NaeSmith)

Näf (see Neff)

Naff (see Neff)

Nafzger
Nafzger Heritage News
1390 Wincanton
Deerfield, IL 60015
Ray Noftsger
Pub. *Nafzger Heritage News*, quarterly,
$12.00 per year subscription; (includes
Noftzger)

Naish (see Nash)

Naismyth (see NaeSmith)

Nakama (see McCune)

Naley (see Naly)

Nance (see Bagley)

Nantooth (see Cooper)

Napier (see Bloss, Frasher)

Napier
*Clan Napier in North America
Kilmahew Route 2, Box 614
Ramer, AL 36069-9245
Phone (334) 281-0505
Lt. Col. John H. Napier, III, Lieutenant
to the Chief
Pub. *Sans Tache*, annually; (includes
Napier family)
$15.00 per year membership

Narsh (see Nash)

Nase (see Weimar)

Nash (see Sullivan Surname Exchange, Album, Corson, Covert)

Nash
Nash Notations
14945 Gale Avenue
Hacienda Heights, CA 91745
Phone (818) 333-5917
Lois Hayes Culver
Pub. *Nash Notations, Information Exchange for Nash, Nashe, Naish, Narsh, Nass Families Everywhere*, quarterly, $14.00 per year subscription

Nash
*Nash Family Association
2701 Church Street
Modesto, CA 95357
Phone (209) 526-9867
LaVonne Houlton, Editor and Branch Representative
Pub. *Nash Family Newsletter*, four to five times per year, $8.50 per year subscription; (includes descendants of Aslak Anudsen Vasshus and Margit Tarjesdatter Vinje-Rui, Telemark, Norway; Nash family from Norway)
Reunion

Nash
Nash
2942 Missouri Drive
Colorado Springs, CO 80909-3113
Kimberly Patton Straight
Pub. *Nash*, quarterly, $14.00 per year subscription

Nash
*Thomas Nash Descendants Association (TNDA)
2733 Runningbrook Lane
Dallas, TX 75228-4304
Phone (214) 328-4973
Dorothy Nash Roberts
(includes descendants of Thomas and Margery (Baker) Nash of New Haven, Connecticut)
No membership dues

Nashe (see Nash)

Nason (see Corson, Wright)

Nass (see Nash)

Nation
Nation Clearinghouse
PO Box 116
Delavan, IL 61734
Dora Inselmann
Pub. Nation Family Newsletter

Nau (see Sherwood)

Naughton (see Macnachton)

Naugle (see Lush)

Nave (see Neff)

Nay (see The Memorial Foundation of the Germanna Colonies, Lemon)

Naylor (see McCune)

Neal (see Barnes, Brown, Macneil)

Neale (see Rutherford)

Neall (see Brown)

Neaves (see Murray)

Neaville (see Wright)

Nebeker
*Nebeker Family Association, Inc.
2765 Jefferson Avenue
Ogden, UT 84403
Phone (801) 393-5714
Frank Nebeker Terry
$10.00 donation per year membership for family units

Neblett (see Folk Family Surname Exchange)

Neece (see Neese)

Neel (see Neal)

Neeley (see Cowart)

Neeley
Neeley's Seedlings
2114-B N.E. Stapleton Road
Vancouver, WA 98661
Phone (206) 694-1826
George F. Neeley

Neely (see Cowart)

Neeney (see Cian)

Neese (see Haynes)

Neese
Neese Family Association
717 Learydale Terrace
Baltimore, MD 21208
Jack Lamar Neese
Pub. *The Neese Family News*

NeeSmith (see NaeSmith)

Neff (see Adams, Frantz, Smith, Stoner)

Neff
*Neff Family Historical Society, Inc.
PO Box 212
Princeton Junction, NJ 08550-0212
Phone (609) 799-2218; (609) 897-1343 FAX
William A. Neff, President and Editor
Pub. *Neff News*, three times per year (February, May and September); (surname database includes over 30,000 records; includes Neff, Naff, Nave, Naef and Näf, primarily from Canton Zürich, Switzerland)

$8.00 per year membership; international reunion every three years in June outside Zürich

Neher (see Frantz)

Neighly (see Naly)

Neil (see McCune, O'Neil)

Neill (see Covert, Neal, Woodrow)

Neilson (see Gregor, Gunn, Mackay, Macneil, Stewart)

Nein (see Nine)

Neino (see Nienow)

Neinow (see Nienow)

Neish (see Gregor)

Neligh (see Naly)

Nell
*Nell Family Genealogical Society
PO Box 133
Topeka, IL 61567
Phone (309) 535-2977
Jim Nell, President
Pub. *Newsletter*, quarterly
$12.00 per year membership

Nell
*Philip Nell Family Organization
873 North 610 East
American Fork, UT 84003
Phone (801) 756-2176
Douglas Sherman Nell
Pub. *Phillip Nell Family Biannual*, semiannually, $5.00 per year subscription; (includes Bate, Bills, Fisher, Hanson, Maynard, Nell, Nokes, Rishtom and Silcox families)

Nellis
Nellis Family Association
80 Cascade Road
West Henrietta, NY 14586
Richard Moon, President
Pub. *News Letter of the Nellis Family Association*, (includes descendants of William and Christian Nellis)
Reunion

Nelms (see Helm)

Nelson (see Cowart, De La Chaumette, Goodenow, Gregor, Gunn, Hoster, Israelite, Lush, MacFaddien, Mackay, McCune, Pool, Wright)

Nelson
*Our Nelson Family Reunion
PO Box 12080
Dallas, TX 75225
D. C. Nelson
(includes descendants of Ambrus and Martha (Robinson) Nelson of

Baltimore, Maryland, 1670–1730, and related families: Allen, Barney, Billington, Bogardus, Burton, Clark, Cox, Douglass, Eaton, Firmin, French, Green, Grunewald, Himmelberger, Hoffert, Hopson, Huffman, Jefferson, Jones, Kingsley, Merklin, Mills, Pease, Plummer, Redman, Rogers, Schaeffer and Seals)
Annual reunion on the Sunday before Memorial Day at First Christian Church, Mutual, Oklahoma

Nelson
The Nelson Family Newsletter
PO Box 537
Milford, TX 76670-0537
Lela Cooper, Publisher
Pub. *The Nelson Family Newsletter*, quarterly, $16.00 per year subscription

Nelsson (see Nelson)

Nenow (see Nienow)

Nerr
*The Neer Family
4368 Ridgepath Drive
Dayton, OH 45424-4746
Col. Dean C. Davisson
Annual reunion at Mechanicsburg, Champaign County, Ohio

Nesbet (see MacDuff, Nesbitt)

Nesbit (see Dunbar)

Nesbitt (see MacDuff)

Nesbitt
*The Nesbitt/Nisbet Society—North America
321 Dixon Avenue
Pittsburgh, PA 15216
Phone (412) 531-2941; E-mail: pdjones@infobahn.icubed.com
Gail Nesbitt Jones, Secretary-Treasurer
Pub. *N/NS Newsletter*, quarterly (January, April, July and October)
$20.00 per year membership for individuals

Nesmith (see NaeSmith)

NeSmith (see NaeSmith)

Ness (see MacDuff)

Nessmith (see NaeSmith)

NesSmith (see NaeSmith)

Neth (see McCanna)

Netherland
*Netherland Family Society
107 South Holston Drive
Church Hill, TN 37642
Phone (423) 245-6844
Sarah Ann Collins, President

(includes Richard Netherland (1764 Virginia–) and Margaret Woods (1768 Virginia–), resided in Sullivan County, Tennessee)

Neuin (see Nine)

Neumann (see Brucker)

Neusz (see Links Genealogy Publications)

Nevett (see Hotchkiss)

Nevill (see Dunbar, Underwood)

Neville (see Wolverton)

Neville
*Neville-Jones-Giles-Spencer-Harrison Families
2620 MacArthur
Waco, TX 76708
Phone (817) 776-2632
Shepherd Spencer Neville Brown
(includes collateral lines: Blalock, Bush, Carmouche, Cocke, Cross, Davies, DeLee, Oliver, Spight, Ward, Wilcox, etc.)

Nevin (see Macnachton)

Nevitt (see Blackburn)

Newberry (see Folk Family Surname Exchange)

Newberry
*Newberry Family and In-Laws
6600C River Valley Marina
Little Rock, AR 72212-9711
Phone (501) 868-1775
Grant H. Collar, Jr.
(includes Newbury/Newberry line beginning with the marriage of John Newberry and Joanna Swain in 1786 in Columbia, Tyrrell County, North Carolina, also a large group thought to be related to Thomas Newberry and Joane Dabinot of Massachusetts; other Newberry families of unknown kinship: Steven Newberry, Sr., and Sarah Chambers, immigrated through Savannah, Georgia in 1802, went to Tennessee, moved with Bunch family to Newton County, Arkansas, Col. Thomas Newburgh and Mary Boges, whose grandson, James Newbury, immigrated to Pennsylvania in 1734, Benjamine Newberry and Adeline Hurley, whose son, John (1849 Illinois–), settled in Oktaha, Indian Territory (now Oklahoma, John H. Newberry (1861 Arkansas–) and Rebecca E. McCarty, who lived near Heber Springs, Cleburne County, Arkansas, Samuel Newberry and Nancy W. Trantham, a logger who moved about 1869 from Tennessee to Gainesville, Greene County, Arkansas)

Newburgh (see Newberry)

Newbury (see Newberry)

Newby (see The Memorial Foundation of the Germanna Colonies, Garner)

Newcomb (see Lampkin, Underwood)

Newcomer (see Likes, Stoner)

Newell (see Grange, Harvey)

Newhart (see Surname Database)

Newlin (see Mahaney)

Newlin
*Newlin-Bush Saga Association
Star Route 5, #144
Rye, CO 81069
Phone (719) 545-9061
Dorothy Luellen, Secretary

Newlin
Newlin Family Clearinghouse
77 Hollow Road
Quarryville, PA 17566-9491
Harry Hoffman

Newman (see Likes, Miller, Nienow)

Newmyer
*Newmyer Family Heritage Association
Rt. 1
Bethel, MO 63434
Clyde Burch, Secretary
(includes Ball, Bloyd, Burch, Cleaver, Dunseith, Dunseth, Dunsieth, English, Jarvis, Jones, Lippincott, Lute, Magruder, Mottron, Roan, Rhoads, Richardson, St. Clair, Sloan, Strickler and Ziegler)

Newrace
*Phillip Heritage House
605 Benton
Missoula, MT 59801
Phone (406) 543-3495
Ruth Phillip, MAS R.G.
Pub. *Newrace Newsletter*, annually, $10.00 per issue

Newton (see Barnard, Clark, Goodenow, Gant, Garner, Graves)

Newton
Oak Leaf Publishing
22 Creek Road, #64
Irvine, CA 91714
Pub. *Newton Family Newsletter*, bimonthly, $10.00 per year subscription

Newton
Newton-Forsythe Newsletter
5180 West Highway 6
Hastings, NE 68901-7702
Phone (402) 462-5218
Dr. Leo Leroy Lemonds

Pub. *Newton-Forsythe Newsletter*, semiannually (spring and fall), $7.50 per year subscription; (includes descendants of Richard Newton (Sudbury, Massachusetts, 1630s) and George Forsythe (Pennsylvania, 1810); also descendants of Simon Stacy, who arrived at Ipswich, Massachusetts, ca 1637; also selected ancestral names: Baker, Barber, Barrett, Batchelder, Bell, Bogwell, Bozman, Bray, Brockett, Carey, Caryl, Claflin, Clark, Clerke, Coolidge, Davis, Dawes, Day, Dickenson, Drake, Eager, Edwards, Etter, Evans, Fillmore, Ford, French, Gye, Hale, Harris, Harter, Haynes, Hervey, Hosmer, Howe, Hughes, Knight, Lancton, Larkin, Lemonds, Littlehale, Loker, Lurvey, Lyfield, Matchett, Maverick, Owens, Paine, Parsons, Paulet, Plympton, Reynolds, Rogers, Rowe, Rush, Strait, Sutliff, Tucke, Vinson, Ward, Warner, West, Wheelock, Whipple, White, Wilkinson and Worcester)
Reunion every three years

Newton
Family Newton Quarterly
312 Ross Avenue
Hamilton, OH 45013
Jim Newton
Pub. *Family Newton Quarterly*, $10.00 per year subscription

Nezat (see Johnson)

Nial (see Brown)

Niblet (see Folk Family Surname Exchange)

Nice (see Links Genealogy Publications, Gregor)

Nichols (see Anthes, Corson, Golding, Heath, Thorn, Wooldridge)

Nichols (see Sullivan Surname Exchange)

Nichols
*Jesse Clyde Nichols
55 Le Mans Court
Prairie Village, KS 66208
Phone (913) 642-1740
Kay Callison

Nicholson (see McRae)

Nickell (see Anthes)

Nickerson (see Bellon, Holden)

Nickerson
Nickerson
Herring Run Road
North Harwich, MA 02645
Olive Cunningham
Pub. *Nickerson*, semiannually, free
Reunion

Nickerson
*Nickerson Family Association, Inc.
11 Dutch's Way
PO Box 291
South Dennis, MA 02660
Phone (508) 398-3183
Pauline F. Derick, Genealogical Chairman
Pub. *Nickerson Family Newsletter*, annually; (includes descendants of William Nickerson and Anne Busby)
$5.00 per year membership

Nickles (see Golding)

Nickols (see Gibson)

Nicks (see Nix)

Nicodemus
Nicodemus Family Reunion
RD 2, Box 714
Bedford, PA 15522
Judy Nicodemus Kendall, Editor and Publisher
Pub. *Nic in Time: Nicodemus Newsletter*, quarterly, $7.50 per year subscription; (includes family from 1700+ in Germany and Switzerland to the present)

Nicol (see MacNicol)

Nicolson (see MacNicol, McRae)

Niddie (see MacDuff)

Niddy (see MacDuff)

Nidie (see MacDuff)

Nidy (see MacDuff)

Niece (see Lush)

Niel (see Brown)

Nielsen (see Brough, Weaver)

Nielson (see McCune)

Niemier
*Niemier Family
PO Box 333
Colona, IL 61241-0333
Phone (309) 792-4579
Norma J. Ogburn

Nienow
*The Carl Nienow Family Organization
890 Biddle Road, #183
Medford, OR 97504
Phone (541) 772-8352; (541) 772-4316;
  E-mail: dmnineow@wave.net
David Matthew Nienow
Pub. *The Nienow Family Journal*, quarterly (January, April, July and October), $16.00 per year subscription; (includes research on the direct

descendants of Carl Nienow (1821 Germany–) and Bertha Braun (1826 Griefanberg, Germany–), emigrated to the U.S. in 1857, also reports on research regarding other related branches of their descendants and the variant spellings of the surname such as Neinow, Nenow, Nieno and Ninow; also related surnames of Brown, Fury, Hall, Keller, Minkel, Muth, Newman and Westover)

Nikolitsch (see Nikolits)

Nilson (see Smith)

Nilson
*Nils Nilson Family Organization
2905 Craig Drive
Salt Lake City, UT 84109
Phone (801) 277-6107
Hollis D. Smith

Nilsson (see Nelson)

Nims (see Goodenow)

Nims
Nims Family Association
PO Box 186
Eden, UT 84310-0186
David A. Nims, Secretary
(includes descendants of Godfrey Nims (1650–1705))
$10.00 per year membership, annual reunion in even-numbered years in Old Deerfield, Massachusetts

Nine
Nine/Nein/Neuin Family Reunion
4701 Saint George Street
Reading, PA 19606
Phone (215) 779-3464
Jackie Nein Flamm, Historian
Pub. *9's in America*, annually; (includes Nein, Neuin, Nine)
$5.00 per year membership; $35.00 life membership

Ninow (see Nienow)

Nisbet (see Nesbitt)

Nish (see Gregor)

Nite (see Knight)

Nithsdale (see Maxwell)

Nivenson (see Macnachton)

Nix
Nix/Nicks
6180 Merrywood Drive
Rocklin, CA 95677-3421
Kathleen Stewart
Pub. *Nix/Nicks*, quarterly (February, May, August and November), $12.00 per year subscription

Nix
*Nix/Nicks Family of the South
501 North Smith
Vinita, OK 74301
Dorothy Nix
No cost, send FGS and SASE

Noble (see McCune)

Noderer
Noderer News
1940 Galveston Street
San Diego, CA 92110
Evelyn R. Noderer, Editor
Pub. *Noderer News*, three times per year

Noe (see Noah)

Noeh (see The Memorial Foundation of
the Germanna Colonies)

Noel (see Garner, Lambert)

Noffsinger (see Stoner)

Noftzger (see Nafzger)

Nohl (see Lambert)

Nohl
*Nohl Family
2046 Valley Meadow Drive
Oak View, CA 93022
Phone (805) 649-9044
Sheila McNeil Marrero
(includes the Fred (Friederich) Nohl
family which migrated to Ripon,
Wisconsin, in 1849 from Werdohl,
Sauerland (now Westphalia))

Nokes (see Nell)

Nokes
*John Nokes Family Organization
645 Lasalle Drive
Murray, UT 84123-6827
Phone (801) 266-2575
W. Allan Levorsen, Family Historian
(includes descendants of John Nokes
(ca 1750–1819), especially of the
Champlain Valley)

Nokes
*Horace Nokes Family Organization
2644 West 12420 South
Riverton, UT 84065
Paula Egbert, Family Genealogist

Noland (see Nowlin)

Nolen (see Nowlin)

Nolin (see Lagesse)

Noll (see Cole, Wert)

Nooe (see Noah)

Nooner (see Folk Family Surname
Exchange)

Nope (see Scadlock)

Norberg (see Likes)

Nord (see Peterson)

Norman (see Gower, Johnson, Kunkel,
Loop, McCune)

Norman
*Richard Norman Family Organization
3611 Maine Avenue
Long Beach, CA 90806
Phone (310) 427-1090
James A. Norman

Normile (see Armbruster)

Norris (see Garner)

Norris
*Norris Surname Organization
3 Brazill Lane
Whitehall, MT 59759
Phone (406) 287-3369
Lindia Roggia Lovshin

Norris
*Edward Norris Family Organization
4502 Garden Place, N.W.
Gig Harbor, WA 98335-1426
Phone (206) 851-7742
Tony Norris
(includes descendants of Edward Norris
and Margaret Potts, married 1835 in
Perry County, Ohio)

Norris
Nexus Publications
2207 N.E. 12th Street
Renton, WA 98056
Lynn Wood, Editor
Pub. *Norris Nexus*, quarterly, $20.00 per
year subscription

North (see Heath)

Northcraft (see Lambert)

Northrup
*Northrup Family Researchers
9999 S.E. Frenchacres Drive
Portland, OR 97266
Phone (503) 775-6697
R. T. Howard, Executive Director

Norton (see Davis)

Norton
*Kinseeker Publications
5697 Old Maple Trail
PO Box 184
Grawn, MI 49637
Phone E-mail: AB064@taverse.lib.mi.us
Victoria Wilson, Editor
Pub. *Norton Notes*, quarterly, $10.00 per
year subscription

Norum
The Norum Family Reunion
7344 Marvin Road, N.E.
Olympia, WA 98516
James Bentley Strong, U.S. Contact
Biennial reunion

Norvel (see Norvell)

Norvell
*Norvell Family Organization (NFO)
26925 Cougar Pass Road, Rt. 6
Escondido, CA 92026
Phone (619) 749-2027
Wanda Norvell Flynn, Corresponding
Secretary
Pub. *Norvell Nuggets*, irregularly, free;
(includes all Norville, Norvel, Norvil,
Nowel, etc., in the U.S. from 1600 to
the present; computer database)

Norvell
The Norvell Family Newsletter
227 West Avenue
Canandaigua, NY 14424-1533
John E. Norvell
Pub. *The Norvell Family Newsletter*,
semiannually, $5.00 for two-year
subscription

Norvil (see Norvell)

Norville (see Norvell)

Norwood (see Gant)

Nostrae
Nostrae Familae
PO Box 10969
Saint Louis, MO 63135
Pub. *Nostrae Familae*

Notaro (see Gratta)

Notter (see McCleave)

Novack (see Nowak)

Novak (see Nowak)

Nowack (see Nowak)

Nowak
Nowak-Nowack-Novak-Novack
4801 Woodhall
Detroit, MI 48224-2226
Carol Nowak
Pub. *Nowak-Nowack-Novak-Novack*,
quarterly, $16.00 per year U.S.
subscription, $20.00 per year foreign
subscription

Nowel (see Norvell)

Nowlin (see Folk Family Surname
Exchange)

Nowlin
The Nowlin Newsletter
PO Box 96194
Oklahoma City, OK 73143-6194
Phone (405) 634-0800
Mary K. Nowlin, Editor
Pub. *The Nowlin Newsletter*, quarterly
(February, May, August and
November), $10.00 per year
subscription; (includes variant
spellings: Noland, Nolen, etc.)

Noxon
Noxon Family Association
10305 West Virginia Avenue
Lakewood, CO 80226
Joan Noxon
Pub. *Noxon Talk*, quarterly
$10.00 per year membership

Noyes
*New Canaan Historical Society
13 Oenoke Ridge
New Canaan, CT 06840
Phone (203) 966-1776
Marilyn T. O'Rourke, Librarian
(primarily New Canaan local history, not
genealogical, but features Silliman,
Noyes, Weed surname collections)
$25.00 per year membership for
individuals, $30.00 per year
membership for families

Nucator (see Gregor)

Nuckols (see Nuckolls)

Nudie (see MacDuff)

Nugent (see Johnson)

Nugteren (see Poll)

Nulton
*John Nulton Family Organization
15513 Norman Drive
Gaithersburg, MD 20878
Phone (301) 977-2831
Lynn P. Nulton
(includes descendants of John Nulton of
Winchester, Virginia, probably through
Pennsylvania and New Jersey)

Nunnamaker (see The Memorial
Foundation of the Germanna Colonies)

Nurse (see Towne)

Nussbaum (see Anthes)

Nute (see Corson)

Nutsch (see Reedy)

Nutt (see Macnachton)

Nutter
Nutter Newsletter
3309 Fox Chase Court
Midlothian, VA 23112

Phone (804) 744-2141
Janet Nutter Alpert, Editor
Pub. *Nutter Newsletter*, quarterly, free to
Nutter descendants, $1.00 per issue for
back issues; (includes Hatevil Nutter
line from New Hampshire and New
England, and Christopher Nutter line
from Virginia, Maryland and West
Virginia)

Nutting (see Barnard)

Nuzum
*Nuzum Family Association
801 Sequoia Avenue
Millbrae, CA 94030
Phone (415) 697-9410
Thomas M. Brocher, Historian
Annual reunion

Nydie (see MacDuff)

Nydy (see MacDuff)

Nye (see Wert)

Nye
*The Nye Family of America
Association, Inc.
85 Old Country Road
PO Box 134
East Sandwich, MA 02537
Phone (508) 888-4213 (Benjamin Nye
Homestead); (508) 888-2368
(Curator); (508) 888-1681 (President)
Rosanna Cullity, Curator; Lois Howland,
President
Pub. *The Nye Family Newsletter*,
semiannually
$10.00 per year membership for
individuals; biennial reunion in August
or September of odd-numbered years

Nygaard
Who Are My Cousins?
2524 Oriole Circle
Red Wing, MN 55066-4103
Roger Sween
Pub. *Who Are My Cousins?*, quarterly,
$6.00 per year subscription; (includes
Nygaard, Odegaard and Hovdesven)

Nygren (see Anthes)

Oakes
*Pioneer Publication
PO Box 1179
Tum Tum, WA 99034-1179
Phone (509) 276-9841
Shirley Penna-Oakes
Pub. *Oakes Acorns*, irregularly, $6.00 per
issue plus $1.75 postage for one to
three books, 50¢ for each additional
book

Oakey
James Oakey Family Organization
PO Box 9
Dingle, ID 83233
Phone (208) 847-1284
Jean Oakey Alleman

Oakley (see Nettles)

Oathoudt (see Oothoudt)

Oathout (see Oothoudt)

Oatout (see Oothout)

O'Bannan (see Cian)

O'Behan (see Cian)

O'Beice (see Cian)

Oberbeck (see Orebaugh)

Oberholtzer (see Overholser)

Oblinger
*Oblinger/Oplinger/Uplinger Family
Association
1008 North Poplar Street
Whitehall, PA 18052
Phone (610) 437-2566
Don Oplinger, President

O'Brady (see Cian)

O'Brenan (see Cian)

O'Brennan (see Cian)

O'Breslin (see Cian)

O'Briain (see Cian)

O'Brien (see Blossom Press, Bryan,
Byrom, Cian)

O'Brien
O'Brien Surname Organization
6180 Merrywood Drive
Rocklin, CA 95677-3421
Kathleen Stewart

O'Brien
O'Brien/Diedrich Family Newsletter
5054 Calderon Road
Woodland Hills, CA 91364
Phone (818) 225-8991
Mary D. McKinnon, Editor
Pub. *O'Brien/Diedrich Family
Newsletter*, irregularly, donation for
subscription; (includes descendants
and collateral lines of two couples who
settled in DeKalb County, Illinois:
Patrick O'Brien (1829–1884) of
County Clare, Ireland, and Mary
Sheehan (1837–1903) of County
Kerry, Ireland, and Peter Diedrich
(1826–1900) of Luxembourg and
Catherine Tyson (1836–1919) of
Luxembourg)

O'Brocain (see Cian)

O'Bryant (see Bryan)

O'Cahalan (see Cian)

O'Cahill (see Cian)

O'Callaghan (see Cian)

O'Carney (see Cian)

O'Carol (see Cian)

O Carragher (see Caraher)

O'Carroll (see Cian)

O'Carry (see Cian)

O'Carthy (see Cian)

O'Casey (see Cian)

O'Castles (see Cian)

O'Coghlen (see Cian)

O'Collin (see Cian)

O'Collins (see Cian)

O'Connell (see Cian)

O'Connelly (see Cian)

O'Connor (see Cian)

O'Corcoran (see Cian)

O'Cormacan (see Cian)

O'Corra (see Cian)

O'Corry (see Cian)

O'Cosgrave (see Cian)

O'Cronan (see Cian)

O'Cuill (see Cian)

O'Cullen (see Cian)

O'Cullenan (see Cian)

O'Curry (see Cian)

O'Dallon (see Cian)

O'Dally (see Cian)

O'Day (see Cian)

O'Dea (see Cian)

Odegaard (see Nygaard)

Odekirk (see Ouderkerk)

Odel (see Cian)

Odell (see CTC Family Association, Covert, O'Dell, Smith)

O'Dell (see Cian)

Odell
*Odell Family Association
5526 61st Street East
Bradenton, FL 34203-9745
Phone (813) 756-1318
Joseph L. Smith, President

O'Dell
*The Legacy
875 Lindsten
PO Box 2040
Pinetop, AZ 85935
Phone (602) 367-4262
Kay O'Dell, Editor and Publisher
Pub. *The O'Dell Diggin's*, quarterly,
　$20.00 per year subscription; (includes
　Odell, Odle, all dates and places)
Reunion every three years

Odem (see Odom)

Oden (see Athy, Ogden)

O'Deneen (see Dineen)

Oder (see Oliver)

Oderkirk (see Ouderkerk)

O'Dermod (see Cian)

O'Derry (see Cian)

O'Dinan (see Cian)

O'Dineen (see Dineen)

O'Dinerty (see Cian)

O'Dinneen (see Dineen)

Odle (see O'Dell)

Odlin (see Corson)

O'Dochartaigh
*O'Dochartaigh Family Research
　Association
206 North Linn Avenue
Fayette, MO 65248-1433
Phone (816) 248-3247; (816) 248-1514
Edward M. Dougherty, Family
　Representative
Pub. *From Ireland*
$15.00 per year membership; reunion in
　2000

Odom (see Ogden)

Ellen Payne Odom Genealogy Library
　(see Multi-family Associations)

Odom
Odom Family Association
PO Box 1916
Smyrna, GA 30081
Pub. *Odom Observer*
$15.00 per year membership

Odom
National Odom Assembly
1455 East 52 Place
Tulsa, OK 74105
Phone (918) 742-3893
John D. Denny, Editor
Pub. *NOA News*, quarterly (October,
　January, April and July); (includes
　Odum, Odem and Oldham)
$20.00 per year full membership, $10.00
　per year associate membership, annual
　reunion

O'Donnegan (see Cian)

O'Donnelly (see Cian)

O'Donocho (see Cian)

O'Donoghy (see Cian)

O'Donohoe (see Cian)

O'Donoughe (see Cian)

O'Dooley (see Cian)

O'Doran (see Cian)

O'Driscoll
O'Driscoll Quarterly
437 South Highland Court
Montgomery, AL 36104-5149
Phone (205) 264-2131
Sandra J. Black, Publisher
Pub. *O'Driscoll Quarterly*, (June,
　September, December and March),
　$16.00 per year subscription, free
　queries; (includes Driscal, Driscoll,
　Driskell, Driskill, etc.)

O'Druin (see Cian)

O'Duana (see Cian)

O'Dullahanty (see Cian)

Odum (see Odom)

O'Eark (see Cian)

Oehler (see The Memorial Foundation of
　the Germanna Colonies, Donner)

Oehlschutt (see The Memorial
　Foundation of the Germanna Colonies)

Oerin (see Irwin)

Oeryn (see Irwin)

Oettinger (see Nettles)

O'Felan (see Cian)

O'Fercinn (see Cian)

Officer (see Allison)

Offley (see Rutherford)

O'Finnegan (see Cian)

O'Flanagan (see Cian)

O'Flynn (see Cian)

O'Fogarty (see Cian)

O'Furey (see Cian)

Ogan (see Cian, Ogden)

O'Gara (see Cian)

O'Garra (see Hay)

O'Garrow (see Hay)

Ogborn (see Ogden)

Ogburn (see Ogden)

Ogburn
*Ogburn Family Association
PO Box 333
Colona, IL 61241-0333
Phone (309) 792-4579
Norma J. Ogburn

Ogden (see Lamoreaux)

Ogden
*Ogden Database
1801 Ardath
Wichita Falls, TX 76301
Phone (817) 767-6658
W. Henry Ogden, Jr.
(includes Oden, Odom, Ogan, Ogborn,
Ogburn, Ogden, Osborn and Osburn)

Ogilvie (see Allen)

Ogilvie
Ogilvie Kith and Kin
1850 Case Street
Batesville, AR 72501-5923
Phone (501) 793-6489
Craig Ogilvie, Editor
Pub. *Ogilvie Kith and Kin*, quarterly,
$8.00 per year subscription

Ogilvie
*Ogilvie Surname Organization
150 Brown Street
Saint Clair, MI 48079-4882
Phone (810) 329-9359
George M. Roberts
(includes Ogilvie and Oglesby in the
U.S. and Canada)

Ogle (see Folk Family Surname
Exchange)

Ogle
*Ogle/Ogles Family Association
124 12th Avenue
Indialantic, FL 32903
Jean Godwin

Pub. *The Ogle Genealogist*, annually;
Ogling for Ogles, semiannually
$13.00 per year membership; reunion

O'Gleason (see Cian)

Ogles (see Ogle)

Oglesby (see Folk Family Surname
Exchange, Ogilvie)

Oglethorpe (see Folk Family Surname
Exchange)

O'Grady (see Cian)

O'Guda (see Cian)

O'Gunning (see Cian, Gunnin)

O'Haithchir (see Cian)

O'Halley (see Cian)

O'Hally (see Cian)

O'Hanrahan (see Cian)

O'Hara (see Cian, Rooney)

O'Hara
*O'Hara Family Association
9190 Oak Leaf Way
Granite Bay, CA 95746
Phone (916) 791-0405
Linus Joseph Dewald
(includes descendants of Ed. Rooney and
Marg. O'Hara (ca 1810 County Down,
Ireland–))

O'Hara
*Roger O'Hara Family Organization
20 Rigging Way
Marstons Mills, MA 02648
Phone (508) 420-5310
Thomas M. Whelan
(includes O'Haras of County Sligo,
Ireland)

O'Hare (see Cian)

O'Hay (see Cian, Hay)

O'Hea (see Hay)

O'Heffernan (see Cian)

O'Hegarty (see Cian)

O'Hehir (see Cian)

O'Henery (see Cian)

O'Heron (see Cian)

O'Hickey (see Cian)

Ohler (see Eller)

Ohlschlagel (see The Memorial
Foundation of the Germanna Colonies)

Ohlson (see Bouton)

Ohmart (see Frantz)

O'Hogan (see Cian)

O'Hora (see Cian)

O'Hurley (see Cian)

O'Karrell (see Cian)

O'Kearney (see Cian)

O'Keeffe (see Cian)

O'Keeffee (see McCanna)

O'Keely (see Cian)

O'Kelleher (see Cian)

O'Kennedy (see Cian)

Olan (see Olin)

O'Lanigan (see Cian)

O'Laughlen (see MacLachlan)

O'Laughlin (see MacLachlan)

Olcott (see Beaman)

Olden (see Olin)

Oldham (see Odom)

Olds (see Grant)

O'Leahy (see Lea)

O'Leary (see CTC Family Association,
Cian)

Olford (see Alford)

O'Liddy (see Cian)

Olin
*Olin Family Society
8213 Bailey Lake Road
Waterville, NY 13480-2703
Phone (315) 861-7712; E-mail:
TROlin@InterRamp.com
Thomas R. Olin, Genealogist
Pub. *The OLINews*, semiannually; $5.00
per year U.S. subscription (summer to
summer), $7.00 per year Canadian
subscription; (includes Olan and
Olden, especially descendants of John
Olin (–1742 Rhode Island) married
Susannah Spencer (ca 1680–?))
Annual reunion

Olin
*Rebecca Englesby Olin Family
  Organization
1774 Country Club Drive
Logan, UT 84321
Phone (801) 753-6924
Joyce Elfrena Kalanquin

Oliphant (see Brawley, Sutherland,
  Turner)

Oliphant
*Oliphant Family Group
1177 Deerfield Place
Highland Park, IL 60035
Phone (708) 433-0351
Nancy Jo Stein, Coordinator
(includes Oliphant, Olivant, Olliphint,
  Ollyphant, Olophant, etc., all
  variations)

Oliphant
*The Oliphant Clan and Family
  Association
10 Glen Road
Ringwood, NJ 07456-2331
Phone (201) 962-4584
Steven D. Oliphant, Convenor
Pub. *The Oliphant Clan and Family
  Association Newsletter*, quarterly,
  $15.00 per year subscription

Oliver (see Catlow, Fraser, Neville, Rice,
  Schaffer)

Oliver
*Kinseeker Publications
5697 Old Maple Trail
PO Box 184
Grawn, MI 49637
E-mail: AB064@taverse.lib.mi.us
Victoria Wilson, Editor
Pub. *The Family Series: Oliver*,
  irregularly, $6.50 per year subscription

Oliver
*Oliver Family Reunion
4560 S.W. Luradel Street
Portland, OR 97219-6820
Phone (503) 244-3826
Rebecca Oliver Torland
(includes descendants of Elijah Turner
  Oliver and wife Catharine Oder, and
  their three sons, Hiram Wesley Oliver
  who married Julia Ann McCaleb and
  Maria L. Burt, and came to Oregon
  from Iowa in 1864, Joseph E. Oliver,
  and Eliel Oliver)
Annual reunion

Oliver
*The Oliver Orator
12600 Bissonnet A4-407
Houston, TX 77099
Dede D. Mercer, Publisher
Pub. *The Oliver Orator*, semiannually,
  $20.00 per year subscription; (all
  variations of the surname, worldwide)

Olivier (see Blossom Press)

Olivo (see Johnson)

Olles
*Olles Unlimited
521 Poland Road
Danville, IL 61834
Phone (217) 442-6074
Wanda Mulholland Olles, Author

Ollyphant (see Oliphant)

Olmstead (see Catlow, Olmsted)

Olmstead
Walter Morris Olmstead Descendants
  Reunion
2613 South Newton Street
Sioux City, IA 51106-3412
J. Winn

Olmsted (see Rothenberger)

Olmsted
*Olmste(a)d Family Association
OFA Box 40192
Saint Paul, MN 55104
Phone (612) 487-3672
Marcia "Marty" Lamb, Secretary
Pub. *Tree Leaves: The Family
  Olmste(a)d*, quarterly
  $10.00 per year membership

Olmsted
*Heart of the Lakes Publishing
PO Box 299
Interlaken, NY 14847-0299
Phone (607) 532-4997; (607) 532-4684;
  E-mail: WaltSteesy@aol.com
Walter W. Steesy
Pub. *Olmste(a)d's Genealogy Recorded*,
  irregularly

Olney (see Newbold)

O'Lonergan (see Cian)

Olophant (see Oliphant)

O'Loughlin (see MacLachlan)

O'Loughnan (see Cian)

Olsen (see Blossom Press)

Olson (see Surname Sources, Heath,
  Lush)

Olvera
*The Olvera Family Association
24901 Danafir
Dana Point, CA 92629
Phone (714) 240-2490
Carlos N. Olvera, President
Pub. *Newsletter Flyer*, irregularly, no
  cost; (includes Olvera in Mexico City
  1824–1917 and Spain from 1600)

Olwin (see Ohlwein)

Olwine (see Ohlwein)

O'Lynch (see Cian)

O'Mahoney (see Cian)

O'Mahony (see Cian)

O'Mahony
*The O Mahony Society
3602 Isabell Street
Wheaton, MD 20906-4336
Phone (301) 946-6670
Eileen Mahony McConnell, Mid-Atlantic
  Representative
Pub. *The O Mahony News*, semiannually;
  The O Mahony Journal, annually
$20.00 per year membership; annual clan
  rally in June in Ireland, annual get-
  together in October in the U.S

Oman
Oman Family
PO Box 6163
Los Osos, CA 93412
Phone (805) 528-8013
Rosemary Sylvester Flamion

O'Maolin (see Cian)

O'Mara (see Cian)

O'Meagher (see Cian)

O'Meara (see Cian)

O'Meehan (see Cian)

O'Menhundro (see Futral)

O'Moloney (see Cian)

O'Moore (see Cian)

Omuig
Omuig Surname Organization
22916 Carlow Road
Torrance, CA 90505
Phone (310) 378-3574
Charlene DeLong

Omvig
Omvig Family Organization
22916 Carlow Road
Torrance, CA 90505
Phone (310) 378-3574
Charlene DeLong

O'Neal (see O'Neil)

O'Neil (see Bibee, Cian, Lemon)

O'Neil
The Family Connection
730 East Grand Avenue
Pomona, CA 91766-3643
Jim and Beverly Cothren
Pub. *The Family Connection of the
  O'Neil, Neil, O'Neal Surname*, three
  times per year
$15.00 per year membership

O'Neill (see Cian)

Oney
*The Elwood E. Oney Reunion
RR 1, Box 31
Noxen, PA 18612
(includes descendants of Elwood
Emmanuel[3] Oney (Thomas[2],
Nathaniel[1]) (1891 LaAnna, Pike
County, Pennsylvania–1960 Harveys
Lake, Luzerne County, Pennsylvania)
and his two wives, Mable Anderson
(1895–1918), daughter of George M.
Anderson and Kittie Kocher, and
Bertha Eunice Crispell (1904–1992
Kingston, Luzerne County,
Pennsylvania), daughter of Frederick
Cornelius Crispell and Olive Arminda
Miner; Nathaniel[1] Oney (1804–1888)
and Susanna Beach (1815–1883),
daughter of Benjamin Beach and
Elizabeth Rush; Christopher Miner
(1768 Stonington Township,
Connecticut–) and his wife, Rebecca
(1790 New Jersey–); Simon Anderson
of Lake Township, Luzerne County,
Pennsylvania, and his wife Ura
(–1872))
Annual reunion on the fourth Saturday of
July at Sorber Ranch, Noxen,
Pennsylvania

Ong
*Ong Surname Organization
2221 Christy Place
Herndon, VA 22070
Phone (703) 481-0143; E-mail:
ROng657593@aol.com
Richard A. Ong
(on-line computer access planned for
Ong family)

O'Noonan (see Cian)

Onstead (see Pannill)

Onstrander (see Ostrander)

Oostrander (see Ostrander)

Oostrum (see Van Steenwyk)

Oothout (see Oothoudt)

O'Patten (see Cian)

op den Graeff (see Links Genealogy
Publications)

Op den Graeff (see DeHaven)

op de Trap (see Links Genealogy
Publications)

op de Trapp (see Links Genealogy
Publications)

Op Dyck
Op Dyck Genealogy
2334 Kenwood Avenue
Fort Wayne, IN 46805-2771

Jean Opdycke Dreher, Publisher
(includes Opdycke, Opdyke, Updike,
etc., family that came to America in
1650 from Germany and Holland)

Opdycke (see Op Dyck)

Opdyke (see Op Dyck)

Oplinger (see Oblinger)

O'Quill (see Cian)

O'Quin (see Cian)

O'Quinlevan (see Cian)

O'Quirk (see Cian)

O'Quirke (see Cian)

O'Ragan (see Reagan)

Orchille (see Graham)

Orden (see Roberts)

Ordway (see Wright)

Ordway
Wilson Family Record Depository
169 Melody Lane
Tonawanda, NY 14150-9109
Robert J. Wilson
Pub. *Ordway*, quarterly, $25.00 per year
subscription

O'Reagan (see Reagan)

Orebaugh
*Andreas & Elisabeth Orebaugh
Association
15250 Orebaugh Lane
Helendale, CA 92342
Phone (619) 245-8861
Sarah Orebaugh, Historian Genealogist;
Mirl Orebaugh
(includes descendants of Andreas
Orebaugh (Oberbeck) (ca 1694
Germany–1765 Bucks County,
Pennsylvania) and Elisabeth Drach
(Oberbeck) (–1775 Bucks County,
Pennsylvania))
$7.50 per year membership for families

Oreck (see Oreckovsky)

Oreckovsky
*The Oreck Foundation
6302 East Monterosa
Scottsdale, AZ 85251
Phone (602) 970-1514; E-mail:
resilver@silverw.com
Robert Silver, President
Pub. *The Oreck Family News*, annually;
(includes descendants of Abraham and
Hykeh Oreckovsky (ca 1810) who
came from Novoukrainka, near
Yelisavetgrad (now Kirovograd),
Ukraina, to Duluth, Minnesota)

O'Regan (see Cian)

Orgeron (see Augeron)

Orman (see Behnke)

Orr (see Gregor)

Orrell
Orrell Family Association
145 Sanford Avenue
Catonsville, MD 21228-5140
Phone (410) 788-6882
Reverdy Lewin Orrell, III, Founder
Pub. *Orrell Family Association
Newsletter*, quarterly
$20.00 per year membership; annual
reunion in June

Orrick (see MacDuff)

Orrock (see MacDuff)

Orruein (see Irwin)

Ort (see Hoster)

Ortego (see Johnson)

Orth (see Hoster)

Ortscholz (see Scholz)

Ortstadt
*Ortstadt-Ottstadt-Otstot(t) Organization
5124 North 33rd Street
Arlington, VA 22207-1854
Phone (703) 538-5446
Col. Charles Mathieson Otstot
Pub. *Annual* (includes descendants of
Jost Ortstadt and Emma
Immichenhain, Hessen, 1618)

Orvine (see Irwin)

Orvington (see Irwin)

Orwin (see Irwin)

O'Ryan (see Cian)

Osatrander (see Ostrander)

Osborn (see Jackson, Kahler, Lacy,
Ogden)

Osborn
*Osborn/Cambron Family Association
8505 Glenview Avenue
Takoma Park, MD 20912
Phone (301) 89-6621;
(301) 589-1366 FAX
M. Sandra Reeves
(restricted to descendants of Tom Osborn
and Nancy Means (ca 1828–); also
Lambert and White)

Osborne (see Applebee, Kahler,
McCune, Randall, White)

Osborne
Osborne Offspring
Rt. 1, Box 356
Rockford, WA 99030
Evelyn Osborne Fricke
Pub. *Osborne Offspring*, annually, $6.00
plus $1.00 postage and handling
(Washington residents add 45¢ tax)

Osburn (see Ogden)

Osburn
*Osburn Reunion
PO Box 208
Dufur, OR 97021-0208
Mrs. Billie L. Fagersberg
Annual reunion on the third Sunday of
August at Greenwater Park, just east of
Oakridge, Oregon

O'Scanlan (see Cian)

O'Scully (see Cian)

O'Seasnain (see Cian)

O'Sexton (see Cian)

Osguthorpe (see McCune)

O'Shanahan (see Cian)

O'Shannon (see Cian)

O'Sheedy (see Cian)

O'Slattery (see Cian)

O'Spealain (see Cian)

O'Spellan (see Cian)

O'Spellman (see Cian)

O'Spillan (see Cian)

O'Spillane (see Cian)

Osstander (see Ostrander)

Ostagain (see Cian)

Ostberg (see Holden)

Oster (see Auster)

Osterander (see Ostrander)

Osterberg (see Holden)

Ostertag (see Franciscus)

Ostertag
*Ostertag-Easterday Association of
America
6916 North Michele Lane
Peoria, IL 61614
Phone (309) 692-6461
Mary K. Easterday Shields,
Corresponding Secretary and Treasurer

Pub. *Ostertag-Easterday Newsletter*,
quarterly
$12.00 for six years membership

Ostervanter (see Ostrander)

Ostrancer (see Ostrander)

Ostranck (see Ostrander)

Ostranda (see Ostrander)

Ostrandar (see Ostrander)

Ostrander (see Main)

Ostrander
Ostrander Reunion
Rt. 1, Box 218
Ghent, NY 12075
Phone (518) 828-6097
Peter Ostrander

Ostrander
*Ostrander Family Association, Inc.
133 School Street
Bradford, PA 16701
Phone (814) 368-5981
Lynn H. Ostrander, President; Mrs. Lynn
H. Ostrander, Editor
Pub. *De Bonte Koe* (The Spotted Cow),
three times per year (January, April
and October); (includes descendants of
Pieter Pieterzen of Amsterdam,
married Tryntje van de Lande ca
November 1652, arrived in Nieuw
Amsterdam in 1660; the family name
was changed to Oostrander about
1700, with variants: Onstrander,
Osatrander, Osstander, Osterander,
Ostervanter, Ostrancer, Ostranck,
Ostranda, Ostrandar, Ostrandt,
Ostrandter, Ostronden, Ostronder,
Oustrande, Van Noorstrant, Van
Noortstrande, Van Nostrandt, Van
Nostrant, Van Nostrunt, Van
Oostrander, Vanostran, Van Ostrand
before becoming standardized as
Ostrander)
$20.00 per year membership; biennial
reunion

Ostrandt (see Ostrander)

Ostrandter (see Ostrander)

Ostrem
*Ostrem-Hatlei Family Association
Jente Lane
1420 Hwy 35/64
Houlton, WI 54082
Phone (310) 533-8243 (California); E-
mail: cvelline@aol.com
Bonnie Zimmer, President
Pub. *Newsletter* (includes related
surnames: Brokke, Hopperstad,
Reierson, Skau and Strand from
Norway)
$10.00 per year membership; biennial
reunion in Minnesota

Ostrin (see Goodenow)

Ostroff (see Cohen)

Ostronden (see Ostrander)

Ostronder (see Ostrander)

Ostrov (see Cohen)

Ostrow (see Cohen)

Ostry (see Waterous)

O'Sullivan (see Cian)

Oswald (see MacDuff)

Oswald
*Oswald Surname Organization
2204 West Houston
Spokane, WA 99208-4440
Phone (509) 326-2089
Donna Potter Phillips
Pub. *Oswald Outlines*, irregularly, $7.00
per issue, free queries; (includes
anyone of the surname, any place, any
time)

Othoudt (see Oothoudt)

O'Tirney (see Cian)

O'Toole-Richardson (see Daley)

O'Tracey (see Cian)

Otstot (see Ortstadt)

Otstott (see Ortstadt)

Ott (see Hire)

Otterbach (see Lemon)

Otto
*The Dr. Bodo Otto Association
624 King Street
Nokomis, FL 34275
Jane Carman Heggan, Secretary-
Treasurer
Pub. *Newsletter*, quarterly; (includes
descendants of Dr. Bodo Otto,
successor organization to The James
Henry Mason I Family Organization,
which was disbanded)
Annual reunion at various locations

Ottstadt (see Ortstadt)

Ouderkerk
*The Ouderkerk Family Genealogical
Association
700 Atlanta Country Club Drive
Marietta, GA 30067
Phone (770) 956-9565
H. John Ouderkirk, President
Pub. *Ouderkerk Family Newsletter*,
quarterly; (includes Odekirk, Oderkirk,
Ouderkerk, Ouderkirk, particularly Jan

Janse Ouderkerk-Beverwych, New
Amsterdam (Albany, New York))
$5.00 per year membership

Ouderkirk (see Surname Sources,
Ouderkerk)

Ougan (see Cian)

Ourine (see Irwin)

Ouron (see Irwin)

Ourren (see Irwin)

Ouseley (see Ousley, Owsley)

Ousley (see Ellett, Owsley)

Ousley
*Ousley Genealogical Society
725 Bluegrass
PO Box 4305
Dallas, TX 75208
Phone (214) 330-1635
Monty T. O. Wedell, President/Editor
Pub. *The Ousley Newsletter*,
semiannually, $3.00 per issue;
(includes Ouseley, Owsley, Points and
Poyntz)
$6.00 per year membership, $5.00 per
year associate membership

Oustrande (see Ostrander)

Overall (see Sawyer)

Overall
Overalls All Over
133 Kingwood Drive
Chattanooga, TN 37412
Eudine M. Britton
Pub. *Overalls All Over*, $12.00 per
volume (Tennessee residents add
7.25% tax)

Overby (see Allen, Golding, Stewart)

Overcash (see Brawley)

Overhiser
Overhiser Cousins Society
332 Division Street
Marshall, MI 49068
Martin Overhiser, President
Pub. *Overhiser Highlights*, semiannually
$10.00 per year membership

Overhizer
Overhizer Cousins
1111 North Blue Star Highway
South Haven, MI 49090
Phone (616) 227-3582
Jeanne M. Hallgren

Overholser
*Overholser Family Association
313 Henry Lane
Wallingford, PA 19086
Phone (610) 566-4888

Barbara B. Ford, Editor and Genealogist
Pub. *Overholser Family Bulletin*,
semiannually (February and August);
(includes all German/Swiss families
with this name, over twenty spellings
(Oberholtzer, Overholt, etc.); some
immigrants from Oberholz, near Wald,
Switzerland, into Germany; some early
American research centered on
Lancaster, Bucks and Montgomery
counties, Pennsylvania, and
surrounding areas of Virginia and
Ohio)
Donation for membership

Overholt (see Oberholtzer, Overholser)

Overholtzer (see Oberholtzer)

Overholzer (see Oberholtzer)

Overstreet (see Corson)

Overstreet
Overstreet Clearinghouse
25 Glyndon Drive, #A3
Reisterstown, MD 21136-2025
Dolly Huff

Overton (see Folk Family Surname
Exchange)

Overton
*Folk Family
PO Box 52048
Knoxville, TN 37950-2048
Hester E. Stockton, Owner; Robert
Overton, Editor
Pub. *Overton Observer*, quarterly, $15.00
per year subscription, $5.00 per issue

Oviatt
Oviatt Family Association
23 Forest Street
South Burlington, VT 05401
James F. Haire, Jr.
Pub. *Ovi(a)tt Newsletter*, irregularly

Ovitt (see Oviatt)

Owen (see Golding, Holden,
MacLachlan)

Owen
Owen-Owens
1221 Candice Court
Mesquite, TX 75149
Mary L. House, Editor
Pub. *Owen-Owens*, quarterly, $15.00 per
year subscription

Owen
*The Owen Family Association
Crystal Plaza 809 South
2111 Jefferson Davis Highway
Arlington, VA 22202
Phone (703) 415-1473
C. Owen Johnson, Genealogist-
Newsletter Editor

Pub. *The Owen Newsletter*, bimonthly;
(includes all branches of the Owen
family)
$10.00 per year membership

Owenby (see Folk Family Surname
Exchange)

Owenby
*Folk Family
PO Box 52048
Knoxville, TN 37950-2048
Hester E. Stockton, Owner; Elizabeth
Hill Ownby, Editor
Pub. *Owenby/Ownby Families*, quarterly,
$15.00 per year subscription, $5.00 per
issue; (includes Owensbey)

Owens (see Cian, Freiling, Golding,
Louden, MacLachlan, Newton, Owen)

Owens
Owens/Stuart/Skipper Family
Association
2700 East Cottonwood Road
Dothan, AL 36301
Glenda Owens

Owensbey (see Owenby)

Owings (see LaRue)

Ownbey
Ownbey/Ownby Reunion
Rt. 4, Box 376
Springdale, AR 72764
Ada Lee Shook, Chairman

Ownby (see Folk Family Surname
Exchange, Owenby, Ownbey)

Owsley (see Ousley)

Owsley
*Owsley Family Historical Society
220 Glenwood Avenue, N.W.
Knoxville, TN 37917-5707
Phone (423) 523-2005
Theresa M. Owsley, Membership
Director
Pub. *OFHS Newsletter*, quarterly;
(includes Ousley, Ouseley, Housley,
etc.)
$25.00 per year membership

Owyrn (see Irwin)

Oxley (see Hall)

Oyer
*Oyer Family Research
263 Bakerdale Road
Rochester, NY 14616
Phone (716) 663-1735
Phyllis Smith Oyer, Publisher and
Researcher

Oynie (see Innes)

Pace (see DeLaughter)

Pace
*The Pace Society of America, Inc.
699 West Verna
Jasper, TX 75951
Katherine Pace Baldwin, Treasurer
Pub. *Pace Bulletin*, quarterly; (includes
descendants of Richard and Isabella
(Smyth) Pace of Jamestown by 1620)
$15.00 per year membership; annual
reunion

Packard (see Wright)

Packard
*Packard and Allied Families Association
18 Homestead Path
Huntington, NY 11743
Karle S. Packard, President
(includes descendants of Samuel[1]
Packard and Elizabeth, Samuel[2]
Packard and Elizabeth Lathrop,
Samuel[3] Packard and Elizabeth Edson,
Paul[4] Packard and Sarah Harrington-
Bruce)

Packer
Nathan Williams Packer Family
Organization
1360 East Ninth North
Logan, UT 84321
Phone (801) 752-6466
Gaye Winward
Pub. *Grist Mill Builder-Bridge Builder-
Family Builder*, annually

Padon (see Gillean)

Page (see Corson, Heath, Ross,
Rutherford)

Page
*James Page Family Organization
4259 West 1200 North
Dayton, ID 83232
Phone (208) 747-3588
Helena M. Page
(includes descendants of James Page
(1862 Bountiful, Davis County, Utah–)
and Emma Kemp (1867 East Ruston,
Norfolk, England–))

Page
Family Limbs
6423 S.E. 97th Avenue
Portland, OR 97266-4529
Shirley L. Bodak
Pub. *Page Family Newsletter*, ten times
per year

Page
*Pioneer Publication
PO Box 1179
Tum Tum, WA 99034-1179
Phone (509) 276-9841
Shirley Penna-Oakes
Pub. *Page Pedigree*, irregularly, $6.00
per issue plus $1.75 postage for one to
three books, 50¢ for each additional
book

Paige (see Heath)

Paine (see Calef, Newton, Payne)

Painter (see Folk Family Surname
Exchange, Barnes, Lush)

Paisley (see Gregor)

Paisley
*The Paisley Family Society
2715 170th Street RFD
Newell, IA 50568-7502
Phone (712) 662-4140
Eugenia Paisley Vogel, USA
Commissioner
Pub. *Paisley Journal*, annually; (includes
all spelling variations: Paslay, Pasley,
Passily, etc.)
$15.00 per year membership

Pait (see Pate)

Paite (see Pate)

Palas (see Mueller)

PalinBonville (see De Bonville)

Pallotta (see Richie)

Palm
*Palm Surname Organization
16117 West Lake Burrell Drive
Lutz, FL 33549
Phone (813) 972-2725
John W. Palm
(includes descendants of Carl Palm (1729
Möllenbeck, Schwerin, Mecklenburg,
Germany–))

Palmer (see Blattenberger, Cowart,
Dockery, Goodenow, Heath, Hopkin,
Lewis, McCune, Pessner)

Palmer
*Palmer (NY, Ontario, Canada, Williams
County, Ohio)
653 Perrshing Drive
Walnut Creek, CA 94596
A. Maxim Coppage, Publisher

Palmer
Wilson Family Record Depository
169 Melody Lane
Tonawanda, NY 14150-9109
Robert J. Wilson
Pub. *Palmer*, quarterly, $25.00 per year
subscription

Palsson (see Palson)

Paltiel (see Lewin)

Palumbo
*The Cousins
25 Forest Creek Drive
Dover, DE 19901
Phone (302) 734-3214; E-mail:
LJara@bdsnet.com

Louis V. Jara, Coordinator
Pub. *The Cousins* (Palumbo-Passero
families of Philadelphia and New York
City, early 1900s, including Nicondro
Palumbo)
Annual Cousins Day Reunion in
September at Bellevue State Park in
Wilmington, Delaware

Pangborn (see Pangburn)

Pangbourne (see Pangburn)

Pangburn
Pangburn Letter
5245 Walton Street
Long Beach, CA 90815
Phone (310) 421-9686
Donn E. Wagner, Editor
Pub. *Pangburn Letter*, semiannually,
free; (includes Pangborn, Pangbourne
and Pangman)

Pangman (see Pangburn)

Pankey (see Anthes)

Pannill
Pannill-Onstead-Gotto-Cooley Family
Association
2306 Westgate
Houston, TX 77019
Phone (713) 529-2333
Harold Helm
$25.00 plus pedigree and family group
sheets for membership

Panther (see Dockery)

Paolini (see Blossom Press)

Papen (see Links Genealogy
Publications)

Paraday (see Paradise)

Paradee (see Paradise)

Paradice (see Paradise)

Paradis (see Lagesse)

Paradis
*Paradis Family Reunion
40 U.S. Route 1
Frenchville, ME 04745
Phone (207) 728-4854
Ross Paradis, President
(includes 1,400 U.S. and Canadian
descendants of Pierre Paradis and
Barbe Guyon, who were married at
Montagne, France, 1633, and settled in
Beauport, Canada)

Paradise
Paradise Family Newsletter
PO Box 339
Jackman, ME 04945
Phone (207) 668-7723
Howard Paradise

Pub. *Paradise Family Newsletter*,
irregularly, about annually, $1.00 per
issue; (includes Paraday, Paradee,
Paradice and Paradis)

Parall (see Prall)

Pardee (see Rothenberger)

Pardue
*The Pardue Family Historical
Association
7534 Willow Lane
Falls Church, VA 22042
Norman C. Pardue, Jr., Editor
Pub. *The Pardue Times & Historical
Gazette*

Paren (see Perrin)

Paridis (see Paradise)

Parin (see Perrin)

Paris (see Heath)

Parish (see Joyner)

Parish
*Parish/Parrish Family Reunion
1505 Western Avenue
Glendale, CA 91201-1215
Frank Thomas, Genealogist/Historian
(includes descendants of Thomas Parrish
and Elizabeth Herring, ca 1790)
Reunion

Park (see McRae, Parke, Parks)

Parke
*The Parke Society, Inc.
PO Box 590
Milwaukee, WI 53201
Phone (414) 332-9984 (evenings)
Theodore Edward Parks, Historian
Pub. *Newsletter of the Parke Society*,
three times per year; (includes all
Park/e/s (Park, Parke, Parkes and
Parks lines into North America from
the British Isles)
$15.00 per year membership, $15.00
application fee, $150.00 life
membership; reunion

Parker (see Folk Family Surname
Exchange, Brawley, Heath, Jesse,
Lynch, Martin)

Parker
*Parker Family
32785 Genoa Road
Genoa, IL 60135-8229
Phone (815) 784-5059
Katherine Jane Parker Brown, Editor
Pub. *Parker Pathways*, three times per
year (January, May and September);
(includes descendants of James Parker
(ca 1752 New Jersey?–1835 Illinois)
and Anna Doty (1765 New Jersey–
1830 Illinois))

$15.00 per year membership; reunion of
the descendants of Newman Ellsworth
Parker (1866–1908) and Priscilla Jane
Lackey (1866–1935), Illinois

Parker
*Parker Family of Delmarva Peninsula
Rt. 2, Box 187
Morgantown, PA 19543
Phone (215) 286-9857
Fred L. Williams, III

Parker
*The Parker Reunion
531 Lockshire Road
Columbia, SC 29210
Phone (803) 772-4788
Dalton A. Parker
(includes descendants of Albert Straughn
Parker (son of Phillip Parker and Mary
Lankford) and Letitia Jones Blackburn
(daughter of Robert L. Blackburn and
Eudora Skelton) of King and Queen
County, Virginia)

Parker
*Parker Clearinghouse
1610 Orange Blossom Loop
Laredo, TX 78045
Phone (210) 791-2717; E-mail:
AlvisExch@aol.com
Kathy Patterson

Parker
*Name Game Enterprises
4204 South Conklin Street
Spokane, WA 99203-6235
Phone (509) 747-4903
Mrs. E. Dale Hastin Smith
Pub. *Parker Papers*, irregularly, $5.75
per issue plus $2.00 postage and
handling

Parkes (see Parke, Parks)

Parkhurst (see Myers, Porter)

Parkinson
*James Parkinson Family Organization
430 North 200 East
Spanish Fork, UT 84660
Phone (801) 798-2995
John T. Parkinson
(includes descendants of James
Parkinson (1808, Hunts., England) and
Elizabeth Chattle (1806, Hunts.,
England))
$5.00 per year membership for families

Parks (see Parke)

Parks
*Parks Surname Organization
405 South Main Street
Anna, IL 62906
George E. Parks
(includes James and John Parks,
Revolutionary soldier, of Uniontown,
Pennsylvania, and Ohio; Jacob Rich,
Revolutionary soldier, of North

Carolina and Tennessee; Jordan
Williford, Revolutionary soldier and
pioneer of Virginia, Tennessee, and
Illinois; John Claye 1620 Virginia,
Henry Clay and the Clays of
Kentucky; Robert Kitchell from
England, with descendants in
Connecticut, New Jersey, Ohio and
Indiana)

Parks
*Parks Database
4880 South Farm Road 189
Rogersville, MO 65742-9473
Robert W. Eckert, M.D.
(connected to Simmons)

Parks
Parks/Park/Parkes Family Organization
Rt. 3, Box 123
Trinity, NC 27370
Cheryl Burrow

Parmely (see Heath)

Parmenter (see Goodenow)

Parmenter
Pioneering Parmenters of America
961 North Euclid Street
La Habra, CA 90631
Phone (310) 697-9940
Carolyn F. Wright, Editor
Pub. *Pioneering Parmenters of America*,
quarterly, $15.00 per year subscription

Parogan (see Cian)

Parot (see Parrott)

Parratt (see Parrott)

Parrett (see Parrott)

Parrican (see Cian)

Parrish (see Holden, Parish)

Parrish
Parrish Family Exchange
3719 Meadow Avenue, North
Renton, WA 98055
Mrs. J. H. Ross
Pub. *Parrish Family Exchange*

Parritt (see Parrott)

Parrot
Parrot/Perrotte Family Newsletter
6925 Marilyn Avenue, N.E.
Albuquerque, NM 87109
Dorothy Parrott Drake
Pub. *Parrot/Perrotte Family Newsletter*
(includes descendants of Albert Perrot
and Marie-Louise Letourneau of St.
Philippe de Laprarie, Quebec; variant
spellings: Parot, Parrotte, Payrot and
Perrot)

Parrott
*The P(eiaou)rr(eaoiu)tt Society
HC 3, Box 2
Sudan, TX 79371-9803
Mrs. Evalyn Parrott-Scott, Vice-President
Pub. *Parrott Talk* (includes Parratt,
    Parrett, Parritt, Parrott, Parrutt, Perratt,
    Perrett, Perritt, Perrott, Perrutt, Pirratt,
    Pirrett, Pirritt, Pirrott, Pirrutt, Porratt,
    Porrett, Porritt, Porrott, Porrutt,
    Purratt, Purrett, Purritt, Purrott,
    Purrutt)

Parrotte (see Parrott)

Parrutt (see Parrott)

Parry (see Holden)

Parson (see Macpherson)

Parsons (see MacPherson, Matteson,
    Newton, Pessner, Rowe)

Parsons
*Parsons Family Reunion
48 East New England Avenue
Worthington, OH 43085
A. C. Parsons
Pub. *Parsons' Paragraphs from
    Parchment Valley, A Newsletter for the
    Descendants of Alexis Fink Parsons
    and Phoebe Casto Parsons*, three
    times per year, $6.00 donation for
    subscription; (includes William
    Parsons and his sons Charles and
    Joseph)

Parsons
*William and Ann Sly Parsons Family
    Organization
295 West Union
Manti, UT 84642
Phone (801) 835-9872; (602) 461-9836
David G. Mackey, Vice President
Pub. *Parsons Family Newsletter*, one or
    two times per year; (includes Parsons
    families in Somerset, England,
    Hamilton, Illinois, Manti, Utah, and
    Elgin, Oregon)

Partain (see Folk Family Surname
    Exchange)

Parten
*To Peg a Parten Line
PO Box 5154
Santa Maria, CA 93456-5154
Glenna Parten Vincent, Publisher
Pub. *To Peg a Parten Line*, quarterly,
    $7.00 per year subscription; (includes
    Partin and Parton)

Partin (see Parten)

Partin
Partin Publications
230 Wedgewood
Nacogdoches, TX 75961-5326
Pub. *Partin*, quarterly, $18.00 per year
    subscription

Parton (see Parten)

Partridge (see Clark)

Partridge
Partridge Family Periodical
PO Box 109
Colton, NY 13625
Pub. *Partridge Family Periodical*,
    quarterly, $10.00 per year subscription

Paschall (see Paschill)

Paschill
*Paschill Genealogy Committee
203 Maple Street
Paris, TN 38242
(includes Paschall)

Pasco (see Pasko)

Pascoe (see Pasko)

Paslay (see Paisley)

Pasley (see Paisley)

Passero (see Palumbo)

Passily (see Paisley)

Passmore (see Wedgeworth)

Pastaorius (see Links Genealogy
    Publications)

Patchy (see Cian)

Pate (see MacDuff, McRae, Paulk)

Pate
Pate Pioneers
Rt. 1, Box 123A
Buffalo, TX 75831
Phone (214) 322-5462
Clovis Byars Herring
Pub. *Pate Pioneers*, quarterly, $15.00 per
    year subscription; (includes Pait, Paite
    and Payte)

Patenade (see Patnode)

Patenaude (see Patnode)

Patenotre (see Patnode)

Pateranski
Pateranski Surname Organization
1936 East Fifth Street
Ontario, CA 91764
Greg Legutki

Paterson (see Brown, Gregor)

Patin (see Johnson)

Patnode
Patnode/Patenade/Patenotre
    Clearinghouse
639 Pontiac Road
Oxford, MI 48371

Marie E. Pearce
Pub. *Our Patenaude, Patenotre Fathers*,
    quarterly, $5.00 per year subscription

Patt (see The Memorial Foundation of
    the Germanna Colonies)

Patt
Patt Family Association (Patts, Pett,
    Petts)
2 Off Schoosett Street
Pembrooke, MA 02359
Phone (617) 826-8032
Robert Patt
(mainly an early Rhode Island name back
    to the early to mid 1700s, and earlier
    in Townsend, Massachusetts and lower
    New Hampshire and Maine)

Patten (see McRae)

Patten
*Patten/Patton Exchange
1856 McDade Road
Augusta, GA 30906
Phone (706) 796-7828
Marjorie Abbott Braswell, Editor
Pub. *Patton Exchange Letter P.E.L.*,
    quarterly, queries free to members;
    (includes Patten and Patton)
$16.00 per year membership

Patterson (see Folk Family Surname
    Exchange, Bates, MacLaren,
    McBurney, Woodrow)

Patterson
*Kinseeker Publications
5697 Old Maple Trail
PO Box 184
Grawn, MI 49637
E-mail: AB064@taverse.lib.mi.us
Victoria Wilson, Editor
Pub. *Patterson People*, quarterly, $10.00
    per year subscription

Patterson
*Patterson/Tiner/Lemaster Reunion
3004 Abbott
Alamogordo, NM 88310
Phone (505) 434-1335
Phyllis Rhodes, Sponsor/Editor
Pub. *L-P Record*, quarterly, $2.00 per
    year subscription
Reunion in June of even-numbered years

Pattie (see MacDuff)

Pattison (see Heath, MacDuff)

Patton (see Gillean, MacLaine, Patten,
    Wright)

Patts (see Patt)

Pattullo (see Gregor, MacDuff)

Patural (see Blossom Press)

Paul (see Mackay)

Paul
*John Paul Family Organization, 1770–1828 of Chester County, South Carolina, 1809 of Lincoln County, Tennessee
HCR 62, Box 113A
Flippin, AR 72634-9710
Phone (501) 453-5286
Charlene Gillespie Deutsch, Compiler

Paulet (see Newton)

Paulitz (see The Memorial Foundation of the Germanna Colonies)

Paulk (see Maxwell, Pollock)

Paulson (see Mackay)

Paupard (see Pautard)

Pautard
*Pautard Surname Organization
5833 Dryden
West Palm Beach, FL 33415
Phone (407) 689-8819
Yves Pautard
Pub. *Pautard Families*, irregularly, $1.00 per issue; (includes Potard, Potar, Paupard back to 1571 in the center of France)

Pavarino
*Pavarino Surname Organization
3 Brazill Lane
Whitehall, MT 59759
Phone (406) 287-3369
Lindia Roggia Lovshin

Pawling (see DeHaven)

Paxman (see McCune)

Paxton
*Paxton Surname Organization
7705 Ensley Drive, S.W.
Huntsville, AL 35802-2845
Phone (205) 883-0207
Thomas W. Burns

Pay (see McCune)

Payne (see Lawrence, Wood)

Payrot (see Parrott)

Payson
Payson/Fogler Reunion
Rt. 1, Box 1280
Exeter, ME 04435
Ruth Goff

Payte (see Pate)

Peacock (see Maxwell)

Peacock
*Peacock Family Association of the South
1801 Sixth Avenue
Fort Worth, TX 76110-6404
Phone (817) 924-2574
Donald L. Peacock
Pub. *Peacock Paths*, quarterly; (includes descendants of Samuel Peacock and sons Samuel, John and William, and all southern Peacock lines)
$10.00 per year membership for households, includes three Peacock publications used for research; reunion

Peak (see Black)

Peak
*Peak, Peake Surname Exchange
PO Box 31
Del Mar, CA 92014
Phone (619) 756-3387
Carol J. Snow, Publisher

Peake (see Peak)

Pearce (see Allison)

Pearce
*Francis Pearce Family Organization
341 East Sixth Avenue
Durango, CO 81301
Phone (303) 247-3551
Deora L. Pierce Powell
(includes descendants Frances Pearce or Pierce (1740–1789), of Derry Township, Mifflin County, and son Obediah (1760–1835))

Pearce
*Pearce Organization
4314 S.W. 22nd Street
Ocala, FL 34474-1814
Phone (904) 237-2444
Margaret Pearce Pasteur, Editor
Pub. *Pearce Bulletin*, irregularly
Reunion

Pearcy
Pearcy-Piercy Family Association
9701 North 111th East Avenue
Owasso, OK 74055
Robert D. Pearcy, President
Pub. *Newsletter*, quarterly; (includes Pearcy, Peercy, Percy, Piercey, Piercy, etc.)

Pearl (see Jewett)

Pearman (see Golliher)

Pearson (see Golding, Gregor, Job, Macpherson, MacPherson)

Pearson
Pearsons Places and Things
PO Box 3225
Cullman, AL 35056-0325
Phone (205) 734-3640
Bettina Pearson Higdon Burns
Pub. *Pearsons Places and Things*, quarterly (December, March, June and September), $12.00 per year subscription, queries accepted; (includes Pearson, all spellings)

Pearson
Pearson
3312 East Costilla Avenue
Littleton, CO 80122
Ann Lisa Pearson
Pub. *Pearson*, quarterly, $12.00 per year subscription

Peary (see Perry)

Pease (see Nelson, Pasko, Reynolds)

Peat (see Gregor)

Peattie (see MacDuff)

Peavler
Peavler
6162 South Poplar
Englewood, CO 80111
Phone (303) 740-9051
Betty Lue Jones
Pub. *Peavler*, semiannually, free

Pechelux (see Merier)

Peck (see The Memorial Foundation of the Germanna Colonies, Anthes, Clark)

Peddie (see MacDuff)

Peddie
*Peddie Surname Organization
48 Clark Road
Chester, NH 03036
Phone (603) 887-3820
Janice E. Jeans, Chairperson

Peddycoart
Peddycoart Family Organization
287 Emory Drive
Arab, AL 35016
Jerry N. Peddycoart
Pub. *Peddycoart Family News*, quarterly
$10.00 per year membership

Peddycourt (see Archer)

Peden (see Gillean)

Pedersen (see Petersen, Usher)

Peebles (see Dockery, Hay)

Peek (see Henderson)

Peeples (see Hay)

Peercy (see Pearcy)

Peers (see Lush)

Peery (see Perry)

Peirce (see Barnard)

Pelas (see Blossom Press)

Pell (see Garner)

Pellard
*Pellard Family Association
PO Box 11251
San Bernardino, CA 92423
Phone (909) 864-7869
Peter E. Carr
Pub. *Pellard Newsletter*, annually, no
cost; (includes Pellard of France, all
periods)

Pellegal (see Blossom Press)

Pelletier
Pelletier Reunion
9 Pennwood Road
Winthrop, ME 04364
Robert G. Pelletier
(includes descendants of Guillaume
Pelletier, who arrived in North
America in 1641)

Pellien
*Pellien/Jaeger/Loretan/Steiner/Ross
Society
10435 West Concordia Avenue
Milwaukee, WI 53222
Phone (414) 259-1315;
(414) 771-8827 FAX
Paul Pellien, Vice President
Pub. *Buffalo Root News*, annually

Pemberton (see Meadows)

Pender (see Lynch, Marshall)

Pendland (see Penland)

Pendleton (see Goodenow)

Pendleton
Pendleton Clan
315 East Tenth Street
Baxter Springs, KS 66713-1612
Colleen Hodge Hearon, President and
Historian
Pub. *Pendleton Family Newsletter*,
semiannually
$10.00 per year membership; annual
reunion on second Saturday of June at
Mount Vernon, Missouri

Penfield (see Wright)

Penion (see Cowart)

Penland
*Penland Historical Society, Inc.
3356 S.E. Azalea
Port Orchard, WA 98366
Phone (206) 876-1932
Gordon Penland, President and Publisher
Pub. *Penland Historical Society, Inc.,
Bulletin*, quarterly; (includes Pendland,
Penland and Pentland)
$10.00 per year membership for
individuals, $15.00 per year
membership for families

Penman (see Armstrong, Hutchison)

Penn (see Folk Family Surname
Exchange, Links Genealogy
Publications, Warren)

Pennfeather (see Cian)

Pennington (see Cowart)

Pennington
Pennington Research Association
202 East Lamar Street
Hollis, OK 73550
Fannie M. Mitchell
Pub. *Pennington Pedigrees*,
semiannually; *Pennington Cousins'
Courier*, semiannually
$20.00 per year membership

Pennington
Pennington
1722 Spring Lake Drive
Arlington, TX 76012
Mary A. Kirby, Editor
Pub. *Pennington*, semiannually, $20.00
per year subscription

Penny (see Corson)

Pennybaker (see Folk Family Surname
Exchange)

Penround (see Pyne)

Pentland (see Penland)

Peoples (see Hay)

Peppard
Peppard People
445 East 70th Street
Kansas City, MO 64131
Stan Lawson
Pub. *Peppard People*

Peppard
*Peppard Family Association
PO Box 507
West Salem, OH 44287
Jean Shaffer

Pepper (see Drewry)

Pera (see Andreossi)

Percival (see Jardine)

Percy (see Pearcy)

Perego (see Perrigo)

Peregy (see Perrigo)

Perez (see Blossom Press)

Perigo (see Surname Sources)

Periman
*Periman Pathways Family Association
1314 West Glenn
Springfield, IL 62704

Phone (217) 546-4591
Ida Periman Miller, Newsletter
Coordinator
Pub. *Periman Pathways Newsletter*,
quarterly, $12.50 per year subscription;
(includes all spellings of the name, i.e.
Periman, Perriman, Perryman and
others)

Perin (see Perrin)

Perkin (see Cian)

Perkins (see Brown, Cian, Catlow,
Corson, Gant, Haynes)

Perkins
*Compu-Chart
363 South Park Victoria Drive
Milpitas, CA 95035-5708
Phone (408) 262-1051
Paula Perkins Mortensen
Pub. *Perkins Family Newsletter*,
quarterly, $10.00 per year subscription

Perkins
*Matilda Talbert-DeLaney-Perkins
Interntational
PO Box 167365
Irving, TX 75016-7365
Allie Simmons
Biennial reunion in odd-numbered years

Perkinson (see Bosher)

Perlander (see Blossom Press)

Peron (see Perrin)

Perratt (see Parrott)

Perrett (see Parrott)

Perrigo (see Surname Sources)

Perrigo
Perrigo/Perego/Peregy Family
(887 Pinecreek, Middleville, MI 49333-
9118—summer address)
4918 2 A Street, East (winter address)
Bradenton, FL 33507
Phone (906) 248-5462
Robert E. Bishop

Perriman (see Periman)

Perrin
Perrin Publications
2771 Pinesboro Drive, N.E.
Grand Rapids, MI 49505-3011
Phone (616) 363-3915
Mary Perrin, President
Pub. *Perrin Profiles*, quarterly (March,
June, September and December),
$10.00 per year subscription; (includes
Paren, Parin, Perin, Peron, Perrine,
Perring and Pirren)

Perrine (see Perrin)

Perring (see Perrin)

Perritt (see Parrott)

Perron (see Johnson)

Perrot (see Parrott)

Perrott (see Parrott)

Perrotte (see Parrot)

Perrutt (see Parrott)

Perry (see Folk Family Surname
    Exchange, Dean, Dutcher, Frasher,
    Lewis)

Perry
*Perry and Long Genealogy
2830 Garden Street
North Fort Myers, FL 33917
Phone (941) 995-7417
Elwell H. Perry
(includes descendants of Ezra Perry
    Sandwich from 1646)

Perry
Up! Perry-Scope
Rt. 1, Box 171B
Hermon, NY 13652
Phone (315) 347-3221
Mary Hadlock Smallman, Editor
Pub. *Up! Perry-Scope*, quarterly, $8.00
    per year subscription; (includes Peery,
    Peary, etc.)

Perryman (see Periman)

Pers (see Barnard)

Persel (see Purcell)

Person (see Macpherson)

Persons (see Parsons)

Pessner
*Richard Pessner Family Organization
915 East 1600 South
Mapleton, UT 84664
Phone (801) 489-9877
Beverly Jean Pessner Arbon
(includes related surnames from
    Germany: Gebhard, Goede (Gaede),
    Jahrhau and Krille; and from England:
    Evans, Hibberd, Humphrey, Palmer,
    Parsons and Warner)

Peter (see Gregor)

Peterkin (see Gregor)

Peters (see Links Genealogy
    Publications, Frantz, Gregor, Schaffer)

Peters
Peters/Wallace/Rentz/Moss Family
    Reunion
1926 Williams Avenue
Natchitoches, LA 71457-9701
Mrs. O. Moss Storey

Petersen (see McCune, Peterson)

Petersen
*Caroline Petersen Family Organization
2230 North 4000 West
Delta, UT 84624
Phone (801) 864-3674
Nancy B. Fowles

Peterson (see Boodry, Goodenow,
    Gregor, Kunkel, Newcomb)

Peterson
*Peterson/sen Book
3444 North Wolters
Fresno, CA 93726-5922
Phone (209) 224-9503
Betty V. Dearing, Family Historian
(includes descendants of Peder Hansen,
    Norwegian immigrant, also the
    Johannes Nord family of Rice Lake,
    Wisconsin)
Biennial reunion

Peterson
*Fredrich and Ane M. Peterson Family
    Organization
938 North 450 East
Ogden, UT 84404
Phone (801) 782-9538
Anna Marilda Christensen Sherman
(includes Peterson and Larsen or
    Johansen)

Petri (see Wright)

Petrie (see Barnard, Gregor, Steers)

Pett (see Patt)

Pettey (see Wright)

Petticrew (see Pettigrew)

Pettierie (see Pride)

Pettigrew
Pettigrew-Petticrew-Cochran(e)-Cockrell
    Family Association
2306 Westgate
Houston, TX 77019
Phone (713) 529-2333
Harold Helm
$25.00 plus pedigree and family group
    sheets for membership

Pettijohn (see Folk Family Surname
    Exchange)

Pettijohn
*Dyer Burgess Pettijohn Family
1303 North 39th Street
Nampa, ID 83687

Phone (208) 466-5821
Ann Tomlinson
Reunion every three years

Pettingill
*The Descendants of Richard Pettingell
339 Murray Avenue
Camarillo, CA 93010
Phone (805) 484-0974
Lewis Pettingill, Chairman
Pub. *The Pettingell Newsletter*, quarterly;
    (includes all descendants of the
    surname Pettingill, all variations in
    spelling)
$10.00 per year membership

Pettit (see Rowe)

Petts (see Patt)

Pettus (see Folk Family Surname
    Exchange)

Petty (see Surname Database, Cowart,
    Wright)

Peugh (see Seward)

Pevey (see Antley)

Peyton (see Rutherford, Stone)

Peyton
*The Peyton Society of Virginia
PO Box 128
Rapidan, VA 22733-0128
Phone (703) 672-2943
George Mason Peyton, Secretary
Pub. *The Peyton Society of Virginia
    Newsletter*, semiannually (October and
    February); (regular membership in the
    society restricted to descendants of a
    Peyton living in Virginia in the
    eighteenth century, associate
    membership for research in progress or
    surviving spouse)
$15.00 per year regular or associate
    membership, $200.00 life membership
    for persons under fifty years of age,
    $150.00 life membership for persons
    fifty years of age or older; annual
    meeting on the third weekend of May
    at Aquia Church, Stafford County,
    Virginia

Pfarr (see Pharr)

Pfoutz (see Stoner)

Phegley (see Heath)

Phelps (see Fuller, Wells)

Phelps
*Phelps Connections
3290 Cebada Canyon Road
Lompoc, CA 93436-9675
Phone (805) 736-8627
Margaret Phelps Swanson, Genealogist
    and Editor

Pub. *Phelps Connections*, quarterly
(January, April, July and October),
$17.50 per calendar year subscription
to A. Arnold Sprague, Treasurer, 808
Fairfield Drive, Knoxville, TN 37919-
4109; (includes all Phelps of the U.S.
and Canada from 1630 to the present)
Reunion

Phelps
*Phelps Family Association of America
1002 Queen Street
Camden, SC 29020-3113
Phone (803) 432-8432
Dallas Leroy Phelps, President/Editor
Pub. *Phelps Family News*, monthly,
$20.00 per year subscription; (includes
Felps, Felts and Pheps)

Phelps
John Phelps and Nathaniel Swingley
Descendants
8552 19th Avenue, N.W.
Seattle, WA 98117-3518
G. Merritt

Pheps (see Phelps)

Pherson (see MacPherson)

Philbrick
*Philbrick/Philbrook Family
Organization
PO Box 1431
Ferndale, CA 95536-1431
Phone (707) 786-9358
Joseph L. Philbrick, Ph.D.
Pub. *Phi-Byte:*, quarterly; (includes
English ancestry, Felbrigg/Philbrick/
Filbrick; also computer database of all
Philbrick/Philbrook families since
1635 in the U.S.)
$25.00 per year membership

Philbrook (see Philbrick)

Philby (see Filby)

Philen
*Stone Circle Press
PO Box 941115
Atlanta, GA 30341
Dan L. Philen, Editor and Publisher
Pub. *Philen Family News*, semiannually,
$4.00 per year subscription

Philips (see Phillips)

Phillips (see Catlow, Corson, Cox,
Curnutte, Durham, Gant, Golding,
Goodenow, Hatfield, Heath, Hyatt,
Looney, McCune, Moody, Nettles,
Reeder)

Phillips
Phillips/Fine Family of Cullman,
Alabama
6421 U.S. Highway 31
Hanceville, AL 35077
Delton D. Blalock

Phillips
*Phillips Family Finder
3394 Areca Palm Avenue
Melbourne, FL 32901
Wilam Ingersoll, Editor
Pub. *Phillips Family Finder*, quarterly,
$16.00 per year subscription; (includes
Philips, all dates and places)

Phillips
*Jonathan P. and Thomas Crow Phillips
Family Organization
3735 Hotze Road
Salem, IL 62881
Phone (618) 548-5216
Kirby Phillips, President
(includes descendants of Jonathan P.
Phillips (1799–1856) and Sarah Fowler
(1806 Davidson County, Tennessee-
Centralia, Illinois), and Thomas Crow
Phillips and Eliza Mildred Chadwell)
Annual two-day reunion on the first
weekend of August

Phillips
*Phillips Family Association
1508 West 17
Hutchinson, KS 67501
Phone (316) 662-5906
Donald F. Phillips
Pub. *Phillips News Letter*, quarterly;
(includes Ely, Green County,
Pennsylvania)
$12.50 per year membership

Phillips
*The USA Phillips Families
1927 South Seventh Street
Chickasha, OK 73018
Phone (405) 224-6927
Dale F. Phillips
(includes descendants of George Phillips
and wives Susannah Dyer and Anne
Brown of Greene County, Tennessee,
1829)
Annual reunion

Phillips
Phillips
6204 South Halifax Avenue
Edina, MN 55424-1914
Nancy J. Pennington, President
Pub. *Phillips*, quarterly, $10.00 per year
subscription
Reunion

Phin (see MacDuff)

Phinn (see MacDuff)

Phoenix (see Fenix, Helm)

Phyllips (see Jett)

Piacun (see Blossom Press)

Piatt
*The Piatt Family Newsletter
655 Orange Court
Rockledge, FL 32955

Phone (407) 636-6217
Eleanore Lynn White
Pub. *The Piatt Family Newsletter*,
monthly, $20.00 per year subscription;
(includes all spellings)
Annual reunion on the third week of June
at Dickenson College, Carlisle,
Pennsylvania

Pickens (see Sneed, Wright)

Pickett (see Chamberlain, Piggot)

Pickles (see Duxbury)

Pidgeon
Pidgeon Clearinghouse
236 Villa Road
Twin Falls, ID 83301-8030
Juvanne Clezie

Pieper (see Flowers)

Piepers
Piepers of Wisconsin Family Association
PO Box 75
Emden, IL 62635
Frank Pieper
Pub. *Pieper News*, three times per year

Pierce (see Surname Sources, Hyatt,
Kunkel, Pearce, Waterous)

Pierce
*Sherman N. Pierce Reunion
PO Box 264
Neodesha, KS 66757-0264
Mr. Gene P. Ewert
(includes descendants of Sherman N.
Pierce and Sarah Ann Baughan)
Annual reunion on the fourth Sunday of
June

Pierce
Thomas and Almy (Chase) Pierce
Research
14021 Saddle River Drive
North Potomac, MD 20878
Phone (301) 340-3315
Ronald P. Milberg

Pierce
*George Pierce Family Database
5766 Ozone Circle
Salt Lake City, UT 84118-7725
Phone (801) 969-6727
Geraldine Mae "Jerrye" Shipley Stillman

Piercey (see Pearcy)

Piercy (see Folk Family Surname
Exchange, Pearcy)

Piersol (see Kahler)

Pierson (see Ross)

Pierson
Pierson Reunion
26 Baker's Hill Road
Weston, MA 02193
Christopher D. Pierson
(includes descendants of Darius Pierson
(1766–1823) and Eunice Kitchel
(1766–1863))

Pietrusiewicz
*Pietrusiewicz Family Organization
6423 North Nordica
Chicago, IL 60631
Phone (312) 763-5014
Arthur Pietrusiewicz

Pigg
A Pigg Family Newsletter
Possum Trot Road
Rt. 1, Box 422
Manchester, KY 40962
Pub. *A Pigg Family Newsletter*

Pigniolo (see Blossom Press)

Pignioloa (see Blossom Press)

Pigsley (see Pixley)

Pigsly (see Pixley)

Pike (see Catlow)

Piland (see Peylont)

Pilant (see Peylont)

Pilgrim
Pilgrim
5892 Karen Avenue
Cypress, CA 90630
Rod Bush
Pub. *Pilgrim*, quarterly, $12.00 per year
subscription

Pilkington (see Brown)

Pillon (see Folk Family Surname
Exchange)

Pillow
*Descendants of David Pillow and
Elizabeth (Snider) Mullenax
RD 2, Box 128A
Harrisville, WV 26362
Phone (304) 643-2540
Rev. Donald E. Richards
Annual reunion on the second Sunday of
August in Ritchie County, West
Virginia

Pinckney (see Surname Sources)

Pinegar (see Folk Family Surname
Exchange)

Pineo (see Greenlaw)

Pinion (see Cowart)

Pinkerton (see MacDuff)

Pinkerton
*Pinkerton Surname Organization
7709 Persimmon Tree Lane
Bethesda, MD 20817
Phone (301) 365-0607
Capt. Richard Pinkerton
(restricted to U.S. families (affiliated
with Pinkerton Surname Organization,
Columbia, Missouri))

Pinkerton
*Pinkerton Surname Organization
1014 Westport Drive
Columbia, MO 65203-0744
Phone (573) 445-2052
Marjorie J. Pinkerton
(restricted to non-U.S. families)

Pinney (see Johnston)

Pinney
*Pinney Depository
575 Stone Jug Road
Lewisberry, PA 17339-9178
Phone (717) 432-2611
Neil V. McGahen
(all branches and emigrants)

Pinson (see Clark, Futral, Golding)

Piotrowski
*Piotrowski Surname Organization
3084 Lakeshore Road
Manistee, MI 49660
Donald Harter, Jr.

Piper (see Murray)

Pipkin
*Pipkin Family Association
2023 Lawrence
Leavenworth, KS 66048
Phone (913) 682-1717
William Phillip Pipkin, Editor
Pub. *Pipkin Family Association
Newsletter*, bimonthly
$5.00 per year membership

Pirratt (see Parrott)

Pirren (see Perrin)

Pirrett (see Parrott)

Pirritt (see Parrott)

Pirrott (see Parrott)

Pirrutt (see Parrott)

Pitcairn (see Graham, MacDuff)

Pitman
Pitman/Pittman Newsletter
2116 Shady Brook Drive
Bedford, TX 76021
Phone (817) 267-1645
Frances Pittman Malcolm

Pub. *Pitman/Pittman Newsletter*,
quarterly, $15.00 per year subscription
Reunion

Pitre (see Johnson)

Pittenger (see Pigg)

Pittenger
*Nicholas Thomas Pittenger Family
Organization
4840 Wyandot
Denver, CO 80221
Phone (303) 433-3769
Mary E. Tudder, Family Genealogist
(includes Pittenger, Hettrick, Roberts of
Pennsylvania 1800, Virginia 1825,
West Virginia 1798, Indiana 1829,
Illinois 1837, Colorado 1902)
SASE

Pittenweem (see MacDuff)

Pittman (see Lynch, Pitman)

Pittman
*Pittman Family History
1041 Ven Villa Road
Marietta, GA 30062-2901
Phone (770) 971-2411
B. E. Pittman
(includes descendants of William
Dahlonegy Pittman (1814–1902),
oldest child of Edward Pittman (1785–
1861) and Temperance Barker Pittman
(1800–1863))

Pittman
Pittman National Reunion
Rt. 1, Box 227
Tylertown, MS 39667
James C. Pittman

Pitts (see Corson)

Pitts
*Pitts Family Reunion (Descendants of
John Pitts 1783)
PO Box 22
Hermitage, MO 65668
Phone (417) 745-6770
Leo H. Pitts
Pub. *Pitts Family Newsletter*,
semiannually
$5.00 per year membership

Pitts*
Pitts Organization
2616 West Jean
Springfield, MO 65803

Pittsley (see Pixley)

Pixlee (see Pixley)

Pixley
*Pixley Family Association
517 Camellia Lane
Vero Beach, FL 32963

Phone (407) 231-5536; E-mail:
  75273.2651@compuserve.com
Clifford Reuter, Editor and Publisher
Pub. *Pixley Press*, bimonthly; (includes
  Pigsley, Pigsly, Pittsley, Pixlee)
$6.00 per year membership

Place
*Edward Place and John Place/Maria and
  Margaret Fenniger Family Association
704 Engelwood Avenue
Waterloo, IA 50701-6134
Phone (319) 233-0251
Bev Place Jenson
(includes descendants of Edward Place
  and his wife, Maria Louisa Fenniger,
  John Place and his wife, Margaret
  Fenniger)

Plain (see Stoner)

Plaisance (see Augeron)

Plamann (see Kunkel)

Plank (see Dean, Sutter)

Plantagenet (see Folk Family Surname
  Exchange)

Plarr (see Wagner)

Plasse (see Waters)

Platt (see Rothenberger)

Platt
*Platt Family Association
132 Platt Lane
Milford, CT 06460
Phone (203) 878-6094
Richard N. Platt, Jr., President
Pub. *Platt Newsletter*, quarterly;
  (includes descendants of Richard Platt
  (1604–1685) of Ware, Hertfordshire,
  England, and Milford, Connecticut,
  and Mary Wood; also Thomas Platt (ca
  1690–1742) of Burlington, New
  Jersey)
$10.00 per year membership, $15.00 per
  year membership for families

Plattenberger (see Blattenberger)

Plauche (see Johnson)

Playfair (see MacDuff)

Pleasants (see McRae)

Plejtes (see Links Genealogy
  Publications)

Ploetz (see Schaffer)

Plomer (see Plummer)

Plum (see Plummer)

Plumb (see Clark, Plummer)

Plumb
Plumb Orchard
34080 West 86th Trail
DeSoto, KS 66018
Phone (913) 585-3160
Ken Plumb

Plumer (see Plummer)

Plummer (see Blossom Press, Nelson)

Plunket (see Cian)

Plunkett (see Cian, Plunket)

Plutko
Plutko Family Newsletter
6862 Palmer Court
Chino, CA 91710-7343
Ray Plutko, Family Historian
Pub. *Plutko Family Newsletter*, annually,
  no charge

Plymale (see Anthes)

Plymer (see Plummer)

Plympton (see Newton)

Poage
Poage Papers
13546 Dahlia Court
Rosemount, MN 55068-3378
Jeff Williamson, Editor
Pub. *Poage Papers*, three times per year,
  $12.00 per year subscription

Poague (see Pollock)

Poalk (see Pollock)

Poalke (see Pollock)

Pobst (see Pabst)

Pobst
Pobst-Richardson Family Reunion
45 Hudgins Road
Poquoson, VA 23662-2001
Phone (757) 868-9346
Lucille R. McMillan, Publisher
(includes descendants of Charles Elisha
  Pobst (1842–1929) and Maria
  Elizabeth Moomaw (1843–1904), also
  of James Muse Richardson (1815–
  1895) and Narcissa T. Wills (1816–
  1893)
Annual reunion in Thaxton, Virginia

Pocahontas (see Rolfe)

Pockhoy (see Links Genealogy
  Publications)

Pocock
*Pocock Surname Organization
6750 East Main Street, #106
Mesa, AZ 85205-9049
Warren D. Steffey

Poe
Poe Pages
Rt. 2, Box 671
Grangeville, ID 83530-9635
Phone (208) 983-0515
Anne Long
Pub. *Poe Pages*, irregularly, $6.50 per
  year (Idaho residents add 5% sales
  tax); (includes Powe)

Poe
*Poe/Hamilton and Allied Families
4252 Eagle Lake Drive
Indianapolis, IN 46257
Sherry Milnamon
(includes descendants of George Jacob
  Poe (1715–1762) of Maryland)
Reunion every five years on the third
  Sunday of August

Pogue (see Pollock)

Poindexter (see Andrews)

Poindexter
Poindexter Family Organization
Rt. 3, Box 123
Trinity, NC 27370
Cheryl Burrow

Poindexter
Poindexter Descendants Association
  (Poingdestra)
5378 East 26th Street
Tulsa, OK 74114
Richard Colby Poindexter, Sr., President

Poingdestra (see Poindexter)

Points (see Ousley)

Poisson (see Possien)

Pole (see Mackay)

Poleson (see Mackay)

Politano (see Gratta)

Polk (see Maxwell, Pollock)

Polk
Polk Family Reunion
(James K. Polk Home, West Seventh
  Street—location)
PO Box 741 (mailing address)
Columbia, TN 38401
Phone (615) 388-2368
Mrs. J. L. Whiteside, Genealogy
  Chairman
(includes Polk, any date, any place)
Biennial reunion in even-numbered years

Polk
*Polk Family
550 Farmers Road
Brenham, TX 77833-9131
Phone (409) 830-9199
Burney Parker, Jr., Coordinator

Polk
Bridges and Trails
5139 Hacienda Drive
San Antonio, TX 78233-5424
Nancy L. King, Editor
Pub. *Bridges and Trails*, quarterly,
$15.00 per year subscription, $4.00 per
issue, queries accepted; (includes Polk,
Polke, Poulk and Poulke families in
America from 1672)

Polke (see Polk, Pollock)

Poll
Poll Family Association (Aaldericnk-
Nugteren-Ryerkerk)
349 Ethel Drive
Nicholasville, KY 40356
Justin Poll

Pollard (see Likes, Mackay)

Polley (see Surname Sources)

Pollock (see Maxwell)

Pollock
James and Rachel Pollock Family
Reunion
PO Box 116
Mansfield, IL 61854
Phone (217) 489-5781
Helen Folk
Annual reunion on the last Sunday of
July at Salem, Indiana

Pollock
*Clan Pollock
1271 Saint Clair Drive
Middletown, KY 40243
Phone (502) 245-0091
Richard H. Pollock, President
Pub. *The Pollag*, quarterly; (includes
Paulk, Poalk, Poalke, Pogue, Polk,
Polke, Pollock, Pollok, Pook, Poolke
and Poulk, originally from
Renfrewshire, Scotland)
$10.00 per year membership

Pollock
*Lineage Search Associates
7315 Colts Neck Road
Mechanicsville, VA 23111-4233
Phone (804) 730-7414 (8:00 A.M.–10:00
P.M.); (800) 728-1935; E-mail:
pollockme@aol.com
Michael E. Pollock, President
Pub. *Pollock Potpourri*, quarterly, $12.50
per year subscription; unlimited free
queries for subscribers, $1.00 per
query for all others; (includes Poague,
Polk, Pogue, Paulk, etc., with many
Scottish lines descending from Fulbert
de Pollock)

Pollok (see Maxwell, Pollock)

Polly (see Sullivan Surname Exchange)

Pomeroy (see Clark, Wright)

Pomfrett (see Folk Family Surname
Exchange)

Pomroy (see Folk Family Surname
Exchange)

Poncy (see Pontius)

Pond
Pond Papers
13546 Dahlia Court
Rosemount, MN 55068-3378
Jeff Williamson, Editor
Pub. *Pond Papers*, three times per year,
$12.00 per year subscription

Ponder
*Ponder Clearinghouse
2881 Pruneridge Avenue
Santa Clara, CA 95051
Phone (408) 248-4970
Robert Gardner, Researcher

Ponthieu (see Johnson)

Pontious (see Pontius)

Pontius
*Pontius Family Association
2009 Garden Drive
Niskayuna, NY 12309-2309
Phone (518) 374-1965; (518) 374-4453
(FAX)
James W. Pontius, Archivist
Pub. *Bridge Builder*, semiannually;
Pontius Family Association Newsletter,
quarterly; (includes Poncy, Punches,
Pontious, Pontzius and all other
spellings in the U.S. and Germany)
$7.50 per year membership, $14.00 for
two years membership, $20.00 for
three years membership, $3.00 per
year for junior membership (under 21,
does not include publications)

Pontzius (see Pontius)

Pook (see Pollock)

Pool (see Evans)

Pool
Edward Pool of Muddy Creek, NC,
Family Association
4550 Sardis Church Road
Macon, GA 31206
Phone (912) 788-1489
William L. Poole, Historian
Annual reunion on the fourth Sunday of
July at Galax, Virginia

Pool
*William Wesley Pool/Poole Family
Organization
4406 Medford Lane
Tifton, GA 31794
Phone (912) 386-0520
Connie P. Bozeman
(includes interest in descendants of
William Wesley Poole (1820 SC–?),

son of Nancy Poole (–Jackson, Butts
County, Georgia), and his wife Jane
Nelson (1828–?) of Butts, Marion and
Schley counties, Georgia, and their son
John Wesley Pool, who went to Texas
and was never heard from again)
Annual reunion on the second Sunday of
August

Poole (see Pool)

Poolke (see Pollock)

Poovey (see Moser)

Pope (see Emery, Moser, Pabst)

Pope
Pope Family Association
718 Sims Avenue
Saint Paul, MN 55106
Phone (612) 771-7060
Wiley R. Pope
Pub. *Pope Family Register*, quarterly
$6.00 per year membership

Popich (see Blossom Press)

Poppy (see Clark, Likes)

Porche (see Johnson)

Poret (see Johnson)

Porratt (see Parrott)

Porrett (see Parrott)

Porritt (see Parrott)

Porrott (see Parrott)

Porrutt (see Parrott)

Port (see Heath)

Porteous (see Porterfield)

Porter (see Sullivan Surname Exchange,
Brown, Macnachton, McCune,
Onsager, Sawyer)

Porter
*Nancy L. Childress Services
3709 West Gardenia
Phoenix, AZ 85051-8266
Phone (602) 841-7478
Nancy L. Porter Childress, Owner and
Editor
Pub. *Porter Settlements*, quarterly,
$12.00 per year subscription

Porterfield (see Allison, Helm)

Porterfield
Porterfield-Porteous-Cunningham-
Lockhart Family Association
2306 Westgate
Houston, TX 77019
Phone (713) 529-2333

Harold Helm
$25.00 plus pedigree and family group
   sheets for membership

Portman (see McCleave)

Posey (see Gray, Wapello)

Posey
Posey
275 West 1200 North
Orem, UT 84057-2610
Robert Posey
Pub. *Posey*, quarterly, $25.00 per year
   subscription

Possan (see Possien)

Possien
*Possien Surname Database
45 First Street
Pequannock, NJ 07440
Donald C. Possien
(includes descendants of Joseph Louis
   Possien who arrived in New York City
   in 1855 from Le Havre, France;
   variants: Poisson, Possan, Pouchin,
   Poussin, Poussineau, Fish)

Postell (see Dockery)

Potar (see Pautard)

Potard (see Pautard)

Pottenger
Pottenger/Pottinger Reunion
937 Parkway Drive
Louisville, KY 40217
Phone (502) 634-0969
Mary Pottinger Barr
(includes descendants of immigrant John
   Pottenger (1662–1735) of Prince
   George's County, Maryland)
Annual reunion on the second weekend
   of October

Pottenger
Pottenger Family of Southwest Ohio
5463 Schiering Drive
Fairfield, OH 45014
Frank Steig, Jr.

Potter (see Barnes, Corson, Goodenow)

Potter
*Potter Family Organization
5697 Millstone Drive
Boise, ID 83714-1645
Phone (208) 375-5060
Halford F. Potter

Potter
Potter Profiles
2204 West Houston
Spokane, WA 99208-4440
Phone (509) 326-2089
Donna Potter Phillips
Pub. *Potter Profiles*, irregularly, $7.00
   per issue

Potthast
Potthast
Whispering Oaks
5821 Rowland Hill Road
Cascade, MD 21719-1939
Phone (301) 416-2660
Victor Gebhart, President
Pub. *Potthast*, annually, $2.00 per issue

Pottinger (see Pottenger)

Potts (see Folk Family Surname
   Exchange, Links Genealogy
   Publications, Brown)

Potts
*The Sylvia Potts Family Organization
7475 S.W. 102nd Avenue
Beaverton, OR 97008-6512
Phone (503) 644-3795
JoAnn Gwinn, Founder
(includes descendants of Lorenzo Potts
   and Hester Milner of Jackson County,
   Ohio, 1850, and James M. Dunham
   and Sylvia Potts of Pike County, Ohio,
   1900–1920)
Send SASE for reply

Pouchin (see Possien)

Poulk (see Polk, Pollock)

Poulke (see Polk)

Pounds (see Harrison)

Poussin (see Possien)

Poussineau (see Possien)

Powe (see Poe)

Powell (see Adams, Cian, Reeder)

Powell
Three Sisters Publications
Rt. 1, Box 201
Green Forest, AR 72638
Pub. *Powell*, quarterly, $10.00 per year
   subscription

Powell
From Generation to Generation
Rt. 1, Box 147
Buncombe, IL 62912
Melody Tellor, Editor
Pub. *Powell People*, quarterly, $15.00 per
   year subscription

Powell
*Rootdiggers, Inc.
PO Box 85
Roundup, MT 59072
Phone (406) 323-1047; (406) 323-1641
Norma J. Powell Jeffery
(includes descendants of Charles and
   Rebecca (Conger) Powell)

Powell
*The Powell Memorial Society
7050 S.E. Morrison
Portland, OR 97215
April Ober
(includes descendants of three brothers
   and a sister: John Alkire Powell (and
   wife Savilla Smith), Noah Powell (and
   wife Mary Smith), Alfred Powell (and
   wives Sarah Bracken, Hannah Goble
   Shirrell, Abigal Lane, and Mary
   Cooper Churchill), and Lucinda
   Powell (husband Anthony Propst), who
   came to Oregon in 1851 and 1852
   from Menard County, Illinois)
Annual reunion on the fourth Sunday of
   June in Oregon

Powell
*James Powell Family Organization
5448 Colter Drive
Kearns, UT 84118
Phone (801) 969-2373
Tyrone T. Powell, President
(includes Powell, 1682–1852 of
   Pennsylvania, North Carolina,
   Missouri, Iowa and Utah; Musgrave,
   1720–1770 of Pennsylvania and North
   Carolina)

Powell
*Powell Surname Organization
James Quaintance Powell Family
   Organization
6262 South Westridge
Murray, UT 84107
Phone (801) 266-4904
Mary L. S. Putnam

Powell
Powell Pursuit
323 Cedarcrest Court East
PO Box 779
Napavine, WA 98565-0779
Phone (360) 262-3300
Ruby Simonson McNeill
Pub. *Powell Pursuit*, irregularly, $5.75
   plus $2.00 postage per issue

Power (see Cian)

Powers (see Goodenow, Johnson, Ross)

Powers
Parker Talbot Powers Descendants
   Association
PO Box 157
Knightsen, CA 94548
Carolyn Sherfy

Powers
Powers-Gambler-Tuckahoe-Kimball
   Family Association
2306 Westgate
Houston, TX 77019
Phone (713) 529-2333
Harold Helm
$25.00 plus pedigree and family group
   sheets for membership

Poyntz (see Ousley)

Praa (see Prall)

Praal (see Prall)

Prael (see Prall)

Prahl (see Prall)

Prall
*Prall Family Association
14104 Piedras Road, N.E.
Albuquerque, NM 87123-2323
Phone (505) 299-8386
Richard D. Prall, Editor
Pub. *The Prall Newsletter*, quarterly;
(includes De Prael, DePraelles, de
Praulle, Du Prael, Parall, Praa, Praal,
Prael, Prahl, Praul, Praulx, Prawl,
Prayle, Preaulx and allied families,
almost all descending from Arendt
Jansen Prall (ca 1627–1725 Staten
Island, New York))
$12.00 per year membership

Prater
Praters in My Pocket
12600 Bissonnet A4-407
Houston, TX 77099
Dede D. Mercer, Publisher
Pub. *Praters in My Pocket*, semiannually,
$20.00 per year subscription; (all
variations of the surname, worldwide)

Prather (see Kunkel)

Prather
Prather Bulletin
PO Box 206
Chillicothe, MO 64601
Elizabeth Prather Ellsberry
Pub. *Prather Bulletin*, bimonthly

Pratt (see Gant, Goodenow, McLouth)

Pratt
Pratts of Maryland Family Association
239 Bloor Street
Conneaut, OH 44030-2016
Ann Grant

Pratt
*Richard Pratt (d. 1822) Family of Bibb
County, Alabama
PO Box 582
Hurst, TX 76053
Phone (817) 282-5293
Chester R. Johnson, Genealogist
Annual reunion on the fourth of July at
Schultz Creek Baptist Church in Bibb
County

Pratuch
*Pratuch Family
PO Box 178
Merrifield, VA 22116-0178
Thomas G. Pratuch, Publisher

Praul (see Prall)

Praulx (see Prall)

Prawl (see Prall)

Pray (see Rutherford)

Pray
*International Pray Family Association
Lionside Business Services, Inc.
RR 2, Box 726
East Lebanon, ME 04027
Phone (207) 457-1482
Donald Everett Pray, Editor, Trustee and
Temporary President
Pub. *Pray Family Newsletter*, three times
per year (March, July and November)
$12.00 per year membership

Prayle (see Prall)

Preator
*Preator/Ault Family Organization
957 Gregory
Peculiar, MO 64078
Phone (816) 779-6333
Richard Preator

Preaulx (see Prall)

Preaux (see Priddy)

Preddy (see Priddy)

Predmore
*Predmore/Pridmore/Pridemore/
Pregmore Association
545 Jefferson
Kimberly, ID 83341
Phone (208) 423-4293
Howard Johnston, Secretary
Pub. *Predmore/Pridmore/Pridemore/
Pregmore Association Journal*,
quarterly; (includes Prigmore)
$20.00 per year membership

Preece (see Allen)

Pregmore (see Predmore)

Prejean (see Johnson)

Premak (see Primak)

Premm
*Premm Family Association
9190 Oak Leaf Way
Granite Bay, CA 95746
Phone (916) 791-0405
Linus Joseph Dewald
(includes descendants of Eliz. Premm
and John Eyanson (Ironson, I'anson,
etc.) (ca 1720–))

Premock (see Primak)

Prentice
*Descendants of Valentine Prentice
9190 Oak Leaf Way
Granite Bay, CA 95746
Phone (916) 791-0405

Linus Joseph Dewald, Editor
Pub. *Valentine Prentice Newsletter*,
semiannually, free to donors of $25.00
or more to our PROVE fund; (includes
all descendants of Valentine Prentice,
who immigrated in 1631 to Boston)

Prescott (see Rothenberger, Wright)

Prescott
*Ward Publishing Company
42 Larchmont Road
Asheville, NC 28804-2446
Phone (704) 254-3311; E-mail:
dclineward@aol.com
Doris Cline Ward, Owner and Editor
Pub. *Prescotts Unlimited*, quarterly
(March, June, September and
December), $10.50 per year
subscription, $4.00 per issue; (any
Prescotts, including ancestries of John
Prescott of Massachusetts, James of
New Hampshire, and John of Virginia)

Preslar (see Presley)

Presley
Presley/Preslar/Pressly Family Research
Association
1924 Dakota, N.E.
Albuquerque, NM 87110
Phone (505) 256-9041
Edwin C. Dunn, President
Pub. *The Presley/Preslar/Pressly
Newsletter*, quarterly, $10.00 per year
subscription; (includes Bressler,
Pressler, Priestley and Pursley)

Pressler (see Presley)

Pressly (see Presley)

Preston (see MacDuff, Tanner)

Preston
Preston Scoop
106 Mikel Court
Summerville, SC 29485
Doris J. O'Brien
Pub. *Preston Scoop*, bimonthly, $10.00
per year subscription

Pretty (see Priddy)

Prevost
*Association of Prevost-Provost Families
of America (Eastern)
L'Association des Prévost et Provost
d'Amérique
709 North Poplar Street
Creston, IA 50801-1740
Dr. Richard L. Provost, Membership
Secretary
Pub. *Le Prévostal*, quarterly; (includes
Preveaux, Prevo, Prévost, Prevot,
Prost, Proveaux, Provo, Provoost and
Provost, Provot)
$20.00 per year membership

Prewitt (see Pruitt)

Pribbenow (see Pribbeno)

Price (see Harless, McCune, Wert)

Price
Peneul Price and Jane Bryson
  Descendants Association
1545 Parish Place
Jacksonville, FL 32205
Phone (904) 388-3286
Marian Price Hart
(includes allied families of Beaty, Sadler
  and Bryson)
Annual reunion in September in
  Lincolnton, Georgia

Prichard (see Bagley)

Prickett (see Springer)

Priday (see Priddy)

Priddy (see Folk Family Surname
  Exchange)

Priddy
*Priddy Family Association
1015 Saint John Road
Elizabethtown, KY 42701
Phone (502) 737-8846
Pastor Fred G. Butler
(includes Priddy, Butler, Riggs, Choate,
  Bagwell and 200 other allied names)

Priddy
*Folk Family
PO Box 52048
Knoxville, TN 37950-2048
Hester E. Stockton, Owner; Vadie Priddy,
  Editor
Pub. *Priddy Press*, quarterly, $15.00 per
  year subscription, $5.00 per issue;
  (includes Preaux, Preddy, Pretty, Pride,
  Prideaux, Purdy)

Priddy
*Stockton Seekers
PO Box 52048
Knoxville, TN 37950-2048
Hester E. Stockton
Annual reunion in June at the Red River
  Valley Fairgrounds, Paris, Texas

Priddy
*Priddy People
PO Box 52048
Knoxville, TN 37950-2048
Hester E. Stockton
(includes all Preddy, Priday, Priddy,
  Prideaux, Pritty)
Annual reunion in June at the Red River
  Valley Fairgrounds, Paris, Texas

Pride (see Priddy)

Pride
*Pride Family Reunion
6611 West Mill Road
Evansville, IN 47720-2037
Phone (812) 963-5145
Margaret Pride, Chairman

Prideaux (see Priddy)

Pridemore (see Predmore)

Pridmore (see Predmore)

Priest
Priest
8210 North Seven Mile
Mesick, MI 49668
Jolene Kelly Pillars
Pub. *Priest*, quarterly, $18.00 per year
  subscription

Priestley (see Presley)

Prigmore (see Predmore)

Primack (see Primak)

Primak
*Primak Family Association
8505 Glenview Avenue
Takoma Park, MD 20912
Phone (301) 89-6621;
  (301) 589-1366 FAX
Barbara Levitz, Family Genealogist
(includes descendants of Primak family
  from White Russia, Vinnitsa,
  Havrilovka; includes Primack, Premak,
  Premock, Prymak, Spielberg and
  Spiel'berg)

Primrose (see Folk Family Surname
  Exchange, MacDuff)

Prindle (see Mueller)

Pringle (see Brengle)

Prior (see Lush)

Pritchard (see Moody, Preece, Pritchett)

Pritchett (see Pryor)

Pritchett
*Pritchett/ard Surname
PO Box 452
Many Farms, AZ 86538
Doris Melissa Pritchett Horlacher,
  Author, Researcher, Compiler,
  Publisher and Marketer
(includes descendants of Obediah, Sr.,
  and Margaret Pritchett/ard of Saint
  George Parish, Harford County,
  Maryland)

Pritty (see Priddy)

Probst (see Brown)

Proctor
Proctor Family Organization
8 Surrey Lane
West Peabody, MA 01960
A. Carlton Proctor
Pub. *Proctor Family Newsletter*,
  quarterly
$5.00 per year membership

Propst (see Powell)

Prosie (see The Memorial Foundation of
  the Germanna Colonies)

Prouce (see Prowse)

Proud (see Kunkel)

Proudfoot
*The World Proudfoot Genealogical
  Society
8702 Galena Drive
El Paso, TX 79904
Phone (915) 755-6684
Dorsey and Muriel Proudfoot
$3.00 per year membership for
  individuals, $6.00 per year
  membership for couples

Prouse (see Prowse)

Prouty
*Prouty Register
18538 Westlawn Street
Hesperia, CA 92345-6924
Ethel Mae Castelli, Secretary
Pub. *Newsletter*, quarterly
$3.00 membership

Provost (see Wright)

Prowse
Prowse Family History News
3417 Mansfield Road
Falls Church, VA 22041-1407
Norman J. Reid
Pub. *Prowse Family History News*,
  quarterly, $6.00 per year subscription;
  (includes Prouse and Prouce)

Prucheti (see Andreossi)

Prudhomme (see Johnson)

Prudhomme
Prudhomme Family Newsletter
PO Box 13548
Saint Louis, MO 63138
Maryann Schirker
Pub. *Prudhomme Family Newsletter*,
  quarterly, $25.00 per year subscription

Pruett (see Pruitt)

Pruit (see Eaves)

Pruitt (see Burrell)

Pruitt
*Pruitt Surname Organization
7705 Ensley Drive, S.W.
Huntsville, AL 35802-2845
Phone (205) 883-0207
Thomas W. Burns

Pruitt
*Pruitt/Prewitt Family Association
1800 N.W. 81st Street
Des Moines, IA 50325

Richard A. Pruitt
Pub. *Prewitt-Pruitt Newsletter*,
   semiannually (June and January)
$2.00 per year membership

Pruitt
*Pruitt/Black Family Reunion
124 Bent Tree Trail
Burleson, TX 76028
Phone (817) 295-6938
Mike Pruitt
(includes descendants of James Black,
   the blacksmith from Washington,
   Arkansas, who made the famous
   Bowie knife; database of 40,000 to
   50,000 Pruitt, Prewitt, Pruett names
   from all over the U.S. from 1700)

Prussia (see Lush)

Pruyn (see Barnard)

Pryde (see Pride)

Prymak (see Primak)

Pryor
*Pryor Clearinghouse
207 Auburn Drive
Dalton, GA 30720
Phone (706) 278-1504
Joseph Wiley Reid
(1400–1890 period)

Pryor
Courier Publications
PO Box 1284
Natchitoches, LA 71458-1284
Annette Carpenter Womack
Pub. *Pryor Family Courier*, quarterly,
   $10.00 per year subscription

Puckett (see Baughman, Graham)

Puffer (see Bassett)

Pullen (see Rutherford)

Pulley (see Lemon)

Pulliam
*The Pulliam Point
12600 Bissonnet A4-407
Houston, TX 77099
Dede D. Mercer, Publisher
Pub. *The Pulliam Point*, semiannually,
   $20.00 per year subscription; (all
   variations of the surname, worldwide)

Pulsipher (see Terry)

Pumphrey
The Pumphrey Family Association
809 Saint Dunstans Road
Baltimore, MD 21212
Phone (410) 433-0293
Patricia A. Pumphrey

Pumphrey
Pumphrey
2116 Holland Corner Road
Suffolk, VA 23437
Galen M. Pumphrey
Pub. *Pumphrey*, semiannually, $4.00 per
   year subscription
Biennial reunion in the Baltimore,
   Maryland, area

Punches (see Pontius)

Pund (see Miehls)

Purcell (see Cian, Montague, Rebele)

Purcell
*Purcell Family of America Genealogical
   Association
3929 Southview Avenue
Dayton, OH 45432-2121
Phone (513) 426-0460
Alice Crist Purcell, Editor
Pub. *Purcell Family of America
   Genealogical Association Journal*,
   quarterly (January, April, July and
   October, with index in October);
   (includes Persel, Pursel, Pursell,
   Pursley, etc.)
$15.00 per year membership

Purdy (see Daley, Priddy)

Purgley (see Blossom Press)

Purinton (see Chase)

Purratt (see Parrott)

Purrett (see Parrott)

Purritt (see Parrott)

Purrott (see Parrott)

Purrutt (see Parrott)

Pursel (see Purcell)

Pursell (see Purcell)

Pursley (see Presley, Purcell, Warren)

Purviance
*Purviance Family News and Notes
105 Washington Avenue, Space 29
Yakima, WA 98903
Phone (509) 575-0776
Elsie Eschbach, Co-editor
Pub. *Purviance Family News and Notes*,
   quarterly

Putman (see Allison, Golding)

Putman
Putman Family Organization
7526 Sixth Street
Rio Linda, CA 95673
Phone (916) 991-5597
Pub. *Putman Family*

Putman
*The Putman Family Newsletter
315 East Grant Street
Caro, MI 48723
Mark R. Putman
Pub. *The Putman Family Newsletter*,
   bimonthly, $15.00 per year
   subscription
$5.00 and SASE for search of database

Putnam (see Scott)

Putterbaugh (see Metzgar)

Putterbaugh
Putterbaugh/Butterbaugh Exchange
616 West High Street
Portland, IN 47371
Wilbur Linder
Pub. *Putterbaugh/Butterbaugh
   Newsletter*

Pyatt (see Graham)

Pye (see Graham)

Pyland (see Peylont)

Pylant (see Peylont)

Pylant
Pylant
1501 Road Camp Road
Ruston, LA 71270
Delaine M. Pylant
Pub. *Pylant*, semiannually, no charge
Reunion

Pyle (see Dawson, McRae, Way)

Pyles (see Bloss)

Pyne
*Pyne Family Descendants
7997 Windsail Court
Frederick, MD 21701
Phone (301) 695-3935
Frederick W. Pyne, Family Genealogist
Pub. *Letter*, irregularly; (includes English
   and American descendants of John
   Pyne (1533–1572) and Honor
   Penround of East Down, Devon)

Pyott (see Graham)

Pyper (see Murray)

Pyron (see Harris)

Pyron
*Pyron Reunion
5250 Helene Cove
Memphis, TN 38117
(includes descendants of William Riley
   Pyron (1824–1907))
Biennial reunion in Tennessee

Quackenbush
*Quackenbush Surname Organization
7024 Morgan Road
Greenwell Springs, LA 70739
Phone (504) 261-5515
Serena Abbess Haymon
(includes all spellings in Texas and the
    South)
No charge, registration required

Quaile (see Cian)

Quain (see Cian)

Quarals (see MacDuff)

Quarles (see Folk Family Surname
    Exchange)

Quarles
*Folk Family
PO Box 52048
Knoxville, TN 37950-2048
Hester E. Stockton, Owner; Aaron
    Quarles, Editor
Pub. *Quarles Queries*, quarterly, $15.00
    per year subscription, $5.00 per issue

Quarral (see MacDuff)

Quarrel (see MacDuff)

Quarrels (see MacDuff)

Quatrocchio (see Blossom Press)

Quatroy (see Blossom Press)

Quay (see Mackay)

Quealy (see McCune)

Queen (see Bloss

Queram (see Quiram)

Querelle (see Coryell)

Quesenberry (see Cox)

Quey (see Mackay)

Quick
Descendants of George R. and Mary L.
    (Drown) Quick Reunion
318 North Birchwood
Fremont, NE 68025
Norma J. Schutt

Quillen (see Kettenring)

Quilty (see Cian)

Quimby (see Corson)

Quinn (see McCune)

Quinteros (see Johnson)

Quiram
*Quiram Family Reunion
RR 1, Box 56A
Elysian, MN 56028
Phone (507) 362-8886
Noel Quiram
Biennial reunion at Waterville,
    Minnesota

Quiram
Quirams Unlimited
1040 East McCanse
Springfield, MO 65803-3613
Phone (417) 833-2814
Glen Gohr, Editor
Pub. *Quirams Unlimited*, semiannually,
    donation for subscription; (includes the
    surname Quirams and all variants of
    the name—Kwiram, Kwirant, Queram,
    Quirant, etc.—a German name which
    originated in eastern Germany, now
    Poland; some of this family migrated
    into Russia, Brazil and Canada)

Quirant (see Quiram)

Quirk
*Quirk(e) Surname Organization
2310 Juniper Court
Golden, CO 80401-8087
Phone (303) 526-1319
Terence T. Quirke, Jr., Ph.D., C.G.,
    Proprietor
(pre-1900, Ireland)

Quirke (see Quirk)

Quittner
*Clifford James Quittner Family
    Organization
1389 Kinsport Lane
San Jose, CA 95120
Phone (408) 268-5026
Linda Remund Quittner
Pub. *Quittner Family Organization*,
    irregularly
$10.00 per year membership for families

Quivey (see Withy)

Rabalais (see Johnson)

Rabb
*Rabb
510 Lakewood Circle
Colorado Springs, CO 80910
Phone (719) 574-4115
Victor Wegenhoft

Rabenhorst (see Hinz, Sager)

Rabun (see Gillaspie)

Racer (see The Memorial Foundation of
    the Germanna Colonies)

Rackett
*Rackett Family
1119 Hedgewood Lane
Niskayuna, NY 12309-4602

Phone (518) 377-8938
Bette Innes Bradway, C.G.
Exchange of data

Radabaugh (see Buzzard)

Radcliff (see Ratcliff)

Radel (see Wert)

Rademacher (see Cole)

Rader (see Surname Database)

Rader
*Rader Association
2633 Gilbert Way
Rancho Cordova, CA 95670-3513
Phone (916) 366-6833; E-mail:
    raderjim@msn.com; Website: http://
    pages.prodigy.com/ca/raderjim/
    raderjim.html
James Lee Rader
Pub. *Rader Ramblings*, quarterly;
    (includes worldwide Rader/Raeder/
    Reader/Röder/Roeder/Roeter/Roether/
    Röter/Röther/Rötter database with over
    15,000 individuals and 4,000
    marriages)
$15.00 per year membership; Roeder
    reunion in Pennsylvania

Radford (see Brawley, McNeely,
    Dockery)

Radibush (see Roudabush)

Radloff (see Borchardt)

Radue (see CTC Family Association,
    Sager)

Rae (see Folk Family Surname
    Exchange, MacRae, Ray)

Raeder (see Rader)

Raffe (see Barber)

Ragan (see Reagan)

Ragas (see Blossom Press)

Ragatz (see Linck)

Ragsdale (see Folk Family Surname
    Exchange, Allison, Andrews, Anthes,
    Johnson)

Ragsdale
Ragsdales of America
PO Box 3793
Santa Cruz, CA 95063
E-mail: NonaW@aol.com
Nona Williams, Editor
Pub. *Ragsdales of America*, quarterly,
    $15.00 per year subscription, queries
    accepted

Ragsdale
*Folk Family
PO Box 52048
Knoxville, TN 37950-2048
Hester E. Stockton, Owner; Rebecca
    Ragsdale, Editor
Pub. *Ragsdale Register*, quarterly, $15.00
    per year subscription, $5.00 per issue;
    (includes Ragsdell and Ragsdill)

Ragsdell (see Ragsdale)

Ragsdill (see Ragsdale)

Ragsdille (see Johnson)

Railsback (see The Memorial
    Foundation of the Germanna Colonies)

Railsback
Railsback Descendants Association
Rt. 1, Box 222
Reagan, TX 76680
D. Cox

Rain (see Rainey)

Raine (see Holden, Rainey)

Raines (see Rainey)

Rainey
Rainey Times
Rt. 4, Box 56
Sulphur Springs, TX 75482
Phone (903) 885-3523;
    (903) 439-1081 FAX
Marynell Bryant, Editor
Pub. *Rainey Times*, annually, $20.00 per
    year subscription; (includes Rain,
    Raine, Raines, Rains, Rainy, Raney,
    Ranney, Rayne, Rennie, etc.)
Biennial Rainey/Raney Research
    Conference in even-numbered years

Rains (see Louden, Rainey)

Rainwater (see Folk Family Surname
    Exchange, Haynes)

Rainwater
Rainwater Researcher
24406 McBean Parkway, #111
Valencia, CA 91355-1974
Robert Albert, Jr.
Pub. *Rainwater Researcher*, three times
    per year, $15.00 per year subscription

Rainy (see Rainey)

Raith (see MacDuff, MacRae)

Raley (see Miles)

Rall (see McCune)

Ralston (see Holloway)

Ramage
*The Ramage Association
7570 East Speedway, #509
Tucson, AZ 85710
Phone (602) 296-4377
William Ray and Ann Ramage
Pub. *On the Ramage Trail*, quarterly

Ramba (see Rambo)

Rambaud (see Rambo)

Rambeau (see Rambo)

Rambo (see Emery)

Rambo
*The K.A.R.D. Files
19305 S.E. 243rd Place
Kent, WA 98042-4820
Phone (206) 432-1659
Judy K. Dye, Owner
Pub. *Rambo References*, irregularly,
    $6.00–$7.00 per volume (Washington
    State residents add 8.2% sales tax);
    (includes Ramba, Rambaud, Rambeau,
    Ramboe, Rambough, Rambow,
    Rombough and Rumbo)

Ramboe (see Rambo)

Rambough (see Rambo)

Rambow (see Rambo)

Ramer (see Raymer)

Ramey (see Garner)

Ramey
Ramey Ramblings
1160 East Avenue J-12
Lancaster, CA 93535
Phone (805) 942-8762
Gary and Melinda Ramey
Pub. *Ramey Ramblings*, annually, $6.00
    per year subscription; (includes
    Ramey, Remy and Rhamy)

Ramsay (see MacDuff, Ramsey)

Ramsay
Ramsay Clan Society
7493 Zachary Taylor Highway
Unionville, VA 22567
Phone (703) 854-5645
Tom Harding, President
Pub. *Clan Ramsay Newsletter*, quarterly;
    (includes Dalhousie, Ramsey)

Ramsey (see Cowart, Evans, Heath,
    McBurney, Ramsay)

Ramsey
Clan Ramsey of North America
434 Skinner Boulevard
Dunedin, FL 34698-4938
David F. Ramsey, Membership Secretary
Pub. *Ramsay Report*, quarterly
$15.00 per year membership

Ramsey
*Ramsey Surname Organization
1039 Hood Avenue
Jacksonville, FL 32254-2303
Phone (904) 387-1040
Jettie Cecil Ramsey

Ramsey
Ramsey Newsletter
4850 Parkton Place
Florisant, MO 63033
Gwyn Ramsey
Pub. *Ramsey Newsletter*, quarterly

Ramsey
*Ramsey/Ramsay Repository
11702 N.E. Sunset Loop
Bainbridge Island, WA 98110-1219
Phone (360) 842-4896
C. E. "Chuck" Munat

Ranc (see Ronk)

Ranck (see Ronk)

Ranck
*John Phillip and John Michael Ranck/
    Rank Family Reunion
300 Valleybrook Drive
Lancaster, PA 17601
Phone (717) 569-5936 (editor);
    (717) 964-1848 (president)
Harriet Ranck, Editor; Rev. Park Ranck,
    President
Pub. *The Ranck Reporter*, semiannually
Donation for membership

Rand
Rand Family Reunion
5612 S.E. Oetkin Road
Milwaukie, OR 97267
Leah M. Brown
(includes descendants of John Clay Rand
    (son of David and Emily (Hays/Hayes)
    Rand, descendant of Frances Rand,
    who immigrated from England in 1631
    and settled in New Hampshire) and his
    wife, Sarah Abbot Meacham (daughter
    of Chadwell and Mary (Lee)
    Meacham), who came to Oregon from
    Minnesota about 1883)

Randall (see Folk Family Surname
    Exchange, Heath, MacDuff)

Randall
*Chronicles of Christopher C. Randall
52024 Ocotillo Drive
Wickenburg, AZ 85390
Phone (520) 684-5816
Sharon J. Pearson, Family Historian
(includes descendants of Christopher C.
    Randall (1808 Vermont or New York–
    1856 Dekorra, Wisconsin) and Mary
    Safronia Osborne (1815 Attica, New
    York–1899 Poynette, Wisconsin), also
    Thomas Augustus Moungey (ca 1830
    Ireland or England–) and Isabella
    Josephine Smailla (1831 Scotland–
    1915 Poynette, Wisconsin))

Randall
*Randall Surname Organization
7024 Morgan Road
Greenwell Springs, LA 70739
Phone (504) 261-5515
Serena Abbess Haymon; Morris Randall
(includes descendants of Johnston
    Randall of Mississippi, Georgia and
    Pennsylvania)
Reunion

Randall
Randall Family Newsletter
PO Box 13548
Saint Louis, MO 63138
Maryann Schirker
Pub. *Randall Family Newsletter*,
    quarterly, $25.00 per year subscription

Randel (see Folk Family Surname
    Exchange, Johnson)

Randell (see MacDuff)

Randle (see MacDuff)

Randleman
Randleman/Rendleman/Rentleman
    Reunion
651 Sherwood, N.E.
Corvallis, OR 97330
Mrs. Billie Snead Webb
Pub. *Randleman/Rendleman/Rentleman
    Newsletter*

Randles (see Anthes, MacDuff)

Randolph (see Folk Family Surname
    Exchange, Clark, Johnson, MacDuff)

Raney (see Rainey)

Rangila (see McCune)

Rank (see Ranck, Ronk)

Rankan (see Gillean)

Rankin (see Clark, Lush)

Ranleillor (see MacDuff)

Ranlellor (see MacDuff)

Ranney (see Rainey)

Ranney
The Ranney Roots
PO Box 580
Naples, NY 14512
Phone (716) 374-6153; (716) 374-5655
    FAX
Hank Ranney, Co-Editor/Publisher
Pub. *The Ranney Roots: A Newsletter of
    the Ranney Family*, quarterly, $10.00
    per year subscription; (includes
    descendants of Thomas and Mary
    Ranney (1650–1690) of Cromwell,
    Connecticut)
Reunion

Ransom (see Allen, Corson)

Ransom
*Daniel Roy Ransom Family
    Organization
6771 Gardenia Avenue
Long Beach, CA 90805
Phone (310) 422-2323
Mary Vance

Rape (see Reeb)

Rapp (see Surname Database)

Rardin (see Waltermire)

Rasmuson
*Nils Gunnar Rasmuson Family
    Organization
13206 Wilton Oaks Drive
Silver Spring, MD 20906
Phone (301) 942-3856
Dale M. Rasmuson, Representative
(includes Rasmuson and allied families
    in Malmohus and Kristianstadsläns,
    Sweden, 1600–1900)

Rasmussen (see Johnson, Sorenson)

Ratcliff
*Richard Ratcliff Genealogical Society,
    Talbot Co., Maryland
1201 West Missouri
Midland, TX 79701
Jane Clancy Debenport, President/
    Publisher
Pub. *Richard Ratcliff Genealogical
    Society Bulletin*, quarterly, $10.00
    donation per year for subscription;
    (includes Radcliff, Ratliff)

Rathbone (see Rathbun)

Rathbone
Wait Rathbone Newsletter
3870 Barren River Road
Bowling Green, KY 42101
Pub. *Wait Rathbone Newsletter*, annually

Rathbun
*Rathbun Family Association
11308 Pope's Head Road
Fairfax, VA 22030-4614
Phone (703) 278-8512
Frank H. Rathbun, President
Pub. *Rathbun-Rathbone-Rathburn
    Family Historian*, semiannually
    (spring and fall); (most families of this
    name are descendants of John and
    Margaret (Acres) Rathbun, early
    settlers of Block Island, Rhode Island,
    in the late 1600s)
$12.00 per year membership; reunion

Rathburn (see Rathbun)

Rathke (see Griepp)

Ratliff (see Hatfield, Ratcliff)

Ratrie (see Anthes)

Rattan (see Rutan)

Rau (see Surname Database)

Raub (see Surname Database)

Raubenolt (see Likes)

Rauh (see Rowe)

Rauk (see Rook)

Rausch (see Roush)

Rawlings (see Rawlins)

Rawlins
*The Rawlin(g)s-Rollin(g)s Family
    History Association
4918 Kenneth Avenue
Carmichael, CA 95608
Phone (916) 482-8261
Katherine Rawlings, Editor and Founder
Pub. *The Rawlin(g)s-Rollin(g)s Family
    History Association*, quarterly (March,
    June, September and December);
    (includes all other spellings, of which
    there are many)
$7.50 per year membership

Rawls (see Emery, Warren)

Ray (see Folk Family Surname
    Exchange, Ammons, Ellett, Gant,
    MacRae, Scott)

Ray
John Ray of Georgia Descendants
Ray's Genealogical Services
1008 East Second
PO Box 482
McCook, NE 69001
R. Ray
Pub. *(Rhea, Rae, Rea, Wray, Raye and
    other various spellings) Newsletter*,
    quarterly, $10.00 per year subscription

Ray
Joseph Ray and Mary Fouts Reunion
2606 Culver
Midland, TX 79705
Phone (915) 694-0101
Mrs. Fran Hoerster
Pub. *Joseph and Mary Ray Reunions
    Newsletter*, quarterly
$10.00 per year membership

Rayburn (see Hall)

Raye (see Ray)

Raymer
Raymer Family Association
405 Austin Raymer Road
Bowling Green, KY 42101-9302
Lloyd M. Raymer, President
Pub. *Raymer (Ramer) Roots*,
    semiannually
$6.00 per year membership

Raymer
Raymer-Roemer
Whispering Oaks
5821 Rowland Hill Road
Cascade, MD 21719-1939
Phone (301) 416-2660
Victor Gebhart, President
Pub. *Raymer-Roemer*, annually, $2.00 per
issue

Rayne (see Rainey)

Rea (see Chaney, MacRae, Ray, Way)

Read (see Goodenow, Likes, Reed)

Reader (see Rader)

Readie (see MacDuff)

Reading (see The Memorial Foundation
of the Germanna Colonies)

Ready (see MacDuff, Reedy)

Reagan
Reagan Family Association
PO Box 834, University Station
Knoxville, TN 37996-4800
James S. Cotham; A. M. Reagan
Pub. *Reagan Family Journal*, quarterly;
(includes O'R(e)agan, Ragan, Regan
and Rigan)
$10.00 per year membership

Reap (see Reeb)

Reap
Reap/Reep Family Association
PO Box 683
800 Williams Street
Kings Mountain, NC 28086
M. Huitt Reep
Pub. *Newsletter*, annually
Biennial reunion

Reasoner
Reasoner Family Association
1710 Van Stone Drive
Rockford, IL 61111
Phone (815) 654-0452
William Edmundson, President
Pub. *Reasoner Family Bulletin*,
irregularly
$8.00 per year membership

Reasor
*Reasor Surname Organization
2815 Beachwood Lane
South Bend, IN 46615
Miss Leslie Howard
(includes Reasors who came to Saint
Joseph County from Dayton, Ohio, in
1858)

Reath (see MacRae)

Reaves (see Reeves)

Reay (see Mackay)

Rebe
Rebe
Whispering Oaks
5821 Rowland Hill Road
Cascade, MD 21719-1939
Phone (301) 416-2660
Victor Gebhart, President
Pub. *Rebe*, annually, $2.00 per issue

Rebele
*R. Associates
901 Pine Tree Point
Swanton, MD 21561-9736
Carl Purcell Rebele
(includes Bonan, Köenig, Purcell, Rebele
and Smith)

Reber
*Reber Surname Exchange
3385 South Bluff Road
Syracuse, UT 84075
Phone (801) 773-0531
Helga Reber Willie, Researcher

Reckart
Reckart Family Association
119 North Alleghany Street
Cumberland, MD 21502
Stephan Lawson
Pub. *Reckart Family Register*

Rector (see The Memorial Foundation of
the Germanna Colonies)

Redd
*Lemuel Hardison Redd Family
Organization
PO Box 306
Monticello, UT 84535
Phone (801) 587-2576
J. Whitney Redd, President
(includes Utah Redd families and their
progenitors)

Reddell (see Ross)

Reddick
*Reddick (Redick, Riddick, Ruddick)
Family Association
5450 Whispering Oak Way
PO Box 757
Paso Robles, CA 93447-0757
Phone (805) 238-2316
Richard D. Reddick, Editor
Pub. *Rddk Roster*, biannually (June of
even-numbered years)

Redford (see Innes)

Redfore
The Redford Family Newsletter
19110 Doveton
Spring, TX 77388
Pub. *The Redford Family Letter*

Redick (see Reddick)

Redman (see Corson, Nelson)

Redmond (see Broadfoot)

Redmond
*Redmond Family Reunion
413 Lake Road
Waynesboro, VA 22980
Phone (540) 949-7075
Melvin Redmond, Historian

Rednock (see Graham)

Redre (see Dietwiler)

Reece (see Gibson)

Reece
Reece's Pieces
12600 Bissonnet A4-407
Houston, TX 77099
Dede D. Mercer, Publisher
Pub. *Reece's Pieces*, semiannually,
$20.00 per year subscription; (all
variations of the surname, worldwide)

Reed (see Folk Family Surname
Exchange, Austin, Bodine, Carlton,
Collette, Cox, Donnachaidh, Heath,
Johnson, Joyner, Simpson, Wright)

Reed
*Benjamin Reed/Reid Family
Association
5631 Biscayne Boulevard
Miami, FL 33137-2634
Phone (305) 757-4966
Dora Reid Fieber, Secretary
(includes descendants of Benjamin Reid
(1782–1864) and Mary Prall who were
married in Kentucky and died in
Edwards County, Illinois, having been
from Pennsylvania, Maryland and New
Jersey)

Reed
Reed Organization
16677 Carlisle
Detroit, MI 48205
Deanna Shukwit

Reed
Reed Organization
434 Oak Street
Rochester, MI 48307-1927
Russel J. Reed

Reed
The Reed Review
12600 Bissonnet A4-407
Houston, TX 77099
Dede D. Mercer, Publisher
Pub. *The Reed Review*, annually, $20.00
per year subscription; (all variations of
the surname: Reid, etc., worldwide)

Reed
Michael Reed Family Association
316 North Eighth Street
Temple, TX 76501
D. Reed

Reed

*Reed Reunion
Rt. 2, Box 506
Floyd, VA 24091
Phone (540) 745-2314
Maynard G. Hylton
(includes descendants of W. Paris Reed
and Druzillia Reed-Reed)
Biennial reunion in even-numbered years
at the Laurel Branch Church of the
Brethren at Floyd, Virginia

Reed

*Family Publications
5628 60th Drive, N.E.
Marysville, WA 98270-9509
E-mail: cxwp57a@prodigy.com
Rose Caudle Terry, Publisher
Pub. *Reed Roots*, two to four times per
year, $8.95 per volume subscription,
plus $1.50 postage per order; (includes
Read, Reid, etc., all spellings, all
nationalities)

Reeder (see Hynton, Kimmel)

Reeder

*John Reeder Family Association, 1630
Boston, Mass.
PO Box 13302
Tampa, FL 33681-3302
Ernestine Siegel, B.A., Director
(includes descendants of John Reeder I
who came to America aboard the
Arbella in 1630 and helped to found
Springfield, Massachusetts, in 1636,
and was later in New Haven,
Connecticut, Stratford (now
Bridgeport), Connecticut, Middleburgh
(Newtown), Long Island, and Pavonia
(near Rahway), New Netherlands
Colony, married Hannah Thorpe and
Margaret who was called Mrs. Samuel
Toe at her death; also allied families:
Adams, Bainbridge, Bean, Biles,
Burroughs, Firman, Green,
Hendrickson, Howell, Hunt, Isaacks,
Ketchum, Locke, Mershon, Phillips,
Powell, Robinson, Scudder, Smith,
etc.)
No membership fee

Reeder

*Purley Louis Reeder Family
Organization
4851 South 600 West
Ogden, UT 84405-6008
Phone (801) 479-7625
J. Allen Reeder
(includes descendants of Purley Louis
Reeder and Kate Cowdery)

Reedy (see Kunkel)

Reeks

*Ancestors of Reeks and Rogers,
Christchurch, Dorset, England
2013 Westover Drive
Pleasant Hill, CA 94523

Phone (510) 934-9416
Lindsay S. Reeks, Publisher

Reep (see Reap)

Reep

*Reep Family Association, Inc.
PO Box 113
Bladensburg, MD 20710-0113
Phone (301) 927-7241
James W. Reep, Historian-Archivist and
Newsletter Editor
Pub. *Reep Family Review*, semiannually
(April and October) with special
biennial reunion issue
$5.00 per year membership; biennial
reunion

Reeves (see Brothers, Moore, Robinson)

Reeves

*Reeves/Mulinax Family Association
8505 Glenview Avenue
Takoma Park, MD 20912
Phone (301) 89-6621; (301) 589-1366
FAX
M. Sandra Reeves
(restricted to descendants of John H.
Reeves (1836 South Carolina–) and
Hannah H. Mulinax (1838 North
Carolina-) of South Carolina, North
Carolina, Georgia and Alabama; also
Hawks)

Reeves

Reeves-Reaves-Etc.
849 Rutland Drive
Southaven, MS 38671
Barry L. Reeves
Pub. *Reeves-Reaves-Etc.*, bimonthly,
$20.00 per year subscription

Regan (see Reagan)

Regnier (see Lagesse)

Rehklau (see Buechele)

Rehlich (see Lambert)

Reiach (see MacDuff)

Reich (see Wright)

Reich

Reich Family Association
514 Kirkwood Lane
Camden, SC 29020-2410
Merrill Reich, Family Representative

Reid (see Cook, Donnachaidh, Golding,
McCormick, Mueller, Reed)

Reid

Reid Family Data
PO Box 488
Due West, SC 29639-0488
Elizabeth Reid Austin
Pub. *Reid Family Data*, quarterly, $8.00
per year subscription, $2.00 per issue;

(includes descendants of Theodore
Henderson Reid and Sarah Barksdale
Harvey Reid)
Annual reunion on the second Sunday of
August in Franklin County, Alabama

Reidford (see Innes)

Reierson (see Ostrem)

Reifsnyder

*Reifsnyder and Related Spellings:
Achtung! Family Association
2696 Edgehill Road
Cleveland, OH 44106-2806
Phone (216) 371-3561; E-mail:
fs332@cleveland.freenet.edu
Jim Walton, President
$30.00 plus FGS or donation for life
membership

Reigart (see Hoster)

Reigel (see Kimmel)

Reikofski (see Voss)

Reimer

*Reimer Genealogy Center Worldwide
Box 121, Fawn Ridge Road
Warrensburg, NY 12885-0121
Arthur A. Reimer, Director
(includes Reimer, Remer and all forty-
five ways of spelling surname, as well
as Ballschnider, Winter, Sendzek, etc.,
in Pommern, Silesia, Brandenburg,
East and West Prussia, Poland, etc.)
Free information, send family group
sheet and SASE (no personal visits)

Reimschussel

*Reimschussel Surname Organization
495 South 900 East
Provo, UT 84606
Phone (801) 377-2662
Helen Reimschussel Anderson,
Genealogist
(includes descendants of Johann Anton
Ignatz Reimschussel (1813 Kniegnitz,
Schlesien, Prussia–1889 Nicolstadt,
Schlesien, Prussia) and Anna Rosina
Pauser (1815 Datzdorf, Jauer,
Schlesien, Prussia–1897 Wahlstatt,
Schlesien, Prussia))

Reinbold

*Ernst Ludwig Reinbold Family
Organization
998 Bloomington Drive South
Saint George, UT 84790-7585
Phone (801) 673-6314
Carolyn Reinbold
(includes descendants of Ernst Ludwig
Reinbold (by 1748) and his wife
Christina Hendrick/s)

Reinhardt (see Shurtleff)

Reinmüller (see Surname Database)

Reisinger (see Risinger)

Reister (see Messner)

Reith (see MacDuff)

Reitzi (see Brucker)

Reller (see Lush)

Remel (see Johnson)

Remer (see Reimer)

Remick (see Corson, Hoster)

Remund
*Clive Ott Remund Family Organization
1389 Kinsport Lane
San Jose, CA 95120
Phone (408) 268-5026
Linda Remund Quittner

Remy (see Ramey, Rutherford)

Ren (see Wren)

Rendall (see MacDuff)

Rendell (see MacDuff)

Render (see Album)

Rendle (see MacDuff)

Rendleman (see Randleman)

Renfrew (see Gregor)

Rennie (see Rainey)

Rennison
Rennison Ramblings
340 Hazel Avenue
Saint Louis, MO 63119-4267
Phone (314) 962-0025
Frances Doutt Smith
Pub. *Rennison Ramblings*, three times
per year, donation for subscription;
(for all Rennisons, but especially
descendants of John Rennison (1779
England–1844) and Jane Creighton
(ca 1777 England–), immigrated to
America 1820, settled Cooper County,
Missouri)

Rennollet
*Paul Rennollet Family Organization
333 West Wayne Street
Lima, OH 45801
Phone (419) 227-2876
Phyllis Mast Leech, Historian
(includes Renolet, etc.)
Biennial reunion

Renolet (see Rennollet)

Rentleman (see Randleman)

Rentsch
*Rentsch-Herold Family
1721 North Palm Avenue
Upland, CA 91786-1957
Phone (909) 981-5741 (days); (909) 981-
3558 (evenings)
Mary Burney Matreyek
Pub. *Rentsch-Herold Family Newsletter*,
three times per year, $3.00 per year
subscription; (includes descendants of
Johan Rentsch (1836 Trub,
Switzerland–), married 1857 to Maria
Rothlisberger (1835–1907), settled in
Laurens, Iowa in the 1880s)

Rentz (see Peters)

Repass
Repass Family Newsletter
PO Box 505
Wytheville, VA 24382
Beverly Repass Hoch, Editor
Pub. *Repass Family Newsletter*,
semiannually, $10.00 per year
subscription; (includes descendants of
Hans Jacob Rippas and Anna Gerber)

Repath (see Blossom Press)

Reph (see Reeb)

Retan (see Rutan)

Retherford (see Tidwell)

Reuel (see MacDuff)

Rex (see Surname Database)

Rextroat
Rextroat Family Newsletter
708 South Maple
Ellensburg, WA 98926
Evelyn Cox
Pub. *Rextroat Family Newsletter*,
quarterly

Reyn (see Rhines)

Reynolds (see Cian, Futral, Gant,
Hatfield, Newton, Rutherford)

Reynolds
*Kinseeker Publications
5697 Old Maple Trail
PO Box 184
Grawn, MI 49637
E-mail: AB064@taverse.lib.mi.us
Victoria Wilson, Editor
Pub. *Reynolds Records*, quarterly, $10.00
per year subscription

Reynolds
*Reynolds Family Association
4004 Javins Drive
Alexandria, VA 22310
Phone (703) 960-1782

Sybil R. Taylor, Vice President,
Publications, and Editor
Pub. *Reynolds Recollections*, bimonthly;
(includes American progenitors: John
Reynolds 1650 and Ann Holbrook of
Weymouth and Stonington,
Connecticut; Robert 1630 and Mary of
Boston, Massachusetts; William 1634
and Alice Kitson of Duxbury,
Massachusetts, and Cape Porpoise,
Maine; James 1643 and Deborah of
North Kingstown, Rhode Island; John
1650 and Sarah Backus of Saybrook,
Lyme and Norwich, Connecticut;
_____ Reynolds 1725 and _____
Crook of Washington County,
Maryland; Christopher 1622 and
Elizabeth of Isle of Wight, Virginia;
Henry 1676 and Prudence Clayton of
Lancaster County, Pennsylvania;
Electius 1678 and Mary Pease of
Salem and Middleboro, Massachusetts;
John 1634 and Sarah of Watertown,
Massachusetts, Wethersfield and
Stamford, Connecticut; John 1682 of
Delaware; Richard 1708 and Mary
Capers, Benjamin and Mary, and
William of St. Helena's Parish, South
Carolina; John 1708 and Elizabeth of
Kent County, Delaware; Katherine
1635 and Edward Starbuck of Dover,
New Hampshire and Nantucket Island;
Thomas 1637 and Mary of Isle of
Wight, Virginia; William 1640 and
Ann Harrison of York County,
Virginia; John 1660 and Naomi
Latimer of Wethersfield, Connecticut;
Thomas 1652 and Susan Snead of
York County, Virginia; James 1784 and
Mary Bannon, Margaret and Andrew
Forgey, Ellen and _____ McDaniel of
County Louth, Ireland, and Knox
County, Tennessee; William 1850 and
Rebecca Tawn of Moulton, England,
and Grinnell, Iowa; Frederick Thomas
1920 and Rosa Annie Jones of London
and New York City; Thomas 1837 and
Mrs. Agnes (McCulloch) Cardwell of
Armagh, Ireland, and Bergen County,
New Jersey; Thomas 1886 and Bigham
Stuart of Scotland and Scranton,
Pennsylvania; James (to 1703) and
Mrs. Susanna Reynolds of Essex
County, Virginia)
$10.00 per year membership; reunion

Rhamy (see Ramey)

Rhamy
*Rhamy Reunion
PO Box 733
Stillwater, OK 74076
Bea Rhamy; Alline Anderson

Rhea (see Kettenring, Ray)

Rheutan (see Rutan)

Rhind (see Lindsay)

Rhinehart
*Rhinehart Family Reunion
1080 North Holliston
Pasadena, CA 91104
Phone (818) 794-7973
Kathryn Rhinehart Bassett
(includes ancestors and descendants of
    Frederick Rinehart (1788
    Pennsylvania–) and Catherine Burrell
    (1787 Pennsylvania–))
Donation for membership; biennial
    reunion in August of odd-numbered
    years in Muncie area of Indiana

Rhines (see Gotham)

Rhines
Rhines/Kepple Family Organization
Rt. 2, Box 192
Kane, PA 16735
Flora Rhines Powell
Reunion only

Rhines
*Rhines Family History
Rt. 1, Box 45
Utica, PA 16362
Mrs. Lyril Rhines Banister, Publisher
(includes descendants of Christopher
    Columbus Rhines (Reyn), mainly
    through his grandson, George Stean
    Rhines, who married Frances Keppel)

Rhoads (see Newmyer, Stoner)

Rhoads
*Rhoads Family
10435 Tullymore Drive
Adelphi, MD 20783
Phone (301) 434-8034
Catherine M. Rhoads

Rhoda (see Stowell)

Rhodes (see Surname Sources, McGrath,
    Roades, Rutherford, Stoner)

Rhodes
Rhodes
133 Montclair Loop
Daphne, AL 36526-8151
Craig Rhodes
Pub. *Rhodes*, quarterly, $12.00 per year
    subscription

Rhodes
*Rhodes Family Database
Rt. 1, Box 37
Concord, NE 68728
Phone (402) 584-2407
Marlys McGrath Rhodes Rice, Historian
(database includes all Rhodes families)

Rhonemus (see Hieronymus)

Ribble
Ribble-Darlington-DeFrance-Arnett
    Family Association
2306 Westgate
Houston, TX 77019

Phone (713) 529-2333
Harold Helm
$25.00 plus pedigree and family group
    sheets for membership

Ribble
*Ribble of New York, New Jersey,
    Virginia and Kentucky Descendants
108 Wood Drive
Kerrville, TX 78029
Phone (210) 257-8249
June Anne Ribble Landreth

Ribich
*Ribich Surname Organization
3 Brazill Lane
Whitehall, MT 59759
Phone (406) 287-3369
Lindia Roggia Lovshin

Rice (see Barnes, Davis, Goodenow,
    Lush, McCune, McGrath, Miller)

Rice
Rice/Royce Database
49 Seaside Avenue
Westbrook, CT 06498
Phone (203) 399-9273
Margaret Buckridge Bock
(includes descendants of John of
    Dedham)

Rice
*James Rice Family Organization
2532 Smith Road
American Falls, ID 83211
Phone (208) 226-7854
Gary L. Wiese, President
(includes allied surnames of Bailey,
    Burden, Murrell, Oliver and Whally)

Rice
Rice-Smith Newsletter
17720 New Market Road
Dearborn, MO 64439-9720
Lois J. Phillips Foster
Pub. *Rice-Smith Newsletter*, annually
    (January)

Rice
*Fleming Bailey Rice Association
PO Box 116
Moberly, MO 65270-0116
Phone (816) 263-7576; E-mail:
    kcecyr@mcmsys.com
Karl Rice, Genealogist
(includes descendants of Fleming Bailey
    Rice (1803–1879) and Eliza Shumate
    (1806–1871))

Rice
*The Edmund Rice (1638) Association,
    Inc.
24 Buckman Drive
Chelmsford, MA 01824
Phone (508) 256-7469
William H. Drury, Treasurer and
    Membership Chairman
Pub. *Edmund Rice (1638) Association
    Newsletter*, quarterly; (deals

exclusively with descendants of
    Edmund Rice (1594–1664) who came
    to this country in 1638 and founded
    Sudbury and Marlborough,
    Massachusetts)
$10.00 per year membership for
    individuals

Rice
*Alice Rosina Smith Rice Family
    Organization
2717 N.E. 148th Street, #7R
Vancouver, WA 98686-1576
Phone (360) 573-8563
Richard E. Sellick, President
(includes allied surnames of Maslen,
    Murrell and Smith)

Rich (see Clark, Goodenow)

Rich
*The Rich Family Association
PO Box 142
Wellfleet, MA 02667
Phone (508) 432-5418 (President's home
    in Harwich Port)
Robert L. Park, President/Treasurer
Pub. *Kinfolk*, three times per year
$12.00 per year membership for
    individuals, $12.00 per year
    membership for families

Richards (see Corson, Likes, Moore)

Richards
John Richards and Catherine Harry
    Descendants
3847 46th, N.E.
Seattle, WA 98105
Jean Richards Timmermeister
Pub. *Richards Ramblings*

Richardson (see Buchanan, Clark,
    Dawson, Forester, Guild, Hopkin,
    Newmyer, Probst, Rutherford, Tate)

Richardson
*Richardson Heritage Society
944 South "G" Street
PO Box 123
Broken Bow, NE 68822
Phone (308) 872-2167
Harry Marcus Richardson, Editor
Pub. *Richardson Family Researcher and
    Historical News*, quarterly (March,
    June, September and December);
    (includes Buck, Calmes, Chrisman,
    Dale, Deatherage, Downey, Eastham,
    Gross, Hite, Lovell, McCarty, Moore,
    Murphy, Waller and Wilburn)
$10.00 per year membership

Richarme (see Blossom Press)

Riche (see Johnson)

Richelieu
*Richelieu/Vix Families Society
HCR 32, Box 170
West Bath, ME 04530-9505

Phone (207) 443-4530
Charles F. Richelieu

Richey (see Garner, Gunnin, McRae)

Richmond
Richmond Family
136 East Avenue 37
Los Angeles, CA 90031
H. Richmond
Pub. *Richmond Family*

Richner (see Bolliger)

Richter (see Sager)

Rickel
Rickel Family Association
Rt. 2, Box 97
Warsaw, IN 46580
Cloice E. Metzgar

Ricker (see Corson, Wright)

Rickey
*Rickey Family Association
235 15th Street, N.E. (address April 1 to
    November 1)
Salem, OR 97301-4228
Phone (503) 363-4389
Stanton M. Rickey, Editor
Pub. *Rickey Roots and Revels*, quarterly
$10.00 per year membership; reunion

Rickner (see Scott)

Ricks (see Saye)

Ricouard (see Blossom Press)

Riddick (see Reddick)

Riddle (see Beavers, Likes, McCune)

Riddoch (see Gregor)

Rider (see Sullivan Surname Exchange,
    Johnson)

Ridgeway (see Wright)

Rieder (see McCanna)

Riegle (see Wert)

Riess (see Arthur)

Rife (see Reiff)

Riffe (see Reiff)

Rigan (see Reagan)

Rigby (see Roskelley)

Riggle
*George Riggle and Mary Edwards
    Family Reunion
138 Wheatland Avenue
Logansport, IN 46947
Verna L. Warfield

Riggs (see Priddy)

Rigney
*Rigney-Lindsey Reunion
114 Lee Street
Radford, VA 24141
Phone (703) 639-4500
Bernice Phillips
(includes descendants of Kelly Isaac
    Rigney and Annie Lindsey-Rigney)
Annual reunion at Claytor Lake State
    Park

Riker (see Ryker)

Riker
Riker-Ryker
1508 North Rykers Ridge Road
Madison, IN 47150-9192
Pub. *Riker-Ryker*, quarterly, $10.00 per
    year subscription
Reunion

Riley (see Folk Family Surname
    Exchange, Brooks, Heath)

Rima
*The Rimas
7 Prescott Road
Lynn, MA 01902
Steve Rima

Rinck (see Rink)

Rinehart (see The Memorial Foundation
    of the Germanna Colonies, Rhinehart,
    Stoner)

Riner (see The Memorial Foundation of
    the Germanna Colonies)

Rinesmith (see Likes)

Ring (see Cian)

Ringle (see CTC Family Association)

Ringo
*Ringo on Computer
3701 Cross Creek Road
Santa Rosa, CA 95403
Phone (707) 523-2044
Robert B. Ringo

Ringo
*Ringo Family Research Group
312 Ivanhoe Avenue
Eugene, OR 97404
Phone (541) 689-6323
May Ringo King, Secretary
(includes allied Britton and Cummins
    families 1820–1860)
Annual reunion in August at Ringo
    Century Farm, Clackamas County,
    Oregon

Rinker (see Surname Database)

Rinker
*Rinker Family Association
8317 South Middle Road
Mount Jackson, VA 22842-2832
Phone (540) 477-3428; (540) 477-3428
    FAX; (540) 333-3737 Cellular
Daniel Warrick Burruss, II
(includes descendants of Jacob, Casper
    and Henry Rinker, the immigrants who
    settled in the northern Shenandoah
    Valley of Virginia)
No membership dues; annual reunion on
    the third Saturday of July

Ripley (see Barnes)

Ripley
Ripley
6180 Merrywood Drive
Rocklin, CA 95677-3421
Kathleen Stewart
Pub. *Ripley*, quarterly, $12.00 per year
    subscription

Rippas (see Repass)

Rippy (see Gant)

Riseley (see Risley)

Risener (see Wiler)

Riser (see Rizer)

Rishtom (see Nell)

Rising
Rising Family Association
24 Ralph Stubbs Road
Randolph, MA 02368-3656
Gale Bunner
Pub. *Rising Family Association*, annually
    (June)
$5.00 membership per family

Risinger (see Folk Family Surname
    Exchange)

Risk (see Buchanan)

Risley
*The Risley Family Association, Inc.
PO Box 552
Clarkson, NY 11430-0552
Phone (716) 637-6419
Roy D. Goold, President
Pub. *The Risley Record*, quarterly;
    (includes Wrisley, Rizley, Riseley,
    descendants of Richard Risley, Sr.
    (1610–1648) of England and Hartford,
    Connecticut)
$10.00 per year membership for the first
    year and $6.00 thereafter; annual
    reunion

Ritches (see Gunnin)

Ritchhart (see Richhart)

Ritchie (see Hay)

Rittenhouse (see Links Genealogy Publications)

Rittenhouse
Rittenhouse Family Newsletter
10490 Frontenac Woods Lane
Saint Louis, MO 63131-3423
E. Mark Haacke, Editor
Pub. *Rittenhouse Family Newsletter*, semiannually, $15.00 per year subscription
Reunion

Rittenhuysen (see Links Genealogy Publications)

Ritter (see Surname Database, Johnson)

Rivard
Rivard Family Newsletter
PO Box 13548
Saint Louis, MO 63138
Maryann Schirker
Pub. *Rivard Family Newsletter*, quarterly, $25.00 per year subscription

Rizer
Rizer/Riser Research
1527 Benson Drive
Dayton View Triangle
Dayton, OH 45406-4515
Kathleen Rizer
Pub. *Rizer Research*, two or three times per year, $1.00 per issue; (dedicated to identifying the ancestors and descendants of Martin Rizer of Virginia and Maryland)

Rizley (see Risley)

Roach (see Catlow, Heath, Rutherford)

Roades
Roades-Ketchum-Rhodes-Helmsley Family Association
2306 Westgate
Houston, TX 77019
Phone (713) 529-2333
Harold Helm
$25.00 plus pedigree and family group sheets for membership

Roadman (see Rodman)

Roan (see Cian, Newmyer)

Roark (see Leland, Merier)

Robb (see Robison, Stewart)

Robb
The Robb Family Genealogical Society
2144 150th Avenue, N.E.
Ham Lake, MN 55304-2647
Jeff Walt Robb
Pub. *The Robb Family Journal* (includes any and all Robb immigrants, Robb family tree storehouse)

Robb
Robb Relatives
421 Kemmerer Road
State College, PA 16801
Phone (814) 237-6447
Barbara Robb Kabel
Pub. *Robb Relatives*, semiannually (February and October), $5.00 per year subscription, free queries; (all Robbe-Robbs welcome, especially descendants of William Robb/Robbe (1692–1769) of Peterborough, New Hampshire)

Robbe (see Robb)

Robbie (see Donnachaidh)

Robbins (see Brawley, Clinton, Robertson, Robinson, Robison, Saye)

Robbins
Robbins Journal
PO Box 2361
Kirkland, WA 98033
Phone (206) 823-0200
Kevin K. Mittge
Pub. *Robbins Journal*, quarterly, $6.50 per year subscription; (includes Robins)

Roberson (see Johnson, Robinson, Robison)

Roberts (see Corson, Dockery, Donnachaidh, Forester, Heath, Herrell, Hilton, Likes, Lush, Newcomb, Pittenger, Robertson, Robison, Scott, Wright)

Roberts
Roberts and Smith Reunion
8412 Grandview Lane
Overland Park, KS 66212
Mrs. A. F. Cooper
Reunion every three years in Harrison, Arkansas

Roberts
*Roberts Surname Organization
150 Brown Street
Saint Clair, MI 48079-4882
Phone (810) 329-9359
George M. Roberts

Roberts
Roma Publishing
5560 Gibson Road
Vicksburg, MS 39180
Pub. *Roberts Register*, three times per year

Roberts
Wilson Family Record Depository
169 Melody Lane
Tonawanda, NY 14150-9109
Robert J. Wilson
Pub. *Roberts*, quarterly, $25.00 per year subscription

Roberts
*Roberts Family Tree
315 Waldheim Drive
Ambler, PA 19002-2425
Phone (215) 646-6556
Jean C. Roberts Harris
(John and Sarah Roberts, from Northampton, England, to Burlington County, New Jersey, 1677 on the *Kent*)
Reunion in Moorestown, New Jersey

Roberts
*Roberts Reunion
Iaegar, WV 24844
Phone (304) 938-2671
Mrs. Oscar Roberts
(mainly the descendants of Owen Roberts)
Annual reunion on the fourth Sunday of July at Panther State Park, outside Iaegar, West Virginia

Robertson (see Folk Family Surname Exchange, Donnachaidh, MacDuff, McCullah, Robinson, Robison)

Robertson
*Descendants of William Robertson of Londonderry, New Hampshire
19441-133 Business Center Drive
Northridge, CA 91324
Phone (818) 886-7830
Roger E. Robertson, Genealogist
Pub. *Robertson-Woodend Newsletter*, irregularly, no cost; (includes descendants of William Robertson (1703–1790) and wife, Margaret Woodend (1705–1785), who emigrated from Northern Ireland to Londonderry, New Hampshire, in 1730)

Robertson
Robertson Quarterly Roundup
509 Commanche Trail
Frankfort, KY 40601-1751
Joy Van Curon Blanton, Editor and Publisher
Pub. *Robertson Quarterly Roundup*, $10.00 per year subscription, $3.50 per issue; (includes Robison, Robbins, Robeson, Roberts, etc.)

Robertson
*Name Game Enterprises
4204 South Conklin Street
Spokane, WA 99203-6235
Phone (509) 747-4903
Mrs. E. Dale Hastin Smith
Pub. *Robertson Report*, irregularly, $5.75 per issue plus $2.00 postage and handling

Robeson (see Robertson, Robinson)

Robeson
*John Robeson and Mary Mettlin Descendants
8500 Camille Drive, S.E.
Huntsville, AL 35802-3408
Phone (205) 881-0906
Vernon S. Robeson, Secretary

Robey (see Athy, Likes)

Robey
Robey/Robie/Roby Family Association, Inc.
20307 Beaconfield Terrace
Germantown, MD 20874-3094
Phone (301) 540-8231
Joy Robey Klingaman, Secretary-Treasurer
Pub. *Newsletter*, semiannually; (includes descendants of Jean Roby, who came to America from Quebec in the 1870s, of a Polish family which shortened its name to Robie, of four closely related men from the Roby family of Castle Donington, England, who settled in New England, etc.)
$20.00 per year for family membership; reunion

Robichaud (see Johnson)

Robicheaux (see Johnson)

Robidoux (see Lagesse)

Robie (see Robey)

Robinet (see Carley)

Robinett
*Robinett Family Association of America
4745 South Atlantic, #506
Ponce Inlet, FL 32127-7134
Phone (904) 761-6783
James M. Robinett, Historian
Pub. *Robinett Family Association News and Journal*, quarterly (January, April, July and October); (includes Robinette, Robnett)
$15.00 per year membership

Robinette (see Robinett)

Robins (see Robbins)

Robinson (see Blossom Press, Surname Sources, Arthur, Black, Goodenow, Gunn, Johnson, Kunkel, Lemon, Mowreader, Nelson, Reeder, Robertson, Robison)

Robinson
Robinson/Rolls Families
6421 U.S. Highway 31
Hanceville, AL 35077
Delton D. Blalock

Robinson
*Tye Robinson's Descendants
8505 Glenview Avenue
Takoma Park, MD 20912
Phone (301) 89-6621;
   (301) 589-1366 FAX
M. Sandra Reeves
(restricted to relatives of Union veteran of Shiloh, Tye Robinson, and Nancy Bell of Tennessee and Mississippi; also Bullard, Reeves and Thomas)

Robinson
Robinson/Robison Researcher
PO Box 661
Waynesville, OH 45068
Frank H. Robison
Pub. *Robinson/Robison Researcher*, quarterly, $7.00 per year subscription

Robinson
Robinson Search
PO Box 730
Pacific City, OR 97135
Pub. *Robinson Search*

Robinson
Genealogical and Historical News
369 East 900 South, Suite 247
Salt Lake City, UT 84111
R. D. Bradshaw, Editor
Pub. *Robinson, Roberson, Robertson, Robison of Virginia Letter*, quarterly, $10.00 per year subscription

Robinson
*Charlotte Robinson Family Organization, 1837–1841 of Tennessee, 1841 of Illinois)
HCR 62, Box 113A
Flippin, AR 72634-9710
Phone (501) 453-5286
Charlene Gillespie Deutsch, Compiler

Robinson
*John Robinson/Ann Gregson Family Organization
825 West 600 South
Logan, UT 84321
Phone (801) 753-5108
E. Wayne Robinson, President
Pub. *The Mountain Robin*, quarterly
$10.00 per year membership

Robinson
*John Rowlandson Robinson Family Organization
454 South 100 East #11
Saint George, UT 84770
Phone (801) 674-2136
Cleo Edwards, Family Genealogist
(includes descendants of John Rowlandson Robinson, Sr. (1815 Dubgarth, Clapham, Yorkshire, England–) and wives Alice Coupe (1818 Haslingden, Lancashire, England–) and Jane Coupe (1832 Haslingden, Lancashire, England–))
Biennial reunion in even-numbered years on the Saturday closest to March 6

Robinson
*Robinson Registry
Hewick Plantation
PO Box 82—VSH 602/VSH 615
Urbanna, VA 23175-0082
Phone (804) 758-4214; (804) 758-4080 FAX; E-mail: Hewick@aol.com, Prodigy (GZKQ12A), Compuserve 103175,3656
Helen Nichols Battleson, Editor

Pub. *Robinson Family Journal*, semiannually (October and April), $22.00 per year subscription; (including descendants of Christopher Robinson (1645–1693) of Yorkshire, England, and Middlesex County, Virginia; variants: Robbins, Roberson, Robertson, Robeson and Robison)

Robison (see Ammons, Donnachaidh, Gunn, Robertson, Robinson)

Robison
*The R's Relatives
2070 Dutch Slough Road
PO Box 547
Bethel Island, CA 94511
Phone (510) 684-2117;
   (510) 684-9610 FAX
Robert D. "Bob" Gromm, Editor-Publisher
Pub. *The R's Relatives*, quarterly, $12.00 for four issues; (includes all various spellings Robb, Robbins, Roberson, Roberts, Robertson, Robinson, Robison, Robson, etc., all sons of Rob)

Robnett (see Robinett)

Robson (see Donnachaidh, Gunn, Robison)

Roby (see Robey)

Roby
Roby
Whispering Oaks
5821 Rowland Hill Road
Cascade, MD 21719-1939
Phone (301) 416-2660
Victor Gebhart, President
Pub. *Roby*, annually, $2.00 per issue

Rockafellow
Rockafellow Family Association
12879 Croftshire Drive
Grand Blanc, MI 48439-1543
Phone (313) 694-2932
Max E. Rockafellow, Family Genealogist
Pub. *Ancestry of the Rockafellow Family*, annually

Rockenbach (see Catlow)

Rocket
*Rocket(t)/Rockette Association
13033 Caminito Dos Amantes
San Diego, CA 92128-1722
Phone (619) 438-8428
Charles Whitlock Rockett

Rockett (see Rocket)

Rockette (see Rocket)

Rockstad
*Rockstad Family Association
3947 Lakewood Avenue
White Bear Lake, MN 55110
Phone (612) 429-5572

Ruth Gibson, Genealogist
(includes Rockstead, Rogstad, Rokstad)

Rockstead (see Rockstad)

Rockwell
John Rockwell and Sarah Wilcox
   Reunion
1116 Grant Street
Ypsilanti, MI 48197
Phone (313) 483-3236
Doris Milliman, Secretary-Treasurer
Pub. *Rockwell News*, semiannually, $4.00
   per year subscription

Rod (see Lemon)

Roddham (see Rodman)

Rodeheaver (see The Memorial
   Foundation of the Germanna Colonies)

Roden (see McLouth)

Rodenbough (see Roudabush)

Röder (see Rader)

Rodes (see Schindel)

Rodgers (see Surname Database, Rogers,
   Scott)

Rodgers
*Abraham Rodgers and Anna Ferguson
   Family Organization
1450 North 1180 East
Shelley, ID 83274
Phone (208) 523-0847
Vicki Lee Smith, Representative
(includes descendants of Abraham
   Rodgers (1836 Iowa–1911
   Washington) and Anna Ferguson (1840
   Iowa–1903 Washington))
Meeting once every three years

Rodi (see Blossom Press)

Rodman
Rodman-Roadman-Roddham-Rothman
   Family Association
2306 Westgate
Houston, TX 77019
Phone (713) 529-2333
Harold Helm
$25.00 plus pedigree and family group
   sheets for membership

Roe (see Rothenberger, Rowe)

Roe
*Roe Cousins Family Reunion
9240 Werner Drive
Kewaskum, WI 53040
Phone (414) 626-2696
Dean H. Roe, Publisher
(includes descendants of Benjamin Roe
   and Halsey Roe)
Annual reunion in June near the
   Whitewater, Walworth County,
   Wisconsin, area

Roecklein (see Likes)

Roeder (see Surname Database, Rader)

Roehr (see Clark)

Roelofs (see Rutherford)

Roemer (see Surname Database,
   Dittmann)

Roeter (see Rader)

Roether (see Rader)

Rogers (see Surname Database, Arthur,
   Bodine, Brawley, Brown, Coward,
   Nelson, Newton, Reeks, Rutherford,
   Scott, Shurtleff, Silvers)

Rogers
*Joseph Knight Rogers Family
   Organization
1832 North Barkley
Mesa, AZ 85203
Phone (602) 835-0705
J. M. Denham
(includes allied families of Collins,
   Gardner, Hows, Marston, Sinclair and
   Stratton)

Rogers
*Thomas Rogers Society, Inc.
1208 Maple Avenue
Evanston, IL 60202-1217
Phone (847) 328-7031
Mrs. George Clark Frederick, President
Pub. *Newsletter*, three times per year;
   (includes descendants of Thomas
   Rogers, a signer of the Mayflower
   Compact 1620)
Application fee, annual or life
   membership; triennial meeting in
   September in Plymouth, Massachusetts

Rogers
*Rogers Clan
Highway 87 North
PO Box 340
Burkeville, TX 75932
Phone (409) 565-4751
Helen Rogers Skelton

Rogers
*Rogers Roots
1321 Gum Tree
Huffman, TX 77336
Phone (713) 324-3797
Molly Bateman Reigard, Editor
Pub. *Rogers Roots*, quarterly, $15.00 per
   year subscription; (includes Ro(d)gers,
   mostly southern, with a few northern
   lines)

Rogers
Rogers Research Data
323 Cedarcrest Court East
PO Box 779
Napavine, WA 98565-0779
Phone (360) 262-3300

Ruby Simonson McNeill
Pub. *Rogers Research Data*, irregularly,
   $5.75 plus $2.00 postage per issue;
   (includes Rodgers)

Rogge (see Rugg)

Roggia
*Roggia Surname Organization
3 Brazill Lane
Whitehall, MT 59759
Phone (406) 287-3369
Lindia Roggia Lovshin

Rogstad (see Rockstad)

Rohde (see Lush)

Rohrbach
*Rohrbach Genealogy
PO Box 250
Rockport, ME 04856-0250
Phone (207) 236-6565
Lewis Bunker Rohrbach, C.G.
(includes Rohrbach, all time periods, all
   locations, 30+ spellings)

Rohrer
The Rohrer Families
Rt. 1, Box 96
Arlington, KY 42021

Rojas (see Blossom Press)

Rokstad (see Rockstad)

Roland (see Likes)

Rolfe
*The Pocahontas Foundation
PO Box 431
Berryville, VA 22611
Phone (540-955-1428
Stuart E. Brown, Jr., Executive Director
(includes descendants of Pocohontas,
   who married John Rolfe)

Roller (see Grant)

Roller
*The Roller Family Association
8213 Hamilton
Overland Park, KS 66204
Phone (913) 381-9758
Brenda Taylor
Pub. *The Roller Family Association
   Newsletter*, semiannually (January and
   July)
$5.00 per year membership

Rollings (see Rawlins)

Rollins (see Rawlins)

Rolls (see Robinson)

Roman (see Folk Family Surname
   Exchange)

Rombough (see Rambo)

Römer (see Surname Database)

Romeus (see Hieronymus)

Romich (see Romig)

Romig
*Romig/Romich Family Association
219 North Leonard Street
Green Springs, OH 44836
Phone (419) 639-2358
Lisa Alcala
Pub. *Romig Reflections*, three times per
year (winter, fall and spring)
$4.50 per year membership

Rondey (see Blossom Press)

Rongnion (see Runyan)

Ronk (see Hudlow)

Ronk
Ronk and Showalter Database
4301 Deer Lakes
Wichita, KS 67210-1650
Brenda Robertson
(includes Ranc, Ranck, Rank and Ronk
family which left Paris for Germany,
then settled in Pennsylvania)

Ronquillo (see Blossom Press)

Rook (see Folk Family Surname
Exchange)

Rook
*Folk Family
PO Box 52048
Knoxville, TN 37950-2048
Hester E. Stockton, Owner; Lizzie and
Clara Rook, Co-Editors
Pub. *Rook Roots*, quarterly, $15.00 per
year subscription, $5.00 per issue;
(includes Rauk, Rooke, Rookes,
Rooks, Ruark and Ruck)

Rook
*Rook Reunion
PO Box 52048
Knoxville, TN 37950-2048
Hester E. Stockton
(includes all Rook, Rooke, Rookes,
Rooks and Ruark)
Annual reunion in June at the Red River
Valley Fairgrounds, Paris, Texas

Rooke (see Folk Family Surname
Exchange, Rook)

Rookes (see Rook)

Rooks (see Rook)

Roome
*Roome Surname Organization
150 Brown Street
Saint Clair, MI 48079-4882
Phone (810) 329-9359

George M. Roberts
(includes families from Ontario, U.S.A.,
England)

Rooney (see Dwyer, O'Hara)

Rooney
*Rooney Family Association
9190 Oak Leaf Way
Granite Bay, CA 95746
Phone (916) 791-0405
Linus Joseph Dewald
(includes descendants of Ed. Rooney and
Marg. O'Hara (ca 1810 County Down,
Ireland–))

Roop (see Stoner)

Roop
*Roop-Royer Family
10715 Moosberger Court
Columbia, MD 21044
Phone (410) 531-6020
Richard R. Weber, Historian
(database with over 7,000 names,
especially descendants of John and
Christian Rupp of Lancaster County,
Pennsylvania by the 1750s, and many
Rupps who came to Maryland about
1800 and spelled the name Roop)
Annual reunion in September in
Maryland

Roose
Roose/Ruoss National Family Reunion
(Ruse/Ruiz/Russ)
2207 West Virginia Avenue, Apartment A
Dunbar, WV 25064
Phone (304) 768-1647
Sylvia Kelly

Root (see Barnes, Wright)

Root
*Solomon Francis Root Family
Organization
1144 Palisades Drive, N.W.
Albuquerque, NM 87105-1230
Phone (505) 831-2838
Martha Lane Root Brink, Editor
Pub. *The Flourishing Roots*,
semiannually; (includes descendants of
Solomon Francis Root (1826
Middlefield, Massachusetts–1915 West
Roxbury, Massachusetts) and Amanda
Lane (1839 Gloucester,
Massachusetts–1918 West Roxbury,
Massachusetts))
$1.50 per year membership

Roote (see Barnard)

Roots
Roots Family Organization
PO Box 160185
Austin, TX 78716
Phone (512) 263-5226
Ann Jones, Editor
Pub. *Roots Roots*, irregularly, $3.00 per
issue

Roper
*John William Roper Database
4392 South 1300 West
Salt Lake City, UT 84123
Phone (801) 261-4414
Marianne Roper Van Beekum
(includes descendants of John William
Roper and Suzanna Smith, who were
married in 1831)

Rordin (see Waltermire)

Rosano (see Gratta)

Rose (see Campbell, Clark, Dockery,
MacFaddien, Smith, Tidwell)

Rose
*Rose Family Association
1474 Montelegre Drive
San Jose, CA 95120-4831
Phone (408) 268-2137
Christine Rose, C.G., C.G.L., F.A.S.G.,
Editor
Pub. *Rose Family Bulletin*, quarterly;
Rose Association Newsletter, quarterly;
(includes Rose, all nationalities,
nationwide)
$20.00 per year membership includes
both periodicals; reunion

Rose
*Clan Rose Society of America
629 Mohican Trail
Wilmington, NC 28409
Phone (919) 395-5697
Kirk D. Rose, Convener
Pub. *Clan Rose Society of America
Newsletter*, quarterly; (from the U.S.)
$15.00 per year regular membership

Rose
The Israel Rose Family Association
221 S.E. 12th Avenue, Apartment 8
Hillsboro, OR 97123-4392
Julie Jones
(includes descendants of the family
which came in the wagon train of 1862
to eastern Oregon and eastern
Washington)
Annual reunion on third Saturday and
Sunday of August

Rose
*Hulda Jane Rose Lester Family
Organization
PO Box 1084
Welch, WV 24801
Phone (304) 436-6677
Carrie Marie Lester Smith, Organizer
(includes descendants of Mr. France Rose
(1753–after 1860))

Rose
Hiram Rose (Rowell), Jr. Descendants
400 West 6th Avenue
Cheyenne, WY 80758
Margi S. Bagley, Family Historian

Roseberry
Roseberry Family Organization
925 East Sixth Avenue
Mesa, AZ 85204
N. Dees
Pub. *Roseberry Family Newsletter*

Roseborough
*Roseborough Surname Organization
George McIntosh Family Organization
PO Box 284
Belgrade, MT 59714-0284
Phone (406) 656-0979
Irma Jane Mauger

Rosebrooks
*Walter Lyman Rosebrooks Descendants,
    New England
PO Box 67
Columbia, CT 06237-0067
Phone (203) 228-0080
Mrs. Marion Rosebrooks Emmons,
    Family Researcher

Roseman (see Moser)

Rosenberger (see Shaull)

Rosenblatt
*Rosenblatt Surname Organization
199 Commodore Drive
Milledgeville, GA 31061
Phone (912) 968-7425
Richard Bialac

Rosenblum (see Israelite)

Rosener (see Tasset)

Rosenow (see Mandel)

Rosier
Journal of Rosier Families
2305 East Indian Trail
Chandler, OK 74834
Gerald Hoover
Pub. *Journal of Rosier Families*

Ross (see Album, Bloss, Corson, Heath,
    Muir, Pellien, Stewart, Wedmore,
    Wigelius)

Ross
Oak Leaf Publishing
22 Creek Road, #64
Irvine, CA 91714
Pub. *Ross Family Newsletter*, bimonthly,
    $10.00 per year subscription

Ross
*Ross and Kin Update
250 Garrard Boulevard
Richmond, CA 94801-3423
Phone (510) 235-8716
Vera L. Dean, Researcher, Author,
    Compiler and Publisher
(includes research on Cook and Martin
    families of Wayne County, Tennessee,
    and Adams, Arnold, Brooks, Cole,
    Cook, Curtis, Dean, Dickey, Fryer,

George, Hamm, Horton, Lively,
    Maddix (any spelling), Martin, Meeks,
    Page, Powers, Reddell, Ross,
    Standridge, Thompson, Ward, Watts,
    Wilson, Yates and Young families in
    Newton, Pope and Searcy counties,
    Arkansas)

Ross
Ross Reunion
Rt. 1, Box 221
Rochester, IL 62073
D. M. Ross
Annual reunion on the third Sunday of
    September in Springfield, Illinois

Ross
Ross Family Association
2508 Airway Road
Muncie, IN 47304
Dolores Black Rench, Secretary
(includes descendants of Jasper and
    Elizabeth Milliken Ross)
Annual reunion on the second Sunday of
    June in Aurora City Park, Aurora,
    Indiana

Ross
*Jesse Ross Family Organization
14613 Park Avenue Extension
Meadville, PA 16335
Phone (814) 724-3551
Robert H. Ross
(includes descendants of Jesse Ross
    (1781 New Providence,
    Massachusetts–1863 Chittenden
    County, Vermont) and Eunice Burr)

Ross
*Clan Ross Association of the United
    States, Inc.
5430 South Fifth Street
Arlington, VA 22204
Phone (703) 671-5210
Marilyn Ross, F.S.A. Scot, Membership
    Secretary
Pub. *Clan Ross Newsletter*, quarterly
    (includes Anderson, Andison,
    Andrew(s), Corbet(t), Crow(e), Croy,
    Deas, Denoon, Dingwall, Duthie, Fair,
    Fear(n), Gillanders, Hagart, Haggart,
    Lockhart, MacAndrew, McCullie,
    McCulloch, McLullich, MacTaggert,
    MacTear, MacTier, MacTyre, Mitchell,
    Taggart, Tarrell, Tullo, Tulloch, Vass,
    Wass and Waters)
$20.00 per year membership

Ross
*Lauri-Lines
South 2827 Ivory
Spokane, WA 99203
Phone (509) 624-0533
Laurine Mae Palmerton Logsdon
Pub. *Ross Records and Lines*, irregularly,
    $6.00 plus $1.75 postage and handling
    or $2.75 foreign postage and handling
    (Washington State residents add 63¢
    tax)

Rossiter (see Alsop)

Rostock (see Kunkel)

Rostron
*Mary Ann Rostron Family Organization
PO Box 383
Lehi, UT 84043
Verona Blackham Balle

Röter (see Rader)

Röther (see Rader)

Rothermel
*Rothermel Family Association
Rt. 1, Box 178
Mohrsville, PA 19541
Phone (215) 488-6079
Florence Heydt, Historian

Rothlisberger (see Rentsch)

Rothman (see Rodman)

Rötter (see Rader)

Roudabugh (see Roudabush)

Roudabush
Rt. 10, Box 28
Harrisonburg, VA 22801
Phone (540) 867-5257
Rev. Andrew Eggman, Jr.
(includes descendents of Jacob
    Roudabush and Malinda Andes who
    married in Rockingham County,
    Virginia, in 1843; variant spellings:
    Radibush, Rodenbough, Roudabugh,
    Roudebush, Roudenbush, Rouderbush,
    Roudinbush, Routenbush,
    Rowdenbush, Ruebush)

Roudebush (see Roudabush)

Roudenbush (see Roudabush)

Rouderbush (see Roudabush)

Roudinbush (see Roudabush)

Roughan (see Cian)

Roundy (see Allen)

Roundy
*Shadrach Roundy Family Organization
PO Box 114
Fredonia, AZ 86022
Phone (520) 643-7198
Clorene Roundy Hoyt

Rounsville
Rounsville Family Organization
535 North Luce Road
Ithaca, MI 48847
Mary E. Strouse

Rous
*The Rous, Rouse, Rowse family from

Devon England
8313 Highway 19
Cross Plains, WI 53528
E-mail: jcstreet@facstaff.wisc.edu
John C. Street
(includes any time period)

Rouse (see The Memorial Foundation of
the Germanna Colonies, Bodine, Rous)

Rousse (see Blossom Press)

Rousseau (see Johnson)

Rousselle (see Blossom Press)

Routenbush (see Roudabush)

Routt
Routt
1155 Weyburn Lane, #1
San Jose, CA 95129-3613
Patrick L. McCurdy
Pub. *Routt*, semiannually, $5.00 per year
subscription

Row (see Rowe)

Rowden
Rowden Family Association
1 Kingston Drive
Springfield, MO 62702
Pub. *Rowden Family Newsletter*,
annually
$16.00 per year membership

Rowdenbush (see Roudabush)

Rowe (see Miehls, Newton)

Rowe
*Annie Lane Memorial Genealogical
Organization (ALMGO)
c/o 1775 Conrad Avenue
San Jose, CA 95124
Phone (408) 264-5326
Milton Lane, President
Pub. *ALMGO Newsletter*, annually;
(ancestors and descendants of Percy
Lane, who was married in 1904 in
Maine to Annie Rowe, and of John
Kendall, who was married in 1902 in
Maine to Eunice McAllister)
Dues

Rowe
*Rowe Family Association
401 Spruce Street
Dowagiac, MI 49047-1054
Phone (616) 782-8848
Shirley Chennault

Rowe
Rowe Register
11 Rand Road
North Barnstead, NH 03225
Phone (603) 776-6996
Richard Herbert Tivey
Pub. *Rowe Register*, quarterly, $35.00 per
year subscription; (includes Rauh, Roe

and Row)
$50.00 per year active membership

Rowe
*Rowe Family Names
819 North Ladd Court
East Wenatchee, WA 98802
Phone (509) 884-3004
Allene Rowe Zitting, First Officer
(includes descendants of Alonzo Lincoln
(ca 1822 Massachusetts–) and
Catherine Compton (ca 1827 possibly
Missouri–), also allied surnames: Baer/
Behr, Compton, Curtis, Dial, Dowis,
Fimple, Harris, Lincoln, Midkiff,
Parsons, Pettit, Rowe/Roe, Sprinkle,
Thacker, Turley, Wood)

Rowell (see Rose)

Rowell
*Rowell Foundation
645 Sabine
P.O.D.-A
Orchard, TX 77464
Phone (409) 478-7190
W. Douglass Rowell, III
Pub. *Newsletter*, irregularly

Rower (see Dietwiler, Miehls)

Rowland (see Holden)

Rowle (see Rowley)

Rowlee (see Rowley)

Rowlett (see Folk Family Surname
Exchange)

Rowley (see Goodenow)

Rowley
Rowley Researcher
9 Horicon Avenue
Glens Falls, NY 12801
Phone (518) 792-1726
Ernst Spencer
Pub. *Rowley Researcher*, annually;
(includes Rowle, Rowlee and Rowly)

Rowly (see Rowley)

Rowse (see Rous)

Rowzee (see Folk Family Surname
Exchange)

Roy (see Donnachaidh, Gregor, Johnson,
Lagesse, MacGillivray, Roye)

Royce (see Fisher, Rice)

Royds (see MacDuff)

Royer (see Frantz, Roop, Stoner)

Royer
Royer Family Association
South 1813 Warren

Veradale, WA 99037
Susan Ingalls

Ruark (see Rook)

Ruby (see Howard)

Ruck (see Rook)

Rucker
Rucker Ruckus
1516 Elliot Drive
Jeffersonville, IN 47130
Mary Rucker Snyder
Pub. *Rucker Ruckus*, quarterly

Rudd (see Lush)

Rudd
*Rudd Family Research Association
461 Emerson
Chula Vista, CA 91911
Phone (619) 422-4445
Norman N. Rudd, Co-founder
Pub. *Newsletter*, semiannually (May and
November); (includes descendants of
Gordon Rudd and Alicia Wellwood,
who had nine children 1809 to 1831 in
Queens County, Ireland)
$8.00 per year membership for
individuals, $12.00 per year
membership for families

Ruddick (see Reddick)

Rudisill (see Schindel)

Rudland (see Harmon)

Rue (see Cox, Movius)

Ruebush (see Roudabush)

Ruegg (see Rugg)

Ruff
Ruff/Stevens Family Organization
27491 Clearlake Drive
Canyon Country, CA 91351-3610
Bonner Ruff

Ruffcorn (see Likes)

Rug (see Rugg)

Rugeley
*Rugeley Family Association
7614 River Point Drive
Houston, TX 77063
Phone (713) 465-8228 (home); (713)
526-5511 (office)
Dr. and Mrs. W. Rugeley, Livesay
Pub. *RUGFAN* (RUgeley Family
Association Newsletter) (includes
descendants of John Rugeley who
came to Texas in 1842, son of the
original immigrant, Col. Henry
Rugeley, who settled in South
Carolina about 1765, and whose line has been
traced back to 1154 in England)

$10.00 donation per year membership for households

Rugg
*Rugg Archives
PO Box 332
Granville, OH 43023-0332
John Daily Rugg, Director of Research
(includes Rugg, Rugge, Rug, Ruegg and
    Rogge surnames, especially Rugg from
    Pennsylvania since 1790)
No charge

Rugge (see Rugg)

Ruggles (see Surname Sources)

Rugh
*Rugh Family Reunion
579 Monte Vista Drive
Greenwood, IN 46143
Welden Rugh

Ruiz (see Blossom Press, Roose)

Rule (see MacDuff, Turnbull)

Rumbley (see Surname Sources)

Rumbo (see Rambo)

Rumford
*Rumford Surname Organization
3 Brazill Lane
Whitehall, MT 59759
Phone (406) 287-3369
Lindia Roggia Lovshin

Rumley (see Surname Sources)

Rumple (see Brawley)

Rumplemouser (see Shaull)

Runciman (see Laing)

Runion (see Runyan)

Runkle
*Runkle Family Association
11 Runyon Court
Tuckerton, NJ 08087
Phone (908) 782-6155
Jane B. Duffy, Historian
Pub. *Runkle Family Association
    Newsletter*, semiannually
$20.00 per year membership

Runtermann (see Sorenson)

Runyan
*Runyan Reunion
Rt. 1, Box 7
Bonnerdale, AR 71933
Marie Runyan Wright, Publisher
(includes descendants of Vincent
    Rongnion (1645–1713), a Huguenot
    who came from France ca 1666 and
    married Ann Martha Boutcher,
    daughter of John Boutcher (1625–), a

Huguenot; also Runion, Runyon
    variant spellings)

Runyon (see Hatfield, Runyan)

Ruoss (see Roose)

Rupe (see Scott)

Rupp (see Roop)

Rupp
*Pennsylvania-German Rupp Family
107 West Sunhill Road
Manheim, PA 17545
Phone (717) 665-5869
D. Ernest Weinhold
(especially descendants of the very early
    immigrants who settled in northeast
    Lancaster County, Pennsylvania, and
    nearby areas)

Ruse (see Roose)

Rusel (see Russell)

Rush (see Garner, Kunkel, Newton,
    Oney)

Rush
*Rush Family Association
6062 Lake Nadine Place
Agoura Hills, CA 91301-1421
Phone (818) 991-7691; E-mail:
    s_selmer@sageepub.com or
    76070.511@compuserve.com or
    JSVS92A@prodigy.com
Susan Selmer
Pub. *Newsletter*, quarterly, free queries;
    (worldwide database)
$16.00 per year membership

Rush
Rush Family Organization
44540 Gratiot
Mount Clemens, MI 48043
Phone (313) 463-7422
Patricia Rush Gilbert
Pub. *The Rush News*, quarterly
$5.00 per year membership

Rushton (see Weatherbee)

Rusich (see Blossom Press)

Rusk (see Buchanan)

Rusk
*The Rusk Family Organization
3802 Goldfinch Drive, S.E.
Lacey, WA 98503-7126
Phone (360) 493-2065
Dorothy Lee Palmer, Editor
Pub. *Rusk Roundup*, semiannually;
    (includes Rusk/Ruske, worldwide)

Ruske (see Rusk)

Russ (see Roose, Rust)

Russel (see Russell)

Russell (see The Memorial Foundation
    of the Germanna Colonies, Album,
    Corson, Lush)

Russell
Russell Register
4041 Pedley Road, #18
Riverside, CA 92509
Phone (714) 685-8936
Frances R. Nelson, Editor
Pub. *Russell Register*, quarterly, $17.00
    per year subscription

Russell
*Roots Researchers
East Smith
Springfield, MO 65802
Phone (417) 833-4282
Judith A. McClung, Editor
Pub. *Russell Relatives and Ballengee
    Trails*, three times per year, $6.00 per
    year subscription

Russell
*Russell Surname Organization
Charles Lyman Russell Family
    Organization
HC 34 Box 38
Caliente, NV 89008
Pamela Russell Jensen
No cost

Russell
Russell
2873 Mercedes
Odessa, TX 79764
Shirley Shumate
Pub. *Russell*, quarterly, $20.00 per year
    subscription

Russon (see McCune)

Rust (see Folk Family Surname
    Exchange, LaRue)

Rust
*Folk Family
PO Box 52048
Knoxville, TN 37950-2048
Hester E. Stockton, Owner; Janet Rust
    Stinnett, Editor
Pub. *Rust Families*, quarterly, $15.00 per
    year subscription, $5.00 per issue;
    (includes Russ)

Rutenschroer
*Rutenschroer Reunion
79 Drakes Ridge
Bennington, IN 47011
Phone (812) 427-3914
Ellyn R. Kern
Pub. *Rutenschroer Reunion*, $6.00 for
    four issues; (includes descendants of
    Adam and Sophia Rutenshroer, who
    arrived in the U.S. about 1840 and
    settled in Delhi Township, Hamilton
    County, Ohio)

Rutherford (see Tidwell)

Ruton (see Rutan)

Ruttan (see Rutan)

Rutter (see Links Genealogy
    Publications)

Ryan (see Christopher)

Ryder (see Ryther)

Ryerkerk (see Poll)

Ryker (see Riker)

Ryker
Ryker-Riker Historical Society, Inc.
Rt. 2, Ryker's Ridge
Madison, IN 47250
Geneva Cull
$10.00 per year membership

Ryker
Ryker/Riker Family Reunion
4000 N.E. 59th Terrace
Kansas City, MO 64119
Mary Ryker Aleg

Rylander (see Blossom Press)

Rymal (see McCune)

Ryther
Ryther Reunion
HC 06, Box 231
Park Rapids, MN 56470
Will Ryther
(includes descendants of George C.
    Ryther (Ryder) and Margaret Dalton)

Sabean (see Sabin)

Sabin (see Corson, Wright)

Sabin
*The Sabin Association
13380 South Highway 211
PO Box 577
Molalla, OR 97038
Phone (503) 829-7444
Patricia Sabin Torsen, President
Pub. *Sabin/Sabine/Sabean Genealogical
    Newsletter*, quarterly (April, July,
    October and January); (includes
    descendants of William Sabin of
    Rehoboth)
$15.00 per year membership for
    individuals

Sabin
*David and Elizabeth Dorwart Sabin
    Family Organization
1937 South Main Street
Orem, UT 84058-7409
Phone (801) 225-7218
Lee D. Hansen, President
(includes descendants of David Sabin
    and his wife, Elizabeth Dorwart, of
    Lancaster, Pennsylvania and Utah)

Sabine (see Corson, Sabin)

Sackett (see Alsop, Heath)

Sadeen (see Moody)

Sadler (see Price)

Safley
*Safley/Saufley/Sofley Clearinghouse
762 County Road 502
Monette, AR 72447-9113
Phone (501) 486-2234
Joyce Hambleton Whitten
Queries for SASE

Sage (see Weimar)

Sage
*Sage Family Organization
8205 Schribner Road
Wayland, NY 14572
Phone (716) 728-5683
James R. Sage, Family Representative
(includes all Sage and allied families for
    Sage Genealogy revision to be
    published about November 1996)

Sager (see Bechtel)

St. Ann (see Blossom Press)

St. Clair (see Newmyer, Sinkler)

St. Gemme (see Beauvais)

St. George (see McCanna)

Saint John
Saint John Family Register
2190 Camino Largo Drive
Chino Hills, CA 91709
Trish Elliott Collins
Pub. *Saint John Family Register*

St. Philip (see Blossom Press)

St. Romain (see Johnson)

Salinovich (see Blossom Press)

Salisbury (see Barnard)

Sallee (see Kahler)

Salmon (see Templin)

Salmon
*Salmon Family Association, Inc.
2055 Seven Lakes South
Seven Lakes, NC 27376
Phone (910) 673-1607
Franklin B. Tucker, President
(includes descendants of Revolutionary
    War soldier Capt. Peter Salmon (1740–
    1825) of Mount Olive, New Jersey)

Saltoun (see MacDuff)

Salvant (see Blossom Press)

Salyer
Salyer Family Newsletter
Rt. 3, Box 265 AA
Ferrum, VA 24088
Kermit W. Sayler
Pub. *Salyer Family Newsletter*

Sampson (see Clark, Corson, Holden)

Sampson
*Sampson Surname Organization
3 Brazill Lane
Whitehall, MT 59759
Phone (406) 287-3369
Lindia Roggia Lovshin

Samuel
*Samuel Family Depository
7805 Linda Lane
Anchorage, AK 99518
Phone (907) 344-9581
Barbara C. Samuels
Pub. *Samuel Searcher*, quarterly, free

Samuels (see Folk Family Surname
    Exchange)

Samuelson (see Wigelius)

Sanborn (see Corson)

Sanborn
Sanborn
7031 Leawood Street
Kalamazoo, MI 49002-4081
Elmer Corliss Sanborn
Pub. *Sanborn*, semiannually
$6.00 per year membership

Sandau (see Cordes)

Sandefur (see Taylor)

Sanders (see Barnard, Carpenter, Hall,
    Job)

Sanders
*William Sanders Family Organization
PO Box 476
Energy, IL 62933-0476
Floyd Davis
(includes descendants of Mariah and
    William Sanders (South Carolina–1830
    Chetham County, Tennessee), possibly
    the brother of Andrew, son of Isaac,
    and grandson of William Sanders and
    his wife Sarah)
Annual reunion in central part of the
    states (southern Illinois or southeast
    Missouri)

Sanders
Sanders
1408 North Cheyenne Drive
Richardson, TX 75080
Mary Hall-Marshall
Pub. *Sanders*, quarterly, $15.00 per year
    subscription

Sanderson
Sanderson-Saunderson
1408 North Cheyenne Drive
Richardson, TX 75080
Mary Hall-Marshall
Pub. *Sanderson-Saunderson*, quarterly,
$15.00 per year subscription

Sandford (see MacDuff)

Sandilands (see Douglas, MacDuff)

Sandison (see Gunn)

Sandlin (see Douglas)

Sands (see MacDuff)

Sands
*Sands Family Organization
711 Kensington Avenue
Flint, MI 48503
Phone (313) 234-8574
Phyllis S. Kitson
Pub. *Sands Sentinel*, monthly, free

Sanford (see Folk Family Surname
Exchange, Rutherford)

Sanford
*Sanford Families Association
PO Box 843
Aberdeen, WA 98550
Phone (206) 533-0781
Franki Loring, Editor
Pub. *Sanford Et All*, quarterly; (includes
Sanford and allied families
$10.00 per year membership

Sanks
Sanks Connection
137 North Birdsey Street
Columbus, WI 53925
Phone (414) 623-2251
Robert R. Sanks, Editor
Pub. *Sanks Connection*, annually
(February), free

Sant (see Covert)

Sapp
*Sapp Family Association
712 N.W. 95th Terrace
Gainesville, FL 32607
Phone (352) 332-2065; (352) 392-2161
ext. 164
Mitchell E. Sapp, Editor
Pub. *The Sapp Family Association
Newsletter*, quarterly (January, April,
July and October)
$15.00 per year membership; reunion

Sappington
*Sappington, Family History
Sappington's of America Gathering
2809 Mills Road
Prescott, MI 48756-9509
Phone (517) 873-5191 (home);
(517) 345-0711 (work)
Mary Ellen Sappington Good, Historian
Pub. *Newsletter*, annually

Sargent (see Catlow, Harpole, Heath)

Sargent
*Phillip Heritage House
605 Benton
Missoula, MT 59801
Phone (406) 543-3495
Ruth Phillip, MAS R.G.
Pub. *Sargent Newsletter*, annually
$5.00 per year membership

Sarine
Sarine-Sirrine-Surine Family Newsletter
2521 West Needmore Highway
Charlotte, MI 48813
Phone (517) 543-3021
Debra Stadel Eddy, Family Historian
Pub. *Sarine-Sirrine-Surine Family
Newsletter*

Sarnecke (see Newcomb)

Sartain
Sartain Family Newsletter
PO Box 543
Jerome, ID 83338
George Atwood
Pub. *Sartain Family Newsletter*

Sass (see Werner)

Sassaman (see Sossoman)

Sassaman
*Sassaman/Sossaman/Sossomon Family
Association
868 Pippin Avenue
Sunnyvale, CA 94087
Phone (408) 739-6089
James E. Sosaman, Family Historian
Pub. *Sassaman/Sossaman/Sossomon
Family News*, three times per year
$5.00 per year membership

Sassoman (see Sossoman)

Satterfield (see Job)

Satterthwaite (see Lynch)

Satterwhite
*Nall News Publishing Company
PO Box 2186
Willingboro, NJ 08046-2186
Josephine Crittenberger-Nall, Editor-
Publisher
Pub. *Satterwhite Searches*, quarterly,
$16.00 per year subscription

Satyrs (see Rutherford)

Saucier (see Johnson)

Sauerman
Sauerman
Whispering Oaks
5821 Rowland Hill Road
Cascade, MD 21719-1939
Phone (301) 416-2660
Victor Gebhart, President
Pub. *Sauerman*, annually, $2.00 per issue

Saufley (see Safley)

Saum
Saum Newsletter
300 Ohio Street
Jackson Center, OH 45334
Verna Geer Taglieber
Pub. *Saum Newsletter*, quarterly

Saunders (see Sanders)

Saunders
Saunders
1408 North Cheyenne Drive
Richardson, TX 75080
Mary Hall-Marshall
Pub. *Saunders*, quarterly, $15.00 per year
subscription

Saunderson (see Sanderson)

Sausaman (see Sossoman)

Sauve (see Haling)

Savage (see Album, Friend, Hyatt, Scott,
Worthy)

Savage
Dr. John Mulkey Savage Descendants
Organization
832 Bentley Street
Monmouth, OR 97361-9732
Phone (503) 838-6154
Ruth I. Savage Thompson, Family
Representative
(includes descendants of Dr. John
Mulkey Savage and Jane Wait/Waite,
who came to Oregon in 1850 from
Missouri)
Reunion

Savary (see Savory)

Savery (see Savory)

Savil (see Rutherford)

Savoie (see Blossom Press)

Savory (see Mullicken)

Savory
Savory Family Organization
85 Main Street
Groveland, MA 01834-1413
Brian Smith, Family Representative
(includes Savary, Savery and Savory
families of Bonin Islands and New
England)

Savoye (see Johnson)

Sawin
*Sawin Society
82 Humiston Drive Extension
Bethany, CT 06524-3174
Phone (203) 393-0657
Beverly Sawin Davie, Editor
Pub. *Sawin Society Newsletter*, three
times per year; (original ancestor, John

Sawin[1], arrived from Boxford, Suffold County, England in 1641, settled Watertown, Massachusetts)
$5.00 per year membership

Sawyer
*Sawyer Family Association
1111 Simpkins Road
Napa, CA 94558
Phone (707) 255-9508
Mrs. Billie Borders, Editor
(includes Sawyer, Greathouse, Hite, Hyde, Morton, Overall, Whitaker and Whitehead)

Sawyer
*History Books
Drawer 279
Belpre, OH 45714
Herbert L. Roush,Sr.
(family genealogical printouts resulting from the author's research of the life of Nathaniel Leonard Sawyer (1757–1813), one of the unknown adventurers who helped settle the Northwest Territory: Ebenezer Porter, Lydia Sawyer Walker, Sarah Sawyer Browning, John Leonard Sawyer, Porter Sawyer, Mary Frances Sawyer Stewart, Harriot Sawyer Humphrey, Benair Clement Sawyer, Samuel Thompson Sawyer)

Sawyer
Sawyer Reunion
221 S.E. 12th Avenue, Apartment 8
Hillsboro, OR 97123-4392
Julie Jones
(includes descendants of James A. Sawyer and Parmelia Cummings)

Saxby (see Heath)

Saye
*Saye Family Association
2750 South Maryland Parkway
PO Box 15070
Las Vegas, NV 89114
Phone (702) 732-2233 (business); (702) 225-5599 (home); (702) 731-2813 (FAX)
Patricia A. Saye-Barcus, Family Representative
Pub. *Whadda Ya Say, Saye*, quarterly, $5.00 per year subscription; (includes related families of Barnes, Elliott, Gardner, Hodge, Kennett, Ricks, Robbins and Swain)
$20.00 per year membership

Sayler (see Stoner)

Scadlock
*Scadlock Association
535 North Harding Road
Modesto, CA 95351
Phone (209) 571-3902
Gerald Allen, Historian and Publisher-Editor-Secretary

Pub. *Scadaddles*, annually (May); (includes Scadlock, Nope, Jarrett, Goss, Duval)
$10.00 per year membership

Scagel (see Scaggel)

Scagell (see Scaggel)

Scaggel
*Descendants of Christopher Scaggel
1663 Barton Drive
Eugene, OR 97404
Phone (503) 688-1528
Macie Bryan Evans
Pub. *The Schedule*, annually (December), no charge; (tracing descendants of Christopher Scaggel of Rye, New Hampshire in 1720, variant spellings: Scagel, Scagell, Sceggel, Schagel and Sedgell)

Scaife
*Scaife Surname Organization
3 Brazill Lane
Whitehall, MT 59759
Phone (406) 287-3369
Lindia Roggia Lovshin

Scaith (see Shaw)

Scalf (see Bloss)

Scallon (see Johnson)

Scarabin (see Blossom Press)

Scarborough (see MacFaddien)

Scarce
*Scarce/Scearce Family Organization
3607 Arlington
Lawton, OK 73505
Phone (405) 355-7432; (405) 355-7053 FAX; E-mail: bfwf02a@prodigy.com
Aulena Scearce Gibson
Pub. *Searce/Scarce Newsletter*, quarterly; (includes families from the early U.S.)

Scarlett (see Cranston)

Scarlett
*Scarlett Surname Organization
PO Box 8072
Longview, TX 75607-8072
Ben R. Reynolds

Scearce (see Scarce)

Sceggel (see Scaggel)

Schaarschmidt
*Schaarschmidt Family Association/Data Bank
PO Box 75
Moran, WY 83013
Phone (307) 543-2420
John Sharsmith
(includes descendants of Johann Nikolaus Schaarschmidt, son of Anton

Daniel Schaarschmidt (1782–1865), also Scharschmidt)

Schackelford (see Ammons)

Schad (see Heath)

Schade (see Arthur)

Schaedel (see Schindel)

Schaefer (see Shafer)

Schaeffer (see Nelson, Shafer)

Schafer (see Shafer)

Schaff (see Kinney)

Schaffer (see Shafer)

Schaffer
*Schaffer Family Organization
2750 South Maryland Parkway
PO Box 15070
Las Vegas, NV 89114
Phone (702) 732-2233 (business); (702) 225-5599 (home); (702) 731-2813 (FAX)
Patricia A. Saye-Barcus, Family Representative
Pub. *The Schaffer Saver*, quarterly, $5.00 per year subscription; (includes related families of Bading, Graef, Oliver, Peters and Ploetz)
$20.00 per year membership

Schagel (see Scaggel)

Schaiman (see Israelite)

Schalton (see Sheldon)

Schaper (see Bodeker)

Scharf (see Kettwig)

Scharschmidt (see Schaarschmidt)

Schartzer
*BGM Publications
28635 Old Hideaway Road
Cary, IL 60013-9726
Phone (847) 639-2400
Betty G. Massman, Editor and Publisher
(research on the Shartzer/Shertzer surname)

Schaubel (see Surname Database)

Schaup (see Sharp)

Schawb (see Fries)

Schayot (see Blossom Press)

Scheib
*BGM Publications
28635 Old Hideaway Road
Cary, IL 60013-9726

Phone (847) 639-2400
Betty G. Massman, Editor and Publisher
Pub. *Durch Die Fensterscheibe "Thru
   the Windowpane" for the Scheib,
   Shipe, Shive (et var) surname*,
   quarterly, $18.00 per year subscription;
   (written in English)

Scheible
*Johann Andreas Scheible Family
816 North Chester
Monticello, AR 71655
Phone (501) 367-2348
Frieda Scheible Fischer, Co-organizer
Donation for membership; annual
   reunion on Memorial Day weekend in
   even-numbered years at Bethany
   United Church of Christ, Berger,
   Missouri

Scheibler (see Likes)

Scheladen (see Sheldon)

Scheladin (see Sheldon)

Scheladon (see Sheldon)

Schelden (see Sheldon)

Scheldon (see Sheldon)

Schell
*Schell/Shell Clearinghouse
PO Box 335
Owenton, KY 40359-0335
Doris Shell Gill, Genealogist and Family
   Historian
$5.00 for query

Schelle (see Shelly)

Schelten (see Sheldon)

Scheltin (see Sheldon)

Schelton (see Sheldon)

Scheltun (see Sheldon)

Schenck
*Schenck Family History Association
22845 N.E. Eighth Street, #125
Plainfield, NJ 07063
Mary H. Slawson, Secretary
(includes Schanck, Van Nortwick, Van
   Noordwick, Hennessy, Johnson, Van
   Kouwenhoven/Conover and Fuller
   direct lines; more than 200,000 linked
   names, portions of 52 generations, as
   well as journals, biographies, pictures,
   maps, wills, Bible plates, war records,
   etc.)

Scherer (see Surname Database)

Scherer
August Scherer Family Organization
17841 Anthony
Country Club Hills, IL 60478
Phone (312) 798-7647
George Scherer

Scherer
Scherer Family Reunion
215 Spanish Oak Drive
Clinton, MS 39056-5839
Mary Scherer, Family Genealogist

Scherkes (see Links Genealogy
   Publications)

Schertzer (see Schartzer)

Schexnayder (see Johnson)

Schicker (see Dietwiler)

Schilden (see Sheldon)

Schilling (see Klewer, Sheely)

Schilter (see Rothenberger)

Schimpfessel
*Schimpfessel Family Association
9190 Oak Leaf Way
Granite Bay, CA 95746
Phone (916) 791-0405
Linus Joseph Dewald
(includes all phonetic variations:
   Schimpfessel, Shimfesel, Shimpfessel,
   etc.)

Schindel
Schindel-Shindel-Shindle Reunion
27 Webster Street
Westminster, MD 21157-5521
Phone (410) 857-9185
(includes descendants of Georg Friedrich
   Schindel (1724–1804) and Maria
   Barbara Hamm (1725–1797) of
   Lancaster County, Pennsylvania
   (1748–1775), and York County,
   Pennsylvania (1775–1805); George
   Shindle (1753–1821) and Elizabeth
   Hambright of Lancaster County,
   Pennsylvania (allied families: Rudisill
   (Washington County, Maryland),
   Shreiner, Metzger); Anna Maria
   Schindel (1755–1828) and George
   Hambright of Lancaster County,
   Pennsylvania; Elizabeth Schindel
   (1757–) and Frederick Schaedel/
   Shettel of York County, Pennsylvania;
   Ludwig Schindel (1759–1830) and
   Elizabeth Wilt of Franklin County,
   Pennsylvania, and Washington County,
   Maryland; Frederick Shindel (1760–
   1815) and Gertrude Windemeyer of
   York County, Pennsylvania (allied
   family: Lichtenberger); Susanna
   Schindel (1769–1862) and Jacob
   Rudisill of Nelson County, Virginia
   (allied families: Rodes, Smith, Miller))

Biennial reunion in August of even-
   numbered years in Washington County,
   Maryland, or Franklin County,
   Pennsylvania, areas

Schirley (see Shirley)

Schlagel (see Schlegel)

Schlegel (see Savage)

Schlegel
*Schlegel/Schlagel Family Association
731 Firing Center Road
Yakima, WA 98901
Phone (509) 248-3672
Bette Schlagel Rogers, Family Historian/
   Reunion Organizer
(includes Schlegels from Sonneborn,
   Prussia, Germany, 1850, to Ontario,
   South Dakota and Washington State;
   name spelling changed in Ontario)
Reunion

Schleger (see Bodeker)

Schlem (see Schliem)

Schley (see Sager)

Schliem
*Schliem-Schlem Family Reunion
PO Box 238
302 East Prospect Street
South Wayne, WI 53587
Phone (608) 439-5418
Earl Schliem, Historian and Vice-
   President
Donation for membership; annual
   reunion on the first Sunday of August
   in South Wayne Shelter House, South
   Wayne, Wisconsin

Schlotzhauer (see Kunkel)

Schmalz (see Lush)

Schmeiser (see Smyser)

Schmeisser (see Smyser)

Schmidt (see Drury, Kelm, Kinney,
   Koehn, McCune)

Schmidt
Schmidt
821 South First Street
Princeton, IL 61356
Pub. *Schmidt*, quarterly, $15.00 per year
   subscription

Schmitz (see Dietwiler)

Schmoe
Schmoe Family Organization
764 North Spring Valley Parkway
Elko, NV 89801
Judy Swett
Pub. *Schmoe Family Newsletter*

Schmucker
*Schmucker-Smoker-Smucker Family
  Association
2513 College Avenue
Goshen, IN 46526
Phone (219) 534-0841
John R. Smucker, President
Pub. *Schmucker-Smoker-Smucker
  Newsletter*, annually; (includes
  descendants of Christian Schmucker,
  immigrant of 1752)
Donation for membership; reunion every
  five years

Schnabel
*Schnabel Family Association
422 Oak Glen Drive
Ballwin, MO 63021
Phone (314) 394-8621
Jeani Schnabel Ward, Historian
Pub. *Ein Schnabel Für Nachrichten (A
  Nose for News)*, quarterly
$7.00 per year membership

Schnaible
Schnaible Clearinghouse
641 Lewis Road
San Jose, CA 95111
Cynthia Dean

Schneekloth (see Wiese)

Schneider (see Kettenring, Snider,
  Snyder, Wert)

Schneider
*BGM Publications
28635 Old Hideaway Road
Cary, IL 60013-9726
Phone (847) 639-2400
Betty G. Massman, Editor and Publisher
Pub. *Schneider Connections for the
  Snyder, Snider, Schneyder (et var)
  Surname*, quarterly, $18.00 per year
  subscription

Schneider
Schneider Family Newsletter
5827 Granville
Sylvania, OH 43560
Mr. Schneider
Pub. *Schneider Family Newsletter*,
  monthly, $16.00 per year subscription

Schneider
*Johannes Michael Schneider
  Descendants
1001 Sierra Road
Newport, TN 37821-6006
Phone (423) 625-9325
Dorothy P. Brawley
Biennial reunion on the third Saturday of
  October in even-numbered years at the
  New Ebenezer Retreat Center, Rincon,
  Georgia

Schnetzer (see Schulmerich)

Schneyder (see Schneider)

Schnider (see Usher)

Schnigter (see Doeckel)

Schnitzer (see Schulmerich)

Schnoor (see Snoor)

Schnuck (see Snook)

Schnug (see Wert)

Schobe (see Scoby)

Schoenberger (see Blossom Press,
  Shinebarger)

Schoff (see Brown)

Schofield (see Scovil)

Schofiell (see Scovil)

Scholdin (see Sheldon)

Scholdun (see Sheldon)

Scholl (see Cole, Custer)

Scholten (see Sheldon)

Schooley
Trails of Our Fathers
Box 77
North Whitefield, ME 04353
Phone (207) 549-7140
James B. Schooley

Schoonmaker
*Schoonmaker Family Association of
  Huguenot Historical Society of New
  Paltz, New York
PO Box 121
New Paltz, NY 12561
Phone (914) 255-7311 (Tue & Thur
  9:00–4:00)
Carol Johnson
Pub. *The Schoonmaker Family*, (includes
  descendants of Hendrick Jochemcz
  Schoonmaker, also Shoemaker)
$10.00 per year membership

Schoonover
*The Schoonover Clearing House
PO Box 647
Shasta, CA 96087

Schovill (see Scovil)

Schoville (see Scovil)

Schrader (see Cole)

Schrader
Schraders of DeKalb County, Illinois
1220 Hillcrest Avenue
PO Box 446
Livermore, CA 94550
Phone (415) 449-7888
Barry Schrader

Schrand (see Olthaus)

Schreiber*Florida
Schreiber-Scriba
775 North Powerline Road
Deerfield, FL 33442
Phone (305) 428-9443
Ernest H. Kraemer
Pub. *Schreiber-Scriba*

Schroyer (see Friend)

Schubdrein (see Shuptrine)

Schuessler (see Reedy)

Schulden (see Sheldon)

Schuldin (see Sheldon)

Schuldun (see Sheldon)

Schulten (see Sheldon)

Schultheiss
Jacob Schultheiss Family Association
Rt. 2, 2491 South Seminole Highway
Madison, WI 53711
Phone (608) 271-3577
Mrs. J. Vincent Dunn

Schultz (see Holtz

Schulz
*Schulz and Marks Reunion
PO Box 367
Buchanan Dam, TX 78609
Phone (512) 793-2623
Maxine Sullivan Smith
(includes descendants of Mr. and Mrs.
  J. F. Schulz of Addicks, Texas)
Annual reunion on the last Sunday of
  April

Schumacher (see Links Genealogy
  Publications, Ammons, McLouth)

Schupp
*Schupp/Shupp/Shup Family Reunion
444 Roosevelt Avenue
Glendora, NJ 08029
Phone (609) 931-1890
Atwood James Shupp

Schuster (see Kunkel)

Schut (see The Memorial Foundation of
  the Germanna Colonies)

Schuyler
*Schuyler Family Reunion
Friends of Schuyler Museum
32 Catherine Street
Albany, NY 12202
Phone (518) 434-0834
Lois H. Dillon, President

Schwabb (see Swab)

Schwaner (see Schwanner)

Schwartz (see Hoster)

Schwartz
Descendants of Lieb and Louis Schwartz
240 West End Avenue
New York, NY 10023
Eileen Polakoff

Schwartzlaender (see Swartzlander)

Schwartzländer (see Swartzlander)

Schweissfurth (see Lemon)

Schwenck (see Swing)

Schweppe
Schweppe Family Association
3661 Blue Goose Road
West Bend, WI 53095
Esther Auer

Schwing (see Swing)

Schwoder (see Maier)

Scobe (see Scoby)

Scobee (see Scoby)

Scobel (see Blossom Press)

Scobey (see Scoby)

Scobie (see Mackay, Scoby)

Sconce (see Folk Family Surname
Exchange)

Scott (see Folk Family Surname
Exchange, Sullivan Surname
Exchange, Benn, Burnham, Hatfield,
Jardine, Lee, MacDuff, McCune,
Rutherford)

Scott
Kenma Publishing Company
1911 Conlin Avenue
Evansville, IN 47714-4248
Kenneth Gene Lindsay
Pub. *Scott Scanner*, quarterly, $17.95 per
year subscription

Scott
*Scott/Skaggs/Hill/Wilson Family
Organization
1132 North Tela Drive
Oklahoma City, OK 73127-4308
Phone (405) 789-2842
Pauline Carlton Fletcher, Secretary and
Genealogist
(computer database uses Quinsept™,
PAF™ and Reunion™)
Annual reunion

Scott
*Clan Scott Society
PO Box 13021
Austin, TX 78711
David M. Scott, Membership Secretary

Pub. *The Stag & Thistle*, quarterly
$25.00 membership the first year, $20.00
per year membership thereafter

Scott
*Joseph Lee Scott Family Organization
PO Box 33
302 North Randall
Bronte, TX 76933
Phone (915) 473-5331
Brenda Scott Hines
(includes data on Anderson, Appling,
Baggett, Bowen, Byars, Cameron,
Cooper, Daniel, Doshier, Elrod,
Fendley, Hines, Hood, Jameson,
McEachern, McGee, Putnam, Ray,
Roberts, Rodgers, Rogers, Savage,
Sharp, Shirley, Stanley, Strickland,
Stroud, Thomas and Warr families)
Annual reunion in June in Bronte, Texas

Scott
The Scott Searcher
12600 Bissonnet A4-407
Houston, TX 77099
Dede D. Mercer, Publisher
Pub. *The Scott Searcher*, semiannually,
$20.00 per year subscription; (all
variations of the surname, worldwide)

Scott
*The Scott One-Name Study
Rt. 1, Box 15A
Lovettsville, VA 22080-9703
Phone (540) 822-5292
Craig Roberts Scott, C.G.R.S., FSA Scot,
Clan Scott Genealogist
Pub. *The Scott Genealogical Quarterly*,
$22.00 per year subscription

Scovel (see Scovil)

Scovil
*Scovil(l)(e) Database
6025 Riverwood Drive
Atlanta, GA 30328-3732
Phone (404) 256-1925; E-mail:
74761.2054@compuserve.com
Roger M. Scovil
(includes Schofield, Schofiell, Schovill,
Schoville, Scovel, Scovil, Scovill,
Scoville descendants of John and
Arthur Scovell of Connecticut ca 1660
(some 7,500 names))

Scovill (see Scovil)

Scoville (see Barnes, Scovil)

Scoville
*Scoville Family Clearinghouse
87 Carter Lane
Plantsville, CT 06472
Janice Falvey, Family Historian
(includes descendants of Arthur Scoville,
immigrant ancestor, with concentration
on those lines in Litchfield County,
Connecticut)

Scowcroft (see McCune)

Scowden (see Dougan)

Scriba (see Schrieber)

Scrimgeour (see MacDuff)

Scruggs
*Scruggs Family Association
4228 Old Leeds Lane
Birmingham, AL 35213-3314
Phone (205) 871-3017
Dr. B. Q. Scruggs, Jr., Secretary
Pub. *Searching for Scruggs*,
semiannually (spring and fall), free
queries; (includes Scruggs and allied
families)
$25.00 per calendar year membership;
reunion

Scrymgeour (see MacDuff)

Scudder (see Reeder)

Scudder
*Scudder Association, Inc.
731 Bennington Road
Francestown, NH 03043
Phone (603) 547-2545
Mrs. Cy Sherman, Secretary
Pub. *Scudder Searches*, at least
semiannually; *Newsletter*, at least
semiannually
$15.00 per year membership

Scudder
Scudder Association
432 Hillside Place
South Orange, NJ 07079
V. Scudder

Scurlock (see Blanton, Spurlock)

Seager (see Johnston)

Seagler (see Segler)

Seal (see Cell)

Seal
Seal, Seale, Seals Clearinghouse
113 La Porte Drive
Chattanooga, TN 37415-1304
Deborah Hebert

Seale (see Cell, Seal)

Seals (see Clark, Nelson, Seal)

Searcy
*Spencer B. Searcy Descendants
Organization
Rt. 2
Pattonsburg, MO 64670
Phone (816) 367-2129
Noranne Searcy, Historian
(includes descendants of Spencer B.
Searcy (1814–) and Nancy Wilkinson
(1816–))
Copying and postage costs

Searcy
Surnames, Limited
RR 3, Box 59
Muleshoe, TX 79347-9208
Pub. *Searching for Searcy's*, irregularly,
$8.00 per issue

Searfoss (see Serfass)

Sears (see Catlow, Cronn)

Sears
*Sears Family Association
2027 Stoneridge Lane
Duncan, OK 73533
Phone (405) 252-6049
L. Ray Sears, III, President
Pub. *Sears Family Association
Newsletter*, semiannually; (includes
descendants of Richard and Dorothy
Sears of Plymouth Colony (Cape Cod),
1639)
$10.00 per year membership

Seath (see MacDuff)

Seaton (see Broadfoot)

Seaton
James Seaton (1723–1787) Descendants
Family Association
PO Box 4338
Balboa, CA 92661
Phone (714) 650-8739
Scott Montgomery Seaton
(includes Seton)

Seaton
*Seaton Surname Organization
17308 92 Avenue, N.E.
Bothell, WA 98011
Bruce D. Seaton
(largest database on Seatons in America,
also database on Great Britain)

Sebastian (see Wiler)

Sebesy (see Apáthy)

Sebring (see Archer)

Sechrist (see Segrist)

Secoy
*Lazarus and Mary Secoy Descendants
Organization
438 Woodland Drive
Nitro, WV 25143-1060
Phone (304) 755-4728
Kenneth F. Robbins, Historian
Pub. *Descendants of Lazarus and Mary
Secoy*, irregularly; (Lazarus (1777 New
Hampshire–1852 Carthage Township,
Athens County, Ohio) and Mary (1780
Connecticut–1854 Carthage
Township), first settled in Troy
Township, Athens County)
No membership fee; annual reunion on
Labor Day in Athens, Ohio

Secrest (see Folk Family Surname
Exchange, Segrist)

Sedgell (see Scaggel)

Seed
Free Exchange—All Seeds
209 Cresthaven Drive
Vincennes, IN 47591-3854
Terry L. Earnst, Family Historian

Seefeld
*Seefeld/t Reunion
1 Pahokee Lane
Destin, FL 32541-4419
Phone (904) 654-1837
Mary Jane Johnson, Reunion Historian
Pub. *Seefeld/t Reunion Newsletter*,
annually; (includes descendants of
Christian Friedrich Seefeld (1788–
1863) and Anna Sophia Kobs (1792–
1837) of Plantikow, Kreis Naugard,
Pomerania)
Annual reunion last Sunday of July at
Riverhill Park, Kewaskum, Wisconsin

Seefeldt (see Seefeld)

Seeley
Seeley Newsletter
1045 West 19th Street
Lawrence, KS 66014
Hank Seeley
Pub. *Seeley Newsletter*

Seeley
Seeley Genealogical Society
613 Glendale Avenue
Lansing, MI 48910-4614
Robert G. Cox, Editor; Donald Eff
Pub. *Seeley Genealogical Society
Newsletter*, quarterly
$8.00 per year membership (beginning
September 1); reunion every three
years

Seeley
Seeley/Seelye National Reunion
RR 1, Box 314B
Hudson Falls, NY 12839-9732
Marshall B. Seelye, President
Pub. *Seeley Genealogical Society
Newsletter*, quarterly
$8.00 per year membership; reunion
every three years

Seelye (see Seeley)

Seering (see Sager)

Seers (see Catlow)

Seese (see Maust)

Seggie (see MacDuff)

Seggy (see MacDuff)

Segler
Segler/Seigler/Seagler/Sigler Family
Organization
28411 59th Avenue, South
Kent, WA 98032
Phone (206) 852-4557
Carolle Berry
Pub. *Segler, Seagler, Seigler, Sigler
Researchers Exchange*, bimonthly
$6.00 per year membership

Segrist
*Hans/Henry Segrist Family
Organization
145 New Haven Drive
Urbana, OH 43078
Phone (513) 653-6500
Arlene J. Secrist
(includes descendants of Hans/Henry
Segrist (Siegrist, Secrest, Sechrist),
who arrived from Switzerland in 1750
and was married in 1762 by Rev.
William Stoy of First Reformed
Church, Lancaster, Pennsylvania, to
Sarah Kuehner, and whose first child,
John Henry, was born 1763)

Seigler (see Segler)

Seigmann (see Sigman)

Seimen (see Links Genealogy
Publications)

Seip (see Surname Database)

Seith (see Shaw)

Self (see Beckham)

Self
Self Family Newsletter
106 Northside Drive
Calhoun, GA 30701
Daniel C. McCarthy
Pub. *Self Family Newsletter (Selph/
Selfe)*, quarterly, $10.00 per year
subscription

Selfe (see Self)

Sell (see Cell)

Sellards (see Bloss)

Sellars (see Sellers)

Sellen (see Links Genealogy
Publications)

Sellers (see Links Genealogy
Publications, Everett)

Sellers
Sims Publishing
2033 66th Avenue
Sacramento, CA 95823
M. Sims, Editor
Pub. *Sellers Letters*, annually or more
frequently, $15.00 per volume;
(includes Sellars, Cellar and Zellers)

Sellin (see Movius)

Sells (see Cell)

Selph (see Self)

Selvage
Selvage and Selvidge Families of
    America
710 Red Oak Lane
Columbia, MO 65203
Website: http://www.missouri.edu/-
    physcp/genealogy.html
Charles J. Peterson

Selvidge (see Selvage)

Senior
*Senior Family in America Association
1516 Mesa Avenue
Colorado Springs, CO 80906
Phone (719) 473-0122
Colonel Dennis F. Keegan
(descendants of William Senior (born in
    the late 1700s in England), and
    exchanging information on all Senior
    families originating in Great Britain,
    originally from Spain)

Senter (see Center)

Sercovich (see Blossom Press)

Servas (see Serfass)

Setchfield (see Holmes)

Seth (see Shaw)

Seton (see Broadfoot, Seaton)

Settle (see Wright)

Settle
*The Settle-Suttle Family
2890 Corvallis Crescent
Indianapolis, IN 46222
Phone (317) 291-8631
Christine Settles-Contos

Setzer (see Moser)

Setzer
*Setzer Clearinghouse
1328 East Hermosa Drive
Tempe, AZ 85282-5719
Phone (602) 491-2877
Gloria Kay Vandiver Inman
(includes only insignificant spelling
    variations)

Sevier
*Sevier Family Association
2900 Connecticut Avenue, N.W.,
    Apartment 332
Washington, DC 20008
Phone (202) 667-3246
Nancy Sevier Madden, Historian
(includes descendants of Valentine Sevier
    (1712–1803) of St. Giles Cripplegate

Parish, London, England, Rockingham
County, Virginia, and Carter County,
Tennessee)

Seward
*Seward Family Association
Painted Hills, Box 253
Martinsville, IN 46151
Max A. Seward

Seward
Watson Clark Seward Descendants
400 West 6th Avenue
Cheyenne, WY 80758
Margi S. Bagley, Family Historian

Sewell (see Copeland, Hardwick)

Sexson (see Williams)

Sexton (see McCanna)

Seybold (see MacDuff)

Seylar
*Seylar Family Association
210 Cliff Turn
Falling Waters, WV 25419-9530
Phone (304) 274-3104
Larry D. Kump

Seymour (see Stowe)

Shackelford
*The Shackelford Quarterly
PO Box 69
Grandin, FL 32138
Laura Tully
Pub. The Shackelford Quarterly,
    (January, April, July and October),
    $15.00 per year subscription

Shackleton (see Farnes)

Shadduck (see Sullivan Surname
    Exchange)

Shadowens (see Gibbs)

Shafer (see The Memorial Foundation of
    the Germanna Colonies)

Shafer
*Shafer Family Association
141 Hudson Avenue
Chatham, NY 12037
Phone (518) 392-4544
Herman W. Witthoft, Sr.
Pub. The Shafer Family, annually;
    (includes Schoharie County Shafers,
    descendants of Johannes Schaffer (ca
    1664 Germany–) and Maria Elizabeth
    Schaffer (1664–1749), also Schaefer,
    Schaeffer, Schafer, Schaffer, Shafer,
    Shaffer, Shaver)
No membership dues

Shaffer (see Shafer)

Shaffers (see Likes)

Shafran
*Shafran Surname Organization
199 Commodore Drive
Milledgeville, GA 31061
Phone (912) 968-7425
Richard Bialac

Shaklee
*Peter Shaklee Family Organization
14901 North Pennsylvania Avenue, #369
Oklahoma City, OK 73134-6072
Phone (405) 755-8921
William E. Shaklee, President
Pub. Descendants of Peter Shaklee
    (1756–1834), quarterly
$7.00 per year membership

Shalibo (see Charlebois)

Shambaugh
*Shambaughs International, Inc.
1913 68th Street
Des Moines, IA 50322-5866
William H. Shambaugh, Treasurer
Pub. Shambaugh Families Newsletter,
    quarterly
$6.00 per year membership; annual
    reunion

Shankland
*Robert Shankland Family Organization
2048 Forest Park Drive
Jackson, MI 49201
Phone (517) 783-6742
Ronald Lee Shankland
(includes Shanklin and Shankland of
    County Donegal, Ireland, 1612 to the
    present)

Shanklin (see Shankland)

Shanks
*Shanks Family Association
4085 Pleasant Valley Road
West Bend, WI 53095-9271
Phone (414) 644-6562
Dwight A. Shanks
Pub. Shanks Newsletter, semiannually;
    (includes descendants of Thomas
    Shanks (1726–1806), who came to
    America in 1747)
$12.00 per year membership

Shannon
*Shannon Searchers
3413 Fernwood Lane
Shreveport, LA 71108
Phone (318) 686-3112
Joyce Shannon Bridges, Editor
Pub. Shannon Searchers, bimonthly,
    $10.00 per year subscription

Shapiro (see Leopold)

Shapleigh (see Shapley)

Shapleigh
*The Shapleigh Family Association
PO Box 146
Kittery, ME 03904-0146

Phone (860) 643-5652 (in Connecticut)
Ruth Shapleigh-Brown, President
Pub. *The Shapleigh Chronicles*, annually;
(includes descendants of Alexander
Shapleigh (1561–1650) of Kingsweare,
Devon, England, ship owner, merchant
and tradesman, who came to the
Kittery, Maine/Portsmouth, New
Hampshire area in the 1630s)
$10.00 per year membership for families
with children under 18; annual reunion
in August

Shapley
The Shapley Connection
PO Box 83-2130
Richardson, TX 75083-2130
Phone (214) 562-1058
Dr. Brian J. L. Berry, Editor
Pub. *The Shapley Connection: A
Newsletter Devoted to the History and
Genealogy of the Shapley Family and
Its Connecting Lines*, annually;
(includes Shapleigh, Shappley and
Shepley)

Shappley (see Shapley)

Sharbono (see Charbonneau)

Sharkey (see Shirkey)

Sharley (see Shirley)

Sharp (see Allison, Scott)

Sharp
*Merrill John Sharp Family Organization
1503 Top-o-Hallow Road
Ames, IA 50010
Phone (515) 233-1285
Mr. Merrill Kim Sharp
Pub. *Sharp Notes*, semiannually, free;
(includes descendants of Merrill John
Sharp (1940–1990), physician of
Pocatello, Idaho)

Sharp
*The Sharp-Schaup Family in America
940 S.W. 50th Street
Oklahoma City, OK 73109
Phone (405) 632-0802
Edith Wallis Poole, Executive Director
Pub. *Sharp Points (Schaup, etc.)*,
quarterly
$10.00 per year membership or $12.00 to
receive annual index

Sharp
*Christian Sharp Descendants
Association
White School Road
Rt. 1, Box 710
Honey Brook, PA 19344-9753
Phone (215) 273-3241
James E. Frey

Sharpe (see Stewart)

Sharphouse (see Jackson)

Sharples (see Chippendale)

Sharpless (see Way)

Sharr
Sharr Family Organization
PO Box 124
Burlington Junction, MO 64428
Phone (816) 725-4783
Florence Flanary, Editor
Pub. *Sharr Family Newsletter*, annually
(August), free

Shatswell (see Barnard)

Shattuck (see Wright)

Shaub (see Scoby)

Shaull
Shaull, Slaymaker, Shedenheim,
Rosenberger, Rumplemouser Reunion
2535 Grandview
Des Moines, IA 50317
Phone (515) 262-1119
Mildred Shaull Rudasill

Shaumberger (see Shinebarger)

Shaver (see Heath, Shafer)

Shaver
*The Shaver Family Association
283 CR1
Westerlo, NY 12193
Catherine S. Latham, President
Pub. *Annual Family Reunion Letter*
(includes descendants of George
Shaver and Jane Mulford, Town of
Fulton, Schoharie County, New York)
Donation for membership; annual
reunion

Shaver
Shaver Cousins
246 Galahad Street
North Salt Lake City, UT 84054
Evelyn Norris

Shaw (see Chattan, MacDuff)

Shaw
*Robert K. and Mary Lou Shaw Family
Organization
5370 Nugget Road
Fair Oaks, CA 95628
Phone (916) 961-5271
Robert K. Shaw
Pub. *Shaw Family Monthly*

Shaw
*Clan Shaw Society
230 Rolling Road
Gaithersburg, MD 20877
Phone (301) 774-4377 (President);
(301) 926-0405 (Genealogist)
Mr. Meredith L. Shaw, President/
Membership; Janet Manuel,
Genealogist

Pub. *The Dagger*, quarterly; (includes
Ayson, Adamson, Esson, MacAy,
MacHay, Scaith, Seith, Seth, Shay,
Sheach, Sheath, Shiach and Skaith)
$15.00 per year membership for
individuals, $20.00 per year
membership for families, $25.00 per
year sustaining membership; annual
reunion various locations in the U.S.

Shaw
Shaw Newsletter
3615 McKamy Oaks Trail
Arlington, TX 76017
Phone (817) 468-4556
Joan Owens Lamb, Editor
Pub. *Shaw Newsletter*

Shaw
*Elizabeth Jane Shaw Family
Organization
1774 Country Club Drive
Logan, UT 84321
Phone (801) 753-6924
Joyce Elfrena Kalanquin

Shawn (see Shoun)

Shay (see Shaw)

Sheach (see Shaw)

Shearer (see MacDuff)

Shearin (see Gant)

Sheath (see Shaw)

Shedenheim (see Shaull)

Sheehan (see Griffin, O'Brien)

Sheehy (see Devine)

Sheeley (see Sheely)

Sheely
*Sheel(e)y/Schilling Descendants Family
Reunion
Rt. 1, Box 64
Worden, MT 59088
Phone (406) 967-4723
Shirley Fisher, Family Historian
(includes Sheely, Sheeley and Schilling
from Germany, Indiana, Iowa and
South Dakota)
Annual reunion

Sheera (see Cian)

Sheerer (see MacDuff)

Sheesley (see Wert)

Sheets (see Cairer)

Sheible (see The Memorial Foundation
of the Germanna Colonies)

Sheibley (see The Memorial Foundation of the Germanna Colonies)

Sheibly (see The Memorial Foundation of the Germanna Colonies)

Shelby
*Shelby Exchange
809 South Walnut
PO Box 536
Freeman, SD 57029
Phone (605) 925-7186
Carol Peterson, Editor/Publisher
Pub. *Shelby Exchange*, quarterly, $12.50 per year subscription; (all Shelby families in the U.S. and Wales)

Shelden (see Sheldon)

Sheldon (see Clark, Hall)

Sheldon
*The Sheldon Family Association, Inc.
23918 Wolf Road
Bay Village, OH 44140
Phone (219) 432-2362 (President's home in Fort Wayne, Indiana); (216) 871-9420 (Second Vice President)
Rose Sheldon Newton, President; Keith M. Sheldon, Second Vice President, Genealogy Chairman
Pub. *The Sheldon Family Association, Inc. Quarterly*, (January, April, July and October); (includes descendants of colonial Sheldons: Godfrey Sheldon (1671–) and Alice Frost of Bakewell, Derby, England, Scarborough, Maine, and Salem, Massachusetts; Isaac Sheldon (ca 1629–) and wives Mary Woodford and Mehitable Gunn, of England, Windsor, Connecticut, and Northampton, Massachusetts; John Sheldon (ca 1630–) and Joanna Vincent of England and Providence, Rhode Island; John Sheldon (ca 1630–) of Narragansett and South Kingstowne, Rhode Island; spelling variations: Chelden, Cheldon, Cheldun, Chelton, Cheltun, Childen, Childin, Childon, Childun, Chilten, Chilton, Chiltun, Cholden, Choldin, Choldun, Schalton, Scheladen, Scheladin, Scheladon, Schelden, Scheldon, Schelten, Scheltin, Schelton, Schelton, Scheltun, Schilden, Scholdin, Scholdun, Scholten, Schulden, Schuldin, Schuldun, Schulten, Shelden, Sheldun, Shelton, Sheltun, Shilden, Shildin, Shildon, Shilton, Shiltun, Sholden, Sholdin, Sholdon, Sholdun, Sholten, Shulden, Shulten, Shultin, Shulton, Shultun, etc.)
$10.00 per year membership, $15.00 one-time filing fee, $200.00 life membership

Sheldun (see Sheldon)

Shell (see Corson, Merier, Schell)

Shell
Shell
Whispering Oaks
5821 Rowland Hill Road
Cascade, MD 21719-1939
Phone (301) 416-2660
Victor Gebhart, President
Pub. *Shell*, annually, $2.00 per issue

Shellenberger
*Shellenberger Surname Organization
3 Brazill Lane
Whitehall, MT 59759
Phone (406) 287-3369
Lindia Roggia Lovshin

Shelley (see Shelly)

Shelly
*Shelly Families of PA (Schelle, Shelley)
13200 Doty Avenue, #220
Hawthorne, CA 90250
Elayne Alexander, Head of Research
(includes Schelle, Shelley, Shelly families of Pennsylvania, from 1720 to the present)
No cost

Shelton (see Folk Family Surname Exchange, Cowart, Golliher, Sheldon)

Sheltun (see Sheldon)

Shepard (see Beaman)

Shepard
*Ralph Shepard Family Organization
1672 Foresta Court, N.E.
Atlanta, GA 30341
Phone (404) 457-6644
Joseph E. Shepard, Researcher
Pub. *Ralph Shepard Family Organization Information Newsletter*, quarterly, free; (includes descendants of Ralph Shepard and Thanks Lord (1635+))

Shepherd (see Bodine)

Shepherd
The Shepherd Flock
191 Ephrata Avenue, N.W.
Soap Lake, WA 98851
June Gemmer Ponis
Pub. *The Shepherd Flock*, semiannually, $12.00 per year subscription, queries free to subscribers; (includes Sheppard and all variations of spelling, any time, any place)

Shepley (see Shapley)

Sheppard (see Shepherd)

Sheppard
The Descendants of Michael and Mary Sheppard
HCR Box 78
Bowdle, SD 57428
Judy Sheppard Huber

Sherar (see MacDuff)

Sherbon
*Sherbon and Cattermole Relatives Reunion
2632 N.W. 12th Street
Oklahoma City, OK 73107
Phone (405) 524-0305
James Eldon Vaughn
Annual reunion on the first Sunday of June in Oklahoma

Sherbondy
Sherbondy Family Association
6509 West 102nd Street
Overland Park, KS 66212
Jeffrey D. Sherbondy
Pub. *Sherbondy Beacon*, three times per year
$8.00 per year membership

Sherer (see Surname Database, Banks, Roberts)

Sherfey (see Sherfy)

Sherfy
Sherfy/Sherfey Family Organization
PO Box 157
Knightsen, CA 94548
Carolyn Sherfy

Sherk
Sherk/Shirk Reunion
12921 Prince Circle
Broomfield, CO 80020-5421
R. Sherk

Sherley (see Shirley)

Sherman (see Barnard, Brown, Clark, McCune, Wright)

Sherman
Sherman Family Organization
626 Black Rock Road
Bryn Mawr, PA 19010
Phone (215) 525-8929
Robert Carl Fraunberger, C.G., President
Pub. *Sherman Family Newsletter*, irregularly, free for SASE

Sherman
Wade-Smith Genealogy Service
Rt. 7, Box 52
Llano, TX 78643
Evelyn Wade
Pub. *Sherman Folks*

Sherrill (see Brawley, Perkins)

Sherwin (see Heath)

Shettel (see Schindel)

Shiach (see Shaw)

Shick (see Sullivan Surname Exchange, Likes)

Shields (see Surname Sources, Groendyke, Ziegler)

Shilden (see Sheldon)

Shildin (see Sheldon)

Shildon (see Sheldon)

Shilton (see Sheldon)

Shiltun (see Sheldon)

Shimenson (see Israelite)

Shimer (see Von Steuben)

Shimfesel (see Schimpfessel)

Shimon (see Sager)

Shimp
Shimp Family Clearinghouse
77 Hollow Road
Quarryville, PA 17566-9491
Harry Hoffman

Shimpfessel (see Schimpfessel)

Shinall (see Chenault)

Shinault (see Chenault)

Shindafer (see Shintafer)

Shindel (see Schindel)

Shindle (see Schindel)

Shinebarger
Shinebarger/Schoenberger/Shaumberger Genealogy News
2519 Covert Road
Flint, MI 48506
Mrs. Wilson Carb
Pub. *Shinebarger/Schoenberger/ Shaumberger Genealogy News*

Shintafer
Shintafer Searches
6035 S.W. Wilbard Street
Portland, OR 97219
Carolyn Bergeron
Pub. *Shintafer, Shindafer Family Newsletter*

Shipe (see Scheib)

Shipley (see Sullivan Surname Exchange, Hanks, Rutherford)

Shipley
The Shipley Family Newsletter
2152 Victoria Drive
Clearwater, FL 34623
Barbara Howe, Editor/Publisher
Pub. *The Shipley Family Newsletter*, quarterly (winter, spring, summer and fall), $12.00 per year for subscription; (includes Shipleys and those who married Shipleys)

Shipley
*Shipleys of Maryland
7650 Red Fox Trail
Hudson, OH 44236
Phone (216) 653-6024
Rev. Dr. Richard L. Shipley, President
Pub. *Newsletter*, irregularly
Annual reunion

Shipman (see Moore)

Shire (see Likes)

Shirely (see Shirley)

Shires (see McPherson)

Shirk (see Sherk)

Shirky (see Shirkey)

Shirley (see Gant, Scott)

Shirley
*Shirley Association
10256 Glencoe Drive
Cupertino, CA 95014
Phone (408) 255-8511
Betty Shirley
Pub. *Shirley Newsletter*, quarterly; (includes Schirley, Sharley, Sherley, Shirely, Shirley and Shurely)
$20.00 per year membership; reunion

Shirrell (see Powell)

Shive (see Scheib)

Shively
Shively Newsletter
Rt. 5, Box 364
Falmouth, KY 41040-9235
Alice Shivley Freed, Owner
Pub. *Shively Newsletter*, quarterly, $6.00 per year subscription; (includes all spellings)

Shivers
Shivers
802 Camille Drive
Longview, TX 75605
Glydie Ann Nelson
Pub. *Shivers*, quarterly, $7.50 per year subscription

Shobe (see Scoby)

Shockey
*Shockey Family Memorial Fellowship, Inc.
Rt. 2, Box 126-D
Berkeley Springs, WV 25411
Phone (304) 258-5616
Marie F. Shockey, Genealogist/Editor
Pub. *Shockey Newsletter*, annually (March or April), $1.00 per year subscription
$5.00 per year membership

Shockney (see Frazier)

Shoell (see Custer)

Shoemaker (see Links Genealogy Publications, Surname Database, Brawley, Schoonmaker)

Shoemaker
The Shoemaker Signpost
12600 Bissonnet A4-407
Houston, TX 77099
Dede D. Mercer, Publisher
Pub. *The Shoemaker Signpost*, semiannually, $20.00 per year subscription; (all variations of the surname, all over the world)

Shoff (see Brown)

Sholden (see Sheldon)

Sholdin (see Sheldon)

Sholdon (see Sheldon)

Sholdun (see Sheldon)

Sholten (see Sheldon)

Shomers
*Shomers/Schomers Family Organization
4240 N.W. 36 Way
Fort Lauderdale, FL 33309
Phone (305) 486-0942
David W. Shomers, President
Pub. *Schomers Journey to America* (includes descendants of Eberhard and Catherine Shomers, 1845 Buffalo, New York)
$19.00 per year membership

Shook (see Surname Database)

Shoolbread (see MacDuff)

Shoop (see Wert)

Short (see Anthes, Hutchison)

Short
Short Stuff
2190 Camino Largo Drive
Chino Hills, CA 91709
Trish Elliott Collins
Pub. *Short Stuff*

Shoun
Shoun-Shown-Shawn
422 South Walnut Avenue
Temple, OK 73568
Ed Miller
Pub. *Shoun-Shown-Shawn*, quarterly, $10.00 per year subscription
Reunion

Shoun
SH—N Family Association
402 South Bass
McKinney, TX 75069
LaVerne Graves

(includes descendants of Leonard and
   Barbara (Slemp) Shoun, who came to
   East Tennessee in the late 1790s; also
   Shawn, Shown, etc.)
$10.00 per year membership; reunion

Shoup (see Frantz)

Shove
*Shove Family
21 Abington Road
Rochester, NY 14622
Phone (716) 467-3605
Robert C. Shove, President and Secretary

Showalter (see Hudlow, Likes, Ronk)

Shown (see Shoun)

Shreiner (see Schindel)

Shreiner
Shreiner Family Clearinghouse
77 Hollow Road
Quarryville, PA 17566-9491
Harry Hoffman
SASE

Shrigley
*Shrigley Family Organization
99 Allison Street
Lakewood, CO 80226-1474
Phone (303) 234-0830; (303) 234-0144
Mrs. Shelby W. Shrigley
Pub. *Shrigliana*; (includes all Shrigley,
   Srygley and Srigley)

Shrimplin (see Wood)

Shriver (see Likes)

Shropshire
*The Shropshire Society
1136 Cane Ridge Road
Paris, KY 40361-9329
Phone (606) 987-2964
Mrs. Kenney Shropshire Roseberry,
   President
Pub. *The Shropshire Exchange*, quarterly
   (includes descendants of Oliver
   Shropshire who married Elizabeth
   Ring in 1657 in Marlborough,
   Wiltshire)
$20.00 per year membership

Shugart (see Lemon)

Shulden (see Sheldon)

Shull (see Frantz)

Shulten (see Sheldon)

Shultin (see Sheldon)

Shulton (see Sheldon)

Shultun (see Sheldon)

Shumard (see Atchley)

Shumate
Shumate
Whispering Oaks
5821 Rowland Hill Road
Cascade, MD 21719-1939
Phone (301) 416-2660
Victor Gebhart, President
Pub. *Shumate*, annually, $2.00 per issue

Shunk (see Guss)

Shup (see Schupp)

Shupe
*Shupe Family Organization
1523 Lake Street
Ogden, UT 84401
Dolores Montgomery Hunter
Pub. *Bulletin*, annually

Shupp (see Schupp)

Shuptrine
*Shuptrine Family Database
4851 Royce Road
Irvine, CA 92715-2233
Phone (714) 786-7293
Harry and Bev Jesse Shuptrine
(includes more than 2,200 names of
   Shuptrines who were descendants of
   Daniel and Anna Margretha
   (Maennlein) Schubdrein who were
   both born in the Saarbruecken area of
   Germany in the 1680s; members of his
   family were in the Salzburger
   movement of Protestants who escaped
   from Europe and helped to found the
   village of Ebenezer in Georgia in the
   1750s)

Shurley (see Shirley)

Shurtleff (see Shurtliff)

Shurtliff
Shurtliff Signatures
12600 Bissonnet A4-407
Houston, TX 77099
Dede D. Mercer, Publisher
Pub. *Shurtliff Signatures*, quarterly,
   $20.00 per year subscription; (includes
   Shurtleff and all variations of the
   surname, worldwide)

Shutt
Shutt
Whispering Oaks
5821 Rowland Hill Road
Cascade, MD 21719-1939
Phone (301) 416-2660
Victor Gebhart, President
Pub. *Shutt*, annually, $2.00 per issue

Sibbald (see MacDuff)

Sibball (see MacDuff)

Sibbuld (see MacDuff)

Sibley (see Thorn)

Sickles (see Smith)

Sickman (see Sigman)

Sidey (see MacDuff)

Sidie (see MacDuff)

Sidley (see Anthes)

Sidwell
*Sidwell, Hufstetler/Hufstutler, Gordy,
   Frazee Research
162 Quarter Circle Drive
Nibley, UT 84321
Phone (801) 753-3409 (home);
   (801) 797-1902 (work)
Robert W. Sidwell

Siegmund (see Sigman)

Siemes (see Links Genealogy
   Publications)

Siems
*Siems and Damkroger Families
301 Almond Court
San Ramon, CA 94583
Phone (510) 829-1433
Shirley Siems Terry, Editor and Family
   Historian
Pub. *Branching Out*, semiannually, $5.00
   per year subscription; (computerized
   database of 7,000)

Sigler (see Segler)

Sigman (see Moser)

Sigman
*Sigman Research Report
1341 Teton Drive
El Cajon, CA 92021-1043
Phone (619) 448-7880
Cleo E. Wall, Compiler
Pub. *Sigman Research Report*, quarterly
   (March, June, September and
   December), $17.00 per year
   subscription; (includes Zigman,
   Sigman, Sickman, Siegmund,
   Seigmann, etc., in the U.S. and
   Europe)

Sikes (see Tyre)

Siklost (see Baldman)

Silcox (see Nell)

Silence
Silence Family Organization
Rt. 20, Box 236
Springfield, MO 65803
Bertha Cook, Family Representative
Reunion

Siler (see Louden)

Silk (see Cian)

Silke (see Cian)

Sill (see Cell)

Silliman
*New Canaan Historical Society
13 Oenoke Ridge
New Canaan, CT 06840
Phone (203) 966-1776
Marilyn T. O'Rourke, Librarian
(primarily New Canaan local history, not
genealogical, but features Silliman,
Noyes, Weed surname collections)
$25.00 per year membership for
individuals, $30.00 per year
membership for families

Sills (see Cell)

Silvers
Silvers/Rogers Family Association
9120 Belvoir Woods Parkway, #H-409
Fort Belvoir, VA 22060
Mrs. F. Danforth

Silverstein
*Family Ties
19355 Sherman Way, Unit 1
Reseda, CA 91335-3560
Phone (818) 772-1941; (800) 772-1942;
(818) 772-8816 FAX
Richard H. Hoffman
Pub. *Silverstein & Hofman Family Ties
Newsletter*, three times per year, SASE
for sample issue; (Jewish specialty)

Silverthorn
*Silverthorn(e) Family Association
(USA)
1944 East Valley Road
Santa Barbara, CA 93108-1428
Phone (805) 969-4409
Frank Fremont Reed, Editor-Secretary-
Treasurer
Pub. *History of the Silverthorn Family
Supplement & Newsletter*, annually
$10.00 per year membership

Silverthorne (see Silverthorn)

Silverton (see MacDuff)

Silvester (see MacDuff)

Silz
*Silz Worldwide
3283 Millerfield Road
Macon, GA 31211-2744
Phone (912) 745-0921
James E. Silz
Free, except costs of copies and postage

Simcock
*Simcock/Simcox Family Reunion
PO Box 605
Clearlake Oaks, CA 95423
Phone (707) 998-3592
F. Simcox

Simcox (see Simcock)

Simenson (see Israelite)

Simkins (see Simpkins)

Simkins
*James Simkins and Mary Walker
Family Association
1090 East 700 South, #8
Saint George, UT 84770
Phone (801) 628-3449
H. Morris Simkins

Simmon
Simmon Family Reunion
1200 East Washington
Iowa City, IA 52240
Phone (319) 337-2673
Mrs. John K. Hunter, Genealogist
(includes descendants and ancestors of
Henry Peter Simmon (1793
Meisenheim, Germany–1875 Rock
Island County, Illinois) and Eva
Katharina Gravius (1795–1874);
database on Roots III™)

Simmons (see Franciscus, Gant,
Kinsland, Parks)

Simmons
Thomas J. Simmons and Nora McBurney
Family Organization
4406 Arabella Street
Lakewood, CA 90712
Arthur Barrett

Simmons
Simmons Newsletter
1507 Hazel Court
Lincoln, CA 95648
James Eaton Simmons
Pub. *Simmons Newsletter*, quarterly
(February, May, August and
November), $12.00 per year
subscription

Simmons
Simmons Family Association
Rt. 3, Box 587
Broken Arrow, OK 74014
Frances J. Simmons

Simms (see Folk Family Surname
Exchange, Sims)

Simoneau (see Lagesse)

Simonis
*Simonis Family Reunion
E2753 County Highway C
Iola, IA 54945
Phone (715) 445-3148
Melane Zeitlow, Historian
(includes descendants of Mathias
Simonis)
Annual reunion on the first Sunday of
August at Rosholt, Wisconsin

Simons (see Surname Database)

Simonton
*Simonton Clearinghouse
207 Auburn Drive
Dalton, GA 30720
Phone (706) 278-1504
Joseph Wiley Reid
(1400–1890 period)

Simouneau (see Johnson)

Simpkins (see Alsop, Simkins)

Simpson (see Arthur, Fraser, Frazier,
Fullick, Smith)

Simpson
Simpsons, A Gathering of the Clan
PO Box 3793
Santa Cruz, CA 95063
E-mail: NonaW@aol.com
Nona Williams, Editor
Pub. *Simpsons, A Gathering of the Clan*,
quarterly, $15.00 per year subscription,
queries accepted

Simpson
John Simpson Family Association
Star Rt. 1, Box 442
Shell Knob, MO 65747
Pauline N. Bowman
Pub. *Simpsonette*, quarterly

Simpson
Francis Simpson and America Reed and
Mary Ann Corum Family Organization
W6223 Montgomery Road
Deer Park, WA 99006-9506
Phone (509) 276-6429
Weymeth Simpson, President
Pub. *Simpson Family Newsletter for the
Descendants of Francis Simpson and
His Wives, America Reed and Mary
Ann Corum*, semiannually (June and
December)

Sims (see Folk Family Surname
Exchange, Kirk, Lemon, Syms)

Sims
*BGM Publications
28635 Old Hideaway Road
Cary, IL 60013-9726
Phone (847) 639-2400
Betty G. Massman, Editor and Publisher
Pub. *The Sims Seeker*, quarterly, $18.00
per year subscription; (includes all
Sims families, but especially James
Sims, of Culpeper County, Virginia,
ca 1725)
Biennial reunion in odd-numbered years
in Branson, Missouri

Sinclair (see The Memorial Foundation
of the Germanna Colonies, Rogers,
Sinkler)

Sinclair
*Clan Sinclair Association (USA)
PO Box 158
Worcester, MA 01613-0158

Phone (617) 835-2900;
    (508) 835-2944 FAX
H. S. "Pete" Cummings, Jr., Clan
    Genealogist
Pub. *Notes of the Sinclair Genealogist*,
    quarterly
$10.00 per year membership

Sinclair
*Clan Sinclair Association, Inc. (U.S.A.)
124 North 24th Avenue, East
Duluth, MN 55812
Phone (218) 724-7761
David Sinclair Bouschor, FSA Scot,
    President
Pub. *Yours Aye*, quarterly
$10.00 per year membership for
    individuals, $15.00 per year
    membership for families

Sines (see Friend)

Sinex
Sinex
3631 North Mullen Street
Tacoma, WA 98407
Antoinette W. Sorensen
Pub. *Sinex*, quarterly, $5.00 per year
    subscription
Annual reunion, usually in August

Singer (see Israelite)

Sinkler
*Family Bookshelf
PO Box 339
Beeville, TX 78104-0339
Jean Grigsby, Publisher
Pub. *Sinkler, Sinclair, St. Clair Update*,
    annually, $20.00 per volume

Sinnes (see Casto)

Sinsabaugh (see Johnson)

Sinyard
Sinyard/Bates Family of Alabama
6421 U.S. Highway 31
Hanceville, AL 35077
Delton D. Blalock

Sirowan (see Graham)

Sirrine (see Sarine)

Sirrine
*Isaac Sirrine Family Organization
1237 South Val Vista Drive
Mesa, AZ 85206
Phone (602) 892-3681;
    (602) 965-1350 (work)
Josiah Sirrine
Reunion

Sisko (see Francisco)

Sissing
*Sissing Bi-annual Family Reunion
126 East 39th Street
Holland, MI 49423

Phone (616) 392-2497
William Strating
Reunion in alternating years in Holland,
    Michigan, and Fulton, Illinois

Sisson (see McCune)

Sisson
Sisson Newsletter
2750 Marina Avenue
Livermore, CA 94550
Phone (510) 443-5524
David and Joan Sisson
Pub. *Sisson Newsletter*, quarterly, $15.00
    per year subscription; (includes Sisson
    1608 to the present and numerous
    allied families only as directly
    connected in New England, Virginia,
    the midwest and onward, Waite 1700–
    1860 in New York and Massachusetts)

Sivert (see Links Genealogy
    Publications)

Sivey (see Lambert)

Sjøtun (see Velline)

Skaggs (see Corson, Scott)

Skaggs
Skaggs Connection Newsletter
3130 Pear Harbor
Saint Ann, MO 63074
Phone (314) 423-1301
Sally Heller, Editor
Pub. *Skaggs Connection Newsletter*,
    quarterly (February, May, August and
    November), $18.00 per year
    subscription; (Skaggs and allied
    families)

Skaggs
*Skaggs Family
3308 Linda Drive
Amarillo, TX 79109
Phone (806) 352-0818
Ida M. Lancaster
(includes Skaggs family from 1678 to the
    present, especially descendants of
    Richard Skaggs of Barren County,
    Kentucky)

Skaith (see Shaw)

Skau (see Ostrem)

Skear (see Skeer)

Skeen
Skeen-Skeins-Skenes
1221 Candice Court
Mesquite, TX 75149
Mary L. House, Editor
Pub. *Skeen-Skeins-Skenes*, quarterly,
    $12.00 per year subscription

Skeer
*Skeer Family Organization
515 Weiman Avenue
Ridgecrest, CA 93555
Phone (619) 446-4359
W. Thom Skeer, Researcher
Pub. *Newsletter*, semiannually; (includes
    descendants of Nathan Skeer (?–1844
    Butler County, Pennsylvania) and
    related spellings of Skeers and Skear)
Annual reunion

Skeers (see Skeer)

Skeins (see Skeen)

Skelton (see Haynes, Parker)

Skene
Clan Skene Association
PO Box 452
Betsy Layne, KY 41065
Phone (606) 478-4011
Rev. Atlas D. Hall, Vice President and
    Membership Chairman

Skenes (see Skeen)

Skidmore (see Friend, Wright)

Skiles (see Frantz)

Skinner (see Friend, Gregor)

Skinner
*Skinner Family Association
1936 East Fifth Street
Ontario, CA 91764
Greg Legutki, Editor
Pub. *Skinner Kinsmen Update*, quarterly,
    free queries
$16.50 per year membership

Skipper (see Owens)

Skubinna
*International Association of the
    Skubinna Family
16 Third Street, N.E.
Washington, DC 20002-7312
Phone (202) 675-6685
Dr. Martin L. Skubinna, President

Slade (see Warren)

Slagle (see Smith)

Slagle
*Slagle Family Organization
23516 156th Avenue, S.E.
Kent, WA 98042
Phone (206) 630-5899
Diane Slagle Sheridan, Family
    Genealogist
Pub. *Slagle World*, semiannually;
    (includes descendants in Maryland,
    Pennsylvania, Virginia, North
    Carolina, East Tennessee, Missouri,
    Iowa and Nebraska of Henry Slagle,
    who was married 1786 in Shenandoah

County, Virginia, to Christina Kelchner (Keltner))
$5.00 per year membership

Slains (see Hay)

Slane (see Hall)

Slasor
*George Slasor Family Organization
PO Box 482
Culebra, PR 00775
Jack Slasor
(includes descendants of George Slasor (1793 Scotland–1833) and Annaca Clary (1803–1865) of Guernsey County, Ohio)

Slate
Slate Family of America
3644 Oak Cliff Drive
Fallbrook, CA 92028
Marie Hardy Mills

Slaton
Slaton-Slatton Family Project
3454 Manor Lane, #103
Homewood, AL 35209
Clinton and Rhonda Slayton
Pub. *Slaton-Slatton Family Project*

Slattery
Slattery Journal
2716C DuBois Route
Riverton, WY 82501
Pub. *Slattery Journal*

Slatton (see Slaton)

Slaughter (see The Memorial Foundation of the Germanna Colonies)

Slaymaker (see Shaull)

Sleeth (see Thayer)

Slemp (see Shoun)

Slessor (see Gregor)

Slider (see Goodenow)

Sliger (see Freiling)

Slininger (see Lush)

Sloan (see Newmyer)

Slucter (see The Memorial Foundation of the Germanna Colonies)

Sluss (see Kettenring)

Sly (see Parsons, Schleich)

Slye (see Newcomb)

Slyh (see Schleich)

Smail (see Murray)

Smailla (see Randall)

Smairt (see MacDuff)

Smale (see Murray)

Small (see Corson, Murray)

Small
*Pioneer Publication
PO Box 1179
Tum Tum, WA 99034-1179
Phone (509) 276-9841
Shirley Penna-Oakes
Pub. *Small Siblings*, irregularly, $6.00 per issue plus $1.75 postage for one to three books, 50¢ for each additional book

Smart (see MacDuff)

Smeal (see Murray, Schmehl)

Smick (see Likes)

Smith (see Blossom Press, Family Publications, Folk Family Surname Exchange, The Memorial Foundation of the Germanna Colonies, Sullivan Surname Exchange, Surname Sources, Album, Baker, Barnes, Blair, Bloss, Brawley, Brown, Catlow, Chattan, Clark, Corson, Cowart, Crover, Dean, Farrington, Fox, Frasher, Frazier, Futral, Gipson, Goodenow, Grant, Hatfield, Haury, Heath, Hilton, Jackson, Johnson, Lambert, Leavitt, Lush, Macpherson, MacPherson, McCune, McRae, Ogan, Powell, Rebele, Reeder, Rice, Roper, Schindel, Stone, Stoner, Strode, White, Wilson)

Smith
*Smith/Hedrick Family Association
4553 Highway 158 South
Lake City, AR 72437-8562
Phone (501) 237-8104
Dale Hinshaw McMasters, Family Genealogist
Pub. *Smith Hedrick Newsletter*, quarterly (February, May, August and November); (includes descendants of Joseph and Olive Smith, who were married ca 1770 in Rutland Count, Vermont; also George and Mary Hedrick who were married ca 1804 in Kentucky)
$5.00 per year membership; annual reunion on the second Sunday of July

Smith
*Edwin Woodruff Smith Family Organization
Albert Smith Family Organization
3784 Grove Avenue
Palo Alto, CA 94303
Phone (415) 494-8868; E-mail: krallen@townsend.com
Kenneth R. Allen

(PAF™ database includes ancestors and descendants of Edwin Woodruff Smith (1897–1960) and Ethel Olga Akert Neff (1897–1990) of Utah; also Albert Smith (1854–1931) and Mary Ann Storton (1856–1931) of Harlestone, Northamptonshire, England and Utah)
Non-tax-deductible donation for membership

Smith
Sims Publishing
2033 66th Avenue
Sacramento, CA 95823
M. Sims, Editor
Pub. *Smith Papers*, three times per year, $15.00 per year subscription

Smith
Lewis J. Smith Association, Inc.
1027 Highway 164
Commerce, GA 30529
Fred Wendt, Jr., President

Smith
*James Porter Smith Family Organization
960 Whitehawk Trail
Lawrenceville, GA 30243-4192
Phone (770) 962-0649
James Porter Smith, II

Smith
Amasa Smith and Sarah Bowen and Sarah Sykes Descendants Reunion
PO Box 92
Pleasant Hill, IL 62366
Virginia Hart

Smith
*The Nehemiah Smith Family Association
7007 Connecticut Avenue
Chevy Chase, MD 20815-4935
Phone (301) 986-8659
Walter B. Smith, II, Editor
Pub. *News of the Nehemiah Smith Clan— Founded 1637 at Plymouth, Mass.*, bimonthly, $12.00 per year; (includes descendants of Nehemiah Smith (1606?–1686) of New London County, Connecticut, and Ann Bourne (1616–1685?))

Smith
*Association of the Descendants of Ralph Smith of Hingham and Eastham, MA
9 Burley Street
Danvers, MA 01923
Phone (508) 774-5863
Carol Ann Ferris, Historian and Genealogist
Pub. *Report of the Association of the Descendants of Ralph Smith*, annually; (includes descendants of Ralph Smith (1610 England–), came to America in 1633 aboard the *Elizabeth Bonaventure* out of Hingham, England)
$5.00 per year membership (lineal only)

Smith
*Heritage Trail
704 Berkshire Drive
Hattiesburg, MS 39402-1917
Phone (601) 264-1317
Frances Thornton Smith, Publisher
(includes ancestors and descendants of
    Brashears, Byrd, Durant, Klock,
    Marchand, McGilivary, Smith, Weaver
    and Wecriers, starting in 1540)

Smith
Caleb Smith Family Association
3601 Taylor Road
Clifton Springs, NY 14432-9333
Mrs. Harry Zobel

Smith
*Smithtown Historical Society
(5 North Country Road, Route 25A-
    location)
PO Box 69 (mailing address)
Smithtown, NY 11787
Phone (516) 265-6768
Louise Hall, Director; Bradley L. Harris,
    President
(Richard Smith of Smithtown genealogy)

Smith
Wilson Family Record Depository
169 Melody Lane
Tonawanda, NY 14150-9109
Robert J. Wilson
Pub. *Smith*, quarterly, $25.00 per year
    subscription

Smith
*The Smith-Taylor Connections
2776 County Road 27
Bellevue, OH 44811
Phone (419) 483-2363
Kate L. Jett
(includes descendants of Richard "Rock"
    Taylor (–1703) of Massachusetts, and
    his wife, Ruth Burgess, and Jonathan
    Smith (–1824 Dover Township,
    Cuyahoga County, Ohio) of Beverley
    and Ashfield, Massachusetts, son of
    Joseph Smith)

Smith
*Mathias Smith Family Association
169 Swainford Drive
Heath, OH 43056
Phone (614) 522-1507
Sherwood A. Conner, Historian
(includes descendants of Mathias Smith
    of Milan)

Smith
*Newsletter of the Descendants of James
    and Joel Smith*
2209 Eldridge Avenue
Bellingham, WA 98225-2108
Louella Vaughn Small
Pub. *Newsletter of the Descendants of
    James and Joel Smith and Jane and
    Hannah Adams of Pennsylvania and
    Kosciusko County, Indiana,*

semiannually, $2.00 per year
    subscription
Annual reunion in April

Smith
William Barkley Smith Descendants
    Reunion
2555 Coos Bay Boulevard
Coos Bay, OR 97420-2589
M. C. Higgins

Smith
*Smith-Sickles Families
20100 S.W. Johnson Road
West Linn, OR 97068
Phone (503) 635-2411; (503) 635-2312
Nancy Smith Budrow, Editor
Pub. *Black Coulee News*, three times per
    year, donation for subscription;
    (includes descendants of Henry
    Vansickler and Nancy Rose of Ontario,
    Canada, both born ca 1804; some lines
    of Revolutionary War loyalists who
    fled New York for Canada; other
    Ontario surnames: Clark, Engie,
    Huntley, Smith, Whitaker, Young and
    Zufelt; after leaving Canada prior to
    1885, descendants lived in such areas
    as Michigan, Illinois, Iowa, Colorado,
    Ohio, North Dakota and Montana, and
    now are far-flung)
Reunion

Smith
*Joshua Smith Family
729 South Columbia Drive
Woodburn, OR 97071
Phone (503) 982-2110
Ralph S. Blois

Smith
*Smith Database
247 Cross Hill Road
Easley, SC 29640-8857
Phone (864) 859-2392
Linda Gale Smith Cheek, Publisher
(includes all Smith families)

Smith
Smith Digest
2606 McClintic
Midland, TX 79705-7421
Margaret Semple
Pub. *Smith Digest*, quarterly, $15.00 per
    year subscription

Smith
*Thomas Sasson Smith Family
    Organization
2789 West 12075 South
Riverton, UT 84065-7630
Kairlee D. Graham, President
(includes descendants of Thomas Sasson
    Smith (1818 Junius, Seneca County,
    New York–1890 Wilford, Fremont
    County, Idaho), son of Jeremiah Smith
    and Abigail Demont, and Thomas'
    wife, Amanda Ellen Hollingshead
    (1838 Jobs Settlement, McDonough
    County, Illinois–1903 Lethbridge,

Alberta, Canada), daughter of Isaac
    Hollingshead and Mercy Wilcox)

Smith
*George Done Smith Family
    Organization
2905 Craig Drive
Salt Lake City, UT 84109
Phone (801) 277-6107
Hollis D. Smith
(includes descendants of George Done
    Smith (1889 Smithfield, Utah–) and
    Lucinda Fern Nilson (1891–))

Smith
Olsen Enterprises
3931 South 238th
Kent, WA 98032
Pub. *Smith*, quarterly, $14.00 per year
    subscription; (England and New
    England)

Smithson (see Holden)

Smithson
Smithson Family Exchange Newsletter
235 15th Street, N.E. (address April 1 to
    November 1)
Salem, OR 97301-4228
Phone (503) 363-4389
Addie Smithson Dyal Rickey, Editor/
    Publisher
Pub. *Smithson Family Exchange
    Newsletter*, semiannually, free in
    exchange for data

Smoker (see Schmucker)

Smoot (see Freeman)

Smucker (see Schmucker)

Smurr
Smurr Bulletin
3040 Kishner Drive, Apartment 315
Las Vegas, NV 89109
Phone (702) 734-8489
Mrs. G. Allen Lovell, Editor and
    Publisher
Pub. *Smurr Bulletin*, annually, 75¢ per
    issue

Smyser
*Smyser Family Reunion Committee
2229 Old Colony Road
York, PA 17402-4623
Phone (717) 741-1868
Richard B. and Suzanne B. Hershey,
    Chairpersons
Pub. *Newsletter*, annually, free; (includes
    Schmeisser, Schmeiser and Smyser
    family which homesteaded in York,
    Pennsylvania)
Reunion every three years, alternating
    between the U.S. and Germany

Smyth (see Pace)

Smyth
*Adam Craik Smyth Family
    Organization
PO Box 383
Lehi, UT 84043
Verona Blackham Balle

Snead (see Evitt, Reynolds, Sneed)

Sneary
*Sneary Family Association
20 Harpers Way
Carrollton, GA 30117-5207
Phone (706) 830-6702
Dr. Eugene C. Sneary, Family Historian
Pub. *Sneary Family Association
    Newsletter*, irregularly, donation for
    issue

Sneed (see Dockery)

Sneed
*International Association of Sneeds
7860 Timber Hill Drive
Dayton, OH 45424-1934
J. W. Snead, Jr.
Pub. *Sneed Family Forum* (includes
    Snead, Pickens, McCammon,
    Abercrombie)

Snell (see Frantz, Goodman)

Snell
*Snell-Timmerman-Zimmerman
    Newsletter*
Rt. 1
Little Falls, NY 13365
Phone (315) 823-1129
Edith S. Timmerman, Secretary
Pub. *Snell-Timmerman-Zimmerman
    Newsletter*, semiannually, free to
    members, $2.00 per year subscription
    to others

Snider (see Pillow, Schneider)

Snider
*Snider/Snyder Family Reunion
1164 Catherine Street
Suffield, OH 44260
Phone (330) 628-4435
Robert A. Longbottom, Family
    Genealogist and Historian
(includes descendants of Jacob Snider
    (1732–1790 Berkeley County,
    Virginia)
Annual reunion on the first Saturday of
    August at the Snake Spring Church of
    the Brethren near Everett,
    Pennsylvania

Snider
*Daniel Snider Database
132 South First West
Heber City, UT 84032
Phone (801) 654-1215
Betty Montgomery

Sniffen (see Kniffen)

Snipes
*The Snipes Family of America, Inc.
6317 Birling Drive
Columbus, GA 31909-3277
Phone (706) 563-2318
Peggy P. Allen, Secretary
Pub. *The Snipes Hunter*, quarterly;
    (includes several well-established
    lines, including William Snipes,
    Revolutionary War soldier)
$10.00 per year membership; annual
    national meeting

Snively (see Stoner)

Snodgrass
*Snodgrass Clan Society
8221 Stonewall Drive
Vienna, VA 22180-6947
Phone (703) 560-6631; (703) 560-0462
    FAX
Paul D. Snodgrass, Editor
Pub. *The Mace*, semiannually

Snoke (see Snook)

Snook
*The Snook Newsletter
12924 Fourth Drive, S.E.
Everett, WA 98208
Phone (206) 337-4587
Betty Snook Welliver
Pub. *The Snook Newsletter*, four times
    per year (February, April, June and
    October), $15.00 per year subscription
    (includes all spellings: Schnuck,
    Snoke, Snouck, Snuke, etc.)

Snouck (see Snook)

Snow (see Burnham, Golding)

Snow
Snow-Wicker-Vickers-Snowden Family
    Association
2306 Westgate
Houston, TX 77019
Phone (713) 529-2333
Harold Helm
$25.00 plus pedigree and family group
    sheets for membership

Snow
*Erastus Snow Family Organization
Department of Mathematics
Brigham Young University
Provo, UT 84602
Phone (801) 378-2366; E-mail:
    snowd@math.byu.edu
Dr. Donald R. Snow
(includes family of Erastus Snow (1818
    St. Johnsbury, Vermont–1888 Salt
    Lake City, Utah))

Snowden (see Snow)

Snuke (see Snook)

Snyder (see The Memorial Foundation
    of the Germanna Colonies, Sullivan
    Surname Exchange, Schneider, Snider)

Sockwell (see Elder)

Sofley (see Safley)

Sohlbach (see The Memorial Foundation
    of the Germanna Colonies)

Soileau (see Johnson)

Solde (see Beauvais)

Solis (see Blossom Press)

Sollenberger
*Pennsylvania-German Sollenberger
    Family
107 West Sunhill Road
Manheim, PA 17545
Phone (717) 665-5869
D. Ernest Weinhold
(especially descendants of the very early
    immigrants who settled in northeast
    Lancaster County, Pennsylvania, and
    nearby areas)

Solomon (see Gower, Warren)

Somervell (see Somerville)

Somerville
*The Somerville Family, North American
    House
HC 50, Box 719
Prescott, AZ 86301
Phone (520) 445-0755
David B. Somerville, Family Historian/
    Editor
Pub. *The Star and Scabbard*, at least
    twice per year (before and after the
    reunion); (includes all Somervilles,
    Somervells, etc., descendants of
    Norman ancestor, Sir William
    (Gaulter) de Somerville)
No membership cost; annual reunion

Sonner (see Lambert)

Sonzay (see Daniel)

Sorensen
Sorensen/Christensen Family of Lolland,
    Denmark in America
PO Box 153
West Chicago, IL 60186
Phone (708) 293-3147
Holly S. Sorensen, Family Genealogist

Sorrells
*Sorrells Family of the South
44 Clemson Road
Parlin, NJ 08859
Thelma F. Prince

Sossaman (see Sassaman)

Sossomon (see Sassaman)

Souch (see Bradley, Elford)

Soulant (see Blossom Press)

Soule (see Douglas, Heath)

Soule
*Soule Kindred in America, Inc.
53 New Shaker Road
Albany, NY 12205-3615
Phone (518) 869-8368
Betty-Jean Haner, Treasurer and
    Membership Secretary
Pub. *Soule Newsletter*, quarterly
    (January, April, July and October);
    (includes descendants of George Soule,
    Mayflower Pilgrim)
$15.00 per year membership, $25.00 per
    year sustaining membership, $50.00
    per year patron membership, $200.00
    life membership

Sounds
Claudette's
3962 Xenwood Avenue, S.
Saint Louis Park, MN 55416-2842
Claudette Atwood Maerz
Pub. *Sounds Like*, quarterly, $5.00 per
    year subscription

Souples (see Links Genealogy
    Publications)

Sousich (see Blossom Press)

Southard
*Carl D. Southard Associates, Inc.
Rt. 2, Box 294
Zebulon, NC 27597-9423
Anita W. Southard, Editor
Pub. *The Official Southard Gazette &
    Record*, irregularly, $5.25 per year
    subscription

Souther (see The Memorial Foundation
    of the Germanna Colonies)

Souther
Souther
1014 Kupau Street
Kailua, Oahu, HI 96734
Richard Dennis Souther
Pub. *Souther*, quarterly, $8.00 per year
    subscription

Southerland (see Sutherland)

Southwest Mississippi Family Journal
    (see Multi-family Associations)

Southwick (see Barnard)

Southworth
Southworth Hall
PO Box 480
Burney, CA 96013
Phone (916) 335-2430
Ethel V. Shafer
Pub. *Southworth Hall*

Southworth
*Gilbert de Southworth Family
    Organization
PO Box 456
Ucon, ID 83454-0456
Vernon R. Southworth
Pub. *The Southworth Chronicle* (includes
    descendants of Gilbert de Southworth
    (about 1279–) of Samelsbury Hall,
    Lancaster, England)
Reunion every five years

Sowers
Sowers Family Reunion
1204 Clay Street
Winnfield, LA 71483-2956
W. L. Sowers

Sowle
*Sowle Family Organization
801 East Brownell Street
Tomah, WI 54660
Phone (608) 372-7018
Geraldine Sowle Schlosser, Historian
    (includes descendants of James[5] Sowle
    (1761–1821) and Patience Macomber
    (1769–1859) of Westport,
    Massachusetts, and Danby, Vermont)
No membership fee; reunion every three
    years

Space (see Speace)

Spade (see Spayd)

Spalding (see Holden, Murray)

Spangler (see Surname Sources)

Spannuth
*Spannuth Surname Organization
12 Bonnievale Drive
Bedford, MA 01730
Jim Eggert

Sparger (see Wolfensberger)

Spargur (see Wolfensberger)

Sparks (see Dean)

Sparks
*Sparks Family Association
1709 Cherokee Road
Ann Arbor, MI 48104-4448
Phone (313) 662-5080
Dr. Russell E. Bidlack, Editor
Pub. *The Sparks Quarterly*, (March, June,
    September and December); (all U.S.
    Sparks families, 1607 to about 1900)
$10.00 per year membership

Sparrow (see Chaney)

Sparry (see Chadbourne)

Spaulding (see CTC Family Association,
    Rothenberger, Rutherford)

Speace (see Cummings)

Speace
Speace Family Association (Spease/
    Spece/Specht/Spee)
9710 Kendelwick Drive
Richmond, VA 23236
Mrs. Jessie Speas Barbour
Pub. *Speace/Space/Speas/Spece/Spiek/
    Spees Newsletter*

Speak
*Speak/e/s Family Association
RR 3, Box 3393
Athens, TX 75751
Phone (903) 677-3982
Robert Speake, Archivist/Editor
Pub. *SFA Bulletin*, quarterly; (includes
    descendants of Thomas Speak (1645–
    St. Mary's County, Maryland), wife
    Eliz. Bowling, and sons John
    (innholder, will 1731), and Bowling
    (Charles County, Maryland, will
    1755))
$15.00 per year membership

Speake (see Speak)

Speakes (see Speak)

Speakman
*Family of William Speakman
PO Box 762
Fillmore, UT 84631
Phone (801) 743-6217
Scott Speakman, President
    (includes descendants of William
    Speakman and Isabel Cooper)

Speaks (see Speak)

Spear (see Catlow)

Spear
*Spear Family Reunion
Rt. 3, Box 1720
Madison, FL 32340-9531
Phone (904) 929-2846
Elmer C. Spear
Pub. *Spear News*, annually, free

Spearitt (see Spirit)

Spears (see Folk Family Surname
    Exchange)

Speas (see Speace)

Spease (see Speace)

Spece (see Speace)

Specht (see Speace)

Spee (see Speace)

Speed (see Hickman)

Speedie (see MacDuff)

Speedy (see MacDuff)

Speer (see Stone)

Spees (see Speace)

Speight (see Wooten)

Spelbring
*Spelbring/Spelbrink Family Association
121 North Howard
Croswell, MI 48422
Phone (810) 679-3176
Michael Jackson, President/Archivist

Spelbrink (see Spelbring)

Spence (see Archer, Clark, MacDuff, Neville)

Spence
Hapsburg Press
PO Box 173
Broomfield, CO 80038-0173
Barbara Inman Beall, Editor
Pub. *Spence*, five times per year, $10.00 per year subscription

Spencer (see Folk Family Surname Exchange, Arthur, Williams)

Spencer
Spencer Surname Organization
PO Box 487
Madison, AL 35758
Donald Spencer, Secretary-Treasurer

Spencer
*Spencer Family Historical and Genealogical Society, Inc.
5644 Strawberry Hill Dr., Apt. D
Charlotte, NC 28211
Phone (704) 365-3003; E-mail: vmspencer@aol.com
Virgil M. Spencer, President
Pub. *Le Despencer*, quarterly (February, May, August and November)
$20.00 for first-year membership, $15.00 per year membership thereafter, $18.00 per year foreign membership thereafter; biennial reunion

Spencer
Spencer
912 West Second Street
Fort Worth, TX 76102
Phone (817) 335-3819
Johnibel Roberts
Pub. *Spencer*, semiannually, $5.00 per year subscription

Spengler (see Surname Sources)

Spens (see MacDuff)

Sperry (see Hyatt)

Spess (see MacDuff)

Spiegle
Spiegle Family of Alabama
6421 U.S. Highway 31
Hanceville, AL 35077
Delton D. Blalock

Spiek (see Speace)

Spielberg (see Primak)

Spiel'berg (see Primak)

Spies (see Cummings)

Spight (see Neville)

Spillman (see The Memorial Foundation of the Germanna Colonies)

Spilman (see The Memorial Foundation of the Germanna Colonies, Cian)

Spink (see MacDuff)

Spinks (see MacDuff)

Spirit
*Spirit Surname Organization
314 Coventry Lane
Manchester, MO 63021-5123
Phone (314) 394-6789
Elizabeth Quinn
(includes Spearill, Spurrett, Spurrit, etc., spelling variations, especially Robert Spurrit (became Spirit in Northumberland) who was from Oxfordshire ca 1780, possibly descendant of Anthony Spurret of Gloucestershire, England, after 1500)

Spissman (see Arthur)

Spittal (see Buchanan)

Splitlog (see Garren)

Spollen (see Cian)

Spowatt (see MacDuff)

Spoyde (see Spayd)

Sprabary (see Sprayberry)

Spraberry (see Sprayberry)

Spradling (see Guthrie)

Spradling
Spradling-Baker Newsletter
5735 East Robinson Road
Bloomington, IN 47408-9377
A. Tom Spradling
Pub. *Spradling-Baker Newsletter*

Sprague
William Sprague Descendants Reunion
10263 Rt. 76
Hammondsport, NY 14840
Phone (607) 868-4892

Verna E. Sprague
(William Sprague of New Jersey)

Sprayberry
*Sprayberry/Spraberry/Sprabary/Etc. Family Association
PO Box 1204
Lamesa, TX 79331
Phone (806) 872-8326 (office); (806) 872-5503 (home)
John P. Spraberry

Springer (see Weimar)

Springer
Springer Families Newsletter
15749 Selwyn Road
Southgate, MI 48195
Mary Alice Lawson
Pub. *Springer Families Newsletter*

Springer
*Friends of the Springer Homestead, Uniontown, PA
1527 Benson Drive
Dayton View Triangle
Dayton, OH 45406-4515
Kathleen Rizer
Pub. *Descendants of Dennis Springer and Ann Prickett*, three or four times per year; (includes 10,000 descendants who married in 1736 in New Jersey and lived in Virginia)
$5.00 per year membership

Sprinkle (see Likes, Rowe)

Sproul (see Holden)

Spurgeon (see Likes)

Spurlock
*Spurlock Family Association
PO Box 811
Blountville, TN 37617-0811
Mrs. Pat Spurlock Ford, President
Pub. *Spurlock Family Quarterly*, (March, June, September and December); (includes Spurlock/Scurlock, anytime, anywhere, and allied lines; ROOTS III™ database, Prodigy™ ID# GSJP03A, Genie™ ID# P.FORD4)
$11.50 per year membership

Spurrett (see Spirit)

Spurrit (see Spirit)

Squair (see MacDuff)

Squarsich (see Blossom Press)

Squier (see Squires)

Squiers (see Squires)

Squire (see MacDuff, McCune, Squires)

Squires
*Myrtle Mariah Squires Family
   Organization
8255 South Krameria Way
Englewood, CO 80112
Phone (303) 290-0998
Mr. Dana M. Floyd
Free

Squires
*Squires Family Association
Rt. 1, Box 427, Highway 89
Danbury, NC 27016-9773
Phone (910) 593-3186
Stanley C. Squires, Editor
Pub. *Squires Newsletter*, annually
   (usually January), $4.00 donation per
   issue; (includes Squier, Squiers and
   Squire)

Staats (see Barnard, Crusan)

Stabler
*Stabler-Stabley Reunion
RR 1, Box 134A
Allenwood, PA 17810-9605
Barbara Stabley, Family Historian
(includes descendants of Christian
   Stabler (1727 Musberg, Germany–
   1783 York County, Pennsylvania) and
   Anna Mary Fritz (1729 Plattenhardt,
   Germany–1800 York County,
   Pennsylvania) with related German
   families of Boeplen, Burckhardt,
   Metzger, Mueller and Stoll)
FGS available for copying fee and
   postage; annual reunion on the third
   Saturday of August

Stabley (see Stabler)

Stack (see Cian, Devine)

Stackhouse
Stackhouse
Whispering Oaks
5821 Rowland Hill Road
Cascade, MD 21719-1939
Phone (301) 416-2660
Victor Gebhart, President
Pub. *Stackhouse*, annually, $2.00 per
   issue

Stacy (see Newton)

Stacy
From Generation to Generation
Rt. 1, Box 147
Buncombe, IL 62912
Melody Tellor, Editor
Pub. *Stacy Stories*, quarterly, $15.00 per
   year subscription

Stadel
*Stadel Surname Exchange
2521 West Needmore Highway
Charlotte, MI 48813
Phone (517) 543-3021
Debra Stadel Eddy, Family Historian

Staehr (see The Memorial Foundation of
   the Germanna Colonies)

Staffeldt
Staffeldt
9452 East Conquistadores Drive
Scottsdale, AZ 85255
Arnold M. Gavin
Pub. *Staffeldt*, monthly, free with
   submission of family information

Stagner (see Likes)

Stahl (see Cummings)

Staige (see Athy)

Staiger
*McCullah-Wasson Family Reunion
2344 Staiger Road
Billings, MO 65610
Phone (417) 258-7292
Jane Staiger
Pub. *Newsletter*, annually (April);
   (includes descendants of Alexander
   McCullah (1793 Wythe County,
   Virginia–1856) and Lucy Robertson
   (1799 Cooke County, Tennessee–
   1849), and Sir David Wasson (1776
   Ardstraw, Tyrone County, Ireland–
   1850) and Flora Graham (1781
   Scotland–1865))
Reunion

Stalham (see Williams)

Stalker (see Gregor)

Stalling (see Cook)

Stambaugh
*Stambaugh Surname Organization
137 Lorenzi, South
Las Vegas, NV 89107
Phone (702) 877-2438
Juanita Mae McGaughey Clark

Stamper (see Burton)

Stamper
*Stamper Clearinghouse
1328 East Hermosa Drive
Tempe, AZ 85282-5719
Phone (602) 491-2877
Gloria Kay Vandiver Inman
(includes only insignificant spelling
   variations)

Stanbridge (see Stembridge)

Standard (see Folk Family Surname
   Exchange)

Standifer (see Album)

Standridge (see Ross)

Standridge
Standridge Kith an' Kin
6525 Magnolia Drive
Mabelvale, AR 72103

R. P. Baker
Pub. *Standridge Kith an' Kin*,
   occasionally, free to descendants, free
   queries; (includes Standridge, Wallace,
   Wallis, Wallas, descendants of James
   Standridge (1755–1837), a
   Revolutionary War veteran)
Reunion

Stanley (see Scott)

Stanley
Stanley Stepping Stones
26 Orchard Place
Muncie, IN 47305
Phone (317) 289-1447
Cheryl K. Manlove
Pub. *Stanley Stepping Stones*, quarterly,
   $10.00 per year subscription, free
   sample issue for SASE with 52¢
   postage

Stanley
The National Stanley Family Association
37125 Windy Hill Lane
Solon, OH 44139
Sue Stanley Chang, Secretary/Treasurer
Pub. *Stanley News*, quarterly
$10.00 per year membership for
   individuals, $25.00 for three-year
   membership for individuals, $125.00
   life membership for individuals

Stansbury
Stansbury Society
8606 Pleasant Plains Road
Towson, MD 21204
Stuart D. Jessop
Pub. *Stansbury Society Newsletter*,
   quarterly

Stanton (see Brown, McRae)

Stanton
*The William T. and Annie Mary (Durst)
   Stanton Reunion
6042 Hunt Club Road
Baltimore, MD 21227
Phone (410) 796-0557
Sara Stanton Jarrett
(includes Stanton and Durst of
   Grantsville, Garrett County, Maryland,
   and related ancestors and descendants
   as well as other related families such
   as Broadwater, Engle, etc.)
Annual reunion on the second Sunday of
   August in Grantsville, Garrett County,
   Maryland

Stapel (see Staples)

Staple (see Staples)

Staples (see Armstrong, Corson)

Staples
*Staples Family History Association
1570 Waterwitch Drive
Orlando, FL 32806
Phone (407) 851-9489

James C. Staples, President
Pub. *Staples Family History Association Newsletter* (includes Stapel, Staple)

Stapleton (see Cian, McCanna, Witcraft)

Starbuck (see Reynolds)

Stark (see Surname Sources, Donnachaidh, MacDuff)

Stark
Asa Lafitte Stark Family Association
239 Deerfield
Houston, TX 77022-6103
Phone (713) 697-7874
Mary Stark, Historian

Starke (see Surname Sources, Arthur)

Starkey (see Goodenow)

Statler
Statler-Stetler-Stotler Clearinghouse
1317 34th Street
Sacramento, CA 95816-5325
Sandra J. Hall
Pub. *Statler, Stetler, Stotler Newsletter*, quarterly, $12.00 per year subscription

Statmates (see Kepple)

Stature (see The Memorial Foundation of the Germanna Colonies)

Staub (see Baldman)

Stauch (see Stough)

Staudt
*Staudt-Stoudt-Stout Reunion
46 West Broad Street, #A
Reading, PA 19607-2540
Phone (215) 777-4814
Beulah Stoudt Follmer, Corresponding Secretary
Reunion in Umbenhauss Park, Bernville, Pennsylvania

Stauffer (see Millet)

Staymates (see Kepple)

Stearns (see Lush)

Stebbins (see Wright)

Steckman (see Stockman)

Steed (see McCune)

Steel
*John Steel Family Organization
900 Wellsford Road
Modesto, CA 95357
Phone (209) 523-2239
Grace Brown Steele, Secretary

Steele (see Arthur, Carley, Jamison, Wright)

Steele
Descendants of Fielding Steele and Jane Isabel Brooks, Saint Clair, Illinois
25 North Center
Trenton, UT 84338
Gerri L. Ball

Steere
*The Steere Family Association, Inc.
216 Highland Avenue
Warwick, RI 02886
Phone (401) 884-5173
Elizabeth H. Clarke, Registrar
Pub. *Steere Family Reunion Notice* (includes descendants of John Steere of Providence, Rhode Island, 1660)
Annual reunion on the third weekend of August

Steerheim (see Stierheim)

Steerhime (see Stierheim)

Steever (see Stieber)

Steffel
Steffel Chronicle
16 Fairway Drive
Eustis, FL 32726
Richard S. Steffel
Pub. *Steffel Chronicle*, quarterly

Steffey
*L. Dean and Iva Steffey Family Organization
6750 East Main Street, #106
Mesa, AZ 85205-9049
Warren D. Steffey, President
Free

Steffy
My Steffy Family Connections
6206 North Hamilton Road
Peoria, IL 61614
Phone (309) 691-3680
Gerald R. Steffy
Pub. *My Steffy Family Connections* (includes Ulrich and Anna Mari Steffy)

Steger
*Steger Family Lines
12717 Gores Mill Road
Reisterstown, MD 21136
Phone (410) 833-5416
William F. Steger, Editor
Pub. *Steger Family Newsletter*, semiannually, $5.00 per year subscription

Steiermann (see Bentheim)

Steig
Steig Family Association
5463 Schiering Drive
Fairfield, OH 45014
Frank Stieg, Jr.

Steigerwald (see Kunkel)

Steigerwalt
*Steigerwalt Reunion
521 White Street
Bomantown, PA 18030
Phone (610) 852-2725
Burdell Steigerwalt, President and Editor
Pub. *Newsletter*
Annual reunion on the last Saturday of July

Steiner (see Surname Database, Pellien)

Steinersen (see Brown)

Steinmetz (see Kepple)

Steketee
The Steketee Newsletter
PO Box 287
Macatawa, MI 49434
Phone (616) 335-5754; E-mail: stek@macatawa.org
Jerome C. Steketee, Editor
Pub. *The Steketee Newsletter*, donation for subscription

Stembridge
*Stembridge Family Association (Stanbridge/Stonebridge)
1365 Lesley Court
Santa Maria, CA 93454
Phone (805) 922-4313; (805) 346-1156 FAX; E-mail: ccsd62B@prodigy.com
Tina Peddie, President
Pub. *Stembridge Stock*, quarterly
$16.00 per year membership

Stephens (see Archer, Bodine, Stevens)

Stephenson (see Gray, Kunkel, Stevens)

Stepp (see Hardwick, Moser)

Sterett (see Douglas)

Sterheim (see Stierheim)

Sterling (see Folk Family Surname Exchange, Gregor)

Sterling
*Sterling Surname Organization
7024 Morgan Road
Greenwell Springs, LA 70739
Phone (504) 261-5515
Serena Abbess Haymon
Pub. *Sterling Surname Organization*, annually (January); (includes descendants of James Sterling and Margaret McCoy of southwest Mississippi)
$5.00 per year membership

Sterne (see Brown)

Sterner (see Surname Database)

Stetler (see Statler)

Stetson (see Cummings)

Stetson
Stetson Kindred of America, Inc.
60 Sheridan Street
Brockton, MA 02402-2852
James Hoban, Genealogist
Pub. *The Kindred Spirit*, about three
times per year
Annual reunion on the third weekend of
August in Norwell, Massachusetts

Steuart (see MacDuff)

Stevens (see Brown, Heath, Holden,
Hynton, Ruff, Rutherford, Willis)

Stevens
Stevens Stephens Stevenson Stephenson
653 Perrshing Drive
Walnut Creek, CA 94596
A. Maxim Coppage, Publisher
Pub. *Stevens Stephens Stevenson
Stephenson*, quarterly, $10.00 per year
subscription

Stevens
*Vincent Stevens Family Organization
422 Wayne Street
Hollidaysburg, PA 16648
Phone (814) 695-3105
Marion Joan Pressler
(includes descendants of Vincent Stevens
(1745–1843) and Ruth Lane (1750–
1839))

Stevens
*Stevens Database
6609 Montana Lane
Vancouver, WA 98661-7436
Wilson E. Stevens
(includes Bluemel, Eskridge, Stevens and
Voss families, especially Lyman
Stevens (1812–) and his wife, Martha
Durfee (1813–) and their ancestors)

Stevenson (see Armstrong, Stevens)

Stevenson
William Stevenson Descendants
127 West Glaucus Street, #D
Leucadia, CA 92024
R. Stevenson

Stever (see Stieber)

Steward (see Stewart)

Stewart (see Boney, Bosher, Brackett,
Cian, Dawson, Hoster, Kintigh, Lush,
MacDuff, McArdle, Sawyer, Warren,
Wright)

Stewart
Stewart/Steward
6180 Merrywood Drive
Rocklin, CA 95677-3421
Kathleen Stewart
Pub. *Stewart/Steward*, quarterly
(February, May, August and
November), $12.00 per year
subscription

Stewart
*The Clan Stewart Society in America
111 Masonic Avenue
Monroe, LA 71203
Phone (318) 343-7305
M. Monroe Stewart, Membership
Chairman
Pub. *Fesse Chequy*, quarterly; (meaning
Checkered Band; includes branches,
septs and family affiliations: Boyd,
Denniston, France, Francis, Kelso,
Lennox, Lisle, Lombard, Lyle,
Mentieth, Moodie, Stuart; Stewart of
Atholl: Conacher, Cruickshank(s),
Dickey, Duilach, Garrow, Gray,
Larnach, MacGarrow, MacGlashan;
Stewart of Appin: Carmichael, Clay,
Combich, Combie, Conlay, Donlevy,
Leay, Levack, Livingston(e), Lorne,
MacColl, MacCombe, McCombich,
MacDonleavy, MacLeay, MacLew,
MacMichael, MacNairn, MacNucator,
MacRob, Mitchell, Mitchelson, Robb,
Walker; Stuart of Bute: Ballantyne,
Caw, Fullerton, Glass, Hunter,
Jamieson, Lewis, Loy, MacCamie,
MacCaw, MacCloy, McCurdie,
MacElheran, MacKerron, MacLewis,
MacLoy, MacMunn, MacMurtrie,
Malloy, Milloy, Munn, Neilson,
Sharpe; Stewart of Galloway:
Carmichael, MacMichael)
$15.00 per calendar year membership

Stewart
*Descendants of Daniel and Rebecca
Stewart
126 South Adams Street
Rockville, MD 20850-2324
Phone (301) 424-6062
Gordon C. Baker, Historian
(includes descendants of Daniel Stewart
(1825–1887) and Rebecca Blosser
Stewart (1831–1902), residents of
Stewartstown, West Virginia)
Annual reunion on the third Saturday of
August in Morgantown, West Virginia

Stewart
The Stewart Newsletter
PO Box 245
Novinger, MO 63559
Phone (816) 488-6616; (816) 488-6885
FAX; E-mail:
Jethomas@Vax2.Rain.Gen.MO.Us
Janet E. Thomas, Publisher/Owner
Pub. *The Stewart Newsletter*, three times
per year (January, May and
September), $20.00 per year
subscription in the U.S., $25.00 per
year subscription outside the U.S.; *The
Stewart Connection*, quarterly, sent
free to subscribers of *The Stewart
Newsletter*, unlimited queries accepted;
(for the Stewart lineage, with all
variations of spelling)

Stewart
*Walter Stewart Family
6336 Briarwood Road
Columbia, SC 29206

Phone (803) 782-1464
Mary S. Rawlinson
Pub. *Family Newsletter*, annually;
(includes descendants of Walter
Stewart (–1825 Laurens County, South
Carolina) and wives Mary Ross
(–1810) and Isabel Bobo (–1843))
$2.00 per year membership

Stieber
*Stieber Database
214 East Jennings Avenue
South Bend, IN 46614
Phone (219) 291-6336
Rolland A. Steever, Family Researcher
(includes Steever, Stever and Stover
especially family of Upper Paxton
Township, Dauphin County,
Pennsylvania, from pre-Revolutionary
to post-Civil War times, and other
Stiebers who emigrated from Baden,
Germany)

Stiens
*Stiens-Feipel Family History
6588 Onarga
Chicago, IL 60631
Ms. Marion Stiens

Stierheim
*Stierheim Family in America
813 S.W. Alder Street, #700
Portland, OR 97205-3115
Phone (503) 243-2652
Richard D. Brainard, Family Historian
and Publisher
(includes Stierheim, Steerheim,
Steerhime, Sterheim, etc.)
No charge

Stiffler (see Likes)

Stiger (see Cunningham)

Stigler (see The Memorial Foundation of
the Germanna Colonies)

Stiles (see Brown, Heath)

Stiles
*Stiles Family of America and Affiliated
Families
1790 Stiles Road, RFD 1
Penn Yan, NY 14527-9640
Phone (315) 536-6881
Leon N. Stiles, Historian
Pub. *The Stiles Family and Affiliated
Families Newsletter*, at least annually;
(includes data on 20,000 affiliated
Stiles/Styles families and their
descendants, worldwide, through
female as well as male lines)
$10.00 per year membership for
individuals, $200.00 life membership

Still (see Garner)

Stillians
Hapsburg Press
PO Box 173
Broomfield, CO 80038-0173

Barbara Inman Beall, Editor
Pub. *Stillians*, five times per year, $10.00
  per year subscription

Stillson (see Stilson)

Stillwell (see Rutherford, Stilwell)

Stilson (see Aldrich, Barnard)

Stilson
Stilson/Stillson Reunion
8110 S.W. Wareham
Portland, OR 97223
Phone (503) 246-1555
Christie Stilson
(includes descendants of Vincent Stilson
  of Marblehead, Massachusetts,
  ca 1646)
Reunion

Stilwell (see Heath)

Stilwell
Stilwell Stillwell What the 'L'
820 South Clark Street
Visalia, CA 93292-2904
Alice Stilwell, Publisher/Editor
Pub. *Stilwell Stillwell What the 'L'*,
  bimonthly, $16.00 per year
  subscription; (includes Stilwill)

Stilwill (see Stilwell)

Stimpson (see Corson)

Stimson (see Corson)

Stinesyfer (see The Memorial
  Foundation of the Germanna Colonies)

Stinnett (see Folk Family Surname
  Exchange)

Stinnett
*Folk Family
PO Box 52048
Knoxville, TN 37950-2048
Hester E. Stockton, Owner; Phillip
  Wayne Stinnett, Editor
Pub. *Stinnett Families*, quarterly, $15.00
  per year subscription, $5.00 per issue;
  (includes Stinnette)

Stinnette (see Stinnett)

Stipe (see Wright)

Stipelcovich (see Blossom Press)

Stires
*Stires Family Association
Rt. 2, Box 3249
Livermore Falls, ME 04254
Phone (207) 897-4222
W. Dennis Stires
Pub. *Stires Family Newsletter*, monthly
$10.00 per year membership

Stirk (see MacDuff)

Stirks (see MacDuff)

Stirling (see Armstrong)

Stith (see Corson)

Stockbridge
*Stockbridge Reunion
9 Fair Court
Sumter, SC 29150-3244
Phone (803) 773-5005
John M. Stockbridge
(includes descendants of David
  Stockbridge (1749–1832) and Patience
  Bartlett (1752–1806) of North Hadley,
  Massachusetts)
Free

Stockfleth (see Blossom Press)

Stockman
*The Stockman Family
PO Box 250
Silver City, NM 88062-0250
Phone (505) 388-4054
Lee T. Stockman
Pub. *Stockman Family Newsletter*,
  quarterly; $10.00 per year
  subscription; (includes Stockman,
  Stuckman, Steckman, etc., and related
  families in the U.S., generally, with
  emphasis on those of German origin)
Annual reunion in even-numbered years
  in Silver City, New Mexico, and in
  odd-numbered years in both Texas and
  California

Stockton (see Folk Family Surname
  Exchange, Grant)

Stockton
British Stockton Database
19 Brompton Court
Bloomington, IL 61704
(1500s and 1600s)

Stockton
*Folk Family
PO Box 52048
Knoxville, TN 37950-2048
Hester E. Stockton, Owner and Editor
Pub. *Stockton Links*, quarterly, $15.00
  per year subscription, $5.00 per issue;
  (includes deStockton, Stocton and
  Stoughton)

Stocton (see Stockton)

Stoddard (see Goodenow)

Stoddard
Stoddard Family Association
PO Box 434
Elmhurst, IL 60126
Phone (630) 617-4906
John H. Stoddard, Editor
Pub. *The Stoddard Tribeloid*, quarterly;
  (includes Stoddart, Stodder, Studdart,
  etc.)
$10.00 per year membership

Stoddart (see Stoddard)

Stodder (see Stoddard)

Stoever (see The Memorial Foundation
  of the Germanna Colonies, Stieber)

Stokely
*Stokely National Reunion
100 Parkview
Kilgore, TX 75662

Stokes (see Clark, Jelly)

Stokes
The Stokes Family Quarterly
18435 South Mission Hills
Baton Rouge, LA 70810
Phone (504) 756-2303
Alton T. Moran, Editor-Publisher
Pub. *The Stokes Family Quarterly*,
  $12.00 per year subscription

Stoll (see Stabler)

Stoltz (see The Memorial Foundation of
  the Germanna Colonies, Surname
  Database)

Stolz (see Surname Database)

Stone (see Allen, Bailey, Banks, Brooks,
  Cian, Crover, Goodenow, Hilton,
  Hyatt, Hynton, Johnson, Ross,
  Rothenberger, Stewart, Warren)

Stone
Stone
1214 Julie Street
Weatherford, TX 76086-6039
Betty Gerth
Pub. *Stone*, quarterly; (includes
  descendants of James and Elizabeth
  Guest Stone)
$10.00 per year membership

Stonebridge (see Stembridge)

Stonecipher (see The Memorial
  Foundation of the Germanna Colonies)

Stoner (see Jones)

Storey (see Cian, Story)

Storie (see Story)

Stormont (see MacDuff)

Storrs
*Storrs Family Reunion
PO Box 67
Columbia, CT 06237-0067
Phone (203) 228-0080
Marion R. Emmons
(includes descendants in the U.S. and
  New Zealand of Samuel Storrs
  (England-Mansfield, Tolland County,
  Connecticut), and his second wife,

Esther/Hester Agard/Egard, whom he
married in Massachusetts)
Donation for membership; annual
reunion each August in Connecticut

Storton (see Smith)

Story
Story Source
2732 Pleasant Valley Drive
Cantonment, FL 32533
Phone (904) 968-2945
Elizabeth Story Moore, Editor
Pub. *Story Source*, quarterly, $20.00 per
year subscription; (includes Storey,
Storie, etc.)

Storze (see Surname Database)

Stotler (see Statler)

Stouch (see Stough)

Stoudt (see Staudt)

Stouffer (see Stoner)

Stoughton (see Stockton)

Stout (see Garner, Staudt)

Stout
German Stout Family
1840 Torresdale Avenue
Philadelphia, PA 19124
Rev. Edmond Stout

Stout
*English Stout Family
8507 Inverness Drive, N.E.
Seattle, WA 98115
Phone (206) 524-0216
Oliver O. Stout, Genealogist

Stoutzenberger (see Franciscus)

Stovall (see Brodnax)

Stovall
*The Stovall Family Association, Inc.
5000 Rock River Drive
Fort Worth, TX 76103-1226
Phone (817) 457-5383
Lyle Keith Williams, Editor
Pub. *The Stovall Journal*, quarterly;
(includes descendants of Bartholomew
Stovall and Anne Burton who first
settled in Virginia in 1684; database
contains some 79,000 names)
$15.00 per year membership; national
reunion every three years

Stover (see The Memorial Foundation of
the Germanna Colonies, McLain,
Stoner)

Stover
Stover Family Association
204 Medcon Court
Cary, NC 27511
S. Stover

Stow
*Stow(e) Surname, Associates
Thomas Josiah Stow Family
Organization
57 West Guest Avenue
Salt Lake City, UT 84115
Phone (801) 262-2894
Mrs. LaVerne Stowe Sorensen
(includes descendants of Thomas Josiah,
Nathaniel and Elizor (or Ebenezer)
Stow (late 1600s–1700s, of
Connecticut, New Hampshire, and
Massachusetts), presumed descendants
of Thomas Stow(e) of Lancashire,
England)
No fee

Stowe (see Jett)

Stowe
Stowe-Day Foundation
77 Forest Street
Hartford, CT 06105
Phone (203) 522-9258
Pub. *Stowe Foundation Bulletin (includes
Beecher, Hooker, Seymour, Day)*

Stowell
*Stowell Surname Organization
712 Hoff Drive
Blackfoot, ID 83221
Phone (208) 785-2374
Melody Thompson Clegg
(includes descendants of James E.
Stowell (1893) and Marie L. Rhoda
(1894))

Stowers (see Haynes)

Straight (see Freeland)

Strain
*Strain Family Registry
PO Box 11
Dahlonega, GA 30533-0011
Phone (706) 864-6230
J. C. Parker, Ph.D., Historian and
Registrar
(includes Strain, Bandy and Harris
families)

Strait (see Newton)

Stramba (see Stremba)

Strand (see Ostrem)

Strang (see MacDuff)

Strange
Strange Branches and Twigs
5373 Sunset Avenue
Indianapolis, IN 46208
Clover Strange Hankins
Pub. *Strange Branches and Twigs*,
quarterly, $10.00 per year subscription

Stratton (see Heath, Rogers)

Straughton (see McCleave)

Strauss (see Surname Database)

Strawn (see Austin, Likes)

Strayer
*Strayer Family Reunion
PO Box 14102
Columbus, OH 43214
Phone (614) 459-0783; (614) 845-4205
Jerry R. Strayer
Pub. *The Heir Loom*, semiannually
(includes all Strayer descendants)
$3.00 per year membership; annual
reunion on first Sunday of August at
the Salem Recreational Center, Dover,
Pennsylvania, at 1:00 P.M.

Streator (see Hyatt)

Streepers (see Links Genealogy
Publications)

Street (see Hatfield, Wapello)

Street
*Street Family
4538 Hockaday Drive
Dallas, TX 75229
Phone (214) 351-3843
Betty Street, Family Genealogist
(includes Capt. John Street and Hannah
Waddy of Virginia, early 1700s)

Streeter
*Streeter Family Association
209 The Meadows, Enfield, CT 06082
(May to October address)
26A Fisherman's Cove, Ocean Reef Club
(November to May address)
Key Largo, FL 33037
Phone (203) 741-3630 (May–October);
(305) 367-4013 (November–May);
(305) 367-4565 FAX (November–
May)
Joan Streeter Vincunas, Secretary
Pub. *Streeter National Newsletter*,
semiannually (May and November)
$12.00 per year membership

Stremba
Stremba/Stramba Newsletter
526 South Tenth Street
Reading, PA 19601
Rose Stremba Michalak
Pub. *Stremba/Stramba Newsletter*

Streypers (see Links Genealogy
Publications)

Stribling (see Lemon)

Strickland (see Dunbar, Hardwick,
Scott)

Strickland
Strickland Query and Answer Exchange
3812 Lafayette
Fort Worth, TX 76107
Pub. *Strickland Query and Answer
Exchange*

Strickler (see Newmyer)

Stringer (see Gregor)

Stringfield (see Blossom Press)

Stripgen (see Strippgen)

Strock
*Strock Family Association
2445 Ridgeview Lane
Poland, OH 44514-2545
Phone (330) 757-2715
Donn Vernon Strock and Sara Hill Strock

Strode (see Athy)

Stroehm
*Record Depository
81 Hawthorne Avenue
Pocatello, ID 83204
Phone (208) 232-6008
Maja Stroehm Peck
(includes descendants of Josef Stroehm
(Strom) in the U.S. and in Oberweier,
Rotenfels, Muggensturm, Rastatt,
Baden-Baden, and Wuertenberg,
Germany, from 1600 to the present)

Stroh (see Reeb)

Strohm (see Hoster)

Strom (see Stroehm)

Stronach (see Cameron)

Strong (see Clark, MacDuff)

Strong
Strong Family Newsletter
PO Box 13548
Saint Louis, MO 63138
Maryann Schirker
Pub. *Strong Family Newsletter*

Strong
*Strong Family Association of America,
Inc.
156 Maple Drive
Trafford, PA 15085-1435
Phone (412) 372-2313; (412) 372-5290
Dianne Strong Runser, Corresponding
Secretary
Pub. *Together We Are . . . Strong*,
quarterly (March, June, October and
November), $10.00 per year
subscription or membership for
individuals
$15.00 per year membership for families,
$150.00 life membership for
individuals, $200.00 life membership
for families; annual reunion on the
third weekend of August

Strother
*William Strother Society, Inc.
(2700 Gulf Boulevard, Unit #1, Belleair
Beach, FL 346343—winter address)

710 Big Bend Road (summer address)
Barboursville, WV 25504
Phone (813) 596-0058 (Florida)
Robin T. Hite, Genealogist
Pub. *Houses of Strother*

Stroud (see Scott, Tate)

Strouse (see Likes)

Strow (see Reeb)

Struckers (see Likes)

Strunk (see Strunck)

Stuart (see Brackett, Cian, Johnston,
MacDuff, Owens, Reynolds, Stewart)

Stubbings (see Jardine)

Stubbs (see Dawson, McRae)

Stubbs
*Descendants of Richard Stubbs, Hull,
MA, 1642
2596 Whitehurst Road
DeLand, FL 32720
Phone (904) 734-2813
Marjorie Stubbs Heaney, Family
Genealogist-Editor
Pub. *The Stubbs Schooner of News*,
annually (February)
Donation for membership

Stubbs
Missing Links
Rt. 4, Box 184
Saint Maries, ID 83861
Pub. *Stairs to Stubbs*, quarterly, $8.50 per
year subscription

Stuber (see Surname Database)

Stuckey (see Herrington, McGee)

Stuckman (see Stockman)

Studdart (see Stoddard)

Studebaker (see Frantz)

Studebaker
*The Studebaker Family National
Association
6555 South State Route 202
Tipp City, OH 45371-9444
Phone (513) 667-4451, ext. 246;
(513) 667-9322 FAX
Ruth E. Studebaker, President-Executive
Secretary
Pub. *The Studebaker Family*, quarterly;
(includes descendants of Clement
Heinrich Peter Studebaker, from the
Palatinate, Germany, to America,
1736)
$15.00 per year membership, $175.00
life membership; reunion

Studer
Jacob Studer Family Database
1411 West 995 North
Lake Village, IN 46349
Phone (219) 992-3579
Ruth Studer

Stuebing
*Stuebing Family
46 Hamilton Drive
Warminster, PA 18974
H. G. Stuebing
(Pennsylvania, New Jersey and Delaware
from 1682 to the present)

Stuell (see The Memorial Foundation of
the Germanna Colonies, Lemon)

Stukey (see Main)

Stull
*Stull Family Association
81 Highland Avenue
Belleville, OH 44813
Phone (419) 886-3572
J. Fred Stull

Stump
*Stump Family Association
10 South 445 Glenn Drive
Burr Ridge, IL 60521-6858
Phone (708) 325-3208
Dr. Eric C. Stumpf, President and Editor
Pub. *Sump/Stumpf Shoots*, quarterly,
$5.00 per year subscription; (includes
descendants of Johann Georg Stump
who came to America in 1710, lived in
Schoharrie Valley, New York, and
Lancaster, Berks and Lebanon
counties, Pennsylvania)

Stumpf (see Stump)

Sturdivant (see Emery)

Sturgeon (see Maxwell)

Stutts (see Boney)

Styles (see Stiles)

Suddarth (see Casto)

Suggs (see Bagley)

Sullens
*Sullens/Sullins Clearinghouse
110 Roberta Road
Huntsville, AL 35802
Phone (205) 881-3574
Samuel L. Sullins, Jr.
(includes family of Halifax County,
Virginia, 1740–1800)

Sullivan Surname Exchange (see Multi-
family Associations)

Sullivan
*Kinseeker Publications
5697 Old Maple Trail
PO Box 184
Grawn, MI 49637
E-mail: AB064@taverse.lib.mi.us
Victoria Wilson, Editor
Pub. *The Family Series: Sullivan*,
    irregularly, $6.50 per year subscription

Summers (see Emery, Lindsay, Smith)

Summers
Summers Family Organization
20679 Old Farm Road
Benton, IL 62812
Pub. *Summers: Whose? News? Clues?*,
    irregularly

Sumner (see Lindsay)

Sumner
*John Sumner Family Organization
Thomas Sumner Family Organization
PO Box 12
Lindrith, NM 87029
Phone (505) 774-6512
Harold Sumner
Dues; reunion by invitation only

Sumner
*Sumner Family Association
62 Sandbury Drive
Pittsford, NY 14534-2636
Phone (716) 334-2989
Charles H. Sumner, Director
Pub. *Annual Letter*
$5.00 per year membership

Sumnicht (see Sager)

Sumwalt (see Zumwalt)

Sunday (see Kunkel)

Sunderhaus (see Wilson)

Supplee (see DeHaven)

Supplees (see Links Genealogy
    Publications)

Surette
*Surette Genealogy
148 Robbins Road
Arlington, MA 02174
Phone (617) 648-2443
Stephen G. Surette

Surine (see Sarine)

Surnam (see Woolley)

Surname Sources (see Multi-family
    Associations)

Sutherland
*Clan Sutherland Society of North
    America
1509 21st Avenue
Rock Island, IL 61201

Phone (309) 786-5777
Jock R. Sutherland, Genealogist
Pub. *The Dunrobin Piper*, monthly; (not
    a genealogical publication, includes
    septs: Cheyne, Duffus, Gray, Federith,
    Mowat and Oliphant)
$15.00 per year membership, $5.00
    membership application

Sutherland
Collier Research
PO Box 371883
El Paso, TX 79937
Phone (915) 595-2725
Timothy P. Biarnesen, Editor
Pub. *Sutherland/Southerland Quarterly*,
    $20.00 per year subscription

Sutherland
William Sutherland (of Pictou) Clan
N.E. 24170 Highway 3, Apartment 18
Belfair, WA 98528
John A. Sutherland

Sutliff (see Newton)

Sutphin (see Lambert)

Sutten (see Kunkel)

Sutter
*Sutter-Ulrich-Plank Family Association
1270 Highway 9
Lansing, IA 52151-7613
Phone (319) 568-3802
Randy Hamman, Secretary-Treasurer
Pub. *SUP Family History*, $11.00 per
    issue
Annual reunion on the fourth Sunday of
    June at Monona, Iowa

Suttle (see Settle)

Sutton (see Cian, Sutten)

Sutton
Sutton
1921 Baldy Lane
Evergreen, CO 80439-9444
Jim Sutton
Pub. *Sutton*, quarterly, $15.00 per year
    subscription, $18.00 per year overseas
    subscription

Sutton
Sutton Seeker
East 13124 Nixon
Spokane, WA 99216
Joanne M. Elliott
Pub. *Sutton Seeker*, $5.00 plus $1.00
    postage per issue

Swab
*Swab Family Reunion
1215 Harper Avenue
Woodlyn, PA 19094-1211
Phone (610) 833-5223
James J. Swab, Director
(includes descendants of Johannes
    Schwab (1720–1785), also Swabb)

Swabb (see Swab)

Swadley
*Swadley Family Association
9535 Elvis Lane
Seabrook, MD 20706
Phone (301) 577-6482
June Swadley Provini

Swaim (see Folk Family Surname
    Exchange, Farrington)

Swain (see Corson, Newberry, Saye)

Swan (see Folk Family Surname
    Exchange, Brothers, Dobie, Gunn)

Swaner (see Schwanner)

Swanger
Swanger Family Helper
505 Cambridge
Victoria, TX 77901
Melissa Swanger
Pub. *Swanger Family Helper*, quarterly,
    $8.00 per year subscription

Swank (see Frazier)

Swann (see Gunn, Nettles)

Swanner (see Schwanner)

Swanney (see Gunn)

Swanson (see Clowees, Gunn)

Swanton
*Swanton Family History Worldwide
RR 2, Box 670
Wiscasset, ME 04578-9629
Louise M. Swanton

Swartslander (see Swartzlander)

Swartz (see Likes, McCue, Schwartz)

Swartzlander
*Swartzlander Descendants
126 Beaver Avenue
PO Box 279
West Sunbury, PA 16061-0279
Phone (412) 637-2915
Ronald E. Swartzlander, Editor/Publisher
Pub. *The Swartzlander Descendants/Die
    Schwartzländer Nachkommen*, three
    times per year (April, August and
    December), $5.00 per year
    subscription, $2.50 per issue; (includes
    Swartzlander, Swartslander,
    Schwartzlaender, etc., families in
    North America and Germany;
    American progenitor Johann Philipp
    Schwartzländer (1723–ca 1794),
    arrived at Philadelphia from Steinhart,
    Middle Franconia, in 1752 and settled
    in New Britain, Bucks County,
    Pennsylvania, and married Maria
    Magdalena Petzel and Maria Agnes
    Trost)

National biennial reunion on the Sunday
of Labor Day weekend in even-
numbered years; Pennsylvania reunion
same weekend other years

Swarz
*Schwarz Family
532 North Main Street
Wayland, MI 49348
Barbara Schwarz-Sprik, Genealogist

Swasey
*Swasey Family Society
25034 180th Avenue, S.E.
Kent, WA 98042
Phone (206) 630-8659
Clyde W. Downing, Publisher
Pub. *Swasey Family Society*, quarterly
(January, April, July and October),
$12.00 per year subscription, $3.50 per
issue, free queries; (includes all
Swasey, Swasy, Swayze, Sweazey,
Sweesey, Sweesy, Sweezey, Swesey,
Swezey, Swezy, etc., in the U.S. and
Canada, most of whom are
descendants of John[1] Swasey who
came to America in 1629 and settled in
Salem, Massachusetts Bay Colony)

Swasy (see Swasey)

Swayze (see Swasey)

Sweaney (see Looney)

Sweazey (see Swasey)

Swecker
*Swecker Family Reunion
309 Elmhurst Street
Morgantown, WV 26505
Phone (304) 599-0368
Jonas Swecker

Sweesey (see Swasey)

Sweesy (see Swasey)

Sweeton
*Arthur Worth Sweeton Family Reunion
PO Box 158
6 Humphrey Road
Canton Center, CT 06020-0158
Phone (860) 693-4027
Arthur W. Sweeton, III
(ancestors and descendants of Arthur
Worth Sweeton (1859–1928) of North
Canton, Connecticut)
Annual reunion on the first Sunday in
August

Sweezey (see Swasey)

Swepson (see Boyd)

Swesey (see Swasey)

Swezey (see Swasey)

Swezy (see Swasey)

Swickard (see McConnell)

Swift (see Barnard)

Swindell (see The Memorial Foundation
of the Germanna Colonies)

Swinehart
Swinehart Family Clearinghouse
77 Hollow Road
Quarryville, PA 17566-9491
Harry Hoffman

Swing
Swing Family Newsletter
103 West Alabama
Houston, TX 77002-9603
Pub. *Swing Family Newsletter*,
semiannually (spring and autumn),
$5.00 per year subscription; (includes
Schwing and Schwenck)

Swingle (see Anthes)

Swingley (see Phelps)

Swinnerton
The Swinnerton Society
216 Moreton Bay Lane, Apartment 6
Goleta, CA 93117-2236
H. Norman Swinnerton, Vice President,
U.S.A.
Pub. *Swinnerton Family History*,
quarterly (March, June, September and
December), $8.00 per ten-issue volume
subscription (up to $20.00 according to
rate of exchange to pounds sterling)

Swope
*Swope Family
2609 Keddington Lane
Salt Lake City, UT 84117-4562
Phone (801) 278-2230
Winifred Morse McLachlan, Genealogist
(includes descendants of Jacob Schwob
(1709 Bennwil, Baselland,
Switzerland–), who settled in Lebanon
(now North Lebanon) Township,
Lancaster (now Lebanon) County,
Pennsylvania, and his wives, Maria
Schwob of Bennwil and Elisabeth; Jost
Schwab (1656 Sinsheim, Baden,
Germany–) and Anna Katharina
Wolfhardt (1663 Bühren, Baden,
Germany–), emigrated to Lancaster
County, Pennsylvania, in 1720)
$2.00 per year membership; annual
reunion on the last Sunday of June at
Trinity Tulpehocken United Church of
Christ on Old Route 422 east of
Myerstown in Millardsville, Lebanon
County, Pennsylvania

Sykes (see Smith)

Sylve (see Blossom Press)

Sylvester (see Johnson, MacDuff)

Symes (see Syms)

Symington (see Douglas)

Symms (see Sims)

Syms
*Syms/Sims/Symes Surname
Organization
150 Brown Street
Saint Clair, MI 48079-4882
Phone (810) 329-9359
George M. Roberts
(includes families of the U.S. and
Canada)

Syras (see MacDuff)

Syrcle (see Zirkle)

Tabar (see Taber)

Tabb (see Edwards)

Taber (see Jay)

Taber
*Taber/Tabor Database
PO Box 8713
Hot Springs, AR 71910-8713
Phone (501) 922-3355; (501) 922-6736
FAX; E-mail:
104106.53@compuserve.com
Ruthe Taber Boetcker, Editor
Pub. *The Taber Tree*, quarterly, $10.00
per year subscription (includes
descendants of Philip Taber (ca 1605–
1672, varient spellings Tabar and
Tabor)

Tabony (see Blossom Press)

Tabor (see Allison, Dean, Taber)

Tacker (see Album)

Tacket (see Tackett)

Tackett (see Dean)

Tackett
*The Tackett Family Association
1830 Johnson Drive
Concord, CA 94520
Phone (510) 680-0383
Jim W. Tackitt, President/Editor
Pub. *The Tackett Family Journal*,
quarterly; (includes descendants of
Lewis Tacquett (ca 1680–1743) from
France to Stafford County, Virginia;
alternate spellings, Tacket and Tackitt)
$12.50 minimum per year membership;
annual reunion in Pike County,
Kentucky

Tackitt (see Tackett)

Taenzler (see Wagner)

Taft (see Mueller)

Taft
*Taft Family Association
3119 Heatherwood
Yarmouth Port, MA 02675-1457
R. T. Messinger, Editor
Pub. *Taft Tree Talk*, semiannually
$5.00 per year membership

Tagg (see Montague)

Taggart (see Ross)

Taggart
*George Washington Taggart Family
   Organization
PO Box 1836
Tahoe City, CA 96145
Phone (916) 583-3935
Jeanette Taggart Holmes
Pub. *Newsletter*, semiannually
Donation for membership

Tague (see Montague)

Taintor (see Clark)

Taisey (see Heath)

Talbert (see Baughman, Kahler, Perkins)

Talbot (see Athy, Talbert, Rutherford)

Talbot
*John Talbot Family Organization
1910 Rosewood Street
Vista, CA 92083
Phone (619) 598-9111
Warren Talbot
(includes descendants of John Talbot
   (1850 near Lancashire, Preston,
   England–1915 Roberts, Illinois), was
   brought to Peoria, Illinois, in 1858 and
   placed on an "orphan train," son of
   William and Mary, full brother of
   Thomas, who eventually married and
   died in Harvey, Illinois, and half-
   brother of Roger, who moved to
   Indiana)

Talbott (see Holden)

Talbutt (see Talbot)

Taliaferro (see Marshall)

Taliancich (see Blossom Press)

Taliferro (see Delashmutt)

Tallent
Tallent Family Association
515 Garrison Court, S.W.
Concord, NC 28025
William J. Tallent, President and
   Newsletter Publisher
Pub. *Searching for Tallent (However you
   spell it)*, quarterly, $5.00 per year
   subscription
$10.00 per year membership; annual
   reunion

Talley (see Holden)

Tally (see Talley)

Talmage (see Wheeler)

Tam (see MacThomas)

Tamany (see Cian)

Tams (see McCune)

Tanner (see The Memorial Foundation
   of the Germanna Colonies)

Tanner
Tanner Family Organization
2320 South Cypress Bend Drive, #D204
Pompano Beach, FL 33069-4413
D. Thomas Stone

Tanner
*Wave Deforest Tanner Family Database
PO Box 9
Harlem, MT 59526
Phone (406) 353-2427
Lorene A. Kirkaldie
(includes descendants of Wave Deforest
   Tanner's parents, John C. Tanner (1838
   Mayville, Chautaqua County, New
   York–1914 Erie, Erie County,
   Pennsylvania), son of Nicholas and
   Esther Mills Tanner, and John C.
   Tanner's wife Nellie Esther (or
   Elizabeth) Cottrell (1840–1908
   Fairview, Erie County, Pennsylvania),
   daughter of John and Mary Preston
   Cottrell)

Tanner
*William Tanner Family Organization
222 East Sunset
Riverton, WY 82501
Phone (307) 856-0950
Jeanie Tanner
(database includes all Tanners connected,
   as well as the family of William
   Tanner, 1660 Rhode Island, and his
   children, William, Mary, Benjamin,
   Thomas, Avis, John, Francis, Nathan,
   Anna, Rebecca, Elizabeth and Abigail)

Tapp (see The Memorial Foundation of
   the Germanna Colonies)

Tappin (see Clark)

Taranto (see Toronto)

Tarbert (see Torbet)

Tarbet (see Torbet)

Tarne (see Surname Sources)

Tarrell (see Ross)

Tarril (see Chattan)

Tarry (see Musson)

Tarvin
Tarvin Family Association
37 West Ridgewood Avenue
Ridgewood, NJ 07450
Phone (201) 444-0698
Sarah T. Tarvin
Pub. *Tarvin Family Lifeline*, two to three
   times per year
$12.00 per year membership for
   individuals, $20.00 per year
   membership for families

Tasset
*Tasset Tree Trunks
PO Box 1872
Dodge City, KS 67801-1872
Laura Tasset Koehn, President
(includes research on John Henry Tasset
   and Maria Carolina Rosener)

Tassin (see Johnson)

Tate (see Johnson)

Tate
Tate-Richardson-Stroud-Dillard Family
   Association
2306 Westgate
Houston, TX 77019
Phone (713) 529-2333
Harold Helm
$25.00 plus pedigree and family group
   sheets for membership

Tattrie (see Weatherbee)

Tatum (see Job)

Tavaude (see Dragoo)

Tavney (see Cian)

Tawn (see Reynolds)

Tayler (see Garner)

Taylor (see Folk Family Surname
   Exchange, Album, Arthur, Cameron,
   Corder, Farrington, Fowlkes,
   Franciscus, Furse, Goodenow, Gregor,
   Holden, Lemon, Lush, Lynch,
   McCune, Nettles, Smith, Valentine,
   Way, Wiler, Wright)

Taylor
*Taylor Family Association
18002 North 12th Street, #30
Phoenix, AZ 85022
Nani Mercer Neal
Pub. *Taylor Surname Newsletter*,
   quarterly, $20.00 per year subscription

Taylor
*Taylor Book
969 North Reed Station Road
Carbondale, IL 62901
Inez Taylor, Publisher

Taylor
Wilson Family Record Depository
169 Melody Lane
Tonawanda, NY 14150-9109
Robert J. Wilson
Pub. *Taylor*, quarterly, $25.00 per year
subscription

Taylor
Furman V. and Eliza C. Taylor Family
Organization
Valley View Park, Lot 57, Rt. 3
Dallas, PA 18612
Sarah Taylor
Reunion

Taylor
*Taylor-Armstrong Family Association
9100 Highway 2181, Lot 38K
Denton, TX 76205
Phone (817) 566-6605
Virginia Morse
Pub. *Taylor-Armstrong Treasures*, three
times per year
$15.00 per year membership; annual
reunion on the third Saturday of July

Taylor
Collier Research
PO Box 371883
El Paso, TX 79937
Phone (915) 595-2725
Timothy P. Biarnesen, Editor
Pub. *Taylor Quarterly*, $20.00 per year
subscription

Taylor
*A. J. Taylor Family Organization
6070 South Clara Drive
Salt Lake City, UT 84118
Phone (801) 969-9110
Beth Taylor
(includes descendants of William Taylor
(1802 Adlestrop, Gloucester,
England–) and Elizabeth Wardle (1812
Lapworth, Hockleyheath, England–))

Taylor
*Taylor Tracing Tribe
Rt. 1, Box 417
Charlotte Court House, VA 23923-9891
Phone (804) 248-5754
Rev. Cecil Robert Taylor
Pub. *Taylor Talk*, $12.95 per year
subscription; (plans and conducts
seminars and courses on genealogical
research, and searches for Taylor
graves and cemeteries, cleaning them,
repairing markers and tombstones and
replacing them when funds are
available)

Taylor
Taylor Family Association
14333 Aldengate Road
Midlothian, VA 23113
Anne Hale Kellam

Taylor
*Nathaniel C. and Lucy Ann Sandefur
Taylor Descendants Reunion
605 Fir Street
Coulee Dam, WA 99116
Phone (509) 633-2208
Carl E. Gwynn, Secretary
(includes surnames Taylor in Tennessee,
Mann, Miller, Mullinax and Doughty)
Biennial reunion in even-numbered years
on the second weekend of August in
Greenwood County, Kansas

Taylor
Taylor Made for Us
323 Cedarcrest Court East
PO Box 779
Napavine, WA 98565-0779
Phone (360) 262-3300
Ruby Simonson McNeill
Pub. *Taylor Made for Us*, irregularly,
$5.75 per issue plus $2.00 postage

Tea
*The Tea Family Organization
752 Gran Kayman Way
Jamaica Isle
Apollo Beach, FL 33572-2438
Phone (813) 645-6562
Charles L. Tea
Pub. *The Tea Chronicles* (includes related
families: Bondurant, McClain,
Munsell, etc.)

Teachenor (see Tichenor)

Teacher (see Moody)

Teagle
*The Teagle Family
7500 Lester Road, Apartment 46-2
Union City, GA 30291-2350
Winton Teagle, Publisher
(includes descendants of Nathaniel
Teagle (–1708) of Talbot County,
Maryland, through Virginia to Union
County, South Carolina, with branches
in Gwinnett and Meriwether counties,
Georgia)

Teague (see Additon)

Teare (see Behnke)

Tearl (see Thorn)

Teas (see Clark)

Teasdale (see Hutchison)

Tebbs (see Covert)

Tedford
Tedford/Telford
6180 Merrywood Drive
Rocklin, CA 95677-3421
Kathleen Stewart
Pub. *Tedford/Telford*, quarterly (February,
May, August and November), $12.00
per year subscription

Tedlock (see Tatlock)

Teed
*The Teed Family Association
3982 Trotwood Drive
Lake Havasu City, AZ 86406
Phone (520) 680-6257
Sally Teed Foust, Editor
Pub. *The TEED Family Tree: Preserving
and Printing Genealogy and History
For Future Generations*, quarterly;
free queries
$20.00 per year membership

Teison (see Links Genealogy
Publications)

Teissen (see Tyson)

Teitelbaum
*Teitelbaum Surname Database
13442 93rd Avenue, North
Maple Grove, MN 55369-9740
Phone (612) 494-6694
Sherry Constans-Kaiserlik

Tekulvie (see McCune)

Telford (see Farrington, Tedford)

Telley (see Talley)

Telly (see Talley)

Telnes (see Links Genealogy
Publications)

Templeton (see Arthur, Haws)

Templin
*The Templin Family Association
2256 River Oak Lane, S.E.
Fort Myers, FL 33905
Phone (813) 694-8347
Ronald R. Templin, Family Genealogist
(includes descendants of James Templin
and Mary Salmon of Chester County,
Pennsylvania, and Ross County, Ohio)

Templin
*Templin Family Association
7006 S.E. 21st Avenue
Portland, OR 97202
Phone (503) 236-0549
Cynthia M. B. Drayer, Genealogist/
Historian
Pub. *Templin Family Association*, one or
two times per year
$12.00 per two years membership;
biennial reunion in even-numbered
years

ten Broeck (see Barnard)

Tennant (see MacDuff)

Tennis (see Links Genealogy
Publications)

Terrell (see Folk Family Surname
Exchange)

Terrell
Terrell Society of America, Inc.
7701 Park Vista Circle
Charlotte, NC 28226
Phone (704) 541-1857
Mrs. Pat Terrell Walker, Correspondence
    Secretary
Pub. *Terrell Trails*, quarterly
$12.00 per year membership

Terrill
Descendants of Roger Terrill
    Corresponding Society
PO Box 589
Hudson, IL 61748-0589
Nancy Tyrrell Theodore, Executive
    Director/Research Coordinator
Pub. *DOR (Descendants of Roger)
    Newsletter*, quarterly
$10.00 per year membership

Terwilliger
Terwilliger Family Association
(Huguenot Historical Society, New Paltz,
    New York)
2100 Gull Avenue
McAllen, TX 78504-3925
Phone (512) 631-1585
Gordon L. Terwilliger

Teter (see The Memorial Foundation of
    the Germanna Colonies)

Tevebaugh
*Tevebaugh/Teverbaugh Surname
    Organization
217 Grand Avenue
Grand Haven, MI 49417
Phone (616) 842-6121
John Leslie Tevebaugh
Item cost plus postage for family data
    and articles

Teverbaugh (see Tevebaugh)

Thacker (see Rowe)

Thain (see Garner)

Thallion (see MacDuff)

Thallon (see MacDuff)

Thatcher (see Links Genealogy
    Publications)

Thayer (see Harvey)

Thayer
*Thayer Families Association
PO Box 12
Braintree, MA 02185-0012
Phone (617) 328-8236
Raymond A. (Rick) Thayer, Secretary/
    Treasurer
Pub. *Thayer Quarterly* (includes
    descendants of Thomas (1637, settled
    Braintree), his brother Richard (1640/
    41, settled Braintree) and Nathaniel
    (1660, settled Taunton) Thayer who

migrated to America ca 1640 from
    Thornbury, Gloucestershire (now Avon
    County), England)
$15.00 per year membership

Thayer
*Spencer Thayer and Sally Butler
    Reunion
123 North Grove Street
Bowling Green, OH 43402
Phone (419) 352-4940
Lolita Guthrie

Theal (see Theall)

Theall
Theall/Theal Family Organization
Rt. 5, Box 53
Laconia, NH 03246
S. Theall

Thedes
Thedes Newsletter
2603 Marlow Road
Santa Rosa, CA 95401
Mr. Chesnik
Pub. *Thedes Newsletter*

Theison (see Links Genealogy
    Publications, Tyson)

Theobald (see MacDuff)

Therriot (see Johnson)

Theunissen (see Middaugh)

Thibodeaux (see Johnson)

Thienemann
Thienemann Newsletter
205 Cornwallis Drive
Lynchburg, VA 24502-2732
Phone (804) 237-4963; (804) 847-4156
    FAX; E-mail: keithth@aol.com
Keith G. Thienemann
Pub. *Thienemann Newsletter*, annually,
    free; (published in English; includes
    Dienemann and Duhnemann)
Reunion

Thom (see MacThomas)

Thomas (see The Memorial Foundation
    of the Germanna Colonies, Album,
    Bigaouette, Dean, Foley, Gant,
    Guthrie, Job, Jones, Likes, Louden,
    MacThomas, McCanna, Robinson,
    Scott, Stoner)

Thomas
Ddesign
Thomas Research Center
5423 El Camino
Columbia, MD 21044
Pub. *Thomas Research*, quarterly;
    (largest Thomas database in existence)
$15.00 per year membership, $28.00 for
    two years membership, includes
    unlimited computer searches,
    unlimited queries

Thomas
*Descendants of Asa Thomas Reunion
PO Box 245
Novinger, MO 63559
Phone (816) 488-6616; (816) 488-6885
    FAX; E-mail:
    Jethomas@Vax2.Rain.Gen.MO.Us
Roger Thomas
(includes descendants of Asa Thomas,
    the first settler of Milford, Iroquois
    County, Illinois, in 1830, with children
    settling in Milford or close by in
    Iroquois County)
Annual reunion at the Railroad Station in
    Milford, Illinois

Thomason (see Brooks)

Thomason
Thomason Newsletter
595 Idylwood Drive, S.E.
Salem, OR 97302
Phone (503) 362-1035
Carol M. Jacobson, Editor
Pub. *Thomason Newsletter*, quarterly,
    $13.00 per year subscription; (includes
    Thomasson)

Thomasson (see Thomason)

Thomasson
*Thomasson Traces
19 Magnolia Drive
Newnan, GA 30263
Phone (404) 251-0612
Marjorie B. Malloy
Reunion

Thompkins (see Jett)

Thompson (see CTC Family
    Association, Folk Family Surname
    Exchange, Allison, Brawley, Cairer,
    Clowes, Franciscus, Frasher,
    Goodenow, Hatch, Hatfield, Heath,
    Jackson, Lush, Mael, McCune,
    McKee, Robbins, Ross, Thomson,
    Wiler)

Thompson
Thompson Family Organization
5930 River Run Drive
Cottonwood, AZ 86326
James William Thompson, Family
    Representative
Reunion

Thompson
Thompson Trails Quarterly
2190 Camino Largo Drive
Chino Hills, CA 91709
Trish Elliott Collins
Pub. *Thompson Trails Quarterly*, $14.00
    per year subscription

Thompson
*James and Martha Thompson (Pelham)
    Database
13265 Webster Avenue
Savage, MN 55378

Phone (612) 894-5970
Dennis J. Thompson
Pub. *Thompson Family Tree*, annually,
postage for issue; (includes
descendants of James and Martha
Thompson of Pelham, Massachusetts,
1709–1992, with branches for
Wisconsin, Minnesota and California
descendants)

Thompson
*Granville "Carell" Thompson
Descendants
HC-66, Box 79
Indian Valley Road
Radford, VA 24141
Phone (540) 789-4444
Sylvia Thompson Cox
Annual reunion at the Dugspur Rescue
Squad Building, Dugspur, Virginia

Thompson
Nexus Publications
2207 N.E. 12th Street
Renton, WA 98056
Lynn Wood, Editor
Pub. *Thompson Nexus*, quarterly, $20.00
per year subscription

Thoms (see MacThomas)

Thomson (see Arthur, MacThomas,
McCrea)

Thomson
Thomson-Thompson-Tomson
Rt. 1, Box 10
Armstrong, MO 65230
Lewis Nelson Thompson
Pub. *Thomson-Thompson-Tomson*, three
times per year, $12.00 per year
subscription

Thonymys (see Surname Database)

Thorn
*Thomas Thorn and Mary Ann
Downman Organization
2421 North 750 East
Provo, UT 84604-4014
Phone (801) 375-4390
Margaret Fawson Talbot, Research
Coordinator
Pub. *Newsletter*, annually (December);
(includes descendants of Thomas
Thorn (1807–1846) and Mary Ann
Downman (1805–after 1851); also
allied surnames of Gadsden, Hempson,
Hillsdon, Horn, Nichols, Sibley, Tearl
and White of Eaton Bray, Beds,
England)
$30.00 donation per year membership

Thorn
*Thomas Thorn Family Organization
(617 Grand Street, Morgantown, WV
26505—alternate location)
1599 Monaco Circle
Salt Lake City, UT 84121
Phone (801) 278-7708

Eldon B. Tucker, Jr., M.D. (Ret.)
(includes family originally from West
Virginia)

Thornton (see Album, Gant,
Rothenberger, Woodrow)

Thornton
Thomas Thornton Family Bulletin
962 East 2100 North
Logan, UT 84341-1841
Elva Ann Thornton
Pub. *Thomas Thornton Family Bulletin*,
annually

Thorpe (see Reeder)

Thorton
Thorton
1221 Candice Court
Mesquite, TX 75149
Mary L. House, Editor
Pub. *Thorton*, quarterly, $15.00 per year
subscription

Thrash (see Hall)

Thrasher (see Lemon)

Thue (see Velline)

Thurasson (see Kahler)

Thurber
*Thurber Clearinghouse
6358 South Josephine Way
Littleton, CO 80121
Phone (303) 794-0348
Joanne E. Martin
$5.00 search fee, plus copy costs and
postage

Thurgood
*John A. Thurgood Family Organization
1225 West 4575 South
Ogden, UT 84405
Phone (801) 627-2115
Shirley T. Gailey

Thurman
*Thurman Family Association
4201 Wildflower Circle
Wichita, KS 67210
Phone (316) 529-0438
J. Robert Thurman, Historian
Pub. *Newsletter*, annually; (includes
descendants of Powhatten Ellis
Thurman (1811–1890) and Richard
Austin Thurman (1838–1921))
Annual reunion on the third Saturday of
July in Keene, Oklahoma

Thurston (see Underwood, Wright)

Thurston
Shields Publishing Company
PO Box 43
Palos Verdes Estates, CA 90274
Mary Ann Shields
Pub. *Thurston Tracing*, three times per
year, $10.00 per year subscription

Thynne
*Thynne Surname Organization
1257 North Main Street
Centerville, UT 84014-1107
Phone (801) 298-1029
David Bruce Gange

Tibbets (see Corson)

Tibbetts (see Corson)

Tichenor (see Pigg)

Tichenor
Tichenor Family Genealogy Newsletter
RR 4, Box 1016
Napton, MO 65340
Harold A. Tichenor
Pub. *Tichenor Family Genealogy
Newsletter*, irregularly; (includes
descendants of Martin Tichenor of
New Haven Colony as early as 1644,
including Teachenor, Tichinel,
Tichnell, Tishner, Titchenal, Titchenell
and Titchnell)

Tichinel (see Tichenor)

Tichnell (see Tichenor)

Tickle
*Tickle Reunion
1603 Frosty Lane
Salem, VA 24153
Phone (540) 389-0435
Noah M. Tickle, Jr.
Annual reunion on the last Sunday of
July

Tiddy
*Tiddy Family History Society
542 Old Main Street
Rocky Hill, CT 06067-1512
Phone (860) 529-4370
Thomas C. Gross
(includes Tiddy worldwide, especially
descendants of family originating in
Cornwall, England, ca 1630)

Tidwell
*Tidwell, Ledford Database
2913 Roane State Highway
Harriman, TN 37748
Phone (423) 882-7944
Howard Tidwell
(exchanges family group sheets on
Tidwell, Ledford, McGlothin, Rose,
Wakefield, Retherford, Rutherford,
McCurry, Hollis, Goodrum and
Wetherby; Cherokee/Tidwell relations
in Georgia, Tennessee and Oklahoma;
Kestersons in Georgia and Mississippi)

Tietsoort (see Tietsort)

Tietsort
Tietsort, Tietsoort, Tietsworth Family
Association
14850 23 Mile Road
Albion, MI 49224

Phone (517) 629-2345
Shirley J. Hodges, President
Pub. *The Tietsort Family Newsletter*,
    quarterly
$12.00 per year membership

Tietsworth (see Tietsort)

Tigner (see Jelly)

Tiller (see Jacoby)

Tiller
*Tiller-Tipton Reunion
Country Court Trailer Park
1101 Pocahontas, Trailer #18
Palmyra, MO 63461
Marjorie J. Westmoreland
Annual reunion in Elsberry, Missouri

Tillery (see Folk Family Surname
    Exchange, Covert)

Tillman
Tillman-Moses-Leonard-Isaacson Family
    Association
2306 Westgate
Houston, TX 77019
Phone (713) 529-2333
Harold Helm
$25.00 plus pedigree and family group
    sheets for membership

Tillson (see Tilson)

Tillyer (see Tillier)

Tilson
*Tilson/Tillson Family Association
129 Vassar Road
Poughkeepsie, NY 12603
Phone (914) 462-3338; E-mail:
    naomi@mhv.net
Naomi Van Steenburgh
(includes descendants of Edmund Tilson,
    1638)
Reunion

Tilton (see Corson)

Timmerman (see Olthaus, Snell)

Timmons
The Timmons Family Newsletter
361 Second Street
PO Box 262
Montrose, MN 55363-0262
Phone (612) 675-3457
Bunnie Timmons Runman, Editor
Pub. *The Timmons Family Newsletter*,
    quarterly, donation for current issue,
    $1.00 each for back issues; (includes
    Timmons, any place, line or era,
    1600s–1900s)

Timms
Data Unlimited
4941 Syracuse Drive
Oxnard, CA 93033
Jeanne Hicks, Researcher
(includes Tims)

Tims (see Timms)

Tiner (see Folk Family Surname
    Exchange, Brown, Patterson)

Tiner
*Folk Family
PO Box 52048
Knoxville, TN 37950-2048
Hester E. Stockton, Owner; Lucinda
    Tiner, Editor
Pub. *Tiner Times*, quarterly, $15.00 per
    year subscription, $5.00 per issue;
    (includes Tyner)

Tingen
*Garrett Tingen Descendants: Early
    Settler of Person County, North
    Carolina
822 Camino De Los Padres
Tucson, AZ 85718
Phone (520) 297-6585
Leallah Franklin, Publisher

Tingley
Tingleys-United Association
1244 North Fitch Mountain Road
Healdsburg, CA 95448-4512
Mr. Melbourne Tingley
Pub. *Tingleys—United Association
    Newsletter*

Tinklepaugh
Tinklepaugh Family Newsletter
1011 North Clayton Street
Wilmington, DE 19805
Ms. M. A. Brandi Syfrit
Pub. *Tinklepaugh Family Newsletter*,
    annually

Tinsley (see Golding, Warren)

Tinya (see Baldman)

Tippett (see Cusick)

Tipton (see Tiller)

Tischer (see Arthur)

Tisdale (see Surname Sources)

Tishner (see Tichenor)

Titchenal (see Tichenor)

Titchenell (see Tichenor)

Titchnell (see Tichenor)

Tittsworth (see Davis)

Titus
Leaves of the Titus Tree
PO Box 327
Shasta, CA 96087
Grace McQuown
(includes descendants of William M.
    (1791–1876), Kirby William (1833–
    1917) and Mortimer Dormer (1860–
    1937) Titus)

Toal (see Folk Family Surname
    Exchange)

Toalson (see Tolson)

Todd (see Massey, Wallis)

Todd
Todd's Trees 'n' Twigs
Rt. 1, Box 192
Monmouth, IL 61462
James E. and Sharon L. Todd
Pub. *Todd's Trees 'n' Twigs*, quarterly,
    $10.00 per year subscription

Todd
*The K.A.R.D. Files
19305 S.E. 243rd Place
Kent, WA 98042-4820
Phone (206) 432-1659
Judy K. Dye, Owner
Pub. *The Todd Times*, irregularly, $6.00–
    $7.00 per volume (Washington
    residents add 8.2% sales tax)

Toe (see Reeder)

Tolbert (see Talbot)

Tolbot (see Talbot)

Toler (see Hatfield)

Toler
Toler Trails
9103 Stone Creek Place
Dallas, TX 75243
Tobin D. Toler
Pub. *Toler Trails*
SASE

Tolle
Tolle Family Exchange
10351 16th Street
Garden Grove, CA 92643
Phone (714) 534-7606
Thoren Tolle Meyers, Editor
Pub. *Tolle Family Exchange*, bimonthly,
    $8.00 per year subscription

Tolleson (see Golding)

Tolley (see Talley)

Tolly (see Talley)

Tolman
*Thomas Tolman Family Genealogy
    Center
2937 South Orchard Drive
Bountiful, UT 84010
Phone (801) 292-7745
Loa Don Glade, Genealogist-Researcher
Pub. *Thomas Tolman Family Magazine*,
    semiannually; *Thomas Tolman Family
    Organization Newsletter*, annually;
    (includes descendants of Thomas
    Tolman (immigrated ca 1635) and
    wife, Sarah)
$20.00 per year membership

Tolson
*Tolson/Toalson Surname Organization
Thomas Toalson Family Organization
PO Box 852245
Richardson, TX 75085
Phone (214) 783-9211
Owen Thomas Tolson, III
Pub. *Tolson/Toalson Family History*,
    irregularly, no charge; (includes Tolson
    and Toalson families of Virginia,
    Kentucky and Missouri)

Tomerlin (see Tomlin)

Tomlin
Tomlin Family Newsletter
PO Box 476
Hamshire, TX 77622
Bobbie Thompson
Pub. *Tomlin, Tomerlin, Tomlinson,
    Tumlinson Family Newsletter*, monthly,
    $12.00 per year subscription

Tomlinson (see Tomlin)

Tomson (see Thomson)

Toney
Toney Tribune
411 Avondale Road
Huntington, WV 25705-1524
Melinda Vance, Family Representative
Pub. *Toney Tribune*

Tong (see Clark)

Tonn (see Anthes)

Tonnochy (see Donnachaidh)

Toocker (see Tucker)

Tooley (see Smith)

Toomey (see McGrath)

Toon (see Toone, Tune)

Toone (see Tune)

Toone
Toone, Toon and Tune of America
    Family Association
1375 Baxter Road
Petersburg, VA 23803
Phone (804) 861-2704
Lavern Toone, Historian
Annual reunion in Virginia on the second
    Sunday of August and in Nashville,
    Tennessee, on the second Saturday of
    July

Torbain (see MacDuff)

Torbert (see Torbet)

Torn (see MacDuff)

Toronto
*Joseph Toronto Family Organization
1148 South 350 West
Bountiful, UT 84010
Phone (801) 292-1549 (Mrs. Moody);
    (801) 942-5070 (Mr. Toronto)
Maria Toronto Moody; Joseph Christian
    Toronto
(includes descendants and ancestors of
    Joseph Toronto (Giuseppe Efisio
    Taranto, Italian name) (1816–), son of
    Francesco Matteo Antonio Taranto
    (1782 Palermo, Italy–) and Angela
    Maria Fazio (1789 Trapani, Italy–))

Torr (see MacDuff)

Torrens (see Cian)

Torrey
Oak Leaf Publishing
22 Creek Road, #64
Irvine, CA 91714
Pub. *Torrey Family Newsletter*,
    bimonthly, $10.00 per year
    subscription

Tosh (see Lair, Mackintosh)

Toshack (see MacDuff)

Toth (see Baldman)

Totten
Totten Family Organization
4300 East Holt Boulevard, N #1
Montclair, CA 91763-4107
Jon M. Totten

Tounsley (see Tously)

Toupard (see Blossom Press)

Tower (see Hack)

Towery (see Towry)

Towler (see Stewart)

Towne (see Barnard)

Towne
*Towne Family Association, Inc.
6835 Fisher Road
Ontario, NY 14519-9709
Phone (315) 524-8394
James F. Roome, Executive Secretary
Pub. *About Towne*, quarterly (April, June,
    September and December); (includes
    descendants of William and Joanna
    (Blessing) Towne (married 1620, came
    to America from Great Yarmouth,
    England, and settled in Salem,
    Massachusetts, about 1640) and allied
    families: Bridges, Cloyes, Estey and
    Nurse (including Sara Bridges Cloyse,
    Rebecca Nurse and Mary Esty or
    Easty, who were executed during the
    witchcraft delusion of 1692))

$18.00 per year membership for
    individuals, $5.00 for each additional
    member at the same address, $250.00
    life membership for individuals;
    reunion

Townley (see Gant)

Townsden
*Frances Harriet Townsden Family
    Organization
PO Box 383
Lehi, UT 84043
Verona Blackham Balle

Townsend (see Surname Database, Frary,
    Wright)

Townsend
*Townsend Family Missing Links
    Association
5721 Antietam Drive
Sarasota, FL 34231-4903
Phone (813) 924-9170
Charles Delmar Townsend, Compiler
Pub. *Townsend Missing Links*, bimonthly;
    (includes some 12,000 Townsend and
    Townshend families 1630–1850, all
    areas of U.S. and Canada)
$15.00 per year membership in the U.S.,
    $20.00 per year membership in Canada

Townsend
*The Townsend Society of America, Inc.
14 Glen Street
Glen Cove, NY 11542
Phone (516) 676-4100
Ethel Townsend, Treasurer
Pub. *The Townsend Newsletter*, quarterly;
    (includes Townsend and allied lines)
$10.00 per year membership

Townshend (see Townsend)

Townsley (see Tously)

Towry
Towry/Towery Family of America, Inc.
PO Box 770
Grants Pass, OR 97526
Della Y. Guise, Secretary-Treasurer
Pub. *Towry/Towery Newsletter*, quarterly

Toyn
*David Henry (Harry) Toyn Family
    Organization
560 East Sumac
Provo, UT 84604-1828
Phone (801) 375-5333
Thomas D. Toyn, President
(includes descendants of David H. Toyn
    (1849 England–1938) and Martha Jane
    Davis (1847–), of Gouse Creek, Utah)

Trachsel
*Trachsel/Troxell Family Database
998 Bloomington Drive South
Saint George, UT 84790-7585
Phone (801) 673-6314
Carolyn Reinbold

(includes descendants of Stephan and Barbli Trachsel (ca 1536) of Lenk, Canton of Bern, Switzerland)

Tracht
Tracht Family Reunion
840 North Arlington Heights Road
Arlington Heights, IL 60004
Phone (312) 398-2693
Mrs. Barbara Neff Ivan

Tracy (see Paxton)

Trahan (see Bushore, Johnson)

Trahan
*Gathering of the Trahans of America
Edmundite Community
Saint Michael's College
Box 272, Winooski Park
Colchester, VT 05439
Rev. R. Trahan, SSE
Pub. *La Tralannière* (bilingual), semiannually
$10.00 per year membership

Trail (see MacDuff)

Trail
*Trail Family Association
210 Salt Cave Drive
Greers Ferry, AR 72067
Phone (501) 825-7204
Joyce Dean, Secretary, Treasurer and Editor
Pub. *Hidden Trails*, quarterly; (includes Traile and Traill variations)
$10.00 per year membership; annual reunion on the third Saturday of September

Traile (see Trail)

Traill (see MacDuff, Trail)

Trainer (see MacDuff)

Trainor (see MacDuff)

Trait (see Tritt)

Trammel (see Hines)

Transue (see Surname Database)

Trantham (see Newberry)

Trasey (see Cian)

Trate (see Tritt)

Traut (see Lambert)

Travis (see Clinton)

Traylor (see DeLaughter)

Traylor
*Traylor Exchange
1555 Candlelight Drive
Las Cruces, NM 88011
Phone (505) 522-4552
Cal Traylor
Pub. *Traylor/Trouillart Reference Collection* (includes William Randolph arrived Virginia 1669)

Treadaway (see Blossom Press)

Trease (see Likes)

Treat (see Barnard, Canfield, Corson)

Treder (see Zdroik)

Trefethen (see Gerade)

Trefethen
*Trefethen/Trefren Clearinghouse
135 Clover Lane
Medford, OR 97501-2105
Phone (541) 772-5425
Leitha Trefren
Free

Treffry
Treffry/Trefry Family Reunion
N.W. 225 Ann Street
Pullman, WA 99163
Phone (509) 332-0711
Kaye or Kirsten Straight

Trefren (see Trefethen)

Trefry (see Treffry)

Trent (see Golliher, MacDuff)

Trescott
*William Trescott Family Organization
Rt. 1, Box 48
Pomeroy, WA 99347-9713
Barbara Bartels

Tressler (see Cummings)

Trever (see Fadner)

Trew (see McRae)

Trexler (see Surname Database)

Triboulets
Triboulets Tributaries
PO Box 1538
Wichita, KS 67201-1538
Lela Eitel

Tridle (see Frantz)

Trimble (see Turnbull)

Trip (see Tripp)

Triplett (see Covert, Fisher)

Tripp
Tripp Database
49 Seaside Avenue
Westbrook, CT 06498
Phone (860) 399-9273
Margaret Buckridge Bock

Tripp
Tripp Family Association
7536 Gladstone Avenue
White City, OR 97503-1724
Breffni Whelan, President
(all Tripp, Trip and Trippe surnames)

Trippe (see Corson, Tripp)

Tritt
*Tritt Family Research
4072 Goose Lane, S.W.
Granville, OH 43023-9670
Phone (614) 587-0213
Dr. Donald G. Tritt, President
Pub. *Tritt Family Newsletter*, annually, $1.00 per issue; (includes Tritt, Tritten, Dritt, Trait, Trate family, which originated in Lenk and Saint Stephan in The Obersimmenthal, Switzerland)

Tritten (see Tritt)

Trogdan (see Trogdon)

Trogden (see Trogdon)

Trogdon
*Trogdon Historical Society
712 South Peachtree Avenue
Springfield, MO 65802
Phone (417) 866-6908
Billie L. Mynatt, President
Pub. *Trogdon Genealogy News*, quarterly; (includes Trogdan, Trogden, Troglen, Troglin, etc., descendants of William Trogdon (1722 Rattin Row, Ulverstone, Lancastershire, England), settled in Randolph County, North Carolina)
$15.00 per year membership; annual reunion on the first weekend of June

Troglen (see Trogdon)

Troglin (see Trogdon)

Troisi (see Lambert)

Troller (see The Memorial Foundation of the Germanna Colonies)

Trosclair (see Augeron)

Trott (see Barnard, Farrington, Newcomb)

Trouant (see Trufant)

Trouillart (see Traylor)

Troup (see Douglas)

Trousdell (see Covert)

Trout (see Lambert)

Troutman (see Folk Family Surname Exchange, Brawley)

Trower (see McCune)

Troxell (see Trachsel)

Truant (see Trufant)

Truax (see Du Trieux, Haling)

Trub (see Widrick)

Truex (see Du Trieux)

Truglia (see Gratta)

Trumbull (see Turnbull)

Trump (see Van Trump)

Trusheim (see Shurtleff)

Trygstad (see Wilson)

Tryon
Howard Research
8989 S.E. 32nd Avenue
Milwaukie, OR 97222

Tubb (see Allison)

Tubbs (see Allison)

Tuch (see Movius)

Tuckahoe (see Powers)

Tucke (see Newton)

Tucker (see Foster, Masterson, Warren)

Tucker
Tucker
3605 Bear Cove
Benton, AR 72015
William Sanders Tucker, President
Pub. *Tucker*, quarterly; (includes descendants of George Tucker)
$10.00 per year membership; reunion

Tucker
Tucker/Toocker of Saybrook Database
49 Seaside Avenue
Westbrook, CT 06498
Phone (860) 399-9273
Margaret Buckridge Bock

Tucker
*Pioneer Publication
PO Box 1179
Tum Tum, WA 99034-1179
Phone (509) 276-9841
Shirley Penna-Oakes

Pub. *Tucker Times*, irregularly, $6.00 per issue plus $1.75 postage for one to three books, 50¢ for each additional book

Tueller (see Bodine)

Tufts
*Tufts Kinsmen Project
PO Box 571
Dedham, MA 02027-0571
Phone (617) 296-0997
Herbert F. Adams, Family Historian
(includes all Tufts from 1505 to date, including 32,000 people related to Peter Tufts who immigrated from England in 1638)

Tullar (see MacDuff)

Tuller (see MacDuff)

Tulley (see Talley)

Tullis (see MacDuff)

Tullo (see Ross)

Tulloch (see Ross)

Tullser (see The Memorial Foundation of the Germanna Colonies)

Tully (see Talley)

Tumblin (see Folk Family Surname Exchange)

Tumlinson (see Tomlin)

Tune (see Toone)

Tune
Tune, Toone and Toon Family Association
2530 Valmar Place
Reno, NV 89503-2127
Howard L. Tune

Tunes (see Links Genealogy Publications)

Tungate
Tungate Family Organization
3822 Forest Avenue
Cincinnati, OH 45212
Paul Tungate, Family Representative

Tunis (see Links Genealogy Publications)

Tunnis (see Links Genealogy Publications)

Tupper (see Marshall)

Turasson (see Kahler)

Turban (see Laudon)

Turcan (see MacDuff)

Turcotte (see Wright)

Turk (see McCuistion)

Turk
Turk Reunion
Rt. 1
Detroit, TX 75436
Mr. Johnie Lee
Annual reunion on the first Saturday of October

Turley (see Rowe)

Turley
*Turley Family Association
11500 Henegan Place
Spottsylvania, VA 22553
Phone (703) 972-3432
Mrs. Myles B. Mitchell
(includes descendants of Virginia and Maryland Turleys in early 18th century)

Turlich (see Blossom Press)

Turman
James Lackey Turman Family Organization
158 North 200 West
Logan, UT 84321
Phone (801) 752-8330
Sarah Ann Skanchy, Secretary

Turman
*Turman Annual Reunion
Rt. 1, Box 170
Dugspur, VA 24325
Phone (540) 728-3657
Annual reunion at the Dugspur Rescue Squad Building at Dugspur, Virginia

Turnage
Turnage Family of America
Rt. 1, Box 136
Griffithville, AR 72060
Pub. *Turnage Family Newsletter*

Turnage
*Turnage Family America
9955 Wild Grape Drive
San Diego, CA 92131
Phone (619) 271-1225
Elmo Turnage, Editor
Pub. *Turnage Family Newsletter*, three times per year; (includes Turnidge)
$15.00 per year membership

Turnage
Turnage Family Newsletter
518 South Wilson
Royal Oak, MI 48067-2949
Gordon Turnage
Pub. *Turnage Family Newsletter*, three to four times per year, $10.00 per year subscription

Turnage
*Turnage Family America
9815 East 29th
Tulsa, OK 74129
Phone (918) 622-9422
Cathy Turnage, History Chairman
Pub. *Turnage Family Newsletter*, two or
three times per year; (includes all
descendants of Turnage/Turnidge and
allied families; computer database has
over 35,000 descendants)
$15.00 per year membership for
households

Turnbull
*Turnbull Clan Association
1204 West Lonnquist Boulevard
Mount Prospect, IL 60056
Phone (847) 255-7209
Dorothy Turnbull Berk, Convener
Pub. *The Bull's Eye Bull-e-tin*, quarterly;
(includes Trumbull, Trimble (any
spelling variations) and sept family
Rule)
$15.00 per year membership

Turner (see Corson, Emery, Gant,
Garner, Gregor, Lewis, Mix,
Rutherford, Stewart, Warren)

Turner
*Turner/Helm Family (California)
PO Box 1544
Mariposa, CA 95338
Phone (209) 966-2518
Dorothy O'Brien

Turner
*Kinseeker Publications
5697 Old Maple Trail
PO Box 184
Grawn, MI 49637
E-mail: AB064@taverse.lib.mi.us
Victoria Wilson, Editor
Pub. *Tracing Turner*, quarterly, $10.00
per year subscription, $2.50 for sample
issue

Turner
Turner-Chilcoat-Oliphant-Bates Family
Association
2306 Westgate
Houston, TX 77019
Phone (713) 529-2333
Harold Helm
$25.00 plus pedigree and family group
sheets for membership

Turner
Turner Trails Newsletter
2130 Road 12, N.W.
Quincy, WA 98848
Alcenia Appling, Publisher
Pub. *Turner Trails Newsletter*, quarterly,
$12.50 per year subscription

Turnidge (see Turnage)

Turriff (see Hay)

Tussey
Tussey
1221 Candice Court
Mesquite, TX 75149
Mary L. House, Editor
Pub. *Tussey*, quarterly, $10.00 per year
subscription

Tuthill (see Tuttle)

Tuttle (see Barnes, Beaman, Corson)

Twamley
*Twamley Surname Research
827 Legare Road
Aiken, SC 29803
Phone (803) 649-2680
John F. Twombly
(limited information available from the
U.S., Canada, Ireland and England)

Tweeddale (see Hay)

Tweedie (see Fraser)

Twomey (see Newcomb)

Twyford (see Twiford)

Tye (see Brodhead)

Tyler (see Folk Family Surname
Exchange, Surname Sources, Lemon)

Tyler
*Descendants of Ebenezer Tyler
Newsletter*
745 West First Avenue
Garnett, KS 66032
Juanita Tyler Kellerman
Pub. *Descendants of Ebenezer Tyler
Newsletter*

Tymich (see Waterous)

Tymick (see Waterous)

Tynemouth (see MacDuff)

Tyner (see Folk Family Surname
Exchange, Tiner)

Tyre
*Lewis Tyre Family
PO Box 333
Screven, GA 31560
Phone (912) 579-6383
Mrs. H. R. Tyre
(includes descendants of Lewis Tyre and
Sarah Sikes of Appling County,
Georgia, early 1800s)
Annual reunion in July at Laura Walker
State Park

Tyrell (see Anthes)

Tyson (see Links Genealogy
Publications, O'Brien)

Tyson
Links Genealogy Publications
7677 Abaline Way
Sacramento, CA 95823-4224
Phone (916) 428-2245
Iris Carter Jones, Editor
Pub. *Tyson-Theisen-Teissen (Doors-
Dahrs)*, quarterly, $7.00 per year
subscription

Ugron (see Apáthy)

Uhl (see Clowes, Likes)

Uhlendorf (see Lush)

Uirvine (see Irwin)

Uirwin (see Irwin)

Ullery (see Crumrine, Frantz)

Ulmer
Ulmer Family Newsletter
Rt. 3, Box 228
Maryville, MO 64468
Phone (816) 582-4485
Mary Lou Ulmer Piearson
Pub. *Ulmer Family Newsletter*,
biannually (even-numbered years),
free; (George Ulmer of Scott County,
Indiana)

Ulrey (see Stoner)

Ulrich (see Sutter)

Umfraville (see Clark)

Umhauer
*Umhauer Family Association
PO Box 1464
Round Rock, TX 78680
Phone (512) 255-5603
Nancy U. Decker, Family Representative
Free exchange, no reunion

Umstatd (see Links Genealogy
Publications)

Umstattd (see Links Genealogy
Publications)

Umstead (see Links Genealogy
Publications)

Underhill (see Alsop)

Underhill
*Underhill Society of America, Inc.
107 East Main Street
PO Box 712
Oyster Bay, NY 11771
Gloria B. Tucker, Assistant Secretary
Pub. *Bulletin of the Underhill Society of
America*, annually; *News and Views of
the Underhill Society*, semiannually;
(includes all Underhill families of
North America)

$10.00 per year membership, $25.00 sustaining membership, $100.00 life membership

Underwood (see Barnard)

Underwood
*Paddleford Publishing Company
4484 Pitch Pine Court
Concord, CA 94521-4406
Phone (510) 827-0571
Esther E. Gregory
(includes descendants of Finley L. Underwood and Mahala Dowden, along with research on the following families: Ashford, Beard, Blackburn, Dowden, Ewing, Gore, Harlan, Hartle, Lantz, McBride, Nevill, Newcomb and Thurston)

Ungarretti (see Andreossi)

United Family Reunion Association (see Multi-family Associations)

Upchurch
*Upchurch-Bright Family
125 Scenic Drive
Madison, AL 35758
Phone (205) 971-8909
Pub. *Upchurch-Bright Family Newsletter*

Upchurch
Upchurch Bulletin
PO Box 387
Wentzville, MO 63385-0387
Robert Phillip Upchurch, Editor
Pub. *Upchurch Bulletin*, quarterly, $15.00 per year subscription

up de Graeff (see Links Genealogy Publications)

Updegrove (see Links Genealogy Publications)

Updike (see Op Dyck)

Upham
*Upham Family Society, Inc.
(1703 Phineas Upham House, 255 Upham Street, Melrose, MA 02176-3335—location)
11 Lynde Street (mailing address)
Melrose, MA 02176-4605
Phone (617) 662-2737 (location);
(617) 665-1442 (Treasurer and Vice-President, Membership and Administration)
Robert L. Wadland, Treasurer; Beatrice Wadland, Vice President, Membership and Administration
(includes lineal descendants of John Upham, who came to Weymouth with the Hull Company in 1635)
Annual meeting on the third Saturday of June, usually at the Phineas Upham House

Uplinger (see Oblinger)

Upshaw
*Upshaw Family Association of America
408 Colchester Drive
Stone Mountain, GA 30088
Phone (404) 469-4732
Ted O. Brooke

Uptegrove (see Froeschle)

Urbach (see The Memorial Foundation of the Germanna Colonies)

Ure (see McCune)

Urewens (see Irwin)

Urewing (see Irwin)

Urie (see Keith)

Urowrin (see Irwin)

Urquhart
*The Clan Urquhart Association
56 Waldorf Drive
Akron, OH 44313
Phone (330) 867-1030
Christie B. Urquhart Walsh, Secretary
Pub. *Clan Urquhart Newsletter: North American Branch Newsletter*, semiannually
$15.00 to $20.00 per year membership

Urrwine (see Irwin)

Uruin (see Irwin)

Urven (see Irwin)

Urvens (see Irwin)

Urvin (see Irwin)

Urvine (see Irwin)

Urwain (see Irwin)

Urwaine (see Irwin)

Urwan (see Irwin)

Urwayne (see Irwin)

Urwen (see Irwin)

Urwenn (see Irwin)

Urwens (see Irwin)

Urwin (see Irwin)

Urwine (see Irwin)

Urwing (see Irwin)

Urwins (see Irwin)

Urwung (see Irwin)

Urwyng (see Irwin)

Usher (see McCune)

Usher
*Usher Family Reunion
6687 West Trowbridge Street
Boise, ID 83703-6305
Joan S. Keough, Editor
Pub. *House of Usher*, three times per year (December, April and August); (includes descendants of John Usher (1736 Charlestown, Massachusetts–), a descendant of Hezekiah[3] Usher and Abigail Cleveland, Robert[2] Usher and Sarah Blanchard, Robert[1] and Elizabeth Jagger, and was married in 1766 in Norwich, Connecticut, to Prudence Copp (North Parish, New London County, Connecticut–), but interested in anyone with Usher ancestors, especially John and Prudence's children: John Jr., Abigail, Elizabeth, Susannah, Fanny, Joseph and Aaron Usher, who settled in Cedar Rapids, Iowa, in the 1840s)
$5.00 per year membership; annual reunion on the second Saturday of September at Usher's Ferry Park, Cedar Rapids, Iowa

Usher
*Usher Family Reunion
7632 Douglas Drive, North
Brooklyn Park, MN 55443
Phone (612) 566-7770
Yvonne Wiltsey Pedersen
Pub. *House of Usher*; (includes research on Soloman Wiltsey (1826 New York–) and wife Ellen Ann Harvey (1832–1870) of Iowa; also Dowis, Lazenby, Pedersen and Schnider research)
$5.00 per year membership; annual reunion in Cedar Rapids, Iowa

Ussery (see Folk Family Surname Exchange)

Utterback (see The Memorial Foundation of the Germanna Colonies)

Utz (see The Memorial Foundation of the Germanna Colonies)

Vahey
*Vahey Family Association
6137 S.E. 128th Avenue
Portland, OR 97236
Phone (503) 760-5512
Jack E. Vahey, Researcher
Pub. *The Vahey Vine*, quarterly
$5.00 per year membership

Vail
*Vail Family Reunion
2705 Baldwin Drive
Winnsboro, LA 71295
Phone (318) 435-4154
Shirley Annette Burks Wells, Organizer
(includes descendants of Jeremiah Vail, Sr. (1817 Lancaster County, South Carolina–1887 Bienville Parish,

Louisiana), son of Rachel Funderburk and John Michael Vail, who was the son of William Vale or Vail, a.k.a. William Wilmot (1770–80 Ireland?– before 1820 South Carolina))
Annual reunion on the second Sunday of June at Mount Olive Baptist Church, Quitman, Louisiana

Vain (see MacBean)

Vaine (see MacBean)

Vale (see Vail, Veale)

Valentine (see Folk Family Surname Exchange, Felty, Willcocks)

Valentine
Furman Valentine and Eliza Taylor Family Reunion
Valley View Park, Lot 57, Rt. 3
Dallas, PA 18612
Sarah Taylor

Valet (see Blossom Press)

Valette (see Blossom Press)

van Aaken (see Links Genealogy Publications)

Van Aken
*Van Aken Surname Organization
13104-B Avenue Santa Tecla
La Mirada, CA 90638-3272
Phone (310) 947-9200
Glorya Welch
Pub. *Van Aken/Van Auken Newsletter*, quarterly, $7.00 per year subscription; (includes any spelling)

Van Aken
Van Aken/Van Auken Newsletter
38 Padanaram Avenue, #B18
Danbury, CT 06811-5605
Ann C. Croston, Editor
Pub. *Van Aken/Van Auken Newsletter*, quarterly, $6.00 per year subscription

Van Arsdale
Van Arsdale Newsletter, "Van to Van"
1348 Brushing Grove
Wood River, IL 62095
Marvin VanAusdol
Pub. *Van Arsdale Newsletter, "Van to Van"* (Van Osdol/Van Ausdal)

Van Auken (see Van Aken)

Van Ausdal (see Van Arsdale)

van Bebber (see Links Genealogy Publications)

Van Bergen (see Barnard)

van Bom (see Links Genealogy Publications)

Van Brakel (see Van Brocklin)

Van Buren
*VanBuren/Henke/Mohme Family Organization
420 Sycamore Drive
Waterloo, IL 62298
W. Kohlmeier
No membership fee

Van Buskirk
VanBuskirk/Buskirk Clearinghouse
Rt. 1, Box 192
Monmouth, IL 61462
James E. and Sharon L. Todd
Pub. *Van Buskirk Family Newsletter*, quarterly, $10.00 per year subscription

Van Buskirk
Van Buskirk News
5432 University Avenue
Indianapolis, IN 46219
Phone (317) 359-6907
Robert VanBuskirk, Editor
Pub. *Van Buskirk News*, quarterly (January, April, July and October), $12.00 per calendar year subscription; (includes Buskirk)

Vance (see Folk Family Surname Exchange)

Vance
*Vance Research
6771 Gardenia Avenue
Long Beach, CA 90805
Phone (310) 422-2323
Mary Vance

Vance
*Vance Family Association
612 155th Place, N.E.
Bellevue, WA 98007-4822
Phone (206) 746-9907
Bruce Vance, President and Editor
Pub. *Vance Family Association Newsletter*, quarterly (January, April, July and October); (includes Vance of all origins and variations)
$15.00 per year membership; reunion

Van Cleave
*Van Cleave/Cleve/Cleff/et al
8036 11th Avenue, N.W.
Seattle, WA 98117-4123
Allan Wenzel

Vandapoel (see Vanderpool)

Vandapool (see Vanderpool)

van de Lande (see Ostrander)

Van der Poel (see Vanderpool)

Vander Poel (see Vanderpool)

Vanderpool
*Kin Hunters Genealogical Publications and Research
PO Box 151
Russellville, KY 42276
Montgomery Vanderpool
Pub. *Vanderpool Newsletter*, quarterly (January, April, July and October), $4.00 per issue, $14.00 for four issues, $25.00 for eight issues; (includes Vandapoel, Vandapool, Vanderpoel, Van der Poel and Vander Poel)

Van Der Veer (see Vandiver)

Vanderzee (see Bradt)

Vandeveer (see Vandiver)

Vandevert (see Catlow)

Vandiver
*Vandiver/Vandeveer/Van Der Veer Clearinghouse
1328 East Hermosa Drive
Tempe, AZ 85282-5719
Phone (602) 491-2877
Gloria Kay Vandiver Inman
(includes all variant spellings)

Vane (see MacBean)

VanEpps (see Goodenow)

vanHaaften (see Vermazen)

Van Hooser (see Gibson)

Van Horn (see Likes)

Vaniman (see Frantz)

Van Kouwenhoven
VanKouwenhoven/Conover Family Association
317 Old Deal Road
Eatontown, NJ 07724
Phone (201) 222-7505
Mrs. Donald C. Cook, President
Pub. *The Tidings*, annually

Van Lent (see Lent)

Van Linschoten (see Linschoten)

VanMeter (see The Memorial Foundation of the Germanna Colonies)

Vann (see Vaughan)

Van Noorstrant (see Ostrander)

Van Noortstrande (see Ostrander)

Van Nostrandt (see Ostrander)

Van Nostrant (see Ostrander)

Van Nostrunt (see Ostrander)

Van Nuys
Van Nuys Notes
13546 Dahlia Court
Rosemount, MN 55068-3378
Jeff Williamson, Editor
Pub. *Van Nuys Notes*, three times per
    year, $12.00 per year subscription

Van Oostrander (see Ostrander)

Van Orden (see Maybee)

Van Osdol (see Van Arsdale)

Vanostran (see Ostrander)

Van Ostrand (see Ostrander)

Van Sant (see Van Zandt)

Van Schaick
*Descendants of Cornelis Aertsen Van
    Schaick, Inc.
707 South Gulfstream Avenue, #708
Sarasota, FL 34236
Phone (813) 953-4004
Melwood W. Van Scoyoc, President
Pub. *The Van Schaick Kinfolks Quarterly*
    (includes ancestors and descendants of
    Cornelis Aertsen Van Schaick (all
    spellings))
$9.00 per year membership

VanSickler (see Smith)

Van Steenwyk
*Van Steenwyk Descendants Association
420 East 11th Street, #8
Cedar Falls, IA 50613-3364
Edward Bos, Family Genealogist
(includes descendants of Jan Van
    Steenwyk and Maria Justina
    Ooostrum, who immigrated to the U.S.
    in 1847 and helped found the
    community of Pella)

Van Trump
*Van Trump, Heiney, and Etchingham
    Family Tree
9320 West Utah Avenue
PO Box 260170
Lakewood, CO 80226-0170
Phone (303) 985-3508
George VanTrump, Jr., Family
    Coordinator
(includes Etchingham, Heiney, Heiny,
    Trump and Van Trump families)

Van Valkenburg
National Association of Van Valkenburg
    Family, Inc.
110 East Edison Avenue
New Castle, PA 16101
Phone (412) 658-7061
Margaret E. Sica, Family Genealogist
Pub. *NAVVF News Notes*, quarterly
    (includes Falkenburg, Falkenburgh and
    Van Valkenburgh)
$5.00 per year adult membership, $2.00
    per year junior membership; annual
    reunion

Van Valkenburgh (see Van Valkenburg)

Van Vechten (see Barnard)

Van Vliet (see Drake)

Van Voorhees
*The VanVoorhees Association
2415 Spring Hill Drive
Tom's River, NJ 08755-0987
Phone (908) 886-0426
Manning W. Voorhees, President and
    Editor
Pub. *Van Voorhees Nieuwsbrief*, two to
    three times per year; (includes
    descendants of Steven Coerte (Van
    Voorhees) and wives, Aeltje Wessels
    and Willempie Roelofse Seubering, to
    New Netherlands in 1660 from The
    Netherlands)
$7.00 per year membership

Van Wagoner
Van Wagoner Family Library and
    Archives
8891 Collingwood Drive
Los Angeles, CA 90069
Phone (213) 657-3456
Philo W. VanWagoner, Director

Van Wye
*Van Wye Family History Research
    Center
(22864 Glendon Drive—location)
11875 Pigeon Pass Road, Suite B14-228
    (mailing address)
Moreno Valley, CA 92557
Phone (909) 242-4049; (909) 485-2232
    FAX
Norman A. Van Wye, Director
Pub. *Newsletter*, quarterly; (includes Wye
    1275 Kent, Tnegland/Wales; Arthur
    Van Wye[1] 1730 Holland; all family
    line descendants from 1750 in the
    Americas)
$10.00 per year membership; branch
    reunions and annual east/west family
    jamboree

Van Zandt
*VanZandt Society
128 Hedge Road
Levittown, PA 19056
Phone (215) 946-1744
Sally Van Sant Sondesky, Vice President
    and Historian
Pub. *The Van Zandt Record*, three times
    per year; (includes all descendants of
    any spellings: Van Sant, Van Zant,
    Vanzant, Vinzant, etc.)
$10.00 per year membership

Van Zandt
*Bell Enterprises
PO Box 10328
Spokane, WA 99209
Phone (509) 327-2761
Mary Ann L. Vanzandt Bell, Owner,
    Publisher
Pub. *Van Zandt Ancestors*, irregularly,
    $6.00 plus $1.25 postage per issue

Vanzant (see Van Zandt)

Van Zant (see Van Zandt)

Varguson (see Corson)

Varnado
Varnado Families of America
1002 Hemlock Cove
Brandon, MS 39042-7614
Harrell D. Varnado
(includes Vernadeau)

Varner (see Verner)

Varner
Varner Newsletter
6302 Fairview Drive
Pensacola, FL 32505-2057
Phone (904) 432-5291
Janice B. Palmer, Editor
Pub. *Varner Newsletter*, quarterly, $10.00
    per year subscription; (includes
    Varnon, Varnor, Verner, Vernor, Warner
    and Werner)

Varney (see Burnham, Hatfield)

Varnon (see Varner)

Varnor (see Varner)

Varty (see McCanna)

Varven (see Irwin)

Varvin (see Irwin)

Varvine (see Irwin)

Vass (see Ross)

Vasshus (see Nash)

Vaughan (see Folk Family Surname
    Exchange, Pennock, Vaughn)

Vaughan
Vaughan/Vaughn Report
Rt. 1, Box 2
Dallas, TX 75211
SheRita Vaughn Holbrook
Pub. *Vaughan/Vaughn Report*, three times
    per year, $5.00 per year subscription

Vaughan
Partin Publications
230 Wedgewood
Nacogdoches, TX 75961-5326
Pub. *Vaughan-Vaughn*, quarterly, $20.00
    per year subscription

Vaughn (see Folk Family Surname
    Exchange, Bassett, Cummings, Gant,
    Vaughan)

Vaughn
*Huldah Vaughn Family Organization
Rt. 2, Box 2014
Paul, ID 83347

Mrs. Eunice Harmon
Pub. *Huldah's Helpers*, semiannually;
(includes Vaughan, Harmon, Morgan
families of Erie County, Pennsylvania,
1820–40)
Donation for membership

Vaughn
*Vaugh'a'n Family Association
735 North Dallas
Tulia, TX 79088
Phone (806) 995-3308
Kenneth Gwen Vaughn, Treasurer &
Membership
Pub. *Vaugh'a'n Family Association
Newsletter*, quarterly (February, May,
August and November); (includes any
spelling of name, including Baun, etc.)
$10.00 per year membership (beginning
in January); annual reunion

Vaught (see The Memorial Foundation
of the Germanna Colonies)

Vaught
*Vaught Association of the United States
313 Chamberlain
PO Box 2044
Murfreesboro, TN 37133
Phone (615) 896-0182 (after 8:00);
(615) 890-4822
Anita Vaught Gentry
Free membership, annual reunion

Vaughter (see Vawter)

Vaughters (see Vawter)

Vaus (see Folk Family Surname
Exchange)

Vauter (see Vawter)

Vawter (see Rutherford)

Vawter
*Vawter/Vauter/Vaughter(s) Family
Association
4145 North 900 West
Scipio, IN 47273
Phone (812) 392-2149
Bonita Welch, Editor
Pub. *VVV FA Newsletter-Vawter/Vauter/
Vaughter(s)*, quarterly, free queries
$7.00 per year membership; annual
reunion

Vayn (see MacBean)

Vayne (see MacBean)

Vaynes (see MacBean)

Vclauchlayne (see MacLachlan)

VcQuhewin (see MacLachlan)

Veach (see Veitch)

Veal (see Veale)

Vean (see MacBean)

Veane (see MacBean)

Veasey
Veasey-Veazey
PO Box 353
Zebulon, NC 27597
Ann Veazey Davis
Pub. *Veasey-Veazey*, three or four times
per year, donation for subscription

Veatch (see Veitch)

Veazey (see Veasey)

Vee (see MacBean)

Veech (see Veitch)

Veen (see MacBean)

Veene (see MacBean)

Veile (see Veale)

Veillon (see Blossom Press)

Veirs (see Viers)

Veitch
*Veitch Historical Society
1408 Bexley Cove Lane
Knoxville, TN 37922-5823
Phone (423) 690-9485
William A. Veitch, Vice President of
Membership
Pub. *Veitch Chronicle*, three times per
year (February, May and October);
(includes Veach, Veatch and Veech
descendants of William Le Vache
(1296) through James "The Sheriffe"
Veitch (1628–1685), came to America
in 1651)
$15.00 U.S. funds per year membership

Velline
*Velline Family Association
1109 Felbar Avenue
Torrance, CA 90503
Phone (310) 533-8243; E-mail:
cvelline@aol.com
Chris Velline, Genealogist
Pub. *Newsletter*, irregularly; (includes
related surnames: Fimreite, Sjøtun and
Thue of Norway)
Occasional dues; occasional reunion in
North Dakota or California

Veloz (see Arroyo)

Velty (see Felty)

Veltz (see Felty)

Vencell (see Coverstone)

Vencill
Vencill Clearinghouse
1833 South 246th Place
Des Moines, WA 98198
Peggy Coverstone Vencill

Vengular (see Folk Family Surname
Exchange)

Venters (see MacDuff)

Vere (see Viers)

Veres (see Viers)

Vermason (see Vermazen)

Vermazen
*Vermazen/Vermason Family
Organization
161 Delhi Road
Manchester, IA 52057
Phone (319) 927-2964
John Vermazen
(includes descendants of Aart Vermazen
(1797–) and Gijsbertje vanHaaften
(1812–))

Vernadeau (see Varnado)

Verner (see Varner)

Verner
Verner-Varner-Werner-Ferner Family
Association
2306 Westgate
Houston, TX 77019
Phone (713) 529-2333
Harold Helm
$25.00 plus pedigree and family group
sheets for membership

Vernon (see Way)

Vernon
Vernon Vignettes
116 F British Lake Drive
Greensboro, NC 27410
William A. Vernon
Pub. *Vernon Vignettes*, quarterly

Vernor (see Varner)

Versailles (see Versaw)

Vervine (see Irwin)

Verwayn (see Irwin)

Vestal (see Weathermon)

Via (see Folk Family Surname
Exchange, Viers)

Viah (see Viers)

Vian (see MacBean)

Viar (see Viers)

Viard (see Blossom Press)

Viars (see Viers)

Viau (see Lagesse)

Vicars
Vicars Family Association
1032 South Roosevelt Avenue
Columbus, OH 43209
Phone (614) 235-0546
James M. Vicars, President
Pub. *Vicars Family Quarterly* (*VFQ*) (for descendants of Robert and Lydia Jackson Vicars of Southwest Virginia)
$15.00 per year membership

Vick (see Gant)

Vick
*The Joseph Vick Family of America, Inc.
1244 Seminole Drive
Richardson, TX 75080
Billie Jurlina
Pub. *Newsletter*

Vickers (see Paulk, Snow)

Vidacovich (see Blossom Press)

Vidito
Vidito or Vittitow Database
PO Box 513
Seneca, IL 61360
L. Dwight Vidito

Vidrine (see Johnson)

Viebrock
Viebrock Family Reunion
Rt. 2, Box 402
Lincoln, MO 65338
C. Burnett

Vier (see Viers)

Viereck (see Vierig)

Vierig
*Vierig Surname Organization
Johann Friederich Vierig Family Organization
PO Box 17542
Salt Lake City, UT 84117
Phone (801) 966-3544
David O. Vierig
(includes Viereck)

Viers
*Viers-Veirs-Veres Family Organization
2817 Moulton Drive
Placerville, CA 95667
Phone (916) 626-3090
Lester Hunt
Pub. *Quarterly Newsletter, Viers-Veirs Family Organization*, quarterly; (database includes Vear, Vere, Via, Viah, Viar, Viars, Vier, Vire, Vires, Voire, etc.)

$10.00 per year membership; annual reunion in May at Salt Lake City, Utah (except 1997 in France)

Viets
Viets Clearinghouse
731 South Blaine
Moscow, ID 83843-3722
Dorothy D. Viets Schall
Pub. *Viets Clearinghouse*

Vincent (see Hardwick, Sheldon)

Vincent
Vincent Families
728 Robinson Street
Elmira, NY 14904
Phone (607) 734-8684
Katharine R. Vincent
Pub. *Vincent Families*, quarterly, $5.00 donation per year subscription; (includes Vincents and Vinson)

Vincents (see Vincent)

Vines (see Cowart)

Vinet (see Blossom Press)

Vinje-Rui (see Nash)

Vinnirick (see Kettenring)

Vinson (see Newton, Vincent)

Vinzant (see Van Zandt)

Violette
*Violette Family Association
32 Louise Avenue
Methuen, MA 01844
Phone (617) 688-3268
Rita Violette Lippe

Violette
*Violette Family Association
32 Louise Avenue
Methuen, MA 01844
Phone (617) 688-3268
Rita Violette Lippe

Vire (see Viers)

Vires (see Viers)

Visger (see Kellett)

Visscher (see Barnard)

Visser (see Fisher)

Vittitow (see Vidito)

Vix (see Richelieu)

V'Lechreist (see MacLachlan)

Vogan (see Kunkel)

Vogel (see Maier)

Vogt (see Blossom Press, The Memorial Foundation of the Germanna Colonies, Heath)

Voire (see Viers)

Volinsky (see Israelite)

Voltz (see Surname Database)

Volvoski (see Hoffman)

Volz (see Worch)

Von Alten (see Alten)

Von Bellor (see Ingwerson)

vonBülow
*VonBülow Familie
PO Box 71
Akutan, AK 99553
Phone (907) 698-2350
Virginia Darling
(includes descendants of Godfried deBülow of Germany)

von der Moevius (see Movius)

von Dollonstein (see Gebhard)

VonGaelhausen (see Hegner)

von Lichtenstein (see Gebhard)

von Merkle (see Movius)

von Mövius (see Movius)

Voss (see Stevens)

Voss
*VOLORE/PieOnNeerBIG
Rt. 2, Box 255A-VEVO
Pierce, NE 68767-1401
Verne Voss, Historian
(includes Voss, Lohmeier and Reikofski families (VOLORE is acronym for VOss, LOhmeier, REikofski); also includes descendants of Hans Voss)
Information provided at a nominal cost, plus shipping and handling; Hans Voss Family reunion

Voter
Voter Family History Association
Rt. 1, Box 1460
Phillips, ME 04966
Delmar Voter

Vrowing (see Irwin)

Vruing (see Irwin)

Vruving (see Irwin)

Vruvinn (see Irwin)

Vrvin (see Irwin)

Vrvynn (see Irwin)

Vrwayn (see Irwin)

Vrwayne (see Irwin)

Vrwen (see Irwin)

Vrwin (see Irwin)

Vrwine (see Irwin)

Vrwing (see Irwin)

Vryne (see Irwin)

Vucinovich (see Blossom Press)

Vuskovich (see Blossom Press)

Wacker (see Horning)

Waddell (see Nimmo)

Waddle (see Dunnavant, Nimmo)

Waddy (see Street)

Wade (see Bond, Friend)

Wade
Wade-Smith Genealogy Service
Rt. 7, Box 52
Llano, TX 78643
Evelyn Wade
Pub. *Wade Register*, three times per year,
   $10.00 per year subscription

Wade
*Name Game Enterprises
4204 South Conklin Street
Spokane, WA 99203-6235
Phone (509) 747-4903
Mrs. E. Dale Hastin Smith
Pub. *Wade World*, irregularly, $5.75 per
   issue plus $2.00 postage and handling

Wadsworth (see Hansen)

Wadsworth
George Wadsworth Family Organization
45865 Michell Lane
Indio, CA 92201-3780
Helen Free VanderBeek

Wagley
*Wagley Surname Organization
PO Box 8072
Longview, TX 75607-8072
Ben R. Reynolds

Wagner (see Surname Database, Cole,
   Lush, Myers, Wilhelm)

Wagner
*Jacob H. Wagner Annual Family
   Reunion
1424 Ebenezer Road
Fennimore, WI 53809
Phone (608) 943-6812

Cheryl Lemanski
(includes descendants of Jacob "Jake"
   Henry Wagner (1861 Liberty
   Township, Grant Co., Wisconsin–), son
   of Henry Wagner (1828 Sachsen,
   Meiningen Provice, Germany, on the
   River Werra near Eisfeld, Thuringen,
   Germany–) and Ernestine Taenzler
   (pronounced "Denzler"), daughter of
   Gottfried and Justine Plarr Taenzler,
   and of Jacob Henry's wife Mary
   Frances Hannan)
Annual reunion in September at the
   Livingston Fire Department in
   Livingston, Wisconsin

Wagoner (see Frantz)

Wailey (see Whaley)

Wain (see MacBean)

Waine (see MacBean)

Waiste
Hapsburg Press
PO Box 173
Broomfield, CO 80038-0173
Barbara Inman Beall, Editor
Pub. *Waiste*, five times per year, $10.00
   per year subscription

Wait (see Creyts, McCune, Savage)

Waite (see Likes, Savage, Sisson)

Wakefield (see Gant, McGee, Tidwell)

Wakelin (see MacDuff)

Wakely (see Beaman)

Walburn (see Walborn)

Walch (see Anthes, Walsh)

Walden (see Cowart, Lambert, Louden)

Waldenmeier (see Waltermire)

Waldenmyer (see Waltermire)

Waldrip (see Golding)

Waldron*Utah
*Benjamin Waldron Family Organization
3385 South Bluff Road
Syracuse, UT 84075
Phone (801) 773-0531
Allen S. Willie, Researcher

Waldrop (see Golding)

Waler (see Waller)

Walingford (see Wallingford)

Walke (see The Memorial Foundation of
   the Germanna Colonies)

Walker (see Folk Family Surname
   Exchange, The Memorial Foundation
   of the Germanna Colonies, Surname
   Sources, Arthur, Bassett, Felty,
   Goodenow, Gregor, Hardwick,
   Horning, Joyner, Likes, MacMillan,
   Miller, Rollins, Sawyer, Simkins,
   Stewart)

Walker
*Walker Association
18380 North 600th Road
Adair, IL 61411-9230
Joan Walker Hurst, Editor
Pub. *Newsletter*, three times per year
$10.00 per year membership

Walker
*Descendants of William Walker of
   Botetourt Co., Va. and Reuben Walker
   of Harrison Co., (W.)Va.
23 Elizabeth Street
Coldwater, MI 49036
Phone (517) 278-6167
Pamela D. Myers
(includes descendants of William (–1810)
   and Mary Walker of Fincastle,
   Virginia, and their grandson, Reuben
   (1782 Botetourt County, Virginia–1860
   Harrison County, West Virginia), who
   married Elizabeth Douglas Jamison
   and claimed land in West Virginia by
   1840)

Walker
Pence Publications
11009 East Third Avenue, #93
Spokane, WA 99206-6501
Maxine E. Pence, Editor
Pub. *Walker Footprints*, irregularly, $6.00
   per issue

Wall (see Walls)

Wall
Wall(s)/Wallis
6180 Merrywood Drive
Rocklin, CA 95677-3421
Kathleen Stewart
Pub. *Wall(s)/Wallis*, quarterly, $12.00 per
   year subscription

Wall
Hand Writing on the Walls
1243 Shenandoah Drive
Boise, ID 83712-7454
Phone (208) 344-6136
Ruby L. Ewart, Editor
Pub. *Hand Writing on the Walls*,
   quarterly with annual consolidated
   index, $8.00 per calendar year
   subscription; (includes Wall and Walls)

Wallace (see Holden, Lemon, Peters,
   Standridge, Walsh)

Wallace
Wallace
61 West Sutter Road
Paradise, CA 95969

Mary Dell Wallace
Pub. *Wallace*, three times per year, $5.00
per year subscription
Reunion

Wallace
*Wallace-Wallis-Wallice Connections
4080 West 600 North
Leesburg, IN 46538
Phone (219) 858-9464
Marjorie Priser, Editor

Wallace
Clan Wallace Society Worldwide
PO Box 273
Jonesborough, TN 37659
Tom Wallace, President; Charles B.
Wallace, President Emeritus and
Founder, High Commissioner

Wallach (see MacDuff)

Wallas (see Standridge)

Waller (see Folk Family Surname
Exchange, Richardson)

Waller
*Folk Family
PO Box 52048
Knoxville, TN 37950-2048
Hester E. Stockton, Owner; Edmund and
John Waller, Co-editors
Pub. *Waller Wandering*, quarterly, $15.00
per year subscription, $5.00 per issue;
(includes Waler, deValer)

Wallice (see Wallace)

Wallingford (see Corson)

Wallingford
Old Time Publications
10828 Oakbrook Drive
Omaha, NE 68154-2437
Peggy Wallingford Butherus
Pub. *Wallingford Branches*, $4.50 plus
$1.25 postage and handling
(Washington residents add 7.8% sales
tax); (includes Walingford,
Wallingsford, etc.)

Wallingsford (see Harrell, Wallingford)

Wallis (see Standridge, Wall, Wallace)

Wallis
*James Hearknett Wallis Family
Organization
3287 Joyce Drive
Salt Lake City, UT 84109
Phone (801) 484-1736
Gloria Wallis Rytting, Historian
(includes Wallis and Todd surnames)

Walloch (see MacDuff)

Walls (see Christopher, Wall)

Walls
*Hand Writing on the Walls
15000 N.E. Barbara Boulevard
Claremore, OK 74017-1749
Gladys M. Rogers, Editor
Pub. *Hand Writing on the Walls*,
quarterly (January, April, July and
October), $9.00 per year subscription;
(includes Wall(s), all spellings, all
dates and places)

Walrath
Walrath Family Association
PO Box 906
Bonxall, CA 92003
Phone (619) 758-0150
Reetha Clancy
Pub. *Newsletter*, three to four times per
year
No dues, members send money for
postage if they wish

Walsh (see Welch)

Walsh
Walsh Family Chronicles
PO Box 4503
Chicago, IL 60680
Eugene A. Walsh
Pub. *Walsh Family Chronicles (Welch/
Walch/Wallace)*, quarterly, $5.00 per
year subscription

Walston
Walston World Wide
PO Box 5400, Suite 110
Tyler, TX 75712
Robert E. Walston, Editor
Pub. *Walston World Wide*, irregularly,
$6.00 per issue

Walter (see Buchanan, Forbes)

Walter
*Walter Surname Organization
7705 Ensley Drive, S.W.
Huntsville, AL 35802-2845
Phone (205) 883-0207
Thomas W. Burns

Waltermire
*The Waltermire Family Association
141 Hudson Avenue
Chatham, NY 12037
Phone (518) 392-4544
Doris E. De Vane Wells Waltermire
Witthoft
Pub. *Newsletter* (includes descendants of
George Waltermire (Waldenmyer,
Waldenmeier, Waltermyer, etc.) and
wife Margaretha Rardin (Rordin or
Bardin) of Red Hook/Rhinebeck,
Dutchess County, New York, 1745)
No membership dues; biennial reunion
(even-numbered years), on the first
Saturday of August

Waltermyer (see Waltermire)

Walters (see Forbes, Lush)

Walton (see Behnke, Cantrill, Corson)

Walton
*Byberry Waltons
71 East James Court
Millsboro, DE 19966
Richard L. Walton
Pub. *Byberry Waltons Bulletin*,
semiannually, $3.00 per year
subscription; (restricted to descendants
of four brothers who settled in Byberry
Township, Philadelphia, in 1683)
Annual reunion on the second Saturday
of August at Byberry Meeting House,
Byberry Road, Philadelphia,
Pennsylvania

Waltzer (see Blossom Press)

Wampler (see Stoner)

Wampler
Wampler Family Newsletter
31 Thayer Avenue
Joliet, IL 60432
Mr. Wampler
Pub. *Wampler Family Newsletter*

Wamsley (see Rutherford)

Wanamaker (see Wannemacher)

Wandell (see Alsop)

Wane (see MacBean)

Wanger (see Wenger)

Wannemacher
*Wannemacher/Wanamaker
Clearinghouse
936 Mokulua Drive
Kailua, HI 96734-3108
Jean Gurney Rigler
Free exchange for SASE

Wantz (see Boose)

Wapello
*Chief Wapello's Memorial Park
Association
(¼ mile off Highway 34—location)
8218 Highway 34 (mailing address)
Agency, IA 52530-8071
Mary Gibb
Pub. *Chief Wapello's Memorial Park
Association Newsletter*, annually;
(includes descendants of Joseph
Montfort Street, Indian Agent (1782
Lunenburg County, Virginia–1840
Agency, Iowa), the son of Anthony
Waddy Street and Eliza Maria Posey
(1792 Virginia–1846 Agency, Iowa),
and the descendants of the Sac and
Fox Indian Chief Wapello)
$2.00 per year membership, $25.00 life
membership; annual meeting on the
last Monday of April

Ward (see Bond, Clark, Heath, Neville,
Newton, Ross, Thompson)

Ward
*Ward Family Organization
18002 North 12th Street, #30
Phoenix, AZ 85022
Nani Mercer Neal
Pub. *Ward Surname Newsletter*, quarterly,
    $20.00 per year subscription

Ward
Ward Family Association
Rt. 6, Box 6442
Brenham, TX 77833-4127
Elizabeth Ward Kennedy

Ward
*Elanson Ward Family Organization
9002 Belvoir Woods Parkway, Apartment
    309
Fort Belvoir, VA 22060-2709
Nathaniel P. Ward, Coordinator
(includes descendants of Elanson Ward
    (1791–1852) and Jerusha Van Ness
    (1806–1880), resided in Hamburg,
    New York, before 1830, migrated to
    Rock County, Wisconsin, in 1846)

Wardell (see Alsop)

Warden (see Carley, Ellett, Worden)

Wardlaw (see DeLaughter, MacDuff,
    Maxwell)

Wardle (see Taylor)

Wardner
*Wardner Family Historical Association
9305 North Ivanhoe Street
Portland, OR 97203-2925
Carolyn Wardner Buck, Editor and
    Historian Pro Tem
Pub. *Words on Wardners*, three times per
    year
Quadrennial reunion

Wardrop (see MacDuff)

Wardrup
*Wardrups in America
1411 East 35th Street
Odessa, TX 79762
Phone (915) 367-6603
Deborah Little Shackelford

Ward-Thompson (see Buffum)

Wareham (see Jay)

Wareing (see Blanton)

Warfield (see Surname Sources)

Warford (see Folk Family Surname
    Exchange, Pigg)

Warner (see Barnes, Brodnax, Brown,
    Burlingame, Goodenow, Newton,
    Pessner, Varner)

Warner
John Warner of Framingham Association
205 West Street
Lakeside, CT 06758
Brainerd T. Peck, Historian

Warner
*Kinseeker Publications
5697 Old Maple Trail
PO Box 184
Grawn, MI 49637
E-mail: AB064@taverse.lib.mi.us
Victoria Wilson, Editor
Pub. *Warner, Who, When, & Where*,
    quarterly, $10.00 per year subscription,
    $2.50 for sample issue

Warr (see Scott)

Warren (see Avery, Barnard, Hardwick,
    MacDuff, Montague, Orton, Stewart)

Warren
*Ebenezer Warren Family Association
PO Box 1860
Studio City, CA 91614
Phone (818) 980-1005; E-mail:
    AP471@lafn.org
Karen Mohr
(includes descendants of Ebenezer (1748
    Massachusetts–1824 Massachusetts) of
    Roxbury, served in the Battle of
    Lexington, and Ann Tucker (1751–
    1816 Massachusetts))

Warren
*Warren Research and Publishing
1869 Laurel Avenue
Saint Paul, MN 55104-5938
Phone (612) 644-6581
Jim and Paula Warren, Co-editors
(includes Warren families worldwide)
SASE required

Warren
The Warren Cousins
30 Gurney Street
East Providence, RI 02914-2606
Lura N. Sellew

Warrender (see MacDuff)

Warriner (see Clark)

Washburn (see Pigg)

Washington (see Covert, Dunbar, Gant)

Washington
Washingtons of Pontotoc County,
    Mississippi
2702 Chatworth Street
Memphis, TN 38127
Phone (901) 358-0595
Pauline O. Washington
Reunion

Wason (see Buchanan)

Wass (see Ross)

Wasson (see Corson, Davis, McCullah)

Watchman (see MacDuff)

Waterhouse (see Waterous)

Waterous
*Mattanna Family Organization
PO Box 1926
Sandpoint, ID 83864
Phone (208) 263-0828
Robert J. Waterous
(includes descendants of Charles
    Waterous/Waterhouse of New
    Hampshire (ca 1840–?) and Mary
    Elizabeth Pierce of Illinois (1850–
    1890); John Hannon (ca 1824–?) and
    Bridget Flannery (ca 1824–1889)
    County Clare, Ireland, to Chicago;
    Matthew Ostry (1848–1913) and Mary
    Kundrat (1851–1931) Bohemia to
    Chicago; Ferdinand Tymich (Tymick)
    (1849–?) and Rose (ca 1850–ca 1881)
    Bohemia to Chicago; Martin Pierce
    (ca 1790–?) and Esther (Chapman?)
    (ca 1796–?) Massachusetts to New
    York to Illinois; John Bates Kiron
    (1841–1906) from Ireland to Chicago)
Phone or mail SASE for information

Waters (see Folk Family Surname
    Exchange, Buchanan, Burnham,
    Burrell, Forbes, Ross)

Waters
*Waters Family Reunion
(Waters Farm, Waters Road, Sutton,
    MA—location)
PO Box 267 (mailing address)
Bloomfield, NJ 07003
Phone (201) 672-0418
Betty L. Waters, Co-chairman
Pub. *Newsletter*, three times per year;
    (data base includes 4200 descendants
    of Richard Waters and Joyce/Rejoice
    Plasse Waters)

Waterson
Waterson-Watterson Family Organization
30987 Faircliff Street
Hayward, CA 94544
Jo Anne Monroe

Waterson
Waterson/Watterson Family Reunion
Rt. 1, Box 58
Morgantown, IN 46160
Phone (317) 422-8914
Michael Stifler, Secretary

Wathen
*Wathen Family Organization
2201 Riverside Drive
South Bend, IN 46616-2151
Phone (219) 234-6747; E-mail:
    MRoots95@aol.com
Carol Huebner Collins, Editor
Pub. *Wathen Family Newsletter*,
    quarterly, $15.00 per year subscription;
    (clearinghouse for all Wathens)
Sporadic reunion

Watkins (see Callison, Chapman, Corson, Futral)

Watkins
Willie and Sallie Black Watkins Family, Huntersville, Madison County, Tennessee
555 Westwood
Jackson, TN 38301
Phone (901) 427-9141
Judy Alpha

Watkins
*Watkins Family History Society
PO Box 518
Manitowoc, WI 54221-0518
E-mail: buzzwatk@aol.com; Website: www:http://ourworld.compuserve.com/homepages/watkins_fhs
Buzz Watkins, Newsletter Editor
Pub. *Journal of the Watkins Family*
$20.00 per year membership

Watson (see Album, Buchanan, Forbes, Garner, Hay, LaRue, MacDuff)

Watson
*Watson Family Organization
18002 North 12th Street, #30
Phoenix, AZ 85022
Nani Mercer Neal
Pub. *Watson Surname Newsletter*, quarterly, $20.00 per year subscription

Watt (see Buchanan, Forbes)

Watters (see Buchanan, Forbes)

Watterson (see Waterson)

Wattie (see Forbes)

Watts (see Clark, Forbes, Heath, Lambert, Ross)

Watts
Watts
PO Box 146
Hamilton, KS 66853
Leta Watts Harrell
Pub. *Watts*, quarterly, $12.50 per year subscription
Reunion

Watts
Watts Family Organization
27894 Gail Drive
Warren, MI 48093-4984
Dorothy Challacombe Rowell

Waugh (see Lush)

Waulker (see MacMillan)

Way (see Kunkel)

Way
Way Newsletter
1631 Niagara Avenue
Niagara Falls, NY 14305

Glenn C. Way
Pub. *Way Newsletter*, annually

Wayland (see The Memorial Foundation of the Germanna Colonies)

Wayman (see The Memorial Foundation of the Germanna Colonies)

Wayne (see Casey)

Weak (see Week)

Weant (see Boose)

Wear (see Ware)

Weatherbee
*Weatherbee Family
1360 West Macon Street
Decatur, IL 62522-2704
Phone (217) 423-9081
Carl Weatherbee, Editor
Pub. *Weatherbee Round-Up*, bimonthly; (includes Weatherby, Wetherbee, Wetherby, Witherbee, Witherby, over 80 spellings in the U.S. and England)
Donation for membership

Weatherford (see Elder)

Weatherford
*Weatherford Family Association
531 Majestic Avenue
Bellmawr, NJ 08031
Phone (609) 931-3451
Robert E. Weatherford, Librarian
Pub. *Weather-Watch*, quarterly; (includes all Weatherfords and Weatherford descendants)
$8.00 per year membership

Weatherlee (see Weatherly)

Weatherley (see Weatherly)

Weatherly
Weatherly Family Quarterly
12402 Pantano
Houston, TX 77065
Phone (713) 890-0588
Karen L. Daniel, Editor
Pub. *Weatherly Family Quarterly*, (January, April, July and October), $10.00 per year subscription; (includes Weatherlee(y))

Weathermon
*Christopher Columbus Weathermon Family
5619 East Third Street
Tucson, AZ 85711-1418
Phone (520) 745-2144
Wilmer D. Martin, Organizer
(includes descendants of Christopher Columbus Weathermon and Martha Jane "Patsy" Vestal, married 1825 in North Carolina)

Biennial reunion in even-numbered years on the second weekend of July at a community center west of King City, Missouri

Weathers
Weathers-Withers-Wethers Wanderings
77 Decatur Avenue
Spring Valley, NY 10977-4703
Phone (914) 352-7484
Joseph Weathers, Genealogist
Pub. *Weathers-Withers-Wethers Wanderings*, semiannually (June and December)
$15.00 per year membership

Weaver (see The Memorial Foundation of the Germanna Colonies, Sullivan Surname Exchange, Chaudoin, Cowart, Smith, Wert)

Weaver
Weaver Newsletter
RR 1, Box 72A
Douglas, NE 68344-9801
Donald H. Julifs
Pub. *Weaver Newsletter*, quarterly, $7.50 per year subscription

Webb (see Fraser, Jackson, Kahler, Kindel, Lemon, Rutherford)

Webb
Southeast States Webb Family Association
164 Park Brook Circle
Tallahassee, FL 32301-8914
Phone (904) 222-9900; (904) 656-4779; (904) 893-5539 (Director of Genealogical Research Services); (904) 222-9363 (FAX)
Robert A. Webb, Founder/Executive Director; Thomas B. Webb, Jr., Director of Genealogical Research Services
Pub. *Webb Newsletter*, three times per year; (includes ancestors and descendants of John Webb (1714–1778) of Northampton County, North Carolina)
$10.00 per year membership; reunion June in northeast central Florida

Webb
DeGrass Webb Family Organization
245 North Vine #702
Salt Lake City, UT 84103
Phone (801) 363-0401
Gay P. Kowallis
Pub. *Webb Family*, irregularly; (includes descendants of DeGrass Webb only)
$10.00 per year membership

Webb
Webb Family Association
14333 Aldengate Road
Midlothian, VA 23113
Anne Hale Kellam

Webber (see Aldrich, Brucker, Corson)

Weber (see Surname Database, Lahey)

Weber
Weber-Kaiser Family Newsletter
North 629 Hilly Road
Merrill, WI 54452
Patti Laessig Zimmerman
Pub. *Weber-Kaiser Family Newsletter
from Freudenburg, Germany and the
Surrounding Area Near Trier*

Webster (see Barnes, Barnard, Corson)

Webster
Webster/McCracken Families
120 Doza Creek Road
Marissa, IL 62257
J. L. Cox, Sr.

Weckes (see Crispell)

Wecriers (see Smith)

Wedderburn (see MacDuff)

Wedmore
*The Wedmore Clan
(126 Boca Chica—location)
20 Siesta Village (mailing address)
Weslaco, TX 78596
Phone (210) 969-1103
Virginia Vest Stevens, Family
Representative
Pub. *Newsletter*, seimannually; (includes
descendants of John Wedmore (1780/
90) and Jane Ross of Virginia and
Ohio)
Annual reunion at various locations

Weed (see Catlow)

Weed
*New Canaan Historical Society
13 Oenoke Ridge
New Canaan, CT 06840
Phone (203) 966-1776
Marilyn T. O'Rourke, Librarian
(primarily New Canaan local history, not
genealogical, but features Silliman,
Noyes, Weed surname collections)
$25.00 per year membership for
individuals, $30.00 per year
membership for families

Weedman
Weedman Reunion
8417 Burlingame Road
Louisville, KY 40219
G. L. Theiss

Week
*Week, Weeks, Weekes Family
Organization
191 Ephrata Avenue, N.W.
Soap Lake, WA 98851
June Gemmer Ponis
Pub. *The Weak Link*, semiannually;
(includes Week, Weekes, Weeks and
all variations of spelling, any time, any
place)
$10.00 per year membership

Weekes (see Week)

Weeks (see Dockery, Lynch, McCune,
Week)

Weeks
The Weeks in Review
401 North Eton Street, #107
Birmingham, MI 48009-5946
Vickie Long
Pub. *The Weeks in Review*

Weeks
*Leonard Weeks and Descendants in
America, Inc.
Weeks Avenue
Greenland, NH 03840
Edna B. Weeks, Assistant Treasurer
$5.00 per year membership for
individuals under 21, $10.00 per year
for individuals, $15.00 per year for
families, $25.00 per year for
organizations, $100.00 per year for
sponsors, $250.00 per year for patrons,
$500.00 life membership

Weeks
Leonard Weeks Family Organization
6 Pear Street
Laconia, NH 03246-2542
John F. Weeks

Weeks
Weeks
401 Molly, #206
Caldwell, TX 77836
Helen Bullock
Pub. *Weeks*, semiannually, $10.00 per
year subscription

Weems (see MacDuff)

Weepers (see MacDuff)

Weese
Weese Family Newsletter
6602 Westchester
Houston, TX 77005-3756
Phone (713) 664-3429; (713) 664-2874
Sharline or Charles Boykin
Pub. *"Who's Who", The Weese Family
Newsletter*, three to four times per
year, free for exchange of material

Weethee (see Withy)

Wefel
Wefel Family Association
555 Freeman Road, #91
Central Point, OR 97502
Ralph M. Wefel, Chairman
Pub. *Wefel Across the U.S.A.*,
semiannually; (Wefel families from the
city of Schledehausen, Hannover, who
came to America in the 1830s and
after, locating in Fort Wayne, Indiana)
$15.00 per year membership; reunion

Wehrman
Wehrman Family Reunion
Stover, MO 65078
Edgar Witte

Wehrung
*Wehrung Families of Alsace and
America
702 Irving Avenue
Royal Oak, MI 48067-2879
Phone (810) 543-3065; E-mail:
an563Wdetroit.freenet.org; Website:
http://www.geocities.com/Paris/1947/
and http://www.grfn.org/
Brendan Wehrung, Secretary
(includes Ensminger of Waldnambach
and Diemeringen)

Weidman (see Mueller)

Weidner (see Moser)

Weidner
*Weidner/Widener/Widner/Wydner
Group
PO Box 343
Pine Beach, NJ 08741-0343
M. Kelly
(pre-1900 New Jersey)

Weierbach (see Weyerbacher)

Weierback (see Weyerbacher)

Weimer
*Weimer Genealogical Center
11207 Morris Place, N.E.
PO Box 11546
Albuquerque, NM 87192
Phone (505) 299-6117
Ellen Weimer, Director
Pub. *Weimer Genealogical Newsletter*,
bimonthly, $25.00 per year
subscription; (includes Wimer and
Wymer spellings)

Weingart (see The Memorial Foundation
of the Germanna Colonies)

Weinhold
*Pennsylvania-German Weinhold/
Wineholt Family
107 West Sunhill Road
Manheim, PA 17545
Phone (717) 665-5869
D. Ernest Weinhold
(especially descendants of the very early
immigrants who settled in northeast
Lancaster County, Pennsylvania, and
nearby areas)

Weir (see Buchanan, Macnachton)

Weir
*David Weir Family Organization (1770–
Chester County, South Carolina)
Sarah/Susan B. Weir Family
Organization (1770–1812 Chester
County, South Carolina)
HCR 62, Box 113A
Flippin, AR 72634-9710

Phone (501) 453-5286
Charlene Gillespie Deutsch, Compiler

Weirbach (see Weyerbacher)

Weirback (see Weyerbacher)

Weire (see Rutherford)

Weirebach (see Weyerbacher)

Weireback (see Weyerbacher)

Weirick
*Weirick/Weyrick Surname Organization
10315 South 1540 West
South Jordan, UT 84095
Phone (801) 254-3532
Betty Barney Farnsworth

Weiser
*John Conrad Weiser Family Association
55 Kohler School Road
New Oxford, PA 17350-9415
Phone (717) 624-4106
Pastor Frederick S. Weiser, Secretary
Pub. *Newsletter*, semiannually; (includes
    Weiser/Wysor/Wisser families from
    1475 to the present in Germany and
    the U.S.)
$10.00 per year membership, $100.00
    life membership

Weiss (see Wise)

Weisz (see Baldman)

Welborn
Welborn/Wellbourne/Wilburn
    Clearinghouse
5417 South Boston Place
Tulsa, OK 74105
DeWayne Welborn

Welborn
*Welborn Reunion
102 Deer Run Lane
Greenwood, SC 29646
Phone (803) 229-2120
Gene Welborn
(includes Welborns and related families
    with roots in North and South
    Carolina)
Annual reunion on the first Sunday of
    November at Pelzer Community
    Center, Pelzer, South Carolina

Welch (see Clark, Heath, Lush, Nelson,
    Walsh)

Welch
*Links Genealogy Publications
7677 Abaline Way
Sacramento, CA 95823-4224
Phone (916) 428-2245
Iris Carter Jones, Editor
Pub. *The Fountain*, quarterly, $12.00 per
    year subscription; (includes Walsh,
    Welch, Welsch and Welsh)

Welch
*John Isaac Welch Family Organization
220 Harrison Street
Twin Falls, ID 83301
Phone (208) 734-2141
Cardie B. Northrop
(includes descendants of John Isaac
    Welch (1774 North Carolina–1886
    Tennessee), Thomas Samuel Welch
    (1600s, Pennsylvania), John I. Welch
    (late 1600 to early 1700s, Ireland),
    Thomas Samuel Welch (1749), John
    Isaac Welch (1774, North Carolina),
    James Thomas Welch (1805, North
    Carolina), Thomas Conway Welch
    (1823, North Carolina), Henry Martin
    Welch (1854, Kentucky), including
    alternate spellings: Walsh and Welsh)

Welch
Welch-Elverson-Bentsen-Groff Family
    Association
2306 Westgate
Houston, TX 77019
Phone (713) 529-2333
Harold Helm
$25.00 plus pedigree and family group
    sheets for membership

Weld (see Corson)

Welder (see Heath)

Weliver (see Gregor)

Welker
*Georgina Welker Family Organization
8255 South Krameria Way
Englewood, CO 80112
Phone (303) 290-0998
Mr. Dana M. Floyd
Free

Welker
Samuel Sylvester Welker Family
    Organization
161 West 1500 North
Rexburg, ID 83440
Phone (208) 356-8340
Kay Clark
(includes descendants of Samuel
    Sylvester Welker (1887 Bloomington,
    Bear Lake, Idaho–) and Sophrona
    Ricks (1887-Salem, Madison County,
    Idaho–)

Wellauer
*Wellauer Surname Organization
2845 North 72nd Street
Milwaukee, WI 53210
Phone (414) 778-1224; (414) 2109 FAX
Maralyn A. Wellauer
(includes families from Switzerland)

Wellbourne (see Welborn)

Welles
*Welles Family Association, Inc.
2 Howard Avenue
Shelton, CT 06484

Janet W. Lantowsky, Registrar
Pub. *Wellesprings*, semiannually (fall/
    winter and spring), $3.00 per year
    subscription; (includes descendants of
    Gov. Thomas Welles (1590 Sourton,
    Whichford, Warwickshire, England–
    1660 Wethersfield, Connecticut), 4th
    Colonial Governor of Connecticut, and
    Alice Tomes)
$5.00 per year membership, $10.00 for
    membership application; $100.00 life
    membership; annual reunion on the
    first Saturday in October

Wellman (see Franciscus, Fraser,
    Jackson)

Wells (see Boney, Dean, Garner,
    Goodenow, Holmes, Lynch, MacDuff,
    Stone, Welles)

Wells
Wells Family Association
22916 Carlow Road
Torrance, CA 90505
Phone (310) 378-3574
Charlene DeLong

Wells
*Wells Genealogical Research
4504 Fox Creek Drive
Crystal Lake, IL 60012-1870
Phone (815) 455-9055
Ann L. Wells, Publisher
Pub. *Wells Researcher*, quarterly, $12.00
    per year subscription in the U.S.,
    $16.00 per year subscription in
    Canada, $18.00 or £20 per year
    subscription elsewhere; queries $5.00
    from non-subscribers; (all Wells, no
    restrictions)

Wells
*Wells Family Association
735 North Grove Avenue
Oak Park, IL 60302-1551
Phone (708) 524-0695; (708) 524-0742
    FAX; E-mail: SWells.aol.com
Charles Chauncey Wells, Editor
Pub. *Newsletter*, annually; (includes
    descendants of Jonathan and Sylvia
    Phelps Wells who came to Michigan in
    1835; also interested in Wells family of
    Boston, especially Capt. John Wells)
No membership fee; annual reunion

Wells
*Wells Family Research Association
PO Box 5427
Kent, WA 98064-5427
E-mail: 73424.240@compuserve.com
Orin R. Wells, President
Pub. *The Wells Chronicles*, quarterly;
    (includes all lines, worldwide, all
    variations, all centuries; huge database
    projects)
$12.00 per year membership

Wellwood (see MacDuff)

Welsch (see Welch)

Welsh (see Welch)

Wemyss (see MacDuff)

Wendel (see Lambert)

Wendler
*Wendler/Guetzke Family
4103 South Logan Avenue
Milwaukee, WI 53207
Phone (414) 481-6697
Shirley Scharnoski

Wendling
*Hildebrand Family Organization
512 Parker Avenue
Aurora, IL 60505
Phone (708) 898-6763
Patricia Mosley Torrance, Editor
Pub. *Quarterly* (includes descendants of
Judge Abraham and Anna (Shantz)
Hildebrand)
$16.00 per year membership

Wenger (see Frantz)

Wenger
*Wenger/Winger Reunion
1216 Hillcrest Road
Akron, PA 17501
Phone (717) 859-2396
Jay V. Wenger, President
Pub. *The Wenger Report*, annually,
donation for subscription; (includes
Wanger, Wengerd, Wengert, Whanger,
Wingerd and Wingert)
Reunion

Wengerd (see Wenger)

Wengert (see Wenger)

Wenlock (see Hicks)

Wennrick (see Kettenring)

Wentworth (see Corson)

Wentworth
Wentworth Family Organization
Rt. 3, Box 123
Trinity, NC 27370
Cheryl Burrow

Wentz (see Boose)

Wenz (see Lambert)

Werden (see Worden)

Werli (see Hickman)

Werner (see Varner, Verner)

Werner
*Werner Genealogy Database and
Descendant Addresses
322 Mary Avenue
Westminster, MD 21157

Phone (410) 848-6743
Glenn H. Baer, Editor

Werner
*Seifertshausen to Somerset
1512 Palmer Drive
Fayetteville, NC 28303-3039
Phone (910) 822-1021
Paul E. Werner, Publisher
(includes Werner and Sass family
history)

Werner
*Werner/Sass Family Reunion
1052 Cumberland Street
Bethlehem, PA 18017
Ethel M. Woefel
(includes descendants of Adam Werner
and Anna Catharine Sass who lived in
the Meyersdale, Pennsylvania, area)
Annual reunion on the third Sunday of
July, Glencoe, Pennsylvania

Wert (see Wertz)

Wert
*Wert Family History Association
PO Box 240
Port Royal, PA 17082-0240
Phone (717) 527-2642; (717) 527-2793
FAX
Jonathan M. Wert, Ph.D., President and
Editor
Pub. *The Wert Family History Newsletter*
(includes Wert, Wirt, Wirth and Wertz
surname research, especially
descendants of Johann Adam Wirth
(1727–1806) and Eva Elizabeth
Schnug (1730–1800), resided in Upper
Paxton Township, Dauphin County,
Pennsylvania, after 1763; also related
surnames: Bretz, Deibler, Derk,
Derrick, Enterline, Fetterhoff,
Hoffman, Kitch, Lenker, Loos, Metz,
Miller, Noll, Nye, Price, Radel, Riegle,
Schneider, Sheesley, Shoop and
Weaver)

Wertz (see Wert)

Wertz
Wertz
Whispering Oaks
5821 Rowland Hill Road
Cascade, MD 21719-1939
Phone (301) 416-2660
Victor Gebhart, President
Pub. *Wertz*, annually, $2.00 per issue

Wertz
*Wertz Family Association
2912 12th Street, S.E.
Puyallup, WA 98374-1308
Phone (206) 841-3087
Carolyn Cell Choppin, Editor
Pub. *Wertz Relations*, quarterly, $2.00 per
year subscription, $5.00 for three years
subscription; (includes all Wert(z),
Wirt(s), Wuertz, Wurts, etc., families
of Pennsylvania-German origin)

Wescot (see Wescott)

Wescott
*Wescott Family of Maine and New
Hampshire
3031 Fairfield Street
Ontario, CA 91761
Phone (909) 947-0251
Howard E. Wescott, Jr.
(includes variations Wescot, Wescutt,
Wesket, Westcoate, Westgate, Yescot)
No cost

Wescutt (see Wescott)

Wesket (see Wescott)

Wessel (see Dodenhoff)

Wessels (see Alrichs)

West (see Davis, Newton)

West
William Dudley West Family
Organization
90 Ocean Pines
Berlin, MD 21811-9150
Richard or Betty West
(includes descendants of William Dudley
and Rosamund Allen West)

West
West
19201 Plummer Drive
Germantown, MD 20876
Fran West Powell
Pub. *West*, quarterly, $5.00 per year
subscription
Reunion

West
*West/Powell Family Organization
William Henry West Family Organization
2941 South Palmetto Circle
Saint George, UT 84770
Phone (801) 628-0215
Betty B. Evenson
(includes descendants of West of
Hannibal, Marion County, Missouri,
1890s, and wife Minnie Lee Powell)

Westbrook
*Westbrook Surname Organization
150 Brown Street
Saint Clair, MI 48079-4882
Phone (810) 329-9359
George M. Roberts

Westbrook
Westbrook
6626 South 76 E Avenue
Tulsa, OK 74133
Jack E. Westbrook
Pub. *Westbrook*, irregularly, no charge

Westburn (see MacDuff)

Westcoate (see Wescott)

Westcott
Westcott
PO Box 262
Riverton, CT 06065
Pauline W. Dennis
Pub. *Westcott*, quarterly, $5.00 per year
 subscription
Reunion

Westcott
*The Society of Stukely Westcott
 Descendants of America
2145 Richvale Road
Nashport, OH 43830-9727
Phone (614) 454-1876
Betty W. Acker, Historian
Pub. *The Westcott Family Quarterly*
 (includes descendants of Stukely
 Westcott (1592–1677) and his wife,
 Juliana Marchant, of Rhode Island)
Biennial reunion

Westerfield (see Blossom Press)

Westfall (see Gonsalus-Duk, Wigelius)

Westgate (see Wescott)

Westmoreland (see McCune)

Westmoreland
*Westmoreland Family Reunion
Country Court Trailer Park
1101 Pocahontas, Trailer #18
Palmyra, MO 63461
Marjorie J. Westmoreland
Reunion every three years

Weston (see McRae)

Westover (see Nienow)

Westwater (see MacDuff)

Westwood (see MacDuff)

Westwood
*Temperance Westwood Family
 Organization
1774 Country Club Drive
Logan, UT 84321
Phone (801) 753-6924
Joyce Elfrena Kalanquin

Wethee (see Withy)

Wetherbee (see Weatherbee)

Wetherby (see Tidwell, Weatherbee)

Wetherill
*William Peter Wetherill Ancestors &
 Descendants: Pioneer of Ohio
822 Camino De Los Padres
Tucson, AZ 85718
Phone (520) 297-6585
Leallah Franklin, Publisher

Wetherington
Thomas Wetherington Family
 Organization LDS
6214 Lakeshore Drive
Dallas, TX 75214
J. L. Wetherington

Wethers (see Weathers)

Wethey (see Withy)

Wethy (see Withy)

Wetzel
Wetzel Family Organization
9551 Columbus Avenue
Sepulveda, CA 91343
Mrs. R. S. Hughes

Wev (see Covert)

Weybright (see Stoner)

Weyerbach (see Weyerbacher)

Weyerbacher
*Weyerbacher Descendants
109 Holly Hall, Pineford
Middletown, PA 17057
Phone (717) 944-0296
Warren W. Wirebach, President,
 Weyerbacher Reunion
Pub. *Annual Spring Letter*, free; (includes
 Weierbach, Weierbach, Weirbach,
 Weirback, Weirebach, Weireback,
 Weyerbach, Wierbach, Wierback,
 Wierebach, Wiereback, Wirebach,
 Wireback, Wirebaugh, Wirebeck,
 Wyerbaugher, Wyrebaugh)
Annual reunion on the second Sunday of
 July at Silver Creek Park, Route 412
 between Springtown and Pleasant
 Valley, Bucks County, Pennsylvania

Weygandt (see Boose)

Weymes (see MacDuff)

Weyrick (see Weirick)

Whale (see Chamberlain)

Whaley (see Folk Family Surname
 Exchange, Rutherford)

Whaley
*Folk Family
PO Box 52048
Knoxville, TN 37950-2048
Hester E. Stockton, Owner; Bullhead
 Whaley, Editor
Pub. *Whaley Families*, quarterly, $15.00
 per year subscription, $5.00 per issue;
 (includes Wailey and Whalie)

Whalie (see Whaley)

Whalley (see Whaley)

Whally (see Rice)

Whanger (see Wenger)

Wheadon (see Johnson)

Whealton
*Whealton Family Reunion
Rt. 1, Box 118
Bayboro, NC 28515-9725
Phone (919) 745-3783
Lois Jones
Reunion

Wheatley (see Carley)

Wheeler (see Bosher, Catlow, Cronn,
 Hiscock, Lush)

Wheeler
Wheeler Tracks
9920 N.E. 120th Street
Okeechobee, FL 34972-7453
Frances Scroggins Wheeler, Publisher
Pub. *Wheeler Tracks*, quarterly, $10.00
 per year subscription; (includes the
 descendants of brothers Benjamin and
 Martin Wheeler of Granville County,
 North Carolina)
Annual reunion on the third Saturday of
 June in Nashville, Tennessee

Wheeler
*Kinseeker Publications
5697 Old Maple Trail
PO Box 184
Grawn, MI 49637
E-mail: AB064@taverse.lib.mi.us
Victoria Wilson, Editor
Pub. *Wheeler Writings*, quarterly, $10.00
 per year subscription

Wheeler
Wheeler Cousins Newsletter
2011 East Rosebriar
Springfield, MO 65804
Vivagene Wheeler Headley
Pub. *Wheeler Cousins Newsletter*

Wheeler
Wheeler Family Reunion
442 East Main Street
Geneva, OH 44041
Phone (216) 466-0333
Joanne Neubert

Wheeler
Wheeler Cousins
4060 Mary Lee
Memphis, TN 38116
Phone (901) 332-2109
John T. Wheeler
Pub. *Wheeler Cousins*, quarterly, $3.00
 per year subscription; (includes
 descendants of Arcealus, Benjamin,
 Roland and Thomas Wheeler, all living
 in Bedford County, Virginia 1770–
 1790; also Hudgins and Cortnor
 surnames)

Wheeler
*Wheeler Surname Organization
5892 West 10620 North
Highland
American Fork, UT 84003-9591
Phone (801) 756-0155
Grant H. Iverson

Wheelock (see Newton)

Whelchel (see Folk Family Surname Exchange)

Whetman (see Surname Sources)

Whetnall
*Whetnall Family Association
PO Box 3447
Arlington, WA 98223-3447
Phone (360) 658-1000
Ruth Whetnall, President

Wheway (see Arthur)

Whipple (see Kunkel, Newton, Rothenberger)

Whistler (see Cronn)

Whit (see Harbour)

Whitacre (see Whitaker)

Whitaker (see Lee, McCune, Sawyer, Smith)

Whitaker
*Whitaker Clearinghouse
1328 East Hermosa Drive
Tempe, AZ 85282-5719
Phone (602) 491-2877
Gloria Kay Vandiver Inman
(includes spelling variations: Whittaker, Whitacre, etc.)

Whitcomb (see Catlow, Haws)

White (see Bagley, Blakey, Brawley, Brown, Clark, Evitt, Garstin, Goodenow, Gregor, Haynes, Heath, Jamison, Johnson, McKee, Nettles, Newton, Osborn, Rutherford, Thorn, Woolley)

White
*James White Family (NYC) Organization
PO Box 1860
Studio City, CA 91614
Phone (818) 980-1005; E-mail: AP471@lafn.org
Karen Mohr

White
*White/Lambert Family Association
8505 Glenview Avenue
Takoma Park, MD 20912
Phone (301) 89-6621;
   (301) 589-1366 FAX
M. Sandra Reeves

(restricted to descendants of Henry Jasper White (1788–1875); also Cambron, Means and Osborne)

White
*Topp of the Line
1304 West Cliffwood Court
Spokane, WA 99218-2917
Phone (509) 467-2299
Bette Butcher Topp, Owner/Operator
Pub. *White Press*, irregularly, $5.50 per issue plus $2.00 postage and handling

Whitehead (see Lilly, McCain, Sawyer)

Whitehead
*Whitehead Connection
PO Box 1446
Eunice, NM 88231-1446
Phone (505) 394-2403; (505) 394-2036
Diana Whitehead Noel

Whitelaw (see MacDuff)

Whiteman (see Covert)

Whitener (see Dockery)

Whitescarver (see The Memorial Foundation of the Germanna Colonies)

Whiteside
The Whiteside Whisperings
2130 Road 12, N.W.
Quincy, WA 98848
Alcenia Appling, Publisher
Pub. *The Whiteside Whisperings*, quarterly, $10.00 per year subscription

Whitesides (see Folk Family Surname Exchange)

Whitfield (see Hutchison)

Whitfield
*Whitfield Book Publishing Company
13 Costa Street
San Francisco, CA 94110
Phone (415) 615-7219
Vallie Jo Whitfield, Publisher; Joanne V. Whitfield, Editor
(includes books on Whitfield and Hiner/Heiner)

Whitfield
*Society of Whitfields
412 East Beech Street
Goldsboro, NC 27530
Sadie Whitfield
Annual reunion at the Spring Creek School, three miles west of Seven Springs, North Carolina, corner of NC 111 and Mount Olive-Seven Springs Road

Whitford (see Heath)

Whiting (see Barnard, Cox)

Whitley (see Moody)

Whitlock (see Folk Family Surname Exchange, Bates, Bosher)

Whitlock
*Whitlock Family Association
13033 Caminito Dos Amantes
San Diego, CA 92128-1722
Phone (619) 438-8428
Charles Whitlock Rockett, U.S. contact
Pub. *Whitlock Family Newsletter*, quarterly
$10.00 per year membership

Whitman (see Surname Sources)

Whitmore (see Lambert)

Whitney (see Catlow, Franciscus)

Whitney
*The Ancestors and Descendants of Theodore Roosevelt Whitney
Kennedy House Apartment 1324
1901 Kennedy Boulevard
Philadelphia, PA 19103
Harold C. Whitney, Publisher

Whiton
*Whiton Family Association
PO Box 87
Eastford, CT 06242-0087
Phone (860) 974-0492
Martha Clark, Corresponding Secretary
Pub. *Whiton Family Newsletter*, annually (summer months), free
Annual reunion on the Saturday of Columbus Day weekend

Whitt (see Harbour, Hatfield)

Whittaker (see Whitaker)

Whittemore (see Farrington)

Whittenburg (see Cowart)

Whittier
*Whittier Club of Haverhill and Trustees of J.G. Whittier Birthplace and Whittier Home of Amesbury
Haverhill Public Library
99 Main Street
Haverhill, MA 01830
Phone (508) 373-1588
Donald C. Freeman, Editor
Pub. *Whittier Newsletter*, irregularly, free to educational institutions; (deals exclusively with John Greenleaf Whittier and family, not primarily genealogical)

Whittington (see Johnson)

Whittlesey
*Whittlesey Surname Organization
PO Box 26183
Salt Lake City, UT 84126
Phone (801) 272-3928
Willis S. Whittlesey, III

Pub. *Whittlesey Family Newsletter*, irregularly, at least annually, donation per issue

Whyte (see Gregor)

Whyte-Melville (see MacDuff)

Wichern (see Lush)

Wickel (see Robinson)

Wicker (see Snow)

Wicks (see Heath)

Wickwarre (see Barnard)

Wicoff (see Likes)

Wicuff (see Likes)

Widdison (see McCune)

Widdows
The Widdows Web
106 Park Drive
Cranford, NJ 07016
Donald Widdows
Pub. *The Widdows Web*, quarterly, $5.00 per year subscription

Widener (see Weidner)

Widner (see Weidner)

Widrick
*Widrick (Wüthrich) Surname Organization
PO Box 38
Deer River, NY 13627
Phone (315) 493-4958
Edward R. Widrick
(includes Wüthrich, Wittrig, Widrig, Trub, from Switzerland, La Breit (France))

Widrig (see Widrick)

Wiedeman (see Hall)

Wiedemann (see Hall)

Wieland (see The Memorial Foundation of the Germanna Colonies)

Wierbach (see Weyerbacher)

Wierback (see Weyerbacher)

Wierebach (see Weyerbacher)

Wiereback (see Weyerbacher)

Wiese
*Hermann Julies Wiese Family Organization
2532 Smith Road
American Falls, ID 83211
Phone (208) 226-7854

Gary L. Wiese, President
(includes allied surnames of Dittmer, Flemming, Klein, Loyall and Schneekloth)

Wigfield
*Phillip Heritage House
605 Benton
Missoula, MT 59801
Phone (406) 543-3495
Ruth Phillip, MAS R.G.
Pub. *Wigfield Newsletter*, annually
$5.00 per year membership

Wight (see Evitt)

Wight
*Wight Family Organization
PO Box 295
Fort Ogden, FL 33842
Phone (941) 993-1274
Lois J. Wight
Pub. *Newsletter*, quarterly

Wightman (see Surname Sources)

Wike (see Moser)

Wilbanks
Wil(l)banks Trees
1208 North 85th Place
Scottsdale, AZ 85257-4114
Phone (602) 990-7914; E-mail: rmwiv@getnet.com; Website: http://www.getnet.com/~rmwiv
Robert M. Wilbanks, IV
Pub. *Wil(l)banks Trees*, bimonthly (February, April, June, August, October and December), $5.00 per issue, queries accepted

Wilbore (see Barnard, Freelove)

Wilburn (see Page, Richardson, Welborn)

Wilcox (see Goodenow, Hardesty, McCune, Neville, Rockwell, Ross, Savage, Willcocks)

Wilcox
*Bell Enterprises
PO Box 10328
Spokane, WA 99209
Phone (509) 327-2761
Mary Ann L. Vanzandt Bell, Owner, Publisher
Pub. *Wilcox Excerpts*, irregularly, $6.00 plus $1.25 postage per issue

Wildermuth
*Wildermuth Family Association
2786 Elingfield Road
Columbus, OH 43220
Phone (614) 459-6952
David T. Patterson, Treasurer
(includes descendants of Johan David Wildermuth, owns and maintains Wildermuth Memorial Church, Carroll, Ohio)

Wildey (see Daley)

Wildman (see Lemon)

Wilems (see Links Genealogy Publications)

Wiler
*Agustos Frank Wiler Family Organization
462 Woodrow Avenue
Vallejo, CA 94591
Phone (707) 554-3475
Clydene Williams Cannon
Pub. *Four Lines West*, quarterly, $18.00 per year subscription, discounted to members contributing documented information; (includes Wiler-Risener, Williams-Gore, Taylor-Thompson, Sebastian-Bowles)

Wiley (see The Memorial Foundation of the Germanna Colonies, Corson)

Wiley
*Wiley, Woods, Wyatt Family Organization
1132 North Tela Drive
Oklahoma City, OK 73127-4308
Phone (405) 789-2842
Pauline Carlton Fletcher, Secretary and Genealogist
(computer database uses Quinsept™, PAF™ and Reunion™)

Wilfong (see Moser)

Wilfong
*Wilfong Family Reunion (Descendants of Michael and Mary Hagy)
7224 Southeast Street
Indianapolis, IN 46227
Phone (317) 881-1352
Emalou Burton Garten, Secretary
Reunion

Wilhelm
*Wilhelm Where Are You?
PO Box 1872
Dodge City, KS 67801-1872
Laura Tasset Koehn, President
(includes research on Johann Conrad Wilhelm and Katherine Elizabeth Wagner)

Wilhoit (see The Memorial Foundation of the Germanna Colonies, Gant)

Wilhoit
Wilhoit/Wilhite Connections
Rt. 2, Box 43
Wellsville, KS 66092
Margaret Wilhite
Pub. *Wilhoit/Wilhite Connections*, quarterly, $5.00 per year subscription

Wilkens (see Wilkinson)

Wilkensen (see Wilkinson)

Wilkenson (see Wilkinson)

Wilkerson (see Anthes, Johnson, Pigg, Wilkinson)

Wilkerson
*Wilkerson/Wilkinson Clearinghouse
1605 Holly
Gering, NE 69341
Phone (308) 436-5617
Shirley Weihing

Wilkie (see MacDuff)

Wilkins (see Wilkinson)

Wilkinson (see Mackey, McCune, Newton, Pigg, Searcy, Wilkerson)

Wilkinson
Wilkinson
2937 Coral Strip Parkway
Gulf Breeze, FL 32561-2633
Florence Moore
Pub. *Wilkinson*, quarterly, $15.00 per year subscription

Wilkinson
Wilkinson Connection
PO Box 8003
Janesville, WI 53547-8003
Phone (608) 756-3759
Peggy Rockwell Gleich, Editor
Pub. *Wilkinson Connection*, quarterly (February, May, August and November), $15.00 per year subscription, queries free to subscribers; (includes Wilkens, Wilkensen, Wilkenson, Wilkerson, Wilkins, Wilkinson, etc.)

Wilks (see Grover)

Will (see Gunn)

Willard (see MacDuff)

Willard
*The Willard Family Association of America, Inc.
2 Collier Road
Scituate, MA 02066-4607
Phone (617) 544-3976
Alan C. Spooner, President
Pub. *Newsletter*, semiannually (May and December); (includes descendants of Major Simon Willard, who arrived in Boston in 1634, or of his brother George who arrived ca 1634–1635, or of his sister Margery, wife of Dolor Davis, who arrived in 1634)
$5.00 per year membership for individuals, $10.00 per year patron membership, $100.00 life membership; annual reunion on the last weekend of July or the first weekend of August

Willbanks (see Wilbanks)

Willcocks
The Peter Willcocks Society
PO Box 2047
Olathe, KS 66061
Phone (913) 829-0609
Laird M. Wilcox, Director
(membership limited to descendants of Peter Willcocks (1691–1768); collects information on Willcocks, Willcox, Wilcox and allied families of Crane, Mulford and Valentine)
Donation for membership

Willcox (see Willcocks)

Willcox
*The Willcox Family Reunion
2699 Regency Drive, West
Tucker, GA 30084
Phone (770) 938-3719
Martha S. Albertson, Secretary
(includes descendants of Thomas Willcox and Elizabeth (Cole) Willcox who are buried at Ivy Mills, Pennsylvania)
Annual reunion on the first Sunday of June at Little Ocmulgee State Park, near McRae, Georgia

Wille (see Heath)

Willems (see Links Genealogy Publications)

Willenbrock (see Kregal)

Willenbrook (see Kregal)

Willer (see The Memorial Foundation of the Germanna Colonies)

Willey (see Corson, Dobie)

Willey
*John and Mary Willey (b. ca 1770) of Dickson County, Tennessee
998 Bloomington Drive South
Saint George, UT 84790-7585
Phone (801) 673-6314
Carolyn Reinbold
(includes descendants of Stephan and Barbli Trachsel (ca 1536) of Lenk, Canton of Bern, Switzerland)

Willheit (see The Memorial Foundation of the Germanna Colonies)

Williams (see Blossom Press, Family Publications, Folk Family Surname Exchange, Links Genealogy Publications, Surname Sources, Barnes, Bosher, Clark, Cowart, Dean, Detering, Gant, Golding, Goodenow, Harger, Heath, Kepple, Likes, MacDuff, Martin, McNees, Wiler)

Williams
*Solomon Steele Williams Family Organization
1307 East Evergreen Street
Mesa, AZ 85203

Phone (602) 969-8609
Lawrence A. Williams
Pub. *Solomon Steele Williams & Eliza Ann Miller Bulletin*, irregularly; (includes descendants of Solomon Steel Williams (1833 Fleming County, Kentucky–1926 Horace, Kansas) and Eliza Ann Miller (1838 Darke County, Ohio–1911 Appleton, Missouri), and allied families of Baldwin and Bruen, etc.)
Donation for membership

Williams
*Jacob Williams Family Organization
14835 Frontier Drive
Red Bluff, CA 96080
Phone (916) 529-4580
Mary J. Tasto
(includes descendants of Jacob Williams (1849 Ohio) and Adaline Lewis)

Williams
William Patrick Williams Descendants Organization
1401 Venice Street
Longmount, CO 80501
J. D. Williams

Williams
Williams
PO Box 773
Chipley, FL 32428
Martha McKnight
Pub. *Williams*, quarterly, $4.00 per year subscription

Williams
*James Leonard Williams Family Organization
29 East Portland Avenue
Vincennes, IN 47591
Phone (812) 882-9371
Richard Carl Rodgers, II, Historian/ Archivist
(archival facility collects information on all descendants and ancestors of the family in computer database; descendants of James Leonard Williams (ca 1823 Ohio–) and wives Abby Eliza Bicknell (1832 of Warwick, Kent County, Rhode Island– 1865 Providence, Providence County, Rhode Island), daughter of Hosea Bicknell and Charlotte Ives Spencer, and Mahala P. Anderson (1843 Perry County, Indiana–1871 Cannelton, Perry County, Indiana), daughter of Josiah Anderson and America T. Critchlow)

Williams
*William Patrick Williams Family Organization
313 Mankin, N.E.
Albuquerque, NM 87123
Phone (505) 299-8003
Wanda M. Barnum
(includes descendants of Patrick Williams and Eliza Hogan)
Reunion

Williams
*Williams Family Reunion
420 Fattler Ridge Road
Philo, OH 43771
Phone (614) 674-4255
Shelby Jean Smith, Secretary; Robert F.
  Williams, Co-chairman of the
  Genealogical Committee
Pub. *Williams Family Tabloid* (includes
  descendants of William Francis
  Williams (possibly came from Wales
  to Harrison County, West Virginia, in
  1770) and Alice Fletcher of Wolf
  Summitt, West Virginia, and Morgan
  County, Ohio)
Reunion

Williams
*Williams/Bradford/Brookshire Family
  Organization
1132 North Tela Drive
Oklahoma City, OK 73127-4308
Phone (405) 789-2842
Pauline Carlton Fletcher, Secretary and
  Genealogist
(computer database uses Quinsept™,
  PAF™ and Reunion™)
Annual reunion

Williams
Genealogical and Historical News
369 East 900 South, Suite 247
Salt Lake City, UT 84111
R. D. Bradshaw, Editor
Pub. *Williams of Virginia Family
  Newsletter*

Williams
*Williams Family of Delmarva Peninsula
Rt. 2, Box 187
Morgantown, PA 19543
Phone (215) 286-9857
Fred L. Williams, III

Williams
Thomas Williams Family Organization
555 Westwood
Jackson, TN 38301
Phone (901) 427-9141
Judy Alpha

Williams
Bevers Publications
PO Box 3056
Wichita Falls, TX 76309
Mr. Williams
Pub. *Williams Kissin Cousins*

Williams
*Robert Williams of Roxbury
  Association
Route 4 West, Box 11A
Woodstock, VT 05091-1241
Phone (802) 457-2206
Rev. E. H. Williams, Genealogist and
  Chairman
Pub. *Root & Branch*, quarterly; (includes
  descendants of Robert Williams
  (1607–1693) and his wife, Elizabeth

Stalham, of Roxbury, Massachusetts,
  especially descendants of Capt.
  Phinehas[1] Williams (1734–1820) of
  Mansfield, Connecticut, and
  Woodstock, Vermont)
$10.00 per year membership (beginning
  in January); reunion

Williams
*Pioneer Publication
PO Box 1179
Tum Tum, WA 99034-1179
Phone (509) 276-9841
Shirley Penna-Oakes
Pub. *Williams Wandering*, irregularly,
  $6.00 per issue plus $1.75 postage for
  one to three books, 50¢ for each
  additional book

Williamson (see Family Publications,
  Surname Sources, Gunn, Hatfield,
  Jackson, Lahey, Mackay)

Williamson
Williamson Writings
13546 Dahlia Court
Rosemount, MN 55068-3378
Jeff Williamson, Editor
Pub. *Williamson Writings*, three times per
  year, $12.00 per year subscription

Willie
*James Gray Willie Family Organization
3385 South Bluff Road
Syracuse, UT 84075
Phone (801) 773-0531
Allen S. Willie, President
Pub. *Newsletter*, annually (May)
Biennial reunion on Memorial Day in
  even-numbered years in the LDS
  church in Mendon, Cache County,
  Utah

Willis (see Donshea)

Wills (see Gunn, Probst)

Willson (see Brough, Glasgow)

Wilmarth (see Wilmoth)

Wilmot (see Vail)

Wilmoth (see Golding)

Wilmoth
Wilmoth-Wilmott-Wilmarth-Wilson
  Family Association
2306 Westgate
Houston, TX 77019
Phone (713) 529-2333
Harold Helm
$25.00 plus pedigree and family group
  sheets for membership

Wilmott (see Wilmoth)

Wilscam
William Wilscam of Montreal, Quebec,
  and Valporaiso, Indiana, and His
  Descendants
24 Valley Brook Road
Rocky Hill, CT 06067
Phone (203) 529-1438
Roderick A. Wilscam
Donation for membership

Wilsey (see Grasty)

Wilson (see Ammons, Beard, Brough,
  Caskey, Emery, Fletcher, Frasher,
  Glasgow, Gregor, Gunn, Innes,
  Jackson, Job, Lush, MacFaddien,
  McConnell, Ross, Scott, Wigelius,
  Wilmoth)

Wilson
*Wilson Clearinghouse
207 Auburn Drive
Dalton, GA 30720
Phone (706) 278-1504
Joseph Wiley Reid
(1400–1890 period)

Wilson
Craig Junction Publishers
PO Box 242
Craigmont, ID 83523-0242
Marsha Wilson Bovey
Pub. *The Wilson Courier*, quarterly,
  $12.00 per year subscription

Wilson
From Generation to Generation
Rt. 1, Box 147
Buncombe, IL 62912
Melody Tellor, Editor
Pub. *Wilson Research*, quarterly, $15.00
  per year subscription

Wilson
*Wilson Family Reunion—Riley and
  Loretta Smith Wilson
359 Augusta Drive
Abingdon, VA 24211
Phone (540) 628-9059
Violet Wilson Skorinko

Wilson
Genealogical and Historical News
369 East 900 South, Suite 247
Salt Lake City, UT 84111
R. D. Bradshaw, Editor
Pub. *Wilson of Virginia Family
  Newsletter*

Wilson
The Wilson Society
323 Yettman Drive
Pittsburgh, PA 15239-2229
Dolores Wilson, U.S.A. Representative

Wilson
*The Wilson, Sunderhaus and Trugstad
  Families of Ohio and Michigan
PO Box 893
Lindale, TX 75771-0893

Phone (903) 886-5915
Leland E. Wilson
Biennial reunion

Wilson
Wilson
PO Box 1058
Appomattox, VA 24522
John L. Wilson
Pub. *Wilson*, eight to twelve times per
  year; (includes descendants of William
  and Nellie Wilson)
$20.00 per year membership; reunion

Wilt (see Schindel)

Wiltbank
*John Cleveland Wiltbank Family
  Organization
PO Box 764
Snowflake, AZ 85937-0764
Phone (520) 536-7459
Jerry D. Wiltbank
(includes related surname: Kollock)

Wilts (see Kelm)

Wiltsey (see Usher)
Phone

Wimbs (see MacDuff)

Wimer (see Weimer)

Wimmer
Jacob Wimmer and Jemina Labouteaux
  Family Organization
4325 Butler Circle
Boulder, CO 80303
A. Hill

Wimms (see MacDuff)

Wims (see MacDuff)

Winan (see MacLennan)

Winchester (see Nettles)

Wind (see Wint)

Windemeyer (see Schindel)

Winderweedle
Winderweedle
PO Box 1174
Douglas, AZ 85607
Judy Winderweedle
Pub. *Winderweedle*, bimonthly, $15.00
  per year subscription
Reunion

Windle (see Lambert)

Windmiller
Windmiller Family Reunion
PO Box 92
Pleasant Hill, IL 62366
Virginia Hart

Windsor
*Windsor Family Historical Association
67 West Hill Road
Vestal, NY 13850
Phone (607) 785-5785
Nancy Windsor Waterman
Pub. *Windsor Lines*, irregularly; (includes
  Winsor)

Wine (see Stoner)

Winegar
Winegar Family Association (Winniger/
  Wingar)
318 Jamaica Drive
San Antonio, TX 78227
Phone (210) 674-2535
Richard Cain Winegar, Editor
Pub. *The Winegar Family Newsletter*

Winehold (see Weinhold)

Wineholt (see Weinhold)

Winfield
Winfield Family Association
Rt. 1, Box 353
Riverton, WY 82501
Pub. *Winfield Family Association
  Newsletter*, quarterly

Wing (see Barnes)

Wing
Wing Assembly Representing Maine
  (W.A.R.M.)
Rt. 1, Box 534
Canton, ME 04221
Phone (207) 597-2303
Elwood Wing, Jr., President
Pub. *Wing Family Newsletter*

Wing
*Wing Family of America, Inc.
69 Spring Hill Road
East Sandwich, MA 02537
Phone (316) 744-1638 (President's home
  in Kansas)
Dale E. Wing, President
Pub. *The Owl*, annually, $3.00 per issue;
  (includes descendants of The Reverend
  John Wing of Banbury, England, and
  his wife, Deborah, or their ancestors)
$10.00 per year membership

Wingar (see Winegar)

Wingate (see Corson)

Winger (see Wenger)

Wingerd (see Wenger)

Wingert (see Wenger)

Wingerter (see Hegner)

Wingfield
*Wingfield Family Society
301 Belleview Boulevard
Belleair, FL 34616
Phone (813) 461-4187 (Editor); (813)
  461-1083 FAX; (817) 926-2959
  (Database)
Robert E. Carr, Director and Editor;
  Vance Wingfield, Database
Pub. *Wingfield Family Society
  Newsletter*, quarterly, $4.00 per extra
  issue; (includes descendants of Robert
  De Wingfield, 1087, Suffolk, England;
  45,000+ -name database includes
  Wingfield (all spellings) from 1100 to
  the present)
$25.00 per year membership for all
  persons at a single address

Wingo
Wingo
15 Barrington Road
Nitro, WV 25143
Rose Peterson
Pub. *Wingo*, quarterly, $10.00 per year
  subscription

Winn
Winn/Wynn/Wynne/Wynns Newsletter
221 North Spring Street
Columbus, WI 53925
Addie Wynn Berndt
Pub. *Winn/Wynn/Wynne/Wynns
  Newsletter*, quarterly, $15.00 per year
  subscription

Winney (see Winne)

Winniger (see Winegar)

Winning (see MacLennan)

Winny (see Winne)

Winram (see MacDuff)

Winslow (see Goodenow)

Winslow
*The Historic Winslow House
  Association (1699)
(Webster Street at Careswell Street—
  location)
PO Box 531 (mailing address)
Marshfield, MA 02050
Phone (617) 837-5753
Richard Martinez, President
(includes descendants of Edward and
  Susanna (White) Winslow, Mayflower
  passengers)
$15.00 per year membership for
  individuals, $25.00 per year
  membership for families, $75.00 life
  membership for individuals, $100.00
  life membership for families

Winsor (see Barnard, Windsor)

Winstead
*Winstead National Genealogy/Reunion
1112 Vicksburg Street
Deltona, FL 32725-2942
Phone (813) 935-4338
Rosalie Jaszczak, President
Pub. *Winstead National Genealogy/
Reunion Newsletter*, two or three times
per year; (includes descendants of
Samuel Winstead (1701–1774))
$5.00 per year membership, $100.00 life
membership; reunion

Winsten (see Winston)

Winston (see Folk Family Surname
Exchange)

Winston
Winston Family Organization
Rt. 3, Box 123
Trinity, NC 27370
Cheryl Burrow

Winston
*Folk Family
PO Box 52048
Knoxville, TN 37950-2048
Hester E. Stockton, Owner; James W.
Winston, Editor
Pub. *Winston Families*, quarterly, $15.00
per year subscription, $5.00 per issue;
(includes Winsten)

Wint (see Kessler)

Winter (see Appler, Jordan)

Winters
*John P. Winters Family Organization
4936 State Route 159
Red Bud, IL 62278
Phone (617) 282-2401
Selah E. Moore
Annual reunion on the Saturday before
Memorial Day at Concord Baptist
Church Fellowship Hall, Natural
Bridge, Alabama

Winz
*Winz (Wintz) Surname Organization
2845 North 72nd Street
Milwaukee, WI 53210
Phone (414) 778-1224; (414) 2109 FAX
Maralyn A. Wellauer
(includes families from Switzerland)

Wirebach (see Weyerbacher)

Wireback (see Weyerbacher)

Wirebaugh (see Weyerbacher)

Wirebeck (see Weyerbacher)

Wirt (see Wert, Wertz)

Wirth (see Wert)

Wirts (see Wertz)

Wise
*Adam Wise Family Association
29801 Highview Circle
San Juan Capistrano, CA 92675
Phone (714) 661-4808; (714) 661-8408;
(714) 499-5575 (FAX)
Rachel Hayward, Editor and Publisher
$25.00 per year membership; reunion

Wisee (see Links Genealogy
Publications)

Wisely
*Peter Wisely Family Organization, 1750
of Wythe County, Virginia
HCR 62, Box 113A
Flippin, AR 72634-9710
Phone (501) 453-5286
Charlene Gillespie Deutsch, Compiler

Wisely
*Peter Wisely Family Organization,
1830–1839 of Franklin County,
Pennsylvania, 1839–1861 of Randolph
County, Illinois
HCR 62, Box 113A
Flippin, AR 72634-9710
Phone (501) 453-5286
Charlene Gillespie Deutsch, Compiler

Wiseman
*Wiseman Family Association
22962 Lakeshore Drive
Elkhart, IN 46514-9572
Phone (219) 264-6200
Robert D. Wiseman, Historian
Pub. *The Sapit Journal*, quarterly, $10.00
per year subscription; (includes all
Wiseman families, especially
descendants of Thomas, Philadelphia
County, Pennsylvania 1706 and his
(unproven) son Isaac, Berks County,
Pennsylvania, and Rowan County,
North Carolina)
Annual reunion on the third Sunday of
June at Bob Evans Farm Pavilion, Rio
Grande, Ohio

Wisser (see Weiser)

Witbeck (see Barnard)

Witcraft
Witcraft/Stapleton Reunion
6825 S.E. Clackamus Road
Milwaukie, OR 97222
E. Lionberger

Witham (see Everett)

Witham
Witham Reunion
PO Box 75
North Salem, NH 03073
Phone (603) 893-1192
Richard Noyes, President
(includes descendants of John Witham
(1800–1858) of Vermont and his two
wives, Joanna Morrison and Sarah
Corliss)

Annual reunion on the weekend nearest
the 15th of August at the Vermont
Grange Center in Brookfield

Withee (see Withy)

Witherbee (see Weatherbee)

Witherby (see Weatherbee)

Witheril (see McKee)

Withers (see Folk Family Surname
Exchange, Weathers)

Witherspoon (see MacFaddien)

Witherspoon
*The Witherspoon Family Reunion
Association
402 Campo Drive
Grand Prairie, TX 75051-4908
Phone (214) 264-5220
Claude F. Witherspoon, President
Pub. *The Tie That Binds Newsletter*,
quarterly, $15.00 per year subscription
No membership fee; reunion

Withey (see Withy)

Withhuhn (see Sager)

Withie (see Withy)

Withrow
Withrow Family Association
218 N.W. Kaw Avenue
Bartlesville, OK 74003
Mrs. John D. Kerr
Pub. *Withrow Family Corners
Newsletter*, irregularly
$5.00 per year membership

Withy
*With(e)y, Weth(e)y, Quivey,
McWith(e)y, McWeth(e)y, McQuivey,
Withee, Weethee, Wethee, Withie
Family Ties
1508 Marlborough
Ann Arbor, MI 48104
Phone (313) 973-0936
Barbara Snow
(includes extensive files on any families
of these surnames, including
descendants of James Mackerwithey of
Dedham, Massachusetts)

Witt (see Corson, Harbour)

Witte
Witte Family Reunion
Stover, MO 65078
Edgar Witte

Wittenburg (see Cowart)

Witter (see Holmes)

Witter
Witter/Dunwell Lineage Society
PO Box 157
Knightsen, CA 94548
Carolyn Sherfy

Wittrig (see Widrick)

Witty (see Warren)

Wize (see Wise)

Woenne
Woenne/Wönne Family Association
5823 Ross Street
Oakland, CA 94618
Maxine Bell, Secretary
Free

Woertman (see Workman)

Wofford
*Wofford, Lottie, Brinker Association
7217 Norton
Kansas City, MO 64132
Phone (816) 333-4077
Dorothy Wofford
Pub. *Quarterly Newsletter*

Wohlgemuth (see Kinney)

Wolbers (see Duesing)

Wolcott
*The Society of Descendants of Henry
   Wolcott
62 Weston Road
Weston, CT 06883
Phone (203) 227-8103
Donald Bergquist, Second Vice President
Pub. *Annual Report*
$10.00 per year membership, annual
   reunion on the first weekend of August

Wolf (see Cian, Heath Wolfe)

Wolf
*Kinseeker Publications
5697 Old Maple Trail
PO Box 184
Grawn, MI 49637
E-mail: AB064@taverse.lib.mi.us
Victoria Wilson, Editor
Pub. *Wondering Wolfs*, quarterly, $10.00
   per year subscription; (includes Wolf,
   Wolfe, Woolf, etc.)

Wolfe (see Dubberly, Likes, Wolf)

Wolfenbarger (see Wolfensberger)

Wolfenberger (see Wolfensberger)

Wolfensberger
*Wolfensberger Family Association
6400 North Ann Arbor Terrace
Oklahoma City, OK 73132
Phone (405) 721-4383
Lawrence (Larry) M. Jones, Director

Pub. *Wolfensberger Family Newsletter*
(includes variants Wolfenbarger,
   Wolfenberger, Wolfensperger,
   Wolfersberger, Wolfersperger,
   Wolfinbarger, Sparger, and Spargur)

Wolfensperger (see Wolfensberger)

Wolfersberger (see Wolfensberger)

Wolfersperger (see Wolfensberger)

Wolff (see Wolfe)

Wolfinbarger (see Wolfensberger)

Wolfinger
Wolfinger
14 Brook Drive
Furlong, PA 18925
Audrey J. Wolfinger, Editor
Pub. *Wolfinger*, semiannually, $5.00 per
   year subscription
Reunion

Wolgemuth
Wolgemuth Family Clearinghouse
77 Hollow Road
Quarryville, PA 17566-9491
Harry Hoffman
SASE

Wollard (see McCorkle)

Wolpert
*Wolpert Surname Organization
199 Commodore Drive
Milledgeville, GA 31061
Phone (912) 968-7425
Richard Bialac

Wolsey (see McCune)

Wolston (see Brockway)

Wolverton (see Woolverton)

Wolverton
*Wolverton Reunion
2401 West Rollins Road
Columbia, MO 65203
William Marion Harlan
(includes descendants of Joseph Snapp
   Wolverton (1830–1898))
Annual reunion in the first week of
   August at Moberly, Missouri

Wolverton
Wolvertons Unlimited
1040 East McCanse
Springfield, MO 65803-3613
Phone (417) 833-2814
Glen Gohr, Editor
Pub. *Wolvertons Unlimited*, bimonthly,
   $8.00 per year subscription; (includes
   all Wolvertons/Woolvertons in the
   U.S., Canada and England, with
   special focus on the descendants of
   Charles Woolverton of New Jersey
   (ca 1660–ca 1746), Andrew

Woolverton (ca 1750–ca 1812), Moses
   Hanks (1746–1831) and allied
   families: Dodson, Harris, Littlefield,
   Neville, etc.)

Womack
*Womack and Associated Families
   Genealogy Exchange
PO Box 96
Palmdale, FL 33944
Phone (941) 675-0013
Ray Bryan Womack, Sr.
(includes associated families of Burkhart,
   Gass and Boydston)
Free exchange

Womack
From Generation to Generation
Rt. 1, Box 147
Buncombe, IL 62912
Melody Tellor, Editor
Pub. *Womack Workers*, quarterly, $15.00
   per year subscription

Womack
Courier Publication
PO Box 1284
Natchitoches, LA 71458-1284
Annette Carpenter Womack
Pub. *Womack Family Courier*, quarterly,
   $10.00 per year subscription

Wombles
Wombles-Womble
2615 Huntington Road
Springfield, IL 62703
Darlene Wombles
Pub. *Wombles-Womble*, three or four
   times per year, $10.00 per year
   subscription

Womelsdorf
*Womelsdorf Family Association
2129 West New Haven Avenue, #131
Melbourne, FL 32904
Phone (407) 727-2716
M. Normile
Pub. *Womelsdorf Family Newsletter*,
   quarterly
$8.00 per year membership

Wönne (see Woenne)

Wonse (see Likes)

Wood (see Folk Family Surname
   Exchange, Bosher, Countryman,
   Futral, Gant, Golding, Hess, Krom,
   McCune, Rothenberger, Rowe,
   Warren)

Wood
*Wood Publishing Company
2514 Paul Bryant Drive
Tuscaloosa, AL 35401
Phone (205) 759-2102
Thomas Harold Wood, Editor and
   Publisher
Pub. *The Wood-Woods Family Magazine*,
   quarterly, $25.00 per year subscription

Wood
Wood-Woods Family Magazine
903 Myers Avenue
Columbus, TN 38401
Virginia Wood Alexander
Pub. *Wood-Woods Family Magazine*,
semiannually, $10.00 per year
subscription

Wood
*John Wood Family Organization
1286 Apple Avenue
Provo, UT 84604
Phone (801) 373-9897
Stephen L. Wood, President
(includes descendants of John Wood (ca
1745–1880) of New Jersey, Virginia,
Kentucky, West Virginia, Indiana and
Illinois, and Susannah Shrimplin
(1782–1839) of Pennsylvania, West
Virginia, Ohio, Indiana and Illinois;
also John's sister Elizabeth Wood
(1778–1843), who married James
Cochran ca 1800 and lived in Peas
Township, Belmont County, Ohio; and
John's brother, James Wood (1781
Mason County, Kentucky–1848
Sabula, Jackson County, Iowa), who
married Margaret Payne in Union
Township, Knox County, Ohio)

Wood
*John Peacock Wood Family
Organization
PO Box 352
Tremonton, UT 84337
Phone (801) 257-6197
Dr. Reese B. Mason

Woodard (see Woodward)

Woodard
Woodard Family Association
2106 Creekside Court
Arlington, TX 76013
Phone (817) 496-1606
Don Schimpf

Woodend (see Robertson)

Woodford (see Clark, Sheldon)

Woodhouse (see Hyatt)

Woodhull
*Nall News Publishing Company
PO Box 2186
Willingboro, NJ 08046-2186
Josephine Crittenberger-Nall, Editor-
Publisher
Pub. *Woodhull Roots and Branches*,
quarterly, $16.00 per year subscription

Woodin
Woodin Family Newsletter
11292 Ile Road
Chardon, OH 44024
Martha Christian

Pub. *Woodin Family Newsletter*,
annually, $1.00 per issue; (includes
descendants of Aaron G. Woodin)

Woodlief
*Woodlief-Woodliff Family Association
7858 Forest Hill Avenue
Richmond, VA 23225-1931
Fred P. Woodlief, Jr.
(includes descendants of John Woodliffe
(1584–1637))

Woodliff (see Woodlief)

Woodruff (see Barnes, Johnson)

Woodruff
*Wilford Woodruff Family Association
Richard Price & Associates
57 West South Temple Street, Suite 300
Salt Lake City, UT 84147
Richard W. Price, Family Genealogist
(includes descendants of Wilford
Woodruff (1807 Farmington, Hartford
County, Connecticut–))

Woodruff
Woodruff Family History Exchange
PO Box 9395
Anaheim, CA 92812-7395
Margaret E. Morrissey
Pub. *Woodruff Family History Exchange*

Woods (see Folk Family Surname
Exchange, Brawley, Golding,
MacFaddien, Netherland, Wiley,
Wood)

Woodside (see Stone, Warren)

Woodson (see Golding, Heath)

Woodson
*The Thomas C. Woodson Family
Association, Inc.
1431 Highland Drive
Silver Spring, MD 20910
Phone (301) 495-5997
Patricia James, Editor
Pub. *The Thomas C. Woodson Family
Newsletter*, three times per year
(March, July and November);
(includes descendants of Thomas C.
Woodson (1790–1879) of Shadwell,
Virginia, and Jackson County, Ohio)
$20.00 per year membership; reunion

Woodson
Claudette's
3962 Xenwood Avenue, S.
Saint Louis Park, MN 55416-2842
Claudette Atwood Maerz
Pub. *Woodson Watcher Plus Allied Lines*,
quarterly, $15.00 per year subscription

Woodward (see Gant)

Woodward
*Woodward/Woodard Ancestors of New
England
2013 Westover Drive
Pleasant Hill, CA 94523
Phone (510) 934-9416
Lindsay S. Reeks, Publisher

Woodward
Woodward
718 Big Canoe
Jasper, GA 30143
Linda Geiger
Pub. *Woodward*, quarterly, $8.00 per year
subscription

Woodworth (see Gerade)

Woodworth
Surnames, Limited
RR 3, Box 59
Muleshoe, TX 79347-9208
Pub. *Woodworth Journal*, irregularly,
$8.00 per issue

Woody (see Dockery)

Woody
Woody
61 West Sutter Road
Paradise, CA 95969
Mary Dell Wallace
Pub. *Woody*, three times per year, $6.00
per year subscription
Reunion

Woofter (see Douglass, Lambert)

Wooland (see Pasko)

Wooldridge (see Lush)

Wooldridge
Wooldridge Family Reunion
730 Cherokee Boulevard
Knoxville, TN 37919
Phone (615) 524-7887
Wright W. Frost
(includes descendants of Josiah and
Keziah Nichols Wooldridge of
Kentucky)
Reunion in Mayfield, Kentucky, and
other places

Wooldridge
*Wooldridge Family Organization
Coleman Research Agency
241 North Vine Street, Apartment 1104E
Salt Lake City, UT 84103-1945
Marlene McCormick Coleman
(includes all Wooldridge families)

Woolf (see McCune, Wolf)

Woolford
Woolford
Whispering Oaks
5821 Rowland Hill Road
Cascade, MD 21719-1939

Phone (301) 416-2660
Victor Gebhart, President
Pub. *Woolford*, annually, $2.00 per issue

Woolley (see Haynes)

Woolley
*The Utah Woolley Family
2069 East Yale Avenue
Salt Lake City, UT 84108-1905
Phone (801) 582-3668
Preston Woolley Parkinson, Family
　Historian
(includes descendants of Thomas
　Woolley and Sarah Coppock who were
　married in Philadelphia in 1729; also
　John Woolley (1779 West Chester,
　Pennsylvania–) and Rachel Dilworth
　of Chester County, Pennsylvania)

Woolley
*George Edwin Woolley Family
　Association
A Branch of The Utah Wooley Family
3722 South 1880 East
Salt Lake City, UT 84106
Phone (801) 277-9930
Richard W. Fetzer, President
Pub. *George Edwin Woolley Association
　Newsletter*, semiannually (spring and
　fall); (includes descendants of Thomas
　Woolley and Sarah Coppock who were
　married in Philadelphia in 1729; also
　allied surnames: Ashbridge, Curnock,
　Surnam, White and Worrilow)
$10.00 donation per year membership;
　biennial reunion

Woolverton (see Wolverton)

Woolverton
*Woolverton Mountain Reunion
2349 County Road 4290
West Plains, MO 65775-9810
Phone (417) 256-8035
(417) 256-8035
(includes descendants of William Louis
　Woolverton (1822–1894), for whom
　nearby Woolverton Mountain is
　named)
Annual reunion on Mother's Day, the
　second Sunday of May, at the Formosa
　Community Building, Formosa,
　Arkansas

Wooten
Wooten/Wooton and Related Families
　(Speight/Isles)
3517 A South Stafford Street
Arlington, VA 22206
Phone (703) 379-1092
Richard C. Wooten
Pub. *Wooten/Wooton Newsletter*,
　quarterly

Wooton (see Wooten)

Worcester (see Newton)

Worden
*Worden Family Association
1201 Glendale Street
Midland, MI 48642-5105
Phone (517) 631-7801; E-mail:
　WPPat@aol.com
Patricia C. Worden, Archivist
Pub. *Wordens Past*, quarterly; (includes
　Warden, Werden, etc.)
$10.00 per year membership in the U.S.
　and Canada, $12.00 per year
　membership overseas

Workman (see Golding, MacDuff)

Workman
*Family Publications
5628 60th Drive, N.E.
Marysville, WA 98270-9509
E-mail: cxwp57a@prodigy.com
Rose Caudle Terry, Publisher
Pub. *Workman Branches*, two to four
　times per year, $8.95 per volume
　subscription, plus $1.50 postage per
　order; (includes Woertman, Wortman,
　etc., all spellings, all nationalities)

Worley (see Cowart)

Wormet (see MacDuff)

Worrell
Worrell
PO Box 54054
Phoenix, AZ 85078
Mary Nadine
Pub. *Worrell*, quarterly, $12.50 per year
　subscription

Worrilow (see Woolley)

Worsham (see Brodnax)

Worthington (see Michener)

Worthington
Worthington Descendants Organization
6619 Pheasant Road, Rt. 1, #16
Baltimore, MD 21220
Phone (410) 335-3948
Frances Brengle and Beth Poole
Pub. *Worthington Descendants*, quarterly,
　$15.00 per year subscription

Worthy
Worthy/Savage Family Reunion
Rt. 1, Box 127A
Hazelhurst, MS 39083
Jim Eggleston Haddock

Wortman (see Workman)

Wrage (see Bestman)

Wragg
Wragg Exchange
2523 Karla Drive
Mesquite, TX 75150
Dana Meara
Free

Wray (see Jensen, Ray)

Wren
*Wren Family Association
Ruth Wren Research Service
5809 Tautago
El Paso, TX 79924
Phone (915) 755-0083
Ruth Wren, Editor/Owner
Pub. *Wren Kin Newsletter*, quarterly
　(January, April, July and October);
　(includes Wren/Wrenn/Ren surname
　and kin, from 1600 to the present)
$10.00 per year membership

Wrenn (see Wren)

Wrigglesworth (see Lush)

Wright (see Alsop, Hall, MacIntyre,
　Parker)

Wright
*Wright Database
1940 New Jersey Street
Fairfield, CA 94533
Phone (707) 425-2711; (707) 426-2859
　FAX; E-mail: footprints@ptn.com
Don P. Wright
Pub. *Footprints Of Our Past*, quarterly
　(spring, summer, fall and winter),
　$20.00 per calendar year subscription,
　$6.00 per issue; (includes primarily the
　Wright surname, but also Bliss, Foote,
　Hunt, Lampman, Patton, Pomeroy,
　Ridgeway, Root, Skidmore, Stebbins
　and many more from early New
　England; databases on Adkins, Allen,
　Atkins, Baker, Baron, Bartlett,
　Belknap, Borden, Bramlett, Brown,
　Browne, Bush, Callegan, Callen,
　Carpenter, Carter, Case, Chase, Clark,
　Cook, Cornwall, Crail, Crow, Davis,
　Dilley, Doane, Doyle, Drake, Fay,
　Fuller, Gentry, Gilman, Greenslit,
　Gregory, Griswold, Harbison, Harris,
　Harvey, Hatcher, Hatchet, Hefferon,
　Hendrick, Hill, Holbrook, Holebrook,
　Horn, Houghton, Howell, Hutchenson,
　Jaco, James, Janosik, Johnson, Jordan,
　Keith, Kelvedon, Kelverstone, Kruger,
　Lambert, Lampman, Lee, Lewis,
　Little, Long, Lovelace, Lyle, Martin,
　McBride, McClain, Merrill, Miller,
　Morse, Nason, Neaville, Nelson,
　Ordway, Packard, Penfield, Petri,
　Pettey, Petty, Pickens, Prescott,
　Provoost, Reed, Reich, Ricker,
　Roberts, Root, Sabin, Settle, Shattuck,
　Sherman, Skidmore, Stebbins, Steele,
　Stewart, Stipe, Taylor, Thurston,
　Townsend and Turcotte)

Wright
*Wright Information Center
1511 S.W. 65th Terrace
Boca Raton, FL 33428-7819
Phone (407) 482-7582
Phyllis M. Heiss, Genealogist

(computer database, central depository
  and exchange service)
$15.00 minimum, send SASE for
  brochure

Wright
Claudette's
3962 Xenwood Avenue, S.
Saint Louis Park, MN 55416-2842
Claudette Atwood Maerz
Pub. *Wright Family Workbook*, quarterly,
  $14.00 per year subscription

Wright
Wright Family Newsletter
PO Box 13548
Saint Louis, MO 63138
Maryann Schirker
Pub. *Wright Family Newsletter*, quarterly,
  $25.00 per year subscription

Wright
*Wright Offsprings
PO Box 333
Palisade, NE 69040
Phone (308) 285-3242
Irene Wright
(includes Wright family of Virginia,
  Kentucky, Indiana, 1800s and late
  1770s up)

Wrisley (see Risley)

Wuensch (see Surname Database)

Wuertz (see Wertz)

Wurmbach (see Lemon)

Wurts (see Wertz)

Wüthrich (see Widrick)

Wyant (see Anthes)

Wyatt (see Cairer, Wiley)

Wyckoff
Wyckoff House and Association, Inc.
PO Box 100-376
Brooklyn, NY 11210
Phone (718) 629-5400
Pub. *Wyckoff Bulletin*, annually

Wye (see Van Wye)

Wyerbaugher (see Weyerbacher)

Wylie (see Gunn)

Wyllie (see Gunn)

Wymbs (see MacDuff)

Wymer (see Weimer)

Wymes (see MacDuff)

Wyms (see MacDuff)

Wynn (see Dean, Winn)

Wynne (see Winn)

Wynns (see Winn)

Wyrebaugh (see Weyerbacher)

Wyse (see Wise)

Wysor (see Weiser)

Yadon (see Folk Family Surname
  Exchange)

Yager (see The Memorial Foundation of
  the Germanna Colonies, Lambert)

Yancey (see Eaves)

Yaney (see Guthrie)

Yanez (see Cigarroa)

Yankee (see Cairer, Yankey)

Yankey
Yankey/Yankee/Yankie
5037 Robander Street
Carmichael, CA 95608-0938
Barbara H. Mahoney, Editor
Pub. *Yankey/Yankee/Yankie*, irregularly,
  donation for subscription

Yankie (see Yankey)

Yaple (see Baker)

Yarberg (see Yarbrough)

Yarborough (see Yarbrough)

Yarbro (see Yarbrough)

Yarbrough
*Yarbrough National Genealogical and
  Historical Association, Inc.
PO Box 640
Normal, AL 35762-0640
Leonard Yarbrough, Chairman
Pub. *The Yarbrough Family Quarterly*
  (includes all Yarberg, Yarborough,
  Yarbro and Yarbrough spellings)
$25.00 per year regular membership,
  $15.00 per year voting associate
  membership, $10.00 per year non-
  voting library membership

Yarger (see Jurger)

Yarnall
Yarnall-Yarnell Family
627 S.E. 53rd Avenue
Portland, OR 97215
Phone (503) 236-0742
John Morrison, Researcher

Yarnell (see Yarnall)

Yates (see Folk Family Surname
  Exchange, Carpenter, Kettenring,
  Ross)

Yates
*Folk Family
PO Box 52048
Knoxville, TN 37950-2048
Hester E. Stockton, Owner; Susan
  Mariah Yates, Editor
Pub. *Yates of Yore*, quarterly, $15.00 per
  year subscription, $5.00 per issue;
  (includes Yatts, Yeate and Yeates)

Yatts (see Yates)

Yeager (see The Memorial Foundation of
  the Germanna Colonies, Lambert)

Yeaple (see Jelly)

Yearven (see Irwin)

Yeate (see Yates)

Yeater
*Yeater Cousins Association
431 Norwick Road, S.W.
Cedar Rapids, IA 52404
Phone (319) 396-5348
Lisa L. Kuzela, Editor
Pub. *The Yeater Cousins: For All Yeaters
  and Their Kin*, semiannually
$7.00 for a two-year membership to
  Dorothy Barszcz, Secretary-Treasurer,
  2433 238th Street, Torrance, CA
  90501; annual reunion on the third
  weekend of June

Yeates (see Yates)

Yeats (see Folk Family Surname
  Exchange)

Yeaw
*David Yeaw Family Organization
PO Box 11
Medina, WA 98039
Phone (206) 454-3714
Sylvia E. Wilson, Genealogist

Yeingst (see Yiengst)

Yellowlees (see MacDuff)

Yellowley (see MacDuff)

Yellowlie (see MacDuff)

Yerger (see Jurger)

Yergey (see Yocum)

Yescot (see Wescott)

Yester (see Hay)

Yiengst
Yiengst-Yeingst Family
Rt. 2, Box 145
Gardners, PA 17324
Irene Sterner

Yirwing (see Irwin)

Yivewing (see Irwin)

Yocum
*Yocum and Yergey Surname
  Organization
PO Box 284
Belgrade, MT 59714-0284
Phone (406) 656-0979
Wallace Cyril Mauger

Yocum
*Yocum Surname Organization
3 Brazill Lane
Whitehall, MT 59759
Phone (406) 287-3369
Lindia Roggia Lovshin

Yoder (see Frantz)

Yoder
Yoder Newsletter
PO Box 594
Goshen, IN 46527-0594
Phone (219) 825-9318
Ben F. Yoder, Managing Editor; John W.
  Yoder, Circulation Manager
Pub. *Yoder Newsletter*, semiannually
  (April and October), $3.00 per year
  subscription; (includes Yoders, Yother
  and Yotter)

Yoders (see Yoder)

Yonkin (see Younkin)

Yool (see Yule)

York
York Family Newsletter
3500 Sycamore Drive
Boise, ID 83703
Phone (208) 342-7938
Lois Y. Hamilton
Pub. *York Family Newsletter*, quarterly,
  $4.00 per year subscription

Yost (see Surname Database, Brehm)

Yother (see Yoder)

Yotter (see Yoder)

Young (see Folk Family Surname
  Exchange, The Memorial Foundation
  of the Germanna Colonies, Ansel,
  Barnard, Brawley, Clark, Corson,
  Douglas, Franciscus, Garr, Golding,
  Goodenow, Johnson, Lemon, Lester,
  Likes, McCune, Ross, Smith, Weimar)

Young
*Clan Young
12 Emerson Avenue
Saco, ME 04072
Phone (207) 286-8461; E-mail:
  donjanem@aol.com
Donald Murray Miller, Executive
  Secretary
Pub. *Young Times*, three times per year;
  (includes Young from 1066 in
  Scotland, Ireland, Canada and the
  U.S.)
$15.00 per year membership, £15.00 per
  year membership in England, Scotland
  and Ireland

Young
*Young Surname Organization
347 12th Avenue, North
South Saint Paul, MN 55075-1957
Phone (612) 455-3626
Vicki Young Albu, Editor
Pub. *Born Young*, quarterly, $15.00 per
  year subscription, free queries, index
  by both surname and locality;
  (includes Jung and Yung)

Young
Young Family
509 Cokesbury Lane
Asheville, NC 28803
Norman Young

Youngblood
*The Youngblood (Jungblut) Society of
  America, Inc.
PO Box 270396
Corpus Christi, TX 78427-0396
Phone (512) 850-9268
Carl P. Geyer, Agent
Pub. *The Youngblood News Letter*,
  quarterly, $10.00 per year subscription
  for members; (includes Jungblut
  families from the Hamburg area of
  Germany, or living from 1608 to about
  1680 in England, or near Annapolis,
  Maryland, by 1680)
$35.00 per year membership; biennial
  reunion in even-numbered years on the
  first Sunday after the fourth of July in
  Austin, Texas.

Younger (see MacDuff)

Youngken (see Younkin)

Youngkin (see Younkin)

Younkin
*Younkin Family Association
PO Box 340
Hancock, MD 21750-0340
Phone (301) 678-6999; E-mail:
  fanfare@intrepid.net
Donna Younkin Logan, Publisher
Pub. *Younkin Family News Bulletin*,
  quarterly, $15.00 per year subscription;
  (all Younkin, Youngkin, Youngken,
  Younkins, Yonkin, Junghen families)
Free help; annual summer reunion in
  Pennsylvania

Younkins (see Younkin)

Youse (see Hoster)

Yowell (see The Memorial Foundation of
  the Germanna Colonies)

Yrein (see Irwin)

Yrewing (see Irwin)

Yrvin (see Irwin)

Yrwen (see Irwin)

Yrwens (see Irwin)

Yrwin (see Irwin)

Yrwing (see Irwin)

Yrwyne (see Irwin)

Yuill (see Buchanan)

Yuille (see Yule)

Yule (see Buchanan)

Yule
Yule-Yool-Yuille-Zuil
PO Box 818
Gresham, OR 97030
Estella Yule Pryor
Pub. *Yule-Yool-Yuille-Zuil*, quarterly,
  $10.00 per year subscription

Yung (see Young)

Yunie (see Innes)

Yuratich (see Blossom Press)

Zdroik
*Zdroik/Zdrojewski Family Reunion
1208 North Tenth Avenue
Wausau, WI 54401
Phone (715) 675-6836
Cynthia Guenther
(includes descendants of Joseph
  Zdrojewsk and Anna Treder)
Free

Zdrojewsk (see Zdroik)

Zdrojewski (see Zdroik)

Zearfoss (see Serfass)

Zechmeister (see Brucker)

Zehren (see Lahey)

Zeigler (see The Memorial Foundation
  of the Germanna Colonies)

Zeimantz
*Zeimantz Family Association
920 East 26th
Spokane, WA 99203

Phone (509) 838-6800
John Zeimantz

Zeleny (see Havlik

Zell (see Cell)

Zelle (see Cell)

Zellen (see Links Genealogy
   Publications)

Zeller*Pennsylvania
Zeller Family
c/o Bahney
PO Box 407
Myerstown, PA 17067

Zellers (see Sellers)

Zeltner (see Maier)

Zerkel (see Zirkle)

Zerkle (see Zirkle)

Zibilich (see Blossom Press)

Zickafoose (see Buzzard)

Ziegler (see Newmyer)

Ziegler
*Henry Ziegler Family Organization
PO Box 764
Snowflake, AZ 85937-0764
Phone (520) 536-7459
Dorothy Arlene Ziegler Wiltbank
(includes descendants of Henry Ziegler
   (1831–1899) and Martha Shields
   (1841–))

Ziegler
*Ziegler Surname Organization
137 Lorenzi, South
Las Vegas, NV 89107
Phone (702) 877-2438
Juanita Mae McGaughey Clark

Ziehlke
Ziehlke
Whispering Oaks
5821 Rowland Hill Road
Cascade, MD 21719-1939
Phone (301) 416-2660
Victor Gebhart, President
Pub. *Ziehlke*, annually, $2.00 per issue

Ziev
*Ziev Surname Database
1401 Irving Lane
Burnsville, MN 55337-4385
Phone (612) 894-1312
Sherry Constans-Kaiserlik

Zigman (see Sigman)

Zilliox
*Zilliox/Marshall Family of Clearfield,
   Pennsylvania
4063 Heathersage
Houston, TX 77084
Laela Lindner

Zillman (see Marks)

Zimler (see Laubach)

Zimmer (see Johnson)

Zimmerman (see The Memorial
   Foundation of the Germanna Colonies,
   Sullivan Surname Exchange,
   Rutherford, Snell)

Zingsheim
*Kinseeker Publications
5697 Old Maple Trail
PO Box 184
Grawn, MI 49637
E-mail: AB064@taverse.lib.mi.us
Victoria Wilson, Editor
Pub. *Zingsheim Times*, quarterly, $3.00
   per year subscription

Zirkel (see Zirkle)

Zirkle
*Zirkle Family Historical Association
3691 South Middle Road
Quicksburg, VA 22847-1222
Blair Zirkle, Vice President; Jack Zirkle,
   President
Pub. *Z.F.H.A. Newsletter*, three to four
   times per year; (includes Circle,
   Syrcle, Zerkel, Zerkle, Zirkel and all
   variants from Germany through
   America; also descendants of Ludwig
   and Eva Zyrkle, 1500–1900s)
$15.00 per year membership; reunion

Zollicker (see Cairer)

Zollicoffer (see The Memorial
   Foundation of the Germanna Colonies)

Zondervan (see Frazier)

Zook (see Likes)

Zornes (see Pack)

Zufelt (see Smith)

Zug (see Frantz)

Zuil (see Yule)

Zuill (see Buchanan)

Zulauf (see Heath)

Zulpo
*Zulpo Family (Recoaro, Italy) of Rosati,
   MO
7430 Leslie Drive
Edwardsville, IL 62025-7736
Phone (618) 656-2299
Elsie M. Wasser
Annual reunion on the second Saturday
   of August at Saint James Memorial
   Park, Saint James, Missouri

zum Fanghus (see Fankhauser)

Zumwalt
Zumwalt/Sumwalt Genealogical
   Association
3105 N.E. 85th Avenue
Portland, OR 97220
Phone (503) 254-4776
Jax Zumwalt
Pub. *Quarterly*
$10.00 per year membership

Zurier (see Leopold)

Zuvich (see Blossom Press)

Zwigart
Zwigart Association of America
901 Whitesides Court
Lake Lure, NC 28746
Mr. Gill
Pub. *Zwigart*, quarterly
$5.00 per year membership

Zyrkle (see Zirkle)

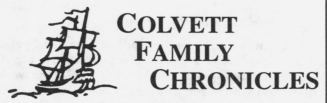

Announcing . . .

The 5th Edition of

GENEALOGICAL & LOCAL HISTORY BOOKS IN PRINT

Family History Volume

Compiled and Edited by Marian Hoffman

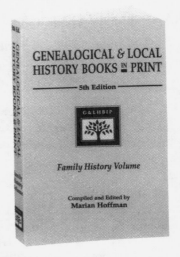

Now published under the imprint of the Genealogical Publishing Company, *Genealogical & Local History Books in Print, Family History Volume,* is at last available in a 5th edition, the first new edition to be published in over ten years! GPC's acquisition of this celebrated finding tool means that the most important bibliographical reference book for genealogists is now published by the major book publisher in the field of genealogy.

First published in 1975 in a single volume of 5,000 entries, *G&LHBIP* grew to three volumes and 30,000 entries by the 4th edition of 1985, with supplements published in 1990 and 1992 containing an additional 10,000 entries. The continuing proliferation of genealogical books in print, however, has made the publication of a mammoth catalogue somewhat unmanageable, so the decision has been taken to publish the new edition in parts, starting with the *Family History Volume,* which is offered here complete in itself. (The remaining volumes of *G&LHBIP*—covering general reference books and locality sourcebooks—will be published in due course.)

This new *Family History Volume* contains listings of available family histories, both as individual works and compilations; it also includes listings of pedigrees, biographies, and family newsletters in print. In addition, it contains the names and addresses of all vendors (authors/publishers, etc.), a comprehensive surname index, space advertisements, and an index to advertisers. With this volume, researchers will know instantly what family histories are available for sale and where they can be bought. And since the first step in genealogical research is to find out what work has already been done on a given family, the *Family History Volume* should be the first place to stop as well as the first place to shop.

Divided into two parts—family histories and compiled genealogies—the *Family History Volume* contains a total of 4,634 entries. Alphabetically arranged by family name, each entry identifies a published family history that is available and in print. Typically, entries give the full title of the work, the author, date of publication, whether indexed or illustrated, in cloth or paper, number of pages, selling price, and vendor number. Vendors are listed separately in the front of the book, both numerically and alphabetically (a happy improvement over previous editions of *G&LHBIP*), with addresses and special ordering information conveniently provided.

In addition, many entries indicate the principal surnames covered in the work (other than those in the title), and all surnames cited, whether in the title of the work or in the body of the entry, appear in the index, where they are keyed to the book number (books are numbered sequentially from 1 to 4,634). An easier or more convenient method of locating books can hardly be imagined!

Yet another improvement over previous editions is the inclusion of a separate section of compiled genealogies. Although occupying only a fraction of the book, this new section nevertheless makes an attempt to list all multifamily compendia in print. Typically, multi-family compendia cover family histories on a regionwide, countywide, or statewide basis. Books such as Boddie's *Historical Southern Families* and Jacobus's *History and Genealogy of the Families of Old Fairfield* fall into this category, and they are grouped here in this new section for the convenience and pleasure of the researcher.

477 pp., indexed, paperback. 1996. **$25.00** plus $3.50 postage & handling. Maryland residents add 5% sales tax; Michigan residents add 6% sales tax.

VISA & MasterCard orders: phone toll-free 1-800-296-6687 or FAX 1-410-752-8492

Genealogical Publishing Co., Inc. / 1001 N. Calvert St., Baltimore, Md. 21202

TIDEWATER VIRGINIA FAMILIES:
A Magazine of History & Genealogy

An Independent Quarterly Publication
Edited by Virginia Lee Hutcheson Davis.

Presenting research in the Virginia counties of Caroline, Charles City, Elizabeth City, Essex, Gloucester, Hanover, Henrico, James City, King George, King & Queen, King William, Lancaster, Mathews, Middlesex, New Kent, Northumberland, Richmond, Warwick, Westmoreland and York.

Current subscription: $24.00/year US.
Subscribe anytime during volume year and receive all four issues
Earlier volumes (4 issues each): $25.00 per vol.
Canada/overseas add $5.00 to each subscription.

Tidewater Virginia Families
316 Littletown Qtr, Williamsburg, VA 23185-5519
Telephone (757) 220-4888

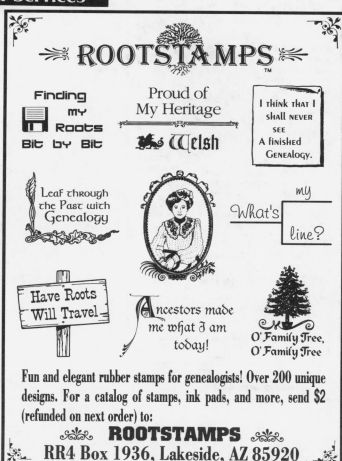

CLEARFIELD COMPANY'S BEST SELLERS

GENEALOGY AND COMPUTERS FOR THE COMPLETE BEGINNER
A Step-by-Step Guide to the PAF Computer Program, Automated Data Bases, Family History Centers, and Local Sources
Revised Second Edition
Karen Clifford

Karen Clifford's *Genealogy and Computers for the Complete Beginner* not only explains how to use the computer as you embark on your family history odyssey but also introduces you to the vast resources of the leading genealogical institution in the world, the Church of Jesus Christ of Latter-day Saints. Perhaps the most important feature of Karen's book is its user-friendliest explanation of the Personal Ancestral File software program (PAF) developed by the LDS Church, the most popular genealogical program in the world. PAF, of course, was designed to be used with the International Genealogical Index, the Family History Library Catalogue, and other data bases of the LDS Church. *Genealogy and Computers for the Complete Beginner* not only explains their various uses but also teaches you how to access them with a minimum of hassle via the Church's local Family History Centers throughout the U.S. This new edition also includes updated sections on census research, "self-tests" at the end of each chapter, and Family History Library handouts.

Revised 2nd ed. 8 1/2" x 11". 282 pp., indexed, paper. 1995. **#9102.** $32.50

GENEALOGY AND COMPUTERS FOR THE DETERMINED RESEARCHER
Revised and Expanded Edition
Karen Clifford

Genealogy and Computers for the Determined Researcher is the dynamic sequel to Karen Clifford's popular introductory guidebook, *Genealogy and Computers for the Complete Beginner*. Here Karen shows the researcher how to immerse himself in the latest version of PAF (Version 2.31) and explains how to construct a genealogy via the computer while undertaking more complex research problems.

One of the most important features of *Genealogy and Computers for the Determined Researcher* is its series of seventeen PAF tutorials that are designed to train you to get the most out of your computer as a research tool. After you've mastered the tutorials, you'll understand why thousands of genealogists have come to depend on PAF to assemble and manage their findings. Accompanying the book itself is a floppy disk for your use in completing the tutorials. Other sections of the *Determined Researcher* go over a variety of genealogical source records not covered in the *Complete Beginner*, including land, probate, military, and emigration/immigration records, as well as records found in periodicals and newspapers. Twenty percent larger than the previous editon, *Genealogy and Computers for the Determined Researcher* now features new or expanded coverage of pre-1850 U.S. census records, Native American genealogy, migration patterns, and the genealogical impact of customs.

Revised and expanded ed. 8 1/2" x 11". 355 pp., indexed, paper. 1995. **#9108.** $39.95 (Includes floppy disk).

GENEALOGY AND COMPUTERS FOR THE ADVANCED RESEARCHER
Pulling it All Together
Karen Clifford

The contents of the concluding volume in Karen Clifford's popular series of informal home-study textbooks for the genealogist fall into two main categories: (1) advanced research techniques and (2) producing a finished family history. Advanced research techniques refer to gathering background information by way of oral histories, evaluating original documents, contracting out research, hunting for ancestors overseas, compiling family health histories, and preparing a video family history. In the second part of the *Advanced Researcher*, Mrs. Clifford shows you how to define the objectives of your research project in terms of which families to write about, the nature of your audience, and the length of your composition. While this volume, like all of her books, has been updated to be used with Personal Ancestral File (PAF) Version 2.31, it also shows you how to use the highly regarded word processing software, WordPerfect, to accomplish your objectives. Still other chapters teach computer-assisted research techniques and book design from page layout to book binding, as well as demonstrate how to scan materials into your family history, convert PAF data to a formal family history, publish the final product, and much, much more.

Genealogy and Computers for the Advanced Researcher is the user-friendly book you've been waiting for to take your genealogical research to new heights, or to bring it to a successful close.

8 1/2" x 11". 347 pp., illus., indexed, paper. 1995. **#9106.** $39.95

A GENEALOGIST'S REFRESHER COURSE
2nd Edition
Judy Jacobson

A Genealogist's Refresher Course is less a how-to book than a collection of first-hand experiences, do's and don'ts, and privileged information. The author emphasizes the importance of verifying our findings against the original (primary) sources, and not relying on secondary, or published, accounts as the foundation for our genealogies. One of the most valuable chapters in the book contains a list of nearly 100 different kinds of sources of genealogical information, including anniversary announcements, bank statements, business licenses, memorial cards, health records, medals, newspaper clippings, subpoenas, and many other record categories that genealogists may fail to consult. Still other chapters discuss how to acquire rare or used books and when and how to hire a professional genealogist. In a word, this is a unique genealogy refresher course! The second edition, besides incorporating corrections to the original work, features one new chapter on the records of lineage, hereditary, and other special organizations and a second on how to find used books crucial to your research.

2nd ed. 96 pp., paper. 1996. **#9156.** $12.00

WRITE THE STORY OF YOUR LIFE
Ruth Kanin

Write the Story of Your Life is the best introduction to writing autobiography ever set into type. Through specific exercises, psychological insights, apt quotes, personal examples and suggested readings, Kanin provides an extensive tour of the creative process. "*Write the Story of Your Life*…must rank as the most comprehensive, definitive, and finest book yet published on the subject."—Alex Haley, author of *Roots*.

219 pp., paper. (1981), repr. 1995. **#3135.** $14.95

POCKET GUIDE TO IRISH GENEALOGY
Brian Mitchell

By skillfully blending case studies, maps, charts, and his own mastery of the subject, Mitchell has managed to convey the basics of Irish genealogical research in scarcely sixty pages. Following introductory chapters on the background to research on the American side, the author describes the nature and uses of all significant record sources in Ireland. Other important chapters explain the differences between the various administrative divisions of Ireland and list all major Irish record offices and heritage centers. In short, if you need a handy roadmap to genealogical research in Ireland, look no further.

63 pp., maps, paper. (1991), repr. 1993. **#9240.** $9.95

ORDER FORM • Clearfield Company, 200 E. Eager Street, Baltimore, MD 21202 • (410) 625-9004

Please send me the following books:

Item #	Title	Price

❑ Enclosed is a check/money order for $ _____

made out to **Clearfield Company**.

❑ MasterCard/Visa # _____

Exp. Date _____   Amount $ _____

Signature _____

Name _____

Address _____

City _____ State _____ Zip _____

Postage & Handling: One book $3.50; each additional book $1.25.
Maryland residents add 5% sales tax; Michigan residents add 6% sales tax.

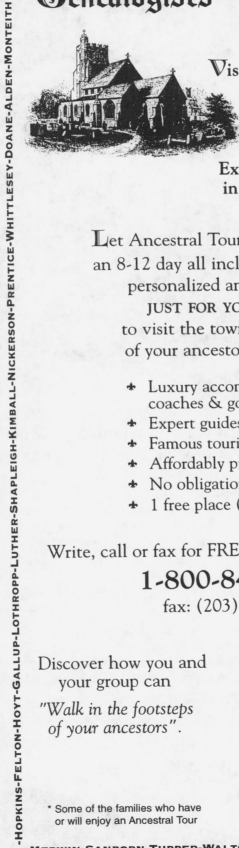